Education Policy

The International Library of Comparative Public Policy

Series Editor: B. Guy Peters
Maurice Falk Professor of American Government and Chair, Department of Political Science, University of Pittsburgh, USA

1. Industrial Policy
   Wyn Grant
2. Urban and Regional Policy
   Jon Pierre
3. Policy Evaluation: Linking Theory to Practice
   Ray C. Rist
4. Budgeting and the Management of Public Spending
   Donald J. Savoie
5. Science and Technology Policy
   Sheila Jasanoff
6. Economic Policy (Volumes I and II)
   Paul F. Whiteley
7. Health Policy
   J.W. Björkman and C. Altenstetter
8. Tax Policy
   Sven Steinmo
9. Criminal Justice Policy
   Jodi Lane and Joan Petersilia
10. Transport Policy
    Kenneth J. Button and Roger Stough
11. Environmental Policy (Volumes I and II)
    Wolfgang Rüdig
12. Education Policy
    James Marshall and Michael Peters

Future titles will include:

Privatization and Public Policy
Vincent Wright and Luisa Perrotti

Agricultural Policy
Wyn P. Grant and J.T.S. Keeler

Defence Policy
Lawrence Freedman

Wherever possible, the articles in these volumes have been reproduced as originally published using facsimile reproduction, inclusive of footnotes and pagination to facilitate ease of reference.

Education Policy

Edited by

James Marshall

Professor of Education
University of Auckland, New Zealand

and

Michael Peters

Associate Professor of Education
University of Auckland, New Zealand

THE INTERNATIONAL LIBRARY OF COMPARATIVE PUBLIC POLICY

An Elgar Reference Collection
Cheltenham, UK • Northampton, MA, USA

Published by
Edward Elgar Publishing Limited
Glensanda House
Montpellier Parade
Cheltenham
Glos GL50 1UA
UK

Edward Elgar Publishing, Inc.
136 West Street, Suite 202
Northampton
Massachusetts 01060
USA

A catalogue record for this book is available from the British Library.

Library of Congress Cataloguing in Publication Data

Education policy / edited by James Marshall and Michael Peters.
(The international library of comparative public policy: 12)
Includes bibliographical references and index.
1. Education and state. 2. Educational sociology. 3. Education—Economic aspects. 4. Critical pedagogy. I. Marshall, James (James D.), 1948– . II. Peters, Michael (Michael A.), 1948– . III. Series. IV. Series: An Elgar reference collection.
LC71.E32 1999
379—dc21 99-39711
CIP

ISBN 1 85898 792 X

Printed and bound in Great Britain by MPG Books Ltd, Bodmin, Cornwall

Contents

Acknowledgements

The editors and publishers wish to thank the authors and the following publishers who have kindly given permission for the use of copyright material.

American Educational Research Association for articles: Carlos Alberto Torres (1995), 'State and Education Revisited: Why Educational Researchers Should Think Politically About Education', *Review of Research in Education*, Chapter 6, **21**, 255–331; Geoff Whitty (1997), 'Creating Quasi-Markets in Education: A Review of Recent Research on Parental Choice and School Autonomy in Three Countries', *Review of Research in Education*, Chapter 1, **22**, 3–47.

American Political Science Association for article: John E. Chubb and Terry M. Moe (1988), 'Politics, Markets, and the Organization of Schools', *American Political Science Review*, **82** (4), December, 1065–87.

Blackwell Publishers Ltd for articles: Howard Glennerster (1991), 'Quasi-Markets For Education?', *Economic Journal*, **101** (408), September, 1268–76; Tony Edwards and Geoff Whitty (1992), 'Parental Choice and Educational Reform in Britain and the United States', *British Journal of Educational Studies*, **XXXX** (2), May, 101–17; John Fitz, David Halpin and Sally Power (1994), 'Implementation Research and Education Policy: Practice and Prospects', *British Journal of Educational Studies*, **XXXXII** (1), March, 53–69; Gary McCulloch (1997), 'Privatising the Past? History and Education Policy in the 1990s', *British Journal of Educational Studies*, **45** (1), March, 69–82.

Nicholas C. Burbules and Thomas A. Callister, Jr. for their own article: (1999), 'A Post-Technocratic Policy Perspective on New Information and Communication Technologies for Education', 1–10.

Caddo Gap Press for article: Peter L. McLaren (1997), 'Unthinking Whiteness, Rethinking Democracy: Or Farewell to the Blonde Beast; Towards a Revolutionary Multiculturalism', *Educational Foundations*, Spring, 5–39.

Carfax Publishing Ltd for articles: A.H. Halsey (1993), 'Trends in Access and Equity in Higher Education: Britain in International Perspective', *Oxford Review of Education*, **19** (2), 129–40; Phillip W. Jones (1997), 'Review Article: On World Bank Education Financing – World Bank (1995) *Policies and Strategies for Education: A World Bank Review* (Washington DC, World Bank)', *Comparative Education*, **33** (1), March, 117–29; Sandra Taylor (1997), 'Critical Policy Analysis: Exploring Contexts, Texts and Consequences', *Discourse: Studies in the Cultural Politics of Education*, **18** (1), April, 23–35; Simon Marginson (1997), 'Subjects and Subjugation: The Economics of Education as Power-Knowledge', *Discourse: Studies in* *the Cultural Politics of Education,* **18** (2), August, 215–27; Hilary Janks (1997), 'Critical Discourse Analysis as a Research Tool', *Discourse: Studies in the Cultural Politics of Education,* **18** (3), December, 329–42.

Eve Coxon for her own article: (1999), 'The Politics of "Modernisation": Education Policy-Making at the Periphery', 1–21.

Dunmore Press for excerpt: Graham Hingangaroa Smith and Linda Tuhiwai Smith (1996), 'New Mythologies in Maori Education', in Paul Spoonley, David Pearson and Cluny Macpherson (eds), *Nga Patai: Racism and Ethnic Relations in Aotearoa/New Zealand,* Chapter 12, 217–34, 289–90.

Educational Theory and the Board of Trustees of the University of Illinois at Urbana-Champaign for article: Colin Lankshear (1998), 'Meanings of Literacy in Contemporary Educational Reform Proposals', *Educational Theory,* **48** (3), Summer, 351–72.

Falmer Press (Taylor and Francis Group) for excerpts: Michael Peters and James Marshall (1996), 'Educational Policy Analysis and the Politics of Interpretation', in *Individualism and Community: Education and Social Policy in the Postmodern Condition,* Chapter 8, 137–52 and references; Susan L. Robertson (1996), 'Teachers' Work, Restructuring and Postfordism: Constructing the New "Professionalism"', in Ivor F. Goodson and Andy Hargreaves (eds), *Teachers' Professional Lives,* Chapter 2, 28–55.

Harvard Educational Review for articles: R.W. Connell (1994), 'Poverty and Education', *Harvard Educational Review,* **64** (2), Summer, 125–49; Amy Stuart Wells and Irene Serna (1996), 'The Politics of Culture: Understanding Local Political Resistance to Detracking in Racially Mixed Schools', *Harvard Educational Review,* **66** (1), Spring, 93–118.

International Labour Review for article: Martin Carnoy (1995), 'Structural Adjustment and the Changing Face of Education', *International Labour Review,* 134 (6), 653–73.

Allan Luke, Bob Lingard, Bill Green and Barbara Comber for their own article: (1999), 'The Abuses of Literacy: Educational Policy and the Construction of Crisis', 1–25.

Macmillan Education Australia for excerpt: David Hogan (1997), 'The Social Economy of Parent Choice and the Contract State', in Glyn Davis, Barbara Sullivan and Anna Yeatman (eds), *The New Contractualism?,* Chapter 9, 119–36 and references.

Open University Press for excerpt: Stephen J. Ball (1994), 'What is Policy? Texts, Trajectories and Toolboxes', in *Education Reform: A Critical and Post-Structural Approach,* Chapter 2, 14–27 and references.

Oxford University Press for excerpt: Roger Dale (1997), 'The State and the Governance of Education: An Analysis of the Restructuring of the State–Education Relationship', in A.H. Halsey, Hugh Lauder, Phillip Brown and Amy Stuart Wells (eds), *Education: Culture, Economy, and Society,* Chapter 17, 273–82.

Teachers College Record for articles: John U. Ogbu (1994), 'Racial Stratification and Education in the United States: Why Inequality Persists', *Teachers College Record*, **96** (2), Winter, 264–98; Michael W. Apple (1993), 'The Politics of Official Knowledge: Does a National Curriculum Make Sense?', *Teachers College Record*, **95** (2), Winter, 222–41.

Triangle Journals Ltd for article: Bob Lingard and Barbara Garrick (1997), 'Producing and Practising Social Justice Policy in Education: A Policy Trajectory Study from Queensland, Australia', *International Studies in Sociology of Education*, **7** (2), 157–79.

Journal of Advanced Composition, University of South Florida for article: Henry A. Giroux (1997), 'Where Have All the Public Intellectuals Gone? Racial Politics, Pedagogy, and Disposable Youth', *Journal of Advanced Composition*, **17** (2), 191–205.

Taylor and Francis Ltd for articles: John A. Codd (1988), 'The Construction and Deconstruction of Educational Policy Documents', *Journal of Education Policy*, **3** (3), 235–47; Jenny Ozga (1990), 'Policy Research and Policy Theory: A Comment on Fitz and Halpin', *Journal of Education Policy*, **5** (4), October–December, 359–62; Jane Kenway with Chris Bigum and Lindsay Fitzclarence (1993), 'Marketing Education in the Postmodern Age', *Journal of Education Policy*, **8** (2), 105–22; Patrick Fitzsimons and Michael Peters (1994), 'Human Capital Theory and the Industry Training Strategy in New Zealand', *Journal of Education Policy*, **9** (3), 245–66; Phillip Brown and Hugh Lauder (1996), 'Education, Globalization and Economic Development', *Journal of Education Policy*, **11** (1), 1–25; Thomas S. Popkewitz (1996), 'Rethinking Decentralization and State/Civil Society Distinctions: The State as a Problematic of Governing', *Journal of Education Policy*, **11** (1), 27–51; Mark Olssen (1996), 'In Defence of the Welfare State and Publicly Provided Education: A New Zealand Perspective', *Journal of Education Policy*, **11** (3), 337–62.

University of Wisconsin Press for article: Mark Blaug (1989), 'Review of *Economics of Education: Research and Studies* Edited by George Psacharopoulos. Oxford: Pergamon Press. 1987. 482 pp.', *Journal of Human Resources*, **XXIV** (2), Spring, 331–5.

Every effort has been made to trace all the copyright holders but if any have been inadvertently overlooked the publishers will be pleased to make the necessary arrangement at the first opportunity.

In addition the publishers wish to thank the Library of the Cheltenham and Gloucester College of Higher Education, the Library of the London School of Economics and Political Science and the Marshall Library of Economics, Cambridge University for their assistance in obtaining these articles.

Preface

We were delighted to be invited by Guy Peters, after he read our *Individualism and Community: Education and Social Policy in the Postmodern Condition* (Falmer Press, 1996), to edit a collection on education policy for the Edward Elgar series on Comparative Public Policy.

As there must always be a gap between the selection of material and its publication in print, we not only provide a summary of policy studies in education in the first chapter, including a brief history of the state of the 'art', but also a brief introduction to the papers in this collection. In our chapter (Chapter 6) we return to works published before the decade 1986–96 to summarize some of the more recent moves in policy. Most of the papers also come from this period. There are exceptions, as some papers (Chapters 25, 36 and 37) have been specially commissioned and some were written and published after 1996. We are grateful to the authors of those papers which were written specially for the collection. The introduction to papers and the commissioned chapters is designed to illustrate the rapid changes that are taking place in educational policy at the end of this millennium.

As always there are a number of people to thank and acknowledge. We would like to thank Guy Peters for his editorial guidance and Nicky Mills at Edward Elgar for her forbearance in the time it took us to get this collection together. We would like to thank all the contributors. Finally, we would like to acknowledge our education policy students at the University of Auckland who, over the years, have provided us with the ideal conditions to 'test' our 'selections', our rationales and our policy approaches.

James Marshall
Michael Peters

The University of Auckland
May 1999

Studies in educational policy at the end of the millennium

James Marshall and Michael Peters

Introduction

If the world's economy has been adjusted in the 1990s to harness the power of rapidly changing technologies, it is also the case that education systems and knowledge, including its transmission, have undergone considerable changes as a result of major changes in educational policy. In the last decade education policy has been directed increasingly towards ensuring that states and economies are able to respond instantly and efficiently to changes in technologies and in the associated realms of knowledge production and national innovation systems. A state remains 'strong' thereby because of its capacities or skills in those mercurial fields, and in the skills which its 'bureaucrats' and professionals possess in maintaining and legitimating the activities and practices – the policies – of that state in obtaining and maintaining efficiency. Put bluntly, science and law are legitimated on the basis of efficiency, and efficiency, in turn, is legitimated on the basis of science and law. This is of course self-legitimating (Lyotard, 1984), if not viciously circular.

And yet the state also remains strong when it has the narrative skill and spin-doctoring to ensure that its policies are accepted as 'truths'. Arguably it will only remain strong if it can ensure that its policy meta-narratives are accepted as true. On a simplistic (and positivistic) view of truth as correspondence to reality, then a state will remain strong when its policies 'correspond' to reality (whatever that is). So, if the state, or its authorities, or its ministries, can change 'reality' to correspond to its policies, then the circle is closed. The state legitimates its 'true' policies because they now correspond to reality. Here the modern notions of policy analysts in government ministries and departments and the spin-doctors of leading politicians become very important, for they possess resources, narrative authority and media power to formulate and articulate the truths of government.

If new policies have explicit economic thrusts – the managerial thrust is also essentially economic because of its over-riding concerns with efficiency – it would be a mistake to see them merely as extensions of the earlier applications of economic theory to education in the 1950s and 1960s. Earlier the emphasis was on grand-scale economic theory, so that investment in education was seen as a part of a larger-scale economic model which was applied to the whole economy, and in which education was but a part of the overall investment. There was an overall theoretical, practical and politico-economic view of the economy which was holistic, and which not only provided a model for 'how' to proceed in the management of business, but also provided the conditions for the application of an economic model. Associated with this approach was an emphasis on a scientific or an empirical–analytical method of analysis, which arguably remains dominant in Western analyses of educational policy. But serious questions need to be raised about the scientific credentials of economics (see section II).

However, the restructuring of state education systems in many Western countries during the last two decades has involved a significant shift towards a 'new managerialism', which has drawn theoretically, on the one hand, on new institutional economics, most notably on public choice theory, agency theory and transaction cost analysis, and, on the other hand, on the model of corporate managerialism and private sector management styles. When we look more closely at these associated theories we can note a shift from a broad notion of an investment in education to a similarly broad notion of investment in human capital, and a new view about these investments, namely that they have to be managed if not governed (see section III). Perhaps the shift here is between two versions of education as an investment in human capital: a liberal, developmental, modernizing view based upon appropriate state investment, as opposed to a neo-liberal, modernizing view based upon 'forced' private investment where the education consumer must invest in him- or herself, especially at the tertiary level.

In this introductory chapter we will deal with some of these issues under four headings: first we will put forward a brief overview of educational policy analysis; second, we will raise questions concerning methodological issues in policy studies; third, we will examine educational policy in this new era of economic managerialism; and, finally, we will provide a brief overview to the papers in the collection and how they fit into the schema of categorization that we have imposed upon the selected articles.

I Educational Policy: A Brief Overview

The Demise of Localism

At one time education policy was conceived, articulated and rested in the local domestic, and perhaps obscure, domain of nation states or, within such entities, in particular ethnic/cultural groups. As Heyneman (1990: 467) observes:

> In the 1960s, it was popular to believe that education was a local endeavour: that it was heavily influenced by local culture and by local political objectives. To a large extent this was correct. But since the 1960s we have learned that there are also universalistic issues and dilemmas in the field of education, characteristics which transcend country categories.

These issues are said by Heyneman to be 'genuinely international issues', as of much concern in OECD countries as in developing countries. Arguably, the issues which he lists do not transcend national, ethnic or cultural boundaries. If they do so this may only be because these 'universalistic' issues had to be formulated in accordance with certain rules, and they had to be transmitted and learned in a certain technocratic and universalistic manner so as to make those issues universalistic, and to make universalistic judgements possible. In other words there are universalistic 'definitions', which reside in a context of universalism and which are assumed both to be meaningful and to be applicable universally. Whether they are the definitions of significant and important educational issues for particular local endeavours is, of course, another matter.

What is necessary to consider educational issues as universalistic is a discourse which permits the possibility of the truth and falsity of universalistic statements either surrounding these issues or formulated within such issues. As argued above, this requires either explicit or implicit definitions of key concepts – 'the empowered person', 'the autonomous person', 'the free chooser', 'the consumer' or 'customer' and so on, or it supposes an acceptance of an apparently neutral language, or a *lingua franca*, in which such concepts are sufficiently ill-defined to permit an 'easy' reading and an 'understanding', or they are assumed to have a common-sense meaning. Here the neo-liberal notions of 'freedom', 'choice' and 'devolution' are clear examples. In fact these are all highly contested concepts and contestable concepts (on 'autonomy' and 'choice', see Marshall, 1996; Peters and Marshall, 1996), and do not carry the certainty or authority of accepted and universalistic meaning, as much of the educational reform literature seems to assume.

Furthermore, it is not at all obvious that definitions of these concepts (or is it words?), or that definitions of other major issues such as selection, subject matter, quality, equity and the status of teachers, can be universalized beyond 'local' and particular social, cultural and ethnic contexts. They can be extended only when assumptions about universalizing the definitions involved are made in advance. This is what, we suggest, must always be the case. But that is not the immediate concern here so much as the extent to which education is no longer conceived as particular, if not idiosyncratic, to a domestic domain, for it has now been turned into a strategic factor in the efficiency of national economic policies. No doubt the identification of universalistic transnational characteristics of education and the intensification of cross-national research, albeit in the search for 'truth', for comparative knowledge and understanding, have provided the data and the groundwork, if not fostered a general worldwide trend of the subsumption of educational systems under the general demand for the efficiency of social systems or states. Jean-François Lyotard (1984) talks here of 'performativity', or the subsumption of education to the efficient functioning of the social system. According to Lyotard, education is no longer concerned with the pursuit of ideals such as that of personal autonomy, emancipation or leadership by an educated ideal, but instead with the means, techniques or skills that both contribute to the efficient operation of the state in the world market and contribute to the maintenance of an internal cohesion and legitimation of the state (see Peters, 1995). However, this requires individuals of a certain kind – not Kantian autonomous persons but, perhaps, Foucault's (1979a, b) normalised and governable individuals. It also requires particular roles for individuals and the state, and a particular relationship between the state and individuals, which ensures not only the security and economic well-being and power of the state, but also the welfare and well-being of the population. But what kind of relationship might that be?

Changes in Policy

Governments, wresting with economic and social problems and difficulties and the general well-being of populations, advance policies and programmes which, if they are to be accepted and implemented by bureaucrats, must be seen by the populace in question as involving appropriate attempts to address their problems, issues and well-being. They must be seen in some sense as being true. But governments can no longer intervene forcefully in the lives of individuals (except perhaps in times of war). If they are to intervene it must instead be indirectly, by such processes as guidance, persuasion or subtle manipulation, if their truths are to be accepted and endorsed. Increasingly, governments have abandoned threats, constraints and bribes – sticks and carrots – in attempts to achieve their socio-political ends through the 'truths' which they articulate. As Rose (1989: 10) says, 'It [government] achieves its effects not through the threat of violence and constraint, but by way of the persuasion inherent in its truths, the anxieties stimulated by its norms, and the attraction exercised by the images of life and self it offers (our enclosure).' Such truths are to be found in policies. Policy, conceived as how the truths of government are formulated and articulated and what they are articulated upon, has become very important for governments. Policy analysis, in turn, involves itself with judgements or evaluations of 'the nature, causes and effects of alternative public policies' (Nagel, 1980: 391) or of existing or proposed policies. It is therefore concerned with evaluating claims to truth. The relationship between policy and policy analysis has been expressed thus: 'policy studies, and the analysis associated with them, aim to empower humans to undertake more effective collective action to solve or reduce significant policy problems. Toward this end, policy analysis places special emphasis on the use of reason and evidence to choose the best policy' (Boyd and Plank, 1995: 1835). Here policy analysis is seen as an integral part of formulating, articulating and implementing policy, and not merely as a way of analysing and understanding policy, post fact so to say. But it is also a typical liberal view of the role of the social sciences as being liberating or as improving the human condition. Several questions need to be raised about this kind of account. In relation to the above account the following questions, at least, can be raised.

First, in this analysis of significant social problems, what counts as *the* policy problem? Whose definition applies? And what counts as evidence, reason and truth? If government is to persuade us of the importance of its 'truths', what are the criteria for truth to which appeal is made? What does it mean to empower human beings? Empowerment has a particular rhetorical ring to it, recalling critical theorists, and, in education in particular, the writings of Paulo Friere and Henry Giroux. Further, who is empowered: is it individuals or groups? What counts as effective action: is it the outcome of the praxis of people immersed in a form of critical literacy, or is it the 'catallaxy' caused by the removal of constraints for utility maximizers to exercise unlimited free choice in the free market? And what is collective action: is it the aggregates of individual actions of members of a group, or something 'done' by the group as a group or coherent whole?

If different answers can be given to these questions does that imply a different view of the best policy? Such issues must be raised and discussed in any introduction to a collection on educational policy for, at least, education is itself concerned with the development of individuals, the development of rationality, and the discovery and transmission of truth. In other words, education is especially under the spotlight of policy appraisal, for educational policy must itself be subject to the same criteria as in education, as to what counts as evidence, reason and truth, and what counts as acceptable pedagogical practices.

Globalization

We can note in the last two decades a move away from small-scale communities towards a notion of a global village. This involves a move towards a technical and elitist cultural base which, if it is universalistic, reeks of an imposed cultural imperialism driven by market forces.

Tied to neither time nor place this cultural base, while drawing upon heterogeneous cultures, so anaesthetizes them that we are presented with standardized context-free packaged commodities (Peters and Lankshear, 1996). According to Smith (1990: 176), a globalized culture:

> would operate at several levels simultaneously: as a cornucopia of standardised commodities, as a patchwork of denationalised ethnic or folk motifs, as a series of generalised 'human values and interests', as a uniform 'scientific' discourse of meaning, and finally as the interdependent system of communications which forms the material base for all other components and levels.

We have already noted the move towards a universalistic approach towards educational issues, problems and policies, and the diminished local domestic concerns and inputs to educational policy. In so far as educational policy becomes universalistic, in so far as its discourse is universal and 'scientistic', and in so far as it is underpinned by both a universalistic telecommunications system and a uniform *lingua franca* of, say, Microsoft, then globalization of education may not be far away, as standardized context-free packages are delivered in the name of education.

But education is also concerned with the development or finding of identity. It is not just that involvement with electronic writing will affect our notions of identity (Marshall, 1996), but also that the young are now faced with growing up in a globalized market of commodities. Identity in part will consist in how they individually position themselves as consumers in this world market of Burger King or the Ritz, Beethoven or Elton John, Just Jeans or Gucci, silk or corduroy, and ... No longer will the role of home, the local and the domestic, be so powerful in the constitution of identity as we enter what has been described as a 'McDonaldization' of culture (Ritzer, 1993).

One is reminded here of the dangers hinted at so much earlier by Max Weber and his metaphor of the iron cage. But is the iron cage upon us, a *fait accompli*, or is it but a danger, something that may come to pass? Whether cultural studies, and poststructuralism and postmodernism, with their emphases on diversity, their incredulity towards meta-narratives and their rejections of universal and totalistic accounts of rationality, can avert the worst excesses of globalization, remains to be seen.

II Methodological Issues

Policy Analysis

As a field of enquiry policy analysis has proved itself receptive to the various methodological developments which have characterized the social sciences as a whole since the early 1970s. Policy analysis involves evaluation and must share certain features with general theories of evaluation. In education, the major theoretical shift in evaluation theory was from a scientific or macro theory to a humanistic account, or micro theory, approach. Merely to categorize educational policy as moving from a science to an art or craft, because of concern over the effectiveness of macro policies and a consequent shift to micro policies (as in Boyd and Plank, 1995), may be to see the history of educational policy analysis as merely being similar to accounts of evaluation in education. In evaluation theory the application of grand theory was seen as too broad and too general to produce particular solutions to particular problems. Instead humanistic case study approaches to evaluation concentrated on the local and particular, proposing workable solutions to problems within 'localized' constraints. This view of policy studies as being either scientific or art, or as being of macro or micro form, is limited, because in part it ignores the contributions to policy studies of theoretical moves in the social sciences. Furthermore, it tends to reduce discussion to issues of theoretical and experimental methodologies, thereby excluding discussions of such things as the policy context and the ends and interests which may be served by various components of a policy.

We will touch briefly upon these issues. It is possible to identify at least three earlier approaches in policy studies which paralleled 'developments' in the social sciences. There was an earlier scientistic or positivistic phase where, if policy questions were seen as scientific, the policies and analyses were phrased in predominantly technical or administrative terms. This was to be superseded by humanistic approaches, first by hermeneutics and then by critical modes of analysis (Callaghan and Jennings, 1985). Some discussion of these approaches is needed.

Scientism and its Traditional Critics

In this section we outline the more traditional criticisms of scientistic approaches to policy. We note the standard philosophical criticisms of positivistic science, which do not necessarily involve an abandonment of a scientific approach to policy, before turning to hermeneutics and critical theory.

First there are a number of dubious and questionable philosophical assumptions that underlie and permeate the scientistic approach. These are normally referred to as 'positivistic', and include the notion of an objective truth; that scientists discover truth as spectators of a world which is essentially a given; the methodological unity of the sciences; reductionism; the fact/value distinction; and the observation/theory distinction.

These assumptions have been subject to intense intellectual criticism since World War II, from which time the social sciences began to blossom. (There can be little doubt that knowledge acquired in World War II was a major contributor to this.) For example, Willard Quine (1961) attacked fundamental philosophical distinctions underlying empiricism; Wilfred Sellars (1963) the myth of the given; Norman Hanson (1958) and Karl Popper (1959) the theory/observation (or Kerry fact) distinction; Popper (1959, 1963) the notion that scientists discovered truth; Thomas Kuhn (1962), in a work tremendously influential in both science and the social sciences (contrary to Kuhn's objections to the extension of his ideas to the latter), argued that the important considerations which affected science were sociological/historical in nature, thereby casting serious doubt upon the fact/value distinction in science and the notion of the epistemic authority of science; John Dewey (as early as 1916), and more recently R.F. Holland (1980), attacked the spectator theory of knowledge and the poverty-stricken notion of pedagogy which must accompany it; and finally, recent work throughout the philosophy of science discredits the notion that there is something which can be called the 'scientific method'.

Jürgen Habermas (1971) provided one of the strongest attacks on positivist epistemology. Indeed, it was Habermas who coined the term 'scientism', which he defines as 'science's belief in itself: that is, the conviction that we should no longer understand science as just one form of possible knowledge, but rather must identify knowledge with science' (1971: 4). Habermas' (1971) central argument against positivism is that it takes one form of knowledge – that is, the empirical–analytical – and treats it as the universally valid measure for all knowledge, and even for rationality itself. The positivist interpretation of science presents a technical or instrumental rationality behind a facade of value-freedom in a way that renders it incapable of justifying its own interests.

Thomas McCarthy (1978: 6) summarizes Habermas' position thus:

> The limitation of reason, at the level of theory to the disinterested employment of the scientific method, and, at the level of practice, to the predictive and technological application of the empirical knowledge that results, renders positivist philosophy incapable of justifying its own interest. If all values are subjective, if practical orientation in life is ultimately beyond rational justification, then the positivist commitment to science and technology and its opposition to dogmatism and ideology is itself subjective and rationally unjustifiable (that is, dogmatic). If, on the other hand, the interest in enlightenment is itself rational then reason harbors a practical interest and cannot be exhaustively defined in terms of science and technology.

As Martin Heidegger (1977) has argued, any social theory or research based on a technical or instrumental interest will be inherently manipulative, if not destructive of human beings. For Heidegger, even science distorts nature, as the scientist is him- or herself a human construction and thus will represent reality to him- or herself, qua scientist, in a particular way. Technology, with its inveterate thrust to 'control and conquer' whatever it confronts, to seize it for its own use, is even more manipulative.

Social theory modelled on the positivist account of science is, of course, open to the same criticisms. Of interest here also are the criticisms of Popper's extension of his ideas on science to the area of the social sciences at a sociological conference at Tübingen in 1961 (Popper, 1976). Indeed Popper, who had vigorously attacked logical positivism, was himself to be classified as having positivist tendencies in a vigorous debate between himself and Theodor Adorno at that conference (Adorno *et al.*, 1976).

It is not difficult to see how Habermas' basic epistemological criticism can be applied in the area of the social sciences, in relation to the fundamental fact/value distinction. Habermas, and his colleague Karl-Otto Apel (1980), provide arguments for the notion that dialogue is a fundamental presupposition for all monological systems of discourse. They both point out that scientists have to be able to understand one another, not only in order to reach agreement but also in order to disagree and continue discussions in some orderly manner. Apel (1980) in particular, has gone to great lengths to discredit 'methodological solipsism'. Buttressed with Wittgensteinian arguments from philosophy of language and C.S. Peirce's notion of community, he shows the logical absurdity inherent in the idea that one person alone could, even in principle, practise science, or indeed any intellectual discipline.

Experimental methodology was a major topic of discussion in education with critics, for example in evaluation (e.g. Weiss, 1972), emphasizing that the complexity of reality was not caught by the idealization and abstraction of complex outcomes into 'simple' quantified notions which can be tested. Full justice was not done to other factors. In the humanistic model the scientist experiment, especially in its traditional form (Fairweather, 1980), is not acceptable, objecting to the manipulation of people in treatment and control groups. From the humanistic position, if people are assigned to groups, that is because the policy and treatments are already operating and are not introduced by the evaluator in the call of research. The focus is the total complex scene (Parlett and Hamilton, 1978), where, in evaluation, case studies describe this complexity through the eyes of evaluators, developers, participants and clients. Given these assumptions, few preconceptions can be made about methodology.

Some proponents of this approach reject objectivity in the scientistic sense outlined, believing that scientific approaches to rationality do not give insight into the description and explanation of programmes designed by human beings for human beings as participants. In Habermasian terms, the presuppositions for these descriptions and explanations must take account of the practical interests of all participants, and if reason is ultimately bound up with those interests, the fact/value distinction is called into question, as is also the scientistic notion of objectivity.

This of course raises the general issue of how human behaviour is to be described and understood, for many believe that human behaviour is best known and understood without scientific concepts and methodology. Here one of the most outspoken critics was Ludwig Wittgenstein (1953), who, drawing upon such distinctions as those between reasons and causes, agency and determinism, and ordinary and scientific languages, argued that notions such as pain are properly understood by our knowledge of how the concept of pain and statements such as, 'I am in pain' and 'He is in pain' operate in our ordinary language. Put another way, psychological concepts such as pain, thinking and reading do not refer to inner mental states which can be described and theorized by such people as psychologists in order to *understand* the concept of pain. There may be such inner mental states but that is irrelevant. Human behaviour, including language use, is rule-following according to Wittgenstein; it reveals a form of life and it is not caused.

Perhaps the most well-known Wittgensteinian critique of the social sciences is that of Peter Winch. His *The Idea of a Social Science* (1958) is highly critical of traditional scientific understandings of human action given by anthropologists and sociologists. His Wittgensteinian central claim is that to understand a language is to understand a form of life. In sociology Max Weber talked of understanding as *verstehen*, and Simon (1945), Gouldner (1954), Davis (1969), Bull (1980) and Benson (1983) provide early examples of the use of rule-following in social policy.

Poststructuralist Critiques

According to Mark Poster (1989) the term 'poststructuralism' was coined by North American academics to catch or capture the work of a quite diverse group of French intellectuals, including Jean Baudrillard, Gilles Deleuze, Jacques Derrida, Michel Foucault and Jean-François Lyotard. We use the term here because, thus defined, it implies no general characteristics and thereby avoids further confrontation or assimilation with the even more difficult term 'postmodernism'. It is, however, possible in relation to educational policy to identify some common themes (Lyotard, 1984; see further, Peters and Marshall, 1996).

First, there is the rise of new social movements (Habermas, 1982), which cannot be characterized as being dependent upon some overlying notion of liberation and/or empowerment, or as being reducible to some notion such as the social relations of production. Not only are these rejected but also those social and political theories in which individualism is prominent, if not paramount. What is common to these new movements is a reaction against individualism, with its accompanying modes of oppression, and a search for new forms of collectivity – as evidenced, for example, in the French students' and workers' revolutions of 1968. Habermas (1981) argues that these conflicts against oppression have arisen not so much in traditional areas of material production and reproduction, but in the areas of the cultural, of socialization and of social integration. These are essentially attempts to resist the penetration of the life worlds of people – here the notions of universal educational issues and the practices of the OECD and World Bank (with its 'fish hook' loans) in a thrust towards globalization must be seriously questioned. One outcome of this critique in educational policy would be a return of its base to a local terrain.

Second, there have been a number of critiques of the notion of reason being absolute and universal. Instead of a totality of reason we have, according to the poststructuralists, a plurality of reasons. Lyotard was to call for 'a war against totality' and Foucault was to refer to Sartre sarcastically, as the last great philosopher of the 18th century, who believed in a totalizing universal world view of reason. No doubt this is a Nietzschean-inspired philosophy (Deleuze, 1962), but it does question the themes of universal questions and universal solutions, and would also require a return of educational policy to a particular cultural base.

The third strand of poststructuralism which we will consider is that of the decentring of the subject. Here the French poststructuralists are in agreement with Habermas that the philosophy of consciousness – or subject-centred reason, or the metaphysics of self-presence – is exhausted, if not dead. By this is meant a rejection of the Cartesian individual subject as the endower of meaning and as the basis of epistemological certainty. This has led for these philosophers to a bankruptcy of liberal notions of freedom and emancipation. In particular, this attack on the subject is also an attack upon certain Cartesian and empirically based accounts of epistemology. For example, is the individualistic autonomous chooser of neoliberal economic theories a given – an actual facet of human experience – or is he or she a prescription of how we ought to be? Habermas, and Dewey before him, especially in educational philosophy and theory (Dewey, 1916), attempted to counter such ontological, epistemological and ethical notions of the individual subject. The notion of the individual chooser as the basis of both economic theory and new public management in education is, then, heavily value-laden (Marshall, 1996).

Finally, we can note the emergence of very strong objections by cultural and ethnic groups to being controlled and/or oppressed by others. There have been the long-term struggles by colonials against 'mother' states (e.g. the USA, India and South Africa), the oppression of indigenous peoples against over-riding immigration from former colonial powers (e.g. the USA, South Africa, New Zealand and Australia – none of these struggles have been similar), the breakups of power blocks (e.g. Habsburg, the Commonwealth, the USSR and Yugoslavia), and the struggles within ethnic or culturally homogeneous communities for recognition or release from oppression (women, gays, children, etc.). These struggles can be termed the 'politics of difference', but the politics involves the struggle for the recognition and acceptance of difference as being a positive aspect of human affairs and not something to be over-ridden, constrained or suppressed. While Derrida is both Jewish and Algerian, many of the poststructuralists were involved in supporting and promoting the importance of the recognition of difference and the importance of both detecting difference (a cognitive task) and respecting difference (an ethical requirement). Poststructuralism, therefore, provides a fertile ground for a critique of universalistic assumptions and approaches to educational policy. Its promise for educational policy has yet to be fully understood or developed.

Economics and Science

Serious questions need to be raised about the scientific status of economics. By this we mean questions about economics which involve a view of science which is not scientistic or positivist in the senses outlined above, but which make claims to being rational. (Thus we will not consider here the views on science of Thomas Kuhn and Paul Feyerabend.) We will start from the view of science propounded by Popper in his *Logic of Scientific Discovery* (1959) because: (a) Popper attacked logical positivism; (b) he discussed economics in his voluminous works; and (c) his work was taken up by economists (De Marchi, 1988: 4), including, most notably, by his friend and colleague Friedrich von Hayek. We can deal only briefly with these issues here (see further the edited collection on Popper and economics, De Marchi, 1988).

The essence of Popper's view is his account of falsification. Scientists do not 'discover' truths (particularly not by induction) and indeed cannot establish truth in science but, instead, they can falsify hypotheses and accepted truths. Science progresses, then, by vigorous, but not naïve, attempts to falsify. It is an asymmmetry that counterpoises the logic of falsifiability (requiring only one counterclaim) against the logic of verification (which assumes a universe that is never closed). But Popper also uses this notion of falsification to distinguish between theories which are scientific and those which are non-scientific. Those theories which cannot in principle be falsifiable are not, according to Popper, scientific. It is important here to note that Popper's criteria are epistemological, that is, concerned with truth. And it is the truths of policies which is of major concern here.

Popper himself backed away from applying strict demands for falsification to economics. That was because of a lack of numerical constants in the economic environment. In other words, there are central elements in economics not open to quantification, which place severe constraints upon predictions and testing, and therefore call into question the scientific status of economics and the notion of truth in economics. This can be put more strongly: 'Economics is not value free. That means that the choices we make about theories and policies in economics invariably reflect our preferred notions of how the world is constituted ... [this leaves] ... the basic theories themselves immune to test results' (De Marchi, 1988: ix).

Another major rationalist approach in philosophy of science is that of Imre Lakatos (1976), Popper's follower. Lakatos argued that scientific theories possess both a hard core of primary or major hypotheses, and a surrounding belt or soft core of secondary or auxiliary hypotheses, which can be amended or abandoned without a need to reject the main hard core of the theory. Testing and falsification are to be directed at the soft core and not at the hard core, which remains more or less inviolate. Thereby the theory can be retained. The notion of an inviolate hard core from which testing is deflected may have some appeal to economics, especially if the hard core is to contain the preferred and value-laden assumptions which seem to be essential to economic theories. But where there are normative assumptions in the hard core – about the way the world should be – that may be to place in question the alleged scientific status of economics. But suppose one believed that both science and economics are value-laden: what then?

McCloskey (1986, 1994) argues that both science and economics involve the use of metaphor: 'People who scrutinize the hard facts about things in science come to the conclusion that the facts are constructed by artful words ... In economic science the very statistics are grounded in values, though no less scientific on that account' (McCloskey, 1994: 60). McCloskey goes on to argue that economics as a science uses the whole 'rhetorical tetrad – the facts, logics, metaphors, and stories necessary for completed human reasoning' (McCloskey, 1994: 61).

While the conclusion is that both economics and the 'hard' sciences are both value-laden and use metaphor, the point here is that economics is not just hard logic and facts. Instead, both science and economics are based upon values and use metaphor to persuade or convince rational people:

> The idea that fact and logic are by themselves enough for science puts one in mind of the ... expression, 'a few bricks short of a load'. The program over the past fifty years of narrowing down our arguments in the name of rationality was a few bricks short of a load. The experiment in getting along with fewer than all the resources of human reasoning was worth trying and had plenty of good results. To admit now that metaphor and story matter also in human reasoning does not entail becoming less rational and less reasonable. On the contrary, as I have said, it entails becoming more rational and more reasonable, because it brings more of what persuades serious people under the scrutiny of reason. (McCloskey, 1994: 63–4)

To recognize values and metaphors in economics is also to see it as a story or narrative, and not value-free. As a value-laden story or narrative, however, it must compete with other value-laden stories and narratives, as it has no epistemologically privileged position.

As there is much talk of a return to Keynesian economic theory in Northern European politics (e.g. see *The Guardian Weekly*, October/November 1998), perhaps Keynes should have the last comment here: 'Economics is a science of thinking in terms of models joined to the art of choosing models which are relevant to the contemporary world' (Keynes, 1971: 295). Yet the positivistic analytical–empirical model is still important, and occurs in the major shifts which have occurred in policy towards 'new managerialism'.

III New Managerialism and Governmentality

The Restructuring of Educational Systems

In the Western world we are witnessing a restructuring of state education systems away from an emphasis on administration and policy – their formulation and articulation – to an emphasis on management. Arguably, this also represents a major shift to a particular kind of policy framework. This new policy framework can be called the 'new managerialism'. It has drawn theoretically, on the one hand, on the model of corporate managerialism and private sector management styles, and, on the other hand, on public choice theory and new institutional economics, most notably agency theory and transaction cost analysis. A specific constellation of these theories is sometimes called 'new public management', which has been very influential in the United Kingdom, Australia, Canada and New Zealand (Peters, Marshall and Fitzsimons, 1999 forthcoming). These theories and models have been used both as the legitimating basis and instrumental means for redesigning state educational bureaucracies, educational institutions and also, albeit surreptitiously, the public policy process itself.

In the cries of choice and decentralization, there has been a major decentralization of management control from the centre (government departments and ministries) to individual institutions. This has been legitimated by a new type of contractualism – often referred to as the doctrine of 'self-management' – and has been coupled with new accountability and funding structures. At the same time there has been a disaggregation of large state bureaucracies into (more or less) autonomous agencies, a clarification of organizational objectives, and a separation of policy advice and policy implementation functions. Thus in education in New Zealand the new Ministry of Education provides policy advice to the Minister, and institutions are left with the problems of implementation and such things as the purchasing of advice and resources from contestable privatized agencies. There has also been a shift from input controls to quantifiable output measures and performance targets, along with an emphasis on short-term performance contracts, especially for chief executive officers and senior managers. In the interests of so-called productive efficiency and choice, the provision of educational services has been made contestable, and, in the interests of so-called allocative efficiency, state education has been marketized and substantially privatized.

The Central Tenets of New Managerialism

James Buchanan's and Gordon Tullock's (1965) public choice theory applies the methods of economics to the study of political and administrative behaviour. Two major elements which are identified are the catallactics approach to economics (or catallaxy, as Hayek terms it) and the classical *homo economicus* postulate concerning individual behaviour. 'Catallactics' is the study of institutions of exchange and rests upon the principle of spontaneous order. It is most thoroughly developed in the work of Hayek, where order in society involves a spontaneous formation and a tendency to equilibrium, given by the economic theory of market exchanges. In Hayek's account we should note also:

- the 'invisible hand' thesis that social institutions arise as a result of human action but not from human design;
- the thesis of the primacy of tacit or practical knowledge – a thesis which maintains that knowledge of the social world is embodied in practices and skills and only secondarily in theories.

Interventionist politics is to be abandoned. Instead, if reform in economic policy is desired, then we should look to the rules through which economic policy decisions are made; that is, look to the constitution itself. Thus, 'to improve politics it is only necessary to improve or reform the rules, the framework within which the game is played ... A game is described by its rules, and a better game is produced only by changing the rules' (Buchanan, 1986: 22).

The main innovation of Buchanan and the public choice school is to apply Hayek's notion of spontaneous order beyond simple exchanges (two commodities/two persons) to complex exchanges. An outcome of this is the removal of 'politics' from all contractural exchanges because contractural arrangements, having been agreed upon by both parties, are no longer conceived as being political.

New Public Management

'New public management' (NPM) has a history that can be traced at least to cameralist ideas, and such ideas underlay administrations in Europe in the early 18th century (Hood, 1990: 205; cf. Foucault (1979a) on cameralism). The main features of NPM can be characterized (Boston, 1996: 108) as:

- an extensive use of written contracts and performance agreements;
- a reliance on short term employment contracts;
- an emphasis on economic rewards and sanctions;
- a reduction in multiple accountability relationships;
- a minimizing of opportunities for ministerial discretion in the detailed operation of government agencies;
- the institutional separation of the funding agency from the provider;
- the separation of advisory, delivery and regulatory functions;
- an introduction of accrual accounting;
- capital charging;
- a distinction between the state's ownership and purchasers' interests;
- a distinction between outcomes and outputs;
- an accrual-based appropriations system;
- an emphasis on contestable provision and contracting out for service.

Hood (1990) gives several possible explanations for the rise of NPM in the late 1980s. The first is that NPM could be interpreted simply as a 'mood swing' or passing fad. Second, NPM could be interpreted as a 'new-look form of Treasury control with a set of doctrines fastened upon the financial by central controlling agencies to destroy the administrative bases of the public welfare lobby and to increase their own power vis-a-vis the professionalised line departments' (Hood, 1990: 206). Third, 'parts of NPM could be seen as reflecting a new political campaign technology – the shift to public policy based on intensive opinion polling which is part of the new machine politics style' (Hood, 1990: 206). Fourth, NPM could reflect a 'new client politics', the advent of a new, easily mobilizable coalition whose collective self-interest drives a policy boom. This is sometimes referred to as the development of the new elite aiming at increasing its own powers of patronage and consisting of management consultants, financial intermediaries, insurance companies and other groups that have a clear interest in privatization and contracting out. It is these people who give policy advice to government on what the rationality of government should be. Fifth, NPM could be interpreted as an administrative reflection of that broader set of social changes triggered by 'post industrialism' or 'post Fordism'. Of the five possible explanations of the rise of NPM, the fifth is, according to Hood (1990: 207), the most complete, though in New Zealand, which has perhaps taken NPM the furthest, there has never been a 'Fordist' means of production.

A major concern in the change to NPM is in public (or civil) service ethics, loyalty to the service as a whole and resilience to political crisis: political accountability involves much more than achieving 'one line' results. Another concern is over the limits of the NPM revolution. There seems to be no end to the individualizing and atomization process, and Hood even envisages the possibility of selling government administrative positions so that the purchaser could then invest in the successful discharge of their duties. Into which sector should high salaries go? So what kind of public service is NPM aiming to produce?

Governmentality

Elsewhere we have employed Michel Foucault's (1979a) notion of governmentality to argue that this 'new managerialism' functions as an emergent and increasingly rationalized and complex neo-liberal technology of governance that operates at a number of levels: the individual ('the self-managing student' and teacher), the classroom ('classroom management techniques'), the academic programme (with explicit promotion of the goals of self-management), and the school or educational institution (self-managing institutions) (Peters, Marshall and Fitzsimons, 1999). Construing self-management as a form of neo-liberal governmentality in Foucault's sense, and focusing upon the first and the last of these levels, that is, on the relations between individual and institutional self-management (understood in the literature as the doctrine of self-management) is fruitful for a 'feel' as to where educational policy is headed. One of the major tenets of 'new managerialism' is that, as there is nothing distinctive of education, it can be conceptualized and managed like any other service or institution, and the 'offerings' of institutions commodified like any other item on a supermarket shelf. Part of the 'success' of the globalized 'new managerialism' lies precisely in its claims for these generic aspects: its applicability to all spheres of administration and its homogenization of all technical and institutional problems as management problems. There are also appeals in NPM to its alleged scientific status. Similar questions must be raised here as have been raised above about the scientific status of economics.

New managerialism, however, shares many features with the notion of 'governmentality'. Foucault (1979a) uses the term 'governmentality' to mean the art of government or 'reason of state' and, historically, to signal the emergence of distinctive types of rule that became the basis for modern liberal politics. Starting from the series security, population, government, Foucault claims that there was an explosion of interest in the 'art of government' in the 16th century which was motivated by diverse questions: the government of oneself (personal conduct); the government of souls (pastoral doctrine); and the government of children (problematic of pedagogy). He says that the problematic of government can be located at the intersection of two competing tendencies – state centralization and a logic of dispersion. This is a problematic which poses questions of the 'how' of government, rather than its legitimation, and seeks 'to articulate a kind of rationality which was intrinsic to the art of government without subordinating it to the problematic of the prince and of his relationship to the principality of which he is lord and master' (Foucault, 1979a: 7). It was only in the late 16th and early 17th centuries that the art of government crystallized for the first time around the notion of 'reason of state' understood in a positive sense, whereby how the state is governed accords with rational principles that are seen to be intrinsic to it. In charting this establishment of the art of government, Foucault thus details the introduction of 'economy' into political practice (understood as 'the correct manner of managing goods and wealth within the family' (Foucault, 1979a: 10)).

Foucault concentrates his analytical energies on understanding the pluralized forms of government, its complexity and its techniques. Our modernity, he says, is characterized by the 'governmentalization' of the state. He is interested in the question of how power is exercised and, implicitly, he is providing a critique of the contemporary tendencies to overvalue the problem of the state and to reduce it to a unity or singularity based upon a certain functionality. This substantive feature – the rejection of state-centred analyses – has emerged from the governmentality literature as it has become a more explicit problematic (see, for example, Burchell *et al.*, 1991; Barry *et al.*, 1996). Governmentality meant both governance of self and others for Foucault. But these were selves who were constituted by technologies of domination and technologies of self (Foucault, 1979b, 1980, 1985, 1990).

Foucault's (1979a) research focuses on questions such as 'who can govern?', 'what does governing mean?' and 'who is governed?'. The target of the analysis of governmentality is not 'institutions', 'theories' or 'ideology', but 'practices' – with the aim of grasping the conditions which make these acceptable at a given moment; the hypotheses being that these types of practice are not just governed by institutions, prescribed by ideologies, guided by pragmatic circumstances – but possess up to a point their own specific regularities, logic, strategy, self-evidence and 'reason'. It is, for Foucault, a question of analysing a regime of practices – practices being understood here as places where what is said and what is done, rules imposed and reasons given, the planned and the taken for granted, meet and interconnect.

Governmentality is about critique, problematization, invention, imagination and changing the shape of the thinkable. Governmentality is the relation between self and itself, interpersonal relationships involving some control and guidance, relations within social institutions and community. The notion of governmentality is thus counterpoised to statist conceptions of power, which in Foucault's view erroneously dominate modern understandings of social relations. The theory of power surrounding the modern state is a problem: the state and sovereignty both rely on juridical conceptions of power as a negative or repressive force. The limited conception of power as an institutional and prohibitory phenomenon cannot adequately explain the range of power relations that permeate the body, sexuality and the family, kinship, discourse. Certain forms of managerialism and governmentality share characteristics such as power relations and, to this extent, are connected and overlap. Thus the self as the politically constituted subject of managerialism becomes a relevant domain of research for educational policy.

The theoretical promise of this problematic for the analysis of educational policy can be summarized briefly as follows. First, a neo-Foucauldian approach to the question of governance avoids interpreting liberalism as an ideology, political philosophy or as an economic theory, to reconfigure it as a form of governmentality with an emphasis on the question of how power is exercised. Second, it makes central the notion of the self-limiting state, which, in contrast to the administrative (or 'police') state, brings together in productive ways questions of ethics and technique, through the 'responsibilization' of moral agents and the active reconstruction of the relation between government and self-government. Third, it proposes an investigation of neo-liberalism as an intensification of an economy of moral regulation which was first developed by liberals and not merely or primarily as a political reaction to 'big government' or the so-called bureaucratic welfare state of the postwar Keynesian settlement. Fourth, the approach enables an understanding of the distinctive features of neo-liberalism. It understands neo-liberalism in terms of its replacement of the natural and spontaneous order characteristic of Hayekian liberalism with 'artificially arranged or contrived forms of the free, entrepreneurial and competitive conduct of economic-rational individuals' (Burchell, 1996: 23). And, further, it understands neo-liberalism through the development of 'a new relation between expertise and politics' (Burchell, 1996: 23), especially in the realm of welfare, where an actuarial rationality and new forms of prudentialism manifest and constitute themselves discursively in the language of 'purchaser–provider', 'audit', 'performance' and 'risk management' (O'Malley, 1996).

All of these points – the exercise of power, the development of certain types of moral agent and new forms of moral regulation, the introduction of forms of competition and entrepreneurial conduct, and the role of new managerialism in education – bear heavily upon educational policy.

However, they also bear heavily upon educational research, for if certain policies are to be pursued and if they are to impact upon 'reality', then certain research will provide a basis and support for policy choice as will certain research of policy implementation provide ongoing support for the continuation of policy. If governments are to show that policy accords with reality then research itself must be governed. It must be categorized and classified in certain ways – normalized – so that certain types of research are excluded as being outside the norms of the category of 'research'. We have described an example of this in Marshall and Peters (1995). There we document the course that a particular research programme took, and how the reason of the state asserted and reasserted itself. This research programme was, we believe, genuinely bi-cultural. It offered Maori in New Zealand a proper role in education through the control and examination of their own language – which is presumably their property – but which they still have to purchase in a packaged form, the form of which they resent. What was their property has been packaged within the state education system and, as citizens, they can purchase it. Hence the state has 'fulfilled' its obligations to its citizens because citizenship has become defined or asserted as the right to acquire property. Because this research challenged the accepted norms it was categorized, marginalized and ignored; in short it was governed.

IV The Collection

It is not our intention to provide a detailed discussion of the papers which we have selected. In this introduction we have tried to alert readers in a general manner to a number of historical moves in educational policy, and a number of theoretical positions and issues which have permeated, and at times pervaded, educational policy. We do not wish to pursue these matters by further reading our position into the selected papers because, we believe, they should 'stand' by themselves so that the reader can decide. In any case, our own position on educational policy is in chapter 6 and available more fully in Peters and Marshall (1996). However, there is a rationale for the ordering of the papers selected for this collection.

We have arranged the selection according to five broad categories. In general we believe that these categories catch the positions of the selected papers, without denying that particular papers have components which overlap, or are clearly relevant to, the other main areas or categories. These broad categories are:

- education policy: definition, analysis, criticism and research;
- economics: markets and development;
- education policy and the state;
- race, development and culture;
- social justice, literacy and new technologies.

Education Policy: Definition, Analysis, Criticism and Research (Chapters 1–7)

No collection on education policy can afford to ignore the question of its own self-definition and the ways in which this question (including within policy studies more generally) has shifted quite markedly on the basis of developments in the social sciences and, to a lesser extent, the humanities. For example, the shifts we outlined above indicated major shifts in methodology from positivistic models, to models influenced by hermeneutics, critical theory and, most recently, poststructuralism. We might even suggest, more broadly, a move from 'scientistic' to 'narrative' forms of policy studies in education. Yet despite innovative models and methodologies in education policy studies, states and international agencies have tended to embrace models and methodologies based upon economics, and if there has been an overall shift in state-led education policy from classical liberal economics to forms of so-called 'new growth theory' that emphasize analyses of human capital and the importance of research and development, it has not been a shift that has recognized the innovations occurring often within university environments. One of the features of the neo-liberal policy environment *per se* is the lack of dialogue between state policy practitioners and 'policy intellectuals', as we might call them, who operate most often in the university, where the demands, constraints and accountability of public policy are, perhaps, less acute. This first category, then, concerns itself with questions of definition, analysis, criticism and research.

The section opens with Stephen J. Ball's provocative paper, 'What is Policy? Texts, Trajectories and Toolboxes', in which Ball raises critical questions about the nature of policy, what is a text and how it might be used. Given some understanding of a policy text from Ball's article, John A. Codd then looks at how policy texts are constructed and how, in turn, such texts may need to be deconstructed. Codd emphasizes the importance here of being able to analyse discourse and the importance of reading into policy texts messages perhaps contrary to the overt or explicit intentions of the owners of the texts. Fitz, Halpin and Power then turn in chapter 3 to the important questions of how policy might be implemented in education and the research associated with such implementation. This section then turns to more overtly theoretical issues in relation to education policy studies. In chapter 4, Janks explores how policy research itself can be subjected to critical discourse analysis. Ozga then looks closely at theory in policy research. Finally, Taylor looks in particular at a form of critical policy analysis.

Economics: Markets and Development (Chapters 8–15)

The second category, called 'Economics: Markets and Development', is meant to convey the profound shift that education policy has undergone since the early 1980s in being regarded as an aspect of social policy and a part of the means of social redistribution, with an accent on what we might call education as a 'welfare right', to being considered one of the leading sectors of the economy policy, with an emphasis on privately sponsored forms of human capital investment and pupil or student as consumer.

This section opens in chapter 8, with Mark Blaug's 'Review of *Economics of Education: Research and Studies*', published in 1989 but written early in the start of the decade of the more overt economic management of education by neo-liberal ideology based upon particular forms of economic theory (see above). Brown and Lauder then generalize economic considerations into the emergence, discussed above, of globalization in matters educational. Carnoy looks at the changing face of education under the conditions made explicit by Chubb and Moe in chapter 11 and critiqued by Fitzsimons and Peters in chapter 12. Glennerster then raises questions about the status of markets, or quasi-markets, in education. Marginson, in his paper on the economics of education (chapter 14), follows Michel Foucault on power/knowledge and the subject, and raises important questions on the role of 'new' economic theories on the constitution of the subject. Finally, Whitty rounds off the economics section with an investigation of notions of parental choice and the autonomy of schools under quasi-markets.

Education Policy and the State (Chapters 16–23)

Of course, such a characterization and categorization must be offset and balanced by what can be called state theory in relation to education policy that comprises the third category, which we have simply called 'Education Policy and the State'. Indeed, an element of tedium has crept into international debates over the role and scope of the state, not only within education policy but in all policy realms. The arguments are well known: everywhere neo-liberals have argued that the market represents a superior form of political economy both in moral and efficiency terms, and they have recommended the establishment of market relations as a substitute or replacement for social relations mediated by the state. What this has meant very often is that neo-liberals have traded upon arguments about costs of state intervention, about the inefficiencies of 'big government' and about the corresponding efficiencies of the market in the delivery of social policy. Ideologically speaking, this shift has represented a sacrifice of traditional concerns of the welfare state for policies based upon a notion of equality or equality of opportunity for policies that enhance individual choice construed in consumer terms. Sometimes this has also meant a movement progressively away from a discourse of social rights to consumer rights under the doctrine of 'consumer sovereignty' and the assumed rationality and self-interest underlying a revived *homo economicus*.

Michael W. Apple, in chapter 16, is concerned about the nature of knowledge, what counts as knowledge in the curriculum and what counts as 'official' knowledge. Dale sees the state as concerned with governance and how the relationship between the state and education has been 'restructured' in the recent educational reforms. Edwards and Whitty in chapter 18, and Hogan in chapter 19, return to parental choice, this time in relation to the reforms and the contract state. Olssen takes another tack, defending the welfare state and publicly provided education against the neo-liberal reforms and the 'quasi-privatized' market. In chapter 21 Popkewitz examines the 'promise' inherent in the claims for decentralization which have accompanied the reforms and the 'traditional' distinction which has been believed to hold between state and civil society. If this distinction is contaminated then educational researchers must themselves become political, for research questions and findings can no longer be 'neutral'. Susan Robertson looks at the restructuring of teachers' work in chapter 22, and in chapter 23 Carlos Torres rounds off the section with a discussion of the politicization of educational researchers.

Race, Development and Culture (Chapters 24–31)

The fourth category threatens most the core values of liberalism whether in its traditional Kantian formula or in its more narrow economic instrumental version. Certainly, what we have called 'Race, Development and Culture' encompasses much that historically calls liberalism to account in terms of its mono-lingualism and mono-culturalism. Policies of assimilation and integration have now been recognized for what they are – part of the apparatus of Euro-centrism, particularly in its colonizing phase. Liberal democratic societies increasingly are forced to attend to conceptions of cultural self-determination, cultural maintenance and cultural rights as much as to notions of institutional racism, anti-racist education programmes and forms of international aid that are not overly Euro-centric, in ways unthought of a generation or two ago. Perhaps forms of multiculturalism in the polity, in the political processes and in the policy process have the potential to transform not only conceptions of education policy – and the process itself – but also the entire field of policy, and, at the same time, the movements of indigenous peoples have the narrative power to resist and recast forms of neo-liberal globalization.

First in chapter 24 Kenway, Bigum and Fitzclarence tackle the policies of marketing in a postmodern condition where the politics of racial difference become important. Then Eve Coxon raises questions about modernization, educational development and educational development in relation to the South Pacific, with its histories of church involvement, colonial administrations and more recent 'rule' by such institutions as the World Bank. Phillip W. Jones follows her in chapter 26, looking explicitly at the World Bank and its way of financing education. Giroux (chapter 27), McLaren (chapter 28), Wells and Serna (chapter 29) and Ogbu (chapter 30) look at issues of youth, pedagogy, racial stratification, racial politics and political resistance. Finally, Graham Hingangoroa Smith and Linda Tuhiwai Smith consider the situation of Maori in New Zealand with new ideological myths penetrating education, and ethnic relations, perpetuating racism and underachievement of Maori.

Social Justice, Literacy and New Technologies (Chapters 32–38)

The final category – 'Social Justice, Literacy and New Technologies' – indicates how conceptions of social justice are as much tied up with traditional questions of access and participation as with more modern questions of literacy, especially in relation to the so-called 'new technologies'. Literacy is, of course, not a new issue or policy concern, and clearly the major questions of what kind of literacy and how best to encourage literacy have been with us from the very early days of formal education. And yet these standard questions take on a new hue when the traditional conceptions of functional literacy are challenged and notions of literacy as socio-cultural practices are promulgated and advocated as the basis of relevant education policy. At the same time, the question concerning the new technologies is critical for education policy: is it advocated by state agencies because it appears to provide a cheaper form of delivery of educational courses and programmes, overcoming physical and distance obstacles and reducing the need for teaching staff? Or is it advocated on grounds to do with the needs of learners? How ought the new technologies be introduced into various education sectors? Are there non-technocratic ways of proceeding?

Connell (chapter 32) and Halsey (chapter 33) pursue the theme of social justice, tackling questions respectively of poverty and education, and trends in access to higher education and equity, in Britain. In chapter 34 Lingard and Garrick look at how social justice can be produced and practised in education in Queensland, Australia. On the topic of literacy, Lankshear then provides an overall look at literacy in relation to educational practice and theory, arguing for a socio-cultural approach to literacy studies. Luke, Lingard, Green and Comber in chapter 36 look at the politics of literacy and, in particular, how the construction of state 'crises' in literacy has been used as grounds for the restructuring and redirection of state schooling. In chapter 37 Burbules and Callister propose a post technocratic approach to education policy for the new 'mode of information' and associated technologies in education. The final chapter by McCulloch – 'Privatizing the Past?' – provides a concluding summary from a British perspective of history and education policy in the 1990s.

As education at all levels becomes crucially important to nations that define themselves in terms of the 'knowledge society', the 'information society' or 'information economy', education policy – its definition, its methodologies, its professionalization and its pedagogies – also becomes critical. We hope that this collection goes some way to satisfying the demand for text that addresses some of the most important issues as we move into the new millennium.

References

Adorno, Theodore, *et al.* (1976), *The Positivist Dispute in German Sociology*, trans. Glyn Adey and David Frisby, London: Heinemann.

Apel, K.-O. (1980), *Towards a Transformation of Philosophy*, London: Routledge and Kegan Paul.

Benson, J.K. (1983), 'Interorganizational Networks and Policy Sectors', in D. Rogers and D. Whetter (eds), *Interorganizational Coordination*, Ames: Iowa State University Press.

Boston, Jonathan (1996), 'Origins and Destinations: New Zealand's Model of Public Management and the International Transfer of Ideas', in P. Weller and G. Davis (eds), *New Ideas, Better Government*, Sydney: Allen & Unwin, pp. 107–31.

Boyd, W.D.L. and D.N. Plank (1995), 'Educational Policy Studies: Overview', *International Encyclopedia of Education* (2nd edn), Vol. X, Oxford: Pergamon Press.

Buchanan, James (1986), *Liberty, Market and State: Political Economy in the 1980s*, Brighton, Sussex: Wheatsheaf Books.

Buchanan, James and Graham Tullock (1965), *The Calculus of Consent: Logical Founcations of Constitutional Democracy*, Ann Arbor: University of Michigan Press.

Bull, D. (1980), 'The Anti-Discretion Movement in Britain: Fact or Phantom?', *Journal of Social Welfare Law*, 65–83.

Burchell, G. (1996), 'Liberal Government and Techniques of the Self', in Andrew Barry, Thomas Osborne and Nikolas Rose (eds), *Foucault and Political Reason*, London: U.C.L. Press, pp. 19–36.

Burchell, G., C. Gordon and P. Miller (1991), *The Foucault Effect: Studies in Governmentality*, London: Harvester Wheatsheaf.

Callaghan, D. and Jennings, B. (eds) (1985), *Ethics, the Social Sciences and Policy Analysis*, New York: Plenum Press.

Davis, K.C. (1969), *Discretionary Justice*, Baton Rouge: Louisiana State University Press.

De Marchi, Neil (1988), *The Popperian Legacy in Economics*, papers presented at a symposium in Amsterdam, December 1985, Cambridge: Cambridge University Press.

Deleuze, Gilles (1962), *Nietzsche and Philosophy*, Paris: Presses Universitaires de France (trans. Hugh Tomlinson), and London: Athlone Press (1983).

Dewey, John (1916), *Democracy and Education*, New York: Macmillan.

Fairweather, G.W. (1980), 'Community Psychology for the 1980s and Beyond', *Evaluation and Program Planning*, **3**, 245–50.

Foucault, Michel (1979a), 'Governmentality', *Ideology and Consciousness*, **6**, 1–26.

Foucault, Michel (1979b), *Discipline and Punish: The Birth of the Prison*, trans. Alan Sheridan, New York: Vintage Books.

Foucault, Michel (1980), *The History of Sexuality*, Vol. 1, New York: Vintage.

Foucault, Michel (1985), *The Use of Pleasure: The History of Sexuality*, Vol. II, New York: Vintage.

Foucault, Michel (1990), *The Care of the Self: The History of Sexuality*, Vol. III, Harmondsworth: Penguin.

Gouldner, A.W. (1954), *Patterns of Industrial Bureaucracy*, Glencoe, Il.: Free Press.

Habermas, Jürgen (1971), *Knowledge and Human Interests*, trans. J. Shapiro, Boston: Beacon Press.

Habermas, Jürgen (1981), 'Modernity versus Postmodernity', *New German Critique*, **22**, 3–14.

Habermas, Jürgen (1982), 'New Social Movements', *Telos*, **49**, 31–7.

Hanson, Norman (1958), *Patterns of Discovery*, Cambridge: Cambridge University Press.

Heidegger, Martin (1977), *The Question of Technology*, trans. William Lovitt, New York: Harper and Row.

Heyneman, S.P. (1990), 'The World Economic Crisis and the Quality of Education', *Journal of Educational Finance*, **15** (4), 456–69.

Holland, R.F. (1980), *Against Empiricism: On Education, Epistemology and Value*, Oxford: Blackwell.

Hood, C. (1990). 'De-Sir Humphreyfying the Westminster Model of Bureaucracy: A New Style of Governance?', *Governance: An International Journal of Policy and Administration*, **3** (2), 205–14.

Keynes, John Maynard (1971), *Collected Writings*, Vol. XIV, London: Macmillan.

Kuhn, Thomas (1962), *The Structure of Scientific Revolutions* (2nd edn), Chicago: Chicago University Press.

Lakatos, Imre (1976), *Proofs and Refutations*, Cambridge: Cambridge University Press.

Lyotard, J.-F. (1984), *The Postmodern Condition: A Report on Knowledge*, Theory and History of Literature, 10; Minnesota: University of Minnesota Press.

Marshall, James D. (1996), 'Education in the Mode of Information: Some Philosophical Issues', in Frank Margonis (ed.), *Philosophy of Education 1996*, Urbana, Il.: Philosophy of Education Society.

Marshall James D. and Peters, Michael (1995), 'The Governance of Educational Research', *Australian Educational Researcher*, **22** (2), 107–20.

McCarthy, Thomas (1978), *The Critical Theory of Jürgen Habermas*, Cambridge, Ma.: MIT Press.

McCloskey, D. (1986), *The Rhetorics of Economics*, Brighton, Sussex: Wheatsheaf.

McCloskey, D. (1994), *Knowledge and Persuasiòn in Economics*, Cambridge: Cambridge University Press.

Nagel, S.S. (1980), 'The Policy Studies Perspective', *Public Administration Review*, **40**, 391–6.

O'Malley, P. (1996), 'Risk and Responsibility', in A. Barry, T. Osborne and N. Rose (eds), *Foucault and Political Reason: Liberalism, Neo-liberalism and Rationalities of Government*, London, UCL Press, pp. 189–208.

Parlett, N. and Hamilton, D. (1978), 'Evaluation and Illumination: A New Approach in the Study of Innovatory Programs', in D. Hamilton *et al.* (eds), *Beyond the Numbers Game*, Berkeley, Ca: McCutcheon.

Peters, Michael (ed.) (1995), *Education and the Postmodern Condition*, Foreword by Jean-François Lyotard, Westport, Ct and London: Bergin & Garvey.

Peters, Michael and Lankshear, Colin (1996), 'Postmodern Counternarratives', in Henry A. Girouz, Colin Lankshear, Peter McLaren and Michael Peters, *Counternarratives: Cultural Studies and Critical Pedagogies in Postmodern Spaces*, New York: Routledge.

Peters, Michael and Marshall, James (1996), *Individualism and Community: Education and Social Welfare in the Postmodern Condition*, London: Falmer Press.

Peters, Michael, Marshall, James and Fitzsimons, Patrick (1999), 'Managerialism and Educational Policy in a Global Context: Neoliberalism, Foucault and the Doctrine of Self-Management', forthcoming in Nicholas Burbules and Carlos Torres (eds), *Golobalisation and Educational Policy*, New York: Routledge.

Popper, Sir Karl (1959), *The Logic of Scientific Discovery*, London: Routledge and Kegan Paul.

Popper, Sir Karl (1963), *Conjectures and Refutations: The Growth of Scientific Knowledge*, London: Routledge and Kegan Paul.

Popper, Sir Karl (1976), *The Logic of the Social Sciences*, in Adorno *et al.* (1976).

Poster, Mark (1989), *Critical Theory and Poststructuralism*, Ithaca: Cornell University Press.

Quine, W.V.O. (1961), *From a Logical Point of View*, Cambridge, Ma: Harvard University Press.

Rose, N. (1989), *Governing the Soul: The Shaping of the Private Self*, London: Routledge.

Ritzer, George (1993), *The McDonaldization of Society: An Investigation into the Changing Character of Social Life*, Newbury Park, Ca: Fine Forges Press.

Sellars, Wilfrid (1965), *Science, Perception and Reality*, London: Routledge.

Simon, H.A. (1945), *Administrative Behaviour*, Glencoe, Il.: Free Press.

Smith, Anthony (1990), 'Towards a Global Culture', *Theory, Culture and Society*, **7** (2–3), 172–92.

Weiss, Carol (1972), *Evaluation Research*, Englewood Cliffs, NJ: Prentice Hall.

Winch, Peter (1958), *The Idea of a Social Science*, London: Routledge and Kegan Paul.

Wittgenstein, Ludwig (1953), *Philosophical Investigations*, Oxford: Blackwell.

Part I
Education Policy: Definition, Analysis, Criticism and Research

[1]

What is policy? Texts, trajectories and toolboxes

This chapter is an exercise in theoretical heurism. It is intentionally tentative and open-ended. I realize that on occasion I resort to aphorism rather than argument. It rests in part on an oddly unfashionable position in educational and sociological research; that is, that in the analysis of complex social issues – like policy – two theories are probably better than one. To put it another way, the *complexity* and *scope* of policy analysis – from an interest in the workings of the state to a concern with contexts of practice and the distributional outcomes of policy – precludes the possibility of successful single-theory explanations. What we need in policy analysis is a toolbox of diverse concepts and theories – an applied sociology rather than a pure one. Thus, I want to replace the modernist theoretical project of abstract parsimony with a somewhat more post-modernist one of localized complexity. This polarization, between parsimony and complexity, and the dilemmas it highlights are very much to the fore in recent debates in the UK about the conception and purposes of 'policy-sociology' (Ozga 1987, 1990; Ball 1990b). Thus, Ozga (1990: 359) suggests that it is important to 'bring together structural, macro-level analysis of education systems and education policies and micro-level investigation, especially that which takes account of people's perception and experiences.' Now that is what I mean by scope and I agree strongly with Ozga's plea. But she goes on to criticize approaches that generate 'a view of policy making which stresses ad hocery, serendipity, muddle and negotiation' (p. 360). Now that is part of what I mean by complexity (or at least one aspect of it) and I disagree with the exclusitory thrust of Ozga's plea. We cannot rule out certain forms and conceptions of social action simply because they seem awkward, theoretically challenging or difficult. The challenge is to relate together analytically the ad hocery of the macro with the ad hocery of the micro without losing sight of the systematic bases and effects of *ad hoc* social actions: to look for the iterations embedded within chaos. As I see it, this also involves some rethinking of the simplicities of the structure/agency dichotomy. This task is one which Harker and May (1993: 177) identify as central to Bourdieu's sociology; that is, 'to account for agency in a constrained world, and show how agency and structure are implicit in each other, rather than being the two poles of a continuum'.

One of the conceptual problems currently lurking within much policy research and policy sociology is that more often than not analysts fail to define conceptually what they mean by policy. The meaning of policy is taken for granted and theoretical and epistemological dry rot is built into the analytical structures they construct. It is not difficult to find the term policy being used to describe very different 'things' at different points in the same study. For me, much rests on the meaning or possible meanings that we give to policy; it affects 'how' we research and how we interpret what we find. Now let me add quickly that I do not exempt myself from these criticisms, although in recent work with Richard Bowe we have tried to be careful and explicit about our understanding and use of the term policy (Bowe and Ball with Gold 1992; see also Chapter 1).

Typically in a piece of writing which begins like this one I would now offer my own definitive version of the meaning of policy, and with a few rhetorical flourishes and a bit of fancy theoretical footwork I would solve all the problems that I have pointed up. But I cannot do that. Or at least I cannot do that very simply. The reason is that I hold my own theoretical uncertainties about the meaning of policy and in current writing on policy issues I actually inhabit two very different conceptualizations of policy. For the time being I will call these *policy as text* and *policy as discourse*. In simple terms the differences between these two conceptualizations are rather dramatic and in sociological terms rather hoary and traditional. But the point I am moving on to is that policy is not one or the other, but both: they are 'implicit in each other'. As an aside, but an important aside, the question 'what is policy?' should not mislead us into unexamined assumptions about policies as 'things'; policies are also processes and outcomes (more of which later).

Policy as text

Here, somewhat under the influence of literary theory, we can see policies as representations which are encoded in complex ways (via struggles, compromises, authoritative public interpretations and reinterpretations) and decoded in complex ways (via actors' interpretations and meanings in relation to their history, experiences, skills, resources and context). A policy is both contested and changing, always in a state of 'becoming', of 'was' and 'never was' and 'not quite'; 'for any text a plurality of readers must necessarily produce a plurality of readings' (Codd 1988: 239). Now this conception is not simply one which privileges the significance of readings of policy by its subjects. While that is important – authors cannot control the meanings of their texts – policy authors do make concerted efforts to assert such control by the means at their disposal, to achieve a 'correct' reading. We need to understand those efforts and their effects on readers and to recognize the attention that readers pay to the writers' context of production and communicative intent (Giddens 1987: 105–7). But, in addition, it is crucial to recognize that the policies themselves, the texts, are not necessarily clear or closed or complete. The texts are the product of compromises at various stages (at points of initial influence, in the micropolitics of legislative formulation, in the parliamentary process and in the politics and micropolitics of interest group articulation). They are typically the cannibalized products of multiple (but circumscribed) influences and agendas. There is ad hocery, negotiation and serendipity within the state, within the policy formulation process.

Now if this sounds like a restatement of the epistemology of pluralism it is not meant to be. There is a difference between agenda control and ideological politics and the processes of policy influence and text production within the state. Only certain influences and agendas are recognized as legitimate, only certain voices are heard at any point in time. The point is that quibbling and dissensus still occur with the babble of 'legitimate' voices and sometimes the effects of quibbling and dissensus result in a blurring of meanings within texts, and in public confusion and a dissemination of doubt. We only have to look at Edwards *et al.*'s (1989, 1992) studies of the assisted places scheme and city technology colleges to see that sometimes it is actually difficult even to identify analytically what a policy is and what it is intended to achieve. These studies also point up a second issue. Policies shift and change their meaning in the arenas of politics; representations change, key interpreters (secretaries of state, ministers, chairs of councils) change (sometimes the change in key actors is a deliberate tactic for changing the meaning of policy). Policies have their own momentum inside the state; purposes and intentions are reworked and reoriented over time. The problems faced by the state change over time. Policies are represented differently by different actors and interests: Kenneth Baker's grant maintained schools scheme as against Margaret Thatcher's; Margaret Thatcher's National Curriculum as against John Major's, Kenneth Baker's, Kenneth Clarke's and Ron Dearing's. At all stages in the policy process we are confronted both with different interpretations of policy, and with what Rizvi and Kemmis (1987) call 'interpretations of interpretations'. And these attempts to represent or rerepresent policy sediment and build up over time; they spread confusion and allow for play in and the playing off of meanings. Gaps and spaces for action and response are opened up or reopened as a result. Thus, the physical text that pops through the school letterbox, or wherever, does not arrive 'out of the blue' – it has an interpretational and representational history – and neither does it enter a social or institutional vacuum. The text and its readers and the context of response all have histories. Policies enter existing patterns of inequality, e.g. the structure of local markets, local class relations. They 'impact' or are taken up differently as a result (see Ball *et al.* (1993a) on the middle-class use of local education markets). Policy is not exterior to inequalities, although it may change them; it is also affected, inflected and deflected by them.

Some texts are never even read firsthand. An ongoing study of the maths National Curriculum has found that 7 per cent of its sample of maths teachers have never read any National Curriculum documents (Brown 1992); an ongoing study of assessment at Key Stage 1 finds that a significant number of teachers in the 32 case study schools fundamentally misunderstand the premises and methods of School Attainment Tasks and teacher assessment and have employed these misunderstandings to organize their classroom practice (Gipps and Brown 1992). Confusion begets confusion. But there may often be key mediators of policy in any setting who are relied upon by others to relate policy to context or to gatekeep, e.g. headteachers (Wallace 1988) or heads of department (Bowe and Ball with Gold 1992). And certain policy texts may be collectively undermined (e.g. the 1993 teacher unions' stand against national testing for 14-year-olds and the publications of school test results for 7- and 14-year-olds) or may generate mass confusion and demoralization. Pollard (1992: 112) provides a very good example of both the mediation and delegitimation of a text: the Schools Examination and Assessment Council *Guide to Teacher Assessment* (1990).

> This document, which was intended to provide INSET support to schools, seriously failed to connect with primary teachers' views about learning or with the practicalities of the circumstances in which they work. For instance, it was suggested that 'lessons' are planned with direct reference to Attainment Targets and suggested, unproblematically, that the National Curriculum has set out the order in which children would learn. To teachers and advisers who retained child-centred beliefs and an awareness of the diverse patterns by which children learn, this was like a red rag to a bull. There was also enormous hilarity and anger over the impracticality of many of the suggestions which were made. In particular, the authors of the materials seemed to have no awareness of the demands of teaching with large class sizes and made a number of simplistic and naive suggestions. The credibility of the document was thus heavily undercut. SEAC was then humiliated by an article on the materials by Ted Wragg in *The Times Educational Supplement* entitled 'Who put the "Ass" in Assessment?' and a large number of schools and LEAs actively discouraged the circulation or use of the *Guide*.

None the less, policies *are* textual interventions into practice; and although many teachers (and others) are proactive, 'writerly', readers of texts, their readings and reactions are not constructed in circumstances of their own making. Policies pose problems to their subjects, problems that must be solved in context. It may be possible for some to 'hide' from policy but that is rarely a common option. I must be very clear, policy 'matters: it is important, not the least because it consists of texts which are (sometimes) *acted on*' (Beilharz 1987: 394). The point is that we cannot predict or assume how they will be acted on in every case in every setting, or what their immediate effect will be, or what room for manoeuvre actors will find for themselves. Action may be constrained differently (even tightly) but it is not determined by policy. Solutions to the problems posed by policy texts will be localized and should be expected to display ad hocery and messiness. Responses must be 'creative'; but I use the term carefully here and in a specific sense. Given constraints, circumstances and practicalities, the translation of the crude, abstract simplicities of policy texts into interactive and sustainable practices of some sort involves productive thought, invention and adaptation. Policies do not normally tell you what to do, they create circumstances in which the range of options available in deciding what to do are narrowed or changed, or particular goals or outcomes are set. A response must still be put together, constructed in context, offset against other expectations. All of this involves creative social action, not robotic reactivity. Thus, the enactment of texts relies on things like commitment, understanding, capability, resources, practical limitations, cooperation and (importantly) intertextual compatibility. Furthermore, sometimes when we focus analytically on one policy or one text we forget that other policies and texts are in circulation, and the enactment of one may inhibit or contradict or influence the possibility of the enactment of others (I could illustrate most of these points with data from our Education Reform Act study; Bowe and Ball with Gold 1992). And the more ideologically abstract any policy is, the more distant in conception from practice (as in the example above), the less likely it is to be accommodated in unmediated form into the context of practice; it confronts 'other realities', other circumstances, like poverty, disrupted classrooms, lack of materials, multilingual classes. Some policies change some of the circumstances in which we work; they cannot change all the circumstances. Riseborough (1992), in a detailed analysis of the policy responses of one primary headteacher, draws our attention to the importance of 'secondary adjustments' in teachers' engagement with policy: 'teachers can create, through a repertoire of individual and collective, "contained" (i.e. "fitting in without introducing pressure for radical change") and "disruptive" (i.e. attempts to radically alter the structure or leave) strategies, an empirically rich underlife to policy intention' (p. 37). Generally, we have failed to research, analyse and conceptualize this underlife, the 'secondary adjustments' which relate teachers to policy and to the state in different ways. We tend to begin by assuming the adjustment of teachers and context to policy but not of policy to context (see Chapter 1). There is a privileging of the policy maker's reality. The crude and over-used term 'resistance' is a poor substitute here, which allows for both rampant over-claims and dismissive under-claims to be made about the way policy problems are solved in context. I also want to avoid the notion that policy is always negatively responded to, or that all policies are coercive or regressive. Some emancipatory policies are subject to creative non-implementation (education history is littered with examples). And some policies may be deployed in the context of practice to displace or marginalize others (see Troyna 1992).

In all this discussion of interpretation and creativity I am not trying to exclude power. Textual interventions can change things significantly, but I am suggesting that we should not ignore the way that things stay the same or the ways in which changes are different in different settings and different from the intentions of policy authors (where these are clear). Power, as Foucault points out, is productive: 'relations of power are not in superstructural positions, with merely a role of prohibition or accompaniment; they have a directly productive role, wherever they come into play' (Foucault 1981: 94). Policies typically posit a restructuring, redistribution and disruption of power relations, so that different people can and cannot do different things; again 'relations of power are not in a position of exteriority with respect to other types of relationships (economic processes, knowledge relationships, sexual relations), but are are immanent in the latter' (Foucault 1981: 94). Power is multiplicitous, overlain, interactive and complex, policy texts *enter* rather than simply change power relations: hence, again, the complexity of the relationship between policy intentions, texts, interpretations and reactions. From a rather different theoretical starting point Offe (1984: 106) offers a similar view:

> the real social effects ('impact') of a law or institutional service are not determined by the wording of laws and statutes ('policy output'), but instead are generated primarily as a consequence of social disputes and conflicts, for which state policy merely establishes the location and timing of the contest, its subject matter and 'the rules of the game'. In these cases of extra-political or 'external' implementation of social policy measures state social policy in no way establishes concrete 'conditions' (for example, the level of services, specific insurance against difficult living conditions). Instead, it defines the substance of conflict and, by differentially empowering or dis-empowering the relevant social groups, biases the extent of the specific 'utility' of the institutions of social policy for these groups.

What Offe is saying, I think, is that practice and the 'effects' of policy cannot be simply read off from texts and are the outcome of conflict and struggle between 'interests' in context. (The use of the market form within policy and the relative advantage that this allows middle class families to achieve is a case in point; see Chapter 7.)

Thus, I take it as axiomatic that there is agency and there is constraint in relation to policy – this is not a sum-zero game. Policy analysis requires an understanding that is based not on constraint *or* agency but on the changing relationships between constraint *and* agency and their inter-penetration. Furthermore, such an analysis must achieve insight into both overall and localized outcomes of policy.

But I also want to use this quotation as a transition point in order to move on to the *other* things I want to say about policy. First, I want to take up the point made that state policy 'establishes the location and timing of the contest, its subject matter and "the rules of the game".' This, I think, highlights the importance of policy *as* and *in* discourse. Second, I want to return to the problem of the 'effects' of policy.

Policy as discourse

In the above there is plenty of social agency and social intentionality around. Actors are making meaning, being influential, contesting, constructing responses, dealing with contradictions, attempting representations of policy. Much of this stuff of policy can be engaged with by a realist analysis in the different contexts of policy. But perhaps this *is* a new pluralism. Perhaps this *is* caught within an ideology of agency; by dealing with what is or can be done it misses what Ozga calls 'the bigger picture'. In other words, perhaps it concentrates too much on what those who inhabit policy think about and misses and fails to attend to what they do not think about. Thus we need to appreciate the way in which policy ensembles, collections of related policies, exercise power through a *production* of 'truth' and 'knowledge', as discourses. Discourses are 'practices that systematically form the objects of which they speak . . . Discourses are not about objects; they do not identify objects, they constitute them and in the practice of doing so conceal their own invention' (Foucault 1977: 49). Discourses are about what can be said, and thought, but also about who can speak, when, where and with what authority. Discourses embody the meaning and use of propositions and words. Thus, certain possibilities for thought are constructed. Words are ordered and combined in particular ways and other combinations are displaced or excluded. 'Discourse may seem of little account', Foucault (1971: 11–12) says, 'but the prohibitions to which it is subject reveal soon enough its links with desire and power.' But discourse is 'irreducible to language and to speech' (Foucault 1974: 49), it is 'more' than that. We do not speak a discourse, it speaks us. *We are* the subjectivities, the voices, the knowledge, the power relations that a discourse constructs and allows. We do not 'know' what we say, we 'are' what we say and do. In these terms we are spoken by policies, we take up the positions constructed for us within policies. This is a system of practices (marketing one's courses, promoting one's institution) and a set of values and ethics (forcing unproductive colleagues to take early retirement so that they do not have to be counted in the departmental performativity returns). 'Discourses get things done, accomplish real tasks, gather authority' (Said 1986: 152). And we have to note the decentring of the state in this: discourses are non-reductionist. The state is here the product of discourse, a point in the diagram of power. It is a necessary but not sufficient concept in the development of an 'analytics of power' – 'The state can only operate on the basis of other, already existing power relations' (Rabinow 1986: 64), like racism and like patriarchy. I am not arguing that the state is irrelevant, or that is should not play a key role in policy analysis (see Ball 1990b). But serious attention needs to be given to the play of state power within 'disaggregated, diverse and specific (or local) sites' (Allan 1990) and to the ways in which particular fields of knowledge are sustained and challenged in these settings, around particular 'events'.

In Foucault's terms we would see policy ensembles that include, for example, the market, management, appraisal and performativity as 'regimes of truth' through which people govern themselves and others. This is based upon the production, transformation and effects of true/false distinctions (Smart 1986: 164) and the application of science and hierarchisation to 'problems' in education – like standards, discipline, the quality of teaching, efficient use of resources. These new 'sciences' of education are inhabited, disseminated and legitimated by a set of 'specific' intellectuals: the Spinks and Caldwells, Sextons, Hargreaves and Hopkins, and Fidlers and Bowles (see Chapter 6). The point of all this is that an exclusive focus upon 'secondary adjustments', particularly if this takes the form of 'naive optimism', may obscure the discursive limitations acting on and through those adjustments. We may only be able to conceive of the possibilities of response in and through the language, concepts and vocabulary which the discourse makes available to us. Thus, Offe may be right in stressing that struggle, dispute, conflict and adjustment take place over a pre-established terrain. The essence of this is that there are real struggles over the interpretation and enactment of policies. But these are set within a moving discursive frame which articulates and constrains the possibilities and probabilities of interpretation and enactment. We read and respond to policies in discursive circumstances that we cannot, or perhaps do not, think about. Also embedded in this is the intellectual work done on and in the 'politics of truth' by the advocates and technicians of policy change, and the 'will to power' and desire of those who find themselves the beneficiaries of new power relations, where power is 'exercised in the effect of one action on another action' (Hoy 1986: 135). 'Power may be understood in the first instance as the multiplicity of force relations in the sphere in which they operate and which constitute their own organization' (Foucault 1981: 92) (see Chapter 4 with regard to this). Thus, in these terms the effect of policy is primarily discursive, it changes the possibilities we have for thinking 'otherwise'; thus it limits our responses to change, and leads us to misunderstand what policy is by misunderstanding what it does. Further, policy as discourse may have the effect of redistributing 'voice', so that it does not matter what some people say or think, and only certain voices can be heard as meaningful or authoritative.

Now the danger here, of course, is that of 'naive pessimism'. As Jameson (1984: 57) puts it,

> the more powerless the reader comes to feel. In so far as the theorist wins, therefore, by constructing an increasingly closed and terrifying machine, to that very degree he [*sic*] loses, since the critical capacity of his work is thereby paralyzed, and the impulses of negation and revolt, not to speak of those of social transformation, are increasingly perceived as vain and trivial in the face of the model itself.

But in practice in complex modern societies we are enmeshed in a variety of discordant, incoherent and contradictory discourses, and 'subjugated knowledges' cannot be totally excluded from arenas of policy implementation (see Riseborough 1992). 'We must make allowance for the complex and unstable process whereby discourse can be both an instrument and an effect of power, but also a hindrance, a stumbling block, a point of resistance and a starting point for an opposing strategy' (Foucault 1981: 101). But we do need to recognize and analyse the existence of 'dominant' discourses, regimes of truth, erudite knowledges – like neo-liberalism and management theory – within social policy. At present I can offer no satisfactory closure on the issue of policy as discourse except, weakly perhaps, to reiterate my earlier point about needing more than one good theory to construct one half-decent explanation or account. (I tried this composite theory approach in my (1990b) study of the politics of educational reform in the UK.)

Policy effects

I want now to take up some problems remaining in the first section of the chapter in a different way. That is, by exploring how we might begin to conceptualize policy effects in a way that is neither theoretically high-handed nor trivializing. This also takes me back to my disagreement with Ozga, noted above, about the nature of localized responses to policy as being *ad hoc*, serendipitous etc. In this respect both those writers who celebrate agency and their critics misunderstand, or are at least imprecise about, what might be meant by the effects or impact of policy. I want to distinguish initially between the generalities and specifics of policy effect.

Again I want to make myself clear: the earlier discussion of policy texts is not intended to convey a conception of policy effects as typically minimal or marginal. It is not that policies have no effects, they do; it is not that those effects are not significant, they are; it is not that those effects are not patterned, they are. But to reiterate, responses (as one vehicle for effects) vary between contexts. Policies from 'above' are not the only constraints and influences upon institutional practice. One difficulty in discussing effects is that the specific and the general are often conflated. The general effects of policies become evident when specific aspects of change and specific sets of responses (within practice) are related together. A neglect of the general is most common in single-focus studies, which take one change or one policy text and attempt to determine its impact on practice. Taken in this way the specific effects of a specific policy may be limited but the general effects of ensembles of policies of different kinds may be different. I would suggest that in the UK at least (probably also in the USA, Canada, Australia and New Zealand), the cumulative and general effects of several years of multiple thrusts of educational reform on teachers' work have been profound. Here teachers' work is a general category which encompasses a variety of separate reforms related to curriculum, assessment, performativity, organization, pay and conditions (see Chapter 4). Again, though, such a generalization has to be handled carefully in at least two senses. (a) There is a danger of idealizing the past and portraying a situation in which teachers once had autonomy and now do not (again this is not a zero-sum issue). A formulation like that of Dale (1989b) of a shift from licensed to regulated autonomy is a useful tool in thinking about this. What he attempts to capture is a qualitative shift from one kind of autonomy to another; thus he has to specify the different characteristics of the two kinds. (b) The generalization will not encompass the experience of all types of teachers in all types of situation. Two examples. Teachers in the UK who find themselves in over-subscribed schools of high reputation, which can thus select students, may find their conditions of work and freedom for manoeuvre very different from teachers in under-subscribed schools of poor reputation, which must take what students they can get and will be funded at a lower level accordingly. Furthermore, the recent changes in the UK have had very different implications for classroom teachers and headteachers. The latter, in some respects, and also depending on which schools they are responsible for, find their freedom for manoeuvre and powers in relation to erstwhile colleagues enhanced rather than diminished. They are beneficiaries, at least to an extent, in the redrawing of the diagram of power (see Chapter 6). This kind of attention to policy 'effects' also highlights some other difficulties inherent in the 'policy as text' perspective. A concentration upon the interpretational responses of individual actors can lead to a neglect of the compound and structural changes effected by state policies. In particular, such a focus may lead to a neglect of the pervasive effect of institutional reconfiguration (see Chapters 4 and 5).

But there is a further important distinction to be made in regard to effects, a distinction between what might be called first order and second order effects. First order effects are changes in practice or structure (which are evident in particular sites and across the system as a whole), and second order effects are the impact of these changes on patterns of social access, opportunity and social justice. Walker (1981: 225) articulates the distinction thus:

> the essential aspect of *social* policies is their distributional implications or outcomes. Social policies may be made implicitly or explicitly, by a wide range of social institutions and groups, including the state. The task of social policy analysis is to evaluate the distributional impact of existing policies and proposals and the rationales underlying them. In such analyses attention will be focussed . . . on the behaviour of organisations, professionals and classes in order to balance descriptions of the institutional framework through which the welfare state is administered with analysis of the social production and maintenance of inequality.

One important analytical strategy which provides a mechanism for linking and tracing the discursive origins and possibilities of policy, as well as the intentions embedded in, responses to and effects of policy, is that employed by Edwards *et al.* (1989, 1992) in their APS (assisted places scheme) and CTC (city technology colleges) studies. They are what I would call policy trajectory studies. They employ a cross-sectional rather than a single level analysis by tracing policy formulation, struggle and response from within the state itself through to the various recipients of policy. Richard Bowe and I have attempted to give some conceptual structure to the trajectory method by adumbrating three contexts of policy-making (Bowe and Ball with Gold 1992): *the context of influence, the context of policy text production and the context(s) of practice.* Each context consists of a number of arenas of action – some private and some public. Each context involves struggle and compromise and ad hocery. They are loosely coupled and there is no one simple direction of flow of information between them. But in theoretical and practical terms, this model requires two further 'contexts' to make it complete. First, we must add the relationship between first order (practice) effects and second order effects; that is, *the context of outcomes.* Here analytical concern is with the issues of justice, equality and individual freedom. Policies are analysed in terms of their impact upon and interactions with existing inequalities and forms of injustice (see Chapter 7). The question of the fifth context is then begged, *the context of political strategy*; the identification of a set of political and social activities 'which might more effectively tackle inequalities' (Troyna 1993: 12). This is an essential component of what Harvey (1990) calls *critical social research* or the work of those Foucault calls 'specific intellectuals', which is produced for strategic use in particular social situations and struggles. As Sheridan (1980: 221) puts it: 'the Foucauldian genealogy is an unmasking of power for the use of those who suffer it'. This is what Foucault calls 'the real political task' in our society, 'to criticize the working of institutions which appear to be both neutral and independent, and to criticize them in such a manner that the political violence which has always exercised itself obscurely through them will be unmasked so that we can fight them' (in Rabinow 1986: 6). But Foucault's method also carries stark messages for the over-ambitious researcher/reformer; for the genealogical method, Sheridan (1980: 221) goes on to say, 'is also directed against those who would sieze power in their name'.

References

Allan, J. (1990). 'Does feminism need a theory of "the state"?', in Watson, S. (ed.) *Playing the State: Australian Feminist Interventions,* Sydney, Allen and Unwin.

Ball, S. J. (1990b). *Politics and Policy Making in Education*, London, Routledge.

Ball, S. J. (1993a). 'Education markets, choice and social class: the market as a class strategy in the UK and US', *British Journal of Sociology of Education,* 14 (1), 3–19.

Beilharz, P. (1987). 'Reading politics: social theory and social policy', *Australia and New Zealand Journal of Sociology*, 23 (3), 388–406.

Bowe, R. and Ball, S. J. with Gold, A. (1992). *Reforming Education and Changing Schools*, London, Routledge.

Brown, M. (1992). National Curriculum Mathematics – National Evaluation, personal communication.

Codd, J. (1988). 'The construction and deconstruction of educational policy documents', *Journal of Education Policy*, 3 (5), 235–48.

Dale, R. (1989b). *The State and Education Policy*, Buckingham, Open University Press.

Edwards, T., Fitz, J. and Whitty, G. (1989). *The State and Private Education: an Evaluation of the Assisted Places Scheme*, London, Falmer.

Edwards, T., Gewirtz, S. and Whitty, G. (1992). 'Whose choice of schools? Making sense of city technology colleges', in Arnot, M. and Barton, L. (eds) *Voicing Concerns*, Wallingford, Triangle.

Foucault, M. (1971). *The Order of Discourse*, Paris, Gallimard.

Foucault, M. (1974). *The Order of Things*, London, Tavistock.

Foucault, M. (1977). *The Archeology of Knowledge*, London, Tavistock.

Foucault, M. (1981). *The History of Sexuality, Vol. 1*. Harmondsworth, Penguin.

Giddens, A. (1987). *Social Theory and Modern Sociology*, Cambridge, Polity Press.

Gipps, C. and Brown, M. (1992). National Assessment in Primary Schools Project, Seminar Paper, Institute of Education, University of London.

Harker, R. and May, S. A. (1993). 'Code and habitus: comparing the accounts of Bernstein and Bourdieu', *British Journal of Sociology of Education*, 14 (2), 169–79.

Harvey, L. (1990). *Critical Social Research*, London, Allen and Unwin.

Hoy, D. (1986). 'Power, repression, progress: Foucault, Lukes and the Frankfurt School' in Hoy, D. (ed.) *Foucault: a Critical Reader*, Oxford, Blackwell.

Jameson, F. (1984). 'Postmodernism or the cultural logic of late capitalism', *New Left Review*, 147, 61–84.

Offe, C. (1984). *Contradictions of the Welfare State*, London, Hutchinson.

Ozga, J. (1987). 'Studying education policy through the lives of policy makers', in Walker, S. and Barton, L. (eds) *Changing Policies. Changing Teachers*, Milton Keynes, Open University Press.

Ozga, J. (1990). 'Policy research and policy theory: a comment on Fitz and Halpin', *Journal of Education Policy*, 5 (4), 359–62.

Pollard, A. (1992). 'Teachers' responses to the reshaping of primary education', in Arnot, M. and Barton, L. (eds) *Voicing Concerns*, Wallingford, Triangle.

Rabinov, P. (1986). *The Foucault Reader*, Harmondsworth, Penguin.

Riseborough, G. (1992). 'Primary headship, state policy and the challenge of the 1990s', *Journal of Education Policy*, 8 (2), 123–42.

Rizvi, F. and Kemmis, S. (1987). *Dilemmas of Reform*, Geelong, Deakin Institute for Studies in Education.

Said, E. (1986). 'Foucault and the imagination of power', in Hoy, D. (ed.) *Foucault: a Critical Reader*, Oxford, Blackwell.

Sheridan, A. (1980). *The Will to Truth*, London, Tavistock.

Smart, B. (1986). 'The politics of truth and the problem of hegemony', in Hoy, D. (ed.) *Foucault: a Critical Reader*, Oxford, Blackwell.

Troyna, B. (1992). '"The hub" and "the Rim": how LMS buckles antiracist education', paper presented at the 8th ERA Research Network Seminar, 12 February.

Troyna, B. (1993). 'Critical social research and education policy', paper presented to the Conference on New Directions in Education Policy Sociology, 30–31 March.

Walker, A. (1981). 'Social policy, social administration and the social construction of welfare', *Sociology*, 15 (2), 255–69.

Wallace, M. (1988). 'Innovation for all: management development in small primary schools', *Education Management and Administration*, 16 (1), 15–24.

[2]

J. EDUCATION POLICY, 1988, VOL. 3, NO. 3, 235–247

The construction and deconstruction of educational policy documents

John A Codd
Massey University, Palmerston North, New Zealand

This article begins with a critique of the traditional technical-empiricist approach to policy analysis in which official documents issued by agencies of the state are interpreted as expressions of political intention, that is as proposed courses of action to be discussed by the public before being implemented as official policy. It is argued that this traditional approach to policy is based upon idealist assumptions about the nature of language itself which take it to be a transparent vehicle for the transmission of information, thoughts and values. An alternative approach to the analysis of policy documents is outlined based on theories of discourse that have been developed from within a materialist conception of language. It is suggested that some policy documents legitimate the power of the state and contribute fundamentally to the 'engineering' of consent. Such texts contain divergent meanings, contradictions and structured omissions, so that different effects are produced on different readers. An important task for policy analysis is to examine those effects and expose the ideological processes which lie behind the production of the text. Thus, it is suggested that the analysis of policy documents could be construed as a form of textual deconstruction.

Introduction

For a long time, the field of policy analysis has been fraught with argument over its purposes and methods. What began as a 'policy orientation' within social science (Lasswell 1951) was later elevated by some proponents to the level of 'a new supra discipline' (Dror 1971: ix). A widely accepted view, however, takes policy analysis to be a multidisciplinary field that cuts across existing specializations to employ whatever theoretical or methodological approach is most relevant to the issue or problem under investigation. According to Ham and Hill:

> . . the purpose of policy analysis is to draw on ideas from a range of disciplines in order to interpret the causes and consequences of government action, in particular by focusing on the processes of policy formulation. (Ham and Hill 1984: 11)

Policy here is taken to be any course of action (or inaction) relating to the selection of goals, the definition of values or the allocation of resources. Fundamentally, policy is about the exercise of political power and the language that is used to legitimate that process. Policy analysis is a form of enquiry which provides either the informational base upon which policy is constructed, or the critical examination of existing policies. The former has been called analysis *for* policy, whereas the latter has been called analysis *of* policy (Gordon *et al.* 1977: 27).

Analysis *for* policy can take two different forms: (*a*) *policy advocacy* which has the purpose of making specific policy recommendations; and (*b*) *information for policy* in which the researcher's task is to provide policy-makers with information and data to assist them in the revision or formulation of actual policies.

Analysis *of* policy can also take two different forms: (*a*) *analysis of policy determination and effects*, which examines 'the inputs and transformational processes operating upon the construction of public policy' (Gordon *et al.* 1977: 28) and also the effects of such policies on various groups; and (*b*) *analysis of policy content*, which examines the values, assumptions and ideologies underpinning the policy process.

The central focus of the following discussion is on the analysis of policy content, more specifically, the analysis of the content of policy documents. It is argued that such documents should be regarded as texts which are capable of being decoded in different ways depending upon the contexts in which they are read. It is suggested, moreover, that policy analysts can use some of the methods and theories of textual analysis that have been developed and refined within the field of literary criticism to examine the language content of policy documents. The discussion begins by challenging the dominant account of how official documents function within the policy formation process and questions the theory of language that it presupposes. An alternative approach, derived from a materialist theory of discourse, is then outlined. It is suggested that such an approach to the analysis of policy documents could be construed as a form of textual deconstruction in which ideological effects can be critically examined.

The state and educational policy

The orthodox liberal view of education and society emphasizes the role that schooling plays in promoting social mobility. Within this view, the state has a neutral function to protect the interests of all members of society by a system of universally accepted rules and regulations. Accordingly, the state will promote policies which are in 'the public interest' and whether or not individuals take advantage of those policies is assumed to be a matter that is largely their own responsibility. In this view, the overriding purpose of state policies is to provide an equitable means for the distribution of social goods (such as education) among competing groups on the basis of their needs or deserts. This is a view which, in New Zealand, we have seen exemplified in the writings of Renwick (1986). In recent years, however, this conception of the state has been criticized increasingly from a neo-Marxist point of view (Shuker 1987) in which it is argued that the capitalist Welfare State basically serves the interests of dominant groups within society. Within this critical tradition, Claus Offe's (1984) analysis of the welfare state provides some insights into the purposes, effects and necessary contradictions of many current and proposed government policies.

Offe argues, contrary to the claims of state-derivationist and structural-Marxist theories, that Welfare State policies do not necessarily or automatically serve the interests of the capitalist class. In his view, 'what the state protects and sanctions is a set of institutions and social relationships necessary for the domination of the capitalist class' (Offe 1984: 120) but it nevertheless seeks to implement and guarantee the collective interests of all members of society. In other words, the state works in the interests of the capitalist mode of production rather than exclusively in the interests of one class. In particular, it works to support the process of capital accumulation by providing a context in which the continued expansion of capital is accepted as legitimate. Moreover, the political power of the state depends, indirectly, on the private accumulation of capital which, through taxation, provides the state with its resources. The exercise of this power is legitimated through the democratic processes of election and representation. However, according to Offe, the state's role in the process of capital accumulation, while necessary to advanced forms of capitalism, produces a number of fundamental contradictions at the policy level. These contradictions frequently lead to the failure of policies in areas such as education but they often remain unrecognized because of the language in which such policies are couched. Thus, policies are produced in response to the failure of other policies leading to what Offe refers to as crises of crisis management. Examples within education can be identified in policies relating to assessment and credentialism, transition education and decentralization of curriculum control.

Offe's theory goes a long way towards explaining why the state has a particular interest in promoting public discussions of educational policy such as that which has been recently evidenced in New Zealand by *The Curriculum Review* (1987). Such discussion has become an accepted part of what is called 'the democratic process' through which people come to believe that the policies of the state are the result of 'public consent' rather than necessary forms of social control and crisis management. In other words, if people believe that political decisions are the result of public discussion, and if they have the right to contribute to that discussion, then they are most likely to accept rather than resist existing power relationships.

Because the state has a particular interest in promoting public discussion of educational policy, its agencies produce various policy documents which can be said to constitute the official discourse of the state (Codd 1985). Thus, policies produced by and for the state are obvious instances in which language serves a political purpose, constructing particular meanings and signs that work to mask social conflict and foster commitment to the notion of a universal public interest. In this way, policy documents produce real social effects through the production and maintenance of consent. These effects, however, remain unrecognized by traditional forms of policy analysis which are derived from an idealist view of language and enshrined within technical-empiricist view of policy-making.

The technical-empiricist approach to policy-making

Policy documents are generally interpreted as expressions of political purpose, that is as statements of the courses of action that policy-makers and administrators intend to follow. Within this view, the analysis of a policy document becomes a quest for the authorial intentions presumed to lie behind the text. It is a form of analysis which is frequently part of an instrumentalist approach to the whole policy-making process. Discrete functions are assigned to the policy researcher (who is a disinterested provider of information), the policy-maker (who produces the policy), and the policy recipient (who interprets or implements the policy). The document itself is regarded as a vehicle of communication between these agents within the process.

The traditional view of policy-making is a technical-empiricist one in which the researcher or social scientist is expected to produce a body of knowledge encompassing various factual explanations and causal connections which policy-makers may then draw upon in the formulation of policy proposals and the writing of policy documents. The policy researcher produces the general laws and theories relating to the structures which govern educational processes, while the policy-maker must then decide the 'best means' of achieving certain predetermined goals. Thus, policy analysis is relegated to a totally instrumental function, succinctly described by Fay in the following terms:

> A policy science is supposed to be a device for organizing political thought in a rational way, merely a method for clarifying empirical relationships among alternative actions and for sorting out their likely consequences, and a procedure for making 'correct' decisions; as such, it is supposed to be employable by anyone, regardless of his political views, for any end whatsoever, and its results are supposed to be impartial in the sense of not being dependent upon the particular evaluations of the policy scientist for their truth. (Fay 1975: 57)

Expressed simply, the technical-empiricist view of policy formation treats educational provision as a set of means to given ends. These ends are expressions of educational aims and belong within the domain of values. How we might go about achieving them is a question for research and belongs within the domain of facts. Thus it is assumed that there are alternative means available to given ends and that the proper role for research is in evaluating the effectiveness and efficiency of alternative means for attaining the chosen ends. It is assumed that research (with its objective methods of data collection and theory validation) provides scientific knowledge about the means available and their relative effectiveness under different circumstances.

Within a technical-empiricist approach to educational policy-making, policy statements or documents relate educational intentions, in the form of values and goals, to factual information resulting from research. These statements must then be interpreted by those who would either discuss or implement the policy. This can be represented diagrammatically as in figure 1.

Because policy documents are construed as *expressions* of particular information, ideas and intentions, the task of analysis becomes one of establishing the *correct* interpretation of the text. When there is controversy surrounding the meaning of a document, it is assumed that some readers have misunderstood what was meant. One of the tasks of the policy analyst within this approach therefore, is to clear up such confusions and establish an authoritative interpretation. However, in the next two sections it is argued that such a task is founded upon mistaken idealist assumptions about both the nature of intentions and the nature of language itself. It is subsequently argued that these assumptions are widely held because they belong within a liberal humanist ideology which is largely successful in masking fundamental contradictions behind the rhetoric of many state policies.

The intentional fallacy

To assume that policy documents express intentions is to subscribe to a version of what in literary criticism has come to be known as the *intentional fallacy* (Wimsatt and Beardsley 1954). In essence, this particular version of the fallacy holds that the meaning of a literary text corresponds to what the author *intended*, that is the text is taken as being *evidence* of what the

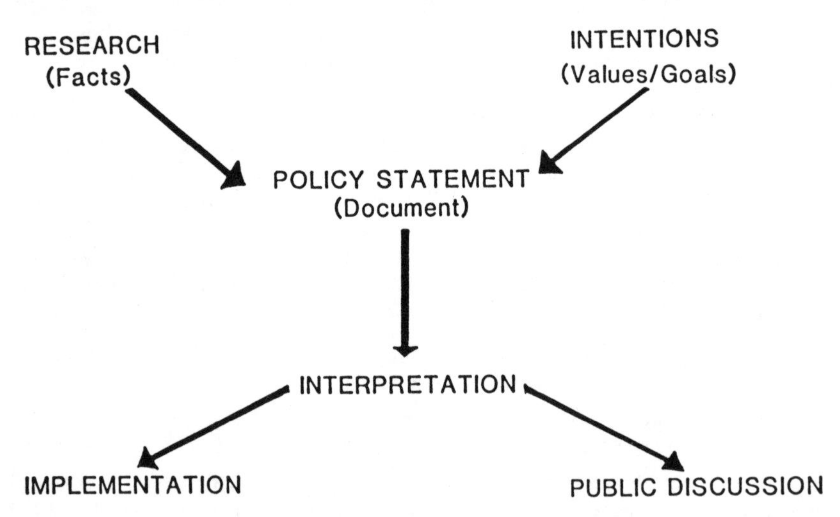

Figure 1. Technical-Empiricist Model of Policy Analysis

author intended to express. As Lyas (1973) points out, the fallacy can be shown to derive from an idealist confusion about the relevant sense of 'intention'. First, it is a mistake to think of intentions as private mental events (arguments which show this to be a mistake can be found in Wittgenstein's *Philosophical Investigations*, 1953). Second, intentions are not the same as 'statements of intention' (people can be mistaken about their own intentions). Third, we must distinguish between an intention in the sense of a prior plan or design and an action that is done *intentionally*. In short, it is the adverbial sense of intention, rather than the nominal sense, that is relevant to the interpretation of texts. The crucial point, however, is that nothing can be said about an author's intentions apart from various features of the text itself and the context in which it is interpreted. As Fay points out:

> Intentional explanations . . . make sense of a person's actions by fitting them into a purposeful pattern which reveals how the act was warranted, given the actor, his social and physical situation and his beliefs and wants. An intention is no more 'behind' the action than the meaning of the word is 'behind' the letters of which it is composed, and it is no more an 'invisible mental cause' of an act than is a melody the invisible cause of the pattern of notes that we hear at a concert. (Fay 1975: 73–4)

The place of intentional explanations in literary interpretation was first challenged by a group of literary critics in the 1940s and 50s who have come to be associated with what is called the 'New Criticism' (Simonson 1971). These critics insisted upon what they called 'the autonomy of the text' which implied that the meaning of a text could not extend beyond the literary object itself. Some structuralists went even further, insisting upon a complete negation of the concept of authorship within literary analysis. Roland Barthes, for instance, has argued that:

> . . . .a text is not a line of words releasing a single 'theological' meaning (the 'message' of the Author-God) but a multi-dimensional space in which a variety of writings, none of them original, blend and clash. (Barthes, 1977: 146)

Barthes goes even further when he adds that:

> . . . .a text's unity lies not in its origin but in its destination . . . .the birth of the reader must be at the cost of the death of the Author. (Barthes 1977: 148)

Another influential literary critic, Northrop Frye (1957) has also totally rejected the invocation of the author as any guarantee that a text can have a single meaning. What this means, essentially, is that for any text a plurality of readers must necessarily produce a plurality of readings.

Now, it should be recognized that there has been considerable debate about the nature of intentional explanations in literary criticism, and their significance for the validity of interpretation (Hirsch 1967). Nevertheless, there are important implications here for policy analysis, given that many policy documents do not even have single identifiable authors and are inevitably addressed to a plurality of readers. Instead of searching for authorial intentions, perhaps the proper task of policy analysis is to examine the differing effects that documents have in the production of meaning by readers. This would involve a form of discourse analysis developed within a materialistic theory of language. Before examining the implications of such an approach, however, it is necessary to consider the linguistic assumptions behind the traditional technical-empiricist approach to policy-making.

Linguistic idealism

Attempts to analyse policy documents by explicating the ideas within them and clarifying their intended meanings, presuppose a theory of language which may be called idealist because of the posited relationships between words, thoughts and things. These relationships were illustrated diagrammatically by Ogden and Richards (1923: 11) in what has come to be called 'the semiotic triangle' (see figure 2).

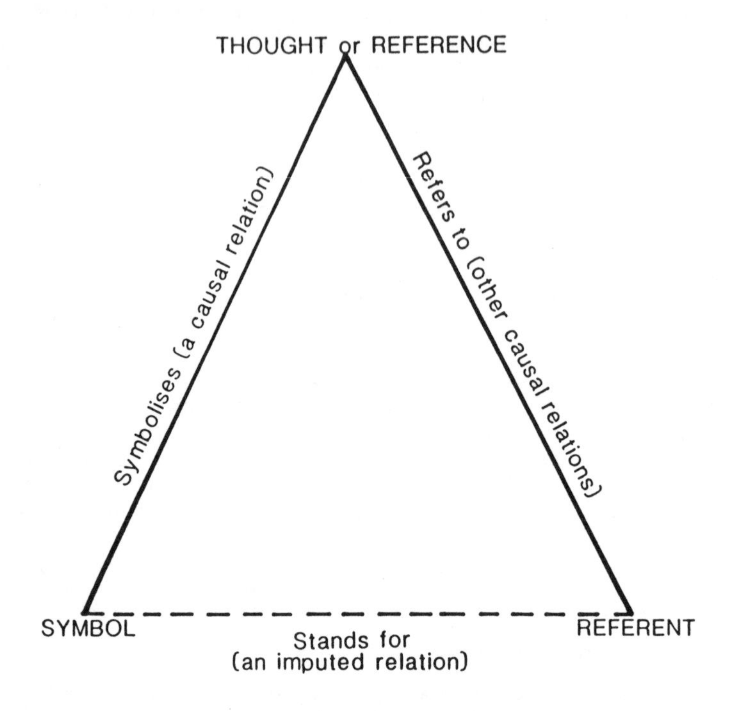

Figure 2. The Semiotic Triangle

Ogden and Richards argued that language bears an indirect relationship to the real world, one which is imputed because it is mediated by thought. The relationship between language and thought is direct and causal. Moreover:

> When we speak, the symbolism we employ is caused partly by the reference we are making and partly by social and psychological factors – the purpose for which we are making the reference, the proposed effect of our symbols on other persons and our own attitude. When we hear what is said, the symbols both cause us to perform an act of reference and to assume an attitude which will, according to circumstances, be more or less similar to the act and the attitude of the speaker. (Ogden and Richards 1923: 10–11).

Given these relationships, conceptual truth becomes a matter of the correctness of language in expressing what is thought and the adequacy of the language in producing a concurrence of thought in a suitable interpreter. Thus, within this theory of language, symbolic truth (coherence) is distinguished from referential truth (correspondence). Ogden and Richards define symbolic (or conceptual) truth as follows:

> A true symbol = one which correctly records an adequate reference. It is usually a set of words in the form of a proposition or sentence. It correctly records an adequate reference when it will cause a similar reference to occur in a suitable interpreter. It is false when it records an inadequate reference. (Ogden and Richards 1923: 102)

This means that a proposition can be empirically false and yet also be a correct expression of what the speaker thought. Conceptual clarity is not dependent on empirical truth and Ogden and Richards make the point that:

> It is often of great importance to distinguish between false and incorrect propositions. An incorrect symbol is one which in a given universe of discourse causes in a suitable interpreter a reference different from that symbolized in the speaker. (Ogden and Richards 1923: 102)

This is the conception of language implicit in the work of policy analysts who seek to clarify the meaning of policy documents. The main point of their work is to make language transparent through correct use in order to produce commensurability of meaning amongst different readers of the text. Essentially, this kind of policy analysis takes language to be a transparent vehicle for the expression of experience. It is a view of language in which:

> Our concepts and our knowledge are held to be the product of experience (*empiricism*), and this experience is preceded and interpreted by the mind, reason or thought, the property of a transcendent human nature whose essence is the attribute of each individual (*idealism*). (Belsey 1980: 7).

What this empiricist-idealist view of language is unable to take into account, however, is that language itself is a sphere of social practice and is necessarily structured by the material conditions in which that practice takes place. This requires an alternative conception of language which recognizes that words, whether in speech-acts or texts, do more than simply name things or ideas that already exist. It requires a conception of how the use of language can produce real social effects, and how it can be political, not only by referring to political events, but by itself becoming the instrument and object of power. In particular, if it is to inform the analysis of policies produced by and for the state, it requires a conception of how language produces ideological effects by suppressing the contradictions of people's experience in the interests of preserving the existing social formation. Such a materialist conception of langauge has emerged within theories of discourse which can be traced back to the pioneering work of the French linguist, Ferdinand de Saussure.

Theories of discourse

Saussure's work has had a major influence on the structuralist tradition which adheres to the view that language precedes experience at some levels, making the world intelligible by differentiating between concepts. While this is not the place for a detailed account of structuralist theories of language, it shall suffice to say that this tradition has totally rejected the idea that language symbolizes the reality of an individual's experience and *expresses* that reality in a discourse which enables other individuals to recognize it as true.

Saussure challenged the notion that words express pre-existent ideas and the assumption that language can be reduced to a naming process. He argued that language is not simply a static set of signs through which individual agents transmit messages to each other about an externally constituted world of 'things'. Rather, language is a set of social practices which makes it possible for people to construct a meaningful world of individuals and things. In his pioneering work, Saussure distinguished between *langue* (the normative rules or conventions of language) and *parole* (the actual utterances made by speakers in concrete situations).

In opposition to idealist theories of language, Saussure argued that the linguistic sign unites, not a thing and a name, but a concept and a sound image. This is not a causal relationship, but rather, as Saussure pointed out:

> The two elements are intimately united, and each recalls the other. Whether we try to find the meaning of the Latin word 'arbor' or the word that Latin uses to designate the concept 'tree', it is clear that only the associations sanctioned by that language appear to us to conform to reality, and we disregard whatever others might be imagined. (Saussure 1974: 66–7)

Saussure argued that language is a product of social forces. It is *both* an arbitrary system of signs *and* a domain of socially constituted practices. Like any other social institution it will change over time but always within social and temporal limits. Such limits, or structures, both enable and at the same time check the amount of choice that is available to a community of language users.

> Language is checked not only by the weight of the collectivity but also by time. These two are inseparable. At every moment solidarity with the past checks freedom of choice. We say *man* and *dog* because our predecessors said *man* and *dog*. This does not prevent the existence in the total phenomenon of a bond between the two antithetical forces – arbitrary convention by virtue of which choice is free and time which causes choice to be fixed. Because the sign is arbitrary, it follows no law other than that of tradition, and because it is based on tradition, it is arbitrary. (Saussure 1974: 74)

Saussure's work was to prepare the way for a materialist theory of language in which the term *discourse* has come to be used to embody both the formal system of signs *and* the social practices which govern their use. In this sense, *discourse* refers not only to the meaning of language but also to the real effects of language-use, to the materiality of language. A discourse is a domain of language-use and therefore a domain of lived experience. It can be ideological in the Althusserian sense because it can become an unconscious, taken-for-granted 'system of representations' (Althusser 1969: 231–236). This form of ideology is *inscribed in* discourse rather than symbolized by it, in other words, it is not synonymous with a set of doctrines or a system of beliefs which individuals may choose to accept or reject. As Catherine Belsey points out:

> A discourse involves certain shared assumptions which appear in the formulations that characterize it. The discourse of common sense is quite distinct, for instance, from the discourse of modern physics, and some of the formulations of the one may be expected to conflict with the formulations of the other. Ideology is *inscribed in* discourse in the sense that it is literally written or spoken *in it*; it is not a separate element which exists independently in some free-floating realm of 'ideas' and is subsequently embodied in words, but a way of thinking, speaking, experiencing (Belsey 1980: 5)

Because people participate in a range of discourses (political, scientific, religious) there are manifold ways in which they can signify and represent the conditions of their lived experience. But this does not separate discourse from subjective experience. Rather, discourse itself is constitutive of subjective experience and is also a material force within the construction of subjectivity (Macdonell 1986).

The point has been made earlier that theories of discourse are centrally concerned with the relationship between language and ideology. In this sense, ideology includes all the ways in which meaning (signification) serves to sustain relations of domination (Thompson 1984). To explain this further, it is necessary to invoke the notion of discursive power. Only within a materialist view of language is it possible to show how discourse can mediate the exercise of power, for it must go beyond the meaning of what is said to the act of saying it. As Bourdieu has stated:

> Language is not only an instrument of communication or even of knowledge, but also an instrument of power. One seeks not only to be understood but also to be believed, obeyed, respected, distinguished. (Bourdieu 1977: 648)

To understand how language can be an instrument of power it is necessary to extend the concept of power itself. At one level, power can be readily understood as coercive force or restraint. What is much more difficult to comprehend is the idea of power being exercised through consent, through what Gramsci called 'ideological hegemony'. To recognize power in terms of sovereignty or exploitation is less problematic than to recognize the forms of power which penetrate consciousness itself. These latter forms of power are normatively exercised within structures of distorted communication and false constructions of social reality. As institutionalized forms of domination they constitute pervasive expressions of power without normally being recognized as such by those who are affected. These are the micro-technologies of power that have been studied with such acute concentration in the work of Michel Foucault.

While rejecting the orthodox Marxist distinction between knowledge and ideology, Foucault has advanced the view that all knowledge is a product of power relations. Within this view, he has developed a non-economic analysis of power and power relations (Smart 1983). Rather than being a possession or commodity, power is exercised through dispositions, techniques, examinations and discourses. Foucault argues that:

> In a society such as ours, but basically in any society, there are manifold relations of power which permeate, characterize and constitute the social body, and these relations of power cannot themselves be established, consolidated nor implemented without the production, accumulation, circulation and functioning of a discourse. There can be no possible exercise of power without a certain economy of discourses of truth which operates through and on the basis of this association. (Foucault 1980: 93)

The power that is exercised through discourse is a form of power which permeates the deepest recesses of civil society and provides the material conditions in which individuals are produced both as subjects and as objects. It is this form of power which is exercised through the discourses of the law, of medicine, psychology and education.

In most modern societies, the education system is controlled by the state, but it works to maintain relations of power throughout the society as a whole. For this reason, the official discourse of the state relating to educational policies (eg., core curriculum, transition education, systems of assessment or school management) are obvious instances in which discourse becomes the instrument and object of power. But discourses operate at a number of levels within educational institutions. Teachers, for example, have their own craft discourse relating to pedagogical practice. This discourse will impose limits upon what is possible in areas of classroom organization control and discipline, or the assessment of learning. More importantly, however, the whole schooling process is an apparatus for the distribution, appropriation and stratification of discourses. Foucault writes about schooling in the following way:

> But we know very well that, in its distribution, in what it permits and what it prevents, it follows the lines laid down by social differences, conflicts and struggles. Every educational system is a political means of maintaining or modifying the appropriation of discourses, with the knowledge and power they bring with them. (Foucault 1972: 46)

In addition to these discourses embodied in school curricula, there are many theoretical discourses *about* educational phenomena which have been instrumental in the exercise of power and have had far-reaching effects upon the institution of schooling. The discourse of psychometrics, for instance, is an obvious case in point (Rose 1979, Gould 1981). During a period of 50 years, the language of mental measurement has penetrated the craft discourse of teachers and shaped their practices. A critical analysis of such discourse seeks to expose the connections between psychometric theories and administrative practices, revealing the effects of using this form of technical language to legitimate the exercise of power.

Deconstructing policy documents: the case of 'The Curriculum Review'

The deconstruction of official discourse, in the form of documents, reports and policy statements, treats such texts as cultural and ideological artifacts to be interpreted in terms of their implicit patterns of signification, underlying symbolic structures and contextual determinants of meaning (Burton and Carlen 1979). Policy documents in this kind of analysis do not have a single authoritative meaning. They are not blueprints for political action, expressing a set of unequivocal intentions. They are ideological texts that have been constructed within a particular historical and political context. The task of deconstruction begins with the explicit recognition of that context.

In New Zealand during the 1980s much of the public discussion about education has focused on policies concerning the official, or 'core' school curriculum. In March 1984, a major controversy arose when the politically conservative Minister of Education at that time released a policy document (*A Review of the Core Curriculum for Schools*) allowing a period of only eight weeks for public comment and formal submissions. Among other proposals, the policy contained a list of 'basic' subjects which schools would be compelled to teach for stipulated minimum periods of time. Teachers' organizations, academic commentators and spokespeople on the political 'left' condemned the document for what were perceived to be its restrictive and anti-democratic implications.

Coincidentally, at the height of this controversy, the government called a 'snap' election and, perhaps predictably, with public attention already focused on the core curriculum for schools, education became an election issue. The opposition Labour Party pledged to 're-open' the discussion and to extend the opportunities for consultation and participation. Labour won the election on 14 July 1984 and the new Minister of Education announced that the review of the core curriculum for schools would be re-opened and would involve wide public discussion.

The Committee to Review the Curriculum for Schools was set up by the Minister in November 1984. During the following year, a series of issue booklets were distributed to stimulate and focus public discussion. In this phase of the review, more than 21,500 responses were received from individuals and groups, including students, parents, school committees, boards, teacher organizations, Maori and Pacific Island groups, and community education organizations. A draft report was released in August 1986 and a further 10,000 responses were received. The final document, entitled *The Curriculum Review*, was released in March 1987. It has subsequently been lauded by the political 'left' while invoking strong criticism from the 'right' for its 'liberal and costly' proposals.

The Curriculum Review is a 128 page policy document divided into two main sections. The first section sets out the policy and the second is largely descriptive of the review process itself. Considered as a whole, the document is constructed within an ideological framework of liberal humanism which enables the text to be read in different ways by readers who occupy different social locations. Belsey describes the main assumptions upon which such a framework rests:

> The ideology of liberal humanism assumes a world of non-contradictory (and therefore fundamentally unalterable) individuals whose unfettered consciousness is the origin of meaning, knowledge and action. It is in the interests of this ideology above all to suppress the role of language in the construction of the subject, and to present the individual as a free, unified autonomous subjectivity. (Belsey 1980: 67)

Within this kind of ideology, policy texts such as *The Curriculum Review* are constructed as determinate representations (i.e, they claim to convey intelligible relationships between elements of social reality). Hence, the document opens with a statement which focuses on the individual learner and projects an image of social harmony surrounding the institution of schooling.

> The learner is at the heart of all educational planning. Learning is the distinctive purpose of schools. Learning happens best when there is an active partnership of students, teachers, families, and the community. (*The Curriculum Review*, 1987: 8)

The document asserts that a national common curriculum should 'be given status by regulation' and that 'each school have responsibility to develop a school curriculum which is consistent with the national common curriculum'. In other words, the document presents simultaneously proposals which can be interpreted as representing *both* centralization and decentralization of control. There is a strong emphasis on school and community based planning of the curriculum while, at the same time, it is stated that each school's curriculum 'must be agreed to by the schools' managing body, and approved by the district senior inspector' (p. 21). Nowhere in the document is the possibility of conflicts of interest discussed and the fundamental contradiction between autonomy and control is not addressed directly.

One of the central tasks for the critical analysis of a document such as *The Curriculum Review* is a deconstruction of its text which focuses on the processes of its production as well as on the organization of the discourses which constitute it and the strategies by which it masks the contradictions and incoherences of the ideology that is inscribed in it. The process of deconstruction of policy texts is an objective process because such texts contain within themselves an implicit critique of their own values.

The values that are central to *The Curriculum Review* are explicitly presented within the 15 basic principles upon which the national common curriculum is to be developed. These principles signify an ideal set of conditions which prescribe that the curriculum shall be: common to all schools; accessible to every student; non-racist and non-sexist; able to ensure significant success for all students; whole; balanced; of the highest quality for every student; planned; co-operatively designed; responsive, inclusive, enabling, enjoyable. These values presuppose the existence of a social context in which it is possible for all individuals to gain maximum fulfilment – a society which is non-competitive and where unlimited resources can be distributed to all on an equal basis. Such a society, of course, does not exist outside the liberal-humanist ideology within which it is conceived. The implicit critique of this ideology is signified by the document's total lack of any specific reference to a social context in which there are major structural inequalities and where there is fierce competition for finite resources. Nowhere does this document contain language which would draw the attention of the reader to the current fiscal crisis, the unequal distribution of power or the economic imperatives of a segmented labour market. The internal contradiction is brought into sharp focus by the small section of the document presented under the heading 'Economic Implications'. Here it is stated that:

> Some of the resources needed to implement the recommendations of this review already exist; others will need to be developed, and some of these have considerable financial implications. (*The Curriculum Review* 1987: 20)

This can be read as an *understatement* which draws attention to the impossibility of achieving what the 15 principles prescribe. Such a reading however, which is a deconstruction of the text's explicit meaning, requires a new process of production of meaning by the reader.

The above example serves to illustrate how the process of deconstruction can be used in the analysis of a policy document such as *The Curriculum Review*. This process needs to distance itself from the imaginary coherence of the text, examining its discourse and viewing it not as a vehicle for communicating 'information' or transmitting 'a plan of action', but as an ideologically constructed product of political forces. Because it is unable to produce a coherent and internally consistent representation of a contradictory social world, the policy text, in spite of itself, embodies incoherences, distortions, structured omissions and negations which in turn expose the inability of the language of ideology to produce coherent meaning. Deconstructive analysis would focus on the process of production of the text as well as on the organization of the discourses which constitute it and the linguistic strategies by which it masks the contradictions and incoherences of the ideology that is inscribed in it. The purpose of deconstructing policy texts is to ascertain their actual and potential effects upon readers, rather than to establish the intended meaning of their authors. As Belsey points out:

> The aim is to locate the point of contradiction within the text, the point at which it transgresses the limits within which it is constructed, breaks free of the constraints imposed by its own realist form. Composed of contradictions, the text is no longer restricted to a single, harmonious and authoritative reading. Instead it becomes *plural*, open to re-reading, no longer an object for passive consumption but an object of work by the reader to produce meaning. (Belsey 1980: 104)

Empirical evidence of a policy document's plurality of meaning can be readily obtained from an examination of the comments made about it by various categories of reader. The widely differing comments made about *The Curriculum Review*, for example, by representatives of teachers' and parents' organizations, politicians, various conservative (and liberal) pressure groups and, most notably, The Treasury, demonstrate the wide spectrum of interpretations that such a text can elicit. The aim of discourse analysis is not to prove which of these readings is *correct* but to consider them *all* as evidence of the text's inherent ideological ambiguities, distortions and absences. In this way, it is possible to penetrate the ideology of official policy documents and expose the real conflicts of interest within the social world which they claim to represent.

Conclusion

In surveying the field of policy analysis a decade ago, Dye suggested that it was a weakness of such analysis that it concentrated 'primarily upon activities of governments, rather than the rhetoric of governments' (Dye 1976: 21). What were needed, however, were methods appropriate to this new task. This article has gone some way towards outlining an alternative approach to the analysis of policy documents based on theories of discourse.

References

ALTHUSSER, L. (1969) *For Marx*, trans. B. Brewster, (London: Penguin).
BARTHES, R. (1977) 'The death of the author' in *Image-Music-Text* (Glasgow: Fontana/Collins). (Originally published in French.)
BELSEY, C. (1980) *Critical Practice* (London: Methuen).
BOURDIEU, (1977) 'The economics of linguistic exchanges', *Social Science Information*, 16(6), pp. 645–668.
BURTON F. and CARLEN, P. (1979) *Official Discourse* (London: Routledge & Kegan Paul).
CODD, J. A. (1985) 'Images of schooling and the discourse of the state' in J. Codd, R. Harker and R. Nash (eds.) *Political Issue in New Zealand Education* (Palmerston North: Dunmore Press) pp. 23–41.
DROR, Y. (1971) *Design for Policy Sciences* (New York: Elsevier).
DYE, T. R. (1976) *Policy Analysis* (Alabama: University of Alabama Press).
FAY, B. (1975) *Social Theory and Political Practice* (London: Allen and Unwin).
FOUCAULT, M. (1972) *The Archaeology of Knowledge* (London: Tavistock).
FOUCAULT, M. (1980) 'Two lectures', in C. Gordon (ed.) *Power/Knowledge: Selected Interviews and Other Writings 1972–1977* (Brighton: Harvester Press) pp. 78–108.
FRYE, N. (1957) *Anatomy of Criticism* (Princeton: Princeton University Press).
GORDON, I., LEWIS, J. and YOUNG, K. (1977) 'Perspectives on policy analysis', *Public Administration Bulletin*, 25, pp. 26–35.
GOULD, S. J. (1981) *The Mismeasure of Man* (London: Penguin).
HAM, C. and HILL, M. (1984) *The Policy Process in the Modern Capitalist State* (Brighton: Harvester Press).
HIRSCH, E. D. (1967) *Validity in Interpretation* (New Haven: Yale University Press).
LASSWELL, H. (1951) 'The policy orientation', in D. Lerner and H. Lasswell (eds.) *The Policy Sciences* (Stanford: Stanford University Press) pp. 3–15.

LYAS, C. (1973) 'Personal qualities and the intentional fallacy', in G. Vesey (ed.) *Philosophy and the Arts* (London: Macmillan) pp. 194–210.

MACDONELL, D. (1986) *Theories of Discourse* (Oxford: Blackwell).

OFFE, C. (1984) *Contradictions of the Welfare State* (London: Hutchinson).

OGDEN, C. K. and RICHARDS, I. A. (1923) *The Meaning of Meaning* (London: Routledge & Kegan Paul).

RENWICK, W. L. (1986) *Moving Targets* (Wellington: NZCER).

REPORT OF THE COMMITTEE TO REVIEW THE CURRICULUM FOR SCHOOLS (1987) *The Curriculum Review* (Wellington: Government Printer).

REVIEW OF THE CORE CURRICULUM FOR SCHOOLS (1984) (Wellington: Department of Education).

ROSE, N. (1979) 'The psychological complex: mental measurement and social administration', *Ideology and Consciousness*, 5, pp. 5–68.

SAUSSURE, F. (1974) *Courses in General Linguistics* (London: Fontana/Collins). (Originally published in French 1916.)

SHUKER, R. (1987) *The One Best System* (Palmerston North: Dunmore Press).

SIMONSON, H. P. (1971) *Strategies in Criticism* (New York: Holt, Rinehart and Winston).

SMART, B. (1983) *Foucault, Marxism and Critique* (London: Routledge & Kegan Paul).

THOMPSON, J. B. (1984) *Studies in the Theory of Ideology* (Cambridge: Polity Press).

WIMSATT, W. and BEARDSLEY, M. (1954) 'The intentional fallacy', in W. K. Wimsatt (ed.) *The Verbal Icon* (London: Methuen) pp. 3–18.

WITTGENSTEIN, L. (1953) *Philosophical Investigations*, trans. G. E. M. Anscombe, (Oxford: Blackwell).

[3]

British Journal of Educational Studies
Vol XXXXII No 1, March 1994 ISSN 0007–1005

IMPLEMENTATION RESEARCH AND EDUCATION POLICY: PRACTICE AND PROSPECTS

by John Fitz, *School of Education, University of Wales Cardiff,* David Halpin, *Department of Education, University of Warwick, and* Sally Power, *Department of Education, University of Warwick.*

ABSTRACT: This paper offers a brief guide to implementation research and some of the conceptual and methodological issues it raises. In the course of reviewing investigations of the import of aspects of the 1988 Education Reform Act, it also considers the issues posed for education policy studies in a context where the 'centre' is connected to a dispersed and differentiated periphery.

Key words: Formulation, Implementation, Policy Cycle

1. Introduction

Implementation research is broadly concerned to investigate the structures and processes within which policy objectives are put into practice. It has been an established branch of political science for at least two decades. That body of work, however, has rarely informed the analysis of education policy. It is against that background that this paper offers a brief guide to implementation research and to some of the conceptual and methodological issues it raises.

The paper is organized into three sections. The first section reviews some of the theoretical and methodological properties of the so-called 'top down' and 'bottom up' approaches to implementation research.

The second section is a selective account of implementation research as it appears in some recent analyses of English education policy, including our own research on grant-maintained schools. It notes that little systematic distinction is made between policy formulation and policy implementation.

Section three reviews a range of research which focuses on the impact of the 1988 Education Reform Act. It moves on to consider the issues posed for policy research in a context where the 'centre' is connected to a diverse, dispersed and differentiated periphery.

2. Implementation Research and the Policy Process

Implementation studies were born out of adversity[1]. The 'first wave' of implementation research was North American, and was broadly concerned to understand why a series of Federally funded programmes, launched in the 1960s, were relatively ineffective (Ham and Hill, 1984). Their geist is appropriately conveyed by a sub-title to one of the early studies of policy implementation:

> How Great Expectations in Washington are Dashed in Oakland: or Why It's Amazing that Federal Programmes Work At All, This Being the Saga of the Economic Development Administration as told by two Sympathetic Observers Who Seek to Build Morals on the Foundations of Ruined Hopes. (Pressman and Wildavsky, 1973, quoted in Ham and Hill, 1984 p. 97).

These 'top down' studies (Sabatier, 1986) characteristically focused on the implementation of policies developed at the centre in local or 'street level' environments. The research was primarily concerned to identify the conditions which would maximize the translation of policy objectives into practice. These studies also sought to redress the relative neglect of research into policy execution and management, particularly in the field of political science, which hitherto had primarily concerned itself with policy formulation.

The 'top down' approach conceived policy formulation and policy implementation as two distinct phases within the policy process and organized research around them, thus confirming the distinction. That tendency was further advanced by the construction of models, structured around successive 'stages' of the policy implementation process, that aimed to map 'linkages', 'veto points' or 'decision points' involved in policy development (e.g. Sabatier and Mazmanian, 1981). Inferences were drawn between the number of linkages in the policy process and the likelihood of a policy being implemented successfully.

By virtue of making the distinction between policy formulation and policy implementation, 'top down' studies tended to render the policy process as hierarchical and linear. In the USA, for example, this reflects divisions within the policy community, particularly at the Federal level. Here, there are clear divisions between political appointees, who see their role as policy formulators, and career public servants whose primary role is to implement policy (Heclo, 1984).

Moreover, it is an approach which corresponds in structure to the constitutional separation of powers between Federal and state governments. While the first wave of implementation researchers modified their models in response to internal critique and to empirical testing (Sabatier, 1986), the centre-focused, hierarchical framework within which the studies were conducted were seen as obstacles by the second wave of implementation researchers. They sought to address implementation research from the 'bottom up'[2].

There are several strands within 'bottom up' implementation research and these may co-exist within one particular study. It is an approach, however, which emphasises the importance of the 'street level' bureaucrats and locally based organizations to the success or otherwise of policy implementation. These, it is argued, are the institutions, organizations and actors considered to be most closely involved in the lives of target groups and individuals and, it is they, through their interaction with consumers, who determine the extent to which policies are rendered effective.

The shift in focus from 'top' to 'bottom' had two important consequences for the organization of implementation research. The first was a change in the unit of analysis. The second concerned the methods of enquiry, particularly how and where implementation research was to be conducted.

Hjern and Hull (1982), for example, argue that the 'constitution' (formal authority structures, the legislature, the legal system and public administration) was the unit of analysis of 'top down' research. In effect, this limited the number and kind of participants considered to be part of the policy process, both being determined by the range of 'legitimate' authority structures within any given system. They proposed that the 'policy system' should be substituted as the object of enquiry. For these authors, therefore:

> The methodological imperative for describing a policy system is to identify the policy makers who populate it in order that its goals, environments and resources become determinate (Hjern and Hull, 1982 p. 106).

Their larger purpose was to expand the number of organizations, groups and individuals considered as participants in the policy process. They argued that this would also 'democratise' implementation research through the inclusion of actors, organizations and individuals 'outside' the authority structures as legitimate actors. Moreover, as more participants were assigned an active role in the process, sustaining any clear-cut distinction between 'formulation' and 'implementation' became more problematic, as the number of sites where policy was interpreted and acted on increased.

Within this general reconceptualization of implementation research there were divergent forms of investigation. There were, for example, studies of single policies and their impact in local settings. Other enquiries focused on 'street level' bureaucrats or target groups and sought their views on a raft of policies and their articulation to actors' everyday lives. Here, enquiries were concerned to identify the relative importance actors attach to a variety of policies and to their prioritization of policies that influence their lives. Although this was a rather more indirect study of implementation, it had the advantage of screening out the intentions of policy advocates in order to yield more consumer-orientated accounts of policy effectiveness[3].

Clearly, there are limitations to 'bottom up' research. Sabatier (1986) notes three difficulties. First, it is likely to over-emphasize the ability of the periphery to frustrate the centre's intentions. Second, its focus on present participants in the policy process tend to overlook policy developments in the past and the influence of earlier (and different?) participants. Third, in making the perceptions and activities of participants paramount, it is in danger of leaving unanalysed 'social, legal and economic factors which structure the perceptions, resources and participation of those actors' (Sabatier, 1986 p. 35).

The last point is important when seeking to understand why policies produce 'winners' and 'losers'. Moreover, in the context of societies structured around a combination of capitalist production relations and liberal democratic institutions, the macro factors Sabatier refer to also underpin explanations as to why a variety of policies, over time, are likely to produce the same sets of 'winners' and 'losers' (e.g. Bourdieu, 1977; Land, 1978).

This brief account of the first two waves of implementation research inadequately represents the diversity of types of study within the two approaches. Neither does it do justice to the sophisticated attempts at model building and conceptualization of the implementation process nor report sufficiently on the extension application of these models to specific policies. For analytical purposes it also suggests there was a clear sequence in kinds of implementation research, where, in practice, there has been considerable overlap between the two. Nevertheless, in drawing attention to the importance of implementation as an important challenge to academics, implementation researchers operating within mainstream social science have, by implication, identified issues which ought also to be the concern of education policy research.

Some of these matters, such as the distinction between 'formulation' and 'implementation', the relative power of the centre to impose its will on local agencies, and whether the focus should be 'constitutional' structures or 'policy systems' are especially relevant and will be taken up below.

3. Implementation Research and Education Policy Studies

Although there has been a considerable expansion in the study of policy-making in education in recent years, very few researchers have cited or built on previously existing studies of implementation. One exception is Charles Raab, but his area of research and publication has been broadly construed as 'political science' (e.g. Raab, 1992a). There is more than a family resemblance, however, between the ways in which implementation researchers have gone about their work and the approaches adopted by those engaged in education policy analysis.

Both sets of researchers show a clear preference for qualitative methods of enquiry. In education, this has generally involved documentary and archive research, followed by interviews with policy makers, implementers and recipients, combined, in some cases, with observation of groups making and taking decisions over extended periods of time (e.g. Brehony and Deem, 1991). The purpose here, as Raab notes, is to understand actions and motives from the inside (Raab, 1992 p. 12). A danger in this approach, however, is the investigation can become locked into the discourse of participants in the policy process and disregard or underplay larger economic, political and administrative factors which also shape policy development (see Ozga, 1990). But, equally, different strategies have been suggested for moving beyond it. Ozga, for example, indicates the importance of locating policy-makers within a wider social context (Ozga, 1987). In the case of 'the powerful', this includes mapping shared class membership and backgrounds in particular schools and universities, and extended family and other social connections. Thus, the explanation of why some policies and values are promoted, and others are not, involves reference to sites outside the direct processes and procedures of education policymaking (Gewirtz and Ozga, 1990). For Raab, 'interviewing and close observation' are the methods which yield the data for the analysis of 'the network of interacting actors' (Raab, 1992b, p. 12). In Raab's case, it is 'the network', as well its individual members, which is the focus of policy determination and dissemination. In general, then, however diverse the research techniques and theoretical orientations, recent studies of education policy have shown a strong preference for 'getting inside' the policy process.

As to the policy process itself, however, education policy studies, particularly those which have focused in depth on single policies, employ the terms 'formulation' and 'implementation' but without theorizing any distinction between them. (e.g. Dale, 1990; Edwards, Fitz and Whitty, 1989). In these examples, 'formulation' and 'implementation' appear as relatively unproblematic stages within the narration of the policy process. In addition, they also denote stages around which data collection and analysis was organized. These terms have been employed generally to describe two different kinds of activity: the making and the execution of policy. On examination, however, and certainly in the above studies of education policy, these differences are difficult to sustain in any meaningful and systematic way.

The Assisted Places Scheme study, is one example of the difficulty of maintaining this distinction (Edwards, Fitz and Whitty, 1989). Chapter three of the study is titled, 'Formation and Implementation'. In narrative terms, it tells us how the Scheme was embodied in legislation after the 1979 General Election. Specifically, it reports on the administrative details arrived at after negotiations had taken place between the policy's advocates, civil servants and bodies representing the independent school sector. It concludes at the point where individual schools invited to participate in the Scheme agreed contracts with the Secretary of State for the provision of assisted places.

From the political science perspective, this account of the construction of the administrative details of the Scheme is compatible with the formulation stage of the policy. In the chapters which follow, there is a detailed exploration of the various ways in which independent schools responded to the policy and, how their decisions affected neighbouring schools recruitment patterns. They also explore the extent to which the schools involved helped to maintain or change patterns of social and cultural reproduction. The study contains, therefore, a 'meso' level analysis of institutional change, and a 'macro' level investigation of cultural capital, family arrangements, occuptional background and their articulation with school choice.

The Assisted Places study is an important piece of research because its co-directors, Whitty and Edwards, devised a framework to evaluate education policy with replicable properties which could be employed in respect of other educational policies. In this respect, it is similar in purpose to implementation research developed within political science.

Broadly speaking, it is a 'top down' framework, the aim of which is to evaluate the process of implementation and impact of a policy at the periphery which was previously devised at the centre. However, the detailed local studies of parents' and pupils' choice of schools are compatible with key features of 'bottom up' implementation research. Nevertheless, its more general concern, to evaluate the contrasting predictions made about the policy's likely effects, emphasises its 'top down' qualities. Moreover, by starting out from people's predictions, this mode of enquiry cleverly avoids the problem of researchers importing their own arbitrary criteria into the evaluation of policy.

If anything, it lacks an *abstract* modelling of the policy process, i.e. what activities comprises 'formulation' and how these are different from, and relate to, 'implementation' activities. To reiterate, however, the Assisted Places researchers are not alone here.

By contrast, Ball and Bowe conceptualize the policy process in ways which seek to move beyond the traditional use of formulation and implementation. Against a state control model within which policies issue from the centre and develop in ways which increase state control over all aspects of education, Ball and Bowe propose to interpret:

> . . . the policy process [as] a good deal more complex than this, and that there is a dialectical process in which the 'moments' of legislation (the Act), documentation (from the NCC, the DES, etc) and 'implementation' (the work of teachers) may be more or less loosely coupled (Ball and Bowe, 1992, p. 98).

The 'moments' are coupled via the creation and interpretation of policy texts operating and producing effects with in a cycle. The separation of 'formulation' and 'implementation' of policy is displaced by the conception of policy generated and implemented 'within and around the (educational) system' (Ball and Bowe, op cit, p. 100). Micro-political processes and the practitioners engaged in it are thus important both to the advance of policies and their outcomes because practitioners, distanced from the centre, have the capacity to 'recontextualize' intended and actual policies. Ball and Bowie continue:

> It is our contention that it is in the micro-political processes of the schools that we begin to see not only the limitations and possibilities state policy places on schools but, equally, the limits and possibilities practitioners place on the capacity of the state to

reach into the daily lives of schools. (Ball and Bowie, 1992, p. 101).

These propositions strike a careful balance between the centre's power to disseminate policy and the practitioners' capacities to interpret policies in ways and directions not anticipated by their authors. It also bears the characteristics of 'bottom up' approaches outlined earlier and is, therefore, subject to some of the criticisms directed at that form of research. In other respects, however, 'implementation' is rendered as a complex, creative and important 'moment' in the cycle, in which practitioners are conceptualized as meaningfully interpreting, rather than simply executing, policy which has been 'handed down'. It also provides a way of seeing how the micro-politics of the policy might force policy adjustments or modifications at the centre. In the contemporary English context, however, one senses that the recursive possibilities of the policy cycle may be more rhetorical than real. While a study of the implementation of the National Curriculum suggests that the periphery has considerable power to reinterpret and frustrate the centre's objectives Grant Maintained (GM) schools policy, on the other hand, as we shall stress shortly, can be interpreted as an example of the capacity the centre has to create and recreate a framework to optimize the implementation of its policies. Indeed, as Ball and Bowe acknowledge, there is strong evidence of successive administrations taking powers to drive policy in education from the centre. The general redirection of resources away from block grants, to centrally defined initiatives (the Technology Schools Initiative is one recent example) exemplifies the centre's capacity to exert direct influence on the periphery in a variety of ways.

Moreover, successive Tory governments have demonstrated their willingness to demobilize networks of influence, including key bureaucracies, which were once seen as crucial to the implementation of education policy. It has, for example, redefined the composition of governing bodies, and empowered parents, via ballots, to take schools out of the control of local authorities. Indeed, recent governments have not only crafted policy, but also created instruments intended to maximize the possibility of their execution. The 1988 Education Reform Act is as much about restructuring institutions – defining new goals, delineating fields of operation and reconstituting membership of the policy community – as it is about promulgating substantive education policies. This, in turn, has been reflected in the concerns of education policy research which has focused on the implementation and evaluation of impact of the reforms legislated in the Act, including our own investigations into the GM schools policy.

IMPLEMENTATION RESEARCH AND EDUCATION POLICY

4. The Education Reform Act and Implementation Research

As two commentators recently noted, institutional reform has one considerable benefit for policy makers:

> Political actors of course are not unaware of the deep and fundamental impact of institutions, which is why battles are so hard fought. Reconfiguring institutions can save political actors the trouble of fighting the same battle over and over again (Thelen and Steinmo, 1992 p 12)

In the case of GM schools policy, institutional reconfiguration was one of the key objectives. City Technology Colleges, the National Curriculum and its assessment procedures, and local management of schools also have a similar purpose. In implementation terms, therefore, it is not just a case of evaluating the extent to which centrally formulated policies are adopted or deflected at the periphery, rather it is the case that research has to engage as well with newly created or restructured institutions and institutional relations, the purpose of which, in part, is the efficient delivery of educational reforms.

In addition, recent policy research has also been confronted by the problem of studying 'policies in motion' (Edwards, Gewirtz, and Whitty, 1992), that is policies which have undergone considerable adjustments since their introduction. GM schools policy is an example of this. We use this as one instance of a policy which involves restructuring educational provision and one which has been considerably adjusted in the course of its development.

Although the idea of schools leaving the control of, or 'opting out' of, LEA control did not originate within the Department of Education and Science (DES), the policy was the product of a 'policy loop' involving ministers and civil servants (Fitz and Halpin, 1991). That is to say, there were political and bureaucratic 'moments' in the policy's development. Conceptually, the political and bureaucratic arenas can be considered in terms of Bourdieu's 'fields' (Bourdieu and Wacquant, 1992). They are defined relationally: by '*positions*' (eg parties, satellite agencies, the legislature, the executive etc.); by *procedures* specific to each field: by *actors* endowed with particular habituses; by *struggles* for control over contrasting forms of 'symbolic violence' and 'coercive norms'; and by different forms of '*symbolic capital*'. The fields are further consolidated by the logics employed by actors in defining the objects of their struggles and by the values they sustain and promote[4].

Initially, at least, GM schools policy bore a substantial civil service imprint. Its failure to achieve the radical intentions of the New Right has to be seen in the light of DES officials creating an administrative framework guided by the principle that the policy had to be formulated in ways such that its effectiveness could be demonstrated. For example, differences between GM and locally managed (LEA) schools were minimized in order to demonstrate the managerial efficiencies and educational benefits of school autonomy. Thus is was intended that GM status would confer no financial advantage on any school which opted out, and therefore it was intended that GM and locally managed schools would compete, in resource terms, on a level playing field. Additionally, GM schools were required to teach the National Curriculum and participate fully in the associated assessment procedures. Moreover, the requirement that schools would not be allowed to change their admissions policies within five years of incorporation was included, not only to preserve diversity of choice, but as a further opportunity to monitor the effects of increased autonomy on school performance over a period of time. Other features, such as the early proposal to limit GM status to schools with more than 300 pupils, were compatible with ministers', and civil servants' interests. The former Education Secretary, Kenneth Baker, wanted a few high profile demonstrations of the benefits conferred by grant-maintained status. For the DES, the measure limited the expansion of the department's responsibilities and thus any consequent increase in personnel.

While the administrative arrangements for GM status served to advance some of the objectives of the political field, notably to introduce diversity and competition into the system, many of the policy details originated in the administrative field and some of these undermined some of the more ambitious intentions of politicians. For example, the particular kind of autonomy granted to GM schools fell far short of the kinds of self-governance promoted by the New Right in Britain and enjoyed by similar schools in Europe and the USA (e.g. Mason, 1992; Chubb and Moe, 1990). Unlike City Technology Colleges, they were not established as centres of innovation (Edwards, Gewirtz and Whitty, 1992). Indeed, it was not clear, initially, what advantages GM status offered to schools that would make them distinctively different to schools operating under LMS arrangements. This is one of a number of factors which may have influenced the scale and pace of opting out. Certainly, schools have not left local authorities in the number confidently predicted by the policy's advocates. Consequently there has been increasing government anxiety about numbers of GM schools, particularly in relation to the public's perception of the policy's success. Certainly, the scale and pace of opting out has caused legitimation problems for the government, brought about largely by the 'numbers' discourse which has dominated the political field from the time the first GM schools opened. 'Success' or 'failure' of the policy has been construed primarily in terms of number of ballots held, applications for grant maintained status and the number of schools operating as GM establishments. Successive Education Secretaries have therefore sought to make GM status more financially attractive. Indeed, the key principle of implementation has now been reversed. Measures have been introduced to encourage schools to opt out and to promote autonomously incorporated schools as the 'natural organizational model' for the delivery of education. Struggles within the political field have thus redefined policy objectives, and these, in turn, have been addressed by the bureaucratic field where adjustments have been made to the administrative framework.

These specific policy adjustments have taken place within an institutional structure created in large part by the 1988 Education Reform Act in which it has become increasingly difficult to thwart detailed control of education by the political field. The long-run exclusion of LEAs, teachers and their respective associations from consultations about policy and their replacement by 'the new magistracy' (Stewart, 1992, p. 7) of non-elected, ministerially nominated agencies has increased the capacity of the centre to drive policy.

The narrative account we present here draws on documentary analysis and interview-based fieldwork in Whitehall, LEAs, schools and also home based parental interviews. This research led us to conclude that the GM schools policy diminished seriously some LEAs capacity to plan education provision. We also demonstrated that schools seeking GM status did so for a variety of reasons other than the independence associated with opting out, and that they were having very limited effects on parents' perception of choice and actual control of schools. We noted, too, that the increased autonomy enjoyed by GM schools had not been translated into new or different styles of teaching and learning (see Fitz, Halpin & Power, 1993). In many respects, then, our research is conventional implementation research. However, the significant reforms to the policy in the course of our investigations required us to engage throughout with the changing contours of the policy process. Thus, data gathered at the implementation phase were employed in our interviews with those publicly defined as the policy makers, advocates and critics. This, in turn, influenced our narrative account of the policy's progress and also our analysis of the policy's contribution to the reconfiguration of institutions in the education system. As it appears in our work, therefore, implementation research is part of the extended project of getting 'inside' the policy process with the larger purpose of understanding how its complexities relate to, and are influenced by, its economic, social and educational context.

Some of the concerns and the features of our own research has its reprise in numerous other studies of the 1988 Education Reform Act. The volumes edited by Coulby and Bash (1991) and Simkins, Ellison, and Garrett (1992) are indicative, though by no means comprehensive, of the range of work that has been undertaken or is in progress. The researchers in these volumes are concerned to move beyond commentary and critique towards detailed empirical studies of the impact of the Reform Act's measures. That does not mean, however, that ideological analysis has diminished. On the contrary, in both collections the implementation process is variously interpreted as evidence of 'centralization' or, 'privatization' or concerted attempts to foster markets and market principles at the heart of educational provision. Of equal concern are the traditional themes of the sociology of education, namely the extent to which the 1988 Education Reform Act is fostering differentiated educational institutions and thus sustaining and reproducing existing social and educational inequalities. Rather more numerous, however, are 'impact studies', that is, more narrowly focused, empirical investigations which report on the impact of the Act in local settings and on educational institutions.

Some are ambitious in their scope, research design, and the conceptual framework employed to discuss the effects of educational reform. Stewart Ranson's study of the changes wrought by the Act on LEAs is one prominent example (Ranson, 1992). Based on empirical work in four areas, it explores how historic perspectives, management style, organizational features and views of the public influence LEAs' responses to the opportunities and the challenges presented by recent legislation. Ranson's work is very close in some respects to the kinds of implementation research discussed above. However, in this study he is not so much concerned to develop models of those LEAs most likely to adopt centrally determined values, rather to argue that the Act has provided a general framework in which LEAs, influenced by existing organizational features and value orientations, develop distinctive modes of operation.

Other implementation research in these volumes is distinguished by the extent to which it reports from 'the inside' of the policy process. Thus, in contrast to our own studies, Deem and Wilkins write about opting out as key participants in the decision-making process which led to a school seeking GM status (Deem and Wilkins 1992). This is an unusual account by two researchers, one of whom had extensive management experience in LMS schools prior to his school seeking and gaining GM status. In this light, the claims they make for the advantages of GM status, and for school autonomy in general, present some difficulty for those wedded to the idea of continuing LEA control of schools. Whether or not some of the attractions of GM status will be so appealing if and when its financial advantages are reduced or disappear remains to be seen.

A feature of current policy research in education is the degree to which it is case-study based. There are numerous examples in the Simkins *et al.* volume (1992). Some focus on single institutions, others involve cross-site comparisons. Of the latter, Marren and Levacic's study (1992) focuses on spending decisions in eleven schools operating devolved budgets for the first time under LMS. They demonstrate that under the formulae employed to distribute financial resources to schools there are winners and losers, and within schools the same pattern obtains. The study can also be interpreted as evidence both of the extent to which managerialism has permeated into the fabric of educational institutions and of the changing role of the headteacher, from leading educational professional to steward of the budget.

These case studies report on the effects of restructuring at 'street level'. From the 'inside' they demonstrate the degrees of adaptation of, and resistances to, the broad ideological project which stands at the centre of the 1988 Education Reform Act. They also remind us of the diversity of practice even between and within institutions which, on the surface, are broadly similar in their organization and purpose. This may give some support to those who would argue that the system is now so diverse, and responses to the Act are so multifarious, that perhaps we need to look in new ways at the system. For example, the meta-narrative which underpins the very idea of 'implementation', linearly structured around policy formulation at the centre, followed by its introduction, adoption or deflection at the periphery, ought to be revised or replaced. In its place, we may need to think of devising a conceptual framework which gives prominence to a fragmented, market orientated social and educational system, that is increasingly difficult to control from the centre.

In this light, it may therefore be worth considering the work of those theorists, such as Kenway and her colleagues, who explore the articulation of postmodernist tendencies with education policy-making (Kenway, Bigum and Fitzclarence, 1993). Amongst the things they draw attention to is the importance of modern global communication systems and the potential they have for dissolving boundaries between nation states and between national and local contexts. In these circumstances, implementation research, particularly in education policy, needs to engage more than it has thus far with the creation of information systems which have enabled governments to communicate directly with its policy 'consumers'. It might well be that implementation research has to engage more with the nature, pattern and direction of information flows which effectively account for the scale and the pace of policy take-up[5]. The notion of implementation research thus may need to expand its conventional interests in the identification of 'decision points', tracing networks of actors, or mapping policy communities. It will need to embrace further the (changing) systems which channel communications between individuals, communities and agencies and how these shape the way one relates with the others. This approach not only opens up new questions about the relative effects, and effectiveness, of policies but also raises interesting questions about who is empowered by them and who is not.

5. Conclusion

There is very little agreement within policy studies about precisely what constitutes 'implementation'. The most we can say about much of the research reported above is that it has a shared interest to get inside a process within which policy objectives are translated into practice. Educational policy studies, however, have indicated the extent to which it is difficult to distinguish conceptually between practices, formally or analytically, described as 'formulation' and 'implementation'.

On the other hand, there are marked differences in the purposes researchers attach to their investigations. While some of the earlier studies were instrumentally concerned to discover the conditions under which policy objectives could be most perfectly realized, other studies, including recent policy analysis in education, are broadly academic in orientation. Their focus has been on 'what takes place' (Lane, 1993) and why. These studies, organized around the narration and historical analysis of a single policy, are, in the case of education, further analyzed in terms of its differential impact on social classes, groups and individuals. But they are also academic in another sense: they have been conducted in the knowledge that the state is unlikely to be persuaded by, or to act on, any of their findings, however relevant.

6. Notes

1. For an overview of 'top down' studies, see Sabatier (1986). See also Ham and Hill (1984) and Lane (1993) for a critical review.
2. For examples of 'bottom up' research, see *The European Journal of Political Research*, 10 (1982), a special issue devoted to implementation.
3. One example of this approach in education is the 'micro markets' study by Stephen Ball, Richard Bowe and Sharon Gewirtz at King's College, London. This study is investigating 'on the ground' many different aspects of the operation of the Education Reform Act.
4. For a fuller account of this conceptual framework and its application to GM schools policy, see 'Implementation and education policy', unpublished paper presented to New Directions in Education Policy Sociology Conference, Southampton, 30–31 March 1993.
5. Roger Dale's conception of 'carriers' of policy is one move in this direction. It forms part of an analysis which seeks to explore the processes which lead to the 'globalization' of education policies (see Dale, 1992 p 29).

7. References

BALL, S. J. (1990) *Politics and Policy Making in Education* (London, Routledge).

BALL, S. J. and BOWE, R. (1992) Subject departments and the 'implementation' of National Curriculum policy: an overview of the issues, *Journal of Curriculum Studies*. 24 (2), 97–115.

BOURDIEU, P. and PASSERON, J. C. (1977) *Reproduction in Education, Society and Culture* (London, Sage).

BORDIEU, P. and WACQUANT, L. (1992) *An Invitation to Reflexive Sociology* (Cambridge, Polity Press).

BREHONY, K. and DEEM, R. (1990) Charging for free education: an exploration of a debate in school governing bodies, *Journal of Education Policy*, 5, 333–345.

COULBY, D. and BASH, L. (eds.) (1991) *Contradiction and Conflict: the 1988 Education Act in Action* (London, Cassell).

CHUBB J. E. and MOE, T. (1990) *Politics, Markets and America's Schools* (Washington, Brookings Institution).

DALE, R. (1992) What do they know of England? Paper presented to the ESRC Seminar: Methodological and Ethical Issues Associated with Research into the 1988 Education Reform Act, University of Warwick, 29 April.

DALE, R. et al (1990) *The TVEI story, policy, practice and preparation for the work force* (Milton Keynes, Open University Press).

DEEM, R. and WILKINS, J. (1992) *Governing and managing schools after ERA: the LEA experience and the GMS alternative*. In SIMKINS, T., ELLISON, L. and GARRETT, V. (Eds) (1992) *Implementing Educational Reforms: the early lessons* (Harlow, Longman/BEMAS).

EDWARDS, T., GEWIRTZ, S. and WHITTY, G. (1992) Researching a policy in progress: the city technology college initiative, *Research papers in Education*, 7 (1), 79–104.

EDWARDS, T., FITZ, J. and WHITTY, G. (1989) *The State and Private Education: An Evaluation of the Assisted Places Scheme* (Basingstoke, Falmer).

IMPLEMENTATION RESEARCH AND EDUCATION POLICY

FITZ, J. and HALPIN, D. (1991) From a 'sketchy policy' to a 'workable scheme': the DES and grant-maintained schools policy, *International Studies in Sociology of Education*, 1, 129–151.

FITZ, J., HALPIN, D. and POWER, S. (1993a) *Grant-Maintained Schools: Education in the Market Place*. (London, Kogan Page).

FITZ, J., POWER, S. and HALPIN, D. (1993b) Opting for grant-maintained status: a study of policy-making in education *Policy Studies*, 14 (1), 4–20.

GEWIRTZ, S. AND OZGA, J. (1990) Partnership, pluralism, and educational policy: a reassessment, *Journal of Education Policy*, 5 (1), 37–48.

HALPIN, D. and FITZ, J. (1990) Researching grant-maintained schools, *Journal of Education Policy*, 5 (2), 167–180.

HAM, C. and HILL, M. (1984) *The Policy Process in the Modern Capitalist State* (London, Harvester).

HECLO, H. (1984) In search of a role: America's higher civil servants. In SULEIMAN, E. (ed) *Bureaucrats and Policy Making* (New York, Holmes and Meier).

HILLGATE GROUP (1986) *Whose Schools? A Radical Manifesto* (London, Hillgate Group).

HJERN, B. and HULL, C. (1982) Implementation research as empirical constitutionalism, *European Journal of Political Science*, 10, 105–115.

KENWAY, J., BIGUM, C. and FITZCLARENCE, L. (1993) Marketing education in the postmodern age, *Journal of Education Policy*, 8 (2), 105–122.

LAND, H. (1978) Who cares for the family? *Journal of Social Policy*, 7 (3), 257–284.

LANE, J-E. (1993) *The Public Sector, concepts, models and approachs* (London, Sage).

MARREN, E. and LEVACIC, R. Implementating local management of schools: the first five years. In SIMKINS, T., ELLISON, L. and GARRETT, V. (Eds) (1992) *Implementing Educational Reforms: the early lessons* (Harlow, Longman/BEMAS).

MASON, P. (1992) *Independent Education in Europe* (London, ISIS).

NO TURING BACK GROUP (1986) *Save Our Schools* (London, Conservative Central Office).

OZGA, J. (1987) Studying education through the lives of policy-makers: an attempt to close the macro-micro gap. In L. BARTON and S. WALKER (eds), *Changing Policies, Changing Teachers: new directions in schooling* (Lewes, Falmer Press).

OZGA, J. (1990) Policy research and policy theory: a comment on Halpin and Fitz, *Journal of Education Policy*, 5, 359–362.

PRESSMAN, J. and WILDAVSKY, A. (1973) *Implementation* (Berkeley, University of California Press).

RAAB, C. (1992a) Taking network seriously: education policy in Britain, *European Journal of Political Research*, 21 (1–2), 69–90.

RAAB, C. (1992b) Where are we now: some reflections on the sociology of education. Paper presented to ESRC Seminar on Methodological and Ethical Issues Associated with the Education Reform Act, University of Warwick, 29 April.

RANSON, S. (1992) LEA responses to the Education Reform Act. In SIMKINS, R., ELLISON, L. and GARRETT, V. (Eds) *Implementing Educational Reforms: the early lessons* (Harlow, Longman/BEMAS).

SABATIER, P. and MAZMANIAN, D. (1981) Implementation of public policy: a framework of analysis. In D. MAZMANIAN and P. SABATIER (eds) *Effective Policy Implementation* (Lexington, D. C. Heath).

SABATIER, P. (1986) Top-down and bottom-up approaches to implementation research, *Journal of Public Policy*, 6 (1), January–March, 21–48.

SEXTON, S. (1987) *Our Schools – A Radical Policy* (Warlingham, Institute of Economic Affairs).

SIMKINS, T., ELLISON, L. and GARRETT, V. (Eds) (1992) *Implementing Educational Reforms: the early lessons* (Harlow, Longman/BEMAS).

STEWART, J. (1992) Accountability to the Public. Paper presented to the European Policy Forum, Westminster Conference, December.

THELEN, K. and STEINMO, S. (1992) Historical institutionalism in comparative politics. In S. STEINMO, K. THELEN and F. LONGSTRETH (Eds) *Structuring Politics, Historical Institutionalism in Comparative Settings* (Cambridge, Cambridge University Press).

Correspondence:
Dr John Fitz
School of Education
University of Wales Cardiff
PO Box 922
Cardiff CF2 4YG

[4]

Discourse: studies in the cultural politics of education, Vol. 18, No. 3, 1997

Critical Discourse Analysis as a Research Tool

HILARY JANKS, *University of the Witwatersrand, Johannesburg, South Africa*

Critical discourse analysis (CDA) stems from a critical theory of language which sees the use of language as a form of social practice. All social practices are tied to specific historical contexts and are the means by which existing social relations are reproduced or contested and different interests are served. It is the questions pertaining to interests that relate discourse to relations of power. How is the text positioned or positioning? Whose interests are served by this positioning? Whose interests are negated? What are the consequences of this positioning? Where analysis seeks to understand how discourse is implicated in relations of power it is called critical discourse analysis.

Fairclough's (1989, 1995) model for CDA consists of three interrelated processes of analysis which are tied to three interrelated dimensions of discourse. These three dimensions are:

1. the object of analysis (including verbal, visual or verbal and visual texts);
2. the processes by which the object is produced and received(writing/speaking/designing and reading/listening/viewing) by human subjects;
3. the socio-historical conditions that govern these processes.

According to Fairclough each of these dimensions requires a different kind of analysis:

1. text analysis (description);
2. processing analysis (interpretation);
3. social analysis (explanation).

What is useful about this approach is that it enables the analyst to focus on the signifiers that make up the text, the specific linguistic selections, their juxtapositioning, their sequencing, their layout. However, it also requires that the historical determination of these selections is recognised in order to understand that these choices are tied to the conditions of possibility. This is another way of saying that texts are instantiations of socially regulated discourses and that the processes of production and reception are socially constrained. Why Fairclough's approach to CDA is so useful is that it provides multiple points of analytic entry. It does not matter which kind of analysis one begins with, as long as they are all included and are shown to be mutually explanatory. It is in the interconnections that the analyst finds interesting patterns and disjunctions that need to be described, interpreted and explained.

In this article I demonstrate how to use this three-part analytic model for working with

0159-6306/97/030329-14

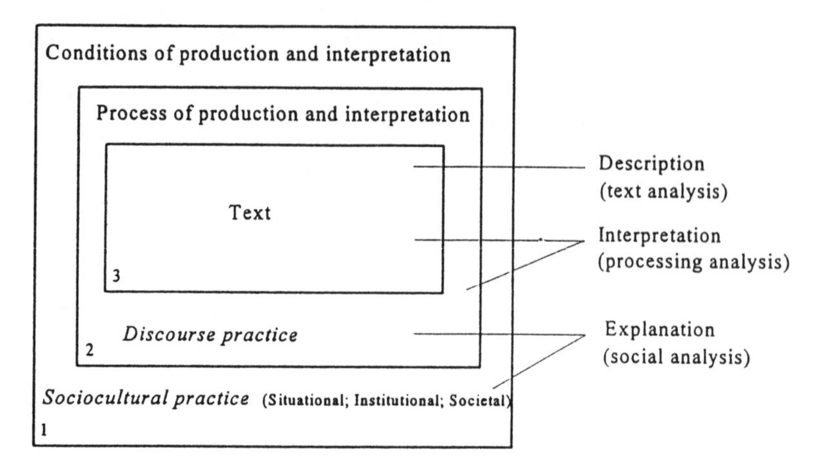

Figure 1. Fairclough's dimension of discourse and discourse analysis.

a text. However, one of the weaknesses of verbal accounts is that words cannot be presented as a gestalt: words march in rows one after the other, structured into a meaningful order. Analysis is not always as tidily linear. Fairclough tries to capture the simultaneity of his method of CDA with a model that embeds the three different kinds of analysis, one inside the other. See Figure One (Fairclough, 1995, p. 98).

The embedding of the boxes emphasises the interdependence of these dimensions and the intricate moving backwards and forwards between the different types of analysis. It is easier to capture the interdependence of Fairclough's boxes if one thinks of them three-dimensionally, as boxes nesting one inside the other rather than as concentric circles. This three-dimensional image enables one to understand that an analytic move to examine a single box necessarily breaks the interdependence between the boxes and requires subsequent moves which re-insert that box into its interconnected place. The focus on any one box, therefore, has to be seen as a relatively arbitrary place from which to begin. A technique that I use, in the initial stages of working with a text, is to draw three large, empty embedded boxes. I record my analytic comments in the appropriate box as they occur. This enables me to work with the different types of analysis simultaneously rather than sequentially and facilitates the drawing of linking lines across the boxes to stress interconnections.

Engaged and Estranged Reading Positions: reading with and against a text

Looking at a text critically is not very difficult when we disagree with it—when the positions that it offers to us as readers are far removed from what we think and believe and value. In cases where we begin from a position of estrangement or alienation from the text it is easier to read against rather than with the text. The interests served by the text may be apparent; the reader may even be at the receiving end of the consequences entailed and might have little difficulty in questioning the text.

Where the naturalisations in a text are not natural for us as readers or listeners, we are at an advantage in that this teaches us that what texts construct are only versions of reality. In South Africa large-scale shack settlements which had existed in the same place for at least a generation were referred to by the apartheid State as 'squatter camps'; whereas the Bantustans, which many urban dwellers had never even visited, were designated as 'homelands' to which they could be 'repatriated'. People did not need degrees in CDA to know where home was. Their lived experience deconstructed the language of apartheid. Readers who do not share the codes of the text are an important CDA resource in teaching and in research for reading against the grain. Often these readers are the very people who are labelled as disadvantaged or lacking the cultural capital for dominant literacy, that is for producing dominant readings of a text from the position of the ideal reader. This labelling implies an assimilationist model of literacy, where readers are expected to identify with the textual positionings, rather than a critical model, which requires them both to engage with and to question these positions.

A range of factors, both textual and non-textual, structure the reader's engaged–estranged location in relation to any particular text. Each on its own is a form of entrapment. Engagement without estrangement is a form of submission to the power of the text regardless of the reader's own positions. Estrangement without engagement is a refusal to leave the confines of one's own subjectivity, a refusal to allow otherness to enter. Without the entry of the other, can we be said to have read the text at all?

There are many factors that tip the scales in favour of engagement. These include: the reader cooperatively reading to make sense of the text (Grice, 1975; Smith, 1971); the writer writing so as to constrain possible interpretations, surreptitiously structuring the subjectivity of the ideal reader (Scholes, 1985); and the teacher privileging 'particular reading positions and practices from the many that are available or imaginable' (Freebody *et al.*, 1991, p. 445) so that students learn a 'singular way of reading a text properly' (Freebody *et al.*, 1991, p. 442). Cooperation, textual power and institutional practices favour engagement. In reading with the text, readers start by identifying with the 'preferred readings' (Hall, 1980) constructed by the text and then move deliberately to resist the text's apparent naturalness. The theory and practice of CDA suggests strategies that enable this deliberate move and argues the need for reading against the text to counterbalance reading with the text.

CDA: where to begin?

When I want to do a thorough critical discourse analysis, I usually begin with a text (among many). I see how far I can get with a single text and then try to fill in the gaps and unanswered questions and hypotheses raised by this limited and arbitrary entry point. What I am ultimately looking for are patterns that I can use to establish hypotheses about discourses at work in society. I then try to confirm or disconfirm these hypotheses by looking for other related texts. This enables me to discover questions that need answering with regard to the social relations and discourses instantiated in this text and others connected to it. I tend to work from text to discourse(s)—I begin with textual analysis (Fairclough's box 3), always aware that this is only one lens through which to consider the data and that the other lenses are essential to provide other perspectives.

The text that I will analyse to illustrate this method of CDA is an advertisement for the Standard Bank's Domestic Promise Plan which appeared in the *Weekly Mail and Guardian* in 1994 (see Figure Two).

Figure 2.

Text Analysis

In unpacking a text it is important to remember that it is never possible to read meaning directly off the verbal and visual textual signs. This is well illustrated by reference to this particular text. Here the narrator, presumably the woman in the visual text who is named as a 'domestic' in the linguistic text, is wondering what will happen to her when she is old and the baby, baby Jay, does not need her anymore. Whose baby is baby Jay? South Africans familiar with the discourse of 'maids and madams' (Cock, 1980; and the cartoon strip 'Madam and Eve') are likely to assume that the baby is the employer's baby whom the domestic worker is employed to care for. Such an assumption would account for the worker's fear that when the baby no longer needs her she will be out of work. Many Australian readers that I have worked with, drawing their interpretation from the discourse of ageing and women's fears of not being needed once the children have grown up, assume that the worker is thinking about her own baby. The different discourses available for readers to draw on provide different conditions for the reception of this text in these two different contexts (Fairclough's box 1). Without reference to the context of production and reception (Fairclough's box 2) it is not possible to favour either of these readings on the basis of close textual analysis alone. This is not to say that some textual features—the baby's name, visual clues such as what the domestic worker is wearing while baby Jay is sleeping—used in conjunction with contextual knowledge, cannot be used as evidence to support one or other of these interpretations. Recognising the limitations of textual analysis, I will use it as a heuristic device, a place to begin. Towards the end of the paper I will consider a different possible entry point.[1]

Analysing the Visual Signs

The Standard Bank advertisement for its Domestic Promise Plan includes a visual text depicting a domestic worker, dressed in what could be an overall and scarf, staring pensively out of an open window, her face lit by the light from the window. The pensiveness is evoked by the position of her hand cupping her chin in the pose associated with Rodin's *Thinker*. The burglar bars on the window are suggestive of imprisonment but they are also shaped in the form of the cross. The cross could be seen to reinforce the suggestion of suffering created by the bars and to underscore the sense of hope created by the light that comes from outside. This hope is lexicalised as a 'promise' in the form of a retirement scheme for domestic workers. This link is established visually by the blue tints of the picture and the use of royal blue to surround the logo and the words 'Standard Bank', placed centrally at the bottom of the advertisement. The full blue of the logo compared with the muted blue tints in the picture creates a shift from uncertainty to certainty as one moves from the picture to the bank and its promise. In semiotic terms the logo has a higher modality (Kress & van Leeuwen, 1990, p. 51). These colours are not captured in the black and white reproduction of the advertisement in Figure Two.

There are other important aspects of the visual text. The woman in the text is not looking at the viewer. The picture therefore 'does not demand that the viewer enter into an imaginary social relation' with the woman (Kress & van Leeuwen, 1990, p. 28). Instead she is presented as an object for the viewer's contemplation. The shot is a close-up, which suggests the viewer's intimate knowledge of the woman. This is supported by the narratavised linguistic text which enables the viewer/reader to intrude on the woman's thoughts.

The composition of the overall text (including both visual and verbal signs) has interesting features on both its vertical (top–down) and horizontal (left–right) axes. On the vertical axis the text is divided into two parts. The top part, in which the picture of the woman occupies half of the overall text, dominates. The soft tints, the pensive pose, and the fact that from a Western left–right orientation the woman seems to be looking backwards create uncertainty in semiotic terms.

The woman's hand, which cups the lit half of her face, divides the top half of the page down the middle on the horizontal axis. The hand leads the viewer's eye down to the column of linguistic text immediately below it. This column is different from the other two columns of print on either side of it: it appears in a shaded box; it has a different typeface and a larger font; there is larger spacing between the lines; the Standard Bank logo, the name of the policy and a slogan are placed centrally below this column. The force of this focusing directs the eye from the picture to this column of print, thus setting up a preferred reading path. This pull to the middle column of print is offset by a tendency to start with the left-hand column of print because of the left–right reading orientation developed as a habit of Western literacy. Which of these pulls is stronger would I suspect be influenced by one's purpose for reading. If one were reading closely in order to do a textual analysis one would be more likely to begin on the left with the first column. If one were flipping through the newspaper, not really intending to read the advertisement at all, the middle column might be more likely to catch the eye.

Analysing the Verbal Signs

In the middle column, the verbal text sets up a dichotomy between knowing and not knowing, which reinforces questions relating to the woman's uncertainty or certainty raised in the visual text. The first paragraph is structured around what 'I' knows and the second states what 'I' does not know. This pattern of certainty and uncertainty is reinforced by the organisation of the columns on either side of the shaded central block. To the left we are mainly (but not exclusively) presented with the domestic worker's uncertainty, 'I wonder where I'll be sleeping when I am too old to work', 'Something or other about a retirement policy', 'But what happens to me when Jay doesn't need me anymore?' To the right we are told why the worker can 'stop worrying'; how because everything has 'been taken care of she can say 'I turned back to the window. And for the very first time I could see a lot further than my sixty-fifth birthday'.[2] The patterns of certainty and uncertainty are also not distributed equally among the participants: the worker, the employer, the baby and the bank. The employer and the bank have certainty, the worker does not, and the baby asleep is neither certain nor uncertain. The employee's uncertainty is such that 'peace of mind about retirement' is something that an employer is able to 'give' to a worker.

If one starts with the middle column, the reader is left to work out who 'I' is from the weight of the visual text and the rules of deixis, whereby 'I' is the woman in the picture. This reading is confirmed by the column of print on the left where 'I' is said to 'stare out of the window'. With either reading path, the use of the first-person narrative is firmly established. This works to humanise the domestic worker as a subject and a potential agent. She is a person with worries about her old age. It also suggests that domestic workers who can identify with this narrative are the likely addressees for this text. The last sentence 'Why not give your domestic peace of mind?' therefore constitutes an unexpected switch of addressee to the employer. But the 'you' does not have a stable referencing function. In the slogan 'with us you can go so much further' the 'you' seems to suggest the beneficiary of the Standard Bank's services, in this instance the worker. This text's ambivalence in relation to the addressee is significant, and seems to reflect an uncertainty with regard to the changing position of 'domestics'. These shifts manifest as discoursal shifts from a paternalistic discourse of 'domestics' as servants who need to be cared for, to a liberal discourse of workers as independent human beings with needs, and possibly to a labour discourse of workers' rights.

While the use of personal narrative moves against the dehumanising and othering discourse of apartheid racism, the construction of the woman as an object of our gaze in the visual text does not. Neither does the pattern of lexicalisation. The employer, Mrs Lambert, and the baby, Jay, are both named. Only the domestic worker is not dignified with a name. This indignity is compounded by the failure even to nominalise her. Her status as a worker is reduced to an attribute—'domestic worker' (attribute + nominal) is thus reduced to 'domestic'. If she is a domestic worker, then Mrs Lambert is a domestic employer, but she is not lexicalised by either her attribute 'domestic' or by her status, 'employer' because she is identified by her name. The advertisers avoid the earlier lexicalisations of 'girl', 'servant' and 'maid' and capitalise on liberal reconstructions. But they stop short of labour discourse. The selection of 'domestic' as a nominal seems to be a reduction of 'domestic worker' the lexicalisation used by the Domestic Workers' Union.

Different lexical selections can signal different discourses (colonial, liberal, labour discourses). Most texts are hybrids, which draw on more than one discourse. I argue that the specific hybridity of this text provides evidence for values in transition. It shows the tenacity of existing discourses at work in society and the struggle of alternative discourses to emerge. Textual instantiations capture the clash of discourses and demonstrate ideological forces at work to produce a different hegemony.

It is easy to show the power of the racist discourse of paternalism if one does a transitivity analysis of this text. Before turning to a transitivity analysis, it is important to make explicit the means I have used to produce the verbal analysis thus far. Essentially I work with a check list based on Halliday's *Introduction to Functional Grammar* (1985). This is also the basis for Fairclough's key questions for text analysis (1989, pp. 110–111). In simple terms one has systematically to examine:

1. lexicalisation;
2. patterns of transitivity;
3. the use of active and passive voice;
4. the use of nominalisation;
5. choices of mood;
6. choices of modality or polarity;
7. the thematic structure of the text;
8. the information focus;
9. cohesion devices.

These are Halliday's grammatical resources for ideational, interpersonal and textual meanings. What one is looking for are patterns that emerge across these linguistic functions which confirm or contradict one another. So, for instance, the pattern of certainty/uncertainty, essentially an analysis of modality and polarity, establishes a hierarchy of power which is confirmed by the naming practices and the transitivity analysis. An examination of cohesion which, amongst other things, requires one to look at how pronouns are used to refer, reveals that the reference system is not stable. This instability does not surface elsewhere in the textual analysis and can only be understood by using the other dimensions of CDA, as I will show later. Because it is difficult to know what aspect of the grammar is going to be most fruitful in the analysis of a particular text, I find it essential to examine all aspects. Often the analysis of the separate elements produces patterns that are confirmed across the elements. As it is not possible to include a detailed analysis of every aspect in this article, I demonstrate the kind of systematicity required by focusing on transitivity. Transitivity was chosen because of all the grammatical aspects I analysed, it yielded the most fruitful data for this text.

In his *Introduction to Functional Grammar* Halliday (1985) explains transitivity as follows:

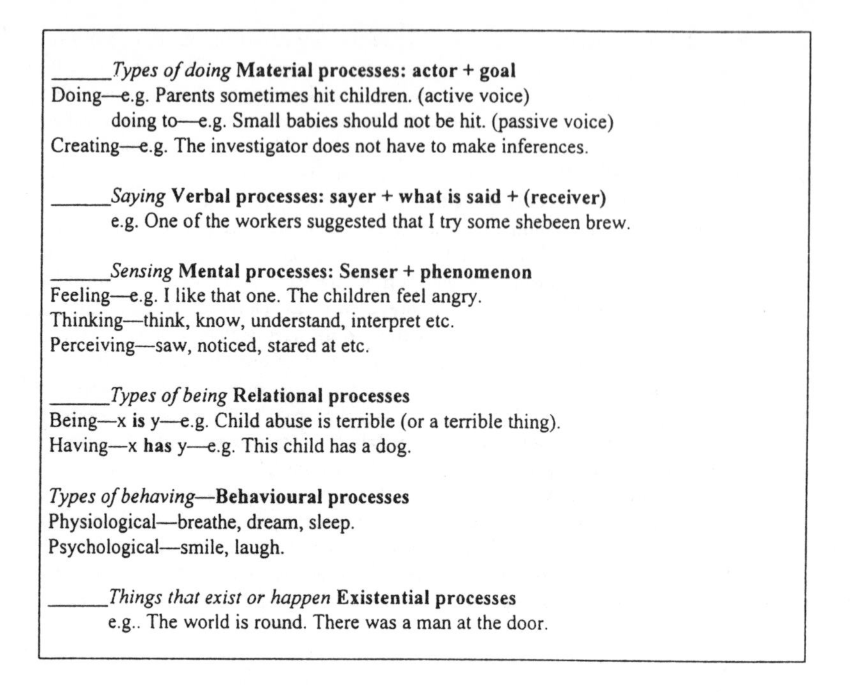

______*Types of doing* **Material processes: actor + goal**
Doing—e.g. Parents sometimes hit children. (active voice)
doing to—e.g. Small babies should not be hit. (passive voice)
Creating—e.g. The investigator does not have to make inferences.

______*Saying* **Verbal processes: sayer + what is said + (receiver)**
e.g. One of the workers suggested that I try some shebeen brew.

______*Sensing* **Mental processes: Senser + phenomenon**
Feeling—e.g. I like that one. The children feel angry.
Thinking—think, know, understand, interpret etc.
Perceiving—saw, noticed, stared at etc.

______*Types of being* **Relational processes**
Being—x **is** y—e.g. Child abuse is terrible (or a terrible thing).
Having—x **has** y—e.g. This child has a dog.

Types of behaving—**Behavioural processes**
Physiological—breathe, dream, sleep.
Psychological—smile, laugh.

______*Things that exist or happen* **Existential processes**
e.g.. The world is round. There was a man at the door.

Figure 3. The system of transitivity in the clause: summary of types with examples.

> A fundamental property of language is that it enables human beings to build a mental picture of reality, to make sense of their experience of what goes on around them and inside them ... Our most powerful conception of reality is that it consists of 'goings-on': of doing, happening, feeling, being. These goings on are sorted out in the semantic system of the language, and expressed through the grammar of the clause. (p. 101)

Amongst other things the clause evolved to express the

> ... reflective, experiential aspects of meaning. This ... is the system of TRANSITIVITY. Transitivity specifies the different types of processes that are recognised in the language and the structures by which they are expressed. (p. 101)

Halliday's grammar proposes six different processes or kinds of transitivity (see Figure Three). To do a transitivity analysis it is necessary to identify every verb and its associated process. It is then necessary to identify patterns in the use of these processes. So Luke (1988) in analysing early readers notices a pattern in which the child characters Dick and Jane are only given material and verbal processes. From this he concludes that children are represented as allowed only to do and to say; they are not allowed to think (mental processes) and to be (relational processes).

Figure Four provides a transitivity table for the Standard Bank's Domestic Promise Plan advertisement, showing transitivity arranged according to three participants: Mrs Lambert, the domestic, Baby Jay. What is interesting here is not that (like Dick and Jane)

Mrs Lambert Activity	*Mrs Lambert* Process	*The domestic* Activity	*The domestic* Process	*Baby Jay* Activity	*Baby Jay* Process
spoke	verbal	stare	mental	is sleeping	behavioural
showed	material	wonder	mental	does not need	mental
told	verbal	will be sleeping	behavioural	has	relational
was putting	material	am	relational		
smiled	behavioural	know	mental		
said	verbal	could take	material (but only with permission)		
said	verbal	worrying	mental		
taken care of	material	turned	material		
give	material	could see	mental		
call	verbal	know	mental		
		know	mental		
		to prepare	material		
		don't know	mental		
		am	relational		

Figure 4. Transitivity processes in the Standard Bank advertisement for its Domestic Promise Plan.

Mrs Lambert is constructed with predominantly material and verbal processes and the domestic worker with largely mental and relational processes. There is nothing intrinsically superior or inferior about material, mental, verbal or relational processes. In this context, however, constructing the domestic worker with few material processes suggests that she is unable to act except with the permission of or in the service of her employer. It is as if agency is granted her by her employer. Her employer, on the other hand, acts and speaks at will. The domestic worker says nothing. She has no overall processes and is caught in a one-way conversation, at the receiving end of Mrs Lambert's speech. What is particularly interesting, however, is the patterned alignment between the domestic worker and the baby. They are the only participants whose processes are mental, behavioural and relational. Thus in the transitivity structure one can see the domestic worker constructed as a baby who needs to be 'taken care of'. The transitivity analysis reveals the infantalisation of human subjects which is the result of paternalism.

Discourses at Work in the Context

How does this pattern of transitivity happen? Should we imagine advertising copy-writers deliberately working out a careful alignment between the transitivity processes selected for the adult worker and for the baby in her care? CDA, which requires that we consider the social conditions that affect textual production, can suggest a fruitful line of enquiry. It leads me to hypothesise that the discourse of paternalism/infantalisation continues to exist in South Africa as a resource that is available for text producers to draw on when they write. 'Draw on' suggests conscious volition or deliberate choice. This may in fact be the case—one in which the advertisement writers choose to use a racist/paternalistic discourse. Using a Foucauldian perspective, I would rather argue that as members of a society we are constituted in and by the available discourses and that they speak through us—it is as if the discourse of racist/paternalism chooses the advertisement writers. I base this argument on the transitivity analysis. Transitivity is not as easily visible to producers and readers as other linguistic features because of the complexity of its encoding. Lexical selection in the verb has to be related to syntactic extensions, to participants and to processes. In addition one has to trace the patterns of use across participants. Deconstructive analysis of transitivity is a layered and complex process. It is not something that one can 'see' or 'feel' by just looking carefully at a text. I would argue that because transitivity is less obvious, deeper in the syntax, it suggests less conscious control by the writer and it requires more conscious effort for the reader to analyse it.

Examples of more obvious linguistic selections that are easier to recognise and monitor include the way in which the participants are named (discussed earlier) and the use of the passive construction. In 'It's all been taken care of', the deleted agent is presumably the employer who acts on behalf of her employee without her full consent or understanding, the latter shown by 'Something or other about a retirement policy'. This worker, constructed as unable to take care of herself, is elsewhere in the text shown as capable of performing highly complex and responsible tasks (looking after the employer's sick child and preparing a meal for twelve people). Here one might wish to argue that the advertiser needs to construct the domestic worker as having no agency in order to ensure that the employer, who is more likely to accept that individuals (rather than the State) have to take responsibility for their financial security (the basic premise on which the insurance industry is based), will buy such a policy on behalf of her employee.

It was precisely at this level of linguistic selection that it was possible earlier in the article to suggest that the writer was conscious of avoiding old apartheid-speak. In addition, the apparent ambiguity in the selection of pronouns suggests that the text does not have a stable addressee. These linguistic selections provide intimations that this text is complex and shifting rather than simply being locked in to old discourses. But text analysis alone cannot take us far enough and we need to bring the other dimensions of discourse analysis into focus.

Interpretation: analysing the processes of production and reception

Fairclough refers to the situational context and the intertextual context as central to the process of interpretation. In terms of the situational context it is useful to ask questions about time and place. Could this text have been produced earlier than 1994? Is it simply an old apartheid text? Could this text have been produced outside South Africa? What contextual factors influenced the production and interpretation of this text?

We have already seen how the advertisement constructs retirement policies and relatedly the provision of pensions within a discourse of employer goodwill and not within a discourse of workers' rights. The new labour statutes, notably the Basic Conditions of Employment Act 3 of 1981, were only extended to domestic workers in 1994 (the year in which this text was produced). These statutes provide domestic workers with some protection against unfair labour practices for the first time. They require contracts, lay down the number of hours that an employee can be expected to work and they legislate for overtime pay. What is not included are a minimum wage and conditions of service. That there is no legislated right to a pension from one's employer is what is relevant to the discussion in this paper. Although the discourse of goodwill ties the advertisement to a discourse of paternalism, what is new is the idea that domestic workers should have improved conditions of service. I can therefore hypothesise that there were no equivalent advertisements in the 1980s as financial security for domestic workers in their old age was not yet on the social agenda. This advertisement shows an awareness on the part of the Standard Bank that there is now a whole new market for its policies which could not previously be tapped. This notion of provision is possibly a first step in the direction of entitlement and is certainly an idea around which a union could mobilise its members. These hypotheses provide the basis for interesting research questions. When did such advertisements first appear? Is the 1994 date of the new labour statutes and this policy coincidental or deliberate? How will the issue of pensions for domestic workers change over time? Will pensions ever become a legal obligation on the part of employers?

The Standard Bank becomes an obvious place to look for additional data in terms of the intertextual context. Bingo! The bank has a brochure for this Domestic Promise Plan (still available from the bank in 1997) and there is a great deal of intertextual similarity between it and the advertisement under discussion. In the brochure the visual text of the woman is repeated, but this time the shot is less close up, she is facing to the right, and the burglar bars are extended so that they no longer form a cross. Her youth and the possibility of 'promise' are established by comparison with the visual on the front cover of the brochure, in extreme close-up, of a much older man holding his or her face with both hands in a symbolic gesture of hopeless despair. In the brochure there is no ambiguity about the addressee; it is unequivocally the employer as can be seen from the following quotations from the brochure.

> How often do we consider that the unemployment benefits, medical aid and pension schemes which we take for granted from our employers are not available to our domestic staff? (p. 3)
>
> Your employee will become the sole owner of his/her Domestic Promise Plan. (p. 5)
>
> Why not give your employee peace of mind about retirement? Simply complete the attached application form and mail it in the envelope provided. (p. 8)

In the brochure there is a great deal of hybridity in the lexicalisation. Workers are referred to as 'domestic staff', 'your employee', 'your domestic', 'maid', 'gardener'. Most references are to the reader as an 'employer' and to domestic staff as 'employees'. That this new market for insurance policies is tied to changes in the situational context is made explicit by six pages in the brochure (as many as for information on the policy itself) which 'gives an overview of the new legislation applying to your domestic employees—formulated for your interest' (p. 9). This includes information about salaries and wages, hours of work, meal intervals, annual leave, sick leave, overtime, Sunday work, public holidays, termination of employment and what you as an employer need to do (pp. 10–14). Buying your worker a Domestic Promise Plan is thus textually linked to the new conditions of service for domestic workers and to post-apartheid labour conditions. In case this alienates prospective policy purchasers, the Standard Bank distances itself from this legislation in the closing sentence of the brochure: 'For now the most important thing is not to over-react. Good working relationships, founded on fairness and honesty, will endure in spite of legislation' (p. 14).

It thus simultaneously promotes and undercuts this legislation. The text locates itself in contradictory positions, so that the bank can have it both ways. This accounts for the other signs of textual hybridity.

Textual Hybridity

Hybridity is a fruitful area for CDA to investigate because it is here that the different interests are played out. Of the many different discourses available in the society to be drawn from, different texts privilege different ones. The privileging of discourses works to serve particular interests.

For example, in South Africa there are different discourses of ageing. In many African communities old people are respected and valued; the extended family system provides young people with a measure of security for their old age (albeit tied to a system of patriarchal rights and obligations). This is not to suggest that people who work should not have financial rights on retirement. It does, however, raise questions about whether a domestic worker is likely to stand at the window worrying about her old age (rather than, say, how she will pay her children's school fees or afford to buy a house). These concerns seem to arise more from Western discourses of ageing, in a culture that venerates youth and associates old age with redundancy and insecurity. The reference to the woman wondering 'what happens when baby Jay doesn't need me anymore', although not a reference to her own baby, is clearly drawn from a discourse of ageing which relates to the nuclear family and the 'empty nest' syndrome not really experienced in extended families where old people often care for their own grandchildren and other young children. Researchers can learn to analyse the interests at work in the privileging and backgrounding of different discourses. In this text it is clear that a Western discourse of ageing is more likely to sell retirement policies.

Explanation: social analysis

Volosinov says that:

> ... the inner dialectic quality of the sign comes out fully in the open in times of social crises or revolutionary changes. In the ordinary conditions of life, the contradiction embedded in every ideological sign cannot emerge fully because the ideological sign in an established, dominant ideology is always somewhat reactionary and tries, as it were, to stabilize the preceding factor in the dialectical flux of the social generative process, so accentuating yesterday's truth as to make it appear today's. (1973, p. 24)

South Africa is in just such a period of revolutionary changes. The sign is clearly unstable. It is interesting to note that the signifiers are constantly shifting. 'Squatter camps', terminology used to signify the illegality and the impermanence of shack settlements, are now referred to as 'informal settlements', with the root word 'settle' implying a recognition of permanence. Mandela's household staff

> ... consists of 61 cleaners, three food service aides, eight household aides, a general foreman, a storekeeper, three household managers, one guest house

> manager, two household supervisors and two household controllers. (*Weekly Mail and Guardian*, March 1996, p. 8)

He appears to have no domestic workers.

When the sign is unstable it is possible to see the workings of ideology. Ideology is at its most powerful when it is invisible, when discourses have been naturalised and become part of our everyday common sense. This is what results in writers using a discourse of paternalism unconsciously, because it is available. By being there, it and the other available discourses constitute our identities and our constructions of the world. In a time of change, new discourses become available offering us new subject positions from which to speak and read the world. The conditions of text production and text reception are gradually transformed.

If this explanation is correct then the analysis of this text leads to really interesting possibilities for further critical discourse analysis. The text analysis has generated a hypothesis that hybridity, in which pre-transformation and post-transformation discourses appear simultaneously in texts, is a feature of South African discourse in the 1990s. This suggests further research in which one could track the development of this hybridity across texts over a period of time until the society stabilises. One could begin to ascertain whether the hybridity is widespread or tied to specific genres or specific text producers. It might even be possible to watch the formation of a new discursive hegemony that replaces the old.

The starting point for this article was text analysis. It has led to the formulation of new research questions, the starting point for which is in the processes of production and reception, and the socio-historical conditions which govern them. But in the same way that textual analysis brought us to this new beginning, to these new questions, this enquiry will require a return to text analysis. The researcher will need to describe and interpret the new texts that the research questions lead to. The strength of CDA is that the different dimensions of analysis that it offers provide the means both for producing research questions and for analysing data. As such, it is an extremely important research tool.

Correspondence: Hilary Janks, Department of Applied English Language Studies, University of the Witwatersrand, PO Wits 2050, Johannesburg, South Africa.

NOTES

1. I am grateful to my 1996 AELS 3 students for this observation.
2. How much future financial security one can buy for R30 per month is also an important question. The small amount raises some questions about whether or not Mrs Lambert is correct in telling her worker that she 'can stop worrying'.

REFERENCES

COCK, J. (1980) *Maids and Madams* (Cape Town, David Phillip).

FAIRCLOUGH, N. (1989) *Language and Power* (London, Longman).

FAIRCLOUGH, N. (1995) *Critical Discourse Analysis* (London, Longman).

FREEBODY, P., LUKE, A. & GILBERT, P. (1991) Reading positions and practices in the classroom, *Curriculum Inquiry*, 21(4).

GRICE, H.P. (1975) Logic and conversation, in: P. COLE & J.L. MORGAN (Eds) *Syntax and Semantics III: speech acts* (New York, Academic Press).

HALL, S. (1980) Encoding/decoding, in: *Culture, Media, Language* (London, Hutchinson).
HALLIDAY, M.A.K. (1985) *An Introduction to Functional Grammar* (London, Edward Arnold).
KRESS, G. & VAN LEEUWEN, T. (1990) Reading Images (Victoria, Geelong, Deakin University Press).
LUKE, A. (1988) *Literacy, Textbooks and Ideology* (London, Falmer Press).
SCHOLES, R. (1985) *Textual Power* (New Haven, Yale University Press).
SMITH, F. (1971) *Understanding Reading: a psycholinguistic analysis of reading and learning to read* (New York, Holt, Rinehart & Winston).
VOLOSONIV, V.N. (1973) *Marxism and the Philosophy of Language*, L. MATEJKA & I.R. TITUNIK (Trans.) (New York, Seminar Press).
Weekly Mail and Guardian (1996) March, p. 8.

[5]

J. EDUCATION POLICY, 1990, VOL. 5, NO. 4, 359–362

Policy Research and Policy Theory: a comment on Fitz and Halpin[1]

Jenny Ozga
Bristol Polytechnic

This note is primarily intended as a commentary on John Fitz and David Halpin's 'Researching Grant Maintained Schools', but it would be unfair to put the onus for what follows exclusively on their shoulders. It was not that paper alone, but the extent to which that paper might be representative of a trend in education policy studies of Education Reform Act (ERA) and post-ERA developments which concerned me. Other contributory factors were McPherson and Raab's (1988) 'Governing Education', to which they refer, David Hargreaves excoriation of sociologists at the Newman/Westhill conference in 1989, where *Governing Education* also featured largely, and a number of research papers, including those on City Technology Colleges (CTCs), recently presented to the ERA research network seminar, an earlier meeting of which saw the first appearance of the paper by Fitz and Halpin.

The contents of this note are also, of course, shaped by my own preoccupations, and may be idiosyncratic. Those preoccupations concern the need to bring together structural, macro-level analysis of education systems and education policies and micro-level investigation, especially that which takes account of people's perceptions and experiences. Evidence of the long-standing preoccupation, and of the complexity of the problem and slow progress made in working on it may be found in Ozga (1987) and Gewirtz and Ozga (1990). A further important explanation of the source of my concern about this trend in education policy research lies in my work on the Open University's course Policy-making in Education, which attempts to introduce students to ways of understanding education policy, primarily through a comparison of alternative theoretical frameworks.

I have spent so long explaining the background to my comments because I am well aware that it is easy to criticize people for their failure to do what they did not set out to do. I appreciate that Fitz and Halpin set themselves limits in their paper, that it was a seminar paper intended to promote discussion rather than a comprehensive model for research, and that the diverse backgrounds of the audience at the seminar where it was originally delivered needed to be taken account of. There are very large sections of the paper with which I do not take issue – most of the last half of it, in fact. The problem for me lies more with what is not included. They suggest that there are five aspects of the Grant Maintained (GM) Schools initiative which need further research. These are:

- (i) comparisons with similar initiatives in other countries;
- (ii) historical and ideological antecedents of the policy
- (iii) detailed case studies which locate GM schools as study of the implementation of the ERA;
- (iv) investigation of educational change and the formation of state education policy;

(v) investigation of the numbers of GM schools.

In introducing these five headings, the authors indicate the need for 'detached analysis' and their concern to explore the extent to which this particular policy is part of a coherent policy or just an example of 'ad hocery'.

The content and style of the discussion, and particularly the weight given to the accumulation of information about GM schools reminded me of case studies of education policy-making from a pre-ERA era, in particular those produced in the early 1970s by Saran (1973) or Fenwick (1976). Their main characteristic was the richness of the picture they presented, and the detail of their description. This was linked to their very limited – sometimes totally absent – consideration of broader issues, such as what part their detailed account of a specific issue played in the creation of a bigger picture, and what theoretical perspective informed their studies. If there was a perspective, it often derived from Kogan (1975). Kogan's concern to explore people's experience of current educational change is quoted approvingly by Fitz and Halpin, and, indeed, his work underpins *Governing Education*. It should be recognized, however, that Kogan's concern with people's perceptions of change derives from a view of policy-making which stresses ad hocery, serendipity, muddle and negotiation. The evidence of diversity and autonomy that he finds, and that characterize studies influenced by his work, is hardly surprising. All that work has contributed to the development of an orthodoxy about post-war education policy-making in England and Wales which stresses partnership, local autonomy, diversity, local education authority and teacher power, and so on. Because our perceptions of that period are so imbued with pluralist interpretations which look like mere descriptions, we lose sight of the coherence of education policy, its essentially differentiated nature, its consistent functions and attendant contradictions. The dangers of an overemphasis on diversity and devolution are especially strong now, after ERA.

When, in the 1970s, sociologists of education began to take an interest in education policy, they came to it from within the 'new' sociology of education, and produced analyses which neglected or denied agency and consciousness. They were, accordingly, severely criticized by the pluralists, while much of their black box view of education was also questioned by ethnomethodologists. But while it is all very well to recognize the validity of critiques of the functionalist nature of some of these explanations of education policy, and necessary to give credit to the experiences and actions of pupils, teachers and individual policy-makers (and I have argued for all these), there is, perhaps, a danger that we are moving too far in one direction, encouraged by the current climate to keep well away from agendas which focus on theorizing the role of the state in education, preoccupied instead with gathering rich descriptions, without sufficient thought to the nature of the thing to be described.

This is my major concern in relation to Fitz and Halpin and in relation to the work to which they refer. I endorsed *Governing Education* (on the cover!) because I think it does make a valuable contribution to an area where we knew very little, and it uses the experiences and understandings of policy-makers themselves. But it remains, for me, largely a missed opportunity, using the diversity of recollection to produce a model of policy-making which is indeterminate. As Grace (1989) has pointed, out, following C. Wright Mills, the methodological approaches of liberal pluralism will inevitably produce indeterminate conclusions. He goes on; 'McPherson and Raab do *not* relate the "Micro politics of personal relationships to a wider analysis of power" which is their stated intention, because the wider analysis of power is largely absent' (p. 92).

I believe that we need that analysis as a precondition of carrying out the detailed, information gathering work that most of Fitz and Halpin's paper is taken up with. The frameworks of explanation that were developed in relation to the role of the state in education policy remain powerful and valid, though we now recognize that the picture is more complex and contradictory than we thought at first. State-centred theory is perfectly capable of accommodating complexity and difference, it is only in its caricatured form that it appears to produce overdetermined and deterministic explanations.

This brings me to my final point, which is that a further trend in sociologically informed studies of education policy has been to emphasize the contradictory nature of much current policy-making, its messiness and illogicality – this is particularily evident in discussions of the apparent contradiction between centralization and devolution in education policy. As a consequence it is assumed that state centred/Marxist explanations are invalid, and some form of quasi-systems theory combined with pluralism (stressing client and consumer orientation) is invoked. This sometimes combines with uneasiness about forms of analysis which are apparently hostile to the consumer/client, and fail to recognize the benefits they may enjoy from particular policies like GM schools and CTCs. This uneasiness is, again, a reflection of past practice, and of a limited view of the capacity of state-centred analysis.

Explanations of education policy which take as their starting point the role of the state are inherently concerned with the contradictory nature of the demands made on the state, and by the tensions caused by the requirement upon it to deal simultaneously with these requirements. From within that theoretical framework, certain areas of investigation follow, for example the need to investigate the source, scope and pattern of any education policy, the operation of the state apparatus, its internal contradictions and conflicts, the historical antecedents of policy structure, content and culture. Those investigations, must, of course be informed by individuals' perceptions and experiences, and the informing framework must be interrogated by such material and tested against it. Otherwise we shall continue to dismantle and describe all the parts of the machine without being able to explain either how it works or what it is for.

These are hardly original arguments, indeed they have a long history. Their repetition is justified, I think, because of the challenge that we face in explaining education policy in a period of change, and because of the temptation, in a climate which is hostile to views of the world which conflict with its own, to get on with the very necessary task of capturing what is going on, rather than attempting to create an ordered and logical analysis of it. But we must do both, and must not assume that the inherent contradictions of current policy vitiate explanation. Quite the reverse.

I will conclude by indicating what might be done. Roger Dale's recent paper on CTCs (Dale 1990) provided a model of the kind of analysis of policy source and scope, within a state centred framework, that I discussed above. It has little or nothing on pattern, but a good deal of that is becoming available through the kind of work that Fitz and Halpin argue for, carried out in relation to the CTCs by Tony Edwards, Sharon Gewirtz and Geoff Whitty, and also by Geoff Walford and Henry Miller, and reported to a recent meeting of the ERA research network. That material could be used to explore and interrogate the theoretical framework developed by Dale. Work like this does not deny the need for detailed case study, but gives such work an explanatory purpose. Without it we will be busy but blind.

Note

1. Fitz, J. and Halpin, D. (1990) 'Researching Grant Maintained Schools', *Journal of Education Policy*, 5 (2), pp. 167–180

References

DALE, R. (1990) 'The Thatcherite Project in education; the case of the City Technology Colleges', *Journal of Critical Social Policy*, 49 (3), pp. 26–33.

FENWICK, K. (1976) *The Comprehensive School 1944–1970* (London: Methuen).

GEWIRTZ, S. and OZGA, J. (1990) 'Partnership, pluralism and education policy: a reassessment', *Journal of Education Policy*, 5 (1), pp. 37–48.

GRACE, G. (1989) 'Education policy studies; developments in Britain in the 1970s and 1980s', *New Zealand Journal of Educational Studies*, 24 (1), pp. 87–95.

KOGAN, M. (1975) *Educational Policy-making* (London: George Allen and Unwin).

MCPHERSON, A. and RAAB, C. (1988) *Governing Education; a Sociology of Policy Since 1945* (Edinburgh: Edinburgh University Press).

OZGA, J. (1987) 'Studying education through the lives of policy-makers; an attempt to close the micro-macro gap' in L. Barton, and S. Walker, (eds) *Changing Policies, Changing Teachers* (Lewis: Falmer Press).

SARAN, R. (1973) *Policymaking in secondary Education* (Oxford: Avendon Press).

Abstract

This short paper was produced in response to David Halpin and John Fitz's 'Researching Grant Maintained Schools', which is seen as indicative of a trend within education policy research towards the accumulation of detailed case study and the relative neglect of theoretical analysis. The different – and sometimes conflicting – research traditions in education policy are briefly summarized, and the factors contributing to the encouragement of pluralist approaches discussed. The paper concludes by arguing the case for analysis of education policy from within a state-centred perspective, in combination with detailed investigation of policy implementation.

[6]

Educational Policy Analysis and the Politics of Interpretation

Introduction

Policy analysis as a field of enquiry has proved itself receptive to the methodological developments which have characterized the social sciences as a whole since the early 1970s. It has passed through a positivistic phase where policy problems were seen in predominantly technical or administrative terms to admit the relevance of hermeneutical and critical modes of analysis (Callaghan and Jennings, 1985).

A number of authors in the area of educational policy have recently reviewed the assumptions and 'technicist' values motivating mainstream policy analysis. Goodson (1986) for instance, refers to the collapse of holistic planning in the field of education and emphasizes the importance of the social context. He proposes an 'hermeneutical' model of policy as a complex message (1986, p. 6): 'whose meaning like that of any message becomes increasingly scrambled for decoders in direct proportion to the number of "unfamiliar" concepts onto which its phrases are mapped'.

Prunty (1985) criticizes current trends in educational policy analysis and proposes an alternative framework based on critical social theory. His criticisms of existing policy analysis in education, in part, are that the term 'policy science' gives the enterprise a 'false precision' and obscures value, ethical and political implications, especially when problems are viewed as 'technical' ones capable of technical or administrative solutions. He advocates a form of policy analysis which is 'educational' in its terms of reference, taking account of the critical theories of authors like Bowles and Gintiss, Bernstein, Young and Willis, from which he infers these basic suppositions: policy analysis ought to be critical in intent, where analysts strive to expose sources of domination and repression; and ethical in nature, where persons are treated as ends in themselves.

The notions of problem formulation and the importance of the context were emphasized by the founding fathers of policy analysis (e.g., Lasswell, 1971). In more recent accounts of hermeneutical models attention has shifted from the simple demands to recognize the importance of context both in the formulation of problems and in the activity of policy analysis more generally, to emphasizing the fact that interpretation is an inherently politically loaded activity. The 'politics of interpretation' has become the new desideratum of a diverse set of post-empiricist and postmodernist thinkers. Yet it is not clear whether a 'politics of interpretation' ought to be considered as a form of ideological and cultural life, or whether it ought to be construed as a reflection on the processes of interpretation (Mitchell, 1982).

The notion of a 'politics of interpretation' is central to analysing policies as 'texts'. It need not simply result in the negative activity of unmasking ideology, conceived of as false claims to neutrality. It may also serve as the affirmation of a set of shared values of a community, or as an 'agenda for progressive action, a conception of interpretation as the liberation of suppressed or forgotten meanings, or as the envisioning of new meanings which may give direction to social change' (Mitchell, 1982, p. vi.).

Indeed in the formulation outlined in this chapter, the negative moment of unmasking, of explicating the rules, norms and interests which underlie what we have termed 'the evaluative context' is but a prelude to the articulation of new and progressive perspectives which can serve an emancipatory interest and open the way to the search for a well defined social problem in policy analysis.

In Chapter 7 we elaborated a Wittgensteinian-inspired philosophical model *and* theory of evaluation. The logical model, on our account, comprised five categories. Among them figured the category of *context*. On the basis of a Wittgensteinian account of rules and rule-following we argued 'that human activity is fundamentally and essentially evaluative for rules or agreement in shared practices are the basis for evaluation', and we attempted to demonstrate that formal evaluation of a programme or policy took place in a context already constituted by values, norms and interests.

In other words, we argued that there are sets of pre-existing rules which function as implicit standards for describing and judging what is to count as behaviour of a certain type, and that these implicit rules comprise the *context* against which any formal analysis or evaluation must take place.

In the theory proposed we focused on the conceptual primacy of the *learning community*, and sketched the defining characteristics of the ideal learning community. The learning community was construed in both theoretical and practical terms as a means by which a society can review, improve and develop policies, programmes and practices. Closely tied to the emancipatory intent of such a community we foreshadowed a procedure or a practical tool and logical first step for making explicit the evaluative context in terms of its implicit rules and assumptions.

The notion was developed in terms of a series of five overlapping phases, each designed to raise progressively broader questions concerning the interpretation of the relation of the 'received' problem to its context. The first phase was designed to isolate 'the problem' within the wider 'policy context' in order to explicate the 'official' values and interests behind 'received' definitions and to trace the history of 'the problem' in official discourse. The object of the second phase was to investigate how rules establish the context and provide parameters within which definitions can be formulated or excluded. The third phase, concerned with the wider political and economic context, sought to identify 'enabling' or 'disabling' structures governing the acceptance and rejection of policies and programmes. Fourth, under the banner of 'the public interest' (understood as minimally involving some notion of collective good), we proposed a form of conceptual analysis as the means for locating key political concepts and policy terms within their theoretical paradigms. The last and final phase sought potential working definitions of 'the problem' identifying and rejecting those accounts which 'blame the victim' or obfuscate wider issues.

The procedure was developed, applied in practice, and refined in a practical project on programme evaluation and policy development. This project was devised by the New Zealand State Services Commission to meet a strong demand by government departments for a senior officers' course on programme evaluation and policy development (State Services Commission is one of two governmental control departments, along with Treasury, and has overall responsibility for the training of government officers). The project ran from end-July 1985 to mid-May 1986 and required eighteen officers from six departments to produce plans for the development or evaluation of a programme or policy (actual or proposed). In all cases programmes or policies were developed — some to an advanced stage with submissions to prime audiences and actual implementation (Marshall and Peters, 1986).

The project involved teams of officials organized on a departmental basis participating in a series of formal sessions presenting a current policy or programme under review or for development. During formal sessions of the course (a total of six days organized over a period of nine months) each team presented its plans. These plans were presented initially in the form of an issue paper, and subsequently subjected to collegial discussion, analysis and refinement. The framework of our procedure for analysing the evaluative context as a major theoretical input to the course, provided an initial and ongoing basis for analysis.

Participants acknowledged the usefulness of this procedure as a practical working tool stressing its value in both clarifying the operating concepts, values and underlying assumptions of programmes and policies (which in and of itself had a surprising pay-off for more technically oriented questions concerning their implementation and administration), and identifying different (sometimes contradictory) descriptions and definitions elicited from major stakeholders. Regarding the latter point, the procedure proved a successful tool for identifying and isolating potential areas of contestation between stakeholders and for tracing the theoretical and/or value origin of these differences. Participants, for instance, commented on the 'distance' between centralist values of departmental administration focusing on economy, efficiency, measurability and at times expediency, in terms of formulation of problems and design of programmes and policies, versus the values of recipient or target populations.

Individualism and Community

Whilst the reactions of these participants — senior public servants — was important, further evaluation of its utility as a practical tool was required. The opportunity for a further evaluation of this procedure — what we now prefer to call 'analysing the evaluative context' — was provided in a new project concerning Maori education in New Zealand. (The Maori people — te tangata whenua — are the indigenous inhabitants of Aotearoa (New Zealand)). As a result of our involvement in this new project our original notion of this procedure underwent a further set of developments.

This chapter, then, is concerned with the theoretical development of a practical set of guidelines as a means for analysing and critiquing programmes and policies. It adopts and develops a problem oriented approach focusing on the *context* in which problems can be sited and it makes explicit the rules, norms and interests that structure and may underlie that context. In the next section we review some of the classical texts on approaches to social policy problems, particularly those approaches which seek the relevance of a notion of contextuality. We also argue for an approach to the search for a well-defined problem and its relevance to both the making and evaluation of social policy. In the following section we formalize the set of practical guidelines as developed to date. In the final section we exhibit the use of this tool in a recent project.

Problem Orientation and the Importance of Context

It is curious, indeed, that in the wake of positivism some theorists have sought a hermeneutical reading of policy analysis at much the same time that *others* have re-discovered the importance of questions of contextuality in the founding fathers. Torgenson (1985), for instance, provides us with an account of Harold Lasswell's contextual orientation in policy analysis. Contextuality is the first of three principal attributes laid down by Lasswell (1971, p. 4) for the policy sciences, along with problem-orientation and methodological diversity. He further suggests that an adequate strategy of problem-solving encompasses five intellectual tasks, including: goal clarification; trend description; analysis of conditions; projection of developments; invention, evaluation and selection of alternatives. Neither is this emphasis on contextuality confined to Lasswell. It is clearly evident in Merton and Nisbet (1961). Following Max Weber, Merton asserts that the choice of problems has 'value-relevance' (Wertbeziehung) and further states: 'Moral issues inhere in the very formulation of problems for sociological research' (Merton, 1961, 2.4). Nisbet (1961, 72a) repeats Merton's maxim that social problems are inseparable from contexts, but both adopt a Weberian approach to the issue of 'value-neutrality' in the social sciences: the very normative framework of science with its institutional commitment to the values of truth etc., makes objectivity possible. The lesson, by comparison, that many postmodernist theorists teach us is that 'objectivity' in the social sciences is an illusion, particularly in those cases where such sciences purport to provide guidance in solving *social* problems (Diesing, 1982). In other words, the values that researchers hold, the paradigms they operate from, and the ideological perspectives which guide them in the selection of a problem as a *social* problem and thereafter throughout the research process, exert powerful influences on professional *choices* researchers make during the course of inquiry. In the emergence of (and transition to) a hermeneutical model of inquiry in the social and policy sciences, interpretation has, itself, come to be seen as an inherently politically loaded activity.

In traditional approaches, in both policy analysis and related activities such as policy evaluation and development, a problem-solving process is often adopted, and there is an emphasis in the early or initial phases of this process to define the problem. For example, in the area of social policy research a conventional problem-solving process is often used to describe various phases of policy. Normally, it begins with the phase of problem specification (e.g., see Dluhy, 1981, p. xxii–xxiii), and then moves through the phases of development and structuring of alternatives, ratification and acceptance of proposals, policy implementation, and evaluation. The approach is widely adopted. It is seen as an early and crucial stage in various models proposed under the banner of action research (Peters and Robinson, 1984) and in the development of more 'democratic' methodologies, e.g., participatory research (see Brown, 1985).

Often it is conceived of as an essentially linear process which does not see the definition of a problem as open to interpretation, or as involving a series of iterative feedback cycles (the hermeneutical circle or spiral) in which the definition may undergo considerable shifts in meaning. Indeed, it may be the case in practice that the problem cannot be defined, or can be defined only according to contradictory interpretations, or that preliminary definitions will need to undergo considerable shifts as data collection proceeds and is analysed and interpreted.

Perhaps Habermas, more than anybody else, is responsible for justifying the primacy of a *critical hermeneutics* against the sway of positivistic methodology, arguing that social science can be called upon as an auxiliary science in national administration *only* if it is supplemented by a hermeneutical social science that elucidates the rational ends and interests to be served. Others, following Habermas' lead, have directly questioned the metaphor of social engineering, arguing that its fundamental flaw is that it side-steps the centrality of questions of power and interest in social policy formation.

The movement in philosophy of science away from logical and 'internal' models of rationality to the positive recognition of the historical norms and interests which permeate scientific institutions is also a movement which has explicitly turned to hermeneutics — to the model of the text and the recognition of context. Bauman (1987) significantly charts a shift in the position of intellectuals from one as 'legislators' on opinions for the rest of the community in the modern age, to one as 'interpreters' in the age of postmodernism, representing different standpoints in relation to one another.

The history of the sociologizing of knowledge — epigrammatically, knowledge as social belief (Durkheim); knowledge as rule-following (Wittgenstein); knowledge as ideology (Mannheim and Marx) — has its recent developments in the work of numerous scholars, including Robert K. Merton, Peter Winch, Stephen Toulmin, Karl-Otto Apel, Mary Douglas and Richard Rorty. Such work offers a broad methodological warrant for viewing any attempt to provide a problem orientation in applied social sciences as seriously deficient should it exclude the consideration of context — the milieu or environs of the text or the text-analogue.

In the field of policy analysis defining the problem is both an interpretive and inherently politically loaded activity. Practitioners are frequently confronted with the dilemma of serious incompatibilities between rival accounts or interpretations of what constitutes 'the problem'. Discrepancies are often most serious, in some cases unresolvable, when practitioners are faced with interpretations of a problem proposed by policy-makers on the one hand and those of recipient populations on the other.

Only by beginning with a problem and the search for a well-defined problem (i.e., one that is identified and defined within the full socio-historical context), can policy analysts defend themselves against criticisms of serving centralist and bureaucratic values, or of being motivated by a technocratic imperative.

In the view which we propose the 'evaluative context' is of central importance. By this we mean the already sets of pre-existing rules which comprise a context against which any formal evaluation takes place. The evaluative context is itself *evaluative* as it has built into it an evaluative texture which reflects the community of interests involved and which is, perhaps, most clearly exemplified in the rules that structure various subcommittees, institutions and organizations; and, in particular, the rules, explicit and implicit, that structure any policy/programme development or evaluation. It is these rules, descriptive of reality, which must be identified, made explicit, and assessed, in the process of analysing the evaluative context.

The extensive literature on rules and rule-following in social theory cannot be tracked out here in detail. It traverses the territory of linguistics (Chomsky), structuralist anthropology (Lévi-Strauss), moral and legal philosophy (e.g., Toulmin, Baier, Hart, Rawls), interpretive sociology/anthropology (e.g., Garfinkel, Douglas), philosophy of social science (Winch) and, of course, philosophy of language (Wittgenstein) and social policy. We are not maintaining that the notion of rule at stake among these disciplines is one of uniform use because the distinctions in use are many and varied (Shwayder, 1965; Twining and Miers, 1976). But of special note is Giddens' (1976) attempt in social theory to understand the problem of the production and reproduction of structures in society by recourse to a Wittgensteinian analysis of rule-following. Giddens' (1976) Wittgenstein-inspired rule-following account, and his attendant notion of 'structuration', is important for it provides a general conceptual framework for understanding human social activity in a way that avoids the structure-agency problem.

Educational Policy Analysis and the Politics of Interpretation

Habermas' (1971, 1979) notion of 'communicative action' owes something to Wittgenstein, Austin and speech-act theory. While Habermas talks of binding consensual norms rather than rules in the context of communicative action, the intent is similar. Further, in his theory of the ideal communicative community, where at the level of discourse the implicit validity claims of *comprehensibility, truth, rightness*, and *veracity* can be discursively redeemed in the realm of pure argumentation, an analysis is offered whereby the concepts of rules and interests are theoretically aligned.

In our own approach to evaluation Wittgensteinian influences have occurred at three levels; first, in outlining a general philosophical model of evaluation (though we believe this model to hold independently of its particular Wittgensteinian derivation); second, in developing our particular theory of evaluation, which is centered on the ideal learning community; and, third, in the identification of rules, governing the *evaluative context*, which are at a level which is no longer theoretical but practical.

Analysing the Evaluative Context

The problem, as a thing thrown or put forward (in the original Greek sense) or as a difficult question posed for solution (in common parlance), emerges and is shaped as a result of intellectual activity and becomes the focus for learning and research. It is, however, only an historical and provisional starting point, for in order to fully articulate and define a problem, its first tentative outline must be related back to an understanding of the problem-context and forward to the anticipation of action.

This *dialectical* process of siting the problem in its context and in regard to strategic action permits a 'reading' — possibly diverse readings — of the problem (the part), and in relating it back to its context (the whole) and forward to its strategic solution (the new whole), the problem itself will undergo changes in its definition.

In other words, what we are asserting here is that for the entire duration of the learning (research) process the stage of defining the problem is never surpassed: it remains an integral part of the learning process through to its successful resolution, and thereafter, in monitoring the continued effects of strategic action.

The conceptual element, emphasizing the reflective and reflexive characteristic of the learning (research) process as it is brought to bear on a problem and its context, is always with us. This is one reason for beginning, temporally and logically, with the problem and its initial and tentative definition: it stresses the vital importance of the conceptual element in investigating and transforming social reality.

In what follows we put forward in schematic form the notion of analysing the evaluative context. It is presented in five related stages (A through to E), each of which, in successive turns, is designed to raise broader and broader questions. The stages begin with a view of the problem in the immediate policy context and finally return to a provisional definition of the problem. The five stages constitute, effectively, a feedback loop the purpose of which is to site a problem with regard to its context. It performs this task by adopting the critical attitude: each stage has listed within it a series of questions designed to challenge the 'received' definition and its underlying set of values and assumptions. Only by attempting to provide answers to such questions is the problem properly sited according to its context. We acknowledge that it is not an easy task (who said social science research was easy?) and that it is likely to challenge not only the 'received' definition but also official views and, not least, the policy analyst's or evaluator's own theoretical sensibilities.

By siting the problem in its context we hope to be able to take account of the way certain sets of values and assumptions, often masked as neutral, intrude into analysis and definition, predominating at the expense of other, and possibly, opposing sets. This methodological tool will help analysts, evaluators and/or researchers to become aware of the extent to which social problems have a history of definition in official and intellectual discourse and how this history, as an inherited residue, often distorts the production of a well-defined problem, predisposing us towards one set of values rather than another. It aims also to prevent the fragmentary and segmented nature of definition and analysis, allowing, at a critically early stage, the fullness of a contest to help frame a problem.

It should be noted that the framework or schema of questions presented below is suggested as a means of criticizing and exposing the contradictions and limits of policies. It is meant to be used creatively. The authors do ***not*** believe that such a framework is to be followed mechanically as an algorithm. Rather it is to be seen and used as a set of flexible guidelines.

The 'Received' Problem and the Policy Context

A problem does not 'officially' exist in isolation but in a network defined by a policy context. The policy context is, itself, a network of policies and programmes which contribute to the definition of a set of related problems. This is where the problem in question is to be sited initially; by reference to the received definition of concepts, the underlying values, assumptions and interests which determine the policy context and thereby identify a problem under a certain description. It is important to realize that this context is not static but, rather, has evolved historically from earlier contexts and earlier definitions of 'the problem'.

1 What is the 'received' definition of the problem?
2 What is the network of related problems?
3 What is the policy context? (i.e., the network of associated policies or programmes)

Educational Policy Analysis and the Politics of Interpretation

4 How are the key terms defined in the policy context?
5 What are the values and assumptions underlying the context?
6 How has this context evolved *historically*?
7 What is the history of 'the problem' in official discourse?
8 Whose interests are best served by the 'received' definition of the problem?

Identifying the Rules

The rules are those practices which comprise behaviours of a certain type, definitive of a community, and the expressions of which may be articulated in such things as constitutions, laws, written rules (including precedents), stated policies, manuals, and directions from supervisors (written or verbal), though they may have to be 'derived' from established practices, precedents and acknowledged procedures. These rules establish the context and provide parameters within which definitions can be formulated or *excluded*.

9 Which rules are directly related to the 'received' definition of the problem?
10 What is the status of such rules?
11 Do these rules have explicit interpretations?
12 What possible definitions of the problem are excluded by these rules, or by particular 'established' interpretations of these rules?
13 What are the underlying values and assumptions of these rules (i.e., whose interests are best served by them)?

The Community of Interests and the Wider Socio-political Context

While the immediate rules establish a context and provide parameters in which definitions of problems can be formulated *or* excluded, there are wider political and economic structures which, in large part, constrain and determine the acceptance and rejection of policies and programmes. These structures can be seen as enabling or disabling in terms of the interests of different communities.

14 What *constraints* are posed by governmental and fiscal policies?
15 What *preferences* are expressed or indicated by governmental and fiscal policies?
16 Which community interests, responses and reactions have been expressed? Which have not?
17 How do various community and pressure groups view the problem? e.g., What definitions do they, or would they, hold?
18 Are there common or universalisable emancipatory interests?

Individualism and Community

Paradigm Context and the Public Interest

The terms 'public interest' and 'in the public interest' minimally involve some notion of the collective social good. State action in the public interest implies a form of intervention taken on behalf of the whole community, against private or sectional interests, to improve the access of disadvantaged groups to goods and services. The evaluation of programmes and policies designed to serve the public interest thus necessarily requires examination of the economic and political context for policy decisions which are taken within this content and reflect the terms which constitute it. Such terms for instance, as 'freedom', 'equality', 'social needs', 'market' and 'class' are the main sorts of concepts that frame the context, but these are essentially contestable in that the same concepts may stand under different, perhaps contradictory interpretations, depending upon the theory or paradigm adopted. In other words, these concepts are theory-laden and the same term or 'concept' may be used in the service of contradictory theses. In evaluating or analysing programmes and policies put forward in the public interest it is therefore necessary to identify the main concepts used and the theory(ies) and paradigms they stand under (often this amounts to mapping the relations between concepts and clarifying assumptions).

19 What are the main concepts used?
20 How are these concepts used?
21 What are the relations between these main concepts?
22 What theory(ies) do they help to constitute or legitimate?
23 In the theory(ies) identified what assumptions are made regarding the relations between 'freedom' and 'equality', etc?
24 In the theory identified what assumptions are made concerning the role of the State?
25 What implications do the assumptions (in 23 and 24) have for policy proposals?

The Provisional Definition of the Problem

This process which has aimed at examining the 'received' definitions of social problems and main concepts within their wider context, eventually leads back to the provisional definition of the problem, and acts as a final checking or filtering phase.

26 What are the potential working definitions of the problem?
27 Which definitions exhibit an individualistic bias (e.g., 'blaming the victim')?
28 Which definitions suggest ameliorative solutions?
29 Which definitions contribute to segmented, fragmented and/or 'isolated' solutions?

30 Which definitions obfuscate wider political and economic issues?
31 To what extent are emancipatory interests ideologically suppressed in the working definition of the problem?

We refer here to a *provisional* definition of the problem. Yet the stated aim was the search for a well-defined problem! A provisional definition may become, in the iterative cycle, a new received definition or be accepted as a well-defined problem. But even then this is never a final nor a fixed definition and, indeed, it may cease to be a well-defined problem as the evaluative context shifts either from interaction with any programme or policy designed to 'solve' this problem, from other wider or major policy shifts, or from the collection and analysis of data. Our claim for the framework outlined above is that it has a constructive use not only in the review and development of programmes and policies but also in terms of their critique.

The five step procedure provides the evaluator with a clear, normative stance which is based upon an interest in emancipation and which is critical in intent. The procedure is an hermeneutical one, designed to produce a well-defined problem by explication of the norms, rules and interests which structure the context within which the problem is formulated or defined.

Hence the client's definition of the problem *may* differ from that arrived at by this process. But this is not necessarily so. However it would be the case where the client's definition is revealed as being narrow and technicist and, to some degree, at odds with that of the community or target population.

The hermeneutical five step process of explicating the context is designed to highlight differences amongst stakeholders in the definition of the problem. It is a process which is also designed to take account of these differences in arriving at a provisional definition of the problem on the basis of historical evidence and conceptual analysis. The provisional definition remains at the heart of the evaluation research process, open to empirical testing throughout the project.

To Reo o te Tai Tokerau

The methodology of what we call 'analysing the evaluative context' was developed initially in a policy development project for the New Zealand government (Marshall and Peters, 1986) It was subsequently refined and fine tuned in two further projects on Maori education (Peters and Marshall, 1988c; 1989; 1990). The methodology has been used by practising policy analysts and theorists in New Zealand, most notably by Penetito (1988) and Penetito *et al.* (1991) as part of the review methodology developed for the newly established Education Review Office in New Zealand, which has responsibility for monitoring performance and outcomes of schools and other agencies.

As there is insufficient space here to comment on all the projects and developments we will confine our attention to the use of the methodology in

Individualism and Community

one project — Te Reo O Te Tai Tokerau. Here we are simply concerned to briefly introduce the project so as to demonstrate the application of our procedure of analysing the evaluative context and the crucial role that our procedure came to play in developing a well defined problem with which to begin.

The history of policy toward education of the Maori people in New Zealand has been ethnocentric in its approach, based on unexamined assumptions of the cultural superiority of the pakeha which has extended as much into related issues of research and evaluation, as it has into policy decision-making. This history can be seen in an 'assimilationist' approach to race relations which predominated up until the late 1950s and in the focus on a policy of 'integration' implicitly based on a notion of 'cultural deprivation' during the 1960s and early 1970s. Thereafter followed a transitional period where emphasis was shifted from 'cultural deprivation' and 'the problem of the Maori child' to a concept of 'cultural difference'. Finally, we have entered an era dominated by the attempt to formulate a 'multicultural' policy. Most recently, there have been some signs that we are moving into a policy era of 'bi-culturalism', most as a result of Maori initiatives.

Within education policy Maori language has generally suffered the fate of most minority languages: its attrition through the depletion of native speakers. These effects can be seen clearly in the senior secondary school where Maori language has been 'controlled' within a monocultural schooling system.

For instance, only 2,500 candidates out of the 50,000 15-year-old New Zealanders who sit Maori for School Certificate (the national examination taken in the third year of the secondary school — age 16), elect to take Maori. A major obstacle to the wider acceptance of Maori as a subject, let alone a teaching medium, in secondary schools has been the scaling system. Others, including Professor Ranginui Walker and Mr Bernard Gadd, have criticized the monocultural bias of the School Certificate English paper in 1971, pointing out the 'institutionalized racism' of the education system by reference to the 'complex gate-keeping system' operating with the School Certificate subject-hierarchy pass-rate.

Another factor which inhibits the growth of Maori as a living language is the fact that while Maori is traditionally an oral language, the emphasis in School Certificate is predominantly on Pakeha skills of reading and writing. Oral Maori has for over a decade been a component of School Certificate Maori.

Te Reo O Te Tai Tokerau originated in development work by the Department of Education (now Ministry of Education) on School Certificate Maori. This development work must be seen against other expressed concerns for fairness and justice. The Maori Language Syllabus Committee in a report of 12 August 1986, expressed reservations concerning mark adjustments and distribution policies despite the raising of the median to 52 (same as School Certificate English) and the reporting in grades. The School Certificate Examinations Board asked the Committee to consider the possibility of a criterion-based achievement system, total internal assessment and reporting oral and written components separately. A school survey in March 1985 revealed almost total support for increasing the weighting for the oral component and a substantial minority wanted to increase marks allotted for Oral Maori still further. In October 1985 an interim amendment to School Certificate Maori increased the oral component from 15 to 25 per cent. The then Education Department's development project had:

- produced five levels which were defined in Maori and used to guide assessors;
- established training for the assessors;
- re-designed the oral test;
- resulted in three moderators being appointed to monitor standards in Maori; and
- began to explore means by which class teachers' involvement in the assessment may be increased.

The Te Reo O Te Tai Tokerau Project was the use of all of these strategies in the Tai Tokerau region of New Zealand (i.e., Northland, a province comprising some eighteen state secondary schools). Specifically the Department expected of the project information on: the effectiveness of assessor training; the reliability of teacher assessment; the practicalities of moving candidates to central venues and the effects on candidates; the appropriate forms of moderation for Oral Maori; the costs associated with various approaches to moderation.

The first approach to the project was in terms of analysing the evaluative context, a subject to which we now turn. Within the first category — the problem context — we were presented, *we believe*, with essentially this received definition, or official definition, of the problem: 'The problem that confronts those responsible for the School Certificate Examination in Maori is to increase both the proportion of the oral component and teacher involvement in the assessment process but, at the same time, to maintain the precision of assessment that typifies the School Certificate examination as a whole.'

The problem is deeply embedded in the history of race relations in New Zealand. It should also be noted that the potential contribution that an increase in the amount of oral Maori in this examination could make to the survival of wide use of Maori is considerable. The problem then is at the cutting edge and is clearly related to broader Maori language and educational policies and, more deeply, to power issues that have surfaced explicitly recently, but which can be retraced to the Treaty of Waitangi. The School Certificate Examination is not without problems itself; particularly on questions of internal assessment and the scaling procedures adopted on this, essentially, norm referenced examination.

The historical context and the official discourse permitted us to identify values and assumptions underlying the evolution of this problem. There have been progressive shifts in research and policy from 'the Maori problem' to the alleged deficiency of 'the Maori child', to the acknowledgment of cultural differences and, recently, the acknowledgment of cultural biases in the public education system. At each point key terms such as 'cultural deprivation' and 'cultural difference' were used to formulate the Pakeha (white mono-cultural) 'answer' to the problematization of an isolated and fragmented social reality. In each case the problem of Maori education was defined in terms of mono-cultural and often imported social theory which ignored Maori/Pakeha social relations and the wider political and economic contexts. Equally at each point we can identify changes in these values and assumptions.

At this stage then the question must be raised as to whether this definition of the problem still serves mono-cultural interests. The rules governing this definition of the problem are essentially those encapsulated in current Education Acts and the discretionary power conferred upon officers of the Ministry of Education by the Act and associated legislation, Orders in Council etc. But these rules have changed over time also. At one point in time Maori was not permitted to be spoken in schools. Maori were required to speak English and punished if they spoke their mother tongue. In particular for now there are rules governing the 'ownership' of School Certificate Maori, the conduct of such exams, what counts as knowledge, teaching and, even, a *school.* Again these reflect in essence a mono-culturalism, and not Maori practices and discourse. From this definition of the problem the rules governing the practice of the oral Maori examination will not be those of a People not merely of different culture, but heavily steeped in an oral tradition, with an emphasis on group dialogue and decision making and with different conceptions of communication than those employed, say, in the oral interview of a Pakeha student in an examination of French as a second language. Definitions of the problem of examining oral Maori which are based upon Maori culture may then be excluded by the rules underlying the 'official' definition.

The questions under the wider political and economic context invited us to consider this problem in relation to the fact that Maori is not merely *taonga* (prized possession) but also, now, an official language; to the increasing political importance of the Waitangi Tribunal; and to the perceived importance of the resurgence of Maori language in the empowering of Maori people. Narrowly hived off under the aegis of matters educational the fate of Maori language may be to fail to receive the impetus which some see as necessary if it is to survive. There are of course language and cultural variations between regions and the 'local' control of language becomes of paramount importance.

In the economic sphere the New Zealand economy has undergone a massive restructuring spurred by the neo-liberal economic policies of Labour and National administrations. Under these policies government trading departments have been first corporatized and then privatized, and the market environment deregulated so that they must compete in the private sector. Crown land, over much of which there are disputed Maori land claims, would have, no doubt, been sold off as corporations attempt to realize on assets had it not seen massive Maori protest. Effects of corporatization, privatization, deregulation, and cutbacks of government staff have resulted in heavy further unemployment for Maori, especially in rural areas where they are being further marginalized.

Under these economic policies it would seem unlikely that Maori, recognized as it is as an official language, will be used in the day to day conduct of government affairs (except as already legitimized in the courts). Already there have been calls for a return to one official language — English.

These structural economic changes would seem to be inimical to Maori language and the effect upon the Ministry of Education of calls for greater efficiency, cost-effectiveness and user-pays principles *may* be to reinforce this definition of the problem and incline the solution towards the status quo — i.e., centralized mono-cultural control.

Within the category of the public interest the key concept is that of bi-culturalism. As we have seen above there has been a shift from openly assimilationist policies to policies based upon the recognition of cultural differences. Recognizing differences is one thing, but if the efforts of education do not aim beyond the need to develop in Maori pupils notions of self-esteem and the capacity to survive in, and cope with, mono-cultural domination then there will be no structural changes to this domination. Teaching Pakehas (non-Maori) to be nice to Maoris whilst ensuring continued domination is the outcome of concepts of multi-culturalism which do not challenge the social relations of the education system. Being aware of and sensitive towards cultural issues without addressing questions of resources and power, leaves the dominant structures and institutions unaltered. The concept of bi-culturalism imbedded in principles of justice, social need and power sharing would be one which acknowledged the need for control of education for Maori by Maori. Concern that this may lead to 'ghettoizing', as it may be in England where some ethnic communities are retreating behind ethnic walls (Aspin, 1987), must be tempered by the realization that there is a sense in which Maoris are already ghettoized by racist structures and institutions, including education, which have involved them in their own cultural disenfranchisement.

We are now in a position to look at a redefinition of the problem. Seen from a concept of bi-culturalism which identifies power structures and which will lead to Maori control of its own education, the provisional definition becomes something like this: 'How to conduct the oral interview in School Certificate Maori so that; Maori knowledge and cultural norms are adhered to; it is seen as legitimate by Maori; and it accords with the standards of precision that typifies the examination.'

This represents quite a marked shift in the problem. Whereas the evaluators were asked to comment on the appropriate forms of moderation for oral Maori, they were not asked to comment specifically upon the form that the oral interview should take. There are different values governing communication for Maori which have strong implications for the conduct of the oral interview as a form of assessment of Maori language. The evaluation problem then is no longer one of merely judging consistency between numbers of assessments of pupils. This problem remains of course but if things Maori are to structure the form and conduct of the oral interview then there will be a need to convince those responsible for the conduct of School Certificate Examinations that precision, accuracy and fairness are being safeguarded.

Our view of evaluation as education — the attempt to review, improve and develop policies and practices — is well suited to overcoming this dilemma. On this case, perhaps, the Ministry of Education, may need to accept a different definition of the problem. There is, of course, a variety of opinions held by officers within the Ministry so that perhaps this provisional definition will be recognized as the problem, or as a conjoint and closely associated problem. What will be crucial here is the concept of bi-culturalism. For any State Ministry of Education it must be difficult, if not impossible, to countenance ownership of one of its curriculum offerings by others than the Ministry, and partnership may be the best possibility. The major educational problem then for the evaluators is the promotion of a concept of bi-culturalism that is empowering for Maori people.

The guidelines of contextual analysis then can be seen as an important analytical tool in the identification of different possible definitions of the problem and, in this case, the framing of policy that is empowering for Maori in a way in which the mere shift in the allotment of marks for School Certificate Maori and the increased involvement of Maori in assessment is not.

This procedure of contextual analysis played an important part in the project Te Reo O Te Tai Tokerau. It provided a conceptual and historical tool which was developed within the context of a theory of evaluation as a form of community empowerment. It has been used to good effect, as a crucial research stage, in subsequent and related projects by us (see Peters and Marshall, 1990) and by others (e.g., Penetito, 1988; Penetito, Thear and Glasson, 1991).

References

ASPIN, D. (1987) '"Critical openness" as a platform for diversity: towards an ethic of belonging', in O'KEEFE, B. (Ed) Building Walls or Building Bridges: Schools for Tomorrow, Barcombe, Falmer Press.

BAUMAN, Z. (1987) *Legislators and Interpreters: On Modernity, Postmodernity and Intellectuals*, Cambridge, Polity Press.

BROWN, L.D. (1985) 'People centered development and participatory research', Harvard Educational Review, **55**, 1, pp. 64–75.

CALLAGHAN, D. and JENNINGS, B. (Eds) (1985) *Ethics, the Social Sciences and Policy Analysis*, New York, Plenum Press.

DIESING, P. (1982) *Science and Ideology in the Policy Sciences*, New York, Aldine.

DLUHY, M.J. (1981) 'Introduction: The changing face of social policy', in TROPMAN, J.E., DLUHY, M.J. and LIND, R.M. (Eds) *New Strategic Perspectives on Social Policy*, New York, Pergamon Press, pp. xi–xxviii.

GIDDENS, A. (1976) *New Rules of Sociological Method*, London, Hutchinson.

GOODSON, I. (1986) 'Policy in social context: Collapse of holistic planning in education', *Journal of Education Policy*, **1**, pp. 5–22.

HABERMAS, J. (1971) Knowledge and Human Interests, Shapiro, J. (Tr), Boston, Beacon Press.

HABERMAS, J. (1979) *Communication and the Evaluation of Society*, MCCARTHY, T. (Tr), London, Heinemann.

LASSWELL, H.D. (1971) *A Pre-View of Policy Sciences*, New York, Elsevier.

MARSHALL, J.D. and PETERS, M.A. (1986) 'Evaluation and education: Practical problems and theoretical perspectives', *New Zealand Journal of Educational Studies*, **21**, 1.

MARSHALL, J.D. and PETERS, M.A. (1986) *Report on the Programme Evaluation and Policy Development Project*, NZ State Services Commission, Training and Development Branch, p. 220.

MERTON, R.K. (1961) 'The Sociology of social problems', in MERTON, R.K. and NISBET, R. (Eds) *Contemporary Social Problems*, New York, Harcourt Brace Jovanovich, pp. 3–44.

MERTON, R.K. and NISBET, R. (1961) (Eds) *Contemporary Social Problems*, New York, Harcourt Brace Jovanovich.

MITCHELL, W.J.T. (1982) 'Editor's introduction: The politics of interpretation', *Critical Inquiry*, **1**, pp. iii–viii.

NISBET, R. (1961) 'The future and social problems', in MERTON, R.K. and NISBET, R. (Eds) *Contemporary Social Problems*, New York, Harcourt Brace Jovanovich, pp. 729–55.

PENETITO, W.T. (1988) 'Maori education for a just society', in *Report of the Royal Commission on Social Policy*, **4**, Wellington, Government Printer.

PENETITO, W.T., GLASSON, J. and THEAR, L. (1991) 'Review methodology: Keeping it simple while engaging with complexity', Paper presented to 13th National Conference of New Zealand Association for Research in Education, Dunedin, 28 November–1 December.

PETERS, M.A. and MARSHALL, J.D. (1988c) 'Te reo o te Tai Tokerau: Community evaluation, empowerment, and opportunities for oral Maori language reproduction', in *Report of the Royal Commission on Social Policy*, Vol. 3, Pt. 2, *Future Directions*, Wellington, Government Printer, pp. 705–43.

PETERS, M.A. and MARSHALL, J.D. (1989) *Nga Awangawanga Me Nga Wanata A Te Iwi O Te Tai Tokerau: Final Report of the Project, Issues Concerning the Schooling and Retention of Maori Secondary School Students in Northland*, Department of Education, Wellington, NZ

PETERS, M.A. and MARSHALL, J.D. (1990) 'Education, the New Right and the crisis of the welfare state in New Zealand', *Discourse*, **11**, 1, pp. 77–90.

PETERS, M.A. and ROBINSON, V. (1984) 'The status and origin of action research', *Journal of Applied Behavioural Science*, **20**, 2, pp. 113–24.

PRUNTY, J.J. (1985) 'Signposts for a critical educational policy analysis', *Australian Journal of Education*, **29**, 2, pp. 113–40.

SHWADER, D.S. (1965) *The Stratification of Behaviours*, London, Routledge and Kegan Paul.

TORGENSON, D. (1985) 'Contextual orientation in policy analysis: The contribution of Harold D. Lasswell', *Policy Sciences*, **18**, pp. 241–61.

TWINNING, W. and MIERS, D. (1976) *How to Do Things with Rules*, London, Weidenfeld and Nicolson.

[7]

Discourse: studies in the cultural politics of education, Vol. 18, No. 1, 1997

Critical Policy Analysis: exploring contexts, texts and consequences

SANDRA TAYLOR, *School of Cultural and Policy Studies, Queensland University of Technology, Australia*

Introduction

Little attention has been given to research methodology in the educational policy literature and, as Ball (1990, p. 9) has noted, the field of policy analysis has been dominated by commentary and critique rather than empirical research. It would appear that methodological questions about what 'data' are needed for analysis and how that material is collected have been less important in critical policy work than the theoretical frameworks which are used and the questions which are asked. There is, however, an extensive body of literature in the US dealing with policy 'evaluation' and 'implementation studies'. Much of this literature is managerialist, technicist and uncritical in approach, although a more critical literature has emerged in recent years (see, for example, Hawkesworth, 1988; Deleon, 1994). In the British context, Halpin and Troyna's (1994) edited collection has helped to redress the lack of concern for methodological issues within the field. In this paper I will review recent developments in methodology in policy analysis with particular emphasis on the influence of theories of discourse. Examples from recent Australian research will be used to illustrate the application of theories of discourse in education policy analysis, and the paper concludes by suggesting some requirements for education policy research which is both critical and political.

Ozga (1987) has termed the field of inquiry in education policy analysis 'policy sociology', which she describes as 'rooted in the social science tradition, historically informed and drawing on qualitative and illuminative techniques' (p. 144), and this term has been adopted by many policy researchers. Grace (1987) refers to 'policy scholarship', while the American literature refers to the 'policy sciences'—a term first used by Lasswell in 1949 (Deleon, 1994, p. 77). Troyna (1994, pp. 81–82), however, rejects any dichotomy between policy sociology and other approaches using a social science perspective, basically because he believes that the former under-emphasises feminist and anti-racist work and fails to produce studies which have a 'strategic edge'. Troyna (1994) wishes to emphasise the linkages between critical policy analysis and critical social research, and argues that critical social research is interested not only in what is going on and why, but

0159-6306/97/010023-13

is also concerned with doing something about it. Drawing on Harvey (1990), Troyna stresses that 'Critical social research includes an overt political struggle against oppressive social structures' (p. 72). Taking into account these concerns, my preferred term is 'critical policy analysis' (Prunty, 1985), a term which is also quite widely used in the field, particularly in Australia.

Leaving aside the question of terminology, Codd has argued that for some time 'the field of policy analysis has been fraught with argument over its purpose and methods' (1988, p. 235), and continues:

> A widely accepted view, however, takes policy analysis to be a multi-disciplinary field that cuts across existing specialisations to employ whatever theoretical or methodological approach is most relevant to the issue or problem under investigation. (1988, p. 235)

Further, in a review of recent qualititative research in policy in the UK, Maguire and Ball (1994) comment that, in general, policy studies appear to be methodologically unsophisticated, with issues of language and meaning taken for granted. Elsewhere, writing of his aim to capture the 'messiness' and complexity of the policy-making process in his research on the 1988 Education Reform Act in Britain, Ball (1990) comments that, 'The changing processes of policy making in education over the past ten years have, to a great extent, outrun the development of relevant analysis and conceptualisation' (p. 7), and 'the conceptual tools seem blunt and irrelevant' (p. 8).

Gillian Fulcher (1989) made a similar point in relation to her research on integration policies in Victoria. Fulcher writes of her search for a theoretical model in the policy literature to use in her research, and her surprise in finding the inadequacy of most of that literature and that most of it conveyed 'no sense of the political struggles involved in developing and implementing policy' (1989, p. 3). As Fulcher (1989, p. 3) put it: 'The discrepancy between the literature and the political reality I saw, encouraged me to be sceptical of most of the conceptual and theoretical platforms the literature offered'.

There was, it seems, some sort of *impasse* in theory and methodology which was recognised by these writers. However, recent theoretical developments have been useful in highlighting the complexities of policymaking for which the traditional models seemed simplistic, and old conceptual tools seemed too blunt. They have offered 'a new set of tools to begin to try to explain things' (Ball, 1990, p. 18), with new possibilities being opened up through associated methodologies. This has lead to a growing awareness of methodological issues in education policy work, with an increasing emphasis on issues to do with *meaning* and, related, a shift towards exploring the *effects* of policy rather than on policy intentions (Codd, 1988; Ball, 1990). We are also becoming much more conscious of questions of subjectivity (Jansen & Peshkin, 1992) and interpretation (Rizvi & Kemmis, 1987), particularly in interview based studies (Scheurich, 1995); and of the standpoint of the researcher (Smith, 1987).

In general, the problematising of aspects of method in this way seems to be a result of post-modernism 'as a growing intellectual and cultural sensibility' that is influencing academic thought (Schram, 1993, p. 250), as well as, and often related, the impact of feminist approaches to policy analysis. Moving away from these broader developments, I now want to turn to consider the particular influence of theories of discourse on policy analysis and their value for critical policy work.

Theories of Discourse and Policy

While there are various strands within this work and a number of theorists have been influential in policy analysis, all draw to some extent on Foucault's theories of discourse, often complemented by neo-marxist cultural theorists like Gramsci (e.g. Fairclough, 1989; Kenway, 1990). While Thompson (1984) provides a detailed discussion of the various strands contributing to discourse theory, Codd (1988) provides a clear discussion of the theoretical underpinnings to his application of discourse theory to education policy analysis. My own approach has been influenced more indirectly by my work in feminist cultural studies and in feminist policy studies. By using the term 'theories of discourse' I want to adopt a broad—and pragmatic—approach to the interrelated developments in social theory, and reject any tight categorisation of theoretical positions as has been common in much of the recent academic literature.

Central in theories of discourse are language and meaning—aspects which, as has been mentioned, have often been taken for granted in policy analysis in the past. The major explanatory concept used in these theories is: *discourse*. This term was used by Foucault 'to designate the conjunction of power and knowledge' (Kenway, 1992, p. 128), while Meutzenfeldt defines discourse as: 'the complex of ... notions, categories, ways of thinking and ways of communicating that constitutes a power-infused system of knowledge' (1992, p. 4). Meutzenfeldt uses the concept in developing a sociological framework to examine how political processes and policy-making shape and are shaped by both social power relations and the power of the state. This approach is particularly useful for critical policy analysis because it can take account of policy making at all levels, allows for conceptualisation of the state, and highlights the *political* nature of policy making. In addition, it is a dynamic framework which emphasises *culture* as well as *practice*.

Even though policy is not explicitly mentioned in the extract which follows, it can be usefully conceptualised within this framework:

> On one hand, the various projects of state institutions, party politics and social movements draw on the social categories, resources and meanings *[i.e. discourses]* that are made available and reproduced through the culture and practices of the wider society. On the other hand, those same political projects simultaneously impact upon the wider society: they shape social categories, position people within them, and mould the categories of citizenship through which people are brought into particular relationships with the state and politics. (Meutzenfeldt, 1992, p. 2)

Policy, as an aspect of the various political projects of state institutions referred to by Meutzenfeldt, is central in these dynamics.

Fairclough's (1989, 1992, 1993) focus on language as social practice also provides a useful theoretical base for critical policy analysis. Fairclough is interested specifically in the relationship between 'discursive practices, events and texts' on the one hand, and 'wider social and cultural structures, relationships and processes' on the other—in order to explore the linkages between discourse, ideology and power (Fairclough, 1993, p. 135). These linkages are clearly relevant to the exploration of policy documents within broader policy processes.

In my view, discourse theories have enhanced the scope of critical policy analysis in a number of ways. The most obvious influence is the increasing focus on policy documents as *texts*, but discourse theories can also be drawn on to explore policy-making processes within the broad discursive field within which policies are developed and implemented. In other words, they enable valuable fine-grained analyses to be under-

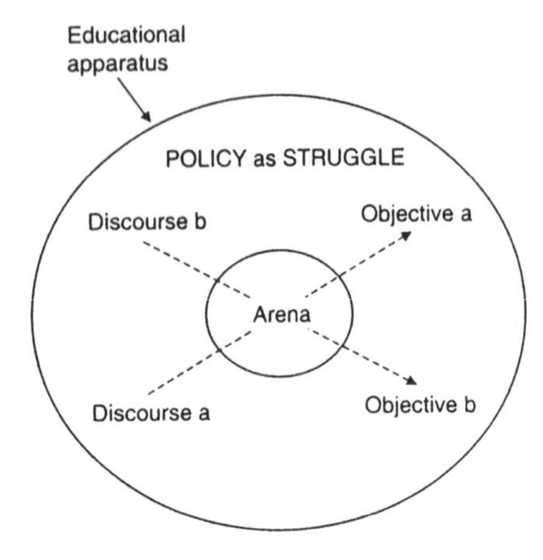

Figure 1. A political model of policy based in a theory of discourse.

Source: Fulcher, 1989, pp. 4, 6.

taken within a broader structural analysis. I have found them useful in my own ongoing work on equity, policy and the politics of change—particularly because of their emphasis on *culture*.

From a discourse theory perspective, *policy making* is viewed as an arena of struggle over meaning, or as 'the politics of discourse' (Yeatman, 1990). The emphasis is placed on policy *processes* and policy is seen as 'struggle between contenders of competing objectives, where language—or more specifically, discourse—is used tactically' (Fulcher, 1989, p. 7). For example, in her study of the development and implementation of integration policy in Victoria, Fulcher found that the 'rights' discourse articulated by parents of students with disabilities conflicted with the discourse of professionalism of the special educators. Struggles such as these are viewed as occurring at all levels and in all arenas of policy making—Fulcher identified policy arenas at six different levels in the Victorian education system, from School Council Subcommittees on Integration to the Regional Board—and are often reflected in the form of tensions and contradictions, or competing discourses, in the resulting policies themselves (Fulcher, 1989).

From this perspective, then, *policy texts* represent the outcome of political struggles over meaning. Codd elaborates on this point (1988):

> ... policy documents can be said to constitute the official discourse of the state (Codd, 1985). Thus policies produced by and for the state are obvious instances in which language serves a political purpose, constructing particular meanings and signs that work to mask social conflict and foster commitment to the notion of universal public interest. In this way, policy documents produce real social effects through the production and maintenance of consent. (p. 237)

However, also central to theories of discourse is the idea that there is no single reading of policy texts. Rather, 'for any text a plurality of readers must necessarily produce a plurality of readings' (Codd, 1988, p. 239). Consequently, Codd suggests that: 'Instead of searching for authorial intentions, perhaps the proper task of policy analysis is to examine the differing effects that documents have in the production of meaning by readers'

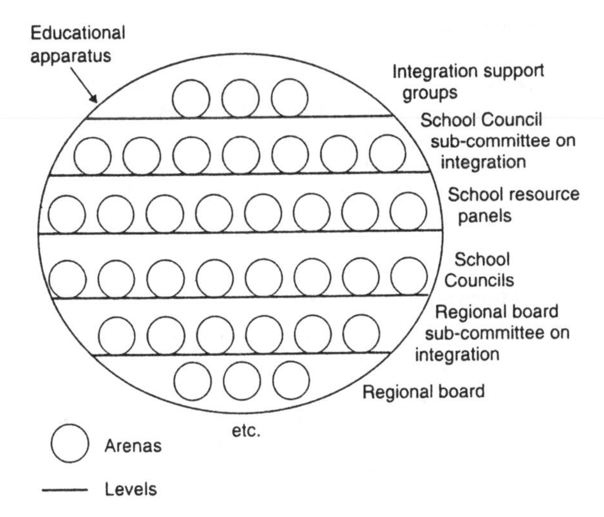

Figure 2. Some examples of policy levels and arenas in the Victorian educational apparatus.

Source: Fulcher, 1989, pp. 4, 6.

(p. 239). Through reinterpretation and recreation, policies may be seen to be: 'continuously constituted and reconstituted through discussion, activities and social relationships' (Rizvi & Kemmis, 1989, p. 15). Further, it is possible to conceptualise policy making as a continuous policy cycle of policy making and remaking in specific sites (Bowe, Ball & Gold, 1992; Ball, 1994). (See also Fulcher (1989) who has a similar view, although she does not use the term *policy cycle.*)

Associated with this theoretical approach is some sort of textual analysis, ideology critique or deconstruction to highlight the constitutive practices texts use. The approach is useful in highlighting values and teasing out competing discourses, both in policy development and policy implementation (to use the old dichotomy). Some fine grained analyses of the use of language in policy texts use a linguistic approach—exploring linguistic strategies used to position readers (Luke *et al.*, 1993), as well as key words used. However, McHoul (1984), in what seems to be one of the first applications of discourse analysis in relation to education policy, distances himself from what he refers to as 'a narrowly formalistic look at the "linguistics" of policy statements' (p. 1). He explains that policy texts 'constitute nodal points or networks of signifying practice generally; networks of discourse which constitute a field of power and knowledge ...' (pp. 1–2). His focus is on texts and textuality: on the 'conditions of possibility' of policy texts—how they come to *be*.

McHoul (1984) analysed Queensland Education Department's Equal Opportunities policy statement and associated documents produced by the conservative Bjelke-Peterson government in 1981; developed as a result of the availability of Commonwealth funding for programs for the education of girls (Lingard, Henry & Taylor, 1987). McHoul showed, using a discourse analytic approach, the contradictions within the policy documents, and how the policy text transformed, incorporated and neutralised feminist discourses. Significantly, this discourse analysis was placed in a broader socio-historical context. As is emphasised by Codd (1988), whose application of discourse analysis to education policy work has been influential in Australia and New Zealand, such fine-grained analyses need to be placed in a broader context: 'Policy documents ... are ideological texts that have been constructed within a particular context. The task of deconstruction begins with the recognition of that context' (pp. 243–244). The following section, which briefly outlines some of the ways in which discourse theory can be used in critical policy analysis, begins with a consideration of the analysis of policy contexts.

Applications in Education Policy Analysis

Discourse theory can be used to explore particular policies in their historical context; tracing how policy 'problems' are constructed and defined and how particular issues get to be on the policy agenda. It is also useful in highlighting how policies come to be framed in certain ways—reflecting how economic, social, political and cultural contexts shape both the content and language of policy documents.

For example, there have been significant changes in how approaches to educational inequality have been framed and in key concepts which have been used in education policies (Rizvi & Kemmis, 1987; Connell & White, 1989). Differences in terminology reflect the particular historical and cultural context, and have implications for the ways in which particular concepts are used and understood. The various concepts which are associated with equity issues are highly malleable—with terms and meanings changing over time and according to the political context: 'Concepts do not remain still for very long. They have wings, so to speak, and can be induced to fly from place to place. It is this context which defines their meaning' (Apple, 1993, p. 49). In Britain, though 'stronger' policy approaches which are directed at structural change have been termed 'anti-racist' and/or 'anti-sexist', 'equal opportunities' is the term which is used to cover the general policy field. In Australia, on the other hand, 'equity' and 'social justice' have come to be used as the 'umbrella' terms to refer to policies which aim to address inequalities in education—reflecting a move towards the notion of 'fairness', which places emphasis on participation as well as outcomes in addressing educational inequalities between social groups. Hence linguistic practices used—which operate at the level of metaphor and symbolism—are relevant for policy making and analysis (Schram, 1993). Policy discourse can be conceptualised as a kind of 'symbolic language' with specific terms such as 'equity' acting as 'condensation symbols' (Troyna, 1994) within the cultural context.

The significance of the *cultural context* for education policy making was highlighted in my research on equity and the Education Reform Act in Britain (Taylor, 1993). I explored the impact of the changing cultural and political context on the 'politics of discourse' relating to 'equal opportunities' policies in Britain and argued that:

> The British experience shows the importance of the cultural, or 'common sense', level in influencing how popular prejudices are taken up and articulated in policies. The Conservatives were able to draw on the deep seated conservatism in British culture to marginalise anti-sexist and anti-racist education and to construct their new policy agenda. (Taylor, 1993, p. 38)

In addition, the conservative popular press were able to pick up and articulate discourses of racism in the community in orchestrating support for the government, and in the process 'equal opportunities' became seen as a 'loony left' issue and discredited. (See Wallace, 1993, on the contribution of the mass media on education policy processes.)

In contrast, in my research with Miriam Henry, the emphasis was more on the impact of the changing *economic and political context* on the way equity issues have been framed, or reframed, in Australian education policy. Labor's approach to gender reform policy was to link together gender equity and economic rationalism in 'an uneasy alliance' (Henry & Taylor, 1993), as a result of Labor's shift towards economic rationalism in the mid to late 1980s. However, we argued that this approach to social justice builds on Australian traditions of reform in which elements of market needs and social reform are intertwined. We traced the impact of this contradictory policy context on the implementation of the *National Policy for the Education of Girls*. As a result of the competing discourses—with economic rationalist discourses dominating—the equity goals of the policy were distorted through a narrowing focus on vocational education and training.

As well as being useful in exploration of policy contexts then, discourse theory can be applied to policy implementation case studies. Given that contradictory contexts and competing interests are reflected in policies as competing discourses, policy effects are by no means certain or predictable. Discourse theories are useful for investigating how policies are *read* and *used* in context; in other words, for documenting the politics of discourse during policy implementation. This kind of focus will be illustrated in more detail in the next section.

Discourse theory can also be used to highlight the workings of the state in policy formulation. (See, for example, Ball's (1990) research on the development of the Education Reform Act, or Kenway's (1992) work on feminism and the state.) My own work on the state and social change (Henry & Taylor, 1993; Taylor, 1993) has been influenced by discourse theory via feminism. We have drawn on feminist accounts of the state which, in line with a focus on the politics of policy processes, emphasise the state as a set of dynamic, historically located and complex processes rather than, simply, a set of institutions. In Burton's words:

> The state is not a thing; it does not exist as a single, monolithic entity. It is a complex of relationships, embodying a certain form of power operating through various institutional arrangements ... The state is a social–political process, the result at any given moment of struggles and demands. (1985, pp. 104–105)

The influence of theories of discourse have resulted in more critical awareness of methodological questions which had previously been taken for granted—particularly in relation to interpretation. In their policy case study of the Participation and Equity Program in Victorian Schools, Rizvi and Kemmis (1987) refer to a scene in *The Life of Brian* to illustrate the problem of interpretation:

> In the film there is a moment when a spectator of the sermon on the mount relays the words of the distant Christ to others still further back in the crowd: 'blessed are the cheesemakers ...', he reports. The interpretation of interpretation causes problems of refraction as messages are relayed across distance, across time, levels of hierarchies, and locations. (p. 15)

These problems clearly have implications for policy-making processes. They also have implications for methodology in critical policy analysis itself as new questions are posed about the validity of ethnographic and other qualitiative methodologies which are often used in policy work (Eisenhart & Howe, 1992; Silverman, 1993).

Questions have also been raised about the ideological nature of policy research

(Schram, 1993; Griffin, 1994), and we have come to see the ways in which our theoretical frameworks help to legitimate particular approaches to policy making. For example, Ball (1990), researching changes in education policy-making processes in Britain following the Education Reform Act, suggested that perhaps theoretical shifts have made the pluralist approach to policy making seem to be inadequate and ideological (pp. 12–13). In this context, research by Gewirtz and Ozga (1990) demonstrated that the notion of 'partnership' in Britain had been working in an ideological way—obscuring the bureaucratic control exerted on education policy making at the local level by central government officers.

There has also been a recent tendency to problematise how policy problems are constructed and how they are framed (see, for example, Beilharz, 1987; Huxley, 1989; Yeatman, 1990; Griffin, 1994). In this context, Schram (1993) shows how social welfare policy in contemporary post-industrial US maintains old distinctions and helps to recreate problems of the past—especially in relation to reproducing women's poverty, and argues that policy helps to construct the reality it confronts. Scheurich (1994), on the other hand, advocates an emphasis in policy analysis on how problems get to be on the policy agenda, and gives this approach the new name of: *policy archaeology.*

Research on the New Post-Compulsory Education and Training Agenda

In this section of the paper I will discuss two examples from my research with Miriam Henry on the new post-compulsory education and training policies in Australia in which our work has been influenced by theories of discourse. Our on-going interest is on equity, policy and the politics of change.

Debates around the Post-Compulsory Education and Training Agenda

Our initial research project on the post-compulsory policies focused on the policy context and the debates around the new agenda (Taylor & Henry, 1994). In terms of the applications to policy analysis discussed in the previous section, the project attempted to link *text with context.* We traced the framing of the policy agenda—resulting from the involvement of the Commonwealth and all state governments, the Australian Council of Trade Unions (ACTU) and the unions, and business and industry—and the way competing discourses were 'stitched together' in the new policies. We also traced the historical antecedents which led to this policy framework. For example, both the government's and the ACTU's agendas build on a mix of utilitarian and more progressive discourses in Australian education, the origins of which we traced and documented.

The various competing interests and discourses involved in policy formulation were explored through an analysis of the media debates in *The Australian* newspaper's weekly 'Higher Education Supplement' through 1992—the year the policies were developed. The main debates were over the following issues: the distinction between education and training and the respective roles of the universities and TAFE colleges; competency based education and training; centralised policy control; and funding and resources. We argued that our analysis of debates revealed new alliances and divisions involving key players and sectors of the post-compulsory system, and highlighted: '... the stretched nature of this policy "umbrella", sheltering as it does a fragile consensus, in turn sheltering a number of disparate and not necessarily compatible interests' (Taylor & Henry, 1994, p. 117).

It was clear that there were underlying tensions within the new vocationalist discourses in the Finn, Carmichael and Mayer reports reflecting these disparate interests (for example, between exponents of liberal education and vocational training, or between fordist and post-fordist assumptions about the workplace), despite the use of key words such as 'pathways' and 'convergence'—which acted in a sense as linguistic markers glossing over the different perspectives of the key players. For example, 'the competencies debate' was complicated by the different strands of competencies involved: competency based training or education; vocational competencies as referred to in the Carmichael Report; and the key competencies as developed by the Mayer committee. The proponents of the new policies argued that the key competencies form the foundation for but are independent of the Australian Vocational Certificate (AVC) Training System—a crucial point, because in much of the education debate the various competency strands were conflated by those, such as the older more traditional universities, who opposed the new agenda.

We argued that the agenda was complex and ambiguous, operating in a multilayered policy field, and offering contradictory possibilities for young people. We suggested that, while limited reforms were possible, the very breadth and ambiguity of the policy agenda might very well exacerbate regressive ends.

Implementation of the Carmichael Report

Following the initial project, we were interested, then, in the impact of this contradictory and ambiguous agenda. In 1993, we commenced research in Queensland aimed at investigating which aspects of the new policies were being picked up 'on the ground' (Henry & Taylor, 1995). Here the focus of our research was on *text and consequences.*

We were interested in examining the broad claim for greater 'inclusiveness' as well as more 'targetted' notions of equity underlying the concern with questions of participation, equity and access for disadvantaged groups in the Carmichael Report and associated documentation. We looked in some detail at four of the projects funded as pilot studies for the introduction of the AVC Training System (referred to as AVC pilots), which in turn involved an examination of the processes surrounding the administration of the pilots. Given our theoretical interest in the dynamics and politics of policy processes, we wanted to explore the administrative and systemic context within which the pilots operated as well as 'on the ground' implementation issues; hence we also examined how equity matters were dealt with within the Commonwealth and state bureaucracies as well as within the projects themselves. Key players involved in initiating or implementing the pilots were interviewed and documentation relating to the pilots was examined. Additionally, we had access to the minutes of state steering committee meetings.

The documents revealed that there is no shortage of rhetoric or strategies for dealing with equity, and our study confirms that there is no shortage of subversive tactics 'on the ground' either. The research highlighted an important dynamic in the change process: the relationship between policy objectives and policy outcomes. The study indicated that slippages between rhetoric and practice were already apparent in the early implementation stages of these policies, and threatened to push the policy agenda in conservative directions. The mediating effects of a complex layering of policy processes, usefully captured by the notion of 'policy refraction' (Freeland, 1981), was notable in this case study. Strongly stated equity objectives at the Commonwealth level became progressively weakened in the ebb and flow of negotiation and in the face of local pressures along the 'policy chain': the perceived urgency of getting the agenda 'up and running'; the constitution of a state steering committee without expertise in or commitment to equity implementation; the masculinist culture of the trades environment; the particular pressures facing schools; and so on. The study showed how the various levels—Commonwealth, state and local—were able to play off against each other in order to avoid responsibility for equity provision.

But slippage between objectives and outcomes is not simply a matter of a 'gap' between policy formulation (rhetoric) and implementation (reality). The notion of competing discourses is also relevant to this analysis. The case study showed how, in the politics of policy implementation, older and powerful meanings may emerge within the new vocationalist discourse. The pilot projects used keywords such as 'pathways', 'equity' and 'convergence' to legitimate fairly traditional versions of vocational education likely to maintain rather than address social divisions. Also embedded in the policies were other competing discourses of regulation and deregulation—the latter a reflection of the economic context which threatened to distort the long term goals of the policies.

We used the notion of 'playing the agenda' in relation to the dynamics of policy making at all levels—highlighting the politics of discourse where new concepts were used strategically to legitimate particular approaches and to attract funds from the 'AVC bucket' for projects which failed to come to grips with the new policies.

Conclusion: linking contexts, texts and consequences

In this concluding section, I will attempt to draw the threads of my argument together and suggest some criteria for approaching education policy research which is both critical and political. In the paper I have examined the influence of theories of discourse on policy analysis and their value for critical policy work. I have discussed a few examples of their application from my own recent research, though these examples are not offered in any way as 'ideal models'. Rather than indicating a deliberate *move* to draw on discourse theory, the research has been more indirectly influenced by discourse theory through feminist cultural studies and feminist policy analysis.

I have argued that discourse theory has allowed us to address the complexity of education policy making through a focus on the 'politics of discourse'. In my view, such an approach is able to contribute to a deeper understanding of how policy-making processes *work* at a fine-grained level. However, to be strategically and politically useful, it is important that such fine-grained analyses are located within a broader context, including an historical context. This seems to be a crucial feature of critical policy analysis, that is, the notion of 'thinking relationally'—where theoretical frameworks are used to place cultural forms within broad patterns of social inequality and relations of domination (Carspecken & Apple, 1992, p. 512). Similarly, Agger (1992) usefully distinguishes between a critical (sociologically based) post-structuralism, where discursive strategies of policy texts are placed in broader context, and a post-structuralism drawn more from literary criticism which does not take account of the broader political context within which texts are generated.

There seems to be general agreement among most policy researchers that there is a need to take account of both 'micro' and 'macro' levels, and that critical work needs to place education policy making within its broad economic, social and historical context. But, rather than maintain the macro/micro dichotomy—or even a macro/meso/micro categorisation—I would want to emphasise the many layered nature of policy making and the importance of exploring the *linkages* between the various levels of the policy process with an emphasis on highlighting power relations. In other words, we need to think about the three aspects included in my title: contexts, texts and consequences. Policy texts need to be analysed within their context and also in relation to their impact on policy arenas in the broadest sense.

There is probably a need too for more comparative work—as advocated by Dale (1994). I have been struck by the ways in which the political contexts within which we work frame our approaches to policy analysis. In Britain, as a result of changes brought about by the Education Reform Act and the marginalisation of sociology as a discipline, policy researchers have probably had fewer opportunities to be involved with policy development than in Australia. Labor governments in Australia have provided opportunities for direct involvement in central policy making at Commonwealth and state levels, and there are also opportunities through the unions, women's movement and other community groups to become involved in policy processes more indirectly. For example, our research on women and training has been used by activists within the unions to push the training reform agenda in progressive ways. As Finch (1984, p. 231) observes, 'one important implication of policy-oriented qualitative research is that it has the potential for engaging the researched as well as the researcher in evaluating the *status quo* and bringing about change'. Thus she reminds us of the need to be concerned about grass roots policy change as well as providing information 'upwards to remote "policy makers"' (p. 231).

In this paper I have avoided becoming involved in the 'state control versus policy cycle debate' (Slee, 1995) which has become artificially polarised and reified in the literature in a way which is not very useful. The so called 'debate' is a tangled web with a number of strands or dimensions caught up in the discussions. As well as the issue of the role of the state (Dale, 1992) versus localised players in specific sites (Fulcher, 1989; Bowe, Ball & Gold, 1992; Ball, 1994) in the development and implementation of policy cycle, there are vestiges of old debates around pluralism/state control, policy making as linear/complex, and the degree to which an analysis is sufficiently strategic or not. There have also been vigorous debates in the literature around the use of post-structuralist approaches in theorising policy which are relevant to the present discussion. Criticisms have been made of the use of discourse theory in policy analysis for under-playing the constraints on policy making (Evans, Davies & Penny, 1994), and Hatcher and Troyna argue that the policy cycle approach 'distorts understandings of the policy process, especially in the relative powers which it assigns to the central apparatus of the state and to the schools' (1994, p. 156). Other writers (Henry, 1993) criticise post-structuralist approaches for their failure to ground fine grained analysis in a material or structural analysis. In this paper I have emphasised the importance of placing fine grained policy analyses in their broader context. In his recent work, which draws on critical theory and ethnography as well as post-structuralism, Ball (1994) makes it clear that he is not neglecting broader power issues, or indeed political questions relating to social justice. Further, he anticipates criticism of his use of what might be seen as incompatible theoretical perspectives, arguing that: 'The critical analyst must take risks, use imagination, but also be reflexive. The concern is with the task rather than with theoretical purism or conceptual niceties' (Ball, 1994, p. 2). This is the position which I have adopted in this paper though I too am aware of the possible problems of eclecticism.

Finally, I think that methodological issues have been side stepped for too long in education policy analysis. More attention should be given to questions of meaning and interpretation—as well as validity, reliability and subjectivity which I have only mentioned briefly. Such attention will strengthen policy research and hopefully produce critical analyses which will be useful in relation to the pursuit of social justice. What is important is an underlying value commitment to social justice, and an analysis which is as rigorous as possible. And we need to remember, in line with the broader conceptualisation of policy as the politics of discourse which I have advocated, that policy research may be used not only by policy makers within the state, but by other interest groups, such as teachers. An understanding of policy processes as the 'politics of discourse' can be very useful to those involved in 'on the ground' struggles in the various arenas of education policy making.

Correspondence: Sandra Taylor, School of Cultural and Policy Studies, Queensland University of Technology, Kelvin Grove Campus, Red Hill, Queensland 4059, Australia.

REFERENCES

AGGER, B. (1992) *Cultural Studies as Critical Theory* (London, Falmer Press).

APPLE, M. (1993) Thinking 'right' in the USA: ideological transformations in an age of conservatism, in: R. LINGARD, J. KNIGHT & P. PORTER (Eds) *Schooling Reform in Hard Times* (London, The Falmer Press).

BALL, S.J. (1990) *Politics and Policy Making in Education: explorations in policy sociology* (London, Routledge).

BALL, S.J. (1994) *Education Reform: a critical and post-structural approach* (Buckingham, Open University Press).

BEILHARZ, P. (1987) Social democracy and social justice, *Australian and New Zealand Journal of Sociology*, 25(1), pp. 85–99.

BOWE, R., BALL, S.J. & GOLD, A. (1992) *Reforming Education and Changing Schools: case studies in policy sociology* (London, Routledge).

BURTON, C. (1985) *Subordination: feminism and social theory* (Sydney, Allen & Unwin).

CARSPECKEN, P.F. & APPLE, M. (1992) Critical qualitative research: theory, methodology, and practice, in: M.D. LE COMPTE, W. MILLROY & J. PREISLE (Eds) *The Handbook of Qualitative Research in Education* (San Diego, Academic Press).

CODD, J. (1988) The construction and deconstruction of educational policy documents, *Journal of Education Policy*, 3(3), pp. 235–247.

CONNELL, R.W. & WHITE, V. (1989) Child poverty and educational action, in: D. EDGAR, D. KEANE & P. MCDONALD (Eds) *Child Poverty* (Sydney, Allen & Unwin).

DALE, R. (1992) Whither the state and education policy? Recent work in Australia and New Zealand, *British Journal of Sociology of Education*, 13, pp. 387–395.

DALE, R. (1994) Applied education politics or political sociology of education?, in: D. HALPIN & B. TROYNA (Eds) *Researching Education Policy. Ethical and Methodological Issues* (London, The Falmer Press).

DELEON, P. (1994) Reinventing the policy sciences: three steps back to the future, *Policy Sciences*, 27, pp. 77–95.

EISENHART, M.A. & HOWE, K.R. (1992) Validity in educational research, in: M.D. LE COMPTE, W. MILLROY & J. PREISLE (Eds) *The Handbook of Qualitative Research in Education* (San Diego, Academic Press).

EVANS, J., DAVIES, B. & PENNY, D. (1994) Whatever happened to the subject and the state in policy research in education?, *Discourse*, 14(2), pp. 57–64.

FAIRCLOUGH, N. (1989) *Language and Power* (London, Polity Press).

FAIRCLOUGH, N. (1992) *Discourse and Social Change* (London, Polity Press).

FAIRCLOUGH, N. (1993) Critical discourse analysis and the marketization of public discourse: the universities, *Discourse and Society*, 4(2), pp. 133–168.

FINCH, J. (1984) *Research and Policy: the uses of qualitiative methods in social and educational research* (London, The Falmer Press).

FREELAND, J. (1991) Where do they go after school?: a critical analysis of one education program for unemployed youth, *The Australian Quarterly*, Spring, pp. 351–373.

FULCHER, G. (1989) *Disabling Policies? A comparative approach to education policy and disability* (London, The Falmer Press).

GEWIRTZ, S. & OZGA, J. (1990) Partnership, pluralism and education policy: a reassessment, *Journal of Education Policy*, 5(1), pp. 37–48.

GRACE, G. (1989) Education policy studies: developments in Britain in the 1970s and 1980s, *New Zealand Journal of Educational Studies*, 24(1), pp. 87–95.

GRIFFIN, C. (1994) *Representations of Youth. The study of youth and adolescence in Britain and America* (Cambridge, Polity Press).

HALPIN, D. & TROYNA, B. (Eds) (1994) *Researching Education Policy. Ethical and Methodological Issues* (London, The Falmer Press).

HARVEY, L. (1990) *Critical Social Research* (London, Allen & Unwin).

HATCHER, R. & TROYNA, B. (1994) The 'policy cycle': a Ball by Ball account, *Journal of Education Policy*, 9(2), pp. 155–170.

HAWKESWORTH, M.E. (1988) *Theoretical Issues in Policy Analysis* (New York, State University of New York Press).

HENRY, M. (1993) What is policy? A response to Stephen Ball, *Discourse*, 14(1), pp. 102–105.

HENRY, M. & TAYLOR, S. (1993) Gender equity and economic rationalism: an uneasy alliance, in: B. LINGARD, J. KNIGHT & P. PORTER (Eds) *Schooling Reform in Hard Times* (London, The Falmer Press).

HENRY, M. & TAYLOR, S. (1995) Equity and the AVC pilots in Queensland: a study in policy refraction, *Australian Education Researcher*, 22(1), pp. 85–106.

HOWELL, D. (1990) Some thoughts on 'researching grant-maintained schools', *Journal of Education Policy*, 5(3), pp. 242–244.

HUXLEY, M. (1989) Reading planning politically, *Arena*, 89, pp. 116–129.

JANSEN, G. & PESHKIN, A. (1992) Subjectivity in qualitative research, in: M.D. LE COMPTE, W. MILLROY & J. PREISLE (Eds) *The Handbook of Qualitative Research in Education* (San Diego, Academic Press).

KENWAY, J. (1990) Education and the Right's discursive politics, in: S. BALL (Ed.) *Foucault and Education. Discipline and Knowledge* (London, Routledge).

KENWAY, J. (1992) Feminist theories of the state: to be or not to be, in: M. MUETZENFELDT (Ed.) *Society State and Politics in Australia* (Sydney, Pluto Press).

LINGARD, R., HENRY, M. & TAYLOR, S. (1987) A girl in a militant pose: a chronology of struggle in girls' education in Queensland, *British Journal of Sociology of Education*, 8(2), pp. 135–152.

LUKE, A., NAKATA, M., SINGH, M. & SMITH, R. (1993) Policy and the politics of representation: Torres Strait Islanders and Aborigines at the margins, in: R. LINGARD, J. KNIGHT & P. PORTER (Eds) *Schooling Reform in Hard Times* (London, The Falmer Press).

MAGUIRE, M. & BALL, S. (1994) Researching politics and the politics of research: recent qualitative studies in the UK, *International Journal of Qualitative Studies in Education*, 7(3), pp. 269–285.

MCHOUL, A.W. (1984) Writing, sexism and schooling: a discourse analytic investigation of some recent documents on sexism and education in Queensland, *Discourse*, 4(2), pp. 1–17.

MCNAY, I. & OZGA, J. (Eds) (1985) *Policy Making in Education: the breakdown of consensus* (Oxford, Pergamon/OUP).

MUETZENFELDT, M. (Ed.) (1992) *Society State and Politics in Australia* (Sydney, Pluto Press).

OZGA, J. (1987) Studying education through the lives of policy makers; an attempt to close the micro-macro gap, in: S. WALKER & L. BARTON (Eds) *Changing Policies. Changing Teachers* (Milton Keynes, Open University Press).

PRUNTY, J. (1985) Signposts for a critical educational policy analysis, *Australian Journal of Education*, 29(2), pp. 133–140.

RIZVI, F. & KEMMIS, S. (1987) *Dilemmas of Reform. The Participation and Equity Program in Victorian Schools* (Geelong, Deakin Institute for Studies in Education).

SCHEURICH, J. (1994) Policy archeology: a new policy studies methodology, *Journal of Education Policy*, 9(4), pp. 297–316.

SCHEURICH, J. (1995) A post-modernist review of research interviewing, *International Journal of Qualitative Studies in Education*, 8(3), pp. 239–252.

SCHRAM, S.F. (1993) Postmodern policy analysis: discourse and identity in welfare policy, *Policy Sciences*, 26, pp. 249–270.

SILVERMAN, D. (1993) *Interpreting Qualitative Data. Methods for Analysing Talk, Text and Interaction* (London, Sage).

SLEE, R. (1995) *Changing Theories and Practices of Discipline* (London, The Falmer Press).

SMITH, D. (1987) *The Everyday World as Problematic. A Feminist Sociology* (Milton Keynes, Open University Press).

TAYLOR, S. (1993) 'Equal opportunities' policies and the 1988 Education Reform Act in Britain: equity issues in cultural and political context, *Discourse*, 14(1), pp. 30–43.

TAYLOR, S. & HENRY, M. (1994) Equity and the new post-compulsory education and training policies in Australia: a progressive or regressive agenda?, *Journal of Education Policy*, 9(1), pp. 105–127.

THOMPSON, J.B. (1984) *Studies in the Theory of Ideology* (Berkeley, University of California Press).

TROYNA, B. (1994) Critical social research and education policy, *British Journal of Educational Studies*, 42(2), pp. 70–84.

WALLACE, M. (1993) Discourse of derision: the role of the mass media within the education policy process, *Journal of Education Policy*, 8(4), pp. 321–337.

YEATMAN, A. (1990) *Bureaucrats, Technocrats, Femocrats. Essays on the Contemporary Australian State* (London, The Falmer Press).

Part II
Economics: Markets and Development

[8]

Review of *Economics of Education: Research and Studies*

Edited by George Psacharopoulos. Oxford: Pergamon Press. 1987. 482 pp.

Mark Blaug

The economics of education as a field of study was born phoenix-like in the early 1960s out of the pioneering work of Gary Becker and Edward Denison and the promotional efforts of Theodore Schultz. In the 1970s, however, came the screening hypothesis and the associated notions of internal and segmented labor markets. At the same time, the emerging problem of stagflation in the industrialized countries and the decline in rates of economic growth in both the First and the Third World sapped confidence in the power of education to promote growth, development, equality and all the other good things of life. The 1980s have seen a deepening pessimism about the importance of education and with it has come a pervasive disillusionment with the economics of education as an area of teaching and research. One might almost go so far as to say that the economics of education now lies dead in the mind of both professional economists and professional educators.

The New Palgrave. A Dictionary of Economics, published last year by Macmillan in four volumes, contains no entry for "economics of education" and refers the reader instead to an essay on "Human Capital" as if the economics of education were merely another name for human capital

The author of this review is a professor in the Department of Economic, Administrative, and Policy Studies in Education at the University of London and at the University of Buckingham.

theory, a proposition which is roughly equivalent to equating labor economics with the marginal productivity theory of wages. However, this failure of the economics of education to be recognized as a specialized field of study in an encyclopedia that will probably remain the standard reference work on economics for the next two or three decades—and this despite the existence of a professional journal exclusively devoted to the subject, *The Economics of Education Review*—merely registers the general sense of boredom of economists with a subject that has remained relatively stagnant for more than a decade.

It is not difficult to find the source of this contempt for the economics of education. The simple fact is that the field has failed to deliver the goods. We are certain that education contributes to economic growth but then so does health care, housing, roads, capital markets, et cetera, and in any case we cannot quantify the growth-enhancing effects of education under different circumstances and we cannot even describe these effects except in the most general terms. We can measure private and social returns to educational investment but since we cannot specify, much less measure, the externalities generated by educated individuals, not to mention the consumption benefits of education, the "social" rate of return to education is a bogus label. But even if the externalities of education were nil, it would still be true that we have been unable to separate the productivity from the screening functions of schooling and hence cannot even say what the social rate of return to education actually means. Is it cognitive knowledge or effective behavioral traits that make educated workers valuable to employers? Is it believable that we can still ask such a question, knowing that the literature does not vouchsafe a firm answer? A subject that after 25 years of study and investigation is unable convincingly to resolve at least some of these issues is not to be taken seriously. And, indeed, it is not taken seriously.

The present volume reprints 88 entries in the ten-volume *International Encyclopedia of Education,* edited by Thorsten Husèn and Neville Postlethwaite (1985). On the whole, these entries are very well done, giving a genuine overview of the economics of education as of the mid-1980s, and the 54 contributors make up a veritable who's who in the subject. This is as sound a mini-textbook in the economics of education as we are likely to have for many years to come. But the fact remains that virtually every one of these articles could have been written in identical terms 10 or even 15 years ago; if the date of publication on the fly-page of the book were lost, only an occasional reference to recently published case studies would tell us that it had in fact been published in 1987, and not in 1977 or even in 1967. Such theoretical and empirical stagnation is to be contrasted with the explosive developments in recent years in, say, health economics, labor economics, macroeconomics, and even microeconomics. The economics of education instead rests on its oars: it does not fructify.

I come not to praise the economics of education but also not to bury it. Economists have much to say about the costing and finance of education that is relevant to current political debates in Europe and America; moreover, so long as the Vocational School Fallacy and the discredited practice of manpower forecasting are alive and well in Africa, Asia, and Latin America—as unfortunately they are—the economics of education will remain a relevant field of specialization, at least for its negative messages. But there is no use in pretending that the antipathy of educators toward economists and the public disdain of economists in current controversies about education are not in part our own fault, reflecting the poor substantive achievements of the economics of education. Many, if not most, of the essays in the volume under review exhibit an alarming air of complacency about the status of the subject, which bodes ill for potential future developments.

For example, both N. L. Hicks on "Education and Economic Growth" (pp. 101–107) and D. B. Holsinger on "Modernization and Education" (pp. 107–10) review a number of studies that have demonstrated the correlation between measures of education and measures of economic growth but they fail to emphasize sufficiently how little we still know about the causal impact of education on either economic growth or modernization. As a case in point, much is made of studies on farmer productivity in developing countries, which conclude that additional years of formal schooling substantially raise both output per acre and output per worker, at least in modernized rural areas (see "Farmers' Education and Economic Performance" by M. E. Lockwood, pp. 110–16). Without casting doubt on the significance of this finding so far as it goes, it is nevertheless misleading to extrapolate it to the rather different setting of large industrial enterprises in advanced countries. By way of contrast, Foster writes with what seems to me to be appropriate circumspection on "The Contribution of Education to Development" (pp. 93–100).

Likewise, there is a tendency in some of the essays to set out a long list of the pecuniary and nonpecuniary benefits of education for both educatees and society at large and to infer from this that there is underspending on education (see L. C. Solomon, "The Range of Educational Benefits," pp. 83–93, and W. W. McMahon, "Consumption and Other Benefits of Education" and "Externalities in Education," pp. 129–37). But apart from the omission of an almost equally long list of negative effects of education, it is the marginal and not the total externalities of an activity that are relevant to arguments about "market failures"; in addition the case for "market failure" must be matched by an examination of "government failure" before drawing conclusions about public support for education. In general, the application of standard welfare economics applied to education is never given its proper due in this volume: only two articles, namely W. W. McMahon on "Externalities" (pp. 133–37) and J. Wiseman on "Public Finance of Education" (pp. 436–39), are devoted to it and it is only mentioned parenthetically in one or two articles. And yet is it of crucial significance in considering all questions of educational finance and government regulation of the education industry.

Human capital theory is explained in numerous entries and extolled in many more (e.g., M. Woodhall, "Human Capital Concepts," pp. 21–24, M. J. Bowman, "On-the-Job Training," pp. 24–29, W. W. McMahon, "Expected Rates of Return to Education," pp. 187–96, M. Woodhall, "Earnings and Education," pp. 209–18, and G. Psacharopoulos, "Earnings Functions," pp. 218–23, and "The Cost-Benefit Model," pp. 342–47) but the failure of human capital theory decisively to disentangle the interrelationships between endowed ability, acquired ability, and educational attainment is consistently underemphasized. In that respect, J. R. Behrman and P. Taubman ("Kinship Studies," pp. 291–98) stand out from all the other contributors because they argue, here as elsewhere, that rates of return on education, calculated in the usual manner, are biased upward because of omitted interactions between ability and schooling. Widening the argument, it is curious to notice how the very explanatory power of earnings functions specified in terms of human capital theory signify different things to different authors. According to Jacob Mincer, about half of the variance in the distribution of earned income is explained by variations in years of formal schooling and work experience; some see this as dramatic confirmation of human capital theory—after all, the entire distribution of individual's earnings is being explained by two or at most three variables—while others argue that this is evidence that factors other than education and training must be important in explaining earnings differentials (compare pp. 163, 221–22, 263).

When we add these hints of doubt to the subversive implications of the screening hypothesis, the empirical status of human capital theory seems much less secure than it appears in many entries in this book. Screening, filtering, credentialism, and the like are clearly expounded by R. McNabb in "Labour Market Theories and Education" (pp. 157–64) and D. R. Winkler provides an incisive review of the inconclusive effort to date to test the screening hypothesis ("Screening Models and Education," pp. 287–91). But the observational equivalence of human capital theory and screening models only encourages still greater caution in respect of human capital theory: the screening hypothesis *could* be true, and if it is, we have all been drawing the wrong conclusions from human capital theory.

Let me draw this review to a close by simply listing the other essays which I can commend on pedagogic grounds: E. A. Hanushek, "Educational Production Functions" (pp. 33–41); F. Orivel, "Educational Technology" (pp. 42–53); L. C. Solomon, "The Quality of Education" (pp. 53–59); S. Rosen, "Job Information and Education" (pp. 179–82); H. G. Grubel, "The Economics of the Brain Drain" (pp. 201–206); R. B. Freeman, "Demand Elasticities for Educated Labor" (pp. 237–39); M. J. Bowman, "Skill Excess and Shortage" (pp. 307–11); J. K. Hinchliffe, "Forecasting Manpower Requirements" (pp. 315–23); and D. W. Verry, "Education Cost Functions" (pp. 400–409). There are a surprisingly small number of weak papers and virtually no aspect of the economics of education does not get a mention somewhere in this book. I noted only one topic, or rather one feature of a topic that was totally neglected. The famous Hansen-Weisbrod demonstration of the alleged inequitable effects of higher education subsidies is alluded to here and there (pp. 6–7, 314) but it is never adequately reviewed anywhere in the volume either in the papers on education and income distribution or in the papers on educational finance. This is very odd and even odder is the absence of any reference when the subject does appear to the intergenerational features of the who pays/who benefits? question; there have been as many as six or seven articles in recent years on precisely that element in the ongoing debate about the role of education in equalizing income distribution.

The most frequently cited author in this book is not Becker, not Denison, not Schultz but the editor, George Psacharopoulos. In part this is due to the fact that he is the author of 13 of the 88 contributory articles and is notoriously fond of citing himself. Nevertheless, even if one removes the self-citations in his prodigious entry in the Name Index, he still emerges as one of the most frequently cited writers in the economics of education. And, indeed, he is the Harry Johnson of the economics of education, whose prolific output has put everyone else to shame. The preparation of *The International Encyclopedia of Education* was a herculean task in which George Psacharopoulos assumed responsibility for all articles falling within the economics of education. The result was a set of entries that has added up to a book that will serve equally well for teaching purposes in departments of economics and in departments of education.

[9]

J. EDUCATION POLICY, 1996, VOL. 11, NO. 1, 1–25

Education, globalization and economic development

Phillip Brown
University of Kent at Canterbury
Hugh Lauder
University of Bath

This paper critically examines two trajectories for economic development under the new global economic competition: the neo-Fordist route of the New Right and the post-Fordist route of centre-left Modernizers. It is argued that both positions are unlikely to achieve economic prosperity and equality of opportunity for all, although there are elements in the Modernizers' programme that are desirable. The Modernizers emphasize the idea of a 'high skill, high wage economy' in which the upgrading of educational standards is seen as central to the delivery of social justice and economic growth. However, their characterization of the relationship between national and global economies is seriously flawed. Their explanation for the economic and social polarization of these societies in terms of the global demand for skill rests on commonly held but inadequate neo-classical economic assumptions. This leads to a paradox in the Modernizers' position. They place education at the heart of their strategy while being unable to explain or address the problem of polarization. Yet, a polarized society will not create high standards of educational achievement for all. This paper seeks to resolve the paradox by providing a more adequate explanation for polarization and, in doing so, establishes a framework for reconciling the aims of equality of opportunity with economic prosperity under the present global economic conditions.

Introduction

Since the first oil shock in the early 1970s western societies have experienced a social, political and economic transformation that is yet to reach its conclusion. At its epicentre is the creation of a global economy that has led to an intensification of economic competition between firms, regions and nation-states (Dicken 1992, Michie and Smith 1995). This globalization of economic activity has called into question the future role of the nation-state and how it can secure economic growth and shared prosperity. At first sight this may appear to have little to do with educational policy; however, the quality of a nation's education and training system is seen to hold the key to future economic prosperity. This paper will outline some of the consequences of globalization and why education is crucial to future economic development. It will also show that despite the international consensus concerning the importance of education, strategies for education and economic development can be linked to alternative 'ideal typical' neo-Fordist and post-Fordist routes to economic development which have profoundly different educational implications.

These neo-Fordist and post-Fordist routes can also be connected to alternative political projects. Since the late 1970s the USA and UK have followed a neo-Fordist route in response to economic globalization, which has been shaped by the New Right's enthusiasm for market competition, privatization and competitive individualism. However, with the election of the Democrats in the 1992 American presidential elections and the resurgence of the British Labour Party there is increasing support

0268–0939/96 $12 · 00

for a post-Fordist strategy. Although much has already been written about the flaws in the New Right's approach to education and national renewal, far less has yet been written on what we will call the 'left modernizers'. It will be argued that whilst the left modernizers present a promising programme for reform *vis-a-vis* the New Right, their account of education, skill formation and the global economy remains unconvincing. Therefore, an important task of this paper is to highlight the weaknesses in the left modernizers' account to show that if post-Fordist possibilities are to be realized, it will be essential for those on the left to engage in a more thoroughgoing and politically difficult debate about education, equity and efficiency in late global capitalism.[1]

Globalization and the new rules of economic competition

The significance of globalization to questions of national educational and economic development can be summarized in terms of a change in the rules of eligibility, engagement and wealth creation (Brown and Lauder forthcoming). First, there has been a change in the rules of eligibility. In the same way that sports clubs run 'closed' events where club membership is a condition of entry, they may also run tournaments 'open' to everyone. Likewise there has been a shift away from the closed or walled economies of the postwar period towards an open or global economy. As a result of this change in the rules of eligibility domestic economies have been exposed to greater foreign competition (Reich 1991, ILO 1995). Changes in the rules of eligibility have also enhanced the power of the multinational corporations (MNCs). The MNCs not only account for a growing proportion of cross-border trade, but are a major source of new investment in technology, jobs and skills. Since the mid-1970s the MNCs have grown more rapidly than the world economy. In 1975, the 50 largest industrial corporations worldwide had sales of US$540 billion and $25 billion in profits. In 1990, sales figures for the top 50 had climbed to $2.1 trillion and their profits had reached $70 billion. In real terms, whereas the US economy was growing at an annual rate of 2.8% (the OECD average was 2.9%), the MNCs' annual sales growth was in the region of 3.5% during the period between 1975 and 1990 (Carnoy *et al.* 1993: 49).

Moreover, the old national 'champions' such as Ford, IBM, ICI and Mercedes Benz have tried to break free of their national roots, creating a *global auction* for investment, technology and jobs. As capital has become footloose, the mass production of standardized goods and services has been located in countries, regions or communities which offer low wage costs, light labour market legislation, weak trade unions and 'sweeteners' including 'tax holidays' and cheap rents. Such investment has significantly increased in the new industrial countries (NICs) such as in Singapore, Taiwan, China and Brazil (Cowling and Sugden 1994). It is estimated that in the 1980s some 700 US companies employed more than 350,000 workers in Singapore, Mexico and Taiwan alone and that 40% of the jobs created by British MNCs were overseas (Marglinson 1994: 64).

In reality, the global auction operates like a Dutch auction. In a Dutch auction corporate investors are able to play off nations, communities and workers as a way of increasing their profit margins, bidding spirals downwards impoverishing local communities and workers by forcing concessions on wage levels, rents and taxes in exchange for investment in local jobs. In order to persuade Mercedes to set up a plant in Alabama, the company received an initial $253 million, with tax breaks over 25 years which have been estimated to be worth an extra $230m. The Swiss Bank Corporation will receive some $120m of incentives over the next 10 years from Connecticut, for moving its US headquarters from Manhattan to the city of Stamford.[2]

In the USA and UK the creation of a global auction has also been linked to the breakdown of the Fordist rules of engagement between government, employers and workers. Although some writers have restricted their definition of Fordism to refer exclusively to the system of mass production, Fordism is a label that can equally be applied to Keynesian demand management in the postwar period referring to the expansion of mass consumption as well as mass production (Lipietz 1987, Harvey 1989). The rapid improvement in economic efficiency which accompanied the introduction of mass production techniques necessitated the creation of mass markets for consumer durables, including radios, refrigerators, television sets and motor cars. In order for economic growth to be maintained, national governments had to regulate profits and wage levels to sustain the conditions upon which economic growth depended. Hence, the development of the welfare state in western industrial societies was seen to reflect efforts on the part of national governments to maintain the Fordist compromise between employers and organized labour. The combination of increased welfare state protection for workers, coupled with full employment and a degree of social mobility, temporarily 'solved' the problem of distribution (Hirsch 1977) under Fordism. The problem of distribution is that of determining how opportunities and income are to be apportioned. Under capitalism this is an ever present problem because it is a system which is inherently unequal in its distribution of rewards and opportunities. However, during the Fordist era the combination of the rewards of economic growth being evenly spread across income levels, increasing social security, occupational and social mobility according to ostensibly meritocratic criteria generated a high degree of social solidarity. However, over the last 20 years the USA and UK have introduced 'market' rules of engagement. Here the nation-state is charged with the role of creating the conditions in which the market can operate 'freely'. Therefore, rather than trying to engineer a compromise between employers and the trade unions the state must prevent the unions from using their 'monopoly' powers to bid-up wages which are not necessarily reflected in productivity gains. Hence, according to the market rules of engagement the prosperity of workers will depend on an ability to trade their skills, knowledge and entrepreneurial acumen in an unfettered global market-place.

Finally, the transformation in western capitalism has entailed new rules of wealth creation. These have undermined the viability of building national prosperity on the Fordist mass production of standardized goods and services.[3] Fordist mass production was based on the standardization of products and their component parts. Many of the tasks previously undertaken by skilled craftsmen, such as making door panels or parts of the car's engine 'by hand', were mechanized by designing jigs, presses and machines able to perform the same operations hundreds, if not thousands of times a day, with the use of a semi-skilled operative. The Fordist production line was characterized by a moving assembly line, where the product passes the workers along a conveyor, rather than the worker having to move to the product as in nodal production. A further feature of Fordism was a detailed division of labour, within which the job tasks of shopfloor workers were reduced to their most elementary form in order to maximize both efficiency and managerial control over the labour process. Hence, Fordism was based on many of the principles of 'scientific management' outlined by Frederick Taylor who offered a 'scientific' justification for the separation of *conception* from *execution*, where managers monopolized knowledge of the labour process, and controlled every step of production.

However, in the new rules of wealth creation economic prosperity will depend on nations and companies being able to exploit the skills, knowledge and insights of workers in ways which can no longer be delivered according to Fordist principles. Enterprises which can deliver a living wage to workers now depend on the quality as much as the price of goods and services, and on finding new sources of productivity and investment. Such 'value added' enterprise is most likely to be found in companies offering 'customized' goods and services in microelectronics, telecommunications, biotechnology, financial services, consultancy, advertising, marketing and the media.[4]

In response to these new rules all western nations, in their domestic economies and foreign affairs, have had to look to their own social institutions and human resources to meet the global challenges they confront (OECD 1989). Lessons learnt from Japan and the Asian Tigers suggest that the 'human side of enterprise' is now a crucial factor in winning a competitive advantage in the global economy. Advantage is therefore seen to depend upon raising the quality and productivity of human capital. Knowledge, learning, information and technical competence are the new raw materials of international commerce:

> Knowledge itself, therefore, turns out to be not only the source of the highest-quality power, but also the most important ingredient of force and wealth. Put differently, knowledge has gone from being an adjunct of money power and muscle power, to being the very essence. It is, in fact, the ultimate amplifier. This is the key to the power shift that lies ahead, and it explains why the battle for control of knowledge and the means of communication is heating up all over the world. (Toffler 1990: 18)

Although such statements greatly exaggerate the importance of knowledge in advanced capitalist economies, without exception, national governments of all political persuasions have declared that it is the quality of their education and training systems which will decisively shape the international division of labour and national prosperity. Therefore the diminished power of nation-states to control economic competition has forced them to compete in what we call the global *knowledge wars*. In Britain, for instance, the National Commission of Education suggests that:

> For us, knowledge and skills will be central. In an area of world-wide competition and low-cost global communications, no country like ours will be able to maintain its standard of living, let alone improve it, on the basis of cheap labour and low-tech products and services. There will be too many millions of workers and too many employers in too many countries who will be able and willing to do that kind of work fully as well as we or people in any other developed country could do it – and at a fraction of the cost. (1993: 33)

But how the problem of education and training policies is understood and how the demand for skilled workers is increased is subject to contestation and political struggle. There is no doubt, for instance, that the introduction of new technologies has expanded the range of strategic choice available to employers and managers. However, this has exposed increasing differences, rather than similarities, in organizational cultures, job design and training regimes (Lane 1989, Green and Steedman 1993). There are few guarantees that employers will successfully exploit the potential for 'efficiency', precisely because they may fail to break free of conventional assumptions about the role of management and workers, and cling to the established hierarchy of authority, status and power. As Harvey (1989) has recognized, new technologies and coordinating forms of organization have permitted the revival of domestic, familial and paternalistic labour systems given that, 'The same shirt designs can be reproduced by large-scale factories in India, cooperative production in the 'Third Italy', sweatshops in New York and London, or family labour systems in Hong Kong' (p. 187). This should alert us to the fact that the demise of Fordism in the West does not necessarily mean that the majority of workers will find jobs which exercise the range of their human capabilities. The interests of employers seeking to maximize profits and workers seeking to enhance the quality of working life and wages remain an important source of cleavage given that it is still possible for companies to 'profit' from low-tech, low-wage operations. There is no hidden-hand or post-industrial logic which will lead nations to respond to the global economy in the same way, despite the fact that their fates are inextricably connected. Indeed, we would suggest that the universal consensus highlighting education and training systems as holding the key to future prosperity has obscured fundamental differences in the way nations are responding to the global economy.

Therefore, while recognizing that some of the key elements of Fordism in western nations are being transformed in the global economy, it is important not to prejudge the direction of these changes which must remain a question of detailed empirical investigation (see Block 1990). For analytical purposes it is useful to distinguish two 'ideal typical' models of national economic development in terms of neo-Fordism and post-Fordism (see table 1). Neo-Fordism can be characterized in terms of creating greater market flexibility through a reduction in social overheads and the power of trade unions, the privatization of public utilities and the welfare state, as well as a celebration of competitive individualism. Alternative, post-Fordism can be defined in terms of the development of the state as a 'strategic trader' shaping the direction of the national economy through investment in key economic sectors and in the development of human capital. Therefore, post-Fordism is based on a shift to 'high value' customized production and services using multi-skilled workers (see also Allen 1992).

In the 'real' world the relationship between education and economic development reveals examples of contradiction as much as correspondence. Moreover, although it is true to say that countries such as Germany, Japan and Singapore come closer to the model of post-Fordism, and the USA and UK approximate neo-Fordist solutions, we should not ignore clear examples of 'uneven' and contradictory developments within the same region or country. It also highlights the fact that there are important differences in the way nation-states may move towards a post-Fordist economy with far-reaching implications for democracy and social justice.

Nevertheless, these models represent clear differences in policy orientations in terms of the dominant economic ideas which inform them and underlying cultural assumptions about the role of skill formation in economic and social development (Thurow 1993). First we will assess the New Right's interpretation of education as part of a neo-Fordist strategy, before undertaking a detailed account of the left modernizers' vision of a post-Fordist high-skill, high-wage economy.

The New Right: education in a neo-Fordist 'market' economy

The New Right interpretation of the Fordist 'crisis' is based on what we call the welfare shackle thesis. In the 19th century it was the aristocracy and the *ancient régime* in Europe who were blamed for 'shackling' the market and free enterprise. In the late 20th century it is the welfare state.[5] The New Right argue that the problem confront-

Table 1. Post-Fordist possibilities: alternative models of national development.

Fordism	Neo-Fordism	Post-Fordism
Protected national markets	Global competition through: productivity gains, cost-cutting (overheads, wages)	Global competition through: innovation, quality, value-added goods and services
	Inward investment attracted by 'market flexibility' (reduce the social cost of labour, trade union power)	Inward investment attracted by highly skilled labour force engaged in 'value added' production/services
	Adversarial market orientation: remove impediments to market competition. Create 'enterprise culture'. Privatization of the welfare state	Consensus-based objectives: corporatist 'industrial policy'. Cooperation between government, employers and trade unions
Mass production of standardized products/low skill, high wage	Mass production of standardized products/low skill, low wage 'flexible' production and sweatshops	Flexible production systems/small batch/niche markets; shift to high-wage, high-skilled jobs
Bureaucratic hierarchical organizations	Leaner organizations with emphasis on 'numerical' flexibility	Leaner organizations with emphasis on 'functional' flexibility
Fragmented and standardized work tasks	Reduce trade union job demarcation	Flexible specialization/multi-skilled workers
Mass standardized (male) employment	Fragmentation/polarization of labour force. Professional 'core' and 'flexible' workforce (i.e. part-time, temps, contract, portfolio careers)	Maintain good conditions for all employees. Non 'core' workers receive training, fringe benefits, comparable wages, proper representation
Divisions between managers and workers/low trust relations/ collective bargaining	Emphasis on 'managers' right to manage'. Industrial relations based on low-trust relations	Industrial relations based on high trust, high discretion, collective participation
Little 'on the job' training for most workers	Training 'demand' led/little use of industrial training policies	Training as a national investment/ state acts as strategic trainer

ing western nations today can only be understood in light of profound changes in the role of government during the third quarter of the 20th century. They assert it is no coincidence that at the same time western governments were significantly increasing expenditure on social welfare programmes, there was high inflation, rising unemployment and economic stagnation (Murray 1984). Western societies have run into trouble because of the extensive and unwarranted interference by the state. Inflation, high unemployment, economic recession and urban unrest all stem from the legacy of Keynesian economics and an egalitarian ideology which promoted economic redistribution, equality of opportunity and welfare rights for all. Hence, the overriding problem confronting western capitalist nations is to reimpose the disciplines of the market.

According to the New Right the route to national salvation in the context of global knowledge wars is through the survival of the fittest, based on an extension of parental choice in a market of competing schools, colleges and universities (Ball 1993). In the case of education, where funding, at least during the compulsory school years, will come from the public purse, the idea is to create a quasi-market within which schools will compete (Lauder 1991). This approximation to the operation of a market is achieved by seeking to create a variety of schools in a mixed economy of public and private institutions. In some cases they will aim at different client groups such as the ethnic minorities, religious sects, or 'high flyers'. This 'variety', it is argued, will provide parents with a genuine choice of different products (Boyd and Cibulka 1989, Halstead 1994). Choice of product (type of school) is seen to be sufficient to raise the standards for all, because if schools cannot sell enough desk space to be economically viable, they risk going out of business. Moreover, the economic needs of the nation will be met through the market, because when people have to pay for education they are more likely to make investment decisions which will realize an economic return. This will lead consumers to pick subjects and courses where there is a demand for labour, subsequently overcoming the problem of skill shortages. Equally, there will be a tendency for employment training to be 'demand led' in response to changing market conditions (Deakin and Wilkinson 1991).

Critics of the marketization of education therefore argue that the introduction of choice and competition provides a mechanism by which the middle classes can more securely gain an advantage in the competition for credentials (Brown 1995). This is because not all social groups come to an educational market as equals (Collins 1979). Cultural and material capital are distributed unequally between classes and ethnic groups. In particular, it is the middle classes which are more likely to have the cultural capital to make educational choices which best advantage their children (Brown 1990, Brown and Lauder 1992). In consequence, the introduction of parental choice and competition between schools will amount to a covert system of educational selection according to social class as middle-class children exit schools with significant numbers of working-class children. The consequence will be that the school system will become polarized in terms of social class and ethnic segregation and in terms of resources. As middle-class students exit from schools with working-class children they will also take much needed resources from those schools and effectively add to already well-off middle-class schools.

What evidence there is about the workings of educational markets suggests that they are far more complex than their critics suggest (Lauder *et al.* 1994). Nevertheless, the evidence so far confirms the prediction that choice and competition tend to lead to social class and ethnic polarization in schools (Willms and Echols 1992, Lauder *et al.* 1994). In nations such as the USA and UK, the overall effect will be to segregate students in different types of school on the basis of social class, ethnicity and religion. The net result will again be a massive wastage of talent as able working-class students once more find themselves trapped in schools which do not give them the opportunity of going to university (Halsey *et al.* 1980). If this is the overall effect then it can be argued that the marketization of education, while appearing to offer efficiency and flexibility of the kind demanded in the post-Fordist era, will in fact school the majority of children for a neo-Fordist economy which requires a low level of talent and skill.

The marketization of education will inevitably have an inverse effect on the ability of nation-states to compete in the global auction for quality inward investment, technology and jobs. Although multinational organizations are always on the look-out to reduce their overheads, including labour costs, investment in 'high-value' products and services crucially depends upon the quality, commitment and insights of the workforce, for which they are prepared to pay high salaries. The problem that nation-states now confront is one of how to balance commercial pressures to reduce labour costs and other overheads whilst mobilizing an educated labour force, and maintaining a sophisticated social, financial and communications infrastructure. This problem has been exacerbated by the fact that the low-skill, high-wage jobs associated with Fordism in North America and Europe are being transplanted to the NICs where labour costs are much lower, leading to a significant deterioration in working conditions in the low-skill jobs remaining in the west (Wood 1994).

In the context of the global auction, the market reforms in education are likely to leave a large majority of the future working population without the human resources to flourish in the global economy. Here the link between market reforms and neo-Fordism is barely disguised in countries which were dominated by New Right governments in the 1980s. The principle objective of economic policy is to improve the competitiveness of workers by increasing labour market flexibility by restricting the power of trade unions, especially in order to bring wages into line with their 'market' value. This philosophy led Britain to reject the Social Chapter of the Maastricht Treaty which provided legislative support for workers, because it was argued that it would undermine Britain's competitiveness in attracting inward investment, despite the poor work conditions this would inflict on employees. In contradistinction, market reforms in education and the economy have ensured the conditions in which highly paid middle-class professionals and élite groups are able to give their children an 'excellent' (*sic*) education in preparation for their bid to join the ranks of Reich's (1991) 'symbolic analysts'.

A different critique, albeit coming to the same conclusions, can be mounted against the introduction of market mechanisms in post-compulsory education and training. A key area of the post-compulsory sector for a post-Fordist economy is that concerned with the education of skilled tradespeople and technicians (Streeck 1989). The New Right has argued that the introduction of market mechanisms into this area will ensure a closer matching of supply and demand for trained labour and hence greater efficiency in the allocation of skilled labour. The argument rests on the assumptions that individuals and employers should bear the cost and responsibility for training. It is assumed that individuals gain most of the benefits from such a training and that they should therefore bear much of the cost (Lauder 1987). Moreover, since they are paying substantially for their training they will choose to train in an area in which there is market demand. In so far as employers should help bear the cost of training and the responsibility for the type of training offered, it is argued that employers are in the best position to assess the numbers of skilled workers required and the kind of skills they should possess. Underlying this observation is an appreciation of employers' short-term interests. Given the assumption that they 'know best' what the levels and nature of skilled labour should be, it follows that they will be reluctant to pay taxes or levies for training undertaken by a third party, such as the state.

While this view, as with other New Right views, is plausible, it has come in for sustained criticism. One of the most cogent is that of Streeck (1989, 1992). He argues that under a free labour contract of the kind found in liberal capitalist societies which gives workers the right to move from one firm to another, skills become a collective good in the eyes of employers. This is because the rewards of training individuals can easily be 'socialized' by the expedient of trained workers moving to another job while the costs of training remain with the original employer. Since employers face a clear risk in losing their investment they are unlikely to invest heavily in training. Streeck argues that, as a result, western economies are likely to face a chronic skill shortage unless the state intervenes to ensure that adequate training occurs.

Moreover, unless there is state intervention employers will reduce the training programmes they do have when placed under intense competitive pressure and/or during a recession. Streeck (1989) notes that in the prolonged economic crisis of the 1970s, western economies, with the exception of Germany, reduced their apprenticeship programmes. In Germany government and trade union pressure ensured that the apprenticeship programme was extended. Two consequences followed: the apprenticeship system helped to alleviate youth unemployment and it contributed to the technical and economic advantage enjoyed by German industry in the early 1980s.

There are further criticisms that can be made of a market-determined training system. From the standpoint of the individual, it is unlikely that those who would potentially enter a skilled trade or technical training, working- and lower middle-class school leavers, could either afford the costs of such a training or take the risks involved. The risks are twofold: first, given the time lag between entering a training programme and completing it, market demand for a particular type of training may have changed with a resulting lack of jobs. In the competitive global market, such an outcome is all too likely. If the training received were of a sufficiently general nature to produce a flexible worker that might be less of a problem. However, in an employer-led training system the pressure will always exist for training to meet employers' specific and immediate needs. The consequence is that such a training system is likely to be too narrowly focused to meet rapidly changing demand conditions. Second, a further point follows from this, namely that the industries of today are likely to be tomorrow's dinosaurs. As a result, employer-led training schemes may not contain the vision and practice required in order to maintain the high skill base necessary for a post-Fordist economy. Clearly the structure of Germany's training system offers an example of an alternative which can begin to meet the requirements of a post-Fordist economy. This, as Streeck (1992) notes, involves a partnership between the state, employers and trade unions. It is a system which ensures that employers' immediate interests are subsumed within a system concerned with medium and longer term outcomes. Therefore the outcome of the reassertion of market discipline in social and economic institutions has been the development of a neo-Fordist economy characterized by insecurity and the creation of large numbers of temporary, low-skilled and low-waged jobs. We have also argued that the appeal to 'self-interest' and 'free enterprise' serves to mask the political interests of the most privileged sections of society. Indeed, the very notion of a national system of education is called into question as professional and élite groups secede from their commitment to public education and the ideology of meritocracy upon which public education in the 20th century has been founded.

Left modernizers: education in a post-Fordist 'magnet' economy

Over the last decade a new centre-left project has emerged in response to the ascendancy of the New Right. These 'left modernizers' reject much that was previously taken for granted amongst their socialist predecessors, contending that the transformaton of capitalism at the end of the 20th century had signficantly changed the strategies that the left needs to adopt in its pursuit of social justice *and* economic efficiency. This involves a recognition that the left must develop a credible response to the global economy, which will include economic policy and management as well as dealing with issues of distribution, equity and social policy (Rogers and Streeck 1994: 138). At the top of their agenda is a commitment to investment in human capital and strategic investment in the economy as a way of moving towards a high-skilled, high-waged 'magnet' economy. Underlying these economic forms of investment is a vision of a society permeated by a culture of learning for it is the knowledge, skills and insights of the population that provide the key to future prosperity. The ideas of the 'left modernizers' are to be found in books such as Reich (1991) and Thurow (1993) in the USA, the Commission on Social Justice (1994) and Brown (1994) in the UK. The ideas represented in these works are also consistent with Democratic politics in the USA and have informed the direction of Labour Party policy in Britain.[6]

The modernizers' account of how to create a post-Fordist economy can be summarized in the following way. It begins with a recognition that it is impossible to deliver widespread prosperity by trying to compete on price rather than the quality of goods and services. They therefore advocate a change in policy relating to investment in both physical and human capital. They advocate what has become known as producer capitalism (Dore 1987, Thurow 1993, Hutton 1995) in which low-cost long-term investment is linked to the development of human capital. Producer capitalism stands in stark contrast with market capitalism in which price and short-term profit are the key criteria for enterprises. Not surprisingly, they reject the assertion made by the acolytes of market capitalism that the only route to prosperity is through the creation of greater market 'flexibility' by lowering labour costs or by repealing labour protection laws. The modernizers see that in the new economic competition making those at the bottom end of the labour market more insecure and powerless against exploitative employers is not the way for workers and nations to confront the challenge of the global auction. They recognize that the provision of a floor of protective rights, entitlements and conditions for workers in the context of the global auction is both socially desirable and economically essential. In practice what this means is reinforcing labour laws against the worst excesses of unscrupulous employers and the vagaries of the global auction. This will include a minimum wage and various forms of government intervention to get the long-term unemployed back to work. For modernizers, this is part of building a new high-trust partnership between government, employers and workers. For they argue that it is only through such a partnership that a high-skill, high-wage economy can be created. The role of the state in such a partnership is that of a 'strategic trader' (Krugman 1993) selecting 'winners' or guiding industrial development where appropriate and, most importantly, providing the infrastructure for economic development. Here the development of a highly educated workforce is seen as a priority.

The importance the modernizers attach to education stems from a belief that the increasing wage inequalities in the USA and UK over the last decade are a reflection of the returns to skill in a global auction for jobs and wages. The essence of this idea was captured by Bill Clinton in a major address on education:

> The key to our economic strength in America today is productivity growth . . . In the 1990s and beyond, the universal spread of education, computers and high speed communications means that what we earn will depend on what we can learn and how well we can apply what we learn to the workplaces of America. That's why, as we know, a college graduate this year will earn 70 per cent more than a high school graduate in the first year of work. That's why the earnings of younger

workers who dropped out of high school, or who finished but received no further education or training, dropped by more than 20 per cent over the last ten years alone.[7]

Hence, for all western societies the route to prosperity is through the creation of a 'magnet' economy capable of attracting high-skilled, high-waged employment within an increasingly global labour market. This is to be achieved through sustained investment in the national economic infrastructure including transportation, telecommunications, R&D, etc. alongside investment in education and training systems. In the modernizers' account it is nevertheless acknowledged that there are unlikely to be enough skilled and well-paid jobs for everyone. However, flexible work patterns are assumed to lead to greater occupational mobility permitting people to move from low-skilled jobs when in full-time study, to high-skilled jobs in mid-career back to low-skilled jobs as retirement age approaches. Of course, such a view depends on substantial mobility in both an upwards and downwards direction (Esping-Andersen 1994). Therefore, in the same way that unemployment is tolerable if it only lasts for a few months, being in a low-skilled, poorly paid job is also tolerable as long as it offers progression into something better.

Education and training opportunities are thus pivotal to this vision of a competitive and just society. For not only can education deliver a high value-added 'magnet' economy but it can also solve the problem of unemployment. However, it is a mistake for nation-states to 'guarantee' employment because this harbours the same kind of vestigial thinking that led to previous attempts to protect uncompetitive firms from international competition: they simply become even less competitive. The only way forward is to invest in education and training to enable workers to become fully employable. In this account, social justice inheres in providing all individuals with the opportunity to gain access to an education that qualifies them for a job. Clearly there is a tension here between the idea of flexibility and the need to guarantee a minimum wage, so protecting labour from exploitation. All the indications are that the modernizers will err on the side of caution and provide what could only be described as minimal protection. In the end, the difference between the modernizers and the New Right on this issue may be marginal although, as we shall see, there are good economic reasons why adequate social protection is desirable.

There are several features of the modernizers' account with which we concur, including the need to introduce a version of 'producer' capitalism, but as a strategic policy for education and economic development it is flawed. Our purpose in exposing these flaws is to set the scene for a more radical and thoroughgoing debate about education, economy and society in the early decades of the 21st century. Our criticisms cluster around four related problems: first, the idea of a high-skilled, high-wage magnet economy; second, whether reskilling the nation can solve the problem of unemployment; third, whether it is correct to assume that income polarization is a true reflection of the 'value' of skills in the global labour market; and finally, the problem of how the modernizers propose upgrading the quality of human resources so all are granted an equal opportunity to fulfil their human potential.

How can a high-skilled, high-wage 'magnet' economy be created?

Their view that the future wealth of nations will depend on the exploitation of leading-edge technologies, corporate innovation and the upgrading of the quality of human resources can hardly be quarrelled with. Nations will clearly need to have a competitive advantage in at least some of the major industrial sectors, such as telecommunications, electronics, pharmaceuticals, chemicals and automobiles (Porter 1990, Thurow 1993). There is also little doubt that this will create a significant minority of jobs requiring highly skilled workers. However, the problem with the modernizers' account is that they assume that highly skilled and well-paid jobs will become available to all for at least a period of their working lives. Indeed, this is an essential tenet of their argument given that they suggest that widening inequalities can be overcome through upskilling the nation and that full employment remains a realistic goal. In other words, the modernizers continue to believe that the labour market can act as a legitimate mechanism (through the occupational division of labour) for resolving the distributional question in advanced capitalist societies.

The plausibility of this account hangs on the idea that the global auction for jobs and enterprise offers the potential for western nations to create 'magnet' economies of highly skilled and well-paid jobs. This is an idea which has obvious appeal to a broad political constituency. It serves to replenish the spirits of those who see the USA following the UK in a spiral of economic decline after a period of global dominance. We are presented with the comforting picture of a global economy which, although no longer likely to be dominated by American and European companies, is characterized by prosperous western workers making good incomes through the use of their skills, knowledge and insights. In reality, however, this characterization represents an imperialist throw-back to the idea that innovative ideas remain the preserve of the advanced western nations, with the possible exception of Japan. Reich, for example, assumes that as low-skilled work moves into the NICs and Third World economies, the USA, the European EU countries and Japan will be left to fight amongst themselves for the high value-added jobs. The problem with this view is that it completely misunderstands the nature of the economic strategies now being implemented by the Asian Tigers, who have already developed economic and human capital infrastructures which are superior to those of many western countries (Ashton and Sung, 1994). This is partly reflected in the international convergence in education systems, at least in terms of expanding their tertiary sectors. Therefore, whilst we should not rule out the possibility that MNCs, when making inward and outward investment decisions, will judge the quality of human resources to be superior in particular countries, it is extremely unlikely that a small number of nations will become 'magnets' for high-skilled, high-waged work.

They have also overestimated the extent to which even the most successful modern economies depend on the mass employment of highly skilled workers. Indeed, an unintended consequence of the massive expansion of tertiary education may be to create a substantial wastage of talent amongst college and university graduates unable to find a demand for their skills, knowledge and insights. This new 'wastage of talent' is likely to be especially acute in countries which have pursued the neo-Fordist trajectory of labour market deregulation, corporate down-sizing and growth of temporary, casual and insecure work – conditions which are hardly conducive to the production of high-quality jobs distinguished by worker autonomy and cognitive complexity.

The difficulty for the modernizers is that by concentrating on the question of skill formation rather than on the way skills are linked to the trajectory of economic development, they obscure some of the fundamental problems, relating to educated labour, that need to be confronted. Piore (1990) has, for example, argued that where labour market regulation is weak, there is no incentive for employers to invest and use the new technology in a way which raises the value added and the quality of work. Rather, weak labour market regulations leads to a vicious circle whereby profit is extracted through sweatshop labour, low wages and low productivity. In effect, what regulated labour markets do is to create an incentive for entrepreneurs to invest in capital-intensive forms of production in order to generate the high value added to pay for the wage levels set by regulated labour markets (Sengenberger and Wilkinson 1995). If Piore is correct then we would expect the patterns of future work to develop along different trajectories depending on the degree to which their labour markets are regulated. While projections of labour supply and occupational change need to be viewed with some scepticism the recent OECD (1994) report on this subject certainly supports Piore's position when the USA is compared with Holland. On all indices of social protection and labour-market regulation Holland provides an example of far greater social protection for workers, yet the vast majority of new jobs being created could be classified as 'skilled' (OECD 1994). In the USA approximately half the jobs being created were in service occupations requiring little formal training. The lesson here is obvious: the route to a high value-added economy must involve an analysis of factors affecting the demand for educated labour. The implicit assumption, harboured by the modernizers, that through investing in the employability of workers, employers will automatically recognize this potential and invest in upgrading the quality of their human resources is clearly naive.[8] The historical record in both the USA and UK shows that while there are firms that recognize investment in people to be vital to the medium-term success of their companies, there are many others who equally recognize that fat profits can still be made off the backs of semi-skilled and unskilled, low-waged workers. Equally, the idea that western nations can compensate for the failings of local employers by attracting inward investment from blue-chip MNCs is clearly not going to be sufficient to move from a neo-Fordist to a post-Fordist economy. Therefore, there seems little doubt that although in some important respects the modernizers will succeed in producing some improvement in the quality of employment opportunities, they will not achieve the goals of post-Fordist development because investment in education and training as the focal point of their policy will not lead to the creation of a high-skill, high-wage economy.

Can reskilling the nation solve the problem of unemployment?

The focus on employability rather than employment also leaves the modernizers accused of failing to offer a realistic return to full employment. Indeed, the high-skill, high-wage route may be pursued at the price of high unemployment. This is because neo-classical economists argue that labour market deregulation is the only way to solve unemployment. The theory is that the regulation of the labour market favoured by the modernizers bids up the price of those in work and discourages employers from taking on more workers. With deregulation the price of labour would fall and employers would 'buy' more workers. The debate over labour-market deregulation has given rise to the view that all advanced societies are now on the horns of a dilemma in terms of unemployment. Either labour markets are deregulated as in the USA, where official unemployment is below 5%, but where there is extensive poverty because wages at the bottom end of the labour market are insufficient to live off, or they are more regulated as in the producer capitalist route pursued by

Germany, but unemployment is higher – as is the compensation paid to the unemployed (Commission of the European Communities 1993, Freeman 1995). The problem this poses to the modernizers is that on the one hand a majority of workers can expect good quality jobs and a reasonable standard of living but the polarization of market incomes avoided by the producer capitalist route is reproduced between those in work and those unemployed. The divisions in society remain but the source is different.

Unemployment, at the low levels achieved during the postwar period, was historically unique, depending on a contingent set of circumstances (Ormerod 1994). Attempting to create similar circumstances for the early part of the 21st century is likely to prove elusive and in political terms something of a hoax perpetrated by political parties who promise it or something close to it. It is, perhaps, for this reason that the modernizers translate full employment into full employability, thereby throwing the onus on the individual to find a job.

If we examine the profiles of several OECD countries, there are two striking observations that can be made. First, GDP has been divorced from employment in the past 20 years, just as growth has not led to a shared prosperity during the same period. In Spain the economy grew by 93% between 1970 and 1992 and *lost* 2% of its jobs (*Financial Times* 2 October 1993). This is in stark contrast with the postwar period when both incomes and jobs were linked to economic growth. Growth delivered an even rise in income for all occupational groups. Second, the trajectories taken by OECD countries in terms of their main indicators – inflation, growth and balance of payments – vary dramatically, yet unemployment remains around or above 7%, in terms of the official statistics, for every country with the exception of the USA and Japan. This includes countries with high levels of growth such as Canada, New Zealand and Australia.[9]

What appears to have happened in the past 25 years is that a set of economic and social force have pushed the lower limit of unemployment up substantially from an OECD average well below 5% in the postwar period to an average well above 7%. Clearly the oil price hikes of the early 1970s had much to do with the initial jump in unemployment but since then a series of contingent factors have conspired to lock unemployment in at this high level. The introduction of new technology, which has enabled machines to replace workers, could have had a significant impact on unemployment for both blue- and white-collar workers as the jobless growth in Spain suggests. Similarly the number of blue-collar jobs lost to the developing nations has added to the problem (Wood 1994). However, these factors have to be placed within the wider context of economic regulation in relation to the global economy. It is worth noting that current economic orthodoxy ensures that interest rates rise with economic growth, thereby potentially choking off further investment in productive capacity and hence employment. It may also reduce demand, especially in countries such as the USA and UK with a high proportion of families with mortgages.

There are two mutually consistent explanations for the link between rising interest rates and growth. The first is that in a deregulated global finance market there is a shortage of investment funds, especially at times of growth. After all, with the potential to invest in developing nations, as well as the developed nations, the competition for investment has increased dramatically. Moreover, in a global economy the business cycles of the developed and developing nations are likely to be more synchronized so that an upturn in the global economy is likely to be met by a global demand for increased investment (Rowthorn 1995). The second is that, within nations, the key instrument for the control of inflation is interest rates. As economies overheat, interest rates are raised by central banks to choke off demand. The use of interest rates to control inflation is claimed to be successful in a way in which other measures tried in the 1970s and 1980s, incomes policies and control of money supply, were not. Again, however, we should note the role of the new global economy in defining the control of inflation as a key element in any successful national competitive strategy. If inflation in any one country rises to appreciably higher levels than in competitor countries, its goods are likely to be priced out of the market. Hence the significance accorded to the control of inflation in a global economy. But the cost of using interest rates to this end is that economies are permanently run under capacity (ILO 1995: 163). The rise in interest rates simply chokes off demand before it can appreciably effect unemployment levels.

More recently, studies have argued that it is declining economic growth and hence demand, among the OECD countries, since 1973 which is the fundamental cause of unemployment (Eatwell 1995, ILO 1995). While the trend in economic growth in all OECD countries has declined (ILO 1995: 133) it is unclear whether raising levels to those in the period between 1960 to 1973 would have the same impact on unemployment now as it did then, as the examples of Australia and Canada show. The problem is that in a global economy, growth may be achieved through exports and the benefits of growth spent on imports rather than home-produced goods. Whereas in the postwar Fordist economies a rise in demand would percolate through the economy, thereby creating jobs, a rise in demand now may simply create jobs in some other part of the world. This may be especially so in countries where increases in incomes are accruing to the wealthy who spend their money on luxury goods from overseas.

The alternative to this macro-analysis of the causes of unemployment is the micro-analysis of some neo-classical economists, who argue that it is labour-market rigidities, of the kind discussed above, especially the power of trade unions and highly regulated labour markets, which cause unemployment and sustain inflation. There are two elements to their explanation. The first is that these rigidities bid up the price of labour and maintain it at a level higher than desirable to clear the labour market of unemployed. The second is that these rigidities allow the 'insiders' who are employed to bid up their wages even when others are unemployed (Lindbeck and Snower 1986). There are two problems with this theory. First, there appears to be no strong relationship between the degree of social protection, labour market regulation and unemployment, with the exception of the USA (although see Freeman 1995). Historically the lowest levels of unemployment, from 1950–73, have been associated with the highest levels of social protection and labour market regulation, while the present period represents one of the lowest levels of protection and regulation and the highest levels of unemployment. Moreover, even within the current period differences between nations relating to regulation, protection and economic performance hardly bear out this thesis. For example, the UK has one of the lowest levels of labour protection in the OECD and an unemployment rate of 8.4% (OECD 1994: 155). In contrast, Holland, which has an above-average level of protection and regulation, has an unemployment rate of 7.3%. Moreover, their inflation rates are not substantially different. Britain has had an annual rate of 2.4% in the past year and Holland 3%. Second, where labour markets have been deregulated they have not brought about a substantial reduction in unemployment. This is certainly the case in the UK and in New Zealand where unemployment is still about 7%.

Overall, it seems extremely unlikely that the problem of unemployment can be solved by any of the conventional remedies and to pretend otherwise merely holds out false promises to a generation of unemployed. The New Right solution was to price people back into jobs. The modernizers' solution is to create a high-skill, high-wage 'magnet' economy. Neither solution is adequate. The New Right solution manifestly has not worked and it threatens a new cycle of low-wage job creation. The modernizers, whilst having a more sustainable approach to global economic competition, have no answer to unemployment. Therefore, the most important conclusion to be drawn from this discussion is that the modernizers lack an adequate account of how all will share in the future prosperity accrued from the investment in education and national economic growth. Unemployment will remain a structural feature of western societies and the 'distributional' question (Hirsch 1977), temporarily solved under Fordism through full employment and the even spread of the fruits of growth across the occupational structure, must now be addressed by the modernizers. Consequently, we argue elsewhere (Brown and Lauder forthcoming) that the distributional problem can only be remedied by the introduction of a 'social wage' and that occupational opportunities will have to be shared. Moreover, the question of unemployment is not only one about social justice, but one of economic efficiency. If the economic fate of nations increasingly depends upon the quality of their human resources, it will not be possible to write off a large minority of the population to an 'underclass' existence. Indeed, the issue of long-term unemployment is part of a wider problem of social and economic polarization. Therefore, we need to examine the modernizers' account of skill and income polarization before asking how those people living in poverty are going to acquire the appropriate skills to get high-skilled, high-waged jobs, when research has demonstrated that social deprivation has a profoundly negative impact on academic performance.

Does income polarization reflect the 'value' of skills, knowledge and insights in the global labour market?

Considerable doubt must be cast on the way the modernizers have understood the 'high skill = high wage' equation. This is important to our discussion because growing income inequalities are seen to reflect individual differences in the quality of their 'human capital'. Here their argument is based on trend data which show a widening of income inequalities. There has been a dramatic increase in income inequalities in both the USA and the UK since the late 1970s. Such evidence is taken to reflect the relative abilities of workers to trade their knowledge, skills and insights on the global labour market. According to the modernizers, as low-skilled jobs have been lost to developing economies with cheaper labour, the wages of less skilled workers in the West have declined. By the same token, in the new competitive conditions described above, those workers who have the skills, knowledge and insights that can contribute to 'value-added' research, production, consultancy or service delivery in the global labour market have witnessed an increase in their remuneration. Hence analysis and remedy are closely related in the modernizers' account: if the reason so many workers are in low-paying jobs, or worse, unemployed is that they lack skills, the solution is to give them the skills. It is an appealing analysis but at best it is based on a partial truth.

If increasing income polarization was a consequence of the neutral operation of the global economy we should find the same trend in all the advanced economies. However, the evidence suggests that the increasing polarization in income is far more pronounced in the USA and UK than in any other OECD country (Gardiner 1993:14; Hills 1995). In Germany there has actually been a decline in income differentials (OECD 1993)!

It could also be expected that if the increased dispersion of income was a result of the changing cognitive and skill demands of work, then nations with the highest levels of technology and investment in research and development would lead the table of income inequalities. Yet, the evidence that does exist suggests quite the opposite. Wood (1994) notes that, 'Japan and Sweden are leaders in applying new technology, while the USA and UK are laggards' (p. 281). He also notes that the work of Patel and Pavitt (1991) suggests that civilian research and development, as a proportion of GDP in the 1980s, was higher in Sweden and Japan than in the USA and UK. Equally, in terms of patenting in the USA, Germany, which experienced declining inequalities of income during this period, greatly outperformed the UK.

One conclusion to be drawn from these considerations is that rather than the returns to skill becoming more responsive to the operation of the global auction, the relationship between skill and income is less direct than the modernizers assume, the reason being that the relationship between income and skills is always mediated by cultural, political and societal factors. This is of course obvious when unpaid child care, undertaken primarily by women, is taken into consideration. Moreover, despite the way skill is used in the current debate about income inequalities and economic performance it has proved extremely difficult to arrive at an agreed definition of skill, which explains why studies comparing labour markets in neighbouring countries such as Germany and France show that the process of training, career progression and reward for skills in intricate, subtle and substantially different in the two countries (Maurice *et al.* 1986). Another study (Dore, 1987) has highlighted differences in the way rewards are distributed for work in the USA as opposed to Japan. In the USA it is assumed by neo-classical economists that there is a direct relationship between skill and income. However, Japanese industry, the exemplar of producer capitalism, has not organized the relationship between skill and income in this way. Rather, it has based income on loyalty to the company and length of service, rather than 'skill' in any pristine sense. As Dore has noted, in Japan there is a remarkable 'lack of consciousness of the market price of a skill' (p. 30). This being the case it could be expected that even if the polarization of income in the USA was a response to the changing demand for skill, this would not be the case in Japan. A further glance at the OECD (1993) data also tells us that while there has been some widening of income differentials in Japan, it does not reflect the polarization characteristic of the USA and UK.

What this evidence suggests is that the modernizers' assumption that by raising skill levels there will be a commensurate increase in income regulated through the global labour market is clearly incorrect. The answer is to be found not in the neutral operation of the global labour market as Reich and others have suggested, but in the way the USA and UK have *responded* to global economic conditions. This response, like the global economy itself, has been shaped by the New Right political projects of Reagan and Thatcher (Marchak 1991). Although the debate about what is distinctive about the USA and UK takes us beyond the confines of this paper, the polarization in income can be explained more convincingly in terms of differences in labour market power rather than returns to skills (although they are not mutually exclusive). A major consequence of market deregulation has been to enhance the power of 'core' workers in down-sized organizations. This is supported by the fact that the most dramatic changes in income distributon are to be found at either end of the income parade. What income polarization in the USA and UK also reveals is the way in which the 'casino' economies of these countries in the 1980s enabled company executives and senior managers, along with those who worked in the financial markets, to engage in 'wealth extraction' rather than the development of sustainable forms of 'wealth creation' (Lazonick 1993). This largely explains why a study reported by Bound and Johnson (1995) found that in the USA a large part of the increase in the returns to a university degree was due to an increased premium put to use in the business and law fields. The wages of computer specialists and engineers actually *fell* relative to those of high school graduates.

But if the rising incomes of the work rich are explicable in terms of 'paper entrepreneurialism' (Reich 1984) and corporate restructuring, can the decline in the wages of the unskilled be explained in terms of the neutral operation of the global economy? In addressing this question there is the problem of measuring the extent to which semi- and unskilled work has been transplanted to the developing nations. One estimate is that up to 1990 changes in trade with the South has reduced the demand for unskilled relative to skilled labour in the North by approximately 20% (Wood 1994: 11). However, it is not only that industrial blue-collar jobs were lost, but the perennial threat of relocation to developing world countries which ensured that wages were depressed for remaining unskilled workers. It is, of course, hard to measure the degree to which this threat has been material in keeping down wages. Nevertheless, it is worth noting that there is little correlation between manufacturing competitiveness and low wages. In the most successful industrial economies Germany and Japan, manufacturing wages are higher than anywhere else. However, New Right governments in the USA and UK took the 'lesson' to heart and helped to drive down wages by labour market deregulation. Estimates for the UK (Gosling and Machin 1993) and the USA (Blackburn *et al.* 1990), for instance, calculate that the decline in unionization in the 1980s accounts for 20% of the increase in wage inequality. In addition, making it easier to hire and fire workers enabled companies to achieve numerical flexibility in terms of their wages bills (Atkinson 1985). At times of economic boom workers could be hired while in times of downturn they could be fired. In Britain, for example, in the last three months of 1994, 74,120 full-time jobs disappeared and 173,941 part-time jobs were created. This is a clear example of how to organize a labour market for short-term expedience, but it also suggests that companies have not only externalized the risks associated with unstable market conditions but also their labour costs, especially among low-skilled workers. In such circumstances it is difficult to see how the modernizers can resolve the problem of widening income inequalities when they are judged to reflect the neutral operation of the global economy.

Indeed, high levels of income inequalities are interpreted by the modernizers as a reflection of educational and corporate inefficiency in a global labour market which can only be narrowed through investment in education and training. If inequalities persist it is because the latter are failing to upgrade the quality of human resources. With respect to national systems of education, inequalities become a useful measure of their effectiveness. However, this raises a set of questions and problems for the modernizers with respect to the social conditions under which education can achieve greater equality of opportunity and higher levels of educational achievement for all. It is to this, fourth, problem that we now turn.

How can the quality of human resources be upgraded where all are granted an equal opportunity to fulfil their human potential?

In answering this question the modernizers recognize that the wealth of nations depends upon upgrading the quality of human resources. They recognize that ways must be found to develop the full potential of a much larger proportion of the population than prevailed in the Fordist era. They point to the need to widen access to tertiary education and to create the institutional framework necessary to offer lifelong learning to all. They also recognize a need to improve overall educational standards as US and UK students appear to be falling behind in international comparative tests. A national commitment to investment in the 'employability' of present and future workers is understood by the modernizers to represent a new social contract between the individual and the state, given that such investment is viewed as a condition for economic efficiency and social justice. However, their interpretation of how equity and efficiency are to be achieved in the global economy is politically impoverished. In part, this is because the question of equity has been subsumed within a debate about how to upgrade the overall quality of education and training systems based on an assumption that domestic inequalities of opportunity are largely irrelevant if a nation can win a competitive advantage in the global knowledge wars, permitting all to compete for high-skilled, high-waged jobs. Therefore, the old national competition for a livelihood, based on the principles of meritocratic competition, is of far less importance than that of how to upgrade the quality of the education system as a whole. Again we find the idea of a high-skill, high-wage magnet economy used to extract the political sting from questions of social and educational inequalities.

The reality is that questions of social justice cannot be resolved through the operation of the global labour market. Indeed, if the creation of a post-Fordist economy depends on a general upgrading of the skills of the labour force, tackling the problem of domestic inequalities in income and opportunities has become *more* rather than less important with economic globalization. There are at least two related reasons for this. First, the use of education and training institutions to raise technical standards for all does not resolve the question of 'positional' advantage (Hirsch 1977). In other words, access to élite schools, colleges and universities, along with the credentials they bestow, remains a key factor in determining labour market power. In addition, if our analysis of income inequalities is correct, labour market power has, if anything, become more important as a result of corporate restructuring and the decline of graduate careers (Brown and Scase 1994). Therefore, the question of social justice will continue to depend on how individual nation states frame the competition for a livelihood.

The question of positional competition has also become more important because there has been a change in the nature of educational selection. Today the institutional expression of a commitment to meritocratic competition in education has been suffocated under the grip of the New Right. A commitment to a unified system of schooling within which students will be educated according to ability and effort has been abandoned in favour of consumer sovereignty based on parental 'choice' and a system of education based on market principles. A consequence of this change in the organization of educational selection from that based on 'merit' to the 'market' (Brown 1995) is, as argued above, that it serves to encourage the creation of underfunded sink schools for the poor and havens of 'excellence' for the rich. Therefore, the school system in both the USA and UK no longer reflects a commitment to open competition but gross inequalities in educational provision, opportunities and life chances. In Washington, DC the wealthy are queuing up to pay as much as $12,000 a year to send their five-year-old children to private schools, while the city is virtually bankrupt and severe cuts to the educational budget are inevitable.[10]

Therefore, although equality of opportunity is recognized as a condition of economic efficiency the modernizers have effectively avoided perhaps the most important question to confront the left at the end of the 20th century, that is, how to organize the competition for a livelihood in such a way that a genuinely equal opportunity is available to all. Avoiding the positional problem by appeals to the need to raise educational standards for all in the global market not only fails to address this question but also offers little insight into how the foundations for social solidarity upon which the institutional expression of meritocratic competition rests, are to be rebuilt. Indeed, their focus on increasing the 'employability' of workers reinforces a sense of the insecure nature of work at the end of the 20th century (Newman 1993, Peterson 1994). It encourages people to watch their backs constantly and to put their child first in the educational and labour market jungle. Without an adequate foundation for material and social security the emphasis on enhanced employability within a culture of competitive individualism becomes translated into the Hobbesian condition of 'all against all'. When education becomes a positional good and where the stakes are forever increasing in terms of income, life-chances and social status, powerful individuals and groups will seek to maximize their resources to ensure that they have a stake in the game by whatever means.[11] Therefore, how the state intervenes to regulate this competition in a way which reduces the inequalities of those trapped in lower socioeconomic groups must be addressed, not only as a matter of economic efficiency but also for reasons of social justice in a post-Fordist economy.

The relationship between equity and efficiency at the end of the 20th century does not only rest on the reassertion of meritocratic competition in education, but on a recognition that the wealth of the nation's human resources is *inversely* related to social inequalities, especially in income and opportunity. Therefore, narrowing such inequalities is likely to be a cost-effective way of investing in human capital, which in turn should lead to improvements in economic efficiency. Hence, we would predict that the polarization of income in nations such as the USA and UK during the 1980s will have led to a wider dispersal of educational achievement than in nations with little or not widening of incomes. We are currently analysing the comparative evidence in order to examine the hypothesis that relative deprivation has an absolute effect on the quality of a nation's human resources (Wilkinson 1994). If our hypothesis proves to be supported by the empirical evidence, it will come as little surprise to sociologists who have consistently found a close relationship between inequality and academic performance.[12] The fact that at least a fifth of children in both the USA and UK now live in poverty is inevitably going to have a detrimental impact on the ability of these children to respond to educational opportunities and to recognize the relevance of formal study when living in neighbourhoods with high unemployment, crime and deprivation. Indeed, the importance of equity to the question of social learning is graphically illustrated in Julius Wilson's (1987) study of the urban underclass in America. He suggests that 'a perceptive ghetto youngster in a neighbourhood that includes a good number of working and professional families may observe increasing joblessness and idleness but he [*sic*] may also witness many individuals going to and from work; he may sense an increase in school dropouts but he can also see a connection between education and meaningful employment' (1987: 56). He goes on to argue that the exodus of 'respectable' middle- and working-class families from the inner-city neighbourhoods in the 1970s and 1980s removed an important 'social buffer' that could deflect the full impact of prolonged and increasing joblessness, given that the basic institutions in the area (churches, schools, stores, recreational facilities, etc.) were viable so long as more economically stable and secure families remained. Hence, the more social groups become isolated from one another the fewer opportunities exist for the kind of social learning which even in the deprived neighbourhoods of US and UK cities could offer role models to children other than those which now exist due to the 'political economy of crack' (Davis 1990).

Moreover, the impact of widening social inequalities is not restricted to children from ghetto or poor backgrounds; it also infects the social learning of the wealthier sections of the population. In a characteristically perceptive discussion John Dewey noted that every expansive period of social history is marked by social trends which serve to 'eliminate distance between peoples and classes previously hemmed off from one another' (1966: 100). At times where the opposite happens it narrows the range of contacts, ideas, interests and role models. The culture of the privileged tends to become 'sterile,to be turned back to feed on itself; their art becomes a showy display and artificial; their wealth luxurious; their knowledge over-specialised; their manners fastidious rather than human' (Dewey 1966: 98).

Hence the view which the modernizers take in assuming that inequalities will narrow once there is proper investment in education and training fails to recognize that the future wealth of nations depends upon a fundamental challenge to inequalities in both income and opportunities. Therefore, the role of the nation-state must increasingly become one of balancing the internal competition for a livelihood with a strategy geared towards upgrading the quality of education for all through a reduction in relative inequalities. Moreover, a commitment to equality of opportunity is not only vital to the life-blood of a high-skill economic strategy, but it provides a clear message to all sections of society that they are of equal worth and deserve genuine opportunities to fulfil their human potential.

Conclusion

The increasing importance attached to education in the global economy is not misplaced in the sense that nations will increasingly have to define the wealth of nations in terms of the quality of human resources among the population. The creation of a post-Fordist economy will depend upon an active state involved in investment, regulation and strategic planning in the economic infrastructure alongside a commitment to skill formation through education and training. We have argued that such an economic strategy is necessary because it is the best way of creating a social dividend which can be used to fund a 'social wage' for all given that the 'distributional' problem can no longer be solved through employment within the division of labour. A social wage which delivers families from poverty thereby becomes an important foundation of a learning society, designed to follow the post-Fordist trajectory to a globally competitive economy and to a socially just society (see Brown and Lauder forthcoming). Hence, if the potential and limitations of educational reform in the creation of post-Fordist economy are to be adequately addressed by the modernizers there is an urgent need for those on the left to grapple with the issues explored in this paper.

Notes

1. This paper develops a number of themes outlined in earlier papers (Brown and Lauder 1992, 1995). It also serves to clarify our interpretation of the relationship between education and post-Fordism which has been criticized by Avis (1993) and Jones and Hatcher (1994).
2. Figures from *Financial Times* Survey 'North American Business Location' 19 October 1994.
3. Antonio Gramsci (1971) used the term Fordism to describe a new system of mass production introduced by the American car manufacturer Henry Ford. Gramsci recognized that the introduction of mass production also required a new mode of social regulation 'suited to the new type of work and productive process' (p. 286). Ford's rise to prominence at the time stemmed from the market success of the Model T motor car which was launched in 1916. The system of mass production enabled him to capture 55% of the US market in the early 1920s by selling the Model T at a tenth of the price of a craft-built car (Braverman 1974, Murray 1989).
4. As it is more difficult for competitors to mass produce the same goods or to offer customers tailored services (see Schumpeter 1961, Collins 1986, Blackwell and Eilon 1991). In such companies improvements in productivity depend upon the 'organic' integration of applied science, technological innovation, free-flow information networks, and high-trust relations between management and multi-skilled workers. The increasing costs of errors, demand for quality control, and for multi-skilled workers with a conceptual grasp of a large section of the production process or office activities has made the specialized division of labour in Fordism a source of organizational inefficiency.
5. The idea of a 'Feudal' shackle is discussed by Hirschman (1986).
6. Given such a diverse range of publications there will inevitably be differences in focus and policy emphasis. The extent to which the Clinton administration in America has attempted to introduce a viable industrial policy has been clearly limited; see Shoch, J. (1994) 'The politics of the US industrial policy debate, 1981–1984 (with a note on Bill Clinton's 'industrial policy')', in D. Kotz, T. McDonough and M. Reich (eds) *Social Structures of Accumulation* (Cambridge: Cambridge University Press).
7. 'They are all our children', speech delivered at East Los Angeles College, Los Angeles, 14 May 1992. The modernizers' view contrasts with the rhetoric, if not the practice, of the New Right. There is clearly a tension between New Right views regarding the expansion of tertiary education and the practice of the Conservative Party in the UK, where there has been a rapid expansion of tertiary provision despite the views of influential theorists and journalists such as Friedman, Hayek and Rees-Mogg, suggesting that it is only an élite that needs a university education. It is also worth noting that, in terms of imagery, the New Right do not present the future in terms of a 'learning society' but an enterprise culture, in which a few outstanding captains of industry and commerce, the Bill Gates and Richard Branson's of this world, are feted as the leaders of an economic renaissance.
8. The floor of protective rights for workers as envisaged by the modernizers is, for example, likely to be too weak to act as an incentive to employers to upgrade the quality of work opportunities. Moreover, see Kuttner's response to Rogers and Streeck (1994).
9. Data compiled from the *Independent on Sunday*'s economic indicators 1994–95.
10. The question of equality of opportunity needs to be addressed head on as it is not only essential to economic efficiency, but to the legitimization of a system of educational and occupational selection which is inherently stratified in terms of income, status, work styles and lifestyles. In postwar western societies the reason why a menial labourer is paid $17,000 and a private sector manager $85,000 was legitimized in terms of the outcome of a meritocratic competition based on individual ability and effort. The commitment to open competition found expression in the idea of the socially-mixed-ability high or comprehensive school. Yes, there remained deprived inner-city districts where children, especially from African-American and Hispanic backgrounds, were clearly not getting equality of opportunity but even here 'head start' programmes were launched to try to create a level playing field.
11. Moreover, for those in lower socioeconomic circumstances their exclusion from decent academic provision is compounded by deindustrialization which has created a rust belt across the heartlands of both the USA and UK, sometimes destroying vibrant communities (Bluestone and Harrison 1982). Therefore, although the modernizers assume greater flexibility in the occupational structure as a response to the employment needs of men and women at different stages of their lives, the reality seems more likely to lead to intensive competition and highly restricted opportunities to enter the professional core and a constant flux restricted to jobs which are low skilled, low waged and inherently insecure. This outcome may well be reinforced by the fact that as employers place a premium on employees with the appropriate social and interpersonal skills alongside their technical know-how, the cultural capital of job-seekers assumes greater importance. Without the financial and social resources

required to invest in cultural capital those from poorer backgrounds who are more likely to attend less prestigious halls of learning will be at a distinct disadvantage (Brown and Scase 1994).

12 For a discussion of the definition of relative deprivation and poverty see Townsend P. (1993) *The International Analysis of Poverty* (New York: Harvester Wheatsheaf).

References

ALLEN, J. (1992) 'Post-industrialism and Post-Fordism'. In S. Hall *et al.* (eds), *Modernity and its futures* (Cambridge: Polity).

ASHTON, D. N. and SUNG, J. (1994) *The State, Economic Development and Skill Formation: A New Asian Model*, Working Paper No. 3 (Leicester: Centre for Labour Market Studies, University of Leicester).

ATKINSON, J. (1985) 'The changing corporation'. In D. Clutterbuck (ed.), *New Patterns of Work* (Aldershot: Gower).

AVIS, J. (1993) 'A new orthodoxy, old problems: post-16 reforms'. *British Journal of Sociology of Education*, 14, 245–260.

BALL, S. (1993) 'Education markets, choice and social class: the market as a class strategy in the UK and the USA'. *British Journal of Sociology of Education*, 14(1), 3–19.

BLACKBURN, M., BLOOM, D. and FREEMAN, R. (1990) 'The declining economic position of less skilled American men'. In G. Burtless (ed.), *A Future of Lousy Jobs?* (Washington DC: Brookings Institute).

BLACKWELL, B. and EILON, S. (1991) *The Global Challenge of Innovation* (Oxford: Butterworth-Heinemann).

BLOCK, F. (1990) *Postindustrial Possibilities: A Critique of Economic Discourse* (Berkeley: University of California Press).

BLUESTONE, B. and HARRISON, B. (1982) *The Deindustrialization of America* (New York: Basic Books).

BOUND, J. and JOHNSON, G. (1995) 'What are the causes of rising wage inequality in the United States?' *Economic Policy Review*, Federal Reserve Bank of New York, 1(1), 9–17.

BOYD, W. and CIBULKA, J. (eds) (1989) *Private Schools and Public Policy* (London: Falmer Press).

BRAVERMAN, H. (1974) *Labour and Monopoly Capital* (London: Jessica Kingsley).

BROWN, G. (1994) 'The politics of potential: a new agenda for Labour'. In D. Miliband (ed.), *Reinventing the Left* (Cambridge: Polity).

BROWN, P. (1990) 'The 'Third Wave': education and the ideology of parentocracy'. *British Journal of Sociology of Education*, 11, 65–85.

BROWN, P. (1995) 'Cultural capital and social exclusion: some observations on recent trends in education, employment and the labour market'. *Work Employment and Society*, 9(1), 29–51.

BROWN, P. and LAUDER, H. (1992) 'Education, economy and society: an introduction to a new agenda. In P. Brown and H. Lauder (eds), *Education for Economic Survival: From Fordism to Post-Fordism?* (London: Routledge).

BROWN, P. and LAUDER, H. (forthcoming) *Capitalism and Social Progress in the Twenty-First Century*.

BROWN, P. and SCASE, R. (1994) *Higher Education and Corporate Realities* (London: UCL Press).

CARNOY, M., CASTELLS, M., COHEN, S. and CARDOSO, F. H. (1993) *The Global Economy in the Information Age* (Pennsylvania: Penn State University).

COLLINS, R. (1979) *The Credential Society* (New York: Academic Press).

COLLINS, R. (1986) *Weberian Sociological Theory* (New York: Cambridge University Press).

COMMISSION OF THE EUROPEAN COMMUNITIES (1993) *Growth, Competitiveness, Employment: The Challenges and Ways Forward into the 21st Century* White Paper, Bulletin of the European Communities 6/93.

COMMISSION ON SOCIAL JUSTICE (1994) *Social Justice: Strategies for National Renewal* (London: Vintage).

COWLING, K. and SUGDEN, R. (1994) *Beyond Capitalism: Towards a New World Economic Order* (London: Pinter).

DAVIS, M. (1990) *City of Quartz* (New York: Verso).

DEAKIN, S. and WILKINSON, F. (1991) 'Social policy and economic efficiency: the deregulation of the labour market in Britain'. *Critical Social Policy*, 11(3), 40–61.

DEWEY, J. (1966) *Democracy and Education* (New York, Free Press).

DICKEN, P. (1992) *Global Shift: The Internationalisation of Economic Activity* (London: Paul Chapman).

DORE, R. (1987) *Taking Japan Seriously* (London: Athlone Press).

EATWELL, J. (1995) 'The international origins of unemployment'. In J. Michie and J. G. Smith (eds), *Managing the Global Economy* (Oxford: Oxford University Press).

ESPING-ANDERSEN, G. (1994) 'Equity and work in the post-industrial life-cycle'. In D. Miliband (ed.), *Reinventing the Left* (Cambridge: Polity).

FREEMAN, R. (1995) 'The limits of wage flexibility to curing unemployment'. *Oxford Review of Economic Policy*, 11(1), 63–72.

GAMBLE, A. (1988) *The Free Market and the Strong State* (London: Macmillan).

GARDINER, K. (1993) A Survey of Income Inequality Over the Last Twenty Years – How Does the UK Compare?, Welfare State Programme No 100 (London: Centre for Economics and Related Disciplines, London School of Economics).

GOSLING, A. and MACHIN, S. (1993) *Trade Unions and the Dispersion of Earnings in UK Establishments, 1980–90*, Centre for Economic Performance Discussion Paper No. 140 (London: London School of Economics).

GRAMSCI, A. (1971) *Selections from Prison Notebooks* (London: Lawrence & Wishart).

GREEN, A. and STEEDMAN, H. (1993) *Education Provision, Education Attainment and the Needs of Identity: A Review of Research for Germany, France, Japan, the USA and Britain* (London: NIESR).

HALSEY, A. H., HEATH, A. and RIDGE, J. (1980) *Origins and Destinations* (Oxford: Clarendon).

HALSTEAD, M. (ed.) (1994) *Parental Choice and Education* (London: Kogan Page).

HARVEY, D. (1989) *The Conditions of Postmodernity* (Oxford: Blackwell).

HENDERSON, A. and PARSONS, T. (eds) (1974) *Max Weber: The Theory of Social and Economic Organisation* (New York: Oxford University Press).

HILLS, J. (1995) *Income and Wealth, Vol 2: A Summary of the Evidence* (York: Joseph Rowntree Foundation).

HIRSCH, F. (1977) *Social Limits to Growth* (London: Routledge).

HIRSCHMANN, A. (1986) *Rival Views of Market Society and Other Essays* (London: Viking).

HUTTON, W. (1995) *The State We're In* (London: Jonathan Cape).

INTERNATIONAL LABOUR ORGANISATION (ILO) (1995) *World Employment* (Geneva: ILO).

JONES, K. and HATCHER, R. (1994) 'Education, progress and economic change: notes on some recent proposals'. *British Journal of Educational Studies*, 42, 245–260.

KRUGMAN, P. (1993) *Peddling Prosperity: Economic Sense and Nonsense in the Age of Diminished Expectations* (New York: W. W. Norton).

LANE, C. (1989) *Management and Labour in Europe* (Aldershot: Edward Elgar).

LAUDER, H. (1987) 'The New Right and educational policy in New Zealand'. *New Zealand Journal of Educational Studies*, 22, 3–23.

LAUDER, H. (1991) 'Education, democracy and the economy'. *British Journal of Sociology of Education*, 12, 417–431.

LAUDER, H. and HUGHES, D. (1990) 'Social inequalities and differences in school outcomes'. *New Zealand Journal of Educational Studies*, 23, 37–60.

LAUDER, H. *et al.* (1994) *The Creation of Market Competition for Education in New Zealand* (Wellington: Ministry of Education).

LAZONICK, W. (1993) 'Industry clusters versus global webs: organisational capabilities in the American economy'. *Industrial and Corporate Change*, 2, 1–24.

LINDBECK, A. and SNOWER, D. (1986) 'Wage setting, unemployment and insider–outsider relations'. *American Economic Review*, 76, 235–239.

LIPIETZ, A. (1987) *Mirages and Miracles: The Crises of Global Fordism* (London: Verso).

MARCHAK, M. P. (1991) *The Integrated Circus: The New Right and the Restructuring of Global Markets* (Montreal: McGill-Queen's University Press).

MARGINSON, P. (1994) 'Multinational Britain: employment and work in an internationalised economy'. *Human Resource Management Journal*, 4(4), 63–80.

MAURICE, M., SELLIER, F. and SILVESTRE, J. (1986) *The Social Foundations of Industrial Power* (Cambridge, MA: MIT Press).

McGREGOR, D. (1960) *The Human Side of Enterprise* (New York: McGraw-Hill).

MICHIE, J. and SMITH, J. G. (eds) (1995) *Managing the Global Economy* (Oxford: Oxford University Press).

MURRAY, C. (1984) *Losing Ground: American Social Policy 1950–1980* (New York: Basic Books).

MURRAY, R. (1989) 'Fordism and post-Fordism'. In S. Hall and M. Jacques (eds), *New Times* (London: Lawrence & Wishart).

NATIONAL COMMISSION ON EDUCATION (1993) *Learning to Succeed* (London: Heinemann).

NEWMAN, K. (1993) *Declining Fortunes* (New York: Basic Books).

OECD (1989) *Education and the Economy in a Changing World* (Paris: OECD).

OECD (1993) *Employment Outlook* (Paris: OECD).

OECD (1994) *Employment Outlook* (Paris: OECD).

ORMEROD, P. (1994) *The Death of Economics* (London: Faber & Faber).

PARKIN, F. (1979) *Marxism and Class Theory: A Bourgeois Critique* (London: Tavistock).

PATEL, P. and PAVITT, K. (1991) 'Europe's technological performance'. In C. Freeman, M. Sharp and W. Walker (eds), *Technology and the Future of Europe* (London: Pinter).

PETERSON, W. (1994) *Silent Depression: The Fate of the American Dream* (New York: W. W. Norton).

PIORE, M. (1990) 'Labor standards and business strategies'. In S. Herzenberg and J. Perez-Lopez (eds), *Labor Standards and Development in the Global Economy* (Washington DC: US Department of Labor).

PIORE, M. and SABEL, C. (1984) *The Second Industrial Divide: Possibilities for Prosperity* (New York: Basic Books).

PORTER, M. (1990) *The Competitive Advantage of Nations* (London: Macmillan).

REICH, R. (1984) *The Next American Frontier* (Harmondsworth: Penguin).

REICH, R. (1991) *The Work of Nations* (London: Simon & Schuster).

ROGERS, J. and STREECK, W. (1994) 'Productive solidarities: economic strategy and left politics'. In D. Miliband (ed.), *Reinventing the Left* (Cambridge: Polity).

ROWTHORN, R. (1995) 'Capital formation and unemployment'. *Oxford Review of Economic Policy*, 11(1), 26–39.

SABEL, C. F. (1982) *Work and Politics* (Cambridge: Cambridge University Press).

SCHUMPETER, J. (1961) *The Theory of Economic Development* (New York: Oxford University Press).

SENGENBERGER, W. and WILKINSON, F. (1995) 'Globalization and labour standards'. In J. Michie and J. G. Smith (eds), *Managing the Global Economy* (Oxford: Oxford University Press).

SNOWER, D. (1995) 'Evaluating unemployment policies: what do the underlying theories tell us?'. *Oxford Review of Economic Policy*, 11, 110–135.

STREECK, W. (1989) 'Skills and the limits of neo-liberalism: the enterprise of the future as a place of learning'. *Work, Employment and Society*, 3, 90–104.

STREECK, W. (1992) *Social Institutions and Economic Performance* (London: Sage).

THUROW, L. (1993) *Head to Head: The Coming Economic Battle Among Japan, Europe and America* (London: Nicholas Brealey).

TOFFLER, A. (1990) *Powershift* (New York: Bantam).

WILKINSON, R. (1994) *Unfair Shares: The Effect of Widening Income Differences on the Welfare of the Young* (Ilford: Barnardo's Publication).

WILLMS, J. and ECHOLS, F. (1992) 'Alert and inert clients: the Scottish experience of parental choice of schools'. *Economics of Education Review*, 11, 339–350.

WILSON, W. (1987) *The Truly Disadvantaged* (Chicago: University of Chicago Press).

WOOD A. (1994) *North–South Trade, Employment and Inequality: Changing Fortunes in a Skill-Driven World* (Oxford: Clarendon).

International Labour Review, 1995, Vol. 134, No. 6

Structural adjustment and the changing face of education

Martin CARNOY *

The world economy has undergone sweeping changes in the time of a generation. The changes reflect the increased globalization of economic activities, growing competition among nations for markets and the widespread impact of the information and communications revolution. Higher productivity and economic growth are increasingly dependent on the application of knowledge and information to production of goods and services, and such knowledge is increasingly science-based. This is not an entirely new phenomenon, since knowledge has always been a key factor in the organization and fostering of economic growth. But as economies become more complex, consumption becomes more varied and competition increases, knowledge and information are more critical to the production and realization process.

All national economies (and subnational regions, industries and most firms) have had to adjust to this new "structural" reality. In the broadest of terms, this is the meaning of structural adjustment. In one analyst's words, "The main objective . . . is to overcome economic crisis and imbalance caused by internal or external shocks and past mismanagement of the economy" (Woodhall, 1991, p. 10). Structural adjustment is normally associated with the correction of imbalances in foreign accounts and domestic consumption (including government deficits) and with the deregulation and privatization of the economy. It is therefore identified with public sector austerity and as a consequence, in many countries, with growing poverty and an increasingly unequal distribution of income, resulting in "reduced government funding for public education programmes, lower personal incomes and family budgets available for education, and an increased focus on encouraging private education initiatives, which only some can afford" (Reimers and Tiburcio, 1993, p. 14).

---

* School of Education, Stanford University, Stanford, California. This article is drawn from the author's contribution to *The impact of structural adjustment policies on employment and training of teachers*, one of two reports being submitted to the First Session of the ILO's Joint Meeting on the Impact of Structural Adjustment on Educational Personnel, to be held in Geneva, 22-26 April 1996.

The adverse impact of economic adjustment on education could not have come at a worse time in the history of developing countries. As information – hence education – assumes a crucial importance in the world economy and society only individuals and countries with a high level of education can cope with the enormous changes taking place. In such circumstances, structural adjustment has made the delivery of education even more difficult in developing countries. In their turn, education professionals have been made to bear much of the burden of these growing difficulties, for which they have often also been blamed.

But structural adjustment as practised in most high-income countries of the OECD and in the newly industrializing countries (NICs) of Asia does not display these features. There the focus of adjustment has been on increased exports, reduced domestic demand, various constraints on government spending and some privatization; with a few notable exceptions, it has not entailed policies that greatly increase inequality or poverty. Rather, many of the richer economies have focused on "self-adjusting" mechanisms to rationalize production and the public infrastructure that serves productive and social functions. Their educational systems have not suffered and, in general, their education professionals have made income gains. In the best of cases, education has improved and teachers have participated in making that improvement happen.

This suggests that there are several categories of structural adjustment. It also suggests that the term "structural adjustment" is commonly used not in its broader sense of reorganizing the structure of production in response to very significant changes in the world economy, but for a particular set of policies. The origins of these policies were as much the political and economic conditions prevailing in the United States in the 1970s as the underlying economic problems of developing countries at that time. The combination of the prevailing political views in the United States with the indebtedness characterizing many developing countries and with inefficiency in the public sector resulted in the emergence of a dominant view of how economies in crisis should reorganize to resume growth. When applied, the policies reflecting this view did indeed increase economic inequality and poverty, without necessarily improving the chances of sustainable development. They also usually meant less emphasis on the role of the public sector in economic growth and cuts in public expenditure on services, including education – precisely at a time when the shift to a world information economy called for increased public investment in education and for more rational, and probably extensive, public intervention and mobilization of resources.

The emergence of this dominant view may be attributed to two factors. The first concerns the initial conditions in those countries least able to adjust to the new international economic order. The simplest way to grasp this situation is to observe that the countries best able to self-adjust already enjoyed conditions consistent with world market competitiveness and had the capacity to respond to rapidly changing technology (Amsden, 1989;

Castells, 1991; Birdsall and Sabot, 1993). These conditions included the capacity to develop and mobilize the knowledge needed to produce new information-based goods and services and to adopt new methods to produce, and sometimes export, traditional industrial and agricultural products more efficiently; a well-organized public service capable of mobilizing and/or providing the framework for private sector organizational and technological responses to change; public education, workers' training, investment in infrastructure and government investment in research and development; and a reasonable national income distribution which could ensure political stability during a process of change.

The less successful countries did not enjoy all or even, in some cases, any of these conditions. In Latin America, for example, a long history of import-substitution industrialization based on high levels of protection for domestic industries and other forms of state intervention, coupled with a highly unequal income distribution, made it difficult to sustain corrective economic policies in the 1970s. By the 1980s, when creditor countries raised interest rates sharply to reduce their own rates of inflation and then cut back foreign lending, Latin American countries were overwhelmed by an enormous debt crisis (Iglesias, 1992). Most African countries found themselves in a similar situation, heavily in debt and faced with rapidly deteriorating terms of trade. Their economies suffered a drain on their capital and negative rates of economic growth in the 1980s – and governments were generally ill-equipped to improve infrastructure, support private sector efforts to export and develop new products and processes or attract foreign investment on reasonable terms. The command economies of the Soviet Union, of its east European satellites and of China also began to flounder in the 1970s as the heavy industry/military basis of economic growth and technological change ran out of steam. Only China was able to promote economic decision-making changes that increased economic growth, mainly in agriculture but also in special industrial zones. The countries in deepest trouble in the early 1980s, therefore, were those which lacked a dynamic export-oriented private sector and which were characterized by heavy public debt and inefficient public services.

The second factor giving rise to the dominant view was the distinct paradigm shift away from Keynesianism and toward neo-liberal monetarism that occurred in many developed countries in the early 1980s – particularly in the United States (Harrison and Bluestone, 1988). This economic policy thinking led to a drastic increase in real interest rates to reduce inflationary tendencies in developed countries and to sharp cuts in foreign loans to developing countries to reduce financial exposure (Iglesias, 1992). At the international level, monetarist thinking also became the dominant paradigm at the International Monetary Fund (IMF) and, to a lesser extent, at the World Bank. When these institutions were called upon to help relieve the debt problems of developing countries, they imposed a set of structural adjustment policies (SAPs) on developing countries that reflected this economic paradigm. At the same time, the reduction of public sector spending and of government regulation became an important condition for developing countries to obtain structural adjustment loans. For their part, most developed countries (including the United States) and the most successful Asian NICs did not reduce government spending, government deficit financing or economic regulation, and many did not reduce the share of the public sector in the gross national product in the 1980s.

Besides a general reduction of public expenditure, structural adjustment loans to developing countries required: the reduction of consumer subsidies (both to bring down government spending and to stimulate exports); the elimination of price controls and drastic lowering of tariffs in order to bring domestic prices in line with world prices; the revision of other trade policies to encourage exports; the revision of fiscal, especially tax, policies to reduce public sector deficits and distortions in the private sector; charging users for public services; the privatization of public enterprises and social services; and the institutional reforms required to provide those services (Woodhall, 1991).

Many elements in this particular array of SAPs were necessary to adjust developing economies to external shocks, to mobilize the resources needed to develop under new world economic conditions and to allocate resources more efficiently. But the critical approaches to the size and role of the public sector that characterized these SAPs and which were evident in the conditions they imposed on loan disbursements ("conditionalities") also tended to be detrimental to public services and investment and to the groups dependent on those services and investment. The SAPs' negative impact on education was particularly harmful because an improvement in labour force skills was vital in view of the new goods, services and production processes needed to be competitive and to stimulate growth in the 1980s and 1990s. According to Andrew Noss, writing for the World Bank, conditionalities in several policy areas have had an important impact on the education sector:

> *Public recurrent and capital expenditures conditionality* addresses the size and composition of the public investment program, as well as the recurrent expenditure allocation, in order to reduce the government budget deficit and rationalize the public expenditure program. *Wages and employment conditionality* focuses on civil service retrenchment and is often implemented through a wage bill or hiring freeze. *Subsidies conditionality* reduces or removes government subsidies in order to correct price distortions, improve economic efficiency and improve the equity and efficiency of subsidy programs through better targeting. *Social policies conditionality* protects vulnerable groups from the impacts of adjustment, especially during the transition period (Noss, 1991, p. 2, referring to Kakwani, Makonnen and Van der Gaag, 1990).

However, maintaining public spending growth did not guarantee an end to the growth of poverty. As recent studies of Latin American countries in the 1980s show, debt-ridden economies could have avoided adjustment policies for many years, but could not have avoided increased poverty or greater income inequality as their economies adjusted to the external shock of the balance-of-payments crisis (Lustig, 1995).

Moreover, the smaller economies with less bargaining power and fewer intellectual resources with which to respond to IMF/World Bank policy recommendations were bound to agree to that particular set of SAPs. In the words of the former President of Costa Rica, Oscar Arias: "A small country like Costa Rica has little choice in such matters" (Carnoy and Torres, 1994, p. 92).

A number of empirical studies, including those carried out by the World Bank, have shown that policies recommended by the IMF and the Bank, particularly in the early and mid-1980s, were associated with increased poverty, increased inequality of income and wealth and slow (or negative) economic growth (for example, Cornia, Jolly and Stewart, 1987; Bello, 1993; Kakwani, Makonnen and Van der Gaag, 1990). Although it is difficult to separate the effects of IMF and Bank recommendations and lending from those of the internal and external conditions that first prompted the need for short- and long-term financing, and although there may have been some successes, there is persuasive evidence that the conditions imposed for these loans were not the most effective recipe for restarting economic growth or for equitably distributing the fruits of growth. In practice, the recipe took much longer to produce recovery and did so at a much higher cost than its proponents had claimed. Whatever the intention behind the imposition of these conditions, the results were almost certain to be a less equal income distribution and reduced access to and lower quality of education for the poor. The conditions also lowered the chances of the poor to benefit from training and skills development in the most favourable circumstances, thus working against broadly based higher-level training systems (Lucas, 1994).

These largely negative effects of SAPs on the supply of and demand for education had become evident by the mid-1980s. When economic recovery in the OECD countries and structural adjustment policies did not produce the expected rapid economic recovery of debt-ridden developing countries, the World Bank reacted in two ways on the education front. First, it increased the amounts available for lending to the education sector by stepping up sector investment loans (SECILs) and sector adjustment loans (SECALs) as well as the more traditional specific investment loans (SILs). Although there were few of them, the SECALs were specifically designed to implement major structural reforms in education (Thomas and Verspoor, 1994). Second, it promoted a particular set of educational reforms, which focused on raising quality without increasing cost, on reducing the public cost per student at various education levels while maintaining quality and, in the same spirit, on raising the private household contribution to education through increased user fees, especially at the higher levels of education.

The overall aims of these two approaches were to mitigate the most adverse effects of structural adjustment on education and to make the education sector more efficient (and equitable) during a period of declining public spending. However, as Reimers and Tiburcio have pointed out, "such good intentions have rarely been put into practice because stabilization programmes have limited government counterpart funds available for such activities. Financing agencies now tend to postpone decisions on educational projects, pending the results of financial and human resource feasibility studies regarding the absorption and management capacities of the educational agency or institution" (1993, p. 14).

The following pages first take up the types of reforms that have been required of the education sector. Then the important question of their impact on the quality of education is addressed. And finally, the possibility of alternative policies for adjustment is considered.

Structural adjustment in the education sector

Changes in the world economy have provoked three kinds of response in the education sector: (a) reforms in response to shifting demand for skills in both the domestic and the world labour markets and to new ideas about organizing the production of educational achievement and work skills – these may be referred to as "competitiveness-driven reforms"; (b) reforms in response to cuts in public sector budgets and private company incomes which reduced the public and private resources available for financing education and training – "finance-driven reforms"; and (c) reforms to improve education's important political role as a source of social mobility and social equalization – "equity-driven reforms".

Competitiveness-driven reforms

The underlying philosophy of such reforms is best captured in the 1992 report of the OECD's ministerial-level Education Committee:

> The "human factor" is fundamental to economic activity, competitiveness and prosperity, whether manifest as knowledge and skills or in the less tangible forms of flexibility, openness to innovation, and entrepreneurial culture. All OECD economies are engaged in a process of structural adjustment and rapid technological development. Employment patterns and workplace processes evolve rapidly. Together, these changes exercise a profound impact on the topography of relevant knowledge and skills and hence on the capacity of individuals, young and old, men and women, to participate in economic life (OECD, 1992, p. 32).

In practice, this philosophy translates into organizational reforms of educational institutions in order to raise the "quality" of their output as measured mainly by students' performance on tests that assess what international curriculum standards suggest students should know by a certain age or grade of school. But quality is often also loosely defined by employers' views of how far the education schools produce is relevant to a changing world of work. For example, employers may regard secondary education as low quality if graduates of that level cannot learn job skills.

The organizational reforms aimed at increasing educational quality may be classified in four categories – decentralization, centralization, improved resource management and improved recruitment and training of teachers.

Decentralization

Municipalities and, in some places, schools, may be given greater autonomy in decision-making on education. One purpose of decentralization is to pass the control of curriculum and teaching methods to local communities and to the principals and teachers of the schools themselves – the assumption being that increased flexibility and control by these groups enable a better fit between educational methods and the clientele served as well as greater accountability for educational results. Reformers reason that if the local educational authorities see themselves as responsible for the delivery of education – and are seen as such – the quality of education will improve (Hannaway and Carnoy, 1993).

An extension of such reforms is public-school choice and the privatization of education (CERI, 1994b; UNESCO, 1993). Parents' choice is influenced to a great extent by conditions they perceive as desirable or undesirable (for example, the social composition of the school student body or because, for religious or educational reasons, they wish more or less curricular pluralism than is already provided); research shows that in fact "parents and children rarely choose schools on the basis of well-informed comparisons of educational quality" (CERI, 1994b, p. 7). Those advocating greater parental choice argue that the threat of "parent exit" would motivate teachers and principals to improve school quality – but there is no direct evidence that this threat of exit improves school performance. Certain school aims associated with effectiveness, such as the instilling of strong leadership or a sense of mission as well as parent involvement, may suffer if more active parents exit from the school. Nevertheless, a major argument in favour of privatization is its positive effect on competition between schools and on school and teacher accountability, hence on school quality (Behrman, 1993; CERI, 1994b; Psacharopoulos, 1994; Psacharopoulos, Tan and Jimenez, 1989).

Centralization

In the United States, for example, where formal education is highly decentralized, reforms have simultaneously called for greater centralization *and* school restructuring (placing greater control in the hands of teachers and principals). Centralization reforms have focused on higher learning standards, in the narrow sense of "a learning standard that an educational programme aims to help learners attain . . ." (UNESCO, 1993, p. 78). In its *Goals 2000* legislation (EFRC, 1994), the United States Congress moved towards requiring students everywhere in the United States to meet certain minimum standards for high-school graduation and towards raising average student achievement to the highest world levels in mathematics and science by the year 2000. Although the United States has not yet introduced national or state tests, a systemic reform aims at a national curriculum and centrally imposed requirements regarding academic achievement – on the grounds that in many of the countries where students achieve high academic levels, centrally imposed standards have raised overall performance.

Improved management of educational resources

Many proposals for improving educational outcomes rely on the introduction of a new "high-yield" approach to resources – which can significantly improve students' achievement at relatively low cost – and on better management and allocation of existing resources in schools. The introduction of high-yield resources implies universal access to school books in countries where pupils have been without textbooks (Lockheed and Verspoor, 1991), peer tutoring in higher-income countries where school supplies are widely available (Levin and Meister, 1986), and a "third television channel" using the full range of communications media available in a given society, in order to reach the "very large numbers of young people and adults who never had an opportunity to receive formal education of any kind, or who dropped out of the formal system before learning anything of value to themselves or society" (UNESCO, 1993, p. 64).

The main focus of "better management" – as reflected in the "effective schools" literature (see Lockheed and Levin, 1993) – is to increase teachers' efforts and powers of innovation and simultaneously to help teachers evolve effective alternative approaches to teaching (Levin, 1994). The aim is to produce high academic achievement with approximately the same set of physical assets and pupil populations as lower-achieving schools. In their defence of the case for increased privatization, advocates of vouchers in the United States and elsewhere have argued that, compared with public schools, privately managed schools are able to achieve higher academic standards whilst using the same or fewer resources because they have greater flexibility in the allocation of teachers' time (Carnoy, 1993). A similar set of arguments have been used to justify voucher plans in developing countries (Behrman, 1993).

Finally, the World Bank puts forward a strong argument (one which also underpins the thrust of the recommendations made at the 1990 World Conference on Education for All in Jomtien, Thailand) that public education in developing countries should focus on expanding and improving basic education because the pay-off – the "social rate of return" to resources invested at that level – is higher than to resources invested at the secondary and higher levels (Psacharopoulos, 1994; World Bank, 1994; Lockheed and Verspoor, 1991). This implies that there is a greater increase in economic productivity and the social good (as measured, for example, by improved children's health and nutrition and lower fertility rates) as a result of public spending on basic education rather than on higher education. By this argument it is socially more "efficient" to invest scarce public resources in the primary level, taking them away from secondary and (particularly) university education. Although this claim is contested (Ryoo, Nam and Carnoy, 1993), it does form the basis for much of the Bank's policy on the education sector.

Improved teacher recruitment and training

According to the OECD, "improving educational quality has become a widespread priority and in this the role of teachers is pivotal . . . Successful reform is realized by and through them" (OECD, 1992, p. 79). The OECD focuses mainly on reforms that would improve the recruitment and retention of high-quality teachers to schools and universities, on pre-service training to make them highly effective "knowledge transmitters", and on in-service training to maintain and develop their skills and interest. The "complex components of the profession's attractiveness" (see OECD, 1992, pp. 81-83) include not only teachers' relative salaries, but how teachers are regarded by society as a whole, the relative isolation teachers feel in their work and the degree to which they are treated as professionals by the education authorities. The latest research on the quality of teaching identifies a number of tangible and intangible factors to do with the individual teacher, the individual school and the broader policies of education authorities. The greatest challenge, according to the OECD, is to find the proper mix of variables at the different levels which "complement and reinforce one another, not conflict and compete" (see CERI, 1994a, pp. 113-117).

The ILO and UNESCO have argued that these issues are just as relevant in developing countries as in the industrialized economies of the OECD. Both organizations and the Joint ILO/UNESCO Committee of Experts on the Application of the Recommendation concerning the Status of Teachers (CEART) have also placed major emphasis on the training, working conditions and salaries of teachers (including those in technical and vocational education and training) as well as on their decision-making role in educational change at the national and the local levels; indeed, they consider these to be central to the improvement of quality in education (ILO/UNESCO, 1989 and 1994).

On the basis of empirical studies relating academic achievement to school inputs and pupils' socioeconomic background (school production function analysis), the World Bank argues strongly that the most effective way of improving pupil learning is to step up teachers' education in their subjects, and to provide less pre-service and more in-service training (Lockheed and Verspoor, 1991; World Bank, 1990). Bank analysts correctly describe current teachers' education programmes in developing countries as being of poor quality and badly in need of reform. Yet few Bank loans have included any requirements to improve pre-service training. Rather, the emphasis has been on recruiting teachers with little or no pre-service training and then giving them in-service training.

Finance-driven reforms

Of all the international agencies, the World Bank is the main advocate of "finance-driven" reforms. This should surprise no one. The Bank is a financial institution, and its concern with development arises partly because of its interest in reducing the cost of public service delivery. Policies over the past decade have focused on three areas of reform: (a) the shift of public funding for education from higher to lower levels of education; (b) the privatization of secondary and higher education in order to expand those levels; and (c) the reduction of costs per pupil at all levels of education, chiefly through control of the growth of salary costs by lowering qualification requirements, by increasing class size in primary and secondary education where student/teacher ratios are under 45 and/or by a more intensive use of teachers (multi-grade and multi-shift classes) (Farrell, 1993; Psacharopoulos, Tan and Jimenez, 1989; World Bank, 1990). In brief, this involves the following.

Shifting public funding from higher to lower levels of education

Higher education involves high costs and basic education relatively low costs. In many countries, public university education costs are heavily weighted toward non-teaching and non-research expenditures, such as student subsidies and administrative costs. Classroom space is often underused and many faculties operate with small numbers of students and diseconomies of scale. All this raises questions about the efficiency of public universities in many of the countries where they receive a high proportion of public resources. Further, in many of these same countries basic education is of low quality and drop-out rates are high. Shifting spending, it is argued, would enhance opportunities for large numbers of primary-school students, rather than subsidize students from an elite group whose families could mostly bear the costs of their university education.

The privatization of secondary and higher education

The principal argument for privatizing higher levels of education is that, given projected increases in demand in many countries, public funds will be insufficient to finance the expansion of secondary and higher education. So, for education to expand at those levels, developing nations will have to rely on students' families to finance a high proportion of school costs. This privatization may be carried out in two ways: (a) by allowing the creation of far more accredited private secondary schools and universities; and (b) by limiting the public assistance given to all schools (including public ones) and increasing fees charged to students to cover the gap between the cost per student and public assistance per student. International financial institutions have also focused on increasing community contributions to schools, both pecuniary and non-pecuniary. All these reforms basically advocate increased financing of schooling through user fees, whether the users be the community or individuals. The more privatized the level of schooling, the greater the user fee component in its funding. For efficiency and equity reasons, the World Bank has argued that the higher the level of schooling the greater should be the user-fee proportion of total financing.

The reduction of cost per student at all schooling levels

The World Bank's key proposals to reduce the public cost of schooling at all levels include: holding down the overall salary bill, increasing class size and making greater use of teaching in shifts. On the basis of a study of a number of school production function estimates relating pupil achievement to a series of school inputs, and taking pupils' socioeconomic background into account, Bank analysts conclude that the pupil/teacher ratio has essentially no effect on pupil achievement when class sizes range from 20 to 45 pupils per teacher (see, for example, Farrell and Oliveira, 1993; Fuller, 1985; Lockheed and Verspoor, 1991; Harbison and Hanushek, 1992; World Bank, 1990). In most developed and many developing countries, the average ratio is well below 45, although class sizes may exceed that ratio in the urban areas of many low-income countries. According to the Bank, countries with fewer than 45 pupils in a class could save significant public resources by increasing class size over time and also by using double or triple shifts. This would reduce the demand for teachers and allow for much more public spending on "high-yield, low-cost" resources (such as books and other supplies, or in-service training) that complement and enhance good teaching. Removing the link between teachers' salary levels and civil-service scales and reducing the requirements on formal qualifications would, it is maintained, free additional resources.

Equity-driven reforms

The shift of public spending from higher to lower levels of education and many of the competitiveness-driven reforms discussed above have been justified on the grounds of equity. They are also supposed to help education serve as an instrument of social mobility. For example, the Bank has consistently argued (with empirical support) that free public university education is a subsidy for higher-income groups at the expense of the poor (see Psacharopoulos, 1994, for an update on returns to education). A shift of public resources from higher levels of education to primary (basic) education implies favouring low-income groups over high-income groups in the delivery of educational services.

The main equity-driven reforms in developing countries are designed to achieve the following.

(a) To provide the lowest-income groups with high-quality basic education, especially the large number of youths and adults who do not currently have access to basic skills. The 1990 World Conference on Education for All was organized by the United Nations Development Programme, UNESCO, UNICEF, and the World Bank to focus attention on the equity implications of the challenges arising from the need to expand basic education in developing countries (WCEFA, 1990a and b). Some of the reforms proposed were financial, but many sought to improve the quality of teaching, to increase the time teachers spend in schools, to make school supplies available to children from low-income families and to improve school curricula. Some agencies, including UNESCO, have also recommended special educational programmes, such as distance learning and non-formal education (UNESCO, 1993).

(b) To reach certain groups who lag behind educationally, e.g. women and rural populations. There is particular concern about women's education because of the crucial role that women play in economic development, social change, raising children and decisions about fertility. High fertility rates and low life expectancies at birth are both associated with high rates of female illiteracy (UNESCO, 1993; Carnoy, 1992). Rural populations in developing countries traditionally receive much less education – in terms of both quality and quantity – though most countries would benefit from investing in education to increase agricultural productivity for their continued economic development.

In OECD countries, equity-driven reforms tend to be targeted at particular students throughout the educational system who are "at risk" (i.e. on low incomes) or who have special needs, and to focus on reforms to increase their success at school. These include special programmes aimed at improving retention and student achievement, including special, multicultural and bilingual ones for speakers of minority languages and "head-start" early-education programmes, and programmes for transition from school to work which combine school curricula with apprenticeship training and after-school activities designed to increase pupil motivation and parent involvement. The reforms often include special training for the teachers involved.

Conflicts between reforms

Whereas all countries have proposed – and sometimes implemented – all three types of reforms in the context of structural adjustment, the OECD countries and most of the Asian NICs have tended to focus on competitiveness-induced reforms. Some OECD countries, such as Australia, Canada, New Zealand, the United States and many European countries, have also emphasized equity-driven reforms. The heavily indebted countries of Latin America and Africa have been obliged to focus almost exclusively on finance-induced reforms.

This holds true even in the case of a specific reform. A good example is school decentralization. In OECD countries, school decentralization reform focuses primarily on shifting management control over schools rather than expenditure cuts. In Africa, Latin America, and even the rapidly growing countries of Asia, the main objective of decentralization is to shift government's financial management responsibility, including the negotiation of teachers' salaries, on to state and local jurisdictions – thus reducing central government spending and public spending in general.

Despite the competitiveness and equity justification for all finance-driven reforms associated with structural adjustment policies, such reforms tend to have economic and educational effects which fail to increase (indeed which can even undermine) educational quality and equity. Despite calls to reduce public spending on higher education and increase spending on primary schooling, in practice when incomes have declined the decreased public spending on education in most countries has forced low-income children out of school. A recent World Bank paper refers to Cornia, Jolly and Stewart (1987) in arguing that: "Because SALs focus on correcting imbalances in the economy and laying the foundations for growth rather than on equity, the particular forms taken by cuts in subsidies, real wages, and real education expenditures have high social costs, at least until the economy begins to grow"; referring to Griffin and Knight (1989) it continues with the argument that "in many Third World countries human development programs are 'savagely' cut and long-term prospects for development diminish while inequality and poverty increase" (Noss, 1991, p. 4).

The combination of economic crisis and structural adjustment results not only in public expenditure cuts but usually also in lowered incomes; in the case of SAPs, it tends to reduce incomes unequally, affecting the poor (although not necessarily all subgroups of the poor) more than those with high incomes. And, concerning education, as these drops in income are accompanied by pressures to replace decreased public spending with increased private contributions to schools (higher user fees or lower subsidies, for example), there is a fall-off in the demand for schooling. The declining health and nutrition standards which may accompany structural adjustment can also reduce attendance at school. On the other hand, higher unemployment rates tend to increase the demand for schooling, especially at secondary and tertiary levels, and to involve a corresponding decline in income.

The case for finance-based reforms is persuasive. In many countries, harsh economic reality dictates that public resources are not – and probably will not become – available to provide a full and reasonably high-quality basic education to all children; meanwhile secondary and higher education are heavily subsidized by the public sector. Low-income countries experiencing slow economic growth must find private resources for higher levels of schooling if they are to provide the skills needed in today's world. High-income countries in a slow-growth world economy also have to allocate public resources more effectively if they are to continue to deliver high-quality public services. Further, the World Bank makes a good case that freely provided education at university and, in some countries, upper-secondary levels unnecessarily subsidizes students whose families generally could afford to contribute substantially towards their education – this at the expense of poorly funded basic education for the mass of children. The Bank also argues convincingly that other savings could be made through a more efficient allocation of resources in the education sector (Lockheed and Verspoor, 1991).

That having been said, however, World Bank policies may themselves be contributing to the shortage of public resources for education. First, structural adjustment loans require the reduction of public sector spending, and every government views educational expenditures as part of that package. Bank analysis has suggested that higher intensity structural adjustment is associated with greater reductions in educational spending (Noss, 1991). Second, even if the Bank has responded to the undesirable impact of structural adjustment policies on education by greatly expanding its lending to the education sector, its conditions for these loans may mean that the public effort in education is reduced in the long run. Indeed, the combination of these policies, including strong recommendations to privatize, reduces the pressure on governments to raise public spending on education.

A particularly disturbing threat to the enhancement of academic achievement is the World Bank's usually implicit (but sometimes explicit) emphasis on specifically reducing public expenditure on teachers' salaries. From a finance-reform perspective, this follows a certain logic, since salaries represent such a high proportion of total public expenditure on education. Bank policy has retreated from its earlier position that reducing teachers' salaries was the *sine qua non* of its finance-based reforms. Moreover, by the beginning of the 1990s, its policy on primary education identified good salaries and benefits, working conditions and career advancement opportunities as important factors in teacher motivation. Recent Bank documents seem to reflect a strong commitment to improving teaching through better recruitment and training (Lockheed and Verspoor, 1991; Farrell and Oliveira, 1993). But because of these overall reforms, teachers have borne the brunt of government attempts to reduce costs – and hence are often perceived as the villains and the cause of the increasing difficulties faced by most countries' schools. The Bank's present focus on privatization, freezing salary costs, and increasing class size continues to give the impression to governments that an increase in teachers' workload and a reduction in their qualifications and pay would not have deleterious effects on pupil performance. Indeed, when teachers resist externally imposed reforms that worsen their teaching conditions, their organizations are singled out as the major obstacle to educational improvement.

Most importantly, however, policies that serve to undermine the value of public education and of public-school teachers ignore the fundamental political realities involved in raising the quality of education. Given that teachers continue to work largely unsupervised behind the closed doors of classrooms, if nations hope to increase the cognitive skills of their young people through education they will have to rely on autonomous, motivated and skilled professional teachers trained in public institutions to do so. Teachers' self-perception, the degree of their commitment to pupils' academic success, their willingness to learn to do their job better and their teaching abilities are all key elements in the production of basic and advanced learning in any society (ILO/UNESCO, 1989; CERI, 1994a). In order to obtain teachers' commitment and involvement, the management system must take their needs into account and involve them in improving the quality of education. Improving teaching skills inevitably requires a heavy dose of public sector involvement, and not just at the basic education level. It is well to remember that the immense United States higher education system is 90 per cent public (United States Department of Education, 1994). Almost everywhere in the world, the training, recruitment and professional development of teachers through in-service training are financed and managed by the public sector. If schools are to be improved, it is the public sector that will be largely responsible, with private education acting as a complement not a substitute (ILO, 1991).

Has the quality of education declined?

Many observers consider that the most important policy concern is whether educational quality declines in countries that cut educational expenditure per pupil. On the basis of case-studies undertaken in Africa and Latin America, Woodhall (1994) concludes that this is indeed what has been occurring. If school production function results are to be believed, however, large increases in class size and reductions in spending on teachers' salaries do not necessarily reduce pupil achievement (Harbison and Hanushek, 1992, cited in Behrman, 1993, who nevertheless points out methodological weaknesses in many of these studies). Such production functions relating school inputs to outputs are estimated with individual pupil data at a single point in time. However, research carried out in the United States on variations in achievement over time suggests that when schools suffer from considerable underfunding – as schools for black children in the southern United States did in the 1940s and 1950s – increased funds lead to improved quality (Card and Krueger, 1992a), and that in turn, such quality changes in education positively affect wages in periods when wages are rising (Card and Krueger, 1992b; Carnoy, 1994).

In the developing countries time series data on school achievement are practically non-existent. The International Educational Assessment has included a number of developing countries, but the data are not available over time. In what represents a rare case, Chile has carried out a longitudinal assessment of its "municipalization" reform of 1980; under this reform, the management of primary schools was turned over to municipalities and a voucher plan implemented, in which the Chilean Government allowed parents to spend for each of their children at a private school the equivalent of the public cost per pupil. This gave rise to large numbers of subsidized private schools. Since that reform and others (e.g. the drastic privatization of the university and secondary levels and its consequent reduction in teachers' salaries) conformed closely with sectoral adjustment conditions imposed by the World Bank, the Chilean assessment can give us some indication of the impact of structural adjustment on school achievement. National examinations in Spanish and mathematics were held for fourth grade pupils in 1982, 1988 and 1990. The Spanish scores rose slightly for middle-class pupils in both subsidized private schools and municipal schools through the period 1982-88, but fell for pupils in fully private schools (only middle- and upper-socioeconomic classes represented) and for lower social class pupils in both subsidized private schools and municipal schools (Prawda, 1993). In each of the three years, middle-class pupils obtained higher scores in the private subsidized schools and lower social class pupils did as well or better in municipal schools (Prawda, 1993; Tedesco, 1992). Average scores were low by international standards. In mathematics, these tendencies were less pronounced in terms of spreading inequity, but otherwise similar: middle-class students seemed to benefit from the reform, but lower social class students did not (Prawda, 1993; Tedesco, 1992). In any case, the gains were modest, even for middle-class students. Furthermore, according to a task force reporting in 1994 on the state of Chilean education, there had been no significant changes made in the 1980s in the curriculum or pedagogy as a result of the 1980 reform (Comité Técnico, 1994). Since a third of all primary-school pupils come from families in the bottom 20 per cent of income-earners, and 56 per cent from the bottom 40 per cent, the decline in test scores for the lowest groups suggests that the reform may have had an adverse effect on the majority of pupils.

A more common (and readily available) indicator of quality change is the proportion of pupils reaching the fourth grade of primary school. However, care must be taken when interpreting this figure, because the success rate can easily be raised by reducing repetition ("staying down") in earlier grades – and repetition is not usually a function of school quality (as many analysts contend) but rather of the number of places available at the next level of schooling. Most countries make their decisions about how many pupils should proceed to the secondary level on institutional and financial grounds, not on whether the achievements of the school-age population at primary level warrant it. Although a rise in the proportion of pupils reaching fourth grade does not necessarily mean an increase in primary-school quality, a decline almost certainly reflects an undesirable trend. Either students' families are facing economic hardship that prevent them from sending their children to school, or the school is raising the financial requirements so much that some children are forced to leave, or yet conditions in the schools are worsening to such a degree that pupils are more likely to repeat and then drop out.

Data for 51 developing countries show that 13 had declining proportions of pupils reaching fourth grade, of which seven were in Africa (UNESCO, 1993, table 5). There is no strict relation between structural adjustment and these changes. Among the 21 African countries for which data were obtainable, in seven (Congo, Côte d'Ivoire, Kenya, Lesotho, Togo, Zaire, Zimbabwe) the proportion reaching fourth grade fell in the 1980s. Three of these countries raised their public spending as a proportion of GNP. In Congo and Côte d'Ivoire, the retention rate declined from the 90-per-cent range to the 80-per-cent range; in other countries, however, the drop was to much lower percentage ranges, indicating that things went from not very good to much worse. Only four countries made substantial gains (Burkina

Faso, Ethiopia, Malawi and Niger). The other ten countries held even. Only four of those did so because they already had over 90 per cent reaching grade four (Botswana, Mauritius, Senegal, United Republic of Tanzania). Significantly, three of the four countries making gains were in the group that had increased public spending as a percentage of GNP, and none of the countries in the negative GNP per capita growth plus growth of public spending/GNP group made gains.

Yet the Latin American data suggest that reduced poverty appears to have a greater effect on the drop-out rates from primary school than does increased spending on education. Brazil, Mexico and Venezuela – all countries with substantial increases in the poverty rate (Lustig, 1995) – reported lower retention rates at fourth grade, but a number of countries made large gains in retention rates. Most of them, including Colombia, Costa Rica and Paraguay, lowered their poverty rates during the 1980s. But that was not true of Chile, which nevertheless made a large gain in the proportion reaching the fourth grade.

The available data on the quality of education therefore send a mixed message on the effects of structural adjustment. Financially-driven structural adjustment measures have not improved average educational performance, and there is some evidence that disparities in performance have increased. From the Chilean data, it appears that for pupils from low-income families (who represent a large proportion of all primary-school students), decentralization, cuts in spending and privatization – all ingredients of structural adjustment – have lowered the quality of their education. If data on pupil achievement were available from other countries in Latin America and Africa hit hard by a combination of deteriorating economic conditions and structural adjustment policies, the results would probably be similar.

Are there alternative approaches?

For many of the countries that began the structural adjustment process in the 1980s the worst is over; economic growth per capita is positive and education budgets are again on the rise in absolute terms. Yet, international agencies committed to public sector austerity continue to push for educational reforms that reflect structural adjustment thinking – and more specifically, public austerity in education. The conceptual legacy of these policies continues and therefore so does its impact on education and teachers – hence the focus in this article on those policies.

The financially-driven educational reform policies responded to certain imperatives of new economic conditions – but did so in a way that tried to "Taylorize" teachers as delivery workers. The reforms met few, if any, of the conditions required to enhance the learning environment in schools. In that sense, they were largely counterproductive to producing and delivering higher quality education.

There is arguably an alternative to that particular model of educational reform. Some countries have reduced public spending as a percentage of

GNP, but because of relatively rapid increases in GNP were able to increase public spending and spending on education. Other countries had (moderate) negative per capita economic growth but were able to maintain per pupil spending in education by allowing their public spending to rise as a percentage of GNP. Many of these countries were able to improve the conditions in schools and to maintain teacher pay while doing so. In those developing countries with positive per capita GNP growth that did not implement traditional structural adjustment policies – mostly in Asia – the main changes that occurred during this period were a lowering of class size, higher teacher salaries, fewer total hours worked per month (Republic of Korea, for example) and increased bonuses for working in rural areas (Indonesia, for example). This is particularly significant because international agencies have given Asian countries as examples of how to deliver high-quality education at low cost per pupil (large class sizes, many hours per month worked by teachers, relatively low teachers' salaries compared to average wages). Indeed, a primary/lower secondary school teacher in the Republic of Korea earned three times the per capita income in 1993 and twice the average income per employed worker. The ratio to average worker income is higher than in most countries in the world, including Japan or the United States (Cox Edwards, 1993; information provided directly by the Ministry of Labour, Republic of Korea). The Republic of Korea and other east Asian countries also reduced their pupil-teacher ratios in the 1980s.

Other developing countries are likely to adopt the same approach as the east Asian countries – i.e. to improve material conditions for education workers – once their economies recover from the influence of high capital costs and low commodity prices. In the context of the east Asian NICs, higher pay appears to be part of an implicit arrangement in which workers' rights to strike or bargain collectively are restricted. The model may be regarded as "traditional industrial", with employed teachers rewarded with a higher standard of living from the greater per capita output generated by the economy as a whole, with little effort given to changing the educational process with the improvement in material conditions and a reduction in class size.

With the focus on financially driven reforms in the 1980s, and the resulting major reductions in teacher salaries and educational materials, it is quite possible that economic recovery in Latin America, and Africa, will result primarily in an Asian-NIC-style financial restoration in the 1990s. There is evidence that such financial restoration is taking place in many countries of Latin America and Africa. Public educational expenditures, and with them teacher salaries, are increasing again. Some countries in Latin America, where teacher salaries fell substantially in the 1980s – for example, Chile, Costa Rica and Mexico – have all increased salaries in the 1990s – even though it took court action in Costa Rica and a democratically elected social-democratic government in Chile to obtain the changes. And, following the financial restoration scenario, little else about education is transformed in this process.

Financial decentralization reforms, e.g. in Latin America, could lead to more teacher participation in educational decision-making. However, this will depend upon the teachers' organizations themselves; they must become much more powerful educational actors at the state and local government levels than they have been at the central government level. In Chile, the return to democracy in 1990 led to the restoration of teachers' bargaining rights and an increased role in educational decision-making at the central government level. This has had a significant impact on the role of teachers in negotiation and consultation at the municipal level. In Mexico, it appears that, on the collective bargaining side, some state teachers' union locals are successfully bargaining for salary "add-ons". But beyond that, there is little evidence yet that financial decentralization has had any implications in Mexico for a different, more participative, model of educational management and delivery. Basically, teachers' material working conditions have improved and their work has become less arduous, but what remains unchanged are assumptions of how education should be organized, learning enhanced and teachers trained and employed. And teachers' participation in this decision-making remains limited.

The alternative model does not preclude financial and managerial efficiency. Indeed, it sets out to attain more for a given amount of resources than do structural adjustment models. The latter are mainly concerned with cutting the cost of schooling, assuming – incorrectly – that school quality does not decline with lower teacher salaries and larger classes. And even if that assumption were correct, the structural adjustment strategy effectively places less emphasis on learning improvement than on learning maintenance at lower cost, even in the longer run.

References

Amsden, Alice H. 1989. *Asia's next giant: South Korea and late industrialization*. New York, Oxford University Press.

Behrman, Jere R. 1993. *The contribution of human capital to economic development: Some selected issues*. World Employment Programme Research Working Paper No. 36, WEP 2-46/WP.36. Geneva, ILO.

Bello, Walden. 1993. *Dark victory: The U.S., structural adjustment and global poverty*. Oakland, CA, Institute for Food and Development Policy.

Birdsall, Nancy; Sabot, Richard. 1993. *Virtuous circles: Human capital, growth and equity in East Asia*. Policy Research Department Paper prepared for the World Bank research project on "Strategies for Rapid Growth: Public Policy and the Asian Miracle". Washington, DC, World Bank.

Card, David; Krueger, Anne. 1992a. "Does school quality matter? Returns to education and the characteristics of public schools in the United States", in *Journal of Political Economy* (Chicago), Vol. 100, No. 1 (Feb.), pp. 1-40.

—;—. 1992b. "School quality and black/white relative earnings: A direct assessment", in *Quarterly Journal of Economics* (Cambridge, MA), Vol. 107, No. 1 (Feb.), pp. 151-200.

Carnoy, Martin. 1994. *Faded dreams: The politics and economics of race in America*. Cambridge, Cambridge University Press.

—. 1993. "School improvement: Is privatization the answer?", in Jane Hannaway and Martin Carnoy (eds.): *Decentralization and school improvement*. San Francisco, CA, Jossey-Bass, pp. 163-201.

—. 1992. *The case for investing in basic education*. New York, UNICEF.

—; Torres, C. A. 1994. "Educational change and structural adjustment: A case study of Costa Rica", in J. Samoff (ed.): *Coping with crisis: Austerity, adjustment and human resources*. Paris, Cassell/UNESCO, Chapter 5.

Castells, Manuel. 1991. *Four Asian tigers with a dragon head: A comparative analysis of the State, economy and society in the Asian Pacific Rim*. Madrid, Instituto Universitario de Sociología de Nuevas Tecnologías, Universidad Autónoma de Madrid.

Centre for Educational Research and Innovation (CERI). 1994a. *Quality in teaching*. Paris, OECD.

—. 1994b. *School: A matter of choice*. Paris, OECD.

Comité Técnico. 1994. *Los desafíos de la educación Chilena frente al siglo 21*. Comité Técnico Asesor del Diálogo Nacional sobre la Modernización de la Educación Chilena designado por S.E. el Presidente de la República. Santiago de Chile.

Cornia, Giovanni Andrea; Jolly, Richard; Stewart, Frances. 1987. *Adjustment with a human face*. Vol. 1. Oxford, Clarendon Press.

Cox Edwards, Alejandra. 1993. "Teacher compensation in developing countries", in Joseph P. Farrell and João B. Oliveira (eds.): *Teachers in developing countries: Improving effectiveness and managing costs*. Washington, DC, World Bank, pp. 53-66.

Education Funding Research Council (EFRC). 1994. *Goals 2000: A national framework for America's Schools*. Arlington, VA, EFRC.

Farrell, Joseph P. 1993. "International lessons for school effectiveness", in Joseph Farrell and João B. Oliveira (eds.): *Teachers in developing countries: Improving effectiveness and managing costs*. Washington, DC, World Bank.

—; Oliveira, João B. (eds.). 1993. *Teachers in developing countries: Improving effectiveness and managing costs*. Washington, DC, World Bank.

Fuller, Bruce. 1985. *Raising school quality in developing countries: What investments boost learning?* Education and Training Series Discussion Paper, Report No. EDT 7. Washington, DC, World Bank.

Griffin, Keith; Knight, John. 1989. "Human development: The case for renewed emphasis", in *Journal of Development Planning* (New York), No. 19, pp. 9-40.

Hannaway, Jane; Carnoy, Martin (eds.). 1993. *Decentralization and school improvement*. San Francisco, Jossey-Bass.

Harbison, Ralph; Hanushek, Eric. 1992. *Educational performance of the poor: Lessons from rural northeast Brazil*. New York, Oxford University Press.

Harrison, Bennett; Bluestone, Barry. 1988. *The great U-turn: Corporate restructuring and the polarizing of America*. New York, Basic Books.

Iglesias, Enrique. 1992. *Reflections on economic development: Toward a new Latin American consensus*. Washington, DC, Inter-American Development Bank.

ILO. 1991. *Final report of the Second Joint Meeting on Conditions of Work of Teachers*. JMEWCT/2/1991/15. Geneva.

ILO/UNESCO. 1994. *Report of the Joint ILO/UNESCO Committee of Experts on the Application of the Recommendation concerning the Status of Teachers*. CEART/VI/1994/12. Geneva, ILO.

—. 1989. *Report of the Joint ILO/UNESCO Committee of Experts on the Application of the Recommendation concerning the Status of Teachers*. CEART/V/1988/5. Geneva, ILO.

Kakwani, Nanak; Makonnen, Elena; Van der Gaag, Jacques. 1990. *Structural adjustment and living conditions in developing countries*. PRE Working Paper WPS 407. Washington, DC, World Bank.

Levin, Henry M. 1994. "Learning from accelerated schools", in James H. Block, Susan Toft Everson and Thomas R. Guskey (eds.): *School improvement programs: A handbook for educational leaders*. New York, Scholastic Books.

—; Meister, Gail. 1986. "Is CAI cost-effective?", in *Phi Delta Kappan* (Bloomington, IN), Vol. 67, No. 10 (June), pp. 745-749.

Lockheed, Marlaine E.; Verspoor, Adriaan M. 1991. *Improving primary education in developing countries*. Oxford, Oxford University Press.

—; Levin, Henry. 1993. *Creating effective schools*. London, Falmer Press.

Lucas, Robert E. B. 1994. "The impact of structural adjustment on training needs", in *International Labour Review* (Geneva), Vol. 133, No. 5-6, pp. 677-694.

Lustig, Nora (ed.). 1995. *Coping with austerity: Poverty and inequality in Latin America*. Washington, DC, The Brookings Institution.

Noss, Andrew. 1991. *Education and adjustment: A review of the literature*. Population and Human Resources Department Working Paper, WPS 701. Washington, DC, World Bank.

Organization for Economic Cooperation and Development (OECD). 1992. *High-quality education and training for all*. Paris.

Prawda, Juan. 1993. "Educational decentralization in Latin America: Lessons learned", in *International Journal of Educational Development* (Oxford), Vol. 13, No. 3, pp. 253-264.

Psacharopoulos, George. 1994. "Returns to investment in education: A global update", in *World Development* (Oxford), Vol. 22, No. 9, pp. 1325-1343.

—; Tan, Jee-Peng; Jimenez, Emmanuel. 1989. "Financing education in developing countries", in *IDS Bulletin* (London), Vol. 20, No. 1, pp. 55-58.

Reimers, Fernando; Tiburcio, Luis. 1993. *Education, adjustment and reconstruction: Options for change*. Paris, UNESCO.

Ryoo, Jai-Kyung; Nam, Young-Sook; Carnoy, Martin. 1993. "Changing rates of return to education over time: A Korean case study", in *Economics of Education Review* (Oxford), Vol. 12, No. 1, pp. 71-80.

Tedesco, Juan Carlos. 1992. "Nuevas estrategias de cambio educativo en América Latina", in *Boletín del Proyecto Principal de Educación en América Latina y el Caribe* (Santiago de Chile), No. 28 (Aug.), pp. 7-24.

Thomas, Christopher; Verspoor, Adriaan M. 1994. *Education sector lending instruments*. Mimeo. Washington, DC, World Bank.

United Nations Educational, Scientific and Cultural Organization (UNESCO). 1993. *World Education Report, 1993*. Paris.

United States Department of Education, National Center for Educational Statistics (NCES). 1994. *Digest of Educational Statistics*. Washington, DC.

Woodhall, Maureen. 1994. "The effects of austerity and adjustment on the allocation and use of resources: A comparative analysis of five case studies", in Joel Samoff (ed.): *Coping with crisis: Austerity, adjustment and human resources*. Paris, Cassell/UNESCO, p. 175.

—. 1991. *Education and training under conditions of economic austerity and restructuring*. Paris, UNESCO, Bureau for the Coordination of operational activities.

World Bank. 1994. *Governance: The World Bank's experience*. Washington, DC.

—. 1990. *Primary education*. A World Bank policy paper. Washington, DC.

World Conference on Education for All (WCEFA). 1990a. *World Declaration on Education for All*. New York, UNDP.

—. 1990b. *Framework for Action to Meet Basic Learning Needs*. New York, UNDP.

[11]

POLITICS, MARKETS, AND THE ORGANIZATION OF SCHOOLS

JOHN E. CHUBB
The Brookings Institution
TERRY M. MOE
Stanford University

We offer a comparative analysis of public and private schools, presenting data from a new national study—the Administrator and Teacher Survey—that expands on the pathbreaking High School and Beyond survey. We find that public and private schools are distinctively different in environment and organization. Most importantly, private schools are more likely to possess the characteristics widely believed to produce effectiveness. We argue throughout that the differences across the sectors are anchored in the logic of politics and markets. This argument derives from our belief that environmental context has pervasive consequences for the organization and operation of all schools and specifically that the key differences between public and private environments—and thus between public and private schools —derive from their characteristic methods of social control: the public schools are subordinates in a hierarchic system of democratic politics, whereas private schools are largely autonomous actors "controlled" by the market.

Virtually all public schools in the United States are governed by democratic institutions of the same basic form. This form is now taken for granted. There is a broad consensus that democratic control of the public schools is a good thing and that democratic control means control through local school boards, superintendents, central office bureaucracies, and corresponding apparatuses at the state and (increasingly) the federal levels. However heated the conflict over educational policy and practice, however intense the struggle for influence and resources, the "one best system" stands above it all (Tyack 1974).

In recent years, educational politics has centered on the quality of the public schools. Long-simmering discontent about declining test scores, loose academic standards, and lax discipline—fueled by a series of national studies—has engendered a widespread reaction against the "rising tide of mediocrity" (National Commission on Excellence in Education 1983), and state legislatures around the country have responded with reforms ranging from stricter academic requirements to merit pay plans for teachers (Doyle and Hartle 1985). Throughout this period, the "one best system" has provided the institutional framework within which problems have been identified and policy responses chosen. It structures criticism and reform, but it is never their target.

Much the same is true within educational research, which has generally taken institutions as given. Studies of school effectiveness have focused directly on the

AMERICAN POLITICAL SCIENCE REVIEW
VOL. 82 NO. 4 DECEMBER 1988

schools, asking about those aspects of organization and immediate environment that explain school performance. Taken as a whole, this work has promoted a loose consensus on factors that appear to enhance effectiveness, among them, clear school goals, rigorous academic requirements, an orderly climate, strong instructional leadership by the principal, teacher participation in decision making, cooperative principal-teacher relations, active parental involvement, and high expectations for student performance (Boyer 1983; Brookover et al. 1979; Goodlad 1984; Powell, Farrar, and Cohen 1985; Rutter et al. 1979; Sizer 1984).

This research has shaped the contours of public debate by suggesting traits good schools ought to have. But it is the institutional system itself, accepted by one and all, that tells us how these desirable features are to be transmitted to the schools: they are to be imposed from above. For many objectives—tougher academic requirements, say—reform simply calls for new legislative or district policy. Not coincidentally, these have been among the more popular reforms. Other objectives are less amenable to formal imposition—cooperative relations within the school, for example. But these tend to be regarded as matters of good management and training, and thus as reforms that can be delegated to the professional side of the control structure. Whether the means are formal or professional, then, the rationale of democratic control is to "make" schools more effective by imposing desirable traits on them (Campbell et al. 1985).

These reforms are likely to fail. To see why, it is useful to begin with a curious feature of the way schools are conventionally understood. Among those who study education, it is received doctrine that schools are open systems and thus products of their environments (Scott and Meyer 1984; Weick 1976). By this logic it should follow that the organization and performance of schools are largely explainable by the environments that surround them. Different types of environments should tend to produce different types of schools. When schools turn out to have undesirable characteristics, the logical culprit is the environment—not the schools.

Yet studies of school effectiveness have rarely taken the environment seriously. They tend to explain poor performance in terms of variables inside and immediately outside the school—and then they turn to our institutions of democratic control to make the necessary changes. Our institutions, however, are core components of the very environment that by open systems reasoning is likely to have caused the problems in the first place. These studies should be asking, What is the relationship between democratic control and the organization of schools? Might there be something inherent in these institutions that systematically promotes organizations of a type no one really wants?

We do not pretend to have all the answers. We do think, however, that institutions are fundamental to an understanding of schools. Here we try to make a plausible case for this view by developing a theoretical argument and presenting some new evidence from a recent survey.

Our basic argument is that the organization of schools is largely endogenous to the system of institutional control in which the schools are embedded. Different systems of institutional control should tend to produce schools with distinctive patterns of characteristics. While we will specify these patterns in some detail, our most general claim is simply that the hierarchy of democratic control, the "one best system," puts its stamp on the organization of our public schools and that this stamp holds the key to school quality and school reform.

Institutional issues are often difficult to explore through empirical research. This is especially true in studying the "one best system." How can we study institutional effects if there is only one, all-encompassing institution? An instructive way to proceed, we believe, is to compare public schools to those schools that fall outside the hierarchy of democratic control: private schools.

That is what we do here. We explore the logic of institutional control in the two sectors and derive implications for schools. This line of reasoning suggests that schools should indeed look different across sectors and, most importantly, that democratic control should inhibit the emergence of "effective school" characteristics. Using data obtained from a representative sample of public and private high schools, we compare them on a range of characteristics commonly associated with effective academic performance. These results consistently suggest that institutions are important determinants of school organization—and that, in consequence, public schools are quite literally at a systematic disadvantage.

Politics, Markets, and Control

Public schools are controlled by democratic authority and administration. The specifics vary from district to district and state to state, but the basic framework is remarkably uniform throughout the country. The private sector might seem to lack any comparable uniformity. Most private schools are affiliated with a church; some are elite preparatory schools; some are military academies; and there are other types as well (Kraushaar 1972). But they all have two important institutional features in common: society does not control them directly through democratic politics, and society does control them—indirectly—through the marketplace. Rather than marvel at diversity, we find it useful to think about schools in terms of these alternative institutions of social control. As a shorthand, we will refer to them as politics and markets.

We want to provide a little background on how these institutions operate and what they imply for schools. We will not yet relate them to specific aspects of school organization. This will be done later when we turn to a discussion of the survey data.

Constituents and Consumers

Popular myth lauds the role of local citizens and their elected school boards in governing the public schools. But the fact is that the schools are not locally controlled and are not supposed to be. The state and federal governments have legitimate roles to play in financing schools, setting standards, and otherwise imposing their own policies. This means that U.S. citizens everywhere, whether or not they have children in school and whether or not they live in the district or even the state, have a legitimate hand in governing each school (Campbell et al. 1985; Wirt and Kirst 1982).

The proper constituency of even a single public school is a huge and heterogeneous one whose interests are variously represented by formally prescribed agents—politicians and administrators—at all levels of government. Parents and students, therefore, are but a small part of the legitimate constituency of "their own" schools. The schools are not meant to be theirs to control and are literally not supposed to provide the kind of education they might want. Public education is shaped by larger social purposes as defined by larger constituencies.

Private schools determine their own goals, standards, and methods. These may reflect the values of owners or patrons, or perhaps a collective such as a diocese. But the market imposes a fundamental constraint. Private schools provide services in exchange for payment, and unless heavily subsidized from the outside, they must please their consumers —students and parents—if they are to prosper. Whatever the constituency of the private school, therefore, it will surely be much smaller and more homogeneous than the democratic constituency of the public school, and students and parents will occupy a much more central position within it.

Exit and Voice

In the private marketplace, educational choice is founded on what has come to be called, following Hirschman (1970), the *exit* option. If parents and students do not like the services they are being provided, they can exit and find another school whose offerings are more congruent with their needs. This process of selection promotes a match between what educational consumers want and what their schools supply. Matching is reinforced by the population effects (Alchian 1950) of selection: schools that fail to satisfy a sufficiently large clientele will be weeded out (or, if subsidized, become an increasing burden).

Selection also forges a strong bond between consumer satisfaction and organizational well-being. This gives schools incentives to please their clientele, as well as to set up *voice* mechanisms—committees, associations—that build a capacity for responsiveness into organizational structure. These incentives, too, promote a match—but they are not necessary for success. A school might rigidly adhere to purist doctrine yet succeed because that is what enough consumers happen to want. Either way, the result tends to be the same: a match.

In the public sector, popular control is built around voice. Exit plays a minimal role. The public school is usually a local monopoly, in the sense that all children living in a given area are assigned to a particular school. This does not eliminate choice, since parents can take account of school quality in deciding where to live. But residential decisions involve many factors in addition to education, and once they are made, sunk costs are high.[1] Low or declining quality need not keep parents from moving into an area, and it is even less likely to prompt existing residents to pick up and leave.

It might prompt them to consider a private school. But here they confront a major disincentive: public schools are free, private schools are not. Due to this cost differential, the perceived value of private schools must far outweigh that of public schools if they are to win students. To put it the other way round, public schools, because they are relatively inexpensive, can attract students without seeming to be particularly good at educating them.

Lacking a real exit option, many parents and students will choose a public school despite dissatisfaction with its goals, methods, or personnel. Having done so, they have a right to voice their preferences through the democratic control structure—but everyone else has the same rights, and many are well armed and organized. Voice cannot remedy the mismatch between what parents and students want and what schools provide. Conflict and disharmony are built into the system.

Autonomy and Control

In the private sector, the exit option not only promotes harmony and responsiveness, it also promotes school autonomy. This is true even for schools that are part of a hierarchy, as the Catholic schools are. The reason is that most of the technology and resources needed to please clients are inherently present at the bottom of the hierarchy—in the school—since educational services are based on personal relationships and interactions, on continual feedback, and on the knowledge, skills, and experience of teachers. The school is thus in the best position to know how to enhance its own organizational well-being. Hierarchical control, or any external imposition, tends to be inefficient and counterproductive.[2]

Organization of Schools

Central direction is important when superiors have an agenda of their own that cannot be pursued simply by pleasing clients. In the private sector, imposition of such an agenda involves a trade-off: if schools are constrained in their efforts to please clients, dissatisfied clients can leave. In some hierarchies—notably, those associated with churches—superiors may consider this an acceptable price; they may prefer "pure" schools to growing, prosperous ones. But it is still a price, one that threatens organizational well-being—and one that in the limit can be fatal. Thus, even if there are higher-order values to be pursued, the exit option discourages tight external control in favor of school autonomy.

In the public sector the institutional forces work in the opposite direction. The raison d'être of democratic control is to impose higher-order values on schools and thus limit their autonomy. Exit is an obstacle to control: when the governance structure imposes a policy on parents and students who disagree, exit allows them to avoid compliance by "voting with their feet," thus defeating the purpose of the policy. But public officials do not have to take exit as a given. They can simply pass laws restricting its availability. While private decision makers value autonomy because it helps them cope with problems of exit, public officials eliminate exit in order to facilitate their imposition of higher-order values.

The drive to restrict autonomy is built into the incentive structures of politicians and bureaucrats. Politicians seek political support by responding to various constituency groups, particularly those that are well organized and active. These include teachers' unions and associations of administrators, but also a vast array of groups representing more specialized interests—those of minorities, the handicapped, bilingual education, drivers' education, schools of education, book publishers, and accrediting and testing organizations, among others. These groups typically have financial or occupational stakes in existing educational arrangements, and their policy positions reflect as much. They all want a share of the public's educational resources. They want to influence educational programs. They want to have a say in how the schools are organized and operated. And politicians are only too happy to oblige—this is the path to political popularity (Masters, Salisbury, and Eliot 1964; Iannaccone 1967; Peterson 1976; Wirt and Kirst 1982).

Bureaucrats play both sides of the governmental fence. Their power rests on the fact that bureaucracy is essential to direct democratic control. The imposition of higher-order values is hardly automatic, particularly given the built-in dissatisfaction of parents and students and the inevitable pressures from teachers and principals for autonomy. Control requires rules and regulations, monitoring, incentive structures, and other means of ensuring that those engaged in the educational process behave as they are supposed to behave. It requires bureaucracy—and bureaucrats.[3]

As public officials they have incentives to expand their budgets, programs, and administrative controls. These are the basics of bureaucratic well-being, and their pursuit is an integral part of the job. But bureaucrats also belong to important interest groups—of administrators, of professionals—that lobby government from the outside (ostensibly) as well. Although traditionally they have portrayed themselves as nonpolitical experts pursuing the greater good, they are in fact a powerful special interest—an interest dedicated to hierarchical control (Knott and Miller 1987; Tyack 1974).

The system, in short, is inherently destructive of autonomy. Politicians have the authority to shape the schools through public policy, and, precisely because they have this authority, they are consistently

American Political Science Review Vol. 82

under pressure from interest groups to exercise it. It is in their own best interests to impose choices on the schools. The same is true of bureaucrats, who have occupational and professional stakes in control: a world of autonomous schools would be a world without educational bureaucrats. Thus, while principals and teachers may praise the virtues of autonomy, the "one best system" is organized against it. Politicians, bureaucrats, and virtually the full spectrum of interest groups tend to see autonomy for what it is: a transfer of power and a threat to their interests.[4]

Purpose and Performance

Public schools are products of public policy. With a huge constituency, there is inevitably dissension over what constitutes "good" policy—and many of the contending groups have their own stakes in public education and are not simply struggling to provide us with "good" policy anyway. Even if they were, there is no guarantee they could implement it very effectively, for bureaucratic control is an inherently difficult and costly means of engineering educational outcomes.

Reform grows naturally out of all this. When important groups signal their dissatisfaction with what the schools are doing, politicians and bureaucrats spring into action. They respond to group demands by doing what they are institutionally empowered and motivated to do: they seek remedies through new policies and new controls. This is the characteristic way in which the public schools are "improved." And because administrative problems, value conflicts, and shifts in power alignments are endemic to the system, reform is a never-ending process.

Private schools operate in a wholly different institutional environment. Reform occurs when schools find it in their own best interests to make adaptive adjustments, when new schools enter the educational marketplace, and when unpopular schools fail. All are closely tied to the interests of parents and students.

Are private schools also likely to be better than public schools? In an important sense, the answer is *yes*. Parents and students who choose a private school are revealing their judgment of quality: the private school is not only better, it is better by an amount that exceeds the cost differential. Since there is clearly an objective basis for their judgment—they directly experience private education and are free to return to the public sector at any time—we have good reason to believe that private schools are in fact more effective at providing the types of educational services their clients care about.

But are they better at the important things schools ought to be doing? This question cannot be answered without substituting our value judgments for those of parents and students. A church school that attracts students on the basis of religious and moral training almost surely outperforms the local public school on this dimension. But this says nothing about their relative effectiveness in transmitting democratic values or an appreciation of cultural diversity. Performance is only desirable if the goals are desirable.

This, of course, is the justification for democratic control. In principle, our institutions are set up to articulate important social goals and to ensure that schools act effectively on them. If private schools do a better job of providing certain services or of pleasing parents and students, this does not mean that society must therefore prefer private to public education. Any evaluation has to depend on a more fundamental judgment about what the schools ought to be doing.

In objective terms the two institutional systems are simply very different, and they give rise to schools that reflect these differences—providing different services in different ways to please different constituencies.

Organization of Schools

Data and Method

High School and Beyond (HSB), first administered in 1980, is the most comprehensive survey of secondary schools to date. The original data base, pertaining to some 60 thousand students in more than one thousand public and private schools, provided a rich source of information about student achievement, attitudes, activities, and family background. This was the empirical foundation for Coleman, Hoffer, and Kilgore's (1982) *High School Achievement*, which set off shock waves in the educational community with its conclusion that private schools are academically more effective than public schools.[5]

High School and Beyond included certain information about the schools, but important aspects of organization and environment were not part of the study. To augment the data base, we helped design the Administrator and Teacher Survey (ATS), which went back to about five hundred HSB schools and administered questionnaires to the principal, a sample of 30 teachers, and selected staff members in each. Their responses tell us a good deal more about the schools as organizations—about their external relationships, their leadership, their structure and goals, their patterns of influence and interaction, and their educational practices. We put the ATS data to use in exploring how education is organized in the public and private sectors.[6]

Because private schools are so diverse, empirical work on student achievement has frequently clarified sectoral comparisons by distinguishing two relatively homogeneous types of private schools in the HSB sample—Catholic and elite—from all the rest. Catholic schools have played the central role in these analyses. They are the majority of private schools, and their students are very similar on socioeconomic and ethnic grounds to students in the public sector. The elite schools are the handful of top private schools in the nation as judged by the proportion of seniors who were semifinalists in the National Merit Scholarship competition. The remaining schools, "other private," vary from tiny religious groupings to large college prep schools.[7] We will maintain these distinctions—and despite their marked diversity, we will expect a uniformity across the three types. For by virtue of their shared institutional context, they should give evidence of something that approaches a common syndrome of organization.

In the analysis, we simply regress each organizational or environmental characteristic against dummy variables representing the three types of private schools.[8] Specifically, if C is the characteristic in question, we estimate the following equation:

$$C = B0 + B1\ \text{Catholic} + B2\ \text{other private} + B3\ \text{elite} + \text{error}.$$

The constant, B0, measures the public school mean on C. *Catholic, other private*, and *elite* are dummy variables taking on the value 1 if the school is of that type, 0 otherwise. B1 measures the difference between the Catholic school mean and the public school mean on characteristic C. B2 and B3 measure the same private-public comparison for the other private and elite categories.

These comparisons are made without the usual laundry list of statistical controls. It is an easy matter to include controls for school size, student background, and countless other factors, but we think it would be inappropriate and possibly very misleading to do so at this point. In estimating relationships among variables, the purpose of statistical controls is to remove covariation due to prior or exogenous influences. An institutional perspective on the organization of schools, how-

American Political Science Review Vol. 82

ever, suggests that all major variables are probably endogenous.

It may be, for instance, that private schools are more likely to exhibit certain characteristics—happy teachers, perhaps —because they tend to be smaller organizations than public schools. But it is no accident that private schools tend to be smaller, since small size is a major basis on which they appeal to students, parents, and teachers. Small size and happy teachers are integral parts of the same syndrome. Similarly, private schools may seem to have desirable organizational traits—more orderly climates, say—because their students come from families that care more about education. But these families have chosen their schools in the first place precisely because they like the way the schools are organized. So what causes what? Do motivated students make for a good school, or do good schools attract motivated students? The most reasonable view is that causality flows both ways and thus that both variables are endogenous.

Analogous arguments apply for virtually any variables of interest. To control for them as though they are exogenous is to remove from the sectoral comparisons—and to remove in a methodologically inappropriate way (via additive terms in recursive equations)—factors that are integrally woven into the very fabric of each system. For now, prudence argues for getting a clear look at how basic aspects of environment and organization differ across sectors. Investigation of the causal structure—and with it, informed thinking about statistical controls—can proceed most usefully once this sort of foundation has been laid.

The Findings

External Authorities

If the operation of politics and markets suggests anything, it is that the control of schools should differ systematically across sectors. Public schools should find themselves operating in larger, more complex governing systems that tend to exert greater influence over school policy, educational practice, and personnel decisions. Private schools should tend to enjoy more autonomy with respect to their structure, goals, and operation. Of course, these tendencies are well documented when they derive from higher levels of government authority: public schools are part of state and federal hierarchies, integrated financially and programmatically, while private schools generally are not (Coleman, Hoffer, and Kilgore 1982). But what about immediate outside authorities? What kind of governing system operates at the local level to distinguish the sectors?

Table 1 presents summary figures on the extent to which the various schools are hierarchically subordinate to school boards or to outside administrative superiors (in the form of a superintendent or central office of some kind). Not surprisingly, virtually all public schools in the sample are governed by both; only two of nearly three hundred schools depart from this pattern. The private sector is far more diverse. Almost all private schools, regardless of type, have a school board of some sort, but often there is no accompanying administrative apparatus. Such an apparatus is quite rare among the elite schools, and nearly half of the "other privates" are similarly unencumbered. It is the Catholic schools that most resemble the publics in this regard, with some two-thirds of Catholic schools having both school boards and administrative superiors; even here, however, there is a good deal of hierarchic diversity by comparison to the public sector. Fully a quarter of the Catholic schools are overseen only by a school board, the Church's reputation for hierarchy notwithstanding.

Because administrative authorities are often absent from the environments of

Organization of Schools

Table 1. Types of Outside Authorities (%)

Outside Authorities Present	Public[b]	Catholic[c]	Other Private	Elite Private
School board and administrators[a]	99.3 (287)	69.0 (20)	52.9 (9)	28.6 (2)
School board only	.0 (0)	24.1 (7)	41.2 (7)	57.1 (4)
Administrators only	.3 (1)	3.4 (1)	.0 (0)	.0 (0)
None	.3 (1)	3.4 (1)	5.9 (1)	14.3 (1)
Total	99.9 (289)	99.9 (29)	100 (17)	100 (7)

Note: Numbers in parentheses are the unweighted number of schools in each sector.
[a]Administrators include superintendent or central office.
[b]Excludes several special public schools oversampled in ATS.
[c]Excludes exclusively black Catholic schools oversampled in ATS.

private schools, many of these schools will operate relatively free from bureaucratic control. But what about the control exercised by the political and administrative authorities that public and private schools often have in common? In Table 2 control by school boards as perceived by principals is compared along five basic policy dimensions: curriculum, instructional methods, discipline, hiring, and firing. The results are striking in their consistency. On all five dimensions school boards in the public sector appear to have more influence over school policy than they do in the private sector, regardless of the type of private school. The differences between public and private are consistently greater (and statistically significant) for personnel and disciplinary policy than for matters pertaining to educational practice and content.[9] They amount on the average to between one and two points on a six-point influence scale. But in view of the uniformity of the overall pattern, there is reason to suspect that even the small estimated differences for curriculum and instruction are indicative of a greater role by school boards in the public sector

Table 2. The Influence of School Boards on School Policies

Areas of Influence	Catholic	Other Private	Elite Private
School board			
Curriculum	-.27 (1.33)	-.24 (1.52)	-.07 (.04)
Instruction	-.03 (.14)	-.003 (.02)	-.03 (.01)
Discipline	-.80 (4.02)	-.35 (2.24)	-1.16 (.56)
Hiring	-.98 (5.16)	-.80 (5.31)	-1.11 (.56)
Firing	-.76 (3.83)	-.41 (2.63)	-.86 (.42)
School board vs. principal			
Curriculum	-.40 (1.96)	-.26 (1.63)	.05 (.03)
Instruction	-.06 (.31)	.41 (2.50)	.17 (.08)
Discipline	-.72 (3.59)	-.28 (1.75)	-.92 (.44)
Hiring	-.97 (4.89)	-.42 (2.67)	-1.30 (.63)
Firing	-1.08 (5.65)	-.72 (4.72)	-1.23 (.62)

Note: Reports regression coefficients and t-scores (in parentheses) for dummy variable regression models in which the dependent variable is standardized.

American Political Science Review Vol. 82

Table 3. The Influence of Administration on School Policies

Areas of Influence	Catholic
Administration	
Curriculum	-1.51 (8.19)
Instruction	-1.01 (5.12)
Discipline	-1.23 (6.39)
Hiring	-1.82 (10.28)
Firing	-2.11 (12.65)
Administration vs. principal	
Curriculum	-1.57 (8.44)
Instruction	-1.23 (6.33)
Discipline	-1.11 (5.66)
Hiring	-1.56 (8.39)
Firing	-2.00 (11.57)

Note: Administration includes superintendent or central office. Table reports regression coefficients and t-scores (in parentheses) for dummy variable regression models in which the dependent variable is standardized.

generally. This is reinforced by the perceived influence of school boards relative to principals. As outlined in the lower half of Table 2, the sectoral differences are repeated and sometimes amplified. Relative to their school boards, private principals play a more autonomous role in setting and implementing policy—especially as it pertains to personnel and discipline—than public principals do.

Relative to their administrative superiors, private principals appear to be similarly autonomous. At least this is true of principals in Catholic schools, the only type of private school with enough administrative supervision to make a comparison with public schools valid and instructive. The figures, presented in Table 3, suggest an interesting conclusion: that the famed Catholic hierarchy (although see Greeley 1977) plays a comparatively small role in governing Catholic schools. On all five dimensions, the influence of administrative superiors is far less in Catholic than in public schools. These differences are again greatest in the area of personnel policy, but here the other policy areas reflect substantial differences as well. When we explore the school's autonomy a bit further by comparing the principal's influence to that of administrative superiors, the same pattern emerges. Relative to administrators, Catholic principals enjoy more freedom than public principals in setting school policy.

To be sure, the differences in school autonomy that seem to distinguish the public and private sectors are based on simple measures of perceived influence and not on actual behavior. But the patterns these measures yield are quite uniform and entirely consistent with our expectations for external control. The authorities that are so ubiquitous in the democratic context of the public school are often simply absent from private school settings—and even when they are an acknowledged part of the private governing apparatus, they play less influential roles in the actual determination of school policy. Private schools, it would appear, have more control over their own destinies.

External Constraints: Choosing the Organization's Staff

Among the controls that any organization seeks to exercise over its operations, perhaps none is as important as control over its staff—in the case of a school, its teachers. To what extent does the school have flexibility in recruiting the kinds of teachers it wants and getting rid of those who do not live up to its standards? We have already seen that public schools are at a disadvantage in this regard, for external authorities have much more influence over hiring and firing in the public sector than they do in the private sector. The sectoral differences are not limited to the role of external authorities, however. They become still more dramatic when we consider two additional constraints on the choice of personnel: tenure and unions.

Tenure systems in public schools are special cases of the civil service systems that exist at all levels of government. Historically, these systems arose to prevent politicians from rewarding their supporters with public jobs. Reformers recognized that the widespread use of patronage was inconsistent with the kind of expertise, professionalism, and continuity so necessary to effective government, and —in a halting process that took decades to accomplish—they brought about the pervasive adoption of civil service systems built around objective qualifications and designed to protect employees judged to be qualified. Tenure is one of these protections (Peterson 1985).

Teacher unions (or "associations"), although initially resisted by politicians wedded to patronage, eventually found political allies of their own. Organized teachers could offer money, manpower, and votes to politicians. In state and local elections, where turnout is typically very low, these are attractive inducements indeed. As teacher unions thrived, they gained not only economic concessions but also contractual guarantees of job security and other limitations on responsibilities that reinforced the protections of the civil service system and introduced wholly new constraints into personnel decisions affecting the local school (Grimshaw 1979).

Although there is nothing to prevent unions from gaining a foothold in private schools nor to keep private schools from adopting tenure and other civil service-like protections, there is nothing comparable to government that drives them in that direction. Whether unions and tenure systems take hold in the private sector is determined much less by politics and much more by markets. Schools may choose to offer tenure and other protections as a means of attracting good teachers, particularly given that public schools offer that benefit. But private schools may also decide, especially if the supply of teachers is high, that they can offer a very attractive set of benefits—such as good students, orderly atmosphere, and collegial decision making—without offering tenure at all. Similarly, as in any market setting, unions may or may not succeed in organizing teachers. But they cannot count on symbiotic relationships with the authorities, as public unions can, to help their cause.

The ATS data suggest that the public and private sectors are in fact enormously different in these respects. While 88% of public schools offer tenure, only a minority of the private schools do: 24% of the Catholics, 39% of the elites, and 17% of the "other privates." Among the schools that do offer tenure, moreover, the proportion of teachers who have actually been awarded it reflects the same asymmetry: 80% of the eligibles in public schools have tenure, while the figure is some 10%-16% lower in the private sector. The differences in unionization are even more substantial. The vast majority of public schools are unionized—some 80%—almost all of them by either the National Education Association or the American Federation of Teachers. In the private sector, by contrast, teachers are rarely represented by unions. Only about 10% of the Catholic schools are unionized, and virtually none of the elites and "other privates" are.

To assess whether school control over personnel is perceptibly constrained by tenure, unions, and other proximate external authorities, we asked principals to evaluate an assortment of potential barriers to hiring excellent teachers and firing incompetent ones. On the hiring side, principals in the two sectors agreed on the severity of several obstacles, including applicant shortages and low pay. But public school principals were far more likely to complain about obstacles administrative in origin: "central office con-

American Political Science Review Vol. 82

Table 4. School Personnel Policy and Process

Personnel Constraints	Catholic	Other Private	Elite Private
Barriers to Hiring			
Too many transfers	−.57 (2.72)	−.56 (3.36)	−.43 (.20)
Central office control	−.51 (2.43)	−.25 (1.51)	−.47 (.22)
Barriers to Firing			
Complex procedures	−.59 (3.35)	−1.47 (10.51)	−1.26 (.69)
Tenure rules	−.93 (5.08)	−1.36 (9.39)	−1.55 (.82)
Hours involved in firing someone	−.85 (4.01)	−.75 (4.47)	−.90 (.41)

Note: Reports regression coefficients and t-scores (in parentheses) for dummy variable regression models in which the dependent variable is standardized.

trol" and "excessive transfers from other schools" (see Table 4).

The obstacles to dismissing teachers for poor performance differ similarly. In the public schools the procedures are far more complex, the tenure rules more constraining, and the preparation and documentation process roughly three times as long (Table 4). The complexity and formality of dismissal procedures is the highest barrier to firing cited by public school principals. For private school principals, of every type, the highest barrier is "a personal reluctance to fire." These responses provide a rather poignant statement of the differences between the sectors: while the public school principal is bound most by red tape, the private school principal is bound most by his or her conscience.

Principals do, of course, have other forms of control over their staffs. They can encourage undesirable staff to resign, retire, or transfer. They can offer good teachers special assignments or relieve them of onerous duties. They can recognize high performance with awards.[10] But none of these practices differs systematically across the sectors. Public principals simply have less power than private principals to mold and manage their teaching staffs.

Even if public superintendents or central offices wanted to delegate such power to the school—and, in general, there is no reason to think they have incentives to do this—many personnel decisions cannot in practice be delegated. Tenure protections are usually guaranteed through laws that are written by school boards or state legislatures, and these laws are then enforced by administrators. Union contracts are typically bargained at the district level, not at the school level, and are enforced from above. Tenure and unionization tend to settle the question of where and how the basic personnel decisions will be made in the public sector. They will be centralized. Schools in the private sector, largely free of such constraints, have far greater flexibility to choose their own members and chart their own paths.

Parents

In most respects, private schools would seem to have ideal parental environments. Parents, after all, have made a positive choice to send their children to a private school, presumably because they care about education and have a high appraisal of the school. And if at any time they change their views, they can simply exercise their exit option. This means that the school is likely to enjoy significant gains: they gain children whose family lives encourage education, and parents

Table 5. Parental Relationships with Schools

Parental Role	Catholic	Other Private	Elite Private
Monitoring students	.90 (4.69)	.43 (2.82)	1.30 (.65)
Expectations of students	1.24 (6.85)	.91 (6.33)	2.62 (1.39)
Involvement in school	.74 (3.81)	.52 (3.39)	.64 (.32)
Cooperativeness	.43 (2.13)	.18 (1.14)	.47 (.22)
Freedom from constraint	.57 (2.81)	.22 (1.35)	.49 (.23)

Note: Reports regression coefficients and t-scores (in parentheses) for dummy variable regression models in which the dependent variable is standardized.

who not only will facilitate school objectives by monitoring homework and the like but will be informed and supportive when they take an active interest in school decision making. Parents who may cause problems on these scores are precisely the ones most likely to drop out of the school's environment voluntarily.

Public schools are not so fortunate. Many of their students come from families that put little or no emphasis on education; the students come to school with poor attitudes and orientations, and the parents do little to facilitate the school's efforts. Because exit is often not a viable option, many parents who do not support the school's goals, methods, or activities will remain in its environment nevertheless; and some—perhaps many—will use the democratic mechanisms at their disposal, as well as interactions with principal and staff, to express their dissent and press for change. Far from gaining sustenance from a supportive parental environment, the public school may often find itself dealing as best it can with conflict, disappointment, and apathy.

Not all public and private schools will neatly fit these molds, of course. But it seems clear that characteristics inherent in the two sectors—characteristics anchored in politics and markets—encourage the kinds of environmental differences outlined here. And results from the ATS study, detailed in Table 5, are consistent with this line of reasoning. Parents in the private sector, regardless of the type of less constrained by the kinds of formal rules and norms that due to democratic governing structures impinge on the flexibility of public school principals.

The operation of politics and markets, then, appears to put public schools at a real disadvantage. Because of forces largely beyond the control of the individual school, parents in the public sector tend to be less supportive of the school's general educational efforts and more likely to promote organizational conflict—and, to make matters worse, the school has less flexibility in seeking solutions to these problems. By comparison, private schools have fewer such problems and yet more flexibility for dealing with them.

Between Environment and Organization: The Principal

The principal operates at the boundary of the organization and is, more than any other single person, responsible for negotiating successfully with the environment

Table 6. Characteristics of School Principals

Characteristics	Catholic	Other Private	Elite Private
Teaching experience	.43 (2.21)	.56 (3.59)	.58 (.28)
Motivations			
Policy control	.61 (3.04)	.46 (2.92)	.31 (.15)
Preference for administrative duties	-.33 (1.63)	-.49 (3.08)	-.14 (.07)
Career advancement	-.69 (3.52)	-.61 (3.91)	-.48 (.23)
Desire further advancement	-.76 (3.95)	-.71 (4.69)	-1.04 (.52)
Leadership as perceived by teachers	.41 (2.12)	.74 (4.84)	.64 (.32)
Instructional leadership	.66 (3.67)	1.28 (8.98)	.82 (.44)

Note: Reports regression coefficients and t-scores (in parentheses) for dummy variable regression models in which the dependent variable is standardized.

—responding to demands and pressures from parents, unions, administrators, and school boards, and dealing with external disruptions such as budget cuts, policy conflicts, and demographic changes. The principal may also hold a key to school effectiveness. Evidence increasingly suggests that educational excellence is promoted by a principal who articulates clear goals, holds high expectations of students and teachers, exercises strong instructional leadership, steers clear of administrative burdens, and effectively extracts resources from the environment (e.g., Blumberg and Greenfield 1980; Brookover et al. 1979; Goodlad 1984).

It is seldom stressed, however, that the school environment can have a lot to say about whether the principal is able to practice these precepts of effective leadership—or, for that matter, is even motivated to practice them. Effective leadership does not simply inhere in the individual filling the role; it is unavoidably contingent upon the demands, constraints, and resources that the principal must deal with. Depending on the nature and strength of these forces, even the "best" principal may have only a marginal effect on school performance. We must also remember that principals do not possess or lack leadership qualities by accident. Both environment and organization tend to ensure that there will be selective attraction to the job: certain schools will tend to attract certain kinds of principals. Similarly, principals will be socialized on the job, and internal and external factors will ensure that principals at distinctly different schools will be socialized differently. Thus, while it is one thing to point to certain qualities that appear conducive to effective leadership, it is quite another to suggest that principals are free to develop them.

It should not be surprising, then, to find differences between public and private school principals, both in terms of their own characteristics and in terms of their performance. Consider first what the ATS data (see Table 6) have to say about how they came to their jobs. Private school principals have quite a bit more teaching experience than their public counterparts —the gap is almost four years for principals in Catholic schools, and over five years for those in the elites and "other privates."[11] This is consistent with the hierarchic organization of public sector education: its career ladder offers teachers early opportunities for moving into a host of subordinate administrative positions (such as assistant principalships), followed by subsequent opportunities for moving up in status and salary. As this implies, principals also come to their jobs with different motivations. Private principals are more likely to stress "control over school policies," while public principals place greater emphasis on "preference for administrative responsibilities," a "desire to further [their] career[s]," and an interest in advancing "to a higher administrative post."

The typical career orientations of principals in the two sectors thus appear to be quite different. Public principals tend to disembark from teaching relatively early, get on an administrative track, and take the job of principal to keep the train rolling. Private principals are scarcely on a track at all. They stay in teaching longer, and their view of the principalship focuses more on its relation to the school than on its relation to their movement up the educational hierarchy.

How the principal performs on the job is a function of many things, not just the values and experiences noted here. They would, however, appear to have a direct bearing on one aspect of performance consistently singled out in the effective schools literature: instructional leadership. Teachers in the ATS study were asked questions about the quality of the assistance they received in regard to instructional problems, and their responses indicate strong differences across the sectors. As judged by their own teachers, private principals are more effective in this important area of leadership than public principals are. Again, this may be due to a variety of factors. But the simple fact that the public principal has far less teaching experience (which itself has roots in his or her distinctive career orientation) is in itself likely to affect rapport with teachers, self-perception of instructional role, and other aspects of the job as they pertain to teaching. It is not surprising to find that instructional leadership is more effective in private schools.

Finally, the ATS teachers were asked to evaluate their principal with regard to a range of leadership-related qualities bearing on knowledge of school problems, communication with the staff, clarity and strength of purpose, and willingness to innovate. Constructing a general index of leadership from these items, we find that by these criteria teachers rate private principals to be better all-around leaders than public principals. This result is more likely to reflect the operation of general environmental conditions than the earlier one on instructional leadership. Principals in the public sector are forced to operate in much more complex, conflictual circumstances in which educational success is more difficult to achieve regardless of the principal's (perhaps considerable) abilities and qualifications. If anything, however, it is plausible to suggest that the public principal's lack of teaching experience and a hierarchic career orientation probably contribute to these leadership problems.

While these findings only begin to scratch the surface, it does appear that public and private school principals are quite different in important respects. They have different backgrounds, different career orientations, and—whatever the true constraints on their performance might be—they are evaluated differently by their teachers: principals in private schools are more highly regarded as leaders.

The Organization: Goals and Policies

Given what we know of their environments, there is every reason to expect that public and private schools should adopt very different orientations toward the education of their students. Because public schools must take whoever walks in the door, they do not have the luxury of being able to select the kind of students best suited to organizational goals and structure—it is the latter that must do virtually all the adapting if a harmonious fit is to be achieved. In practice, this means that the pursuit of educational excellence must compete with much more basic needs—for literacy, for remedial training,

American Political Science Review Vol. 82

Table 7. School Structure

Characteristics	Catholic	Other Private	Elite Private
Goals			
Basic literacy	-1.59 (8.83)	-.83 (5.81)	-1.10 (.59)
Citizenship	-1.12 (6.06)	-1.04 (7.11)	-.96 (.50)
Good work habits	-.92 (4.68)	-.52 (3.37)	-.26 (.13)
Occupational skills	-.89 (4.60)	-.77 (5.01)	-.98 (.49)
Academic excellence	.10 (.48)	.41 (2.57)	.94 (.45)
Personal growth	.47 (2.33)	.12 (.78)	.69 (.33)
Human relations	.24 (1.19)	.11 (.71)	.34 (.16)
General graduation requirements			
English and history	.61 (3.09)	.51 (3.26)	.57 (.28)
Science and mathematics	.34 (1.73)	.88 (5.77)	1.78 (.88)
Foreign language	1.28 (7.88)	1.61 (12.47)	3.33 (1.96)
School-wide homework policy	.13 (.65)	.48 (3.06)	.90 (.44)
Goal clarity	.64 (3.32)	.80 (5.24)	.80 (.40)
Goal disagreement	-.35 (1.80)	-.85 (5.59)	-.55 (.27)

Note: Reports regression coefficients and t-scores (in parentheses) for dummy variable regression models in which the dependent variable is standardized.

for more slowly paced instruction. In addition, there is the hierarchic structure of democratic control to ensure that a range of actors and diverse, often-conflicting interests are brought to bear in decisions about what the public school ought to be pursuing and how. As in other areas of politics, the thrust is toward compromises and "solutions" (see also Powell, Farrar, and Cohen 1985) that reflect the lowest common denominator—and often a great deal of ambiguity and internal inconsistency as well. This is to be expected when an important function of the decision-making process is conflict resolution. The process is unavoidably a political exercise, not an analytical attempt at problem solving.

Private schools are largely unconstrained in comparison, both in the selection of students and in the determination of organizational goals. It is only reasonable to suggest that a given private school is likely to have clearer and more homogeneous goals than a given public school. Aggregate comparisons, however, are more uncertain because the private sector is comprised of so many different types of schools; an elite school will emphasize academic excellence, but a religious or military school may have quite different priorities—although we would still expect them to be relatively clear and homogeneous compared to the publics.

Despite such uncertainties, the comparisons across sectors are quite uniform (see Table 7). In terms of general goals, public schools place significantly greater emphasis on basic literacy, citizenship, good work habits, and specific occupational skills, while private schools—regardless of type—are more oriented by academic excellence, and personal growth. For the most part, these sorts of differenes are what we should expect in view of the more fundamental differences in student bodies and governing structures. Most obviously, public schools would ordinarily find it politically and organizationally very difficult to place high priority on academic excellence.

Whether these goals become reflected in school structure and performance depends on whether they are upheld by specific policies and clearly discerned by the staff. As Table 7 suggests, there are definite differences across sectors in these respects. To begin with, the private schools have more stringent minimum graduation requirements; their students, regardless of track, must take significantly more English and history, science and math, and foreign language than must public students in order to graduate. In science, math, and foreign language the differences range up to two years.

Private schools also have stricter homework policies. This is particularly true of the elites and "other privates," most of which establish schoolwide daily minimums per subject, strongly encourage homework, or, in cases where faculty are overzealous, set daily maximums per subject. In contrast, 90% of all public schools leave the amount of homework entirely up to teachers. Catholic schools fall in between these extremes.

These differences in goals and policies are accompanied by differences in their clarity and their acceptance by organization members—key factors in their translation into organizational action. Private teachers uniformly report school goals as clearer—and more clearly communicated by the principal—than public teachers report. In addition, there is less disagreement among the school priorities reported by teachers in private schools. In general, private schools tend to possess a clarity and homogeneity of educational purpose that does set them apart from public schools, at least on average. They place more emphasis on academic excellence, have stricter graduation requirements, and have tougher homework policies. And their staff members have clearer, more consistent conceptions of what their organizations are supposed to be achieving. These are, of course, stereotypical characteristics of "effective shools." They are also characteristics that, due to the differential operation of politics and markets, would seem extremely difficult for public schools to develop in the same degree.

The Organization: People, Decisions, Operation

What should public and private schools look like on the inside? What might we expect in general about their structures, processes, and personnel? A widely accepted notion in organization theory is that environmental complexity is reflected in organizational complexity (Lawrence and Lorsch 1967). For rather obvious reasons, then, public schools should prove far more complex than their private counterparts; and existing studies indicate that this is actually the case (Scott and Meyer 1984). Moreover, their very complexity of structure and heterogeneity of goals suggest that public schools may often be "loosely coupled," characterized by relatively autonomous centers of activity and decision making. Private schools, on the other hand, would seem to approximate classical notions of organization. They have simpler, more stable, less threatening environments, and goals that are fewer in number, clearer, and more narrowly based—characteristics that facilitate the centralized direction of goal pursuit. This would seem to be consistent with the private schools' reputation for rigid curricula, traditional instructional methods, and strong principals.

A politics-and-markets perspective cannot hope to tell us everything we might want to know about organizational structure and process, but it does tend to point us in a different direction. The critical fact about the public school environment is not just that it is complex but that it literally imposes decisions about policy, structure, personnel, and procedure on the school. Thus, while the school may well adapt to environmental complexity by developing an internal complexity of its own, its range of choice is severely constrained—for a great many potential adaptive adjustments are simply ruled out

American Political Science Review Vol. 82

by environmental fiat. Conversely, the private school is not only blessed with a relatively simple environment but with a much broader range of organizational options in adapting to it.

Consider, in particular, the most crucial agent of organizational performance: the teacher. As we have seen, the public school principal is far less able than the private school principal to staff the organization according to his or her best judgment. The public principal may value expertise, enthusiasm, collegiality, communication skills, creativity, or any number of qualifications related to the school's goals but simply has less power to obtain teachers who possess them or eliminate ones who do not. This should tend to promote staff heterogeneity and conflict. Teachers may reject the principal's leadership, dissent from school goals and policies, get along poorly with their colleagues, or fail to perform acceptably in the classroom—but the principal must somehow learn to live with them. When these teachers are represented by unions, as they normally are, leadership difficulties are magnified and an important wedge is driven between the principal and the staff, a wedge that promotes formalized decision procedures, struggles for power, and jealousies over turf. "Professionalism" takes on new meaning—as a justification for placing decision power in the hands of teachers rather than the principal.

Private schools are not immune from personnel problems and struggles for power. But the principal, having much greater control over hiring and firing, can take steps to recruit the kinds of teachers he or she wants and weed out the rest. It also means that teachers have a strong inducement to live up to the principal's criteria on a continuing basis. By comparison to the public school counterpart, then, the private school principal is in a position to create a "team" of teachers whose values, skills, and willingness to work together tend to mirror those qualifications the principal deems conducive to the pursuit of organizational goals. At the same time, the principal is in a position to make teacher professionalism work for, rather than against, him or her. Without real threat to his or her own authority or control, the principal can encourage teacher participation in decision making, extend teachers substantial autonomy within their own spheres of expertise, and promote a context of interaction, exchange of ideas, and mutual respect.

The data from the ATS study seem to provide strong support for this general line of reasoning. As outlined in Table 8, principals and teachers simply have higher opinions of one another in the private sector. Private principals consistently claim that a larger percentage of their schools' teachers are "excellent," suggesting that they are more confident in the abilities of their own staff members than public school principals are. Private sector teachers, in turn, have better relationships with their principals. They are consistently more likely to regard the latter as encouraging, supportive, and reinforcing; and, as we saw earlier, they have higher regard for their principals as effective organizational leaders.

Private school teachers also feel more involved and efficacious in important areas of school decision making that bear on their teaching. In particular, they feel more influential over schoolwide policies governing the curriculum, student behavior, teacher in-service programs, and the grouping of students of differing abilities. Regarding issues of special relevance to the classroom, they believe they have more control over text selection, course content, teaching techniques, disciplining students, and, in the Catholic schools, determining the amount of homework to be assigned. (The non-Catholic private teachers feel constrained by the schoolwide homework policies identified earlier.) Even on matters of hiring and firing,

Organization of Schools

Table 8. Staff Relations

Characteristics	Catholic	Other Private	Elite Private
Percent excellent teachers	.40 (2.07)	.78 (5.05)	1.16 (.58)
Principal-teacher relations	.44 (2.29)	.90 (5.93)	.96 (.48)
Teacher influence and control			
Student behavior codes	.95 (5.15)	1.00 (6.84)	1.04 (.54)
In-service programs	.32 (1.64)	.77 (5.05)	.41 (.20)
Ability groupings	1.24 (7.20)	1.32 (9.69)	1.37 (.76)
Curriculum	1.01 (5.66)	1.22 (8.59)	1.22 (.66)
Text selection	.66 (3.46)	.78 (5.11)	.74 (.37)
Topics taught	.50 (2.62)	.94 (6.23)	.53 (.27)
Techniques	.70 (3.58)	.40 (2.61)	1.06 (.52)
Discipline	1.34 (7.17)	.46 (3.12)	.83 (.42)
Homework	.63 (3.19)	.33 (2.14)	-1.16 (.57)
Hiring	.54 (2.63)	.38 (2.38)	.93 (.44)
Firing	.55 (2.75)	.16 (1.04)	.21 (.10)
Teacher-teacher relations			
Curriculum coordination	.60 (3.11)	.67 (4.37)	.96 (.48)
Teaching improvement	.60 (3.21)	1.06 (7.21)	1.03 (.53)
Collegiality	.90 (5.34)	1.58 (11.82)	.82 (.47)
Success not beyond personal control	.79 (4.19)	.54 (3.59)	1.23 (.62)
Doing best not waste of time	1.12 (5.39)	.96 (5.85)	1.78 (.82)
Job satisfaction	.57 (3.37)	.54 (4.06)	1.01 (.58)
Teacher absenteeism	.58 (3.00)	.73 (4.74)	.49 (.24)
Lowest teacher salary	-.75 (3.92)	-.86 (5.72)	.39 (.19)
Highest teacher salary	-.76 (3.87)	-.57 (3.65)	.91 (.45)

Note: Reports regression coefficients and t-scores (in parentheses) for dummy variable regression models in which the dependent variable is standardized.

private teachers believe they are more influential—this, despite the almost complete absence of unions in their sector.

Relative harmony between private principals and private teachers is matched by relative harmony among the private teachers themselves. On a personal level, relationships are more collegial in the private sector. Stated in the plain terms of the survey, private teachers are more likely to believe that they "can count on most staff members to help out anywhere, anytime—even though it may not be part of their official assignment" and ultimately that "the school seems like a big family." On a professional level, private teachers give greater evidence of mutual involvement and support. They are more likely to know what their colleagues are teaching, to coordinate the content of their courses, and to observe one another's classes. They also spend more time meeting together for the purpose of discussing curriculum and students.

It is no surprise, then, that private school teachers also feel more efficacious than public school teachers. Unlike their public counterparts, they do not believe their success is beyond their control, and they do not feel it is a waste of time to do their best. Overall, private school teachers are much more satisfied with their jobs. It is no wonder, then, that private school teachers have better attendance records nor that they tend to work for less money. Private school teachers are trading economic compensation and formal job security for superior working conditions, professional autonomy, and personal fulfillment. Public school teachers are doing precisely the opposite.

In short, private schools do tend to look more like "teams." By their own account, teachers have better relationships with principals, are more integrally involved in decision making, interact more frequently and productively with their colleagues, and feel more positively about their jobs and their organization. According to their principals, they are higher-quality teachers as well. As professionals, it appears they are given much greater reign in a private setting, which gives them opportunities to put their ideas and skills to use through a level of active involvement and a sharing of power that teachers in the public sector generally cannot expect. The key to explanation is anchored in a more fundamental feature of the sectors: private leaders have the freedom to chose their own professionals, public leaders do not.

Conclusion

The Administrator and Teacher Survey provides the first opportunity to document public-private differences by means of a large, representative sample of schools, and its findings dovetail nicely with major lines of argument in the education literature. If it is true, as Coleman, Hoffer, and Kilgore (1982) and Coleman and Hoffer (1987) have claimed, that private schools outperform public schools on academic grounds, and if the effective schools research is basically correct in the characteristics it tends to associate with effectiveness, then we should find that private schools disproportionately possess these characteristics.

That is just what we find. Private schools have simpler, less constraining environments of administrators, school boards, and parents. They are more autonomous and strongly led. They have clearer goals and stricter requirements, and they put greater stress on academic excellence. Relations between principals and teachers and among teachers themselves are more harmonious, interactive, and focused on teaching. Teachers are more involved in policy decisions, have greater control over their work, and are more satisfied with their jobs.

We have tried to do more here than present findings and relate them to existing work, however. We have tried to develop an institutional perspective that suggests why schools should be expected to differ across the sectors. This perspective arises from our belief that institutional context has pervasive consequences for the organization and operation of all schools, consequences more far-reaching than most of the literature tends to suggest (Pfeffer and Salancik 1979).

Public schools are products of our democratic institutions. They are subordinates in a hierarchic system of control in which diverse constituency groups and public officials impose policies on local schools. It is no accident that public schools are lacking in autonomy, that principals have difficulty leading, and that school goals are heterogeneous, unclear, and undemanding. Nor is it an accident that weak principals and tenured, unionized teachers struggle for power. These sorts of characteristics constitute an organizational syndrome whose roots are deeply anchored in democratic control as we have come to know it.

Private schools are controlled by society too, but not through politics or bureaucracy. They make their own decisions about policy, organization, and personnel subject to market forces that signal how they can best pursue their own interests. Given their substantial autonomy—and given the incentives for autonomy that are built into the system—it is not surprising to find that principals are stronger leaders; that principals have greater control over hiring and firing; that principals and the teachers they choose have greater respect for, and interaction with, one another; and that teachers—without conflict or formal requirement—are more integrally involved in policy-making. These sorts of characteristics are bound up with one another, and they jointly arise from the institutional environment. Different institutions promote different organizational syndromes.

If this is essentially correct, the standard proposals for reforming public schools are misconceived. It is easy to say, for instance, that schools should have greater autonomy or that principals should be stronger leaders. But these sorts of reforms are incompatible with the "one best system" and cannot succeed. Politicians and bureaucrats have little incentive to move forcefully in these directions. Their careers are tied to their own control over the schools, and they are unavoidably responsive to well-organized interests that have stakes in the system's capacity to impose higher-order values on the local schools. Restricting autonomy is what democratic control is all about.

It is also about power, about who gets to have how much say in the control of schools. Reformist notions that the various actors should work together in the best interest of the schools are doomed by the institutions of democratic control, which guarantee conflict of interest, struggle for advantage, and resort to formally enforced "cooperation." Reforms calling for even the simplest changes—testing veteran teachers for minimum competence, say—will normally fail if they threaten established interests. Their bearing on school effectiveness has little to do with their political feasibility.

Reformers must reckon with the possibility that the measures they support, particularly those arising from the effective schools research, are often inconsistent with our current framework of democratic control. The public schools cannot be anything we might want them to be. They must take organizational forms compatible with their surrounding institutional environments. It may well be, then, that the key to school improvement is not school reform, but institutional reform—a shift away from direct democratic control.

This does not mean that the public schools must be freed from all democratic governance. But it is instructive that the private schools, which are products of an institutional system that decentralizes power to the producers and immediate consumers of educational services, tend to develop precisely the sorts of organizational characteristics reformers want the public schools to have. Some sort of voucher system, combining broad democratic guidance with a radical decentralization of resources and choice, is at least a reasonable alternative to direct control—one that might transform the public schools into different, more effective organizations, while still leaving them truly public.

Even if this or some other alternative is someday shown to have compelling features, however, democracy probably cannot get us from here to there. Any proposal to shift away from prevailing institutions is so threatening to established interests that it stands little chance of political victory. Because a shift in institutional control may be the one reform that makes all the others possible, the uncomfortable reality may simply be that all the others are not possible.

Notes

An earlier version of this paper was presented at the 1987 annual meeting of the American Political Science Association, Chicago. The first draft appeared as the Brookings Institution's Governmental Studies Discussion Paper No. 1.

1. The responsiveness of residential decisions to differences in the quality of public services, includ-

ing education, has been extensively investigated and generally found to be quite imperfect (Rose-Ackerman 1983).

2. This is not to say that intelligent guidance from the center—e.g., about important innovations in curriculum and methods—is unimportant, only that education appears to benefit from a balance of control and autonomy favoring the teachers and the school (e.g., Carnegie Forum on Education and the Economy 1986).

3. On the logic of control and its implications for bureaucratic forms of organization, see, e.g., Williamson 1975. For a review with applications to politics, see Moe 1984. On the historical development of the educational bureaucracy, see Tyack 1974 and Peterson 1985.

4. There are some interesting complications that we cannot dwell on here without getting too far afield. Mayors, for instance, sometimes attempt to avoid the risks and pressures of educational politics by minimizing their own roles and shifting authority to others (e.g., members of the school board). More generally, politicians sometimes find it advantageous to create agencies that are insulated in some measure from political influence, including their own influence. These maneuvers, however, never put an end to politics or political control—and the maneuvers themselves are reversible through subsequent political maneuvers. Through it all, the authority to impose higher-order values is still there, and those with access to it still have incentives to use it to get what they want.

5. This study has been pummeled from all angles. See, e.g., Bryk 1981; Goldberger and Cain 1982; Guthrie and Zusman 1981; Heyns and Hilton 1982; Murnane 1981. It seems to us, however, that the thrust of the Coleman-Hoffer-Kilgore argument has largely withstood these attacks. In more recent research by Coleman and Hoffer (1987) it has also been strongly reinforced.

6. When the ATS data are merged with those from HSB and its follow-ups (the details of which are available from the National Center for Education Statistics), they offer a unique foundation for exploring the connections among environment, organization, and student achievement. That is the purpose of our larger project, of which this paper is a part.

7. Studies of organization, as opposed to student achievement, have dealt almost entirely with public schools. Most of what is known about the organization of private schools is derived from case studies or studies of limited samples (Cibulka, O'Brien, and Zewe 1982; Erickson 1982; Greeley 1966; Peshkin 1986; Sanders 1981). Systematic national surveys are rare (Abramowitz and Stackhouse 1980; Kraushaar 1972).

8. The procedures employed in constructing indexes and measures of the variables are detailed in an appendix available from the authors.

9. Throughout this paper coefficients will be called "statistically significant," or simply "significant," if they satisfy a two-tailed t-test at a probability level of .05. The results for the elite schools will not, however, be evaluated in this fashion. The elite schools are not a sample, but a population—the schools with the most National Merit semi-finalists in 1978. As such, it is arguably inappropriate to make statistical inferences from the "sample" to the population. In any case, the number of elite schools is too small, especially after weighting, to produce t-scores in the necessary range of 2.0.

10. Private schools may also offer merit pay; however, only the "other private" sector makes significantly greater use of it. Catholic schools do not differ from public schools in providing merit pay.

11. Recall that the coefficients reported in the tables are based on standardized measures of the dependent variables. When converted back to their original metric, the coefficients for teaching experience are equivalent to the years reported in the text.

References

Abramowitz, Susan, and E. A. Stackhouse. 1980. *The Private High School Today.* National Institute of Education, Washington.

Alchian, Armen A. 1950. "Uncertainty, Evolution, and Economic Theory." *Journal of Political Economy* 58:211–21.

Blumberg, Arthur, and William Greenfield. 1980. *The Effective Principal: Perspectives on School Leadership.* Boston: Allyn & Bacon.

Boyer, Ernest. 1983. *High School: A Report on American Secondary Education.* New York: Harper & Row.

Brookover, Wilbur B., Charles Beady, Patricia Flood, John Schweitzer, and Joe Wisenbaker. 1979. *School Social Systems and Student Achievement: Schools Can Make a Difference.* New York: Praeger.

Bryk, Anthony S. 1981. "Disciplined Inquiry or Policy Argument?" *Harvard Educational Review* 51:497–509.

Campbell, Roald I., et al. 1985. *The Organization and Control of American Schools.* 5th ed. Columbus, Ohio: Charles E. Merrill.

Carnegie Forum on Education and the Economy. 1986. *A Nation Prepared: Teachers for the Twenty-first Century.* Washington: Carnegie Forum.

Cibulka, James G., Timothy J. O'Brien, and Donald Zewe. 1982. *Inner City Private Elementary Schools.* Milwaukee: Marquette University Press.

Coleman, James S., and Thomas Hoffer. 1987. *Public and Private High Schools.* New York: Basic Books.

Organization of Schools

Coleman, James S., Thomas Hoffer, and Sally Kilgore. 1982. *High School Achievement.* New York: Basic Books.

Doyle, Denis P. and Terry W. Hartle. 1985. *Excellence in Education: The States Take Charge.* Washington: American Enterprise Institute.

Erickson, Donald A. 1982. "Disturbing Evidence About the 'One Best System.'" In *The Public School Monopoly*, ed. Robert B. Everhart. San Francisco: Pacific Institute for Public Policy Research.

Goldberger, Arthur S., and Glen G. Cain. 1982. "The Causal Analysis of Cognitive Outcomes in the Coleman, Hoffer, and Kilgore Report." *Sociology of Education* 55:103–22.

Goodlad, John I. 1984. *A Place Called School: Prospects for the Future.* New York: McGraw Hill.

Greeley, Andrew M. 1966. *The Education of Catholic Americans.* Chicago: Aldine.

Greeley, Andrew M. 1977. "Who Controls Catholic Education?" *Education and Urban Society* 9: 146–66.

Grimshaw, William J. 1979. *Union Rule in the Schools.* Lexington, MA: Lexington Books.

Guthrie, James W., and Ami Zusman. 1981. "Unasked Questions." *Harvard Educational Review* 51:515–18.

Heyns, Barbara, and Thomas H. Hilton. 1982. "The Cognitive Tests for High School and Beyond: An Assessment." *Sociology of Education* 55:89–102.

Hirschman, Albert O. 1970. *Exit, Voice, and Loyalty.* Cambridge: Harvard University Press.

Iannaccone, Laurence. 1967. *Politics in Education.* New York: Center for Applied Research in Education.

Knott, Jack H., and Gary J. Miller. 1987. *Reforming Bureaucracy: The Politics of Institutional Choice.* Englewood Cliffs, NJ: Prentice-Hall.

Kraushaar, Otto F. 1972. *American Nonpublic Schools: Patterns of Diversity.* Baltimore: Johns Hopkins University Press.

Lawrence, Paul R., and Jay W. Lorsch. 1967. *Organization and Environment.* Homewood, IL: Richard D. Irwin.

Masters, Nicholas A., Robert Salisbury, and Thomas H. Eliot. 1964. *State Politics and the Public Schools.* New York: Knopf.

Moe, Terry M. 1984. "The New Economics of Organization." *American Journal of Political Science* 28:739–77.

Murnane, Richard J. 1981. "Evidence, Analysis, and Unanswered Questions." *Harvard Educational Review* 51:483–89.

National Commission on Excellence in Education. 1983. *A Nation at Risk.* Washington: NCEE.

Peterson, Paul E. 1976. *School Politics, Chicago Style.* Chicago: University of Chicago Press.

Peterson, Paul E. 1985. *The Politics of School Reform: 1870–1940.* Chicago: University of Chicago Press.

Peshkin, Alan. 1986. *God's Choice: The Total World of the Christian School.* Chicago: University of Chicago Press.

Pfeffer, Jeffrey, and Gerald R. Salancik. 1979. *The External Control of Organizations: A Resource Dependence Perspective.* New York: Harper & Row.

Powell, Arthur G., Eleanor Farrar, and David K. Cohen. 1985. *The Shopping Mall High School: Winners and Losers in the Educational Marketplace.* New York: Houghton Mifflin.

Rose-Ackerman, Susan. 1983. "Beyond Tiebout: Modeling the Political Economy of Local Government." In *Local Provision of Public Services: The Tiebout Model after Twenty-five Years*, ed. George R. Zodrow. New York: Academic.

Rutter, Michael, B. Maughan, P. Mortimer, J. Ouston, and A. Smith. 1979. *Fifteen Thousand Hours: Secondary Schools and Their Effects on Children.* Cambridge: Harvard University Press.

Sanders, James W. 1981. *The Education of an Urban Minority: Catholics in Chicago, 1822–1965.* New York: Oxford University Press.

Scott, W. Richard, and John W. Meyer. 1984. "Environmental Linkages and Organizational Complexity." Stanford University Institute for Research on Educational Finance and Governance Project Report No. 84-A16.

Sizer, Theodore R. 1984. *Horace's Compromise: The Dilemma of the American High School.* Boston: Houghton Mifflin.

Tyack, David. 1974. *The One Best System.* Cambridge: Harvard University Press.

Weick, Karl E. 1976. "Educational Organizations As Loosely Coupled Systems." *Administrative Science Quarterly* 21:1–19.

Williamson, Oliver. 1975. *Markets and Hierarchies.* New York: Free Press.

Wirt, Frederick and Michael Kirst. 1982. *Schools in Conflict.* Berkeley: McCutchan.

John E. Chubb is Senior Fellow, The Brookings Institution, 1775 Massachusetts Ave., NW, Washington, DC 20036.

Terry M. Moe is Associate Professor of Political Science, Stanford University, Stanford, CA 94305.

[12]

J. EDUCATION POLICY, 1994, VOL. 9, NO. 3, 245–266

Human capital theory and the industry training strategy in New Zealand

Patrick Fitzsimons and Michael Peters
Auckland Institute of Technology and University of Auckland

This paper begins with the assertion that the regime of 'perpetual training'' (Deleuze 1992) will become the new regime and system which now motivates and integrates education and industry in the western world. This notion is located in the national industry training strategy for New Zealand. The first section serves to provide the policy context, focusing on public sector restructuring and the significance of the Employment Contracts Act (1991). The industry training strategy is outlined and described in some detail within the main body of the paper. This strategy is explained in terms of the underlying human capital theory, in particular, with reference to a recent OECD survey of New Zealand's economy and in terms of general workplace reform. The paper then addresses the problems inherent in human capital theory and the way it legitimizes present Government policy in education and training. Human capital theory is the most influential economic theory of education, setting the framework of government policies since the early 1960s. The paper isolates two basic assumptions on which neo-classical, and therefore also human capital theory depends. These assumptions are cast in universal and ahistorical terms. The first is the idea that the economy is an analytically separate realm of society that can be understood in terms of its own internal dynamics. The second key foundation is the assumption that individuals act rationally to maximize utilities. The paper argues that individuals are capable of acting irrationally or in pursuit of goals other than the maximization of utility, and that the economy is influenced by politics and culture, but the strategy of excluding these deviations from the rationality principle is justified wrongly by the effort to identify the core dynamics of an economy. Some comment is given towards the end of the paper about recent experience in the UK of the conceptual and empirical problems of the type that the authors consider are in need of research within New Zealand.

Introduction

> The modulating principle of 'salary according to merit' has not failed to tempt national education itself. Indeed, just as the corporation replaces the factory, *perpetual training* tends to replace the *school*, and continuous control to replace the examination. Which is the surest way of delivering the school over to the corporation. (Deleuze 1992)

Perpetual training is the new rationale for education and training systems in advanced countries, providing the link between education, in the broadest sense, and the economic system. It motivates both policy and practice and, in terms of the prevailing human capital theory presently revitalized by the OECD, perpetual training becomes the basis for a vocational reoriëntation of the education system to meet the needs of the 'new' economy. New Zealand is a prime example. The current New Zealand Prime Minister puts it this way: 'In an economy which is integrated and growing – in an inclusive economy – there must be a place for everyone. And education is the key to participation' (Bolger, quoted in Ministry of Education 1993). Further emphasis on perpetual training is reiterated as the basis of the discussion in the same document, *Education for the 21st Century*:

> Schools can no longer provide people with the specific skills they will need in adulthood, because we can no longer predict what those skills will be. People are going to have to re-train several times through their working lives. If change is constant, education and training must be, too. (Ministry of Education, 1993: 1)

0268–0939/94 $10·00 © 1994 Taylor & Francis Ltd.

The new 'visionary' policy document, which aims to provide the future foundations, goes on to develop and discuss 'desirable outcomes' and 'targets' in terms of a discourse that integrates the workplace into the education system and clearly views education and training – the investment in people as our 'greatest resource' – as the basis for future prosperity and success in international competition.

According to the Government's Industry Skills Training Strategy (Education and Training Support Agency 1992: 3) perpetual training will be available through the promotion of a 'training culture' which is to be developed in New Zealand. This cultural change is expected to bring improvements to industry in the form of a 'highly skilled and adaptable workforce that will match the competitiveness needed in the international market place'. This strategy involves a number of components, including the establishment of the New Zealand Qualifications Authority (NZQA), the Education and Training Support Agency (ETSA), and the enactment of related legislation, in particular, the Industry Training Act (1992). These elements are themselves part of the wider strategy that has been termed by the Government 'Skill New Zealand', which aims at the development of a workplace culture that recognizes the importance of workplace training as an alternative to education in tertiary institutions. Skill New Zealand is part of the wider emphasis on the development of a 'seamless education system', which aims at the integration of all levels of education with training in the workplace and as such represents a comprehensive policy which is intended to reach new and unprecedented levels of system integration and rationalization. This paper is concerned with these policy developments: first, it provides a background for these policy moves within the context of liberalization of the economy and restructuring of the public sector; second, it examines the underlying theory of human capital theory; third, it reviews and critiques the essential elements of Skill New Zealand in terms of the establishment of NZQA, ETSA and the Industry Training Act.

The policy context: economic liberalization and public sector restructuring[1]

Education and training 'reforms' must be understood within the wider context of public sector restructuring, and as a subset of the reforms of the state sector based on the same principles, just as the restructuring of the public sector must be understood as a part of the 'radical' structural economic reform embarked upon by the fourth Labour Government (1984–90). On the whole, the 'experiment' has been both accepted and consolidated by the National administration that succeeded Labour in 1990. To be sure, the commitment by British and American administrations to monetarism and supply-side economics and the general move towards economic liberalization by western governments provided a global context for structural reform in New Zealand. This international development was reinforced by the rapid dissemination of a particular set of theoretical developments in microeconomic theory (to the control departments of the New Zealand bureaucracy, the Treasury and State Services Commission), emphasizing notions of public choice, contestability and property rights. Public choice theory, originating with James Buchanan and Gordon Tullock (1962) in Virginia, represents a renewal of the main article of faith underlying classical economic liberalism. It asserts that all behaviour is dominated by self-interest and its major innovation is to extend this principle to the status of a paradigm for understanding politics. On this view individuals are rational utility maximizers and, while it is accepted that the pursuit of self-interest in the market-place will yield socially desirable outcomes, similar behaviour in politics needs to be structured and controlled in various ways (see Easton 1988, Boston *et al.* 1991).

Criticism of the 'Think Big' projects (which emphasized the failure of a huge public investment programme in the 1970s) was ultimately directed at the nature of *direct* government intervention in the economy. This criticism was to be ritually reiterated later with the break-up of the centrally planned economies of Eastern Europe. It was perceived that New Zealand has performed poorly in terms of productivity and growth since the mid-1970s; there was a record of devaluation, inflation and stabilization attempts, and the *ad hoc* development of a set of 'restrictive' regulatory government interventions since the 1970s (Duncan and Bollard 1992).

Jesson (1992: 37), a left-wing critic and recent Alliance party candidate, argues that Labour, historically a political party of the welfare state and the regulated economy with links to the union movement, on becoming government 'discarded this tradition without warning and became a party of the New Right'. Constitutionally, operating on the basis of a 'thin' political system (a two-party system with a single parliamentary chamber and few checks and balances to the exercise of executive power), the Labour Government pushed through its reforms at an astonishingly rapid rate based on a deliberate 'politics of reform' aimed at neutralizing opposition (Douglas 1989). In the six years to 1990 when Labour was in power it almost completely deregulated the New Zealand economy: it deregulated the financial sector; it terminated subsidies for agricultural products and exports; it abolished import licensing, heavily reduced tariffs, removed controls on international capital, liberalized foreign investment, and floated the exchange rate (Duncan and Bollard 1992: 6).

A review of the role of the state and the 'restructuring' of the public sector was seen as a necessary part of the wider structural economic reform. In particular, the new micro-economic theories argued that state-owned and -controlled trading organizations performed poorly because they were constrained by the institutional environment and lacked the same incentives as the private sector. From the mid-1980s the Government pursued a programme of corporatization and, later, privatization, as twin strategies for improving the efficiency and accountability of state trading departments. Under these strategies social functions were separated out from the commercial functions of state trading organizations and 'managers' were required to run these trading organizations as successful businesses which involved pricing and marketing within performance objectives set by ministers. The new state enterprises, modelled on the private sector each with its own board of directors, were required to operate in a competitively neutral environment. The operating principles were enshrined in the State-Owned Enterprises (SOEs) Act (1986). Nine SOEs were created from former government trading departments on 1 April 1987. Subsequently other SOEs have been created.[2] Under the Act trading departments became state corporations regulated by company law. They are required to be run to make a profit and to be as efficient as their private sector counterparts. User charges have been introduced for government services purchased from the corporations and the SOEs, in the newly established competitively neutral environment, are also required to pay dividends and taxes. Ministers are now 'shareholders', and chief executive officers who have purposely been given the freedom to manage without political interference, must provide a 'statement of corporate intent' and annual reports.

A privatization programme followed corporatization, against an explicit election promise. Advocates of state sector reform had seen corporatization as a preliminary and partial solution (Treasury 1984, 1987, Dean 1989). In general, the arguments for privatization centred on alleged operational weaknesses in the SOE model which arose out of differences from the private sector, e.g., no threat of take-over or bankruptcy, non-shareholding directors, state guarantees and monitoring roles. The Treasury (1987) and the Business Roundtable (Blandy 1988) were the strongest voices in favour of privatization, arguing that a transfer of assets to the private sector would address efficiency shortfalls of the SOEs, help reduce the public debt, continue the process of 'load-shedding', and aid capital accumulation in the private sector. Opposition to privatization came from a variety of sources. Maori contested the Government's right to sell off public assets under the Treaty of Waitangi. Unions not only feared huge redundancies but also critiqued the 'emerging privatized market society' focusing on the way a political debate over the role of the state and democracy had been reduced to, or subsumed by, economic arguments (PSA 1989).

Labour's state asset sales programme, which took place from 1988 to (June) 1990, included 15 major businesses totalling approximately a massive $9 billion. (The sale of Telecom at $4·25 billion in 1990 was the fourth largest global sale that year.) The timing of the sales was problematic. The first sales followed rapidly on the huge stock market crash of 1987 in which a fall in value of over 50% was experienced, and the economy was in deep recession. Also the valuation and marketization processes were open to question. Sale by treaty and tender followed by negotiation was criticized as a process open to political interference. No full market flotations occurred. Many of the agreed asset prices, it has been justly asserted, were much too low: the assets sold off had been greatly undervalued. It is not even clear to what extent the level of public debt was reduced through the privatization programme. Whether the sales programme was in the best long-term interests of New Zealand is another matter.

The reform of the remaining core public sector (i.e., the residual non-SOE public sector) including defence, policing and justice, social services such as health and education, and research and development (among others), was based on two major pieces of legislation: the State Sector Act 1988 and the Public Finance Act 1989. Reforms based on these Acts have been described as 'the most far-reaching and ambitious of any of their kind in the world' (State Services Commission 1991). Christopher Hood (1990: 210), commenting on the Treasury's (1987) treatise, *Government Management* – the basis and inspiration for the reforms – described it as 'remarkable', implying that it was vastly more coherent and intellectually sophisticated than its equivalents elsewhere: 'Neither Canberra nor Whitehall has produced anything remotely comparable in quality or quantity to the New Zealand Treasury's "NPM manifesto".' He cites the cardinal principles of what he terms 'New Public Management', set in place by Treasury: goal clarity, transparency, contestability, avoidance of bureaucratic or provider capture, congruent incentive structures, enhancement of accountability and cost-effective use of information.

The impetus for the reforms was economic efficiency and accordingly the reforms 'focused upon generating improvement by clarifying objectives and allowing managers to manage within a framework of accountability and performance' (State Services Commission 1991: 5). The State Sector Act had two main aims: to redefine the relationship between ministers and permanent heads from one based on the Westminster system (e.g., permanent tenure, independently set remuneration) to one based on a performance contract; and to apply similar labour-market regulations to both state and private-sector employment (Scott *et al.* 1990: 153). Where the State Sector Act made changes in industrial relations and in the appointment and employment of senior managers, the Public Finance Act (1989) clarified the meaning of 'performance' in the Public Service by establishing criteria for monitoring. The reforms of financial management under the Finance Act have followed changes adopted in Britain and

Australia with two important differences: the first is the distinction between purchases and ownership; the second is the distinction between output and outcomes. The tension between the Government's aims as owner of its agencies and its aims as consumer of their outputs can be resolved through the market, i.e., contestability. Chief executive officers are directly responsible for the outputs (the goods and services) produced by their departments and the ministers are responsible for choosing which outputs should be produced and therefore also for the outcomes (the effects of those outputs on the community). The first task of policy advice, according to this model of management, is to identify the connection between the outputs and the outcomes, the trade-offs between different outcomes and the best course for the supply of outputs. The justification for public expenditure is related to the directness and quality of the connection. These two major differences have also influenced methods of appropriation (which are now directly linked to performance), the nature of reporting and the nature of policy advice (Scott *et al.* 1990: 156).

Neo-liberals and advocates of New Right policies in New Zealand have increasingly focused their attention on the rising and apparently irreversible tide of welfare expectations, arguing that the welfare state has evaded both investment and work incentives, and has contributed directly to the economic recession. The combined effects of social policies – inclusing guaranteed minimum wages, superannuation, and the exponential growth of health and education sectors – have allegedly strengthened organized labour *vis-à-vis* capital, augmented wage as against capital goods, and increased state borrowing from itself, leading to a decline of profitability.

Neo-liberals such as the previous Minister of Health, Simon Upton[3] and the then Minister of Social Welfare, Jenny Shipley (now Minister of Health), argued that the so-called perverse effects lead to greater state interventionism in both social and economic terms, but the more the state helps, they argue, the more it will have to help and at diminishing levels of effectiveness. It is alleged that increasing levels of intervention, while leading to the current crisis of an imbalance between state receipts and expenditure, tend in the long term to rob economic liberalism of its vitality. The bottom line is that the perverse effects of economic and social intervention represent to these critics a fundamental threat to individual, political and democratic freedom.

Restructuring of the state was not restricted to the core public sector. The principles of public sector restructuring became the basis for the reorganization of education (Picot 1988), local government and health under the Fourth Labour Government. Throughout the period of public sector restructuring, the bulk of the policy initiatives in education aimed at increasing the skill levels of workers were focused on schools but the problem has now been exported upwards to the post-school level.

The National Government, which came to power in 1990, went further in that the 'residual' public sector was redefined in terms of a more limited or minimal state. This government embarked on the most significant changes to the welfare state since its establishment in the 1930s. The major initiatives have included substantial cuts in benefits and other forms of income support, together with much stricter eligibility criteria, greater targeting of social assistance and changes to the method of targeting, and 'a radical redesign of the means by which the state provides assistance', particularly in the areas of housing, health care and tertiary education (Boston 1992: 1). While the changes have been justified in terms of the need for fiscal stringency, given the country's high external debt and the failure of the previous policy regime, it is clear, as Boston (ibid.) notes, that the changes 'also originate from a marked shift in political philosophy' which focuses on the question of the nature and scope of the state.

The Employment Contracts Act

The National Government, in addition, has committed itself to a privatization programme and to the corporatization of the remaining public sector organizations, including Electricity Companies, Crown Research Institutes and Crown Health Enterprises. Perhaps most importantly the National Government has introduced the Employment Contracts Act (1991) which complements social welfare changes in the sense that it is 'decidedly anti-collectivist in philosophy and intent', shifting as it does 'the focus of labour law from the collective to the individual' (Walsh 1992: 59, 64). The Act, designed to liberalize the labour market through deregulation, focuses on seven components: 'freedom of association'; enterprise bargaining; personal grievance; enforceability of contracts; strike and lock-out rights; the redesign of the Employment Court; a code of minimum wages and conditions. In general, then, it can be argued that the National Government has accepted, continued with and attempted to complete the transformation initiated under the neo-liberal ideology of the Labour Government (Easton 1993).

Since 1894, successive statutes have largely governed the nature of employer–employee relationships in New Zealand. From the Industrial Conciliation and Arbitration Act of 1894 to the Labour Relations Act of 1987 there was a statutory basis for union representation. On this basis, unions, on behalf of their members, entered into types of contracts with employers. These contracts were in the form of awards or collective agreements. A major effect of having a system of awards and agreements was that a relatively uniform set of conditions and wages was created. Terms and conditions of employment were arrived at by agreement between unions and employers or, where there was a dispute, by a judgment handed down by the Arbitration Court. Awards covered such matters as: prescribed duties, rates of pay, leave for training (if any), terms of apprenticeships, hours of work, leave allowed, notice required and so on. A major criticism of the system prior to 1991 was that it was too inflexible, it did not take into account the circumstances of individual workplaces and it was also difficult for an enterprise to introduce new technology.

The Employment Contracts Act changed the basis of industrial bargaining in New Zealand and saw a return to direct bargaining between the employer and employees. Instead of a centralized bargaining system the emphasis is now on decentralized bargaining at the individual enterprise level. Contracts of employment were originally a common law concept developed by the courts, setting out the relationship between an individual employee and an employer. Common law is unwritten law based on judicial decisions. In general, the common law applied only when statutes and specific employment contract arrangements are silent or did not apply to the parties concerned.

Any attempt to come to grips with the factors that led to the Employment Contracts Act must, according to Boxall (Harbridge 1993: 148), deal with the reform agenda of New Zealand managers. Management is no longer the reactive party in the ideological debate over the nature of the employment relationship and the practical regulations of its terms. International commentators emphasize that new product markets are increasingly competitive and deregulated. Management is concerned with rising levels of domestic and international competition. The development of contestable markets generates a need for new types of economic performance. There are now data available which demonstrate that employers in the 1980s sought to make labour relations as flexible as they believed product market conditions demanded (Harbridge 1993: 150). The Employment Contracts Act enables pay and performance on the job to be linked. The key in all of this is flexibility, and decentralization of employment wage bargaining follows as one means of securing that value. Bargaining also extends to new technology, methods of work organization, productivity and product quality and new forms of employee involvement in management. The more progressive unions supported more co-operative relationships with employers (Harbridge 1993: 154). Boxall (in Harbridge 1993) sets out trends which he takes from the literature that reports on the progress of the implementation of the legislation. First, given the new opportunity, management is clearly opting for enterprise and workplace bargaining. Second, management has continued to seek improvements in units costs under the Employment Contracts Act. Third, in the main, management is seeking to replace multiple awards with a single collective contract. Fourth, in terms of employee relations styles, a range of management is emerging.

Under enterprise bargaining, where there are serious commitments by management to increased productivity, this is reflected in the employment contracts' greater training investments (Harbridge 1993: 160–162). These employment contracts may focus on skills and competencies as a means of employees obtaining increases in pay. At each step of the career path, a prescribed set of skills will need to be mastered before progression to the next step is possible. These can be written into employment contracts. The establishment of career paths based on the acquisition of skills is intended to develop not only a highly skilled and adaptable workforce, but also a 'training culture' – an attitude that education is a lifelong process – not a once-off matter to be finished and done with.

Training cannot, however, be imposed rationally when changes in attitude and co-operation are required. From Boxall's (Harbridge 1993) data, it appears that enterprise bargaining is the trend and that, in some workplaces at least, training is seen as an investment and written into employment contracts. The Government's industry training strategy depends for its increases in productivity on training built into industry-wide career paths and portability. This latter option seems to be at odds with the trend towards enterprise bargaining. In order for New Zealand to compete successfully in the global market-place it could be argued that changes to accepted ideas and practices are needed. The precise steps to be taken, however, are far from self-evident. An example of the need for debate can be seen in the following comment from a spokesperson from a major national union organization:

> Before anyone starts to interpret this as a Council of Trade Unions advocacy of enterprise bargaining, let me add that we do not think that there is the remotest prospect of any major lift in the competitiveness of New Zealand production if it is based on the enterprise as the focus of change. (Douglas, quoted in Harbridge 1993: 202)

Douglas (ibid.) criticizes the empirical fact that one outcome of the industry training strategy is that the terrain on which employment contracts are negotiated is the enterprise. The employment contracts that encompass increased skill performance as one basis for enhanced work conditions ought, according to the philosophy of the industry training strategy, to be on an industry-wide basis. It would seem consistent within neo-liberal theory for the notion of rational utility maximization to focus on an enterprise level which is of immediate benefit.

Critique of human capital theory

Human capital theory is the most influential economic theory of western education, setting the framework of government policies since the early 1960s. In the *Wealth of Nations* (1776) Adam Smith formulated the basis of what was later to become the science of human capital. Over the next two centuries two schools of thought can be distinguished. The first school of thought differentiated between the acquired capacities which were classified as capital and the human beings themselves, who were not. A second school of thought claimed that human beings themselves were capital.

The clearest statement of the deficiencies of human capital theory goes to the heart of neo-classical economics. The revival of economic sociology, in particular at the hands of Fred Block (1990: 21), wants to challenge one of the two basic assumptions motivating the methodology of neo-classical economics which rests on two basic building blocks:

> The first is the idea that the economy is an analytically separate realm of society that can be understood in terms of its own internal dynamics. Economists are perfectly aware that economy is influenced by politics and culture, but they see these as exogenous factors that can be safely bracketed as one develops a framework that focuses on purely economic factors.
>
> The second key foundation is the assumption that individuals act rationally to maximise utilities. Here, again, economists are acutely aware that individuals are capable of acting irrationally or in pursuit of goals other than the maximisation of utility, but the strategy of excluding these deviations from the rationality principle is justified by the effort to identify the core dynamics of an economy.

Block (1990) effectively isolates two basic assumptions on which neo-classical and therefore also human capital theory depends. These assumptions are cast in universal and ahistorical terms. Given the facts that they emerged from a body of theory which was first formulated in the 19th century and that they continue to provide the basis for neo-liberal restructuring of the state in the 1980s and 1990s within most western liberal democracies, it is, perhaps, time that these original assumptions were re-examined. Together the two assumptions provide the basis for the model of the self-regulating market which harmonizes transactions for products, labour and capital.

Economic sociology challenges the first assumption by arguing that the society and culture cannot be arbitrarily split off from the economy. Clearly, both the society and culture shape the preferences of individuals in various ways. Social factors also influence the economic transactions between employers and employees. Even the contract itself rests on cultural understandings and the legal framework which is historically determined. The methodological foundations of neo-classical economics obscure the social, cultural and political determinants of economic action. This results in an analysis that is ahistorical and, through a tautological procedure, continually rediscovers the centrality of purely economic notions (Marginson 1993: 25). Based on the false premise of the 'naturalness' of the pursuit of economic gain by human inclinations, the 'economic fallacy' imagines that capitalist societies do not have cultures in the way that primitive or pre-modern societies do. When we recognize that the pursuit of economic self-interest is itself a cultural creation, then it is apparent that we too are ruled by deeply held, but unexamined, collective beliefs. What is at stake is the degree of freedom that societies have in shaping their economic institutions. Evidence from structural anthropology (e.g., Lévi-Strauss 1963) suggests that there is considerable freedom within primitive societies to organize their economies in many ways to meet their needs apart from the most functional means. A kinship system, for example, is one of the foundational economic institutions of primitive societies but, according to Lévi-Strauss (1963: 50), 'a kinship system is an arbitrary system of representations, not the spontaneous development of a real situation'. In studying the organization of a kinship system Lévi-Strauss (1963: 51) argues that, in primitive societies, the fact that a kinship system is an arbitrary arrangement shows that economic necessity does not predict the society's actual social arrangements. Block (1990: 28) says that modern complex societies have potentially considerably more leeway than primitive societies in organizing the division of labour to provide the necessities of life. In opposition to neo-classical claims of the dire consequences that might result from interference with the capitalist market, highly developed societies have developed and used functional substitutes for their necessities that have often proved superior to those that they replaced. Neo-classical restructuring is not therefore the economic necessity that its neo-liberal rhetoric proclaims.

How, then, are we to explain the higher earnings of educated labour? The explanation is connected to the assumption in human capital theory that differences in income must as a general rule reflect differences of social productivity. It is of the essence of neo-classical economics to deny any separability of the process of social production from that of the distribution of the social product (Westoby 1974: 40). Since human capital cannot be bought and sold it is represented by its services and as such cannot be measured directly. Education is also universally admitted to have other effects besides increasing the earnings of individuals. The neo-classical human capital perspective simplifies a wealth of social events that are significant in education and reduces the most qualitatively diverse social, psychological and historical phenomena to a common, quantitative denominator. The ordinary thoughts of individual human beings are ignored even though these are what interpret the culture as it is passed by education from one generation to the next. Interpretations within educational transmission must distort the signification of the society, the economy and culture. The rational human capital educational calculus, however, operates as if there were no other factors.

The return to neo-classical theory, in its attempt analytically to split off the economy as separate from society using the notion of human capital, has missed the history of the significance of some elements of Marx's analysis. For Marx, capital has special significance. For economists it is an unconscious article of faith that the economic behaviour of individuals may be understood independently of the social relations in which they are involved, and the history of those social relations. They first describe the essence of people as economic units – as isolated individuals – and they then bring them into association with other people. Economists view these as aggregation problems but this is to misunderstand them. From a Marxist perspective, prior to being conceptualized separately, individuals are already necessarily constructed by the social relations of which they are part. The relationship of the individual (i.e., the individual who has been *a priori* separated out from society by neo-classical economic theory) as the buyer and seller of commodities is false. The contradiction between individual activity and social relations was analysed by Marx (capital) in the form of the contradiction between use value and exchange value within the commodity. The social relations of production are then analysed separately, but in a disguised form as relations between commodities – labour and capital in general. As long as these two spheres are held separate, contradictions are bound to arise in the attempt to reconcile them. For to derive the characteristics of commodities (their relative price) as they confront the individual, we must have already discovered the social relations of whole classes.

Human capital theory is an impoverished notion of capital. It is unable to understand human activity other than as the exchange of commodities and the notion of capital employed is purely a quantitative one. This misses the point that capital is an independent social force where the creation of social value comes about through its capital accumulation and continual transformation through the circulation of commodities. Under capitalism labour is separated structurally from the means of production. These are concentrated, as commodities and capital, in the hands of an opposing class. The means of production are not only physical but appear in social relations. The individual under capitalism can come to grips with the means of production only through selling his or her labour commodity. The struggle of labourers to improve life's conditions is mediated, then, through the social relations within which they find themselves. Given this explanation, human capital is an abstract form of labour – a commodity – and not capital.

Commodities such as human capital are therefore part of the life cycle of capitalism as a form of labour and not able to be exchanged independently of it.

The second assumption exposed by Block (1990) which is of primary importance to human capital theory is also open to criticism on a variety of grounds. The maximization of rational self-interest, separate from the social group to which the individual belongs, is a central article of faith in human capital theory. A criticism of the rational utility maximizer (Block 1990: 25) suggests that the elevation of self-interest to a position of dominance on which much economic analysis rests is itself a consequence of social arrangements. A further criticism emphasizes the problematic nature of individual rationality. Under conditions of complexity and uncertainty, the gap between rationality in action and perfect rationality can be substantial. What constitutes rational action depends to some degree at least on the context.

In modern human capital theory all human behaviour is based on the economic self-interest of individuals operating within freely competitive markets. Other forms of behaviour are excluded or treated as distortions of the model. Milton Friedman (1962: 100–101), for example, argued that all the benefits of vocational and professional education were received by the individual who was educated. People should therefore be able to invest in the education of the individual and expect the individual to repay the capital when they begin earning. Schultz (cited in Marginson 1993) admitted that even though, within the economic sphere, education could be considered as either consumption or as investment – and they are difficult to distinguish – nevertheless he considered education to be an investment. Becker (cited in Marginson, ibid.) identified the services yielded by 'stocks of human capital' as a tradeable commodity capable of being organized on the basis of market exchange. The Chicago school of economics distinguished between two core hypotheses about human capital theory. The first is that education and training increase individual cognitive capacity and therefore augment productivity. The second is that increased productivity leads to increased individual earnings, and these increased earnings are a measure of the value of the human capital. The social rate of return on capital was also distinguished from the private rate of return. The private rate of return on investment in human capital is calculated by adding benefits derived from education over a lifetime or some shorter period and subtracting the total costs incurred while undergoing education. It is difficult, however, to estimate lifetime earnings. There are two different methods used to estimate the social rate of return on investment in education. The first calculates the net benefits to individuals, subtracts the cost of government funding of education and then adds the externalities – the economic benefits of education that are not captured by individuals. It has, according to Marginson (1993: 40) proved impossible to calculate the value of these externalities. The second method of calculating assumes that it is possible to isolate a series of discrete causes of economic growth which are mutually exclusive. In a growing economy with increasing expenditure on education these assumptions about rates of return were not questioned very closely – correlation assumed the mantle of causation. But questions can be raised. If, for example, as educators claim, education had been responsible for economic growth it was equally plausible for politicians, business leaders and media commentators to argue that it was responsible for the recession (Marginson 1993: 44). Even if appropriate statistical information could be collected and calculated about social trends, the method faces big obstacles even as an operational guide to action. We cannot tell from the statistics collected, for example, whether the benefits calculated are stable, diminishing or increasing at the time of calculation. After the enthusiasm of educationalists in the early period of the 1960s, the relationship between education and the economy had now become a liability. In 1986 the

OECD returned to its original 1961 argument calling for:

> . . . lifting of the overall level of educational attainment, greater technological sophistication in the educational systems, closer relations between education and business, and strengthening of recurrent education and on the job training. The 'human factor is assuming pre-eminence as a factor of production'.

This emphasis on human capital theory features in the industry training strategy.

Industry training, the OECD and human capital theory

The clearest statement of the way human capital theory underlines government thinking has been given by the recent OECD (1993) survey of the New Zealand economy. In terms of structural reform the OECD identifies the following four elements as the basis for the Government's structural policy framework:

> enhancing *labour flexibility* – through regulatory reform in the labour market, as well as raising skill levels by additional investment in education, training and employment schemes, and immigration focused on attracting high-quality human capital;
>
> promoting *participation and self-reliance* – through reforms to the welfare system;
>
> improving the *overall competitiveness* of the economy – through continued supply-side reforms including the legal framework, resource management, and tax policy;
>
> and strengthening *interactional linkages* – by encouraging foreign investment and trade development. (OECD 1993: 55)

The OECD, in the fourth and final section of their survey, identifies human-capital development as the crucial issue. Workforce skills and management are seen as the 'key determinant of economic performance', and human-capital development as a 'factor which enhances labour-market flexibility and facilitates structural adjustment' (p. 69). The OECD argues that, while the educational system and formal qualifications represent significant factors in the fabric of human capital, there are important elements which fall outside these realms. Human capital, in OECD terms, is 'the sum of the skills embodied in its people, with the value of that capital dependent on the opportunities people have to use those skills' (pp. 69–70). Clearly, such a definition is designed also to include workforce skills acquired in the workplace. On this basis the OECD makes a case for the importance of skill development which is deemed to be even more crucial for New Zealand than elsewhere given low participation rates in education, the high proportion of people without formal qualifications, and New Zealand's relatively poor performance in terms of total factory productivity (TFP) growth (i.e., output growth unexplained by additional labour and capital imputs). The OECD report states:

> In the past, benefit structures, a lack of vocational focus in the school curriculum, inadequate integration between different forms of post-compulsory education and training, labour-market regulations, and the highly protected economic environment all led to poor skill development (1993: 103)

The survey identifies not only poor skill development but also skill shortages and skill mismatches as primary constraints facing future economic performance. The present government's education and training strategy is reviewd in this context and it is concluded that the restructuring of the public sector and social welfare, the reform of education and training to date and liberalization of the labour market have improved the environment within which New Zealand develop their skills. The report identifies the four areas where reforms are currently being implemented gradually, namely the qualifications framework, industry training, school management and immigration policy. It concludes by making suggestions for further action: it notes that the pace at which both the framework and national curriculum are established will determine when related reforms of the education and training systems become fully effective. The report recommends greater speed and 'adaptability' over 'detailed prescription'. It identifies scope for a co-ordinating role for government in the move to an industry-led training system and highlights the higher education sector as an area where the reforms have not gone far enough. In the absence of significant private sector competition, the report suggests lower per-student subsidies, the levying of the envisaged capital charge regime, and the elimination of any restraints on competitive practices as the policy means for encouraging the sector to respond to the training needs of industry.

Indeed, as Simon Marginson (1993: 48ff.) has noted effectively, the OECD was responsible for the revision and rediscovery of human capital theory in the late 1980s. Originating from neo-classical economics in the work of J. R. Walsh and, later, that of Milton Friedman and Simon Kutkznets in the 1940s and 1950s, human capital theory was to undergo development in the hands of Theodore Schultz, Jacob Mincer and Gary Becker in the 1960s, when the fundamental claim was that human capital determines the rate of economic growth. Marginson (1993: 40) identifies three phases in the application of human capital theory to government education policy:

> The first phase, in the 1960s, was one of public investment in human capital, dominated by claims about a link between education and economic growth. The second phase was a period of eclipse, in which the earlier policy assumptions were abandoned and the rates of return equations were confined to a modest place with the body of neo-classical theory. The third phase (not completed) saw renewed policy commitment to investment in human capital. But in the free market climate now prevailing, the emphasis is on private rather than public investment.

In this latest phase, of which the policies pursued by the Government are a prime example, education in human capital terms is seen as a source of labour-market flexibility in relation to technological and social change.

Workplace reform

The organization of the workforce in New Zealand has traditionally been characterized as hierarchical. In New Zealand (as in his homeland in America) Frederick Winslow Taylor's (1911) ideas on scientific management became guiding principles of corporation and factory management and, to a large extent, they remain so today.[4] Workers in industry were traditionally separated from management in skills, education and culture. There was a strong demarcation of job skills and very little on-the-job training. In a climate of conflict between unions and employers, unions saw it as necessary that employees belonging to one union should not carry out duties properly belonging in the province of another union. The governing principle was control by management. Many of these conditions are to be reformed. As mentioned earlier, the OECD (1993: 69) sees workforce skills and management as the 'key determinant of economic performance', and human capital development as a 'factor which enhances labour-market flexibility and facilitates structural adjustment'. In keeping with such advice, workplace reform has been introduced recently into New Zealand as part of the new flexible form of capital labour relations in the productive sector. Workplace reform implies breaking down the manual–mental division of labour and is based on the development of a labour process which is marked by multiple tasks, high-skilled tasks, horizontal organization, co-operative responsibility and shared decision making. Workplace reform hinges on the integration of: skills; training; work organization; industrial relations; new technologies, production, service delivery systems and quality programmes. These issues are brought together and co-ordinated within companies and industries through joint management and union consultative committees. Workplace reform is presented by management and unions (NZCTU 1992), as an attempt to alleviate worker alienation through integrating the conception and execution phases of work in the interests of productivity. The Employment Contracts Act is central to the creation of the conditions necessary for the reform of the workplace. Instead of a centralized bargaining system the emphasis is now on decentralized bargaining at the individual enterprise level. Contrary to traditional patterns of union initiatives, management in New Zealand as well as internationally has taken the initiative in labour relations (Harbridge 1993: 149). A range of management behaviour is also emerging that allows for flexibility and demands higher levels of skills and problem solving by both workers and management (Harbridge 1993: 160). The critical issue in organizing the reform of the workplace is how to institutionalize the positive feedback needed about productivity of expanded human capacities. Block (1990: 199) discusses some of the institutional innovations in workplace management being used by some US firms. 'First, the firm must commit itself to providing its employees with career development opportunities and greater employment security. A second set of changes in the workplace centres on the greater democratisation of decision making.' A combination of these principles means that work needs to be redesigned and management structures need to be flattened. This includes devolution of responsibility and accountability for decisions on the conception and execution of work to the worker. Workers are given some control over the implementation of reforms in the workplace, which develops a sense of commitment. Under some versions of workplace reform, there are no pay differentials based on the mere possession of skills – instead, performance pay is introduced. Provision of performance pay within employment contracts is consistent with the notion of performance pay introduced into Skill New Zealand by the Industry Training Act (1992) – an Act that is central to the industry training strategy.

Skill New Zealand

Skill New Zealand is the strategy being implemented by the National Government to establish industry-led skills training linked to the National Qualifications Framework across all industries, including those not covered by traditional apprenticeship arrangements. The strategy is parallel to the senior secondary school and merges into tertiary institutions, universities, polytechnics and colleges of education. The strategy, which will be in place by 1995 (Budget 1993: 14), emphasizes national workplace, competency-based training, 'driven' by industry. The strategy has as its aim the production of a highly skilled workforce at enterprise and industry level to enhance New Zealand's competitiveness. Two desirable outcomes following from this aim are listed by the Ministry of Education (1993: 32); first, a training and qualifications system is needed which is highly responsive to the needs of enterprise and industry; second, New Zealand needs to develop an internationally competitive productive sector with a workforce which is able to respond quickly and effectively to a changing international market-place.

Workplace training is being promoted as an alternative to the traditional provision of education in tertiary institutions although it is suggested that industry training organizations (ITOs) will use some of the capacity of that system. Industry is being asked to lead in settling and monitoring skill standards, and designing and making arrangements for the delivery of such training. All successful training under Skill New Zealand will lead to the National Certificate or the National Diploma. These qualifications are part of the same framework that will bind together all education and training in New Zealand. A range of pathways will be developed in schools, tertiary institutions and in the workplace. A Schools–Industry Links policy will encourage the development of linkages between schools and local enterprises. Skill pathways is a transition measure designed to develop training pathways until Skill New Zealand is in place. The scheme is specifically targeted at 16–20-year-olds and will cover existing youth traineeship commitments. Funding for this part of the scheme will be NZ $7·3 million in order to provide an additional 1100–1500 places. To encourage employers to take on and train such people Skill Start has been introduced which provides a subsidy to employers of $1000 per trainee (up to three trainees). Skill Start is expected to cost $5 million. Together the initiatives represent an $18·4 million increase for Skill New Zealand, taking total funding to $59 million.

Under the Skill New Zealand initiative, the target for the development of ITOs by 2001 is that industries covered by an ITO will employ 60% of the employed workforce. The target for skill standards for the National Qualifications Framework will have been developed by 2001 for 100% of industries. The target for qualifications through training in industry at Qualifications Framework Level 4 or above will be achieved in 2001 by 20% of the current adult population. All of these targets are planned to be achieved within existing planned expenditure in this area (Ministry of Education 1993: 33).

The New Zealand Qualifications Authority

The New Zealand Qualifications Authority (NZQA) was established under the Education Amendment Act (1990) in order to 'establish a consistent approach to the recognition of qualifications in academic and vocational areas' (S. 247). The purpose of NZQA is to co-ordinate an accessible and flexible qualifications system which meets New Zealand's education and training needs and internationally recognized standards. NZQA's main functions are listed in the Education Amendment Act (1990) and can be reduced to four purposes: first, to co-ordinate all qualifications in post-compulsory education and training; second, to set and regularly view standards as they relate to qualifications; third, to ensure that New Zealand qualifications are recognized overseas and overseas qualifications are recognized in New Zealand; and finally, to administer national examinations, both secondary and tertiary.

In order for NZQA to perform these functions, units of learning and qualifications will be registered under the National Qualifications Framework (NQF). The NQF is integral to what the Government refers to as a 'seamless' education system where a person's learning achievements in all parts of education and employment are registered and recognized as part of a national qualification. The NQF will be implemented progressively from 1992 with a target date of 1995 being set for completion. The framework consists of eight levels, with level one being all qualifications up to school certificate level and level eight being postgraduate degrees. National Standards Bodies (NSBs) will be established either by NZQA, or as ITOs under the provisions of the Industry Training Act (1992). It is anticipated by NZQA that NSBs will develop progressively a number of operational roles. The key roles of NSBs are: needs analyses in their sphere of interest; assumption of responsibility for establishing boundaries and qualifications; overseeing the development of Unit Standards in the format required by NZQA for registration in the public domain, undertaking sufficient consultation to ensure a wide acceptance of the standards; assisting in the design, and participating in the operation of, quality management systems;

marketing new qualifications in their sector; and making arrangements for the regular review of standards and qualifications. NZQA will establish a networked national database of student records. The NSBs will be representative of all major users of the relevant units and qualifications and will have a central role in development and maintenance of standards in a field, subfield or domain of the framework. The public process resulting in registration will ensure that the units and qualifications have been endorsed by those who use, grant credit towards or provide recognition of them. This requirement will apply to units which are specific to industries and to more general units and qualifications. A Unit of Learning consists of two parts: the Unit Standard and the Unit Delivery. The two key elements of a Unit Standard are Learning Elements and Performance Criteria. Learning elements (outcomes) are statements of competence (intellectual, practical and attitudinal) to be demonstrated by the learner. Performance criteria are statements which specify the standards to which the activity has to be performed and for which evidence must be gathered. The elements and associated performance criteria form a single entity and, according to NZQA, they should be considered together, as one without the other is meaningless. The Unit Delivery consists of the learning and teaching approaches, content and context, resources and the range of assessments. The Unit Delivery moderation will be guaranteed through a quality assurance partnership that will be set up between NZQA and the training provider concerned, but must satisfy NZQA quality assurance requirements.

Education Training and Support Agency

The Education and Training Support Agency (ETSA) was set up under the Education Amendment Act (1990 S. 271). ETSA has the functions of administering the Training Opportunities Programme (TOPS) and the Primary Industry Cadet Scheme. Other activities and programmes relating to education or training are also able to be determined from time to time by the minister after consultation with interested parties. TOPS is part of the Government's overall education and training strategy and is seen as a 'second chance' for those people who missed out on qualifications in the conventional educational institutions (Ministry of Education 1993: 18). TOPS offers vocational education through schools, polytechnics, private providers, marae (Maori community meeting places) and community-based providers and workplaces (O'Rourke 1993). Under TOPS the emphasis is on 'capability skills which will equip the learner for participation in further education, in the workplace and in adult life generally' (ETSA 1993: 13).

Under TOPS, providers either negotiate or compete for contestable funds by submitting tenders to deliver training under contract to ETSA on a regional basis. Types and levels of training purchased by ETSA are identified by regional plans on the basis of skills identified in the local labour market and of the target group in each region. The contracts between ETSA and the providers set out the outcomes that trainees are expected to achieve. The outcomes sought for individual students are: credits towards national qualifications; progression into further education; employment.

Industry Training Organisations

The Industry Training Act (1992) provides, among other things, for the establishment of Industry Training Organisationds(ITOs). The main purposes of the Industry Training Act (1992) are: providing recognition and funding to ITOs that are setting skill standards for, and administering the delivery of, industry-based training; encouraging and improving industry-based training; repealing the Technicians Training Act (1967) and the Apprenticeship Act (1983), and providing for the continued administration of contracts under those Acts. ITOs have a dual role of setting standards for their industry and oversight of the delivery of training to achieve those standards.

Recognition of an ITO is given by the Board of ETSA (Industry Training Act, S. 5). The Industry Training Act (1992, S. 6) requires that ITOs, either alone or acting with other ITOs, be capable of setting skill standards for their industry in consultation with NZQA. Therefore, where an ITO has been established, it will be the National Standards Body for those standards specific to industry which are registered on the National Qualifications Framework. The Industry Training Act (1992) outlines some key matters that the Board of ETSA must consider in the recognition of an ITO (Industry Training Act 1992, S. 6). Upon application for recognition, the ITO must show that it has the capacity to deliver, assess and maintain and monitor training efficiently, and effectively, to the standard required by NZQA. Among the matters to which the Board of ETSA is to have regard before recognizing an applicant organization are 'the extent to which the organisation represents people engaged in the industry in respect of which the organisation wishes to be recognised' (Industry Training Act 1992: S. 7,a).

The four steps that an ITO goes through in order to set up a training programme are: an industry-wide needs analysis, defining and developing standards; achieving recognition of those standards on the NQF; establishing partnerships with training providers – these may be polytechnics, private training establishments or schools; or developing training programmes themselves for their members. This latter option may include an enterprise setting itself up as a private training provider.

Funding

Recognition of an ITO by ETSA is based strongly on the ability of the ITO to show that it can fund its own operation – *in fact it is the intention of government to have all ITOs completely self-funding within five years*. Under the Industry Training Act, there are no statutory levy provisions for ITOs. Previous training levies have also been repealed. The expectation is that ITOs will be funded mainly by their voluntary members. In the 1992–93 financial year there were two contestable administrative funds available from ETSA for ITOs. The first is an administrative fund (about $7m currently), which is used by the apprenticeship and primary industry cadet schemes, and which may be used to administer other approved training programmes. There is also a training development fund of ($2·5m) set aside for industries mainly to help them identify their skills, needs and standards but not intended as an ongoing source of training funds for an ITO. There will be a small amount of money available from ETSA upon application to set up the ITO. This is to include arrangements for the delivery of training under apprenticeship and technicians' contracts. There is a third contestable fund, the equivalent of $22m, which was to be made available in the 1993 calendar year for ITOs to purchase their off-the-job training requirements from whatever source they choose. The $22m is the estimate of what it costs to run all apprenticeships and primary block courses. It is intended that all off-job training for people in programmes approved by ETSA will be purchased exclusively by ITOs through the operation of this contestable fund. ITOs may choose to use the current polytechnic training facilities or make other arrangements which might include renegotiating training provision with the polytechnics. These negotiations may have implications for polytechnics.

The amount of funding available in any one year is determined by the Government. The 1993 Budget announced a further $18·4 million for the Industry Training Strategy, not all of which will go to ITOs. This increase brings the total budget in this industry training strategy to $59 million. The total expenditure voted on education for 1993–94 on the basis of the Government budget is $4763 million.

The capacity of an ITO to represent the industry, however, and to produce and deliver training, and become independent financially, will necessitate further substantial funding arrangements. Common mechanisms suggest for funding are: levies on commodity use (e.g., a percentage on commodities); unions putting a levy on workers; a percentage of payroll could be collected in this manner to cover the largest possible catchment; a levy on base ingredients; the ITO could develop and sell curricula, certificates, training programmes and materials; companies could donate a flat fee (Fitzsimons 1993). The seeding funding needed to start the ITO is provided by ETSA.

The NQF and industry

NZQA claims that the NQF offers industry accessibility, flexibility, guarantee of standards, work-based training, recognition of prior learning, new qualifications and multi-skilling. Training programmes can be broken down into units, each of which has specified learning outcomes and nationally recognized credits. The framework allegedly provides for the flexible transfer of skills and learning. Standards will be safeguarded by a quality management system, maintained by NZQA in partnership with industry and training providers. The framework will enable skills taught on the job to be recognized in a qualification. NZQA considers that while it is often claimed that New Zealand has a workforce with a low level of skills, it may be more accurate to describe it as workforce with a low level of qualifications (NZQA 1992: 11). They say that there must be recognition of existing skills which people have obtained outside formal systems to enable them to further their training. The recognition of prior learning is still in its infancy in New Zealand. It is meant to remove barriers to career development for many workers. NZQA considers that the NQF will encourage the development of new qualifications because individual enterprises can structure their own qualifications around units of learning. The NQF has been designed to introduce an assessment system which measures achievement against standards. Material published by NZQA to date draws a clear distinction between two main types of assessment: norm-referenced and standards-based with a focus on competency-based standards (Peddie 1992: 21).

The process of implementation of training in industry will typically begin after the development of an ITO for that industry. A target of three years is being set for the redevelopment of all existing qualifications which will continue to be recognized and in time will be restructured to fit into the NQF.

NZQA has proposed a quality management system for national qualifications. Units and qualifications will be registered to ensure that standards are set which are relevant, up to date and acceptable to major user groups. Registration of private training establishments will ensure that basic educational and consumer safeguards are met. Accreditation of providers will ensure that providers have the capacity to deliver the Unit Standards. There will be provision for ongoing moderation of assessment. Consistency of assessment with the required standard will be moderated. Finally, to ensure the effective performance of overall systems for the management of quality, there is a system for auditing quality.

Comment

One purpose of this paper is to locate the NZ Government's industry training strategy within human capital theory. An examination of the language and politics of the industry training strategy is needed. A few comments are given here as an indication of the need for further research on the notion of skills, the relationship between labour markets and education, and the possible response of private industry to training.

The notion of skill probably has many common-sense assumptions but within government discourse it is used unproblematically. The common-sense notion of skill has been challenged severely by Blackmore (1992: 351) who argues that 'the claim that skill is technically defined and neutral masks the ideological and political work that such concepts do when uncritically accepted, in exacerbating the gendered division of labour'. Many questions could also be asked about why training should be the focus for reforms in industry. Drake (1988), for example, compares public policy on vocational training provided by employers in France, the former West Germany and the UK and concludes that:

> Recent experience suggests that the fundamental and long term relations between firms, labour markets and the education system are still far more powerful determinants of training provision than eye-catching and *ad hoc* public interventions in training markets on the basis of new laws. (Drake 1988: 320)

By focusing on skill training in the workplace as the chief means of developing an internationally competitive productive nation the New Zealand Government has ignored what Drake (1988: 311) cites as five possible substitutes for transferable skill training. Companies may be able to: (1) change the product; (2) contract production out; (3) change the task (e.g., by substituting capital for labour); (4) reorganize job contents; or (5) hire skilled workers from the external labour market. The policy context for the construction of competitive markets within New Zealand was explained earlier in this paper. There have been, as a result, shifts in the occupational structure of the workforce and in job contents. There is a desire by the Government that Skill New Zealand be the means of ensuring that workers are trained in the appropriate skills. But if we consider what Drake (ibid.) says above about the broader view of the possible responses by companies to modern market conditions, then we would need to concede that 'there is a long chain of options between structural and technical change and corporate training requirements' (Drake 1988: 312). There are questions also about the advisability of placing responsibility on employers to carry out the skills training especially when there are, as Drake (ibid.) has shown, other options. Coopers and Lybrand (Senker 1990: 121) 'found that there were pervasive negative attitudes to training in the top management of most British firms'. In the same paper Senker (ibid.) reports the efforts of the UK Manpower Services Commission Chairman who wrote to 1000 leading British companies asking them for a response to a range of training issues. Senker (ibid.) reports that the response to the investigation was disappointing and it was suggested that UK company boards 'rarely discuss training because it is not seen as a central issue'. Things are probably not much different in New Zealand companies in what is essentially an international market with similar conditions applying to public and private sector restructuring and management responses. Yet in the UK, as in New Zealand, '(e)mployers themselves must assume active leadership in preparing and maintaining a skilled workforce' (Employment Department quoted in Senker 1990: 122). In the UK there is a 'stunning silence about the role of employers in the need to "be flexible", to "move", to gain new skills and qualifications' (Constable 1992: 93). The industry training strategy in New Zealand is currently being contested by the Labour Party (*NZ Herald*, 12 January 1994: 5). The report states that their view is that the strategy will not work unless there is a mandatory training levy.

The preceding discussion offers us some clues about the possible reason for Senker's (1990: 114) polemical statement that, 'it is difficult to percieve any coherent pattern in Government training policy'. The industry training strategy in New Zealand does not address these and many other issues and assumes that the common-sense notion of skills training controlled by industry is the solution to the unproblematic needs companies have in order for New Zealand to become internationally competitive.

Conclusion

The recent neo-liberal restructuring of the state, particularly in terms of policy formulation in industry training, becomes problematic for the New Zealand Government once the foundational assumptions of neo-classical economic theory are questioned and exposed in their limitations. As Marginson (1993: 52) argues, there is a failure to ground the key assumptions of human capital theory in that the theory has failed to find empirical evidence for the following: education determines productivity, productivity determines earnings, and therefore education determines earnings. Marginson (ibid.) argues that other factors, such as social background, are capable simultaneously of influencing education and earnings. He also notes problems faced by any theory of cognitive outputs, the effects of endowed ability, acquired ability; and educational attainments cannot be distinguished from each other, from the prior characteristics of students, or from the context in which learning takes place. These categories are generally acknowledged in education as being conceptually separate and as having differential effects – e.g., people clearly have different endowed intellectual abilities even before any particular training or education and human capital theory ignores this point. The other categories mentioned – cognitive attainments, acquired abilities, formal educational achievements – have been researched extensively in educational literature for many decades but that literature and its findings have been ignored.[5] Further, Marginson (1993) argues that it is impossible to separate the respective contributions of formal and informal learning. In the workplace there are many determinants of productivity other than education. The correlation between educational and other outcomes is confused with causality. Marginson (ibid.) also argues that studies of entrepreneurs (the so-called exemplars of human capital theory) show that their constraints are fundamentally different from those of industrial workers especially in the choices they have available and the context within which they work. Human capital theory thus assumes an unreal certainty about the connections between education, work and earnings.

In terms of current policy, the New Zealand Government has tended to ignore the debate on the foundational assumptions of human capital theory and its limitations, both conceptual and empirical, particularly in education. There are questions here of the neglect so far of the literature on historical developments within capitalism. There are tensions around the adoption of the OECD approach, which recommends massive increases in participation in tertiary education with no increases in the education budget and with a policy of voluntary funding from industry through ITOs. There are important and fundamental ethical problems in conceiving of people as units of capital. Investment in human capital is fundamentally different from other forms of investment – e.g., people who view themselves as ethically free agents should not and probably do not want to be treated as commodities.

It is imperative that the New Zealand Government provide the necessary funds to investigate at an empirical level the effects of human capital theory in education. The touted gains in terms of 'increased productivity' and new 'modes of flexibility' within the industry training strategy may provide political legitimacy at the level of electioneering rhetoric, but there is as yet no investigation into either the conceptual or empirical issues posed in this paper.[6] Since, as the OECD (1993) report argues, human capital theory in education is fundamental to economic recovery, it is vital that research into the veracity of these economic claims be funded.

This paper began with the assertion that the regime of 'perpetual training' (Deleuze 1992) became the new regime and system which now motivates and integrates education and industry. This notion is evident in the Government's Industry Skills Training Strategy in New Zealand which can be explained in terms of the underlying human capital theory. It is evident in the recent OECD survey of New Zealand's economy and in terms of the general workplace reform undertaken since 1990. Human capital theory and the way it legitimates present government policy in education and training is a clear revival of neo-classical economics. This neo-liberal revival of the main articles of faith underlying neo-classical economics represents an 'innocent' return to history. It is a revival which is not sensitive to history, to the intervening history of the welfare state or to the institutionalized compromise between the demands of capital and labour and the welfare state it represented. The return to the roots of the classical tradition is both naïve and nostalgic in that it attempts to revisit the methodological foundations without revision, amendment or modification. In other words, it is simply a reassertion of the same assumptions of the original 19-century doctrine and raises many unanswered questions.

Notes

1. This section is based on revised material taken from Michael Peters, James Marshall and Bruce Parr (1993) 'The marketization of higher education in New Zealand', *Australian Universities Review*, 36(2), 34–39.
2. The nine SOEs were: Electricity and Coal Corporations (from the Ministry of Energy); NZ Post, Post Office Bank and Telecom (from the former post Office); Land and Forestry Corporations (from NZ Forest Service and the Lands and Survey Department); Airways Corporation; and Government Property Services. Subsequently, the Works Corporation was set up from the old Ministry of Works and Development (1988); the Government Supply Brokerage Company was formed from the old Government Stores Board; public sector superannuation funds were separated from Treasury; the Government Computing services were split from the State Services Commission. Under the National Government the health system has been 'restructured', as has the science policy regime; the larger hospitals have become Crown Health Enterprises and the old Department of Science and Industrial Research (DSIR), along with other science departments, has been broken up into ten Crown Research Institutes.
3. Simon Upton was replaced during 1993 by Bill Birch as Minister of Health by the Prime Minister, Mr Bolger, for 'failing to sell the health reforms'. This kind of language, which was taken up and used uncritically by the media in New Zealand, tends to reduce the widespread and principled opposition to the commercialization and privatization of health to a matter of public relations: if only Upton had employed the right PR firm with the appropriate message or advertising package then he might have 'sold' the 'reforms' to an unaccepting public. On this model democracy itself is commodified and public participation is reduced to sampling through opinion polls.
4. Some current management ideology, e.g. total quality management and flexible specialization, exhibits some of Taylor's principles of increasing employee productivity through analysis and measurement. Taylor's influence is also evident in modern personnel management – job analysis, selection of workers and employee training. Perpetual training through continued investment in human capital to meet changing demands is a logical extension of management's needs for flexible specialization.

5. These topics are part of the curriculum in education and psychology undergraduate and graduate courses at universities. The OECD and New Zealand Government human capital theory approach to education ignores the large volume of research in this area of cognitive psychology and consequently the conceptual and empirical problems which that research exposes.
6. In fact the authors recently requested funding for such a project but, in the words of the New Zealand Ministry of Education, such a project is considered of 'low prority'.

References

BLACKMORE, J. (1992) 'The gendering of skill and vocationalism in twentieth century Australian education', *Journal of Education Policy*, (7) 4, pp. 351–377.

BLANDY, R. (1988) *Reforming Tertiary Education* (Wellington: Business Roundtable).

BLOCK, F. (1990) *Post Industrial Possibilities: A Critique of Economic Discourse* (Los Angeles: University of California Press).

BOSTON, J. (1992) 'Country report. The problems of policy coordination: the New Zealand experience', *Governance: An International Journal of Policy and Administration*, (5) 1, pp. 88–103 (Research Committee on the Structure and Organisation of Government of the International Political Science Association).

BOSTON, J., MARTIN, J., PALLOT, J. and WALSH, P. (eds) (1991) *Reshaping The State: New Zealand's Bureaucratic Revolution* (Auckland: Oxford University Press).

BUCHANAN, J. and TULLOCK, G. (1962) *The Calculus of Consent: Logical Foundations of Constitutional Democracy* (Michigan: Ann Arbor).

BUDGET (1993) (Wellington: Government Printer).

CONSTABLE, H. (1992) 'The Labour Party and the classless society 1991: today's education and training: tomorrow's skills', *Journal of Education Policy*, (7) 1, pp. 91–97.

DEAN, R. (1989) *Corporatisation and Privatisation: A Discussion of the Issues* (Wellington: Electrocorp).

DELEUZE, G. (1992) 'Postscript on the societies of control', *October*, 59, pp. 4–7.

DOUGLAS, R. (1989) *The politics of successful reform*, paper presented to the Mont Pelerin Society.

DRAKE, K. (1988) 'Company and public policies on training: some European experience', *Journal of Education Policy*, (3) 4, pp. 311–321.

DUNCAN, I. and BOLLARD, A. (1992) *Corporatisation & Privatisation: Lessons From New Zealand* (Auckland: Oxford University Press).

EASTON, B. (1988) 'From Reaganomics to Rogernomics', in A. Bollard (ed.) *The Influence of American Economics on New Zealand Thinking and Policy* (Wellington: NZIER).

EASTON, B. (1993) 'From Rogernomics to Ruthanasia', in S. Rees, G. Rodley and F. Stilwell (eds) *Beyond the Market: Alternatives to Economic Rationalism* (Melbourne: Pluto Press).

EDUCATION AND TRAINING SUPPORT AGENCY (1993) *Future Directions for the Training Opportunities Programme* (Wellington: Government Printer).

EDUCATION AND TRAINING SUPPORT AGENCY (1991) *The Government's New Industry Skills Training Strategy* (Wellington: Government Printer).

FITZSIMONS, P. (1993) *The Industry Training Organisation*, Occasional Report to the New Zealand Food and Beveridge Industry Training Organisation (Auckland: Kea Press).

FRIEDMAN, M. (1962) 'The role of government in education', in M. Friedman, *Capitalism and Freedom* (Chicago: University of Chicago Press).

HARBRIDGE, R. (1993) *Employment Contracts: New Zealand Experiences* (Wellington: Victoria University Press).

HOLLY, D. (1974) *Education or Domination?* (London: Arrow Books).

HOOD, C. (1990) 'De- Sir Humphreyfying the Westminster model of bureaucracy: a new style of governance?', *Governance: An International Journal of Policy and Administration*, (3) 2, pp. 205–214 (Research Committee on the Structure and Organisation of Government of the International Political Science Association).

JESSON, B. (1992) 'The disintegration of a Labour tradition: New Zealand politics', *New Left Review*, 194 (March–April) pp. 37–54.

LÉVI-STRAUSS, C. (1963) *Structural Anthropology* (Harmondsworth: Penguin).

MARGINSON, S. (1993) *Education and Public Policy in Australia* (Cambridge: Cambridge University Press).

MCCARTHY, P. (1991) *Negotiating Employment Contracts in New Zealand* (Auckland: CCH New Zealand).

MINISTRY OF EDUCATION (1993) *Education for the 21st Century: A Discussion Document* (Wellington: Ministry of Education).

NEW ZEALAND COUNCIL OF TRADE UNIONS (1992) *Building a Better Workplace* (Wellington: NZCITU).

NZ GOVERNMENT (1993) *Budget* (Wellington: Government Printer).

NEW ZEALAND QUALIFICATIONS AUTHORITY (1992) *The Framework and Industry* (Wellington: NZQA).

NEW ZEALAND QUALIFICATIONS AUTHORITY (1993) *Quality Management Systems for the National Qualifications Framework* (Wellington: NZQA).

NEW ZEALAND QUALIFICATIONS AUTHORITY (Undated) *An Introduction to the Framework* (Wellington: NZQA).

OECD (1993) *Economics Surveys 1992–1993: New Zealand* (Paris: OECD).

O'ROURKE, M. (1993) 'Progress in Implementing the Training Opportunities Programme', *The New Zealand Education Gazette*, (72) 11.

PEDDIE, R. (1992) *Beyond the Norm? An Introduction to Standards-Based Assessment* (Wellington, New Zealand: New Zealand Qualifications Authority).

PICOT, B. (1988) *Administering for Excellence: Effective Administration in Education. Report of the Task Force to Review Education Administration* (Wellington: Government Printer).

PUBLIC SERVICES ASSOCIATION (1989) *Private Power or Public Interest? Widening the Debate on Privatisation*, Proceedings of the NZPSA Conference. (Palmerston North: Dunmore Press).

REES, G., WILLIAMSON, H. and WINCKLER, V. (1989) 'The new "vocationalism": further education and local labour markets', *Journal of Education Policy*, (4) 3, pp. 227–244.

SCOTT, G., BUSHNELL, P. and SALLEE, N. (1990) 'Reform of the core public sector: New Zealand experience', *Governance: An International Journal of Policy and Administration*, 3 (2) pp. 138–167 (Research Committee on the Structure and Organisation of Government of the International Political Science Association).

SENKER, P. (1990) 'Some economic and ideological aspects of the reform of education and training in England and Wales in the last ten years', *Journal of Education Policy*, (5) 2, pp. 113–125.

STATE SERVICES COMMISSION STEERING GROUP (1991) *Review of State Sector Reforms* (Wellington: Government Printer).

TAYLOR, F. W. (1911) *Principles of Scientific Management* (New York: Harper).

TREASURY (1984) *Economic Management* (Wellington, NZ: Government Printer).

TREASURY (1987) *Government Management: Brief to the Incoming Government*, Vol 11: *Education Issues* (Wellington, NZ: Government Printer).

TREASURY (1990) *Briefing to the Incoming Government* (Wellington, NZ: Government Printer).

WALSH, P. (1992) 'The Employment Contracts Act', in J. Boston and P. Dalziel (eds) *The Decent Society? Essays in Response to National's Economic and Social Policies* (Auckland: Dunmore Press), pp. 59–76.

WESTOBY, A. (1974) 'Economists and human capital', in D. Holly (ed.) *Education or Domination?* (London: Arrow Books).

[13]

The Economic Journal, **101** (*September* 1991), 1268–1276
Printed in Great Britain

QUASI-MARKETS FOR EDUCATION?

Howard Glennerster

I. INTRODUCTION

The Education Reform Act 1988 marked a decisive break in the tradition of administering education policy in the United Kingdom. Whereas the post war statutes, notably the 1944 Education Act, fused finance and provision the Act of 1988 separated those functions and introduced elements of a market type mechanism into UK education. (For an outline of the legislation and the principles it embodies see Glennerster, Power and Travers, 1991.) On March 23 1991 the *Economist* urged Americans to adopt a similar set of reforms. If the present Conservative Government is returned to power the principles will be extended further. These changes contain some, but only some, elements of an internal market for education within the state education system. Two separate sets of reforms are being implemented, one relates to schools, the other to higher education.

II. QUASI MARKETS FOR SCHOOLS?

All secondary schools and all but small primary schools will be funded according to a formula the central department has to approve. Any pupil signing on at a local state school will trigger a payment by the local education authority (LEA) to the school which will then be free to administer the resulting budget as it pleases. A proportion of the total sum available for schooling in the LEA will be top sliced and kept by the local authority to provide common services, (special units for disruptive pupils, educational psychologists, inspection and central administration), before the rest is allocated by formula. Local authorities must spend less than 15% of what is called their 'Potential Schools Budget' on these common services. The new devolved system goes by the name, Local Management of Schools (LMS). (For an explanation and analysis of the first phase see Lee 1990). In the case of schools that choose to opt out of local control, (only 60 at the time of writing out of 29,000), the same formula is applied to determine how much they receive in grant from central government. However, this grant is then topped up to compensate such schools for not receiving the LEA's central services.

Parents have the right to choose to which school to send their child and cash follows the child according to the formula. The net effect of these measures resembles the kind of voucher scheme once advocated by Jenks in the United States (Mecklenburger and Hostrop, 1972) which confined vouchers to the state school system. Nevertheless, the new scheme falls short of the full market solution for a number of reasons:

(a) No money can escape to the private sector.

(b) There is no free entry for new providers. Capital expenditure for new places and new schools, will have to be approved by the local authority and the central department in Westminster. Central government's watchdog, the Audit Commission, has been pressing local education authorities to economise by closing more schools. Spare capacity to expand, in order to meet demand, will be limited. There is really no mechanism to replicate free entry on the one hand, or bankruptcy on the other, to keep the market truly competitive.

(c) Choice by parents is limited because in the very same Act the Government required all state schools to follow a common curriculum. One of the persuasive arguments advanced by proponents of the voucher scheme was that parents disagreed about what constituted a good education. That was the case for parental choice (Coons and Sugarman, 1978).

(d) Teachers' salaries, the largest slice of the school budget, are still set on a national salary scale limiting the freedom school managing bodies have to arrange their budgets.

For all these reasons many would like to see the next Government take these reforms to their logical conclusion and formula fund all schools, private and public, direct from central government. Schools would then be left to go bankrupt and other risk takers would enter the market offering new educational services. They would set salaries as they chose. Practical problems aside, what is the theoretical case for and against the existing reforms and their possible extension?

Local Management of Schools

The theoretical case for LMS is that it reduces X-inefficiency (Leibenstein 1966, 1973). Senior managers are ill informed about day-to-day issues. Decisions about book purchases or equipment or staffing, taken in a distant County Hall by those who do not have to suffer the consequences of their actions, are likely to be poor just because information is lost in passing up the chain of command, and the incentives in a central bureaucracy are to simplify allocation rules rather than to reflect local situations. LMS provides a mechanism for determining the optimum range of services that should be provided at a local authority level. The argument is that schools should purchase central services only when they need them and these should be charged at cost. Critics object that these services are needed most by schools in disadvantaged areas, (English as a second language, for example). That objection can be met by the response that formula funding should take account of such factors and leave the school free to decide whether to buy the services or do the work itself.

The theory of decentralised budgeting implies that local managers should have the capacity to set their own salary levels untied by national salary scales. That reasoning has been applied to opted out hospitals which can set their own salary scales. Critics raise two kinds of objections. It is suggested that local bargaining would give an unfair advantage to schools in areas with a low tax base. It would not, of course, if schools were funded in ways that gave schools in deprived areas a higher weighting in the formula and central government either funded schools direct or gave LEAs with such schools additional grant. The second objection is that local bargaining removes from the state a powerful monopsony position in its negotiations with teachers unions. Where the balance of advantage lies in that situation is difficult to judge. Local bargaining may tend to increase the public sector pay bill. This has to be weighed against the efficiency gains of decentralised budgeting. As a minimum compromise the national scales could be made more flexible, permitting local managers to pay teachers more in shortage subjects.

So far, then, the case for local management of schools seems to hold up well to theoretical examination. There is also recent empirical support from a large survey of academic results in US schools where decentralised schooling systems showed better results (Chubb and Moe, 1990). What of the case for extending the principle of the market further? Local decentralised school budgeting is a necessary but not a sufficient condition for a true quasi market.

Competition and Open Enrolment

Efficiency. Advocates of full competition between schools have always argued that the case for state involvement in education only extended to its responsibility to empower parents to buy education, and to ensure that, as future citizens, all children acquired basic skills. Beyond that schools were no different to other service providers (Friedman, 1962; Peacock and Wiseman 1964; West, 1965; Maynard, 1975). Under the UK schools market now emerging, the Government will ensure that an acceptable standard of common education is provided by means of the National Curriculum, assessment tests and a national system of inspection by Her Majesty's Inspectors of Schools which dates back to the mid-nineteenth century. With such enhanced information on output, parents and pupils will be able to judge in an informed way between the services offered by competing schools. The most efficient will gain pupils and resources, the others will decline. This is the traditional form of efficiency competition between producers we hope to find in free markets – 'E' competition for short. It is, however, not the only form of competition we observe.

Selectivity. Health economists are fully aware that the health care market is characterised by another form of competition, selection bias, adverse selection or 'S' competition for short (Akerlof, 1970; Pauly, 1986; Summers, 1989; Barr, 1987). The same is true of insurance markets more generally (Pauly, 1974). An analogous problem arises with schooling, though it is not generally discussed in the same theoretical literature.

It is critically important for any health care provider to exclude high cost, high risk, patients from their group of users or benefit recipients. It is thus not surprising to find that an enormous amount of attention is paid in marketing and in competition with other health care providers, to ensure that a minimum number of these high cost patients are attracted. Schools are in a similar position. Work by Rutter *et al.* (1979) produced elaborate and effective measures of what constituted 'good' secondary schools. Yet, it was still true that, when included with data on pupils' basic abilities and parental background, what went on in the school only explained about 5% of the variance in pupil achievements. An even more detailed longtitudinal study of the differential effectiveness of primary schools in London was able to explain 9% of the variance in pupils' reading achievements and 11% of maths attainments by reference to schools' effects (Mortimore *et al.* 1988). These are higher figures than achieved in comparable American studies but are still relatively small compared to the 64% of variance explained by initial attainment and social background. Any school entrepreneur acting rationally would seek to exclude pupils who would drag down the overall performance score of the school, its major selling point to parents. Any nonselective system of schooling would then be an unstable equilibrium. A process of adjustment would follow, moving towards an equilibrium in which schools would cater for children in different bands of ability, and from different social backgrounds. Some would welcome that result others would not. What economic theory suggests is that a pure internal market between schools would not produce a neutral outcome in this respect.

Poor information, joint products and externalities

So far we have seen that an internal market will, other things being equal, produce a selective system of education, selective according to the attributes that determine school performance most strongly, that is inherited ability and social class. Does this matter? There is still dispute about the research evidence but, on balance, it would seem that the introduction of non-selective schooling in Britain in the 1960's and 1970's did raise the educational outcomes of the schooling system especially for the average and below average child (Glennerster and Low, 1990). Schools with mixed ability intakes also achieve better results than those with restricted ability mixes (Rutter *et al.*, 1979). Because parents are not in a position to know the value added by different schools, standardising for the differential intake schools may have, they will get systematically misleading information about the efficiency of the schools between which they must make choices. It would certainly not be in the interests of the selective schools to reveal this kind of information.

Advocates of the market can reasonably respond that there are ways round all these problems. The formulae for funding schools can be so weighted that schools that take less able children receive more money. This sounds like an answer and has intrinsic equity merit but in this context it assumes that moderate additional resources will produce enhanced exam performance that will bid up the results the school achieves to levels it would have reached if it had not taken the slow learner or working class child. Unfortunately, all the evidence suggests that this is not so. Even when large additional sums have been spent on schools with significant numbers of deprived children the results improve only by small amounts, or in much early research not at all (Coleman, 1966; Rutter, 1979; Hanushek, 1986;). Even if we take the more optimistic results their responsiveness to money spent is so low that we cannot rely on a weighted formula to solve the problem of selection. Indeed there may even be perverse effects to offering schools bribes to take less able or deprived children. US evidence from job training schemes suggests that employers may discriminate against trainees from ethnic backgrounds who carry a financial bonus. The reaction seems to have been – if they have to pay us more to take these people they must be less productive. Employers judged that their differentially low marginal product would more than offset the extra subsidy and they were partly convinced of that precisely because there was a subsidy (Haveman and Palmer, 1982).

Advocates of non-selective education argue that such a system produces externalities of several kinds. A common local school fosters local community ties and helps to reduce social class divisions. This may be disputed. A socially inclusive local education system is incompatible with a socially exclusive one. It would seem that the choice between the two has to be a collective choice. An internal market that was completely unconstrained would inevitably preclude that choice by producing a selective system.

In so far as LEA's did succeed in obtaining a mixed entry to the schools in their area, parents would then be able to judge the relative merits of schools' performance starting from a level, as opposed to a staggered, start. It would be necessary, in any system that enabled choice to take place, for the LEA to produce studies of the relative performance of schools in value added terms taking account of the social and other characteristics of individual schools as the Inner London Education Authority (ILEA) did before it was abolished. Parents would then be free to choose between schools that differed in ways that did not produce negative externalities. They could choose between those that offered more or less formal discipline, religious denominational instruction, single sex schooling, sports or music or any mixture of the above.

Sunk costs

Arguably the best way to learn whether a school fits a particular child is to try it out. That is the way we choose between supermarkets or hairdressers but it is not so easily done with schools just because part of the raw material is the child. Moreover, part of the quality of the education process comes from the child being settled and happy in the school. Frequent changes will disrupt that process and could do long term damage. Parents are therefore being quite rational to show loyalty to the school of their initial choice rather than exercising frequent exits and shopping around strategies. Traditions and an ethos in a school community are assets not easily or quickly gained. For a school to decline and go bankrupt over a long period will cause considerable educational and social costs to the pupils caught up in its demise. New entrants will find it takes a long time to build a new school community. The sunk costs, in short, are high. This is not to deny that useful market signals can be produced by new parents opting for other schools and demand slackening. It does suggest however that simple market pressures will not be enough. Professional advice and support that can identify a school at risk and help it to take corrective action early before decline sets in, are important adjuncts to a more market led system.

The case for a managed market

The case so far has been that schooling has some peculiar characteristics that do not adapt readily to a full market solution. Schooling can be reconciled with an element of market discipline but only with a number of safeguards. These require the local education authority to play a significant role. It would be:

(a) To choose a pattern of education provision, selective or non selective, in line with local parents' collective choice;

(b) To plan a structure of schools in the area. This would take account of expected demographic change and the preferences being revealed in parents' choice of school;

(c) To support schools with a good inspection and advisory service which can diagnose those in trouble and give them special and early support to prevent a long terminal illness before closure;

(d) To provide other services on demand at a market price.

If this were done there would be no case for schools to opt out of a local authority that would have supportive and marketing functions alone. Indeed, schools that did opt out of such a system would only be acting rationally as free riders, trying to avoid the costs that need to be incurred to keep such a system in equilibrium, or to evade the choice of the local community that has determined on non-selective education.

III. HIGHER EDUCATION AND POST SCHOOL TRAINING

How far do similar factors operate in post school education? My contention is that the considerations that apply here are rather different. On balance, the case for applying market type mechanisms is stronger. Yet Government policy has been hesitant and confused. Those aged 16 to 18 are in a transition period of near adulthood. The state does not insist they shall be educated but is unhappy if they are not at least being trained. Government has moved to force those not in work to attend some kind of training by withdrawing rights to social security benefit unless young people enter an approved training programme. It might be better to go the whole way and raise the compulsory school or training age to eighteen. Compulsory education or training linked to job experience could be financed through a basic training voucher. Government policy looks as if it is stumbling in that direction.

From the age of eighteen we are dealing with adults, not parents acting as proxy demanders with the state having some residual role to protect the child and ensure that he or she has enough to become a fully independent individual. The balance between private benefits and public good has shifted by adulthood. The aim of public policy is to ensure that individuals invest optimally in their own human capital and have the resources to do so. The citizenship goals that attach to community schooling become irrelevant as young people want to move away from home.

Selective institutions become the norm and competition between institutions to provide the best or most appropriate courses has always been a feature of higher and further education. The social goal remains that of ensuring that young and older adults alike are not prevented from investing in their own futures and hence the economy's productive capacity. Such is the case for treating post school education as any market commodity.

Markets or quasi markets?

Yet here too there are difficulties. The capital market has never been able to handle human capital efficiently, outside a slave society. Though banks will lend money to students without security they will only do so to a limited extent, insufficient to support an individual through an expensive training, tuition costs included. Only students who could rely on rich parents to secure the risk can finance themselves this way. Hence governments have come to provide free or heavily subsidised higher education. Typically, in Europe, these subsidies have been given to institutions of higher education to reduce their tuition costs. In Britain individuals have been subsidised to cover their living costs too.

Three issues have dominated debate on the finance of higher education ever since the Robbins Committee (UK 1963) reported.

(a) Should state financial support for higher education be given to students or institutions?

(b) Should that support take the form of an outright subsidy or a returnable loan?

(c) Should financial support for teaching be separated from research?

The full quasi market approach would suggest that the state should support students with bursaries not subsidise institutions. Polytechnics and universities should compete for students and their bursaries. This would minimise the X-inefficiencies of universities, free them from centralised regulatory control and potential political control and give students real choice enabling good teaching institutions to prosper. (This case is powerfully argued by Barnes and Barr, 1988.) Students should repay the cost of their support in so far as they derive private gain from the investment. Individuals would weigh the costs of higher education against its expected returns. Government should support fundamental research at those institutions that are doing it well not spread an indirect subsidy thinly, mixed up with the funding of student numbers.

In fact, in 1988, the Government chose not to adopt such an approach but pursued a half-hearted and odd mixture of some elements. In the 1988 Educational Reform Act the funding of institutions was continued, with a tighter form of central control and a contractarian relationship between universities and polytechnics and their funding councils. For example, the University Funding Council introduced a bidding system under which universities were to offer to take so many students at a bid price per student. The lower the price the more likely a university was to get student places funded. There was no way of properly holding the quality constant and no way students' preferences could be exercised since the UFC were essentially continuing to ration entry. The result would have been a kind of internal market but one that provided marked incentives for mediocracy. The true market solution would be for the Government to offer a national scheme of bursaries on a subject by subject basis that would be sufficient to pay for tuition and living costs. It would then be for the student to choose which courses best suited and had the best reputations. At the time of writing the future of higher education funding is uncertain.

Government did opt to move gradually towards a loans system that would replace the present system of student grants bit by bit. New top up loans would be available to supplement lower real grants. The Government argued, with good reason, that one of the obstacles to expanding higher education in a period of severe limits on public expenditure, was the very high unit cost of higher education in the UK and our relatively generous system of student support was one element in that high cost (UK, 1988). Its solution was to introduce a mortgage type repayment scheme that saved minimal amounts of money even in the long run and cost money in the short run, while probably acting as a deterrent to some students as well (Barr, 1989). My own long preferred solution has been a graduate tax which avoids presenting students with a future burden unrelated to their capacity to pay. I will not present the case again (Glennerster *et al.*, 1968) especially since Barr (1989) has done it better.

Government does seem to be moving towards the separate funding of research and teaching. Institutions will compete for research funding as a separate exercise. In its crudest form this approach ignores the extent to which scholarship and the advance of knowledge is a joint product of teaching and research. It is certainly true that no government is likely to be able to support top rate scholarship in every department in every college of higher education in the land, but to try to fund the production of mutton only while someone else, you hope, funds the wool, is likely to produce some odd looking sheep.

IV. CONCLUSIONS

Quasi market solutions make more economic sense for institutions of higher education than for schools. Selection bias is more likely as an outcome of competition between schools than competition on efficiency grounds. Quasi markets will preclude non selective education as a democratic choice for local communities. On the other hand, higher education institutions are already selective and other advantages of competition are greater. The Government has, oddly, made the most muddled moves to extend markets here, giving incentives to mediocrity. The long term strategy should be for Government to give full cost bursaries to students together with a basic living grant in return for an enhanced tax obligation in later life. This could be administered through the social security scheme by adding a code to the individual's social security number.

Centres of scholarly excellence would compete for additional funding on the basis of having a critical mass of original and productive academics. Research councils would also fund research projects, doctoral and post doctoral work, as now. Such a competitive policy would give high quality outcomes not the lowest common denominator as the present one promises to do.

London School of Economics

REFERENCES

Akerlof, G. (1970). 'The market for lemons: qualitative uncertainty and the market mechanism'. *Quarterly Journal of Economics*, vol. 84, pp. 488–500.

Barnes, J. and Barr, N. (1988). *Strategies for Higher Education: The Alternative White Paper*, David Hume Paper No. 10. Aberdeen: Aberdeen University Press.

Barr, N. (1987). *The Economics of the Welfare State*. London, Weidenfeld.

Barr, N. (1989). *Student Loans the Next Steps*, David Hume Paper No. 15. Aberdeen: Aberdeen University Press.

Chubb, J. E. and Moe, T. M. (1990). *Politics, Markets and America's Schools*. Washington, D.C.: The Brookings Institution.

Coleman, J. S. (1966). *Equality of Educational Opportunity*. Washington D.C., Government Printing Office.

Coons, J. and Sugarman, S. (1978). *Education by Choice: the Case for Family Control*. University of California, Berkeley.

Friedman, M. (1962). *Capitalism and Freedom*. Chicago: University of Chicago Press.

Hanushek, E. A. (1986). 'The economics of schooling: production and efficiency in public schools'. *Journal of Economic Literature*, vol. 23, no. 3, pp. 1141–77.

Glennerster, H. *et al.* (1968). 'A graduate tax'. *Higher Education Review*, vol. 1, no. 1.

Glennerster, Howard, Power, Anne and Travers, Tony (1991). 'A new era for social policy: a new enlightenment or a new Leviathan?'. *Journal of Social Policy*, vol. 20, no. 3, pp. 389–414.

Glennerster, H. and Low, W. (1990). 'Education and the welfare state: does it add up?'. In *The State of Welfare* (ed. J. Hills). Oxford: Clarendon Press.

Haveman, R. H. and Palmer, S. (1982). *Jobs for Disadvantaged Workers*. Washington D.C., Brookings Institution.

Lee, T. (1990). *Carving Out the Cash for Schools*, Bath Social Policy Paper No. 17. University of Bath.

Leibenstein, H. (1966). 'Allocative efficiency versus X-efficiency'. *American Economic Review*, vol. 56, pp. 392–415.

—— (1973). 'Competition and X-inefficiency: a reply'. *Journal of Political Economy*, vol. 81, pp. 765–77.

Maynard, A. (1975). *Experiment with Choice in Education*. London, Institute of Economic Affairs.

Mecklenburger, J. A. and Hostrop, R. W. (eds) (1972). *Education Vouchers from Theory to Alum Rock*. Homewood, Illinois.

Mortimore, P. *et al.* (1988). *The Junior School project: Part C Understanding School Effectiveness*, ILEA Research and Statistics Section. London: ILEA.

Pauly, M. V. (1974). 'Overinsurance and public provision of insurance: the roles of moral hazard and adverse selection'. *Quarterly Journal of Economics* vol. 88, pp. 44–62.

Pauly, M. V. (1986). Taxation, Health Insurance and Market Failure in the Medical Economy. *Journal of Economic Literature*, vol. 24, pp. 629–75.

Peacock, A. and Wiseman, J. (1964). *Education for Democrats* Hobart Paper No. 25. London: Institute of Economic Affairs.

Rutter, M. *et al.* (1979). *Fifteen Thousand Hours: Secondary Schools and their Effects on Children*. London: Open Books.

Summers, L. H. (1989). 'Some simple economics of mandated benefits. *American Economic Review*, vol. 79, no. 2, pp. 177–83.

UK (1963). *Higher Education* (the Robbins Report) Cmnd 2154. London: HMSO.

UK (1988). *Top-up Loans for Students* Cm 520. London: HMSO.

West, E. G. (1965). *Education and the State*, London, Institute of Economic Affairs.

[14]

Discourse: studies in the cultural politics of education, Vol. 18, No. 2, 1997

Subjects and Subjugation: the economics of education as power-knowledge

SIMON MARGINSON, *University of Melbourne, Australia*

The Economics of Education

Foucault's explorations of power-knowledge have opened many doors. At the same time, in the studies of discipline and governmentality Foucault strangely neglects the domain of economy, or takes it as a given,[1] despite the centrality of economic relations in government. The work of Foucauldians after Foucault has maintained the curious incuriosity about economy, with some exceptions such as Miller and Rose (1990). Despite this there are many points where the economic aspects of power-knowledge, and the power-knowledge aspects of economy, might be usefully explored, suggesting power-knowledge-economy as a method of investigation (Marginson, 1997b). One matter that bears investigating is the effects in government of the economics of education.

As a system of power-knowledge, the economics of education wears two faces. It is one of the modes of government in education programs. At the same time it is a body of knowledge, a sub-discipline of the academic discipline known as neo-classical economics. The aim in this article is to situate the economics of education historically, in order to situate it politically and open a space for alternative constructions of education. What follows is another critique of the economics of education. It is also a critique of earlier critiques.

Economic Critiques of the Economics of Education

Since the early 1960s when the modern role of the economics of education was established, it has been the object of many critical studies.[2] Yet most critiques of economics of education from outside economics have failed to grapple with its specificity, too readily dismissing neo-classicism and its practical effects as false doctrine, implying that it is without purchase (!) in the real world. Within economics, the neo-classical economics of education has been subjected to withering criticism, especially from the political economy side of the argument. In the second half of the 19th century, neo-classical economists broke from the historical and political traditions of political economy (and achieved world-wide dominance in economics) by focusing on the mathematised problem of choice making in a perfect market. Thus neo-classicism is readily made vulnerable on historical grounds. The assumptions underlying the

0159-6306/97/020215-13

economics of education, like many of the assumptions held dogmatically by neo-classical economics, are loose and unproven, lacking realism and resting on little more than rhetorical support (McCloskey, 1994). It is easy to question these assumptions. Despite this, debate between economists of education and their economic critics has been less conclusive than logic or realism might suggest.

For example, as Maglen (1990) points out, the assumptions in human capital theory that investment in education directly produces increases in the marginal productivity of educated labour, and pay rates are grounded in marginal productivity—assumptions which require free competitive markets in both education and labour if they are to hold—have never been grounded empirically. There is an observable correlation between education and pay, but the association is not universal, and the question of causality is another matter again. Further, human capital theory is unable to eliminate other possible hypotheses linking education and pay rates, such as screening theory, which argues that education augments productivity because it acts as a screening device, signalling to employers the presence of qualities such as intelligence or reliability that denote potential productivity (Blaug, 1976). At the macro level, the evidence for the link between human capital investment and economic growth is patchy. The growth hypothesis wavers every time there is a recession, which drives down the alleged returns on educational investment.

In the 1960s the leading human capital economist in Britain was Mark Blaug. After 20 years of work in the economics of education, Blaug despaired of the scientific effectiveness of human capital theory. He concluded in 1988:

> The simple fact is that the field has failed to deliver the goods. We are certain that education contributes to economic growth but then so does health care, housing, roads, capital markets, *et cetera,* and in any case we cannot quantify the growth-enhancing effects of education under different circumstances and we cannot even describe these effects except in the most general terms. We can measure private and social returns to educational investment but since we cannot specify, much less measure, the externalities generated by educated individuals, not to mention the consumption benefits of education, the 'social' rate of return to education is a bogus label. (Blaug, 1988, p. 332)

Input–output modelling faces another set of problems, also the subject of debate within economics. In most countries the largest part of formal education, especially at the school level, takes the form of non-market production on the terrain of the state. But within the neo-classical framework, unless educational services are sold in a market there can be no conclusive measure of output, or of value added in the course of production, or of efficiency and productivity. The economics of education literally cannot contemplate non-market production and has failed to develop analytical tools with which to deal with it. It uses certain mathematical models to cover the gap in coverage, but these models are either arbitrary (such as shadow-prices) or absurd. For example, when using the 'input method' non-market output is defined as the *costs* of inputs to production, ignoring any value added in the process of production. A complex range of educational effects is collapsed into a single figure for costs. The method generates its own contradictions. When the cost of producing the same educational output is increased, this might suggest that efficiency has declined—yet according to the input method the increase in costs has produced an increase in output with efficiency held constant. Conversely, when the cost of inputs decreases due to an improvement in efficiency, without any reduction in output, the input method automatically registers that output has decreased.

In addition, some neo-classical economists have developed the contrary argument that in non-market production in education, an increase in resource inputs bears *no* necessary relationship to the quantity and/or quality of outputs—suggesting that the increased educational spending demanded by the users of education might be wasted because it produces no educational benefits (for example, Hanushek, 1986). This conclusion follows directly from the neo-classical premise than in non-market production, there is *no economic relationship* between inputs and outputs. For governments wanting to economise in education, the argument has an obvious political utility. Not only does it undermine the case for additional spending, it creates a *prima facie* discursive-political bias to market reform. A positive relationship between spending and outputs can only be created in a marketised system (for example, Porter, 1988).

Within their own terms, the economic critiques of the economics of education are convincing. Nevertheless, the fact must be faced that the impact of these critiques has been negligible. Blaug's early work as a human capital economist is still cited, while his later critique of the economics of education has for the most part been studiously ignored. This is not altogether surprising. What sustains the economics of education is not its internal discursive consistency, but consistency in the relations of power that it supports. It depends not on the empirical realism of its analytical assumptions but the practical realism of the power-knowledge relationship between the economics of education and government. Maglen notes in his critique of human capital theory that despite its discursive weaknesses it continues to enjoy strong support among 'those who formulate public policy and those that advise them', while among economists 'there is a reluctance to question its veracity' (Maglen, 1990, pp. 281–282). The norms and the methods of the economics of education, including their blindspots, are functional for certain purposes and kinds of government. If the economics of education is to be unpicked at its seams, it is also necessary to unpick a part of government. The critique of the economics of education thus becomes also a critique of government. To do this, it is necessary to move not only beyond economics but beyond political economy (which is still economy-centred), to an investigation of power-knowledge-economy.

Discursive Structure and Political History

There are many ways of going about this task, but Foucault's work is particularly useful. Foucault provides two different, intersecting routes to the critique of the economics of education. One route is the investigation of its *discursive structures*, the making visible of the bits and pieces that compose it as a conglomeration of knowledge. The other route is the investigation of its *political history*, of its evolution in the strategies and techniques of government.

In investigating the discursive structures of the economics of education, the *Archaeology of Knowledge* (1972) points to the importance of the key ideas and themes that characterise a discipline (or in this case, a sub-discipline), its recurring concepts, its continuities and breaks, its methods, its derivation in economics and elsewhere, the different schools of thought within it. Foucault talks about the 'positivity' of a discipline, those common elements which characterise its unity through time, that provide the common ground on which its participants might agree or disagree with each other. 'A field in which formal identities, thematic continuities, translations of concepts, and polemical interchanges may be deployed' (Foucault, 1972, pp. 126–127). In the economics of education, the two paradigms of the sub-discipline—education as investment in the formation of individual human capital, and education as the input-output production of human services—are heterogeneous. The first is concerned with education's economic effects in sites outside education, the second with education itself as an economic site. Nevertheless, they share a common master discourse, that of neo-classical economic theory, which enables the two paradigms to be stitched together.

Using these paradigms, the economist focuses on such phenomena as budgetary policy on educational expenditure, the pricing and marketing of educational services, the deployment and management of resources used by educational institutions, and the financial control systems that link institutional managers and government; reconstructing these phenomena as the *objects of knowledge* of the intellectual sub-discipline that is the economics of education. In this manner, using the abstract mathematical reconstructions of reality that characterise neo-classical economics, in which economic phenomena are understood as always-already present, the economics of education is constructed at one and the same time 'as a target area for intervention and a functioning totality to be brought into existence' (Gordon, 1980, p. 245).

Table 1 lists the two paradigms that comprise the economics of education, the objects of knowledge associated with them, and sites in which those objects are deployed. (Details from the Table are referred to subsequently.)

Second, working from Foucault's studies of disciplinary technologies and particularly the later histories of governmentality (Foucault, 1991), the political history of the economics of education can be investigated in terms of the governmental demands on its services, its changing applications in government programs, and its implication in the formulation of those programs. The economics of education was associated with the tasks of government from the beginning. It first appears at the end of the 17th century in the emerging sciences of population management, in the work of the early English political economist William Petty. Petty estimated the value of the 'stock' of a nation's human capital using a forward projection of total wages. He used these aggregated calculations to estimate the economic impact of migration and the effects of war on a nation's wealth (Kiker, 1966). Almost a century later, in 1776 Adam Smith agreed with Petty that one of the elements of the 'fixed capital' of the nation was 'the acquired and useful abilities of all the inhabitants or members of the society', acquired during 'education, study or apprenticeship'. Adam Smith took it further, arguing that this human capital was 'fixed and realised, as it were' in the person (Smith, 1979, p. 377). This enabled the management of the population as human capital to become realised at the level of the individual, while steering away from the notion of collective labour producing collective wealth. Using Adam Smith's formula, the amount of investment in human capital could be regulated at the level of the individual, and each individual could regulate her or his *own* investment in the self. This was the leap in the discursive imagination that made possible the later role of the economics of education in the programs of government and the calculations of individuals, though it was almost two centuries before this developed.

The sudden emergence of modern human capital theory at the end of the 1950s is a remarkable story of discursive politics, in which the two imperatives, the discursive and the political, fed each other. The time was right for the human capital theory construction of education as investment. The educational expansion of the 1960s was driven by a powerful coincidence of phenomena: the long post-war boom and expanding taxation revenues; the dominance of Keynesian notions of national economic management in which neo-classical foundations were joined to the politics of social investment; a rising confidence in government programs and the growth of the public sector; the explosion of white collar and professional employment; the drive for generalised scientific

Table 1. The 'positivity' of the economics of education

Key paradigm in the economics of education	Examples of objects of knowledge	Where these objects are located
Education as investment in human capital: (1) social investment (2) individual investment	(1) Education's contribution to income and GDP, aggregate productive capacity, and economic externalities (2) Education's contributions to individual productivity and earnings, for (a) individuals and (b) corporations	(1) Budgetary policy, especially in education, including funding of institutions, and loans and grants to students (2) Economic exchange in the form of (a) tuition fees paid by students and (b) corporate investments in education
Education as input–output production (the use of education production functions)	Standardised inputs and outputs, product/output measures, shadow prices	In government, aggregate cost savings and policies to increase efficiency
	Measures of educational efficiency (cost per unit of output) and productivity (output per unit of input)	Planning and management, and sub-management, of educational institutions
	Comparison of costs and benefits at (a) systemic level and (b) institutional level	Accountability of managers, particularly in relation to costs and outputs, and maximisation of efficiencies

competence in the face of the Soviet 'threat'; and the burgeoning demand for upward social mobility via education. In many OECD countries in the 1960s expenditure on education as a proportion of GDP more than doubled.[3]

The first modern work in the field, deriving from a mostly Chicago school group of neo-classical economists including Schultz (1960, 1961), Denison (1962), Friedman (1962), Becker (1964/1975) and others, was immediately incorporated into the 1960s programs of state-directed educational expansion (for example Martin, 1964). Human capital theory provided an operational rationality for government programs, and a normative setting for the popular demands for educational opportunities. The early version of the theory had extraordinary impact in both economic literature and the government of education. In the surge of investment in human capital it was impossible to say where government began and economics ended, and also *vice versa*. There was a great outpouring of journal articles, books and technical reports in the human capital framework: Blaug identified 800 items by 1966, 1,350 by 1970 and almost 2,000 by 1976 (Blaug, 1976, p. 827). The theory was embraced by the international agencies, the

OECD and the United Nations Educational, Scientific and Cultural Organisation (UNESCO), and later the World Bank, becoming central to the standardised development strategies used in the third world (Marginson, 1993, pp. 31–54). The economists who wrote the principal academic papers were also consultants to national governments and addressed the OECD and UNESCO conferences. 'The step between economic theory and governmental action has never been so short' as Hirsch was later to remark (1976, p. 46).

Once the economics of education has been investigated in terms of both its discursive structures and its political history, the two strands of analysis can then be brought together. In this way it becomes possible to unravel the workings of the economics of education; to understand it as part of a system of power-knowledge in which the arguments flowing through books and journals can be traced to the problems and requirements of government, while at the same time the body of disciplinary argument 'constantly induces effects of power'. The economics of education is more than a set of words or numbers or claims to truth, but *practices* that 'systematically form the objects of which they speak' (Foucault, 1972, pp. 48–49, 1980, pp. 51–52). Among the 'effects of power' induced by the economics of education is its effects in common sense. Education as investment in human capital, and education as input–output production, constitute more than a technical language of economists. They have also become popular metaphors for education. The claim that 'education is an investment in our children' has been a truism in public debate since the 1960s. The idea that education should produce 'outcomes' and deliver 'value for money' is more recent, but has now become widely understood and accepted.

In the work on governmentality Foucault points to the manner in which the state strategies of managing a population became joined to the technologies for differentiating individuals and shaping their behaviours. Thus the programs of government are implicated in the languages and behaviours of everyday life, so that they shape the formation, and the self-formation, of individuals themselves. The human person is both the object and subject of government. Thus the subject is subjugated (Gordon, 1991; Burchell, 1993; Rose, 1993). To trace these effects and synergies between government, knowledge, public life and popular subjectivities, another kind of critique of the economics of education is required. This might be called a power-knowledge critique. Examples of this kind of critique will now be explored.

Power-knowledge Critique 1: investment in the self

Consider the evolution of human capital theory over the last 35 years. There has not been one unitary human capital theory, but several different waves of human capital theory. All contain the core notion that education is investment in individual human capital. But they each have different methodological focuses, and different implications in government policies and relations of power.

The first wave of human capital theory in the 1960s was used to underpin the massive expansion in education systems, financed by governments. The theory's emphasis fell on the alleged social rates of return flowing from investment in human capital; summarised in a single number, the contribution of education to economic growth. By the mid-1980s, with 'small government' and 'structural adjustment' the order of the day, human capital theory was being refashioned (OECD, 1985). Following a line of theorisation developed in agricultural economics, the OECD argued that the contribution of education to economic growth was not linear or automatic as had previously been proposed,

Table 2. Human capital theory and government, 1960s–1990s

Theory	Main theoretical assumptions	Popular understandings	Governmental practices
First wave human capital theory (1960s)	Education leads to productivity higher to higher wages. Investment in education leads to economic growth.	Education delivers career jobs, status and higher private incomes: hence the demands for greater access to education.	Expansion of education provision, supported by funding. Policies of equality of opportunity to maximise human capital.
Screening theory (1970s/1980s)	Education credentials are a surrogate for individual productivity. Education is a screening device that distributes jobs.	The need to struggle for relative advantage: better credentials provide competitive advantage in the labour market.	Cessation of increases in expenditure. Programs linking education to work. Standardisation of educational qualifications.
Second wave human capital theory (1980s)	Education augments the capacity to handle new technologies and other innovations. Education increases productivity and growth.	The strategic character of personal investment: individual education in 'cutting edge' areas (management, computing etc.) can provide relative advantage.	Selective investment in education in high technology and management areas. Programs to lift generic skills, e.g. in communications and understanding technologies.
Market liberal human capital theory (1980s/1990s)	Individuals invest in education until the costs exceed the expected benefits (mostly	Educational investment and its financing are an individual responsibility:	Programs and policies to secure self managing individual investment in

Table 2.—*continued*

Theory	Main theoretical assumptions	Popular understandings	Governmental practices
	defined as future earnings). The aggregated private individual investments in education, on a market basis, lead to the optimum level of social investment.	individualised investment (private schools, home computing, post-graduate courses) maximises the chances of securing relative advantage.	education: the selective use of student assistance, 'talking up' participation, income contingent fees and loans schemes, etc.

particularly by in the arithmetic methods used by Schultz. Rather, the relationship between education and economic value was mediated by technological change. Investment in education increased the capacity to respond effectively to technological innovations. This set the stage for the new governmental strategies of education–industry links, selective investment in R and D and training, and mass generic skills in communications and information technologies (Bartel & Lichtenberg, 1987; OECD, 1987).

By the early 1990s the free market dogs had barked loud and long, and the human capital caravan had again moved on. Governments were committed to extensive market reforms in education, and with popular desire for post-school education moving towards universal levels, no longer needed to provide full public funding of student places in order to maintain the desired levels of participation. The labour market penalties attached to low levels of educational qualification were bound to maintain demand. Student fees at modest levels no longer appeared to act as a deterrent to the same extent as before, though this varied by sector, institution and course. Many OECD governments introduced partial market reforms, at any and every level of education (Marginson, 1997b). Corresponding to the policy shift, work in human capital theory emphasised private individual investment in education, and there was little interest in social investment and social rates of return. It was striking that in complete contrast to the 1960s, very few economists made arguments for the expansion of public expenditure on education. In 1990 the OECD stated in *Financing Higher Education* that private rates of return provided a 'conceptually sound' basis for analysing demand for education. At the same time it opposed calculations of the social returns to spending on education on the grounds that this approach tended to encourage both the expansion of public spending, and credential inflation. It argued that the human capital data on rates of return to investment in education should be used to fix not the level of government funding, but the level of *private* funding in the form of fees (OECD, 1990, pp. 69–70).

There was more at stake here than the abandonment of the old spending programs. The new emphasis on individualised investment signified the workings of new kinds of education programs in which the key agents were the self regulating individual and the autonomous educational institution. Reliance on the self regulating individual as the subject of government, which had long played a role in liberal government, was enhanced in the 1970s and 1980s by both the collectivist individualism of the identity-based social movements and the high liberal individualism of the New Right. The activist Left emphasised difference and self-realisation; the Right emphasised self-interest and economic choice. The trend to self regulation, with something of a high individualist twist, became actualised in the emerging neo-liberal methods of government.[4] Here the micro-level, individualised version of human capital theory came into its own. Education became understood not so much as a social investment with common ends, but as a process of *investment in the self*, that could be managed by parents and students themselves. Keith Joseph, once Thatcher's Minister for Education, argued that 'self interest is indeed the first duty which a man [sic] owes to his community, so he supports himself and does not depend on others' (Joseph & Sumption, 1979, p. 121). As Colin Gordon puts it, the individual became 'the entrepreneur of himself or herself'. It was becoming part of 'the continuous business of living', to make provision for the preservation, reproduction and reconstruction of our own human capital.

In this framework the responsibility of government lay not so much in financing investment but in providing the conditions under which economically rational decision making could take place. By securing individual investment behaviour in education, governments ensured not only that participation in education would regulate itself, but that labour market outcomes would be partly de-politicised. 'The unexpected political acceptability of renewed mass unemployment can be plausibly attributed to the wide diffusion of the notion of individual as enterprise' (Gordon, 1991, pp. 24, 30, 44–46).

Power-knowledge Critique 2: totalising truth

The same kind of power-knowledge critique can be applied to the input–output 'production function' economics of education. In the application of input–output economics to education, which in most OECD countries first occurred on a large scale in the early to mid-1980s, the universalising character of neo-classical economics came into its own. Using input–output modelling, the complex, heterogeneous work of education institutions could be standardised on a common scale, creating measures of 'total' output. By comparing 'total' output to total money cost, the economist could derive a measure of global efficiency. Using input–output measures an education institution or educational system could be tracked, monitored, structured, deconstructed and reconstructed from a fixed central pivot. Lyotard comments that system controllers and orthodox economists share a common conception of society as a unified totality:

> Traditional theory is always in danger of being incorporated into the programming of the social whole as a simple tool for the optimisation of its performance; this is because its desire for a unitary and totalising truth lends itself to the unitary and totalising practice of the system's managers. (Lyotard, 1984, p. 12)

Here economics met managerial reform. Input–output economics provided a framework for the economisation of educational administration, and the entry of economists and accountants into the management of education programs in place of career professional educators, no longer able to be trusted with scarce public expenditure. Input–output conceptions of education fitted with the positivist and linear conceptions of organisational design that dominated modern management. In this framework, organisations were understood as stable sub-systems with defined boundaries, separable from their external context, while subject to determination from 'outside' or 'above' (i.e. subject to management of the orthodox hierarchical kind).[5] There were costs in this. The very facility of economics in inductive generalisation, on which its claim to universality is based, rested on the violent reduction, the simplification and distortion, of the rich empirical material that it confronted. Neo-classical economics operates a closed horizon. Within its own limits each discipline recognises true and false propositions; but it pushes back a whole teratology of knowledge beyond its margins (Foucault, in Barrett, 1991, p. 143). Extended to new terrain in education and elsewhere, economics worked by colonising or eliminating the non-economic 'other' that was outside and opposite to itself—such as the non-pecuniary individual benefits of education, and its shared collective benefits, which dropped from view. Carlson comments:

> Philosophy of presence works by suppressing the other by force or violence, even while denying that this violence occurs. What appears to be a whole is covertly an economy ... The restricted economy claims a profit—the unified whole—but does so only by concealing a loss—the loss of the Other that is violently suppressed. (Carlson, 1992, pp. 265–266)

Yet again, this power-knowledge relationship was largely immune to the conventional critiques. When applied to the purposes of government and management, the processes of abstraction, simplification and reduction became not as a weakness but a strength. The separation of management from its context and the erasure of much of the 'detail' actually enabled more effective control. On one hand economics had an unrivalled capacity to produce a terse summation of a whole complex department; for example, total output, productivity or efficiency expressed as a single figure. On the other hand, economics could be worked in reverse, subjecting a whole population to fine distinctions on the basis of hierarchies of cost and value, facilitating rationalisation. And by narrowing the formal definition of output to what is measured and valued in market terms, economics reduced the range of popular demands and the scope for politicisation of educational programs.

Conclusion: 'a power to be seized'

The power-knowledge critique enables a new kind of research program in relation to the economics of education; in which the focus of investigation becomes, not its inconsistencies as doctrine, nor the tabulation of its empirical applications, but the power-knowledge effects that it induces. In particular, this critique makes it possible to focus more directly and closely on the effects of the economics of education in systems of power: on the kind of human relations and social systems that it creates; on the kinds of education that it enables, values and promotes; on the educational practices that it excludes or reworks. With this kind of detailed work it also becomes possible to bring onto the agenda resistances and differences to the economics of education, and brings into view other and different kinds of power-knowledge relation, towards the formation of a new 'positivity' in education.

The solution does *not* lie in separating knowledge from power, so as to 'purify' academic economics. The economics of education and its uses are irretrievably tangled together. The economics of education is not a science fallen from grace, begging to be rescued from the gutter of politics. The science of the economics of education has *always* been implicated in government. Far from its science being separated from or opposed to its politics, it is when the economics of education reaches its highest level of scientific precision that it is most effective in normative terms. Becker, who won a Nobel Prize for his refinement of human capital theory, emphasises the normative role of economics. He wants to bring every part of social life within its compass, reconstructing it in terms of economic relations and economised individuals (Becker, 1976, pp. 5–6). The economics of education is not a 'reflection' of power. It is one of the active constituents of power. As Barrett states, 'discourse is not simply a translation of domination into language but is itself a *power* to be seized' (Barrett, 1991, p. 42).

When economic conceptions of education become applied in education programs, they start to produce the very behaviours that economists of education have imagined. Where university research is commercialised, researchers begin to think like entrepreneurs, and the free exchange of knowledge begins to be replaced by the legal alienation of intellectual property. When governments imagine students to be financial investors in their own economic futures, and consistent with this vision, provide student financing in the form of student loans repayable after education, forcing students to take into account their future earnings when choosing their course, more of those students *become* self managing investors in themselves. These economic behaviours are never as complete as the theory imagines. The student subjects also have other identities and behaviours, and no one is ever completely 'governed'. Nevertheless, the point is that joined to government, the economics of education forms the objects of which it speaks. It produces itself as true.

Therefore if there is a problem in the economics of education, as it has evolved in the last 35 years, or so, it is not a problem of true or false, but a problem of *right or wrong*. If the economics of education is true only under certain restricted circumstances, these circumstances are present in parts of the education systems, and are likely to further spread. The question is not whether these behaviours are possible. The questions are whether these behaviours are *desirable*, and whether and how to change that mix of power-knowledge into something else. If this mix is to be changed, it will be necessary to draw on a broader range of disciplines when ordering education institutions; and confine the economics of education to a more modest, less totalising place.

To do this it is necessary to extend self-managing selfhood—that bequest of both the Left and the Right forms of individualism—in new directions, to move outside the orthodox 'government of individualisation' (Foucault, 1982, p. 212) in education, and dispense with those subject positions that the neo-classical economics of education has taught. To develop new forms of subjectivity, and the political and educational circumstances in which they can flourish, it is necessary to explain and to expose to view the existing forms of subjectivity and subjugation. One of the common conditions of subjugation is the economics of education. To criticise it on its own terms is to remain imprisoned within it. The argument of this article has been that it is necessary to understand the economics of education as power-knowledge, in order to move beyond it.

This article was originally prepared as a paper for the 25th annual conference of the Australian Association for Research in Education, 26–30 November 1995, Hobart, Australia. Comments by Colin Symes helped to improve it.

Correspondence: Simon Marginson, Centre for the Study of Higher Education, University of Melbourne, Parkville, Victoria 3052, Australia. Email: s.marginson@cshe.unimelb.edu.au

NOTES

1. What he takes as given is a Marxist political economy. In *Discipline and Punish* (1977) Foucault links the emerging disciplinary technologies to economic developments, using a Marxist political economy. In another well known passage Foucault declared that Marx was part of the fabric of his work:

   > I quote Marx without saying so, without quotation marks, and because people are incapable of recognising Marx's texts I am thought to be someone who doesn't quote Marx. When a physicist writes a work of physics, does he find it necessary to quote Newton and Einstein? ... It is impossible at the present time to write history without using a range of concepts directly or indirectly linked to Marx's thought. (Foucault, 1980, pp. 52–53)

2. The literature critiquing human capital theory and economic rationalism in education is too immense to cite here. See Marginson (1993) for further discussion. Shaffer (1961) provides an early critique of human capital theory incorporating many points later made by educationists.
3. See Marginson (1997a, pp. 9–36) for more a detailed discussion.
4. Rose (1993) calls it 'advanced liberalism'. Another term is 'market liberalism' (Marginson, 1997a, b).
5. Lyotard comments the idea of perfect control of a system, based on perfect knowledge of its workings, had its origins in thermodynamics, in 'the notion that the evolution of a system's performance can be predicted if all the variables are known'. The later evolution of physics and quantum mechanics points to weaknesses in this: notions of randomness, contingency and chaos upset bordered, stable systems. Perfect knowledge and control are found to be impossible (Lyotard, 1984, pp. 12, 53–55; Dow, 1990).

REFERENCES

BARRETT, M. (1991) *The Politics of Truth* (Cambridge, Polity Press).

BARTEL, A. & LICHTENBERG, F. (1987) The comparative advantage of educated workers in implementing new technology, *The Review of Economics and Statistics*, 69(1), pp. 1–11.

BECKER, G. (1964/1975) *Human Capital: a theoretical and empirical analysis, with special reference to education* (New York, Columbia University) (first published in 1964).

BECKER, G. (1976) *The Economic Approach to Human Behaviour* (Chicago, University of Chicago Press).

BLAUG, M. (1976) The empirical status of human capital theory: a slightly jaundiced survey, *Journal of Economic Literature*, 14, pp. 827–855.

BLAUG, M. (1988) Review of 'Economics of education: research and statistics', *The Journal of Human Resources*, 24(2), pp. 331–335.

BURCHELL, G. (1993) Liberal government and the techniques of the self, *Economy and Society*, 22(3), pp. 267–282.

CARLSON, D. (1992) On the margins of microeconomics, in: D. CORNELL, M. ROSENFELD & D. CARLSON (Eds) *Deconstruction and the Possibility of Justice*, pp. 265–282 (London, Routledge).

DENISON, E.F. (1962) *The Sources of Economic Growth in the United States and the Alternatives before Us* (New York, Committee for Economic Development).

DOW, S. (1990) Beyond dualism, *Cambridge Journal of Economics*, 14, pp. 143–157.

FOUCAULT, M. (1972) *The Archaeology of Knowledge* (London, Tavistock Publications).

FOUCAULT, M. (1977) *Discipline and Punish* (Harmondsworth, Penguin).

FOUCAULT, M. (1980) *Power-knowledge* (New York, Pantheon Books).

FOUCAULT, M. (1982) The subject and power, in: H. DREYFUS & P. RABINOW (Eds) *Michel Foucault: beyond structuralism and hermeneutics* (Brighton, Harvester Press).

FOUCAULT, M. (1991) Governmentality, in: G. BURCHELL, C. GORDON & P. MILLER (Eds) *The Foucault Effect: studies in governmentality*, pp. 87–104 (London, Harvester Wheatsheaf).

FRIEDMAN, M. (1962) *Capitalism and Freedom* (Chicago, University of Chicago Press).

GORDON, C. (1980) Afterword, in: M. FOUCAULT, *Power-knowledge*.

GORDON, C. (1991) Governmental rationality: an introduction, in: G. BURCHELL, C. GORDON & P. MILLER (Eds) *The Foucault Effect: studies in governmentality*, pp. 1–52 (London, Harvester Wheatsheaf).

HANUSHEK, E. (1986) The economics of schooling: production and efficiency in public schools, *Journal of Economic Literature*, 24, pp. 1141–1177.

HIRSCH, F. (1976) *Social Limits to Growth* (Cambridge, Harvard University Press).

JOSEPH, K. & SUMPTION, J. (1979) *Equality* (London, John Murray).

KIKER, B.F. (1966) The historical roots of human capital, *The Journal of Political Economy*, 74(5), pp. 481–499.

LYOTARD, J.F. (1984) *The Post-modern Condition: a report on knowledge* (Minneapolis, University of Minnesota Press).

MAGLEN, L. (1990) Challenging the human capital orthodoxy: the education-productivity link re-examined, *The Economic Record*, 66, pp. 281–294.

MARGINSON, S. (1992) Productivity in the non-market services: issues and problems, *Labour Economics and Productivity*, 4(1), pp. 53-71.
MARGINSON, S. (1993) *Education and Public Policy in Australia* (Melbourne, Cambridge University Press).
MARGINSON, S. (1997a) *Educating Australia: government, economy and citizen since 1960* (Cambridge, Cambridge University Press).
MARGINSON, S. (1997b) *Markets in Education* (Sydney, Allen and Unwin).
MARTIN, L., Chair of Committee (1964) *Tertiary Education in Australia*, Volume 1, Report of the Committee on the Future of Tertiary Education in Australia (Canberra, Commonwealth Government printer).
MCCLOSKEY, D. (1994) *Knowledge and Persuasion in Economics* (Cambridge, Cambridge University Press).
MILLER, P. & ROSE, N. (1990) Governing economic life, *Economy and Society*, 19(1), pp. 1-31.
ORGANISATION FOR ECONOMIC COOPERATION and DEVELOPMENT, OECD (1985) *Education in Modern Society* (Paris, OECD).
ORGANISATION FOR ECONOMIC COOPERATION and DEVELOPMENT, OECD (1987) *Structural Adjustment and Economic Performance* (Paris, OECD).
ORGANISATION FOR ECONOMIC COOPERATION and DEVELOPMENT, OECD (1990) *Financing Higher Education* (Paris, OECD).
PORTER, M. (1988) Tertiary education, in Centre for Policy Studies, *Spending and Taxing II: taking stock*, pp. 119-137 (Sydney, Allen and Unwin).
ROSE, N. (1993) Government, authority and expertise in advanced liberalism, *Economy and Society*, 22(3), pp. 283-300.
SCHULTZ, T. (1960) Capital formation by education, *Journal of Political Economy*, 68(6), pp. 571-583.
SCHULTZ, T. (1961) Investment in human capital, *American Economic Review*, 51, pp. 1-17.
SHAFFER, H.G. (1961) Investment in human capital: comment, *American Economic Review*, 52(4), pp. 1026-1035.
SMITH, A. (1979) *The Wealth of Nations* (Harmondsworth, Penguin) (first published in 1776).

[15]

Creating Quasi-Markets in Education: A Review of Recent Research on Parental Choice and School Autonomy in Three Countries

GEOFF WHITTY
Institute of Education, University of London

INTRODUCTION

This chapter will review recent research literature concerning the progress and effects of the currently fashionable "parental choice" and "school autonomy" agendas in contemporary education policy. In discussing *parental choice,* the chapter will be particularly concerned with those policies that claim to enhance opportunities for choice among public schools[1] and those that use public funds to extend choice into the private sector. *School autonomy,* as used here, refers to moves to devolve various aspects of decision making from regional and district offices to individual public schools, whether to site-based professionals, community-based councils, or a combination of both. Advocates of both sets of policies argue that they will enhance the efficiency, effectiveness, and responsiveness of the education system as a whole.

The rationale for considering these two agendas together may need some explanation, especially in the United States, where the provenance of the two reforms is quite different and where, in some respects, they are competing strategies. Thus, for example, Moe (1994) suggests that school-based management is a self-serving reform favored by professional educators and designed to resist demands for the radical alternative of choice, which puts power in the hands of consumers. Yet, while he is critical of site-based management as it is generally practiced in

---

This paper draws on research carried out with support from the Economic and Social Research Council and the Institute of Education, University of London. I am also grateful to the University of Canterbury, Christchurch, New Zealand and the University of Wisconsin-Madison for visiting fellowships that enabled me to review relevant research in New Zealand and the United States respectively. The paper has benefited from visits to institutions and conversations with many individuals in all three countries. Particular thanks are due to Tony Bryk, John Chubb, Bruce Cooper, Fred Hess, Allan Odden, Kent Peterson, Penny Sebring, Amy Stuart Wells and John Witte in the United States; to Liz Gordon and Cathy Wylie in New Zealand; and members of the Parental Choice and Market Forces seminar at King's College London. I am grateful to Michael Apple, Marianne Bloch, Bill Boyd, Jim Cibulka, and Hugh Lauder for their helpful comments on an earlier version of the paper. None of those named should be held responsible for the ways in which I have interpreted their comments.

the United States and of some of the versions of devolution practiced elsewhere, he actually wants schools to have much greater autonomy from public authorities. Schools of choice, argue Chubb and Moe (1992), "are entirely autonomous, and they run their affairs as they see fit" (p. 12). This is what is beginning to happen in two other national contexts in which reforms that foster choice and school self-management are even more in evidence than in the United States: England and New Zealand. In those contexts, the interaction of parental choice and school autonomy within public education systems is beginning to create "quasi-markets" in education.

This review will concentrate on the ways in which these two reforms are contributing to the creation of such quasi-markets and on the implications of such a development. Levacic (1995) suggests that the distinguishing characteristics of a quasi-market for a public service are "the separation of purchaser from provider and an element of user choice between providers" (p. 167). She notes that there usually remains a high degree of government regulation, arguably considerably more than would be favored by Chubb and Moe (1992, p. 13). Most commentators see quasi-markets in education as involving a combination of parental choice and school autonomy, together with a greater or lesser degree of public accountability and government regulation. Partly because all of these elements are not always present in existing reforms, reviewing the research evidence is not a straightforward task.

Nor, indeed, is research evidence necessarily the key issue in debates about school reform. Cookson (1994) has characterized the debate about choice as a "struggle for the soul of American education," indicating quite clearly that the struggle is a highly political one involving conflicting values and interests. Similarly, Henig (1994) comments that "the story of choice-in-practice . . . reminds us that the conflicts that are most compelling and difficult to resolve revolve around questions about the kind of society we wish to become" (p. 116). Thus, terms such as choice and autonomy are used and contested in debates that are about much more than technical issues concerning school effectiveness and systemic efficiency.

Nevertheless, research evidence has itself become an important discursive resource in those debates. Furthermore, evidence from one national context is increasingly being mobilized and recontextualized in another. On the basis of a brief visit to Britain sponsored by *The Sunday Times,* Chubb and Moe (1992) declared the British reforms a qualified success and lamented the way in which the complexities of the American constitution had so far prevented similarly root-and-branch reforms in the United States. Moe (1994) argued that while "it's really quite remarkable how similar the [reform] movements have been in the two countries . . . the difference is, [Britain] actually followed through" (p. 24).

Conversely, a British proponent of increased parental choice (Pollard, 1995a, 1995b) recently gained considerable media attention with the claim that, where choice programs have been introduced in the United States, "they are popular, successful and demanded elsewhere" (Pollard, 1995a, p. 4). He suggested that "many ethnic minority and 'poverty lobby' groups are among the leading advocates of choice, seeing it as a way to escape from inner-city sink schools and the culture of low expectations" (Pollard, 1995a, p. 4). Meanwhile, Sexton (1991), a leading advocate of the market-oriented approach in Britain, has tried to use the smaller New Zealand "system"[2] as a laboratory for his ideas. Reports of the "progress" of reform in one context have thus become resources in the struggle for reform in another. Much the same is true of the use of evidence relating to the problems of reform. For example, Carnoy (1995) has recently cited research on choice in Europe (Ambler 1994) to support arguments against vouchers in the United States.

In view of this, it is as well to state at the outset the particular concerns that I bring to my task. Not only do I write from the perspective of an English commentator, as a sociologist of education I have a particular interest in the relationship between education and social inequality, and this is likely to have influenced the way in which I look at the evidence. It will become clear that, while not denying that parental choice and school autonomy can bring benefits to individual schools and students and even have their progressive moments, my conclusion from the evidence we have to date is that, far from being the best hope for the poor, as Moe (1994) suggests, the creation of quasi-markets is likely to exacerbate existing inequalities, especially in instances in which the broader political climate and the prevailing approach to government regulation are geared to other priorities. This is particularly relevant to the cases on which I focus here, England, New Zealand and the United States, where the debate about these reforms has often become linked to a broader conservative agenda.[3]

As we shall see, it is also possible for similar reforms to be related to rather different political agendas. The different political meanings given to reform are important in judging its significance and assessing its effects. Even in the three countries being considered here, the reforms are being implemented in significantly different social and cultural contexts. Education systems have particular structures and embody particular assumptions that are deeply embedded in their time and place. Halpin and Troyna (1994) argue that "fine-grain detail of their implementation" is necessary before reforms in one context can be used as models for policy-making in another, and much the same might be said about the lessons that can be learned from them (p. 1). As Seddon, Angus, and Poole (1991) point out in an Australian contribution to the literature on school-based management, "decisions at proximal [or school] level are circumscribed by decisions at higher levels" and these higher level frames are likely to differ from context to context (p. 32).

I should also preface my comments with a mention of three more specific limitations of any review of the efficacy of parental choice and school autonomy policies undertaken at this time. First, in all three countries, other, sometimes conflicting reforms are being introduced at the same time. In England, for example, the recent extension of parental choice and school autonomy came in at the same time as a controversial national curriculum and system of national testing at ages 7, 11, 14, and 16. It is therefore virtually impossible to separate out the specific effects of any one of these policies. Second, many of the most ardent neo-liberal advocates of school autonomy and parental choice, such as Sexton in Britain (and, indeed, Chubb and Moe in the United States), argue that the reforms are inadequate because the reformers have so far been too cautious. They suggest that the reforms would have worked better if taken to their logical conclusion: ultimately, perhaps, a fully privatized system with vouchers. Finally, it is actually somewhat early to reach a conclusive judgment about these reforms. Indeed, in Britain, the left has often attacked the right for declaring comprehensive education a failure before it had a chance to get established, but that is now what the left often does in attacking the right's reforms. The right not unreasonably replies that one cannot effect a culture shift overnight and that schools and their communities will really reap the benefits only once they have escaped from the welfare state dependency culture and appreciate that they now have real choices.

Nevertheless, given that most advocates of these reforms tend, with missionary zeal, to herald them as a success and that many conservative politicians are seeking to extend them even before they have been properly evaluated, it is important to consider what can be gleaned from the early research, what sorts of claims it can reasonably be used to uphold, and what lessons might inform future reform efforts. In what follows, I first attempt to contextualize and characterize the nature of the reforms in the three countries. I go on to review research on the effects of school choice in each country and then do the same with research on the effects of school autonomy. In the final section of the chapter, I suggest that there is nothing in the research evidence to support the extravagant claims of the reform advocates but that it is nevertheless likely that some variant of these reforms will continue for the foreseeable future. Yet, in the absence of substantial safeguards, reforms that trade on the "market metaphor" are likely to increase rather than reduce inequalities in education in the circumstances currently prevailing in these three countries. I suggest that there is therefore a need to reassert the role of citizen rights in relation to consumer rights and thus to redress a balance that is veering dangerously toward treating education as merely a private consumption good.

PARENTAL CHOICE AND SCHOOL AUTONOMY IN THREE COUNTRIES

Two of the countries addressed here, England and New Zealand, have national systems of public education, while compulsory education in the United States is primarily the responsibility of individual states. It is also important to bear in mind that the total population of New Zealand is 3.5 million and that of England and Wales[4] is about 50 million, as compared with the population of more than 200 million in the United States. This means that it is easier, though not necessarily easy, to generalize about education policy in the first two of the countries under consideration here. On the other hand, those advocates of choice who argue that it will lead to greater diversity of provision tend to suggest that, prior to the recent reforms, the "one best system" in the United States had produced an unusual degree of uniformity and mediocrity in the public school system as a whole (Chubb & Moe, 1990); however, this has been challenged by Witte (1990).

In England, prior to the 1980s, the vast majority of children were educated in public schools maintained by democratically elected local education authorities (LEAs) that exercised political and bureaucratic control over their schools but also often provided them with considerable professional support. Also within the public school system were most church schools, which received funding from and were accorded varying degrees of autonomy by these LEAs. During the 1970s, the media had begun to focus attention on the supposed failings and "excesses" of schools and teachers, particularly in inner city LEAs controlled by left-wing Labour administrations committed to fostering equal opportunities. After the Conservative "revolution" of 1979, the Thatcher and Major governments set about trying to break the LEA monopoly on public schooling through the provisions of a series of education acts passed in the 1980s and early 1990s. Alongside a national curriculum, designed to impose more central government control over what was taught and to increase public accountability through a national system of testing, other policies sought to enhance parental choice and transfer responsibilities from LEAs to individual schools.

The early legislation of the Thatcher government made only tentative inroads into the powers of LEAs. The 1980 Education Act introduced a number of measures to enhance parental choice among public schools and an assisted places scheme that provided government funding to enable academically able children from poor homes to attend some of the country's elite private schools (see Edwards, Fitz, & Whitty, 1989). In the 1986 act, the individual governing bodies (which all public schools are required to have) were reformed by removing the inbuilt majority of allegedly self-serving local politicians and increasing the representation of parents and local business interests.

In the latter part of the 1980s, the government sought to create new forms of public school entirely outside the influence of LEAs. City technology colleges (CTCs), announced in 1986, were intended to be new secondary schools for the inner city. CTCs, with a curriculum emphasis on science and technology, were run by independent trusts with business sponsors. The latter were expected to provide much of the capital funding but with recurrent funding coming from the central government, although the reluctance of business to fund this experiment meant that the government eventually had to meet most of the capital costs as well (Whitty, Edwards, & Gewirtz, 1993). Subsequently, a clause in the 1988 Education Reform Act offered many existing public schools the opportunity to "opt out" of their LEAs after a parental ballot and run themselves as grant-maintained schools with direct funding from central government. Margaret Thatcher expressed the hope that most schools would eventually take this route.

Meanwhile, local management of schools, another aspect of the 1988 act, gave many of those schools that remained with their LEAs more control over their own budgets and day to day management, receiving funds according to a formula that ensured that at least 85% of the LEA's budget was handed down to schools and that 80% of each school's budget was determined directly by the number and ages of its pupils. This severely limited the extent to which the LEA could provide earmarked funding to counter disadvantage. The funding formula included teachers' salaries, and teachers became *de facto* employees of the governing body, even though most remained *de jure* employees of the LEA.

Open enrolment, which was also part of the 1988 act, went much further than the limited enhancement of parental choice introduced in the 1980 Education Act. It allowed popular public schools to attract as many students as possible, at least up to their physical capacity, instead of being kept to lower limits or strict catchment areas (zoning) in order that other schools could remain open. This was seen as the necessary corollary of per capita funding in creating a quasi-market in education. In some respects, it was a "virtual voucher" system (Sexton, 1987), that was expected to make all schools more responsive to their clients and either become more effective or go to the wall. However, existing rules on admission, based on sibling enrollment, proximity, and so forth, were retained once schools were full, although these rules were more flexible in some areas than others and parents were given enhanced opportunities to appeal.

Although elements of the reforms have been concerned with enhancing both parental "voice" and parental "choice," the emphasis has been firmly on the latter. The 1993 Education Act extended the principles of diversity, choice, and institutional autonomy throughout the school system. It extended local management of schools and the right to opt out to virtually all schools, permitted schools to apply to change their character by varying their enrollment schemes, sought to encourage new types of specialist schools, and made it possible for some private schools to opt in to grant maintained status. While the rhetoric has been largely about devolving power to schools, parents, and communities, the act also created a potentially powerful national funding agency for schools that has taken over the planning function from LEAs where grant-maintained schools are in the majority (Department for Education, 1992).

These measures were widely expected to reduce the role of LEAs to a marginal and residual one over the succeeding few years. However, schools have so far been much more reluctant to opt out of their LEAs than the government anticipated, so the Major government has recently advanced the idea of introducing legislation to make all schools grant maintained. While claiming to have already increased diversity and choice, the prime minister looks forward to the day "when all publicly funded schools will be run as free self-governing schools." He believes in "trusting headmasters (*sic*), teachers and governing bodies to run their schools and in trusting parents to make the right choice for their children" (Anderson, 1995). Comprehensive schools are also to be permitted to introduce selection for up to 15% of their intake without having to apply to change their character.

By contrast with England, New Zealand in the 1980s was a somewhat surprising context for a radical experiment in school reform, let alone one associated with the conservative agenda. Unlike in England and the United States, there was no widespread disquiet about educational standards in the public school system nor were there the vast discrepancies in school performance that contributed to a "moral panic" about urban education in those two countries. The initial reforms were introduced by a Labour government, albeit one that had enthusiastically embraced monetarism and "new public management" techniques in the mid-1980s (Wylie, 1995). The education reforms, which were introduced in October 1989, were based on the Picot Report (Picot, 1988) and the government's response, *Tomorrow's Schools* (Minister of Education, 1988). They led to a shift in the responsibility for budget allocation, staff employment, and educational outcomes from central government and regional educational boards to individual schools. Schools were given boards of trustees, originally composed of parents (but extended in 1991 to encourage the inclusion of businesspeople) who had to negotiate goals with the local community and agree on a charter with the central government.

Because boards of trustees have effective control over establishing their own enrollment schemes when a school is oversubscribed, the New Zealand reforms have ushered in a much more thoroughgoing experiment in free parental choice in the public sector than was introduced in England. Extending choice into the private sector has been slower, but a 3-year pilot study of a targeted individual entitlement scheme, the New Zealand equivalent of the British assisted places scheme, has recently been announced. This has led to claims that "it marks the start of a move towards a voucher system in which schools compete for parents' education dollar" (Wellington *Evening Post,* 9/28/95).

However, Wylie (1994) argues that other aspects of the New Zealand reforms "offer a model of school self-management which is more balanced than the English experience [because they put] a great emphasis on equity . . . on community involvement . . . on parental involvement [and on] partnership: between parents and professionals" (p. xv). Furthermore, neither the costs of teacher salaries nor the costs of some central support services were devolved to individual school budgets, although there have subsequently been moves in this direction since the election of a conservative administration in 1990. Currently, only 3% of New Zealand schools are involved in a pilot scheme for "bulk funding" (or devolution of 100% of their funding, including teachers' salaries), but a "direct funding" option is to be opened up to all schools in 1996 for a trial period of 3 years. Unlike the English funding formulas, according to which schools are funded on the basis of average teacher salaries, the New Zealand scheme will be based on actual teacher salaries and a given teacher-student ratio. Alongside these reforms, national curriculum guidelines were introduced, but these guidelines were far less detailed and prescriptive than the English model and paid more attention to minority Maori interests. On the other hand, an outcome-based approach to national assessment is being phased in, and this could provide central government and employers with a highly controversial alternative mode of accountability and control.

In the United States, Newmann (1993) includes parental choice, greater school autonomy, and shared decision making as among the 11 most popular restructuring reforms. However, given the limited role of the federal government in relation to education, it is much harder to generalize about the nature and provenance of such attempts to enhance parental choice and devolve decision making to schools. Even in the context of America 2000 and Goals 2000, which exhibit something of the same tension between centralizing and decentralizing measures found in England and New Zealand, the role of the federal Department of Education had to be largely one of exhortation. Cookson (1995) suggests that, during the 1980s, President Reagan used it as "a 'bully pulpit' for espousing his beliefs in school choice and local educational autonomy," while George Bush "went further . . . in attempting to reorganize the public school system according to what he believed were sound market principles" (p. 409). This included support for parental choice, self-governing charter schools, and the New American Schools program, which, in the original Bush version, displayed some parallels with the English CTC initiative. Although neither Congress nor the states collectively endorsed this overall approach, the National Governors' Association was an early advocate of choice, and the national educational goals did receive bipartisan support and a modest amount of federal funding.

In Goals 2000, the Clinton administration has taken work on voluntary standards and accountability measures much further in the context of what Cookson (1995) describes as the "new federalism" and "a firm but cautious belief in the efficacy of public institutions" (p. 412). Title III of the Goals 2000: Educate America Act provides support for state and local educational improvement efforts designed to help all students attain high academic standards. Site-based management continues to be seen as one way of contributing to this aim, as does parental and community involvement. Choice, though, has been much less in evidence in the federal rhetoric under the Clinton administration.

Meanwhile, the more significant decisions continue to be made at state and district levels, even if, as Cookson (1995) claims, the authors of Goals 2000 saw the federal government as "crafting, shaping and, to some degree, controlling education throughout the fifty states" (p. 414). While a few states, such as Minnesota, have statewide choice plans, many initiatives have been more local. Wells (1993b) demonstrates the huge variety in origins and probable effects of the various choice plans that have been mooted or implemented in the United States over the past few years. Similarly, Raywid (1994) includes among the specialist or "focus" schools (Hill, Foster, & Gendler, 1990) that she advocates a whole variety of schools with very different origins and purposes. These include longstanding specialty schools, such as Boston Latin School and New York's highly academic Stuyvesant High School; magnet schools associated with desegregation plans; alternative schools, sometimes based on progressive pedagogic principles; and private Catholic schools. The nature and provenance of charter schools and that of site-based management within school districts also vary considerably (Murphy & Beck, 1995; Wohlstetter, Wenning, & Briggs, 1995).

However, despite the variety of different reforms in the United States, there are a number of distinctive styles of reform. Some, such as the Coalition of Essential Schools, have been based on particular educational philosophies, while others have been linked to broader political programs. While desegregation was an early impetus for reform, the impact of the broader ideological context and the changed political context since the 1994 congressional elections may now be rather more important than the "new federalism" of the Clinton administration in determining the current direction of policy. This, together with the particular circumstances of individual states and districts, has ensured that much of the neoliberal and neoconservative momentum of the Reagan and Bush administrations has continued to be reflected in local reform efforts.

Even so, it is often claimed that devolution and choice in the United States continue to enlist significant support from more progressive forces, particularly among those representing people of color. Insofar as such claims are true, this may be partly because the initial criticisms of large urban school bureaucracies in general, and of zoning in particular, were often associated with moves to foster desegregation. Yet, far from reflecting the free play of market forces, initiatives such as magnet schools were as much examples of state intervention as the segregated systems they replaced. And, whatever the fiction of particular court challenges, such initiatives were also as much the product of popular political struggles as of individual market choices.

Nevertheless, the rather mixed evidence on the efficacy and effects of desegregation and magnet schools in the 1980s (Blank, 1990; Moore & Davenport, 1990) has sometimes led to the conclusion that enhanced parental voice and choice, rather than more concerted political intervention, will provide the best chance of educational salvation for minority parents and their children. Moe (1994) goes so far as to claim that the best hope for the poor to gain the right "to leave bad schools and seek out good ones" is through an "unorthodox alliance [with] Republicans and business . . . who are the only powerful groups willing to transform the system" (p 33). For this reason, some aspects of the current reform agenda have developed a populist appeal well beyond the coteries of conservative politicians or even the White populations to which they usually appeal, although some of the more extreme voucher-style proposals, such as that included on the ballot in California in 1994, have been rejected at the polls.

Key icons of the school choice movement, such as controlled choice in Cambridge, Massachusetts and Montclair, New Jersey; the East Harlem "choice" experiment in New York; and the Milwaukee private school "voucher" experiment have certainly had active support among the mainly minority populations of these inner-city school districts. The same is true of some of the better known examples of specialist schools, site-based management and shared decision-making in Miami (Dade County) and New York City and of the establishment of local school councils in Chicago. Whether the research evidence actually justifies such support even in some of these cases, let alone the more ambitious plans of market advocates, is more questionable. It is certainly doubtful whether these policies have brought benefits for minority groups as a whole, even in instances in which they have brought particular benefits for specific communities. To explore these issues further, I now consider the limited evidence that is available on the effects of recent policies to encourage parental choice and school self-management.

RESEARCH ON CHOICE

It is clear that *parental choice* is a term that covers a wide range of different policies, even though there are some strong parallels between developments in New Zealand, England, and the United States. There are also particular concerns within the histories of the three countries that influence the terms in which policies are framed. Thus, as we have seen, race has been a much more influential issue in the United States and New Zealand than it has in England, where a government minister was prepared to dismiss concerns about the potential of choice to produce racial segregation with the statement that her government did not wish "to circumscribe [parental] choice in any way" (in Blackburne, 1988, p. A6). On the other hand, concerns about providing opportunities for the single-sex education of girls have been more prominent in England and New Zealand than in the United States, although David (1993) points out that gender perspectives are "curiously absent" in most of the research on school choice. Also, the controversy about choice in England and New Zealand has focused mainly on transfer between primary and secondary schools, whereas much of the American debate has been concerned with elementary as well as middle and high school choice.[5] Not surprisingly, these different concerns have also influenced the focus of evaluations of the reforms in the three countries. Furthermore, the styles of research adopted have been rather different. Paradoxically, given what I have stated earlier about the scope of the reforms in the different countries, the emphasis in the United States is often on the analysis and reanalysis of large data sets and that in England on in-depth ethnographic research in particular communities. The major New Zealand studies tend to combine quantitative and qualitative methods. Even so, research findings on the effects of choice in the three countries display more similarities than differences.

In England, there has been a considerable amount of research looking both at the "marketization" of public services in general and the impact of policies designed to enhance parental choice in education in particular. These latter studies have focused on the effects of open enrollment and the provision of opportunities for parents to choose from a greater variety of types of schools, particularly at the secondary level, including schools outside of LEA control. While some studies have examined the impact of the choice agenda as a whole (Bowe, Ball, & Gold, 1992; Gewirtz, Ball, & Bowe, 1995; Glatter, Woods, & Bagley, 1995), others, such as those on the assisted places scheme (Edwards et al., 1989), CTCs (Whitty et al., 1993) or grant-maintained schools (Fitz, Halpin, & Power, 1993), have concentrated on the impact of the new choices that have been made available.

In a substantial study of quasi-markets in British social policy, Le Grand and Bartlett (1993) argue that the reforms in education and housing have been rather more successful than those in health and social care. In a local case study of education, Bartlett (1993) found that the reforms had been welcomed by many headteachers (school principals) but less so by other teachers. However, he pointed out that, although parental choice has been increased by open enrollment "the door is firmly closed once a school [is full]. And by encouraging an increasingly selective admissions policy in [oversubscribed] schools open enrolment may be having the effect of bringing about increased opportunity for cream-skimming and hence increased inequality" (Bartlett, 1993, p. 150). Furthermore, he found that "those schools which faced financial losses under the formula funding system tended to be schools which drew the greatest proportion of pupils from the most disadvantaged section of the community" (p. 149). Thus, whatever gains may have emerged from the reforms in terms of efficiency and responsiveness to some clients, there were serious concerns about their implications for equity.

Le Grand and Bartlett (1993) take the view that "cream-skimming" poses the biggest threat to equity in the sorts of quasi markets created by the Thatcher government. This danger is clearly demonstrated in an important series of studies by Ball and his colleagues on the operation of quasi-markets in London. In an early study, Bowe et al. (1992) concluded that schools were competing to attract greater cultural capital and thus higher yielding returns. Subsequently, Gewirtz and Ball (1995; Gewirtz et al., 1995) have shown schools seeking students who are "able," "gifted," "motivated and committed," and middle class, with girls and children from South Asian backgrounds being seen as particular assets in terms of their potential to enhance test scores.[6] The least desirable clientele include those who are "less able" and those who have special educational needs (especially emotional and behavioral difficulties), as well as children from working-class backgrounds and boys, unless they also have some of the more desirable attributes.

In these circumstances, popular schools are tempted to become increasingly selective, both academically and socially, through overt as well as covert methods of selection. Particularly if there is no chance of expanding, they try to capitalize on and enhance the scarcity value of their product. Elite private schools in England did not choose to expand during the 1980s despite the demand for their product by the *nouveau riche* of the Thatcherite era. Although the government has provided the possibility of expansion for successful and popular public schools, some have already indicated that they are not interested in this option because it would threaten the ethos they have developed.

Most studies of education markets confirm that cream skimming is a major issue, although the composition of the cream takes a particular form in English education. Bartlett and Le Grand (1993) suggest that cream skimming involves favoring those clients who will bring the greatest return for the least investment, thus leading to discrimination by providers against the more expensive users. It is sometimes argued that, in education, this would involve going for the middle of the market; the gifted and those defined as having special educational needs will cost more to process. There is certainly evidence of discrimination against children with special educational needs. Bartlett (1993) argues that such discrimination will not occur only if the market price varies with the needs of the client. In other words, funding formulas need to be weighted to give schools an incentive to take more "expensive" children. The current premium paid for children with special educational needs may not be enough if it makes the school less popular with clients who, although bringing in less money, bring in other desirable attributes. Bowe et al. (1992) and Vincent, Evans, Lunt, and Young (1995) give examples of schools making just this sort of calculation. However, the academically able are the "cream" that most schools do seek to attract. Such students stay in the system longer and thus bring in more money, as well as making the school appear successful in terms of its test scores and hence attractive to other desirable clients.

Le Grand and Bartlett (1993) found lack of information a major limitation within quasi-markets as they currently operate in England. Glennerster (1991) suggests that, given the opportunity, most schools will want to become more selective because taking children who will bring scores down will affect their overall market position. This is especially so when there is imperfect information about school effectiveness and when only "raw" test scores are made available, as they currently are in England.[7] Schools with the highest scores appear best even if other schools enhance achievement more.[8]

As long as schools tend to be judged on a unidimensional scale of academic excellence, many commentators have predicted that choice, rather than leading to more diverse and responsive forms of provision as claimed by many of its advocates, will reinforce the existing hierarchy of schools based on academic test results and social class. Walford and Miller (1991) suggest that this will run from elite private schools through CTCs, grant-maintained schools, voluntary aided (church) schools, and a rump of LEA schools providing mainly for children with special educational needs: the ultimate residualized or safety-net provision.

My own research (Edwards et al., 1989; Whitty et al., 1993) suggests that, within English culture, schools judged to be good and hence over-subscribed are most likely to be academically selective schools or formerly selective schools with a persisting academic reputation. They are also likely to have socially advantaged intakes. Although parents may choose new types of schools because they are different from the standard local comprehensive school, that does not seem to lead in England to a truly diversified system.[9] Instead, those parents who are in a position to choose are choosing those schools that are closest to the traditional academic model of education that used to be associated with selective grammar schools. Even new types of schools tend to be judged in these terms. Our research showed that many parents chose CTCs not so much for their hi-tech image but because they were perceived as the next best thing to grammar schools or even elite private schools (Whitty et al., 1993).

In this situation, those *schools* that are in a position to choose often seek to identify their success with an emphasis on traditional academic virtues and thus attract those students most likely to display them. Fitz et al. (1993) have shown that many of the first schools to opt out and become grant maintained were selective, single-sex schools with traditional sixth forms, and this gave the sector an aura of elite status. The Grant Maintained Schools Centre has claimed that the sector's test results demonstrate its academic superiority, even though those results are almost certainly determined by the nature of the intakes of the early grant-maintained schools. Some grant-maintained comprehensive schools have reverted to being overtly academically selective, and only those that have clearly failed on traditional academic criteria are likely to risk deviating significantly from the dominant definition of excellence in their curriculum offering. Power, Halpin, and Fitz (1994) found "no indications of any changes relating to the curriculum or pedagogy" and a renewed emphasis on traditional imagery in the way grant maintained schools presented themselves (p. 29). Furthermore, Bush, Coleman, and Glover (1993) suggested that 30% of the grant-maintained "comprehensive" schools they studied were using covert selection, which is also likely to increase their appearance of academic superiority. In addition, grant-maintained schools have been identified as among those with the highest rates of exclusion of their existing pupils and among the least willing to cater for pupils with special educational needs (Feintuck, 1994).

A recent Australian review of such evidence suggested that "paradoxically, the market exacerbates differences between schools on the basis of class, race, and ethnicity, but does not encourage diversity in image, clientele, organisation, curriculum or pedagogy" (Blackmore, 1995, p. 53). Regardless of the rhetoric of restructuring that stresses diversity, "market status is maintained by conforming to the dominant image of a good school as being well uniformed, well-disciplined and academically successful" (Blackmore, 1995, p. 48). Gewirtz et al. (1995) suggest that one effect of the development of an education market in England has been a narrowing of the "scope" of education, in that "almost exclusive emphasis [has been placed] on instrumental, academic and cognitive goals" (p. 174).

According to Walford and Miller (1991), even some of those intended beacons of an entirely *new* form of excellence, CTCs, may be abandoning that distinctiveness in favor of traditional academic excellence. More generally, in a major empirical study of school parental choice and school response, Glatter et al. (1995) conclude that there is no evidence to date of choice producing greater diversity in the school system and some evidence of a tendency toward greater uniformity, except where there has been additional government funding to foster the development of specialist technology schools. In other words, government intervention, rather than parental choice, has brought innovation on the supply side. With regard to hierarchy, Glatter et al. have found no dramatic movement to date but certainly no evidence that it has been reduced by the reforms.

Thus, in England, the entrenched prestige of traditionally academic education has produced a persistent devaluing of alternatives. The government's claim (Department for Education, 1992) that it is policy neither to encourage nor discourage schools from becoming selective ignores the reality of what is happening, both overtly and covertly, when schools are oversubscribed. If different versions of schooling have very different exchange values in competition for entry to higher education and to privileged occupations, then the high value placed on traditional academic success makes access to it a positional good and therefore one in short supply. Schools seeming to offer the best chance of academic success are likely to be considerably overchosen. In instances in which they are, the producer is empowered, and the consumer must establish fitness for the school's purposes.

As long as the notion of fitness remains a narrow one, it is unlikely that those groups that have traditionally performed poorly within the education system will benefit. Behind the superficially appealing rhetoric of choice and diversity, the reforms are resulting in a reduction in choice for many parents rather than the comprehensive empowerment of consumers that markets are presumed by their advocates to produce. While they may be enhancing the educational performance of some children, and certainly that of those schools in which the more advantaged children are concentrated, they seem to be further disadvantaging many of those very groups that were disadvantaged by the previous system. Our own figures (Edwards et al., 1989) on the failure of assisted places schemes to reach the intended clientele of disadvantaged inner-city families are likely to be repeated in the case of other schools of choice with a strong market appeal, as advantaged parents and advantaged schools search each other out in a progressive segmentation of the market (Ranson, 1993).

Walford (1992a) argues that, while choice will lead to better quality schooling for some children, the evidence so far suggests that it will "discriminate in particular against working class children and children of Afro-Caribbean descent" (p. 137). T. Smith and Noble (1995) also conclude, from the evidence, that English choice policies are further disadvantaging already disadvantaged groups. Although schools have always been socially and racially segregated to the extent that residential segregation exists, Gewirtz et al. (1995) suggest that choice may well exacerbate this segregation by extending it into previously integrated schools serving mixed localities. Their research indicates that working-class children and, particularly, children with special educational needs are likely to be increasingly "ghettoized" in poorly resourced schools.

Such trends are particularly evident in inner London, where admissions policies have been relaxed. The former Inner London Education Authority used to operate a "banding" system that sought to ensure that all schools had a reasonable balance of levels of academic ability among their intakes. A recent study (Pennell & West 1995) has suggested that, in light of the abandonment of this system in many parts of London and an increasing number of autonomous schools operating their own admissions policies, there is a danger of growing polarization between schools. They argue that the new system is serving to reinforce the privilege of "those parents who are able and prepared to negotiate the complexities [of the system] compared with those who are less willing or less able to do so" (p. 14).

The Smithfield Project, a major study of the impact of choice policies in New Zealand, suggests that much the same sort of social polarization is taking place there (Lauder et al., 1994; Waslander & Thrupp, 1995). In another New Zealand study (Fowler 1993), schools located in areas of low socioeconomic were found to be judged negatively because of factors over which they had no influence, such as type of intake, location and problems perceived by parents as linked to these factors. Wylie (1994) too has noted that schools in low income areas there are more likely to be losing students to other schools. If we could be sure that their poor reputation was deserved, this might be taken as evidence that the market was working well with effective schools reaping their just rewards. But, as in England, judgments of schools tend to be made on social grounds or narrow academic criteria and with little reference to their overall performance or even their academic effectiveness on value-added measures. Gordon (1994a) points out that

> schools with a mainly middle class and Pakeha (or, increasingly, Asian) population, tend to achieve better on national examinations because of the high level of "readiness" and motivation of the pupils, and relatively low levels of social problems that impinge on educational processes. (p. 19)

Furthermore, advantaged schools are able to introduce enrollment schemes that "have a tendency to reinforce their social exclusivity" (p. 18). Yet schools perceived to be poor are not actually closing but rather remaining open with reduced rolls, declining funding, and low morale, thus producing a self-fulfilling prophecy.

The current funding regime in New Zealand makes it extremely difficult for schools in disadvantaged areas to break out of the cycle of decline. Yet research studies suggest that many of the differences between schools result from factors largely beyond the control of parents and schools, except the power of advantaged parents and advantaged schools to further enhance their advantage and thus increase educational inequalities and social polarization. Lauder et al. (1995) show that, when schools can choose the students they admit, socioeconomic status and ethnic factors "appear to influence school selection, even when prior achievement has been taken into account" (p. 53). This is not necessarily an argument against choice, but it is clear that procedures for selection to oversubscribed schools need reconsideration. Significantly, the Smithfield Project also found that social polarization between popular and unpopular schools decreased only in the single year in which allocations to oversubscribed schools were based on "balloting" (or drawing lots).

Wylie (1994, 1995) reports that the combination of choice and accountability measures has led to schools paying more attention to the attractiveness of physical plant and public image than to changes to teaching and learning other than the spread of computers. It has also led to increased attention to the information about school programs and children's progress that reaches parents, changes that "are clearly not without value in themselves" (p. 163). But she also notes that "they do not seem able to counter or outweigh factors affecting school rolls which lie beyond school power, such as local demographics affected by employment, ethnicity, and class" (Wylie, 1995, p. 163, citing Gordon, 1994b, Waslander & Thrupp 1995).

In the United States, the early association of public school choice with racial desegregation may have ensured that equity considerations continue to play a greater part in education reform than in England or even New Zealand. Nevertheless, there are considerable concerns about the equity effects of more recent attempts to enhance choice, especially because there is no clear evidence to date of a positive impact on student achievement. Indeed, the claim by Witte (1990) that there were few, if any, acceptable studies of the effects of choice on student achievement remains largely true today, notwithstanding his own pioneering studies in Milwaukee. In what follows, I concentrate largely on research or reanalyses of the effects of choice that have been published since Clune and Witte's (1990a, 1990b) two volume collection.[10]

What evidence there is about the effects of choice policies on student achievement and equity continues to be, at best, inconclusive (Plank, Schiller, Schneider, & Coleman, 1993), despite claims by choice advocates that "the best available evidence" indicates that parental choice can and does work to improve the education of all children, especially low income and minority students" (Domanico, 1990, p. 15). Even some of the more positive evidence from controlled choice districts, such as Cambridge, Massachussetts (Rossell & Glenn, 1988; Tan, 1990) and Montclair, New Jersey (Clewell & Joy, 1990), which seemed to show gradual overall achievement gains, is now regarded by Henig (1994) as methodologically flawed, making it difficult to attribute improvements to choice *per se*. Furthermore, although choice has not always led to resegregation, as its critics feared, improvements in the racial balance of Montclair and Cambridge schools were most noticeable during periods of strong government intervention. Henig goes on to argue that the much vaunted East Harlem "miracle" (Bolick, 1990; Fliegel, 1990) has "escaped any serious effort at controlled analysis" even though it has had a special role "in countering charges that the benefits of choice programs will not accrue to minorities and the poor" (p. 142). Not only have the apparently impressive gains in achievement now leveled off or even been reversed, it is impossible to be sure that the earlier figures were not merely the effect of schools being able to choose students from higher socioeconomic groups outside the area or, alternatively, the empowerment of teachers. Overall, both Henig (1994) and Wells (1993b) conclude from exhaustive reviews that the stronger claims of choice advocates cannot be upheld and that choice needs to be carefully regulated if it is not to have damaging equity effects. It is probably too early to assess how the newest forms of choice, such as those involving charter schools, perform in this respect. However, while Medler and Nathan (1995) suggest that charter schools recruit a high proportion of "at-risk" students, both Becker, Nakagawa, and Corwin (1995) and Grutzik, Bernal, Hirschberg, and Wells (1995) argue that some of the features of these schools, such as the emphasis on parental involvement, may have the effect of excluding students from certain disadvantaged groups.[11]

The evidence with regard to private school choice is also contentious but relevant to the present concerns in view of current demands for an extension of the use of public funds to permit students to attend private schools. Much of the controversy centers around the various interpretations of the data from Coleman's high school studies (Coleman, Hoffer, & Kilgore, 1982) and, in particular, the work of Chubb and Moe (1990). While the data show a consistent but relatively small performance advantage for private schools once background variables have been controlled, some argue that it is a product of their methodology and that any advantage would disappear with the use of more subtle measures of the cultural differences between low-income families using private and public schools (Henig, 1994, p. 144). Lee and Bryk (1993) accuse Chubb and Moe of a circularity in their argument in support of school choice and suggest that their conclusions concerning the power of choice and school autonomy are not supported by the evidence as presented. Nevertheless, Bryk, Lee, and Holland (1993) claim on the basis of their own work that Catholic schools do have positive impact on the performance of low-income families; however, they attribute this at least as much to an ethos of strong community values antithetical to the marketplace as to the espousal of market forces. Critics argue that the socioeconomic status of the clientele of Catholic schools is generally above the average and that the figures are affected by leakage into the public sector in the higher grades (K. B. Smith & Meier, 1995; Witte, Thorn, & Pritchard, 1995).

Witte's evaluation of the controversial Milwaukee private school choice experiment, which enables children from poor families to attend private schools at public expense, concludes in its fourth-year report that "in terms of achievement test scores . . . students perform approximately the same as [Milwaukee Public School] students" (p. 28). However, attendance rates for choice children are slightly higher, and parental satisfaction has been high. For the schools, "the program has generally been positive, has allowed several to survive, several to expand, and contributed to the building of a new school" (Witte, Thorn, Pritchard, & Claibourn 1994, p. 28). Yet some of the stronger claims made both for and against this type of program cannot be sustained by the evidence; the Milwaukee program is small and narrowly targeted and is certainly not a basis on which to judge the probable effects of a more thoroughgoing voucher initiative. Its planned extension to include religious schools is, at the time of writing, the subject of a court challenge.

The Milwaukee program overall has not hitherto been oversubscribed and, although students are self-selected, the schools involved have not been in a position to exercise choice. Elsewhere, the combination of oversubscription and self-selection in explaining apparent performance gains through private school choice suggests that cream skimming is a major issue, as in England and New Zealand. K. B. Smith and Meier (1995) use existing data to test the school choice hypothesis and conclude that "competition between public and private schools appears to result in a cream-skimming effect" (p. 61). They also argue that there is no reason to expect that such effects will disappear in greater competition among public schools, especially because some schools would begin with competitive advantages, an issue they regard as seriously underplayed by Chubb and Moe and other advocates of choice. Indeed, they predict that choice could lead to a "two tier system" (p. 61), similar to that which is developing in England and New Zealand.

There is little in this recent evidence to counter the conclusions of Carnoy (1993) in an overview of historical data about choice in the United States. He argues that choice plans that place an undue emphasis on parental choice will benefit the performance only of high-demand, low-middle-income families and that a large fraction of students, particularly those from low-demand families, are likely to be worse off. This will merely increase the variance in student achievement, with some students decidedly worse off, rather than bringing about the overall improvement envisaged by the exponents of choice.

Wells (1993a) points out that the economic metaphor that schools will improve once they behave more like private, profit-driven corporations and respond to the demands of consumers "ignores critical sociological issues that make the school consumption process extremely complex." Some of those issues are explored further in an important contribution to the sociology of school choice by Wells and Crain (1992). That paper and Wells's own research suggest that many choice plans are based on false assumptions about how families behave in the educational marketplace. This means that competition will certainly not lead to school improvement "in those schools where students end up because they did not choose to attend a 'better' school." Escape from poor schools will not necessarily emerge from choice plans because "the lack of power that some families experience is embedded in their social and economic lives" (Wells, 1993a, p. 48). Anyon (1995) concludes from a study of the difficulty of reform in an urban ghetto school that "the only solution to educational resignation and failure in the inner city is the ultimate elimination of poverty and racial degradation" (p. 89). There is no convincing evidence to date that the provision of notional choices of other schools is a realistic alternative solution for most families.

Adler (1993) has suggested some revisions to current British policies that would take choice seriously but avoid the most unacceptable consequences of recent legislation. His particular proposals include retaining LEAs with a responsibility for formulating admissions policies for all local schools, encouraging schools to develop distinctive characteristics, requiring positive choices on behalf of all children and not only the children of "active choosers," involving teachers and older pupils in making decisions that are not necessarily tied to parental preferences, and giving priority in oversubscribed schools to the applicants who are most strongly supported. However, Walford (1992b) advocates that entry to oversubscribed schools should be based on random selection, an approach that is still used in some schools in New Zealand. In the United States, Wells (1990) argues that equitable choice schemes require clear goal statements; outreach work; information and counseling for parents; a fair, unrestrictive, non-competitive, and equitable admissions procedure; and provision of adequate transportation for students.

Similar safeguards were recommended in an international study of choice policies in England, Australia, the Netherlands, New Zealand, Sweden and the United States. This study concluded that in instances in which there is a dominant model of schooling, choice is as likely to reinforce hierarchies as it is to improve educational opportunities and the overall quality of schooling. It was also argued that demand pressures are rarely sufficient to produce real diversity of provision and that positive supply side initiatives are necessary to create real choice. To avoid reinforcing tendencies toward academic and social selection, popular schools may need positive incentives to expand and disadvantaged groups need better information, better transport, and perhaps even privileged access to certain schools (Organization for Economic Cooperation and Development, 1994). Lauder et al. (1995) point out that the enhanced information and travel funds alone may have little effect on the deep-rooted tendency of families of low socioeconomic status not to seek entry to high-status schools.

RESEARCH ON SCHOOL AUTONOMY

If choice policies without appropriate safeguards tend to empower advantaged parents, and perhaps even more so advantaged schools, what has been the impact of moves toward greater *school autonomy*? In origin, reforms that emphasize school autonomy are less clearly associated with the conservative agenda than parental choice. Yet, although Moe (1994) suggests that choice is a far more potent reform measure than school self-management, school autonomy is necessary to free schools to respond positively to market forces. Similarly, while Domanico (1990) states that "public school choice is not an alternative to school-based management; it is the most effective way of instituting school-based management" (p. 1), he also regards school-based management as "the most promising supply-side educational reform" (p. 2).

As I noted earlier, the extent of school autonomy and school self-management varies not only among the three countries but also within them. In general terms, New Zealand schools have the most autonomy and those in the United States the least. Within England, CTCs and grant-maintained schools have the most autonomy, but even LEA schools, which virtually all now have local management, have considerably more autonomy than U.S. schools with site-based management, including many charter schools (Wohlstetter et al., 1995). In terms of financial management, English schools operating under local management currently have more resources under their direct control than New Zealand schools, apart from those of the latter participating in the "direct funding" trials. Whatever the degree of autonomy, few school principals and teachers would wish to revert to a system of detailed day-to-day control of individual schools by local authorities, regional offices, or school districts. On that measure, the reforms could be (and often have been) judged a success. However, a closer look at the details of the relevant research suggests that there have also been some disturbing consequences of the more extreme forms of devolution found in England and New Zealand.

The major national study of the impact of local management of schools in England and Wales was conducted at Birmingham University, over a period of 3 years, with funding from the National Association of Head Teachers. It was largely based on surveys of headteachers' views, followed by visits to a subsample of schools to interview staff. The study was broadly positive but conceded that direct evidence of the influence of self-management on learning was "elusive." The team's initial survey (Arnott, Bullock, & Thomas, 1992) showed that the vast majority of school principals agreed with the statement that "local management allows schools to make more effective use of their resources." However, a majority also believed that, as a result of local management, meetings were being taken up by administrative issues, which lessened attention to students' learning. They were thoroughly divided on the question of whether children's learning is benefiting from local management. Thus, it was rather unclear as to what their concept of greater effectiveness actually related to.

In the final report of the study (Bullock & Thomas, 1994), the proportion of headteachers making a positive assessment concerning improvements in pupil learning had increased over the previous 3 years; significantly however, this assessment came mainly from those schools that had experienced an increase in funding as a result of self-management. A recent book that draws on a number of different research studies also concludes that, although local management enhances cost-efficiency, there is "a lack of strong theoretical argument and empirical evidence" to show that it improves the quality of teaching and learning, as claimed by the government (Levacic, 1995, p. xi).

The limited evidence there is of improvement at this level seems to be associated with increased funding rather than self-management *per se*. These findings might be expected on the basis of work carried out by Cooper (1994) in the United States suggesting that, as more money is passed down to the instructional context, including paying for better qualified or experienced teachers, there are tangible benefits for pupil performance. However, funding of teachers' salaries in England is done on the basis of average rather than actual salaries and schools whose budgets have been squeezed by the effect of this can therefore expect negative consequences. Furthermore, Cooper's research also suggests that if the funding that is, in fact, passed down to schools does not reach the instructional context (i.e., teachers and classrooms), then its benefits will be more questionable. In England, the linking of self-management with parental choice in the creation of quasi-markets has sometimes meant that resources are diverted into marketing rather than instruction and, indeed, successful marketing becomes essential to protect budgets in future years. Some headteachers may divert funds from the classroom on the basis of a judgment that it is in the best long-term interests of the school; however, there is little evidence of immediate benefits as far as teachers and pupils are concerned.

While the Birmingham team concluded that self-management was broadly a successful reform, they conceded that, before a more definitive conclusion could be drawn, more evidence was needed, particularly on the relationship between resourcing levels and learning outcomes. If that link is a close one, as Cooper suggests, then it argues against the current English funding formula that can reward or punish a school with sharp year-to-year changes in resourcing as a result of changes in school rolls. Indeed, it almost argues for a retreat from an extreme form of pupil-based funding either to funding based on average rolls over a number of years (as the research team suggests) or a return to curriculum led staffing with additional resources for disadvantaged schools. This is particularly important in that the schools most affected by budgetary difficulties—and therefore least likely to report a positive impact on pupils' learning—were often found to be those with pupils from disadvantaged communities. This reinforces the concerns of Le Grand and Bartlett (1993) reported earlier.

Wylie's (1994) study of the fifth year of self-managing schools in New Zealand also identified schools in low-income areas, as well as schools with high Maori enrollments, as experiencing greater resource problems than others. She did not find that this correlated with perceptions of the success of the reforms or with evaluations of the influence of the reforms on pupil learning, and she admits to being puzzled by this. However, apart from in a few pilot schools, New Zealand did not yet have direct funding of teacher salaries, and there remained more opportunities to apply for equity funding, so it may be that the funding differences there are less severe in their impact than those in England.

The English results cited here came mainly from headteacher respondents (i.e., from those responsible for the efficient management of the delegated budget and whose authority has been significantly enhanced by the self-management reform). There is, as yet, no similar study of classroom teachers or pupils. But it may be significant that the relatively few classroom teachers who were interviewed by the Birmingham research team were far more cautious than their headteachers about the benefits of self-management for pupil learning and overall standards. This takes on even more significance when one considers a recent report from school inspectors indicating that 70% of primary headteachers are failing to monitor how well their pupils are being taught. According to this report, "most attempts by heads to evaluate their staff's performance centred on what lessons covered rather than their quality or the standards of children's learning" (Office for Standards in Education, 1994). One has then to be somewhat skeptical about the value of claims by these same headteachers that self-management has improved pupil learning.

A local study by Marren and Levacic (1994; Levacic, 1995), independently funded by the Economic and Social Research Council, also found classroom teachers less positive about self-management than either school governors or headteachers. In this study, headteachers generally welcomed self-management even where their school had lost resources as a result of it, while classroom teachers were far more skeptical about its benefits even in schools that had gained in terms of resources. In New Zealand, Wylie (1994) reports that 41% of teachers, as compared with 46% of principals, believed that the quality of children's learning had improved since the shift to school-based management.

As indicated earlier, one of the difficulties in making sense of the British evidence of decentralization is that budgetary autonomy and school-based management were implemented at the same time as a highly centralizing measure, the National Curriculum and national testing. It is therefore difficult to separate their different effects on teachers' work and pupil learning. Interestingly, however, a recent survey conducted by Warwick University (Campbell & Neill, 1994) on the effects of the National Curriculum on primary school teachers, this time funded by a teachers' rather than a headteachers' union, concludes that there has been no overall improvement in standards but that teachers have been driven to burnout. They found that a 54-hour week was now the norm for teachers of children 4–7 years old, with 1 in 10 working more than 60 hours, and respondents spoke of tiredness, irritability and depression, sleeping badly, increased drinking, occasional crying in the staffroom, and a sense of guilt that they were neglecting their own families. While this has to be seen as coming from a particular pressure group, the research was actually sponsored by one of the least militant unions and one broadly in favor of the reforms.[12]

Studies in New Zealand (Bridges, 1993; Livingstone, 1994; Wylie 1994), where the National Curriculum workload is a less significant factor, have produced similar figures. As a result, New Zealand teachers have reported high levels of stress, declining job satisfaction, and a desire to leave the profession, even in cases in which they believed that the reforms had brought some benefits. Wylie (1994) concluded that New Zealand school communities had probably reached the limit of what they could provide to support the reforms in terms of money and time. Her various surveys for the New Zealand Council for Educational Research show a steady decline in teacher morale since the introduction of the reforms and also "quite a high turnover rate for principals (42% in all the schools in the sample between 1991 and 1993)" (Wylie, 1995, p. 163). New Zealand teachers varied considerably in their views about the influence of the reforms on relationships within the school, but Wylie (1994) herself alerts us to the fact that a significant proportion of them reported some deterioration in their relationship with their principal attributable to the reforms. The growing gap between principals' and teachers' perceptions of the effects of reform found in Wylie's 1993 (Wylie, 1994) survey was even more pronounced in a recent evaluation of the bulk funding trial for teachers' salaries. While principals still saw themselves as curriculum leaders, teachers stressed "the current role as being more of a business manager" (Hawk & Hill, 1994, p. 97). Wylie concludes her own most recent assessment with "the troubling thought" that the reforms "may produce only a small gain for the substantial cost of foregone attention to teaching and learning, within positive, supportive relationships" (Wylie, 1995, p. 163).

Some of the small-scale ethnographic evidence from Britain and New Zealand chronicles in more detail the effects of the intensification of teachers' work and its consequences for industrial relations in schools. One of the ironies in England is that, seemingly, both the devolution of self-management and the centralization of the National Curriculum are having detrimental effects on teacher morale and workload. Bowe et al. (1992) point to real problems with both self-management and the National Curriculum in secondary schools and see these problems as contributing to a growing gulf between senior managers and teachers and a clash between managerial and educational values. Broadbent, Laughlin, Shearn, and Dandy (1993), however, report evidence from other schools that the demands of local management were (initially at any rate) absorbed by a core "coping group" of senior managers whose efforts resulted in the core educational values of the school being relatively unscathed. However, some recent work from New Zealand (Murfitt, 1995) seems to suggest that it is middle managers in secondary schools who experience the greatest pressures, from both above and below.

Marren and Levacic (1994) are not sure whether their own evidence that classroom teachers are more critical of self-management than are senior managers is necessarily evidence of a cleavage in values between teachers and managers. They argue that greater class teacher involvement in financial decision making may be needed if self-management is to result in significant improvements in teaching and learning, but they recognize that there is a contrary view that financial management is a specialized task and that senior management needs to become better at it rather than to share it. Hargreaves (1994) goes further and argues for a formal separation between nonteacher chief executives and headteachers as leading professionals, making an analogy with the health service.[13]

Nevertheless, a key issue arising from the research is to what extent it is possible to give classroom teachers a sufficient sense of involvement in resource management decisions to empower them without diverting them from student-related activities in the same way as had happened to headteachers on the evidence of the Birmingham study. Thus, all of these studies raise some serious questions about the effects of self-management on the nature of the school community. While headteachers themselves often claim that local management has increased the involvement of teaching staff in decision making, a study of the effects of self-management on industrial relations in schools, by Sinclair, Ironside, and Siefert (1993) at Keele University, suggests that the very logic of the reforms is that

> headteachers are no longer partners in the process of educating pupils—they become allocators of resources within the school, managers who are driven to ensure that the activities of employees are appropriate to the needs of the business, and givers of rewards to those whose contribution to the business is most highly regarded.

This claim is more consistent with the conclusions of Bowe et al. (1992) than with those of Marren and Levacic (1994) or even Broadbent et al. (1993).[14]

When schools were managed from a more distant bureaucracy, there was often a sense of headteacher and teachers being the professionals fighting a common cause against the distant bureaucracy. With self-management, there has sometimes been a much sharper sense that the school governors and the senior management team are "management" and the teachers and other staff are the "workers." Halpin, Power, and Fitz (1993) suggest that, in the case of grant-maintained schools, the very process of running a self-managing unit can result in an increase in the distance of headteachers from classroom teachers. In some cases, headteachers themselves are coming under pressure from governing bodies acting like Boards of Directors and one dispute of this nature is before the High Court at the time of this writing.

At the same time, many teachers in self-managing schools are feeling the loss of some of the more positive aspects of being part of a larger concern. In the past, LEA support networks fulfilled an important function in Britain. With the devolution of most funds to individual schools, local teachers' centers and other forms of support have often been removed or reduced in scope, even for teachers in LEA schools operating under local management. This problem can be even more acute in the case of grant maintained schools and CTCs, whose staff can easily become isolated from the broader professional community.

Glatter (1993) argues that the quasi-market model does not preclude partnerships between autonomous schools but that "the environment of heightened competition is now framing all such relationships" (p. 8). He also questions whether, without some kind of semi-permanent infrastructure to promote and facilitate collaboration, the start-up and maintenance costs of partnership may be too great for most schools to contemplate. Citing Fullan (1991) and Louis and Miles (1992), he suggests that the erosion of customary networks and support structures could have very serious consequences, because "as we should know well by now, effective change in schools depends as much on providing support as it does on applying pressure" (Glatter, 1993, p. 9). Levacic (1995, pp. 183–185) gives some examples of the continuation and development of cooperative networks among self-managing schools in particular circumstances. However, the possibilities for this depended on trust, which, in turn, could be influenced by the extent of local competition. Significantly, vertical collaboration between primary and secondary schools seemed more in evidence than horizontal networks among schools serving the same phase.

One source of support for teachers has traditionally been their trade unions. As a result of the reforms, teachers face increased workloads, attempts to use them more flexibly to counter the effects of budget restrictions, divisive approaches to performance-related pay, and the substitution of full-time, permanent, qualified, and experienced staff by part-time, temporary, less qualified less experienced, and, therefore, less expensive alternatives. A recent report by the National Foundation for Educational Research confirms that many of these trends have accelerated since the introduction of local management, particularly in those schools adversely affected by the use of average staffing costs in funding formulas (Maychell, 1994). This, of course, has potential implications not only for teachers' conditions of service but also the quality of education. It also poses new challenges for the teacher unions. The research carried out by Sinclair et al. (1993) suggests that the atomization associated with self-management has not yet entirely succeeded in breaking down the traditional power of teacher unions within the state education system. In this respect at least, many of the district-wide networks are still in place, and legal confusion about who is technically the employer in LEA schools operating under local management means that there are a number of issues that still have to be tested in the courts. However, in some grant-maintained schools and CTCs, where the legal issues are more clear cut, unions are being forced to strengthen their plant bargaining capacity or are being marginalized by management. Only one grant-maintained school has so far derecognized teacher unions and withdrawn from national pay agreements, but some CTCs that operate outside both national and local agreements have established in-house staff associations within individual schools or offered the less militant unions "no-strike" agreements in return for recognition.

There have been suggestions, for example by Kerchner and Mitchell (1988) in the United States and Barber (1992) in the United Kingdom, that the teaching unions need to develop a new mode of operation, sometimes termed *third generation* or *professional* unionism, in which they negotiate educational as well as industrial issues and potentially become partners with management in educational decision making to serve the best interests of learners. Self-management has been seen to pose a threat to traditional styles of trade unionism, but to provide real opportunities for this new version. It could also be a way of giving classroom teachers a voice in management without diverting them from their primary role.

Barber, Rowe and Whitty (1995) mounted a small research project, with funding from a national teachers union, to determine to what extent union representatives in England were actually involved in school-based decision making on the ground. During the 1992–1993 school year, we conducted a survey among a sample of school-based union representatives to discover the extent to which they were involved in decision making about budgets, curriculum, and school development planning. Only about 15% of school union representatives had ever been consulted about the budget, the curriculum, or the school development plan. Our subsequent fieldwork suggested that even these figures exaggerated the extent of genuine consultation, let alone formal involvement of unions in school management.

Given the broader political and industrial context in which the British reforms have been introduced, this is hardly surprising. Nor is it surprising that both unions and management were skeptical about whether greater union involvement in management was feasible in the prevailing circumstances. As in the United States, the labor process more generally has been subject to processes of deskilling, reskilling, intensification, and substitution of labor, the relevance of which to our understanding of education has been clearly demonstrated by Apple (1986, 1993, 1995). In this context, we found little evidence of union representatives participating in issues other than those associated with "second generation unionism," that is, giving advice to members, negotiating with management over grievances, and campaigning on issues related to pay and conditions of work.

Some headteachers stated that playing down their members' interests was a prerequisite to the unions becoming more involved in school development planning, but school representatives pointed to the danger of their unique critical perspective thereby disappearing to the detriment of all concerned. With the potential breakdown of national or even LEA-level bargaining on certain issues, leaving these issues to be resolved at the site level, it is likely to become increasingly important for school representatives to be able to explore the relationship among resources, conditions of service, and educational outcomes at the institutional level. Yet both headteachers and union representatives believed that a central concern with the needs of learners might involve union representatives abandoning their more traditional concerns.

There is a fine line to be drawn between third-generation trade unionism and the sort of collaboration that makes it difficult for unions to bargain for their members' interests. In some CTCs, trade unions were not recognized for bargaining purposes and staff associations lacked any teeth. These CTCs are run by trusts dominated by business sponsors, and they have sometimes been seen as the model for the future: post-Fordist schools for a postmodern society. While pay in these schools was usually at a higher level than other local schools, however, conditions of service were also very different. It is a moot point whether free private health insurance is adequate compensation for longer working hours, fixed-term contracts, performance-related pay, and so forth. Flexibility and claims of enhanced professionalism can sometimes become a cover for exploitation of teachers and worsening conditions of service. And, as Blackmore (1995) points out, the self-managing school often retains "strong modernist tendencies for a top-down, executive mode of decision-making . . . [alongside its] 'weaker' post-modern claims to decentralise and encourage diversity, community ownership, local discretion, professional autonomy and flexible decision-making" (p. 45).

Nevertheless, in New Zealand, a report for one of the teachers' unions has emphasized the considerable potential of shared decision making for enhancing the efficiency and effectiveness of self-managing schools (R. Hill, 1992). As a result, action research on the value of various models of shared decision making is currently being undertaken (Capper 1994). Yet, unless they are handled very carefully, any positive moves in this direction are likely to be stymied by already excessive workloads and the growing tensions between teachers and school principals referred to earlier (Livingstone, 1994; Murfitt, 1995; Wylie, 1995). Indeed, Sullivan (1994) has suggested that lack of consultation with teachers over the reforms may create a low-trust hierarchical system rather than a high-trust collegial one.

In the United States, site-based management within school districts has not generally gone as far as it has in either England or New Zealand, certainly in terms of the bulk funding of teachers' salaries and resources for professional development. It is difficult to generalize about the degree of autonomy in site-based management schools (Ogawa & White, 1994) or even charter schools (Wohlstetter et al., 1995). In many cases, the only significant discretionary funds to be disbursed at the site level come from federal and state funding for disadvantaged students. In some states, even charter schools have to negotiate with local school districts for their resources. In that respect, little of the American experience of site-based management is directly relevant to the claims made by advocates of more radical supply side reforms, and, unfortunately, there is little detailed research yet available on the situation in charter schools.[15] In discussing the available research on site-based management, I shall again concentrate on items that have appeared since the publication of Clune and Witte's (1990a, 1990b) work and the rather pessimistic conclusions of Malen, Ogawa, and Kranz (1990) in that collection.

The rhetoric of reform in the United States has often made far more reference to school-based shared decision making as a way of enhancing teacher professionalism than has hitherto been the case in England, where the reforms have been accompanied by attacks on the integrity of the teaching profession in general and teachers' unions in particular. Yet, although much of the rhetoric of the American reform movement has emphasized the importance of empowering teachers, this has often not come about in practice. In reviewing the failure of many American site-based management initiatives to bring about the expected improvement in school performance, Wohlstetter and Odden (1992) have pointed to a lack of employee involvement in many schemes. Rather than merely devolving budgetary, personnel and curriculum decision making to the school level, they argue for regarding site-based management as a comprehensive governance reform that will involve teachers actively in making changes to curriculum and instruction. Other studies show considerable variations in the extent to which schools have changed in practice (Cawelti 1994) and identify important differences in the meanings given to site-based management by some of the key actors involved (Gibbs 1991). Often, site-based management has been treated as merely "an experiment in governance" shifting power from the central office to the school, while "the consequences of decentralization on student achievement remain unknown" (Carlos & Amsler, 1993).

Few programs have been evaluated in terms of performance, and few evaluations have shown clear achievement gains. Although some studies do show gains, the overall impact has so far been disappointing (Ogawa & White, 1994). Wohlstetter and her colleagues (Mohrman, Wohlstetter, & Associates, 1994; Odden & Wohlstetter, 1995; Wohlstetter & Mohrman, 1993; Wohlstetter & Odden, 1992; Wohlstetter, Smyer, & Mohrman, 1994) have suggested that site-based management will have a positive effect only if it is implemented in accordance with what, drawing on the literature of private sector management, they term the "high-involvement model." This requires teacher involvement in decision making, good information, knowledge and skills, power, and rewards, and Wohlstetter et al. suggest that this last condition has too rarely been met. Robertson, Wohlstetter, and Mohrman (1995) argue that, if such conditions are in place, innovations in curriculum and instruction do take place. Wohlstetter (1995) also suggests that site-based management must be augmented by a range of school-, district-, and state-level strategies that facilitate interactions involving various stakeholders and provide a direction for those interactions.

It seems clear that teacher participation in decision making does not necessarily, of itself, improve outcomes for teachers and students (Taylor & Bogotch, 1994). Marks and Louis (1995) argue that teacher empowerment is a necessary rather than a sufficient condition of instructional improvement and that different modes of empowerment can have different effects. Murphy (1994) suggests that one of the reasons why very few studies have shown clear gains in student achievement is that some of the key conditions for success have not been met and that the effect of site-based management (as in the case of the more radical reforms in England and New Zealand) has too often merely been to place additional administrative burdens on teachers. Even the more participatory forms of teacher involvement in decision-making can have unintended consequences. In Minnesota charter schools, for example, "as much as teachers appreciated being board members and making administrative decisions, wearing two hats required a great deal of time and effort" from which they would eventually require some relief (Urahn & Stewart 1994, p. 51). Even in this context, it may therefore be important to take seriously the political insights of those teachers who resist attempts to engage them in management without addressing the broader meaning and consequences of the reforms (Gitlin & Margonis, 1995).

Some of the contributors to Hannaway and Carnoy's (1993) publication argue that the historical record shows that changes in governance, by themselves, are unlikely to produce major changes in the classroom (Elmore, 1993; Tyack, 1993). Discussing the evidence on shared decision making in the context of employee participation in business corporations, Brown (1993) concludes that participation in decision making "cannot be expected to overcome serious shortcomings [in an organization]. Once schools are at a functional baseline, however, innovative [employee involvement] can be a powerful tool for making continual improvements and maintaining high performance" (p. 229).

Critics of site-based management as currently practiced have usually argued for self-management to be taken further. Some have then argued the need to focus on professional improvement in the instructional context (Guskey & Peterson, in press), while others have called for greater empowerment of local communities. These are not always seen as conflicting strategies, although Raywid (1994) advocates "focus" schools, partly because they do not generally seek to engage the community or parents directly in school governance. This, she suggests, would simply shift the interest group politics of the school district down to the site level, presumably with deadening consequences attributed by Chubb and Moe (1990) to political control of schooling. In some respects, the conclusion of Murphy and Beck (1995) that the "structural focus" of site-based management pulls stakeholders toward issues of governance and organization seems to confirm this fear, although their proposed refocusing on issues of teaching and learning still requires the "deep involvement" of teachers and parents. For Raywid, though, the effectiveness of focus schools derives from the very fact that they are "built around specific educational and ethical principles, not around accommodating the interests of all parties" (P. T. Hill et al., 1990). The site policymakers are the principal and teachers. In Raywid's model, even parents are not really regarded as partners in the educational process, since their empowerment should derive from choice rather than voice in a quasi-market.

By contrast, the recent reforms in Chicago are probably the farthest toward the community empowerment end of the continuum. Elmore (1991) argues that "while the Chicago reform has elements of both regulatory and professional control, it is mainly based on a theory of democratic control." It has seemed to move beyond the notion of school and system improvement through professional empowerment to a model placing far more emphasis on parental and community empowerment in achieving this end. The local school councils in Chicago are the nearest equivalent in the United States to governing bodies in England or boards of trustees in New Zealand. Like the latter, they have a majority of parents and responsibility for a similar proportion of the school budget. Although it was initially suggested that local school councils might hire and fire principals at will, the councils have generally concentrated on buildings and health and safety issues; however, they have sometimes also taken a key role in relation to equal opportunities. The advocacy group Designs for Change (1991) claims that the Chicago reforms "nearly doubled the number of African Americans and Hispanics making educational policy decisions in the United States" (p. 1). However, in a major study of community involvement in American school governance, Lewis and Nakagawa (1995) concluded that most parents in Chicago have assumed supportive "enablement" roles rather than being genuinely empowered by involvement with the local school councils. And, ironically, the few parents on the local school councils who seemed to adopt an "empowerment" stance were White, middle-class men.[16]

A recent report (Sebring, Bryk, & Easton, 1995) suggests that the reforms have brought better ties to the community in a number of Chicago schools without threatening principal and teacher responsibility for professional matters. More than 40% of teachers believed that the reforms had had a positive impact on relations with the community, and this seems to have been the single most significant outcome. About a third reported other changes in practice that might be expected to bring eventual benefits in learning outcomes, but these were concentrated in about a third of elementary schools; the impact of the reforms on high schools has remained hard to discern. Only a quarter of teachers reported that the reforms had so far enhanced the quality of student academic performance, and rather more reported a negative effect on student behavior than a positive one. Although data on students' actual achievement have yet to be made available, and there are considerable technical difficulties in making comparisons (Bryk, Easton, Luppescu, & Thum, 1994), there is likely to be little overall improvement on prereform figures.

Thus, as with other forms of site-based management, the Chicago version seems so far to have changed the form of governance without having the widespread impact on outcomes predicted by its advocates. The ambitious goal of bringing student achievement in Chicago up to national norms within 5 years seems to have been quietly forgotten. Lewis and Nakagawa (1995) suggest that the reform has come "to stand for process rather than outcome" and that "even if reformers alter the indicia of success to equal simply community participation, the Chicago school reform falls short—because participation alone has not led to empowerment in any real terms" (p. 168). They regard it as having had more to do with the politics of racial inclusion and the defusing of conflict and argue that, whatever the intention, "the very participation of the parents legitimizes the professionals' grip on policy making and school operations" (p. 149).

This study seems to lend support to those contributors to Hannaway and Carnoy's (1993) publication who argue that governance reforms in education have more to do with external political conditions than with what happens in schools. For such commentators, "centralization-decentralization debates reflect inevitable, cyclical, unresolvable tensions and contradictions in society and . . . the connection between these tensions and school performance is weak at best" (Hannaway & Carnoy, 1993, p. xii). Furthermore, there seems to be an accumulation of evidence that school autonomy, especially when combined with school choice, is as likely to exacerbate differences between schools as it is to lead to school improvement across the system as a whole. While enabling a few schools to take advantage of their new-found freedom, there is little evidence that school-based initiatives alone can overcome systemwide sociological influences on schooling.

There is also a danger that too much emphasis on the power of individual school faculty members to seek their own salvation will, in some contexts, result only in further damage to the morale of an increasingly exploited work force. Even community empowerment has its limitations in this respect, since communities are far from equally endowed with the material and cultural resources for self-management of their schools, as Gordon (1993, 1995) has demonstrated in the case of New Zealand. Lewis and Nakagawa's (1995) conclusions are even more pessimistic: "even if the model is implemented well, a tall order in and of itself, the exogenous factors that lead to the failure of the minority poor in school . . . would seem to require more than a change in school governance can deliver" (p. 172). Certainly, such a strategy is unlikely to succeed in the absence of other changes.

CONSUMER RIGHTS AND CITIZEN RIGHTS IN PUBLIC EDUCATION

It is clear that the significance of reforms such as those involving parental choice and school autonomy can be properly evaluated only in a broader political context. Pointing to the damaging consequences of particular policies is not necessarily to question the motives of those proposing the reform agenda.[17] Many advocates of choice and school autonomy base their support on claims that competition will enhance the efficiency and responsiveness of schools and thus increase their effectiveness. Many hoped that market forces would overcome a leveling-down tendency that they ascribed to bureaucratic systems of mass education, while others saw them as a way of giving disadvantaged children the sorts of opportunities hitherto available only to those who could afford to buy them through private schooling or their position in the housing market. Yet these hopes are not being realized and are unlikely to be realized in the context of broader policies that do nothing to challenge deeper social and cultural inequalities. Atomized decision making in a highly stratified society may appear to give everyone equal opportunities, but transferring responsibility for decision making from the public to the private sphere can actually reduce the scope for collective action to improve the quality of education for all.

Even so, some aspects of the parental choice and school autonomy agendas are almost certain to outlive current conservative administrations. In some other countries, similar reforms are being advocated and implemented by parties and administrations associated with the political left.[18] In some senses, then, the current interest in devolution and choice may be indicative of tendencies of global proportions perhaps associated with post-Fordism or postmodernity.[19] Such a shift in the nature of education policy and administration reflects a more general repositioning of education in relation to the state and civil society (Whitty, in press). Thus, alongside—and potentially in place of—collective provision by public bodies with a responsibility to cater for the needs of the whole population, there are likely to be increasing numbers of quasi-autonomous schools with devolved budgets competing for individual clients in the marketplace.

However, the effects of such policies will be highly dependent on the broader context in which they are introduced. Although the concept of quasi-market always involves some degree of government regulation, there is disagreement about its nature and extent. In the three countries discussed here, conservative commentators wish to move further toward marketized and even privatized forms of education provision. Indeed, as I indicated earlier, some advocates of devolution and choice have argued that the indifferent performance of the reforms so far is merely evidence that they have not gone far enough.[20] For example, a government Minister responsible for the introduction of the assisted places scheme in England used our research showing that the scheme had failed to attract its target group (Edwards et al., 1989) as a basis for arguing in favor of a full-fledged voucher scheme (Boyson, 1990). Similarly, Chubb and Moe's (1992) major criticism of the British reforms was that the government had "created an open enrollment system in which there is very little to choose from, because the supply of schools is controlled by the LEAs" (Moe, 1994, p. 27). Their solution was that all schools should become autonomous.

Empirical research does not, indeed in principle could not, show that such reforms can never have beneficial effects. Yet, the studies reported here suggest that going further in the direction of marketization would be unlikely to yield major overall improvements in the quality of education and would almost certainly have damaging equity effects. The broad conclusion of these studies seems to be that, although the rhetoric of reform often suggests that the hidden hand of the market will produce the best possible outcome, the reality suggests that this is unlikely to be the case. Nor, apparently, has decentralization to schools and local communities done much to correct inequities in the system. In current circumstances in England, New Zealand, and the United States, not only have the positive benefits claimed for the reforms yet to be forthcoming, research suggests that, far from breaking the links between educational and social inequality, reforms may even intensify these links unless appropriate safeguards are put in place.

Tooley (1995), an articulate British advocate of choice, has argued that the potential of markets in education cannot be properly assessed by looking at the effects of quasi-markets or what he prefers to term "so-called" markets. There is an obvious sense in which this is true, and, to that extent, it is a valid criticism of the conclusions drawn from some of the studies reported here. However, insofar as attempts are being made to justify further moves toward the marketization of education, it is becoming increasingly important to try to model the effects of increasing choice options. Thus, for example, Witte, Thorn, and Pritchard (1995) have undertaken an analysis of the current social composition of private and public schools in Wisconsin and concluded that "an open-ended voucher scheme would clearly benefit households that are more affluent than the average household in Wisconsin." They went on to say that, although some might believe that making vouchers available to everyone would open up private schools to the poor, the opposite argument seems equally plausible. With more money available, private schools that cannot afford to select (e.g., some of the inner city private schools in the Milwaukee choice experiment) could become more selective. The already highly selective schools could then maintain their advantage by demanding add-on payments in addition to vouchers.

Thus, in an inegalitarian society, it seems highly improbable that the sort of "bottom-up" accountability associated with markets, and favored by Chubb and Moe (1992, p. 13), can replace the need for democratic accountability if equity is to remain an important consideration. A telling Carnegie report on school choice (Boyer, 1992) provided a reminder that although the school choice debate was, quite correctly, giving much attention to helping individual families, "American education has, throughout its history, focused not just on the empowerment of individuals but also on the building of community" (p. xviii). If devolution and choice are to produce positive effects throughout the school system and benefit all students, there is an urgent need to provide a counter-balance to the overemphasis on self-interest that is currently fostered by the reforms. Henig (1994) suggests that "the logical coherence, academic legitimacy, and conservative appeal of conventional economic theory results in the market rationale dominating the choice movement in public," but he also observes that "non market rationales account for most of the enthusiasm and support" (p. 194). Furthermore, he claims that "where school choice has appeared most successful—as in some of the many experiments with magnets, magnetized districts, and statewide open enrollment—it has been at the instigation and under the direction of strong and affirmative government action" (p. 193). Cookson (1994) too makes a distinction between market-driven and democratic-driven choice policies.

In their critique of Chubb and Moe (1990), K. B. Smith and Meier (1995) suggest that neither the abolition of democratic control nor the abolition of union power is a prerequisite for tackling the problems of bureaucracy, which are at the heart of many critiques of conventional mass education systems. More specifically, they claim to demonstrate that neither democratic control nor strong teachers' unions correlate positively with the size of bureaucracies in U.S. school districts. Smith and Meier also argue that bureaucracy *per se* may not be the problem institutional theorists claim. Rather, they suggest, it may be poverty that leads to enlarged bureaucracies and to depressed educational performance. Their own book is an argument for extending rather than reducing democratic control of education, although on a rather centralized model.

Carnoy (1993) argues that school site measures are likely to contribute to school improvement only in combination with higher performance demands from central authorities, while Gintis (1995) suggests that government regulation and the market should not necessarily be seen as in opposition. He argues that the choice of educational goals can still be debated in the educational arena and the results implemented through the proper choice of policy tools, which might include devolution and choice with appropriate rules for funding and accrediting schools. Thus, "the use of the market is in this sense an *instrument of* rather than an *alternative to* democratic policymaking" (Carnoy, 1993, p. 510).

All of this means that, whatever gains are to be had from handing decision making to parents and teachers (and they seem to be far fewer than the advocates claim), key decisions about goals and frameworks still need to be made in the broader political arena. The reality is that devolution and choice are occurring as part of a broader political strategy. Certainly, the recent education reforms in Britain have as much to do with transferring power to central government as with giving autonomy to parents and schools, even though the rhetoric accompanying reform often seeks to suggest that education has been taken out of politics as normally understood (Chubb & Moe, 1992). McKenzie (1993) has argued that "British governments have actually increased their claims to knowledge and authority over the education system whilst promoting a theoretical and superficial movement towards consumer sovereignty" and Harris (1993) suggests that this is more generally the case. Thus, the key issues remain political ones that need to be pursued at a political level and that cannot be avoided by technical and administrative solutions.

Even Chubb and Moe (1990), who argue that equality is better "protected" by markets than by political institutions, have to concede that choice of school cannot be unlimited and should not be entirely unregulated. In England and New Zealand, far too much is being left to the market, to be determined by the self-interest of some consumers and the competitive advantages of some schools. Yet, even though much of the American research suggests that the most equitable choice schemes are those that retain considerable degrees of regulation, Chubb and Moe (1992) argue that the British approach is a "lesson in school reform" that the United States should follow. My own view is that, in all three countries, much more attention needs to be given both to mechanisms of regulation and to the most appropriate ways of deciding on them. In Britain, devolution and choice have been accompanied by imposed and draconian accountability measures that mitigate against both professional collegiality and a concern with meeting the needs of disadvantaged students. In New Zealand, the adoption of a new public management accountability framework has had similar, although more muted, effects (Wylie, 1995). While similar developments are in evidence in parts of the United States, the more complex constitutional arrangements derided by Chubb and Moe (1992) have hitherto preserved more opportunities for professional and local democratic input in some areas.

Regulating choice and pursuing equity necessitate the existence of contexts for determining rules and processes for adjudicating between different claims and priorities. This entails the revival or creation of democratic contexts within which such issues can be determined. Unfortunately, however, those public institutions that might act on behalf of the broader interests of the community have been progressively dismantled by new right governments, which means that creating a new public sphere in which educational matters can even be debated—let alone determined—poses considerable challenges. According to Foucault, new forms of association, such as trade unions and political parties, arose in the 19th century as a counterbalance to the prerogative of the state and acted as the seedbed of new ideas (Kritzman 1988). Modern versions of these collectivist forms of association may now need to emerge to counterbalance not only the prerogative of the state, as currently exercised in forms of accountability associated with the new public management, but also the prerogative of the market.

Part of the challenge must be to move away from atomized decision making to the reassertion of collective responsibility without re-creating the very bureaucratic systems whose shortcomings have helped to legitimate the current tendency to treat education as a private good rather than a public responsibility. While choice policies are part of a social text that helps to create new subject positions that undermine traditional forms of collectivism, those forms of collectivism themselves failed to empower many members of society, including women and people of color. Margonis and Parker (1995) point out that the "communitarian metaphors" that are often used to oppose the "laissez-faire metaphors" of the choice proponents fail to take account of institutional racism and the deep structural inequalities in American society that indicate that public education has itself never fostered inclusive communities. Unfortunately, however, they give little indication of what a progressive alternative might look like.

We need to ask how we can use the positive aspects of choice and autonomy to facilitate the development of new forms of community empowerment rather than exacerbating social differentiation. So far, in England, the Labour Party has adopted many rightist policies, while the left has done little yet to develop a concept of public education that looks significantly different from the state education that some of us spent our earlier political and academic careers critiquing for its role in reproducing and legitimating social inequalities (Young & Whitty, 1977). Even if the social democratic era looks better in retrospect, and in comparison with current policies, than it did at the time, that does not remove the need to rethink what might be progressive policies for the next century. As Henig (1994) says of the United States, "the sad irony of the current education-reform movement is that, through overidentification with school-choice proposals rooted in market-based ideas, the healthy impulse to consider radical reforms to address social problems may be channeled into initiatives that further erode the potential for collective deliberation and collective response" (p. 222). In New Zealand, Gordon (1994a) argues for "a policy approach that combines the older social democratic goal of educational comparability across class and ethnic boundaries, with real choice for families" (p. 21).

It is surely necessary to think through alternatives as a matter of urgency since the rhetoric—although not the reality—of some of the recent reforms *has* probably been more responsive than critics sometimes recognize to those limited, but nonetheless tangible, social and cultural shifts that have been taking place in modern societies. A straightforward return to the old order of things would be neither feasible nor sensible. Those approaches to education that continue to favor the idea of a common public school are still faced with the need to respond to increasing specialization and social diversity. Connell (1993) reminds us that

> justice cannot be achieved by distributing the same amount of a standard good to children of all social classes. . . . That "good" means different things to ruling class and working class children, and will do different things for them (or to them).

As Mouffe (1989, 1992) has argued, we need to develop a conception of citizenship, and by implication an education system, that involves creating unity without denying specificity.

In this context, it is possible to see that there may well be progressive moments within policies that foster devolution and choice. Apple (1995) has indicated that, in different political circumstances, education vouchers could be used to radical ends, while Atkinson (1994) sees self-managing schools as a basis for rebuilding communities in blighted inner city areas. This potential was recognized in some of the early moves toward devolution in New Zealand, but the recent evidence from New Zealand, as well as England, suggests that other considerations are currently more dominant. Nevertheless, Wylie (1995) argues that, in New Zealand, new forms of accountability and managerialism may still have "more form than substance" and that other practices and values "can be, and often are, given priority at the 'chalkface' " (p. 163).

Yet it is certainly proving increasingly difficult to realize progressive moments at the school site level in a situation of diminishing resources and when the broader political climate is pointing firmly in the opposite direction. Similarly, in the United States, where it is arguable that equity considerations have continued to mitigate the more extreme forms of marketization in education, "the difficult problem of protecting the conditions that make choice work from erosion due to fiscal and political pressures" (Henig, 1994, p. 169) will undoubtedly pose a considerable challenge to progressive forces within education for the foreseeable future. To that extent, while some forms of devolution and choice may warrant further exploration as ways of realizing the legitimate aspirations of disadvantaged groups, they should not be seen as a panacea for the ills of society or as an alternative to broader struggles for social justice.

NOTES

[1] In this review, I use the term *public school* in the North American sense of publicly funded and publicly provided schools, rather than the English sense of elite private schools.

[2] Hirsch (1995) claims that school autonomy has gone so far in New Zealand that the notion of a public education "system" is fast becoming an oxymoron.

[3] Elsewhere (Whitty, 1989), I have characterized this as a new right agenda that combines a neoliberal commitment to market forces with a neoconservative reassertion of "traditional" values. The balance between these aspects of contemporary conservatism varies among (and indeed within) the three countries under consideration here.

[4] Different education legislation applies to Scotland and Northern Ireland. There are also some minor differences between England and Wales. This review focuses on developments in England, although some of the studies cited also include Wales.

[5] One of the few studies of primary school choice in England is reported in Hughes, Wikeley, and Nash (1990). This study concluded that the majority of parents were not exercising a wide range of choice at that level (see also Hughes, Wikeley, and Nash, 1994).

[6] The growth of the "girl-friendliness" of coeducational schools was one of the unanticipated findings of this research. The research team has also explored the role of single-sex girls' schools in the education market for girls (Ball & Gewirtz, in press).

[7] Although scores on National Curriculum tests are only just becoming available, and their publication has been the subject of a dispute with teacher unions, schools in receipt of public funds were required by the 1980 Education Act to make public the results of school leaving examinations at 16+ and 18+ years. In recent years, these results for all schools have been published in the national press.

[8] It remains to be seen whether the British government's recent and reluctant acceptance that "value-added" measures could be helpful will change that situation. Value-added measures of school effectiveness seek to determine how well a school has performed relative to what might be expected in light of the nature of its clientele, either in terms of prior test scores or socioeconomic status or a combination of such indices.

[9] Although the failure of the reforms to promote more genuine diversity has been exacerbated in the English case by a restrictive national curriculum embodying a particularly narrow and nationalistic notion of British culture (Whitty, 1992), much of the evidence also implicates the way choice operates in a highly stratified society.

[10] Unfortunately, I have not had access to a new collection of studies of choice which is to appear in 1996 (Fuller, Elmore, & Orfield, in press).

[11] This would certainly be consistent with British research (Whitty et al., 1993) suggesting that the definitions of "merit" adopted by CTCs can favor members of some minority ethnic groups over others.

[12] The School Teachers' Pay Review Body reported similar or even higher workloads for headteachers but gave slightly lower figures for classroom teachers (Rafferty, 1994a). The publication of these figures coincided with evidence of a steep rise in the numbers of heads and deputies retiring early (Rafferty, 1994b).

[13] The evidence of recent disputes in the health service suggests that few doctors in National Health Service Trust hospitals in Britain or Crown Health Enterprises in New Zealand would argue that this separation has enhanced their professionality or made it easier for them to make clinical decisions independently of financial considerations.

[14] A new study of local management of schools and its equivalent in Scotland is exploring, among other things, the range of variation in management styles and strategies under devolved management.

[15] But see some preliminary work in Bauman, Banks, Murphy, and Kuczwara (1994); Becker et al. (1995); Datnow, Hirschberg, and Wells (1994); Grutzik et al. (1995); Urahn and Stewart (1994); Medler and Nathan (1995); and Wohlstetter et al. (1995). A major evaluation of charter schools is planned by the federal Department of Education, and the Pew Charitable Trusts are funding a study by Chester Finn and Louann Bierlein at the Hudson Institute.

[16] Blackmore (1995) cites English and New Zealand research by Deem (1990) and Middleton (1992) to make a more general claim that "local school boards in newly devolved systems are generally dominated or chaired by white, professional males, who are positioned to claim to represent the universal interests of a homogeneous parent constituency, the clients and 'the school' " (p. 52; see also Deem, Brehony, & Heath, 1995).

[17] However, the devolution of decision making can serve to divert responsibility for cuts in education expenditures from government to parents and schools (Weiss, 1993), and it can thus have considerable political utility in crisis contexts (Malen, 1994).

[18] In Victoria, Australia in the early 1980s, moves toward devolution were being talked of in terms of progressive ideals of community empowerment, although more recent policies there have been associated with the new right. This was also the case with the multi-accented Picot reforms in New Zealand in the 1980s (Gordon, 1992; Grace, 1991). Similarly, the reforms in Chicago were supported by groups of varying political persuasions (Hess, 1990).

[19] Although these reforms are currently most in evidence in the Anglophone world, interest in such measures is spreading to other parts of the world. Even some of the most

successful education systems of the Pacific Rim and continental Europe are now considering pursuing similar policies, although Green (1994) suggests that this trend is far from universal.

[20] Lauder et al. (1995) suggest that, even if this is the case, the disenchantment of working-class parents with the "false promise" of choice in the current reforms will enter the "wisdom of the working class" and thus inhibit any likelihood that they will become the active choosers envisaged by market advocates even in the future (p. 49).

REFERENCES

Adler, M. (1993). *An alternative approach to parental choice* (National Commission on Education Briefing Paper 13). London: National Commission on Education.

Ambler, J. (1994). Who benefits from educational choice? Some evidence from Europe. *Journal of Policy Analysis and Management, 13* (3).

Anderson, B. (1995, August 24). Major urges nation to seize opportunity. *The Times,* 5.

Anyon, J. (1995). Race, social class, and educational reform in an inner-city school. *Teachers College Record, 97* (1), 69–94.

Apple, M.W. (1986). *Teachers and texts.* New York: Routledge.

Apple, M.W. (1993). *Official knowledge.* New York: Routledge.

Apple, M.W. (1995). *Education and power* (2nd ed.). New York: Routledge.

Arnott, M., Bullock, A., & Thomas, H. (1992, February). Consequences of local management: An assessment by head teachers. Paper presented at the Education Reform Act Research Network, University of Warwick.

Atkinson, D. (1994). *Radical urban solutions.* London: Cassell.

Ball, S. J., & Gewirtz, S. (in press). Girls in the education market: Choice, competition and complexity. *Gender and Education.*

Barber, M. (1992). *Education and the teacher unions.* London: Cassell.

Barber, M., Rowe, G., & Whitty, G. (1995). School development planning: Towards a new role for teaching unions? Mimeograph.

Bartlett, W. (1993). Quasi-markets and educational reforms. In J. Le Grand & W. Bartlett (Eds.), *Quasi-Markets and Social Policy* (pp. 125–153). London: Macmillan.

Bartlett, W., & LeGrand, J. (1993). The theory of quasi-markets. In J. LeGrand & W. Bartlett (Eds.), *Quasi-markets and social policy* (pp. 13–34). London: Macmillian.

Bauman, P., Banks, D., Murphy, M., & Kuczwara, H. (1994, April). *The charter school movement: Preliminary findings from the first three states.* Paper presented at the annual meeting of the American Educational Research Association, New Orleans, LA.

Becker, H. J., Nakagawa, K., & Corwin, R.G. (1995, April). *Parental involvement contracts in California's charter schools.* Paper presented at the annual meeting of the American Educational Research Association, San Francisco, CA.

Blackburne, L. (1988, May 13). Peers back policy on open enrolment. *The Times Educational Supplement,* A6.

Blackmore, J. (1995). Breaking out from a masculinist politics of education. In B. Limerick & B. Lingard (Eds.), *Gender and Changing Education Management.* Rydalmere, New South Wales, Australia: Hodder Education.

Blank, R. (1990). Educational effects of magnet high schools. In W. H. Clune & J. F. Witte (Eds.), *Choice and Control in American Education* (Vol. 2, 77–109). New York: Falmer Press.

Bolick, C. (1990). *A primer on choice in education: Part I—How choice works.* Washington, DC: Heritage Foundation.

Bowe, R., Ball, S., with Gold, A. (1992). *Reforming education and changing schools.* London: Routledge.

Boyer, E. L. (1992). *School choice: A special report.* Princeton, NJ: Carnegie Foundation.

Boyson, R. (1990, May). Review of *The state and private education. Times Higher Education Supplement*, 18.

Bridges, S. (1992). *Working in tomorrow's schools: Effects on primary teachers.* Christchurch, New Zealand: University of Canterbury.

Broadbent, J., Laughlin, R., Shearn, D., & Dandy, N. (1993). Implementing local management of schools: A theoretical and empirical analysis. *Research Papers in Education, 8* (2), 149–176.

Brown, C. (1993). Employee involvement in industrial decision making: Lessons for public schools. In J. Hannaway & M. Carnoy (Eds.), *Decentralization and school improvement: Can we fulfill the promise?* (pp. 202–231). San Francisco: Jossey-Bass.

Bryk, A.S., Easton, J.Q., Luppescu, S., & Thum, Y.M. (1994). Measuring achievement gains in the Chicago public schools. *Education and Urban Society, 26*, 306–319.

Bryk, A.S., Lee, V.E., & Holland, P.B. (1993). *Catholic schools and the common good.* Cambridge, MA: Harvard University Press.

Bullock, A., & Thomas, H. (1994). *The impact of local management of schools: Final report.* Birmingham, England: University of Birmingham.

Bush, T., Coleman, M., & Glover, D. (1993). *Managing autonomous schools.* London: Paul Chapman.

Campbell, J., & Neill, S. (1994). *Curriculum at key stage 1: Teacher commitment and policy failure.* Harlow, England: Longman.

Capper, P. (1994). *Participation and partnership: Exploring shared decision-making in twelve New Zealand secondary schools.* Wellington, New Zealand: Post Primary Teachers' Association.

Carlos, J., & Amsler, M. (1993). *Site-based management: An experiment in governance* (Policy Briefs 20). San Francisco: Far West Laboratory for Educational Research and Development.

Carnoy, M. (1993). School Improvement: Is Privatization the Answer? In J. Hannaway & M. Carnoy (Eds.), *Decentralization and school improvement: Can we fulfill the promise?* (pp. 163–201). San Francisco: Jossey-Bass.

Carnoy, M. (1995, July 12). Is school privatization the answer? Data from the experience of other countries suggest not. *Education Week*, 29–33.

Cawelti, G. (1994). *High school restructuring: A national study.* Arlington: Educational Research Service.

Chubb, J., & Moe, T. (1990). *Politics, Markets and America's Schools.* Washington, DC: Brookings Institution.

Chubb, J., & Moe, T. (1992). *A lesson in school reform from Great Britain.* Washington, DC: Brookings Institution.

Clewell, B.C., & Joy, M.F. (1990). *Choice in Montclair, New Jersey.* Princeton, NJ: Educational Testing Service.

Clune, W.H., & Witte, J.F. (Eds.). (1990a). *Choice and Control in American Education* (Vol. 1). New York: Falmer Press.

Clune, W.H., & Witte, J.F. (Eds.) (1990b). *Choice and Control in American Education* (Vol. 2). New York: Falmer Press.

Coleman, J.S., Hoffer, T., & Kilgore, S. (1982). *High school achievement: Public, Catholic and private schools.* New York: Basic Books.

Connell, R.W. (1993). *Schools and social justice.* Toronto: Our Schools/Our Selves Education Foundation.

Cookson, P.W. (1994). *School choice: The struggle for the soul of American education.* New Haven, CT: Yale University Press.

Cookson, P.W. (1995). Goals 2000: Framework for the new educational federalism. *Teachers College Record, 96* (3) , pp 405–417.

Cooper, B. (1994, April). *Administrative and economic efficiency in education: Using school-site ratio analysis.* Paper presented at the annual meeting of the American Educational Research Association, New Orleans, LA.

Datnow, A., Hirschberg, D., & Wells, A.S. (1994, April). *Charter schools: Teacher professionalism and decentralisation.* Paper presented at the annual meeting of the American Educational Research Association, New Orleans, LA.

David, M.E. (1993). *Parents, gender, and education reform.* Cambridge, England: Polity Press.

Deem, R. (1990). Governing by gender—The new school governing bodies. In P. Abbott & C. Wallace (Eds.), *Gender, power, and sexuality* (pp. 58–76). London: Macmillan.

Deem, R., Brehony, K., & Heath, S. (1995). *Active citizenship and the governing of schools.* Buckingham, England: Open University Press.

Department for Education. (1992). *Choice and diversity.* London: Her Majesty's Stationery Office.

Designs for Change. (1991). *Chicago School Reform, 1,* 1–5.

Domanico, R.J. (1990). *Restructuring New York City's public schools: The case for public school choice* (Education Policy Paper 3). New York: Manhattan Institute for Policy Research.

Edwards, T., Fitz, J., & Whitty, G. (1989). *The state and private education: An evaluation of the assisted places scheme.* London: Falmer Press.

Elmore, R.F. (1991). Foreword. In G.A. Hess (Ed.), *School restructuring Chicago style.* Newbury Park, CA: Corwin.

Elmore, R.F. (1993). School Decentralization: Who Gains? Who Loses? In J. Hannaway & M. Carnoy (Eds.), *Decentralization and school improvement: Can we fulfill the promise?* (pp. 33–54). San Francisco: Jossey-Bass.

Feintuck, M. (1994). *Accountability and choice in schooling.* Buckingham, England: Open University Press.

Fitz, J., Halpin, D., & Power, S. (1993). *Grant maintained schools: Education in the marketplace.* London: Kogan Page.

Fliegel, S., with Macguire, J. (1990). *Miracle in East Harlem: The fight for choice in public education.* New York: Random House.

Fowler, M. (1993). *Factors influencing choice of secondary schools.* Christchurch, New Zealand: University of Canterbury.

Fullan, M. (1991). *The new meaning of educational change.* London: Cassell.

Fuller, B., Elmore, R., & Orfield, G. (Eds.). (in press). *School choice: The cultural logic of families, the political rationality of schools.* New York: Teachers College Press.

Gewirtz, S., & Ball, S.J. (1995, April). *Schools, signs and values: The impact of market forces on education provision in England.* Paper presented at the annual meeting of the American Educational Research Association, San Francisco, CA.

Gewirtz, S., Ball, S.J., & Bowe, R. (1995). *Markets, choice and equity.* Buckingham, England: Open University Press.

Gibbs, G.J. (1991). School-based management: Are we ready? *Intercultural Development Research Association Newsletter, 18* (4).

Gintis, H. (1995). The political economy of school choice. *Teachers College Record, 96,* 493–511.

Gitlin, A., & Margonis, F. (1995). The political aspect of reform: Teacher resistance as good sense. *American Journal of Education, 103,* 377–405.

Glatter, R. (1993, September). *Partnership in the market model: Is it dying?* Paper presented at the annual conference of the British Educational Management and Administration Society, Edinburgh, Scotland.

Glatter, R., Woods, P., & Bagley, C. (1995, June). *Diversity, differentiation, and hierarchy: School choice and parental preference.* Paper presented at the ESRC/CEPAM

Invitation Seminar on Research on Parental Choice and School Response, Milton Keynes, England.

Glennerster, H. (1991). Quasi-markets for education? *Economic Journal, 101,* 1268–1276.

Gordon, L. (1992, April). *The New Zealand state and education reforms: "Competing" interests.* Paper presented at the annual meeting of the American Educational Research Association, San Francisco, CA.

Gordon, L. (1993). *A study of boards of trustees in Canterbury schools.* Christchurch, New Zealand: University of Canterbury.

Gordon, L. (1994a) Is school choice a sustainable policy for New Zealand? A review of recent research findings and a look to the future. *New Zealand Annual Review of Education, 4,* 9–24.

Gordon, L. (1994b). "Rich" and "Poor" Schools in Aotearoa. *New Zealand Journal of Educational Studies, 29,* 113–125.

Gordon, L. (1995). Controlling education: Agency theory and the reformation of New Zealand schools. *Educational Policy, 9,* 55–74.

Grace, G. (1991). Welfare labourism versus the new right. *International Studies in the Sociology of Education, 1,* 37–48.

Green, A. (1994). Postmodernism and state education. *Journal of Education Policy, 9,* 67–84.

Grutzik, C., Bernal, D., Hirschberg, D., & Wells, A.S. (1995, April). *Resources and access in California charter schools.* Paper presented at the annual meeting of the American Educational Research Association, San Francisco, CA.

Guskey, T. R., & Peterson, K.D. (in press). School based shared decision making: The road to the classroom. *Educational Leadership.*

Halpin, D., Power, S., & Fitz, J. (1993). Opting into state control? Headteachers and the paradoxes of grant-maintained status. *International Studies in the Sociology of Education, 3,* 3–23.

Halpin, D., & Troyna, B. (1994, April). *Lessons in school reform from Great Britain.* Paper presented at the annual meeting of the American Educational Research Association, New Orleans, LA.

Hannaway, J., & Carnoy, M. (Eds.). (1993). *Decentralization and school improvement: Can we fulfill the promise?* San Francisco: Jossey-Bass.

Hargreaves, D. (1994). *The mosaic of learning: Schools and teachers for the next century.* London: Demos.

Harris, K. (1993). Power to the people? Local management of schools. *Education Links, 45,* 4–8.

Hawk, K., & Hill, J. (1994). *Evaluation of teacher salaries grant scheme trial: The third year.* Palmerston North, New Zealand: Massey University.

Henig, J.R. (1994). *Rethinking school choice: Limits of the market metaphor.* Princeton, NJ: Princeton University Press.

Hess, G.A. (1990). *Chicago school reform: How it is and how it came to be.* Chicago: Chicago Panel on Public School Policy and Finance.

Hill, R. (1992). *Managing today's schools: The case for shared decision-making.* Wellington, New Zealand: Institute for Social Research and Development.

Hill, P.T., Foster G.E., & Gendler, T. (1990). *High schools with character.* Santa Monica, CA: RAND.

Hirsch, D. (1995, May). The other school choice—how should over-subscribed schools select their pupils? Open lecture presented at the Institute of Education, University of London.

Hughes, M., Wikeley, F., & Nash, T. (1990). *Parents and the national curriculum: An interim report.* Exeter, England: University of Exeter.

Hughes, M., Wikeley, F., & Nash, T. (1994). *Parents and their children's schools.* Oxford: Blackwell.

Kerchner, C., & Mitchell, D. (1988). *The changing idea of a teachers' union.* London: Falmer Press.

Kritzman, L. D. (Ed.). (1988). *Foucault: Politics/philosophy/culture.* New York: Routledge.

Lauder, H., Hughes, D., Waslander, S., Thrupp, M., McGlinn, J., Newton, S., & Dupuis, A. (1994). *The creation of market competition for education in New Zealand.* Wellington, New Zealand: Victoria University of Wellington.

Lauder, H., Hughes, D., Watson, S., Simiyu, I., Strathdee, R., & Waslander, S. (1995). *Trading in futures: The nature of choice in educational markets in New Zealand.* Wellington, New Zealand: Ministry of Education.

Lee, V. E., & Bryk, A. S. (1993). Science or Policy Argument? In E. Rasell & R. Rothstein (Eds.), *School choice: Examining the evidence.* Washington, DC: Economic Policy Institute.

Le Grand, J., & Bartlett, W. (Eds.). (1993). *Quasi-markets and social policy.* London: Macmillan.

Levacic, R. (1995). *Local management of schools: Analysis and practice.* Buckingham, England: Open University Press.

Lewis, D. A., & Nakagawa, K. (1995). *Race and educational reform in the American metropolis: A study of school decentralization.* Albany: SUNY Press.

Livingstone, I. (1994). *The workloads of primary school teachers—A Wellington region survey.* Wellington, New Zealand: Chartwell Consultants.

Louis, K.S., & Miles, M.B. (1992). *Improving the urban high school: What works and why.* London: Cassell.

Malen, B. (1994). Enacting site-based management: A political utilities analysis. *Educational Evaluation and Policy Analysis, 16* (3), 249–267.

Malen, B., Ogawa, R.T., & Kranz, J. (1990). What do we know about school-based management? A case-study of the literature—a call for research. In W. H. Clune & J. F. Witte (Eds.), *Choice and Control in American Education: Volume 2* (pp. 289–342). New York: Falmer Press.

Margonis, F., & Parker, L. (1995). Choice, privatization, and unspoken strategies of containment. *Educational Policy, 9* (4), 375–403.

Marks, H. M., & Louis, K. S. (1995). *Does teacher empowerment affect the classroom? The implications of teacher empowerment for teachers' instructional practice and student academic performance.* Madison: Center on Organization and Restructuring of Schools, University of Wisconsin.

Marren, E., & Levacic, R. (1994). Senior management, classroom teacher and governor responses to local management of schools. *Educational Management and Administration, 22* (1), 39–53.

Maychell, K. (1994). *Counting the cost: The impact of LMS on schools' patterns of spending.* Slough, England: National Foundation for Educational Research.

McKenzie, J. (1993, January). Education as a Private Problem or a Public Issue? The Process of Excluding "Education" from the "Public Sphere." Paper presented at the International Conference on the Public Sphere, Manchester, England.

Medler, A., & Nathan, J. (1995). *Charter schools: What are they up to?* Denver, CO: Education Commission of the States.

Middleton, S. (1992). Gender equity and school charters: Theoretical and political questions for the 1990s. In S. Middleton & A. Jones (Eds.), *Women and education in Aotearoa 2* (pp. 1–17). Wellington, New Zealand: Bridget Williams Books.

Minister of Education. (1988). *Tomorrow's schools: The reform of education administration in New Zealand.* Wellington, New Zealand: Government Printer.

Moe, T. (1994). The British battle for choice. In K. L. Billingsley (Ed.), *Voices on choice: The education reform debate* (pp. 23–33). San Francisco: Pacific Institute for Public Policy.

Mohrman, S.A., Wohlstetter, P., & Associates. (1994). *School-based management: Organizing for high performance.* San Francisco: Jossey-Bass.

Moore, D., & Davenport, S. (1990). School choice: The new improved sorting machine. In W. Boyd & H. Walberg (Eds.), *Choice in education* (pp. 187–223). Berkeley, CA: McCutchan.

Mouffe, C. (1989). Toward a radical democratic citizenship. *Democratic Left, 17,* 6–7.

Mouffe, C. (Ed.). (1992). *Dimensions of radical democracy: Pluralism, citizenship, democracy.* London: Verso.

Murfitt, D. (1995). *The implementation of new right reform in education: Teachers and the intensification of work.* Unpublished Masters Thesis, Education Department, University of Canterbury, Christchurch, New Zealand.

Murphy, J. (1994). *Principles of school-based management.* Chapel Hill: North Carolina Educational Policy Research Center.

Murphy, J., & Beck, L.G. (1995). *School-based management as school reform: Taking stock.* Thousand Oaks. CA: Corwin Press.

Newmann, F. (1993). Beyond common sense in educational restructuring: The issues of content and leadership. *Educational Researcher, 22* (2), 4–13.

Odden, E.R., & Wohlstetter, P. (1995). Making School-Based Management Work. *Educational Leadership, 52* (5), 32–36.

Office for Standards in Education. (1994). *Primary matters: A discussion of teaching and learning in primary schools.* London: Author.

Ogawa, R.T., & White, P.A. (1994). School-based management: An overview. In S. A. Mohrman, P. Wohlstetter, and Associates (Eds.), *School-based management: Organizing for high performance* (pp. 53–80). San Francisco: Jossey-Bass.

Organization for Economic Cooperation and Development. (1994). *School: A matter of choice.* Paris: OECD/CERI.

Pennell, H., & West, A. (1995). *Changing schools: Secondary schools' admissions policies in inner London in 1995* (Clare Market Paper 9). London: London School of Economics and Political Science.

Picot, B. (1988). *Administering for excellence.* Wellington, New Zealand: Government Printer.

Plank, S., Schiller, K. S., Schneider, B., & Coleman, J. S. (1993). Effects of choice in education. In E. Rasell & R. Rothstein (Eds.), *School choice: Examining the evidence.* Washington, DC: Economic Policy Institute.

Pollard, S. (1995a, October 22). Labour's slow learners. *Observer Review,* p. 4.

Pollard, S. (1995b). *Schools, selection and the left.* London: Social Market Foundation.

Power, S., Halpin, D., & Fitz, J. (1994). Underpinning choice and diversity? The grant maintained schools policy in context. In S. Tomlinson (Ed.), *Educational reform and its consequences* (pp. 26–40). London: IPPR/Rivers Oram Press.

Rafferty, F. (1994a, August 5). Alarm at growth of 60-hour week. *Times Educational Supplement,* p. 1.

Rafferty, F. (1994b, September 2). Many more heads leave jobs. *Times Educational Supplement,* p. 9.

Ranson, S. (1993, March). *Renewing education for democracy.* Paper presented at the Institute of Public Policy Research Seminar on Alternative Education Policies, London, England.

Raywid, M.A. (1994). *Focus schools: A genre to consider* (Urban Diversity Series 106). New York: Columbia University, ERIC Clearinghouse on Urban Education.

Robertson, P.J., Wohlstetter, P., & Mohrman, S.A. (1995). Generating curriculum and instructional innovations through school-based management. *Educational Administration Quarterly, 31* (3), 375–404.

Rossell, C. H., & Glenn, C. L. (1988). The Cambridge controlled choice plan. *Urban Review, 20* (2), 75–94.

Sebring, P. B., Bryk, A. S., & Easton, J. Q. (1995). *Charting reform: Chicago teachers take stock.* Chicago: Consortium on Chicago School Research.

Seddon, T., Angus, L., & Poole, M. (1991). Pressures on the move to school-based decision-making and management. In J. Chapman (Ed.), *School-based decision-making and management* (pp. 29–54). London: Falmer Press.

Sexton, S. (1987). *Our schools—A radical policy.* Warlingham, England: Institute of Economic Affairs, Education Unit.

Sexton, S. (1991). *New Zealand schools.* Wellington, New Zealand: Business Round Table.

Sinclair, J., Ironside, M., & Seifert, R. (1993, April). *Classroom struggle? Market oriented education reforms and their impact on teachers' professional autonomy, labour intensification and resistance.* Paper presented at the International Labour Process Conference.

Smith, K. B., & Meier, K. J. (1995). *The case against school choice: Politics, markets and fools.* Armonk, NY: M. E. Sharpe.

Smith, T., & Noble, M. (1995). *Education divides: Poverty and schooling in the 1990s.* London: Child Poverty Action Group.

Sullivan, K. (1994). The impact of education reform on teachers' professional ideologies. *New Zealand Journal of Educational Studies, 29* (1), 3–20.

Tan, N. (1990). *The Cambridge controlled choice program: Improving educational equity and integration* (Education Policy Paper 4). New York: Manhattan Institute for Policy Research.

Taylor, D.L., & Bogotch, I.E. (1994). School-level effects of teachers' participation in decision making. *Educational Evaluation and Policy Analysis, 16* (3), 302–319.

Tooley, J. (1995). Markets or democracy? A reply to Stewart Ranson. *British Journal of Educational Studies, 43* (1), 21–34.

Tyack, D. (1993). School governance in the United States: Historical puzzles and anomalies. In J. Hannaway & M. Carnoy (Eds.), *Decentralization and school improvement: Can we fulfill the promise?* (pp. 1–32). San Francisco: Jossey-Bass.

Urahn, S., & Stewart, D. (1994). *Minnesota charter schools: A research report.* St Paul, MN: Research Department, Minnesota House of Representatives.

Vincent, C., Evans, J., Lunt, I., & Young, P. (1995). Policy and practice: The changing nature of special educational provision in schools. *British Journal of Special Education,* 22 (1), 4–11.

Walford, G. (1992a). Educational choice and equity in Great Britain. *Educational Policy, 6* (2), 123–138.

Walford, G. (1992b). *Selection for secondary schooling* (National Commission on Education Briefing Paper 7). London: National Commission on Education.

Walford, G., & Miller, H. (1991). *City technology college.* Milton Keynes, England: Open University Press.

Waslander, S., & Thrupp, M. (1995). Choice, competition and segregation: An empirical analysis of a New Zealand secondary school market 1990–1993. *Journal of Education Policy, 10,* 1–26.

Weiss, M. (1993). New guiding principles in educational policy: The case of Germany. *Journal of Education Policy, 8,* 307–320.

Wells, A.S. (1990). *Public school choice: Issues and concerns for urban educators* (ERIC/CUE Digest 63). New York: ERIC Clearinghouse on Urban Education.

Wells, A.S. (1993a). The sociology of school choice: Why some win and others lose in the educational marketplace. In E. Rasell & R. Rothstein (Eds.), *School choice: Examining the evidence.* Washington, DC: Economic Policy Institute.

Wells, A.S. (1993b). *Time to choose: America at the crossroads of school choice policy.* New York: Hill and Wang.

Wells, A.S., & Crain, R.L. (1992). Do parents choose school quality or school status? A sociological theory of free market education. In P.W. Cookson (Ed.), *The choice controversy* (pp. 65–82). Newbury Park, CA: Corwin Press.

Whitty, G. (1989). The new right and the national curriculum: State control or market forces? *Journal of Education Policy, 4,* 329–341.

Whitty, G. (1992). Education, economy and national culture. In R. Bocock & K. Thompson (Eds.), *Social and cultural forms of modernity* (pp. 267–320). Cambridge, England: Polity Press.

Whitty, G. (in press). Citizens or consumers? Continuity and change in contemporary education policy. In D. Carlson & M. Apple (Eds.), *Critical Educational theory in unsettling times.* Boulder, CO: Westview Press.

Whitty, G., Edwards, T., & Gewirtz, S. (1993). *Specialisation and choice in urban education: The city technology college experiment.* London: Routledge.

Witte, J.F. (1990). Choice and control: An analytical overview. In W.H. Clune & J.F. Witte (Eds.), *Choice and control in American education* (Vol. 1, 11–46). New York: Falmer Press.

Witte, J.F., Thorn, C.A., & Pritchard, K.A. (1995). *Private and public education in Wisconsin: Implications for the choice debate.* Madison: University of Wisconsin.

Witte, J.F., Thorn, C.A., Pritchard, K.M., & Claibourn, M. (1994). *Fourth year report: Milwaukee parental choice program.* Madison: Department of Public Instruction.

Wohlstetter, P. (1995). Getting school-based management right: What works and what doesn't. *Phi Delta Kappan, 77* (1), 22–26.

Wohlstetter, P., & Mohrman, S.A. (1993). *School-based management: Strategies for success.* New Brunswick, NJ: Consortium for Policy Research in Education.

Wohlstetter, P., & Odden, A. (1992). Rethinking school-based management policy and research. *Educational Administration Quarterly, 28,* 529–549.

Wohlstetter, P., Smyer, R., & Mohrman, S.A. (1994). New boundaries for school-based management: The high involvement model. *Educational Evaluation and Policy Analysis, 16* (3), pp 268–286.

Wohlstetter, P., Wenning, R., & Briggs, K. L. (1995). Charter schools in the United States: The question of autonomy. *Educational Policy, 9,* 331–358.

Wylie, C. (1994). *Self managing schools in New Zealand: The Fifth year.* Wellington: New Zealand Council for Educational Research.

Wylie, C. (1995). Contrary currents: The application of the public sector reform framework in education. *New Zealand Journal of Educational Studies, 30,* 149–164.

Young, M., & Whitty, G. (Eds.). (1977). *Society, State and Schooling.* Lewes, England: Falmer Press.

Manuscript received January 15, 1996
Accepted March 15, 1996

Part III
Educational Policy and the State

[16]

The Politics of Official Knowledge: Does a National Curriculum Make Sense?

MICHAEL W. APPLE
The University of Wisconsin–Madison

Education is deeply implicated in the politics of culture. The curriculum is never simply a neutral assemblage of knowledge, somehow appearing in the texts and classrooms of a nation. It is always part of a *selective tradition*, someone's selection, some group's vision of legitimate knowledge. It is produced out of the cultural, political, and economic conflicts, tensions, and compromises that organize and disorganize a people. As I argue in *Ideology and Curriculum* and *Official Knowledge*, the decision to define some groups' knowledge as the most legitimate, as official knowledge, while other groups' knowledge hardly sees the light of day, says something extremely important about who has power in society.[1]

Think of social studies texts that continue to speak of "the Dark Ages" rather than the historically more accurate and less racist phrase "the age of African and Asian ascendancy" or books that treat Rosa Parks as merely a naive African-American woman who was simply too tired to go to the back of the bus, rather than discussing her training in organized civil disobedience at the Highlander Folk School. The realization that teaching, especially at the elementary school level, has in large part been defined as women's paid work—with its accompanying struggles over autonomy, pay, respect, and deskilling—documents the connections between curriculum and teaching and the history of gender politics as well.[2] Thus, whether we like it or not, differential power intrudes into the very heart of curriculum, teaching, and evaluation. What *counts* as knowledge, the ways in which it is organized, who is empowered to teach it, what counts as an appropriate display of having learned it, and—just as critically—who is allowed to ask and answer all of these questions are part and parcel of how dominance and subordination are reproduced and altered in this society.[3] There is, then, always a *politics* of official knowledge, a politics that embodies conflict over what some regard as simply neutral descriptions of the world and others regard as elite conceptions that empower some groups while disempowering others.

Speaking in general about how elite culture, habits, and "tastes" function, Pierre Bourdieu puts it this way:

Teachers College Record Volume 95, Number 2, Winter 1993

0161-4681-93/9502/222$1.25/0

> The denial of lower, coarse, vulgar, servile—in a word, natural—enjoyment, which constitutes the sacred sphere of culture, implies an affirmation of the superiority of those who can be satisfied with the sublimated, refined, disinterested, gratuitous, distinguished pleasures forever closed to the profane. That is why art and cultural consumption are predisposed, consciously and deliberatively or not, to fulfill a social function of legitimating social difference.[4]

As he goes on to say, these cultural forms, "through the economic and social conditions which they presuppose, . . . are bound up with the systems of dispositions (habitus) characteristic of different classes and class fractions."[5] Thus, cultural form and content function as markers of class.[6] The granting of sole legitimacy to such a system of culture through its incorporation within the official centralized curriculum, then, creates a situation in which the markers of taste become the markers of people. The school becomes a class school.

The tradition of scholarship and activism that has formed me has been based on exactly these insights: the complex relationships between economic capital and cultural capital, the role of the school in reproducing and challenging the multitude of unequal relations of power (ones that go well beyond class, of course), and the ways the content and organization of the curriculum, pedagogy, and evaluation function in all of this.

It is at exactly this time that these kinds of issues must be taken most seriously. This is a period—what we can call the *conservative restoration*—when the conflicts over the politics of official knowledge are severe. At stake I believe is the very idea of public education and the very idea of a curriculum that responds to the cultures and histories of large and growing segments of the American population. Even the commitments of the "moderate" Democratic administration now in Washington embody the tendencies I shall speak of here. In fact, it is exactly *because* there is now a somewhat more moderate administration at a national level that we must think quite carefully about what can happen in the future as it is pulled—for political reasons—in increasingly conservative directions.

I want to instantiate these arguments through an analysis of the proposals for a national curriculum and national testing. But in order to understand them, we must think *relationally*; we must connect these proposals to the larger program of the conservative restoration. I want to argue that behind the educational justifications for a national curriculum and national testing is an ideological attack that is very dangerous. Its effects will be truly damaging to those who already have the most to lose in this society. I shall first present a few interpretive cautions. Then I shall analyze the general project of the rightist agenda. Third, I shall show the connections between national curricula and national testing and the increasing focus on privatization and "choice" plans. Finally, I want to discuss the patterns of differential benefits that will probably result from all this.

THE QUESTION OF A NATIONAL CURRICULUM

Where should those of us who count ourselves a part of the long progressive tradition in education stand in relationship to the call for a national curriculum?

At the outset, I want to make something clear. I am not opposed in principle to a national curriculum. Nor am I opposed in principle to the idea or activity of testing. Rather, I want to provide a more conjunctural set of arguments, one based on a claim that at this time—given the balance of social forces—there are very real dangers of which we must be quite conscious. I shall largely confine myself to the negative case here. My task is a simple one: to raise enough serious questions to make us stop and think about the implications of moving in this direction in a time of conservative triumphalism.

We are not the only nation where a largely rightist coalition has put such proposals on the educational agenda. In England, a national curriculum is now, in essence, mostly in place, first introduced by the Thatcher government. It consists of "core and foundation subjects" such as mathematics, science, technology, history, art, music, physical education, and a modern foreign language. Working groups to determine the standard goals, "attainment targets," and content in each have already brought forth their results. This is accompanied by a national system of achievement testing—one that is expensive and takes a considerable amount of time in classrooms to do—for all students in state-run schools at age seven, eleven, fourteen, and sixteen.[7]

The assumption in many quarters here is that we must follow nations with national curricula and testing—Britain and especially Japan—or we shall be left behind. Yet it is crucial that we understand that we *already* have a national curriculum, but one that is determined by the complicated nexus of state textbook adoption policies and the market in text publishing.[8] Thus, we have to ask if a national curriculum—one that will undoubtedly be linked to a system of national goals and nationally standardized instruments of evaluation (quite probably standardized tests, due to time and money)—is *better* than an equally widespread but somewhat more hidden national curriculum established by state textbook adoption states such as California and Texas with their control of 20–30 percent of the market in textbooks.[9] Whether or not such a national curriculum already exists in a hidden way, though, there is a growing feeling that a standardized set of national curricular goals and guidelines is essential to "raise standards" and to hold schools accountable for their students' achievement or lack of it.

Granted, many people from an array of educational and political positions are involved in calls for higher standards, more rigorous curricula at a national level, and a system of national testing. Yet we must always ask one question: What group is in leadership in these "reform" efforts? This of course leads to another, broader question. Given our answer to the former, who will benefit and who will lose as a result of all this? I shall contend that unfortunately rightist groups are indeed setting the political agenda in education and that, in general, the same pattern of benefits that has characterized nearly all areas of social policy—in which the top 20 percent of the population reaps 80 percent of the benefits[10]—will be reproduced here.

Of course, we need to be very cautious of the genetic fallacy, the assumption that *because* a policy or a practice originates within a distasteful position it is fundamentally determined, in all its aspects, by its origination within that tradition. Take Thorndike. The fact that his social beliefs were often repugnant—with his participation in the popular eugenics movement and his notions of racial, gender, and class hierarchies—does not necessarily destroy at each and every moment his research on learning. While I am not at all a supporter of this paradigm of research—and its epistemological and social implications still require major criticism[11]—this calls for a kind of argument different from that based on origination. (Indeed, one can find some progressive educators turning to Thorndike for support for some of their claims about what had to be transformed in our curriculum and pedagogy.)

Of course, it is not only those who are identified with the rightist project who argue for a national curriculum. Others who have historically been identified with a more liberal agenda have attempted to make a case.[12]

Smith, O'Day, and Cohen suggest a positive if cautionary vision for a national curriculum. A national curriculum would involve the invention of new examinations, a technically, conceptually, and politically difficult task. It would require the teaching of more rigorous content and thus would ask teachers to engage in more demanding and exciting work. Our teachers and administrators, hence, would have to "deepen their knowledge of academic subjects and change their conceptions of knowledge itself." Teaching and learning would have to be seen as "more active and inventive." Teachers, administrators, and students would need "to become more thoughtful, collaborative, and participatory. . . . Conversion to a national curriculum could only succeed if the work of conversion were conceived and undertaken as a grand, cooperative learning venture. Such an enterprise would fail miserably if it were conceived and organized chiefly as a technical process of developing new exams and materials and then 'disseminating' or implementing them."[13]

They go on to say:

> A worthwhile, effective national curriculum would also require the creation of much new social and intellectual connective tissue. For instance, the content and pedagogy of teacher education would have to be closely related to the content of and pedagogy of the schools' curriculum. The content and pedagogy of examinations would have to be tied to those of the curriculum and teacher education. Such connections do not now exist.[14]

The authors conclude that such a revitalized system, one in which such coordination would be built, "will not be easy, quick, or cheap," especially if it is to preserve variety and initiative. "If Americans continue to want educational reform on the cheap, a national curriculum would be a mistake."[15] I could not agree more with this last point.

Yet what they do not sufficiently recognize is that much of what they fear is already going on in the very linkage for which they call. Even more importantly, it is what they do not pay sufficient attention to—the connections between a national curriculum and national testing and the larger rightist agenda—that constitutes an even greater danger. It is this on which I wish to focus.

BETWEEN NEOCONSERVATISM AND NEOLIBERALISM

Conservatism by its very name announces one interpretation of its agenda. It conserves. Other interpretations are possible, of course. One could say, somewhat more wryly, that conservatism believes that nothing should be done for the first time.[16] Yet in many ways, in the current situation this is deceptive. For with the Right now in ascendancy in many nations, we are witnessing a much more activist project. Conservative politics now is very much the politics of alteration—not always, but clearly the idea of "Do nothing for the first time" is not a sufficient explanation of what is going on either in education or elsewhere.[17]

Conservatism has in fact meant different things at different times and places. At times, it will involve defensive actions; at other times, it will involve taking initiative against the status quo.[18] Today, we are witnessing both.

Because of this, it is important that I set out the larger social context in which the current politics of official knowledge operates. There has been a breakdown in the accord that guided a good deal of educational policy since World War II. Powerful groups within government and the economy, and within "authoritarian populist"[19] social movements, have been able to redefine—often in very retrogressive ways—the terms of debate in education, social welfare, and other areas of the common good. What education is *for* is being transformed. No longer is education seen as part of a social alliance that combined many "minority"[20] groups, women, teachers, community activists, progressive legislators and government officials, and others who acted together to propose (limited) social democratic policies for schools (e.g., expanding educational opportunities, limited attempts at equalizing outcomes, developing special programs in bilingual and multicultural education, and so on). A new alliance has been formed, one that has increasing power in educational and social policy. This power bloc combines business with the New Right and with neoconservative intellectuals. Its interests lie not in increasing the life chances of women, people of color, or labor. Rather, it aims at providing the educational conditions believed necessary both for increasing international competitiveness, profit, and discipline and for returning us to a romanticized past of the "ideal" home, family, and school.[21]

The power of this alliance can be seen in a number of educational policies and proposals: (1) programs for "choice," such as voucher plans and tax credits to make schools like the thoroughly idealized free-market economy; (2) the movement at national and state levels throughout the country to "raise standards" and mandate both teacher and student "competencies" and basic curricular goals and knowledge, increasingly now through the implementation of statewide and national testing; (3) the increasingly effective attacks on the school curriculum for its antifamily and anti–free enterprise "bias," its secular humanism, its lack of patriotism, and its supposed neglect of the knowledge and values of the "Western tradition" and of "real knowledge"; and (4) the growing pressure to make the perceived needs of business and industry into the primary goals of the school.[22]

In essence, the new alliance in favor of the conservative restoration has integrated education into a wider set of ideological commitments. The objectives in education are the same as those that serve as a guide to its economic and social-welfare goals. These include the expansion of the free market, the drastic reduction of government responsibility for social needs (though the Clinton administration may mediate this in symbolic and not very extensive—and not very expensive—ways), the reinforcement of intensely competitive structures of mobility, the lowering of people's expectations for economic security, and the popularization of what is clearly a form of Social Darwinist thinking.[23]

As I have argued at length elsewhere, the political Right in the United States has been very successful in mobilizing support *against* the educational system and its employees, often placing responsibility for the crisis in the economy on the schools. Thus, one of its major achievements has been to shift the blame for unemployment and underemployment, for the loss of economic competitiveness, and for the supposed breakdown of traditional values and standards in the family, education, and paid and unpaid work places *from* the economic, cultural, and social policies and effects of dominant groups *to* the school and other public agencies. "Public" now is the center of all evil; "private" is the center of all that is good.[24]

In essence, then, four trends have characterized the conservative restoration both in the United States and in Britain: privatization, centralization, vocationalization, and differentiation.[25] These are actually largely the results of differences within the most powerful wings of this alliance—neoliberalism and neoconservatism.

Neoliberalism has a vision of the weak state. A society that lets the "invisible hand" of the free market guide *all* aspects of its forms of social interaction is seen as both efficient and democratic. On the other hand, neoconservatism is guided by a vision of the strong state in certain areas, especially over the politics of the body and gender and race relations; over standards, values, and conduct; and over what knowledge should be passed on to future generations.[26] Those two positions do not easily sit side by side in the conservative coalition.

Thus, the rightist movement is contradictory. Is there not something paradoxical about linking all of the feelings of loss and nostalgia to the unpredictability of the market, "in replacing loss by sheer flux"?[27]

The contradictions between neoconservative and neoliberal elements in the rightist coalition are "solved" through a policy of what Roger Dale has called conservative modernization.[28] Such a policy is engaged in

> simultaneously "freeing" individuals for economic purposes while controlling them for social purposes; indeed, in so far as economic "freedom" increases inequalities, it is likely to increase the need for social control. A "small, strong state" limits the range of its activities by transferring to the market, which it defends and legitimizes, as much welfare [and other activities] as possible. In education, the new reliance on competition and choice is not all pervasive; instead, "what is intended is a dual system, polarized between . . . market schools and minimum schools."[29]

That is, there will be a relatively less regulated and increasingly privatized sector for the children of the better off. For the rest—and the economic status and racial composition in, say, our urban areas of the people who attend these minimum schools will be thoroughly predictable—the schools will be tightly controlled and policed and will continue to be underfunded and unlinked to decent paid employment.

One of the major effects of the combination of marketization and a strong state is "to remove educational policies from public debate." That is, the choice is left up to individual parents and "the hidden hand of unintended consequences does the rest." In the process, the very idea of education's being part of a *public* political sphere in which its means and ends are publicly debated atrophies.[30]

There are major differences between democratic attempts at enhancing people's rights over the policies and practices of schooling and the neoliberal emphasis on marketization and privatization. The goal of the former is to *extend politics*, to "revivify democratic practice by devising ways of enhancing public discussion, debate, and negotiation." It is inherently based on a vision of democracy that sees it as an educative practice. The latter, on the other hand, seeks to *contain politics*. It wants to *reduce all politics to economics*, to an ethic of "choice" and "consumption."[31] The world, in essence, becomes a vast supermarket.

Enlarging the private sector so that buying and selling—in a word competition—is the dominant ethic of society involves a set of closely related propositions. It assumes that more individuals are motivated to work harder under these conditions. After all, we "already know" that public servants are inefficient and slothful while private enterprises are efficient and energetic. It assumes that self-interest and competitiveness are the engines of creativity. More knowledge, more experimentation, is created and used to alter what we have now. In the process, less waste is created. Supply and demand stay in a kind of equilibrium. A more efficient machine is thus created, one that minimizes administrative costs and ultimately distributes resources more widely.[32]

This is of course not meant simply to privilege the few. However, it is the equivalent of saying that everyone has the right to climb the north face of the Eiger or scale Mount Everest without exception, providing of course that you are very good at mountain climbing and have the institutional and financial resources to do it.[33]

Thus, in a conservative society, access to a society's private resources (and, remember, the attempt is to make nearly *all* of society's resources private) is largely dependent on one's ability to pay. And this is dependent on one's being a person of an *entreprenurial or efficiently acquisitive class type*. On the other hand, society's public resources (that rapidly decreasing segment) are dependent on need.[34] In a conservative society, the former is to be maximized, the latter is to be minimized.

However, the conservatism of the conservative alliance does not merely depend in a large portion of its arguments and policies on a particular view of human nature—a view of human nature as primarily self-interested. It has gone further; it has set out to degrade that human nature, to force all people to conform to what at first could only be pretended to be true.

Unfortunately, in no small measure it has succeeded. Perhaps blinded by their own absolutist and reductive vision of what it means to be human, many of our political "leaders" do not seem to be capable of recognizing what they have done. They have set out, aggressively, to drag down the character of a people,[35] while at the same time attacking the poor and the disenfranchised for their supposed lack of values and character.

But I digress here and some of my anger begins to show. You will forgive me I trust; but if we cannot allow ourselves to be angry about the lives of our children, what can we be angry about?

CURRICULUM, TESTING, AND A COMMON CULTURE

As Whitty reminds us, what is striking about the rightist coalition's policies is its capacity to connect the emphasis on traditional knowledge and values, authority, standards, and national identity of the neoconservatives with the emphasis on the extension of market-driven principles into all areas of our society advocated by neoliberals. Thus, a national curriculum—coupled with rigorous national standards and a system of testing that is performance-driven—is able at one and the same time to be aimed at "modernization" of the curriculum and the efficient "production" of better "human capital" *and* represent a nostalgic yearning for a romanticized past.[36] When tied to a program of market-driven policies such as voucher and choice plans, such a national system of standards, testing, and curricula—while perhaps internally inconsistent—is an ideal compromise within the rightist coalition.

But one could still ask, will not a national curriculum coupled with a system of national achievement testing contradict in practice the concomitant emphasis on privatization and school choice? Can one really do both simultaneously? I want to claim here that this apparent contradiction may not be as substantial as one might expect. One long-term aim of powerful elements within the conservative coalition is not necessarily to transfer power from the local level to the center, though for some neoconservatives who favor a strong state when it comes to morality, values, and standards this may indeed be the case. Rather, these elements would prefer to decenter such power altogether and redistribute it according to market forces and thus tacitly disempower those who already have less power while using a rhetoric of empowering the "consumer." In part, both a national curriculum and national testing can be seen as "necessary concessions in pursuit of this long term aim."[37]

In a time of a loss of government legitimacy and a crisis in educational authority relations, the government must be seen to be doing something about raising educational standards. After all, this is exactly what it promises to offer to consumers of education. A national curriculum is crucial here. Its major value does not lie in its supposed encouragement of standardized goals and content and of levels of achievement in what are considered the most important subject areas, though this of course should not be totally dismissed. However, its major role is in *providing the framework within which national testing can function.* It enables the establishment of a procedure that can supposedly give consumers "quality tags" on schools so that "free-market forces" can operate to the fullest extent possible. If we are to have a free market in education with the consumer presented with an attractive range of "choice," a national curriculum and especially national testing in essence then act as a "state watchdog committee" to control the "worst excesses" of the market.[38]

However, let us be honest to our own history here. Even with the supposed emphasis on portfolios and other more flexible forms of evaluation, there is no evidence at all to support the hope that what will be ultimately and permanently installed—even if only because of time and expense—will be something other than a system of mass standardized paper-and-pencil tests.

Yet we must also be absolutely clear about the social function of such a proposal. A national curriculum may be seen as a device for accountability, to help us establish benchmarks so that parents can evaluate schools. But it also puts into motion a system in which children themselves will be ranked and ordered as never before. One of its primary roles will be to act as "a mechanism for differentiating children more rigidly against fixed norms, *the social meanings and derivation of which are not available for scrutiny.*"[39]

Thus, while the proponents of a national curriculum may see it as a means to create social cohesion and to give all of us the capacity to improve our schools by measuring them against "objective" criteria, the effects will be the opposite. The criteria may seem objective, but the results will not be, given existing differences in resources and in class and race segregation. Rather than cultural and social cohesion, differences between "us" and the "others" will be socially produced even more strongly and the attendant social antagonisms and cultural and economic destruction will worsen. (This will be the case as well with the current infatuation with outcome-based education, a new term for older versions of educational stratification.)

Richard Johnson helps us understand the social processes at work here.

> This nostalgia for "cohesion" is interesting, but the great delusion is that all pupils—black and white, working class, poor, and middle-class, boys and girls—will receive the curriculum in the same way. Actually, it will be read in different ways, according to how pupils are placed in social relationships and culture. A common curriculum, in a heterogeneous society, is not a recipe for "cohesion," but for resistance and the

renewal of divisions. Since it always rests on cultural foundations of its own, it will put pupils in their places, not according to "ability," but according to how their cultural communities rank along the criteria taken as the "standard." A curriculum which does not "explain itself," is not ironical or self-critical, will always have this effect.[40]

These are significant points, especially the call for all curricula to *explain themselves*. In complex societies like our own, ones riven with differential power, the only kind of cohesion that is possible is one in which we overtly recognize differences and inequalities. The curriculum then should not be presented as objective. Rather, it must constantly *subjectify* itself. That is, it must "acknowledge its own roots" in the culture, history, and social interests out of which it arose. It will accordingly neither homogenize this culture, history, and social interest, nor homogenize the students. The "same treatment" by sex, race and ethnicity, or class is not the same at all. A democratic curriculum and pedagogy must begin with a recognition of "the different social positionings and cultural repertoires in the classrooms, and the power relations between them." Thus, if we are concerned with "really equal treatment"—as I think we must be—we must base a curriculum on a recognition of those differences that empower and depower our students in identifiable ways.[41]

Foucault reminded us that if you want to understand how power works, look at the margins, look at the knowledge, self-understandings, and struggles of those whom powerful groups in this society have cast off as "the other."[42] The New Right and its allies have created entire groups as these "others"—people of color, women who refuse to accept external control of their lives and bodies, gays and lesbians, the poor, and as I know from my own biography the vibrant culture of working-class life (and the list could continue). It is in the recognition of these differences that curriculum dialogue can go on. Such a national dialogue begins with the concrete and public exploration of "how we are differently positioned in society and culture." What the New Right embargoes—the knowledge of the margins, of how culture and power are indissolubly linked—becomes a set of indispensable resources here.[43]

The proposed national curriculum of course would recognize some of these differences. But, as Linda Christian-Smith and I argue in *The Politics of the Textbook*, the national curriculum serves to partly acknowledge difference and at the same time to reincorporate it within the supposed consensus that exists about what we should teach.[44] It is part of an attempt to recreate hegemonic power that has been partly fractured by social movements.

The very idea of a common culture on which a national curriculum—as defined by neoconservatives—is to be built is itself a form of cultural politics. In the immense linguistic, cultural, and religious diversity that makes up the constant creativity and flux in which we live, it is the cultural policy of the Right to "override" such diversity. Thinking it is reinstituting a common culture, it is instead *inventing* one, in much the same way as E. D. Hirsch has tried to do in his self-parody of what it means to be literate.[45] A uniform culture never truly existed in the United States, only a selective version, an invented tradition that is reinstalled (though in different forms) in times of economic crisis and a crisis in authority relations, both of which threaten the hegemony of the culturally and economically dominant.

The expansion of voices in the curriculum and the vehement responses of the Right become crucial here. Multicultural and antiracist curricula present challenges to the program of the New Right, challenges that go to the core of their vision. A largely monocultural national curriculum (which deals with diversity by centering the always ideological "we" and usually then simply mentioning "the contributions" of people of color, women, and others), emphasizes the maintenance of existing hierarchies of what counts as official knowledge, the revivifying of traditional Western standards and values, the return to a "disciplined" (and one could say largely masculinist) pedagogy, and so on, and a threat to any of these is also a threat to the entire world view of the Right.[46]

The idea of a "common culture"—in the guise of the romanticized Western tradition of the neoconservatives (or even as expressed in the longings of some socialists)—does not give enough thought, then, to the immense cultural heterogeneity of a society that draws its cultural traditions from all over the world. The task of defending public education as *public,* as deserving of widespread support "across an extremely diverse and deeply divided people, involves a lot more than restoration."[47]

The debate in England is similar. A national curriculum is seen by the Right as essential to prevent relativism. For most of its proponents, a common curriculum must basically transmit both the "common culture" and the high culture that has grown out of it. Anything else will result in incoherence, no culture, merely a "void." Thus, a national culture is "defined in exclusive, nostalgic, and frequently racist terms."[48]

Richard Johnson's analysis of this documents its social logic.

> In formulations like these, culture is thought of as a homogeneous way of life or tradition, not as a sphere of difference, relationships, or power. No recognition is given to the real diversity of social orientations and cultures within a given nation-state or people. Yet a selective version of a national culture is installed as an absolute condition for any social identity at all. The borrowing, mixing and fusion of elements from different cultural systems, a commonplace everyday practice in societies like [ours], is unthinkable within this framework, or is

seen as a kind of cultural misrule that will produce nothing more than a void. So the "choices" are between . . . a national culture or no culture at all.[49]

The racial subtext here is perhaps below the surface, but is still present in significant ways.[50]

There are many more things that could be said. However, one thing is perfectly clear. The national curriculum is a mechanism for the political control of knowledge.[51] Once established, there will be little chance of turning back. It may be modified by the conflicts that its content generates, but it is in its very establishment that its politics lies. *Only by recognizing its ultimate logic of false consensus and, especially, its undoubted hardening in the future as it becomes linked to a massive system of national testing can we fully understand this.* When this is connected to the other parts of the rightist agenda—marketization and privatization—there is sufficient reason to give us pause, especially given the increasingly powerful conservative gains at local, regional, and state levels.

WHO BENEFITS?

One final question remains, one that I hinted at previously. Since leadership in such efforts to reform our educational system and its curriculum, teaching, and evaluative policies and practices is largely exercised by the rightist coalition, we need always to ask "Whose reforms are these?" and "Who benefits?"

This is indeed reform on the cheap. A system of national curricula and national testing cannot help but ratify and exacerbate gender, race, and class differences in the absence of sufficient resources, both human and material. Thus, when the fiscal crisis in most of our urban areas is so severe that classes are being held in gymnasiums and hallways, when many schools do not have enough funds to keep open for the full 180 days a year, when buildings are literally disintegrating before our very eyes,[52] when in some cities three classrooms must share one set of textbooks at the elementary level,[53] it is simply a flight of fantasy to assume that more standardized testing and national curriculum guidelines are the answer. With the destruction of the economic infrastructure of these same cities through capital flight, with youth unemployment at nearly 75 percent in many of them, with almost nonexistent health care, with lives that are often devoid of hope for meaningful mobility because of what might simply be best called the pornography of poverty, to assume that establishing curricular benchmarks based on problematic cultural visions and more rigorous testing will do more than affix labels to poor students in a way that is seemingly more neutral is also to totally misunderstand the situation. It will lead to more blame being affixed to students and poor parents and especially to the schools that they attend. It will also be very expensive to institute. Enter voucher and choice plans with even wider public approval.

Basil Bernstein's analysis of the complexities of this situation and of its ultimate results is more than a little useful here. As he says, "the pedagogic practices of the new vocationalism [neoliberalism] and those of the old autonomy of knowledge [neoconservatism] represent a conflict between different elitist ideologies, one based on the class hierarchy of the market and the other based on the hierarchy of knowledge and its class supports."[54] Whatever the oppositions between market- and knowledge-oriented pedagogic and curricular practices, present racial, gender, and class-based inequalities are likely to be reproduced.[55]

What he calls an "autonomous visible pedagogy"—one that relies on overt standards and highly structured models of teaching and evaluation—justifies itself by referring to its intrinsic worthiness. The value of the acquisition of say, the Western tradition lies in its foundational status for "all we hold dear" and in the norms and dispositions that it instills in the students. "Its arrogance lies in its claim to moral high ground and to the superiority of its culture, its indifference to its own stratification consequences, its conceit in its lack of relation to anything other than itself, its self-referential abstracted autonomy."[56]

Its supposed opposite—based on the knowledge, skills, and dispositions "required" by business and industry and seeking to transform schooling around market principles—is actually a much more complex ideological construction:

> It incorporates some of the criticism of the autonomous visible pedagogy . . . criticism of the failure of the urban school, of the passivity and inferior status [given to] parents, of the boredom of . . . pupils and their consequent disruptions of and resistance to irrelevant curricula, of assessment procedures which itemize relative failure rather than the positive strength of the acquirer. But it assimilates these criticisms into a new discourse: a new pedagogic Janus. . . . The explicit commitment to greater choice by parents . . . is not a celebration of participatory democracy, but a thin cover for the old stratification of schools and curricula.[57]

Are Bernstein's conclusions correct? Will the combination of national curricula, testing, and privatization actually lead away from democratic processes and outcomes? Here we must look not to Japan (where many people unfortunately have urged us to look) but to Britain, where this combination of proposals is much more advanced.

In Britain, there is now considerable evidence that the overall effects of the various market-oriented policies introduced by the rightist government are *not* genuine pluralism or the "interrupting [of] traditional modes of social reproduction." Far from this, they may instead largely provide "a legitimating gloss for the perpetuation of long-standing forms of structured inequality."[58] The fact that one of its major effects has been the depowering and deskilling of large numbers of teachers is not inconsequential as well.[59]

Edwards, Gewirtz, and Whitty have come to similar conclusions. In essence, the rightist preoccupation with "escape routes" diverts attention from the effects of such policies on those (probably the majority) who will be left behind.[60]

Thus, it is indeed possible—actually probable—that market-oriented approaches in education (even when coupled with a strong state over a system of national curriculum and testing) will exacerbate already existing and widespread class and race divisions. "Freedom" and "choice" in the new educational market will be for those who can afford them. "Diversity" in schooling will simply be a more polite word for the condition of educational apartheid.[61]

AFTERTHOUGHTS BY WAY OF A CONCLUSION

I have been more than a little negative in my appraisal here. I have argued that the politics of official knowledge—in this case surrounding proposals for a national curriculum and for national testing—cannot be fully understood in an isolated way. All of this needs to be situated in larger ideological dynamics in which we are seeing an attempt by a new hegemonic bloc to transform our very ideas of the purpose of education. This transformation involves a major shift—one that Dewey would have shuddered at—in which democracy becomes an economic, not a political, concept and where the idea of the public good withers at its very roots.

But perhaps I have been too negative. Perhaps there are good reasons to support national curricula and national testing, even as currently constituted precisely *because* of the power of the rightist coalition.

It is possible, for example, to argue that *only* by establishing a national curriculum and national testing can we stop the fragmentation that will accompany the neoliberal portion of the rightist project. Only such a system would protect the very idea of a *public* school; would protect teachers' unions, which in a privatized and marketized system would lose much of their power; would protect poor children and children of color from the vicissitudes of the market. After all, it is the free market that created the poverty and destruction of community that they are experiencing in the first place.

It is also possible to argue, as Geoff Whitty has in the British case, that the very fact of a national curriculum encourages both the formation of intense public debate about whose knowledge is declared official and the creation of progressive coalitions across a variety of differences against such state-sponsored definitions of legitimate knowledge.[62] It could be the vehicle for the *return* of the political, which the Right so wishes to evacuate from our public discourse and which the efficiency experts wish to make into merely a technical concern.

Thus, it is quite possible that the establishment of a national curriculum could have the effect of unifying oppositional and oppressed groups. Given the fragmented nature of progressive educational movements today, and given a system of school financing and governance that forces groups to focus largely on the local or state level, one function of a national curriculum could be the coalescence of groups around a common agenda. A *national* movement for a more democratic vision of school reform could be the result.

In many ways—and I am very serious here—we owe principled conservatives (and there are many) a debt of gratitude in an odd way. It is their realization that curriculum issues are not only about techniques, about how-tos, that has helped stimulate the current debate. When many women, people of color, and labor organizations (these groups are obviously not mutually exclusive) fought for decades to have this society recognize the selective tradition in official knowledge, these movements were often (though not always) silenced, ignored, or reincorporated into dominant discourses.[63] The power of the Right—in its contradictory attempt to challenge what is now taught, to establish a national common culture, and to make that culture part of a vast supermarket of choices and thus to purge cultural politics from our sensibilities—has now made it impossible for the politics of official knowledge to be ignored.

Should we then support a national curriculum and national testing to keep total privatization and marketization at bay? Under current conditions, I do not think it is worth the risk—not only because of its extensive destructive potential in the long and short run, but also because I think it misconstrues and reifies the issues of a common curriculum and a common culture.

Here I must repeat the arguments I made in the second edition of *Ideology and Curriculum*.[64] The current call to "return" to a "common culture" in which all students are to be given the values of a specific group—usually the dominant group—does not in my mind concern a common culture at all. Such an approach hardly scratches the surface of the political and educational issues involved. A common culture can never be the general extension to everyone of what a minority mean and believe. Rather, and crucially, it requires not the stipulation of the facts, concepts, skills, and values that make us all "culturally literate," *but the creation of the conditions necessary for all people to participate in the creation and recreation of meanings and values.* It requires a democratic process in which all people—not simply those who are the intellectual guardians of the Western tradition—can be involved in the deliberation over what is important. It should go without saying that this necessitates the removal of the very real material obstacles—unequal power, wealth, time for reflection—that stand in the way of such participation.[65] As Raymond Williams so perceptively put it:

> The idea of a common culture is in no sense the idea of a simply consenting, and certainly not of a merely conforming society. [It involves] a common determination of meanings by all the people, acting sometimes as individuals, sometimes as groups, in a process which has no particular end, and which can never be supposed at any time to have finally realized itself, to have become complete. In this common process, the only absolute will be the keeping of the channels and institutions of communication clear so that all may contribute, and be helped to contribute.[66]

In speaking of a common culture, then, we should *not* be talking of something uniform, something to which we all conform. Instead, what we should be asking is "precisely, for that free, contributive and common *process* of participation in the creation of meanings and values."[67] It is the very blockage of that process in our institutions that must concern all of us.

Our current language speaks to how this process is being defined during the conservative restoration. Instead of people who participate in the struggle to build and rebuild our educational, cultural, political, and economic relations, we are defined as consumers (of that "particularly acquisitive class type"). This is truly an extraordinary concept, for it sees people as either stomachs or furnaces. We use and use up. We do not create. Someone else does that. This is disturbing enough in general, but in education it is truly disabling. When we leave the creation of culture to the guardians of tradition, the efficiency and accountability experts, the holders of "real knowledge," or to the Whittles of this world (who will build us franchised "schools of choice" for the generation of profit),[68] we place at great risk especially those students who are already economically and culturally disenfranchised by our dominant institutions.

As I noted at the very outset, we live in a society with identifiable winners and losers. In the future, we may say that the losers made poor "consumer choices" and, well, that is the way markets operate, after all. But is this society really only one vast market?

As Whitty reminds us, in a time when so many people have found out from their daily experiences that the supposed "grand narratives" of progress are deeply flawed, is it appropriate to return to yet another grand narrative, the market?[69] The results of this narrative are visible every day in the destruction of our communities and environment, in the increasing racism of the society, in the faces and bodies of our children, who see the future and turn away.

Many people are able to disassociate themselves from these realities. There is an almost pathological distancing among the affluent.[70] Yet how can one not be morally outraged at the growing gap between rich and poor, the persistence of hunger and homelessness, the deadly absence of medical care, the degradations of poverty? If *this* were the (always self-critical and constantly subjectifying) centerpiece of a national curriculum (but then how could it be tested cheaply and efficiently and how could the Right control its ends and means?), perhaps such a curriculum would be worthwhile after all. Until such a time, however, we can take a rightist slogan made popular in another context and apply it to their educational agenda: "Just say no."

This paper was presented as the John Dewey Lecture, jointly sponsored by the John Dewey Society and the American Educational Research Association, San Francisco, April 1992. I would like to thank Geoff Whitty, Roger Dale, James Beane, and the Friday Seminar at the University of Wisconsin–Madison for their important suggestions and criticisms.

Notes

1 Michael W. Apple, *Ideology and Curriculum*, 2nd ed. (New York: Routledge, 1990); and idem, *Official Knowledge: Democratic Education in a Conservative Age* (New York: Routledge, 1993).

2 See Michael W. Apple, *Teachers & Texts: A Political Economy of Class & Gender Relations in Education* (New York: Routledge, 1988).

3 See Basil Bernstein, *Class, Codes and Control Volume 3* (New York: Routledge, 1977); and Michael W. Apple, "Social Crisis and Curriculum Accords," *Educational Theory* 38 (Spring 1988): 191–201.

4 Pierre Bourdieu, *Distinction* (Cambridge: Harvard University Press, 1984), p. 7.

5 Ibid., pp. 5–6.

6 Ibid., p. 2.

7 Geoff Whitty, "Education, Economy and National Culture," in *Social and Forms of Modernity*, ed. Robert Bolock and Kenneth Thompson (Cambridge: Polity Press, 1992), p. 292.

8 See Apple, *Teachers & Texts*; and idem and Linda Christian-Smith, eds., *The Politics of the Textbook* (New York: Routledge, 1990).

9 Ibid.

10 See Michael W. Apple, "American Realities: Poverty, Economy and Education," in *Dropouts from School*, ed. Lois Weis, Eleanor Farrar, and Hugh Petrie (Albany: State University of New York Press, 1989), pp. 205–23; Sheldon Danzinger and Daniel Weinberg, eds., *Fighting Poverty* (Cambridge: Harvard University Press, 1986); and Gary Burtless, ed., *A Future of Lousy Jobs?* (Washington, D.C.: The Brookings Institution, 1990).

11 See, e.g., Stephen Jay Gould, *The Mismeasure of Man* (New York: W. W. Norton, 1981). Feminist criticisms of science are essential to this task. See, for example, Donna Haraway, *Primate Visions* (New York: Routledge, 1989); Sandra Harding and Jean F. Barr, eds., *Sex and Scientific Inquiry* (Chicago: University of Chicago Press, 1987); Nancy Tuana, ed., *Feminism and Science* (Bloomington: Indiana University Press, 1989); and Sandra Harding, *Whose Science, Whose Knowledge* (Ithaca, N.Y.: Cornell University Press, 1991).

12 See Marshall S. Smith, Jennifer O'Day, and David K. Cohen, "National Curriculum, American Style: What Might It Look Like?" *American Educator* 14 (Winter 1990): 10–17, 40–47.

13 Ibid., p. 46.

14 Ibid.

15 Ibid.

16 Ted Honderich, *Conservatism* (Boulder: Westview Press, 1990), p. 1.

17 Ibid., p. 4.

18 Ibid., p. 15.

19 See Apple, *Official Knowledge.*

20 I put the word "minority" in quotation marks here to remind us that the vast majority of the world's population is composed of persons of color. It would be wholly salutary for our ideas about culture and education to remember this fact.

21 Apple, *Official Knowledge.*

22 Apple, *Teachers & Texts*; and idem, *Official Knowledge.*

23 See Ann Bastian et al., *Choosing Equality* (Philadelphia: Temple University Press, 1986).

24 See Michael W. Apple, *Education and Power* (New York: Routledge, ARK Edition, 1985).

25 Andy Green, "The Peculiarities of English Education," in *Education Limited*, ed. Education Group II (London: Unwin Hyman 1991), p. 27.

26 Allen Hunter, *Children in the Service of Conservatism* (Madison: University of Wisconsin-Madison Law School, Institute for Legal Studies, 1988). Neoliberalism actually does not ignore the idea of a strong state, but it wants to limit it to specific areas (e.g., defense of markets).

27 Richard Johnson, "A New Road to Serfdom?," in *Education Limited*, ed., Education Group II, p. 40.

28 Quoted in Tony Edwards, Sharon Gewirtz, and Geoff Whitty, "Whose Choice of Schools?," in *Voicing Concerns: Sociological Perspectives on Contemporary Educational Reform*, ed. Madeleine Arnot and Len Barton (London: Triangle Books, 1992), p. 156.

29 Ibid. The authors are quoting from Roger Dale, "The Thatcherite Project in Education," *Critical Social Policy* 9 (1989): 4–19.

30 "Introduction to Part Three-Alternatives: Public Education and a New Professionalism," in *Education Limited*, ed. Education Group II, p. 268.

31 Johnson, "A New Road to Serfdom?," p. 68.

32 Honderich, *Conservatism*, p. 104.

33 Ibid., pp. 99–100.

34 Ibid., p. 89.

35 Ibid., p. 81.

36 Whitty, "Education, Economy and National Culture," p. 294.

37 Green, "The Peculiarities of English Education," p. 29.

38 Ibid., I am making a "functional" not necessarily an "intentional" explanation here. See Daniel Liston, *Capitalist Schools* (New York: Routledge, 1988). For an interesting discussion of how such testing programs may actually work against more democratic efforts at school reform, see Linda Darling-Hammond, "Bush's Testing Plan Undercuts School Reforms," *Rethinking Schools* 6 (March/April 1992): 18.

39 Johnson, "A New Road to Serfdom?," p. 79; emphasis in original.

40 Ibid., p. 79–80.

41 Ibid., p. 80. See also Elizabeth Ellsworth, "Why Doesn't This Feel Empowering?" *Harvard Educational Review* 59 (August 1989): 297–324.

42 See Steven Best and Douglas Kellner, *Postmodern Theory: Critical Interrogations* (London: Macmillan, 1991), pp. 34–75.

43 Richard Johnson, "Ten Theses on a Monday Morning," in *Education Limited*, ed. Education Group II, p. 320.

44 See Apple and Christian-Smith, *The Politics of the Textbook*; Apple, *Official Knowledge*; and Whitty "Education, Economy and National Culture," p. 28.

45 Johnson, "Ten Theses on a Monday Morning," p. 319; and E. D. Hirsch, Jr., *Cultural Literacy* (New York: Houghton Mifflin, 1986).

46 Johnson, "A New Road to Serfdom?," p. 51. See also Susan Rose, *Keeping Them Out of the Hands of Satan* (New York: Routledge, 1988).

47 "Preface," in *Education Limited*, ed. Education Group II, p. x.

48 Johnson, "A New Road to Serfdom?," p. 71.

49 Ibid.

50 For a more complete analysis of racial subtexts in our policies and practices, see Michael Omi and Howard Winant, *Racial Formation in the United States* (New York: Routledge, 1986).

51 Johnson, "A New Road to Serfdom?," p. 82.

52 See Apple, *Official Knowledge*.

53 See the compelling accounts in Jonathan Kozol, *Savage Inequalities* (New York: Crown Publishers, 1991).

54 Basil Bernstein, *The Structuring of Pedagogic Discourse: Class, Codes and Control, Volume 4* (New York: Routledge, 1990), p. 63.

55 Ibid., p. 64.

56 Ibid., p. 87.

57 Ibid.

58 Geoff Whitty, "Recent Education Reform: Is It a Post-Modern Phenomenon?" (Unpublished paper presented at the Conference on Reproduction, Social Inequality, and Resistance, University of Bielefeld, Bielefeld, Germany, October 1–4, 1991), pp. 20–21.

59 Compare this to the U.S. experience in Michael W. Apple and Susan Jungck, "You Don't Have to Be a Teacher to Teach This Unit," *American Educational Research Journal* 27 (Summer 1990): 227–51.

60 Edwards, Gewirtz, and Whitty, "Whose Choice of Schools?," p. 151.

61 Green, "The Peculiarities of English Education," p. 30. For further discussion of the ideological, social, and economic effects of such choice plans see Stan Karp, "Massachusetts 'Choice' Plan Undercuts Poor Districts," *Rethinking Schools* 6 (March/April 1992): 4; and Robert Lowe, "The Illusion of " 'Choice'," *Rethinking Schools* 6 (March/April 1992): 1, 21–23.

62 Geoff Whitty, personal correspondence. Andy Green, in the English context, argues as well that there are merits in having a *broadly defined* national curriculum, but goes on to say that this makes it even more essential that individual schools have a serious degree of control over its implementation, "not least so that it provides a check against the use of education by the state as a means of promoting a particular ideology" (Green, "The Peculiarities of English Education," p. 22). The fact that a large portion of the teachers in England have, in essence, gone on strike—*refused* to give the national test—provides some support for Whitty's arguments.

63 See Apple and Christian-Smith, *The Politics of the Textbook*.

64 Apple, *Ideology and Curriculum*, pp. xiii–xiv.

65 Raymond Williams, *Resources of Hope* (New York: Verso, 1989), pp. 35–36.

66 Ibid., pp. 37–38.

67 Ibid., p. 68.

68 See Apple, *Official Knowledge*.

69 Whitty, "Education, Economy and National Culture," p. 290.

70 See the discussion in Kozol, *Savage Inequalities*.

[17]

The State and the Governance of Education: An Analysis of the Restructuring of the State–Education Relationship

Roger Dale

Introduction

The past decade has seen far-reaching changes in the education systems of most Western countries. There is broad agreement at a rather general level about the causes and nature of these changes. They are seen as part of the wider decline of the postwar welfare-state settlement, and that in turn is increasingly linked to changes in the global economy. This explanation is, however, very general, and if we are to make progress in understanding the specifics of any case we need above all to be able to spell out the mechanisms through which these changes have been installed. Of course, considerable and valuable work has been carried out in many countries on these issues which has enabled a fairly broad consensus to develop about the nature of the changes, including shifts away from 'state control' towards 'privatization' and 'decentralization' as the commonest responses to the new problems that education systems are facing. However, there has been little investigation of the precise mechanisms of these schemes, and it frequently appears to be assumed that what is 'privatization' or 'decentralization' in one country is the same in another. Recognizing, though, that education systems have nowhere (with the possible example of Chile) literally been privatized, and that there are numerous and very different possible interpretations of decentralization, delegation, devolution, and so on, should give us pause before assuming that we are talking about the same phenomenon.

What I intend to do in this chapter is to develop a basis for understanding and comparing the restructuring of the education–state relationship in Western societies. This involves isolating and analysing the relationships between the various mechanisms crucial to the new relationships between the state and education. Such an enterprise involves a considerable degree of discussion which, though rather abstract, is necessary if these changes to education are to be mapped and their likely effects in terms of equality, democracy, and participation assessed and compared. It is only if a sound basis for comparision can be developed that we can determine what policies are most likely to be effective in meeting the public aims of education.

In doing this I will argue that far from being weakened, the state's role in the control of education has actually been strengthened, if transformed; however, one very serious consequence of the change in the state's role in education is that the public-good functions of education, of which the state is the only reliable guarantor are being withdrawn. There are two reasons for this. The first and perhaps primary reason concerns the ideological commitments of neo-liberalism, which rejects the view that the state has a significant responsibility in supporting the public-good functions of education. The second is more complex and relates to Offe's (1990) view that in certain policy areas the state's capacity to act is severely limited in the present social and economic context.

Most existing theories of the government and control of education have tended to take for granted that education systems are state-controlled and state-run. The question has been 'why the state and education?' rather than 'whether the state and education'. In *The State and Education Policy* (1989) I argued that the education system, like all state organizations, could not avoid addressing the three central problems confronting the state in capitalist societies; (i) supporting the capital accumulation process, (ii) guaranteeing a context for its continued expansion, and (iii) legitimating the capitalist mode of accumulation, including the state's own part in it, especially in education. The paper by Codd, Gordon, and Harker (Ch. 16) provides one example of the application of this approach.

The fact that these core problems are permanently on the agenda of all Western states provides a framework for comparision, although it does not mean that each state will interpret, address, or seek solutions to those problems in the same way. The core problems set limits to state actions, but they do not determine them wholly; the form of state activity can not be read off from its functions.

The central problematic of this approach remains as important as ever. However, the nature and consequences of changes in the global economy and the development of 'pluralist' societies in which ethnic communities are asserting the right to cultural (if not always political and economic) sovereignty means that this framework for comparision needs development.

Education has been affected both directly and indirectly by the changes in the global economy. The direct impact is clearly seen in the case of those developing countries whose education systems have been shaped increasingly by the lending policies of the World Bank and the demands of 'structural adjustment' (i.e. the diminution of the public sector and the expansion of the private) that organizations like the IMF make conditions of support. More indirect effects are seen in those advanced countries that have been striving to cope with the aggregated effects of the decline of the Keynesian welfare-state settlement to the point where public funding of services like education seems no longer feasible at previous levels.

From State Control to Governance

Some elements of the reaction to these changes have been common to many Western countries. What they amount to is a 'hollowing out' of the state (see Jessop 1993) with the loss of some activities 'upwards' to supranational bodies and the loss of others 'downwards' to sub-national or non-state bodies. Thus we see apparently rather similar moves to various forms of 'decentralization' and 'privatization' of education in many Western countries. We might therefore say that while education remains a public issue, in common with many other state activities its co-ordination has ceased to be (at least formally) the sole preserve of the state or government. Instead it has become co-ordinated through a range of forms of *governance*, among which decentralization and privatization figure prominently. Hirst and Thompson (1995) distinguish the key terms in the following way:

> the tendency in common usage (is) to identify the term 'government' with the institutions of the state that control and regulate the life of a territorial community. Governance—that is, the control of an activity by some means such that a range of desired outcomes is attained—is, however, not just the province of the state. Rather, it is a function that can be performed by a wide variety of public and private, state and non-state, national and international, institutions and practices. (p. 422)

It is crucial to note that the state does not 'go away' in this process. Rather, I will argue that its continuing role as overwhelmingly the major funder and regulator of education enables it to remain very much in the driving seat. True, the nature of the work it does has changed, very broadly speaking, from carrying out most of the work of the co-ordination of education itself to determining where the work will be done and by whom. This devolution and detachment demonstrate strength rather than weakness (albeit over a policy terrain considerably reduced by the consequences of states' changing relationships to the global economy). The comparative theoretical issue then becomes one not so much of witnessing the banishment of the state as of 'locating' it and disaggregating its activities.

The Governance of Education

In focusing on the governance of education two sets of issues must be distinguished: what is involved in the governance of education, and how and by whom these activities are carried out. It is in this area that the assumptions of students of education systems are most starkly revealed. It had been effectively taken for granted, firstly, that 'running education' was a single activity and, secondly, that it was carried out by the state. It is necessary to examine these two issues before the consequences for what does and can go on in schools can be specified.

Much recent work on the economics and politics of the welfare state has distinguished three forms of what is usually referred to as 'state intervention'. These relate to three distinct and separable *activities* involved in welfare policy: how it is *funded*, how it is *provided* (or delivered), and how it is *regulated* (or controlled). It is argued that it is not necessary for the state to carry out all of these activities, while remaining in overall control of education.

These activities have to be co-ordinated, and in line with the hollowing-out thesis it has become common for three major *institutions of social coordination* to be distinguished (see e.g. Thompson *et al.* 1991). Several versions of these distinctions appear, but common to them all is the identification of the state and the market as two of the three key institutions of social co-ordination. The third, community, is always a residual category to the state and market and is conceptualized differently (though usually implicitly) according to the conception of state and market taken.[1] Once again, it should be noted that the 'traditional' assumption has been that all the activities involved in the co-ordination of education were carried out by the state. However, a moment's thought shows us that the state has never done all these things alone; the market and especially the community have been indispensable to the operation of the education systems. The difference now is that the areas of their involvement have been greatly expanded and formalized as the area of direct state involvement has contracted. Combining these two sets of variables into a three-by-three table, then, sheds some new light on the governance of education.

In particular, the table demonstrates the inadequacy of a simple 'public–private' distinction and shows how confusing, even misleading, that distinction can be. Only if and when funding, regulation, and provision were all carried out by the state alone could we speak of a 'public' system. Only if and when they were all carried out by 'non-state' bodies could we speak of a 'private' system, and even then 'private' would have to be interpreted as 'non-state'. Table 17.1, is, therefore, salutory because it begins to show the potential complexity of recent educational reforms and hence the dangers of oversimplified arguments about the 'privatization' or 'marketization' of education. It requires us not only to ask what activities are being privatized or handed over to the market or the community, but what this means. The table also fulfils the aim of providing an initial basis for international comparisons of the nature and effects of educational reform.

Table 17.1. A simple representation of the governance of education

	Coordinating Institutions		
Governance Activities	State	Market	Community
Funding			
Regulation			
Provision/Delivery			

However, in this form the table has rather limited value, largely because the categories are too coarse to register the kinds of changes that have been taking place in education systems in recent years. For instance, in recent years we have seen the state remain as principal funder of compulsory education in the Anglophone-dominated societies while using choice- and market-co-ordinating institutions. But even then there are differences in the purposes or aims underlying choice and market mechanisms, and hence different modes of regulation which determine the rules of the choice regimes and markets that have been created. For example, in England and New Zealand market mechanisms have been introduced with the primary aim of creating efficiency, arguably at the expense of equity. In contrast, a controlled-choice regime has been established in Boston. Here the aim is to reconcile parents' preferences with the provision of socially well-balanced schools. The evidence suggests that socially mixed schools are likely to enhance the educational performance of lower socio-economic-status students, hence there is an equity consideration in this system. In Boston parental choice is, therefore, mediated by a central agency which sorts and reorders the preferences for schools. We can call the differing aims underlying the institutions of co-ordination and the regulatory framework they generate their *modes of operation*.

A further difficulty with Table 17.1 is that it doesn't capture the subtlety and complexity of many of the forms of decentralization that have taken place, such as the changes entailed by the Grant Maintained Schools initiative in England, or the raft of reforms that have enabled much greater inter-school contestability in New Zealand. In both cases the state remains the only (formal) funder and operates a regulatory role, through a National Curriculum and assesment regimes, that is more powerful than has traditionally been the case. At the same time, market modes of contestability between schools have been introduced, while ostensibly schools are governed by community forms of management, through the establishment of Boards of Trustees in New Zealand and Boards of Governors in England.

In comparative terms, therefore, we need to pay very close attention to the complexities of the relationships between governance activities and co-ordinating institutions if we are to assess their effects. In order to do so we need to look more carefully at the governance activities, for it is they which ultimately shape and invest the co-ordinating institutions with specific purposes.

Governance Activities

FUNDING

I will begin by setting out very briefly some different forms taken by funding, regulation, and provision. One useful example of the historic existence of a multiplicity of funding sources in education is the English public (i.e. private) schools. These are funded in part directly by fees paid by parents, i.e. 'privately'. Many are also funded in part by religious or other voluntary organizations, i.e. directly 'community' funded. They also receive various forms of state subsidy—through tax relief on various forms of charitable giving from which they are able to benefit, and through rates relief deriving from their charitable status. Private schools also benefit from direct state funding of the academic and professional education of their teachers. All this makes it difficult to state categorically that we are dealing here with a 'private' institution; in terms of funding British 'private' schools share elements of all three kinds of institution. Funding then can be made up of direct, fee, payments, of direct or tax-subsidized gifts, of direct state funding, of community or parent-raised funds, of international funds for education, whether 'public' (and mediated through state and/or voluntary bodies) or 'private', provided by transnational companies or by international voluntary or 'not-for-profit' organizations, or, of course, by any combination of these sources and types of funding.

It is, though, useful to set out the principles of distribution of funding:

1. Funding may be directed to organizations or to individuals (e.g. in the form of scholarships or vouchers) or to combinations of both.
2. Funding may be available to all members of, and/or organizations within, a given population (a territory for the state, an income bracket or 'pooled insurance risk' for the market, 'recognized members' for the community), or targeted at particular groups or individuals (whether on the basis of virtue—e.g. scholarships—or need, as in the case of compensatory funding).
3. Funding may be made subject to conditions (e.g. some form of payment by results).
4. It may be available only on a competitive basis.
5. It can take the form of grants, loans, investment, or subsidy.

All these principles of distribution of funding, which can be combined into a wide range of alternatives, cross the three sets of institutions. It is only when we focus on the sources of funding that significant variation between the institutions is apparent. So only the state can fund education through taxation, whatever combination of central and local, general and specific taxation may be employed. Taxation remains overwhelmingly the dominant source of educational funding, certainly in the compulsory sector. However, one very important feature of educational funding in recent years has been the state-induced (whether through the stick of reduced state funding or the carrot of increased organizational autonomy) proliferation of 'non-state' funding of education. For instance, in an increasing minority of cases tax-derived funds for educational expansion have been augmented by 'community' (typically religious) funds.[2] We should also note the English City Technology College scheme, however, where the set-up costs of schools were to be met largely by industry (see Whitty *et al.* 1993). User fees continue to grow as a proportion of educational funding in 'state' schools, as well as in the private schools, where they have always been indispensable. In addition to the traditional fundraising activities of parent organizations, schools are increasingly encouraged to profit from their own commercial activities, such as renting out their premises, selling computer programs, or enrolling foreign full-fee-paying students. Sponsorship and donations, from whatever source, take on even greater importance than previously.

The restructuring of funding does not only (and all too frequently) entail 'brute' cuts in the public funding of education and the encouragement to look to other sources of funding, but it also assumes a greater 'efficiency' in the use of funds for education. That is to say, the educational 'reforms' in most Anglophone-dominated societies have affected both the level and the disbursement of funding, and point to the removal of barriers preventing the more 'efficient' use of funds. In practice this has meant efforts to diminish the influence of the 'provider' unions on maintaining existing levels of educational expenditure and pressure, in some cases backed up by legislation (see Dale and Jesson 1994), to have public organizations run more like private ones. Such actions are the source of the widespread view that in recent years education has been to a greater or lesser extent 'deregulated'; this is symbolized in the frequent tendency to shift responsibility for the day-to-day running of schools to the schools themselves.

REGULATION

Perhaps the greatest, and certainly the most important, range of variations comes in the area of regulation. It is the ultimate ability of the state to determine policy and sanctions through law that shapes the whole area of regulation. Together with funding, regulation provides the framework within which provision is possible. Funding and regulation combine in different ways to create the context for educational policy, provision, and practice.

However, it is worth probing this a little more deeply, since, as Prosser (1995) points out, the tendency towards greater marketization and 'privatization' of education seems to be seen by policy-makers as the resolution of technical issues of economic principle which are assumed to be similar in any market-oriented economy, so neglecting the particular constraints of legal and political culture. Part of the point of much economic literature (from which Prosser excepts the public-choice school) is to bracket out such cultural factors in favour of an 'acultural form of rational behaviour' (1995: 509). This emphasizes the crucial point, widely acknowledged since Polanyi's *The Great Transformation*, that markets are in no sense 'natural' institutions, but are always shaped by patterns of state regulation (see Waslander and Thrupp Ch. 29). In looking at what might shape education 'markets', therefore, it is essential to pay close attention to the regulations that frame the attempted move towards them; this includes, of course, 'deregulation', the removal of existing regulations that are perceived to act as barriers to greater consumer choice of schools, and all that it is assumed will flow from it in the way of responsiveness, efficiency, and so forth. Such policies typically seek to remove bureaucratic/democratic controls and minimize the areas over which professionals have discretion.

There are three aspects of the processes by which states have shaped the governance of education that are germane to this discussion. These are deregulation, juridification, and the New Public Management. They are closely linked, though they vary considerably both individually and in the ways they combine; together they provide the framework whereby the state retains, even enhances, its strength while divesting itself of a significant range of activities which will, it is anticipated, also thereby become more efficient and responsive.

In Christopher Hood's words, 'Regulation . . . ultimately comes from government's traditional role in providing a basis for trading, by setting standards and rules for the operation of markets' (1995: 19). However, as both Hood and Majone (1990) point out, there are significant differences between national traditions of regulation. As Majone puts it, 'In Europe there is a tendency to identify regulation with the whole realm of legislation, governance, and social control' (p. 1), whereas in America it refers much more to control over activities by specific regulatory agencies; 'regulation is not achieved simply by passing a law but requires detailed knowledge of, and intimate involvement with, the regulatory activity' (p. 2). Majone argues that 'these differences in meaning reflect significant ideological differences between the American and European approach to the political control of markets' (p. 2). The American system 'expresses a widely held belief that the market works well under normal circumstances and should be interfered with only in cases of market failure, such as monopoly power, negative externalities or inadequate information' (ibid.), whereas the traditional response of most European governments to market failure was not regulation but various forms of direct intervention; where regulation has been employed it has typically been assigned to traditional ministries rather than specialized regulatory agencies.

What we may be witnessing then, alongside economic deregulation and the encouragement of markets which includes education, is not just a move to deregulate but to shift the pattern of regulation much more in the American direction. This is especially clear in the New Zealand case, where, following the 1989 education reforms, not only was formal responsibility switched to individual school Boards of Trustees, but the old multi-purpose Department of Education was split up into a policy-orientated Ministry, and a range of specialist agencies such as the Education Review Office and the New Zealand Qualifications Authority. Bureaucratic generalists were everywhere replaced by agencies set up to regulate particular aspects of a formally deregulated and decentralized system. So talking merely of 'deregulation' does not tell the whole story, either in New Zealand or other countries that have followed a similar policy path.[3]

The second state strategy has been juridification, which may be defined loosely as the use of law in structuring social, political, cultural, and economic life (see Cooper 1995: 507). The effect of juridification has been to remove particular, often politically contentious, issues from the political agenda, making them subject to legal and not political dispute. In this, juridification can be seen to draw on some central precepts of Public Choice theory (see Lauder Ch. 25), which emphasizes the importance of constraining political actors by constitutional means. The creation of Reserve banks with responsibility for controlling inflation, irrespective of, or indifferent to, political consequences is one example of this strategy; legislation requiring a balanced budget is another. This applies not just, for instance, to matters like National Curricula (common though these have become), but to teachers' training, their conditions of service, and the basis on which schools are to be run; this is typically to be based on legislation which, as pointed out above, is designed to enable commercial enterprises to run more efficiently.

The third strategy has been the introduction of various versions of the New Public Management which is the policy expression of Public Choice theory. Its central feature is the stress which it places on the importance of public accountability. As Hood (1995) puts it, 'The basis of NPM lies in . . . lessening or removing differences between the public and the private sector and shifting the emphasis from process accountability towards a greater element of accountability in terms of results' (p. 94). Hood lists seven major elements of the NPM: disaggregation of public organizations; greater competition between public-sector organizations as well as between public and private; greater use of private-sector management practices; greater stress on discipline and parsimony in resource use; a move towards more 'hands-on' management; a move towards explicit and measurable standards of performance for public-sector organizations; and attempts to control public organizations according to preset output measures (ibid. 96–7). A major target of this initiative was the level and use of professional discretion, which many of these measures were designed to routinize. It also entails a 'mainstreaming' of state activities, removing claims to special treatment on the grounds of distinct (and unique) sectoral needs and traditions, for instance that teachers' work, conditions, and patterns of reward are different from those of production workers (see Dale and Jesson 1994).

One consequence of the changes to regulation is the effective creation of two different sets of principles by which regulatory and accountability procedures can be determined. We may call these principles 'rule-governed' and 'goal-governed'. Rule-governed forms of regulation operate *ex ante*, before the fact. They seek to control resource *inputs* to activities and to shape and channel *demands* on them. Agents' discretion is constrained by the *legal framework* within which they operate.

Goal-governed forms, by contrast, are designed to control institutions by means of judging how closely they have conformed to their performance targets. That is, they operate *ex post* and focus on the organization's *outputs*, which they aim to influence by controlling the supply of the organization's products or services. Agents' discretion is constrained by the relevant operational procedures.

It is possible to point to two clear targets of these new patterns of regulation. One has certainly been the assumedly malign effects of provider capture in education. These strategies seem designed to limit the influence of teachers over education, atomizing the system by decentralization, introducing tighter controls over curriculum and assessment, and limiting the scope for the political discussion of education. The other aim has been to create regulatory frameworks that encourage new 'providers' to enter the 'educational market', and it is to this issue that we now turn.

PROVISION AND DELIVERY

I do not intend to spend much space on the question of provision and delivery. One reason for the relatively brief treatment is that, as I have argued above, it is shaped by, and largely results from, those changes in funding and regulation that I have just been discussing. Another is that it has been the subject of far more discussion in the literature than either funding or regulation. In this section, therefore, I want to draw attention to just one of the key dimensions of this governance activity: the way provision relates to the question of entitlement. Ralf Dahrendorf, in *The Modern Social Conflict* (1984), refers to policies that seek to make products and services available to consumers, even if that means they are not available to everyone, while entitlement-based policies place the emphasis on ensuring the widest possible distribution of a basic minimum, even if that means curtailing the range of choice for some. The distinction when applied to education concerns that between consumers and citizens (Ranson 1987; 1993). Market forms of provision which have as their aim efficiency arguably play down or exclude issues of equity. Consumers who have material and cultural capital are likely to gain high-quality educational services while those that do not have these forms of capital may be excluded even from a basic education in inner-city areas with low funding and where schools are experiencing a spiral of decline. In a system of education designed for citizens, an attempt is made through the mechanisms of funding and regulation to ensure that everyone has access to a sound education. The clearest examples of these systems tend to be highly centralized bureaucratic forms of education such as that found in Japan (see Green Ch. 18).

The difficulty with the distinction between consumers and citizens in this context is that it doesn't easily fit with elements of community co-ordination and provision of education. For consumers the principle on which education is provided is that of *ability to pay*. For citizens, education is provided as a *universal entitlement* for all who are citizens of a society. Universalism entails treating all members of a population on the same basis. The relevant population for the state is theoretically the whole population under its jurisdiction. However, as Nancy Fraser (1989) has pointed out more decisively than most, in practice if not in principle states' definitions of the population entitled to benefit from 'universally' provided services do not include every citizen but are typically based on class, gender, and racial categories. However, where the state has failed in living up to the principle of universalism it can be challenged in the public arena, although of course as Nancy Fraser (1994) has also pointed out, the public arena itself is a contestable concept.

For community forms of co-ordination and provision, the principle on which education is provided is *eligibility for membership*. In the case of systems of culturally autonomous schooling, such as Kura Kaupapa (Maori) education, the entitlement is based on a subset of citizens with a particular history and culture. The principle underlying provision, which is based on ensuring that benefits go only to members recognized by the community, is explicitly and intentionally particularistic (i.e. designed to exclude non-members). In terms of changes to the state–education relationship, the emergence of a pluralist society with community education provision is perhaps the most novel aspect of the changes that have taken place. This crucial distinction between the state and community modes can be extended through arguments put forward by the Portuguese sociologist Boaventura de Sousa Santos, whose comments, although he is writing about the Portuguese context, have wider applicability. I take the 'welfare society' formulation he uses to be very close to what I intend by the notion of 'community mode'. A pluralist society distinguished by culturally autonomous education would approximate to De Santos's notion of a welfare society. Funds may be devolved to identifiable groups for education, or, indeed, any other welfare function, but how they are then distributed may then be a matter for those groups. He writes:

> Welfare society is hostile to equality, or at least it does not distinguish as clearly as the welfare state between legitimate and illegitimate inequalities . . . it is hostile to citizenship and legal entitlements, since welfare relations are concrete, multiplex, and based on the concrete long-term reciprocity of sequences of unilateral benevolent actors. (Santos 1991: 39)

This distinction points up the issue of accountability within the new state–education relationship. For the complexity involved in the shift from state control to governance also involves different modes of accountability to different constituencies. Many of the current debates in education over, for example, the marketization of education turn on the question of who education is provided for and who is to be held to account for problems of provision. Underlying these debates is the fundamental question of how the public-good purposes of education relating to democracy and equity can be addressed when the governance of education is so fragmented.

Some readers will detect a paradox in the formulation of this problem, because at the outset it was argued that while the nature of the state–education relationship had changed, state power had increased through the shift from state control to governance. State control of funding, the curriculum, and the teaching profession has clearly been strengthened, as the preceding arguments make clear, but it can also be argued that the state's grip is also tightened by decentralized, multiple modes of accountability.

Accountability and the Limits to State Action

Claus Offe (1990: 247) has argued powerfully that the state's capacity to act effectively is severely limited, particularly 'in policy areas where the passions, identities, collectively shared meanings, and moral predispositions within the "life-world" of social actors (rather than their economic interests) are the essential parameters that need to be changed in order to achieve a solution'. He suggests that there are 'clear absolute limits' to all three forms of governmental intervention that he identifies: regulation, manipulation of fiscal resources, and the use of information and persuasion. Bureaucratic regulation is limited by its inflexibility and by the possibility of powerful interests being able to resist it. Economic forms have little impact on people who 'refuse to act according to some utility-maximizing economic calculus' (p. 247). The value of the use of information tends to fall as people become suspicious that it is being used to manipulate rather than to inform them.

Under these circumstances the ability of a government to keep at a distance from being held accountable can clearly be expedient. In the case of devolution to a community it not only shifts accountability onto the community but it appears a particularly 'potent' solution in cases where shared meanings and moral dispositions count for more than the economic calculus. But we should note that while governments may devolve accountability onto communities, the limitations of this devolution may have more to do with appearances than reality. Culturally autonomous schooling can be seen as a 'licensed departure' of a very limited kind, rather than the actions of a genuinely liberal state in a pluralist society.

The case of devolution to choice regimes and quasi-markets in education appears to be a rather more straightforward response to the inflexibilities of bureaucratic forms of organization identified by Offe. The attempts to introduce greater choice into the allocation of public services, through the creation of quasi-markets, for instance, does indicate that the scope-choice regimes may be greater than a simple profit-motive calculation may suggest, for instance in increasing the responsiveness, effectiveness, and efficiency of services. However, the question of accountability in choice regimes remains open and contentious because, inevitably, choice regimes involve decentralization, and where there are many different loci of power it is more difficult to mark out a clear audit trail to those ultimately responsible, as repeated questions about the scope of ministerial responsibility in the new public sector demonstrate.

Conclusion

While specific community or quasi-market policies may go some way to addressing the 'poverty of policy' as articulated by Offe, while keeping the state firmly in the driving seat, the fundamental problem still remains to be addressed. Overall, the state can be seen to be responding to three different sets of pressures. The first is economic and relates to the changing role of the state in the global economy. The second concerns the shift from a welfare state to a welfare society in which the presumption of universalism has been replaced by new forms of particularism based either on the social-class privileges of material and cultural capital, or on membership of an identifiable group in society. The third concerns the limits of state action in the modern context. The shift from state control to governance in education, with all its attendant complexities, can be explained in these terms.

In this paper I've tried to locate some[4] of the key mechanisms involved in this shift so that a comparative analysis of the various effects of the new state–education relationship can be studied. However, there are some broad trends that are now discernible and their effects can be predicted. Essentially, I want to suggest that the most common broad pattern of state withdrawal has been motivated by a wish to reduce public expenditure, limit the extent of provider capture, encourage possessive individualism (Apple 1982), and improve the efficiency and responsiveness of the education system. What has been less frequently attempted, scarcely attempted at all, in fact, has been a commitment by the state to ensure the perpetuation of the public-good qualities of education that it alone can guarantee. The tasks confronting Western states are twofold. Firstly, they need to address the question of how equality of resources and outcomes can be achieved under a complex system of governance in which particularism rather than universalism is an important guiding factor in the provision of education. Secondly, they need to address the question of how effective democratic accountability can be introduced into the system. By addressing these problems rather than resorting to an expedient arms'-length form of accountability, states would be attempting to resolve the dilemma posed by Offe of how to bring about social change in areas resistant to policy intervention of the traditional kind. In doing so, they may create the basis for shared responsibility for education. Finding answers to these challenges is essential to a civilized society.

Notes

1. In a recent paper I distinguished twenty different combinations of 'state, market and network/community/civil society/the family, etc.' (see Dale 1994)). This is not a trivial matter, as will become clear.
2. See Fowler (1994) on the French case.
3. The rationale for creation of multiple agencies has probably been inspired by the New Public Management, which sees the creation of contestability of advice to government from different agencies as a key to the restructuring of the public sector.
4. For further discussion of the mechanisms which are likely to be influential in the new state–education relationship see Dale (1996).

References

Apple, M. (1982), 'Curricular Form and the Logic of Technical Control; Building the Possessive Individual', in Apple, M. (ed.), *Cultural and Economic Reproduction in Education* (London: Routledge).

Cooper, D. (1995), 'Local Government Legal Consciousness in the Shadow of Juridification', *Journal of Law and Society* 22/4: 506–26.

Dahrendorf, R. (1984), *The Modern Social Conflict* (Berkeley: Univ. of California Press).

Dale, R. (1994), 'Locating "The Family and Education" in the Year of the Family'. Keynote address to Australia and New Zealand Comparative Education Society Conference, Melbourne, December.

—— (forthcoming), *Markets and Education* (Milton Keynes: Open Univ. Press).

—— (1996), *Governance* (Auckland: Education Department, Univ. of Auckland).

Dale, R., and Joce, J. (1992), ' "Mainstreaming" Education: the role of the State Services Commission' in Manson, H. (ed.), *Annual Review of*

Education in New Zealand (Wellington: Victoria Univ.), 2: 7–33.

Fowler, F. C. (1992), 'School Choice Policy in France: Success and Limitations', *Educational Policy*, 6/4: 429–43.

Fraser, N. (1989), *Unruly Practices: Power, Discourse and Gender in Contemporary Social Theory* (Minneapolis: Univ. of Minnesota Press).

—— (1994), 'Rethinking the Public Sphere: A Contribution to the Critique of Actually Existing Democracy', in Giroux, H., and McLaren, P. (eds.), *Between Borders: Pedagogy and the Politics of Cultural Studies* (New York: Routledge).

Hirst, P., and Thompson, G. (1995), 'Globalization and the Future of the Nation State', *Economy and Society*, 24/3: 408–42.

Hood, C. (1994), *Explaining Economic Policy Reversals* (Milton Keynes: Open Univ. Press).

—— (1995), 'The New Public Management in the 1980s: Variations on a Theme', *Accounting, Organizations and Society*, 20/2–3: 93–109.

Jessop, B. (1993), 'Towards a Schumpeterian Workfare State? Preliminary Remarks on post-Fordist Political Economy', *Studies in Political Economy*, 40: 7–39.

Majone, G. (ed.) (1990*a*), *Deregulation or Regulation? Regulatory Reform in Europe and the United States* (London: Pinter).

—— (1990*b*), 'Analyzing the Public Sector: Shortcomings of Policy Science and Policy Analysis', in Kaufman, F. (ed.), *The Public Sector* (New York: de Gruyter), 29–45.

Offe, C. (1990), 'Reflections on the Institutional Self-Transformation of Movement Politics: A Tentative Stage Model', in Dalton, R. J., and Koehler, M. (eds.), *Challenging the Political Order: New Social and Political Movements in Western Democracies* (New York: Oxford Univ. Press), 233–50.

Prosser, T. (1995), 'The State, Constitutions and Implementing Economic Policy: Privatization and Regulation in the UK, France, and the USA', *Social and Legal Studies*, 4: 507–16.

Ranson, S. (1987), 'Citizens or Consumers? Policies for School Accountability', in Barton, L., and Walker, S. (eds.), *Changing Policies, Changing Teachers* (Milton Keynes: Open Univ. Press).

—— (1993), 'Markets or Democracy for Education?' *British Journal of Educational Studies*, 41/4: 333–52.

Santos, B. (1991), *State Wage Relations and Social Welfare in the Semi-Periphery: The case of Portugal* (Universidade de Coimbra: Centro de Estudos Sociaias).

Thompson, G., and Levacic, R. (eds.) (1991), *State, Market and Networks* (London: Sage).

Whitty, G., Edwards, T., and Gewirtz, S. (1993), *Specialisation and Choice in Urban Education: The City Technology College Experiment* (London: Routledge).

[18]

BRITISH JOURNAL OF EDUCATIONAL STUDIES
VOL XXXX NO 2 MAY 1992

PARENTAL CHOICE AND EDUCATIONAL REFORM IN BRITAIN AND THE UNITED STATES

by TONY EDWARDS, *School of Education, University of Newcastle upon Tyne and* GEOFF WHITTY, *Institute of Education, University of London*

What marks out the present crisis of confidence in public schooling in Britain and the United States is not so much the severity of the criticisms as the strident denials that any effective remedies can be found within the existing systems. It is being argued that schools will only improve if education is treated as a private good, to be mediated through the unconstrained interplay of market forces. From this radical perspective, a single mechanism is commonly presented as curing all educational ills. As Ronald Reagan claimed at a 1989 White House 'Workshop on Choice' – 'Choice works, and it works with a vengeance' (cit. Maddaus, 1990, pp. 267–268).

There are formidable difficulties, however, in coming to grips with what it is that 'works with a vengeance' once traditional obstacles to the interplay of supply and demand are removed. 'Choice' is merely a slogan, whatever its popular appeal, if there is no delineation of what the choices are, who can make them and under what constraints, and what are the likely effects of extending choice on existing patterns of educational provision. Indeed, the slogan itself can be an obstacle to rational discussion. Its connotations of freedom and individual responsibility may make it seem self-evidently a 'good thing', requiring no careful justification. Its presentation may then take on the appearance of a faith – of unquestioned assertions about 'the overwhelming superiority' of the 'blind, unplanned, unco-ordinated wisdom of the market' over the 'rational' but ineffective interventions of the state (Joseph, 1976, p. 57). General expressions of belief in individual consumer sovereignty are then likely to be countered with equally ungrounded expressions of collectivist disbelief.

In this paper, we examine some of the underlying assumptions about how a 'free' (or freer) market would operate, drawing on argument and evidence from both Britain and the United States. We begin by considering the conviction that transferring power from the producers of education to its consumers will ensure that schools improve. We then question the assumption that a market system would be more equitable as well as more efficient. Finally, we consider claims that enhanced parental choice will produce greater diversity in educational provision, returning to the principle of equity in relation to the endemic problem of providing forms of schooling which are 'different but equal'.

1. Parental choice and school improvement

'Producer capture' has become a common explanation for the failings of the educational system, a public sector 'monopoly' (or quasi-monopoly) being blamed for a lack of proper accountability to consumers and for the consequent complacency of the 'educational establishment' (Seldon, 1986; Flew, 1988; Cox and Marks, 1989; Peterson, 1990; O'Hear, 1991). At school level, the assigning of pupils by catchment area is seen as freeing schools from having to demonstrate either quality or distinctiveness to earn their keep. A captive market secures them against the discipline of consumer preference because there are insufficient penalties for institutional failure and insufficient rewards for institutional success. From this perspective, the essential strategies for educational improvement are to enable individual parents to compare schools and implement their choice, and to compel schools to deserve their custom. If 'the key to success is having something to offer which other people want', then schools which meet this critical test should prosper; conversely, schools which fail it must not be protected against the consequences of their unpopularity, 'under-enrolment' being simply 'a bureaucratic euphemism for what happens when schools are so bad no-one wants to attend them' (Chubb and Moe, 1990, pp. 29–30). Such schools must improve, or close.

This faith in the survival of the fittest, and in parental choice as the means both of creating the struggle and determining its outcomes, seems to require certain conditions to be met. We begin with some questionable assumptions about the supply side. First, popular and over-chosen schools must be able and willing to expand. If they are not, then less popular schools will recruit the overspill and some thoroughly 'undeserving' schools will survive by default. There is therefore a conflict between parental choice and 'rational' use of resources. If rolls are falling in the system at large, as they fell by a third in English secondary schools during the 1980s, then 'rationalisation' requires that surplus places should be taken out rather than re-allocated. From a market perspective, however, those same places provide the 'room' within which successful schools can grow, and it is inconsistent to urge the elimination of surplus places while at the same time linking the closure of 'failing' schools to the beneficial growth of their meritorious competitors (Taylor, 1990).

'Successful' schools may of course choose not to grow, seeing the costs to their manageability or ethos as outweighing any extra resources which expansion might bring. They may also prefer to sift prospective pupils more carefully. Leading English independent schools, for example, which are often cited to exemplify the bracing effects of a market orientation, have normally used their market appeal to become more selective rather than larger (Edwards et al, 1989a). That successful schools may be enabled to select whom they teach is a consequence of a competitive market which its advocates tend to ignore. We return to it in relation to the equalising of educational opportunity which greater consumer choice is said to create. It also has obvious relevance to the 'improving' effects on schools which are attributed to enhanced parental choice.

Those effects seem to rely on the inter-related assumptions that popular schools are better schools, and that they are better at teaching rather than merely the beneficiaries of having more able and 'teachable' pupils. Yet the correlations between current and prior attainment, and between attainment and pupils' social background, are very high. Thus the academic excellence claimed by at least the leading schools in the English private sector has often been explained away as doing no more than confirm the quality of their intakes. In that context, the Assisted Places Scheme introduced in 1981 to sponsor able children from 'less well-off homes' to attend English (and Welsh) independent schools on publicly-funded scholarships can be seen as further enhancing those schools' academic selectiveness and thereby the examination results on which their market appeal largely depends, at the expense of 'competing' state schools from which those pupils are sponsored to withdraw (Edwards et al, 1989b). Similar doubts arise over whether the better performance of magnet schools owes more to their curriculum specialization, to the parents' stronger commitment to schools they have chosen, or to their capacity to recruit better-motivated and often abler students. While some recruit entirely by student and parent interest, taking all-comers or (where over-chosen) selecting by lottery, others are highly selective on the basis of test scores and previous school reports (Blank, 1990). Similarly, the substantial improvements in literacy and numeracy achieved by Manhattan District 4 schools are explained by Domanico (1989; 1990) as a direct consequence of enhanced parental choice. The explanation is unconvincing without also considering how far those schools' new-found capacity to draw in a different clientele has created a very different student mix, with very different composition effects on performance. Some experiments of this sort have certainly been able to reverse the usual flow of students from inner-city to suburbs.

We have argued that a competitive market in education is likely to enhance some suppliers' capacity to choose. Yet it is usually assumed by its advocates that consumers have to be enabled to move freely between competing suppliers if market forces are to have their salutary effects. The prime target for criticism is therefore the neighbourhood school, the assigning of 'captive' customers being cited by George Bush (in the White House conference mentioned earlier) as the main explanation for the 'self-perpetuating mediocrity' of public schools. In England, the definition of 'open enrolment' in the 1988 Education Reform Act was the culmination of a progressive weakening of designated catchment areas in earlier Conservative Government legislation. Schools can now recruit up to their admission limit as defined in 1979, a date chosen to precede the steep fall in secondary rolls referred to earlier and so leave considerable room for 'successful' schools to benefit from their popularity. Parents can seek a place in any school which is not full by that definition, and Local Education Authorities are unable to intervene on traditional grounds of 'public interest' – for example, to maintain viable numbers in another school and so prevent it falling into a downward spiral of decline. Indeed, the 1988 Act's simultaneous introduction of open enrolment, and of delegated budgets determined largely by pupil numbers, has been seen as such a large step towards creating a competitive market as to make unnecessary the more obviously radical and controversial mechanism of educational vouchers. If the carrying of custom to a 'successful' school and away from a 'failing' school is the essential incentive and deterrent of consumer preference, then all that is required is that an appropriate per capita amount of distributed funding should follow each pupil to the school which is preferred (Ashworth et al, 1988; Sexton, 1987; Taylor, 1990).

There are many circumstances, however, in which enrolment cannot be open. Where applicants exceed the available places, is the school able to make whatever selection it wishes? Or is that freedom constrained by (for example) an obligation to give preference to local applicants or those with siblings already at the school, or by a more general obligation to secure a 'balanced' intake? Magnet schools were first introduced to counter the racially segregated intakes produced by segregated housing. They were intended to exert a 'magnetic' pull across boundaries of race and class, thereby challenging the residential segregation which concentrates 'low income central city students in isolated and inferior schools', and enabling distinctive forms of educational excellence to be achieved even in socially disadvantaged areas (Orfield and Peskin, 1989, p. 27; Cooper, 1987; Clinchy, 1989; Fliegel, 1990). They may be subject to racial and social class quotas, as in other schemes for 'controlling' choice so as to combine the abandonment of attendance zones with a ranking of parental choice so that first-choices may be refused in the wider public interest of securing intakes representative of the racial composition of that local system (Fullinwider, 1989; Alves and Willie, 1989, 1991). Such systemic 'controls' on choice constitute interference in a 'free' market in what is regarded as an overriding public interest. There is an interesting example of such constraint in the British Government's insistence that the new City Technology Colleges in the UK must recruit, from their largely inner-city locations, intakes which are socially and ethnically 'representative of the community they serve' (DES, 1986; Murphy et al, 1990). If they are to demonstrate what can be achieved by inner-city schools, then they cannot be allowed to 'cream off' the ablest children around them without making it certain that any success they achieve will be written off as the consequence of a privileged intake rather than of a distinctive curriculum, ethos, and independence from the LEA. They are therefore the only public sector schools in the UK with exclusive catchment areas, a constraint which their free market advocates regard as an illogical departure from the Government's commitment to free parental choice.

The main demand-side assumption is that choice of school can be freely made and effectively implemented. As Lieberman (1989) notes, free market advocates tend to idealize parents as naturally wise and committed educational consumers who will make a positive choice between real alternatives if they perceive themselves as having effective rather than merely formal rights of entry and exit. Reference to the high proportion of parents who already report having the school of their 'choice', or as not having 'considered' other possibilities, is then likely to be dismissed as merely reflecting traditional arrangements in which possible alternatives have not been highlighted, in which actual choice has been used mainly as a safety valve for those strongly dissatisfied with their local school, and in which many parents determine their choice of school by their previous choice of residence. It also has to be assumed that schools in urban areas will not benefit undeservedly from the inertia effects of being the local school. The tendency of proximity to override more calculative criteria leads some choice advocates to make subsidized transport an essential component in their schemes, since without it some parental preferences cannot be effectively registered and some schools retain an undeserved geographical protection against the effects of their unpopularity. Parents choosing independent or parochial schools may be relatively less likely to cite cost and convenience as their main considerations (Sherman, 1983; Coleman and Hoffer, 1987). But there is also substantial evidence that 'incidence of choice diminishes as the distance of alternative schools from the home diminishes' (Echols et al, 1990, p. 209).

The local school may of course be positively chosen as the educational expression of a cohesive community. The child's own insistence on 'being with my friends' may also have a decisive localising influence on the final decision, that particular diversion from more educationally calculative criteria coming through strongly in our own investigation of parental choice across the private and public sectors (Edwards et al, 1989b). Parents' own criteria also range far beyond strategic calculations about future life chances. Yet it would seem reasonable to argue that parental choice will work most directly to concentrate schools' attention on academic standards if it is shaped largely by that criterion. A recent, substantial Scottish study of how and why parents exercise choice concluded that most 'seem to adopt a humanistic rather than a technological perspective, being less concerned with measurable criteria of product than with the creation of an atmosphere supportive of the child's well-being' and of its 'happiness' (Adler et al, 1989, p. 134). In relation to the use of popularity as a test of school quality, that Scottish study produced evidence of children being placed in schools with better results, but no clear evidence that parents were choosing them for that reason. The 'gaining' schools were old-established and formerly selective, larger, and located in areas with relatively low incidences of unemployment and single-parent and low income families. There was no evidence either that having more able pupils at entry was associated with pupils making greater progress during their time at the school. Great care is taken in school effectiveness research to avoid over-crediting schools for the quality of their intakes, for example by comparing actual attainment with what would be 'expected' of a pupil of that ability from that background. Yet value-added analysis is very difficult to present in public debate about the relative quality of schools, both because of its complexity and because it can be made to seem like a search for excuses for 'poor' performance. Where parents themselves make academic achievement their priority, they may 'prefer schools where the absolute level of attainment is high' to those 'which achieve good progress in attainment' (Smith and Tomlinson, 1989, p. 183). If that is so, it constitutes another source of doubt about whether greater choice works inexorably to raise educational standards. We turn now to doubts about whether it is also so evidently more equitable.

2. Parental choice and equity

Among the benefits claimed for enhanced parental choice are those derived from the process of choosing. It is argued that parents who have little say in where their child goes to school may acquiesce in what is offered to them, but are unlikely to feel much involved in what is too obviously provided from above. Contrasts are then drawn not only with private schools, but with those (mainly suburban) schools which are chosen by prior choice of home location and which the parents may even 'colonise' into publicly-funded schools with effectively restricted access (Hatton, 1986). Even choice 'controlled' by the kind of intake restrictions mentioned earlier is defended as giving responsibility (and dignity) to inner-city parents who would otherwise take no active part in choosing their children's school (Glenn, 1990).

It is at this point that arguments for 'improving' and 'democratising' educational provision tend to run together. All parents have to be empowered with rights of entry and exit if all schools are to be subjected to the discipline of consumer preference. At the same time, there are obvious democratic objections to restricting choice of school to those with the money to pay fees, or choose the location of their home, or work admission procedures to their advantage. Thus Lieberman (1989, p. 231) notes the philosophical turnabout that has led conservatives to argue for vouchers on grounds of equal power rather than merely equal rights. In Britain, the long campaign by the Institute of Economic Affairs to replace public provision by market provision shaped by consumer preference is presented as a democratic substitution of 'corrigible differences in purchasing power which determine access in the market' for 'those incorrigible differences in cultural power' which have brought privileged access to those with the knowledge and self-confidence to work the system. It is argued that the market represents 'true democracy' because the consumer 'votes' every time he or she chooses freely between products and suppliers. If a public education is transformed into something resembling a market through the 'earmarked purchasing power' represented by vouchers or other forms of per capita funding, then 'the dignity of choice and personal responsibility now reserved for the wealthy and articulate' is widely diffused, and the distributive justice of the market replaces the mistaken or ineffective interventions of the state' (Seldon, 1981, p. xxi; 1986, pp. 45–46).

The 'inherent tendency to equalize value for money' attributed to a competitive market (Flew, 1988, p. 4) is also assumed to have equalising effects. Thus President Bush claimed that the traditional zoning of intakes which had condemned all public education to 'self-perpetuating mediocrity' placed 'working poor and low income families at the greatest disadvantage' because it was their schools which have been most protected from having to earn their custom (cit. Maddaus, 1990, p. 28). The most radical mechanism for creating a market has been explicitly presented as a source of positive discrimination. Vouchers can of course be implemented in forms which bring particular benefits to the already advantaged – for example, if they subsidize entry to private schools which charge well above the cash value so as to retain an effective social filter, or if they encourage popular public schools to raise their 'prices' so as to control demand. But they could also vary in value so as to favour poorer families, or so that pupils conventionally regarded as difficult to teach are 'worth' more to schools prepared to specialize in providing for them (Friedman and Friedman, 1980; Levin, 1968). A recent change to the English regulations on Local Management of Schools (Government Circular 7/91), whereby some forms of special educational need can produce 'weighted' pupil units, can be interpreted as a move in this direction. There are strong grounds for scepticism, however, about the general enhancement of parental choice which is assumed to occur in a more open educational market. Particularly questionable are assumptions about the essential equality of consumers once 'real' choice is created by open enrolment.

First, choice of school is not marginal choice. Encouraging or sponsoring the exit of parents from a school they judge to be unsatisfactory may concentrate the minds of teachers and administrators on improvements to ward off further losses. It may also diminish its size sufficiently to reduce drastically opportunities for children left behind, while denying the school effective parental voices for change. Thus some parents' exercise of choice may leave others' choice diminished. From that perspective, the main conclusion of the Scottish research cited earlier was that, while the individual parents who exercised choice tended to boost their children's attainment, the accumulated effects of individual choosing were to increase educational inequalities and social polarisation (Adler et al, 1989, p. 208). That conclusion reflects a complication in assessing school effectiveness long recognised in arguments over (for example) the busing of students to otherwise segregated schools; students are consumers of education, but they are also part of the supply process, so that the exit of some diminishes the chances of others (Murnane, 1990).

Secondly, the effective exercise of choice by individual parents depends on access to relevant information about available schools, and the capacity and confidence to sift it, make a decision, and take whatever follow-up action is needed. Moore's (1990) study of public choice in Chicago contrasts the many parents who did not apply for an option school or did so with little understanding, with the minority who were 'well connected to networks of information and influence' and ready to devote great energy to 'mastering the intricacies of admissions and negotiating the outcomes they wanted'. He describes that minority as being 'typically middle-class'. But there is also some evidence to counter the notion that competence in choosing schools 'wisely' is distributed along social class lines (Bauch, 1989; Adler et al, 1989). Indeed, the striking improvements in school performance achieved in Manhattan's District 4 are cited as demonstrating how parental choice can work in an inner-city area suffering all the disadvantages of urban dereliction (Domanico, 1989).

It must be doubted, however, whether the power of exercising choice is anything like equal where demand so exceeds supply that schools can choose from among their applicants. Magnet schools illustrate that constraint. It is claimed, justifiably, that they offer more open access than do neighbourhood schools in 'superior' neighbourhoods, especially those suburban schools which are 'mostly open only to white families and calibrated to their income' (Metz, 1990, p. 114). But generalisations are difficult. Some are academically selective. Some have their intakes controlled in the ways mentioned earlier. In many districts, they have developed into a network of variously specialized forms of secondary education, recruiting on the basis of pupil and parent interest. Ideally, and provided that it also survives that 'backward policing' of effectiveness which direct accountability to customers is intended to provide, then each 'speciality school' should secure its appropriate 'niche in the market' and attract customers across racial and social class boundaries. In practice, a neat matching of special demand with special supply is not what occurs because parents do not see the alternatives as being different but equal. Elite schools like the Bronx High School of Science can be choosy on such traditional grounds as academic merit or apparent respectability, and it is significant that among the indicators offered by Domanico (1990) for the success of 'public choice' in Manhattan's District 4 is the markedly higher success rate in the competition for entry to such schools. At less rarified levels, doubts persist about whether magnets pass the 'critical equity test' – namely, that their benefits extend to the socially disadvantaged – and about how far their apparent effectiveness is attributable to the best-motivated students in the 'best' schools to the exclusion of those evidently 'at risk' (Alves and Willie, 1987; Moore and Davenport, 1989; Moore, 1991). Similar questions are being asked about city technology colleges in the UK, despite the official requirement to recruit socially 'representative' intakes, since over and above any entry tests of pupil and parent commitment to this new choice of school is the possibility of self-selection acting as a powerful social filter within each 'quota' (Walford, et al, 1991). If choice is likely to be 'disproportionately exercised by motivated and well-informed students and parents' (Rosenberg, 1989, p. 43), it is also likely to be disproportionately available to 'valued customers' where the prestige of particular schools or types of school creates a seller's market.

3. Choice, diversity and hierarchy

Preoccupied with educational improvement, Lieberman (1989) argues that competition is most effective when it involves a standardized product or service because choice is then shaped by relative quality alone. It is more usual, however, to argue that choice works best when it stimulates competition between different models of educational excellence. Greater diversity of provision is therefore commonly presented as both a prior condition for, and a consequence of, enhanced parental choice. In this section of the paper we consider some of the dilemmas which arise. We do so briefly in relation to notions of 'common' schooling and then consider the endemic problem of securing diversity without a hierarchy of institutions which distorts both supply and demand.

Diversity has been officially sponsored within public education, for example, in the promotion of magnet schools and the 'sort of magnet school' represented in England by city technology colleges. The grant-maintained schools created when their parents vote to opt-out of local education authority control are intended by the British Government to add 'a new and powerful dimension to the ability of parents to exercise choice within the publicly provided sector of education' and as providing scope for schools to develop distinctive characteristics and then compete for pupils on that basis (DES, 1987). But the most enthusiastic advocates of choice tend to see, in any system of public provision, tight structural limits on the freedom of schools 'to find some specialized segment of the market to which they can appeal' (Chubb and Moe, 1990, p. 550). That particular rejection of mere reform in favour of wholesale reconstruction assumes that public schools are inevitably standardized through the imposition by public authority of 'higher order values'. Since the exercise of that authority is inevitably contested by various interest groups, and it is necessary to avoid too much disruption after every post-election transfer of power, change has to be confined to what can be accepted or at least tolerated by groups temporarily defeated in that struggle. Striving to avoid giving positive offence produces schools which are thereby unlikely positively to please, and likely to be both mediocre and similar in character. Even, then, the wishes of parents who lack political clout are liable to be disregarded. Thus Arons (1989) argues that 'educational bureaucracies are structurally unable to respect pluralism' because of their obligation to uphold (or at least not depart far from) supposedly 'common' values, which are the values of those who do possess 'clout'.

In sharp contrast, a lack of confidence in the willingness of some public authorities to uphold 'common' values has presented segments of the British Right with a considerable dilemma. Thus Margaret Thatcher complained to the 1987 Conservative Party Conference that opportunities were being snatched away from children, especially in the inner-cities, 'by hard-Left education authorities and extremist teachers' determined to replace 'real' education with political slogans and such aberrations as 'anti-racist mathematics'. The inclusion in the 1988 Reform Act of open enrolment and schools' right to opt-out of Local Authority control were intended to subject what the *Sun* newspaper called 'barmy burgherism' to the restraining influence of parental choice. At the same time, a neo-conservative concern to defend the 'national culture' against alien influence assigned some value to a limited National Curriculum until the disciplining effects of parental 'good sense' had time to work (Hillgate Group, 1987; Whitty, 1989; Ball, 1990, pp. 46–56). Yet in its actual and extensive statutory form, the National Curriculum is open to the obvious objection of being fundamentally incompatible with that 'trust' in the interplay of supply and demand to which the Conservative Government also declares itself committed (Sexton, 1988). And there is one form of demand which some of the Right manage (with difficulty) to combine with their commitment to authoritative transmission of 'national' culture. It reflects what they see as the right of any parents to contain their children's schooling within their own cultural or religious frame of reference, a right which deserved Government encouragement for 'new and autonomous schools . . . including Church schools of all denominations, Jewish schools, Islamic schools and such other schools as parents desire' (Hillgate Group, 1987; Marks 1990). In that context, approving reference is made to the Netherlands because of the state's obligation to support any school which attracts a measure of parental support set sufficiently low to enable religious, ethnic and other minority groups to found and maintain their 'own' schools. Although it is unclear how far the state's acceptance of that funding obligation represents a commitment to cultural pluralism or a well-established accommodation between competing groups too powerful to disregard (Glenn, 1988), it is cited as a model for the 'truly radical' mechanism of voucher systems in which capital costs would be included, thereby avoiding that favouring of existing schools which is inevitable with vouchers valued at (for example) the average recurrent costs of a school place.

More familiar arguments for vouchers to be cashable at public or private schools reflect traditional arguments against a public monopoly of educational provision and, in the United States, traditional defence of private schools as necessary escape routes for dissenters from 'majoritarian politics' (Arons, 1989, p. 68; Rebell, 1989). But the current enthusiasm for parental choice, and for diversifying the form and content of educational provision, has attracted wide-ranging support which cuts across traditional Left-Right divisions. Thus the failures of the public school system in Chicago led to reforms offering choice and devolution being pushed through by an alliance of New Right advocates of individual choice, black groups seeking community control of schools, disillusioned white liberals and some former student radicals of the 1960s (Hess, 1990). In Britain, where social democratic policies have often been perceived as monocultural as well as unduly bureaucratic and alienating, it is claimed that many black parents positively welcome the new opportunities offered by the Reform Act to be closer to their own children's schools (Phillips, 1989). While New Right support for their aspirations can be seen as opportunistic, the aspirations are real. If comprehensive education in England was based on the assumption that social class divisions were the predominant lines of fissure in modern society, new forms of schooling may be partly a response to the changing modes of social solidarity associated with what is sometimes termed 'post-modernity' (Whitty, 1991).

In so far as the various school choice policies reflect growing heterogeneity, fragmentation and difference in modern societies, they may represent much more than an expression of Thatcherite or Reaganite ideology which will fade with changes of government. Indeed, it might be argued that those who cling to traditional social democratic approaches to educational provision are wedded to a conception of equity, defined as equality of treatment, that is now quite inappropriate. Yet the working out of parental choice raises traditional social democratic questions – most obviously, and as formulated by Bob Dunn (Minister of State during the passage through Parliament of the Education Reform Act), whether 'more specialized, differentiated schools' can be promoted 'without any one being regarded as inferior to the others' (*Education* 8 July, 1988).

The conventional sociological view has been that parity of esteem is unlikely between schools which are related to very different levels in higher education and very different segments of the labour market, so that the relative opportunities which parents perceive schools of different types to offer is a powerful constraint on the capacity of parental choice to generate diversity. It is more likely that 'speciality schools' will represent a new form of selective tracking (Moore, 1990). Thus in the New York system of high schools, described by HMI (1989) as 'too specialized and too hierarchical in its structure', it is the most obviously 'academic' of those schools which head the hierarchy. In Britain, and apart from a small, explicitly 'progressive' segment, leading schools in the private sector have offered a single choice – namely, a traditional academic education (Edwards et al, 1989a). They would certainly not support the claim, based on American conditions, that 'major educational innovations ordinarily begin outside the public sector' where they do not have to clear the 'majoritarian hurdle' (Coleman, 1990, p. xviii). It is very much easier to argue in the British context that educational innovation has persistently failed when it has diverged too sharply from the academic model firmly entrenched in the high status private sector and in the more favoured public schools.

Indeed, while greater choice within the public sector is often associated with more differentiated provision, it is also seen from the Right as the most effective defence of traditional academic standards (Sexton, 1987; O'Hear, 1991). It is however, likely to reinforce the prestige of forms of schooling most obviously associated with enhanced life chances. Thus it has been predicted that both city technology colleges and grant-maintained schools will wish to move up the traditional hierarchy of esteem and develop an image which appeals to parents seeking a 'traditional' secondary education for their children (Walford et al, 1991; Fitz et al, 1991). Rather than promoting that positive diversity for which market advocates hope, these reforms would then continue the long history of hierarchy and distinction in English education.

Comprehensive schools were partly intended to break the historic links between particular forms of provision and particular social classes. While the predominantly black and working class populations of the inner cities never gained an equitable share of educational resources under social democratic policies, the abandonment of interventionist planning in favour of the market seems unlikely to solve that endemic problem. Indeed, whatever the intentions of their sponsors, it seems that market-oriented reforms and schools of choice are as likely to reinforce structural inequalities as to challenge them. For those members of disadvantaged groups who are not sponsored out of schools at the bottom of the status hierarchy, either on grounds of exceptional academic ability or alternative definitions of merit such as those favoured by city technology colleges, the new arrangements may thus prove to be a powerful way of reproducing deeply entrenched class divisions. Even if the rhetoric of choice resonates with a positive vision of diversity within a post-modern society, the reforms may, in practice, serve to sustain more familiar patterns of social inequality. At the very most, they are likely to relate to a version of post-modernity that emphasises 'distinction' and 'hierarchy' within a fragmented social order rather than one that positively celebrates 'difference' and 'heterogeneity' (Lash, 1990).

Nevertheless, even if there has been no clear 'post-modernist break' in the nature of either society or schooling, traditional social democratic approaches to education policy which favour the idea of a common school, and usually some version of a common curriculum, will have to find ways of responding to those changes that are taking place in contemporary societies. Furthermore, they will need to respond to both the rhetoric and the reality of diversity and choice. Current approaches to citizenship in terms of 'creating unity without denying specificity' (Mouffe, quoted in Giroux, 1990) present a major challenge for future education policy. Glenn (1987) has taken up this challenge for the public school system in the United States, while in England Donald (1989) has called for approaches based on 'participation and distributive justice rather than simple egalitarianism and on cultural heterogeneity rather than a shared humanity'. He argues that this puts a question mark against the very idea of comprehensive education. While we are not convinced that this is necessarily the case, we do accept the need to rethink some old orthodoxies.

Conclusion

Our purpose in this paper has not been to re-assert old-style collectivist principles, but to question that blend of pessimism and optimism which is so marked a feature of recent advocacy of enhanced parental choice – pessimism about the capacity of public education to change or be changed, and optimism about the capacity of a 'free' educational market to guarantee a raising of standards and a breaking up of the 'monolith' for the benefit of all. We believe that giving priority to individual rights of exit from schools which are considered unsatisfactory may provide additional escape routes for some while undermining the will and capacity to reform those schools which the least advantaged attend. But while the 'right' balance between individual rights and collective goals is a value question, not one which will be decided by the weight of evidence, it is important to examine carefully those operating assumptions about how choice works which are made (often implicitly) by those for whom the benefits of an open market appear self-evident.

References

ADLER, M., PETCH, A. and TWEEDIE, J. (1989) *Parental Choice and Educational Policy* (Edinburgh, Edinburgh University Press).

ALVES, M. and WILLIE, C. (1987) Controlled choice assignments: a new approach to school desegregation, *The Urban Review*, 19(2), 67–86.

ALVES, M. and WILLIE, C. (1990) Choice, decentralization and desegregation: the Boston 'controlled choice' plan. In W. Clune, and J. Witte (eds) *Choice and Control in American Education. Volume 2: The Practice of Choice, Decentralising and School Restructuring* (London and New York, Falmer Press).

ARONS, S. (1989) Educational choice as a civil rights strategy. In N. Devins (ed) (1989) *Public Schools, Private Values* (Barcombe and Philadelphia, Falmer Press).

ASHWORTH, J., PAPPS, I. and THOMAS, B. (1988) *Increased Parental Choice: an economic analysis of some alternative methods of management and finance of education* (Warlingham, Institute of Economic Affairs Education Unit).

BALL, S. (1990) *Politics and Policy Making: explorations in policy sociology* (London, Routledge).

BAUCH, P. (1989) Can poor parents make wise educational choices?. In W. Boyd and J. Cibulka (eds) *Private Schools and Public Policy: international perspectives* (Lewes, Falmer Press).

BLANK, R. (1990) Educational effects of magnet schools. In W. Clune and J. Witte (eds) *Choice and Control in American Education, Vol. 2* (London and New York, Falmer Press).

CHUBB, J. and MOE, T. (1990) *Politics, Markets and America's Schools* (Washington D.C., Brookings Institution).

CLINCHY, E. (1989) Public school choice, *Phi Delta Kappen*, 71(4), 289–294.

COLEMAN, J. (1990) Choice, community and future schools. In W. Clune and J. Witte (eds) *Choice and Control in American Education. Vol. 1, The Theory of Choice and Control in Education* (London and New York, Falmer Press).

COLEMAN, J. and HOFFER, T. (1987) *Public and Private High Schools* (New York, Basic Books).

COOPER, B. (1987) *Magnet Schools* (Warlingham, Institute of Economic Affairs Education Unit).

COX, C. and MARKS, J. (1989) *The Insolence of Office* (London, Claridge Press).

DEPARTMENT OF EDUCATION AND SCIENCE (1986) *A New Choice of School* (London, DES).

DEPARTMENT OF EDUCATION AND SCIENCE (1987) *Grant-Maintained Schools: Consultation Paper* (London, DES).

DOMANICO, R. (1989) *Model for Choice: a Report on Manhattan's District 4* (New York, Manhattan Institute for Educational Innovation, Policy Paper No. 1).

DOMANICO, R. (1990) *Restructuring New York's City's Public Schools: the case for public school choice.* (New York: Manhattan Institute for Educational Innovation, Policy Paper No. 3).

DONALD, J. (1989) Interesting Times, *Critical Social Policy*, 9(3), 39–55.

ECHOLS, F., McPHERSON, A. and WILLMS, D. (1990) Parental choice in Scotland *Journal of Education Policy*, 5(3), 207–222.

EDWARDS, A., FITZ, J. and WHITTY, G. (1989a) Private schools in England and Wales. In G. Walford (ed) *Private Schools in Ten Countries* (London, Routledge).

EDWARDS, A., FITZ, J. and WHITTY, G. (1989b) *The State and Private Education: an evaluation of the Assisted Places Scheme* (Barcombe, Falmer Press).

FITZ, J., HALPIN, D. and POWER, S. (1991) Grant-maintained schools: a third force in education? *Forum*, 32(1), 36–38.

FLIEGEL, S. (1990) Creative non-compliance. In W. Clune and J. Witte (eds) *Choice and Control in American Education, Vol. 2* (London and New York, Falmer Press).

FLEW, A. (1987) *Power to the Parents: reversing educational decline* (London, Sherwood Press).

FLEW, A. (1988) *Education Tax Credits* (Warlingham, Institute of Economic Affairs Education Unit).

FRIEDMAN, M. and FRIEDMAN, R. (1980) *Free to Choose* (London, Secker and Warburg).

FULLINWIDER, R. (1989) The state's interest in racially non-discriminatory education. In N. Devins (ed) *Public Schools, Private Values* (Lewes and Philadelphia, Falmer Press).

GEWIRTZ, S., WALFORD, G. and MILLER, H. (1991) Parents' individualist and collectivist strategies, *International Studies in Sociology of Education*, 1, 173–192.

GIROUX, H. (ed) (1990) *Post-Modernity, Feminism and Cultural Politics* (New York, State University of New York Press).

GLENN, C. (1988) *Why Parents in Five Nations Choose Schools* (Massachusetts, Department of Education, Office of Educational Equity).

GLENN, C. (1990) Parent choice: a state perspective. In W. Clune and J. Witte (eds) *Choice and Control in American Education, Vol. 1.* (London and New York, Falmer Press).

HATTON, E. (1985) Equality, class and power: a case study, *British Journal of Sociology of Education*, 6(3), 255–272.

HER MAJESTY'S INSPECTORATE (1990) *Teaching and Learning in New York City Schools* (London, Her Majesty's Stationery Office).

HESS, G. (1990) *Chicago School Reform: what it is and how it came to be* (Chicago, Panel on Public School Policy and Finance).

HILLGATE GROUP (1987) *The Reform of British Education* (London, Claridge Press).

JOSEPH, K. (1976) *Stranded on the Middle Ground* (London, Centre for Policy Studies).

LASH, P. (1990) *Sociology of Post-Modernism* (London, Routledge).

LEVIN, H. (1968) The failure of the public schools and the free market remedy, *Urban Review*, June, pp. 32–37.

LIEBERMAN, M. (1989) *Privatization and Educational Choice* (London, Macmillan).

MADDAUS, J. (1990) Parental choice of school: what parents think and do. In C. Cazden (ed) *Review of Research in Education* (American Educational Research Association).

MARKS, J. (1990) Let natural justice be done, *Times Educational Supplement*, 17 August.

METZ, M. (1990) Potentialities and problems of choice in desegregation plans. In W. Clune and J. Witte (eds) *Choice and Control in American Education, Vol. 1* (London and New York, Falmer Press).

PARENTAL CHOICE AND EDUCATIONAL REFORM

MOORE, D. (1990) Voice and choice in Chicago. In W. Clune and J. Witte (eds) *Choice and Control in American Education, Vol. 2* (London and New York, Falmer Press).

MOORE, D. and DAVENPORT, S. (1989) *School Choice: the New Improved Sorting Machine* (Chicago, Designs for Change).

MURNANE, R. (1990) Family choice. In W. Clune and J. Witte (eds) *Choice and Control in American Education, Vol. 1* (London and New York, Falmer Press).

MURPHY, R., BROWN, P. and PARTINGTON, J. (1990) *An Evaluation of the Effectiveness of City Technology College Selection Procedures* (A Report to the Department of Education and Science).

O'HEAR, A. (1991) *Education and Democracy: against the educational establishment* (London, Claridge Press).

ORFIELD, G. and PESKIN, L. (1989) Metropolitan high schools: income, race and inequality, *Journal of Education Policy*, 4 (5), 27–54.

PETERSON, P (1990) Monopoly and competition in American education. In W. Clune and J. Witte (eds) *Choice and Control in American Education, Vol. 1* (London and New York, Falmer Press).

PHILLIPS, M. (1988) Why black people are backing Baker, *The Guardian*, 9 September.

REBELL, M. (1989) Values inculcation and the schools. In N. Devins (ed) *Public Values and Private Schools* (Lewes and Philadelphia, Falmer).

REGAN, D. (1990) *City Technology Colleges: Potentialities and Perils* (London, Centre for Policy Studies).

ROSENBERG, B. (1989) Public school choice: can we find the right balance? *American Educator*, 1–14 and 40–45.

SELDON, A. (1981) *Wither the Welfare State* (London, Institute of Economic Affairs).

SELDON, A. (1986) *The Riddle of the Voucher: an inquiry into the obstacles to introducing choice and competition in state schools* (London, Institute of Economic Affairs).

SEXTON, S. (1987) *Our Schools: a Radical Policy* (Warlingham: Institute of Economic Affairs Education Unit).

SEXTON, S. (1988) *A Guide to the Reform Bill* (Warlingham: Institute of Economic Affairs Education Unit).

SHERMAN, J. (1983) A new perspective on state aid to private education, *Phi Delta Kappen*, (May), 654–655.

SMITH, D. and TOMLINSON, S. (1989) *The School Effect: a Study of Multi-Racial Comprehensives* (London, Policy Studies Institute).

TAYLOR, C. (1990) *Raising Educational Standards: a Personal Perspective* (London, Centre for Policy Studies).

WALFORD, G. and MILLER, H. (1991) *City Technology College* (Milton Keynes, Open University Press).

WHITTY, G. (1989) The New Right and the national curriculum: state control or market forces? *Journal of Education Policy*, 4 (4), 329–341.

WHITTY, G. (1991) Recent educational reform: is it a post-modern phenomenon? (Conference on 'Reproduction, Social Inequality and Resistance', University of Bielefeld, October).

Correspondence:
Professor Geoff Whitty
Department of Policy Studies
Institute of Education
University of London
55–59 Gorden Square
London WC1H 0NT

[19]

The Social Economy of Parent Choice and the Contract State

DAVID HOGAN

This chapter pursues a series of what might be called ontological questions about the nature of markets, choice and social action. Please do not get me wrong. For all it's intellectual pretensions, this is not a philosophical essay. Rather, it focuses on the kind of conceptual resources that two very different theories of the economy — neo-classical economics and social economy theory — provide for the analysis of current proposals to transform the political economy of schooling by significantly expanding the opportunities for 'parent choice' and the role of 'educational markets' in the system of school governance. The primary context of my argument is the United States where the parent choice movement has gone from strength to strength over the past decade, fuelled by a volatile mix of often atrociously poor urban schooling, middle class status panic and credentialing anxiety, right-wing Republican hostility to the state, and fundamentalist Christian opposition to godless public schooling and secular humanism. However, the theoretical issues embedded in the parent choice debate apply equally well to Australia, given Australia's long history of state aid to private schools and the current effort to displace the centralised bureaucratic state with the contract state that could very well see the further expansion of contractualist principles extended to schooling in the very near future (McGuire 1994).

The theoretical justification of this displacement is the neo-classical assumption that educational markets are far more effective in promoting student achievement ('productive efficiency') and optimising the satisfaction of parent preferences ('exchange efficiency') than state-based allocative processes. The burden of my argument is that neo-classical theory depends on unrealistic and mischievous assumptions about the nature of markets, preferences and choices, and that the extension of market principles in education is likely to deepen and legitimate existing social divisions within Australia. Indeed, we might think of the US experience of markets in schooling as a cautionary tale, an admonitory parable, of what would likely happen in Australia if it were to extend significantly the role of educational markets in education. This is not to say that contractualist principles are incapable of intellectual justification given certain very strict conditions, although I have doubts about this as well, Anna Yeatman notwithstanding (Yeatman 1995). Rather, it is to argue that contractualist principles cannot be adequately defended by resort to neo-classical claims that a contractualist economy would optimise exchange efficiency or social welfare understood as the satisfaction of consumer preferences.

The Gospel According to Chubb and Moe: The Eschatology of the Market

Until the early 1980s, supporters for parental choice in education typically relied on normative arguments to make their case: that parents had the right to send their children to the school of their choice, that parents were better judges and protectors of their children's interests than the state or its functionaries, and that the principle of equal opportunity required that all parents, irrespective of social background, should have the effective ability to send their children to the school of their choice (Friedman 1962; Coons and Sugarman 1978). But with the publication of the research of James Coleman, Thomas Hoffer and Sally Kilgore on student achievement in the early 1980s, supporters of parent choice began to deploy a powerful new empirical argument to support their case: Catholic schools, and private schools generally, were significantly more successful than public schools in creating effective educational 'communities' and promoting student achievement. It therefore followed that the most effective strategy for increasing levels of school achievement in the nation's schools was to give parents the right and the economic wherewithal to send their children to private schools of their choice (Coleman, Hoffer and Kilgore 1981, 1982; Coleman and Hoffer 1987).

Coleman, Hoffer and Kilgore's argument provoked a storm of criticism and counter-argument throughout the 1980s (Coleman and Hoffer 1987). Then, in the late 1980s, John Chubb and Terry Moe took up Coleman *et al.*'s argument and attempted to give it extra spit and polish by offering a fuller explanation of why private schools appear to be generally more effective than public schools in promoting student achievement (Chubb and Moe 1990). Using an extended version of Coleman *et al.*'s national data base, Chubb and Moe developed two general arguments. First, they argued that school organisation is a function of the school's 'institutional environment' rather than the technical properties of the instructional process or the social demography of the student population (Chubb and Moe 1990: 2). Chubb and Moe then went on to argue that

> the specific kinds of democratic institutions by which American public education has been governed for the last half century appears to be incompatible with effective schooling. Although everyone wants good schools, and although these institutions are highly sensitive to what people want, they naturally and routinely function to generate just the opposite — providing a context in which the organisational foundations of effective academic performance cannot flourish or take root.

As a consequence, 'the problem of ineffective performance is likely to continue' so long as the institutions of direct democratic control continue to register citizen preferences, translate them into school policy, and institutionalise them as organisational practices through centralised bureaucratic means. Efforts to reform public schools that rely on the institutions of direct democratic control to directly supply educational services will inevitably fail; effective schooling cannot be mandated from above by bureaucratic means but will have to be generated from below in a decentralised market system based on parental choice and autonomous schools in a deregulated supply system (Chubb and Moe 1990: 2, 23, 31, 37–44, 188–9).

Chubb and Moe's second general argument centred on the claim that student achievement is a function of school organisation and thus ultimately of the structure of school control. Schools that are subject to relatively high levels of bureaucratic control inhibit or suppress student achievement; schools that are relatively free of bureaucratic control promote student achievement. Public schools are of the former kind, private schools of the latter. Democratic politics in the public school sector diminishes student achievement because democratic politics promotes centralised bureaucratic control and therefore inhibits school 'autonomy', while the structure of governance in the private school sector — a decentralised market system — enhances student achievement. And it does so because private schools have sufficient autonomy from democratic politics and centralised bureaucracy to develop those organisational characteristics necessary for high student performance — an ambitious academic program, strong educational leadership, high levels of teacher professionalism, tight discipline, vigorous tracking and so on. As Chubb and Moe report,

> institutions of direct democratic control promote ineffective school organisations. Driven by politics, these institutions encourage the bureaucratisation and centralisation of school control and discourage the emergence of coherent, strongly led, academically ambitious, professionally grounded, teamlike organisations. Institutions of market control encourage pretty much the opposite.

For Chubb and Moe, the policy implication is quite obvious: educational reform based on 'school autonomy and parent-student choice, rather than direct democratic control and bureaucracy' will transform American education where all other reform efforts have and will fail. Indeed, 'choice is a panacea' (Chubb and Moe 1990: 141, 186, 217).

In effect, Chubb and Moe argued that parent choice and deregulated educational markets would promote two long-term efficiency benefits in education. First, expanding parent choice would increase 'exchange efficiency' in the educational market, and thus the overall level of social welfare, by improving the match between family educational preferences and the supply of schooling. Second, parent choice would significantly increase the 'productive efficiency' of schools by improving student achievement levels, in part by securing a better fit between schools and students ('allocative efficiency') and in part by the ability of market competition to improve the quality of instructional practices in schools ('technical efficiency'). I have argued elsewhere that for a variety of reasons — methodological, analytical, conceptual and empirical — the productive efficiency arguments fails (Hogan 1992). Here I want to take up a series of questions that bear on the issue of exchange efficiency: How do economists demonstrate that a particular policy will improve exchange efficiency? What kind of assumptions do they make? How realistic are they? What is a market and what is consumers' choice?

The Social Ontology of Neo-classical Economics

I will begin these metaphysical inquiries with a little known but I think revealing footnote in intellectual history. It centres on the fact that all the great classical economists, from Adam Smith through David Ricardo and on to Karl Marx, had almost nothing to say about the nature of the market as a social institution — that is, as an institutionalised form of social exchange. Adam Smith, for example, mentions the market once in the 1100-odd pages of *An Inquiry into the Nature and Causes of the Wealth of Nations* in a chapter entitled 'That the Division of Labor is Limited by the Extent of the Market'. Indeed, even this reference is purely nominal, since Smith is entirely preoccupied by the division of labour rather than the market as a system of social exchange (Smith 1976: Vol. 1, Bk 1, Ch. 3). Similarly, David Ricardo, arguably the greatest classical economist of all, has almost nothing to say about the nature of the market (Blaug 1978). Perhaps even more surprisingly, the three volumes of Marx's *Capital*, despite his deep concern with many issues bearing on market relations, contain only one 10-page chapter on social exchange in which he uses the word market only twice — and in passing (Marx 1967: Vol. 1, Ch. 2). And so on through to the present day. Joseph Schumpeter's immensely erudite and very long (some 1200 pages) *History of Economic Analysis*, published in 1954, for example, includes no section on 'the market' nor lists it in a subject index that is 30 pages long (Schumpeter 1954).

If classical economic theorists felt no need to discuss the nature of the market as a social institution, neither do neo-classical economists. What they do instead is focus on the economic functions of the market abstracted from the social economy. To neo-classical economics, markets are impersonal and highly efficient mechanisms for registering and aggregating consumer preferences, allocating goods and services, and equilibrating supply and demand through the operation of the price mechanism that acts as a 'signalling' device to balance the supply and demand of goods and services. When prices 'clear' the market the market attains 'equilibrium' of the supply and demand functions. When this happens, the market maximises 'exchange efficiency' and achieves a condition of 'Pareto optimality' in which no one person can be made better off without making someone else worse off. Indeed, the central defining claim of neo-classical welfare economics is that the performance of social and economic institutions ought to be evaluated according to how well they produce goods and services in accordance with consumers' preferences (Broadway and Bruce 1984; Samuelson and Nordhaus 1985).

The coherence of the neo-classical theory of the market and consumers' choice depends on three sets of assumptions: one set concerns the relationship between preferences and choices, another the logical requirements of rational choice, and the third the nature of market equilibrium. I will describe each briefly.

The foundation of the neo-classical theory of consumer choice is a theory of individual preferences. One might even say that the theory of preferences essentially expresses an underlying social ontology, perhaps even a neo-classical metaphysic, of the form '*Je préfère, donc je suis*' — 'I prefer, therefore I am'. But beyond claiming that the fundamental, irreducible and incontrovertible data of social life are individual preferences, neo-classical theory makes a number of additional claims. It claims, first of all, that preference satisfaction is measured by the principle of utility and that preference satisfaction is subject to the 'law of diminishing marginal utility'. It also claims that preferences are prior to choice: we choose what we prefer. In fact, neo-classical theory insists on (and axiomatically requires) a tight conceptual connection between choices and preferences. Whereas classical demand theory treated the relationship between choice and preference as an empirical matter, neo-classical economists, following a suggestion by Paul Samuelson, define preferences in terms of the binary relations underlying consistent preferences. Indeed, choices are 'revealed preferences' — that is, choices are a direct function of preferences (Samuelson 1938: 1947). To view a consumer's choice is to know her preferences, and that's all one needs to know about the dynamics of choice. Or, to put in terms of first principles, '*Je choisis, donc je préfère*' ('I choose, therefore I prefer'). In addition, neo-classical theory assumes that preferences are 'convex' — that people have a taste for variety in their consumption patterns. Next, neo-classical theory assumes that consumer preferences are independent of prices and incomes — that is, it assumes that consumer's preferences are exogenous to the market and therefore independent of market transactions. And finally, individual market choices are parametric rather than strategic — that is, choices are made in situations in which the constraints are given or parametric rather than in situations characterised by various kinds of interdependencies and reciprocal expectations.

The second principal component of the neo-classical theory of consumer choice is the stipulation of a set of conditions that define 'rational choice'. First, consumers possess full information about the nature of the products in the market. Second, consumers do not choose randomly or capriciously from among their preferences. Rather, for consumers to choose rationally, they have to rank their preferences in such a way that the preference ordering satisfies a set of consistency standards. An ordinal preference statement (for example, A is taller than B and B is taller than C) generates a 'weakly ordered' preference statement. The most important consistency property of weakly ordered preference statements is transitivity (if X prefers A to B and B to C he must also prefer A to C). The logical properties of interval level preference orderings ('strongly ordered' preference statements) are even more demanding, for in addition to the consistency requirements (usually described in the technical literature as completeness, transitivity and consistency) of weakly ordered preference statements, they must also be 'monotonic' and 'continuous'. (Monotonicity is the assumption that 'more is better'.) Third, consumers desire to maximise the satisfaction of their given preferences as measured by a utility function within a given set of constraints. In fact, 'economic man' — homo-economicus — is simply a special, albeit theoretically privileged, prodigy of rational man whose preference statements are not only robustly complete, comparable, consistent, transitive, continuous and monotonic, but self-interested as well. A fourth assumption — that choices are homogeneous across institutions, that is, that choices are institutionally isomorphic — is not, strictly speaking, a necessary condition of rational choice *per se*, but neo-classical economists assume that it characterises rational choices generally (Arrow 1951, 1974, 1987; Arrow and Hahn 1971; Baumol 1965; Becker 1976; Broadway and Bruce 1984; Denzau 1992; Elster 1985, 1986; Hahn 1981; Harsanyi 1977; Kornai 1971; Leibenstein 1976; Samuelson 1938, 1947; Sen 1970, 1982; Sugden 1981; Winch 1971).

In sum, in its fully developed form, the neo-classical theory of consumer choice assumes choices are instrumental in character, institutionally isomorphic, and made by maximising and self-interested actors with full information and exogenously produced and consistent preferences utilising exogenously given factor endowments in a world in which there are no strategic or social interdependencies. That's quite a lot to ask for, and it's not all. In addition, neo-classical economics requires us to agree to a third set of assumptions. In order to prove formally or mathematically that free markets promote exchange efficiency and move to a condition of Pareto optimality, neo-classical theorists also ask us to make a number of simplifying assumptions about the nature of economic (or social) action and the character of market processes. Most standard accounts of general equilibrium theory include at least 10 such assumptions.

1. They assume perfectly free competition between and among consumers and suppliers so that no buyer or seller can influence market price by their own independent action.
2. They assume perfect mobility of buyers and sellers, that is, buyers and sellers must be able to enter or leave the market at will (the first and second conditions together create perfectly elastic demand and supply schedules).
3. They assume complete information about the quality, price and performance of goods and services available in the market, and the cost of this information must be zero.
4. They assume that the products in the market must be homogeneous, that is, standardised and undifferentiated.
5. They assume transaction costs (the cost of bringing goods and services together for exchange, the costs of executing agreements, etc.) must be zero.
6. They assume that enforcement costs (the costs of enforcing contracts and property rights) must be zero.
7. They assume that the good(s) in the market are of a private rather than a public character, where a 'public good' is defined by the presence of two conditions: jointness in supply (jointness of supply exists when the production costs of a good are all fixed and its marginal costs are zero, so that extending consumption rights to more consumers does not detract from the benefits enjoyed by others) and the production of externalities (where the existence of

externalities is signalled by the existence of 'third party' or 'neighbourhood' effects).

8. They assume that the technical coefficients of the production of the good(s) in the market are known and stable.
9. They assume that individual consumers are rational, that they are rational when they have consistent preferences (in particular, the preferences must be transitive, so that if X prefers A to B and B to C he must also prefer A to C), and they seek to satisfy their preferences in a way that maximises their utility.
10. They assume that individual preferences and factor endowments are exogenously given or independent of market transactions.

When all of these conditions are jointly satisfied, markets can simultaneously attain 'equilibrium' of supply and demand and 'optimality' in exchange efficiency (Arrow 1951, 1974; Arrow and Hahn 1971; Broadway and Bruce 1984; Buchanan 1985; Debreu 1959; Hahn 1981; Little 1957; Musgrave and Musgrave 1973; Nell 1980; Samuelson 1947; Samuelson and Nordhaus 1985; Thurow 1983).

To the lay person, these conditions may look suspiciously like the Holy Grail, or perhaps a neo-classical version of the Ten Commandments (Thou shall not have inconsistent preferences, Thou shall not have endogenous preferences, Thou shall not have public goods, Thou shall think of markets as systems of exchange, and so on) for the axiomatically inclined members of the neo-classical sect. But neo-classical economists take them very seriously, and for good reason: without them, they could not construct the abstract and formal mathematical models of market equilibrium. Of course, this not a new departure for economics, since economists have been enraptured by abstract-deductive models of the economy since at least Ricardo and Senior in the search for 'universally applicable hypotheses ... which transcend institutional, systematic and historical variations' (Wilbur and Jameson 1983: 32; see also Bell and Kristol 1981; Blaug 1980). Although critics have pilloried the general equilibrium model as a 'celestial clockwork', the practitioners of neo-classical economics view their models as nothing more — or less — than scientifically rigorous attempts to delineate the fundamental nomological features of economic action in all its forms. The point of economic models, after all, is not so much to offer specific causal accounts or explanations of real world contingencies and processes but to provide a theoretical basis for the accurate prediction of economic behaviour and its outcomes (Friedman 1979). Moreover, this predictive ability is enhanced by the fact that in the last analysis, all behaviour is economic, that is, based on rational calculations of self-interest. In Gary Becker's words, 'the economic approach is a comprehensive one that is applicable to all human behaviour ...' (Becker 1976: 6–8).

I must confess to more than a little discomfort with the astonishing intellectual hubris of Becker's *pax neo-classicus economicus*. For the moment, however, I want to limit my comments to the claim that economic exchanges can be abstracted from social organisation and cultural patterns. My argument in short is that the abstraction of the market from the economy and the economy from society eviscerates the ability of neo-classical economics to offer an empirically grounded and conceptually coherent account of consumer choice and market processes. This is hardly a new criticism; in fact it has long been a central argument of 'economy and society' theorists who focus on identifying the diverse ways in which social action generally and the economic processes particularly are 'embedded' in and constituted by social structure and cultural patterns (Block 1990; Etzioni 1988; Etzioni and Lawrence 1991; Friedland and Robertson 1989; Granovetter 1985, 1989, 1991; Hart 1989; Hirsch, Michels and Friedman 1990; Holton 1992; Moore 1955; Parsons and Smelser 1956; Polanyi 1944; Stinchcombe 1983; Swedberg 1991; Swedberg, Himmelstrand and Brulin 1990; Weber 1978; Zuckin and DiMaggio 1990). Of course, some economists have been aware of this, and have sought to overcome it. A few apostates have even suggested the necessity for a 'behavioural' theory of consumer choice (Earl 1983). But by far and away the most influential responses to the limitations of formal neo-classical theory centre on two efforts. The first is the attempt to develop a more realistic 'economics of information' and a fuller account of transaction costs (Stigler 1961; Coase 1960). The second is the effort to undertake a little cosmetic surgery on rational choice theory by developing a 'thicker' account of rationality than the formal requirements of rational choice itself permits (Simon 1952, 1959, 1969, 1979; March 1986; Elster 1984, 1985; Leibenstein 1976; Kornai 1971). But while their efforts offer more grounded accounts of information imperfections and consumer choice, they fail to successfully reintegrate the market into the economy and the economy into society. While these revisionist efforts capture the informational, consistency and maximising limitations of mere mortals very well, they are not nearly so successful in capturing the socially embedded character of choice or of acknowledging the existence of systemic informational asymmetries in the market between buyers and sellers or that these generally reflect the unequal distribution of 'informational resources' (Etzioni 1988: 158–9). In the educational market, for example, there is a striking variability across different groups in their access to information, in the kind of information they seek, in the nature of the information sources, in their ability to pay the direct and opportunity costs of securing information that is available, in their interest in getting information, and in their ability to process and use the information that they gather (Bredo 1988; Bridge 1978; Bridge and Blackman 1978; Bryck, Lee and Smith 1990; Coons and Sugarman 1978; Elmore 1990; Hogan 1992; Klees 1974; Larson, McCarthy and Buechler 1990; Levin 1990; Olivas 1981). More broadly still, these revisionist efforts fail to deal with two crippling weaknesses of neo-classical theory — the assumption that preferences are exogenous to the market, and the assumption that individuals enter the market with exogenously determined factor endowments.

Endogenous Preference Formation and Social Interdependency

I noted earlier that general equilibrium theory assumes that preferences are exogenously produced and given. That is, neo-classical economics assumes that the formation of preferences takes place outside the sphere of economic action (Gintis 1969; Hahnel and Albert 1991; Etzioni 1991). This assumption is an immensely important principle of social ontology at the heart of neo-classical theory that reflects the underlying neo-classical presumption that nature (or God if your preferences run that way) wired individuals in a way that is consistent with the formal mathematical proofs of neo-classical economic theorems. But be that as it may, neo-classical economists make conscious use of this assumption in at least six or seven ways: it underpins their assumption that the market can be conceptualised as an institutional 'black box' free of any institutional impediments to its self-equilibrating logic; along with other requisite conditions, it allows neo-classical economists to demonstrate mathematically the ability of a perfectly free competitive economy to achieve Pareto optimality; it gives them permission to assume that the causal relationship between preferences and social action is one-directional, that the direction goes from preferences to social action (i.e. that social action is a function of preferences), that choices are revealed preferences, and that the process of preference formation lies outside the market; it allows them to claim that economic change is a function of changing preferences, not vice versa, and that preferences are independent of prices and incomes; it allows them to assume that the market constitutes what David Gauthier terms a 'morally neutral' zone of individual preference satisfaction (Gauthier 1986: Ch. 4); and it allows them to ignore what social theorists have known at least since Rousseau, Mandeville, Hume, Smith and possibly Locke — that markets generate psychological scarcity and multiply desire (Hogan 1989).

However, is the assumption of exogenous preferences valid, and what are the consequences if it is not? Now, there is more than a little evidence to suggest that in the real world of the marketplace, preferences are not produced exogenously, and that they are, at least in part, produced endogenously within and by the market (Gintis 1974). For example, there is substantial empirical evidence, both historical and ethnographic, that individuals adapt their educational aspirations to existing or anticipated opportunities (Bishop 1987; Collins 1979; Connell, Ashenden, Kessler and Dowsett 1982; Erickson 1987; Fine 1991; Ogbu 1973; Weis 1990; Willis 1977). In addition, to assume that the formation of preferences is a purely exogenous process ignores the manifest evidence that human agents engage in the elaborate management of preferences with the aid of a variety of technologies of self-management, including adjusting their preferences to the relevant possibilities in their actual situations. In fact, economists even have coined a useful term for processes of this kind — 'adaptive preference formation' (Sen 1982; Elster 1984, 1985, 1986; March 1986). Further, there is by now a very large literature on status group competition and the anthropology of consumption that underscores the unmistakable social interdependencies of consumption and taste formation (Weber 1978; Collins 1979). The formation of preferences is 'an intensely social process', as Paul DiMaggio points out: 'Tastes reflect relationships among people and symbolic attributes of discrete objects which may be unrelated to the technical characteristics of the objects themselves'. Consequently, 'tastes are not exogenous, but rather to some extent socially determined: that is, consumption decisions are interdependent ...' (DiMaggio 1989: 124, 125).

The problems with the neo-classical position are as much conceptual as they are empirical. Given the sociability of human beings and the constitutive character of choice and social action, institutions, including market institutions, engender preferences and interests by virtue of the forms of social action and practices they promote. Social structures and institutions are not socially neutral sites in which social action just happens to take place. Rather, social structures and institutions thickly structure (but do not determine) individual understandings, preferences, aspirations and expectations, and these in turn shape the particular choices individuals make from among the ensemble of choices they face. Social actions — individual choices, practices and projects — are thus constituted by, and embody the effects of, social structures and market processes. In effect, the relation between social action and social structure is recursive: the choices that individuals make shape in very important ways not only the kinds of preferences that they will acquire, but who and what they will become, the kind of resources they will have access to, the capacities they will develop, the kind of choices they will be able to make and will in fact make in subsequent periods of time, and, in general, the kind of lives that they will lead. Consequently, preferences and action are both socially constructed and mutually determining. Preferences are thus not so much 'exogenously' created as formed through the socially constructed choices that individuals make. As Sam Bowles and Herb Gintis suggest, the problem with the neo-classical theory of social action is 'its inability to deal with the link between action and the formation of preferences'. It is not so much the case that the individual seeks to satisfy existing preferences as 'that the individual is socially constituted in such a way that preferences and action are mutually determining, and hence that preferences are formed through choice' (Bowles and Gintis 1986: 20–1).

I wish to emphasise that the argument here is not about the efficiency of the market as a mechanism to register and aggregate choices. Instead, the argument is about the way in which markets themselves shape preferences and choices. And if this is the case, the neo-classical abstraction of the market from the economy and the economy from society is ill-conceived. In the first place, it means that the very idea that one can independently measure the level of exchange efficiency in a market in terms of the satisfaction of existing preferences is at best nonsensical and at worst a wilful sociological deceit. Furthermore, the market itself is a source of preferences — and value — in more than one sense. Markets, by virtue of their ability to promote the reduction of values to a common metric and 'the commodification of social life', transform 'the discourse through which value is understood and measured and hence preferences formed' and help define the standards by which preferences are judged. 'Economic life is social in more than a frictional sense. A market is not simply an allocative mechanism' Friedland and Robertson conclude. 'A market is also a system for generating and measuring value, for producing and ordering preferences that in turn become embedded in culture' (Friedland and Robertson 1989: 26–7, 32). In effect, markets, by virtue of the ambient processes of cultural production they generate and are constituted by, generate the very standards, including exchange efficiency, that neo-classical economists use to evaluate market outcomes.

In addition, recognising that preferences are shaped endogenously rather than exogenously means that we also cannot assume that choices are 'revealed preferences'. And if that's the case, we open up a vast conceptual (but sociologically interesting) space between preferences and choices, not to mention choices and consent. How are preferences socially constituted? How are processes of preference formation socially stratified? How is preference formation affected by the distribution of market capacities (resources, information, understandings, opportunities)? How do individuals 'manage' preferences and tailor their choices to their market situation? What, in effect, is the sociology of 'adaptive preference formation'? Consequently, the analytical challenge is not so much to model mathematically the ways in which markets register and aggregate 'revealed preferences', but to investigate empirically the complicated interrelationships between processes of preference formation, the distribution of relevant 'market capacities' and choices. Now, the constitutive qualities of economic choices and social action have not gone unnoticed by some economists uncomfortable with the neo-classical assumption of exogenous preference formation. In fact, as early as 1944 Trygave Haavelmo broke the spell, and others have followed suit since. The nub of their argument is that the reflexive and recursive qualities of social action renders economic behaviour constitutive rather than merely instrumental in character, that social action, including economic action, necessarily takes place in particular institutional environments, and that institutional environments unavoidably bias or 'structure' the pattern or 'supply' of economic activity, human development and preference formation in certain directions. Indeed, some economists have attempted to identify the particular mechanisms — 'myopic habit formation', 'adaptive preference formation', 'purposeful preference development', 'internalisation', or 'technologies of self-management' — that underlie the process of endogenous preference formation. For some critics, the formal consequences of endogenous preference formation are so severe that they render the mathematical proof of Pareto optimality in competitive markets entirely out of the question (Elster 1978; Gintis 1969, 1974; Hahnel and Albert 1991).

For others, however, endogenous preference formation is not formally inconsistent with the demonstration of Pareto optimality in competitive markets, although it clearly alters the mathematics. Hahnel and Albert, for example, argue that endogenous preferences can be reconciled to the requirements of Pareto optimality, so long as the proofs assume an institutional black box in a competitive market economy or what I call a 'thin' theory of social action (Hahnel and Albert 1991: 146–62). But if we drop the neo-classical assumption of an institutional black box and assume instead a moderately 'thick' institutional environment, we are not only confronted with endogenous preference formation but also the systematic biasing or 'structuring' of the pattern or 'supply' of economic activity. This, in turn, Hahnel and Albert argue, generates 'snowballing' non-optimal allocations, warps the pattern of human development in particular directions, and even disguises the distortions from the actors (Hahnel and Albert 1991: 162–84). Consequently, since any actual economic system requires a particular kind of institutional environment to function in, and particular institutional environments unavoidably create a bias in the conditions of relative supply of different economic activities, a particular ensemble of economic institutions results in 'snowballing' non-optimal allocations, the warping of the pattern of human development in particular directions, which disguise the distortions from the actors, and 'result in ever increasing losses of potential well-being' (Hahnel and Albert 1991: 182).

What then does endogenous preference formation mean for the welfare economics of parent choice? At the very minimum, it renders the theory of rational choice and the notion of exchange efficiency deeply problematic, empirically and conceptually. Empirically, it means that we cannot calculate the exchange efficiency of educational markets merely in terms of the satisfaction of existing educational preferences. Rather, since endogenous preference formation renders the structure and the pattern of existing educational preferences contingent outcomes of existing market processes and social divisions, it will be necessary to offer a detailed account of the social formation of the existing pattern of educational preferences. It also means that the calculation of the exchange efficiency of future educational markets will be contaminated by the impact of prior processes of preference formation on the structure and pattern of educational preferences. Furthermore, given the recursive and constitutive effects of social action, the patterns of preference formation and exchange efficiency are very likely to be increasingly suboptimal (i.e. inefficient) over time, distorting and contrary to the ability of actors to make informed and 'rational' choices about their own long-term welfare.

But the challenge posed by endogenous preference formation is not just empirical; it is also conceptual. How can markets function as a 'morally neutral' zone of preference satisfaction when markets themselves not only help generate the preferences but also help define the standards by which preferences are judged? That is, how is it possible for the educational market to provide an independent measure of value — preference satisfaction — when the educational market itself is at least partially responsible for the preferences as well as the culturally constructed standard (exchange efficiency) by which they are evaluated? Clearly, exogenous preference formation renders the very idea of exchange efficiency and Pareto optimality circuitous and tautological as a measure of social or individual welfare. In addition, although neo-classical theory justifies market institutions in terms of their contribution to exchange efficiency and exchange efficiency on the basis of exogenous preferences, parent choice advocates recognise that educational choices themselves necessarily involve changes in at least two sets of preferences — the preferences of parents through market competition, and the preferences of children through the choice of school and deliberate instruction. As Herb Gintis suggests, education is a prime example of a conscious attempt to change preferences, or more broadly, individual personalities ... Hence the following problem: Neo-classical theory justifies market institutions on the basis of their contribution to growth and allocational efficiency. The norms of growth and efficiency are in turn justified on the basis of the exogenous-preferences assumption. In view of the empirically-determined importance of education in changing preferences to generate an adequate labor force, the theory then appears involved in a contradiction: the adequate performance of the institutions it recommends requires the invalidation of the assumption on which its recommendations rest (Gintis 1974: 416).

Finally, endogenous preference formation also renders a system of parent choice morally suspect by opening up the possibility of galloping or 'snowballing' individualism. I suppose it is possible that neo-classicists could argue that the kinds of social interdependencies created by human sociability would prevent this. But apart from the fact that to make such an argument would flatly contradict the presupposition of homo-economicus and wreck havoc on general equilibrium theory, human sociability provides no analytical protection for parent choice advocates, since I can think of no imaginable reason why a system institutionally designed to promote competition between parents would at the very same time provide incentives to parents to act in other-regarding ways. If anything, free educational markets are likely to result in snowballing individualism in the educational market and an increasingly pervasive market-based system of social reproduction. And this surely can hardly come as news to neo-classical defenders of parent choice. After all, one of the principal findings of game theory is the recognition of pervasive tensions between individual self-interest and the common good.

Endogenous Factor Endowments and Market Capacities

Neo-classical models of competitive equilibrium also assume that individuals enter the market with exogenously determined factor endowments. That is, neo-classical theory assumes as ontologically given the ownership and possession of relevant factor endowments, no matter how unequal, by individuals when they enter the market as producers or consumers. Consequently, Pareto optimal conditions are quite compatible with any particular distribution of factor endowments and do not promise or entail any redistribution of initial factor endowments. Indeed, Pareto improvements simply entail that, given a particular distribution of factors, no one individual will be made worse off by making someone else better off. By the same token, they do not preclude someone becoming better off so long as no one is made worse off. But to demonstrate mathematically the theoretical ability of the market to attain equilibrium and to demonstrate why social policies that permit markets to function 'autonomously' enhance exchange efficiency and allow the market to attain a Pareto optimum condition, neo-classical economists have to assume as given initial factor endowments. They also insist that while the assumption of exogenous factor endowments simplifies the real world, it is harmless. But why should they simplify the model if they wish to demonstrate the superiority of the model in the real world? Should not its assumptions approximate the real world as much as possible? And far from being 'harmless', a good argument can be made that the assumption of exogenous factor endowments is not harmless at all, but disingenuous and mischievous.

One difficulty centres on the nature of the relevant factor endowments. Neo-classical theory assumes that the relevant factor endowments are land, labour and capital. But that's much too simple. In any kind of market society, the factor endowments that matter most are those that are represented by what Anthony Giddens calls 'market capacities'. In the context of a competitive capitalist economy generally, market capacities take various forms: the private ownership of productive property (i.e. 'capital'), income, wealth (in the form of equity in houses, for example), labour market skills, educational credentials, cultural capital, information, 'habitas', social cognition and 'social capital' (Giddens 1974; Coleman 1990). When individuals enter the market, therefore, they enter in possession of some bundle, big or little, of relevant 'market capacities' that they derived from their families, their schools and their neighbourhoods. How well they do in the marketplace, from the kinds of market choices that they make to the kinds and levels of income and other primary social goods that they earn, will depend on the nature and size of the relevant set of market capacities that they 'own' or have access to. The size and nature of these bundles in turn will be a function of the size and nature of the factor endowments of earlier family/school/neighbourhood market transfers and the ability of successive generations of the family to accumulate and transfer market capacities, whether in the marketplace, in neighbourhoods, in families or in schools.

A second difficulty centres on the nature of the 'economic actor' who neo-classical theorists have enter their theoretical markets. The economic actor of neo-classical economics is an abstract individual unencumbered by the nettlesome contingencies of the real world: while she or he is rational, consistent, self-interested and utility maximising, he or she enters the market with an endogenously determined preference schedule. From a theoretical perspective, therefore, the economic actor is asocial, amoral, classless, raceless, genderless, ageless, tribeless, country-less, even transcultural and transhistorical. In a word, they are everyperson — an abstract individual. The obvious trouble with this is that everyman is no man and everywoman no woman in particular. The 'unencumbered self' is a non-entity, an abstraction, a flight of fantasy, artifice, a neo-classical fiction. In the real world, people enter the market with all manner of contingent characteristics, some of them relatively unimportant, but others deeply and pervasively constitutive. No amount of conceptual huffing and puffing by neo-classical economists can change that. Individuals do not enter the market *tabula rasa*; they enter as individuals socially constituted and endowed within and by families embedded in the social economy: in the social division of labour, in social geography, in the structure of social relations and in the market processes that shape them. Consequently, it makes no sense to think that some of the central factor endowments or market capacities (for example, social cognition, cultural and social capital, education) that individuals enter the market with are, in any significant sense, exogenous to the market. Rather, they are constitutive of individuals when they enter the market and cannot be alienated from them, no matter what conceptual machinery one might use. And if that's the case, it follows that the family — its economy, its social organisation, its projects and practices — just as much as the individual actor, should be the analytical focus of formal theoretical work. But to admit that of course would hopelessly complicate the formal proof of optimising solutions by breaking down the conceptual barrier between the economy and society that neo-classical economics depends on.

A third difficulty centres on what individuals do when they enter the educational marketplace. Neo-classical economics invites us to think of market choices as simple consumption choices. But educational choices are not just simple consumption choices — they are investment choices as well. From the perspective of quality conscious parents, major educational choices — choosing a place of residence, choosing public or private schooling — involve making a major investment decision in a place of residence. As Richard Elmore notes, such decisions are 'lumpy' because of the time, effort and cost involved, and because, once made, they are costly to reverse (Elmore 1988: 83). Buying a house is not the same as buying a pair of jeans or a loaf of bread; indeed, for the vast majority of people it is the single most important investment decision they make. The investment character of educational choices from the perspective of children is even more striking, in that their parents' educational choices have long-term and substantial multiplier effects that have substantial consequences for their economic and social well-being as adults. This is because the market value of the educational credentials they will graduate from high school with will affect the kind of occupation they will enter, the income level they will secure, the kind of work satisfaction they will experience, who they will marry, where they will live, what kind of house and car they will own, and even how many children they will have and what kind of school their children will go to ... and so on. In effect, parent choice involves a choice about the creation — the generation — of particular sets of market capacities that will have a very substantial effect on their children's economic welfare when they enter the labour market. And this is true whether or not parents are active choosers. In a word, major educational choices are not just 'lumpy' but 'super-lumpy'. It is therefore a mistake to view educational choices as mere consumption choices in the shopping mall high school writ large; rather, they are also investments in human capital, cultural property, social capital and competitive advantage. For this reason, if no other, consumption metaphors fail to capture the full economic character of educational choices, whether of the educational choices of parents deciding where to live and what kind of school to send their children to, or of the educational choices students make when they decide what classes to register for or whether to work hard in class.

A fourth difficulty centres on the nature of the reasoning that economic actors employ when they enter the marketplace. For neo-classical economics, economic actors are self-interested agents forever seeking to optimise the satisfaction of their preferences. In effect, self-interested economic actors reason instrumentally to maximise their utilities. Not the least of the difficulties of this view is that it is chronically incapable of handling, without collapsing into hopeless solipsism, the intractable sociability and constitutive character of human culture and the broad range of non-self-interested motives that individual behaviour and social action exhibits, from prudence and anxiety to pride and emulation and then onto sympathy, altruism, trust, commitment, co-operation and loyalty, that enter into human reasoning (Sen 1979, 1982; Taylor 1985, 1989; Bruner 1990; DiMaggio 1989; Geertz 1991; Sahlins 1976, 1991). Like the preferences that they announce, instrumental rationality is a contingent and culturally constructed symbolic schema rather than a fundamental datum of social ontology. While neo-classical economists flatter themselves that custom is merely 'fetishised utility', less parochial observers are likely to agree with Marshall Sahlins (1976: x, viii) that 'culture ... constitutes utility'.

A final difficulty returns us to the fundamental ontological questions that opened this chapter. The difficulty centres on what it is that individuals enter when they 'enter' the 'market'. For neo-classical economics, markets are institutional black boxes that aggregate preferences and balance supply and demand. But this is hardly convincing. Among other properties they have, markets are particular ensembles or configurations of power, social relations, resources, opportunities and rules that are deeply and implacably embedded, in Mark Granovetter's words, 'in social structure, flows of information and influence, networks of social relations, and the exercise of power' (Granovetter 1991: 37; see also Giddens 1984; Friedland and Robertson 1989: 4–16, 29–33). Educational markets, for example, can usefully be thought of as a system of 'opportunity structures' and 'choice sets' in which social action takes place and which is structured by them. Opportunity structures are sets of formal opportunities that define the range of social choices that confront individual actors; 'choice sets' define the effective set of social choices that individuals can make given their relevant market resources or capacities. Choice sets are thus constituted both by the formal structure of opportunity and by the nature of the resources that individuals possess within an opportunity structure. The distribution of these 'resources' or 'capacities' is a function of social structure — the social demography of families, the exercise of state power, and market processes. In the case of parent choice, the kind of educational choices that parents make in educational markets are deeply affected by market-structured opportunities and capacities, from home equity and income level to time, information and the various elements of cultural and social capital — education, skills, sophistication, understandings, energy, effort, sense of efficacy, degree of involvement, networks, support groups and so on — necessary to collect and interpret relevant information and make informed decisions. Like most other market capacities, these are distributed in highly unequal ways throughout the educational market, and differentially transmitted to children through processes of social reproduction (Connell *et al.* 1982).

Markets, then, are not just mechanisms that record and aggregate ontologically prior preferences. Rather, markets are structures of power organised around a system of social (specifically, class) relations that 'structure' social action in determinate ways in which the possession of certain attributes or 'market capacities' advantages some individuals and groups relative to others. Markets are also stratified systems of distribution that distribute fundamental 'primary' social goods — income, wealth, capital, cultural property, authority, respect, even power itself — according to the ownership or control of salient market 'capacities' or 'factor endowments'. And because they do this markets sponsor the creation of recursive relations between situations, choices and preferences: situations shape both preferences and choices, and these recursively structure the nature of situations that confront individual actors. As a consequence, market systems tend to produce class-divided societies and to help 'reproduce' them across time in the absence of countervailing pressures: those individuals that possess the skills, capital or other capacities that the market values and rewards have the means to prosper, while those without do not. In addition, markets, apart from the way they distribute factor endowments or market capacities, also function as mechanisms of social reproduction by virtue of their capacity to generate the various social irrationalities of the social logic of collective action in the educational marketplace, including rampart credentialing inflation and the degradation of educational processes reproduction (Berg 1971; Connell *et al.* 1982; Collins 1971, 1979; Hirsch 1976; Hogan 1996; Olson 1965).

Finally, as both subject (or site) and (object) of social and political action, markets are battlegrounds of social conflict and competing interests, including conflicts over the shape and functioning of the market itself, the system of social mobility, and the distribution of power in its various forms. As a consequence, markets, like most institutions, are political constructions that reflect the distribution of political, economic and cultural power in the society generally. Socially neutral sites of economic exchange for mutual benefit they are not.

Conclusion

It is possible to defend contractualist principles on a variety of grounds: as an expansion of the principle of individual liberty and consent, as a mechanism to improve the productive efficiency of public goods production, as a means of assuring the responsivness and accountability of public goods providers, or as a means of optimising exchange efficiency. In this chapter I have sought to challenge the neo-classical defence of contractualism by denying the usefulness and validity of two assumptions that the neoclassical model of exchange efficiency must necessarily make in order to demonstrate the capacity of markets to maximise welfare. In particular, I have suggested that in the real world of the educational marketplace, educational choices are embedded in, and structured by, social arrangements, including the pattern of social inequalities. Educational choices, like social choices generally, are not socially disembodied acts of pure instrumental cognition but socially constituted in a variety of ways. Further, the embedded and constitutive nature of social action undermines the neo-classical argument that the expansion of educational markets and choice would optimise individual and social welfare. Instead, expanding the role of educational markets is likely to augment, reproduce and legitimate existing social divisions.

None of this is to deny the possibility of mounting a defence of contractualism on other grounds. But, clearly, to defend contractualism by collapsing contract into consent and consent into market choice simply will not do. When all is said and done, basic neo-classical assumptions — the autonomous market, rational choice and homo-economicus, and the use of exchange efficiency objectives as the basis of social policy — rest on a series of sociological fictions and abstractions that are as silly and unfounded as they are dangerous. Indeed, there is a remarkable intellectual homology between neo-classical social ontology (the abstract individual) and metaphysics (the autonomous self-equilibrating market) and the efforts of an earlier generation of rationalist theorists, led by Descartes, to marry a corpuscularian theory of matter derived from Greek atomism to the rise of the new mechanical physics and eventually to a Newtonian image of the universe as a vast celestial clock whose inner workings could be deduced mathematically. The notion that economic action simply reflects the proclivity of self-interested individuals 'to truck and barter', or that the market could be considered an 'autonomous' institution, is an essentially Utopian fantasy that ignores the immensely important role of the modern state and civil society in preventing unregulated market forces from destroying the possibility of social reproduction. A society reduced to calculations of self-interest and instrumental market exchanges would be little more than a 'satanic mill' (Polanyi 1944: Ch. 3). The current attack on the liberal democratic state all rather suggests an attempt to breath life — again — into this Utopian fantasy by ideologues committed to a frontal assault on the social norms, the moral sensibilities, the structures of sociability, the institutional arrangements that support a liberal-democratic society. They appear simply incapable of abiding the possibility that all social relations have not yet been fully reduced to the predictable calculations of homo-economicus and an omnipresent cash nexus in one mutant form or another.

References

Arrow, K. (1951), *Social Choice and Individual Values* (New York: Chapman and Hall)

Arrow, K. (1974), 'General Economic Equilibrium: Purpose, Analytic Techniques, Collective Choice', *The American Economic Review* XVIV(3) (June): 253–72

Arrow, K. (1987), 'Rationality of Self and Others in an Economic System', in R. Hogarth and M. Reder (eds) *Rational Choice: The Contrast Between Economics and Psychology* (Chicago: University of Chicago Press)

Arrow, K. and F. Hahn (1971), *General Equilibrium Analysis* (San Francisco: Holden-Day)

Baumol, W. (1965), *Welfare Economics and the Theory of the State* (Cambridge, MA: Harvard University Press)

Becker, G. (1976), *The Economic Approach to Human Behavior* (Chicago: University of Chicago Press)

Bell, D. and I. Kristol (eds) (1981), *The Crisis in Economic Theory* (New York: Basic Books)

Berg, I. (1971), *Education and Jobs: The Great Training Robbery* (Boston: Beacon Press)

Bishop, J. (1987), 'Why the Apathy in American High schools?', *Educational Researcher* (January–February): 6–10

Blaug, M. (1978), *Economic Theory in Retrospect*, 3rd edn (Cambridge: Cambridge University Press)

Blaug, M. (1980), *Economic Theories, True or False? Methodology of Economics* (Cheltenham: Edward Elgar)

Block, F. (1990), *Postindustrial Possibilities* (Berkeley: University of California Press)

Bowles, S. and H. Gintis (1986), *Democracy and Capitalism* (New York: Basic Books)

Bredo, E. (1988), 'Choice, Constraint and Community', in W. Boyd and C.T. Kerchner (eds) *The Politics of Excellence and Choice in Education* (Philadelphia: The Falmer Press)

Bridge, R. (1978), 'Information Imperfections; the Achilles Heel of Entitlement Plans', *School Review* 86(3): 504–29

Bridge, R. and J. Blackman (1978), *A Study of Alternatives in American Education, Vol. 4: Family Choice in Schooling*, R–2170/4–NIE (Santa Monica, CA: RAND Corp)

Broadway, R. and N. Bruce (1984), *Welfare Economics* (Oxford: Blackwell)

Bruner, J. (1990), *Acts of Meaning* (Cambridge, MA: Harvard University Press)

Bryck, A., V. Lee and J. Smith (1990), 'High School Organization and Its

Effects on Teachers and Students', in W. Clune and J. Witte (eds) *Choice and Control in American Education, Vol. 1: The Theory of Choice and Control in American Education* (Philadelphia: The Falmer Press)
Buchanan, A. (1985), *Ethics, Efficiency and the Market* (Totawa, NJ: Rowman and Allanhead)
Chubb, J. and T. Moe (1990), *Politics, Markets and American Schools* (Washington DC: The Brookings Institution)
Coase, R.H. (1960), 'The Problem of Social Cost', *Journal of Law and Economics* 3: 1–44
Coleman, J. (1990), *Foundations of Social Theory* (Cambridge: The Belknap Press)
Coleman, J. and T. Hoffer (1987), *Public and Private High Schools: The Impact of Communities* (New York: Basic Books)
Coleman, J., T. Hoffer and S. Kilgore (1981), *Public and Private High Schools* (Washington DC: National Centre for Educational Statistics)
Coleman, J., T. Hoffer and S. Kilgore (1982), *High School Achievement* (New York: Basic Books)
Collins, R. (1971), 'Functional and Conflict Theories of Educational Stratification', *American Sociological Review* 36: 1002–19
Collins, R. (1979), *The Credential Society: An Historical Sociology of Education and Stratification* (New York: Academic Press)
Connell, R., D. Ashenden, S. Kessler and G. Dowsett (1982), *Making the Difference* (Sydney: Allen & Unwin)
Coons, J. and S. Sugarman (1978), *Education by Choice* (Berkeley: University of California Press)
Debreu, G. (1959), *Theory of Value* (New York: Wiley)
Denzau, A. (1992), *Microeconomic Analysis: Markets and Dynamics* (New York: Irwin)
DiMaggio, P. (1989), 'Cultural Aspects of Economic Organization', in A. Etzioni and P. Lawrence (eds) *Socio-Economics: Towards a New Synthesis* (Armonk, NY: M.E. Sharpe)
Earl, P. (1983), *The Economic Imagination: Towards a Behavioral Analysis of Choice* (Armonk, NY: M.E. Sharpe)
Elmore, R. (1988), 'Choice in Public Education', in W. Boyd and C.T. Kerchner (eds) *The Politics of Excellence and Choice in Education* (Philadelphia: The Falmer Press)
Elmore, R. (1990), 'Choice as an Instrument of Public Policy: Evidence from Education and Health Care', in W. Clune and J. Witte (eds) *Choice and Control in American Education, Vol. 1: The Theory of Choice and Control in American Education* (Philadelphia: The Falmer Press)
Elster, J. (1978), *Logic and Society* (New York: Wiley)
Elster, J. (1984), *Ulysses and the Sirens: Studies in Rationality and Irrationality* (New York: Cambridge University Press)
Elster, J. (1985), *Sour Grapes: Studies in the Subversion of Rationality* (New

York: Cambridge University Press)

Elster, J. (ed.) (1986), *Rational Choice* (New York: New York University Press)

Erickson, F. (1987), 'Transformation and School Success; The Politics and Culture of Educational Achievement', *Anthropology and Education Quarterly* 18(4) (December): 335–59

Etzioni, A. (1988), *The Moral Dimension: Toward a New Economics* (New York: The Free Press)

Etzioni, A. (1991), 'Contemporary Liberals, Communitarians and Individual Choices', in A. Etzioni and P. Lawrence (eds) *Socio-Economics: Towards a New Synthesis* (Armonk, NY: M.E. Sharpe

Etzioni, A. and P. Lawrence (eds) (1991), *Socio-Economics: Towards a New Synthesis* (Armonk, NY: M.E. Sharpe)

Fine, M. (1991), *Framing Dropouts: Notes on the Politics of an Urban High School* (New York: State University of New York Press)

Friedland, R. and A. Robertson (eds) (1989), *Beyond the Marketplace: Rethinking Economy and Society* (New York: Aldine de Gruyter)

Friedman, M. (1962), *Capitalism and Freedom* (Chicago: University of Chicago Press)

Friedman, M. (1979), 'The Methodology of Positive Economics', in F. Hahn and M. Hollis (eds) *Philosophy and Economic Theory* (Oxford: Oxford University Press)

Geertz, C. (1991), 'Deep Play: Notes on the Balinese Cockfight', in C. Mukerji and M. Schudson (eds) *Rethinking Popular Culture* (Berkeley: University of California Press)

Giddens, A. (1974), *The Class Structure of the Advanced Societies* (New York: Harper Torchbooks)

Giddens, A. (1984), *The Constitution of Society* (Berkeley: University of California Press)

Gintis, H. (1969), Alienation and Power: Towards a Radical Welfare Economics, PhD Dissertation, Economics Department, Harvard University

Gintis, H. (1974), 'Welfare Criteria with Endogenous Preferences: The Economics of Education', *International Economic Review* 15(2), June

Granovetter, M. (1985), 'Economic Action and Social Structure: The Problem of Embeddedness', *American Journal of Sociology* 91(3), November: 481–510

Granovetter, M. (1989), 'The Old and the New Economic Sociology', in R. Friedland and A. Robertson (eds) *Beyond the Marketplace: Rethinking Economy and Society* (New York: Aldine de Gruyter)

Granovetter, M. (1991), 'The Social Constructiuon of Economic Institutions', in A. Etzioni and P. Lawrence (eds) *Socio-Economics: Towards a New Synthesis* (Armonk, NY: M.E. Sharpe)

Hahn, F. (1981), 'General Equilibrium Theory', in D. Bell and I. Kristol (eds) *The Crisis in Economic Theory* (New York: Basic Books)

Hahnel, R. and M. Albert (1991), *Quiet Revolution in Welfare Economics* (Princeton: Princeton University Press)

Harsanyi, J. (1977), *Rational Behavior and Bargaining Equilibrium in Games and Social Situations* (Cambridge: Cambridge University Press)

Hart, K. (1989), 'The Idea of Economy: Six Modern Dissenters', in R. Friedland and A. Robertson (eds) *Beyond the Marketplace: Rethinking Economy and Society* (New York: Aldine de Gruyter)

Hirsch, F. (1976), *Social Limits to Growth* (Cambridge, MA: Harvard University Press)

Hirsch, P., S. Michels and R. Friedman (1990), 'Clean Models and Dirty Hands: Why Economics is Different from Sociology', in S. Zucklin and P. DiMaggio (eds) *Structures of Capital: The Social Organization of the Economy* (Cambridge: Cambridge University Press)

Hogan, D. (1989), 'The Market Revolution and Disciplinary Power: Joseph Lancaster and the Psychology of the Early Classroom system', *History of Education Quarterly* 29(3) (Fall): 381–414

Hogan, D. (1992), 'School Organization and Student Achievement: A Review Essay', *Educational Theory* 42(1) (Winter): 83–105

Hogan, D. (1996), 'To Better our Condition: Educational Credentialing and "The Silent Compulsions of Economic Relations" in the United States, 1830 to the Present', *History of Education Quarterly*, forthcoming

Holton, R. (1992), *Economy and Society* (London: Routledge)

Klees, S. (1974), *The Role of Information in the Market for Educational Services*, Occasional Papers on Economics and the Politics of Education, No. 74–1 (Stanford: School of Education, Stanford University)

Kornai, J. (1971), *Anti-Equilibrium* (Amsterdam: North-Holland)

Larson, C., M. McCarthy and M. Buechler (1990), *Educational Choice: Issues of Policymakers* (Bloomington, IN: Indiana University, Indiana Education Policy Center)

Leibenstein, H. (1976), *Beyond Economic Man: A New Foundation for Micro-Economics* (Cambridge, MA: Harvard University Press)

Levin, H. (1990), 'The Theory of Choice Applied to Education', in W. Clune and J. Witte (eds) *Choice and Control in American Education, Vol. 1: The Theory of Choice and Control in American Education* (Philadelphia: The Falmer Press)

Little, I.M.D. (1957), *A Critique of Welfare Economics*, 2nd edn (Oxford: Clarendon Press)

McGuire, L. (1994), 'Service Delivery Agreements — Experimenting with Casemix Funding and Schools of the Future in Victoria', in J. Alford and D. O'Neill (eds) *The Contract State: Public Management under the Kennett Government* (Geelong: Deakin University Press)

March, J. (1986), 'Bounded Rationality, Ambiguity, and the Engineering of Choice', in J. Elster (ed.) *Rational Choice* (New York: New York University Press)

Marx, K. (1967), *Capital*, F. Engels (ed.) (New York: International Publishers)
Moore, W. (1955), *Economy and Society* (New York: Doubleday)
Musgrave, R. and P. Musgrave (1973), *Public Finance in Theory and Practice* (New York: McGraw-Hill)
Nell, E.J. (1980), 'Cracks in the Neo-Classical Mirror: On the Breakup of a Vision', in E.J. Nell (ed.) *Growth, Profits and Property* (Cambridge: Cambridge University Press)
Ogbu, J. (1973), *The Next Generation: An Ethnography of Education in an Urban Neighborhood* (New York: Academic Press)
Olivas, M. (1981), 'Information Access Inequalities: A Fatal Flaw in Educational Voucher Plans', *Journal of Law and Education* 10(4), October: 441–66
Olson, M. (1965), *The Logic of Collective Action: Public Goods and the Theory of Goods* (Harvard: Harvard University Press)
Parsons, T. and N. Smelser (1956), *Economy and Society: A Study in the Integration of Economics and Social Theory* (London: Routledge and Kegan Paul)
Polanyi, K. (1944), *The Great Transformation* (Boston: Beacon Press)
Sahlins, M. (1976), *Culture and Practical Reason* (Chicago: University of Chicago Press)
Sahlins, M. (1991), 'La Pensee Bourgeoise: Western Society as Culture', in C. Mukerji and M. Schudson (eds) *Rethinking Popular Culture* (Berkeley: University of California Press)
Samuelson, P. (1938), 'A Note on the Pure Theory of Consumer's Behavior', *Economica* 5
Samuelson, P. (1947), *Foundations of Economic Analysis* (Cambridge, MA: Harvard University Press)
Samuelson, P. and W. Nordhaus (1985), *Economics* (New York: McGraw-Hill)
Schumpeter, J. (1954), *History of Economic Analysis* (New York: Oxford University Press)
Sen, A. (1970), *Collective Choice and Social Welfare* (San Francisco: Holden Day)
Sen, A. (1979), 'Utilitarianism and Welfarism', *The Journal of Philosophy* 76(9): 463–89
Sen, A. (1982), *Choice, Welfare and Measurement* (Cambridge: MIT Press)
Simon, H. (1952), 'Theories of Decision Making in Economics and Behavioral Science', *American Economic Review* 49 (June): 253–83
Simon, H. (1969), 'A Behavioral Model of Rational Choice', *Quarterly Journal of Economics*: 99–118
Simon, H. (1979), 'From Substantive to Procedural Rationality', in F. Hahn and M. Hollis (eds) *Philosophy and Economic Theory* (Oxford: Oxford University Press)
Smith, A. (1976), *An Inquiry into the Nature and Causes of the Wealth of Nations*, E. Cannan (ed.) (Chicago: University of Chicago Press)

Stigler, G. (1961), 'The Economics of Information', *The Journal of Political Economy* 59(3) (June): 213–25

Stinchcombe, A. (1983), *Economic Sociology* (New York: Academic Press)

Sugden, R. (1981), *The Political Economy of Public Choice* (New York: Halstead Press)

Swedberg, R. (1991), 'The Battle of the Methods: Towards a Paradigm Shift?', in A. Etzioni and P. Lawrence (eds) *Socio-Economics: Towards a New Synthesis* (Armonk, NY: M.E. Sharpe)

Swedberg, R., U. Himmelstrand and G. Brulin (1990), 'The Paradigm of Economic Sociology', in S. Zuckin and P. DiMaggio (eds) *Structures of Capital: The Social Organization of the Economy* (Cambridge: Cambridge University Press)

Taylor, C. (1985), 'What is Human Agency?', in *Human Agency and Language, Philosophical Papers 1* (New York: Cambridge University Press)

Taylor, C. (1989), *Sources of the Self: The Making of Modern Identity* (Cambridge, MA: Harvard University Press)

Thurow, L. (1983), *Dangerous Currents* (New York: Random House)

Weber, M. (1978), *Economy and Society: An Outline of Interpretive Sociology* (2 vols), G. Roth and C. Wittich (eds) (Berkeley: University of California Press)

Weis, L. (1990), *Working Class Without Work: High School Students in a De-industrializing Economy* (New York: Routledge)

Wilbur, C. and K. Jameson (1983), *An Inquiry into the Poverty of Economics* (Notre Dame, IN: University of Notre Dame Press)

Willis, P. (1977) *Learning to Labor* (London: Saxon House)

Winch, D. (1971), *Analytical Welfare Economics* (Harmondsworth, Middlesex: Penguin)

Yeatman, A. (1995), 'Interpreting Contemporary Contractualism', in J. Boston (ed.) *The State Under Contract* (Wellington: Bridget Williams Books)

Zuckin, S. and P. DiMaggio (1990), 'Introduction', in S. Zuckin and P. DiMaggio (eds) *Structures of Capital: The Social Organization of the Economy* (Cambridge: Cambridge University Press)

[20]

J. EDUCATION POLICY, 1996, VOL. 11, NO. 3, 337–362

In defence of the welfare state and publicly provided education: a New Zealand perspective

Mark Olssen
University of Otago

This paper critically examines the crisis of welfare liberalism with specific reference to New Zealand education in order to speculatively reappraise the central principles upon which a revived welfare state could be constructed and in terms of which publicly provided education can be justified. Specifically it will seek to achieve these goals through a number of interrelated tasks. Firstly, it will examine the claims of neo-liberal theory and argue that contradictions within this theory make its demise likely. To do this it will focus on themes relating to the efficiency of markets, rationality and consumer choice, the state and central planning as well as the issue of liberty. Secondly, in a more positive analysis, it will examine prospects for a return to the welfare state in the near future. This will involve an examination of some important criticisms of the traditional welfare state and an assessment of possible models in terms of which a revived, non-bureaucratic welfare state could be constructed.

There has been a crisis of welfare liberalism in the past decade in New Zealand. The crisis can be seen to originate with the election to office of the Fourth Labour Government in 1984, which saw the introduction of neo-liberal policies in education and social welfare, forcing a reversal of Keynesian economic and social policy, and an assault on the structures and practices of the welfare state.

The crisis itself must be traced to a more deep-seated and global crisis occurring in socialist thought and practice since the Second World War. It has been a crisis of both practice and ideology. At one level the collapse of the communist régimes of eastern Europe can be seen as both the effect of a general ideological crisis of left-wing thought and the cause of its more rapid demise. The collapse of communism has, by association, tainted the respectable left in Western countries. Added to this, the rise of neo-liberalism and of postmodernism has served to undermine the legitimacy of left-wing thought. These developments must themselves be seen in relation to a general post-Fordist diversification of economic and social structure as well as the globalisation of economic, political and cultural life.

The resurgence of neo-liberalism discredited any popular appeal that socialist politics in New Zealand might have had, although even without neo-liberalism they were always only a numerically small proportion of the politically interested population. To a large extent, traditional socialist movements have always struggled for recognition in opposition to the politics of liberalism. What neo-liberalism also effected, however, was to discredit the more moderate policy framework of Keynesianism — leading to a crisis of the welfare state (Joppke 1987). Keynesianism sanctioned a mixed economy and interventionist monetary policy where the role of government and the scope of politics were expanded. As a consequence, during its 'golden years' New Zealand experienced nearly full employment. While Keynesian demand management was the dominant policy framework for more than two decades, from the end of the 1960s it slid into crisis triggered by the general international economic recession of 1974–75, the breakdown of regular exchange rates, the collapse of the profitability of business, and by its inability to maintain full employment. In more general terms, as Offe (1984), Habermas (1975) and O'Connor (1973) explain it, the crisis was a response to the increasing inability to reconcile the problems of capital accumulation with the political processes of democratic management and legitimation.

The neo-liberalism that filled the gap was a revived form of classical liberalism. It critiqued both socialism and the welfare state in one stroke as plagued by the evils of 'statism', 'central planning', and bureaucratic, collective provision. It scolded statist options and posited non-statist alternatives emphasising a greater role for freedom and markets. Socialists and welfare state liberals were outflanked. Many conceded that the emphasis on a state provision had left a lot be desired, that it had been unresponsive to public needs, inefficient in providing for them, and at worst brutal and authoritarian (Martell 1992, 1993, McLennan 1993, Amin 1994).

In the twentieth century, neo-liberal economic doctrines were elaborated by various 'organic intellectuals' in economics, political science and in various business and management studies. Foremost amongst these were the 'Chicago School' of pioneering economic researchers led by Friedrich A. von Hayek (1935, 1944) and Milton Friedman (1962, 1980), and the 'Virginia School' of public choice theorists led by James Buchanan and his researchers at the Virginia Polytechnic's School of Political Science (Buchanan 1960, 1969, 1975, Buchan and Tullock 1962).

Neo-liberals supported the free-market. The associated economic and social policies became central to the state's role in America under Ronald Reagan in the late 1970s, in England under Margaret Thatcher in the 1970s, and in New Zealand under the influence of Roger Douglas, the finance minister of the Fourth Labour Government, in the 1980s. The free-market line's appeal to business was obvious, and, although their ideas seemed extreme, they quickly gathered popular support. The doctrine of monetarism wich entailed restraint of the money supply and the public sector replaced Keynesian demand management throughout OECD countries in the mid 1970s. In addition, and encouraged by international organisations such as the World Bank and the IMF, growth in government was halted in most western advanced economies, the privatisation and commercialisation of the public sector began, and support for income redistribution and universal services became substantially weakened.

This paper will look critically at the crisis of welfare liberalism with specific reference to New Zealand in order to speculatively reappraise the central principles upon which a revived welfare state could be constructed and in terms of which publicly provided education can be justified. It will seek to do this through a number of interrelated tasks. Firstly, it will examine critically the claims of neo-liberal theory, and argue that contradictions contained within these claims make the demise of the theory likely. Specifically, the issues which will be examined include those relating to the efficiency of markets, rationality and consumer choice, the state and central planning, as well as the important issue of liberty. Secondly, in a more positive analysis, I will examine the prospects for a return to the welfare state in the near future. This will involve a two-pronged approach including an examination of some important criticisms of the traditional welfare state and an assessment of alternative possible models in terms of which a revived, non-bureaucratic welfare state could be constructed.

Prior to these tasks, and largely as a scene-setting exercise, this essay will briefly review the rise of neo-liberal policy in New Zealand.

Neo-liberalism and New Zealand education

In the 1984 Treasury brief to the incoming Labour Government, *Economic Management*, new-right theory and strategy in relation to the economy in general was established as necessary in relation to several Treasury arguments. In the 1987 brief, *Government Management* (Vol. 1 and 2), Treasury set forth its arguments in relation to more specific areas. Volume 2 was concerned specifically with education. In this they maintained that education could be analysed in a way similar to any other service (p. 2); that education shares the main characteristics of other commodities traded in the marketplace, and that it could not be analysed successfully as a 'public good' (p. 33); that education should be more responsive to business interests and to the needs of the economy (p. 27); that the existing education system had performed badly despite increased expenditure on it (pp. 6, 16, 18, 140); that teachers and the educational establishment have pursued their own self-interest rather than those of pupils and parents, i.e. they had not been responsive enough to consumer interests and desires (pp. 37–38); that the educational system lacked a rigorous system of accountability, there being a lack of national monitoring procedures or of any satisfactory ways of comparing the effectiveness of schools in order to account for the public resources employed (p. 108); that educational management should be decentralised; that decisions could be more efficiently made at the local rather than at the central level; that under central planning mistakes are more likely, less easy to rectify and more costly (pp. 40–41); and that government intervention and control has interrupted the 'natural' free-market contract between producer and consumer with all that entails for efficient and flexible producer responses to consumer demand (p. 41).

In short, Treasury argued that state-provided and state-controlled education had performed badly and would continue to do so unless radical changes were implemented. The Treasury buttressed its arguments for the necessity of change by reference to 'falling standards', rising mediocrity, and 'provider-capture'. They claimed that these threatened our future as a nation.

The second half of the 1980s saw the introduction of new policies[1] which caused a major revolution in education, resulting in changes in its operation and functioning at the early childhood, primary, secondary and tertiary levels. For the first time in New Zealand's history the conception of education as a commercial investment subject to market conditions has become a reality. The central issue of equality of opportunity which dominated the educational debate up until the end of the Muldoon era gave way to talk about 'efficiency', 'choice' and 'competition'. In 1990, a new Ministry of Education was established, replacing the old Department of Education and its regional offices and boards. A great deal of the administration of education was allocated to individual schools, now fitted out with 'Charters' and 'Boards of Trustees' (BOT) which replaced the old 'Boards of Governors' and 'School Committees'. The new structure increased the responsibilities of individual schools, although whether it increased actual effective control over key issues in education is more questionable and has been challenged (see Bates, 1990; Codd, 1990a, 1990b; Smith, 1991; Gordon, 1992; Kelsley, 1993). At a superficial level, the BOTs were given a whole series of new responsibilities including staff employment, management of the institution's property, and the design and implementation of a charter (based on a contract). The Education Review Office (ERO) and the New Zealand Qualifications Authority (NZQA) were also established. These changes were instituted through the 1989 Education Act, the 1990 Education Amendment Act and the 1991 Education Amendment Act. These Acts also laid the framework for bulk funding for both teachers' salaries and school operations, revoked compulsory registration for teachers, and abolished zoning for schools. In 1991, a 'user pays' system of student fees in tertiary education was introduced which laid the basis for the latter modifications and changes introduced by the National government resulting in the introduction of student loans.

The changes to education which resulted from the 'insertion' of the new right into policy making in New Zealand were motivated by the adherence to the groups most centrally involved — the Fourth Labour Government, Treasury, the State Services Commission — to a particular strain of liberal thought referred to most often as 'neo-liberalism' (Codd, 1990a, 1990b, Marshall and Peters 1990, Peters and Marshall 1990, Peters *et al.* 1994). The central defining characteristic of this new brand of liberalism was that it was seen as a 'revival' of the central tenets of classical liberalism, particularly classical economic liberalism. Notwithstanding a clear similarity between *neo* and *classical* liberal discourse, as Gordon (1991), Burchell (1993) and Marshall (1995) maintain, the two cannot be seen as identical, and an understanding of the difference between them provides an important key to understanding the distinctive nature of the restructuring of education in the 1990s.

Whereas classical liberalism represents a negative conception of state power in that the individual was taken as an object to be freed from the interventions of the state, neo-liberalism has come to represent a positive conception of the state's role in creating the appropriate market by providing the conditions, laws and institutions necessary for its operation. In classical liberalism the individual is characterised as having an autonomous human nature and can practise freedom. In neo-liberalism the state seeks to create an individual that is an enterprising and competitive entrepreneur. In the classical model the theoretical aim of the state was to limit and minimise its role based upon postulates which included universal egoism (the self-interested individual); invisible hand theory which dictated that the interests of the individual were also the interests of the society as a whole; and the political maxim of *laissez-faire*. In the shift from classical liberalism to neo-liberalism, then, there is a further element added, for such a shift involves a change in subject position from '*homo economicus*', who naturally behaves out of self-interest, and is relatively detached from the state, to 'manipulatable man', who is created by the state and who is continually encouraged to be 'perpetually responsive'. It is not that the conception of the self-interested subject is replaced or done away with by the new ideals of 'neo-liberalism', but that in an age of universal welfare, the perceived possibilities of slothful indolence create necessities for new forms of vigilance, surveillance, 'performance appraisal' and of forms of control generally. In this new model the state has taken it upon itself to keep us all up to the mark. The state will see to it that each one of us makes a 'continual enterprise of ourselves' (Gordon, 1991) in what seems to be a process of 'governing without governing' (Rose, 1993).

The state seeks to assure then the conditions for perpetual human responsiveness and flexibility that are advanced most forcefully in modern 'new right' theories such as 'Human Capital Theory', 'Public Choice Theory', 'Agency Theory', 'Cost Transaction Analysis' and the revival of various forms of 'Managerialism'. These theories are variants of neo-classical liberal thought and share its major presuppositions that subjects are economically self-interested; that the economy is separate from the rest of society; that the uncoordinated self-interest of individuals correlates with the interests and the harmony of the whole; that individuals are rational optimisers and are the best judges of their own interests and needs; and that a 'flexible', that is deregulated, labour market provides the same opportunities for people to utilise their skills and therefore optimise their life goals. The fundamental aims of the reforms — to manage education to meet the demands of a more unequal society — is at the same time a spur to individuals to act rationally in the market in order to maximise their own production and profit. Individuals will work harder because they are working for themselves, and by such activity also ensure the optimum allocation of resources in society, maximising consumer satisfaction and total economic welfare.

The failure of market theories

The fundamental untenability of the reform programme in relation to the provision of education and social services relates, I want to argue to shortcomings in the theoretical underpinnings of free-market theory. Neo-liberals seek to justify their policies in championing individual liberty against the excesses of the state in relation to central planning, regulation, and social ownership, as well as the inefficiency and lack of consideration for the rights of the consumer and the individual. Markets, they argue, have distinct advantages over state regulation. The laws of supply and demand operate as indicators of under- and over-supply as well as incentives for producers to produce high-quality, competitively priced goods for which there is an established demand. Markets, claim neo-liberals, overcome the inefficiency and unresponsiveness of central state planning as they decentralise power downwards to enterprises, schools and individual consumers. It is in this way that power is shifted from the state into the hands of individuals or of individual schools.

While many on the left, including welfare liberals and older-style socialists, admit the obvious deficiencies of traditional socialism or of the overcentralisation of state ownership and planning, there are many problems with such a market perspective. Amongst the most important identified in recent research are:

1. Consumer demand cannot be seen as equivalent to social need, and in relation to the latter the market is a poor guide. Markets fail to ensure employment or to ensure, or be centrally concerned with, equality in the distribution of resources (Olssen and Morris Matthews, 1995).
2. Markets are cumulatively and inherently inegalitarian in relation to the distribution of resources in society (Martell, 1992). In relation to education, schools are also increasingly distinguishable in terms of resourcing. Rich schools grow richer while poor schools grow poorer (Gordon, 1993).
3. Markets fail to protect democratic rights, and the neo-liberal advocacy of an unregulated market contradicts some established principles of democratic theory. According to Snook (1995: 64)

> It [neo-liberalism] rejects majority rule because there is no 'general will' but only the pressure of interest groups; and it opposes the equal involvement of all since only negative freedoms are to be protected and those with property have much more to be protected.

4. The market fosters competition at the expense of cooperation, and in fact a market orientation to social and economic policy establishes competition as a central structuring norm of a community. Relatedly, market policies under-emphasise the requirement of cooperation and coordination in society in order for groups and individuals to work together (Martell 1993)
5. Arguments for extending private schooling ignore the 'social benefits' that publicly provided education provides. These benefits are related to issues such as citizenship, tolerance, literacy, and the democratic functioning of a community. As the 'social benefits' of education, they cannot be reduced to individual self-interest, or rendered intelligible within a market perspective (Levin 1989).
6. The consumer cannot be supposed to have perfect foresight or make rational decisions based on perfect knowledge or understanding of the situation as market theory implies. It is highly implausible, as Robert Lane (1993) points out, that all people can be represented as economic agents who can be relied on to make choices that are in all cases rational; that they are infinitely clear-headed about how to go about realising their goals and obtaining their desires; that they are capable of foreseeing all of the consequences of their actions; that they can discover which is the best strategy to service their chosen ends; or that each can experience the necessary feedback to keep their expectations in balance with the objective possibilities. This applies to choices made in relation to education or any other social arena.
7. Individuals will clearly differ in their ability to act rationally in their own self-interests; some will be more successful than others. If this is so, then the welfare state liberal believes that there is no reason to structure society exclusively in the interests of those that can succeed. Indeed, as social democrats from John Stuart Mill to Lord Keynes have argued, there is every reason not to do so because, in the main, human beings are not self-sufficient and fiercely independent but are connected to other people and the structures of social support in various relations of dependence and need (relations which will vary depending upon their age, gender, financial means, race or other factors at a specific time and place). If this is so then the welfare liberals' demand for a state which is not exclusively geared to the self-interests of individuals but is generally committed to an overall conception of the good in the interests of all individuals is more likely to be acceptable to the vast majority of its citizens.

Central to predicting a return to the welfare state is the argument advanced by Polanyi (1969) that the state is the only agency that can correct the failings of the market. In Polanyi's view, the rise of the interventionist state in the late nineteenth and early twentieth centuries was to check the excesses and failures of the market in its unregulated form. He argues that the increasing positive role of the state was not promoted by political arguments for socialism but by more pragmatic considerations related to weaknesses inherent in the market mechanism. As he puts it,

> The antiliberal conspiracy is pure invention. The great variety of forms in which the 'collectivist' countermovement appeared was not due to any preference for socialism or nationalism on the part of concerted interests, but exclusively to the broader range of the vital social interests affected by the expanding market mechanism. This accounts for the all but universal reactions of predominantly practical character called forth by the expansion of that mechanism. Intellectual fashions played no role whatever in that process; there was accordingly no room for the prejudice which the liberal regards as the ideological force behind the antiliberal development. (1969: 16)

From the 1860s there was an expanding range of matters on which state action was taken, including legislation relating to employment (child labour), health and education. Polanyi argues, in fact, that the changes from liberal to collectivist solutions happened without any consciousness of deep-seated ideological and political changes on the part of those engaged in the process in countries as diverse as Prussia under Bismarck, Victorian England and France of the Third Republic. Each passed through a period of economic liberalism characterised by free trade and laissez-faire, followed by a period of antiliberal intervention in regard to public health, factory conditions, child labour, municipal trading, social insurance, public utilities and so on. Intervention in the markets, especially as it related to employment, social services and education, was increasingly designed to influence the quality as well as the quantity of its provision, because in fact the free market proved to be 'a poor guide to the best means of satisfying the real wishes of consumers' (Shonfield, 1965: 226–36). In relation to education, the operations of the market proved to be particularly pernicious for, without a reasonably planned approach, one is driven to reliance upon considerations of economic costs and benefits as criteria for the setting of educational goals with the consequent danger that the determination of educational goals and objectives is taken out of the education realm altogether. The weaknesses of such economic principles were set out by Keynes in his original arguments against free-market policies which he made in an article entitled 'The End of Laissez-Faire' written in 1926.

> It is *not* true that individuals possess a prescriptive 'natural liberty' in their economic activities. There is *no* 'compact' conferring perpetual rights on those who Have or on those who Acquire. The world is *not* so governed from above that private and social interests always coincide. It is *not* so managed here below that in practice they coincide. It is *not* a correct deduction from the Principles of Economics that enlightened self-interest always operates in the public interest. Nor is it true that self-interest generally is enlightened, more often individuals acting separately to promote their own ends are too ignorant or too weak to attain even these. Experience does not show that individuals, when they make up a social unit, are always less clear sighted than when they act separately. (Keynes 1926, cited in Rea and McLeod 1969: 52; emphasis in original)

This statement illustrates the early rejection of market principles by many moderate liberals earlier this century who wanted to reform capitalism rather than abolish it. The real issue as Keynes saw clearly was in seeking to ascertain 'what the state ought to take upon itself to direct by the public wisdom, and what it ought to leave with as little interference as possible to individual exertion' (Keynes, 1926, quoted in Rea and McLeod 1969: 53). His arguments against the minimal state were based on the discovery that there is no tendency towards efficient equilibrium in capitalist markets. Keynes was not the first to recognise this, of course. It had concerned economists in both the liberal and radical traditions — Marx, Hobson, Kalecki and others — before Keynes' idea achieved orthodoxy. Specifically important in relation to the development of western welfare states was his theory of consumption functions, and in particular his argument that the diminishing marginal propensity to consume creates a permanent tendency towards disequilibrium (or at least an inefficient equilibrium) as a result of the inefficient aggregate demand it generates.

The state and central planning

In the twentieth century, at the very time welfare states were being constructed, a variety of counter-arguments against any extended role for the state were being developed by neo-liberal writers. These arguments were both economic and political.

Authors such as Hayek (1935, 1944, 1945, 1960), Friedman (1962, 1980), Buchanan (1960, 1969, 1975) and Nozick (1974) contended that all forms of state action beyond the minimal functions of the defence of the realm and the protection of basic rights to life and property are dangerous threats to liberty which are likely to lead down the 'road to serfdom'.[2]

For Hayek, the proper functioning of markets is incompatible with state planning of any sort, either full-scale socialism or the more limited conception of the welfare state. A full-scale rational socialism is impossible because it would have no markets to guide resource allocation (Mises, quoted in Hayek, 1935). In addition, central planning of any form, he claims, is not practical because of the scale of centralised calculation any effective attempt at allocation would require (Hayek, 1944). Hayek's main arguments against central planning are based on two claims: its inefficiency and the threat to freedom of the individual. It would be inefficient, in Hayek's view, because real knowledge is gained and true economic progress made as a consequence of locally generated knowledge derived from 'particular circumstances of time and place' and the state is not privy to such knowledge (Hayek, 1945: 521). The market then is the mechanism which best allocates resources in society. Planning ignores this localistic character of knowledge and interferes with the market's self-regulating mechanism.

Socialist analyses of the role of markets and state planning in socialist societies depart radically from Hayek's view that planning and markets are incompatible with each other. Studies by Dickinson (1933), Lange (1939), Dobb (1955), Brus (1972), Nuti (1981) and Nove (1983) have argued for the central importance (although not priority) of markets moderated by the state. Nove, in his book *The Economics of Feasible Socialism* (1983), argues against the case for generalised central planning as a desirable or workable alternative in western Europe. He recommends an active market economy moderated by a strong state as well as extensive state social and cooperative property.

Hayek's arguments depend on a sharp dichotomy between markets and planning. For Hayek, mistakes and errors become 'entrenched' in the process of planning. Yet why they should become 'entrenched' rather than be 'correctable', is not clear. The issue is important, for the idea that administrative lethargy and proneness to error are endemic to all forms of planning and are not 'correctable' through internally applied quality controls is fundamental to the concept of 'capture' which has become an important theoretical term used in policy reports throughout the western world, including those introduced post-1984 in New Zealand. In addition, the extent to which Hayek's antipathy for planning is grounded in solid evidence or simply reflects his broader anticommunitarianism is problematic. Empirical studies of the history of planning in Britain, such as Wootton (1945), argue that there is little sign of any road to serfdom, or significant erosion of the liberty of the individual as a consequence of increases in state planning in the period between the two world wars.

Underpinning Hayek's views of markets and planning is the absolute priority he gives to a particular conception of freedom and liberty. As Tomlinson (1990: 40) observes, it is on the issue of liberty rather than inefficiency that Hayek's central objections to statism and communitarianism rest. Liberty is defined by Hayek as the basic feature of social organisation. It is 'the state in which a man is not subject to coercion by the arbitrary will of another or others' (Hayek, 1960 quoted in Tomlinson, 1990: 40). All actions of the state are arbitrary except those that conform to the 'rule of law'. The rule of law embodies the legitimate limits of the state's proper functions and relates solely to the protection of personal property. It is a doctrine concerning the limits of the law aimed at restricting the coercive powers of the state. Freedom is threatened by state activity beyond these limits. For Hayek, as for Nozick (1974), or for that matter most neo-liberals, this effectively excludes all welfare rights as well as rights to a minimum level of sustenance or recipience.

Keynes once commented upon Hayek's work that 'it is an extraordinary example of how starting with a mistake a remorseless logician can end up in bedlam' (quoted in Tomlinson, 1940: 40). The alleged threat of the state rests upon a particular definition of freedom as 'the absence of coercion by the state'. It is a limited and unambitious concept of freedom and is enormously problematic.

First, it focuses on the coercion of the state power, but excludes economic threats to freedom, simply ignoring the fact that most of the significant obstacles to freedom are threatened by the impersonal forces of the labour market rather than the state. Why does not the unintended consequences of the behaviour of the market place count as an infringement of liberty? The answer is Hayek does not want to condemn but rather he wants to celebrate the unintended effects of the market on people's lives. It is only intentional, willed coercion by the state, or by individuals, that can diminish freedom. This theory conveniently has the effect of preserving existing property relations.

Second, although Hayek sees a positive role for the state in constructing the human subject, his concept of freedom as it pertains to the individual is a purely negative one; it allows no notion of freedom *to act*. The concept of negative liberty relates only to the *absence* of coercion. As Isaiah Berlin (1969: 122) puts it,

> Coercion implies the deliberate interference of other human beings within the area in which I could otherwise act. You lack political liberty or freedom only if you are prevented from attaining a goal by human beings. Mere incapacity to attain a goal is not lack of political freedom.

The central characteristics of negative liberty can thus be formally stated: (1) liberty is defined in terms of an absence rather than in terms of any positive capacity of individuals to achieve their objectives, and (2) poverty, illiteracy or unemployment may severely restrict what individuals are able to do but none of these affect one's 'negative liberty'.

Negative liberty can be contrasted with positive liberty. While one offers *freedom from*, the other offers *freedom to*. While individuals are given freedom from state coercion, it does not offer 'equal access to the means of life and the means of labour' (Macpherson 1973: 96). To discuss freedom merely in terms of what it prevents being done to the individual ignores the public significance of many freedoms. By ignoring any conception of positive freedom, it ignores the sense in which people's freedom to act depends on, and presupposes a certain degree of equality in the distribution of societal resources.

Although neo-liberals maintain a sharp distinction between negative and positive liberty, and emphasise only the former, writers such as MacCallum (1967) and Martell (1993) question whether such a separation is viable at all. To be concerned with negative freedom from coercion is also to be concerned with positive freedom from coercion to do whatever one wants to do. If state coercion is removed, but I still lack the opportunity, then freedom is pointless. As Martell (1993: 110) states,

> This makes the idea of liberty a nonsense because a person is just as unfree to pursue a path of action because of the lack of resources they have been left with as a result of their position in the market as they are because the state has deliberately deprived them of a right to do so. One coercion may be more acceptable than another.

Negative liberty is achievable in a strictly inegalitarian society, and means that some have greater capacities to act freely than others. To believe in positive liberty is to maintain that all people should have the resources and capacities to express and realise their freedom in their actions. This would entail a broadly egalitarian society, at least in the sense of offering equality of access, a minimum acceptable standard of living, as well as access to forms of cultural capital such as literacy and numeracy.

A third problem with Hayek's concept of liberty is that it constitutes a purely abstract and formal claim that tells us nothing about what life is like for most people in society most of the time. What people tend to do depends upon the character of the society in which they live and on the conditions they find themselves occupying within it.

A fourth problem with Hayek's concept of liberty is the absolute priority claimed for the freedom of the individual. For socialists and welfare liberals, liberty is one of the desirable attributes of social organisation, and individual self-interest is not necessarily an appropriate basis for collective decisions (Wootton 1945: 11, Tomlinson 1990: 40). In exalting the liberty of the individual, not only does it deny that the state can have purposes and duties other than those arising from the purposes and interests of specific individuals or groups of individuals, but if followed logically as a principle it would prevent the state undertaking projects for or on behalf of communities (e.g. education and health). It is not necessary to deny that there are many specific freedoms whose social value consists in allowing individuals to pursue their own ends nor that the market is not the best means of allocation for many resources. The central issue is how far the liberty of the individual and the market can be extended before choices in certain areas need to be limited because of the undesirable consequences of unrestricted individual liberty on society generally. This might occur, for instance, in relation to allowing such things as unrestricted access to fishing reserves, or in relation to being prepared to tolerate enormous levels of poverty in the society. It may be that under certain conditions a government that refuses to act with regard to the distribution of income and wealth may well be more coercive than a government that attempts redistribution (Hindess, 1990). A more communitarian approach has attractions for all those who think of society as a community independent of individuals and who think of the well-being and liberty of individuals as in some way dependent upon the good or well-being of society. One argument for recognising the importance of society independently of the individuals which constitute it relates to the fact that there are general interests, social benefits and public goods which cannot be identified with the interests of individuals. As a result, then, the protection and promotion of these interests must be the responsibility of the state. That is, in order to protect the liberties of all individuals, the state must act to restrain those forms of actions which would necessarily damage or curtail the liberties of any members of the community through either the intended or unintended actions of the labour market, the state, or any other person(s) or group(s) within society. The state should also act 'positively' to enhance the opportunities of all members of society. State action in relation to the environment (e.g. clean air) or education have been advocated on this ground.

Freedom vs control

Arguments against central planning may be persuasive against the idea of completely centralised decision-making for the entire economy or in situations where the personal political and civil liberties of individuals are not protected in law. Beyond this Hayek's account of planning is simply a caricature. One strategy he uses is to posit a single polarity between the individual and centralised decision making, representing the issue as 'freedom vs control'.[3] The implication is that a market orientation does not advocate a particular form of society but simply indicates a preference for individuals to 'freely' plan their own futures, leaving the constitution of society to take care of itself. Such a view is hardly sustainable. In the first place, society necessarily always takes a substantive form, and the argument by neo-liberals that within its policy formulations it is not implying a particular preferred shape to society, or that it does not advocate the establishment of a 'social good' over and above what individuals desire, does not rule out substantive commitments about what society should be like. In effect, in a theoretical sense the substantive commitments of neo-liberals are as much a holistic blueprint for society as are those of Keynesians or even traditional socialists. As Martell (1992) states, to claim that they are not maing a choice about what form society should take must be seen, in fact, as a choice. If decisions are not made about the desirable shape of society publicly by social interests as a whole but left to emerge from the competitive interactions of individuals then the shape of society will be moulded by a combination of laissez-faire and the influence of powerful interests. In short, the neo-liberals claim that their own social 'plans' are not really 'plans' must be viewed critically. In Martell's own words,

> [It] all sounds very nice until you realise that what it does, in effect, is to let in just another particular substantive vision of society as consisting of the sum total of individuals' preferences over which individuals have no overall control. In this sense [neo-liberalism] is in fact a highly substantive doctrine — one which posits a competitive individualist society immune to overall democratic direction. (Martell, 1992: 156)

Neo-liberals might counter that any alternative to a market society is a monolithic community in which all individuals deny their own individuality for the good of the community. Defenders of market liberal societies like Hayek (1935, 1944) or Popper (1961) represent all alternatives to such an order as forms of monist communitarianism. For Hayek, state planning was a slippery slope leading to full-scale totalitarianism (Hayek 1935: 24, 1944, Chp. 3). As Tomlinson points out, he typically dismisses any midway point between centralised and decentralised planning except 'the delegation of planning to organised industries' (Hayek, 1945 quoted in Tomlinson 1990: 49). For Popper, although concerned more generally with the opposition between liberal individualism and Marxism rather than the technical specifications of the market model, all alternatives to a society based on individual values and exchanges were also represented as forms of authoritarian control or as tending to such control. Methodologically, and in terms of policy analysis and implementation they are 'holists'. In his classic discussion of the principles which underlie an 'open society', Popper argues against 'utopian' or 'holistic' engineering in favour of piecemeal social engineering. Whereas piecemeal engineering favours a pragmatic and limited approach to change based on an awareness of the limits of human knowledge and allowing adequate room for the correction of errors, holistic engineering pursues large-scale social experiments. Popper further suggests that the persecutions in Communist countries were the result of a holist conception of society. The holist, says Popper, believes that society is more than the sum of the individuals who comprise it, which gives a licence to those who wish to curtail the rights and freedoms of the individual in the name of society's greater good (Popper 1961: 76–93).

While Popper's arguments were directed against the Marxist-Leninist régimes of Eastern Europe, it is through such forms of reasoning (aided, abetted and extended by neo-liberals such as Hayek, Friedman and Nozick) that milder forms of democratic socialism and welfare statism have been also discredited. Such arguments must be seen as caricatures. Those who criticise neo-liberal restructuring need not deny the importance of individuality or the regard for liberty or plurality in order to advocate some form of social planning in the interests of the public good. It is perfectly conceivable for individuals to make concessions in the interests of a public good of society as a whole and still maintain a commitment to liberty. In fact, it might be said that it is hardly possible to maintain otherwise. In addition, as I will argue shortly, the 'social good' need not be imposed in any dictatorial sense but can itself be the outcome of a democratically negotiated process. This, one might add, is how it should be.

The anti-statism of the neo-liberal needs careful examination. Is it not possible for individual rights and public goods to exist together and be held in balance? Is there no 'middle-ground' position which excludes the view that any degree of state planning throws us onto the slippery slope to serfdom? Can we not hold that societies exist independently of human beings without thereby committing ourselves to the beliefs about one being more important than another? It would also seem that individuals are socially constructed to a large extent in that they depend for all manner of things on society's opportunity structure. Yet it is possible to hold to this view without denying that liberty and choice are important. We can also hold that all that happens and is important to human beings is not to be explained entirely in terms of individual motivations and actions, and hold nevertheless that its *importance* is to be explained by appeal to the desires and interests of individuals.

Individualism

The individualism of neo-liberalism attests to the extreme nature of its doctrine. In a tradition extending from Hobbes to Locke and onwards, classical liberals gave a moral priority to members of society as individuals, and marked the priority by according them non-legal and natural rights which means that there are things the state cannot do to them even in the interests of society as a whole, and further that their obligations to the state as individuals are limited. In the Lockean conception, both the state and society were viewed as 'artifices', i.e. there is nothing necessary or natural about them. They came into being only by the consent of freely contracting individuals.

The individualism of neo-liberalism can be broken down into three different types: ontological, methodological and political individualism. Ontological individualism holds that only individuals are real and that the individual is 'prior' to society. Methodological individualism is the doctrine that collective phenomena (the state, class, education) can for the purposes of explanation be reduced to statements about individual actions and events, and political individualism holds that social policies and state actions are to be judged good or bad only insofar as they serve the desires and purposes of individual members of society. One problem for neo-liberals is that one can be politically individualist without being committed to ontological or methodological individualism.

At a theoretical level, the neo-liberals' individualism is flawed on the grounds that it relies on a view of the individual which is ontologically suspect and psychologically unrealistic, an ideal which C. B. Macpherson (1962) has called the 'possessive individual'. In this model the individual is held to to be proprietor of his or her own capacities and person, owing nothing to society for them. Not only does the individual own his or her own capacities, but each is morally and legally responsible for herself or himself. The individual is held to be asocial and ahistorical. Such a conception also implies a model of society. Freedom from dependence upon others means freedom from relations with others except those relations entered into voluntarily out of self-interest. Human society for the neo-liberal, as for their classical precursors, is simply a series of market relations between self-interested subjects.

What individualist theories overlook in this regard is the significant sense in which people are socially constructed (Gergen 1985, Hindess 1990, Hacking 1995). Individuals are not the constitutive subjects of social life, and their concerns and objectives depend on a variety of social conditions that are independent of and external to them as individuals. In addition, the concepts, language and forms of thought on which individuals depend, also exist in advance of and separate to them. Hence, as Hindess (1990: 19) points out, there is no particular inherent plausibility to the view that policy decisions by the state should be grounded in the choices of its individuals. In that the concerns and interests of individuals will depend on conditions prevailing in the society, some of which could be defined as 'public goods', there is no reason why the overall interests of individuals could not be addressed by focussing on those *conditions* and in seeking to establish the *structures* necessary for individuals to go about their lives. While the overall ends of state policy would in this case still be for the individuals that constitute the society, the means of fulfilling those ends is not therefore relegated to the decisions of the individuals themselves.

Another point that individualist theories overlook is that there are significant actors other than individuals (Hindess, 1990). There are, for instance, significant corporate actors which are influential members of the economic community. What neo-liberals do is dispute the ontological status of such corporate groups. While they recognise that they exist, they claim that for the purposes of explanation and analysis they can be treated as individuals. As a result, powerful institutional actors such as capitalist enterprises, churches or political parties have no effective, theoretical standing in terms of neo-liberal, political theory. Yet such reductionism is unsatisfactory. As Hindess has put it,

> Reductionism (of methodological individualism) in principle offers no practical guidance. It does not tell us how the actions of say, IBM or the Roman Catholic Church should in practice be reduced to the actions of the relevant individuals. Even if there were a clear sense in which the actions of corporate actors could in principle be reduced to the actions of human individuals we should still have to reckon with the concerns and objectives of corporate actors and what they do in their pursuit. (1990: 26–27)

Alternatives

Towards a reappraisal of socialist principles

If neo-liberal arguments against a positive role for the state are deficient, and if it can be argued, as Polanyi does, that the state's role is necessary in order to remedy the con-traditions of the unregulated market, then what remains to be discussed is problems in the theory and practice of socialism and of welfare states.

There is more than just a theoretical interest in the reappraisal of socialist principles. First, socialist principles and themes have been historically important in the formation of the welfare state. Secondly, various forms of social (state and community) ownership have existed within welfare state societies, and to this extent democratic socialism is not necessarily incompatible with welfare liberalism. As it is by no means vouchsafed that neo-liberal hegemony will survive as the dominant discourse structuring state education policy, a renewal of the discussion on the possibility of a revived welfare state is of considerable importance. Although my interest here is speculative, i.e. relevant to the practical possibilities for New Zealand politics in the year 2000, the theoretical reconsideration of models of socialism emerging now in Britain is a suitable place to start in the attempt to reconstruct the welfare state, and to the central role of public education in such a structure.

Models of socialism

New models of the welfare state which permit the co-existence of social ownership together with a private market sector are premised on anti-statist agendas and draw off both the liberal and socialist traditions, acknowledging both the rich conceptions of rights to be found in liberalism and the commitments to equality and justice in the socialist and welfare state traditions. In this sense it is also acknowledged that forms of social (state and community) ownership are compatible with the welfare state.

Individualist socialism: The notion of 'individualist socialism' is referred to by Martell (1992) to characterise the work of British writers like Roy Hattersley (1987) and Raymond Plant (1988). Essentially Hattersley and Plant offer a socialist conception of liberty supplementing negative with positive liberty, and maintain that all people should have the resources and capacities to express and realise their freedom and actions. According to both Hattersley and Plant, an inegalitarian distribution means that some people have a greater capacity to act freely than others and hence a precondition for positive liberty is that resources should be distributed evenly. Such a theory is not sufficient however. While it is a good socialist theory of liberty, it is not a good theory of the welfare state.

Market socialism and socialism with markets: Welfare state liberals have never disputed an important role that markets play within the economy. By and large, democratic socialists have not manifested any blanket hostility to markets either. Work by Dickinson (1933), Lange (1939), Dobb (1955) and Nove (1983) all supported both a strong state and a strong market. While the socialists preferred social, state and community ownership, the welfare statists opted for a private/public mix.

Views about the role of the market in the welfare state must be distinguished from more recent conceptions about 'market socialism' (Gould 1985, Forbes, 1986, Le Grand and Estrin 1989). Market socialism constitutes a mix of neo-liberal principles and traditional welfare concerns. Their vision of socialism is constituted by a commitment to 'equity' or 'starting-gate equality' (Martell 1992) but has no concern to redress structural imbalances through distributional resources. In Hayekian fashion, it exhibits two key characteristics: the essentialisation of the market, and the priority it gives to individual liberty. In doing this it tends to place the market at the cetre of concern, subverting traditional welfare ideals. Not only do they shortchange important values other than liberty, they also (mis)represent the market as the ideal arena of individual choice and liberty. As a consequence, 'consumer demand' is represented as 'choice' which is confused with 'social need'. Mistakenly believing that markets conform to a model of 'equality of opportunity', they overlook their inherent power inequalities. In short, 'consumer demand' must be kept analytically and theoretically distinct from 'social need'. Consumer demand is skewed by people's ability to pay, and, because it is shaped by unequally distributed purchasing power, market forces are a poor indicator of social need (Martell 1992). Producers will not respond to needs of groups who cannot pay or which translate as weak demands due to differences in purchasing power. Markets breed inequality in relation to prosperity/neglect, high earners/low earners, wealth/poverty, and success/failure (Martell 1992). The extent to which this is so needs to be monitored on an ongoing basis through research by the state.

The traditional welfare state: A return to the 'golden days' of the welfare state once the 'blue wave' is over is seen by many as a likely scenario. This position maintains and hopes that when the new right finally recedes things will return to social democracy as usual (McLennan, 1993: 111). There are pluses and minuses to this prospect. As McLennan puts it, the pluses are that 'looking back on it, corporatism *did* generally raise the status and standards of labour in the state and the welfare state *did* 'provide' for people on a universalist basis' (Ibid. emphasis in original).

The minuses are not insignificant, however. The distributional failures of the old welfare state are well documented. Julien LeGrand's (1982, 1987) studies of the British welfare state claims on the basis of a study of empirical data that the welfare state is not redistributive across class lines but that most redistribution is intra-class and over the course of an individual's life time. In addition, middle and upper classes secured a disproportionate amount in terms of per capita share of the total available equity of state-provided resources and services.

Le Grand's and other similar studies influenced the New Zealand Treasury in preparing their brief to the incoming Labour Government in 1984. As the brief reported,

> A variety of studies (in countries with welfare systems broadly similar to New Zealand's) have concluded that most public expenditure on social services is actually distributed in a manner that favours the middle and higher social (income or occupation) groups, despite its notational targeting at low income groups. (New Zealand Treasury 1984: 259)

This especially applies to education, and it is claimed that the middle classes consume more publicly funded education per capita than the poor.

The New Zealand Treasury uses the theoretical concept of 'capture' to ground their critique of the welfare state. This concept is used both to account for the inefficiencies of existing welfare policies in terms of egalitarian objectives and to advocate a shift to neo-liberal solutions based on the minimal state and individual choice.

Bertram (1988) summarises the Treasury's use of the three forms of capture which they claim have been central in criticisms of the welfare state. These are:

1. *Consumer capture*: which occurs when a group of users of state services secures preferential treatment against the interests of other users;

2. *Provider capture*: which refers to the situation where those who supply state services pursue their own interests at the expense of the interests of consumers;
3. *Administrative capture*: which refers to a situation where government departments not directly involved in the production of state-provided services act to advance their own interests at the expense of the quality of those services.

Bertram then argues that the concept of 'capture' presupposes the neo-liberal's individualist assumptions about society; that it presupposes that the welfare state is a zero-sum game; and that it initiates a critique which discounts externalities, public goods, and economies of scale. In overall terms, the concept is inherently biased and fails 'to distinguish the different particular problems while conveying the unsubstantiated impression that there is some overarching meta problem with the welfare state' (Bertram 1988: 115).

A further problem with critiques of the traditional welfare state relates to controversy over the interpretation of distributional data. In 1985, O'Higgins disputed LeGrand's analysis, arguing that while social welfare spending in Britain has not brought about greater overall equality, between 1975 and 1982 it has *combatted and significantly modified the effects of pressures towards increased inequality*. On this point, Peters and Marshall note that

> this is an extremely important point . . . a crucial matter calling for careful research. It may be that the existing provision for state education in New Zealand has not reduced inequalities of race, class and gender to any significant degree: the salient point for educational researchers is whether the proposed restructuring of educational administration indicated by the Picot Taskforce will diminish or exacerbate existing inequalities. (1988c: 88)

The point is important, not just as regards education but to all social services. Clearly, as Bertram (1988: 163) notes, there were problems with the traditional welfare state. The main three he lists are the distribution or 'targeting' of benefits or resources, the exercise of monopoly power by suppliers of services, and administrative distortions. These problems, I will argue, far from being insolvable can be overcome through the implementation of ongoing quality controls and research as well as a commitment by the state to certain fundamental principles. A commitment by the state to established welfare principles of full employment and a living minimum wage would establish a context for the achievement of essential welfare goals without the need for a cumbersome bureaucracy. A commitment to these principles, in fact, solves most of the problems associated with the administration of the welfare, and, it might be added, with many other problems of the society generally (e.g. crime).

The changing social structure

There have been other, more recent challenges to the notion of the traditional, bureaucratic welfare state from both left and right. While time and space do not enable me to do more than briefly outline their main features, as challenges to the possibility or desirability of a welfare state they can be considered under the following headings:

1. *Fordism-post-Fordism*: This thesis maintains the view that society has remorselessly 'moved on' from the 1960s and 1970s and that the revival of neo-liberal policy reflects the different technological, economic and political developments in the material structure of advanced capitalism. The post-Fordist thesis maintains that the character of work itself is changing away from mass pro-

duction models towards individualised, flexible specialisation. This will result in short-term and frequently changing employment patterns. It involves a complex and interrelated series of changes in the labour process and the overall dynamic of macroeconomic change (Hall 1988, Jessop 1994). The Fordism-post-Fordism thesis is both an economic and cultural thesis. In the cultural orbit it is associated with greater fragmentation and pluralism, the weakening of older, collective solidarities and block identities, and the emergence of new identities associated with greater work flexibility, and the maximisation of individual choices through individual consumption (Hall 1988: 251). It essentially involves theorisation of the process of change over the passing age, the origins of the crisis, and the shape of things to come.

2. *Globalisation*: This refers to the internationalisation of both capital and culture which will diminish the significance and power of national politics, as politics and identity at once become 'both more local and more global' (McLennan 1993: 110). As Stuart Hall (1988) notes, it refers to an economy increasingly dominated by multinationals, and to the rise of computer-based information technologies which diminish the importance of national boundaries, undermine the autonomy of the nation-state, and involve a reorganisation of the state's activities along supra-national lines.
3. *Enterprise culture*: This challenge to the welfare state comes from neo-liberalism and involves the charge that the traditional welfare state constitutes a culture of dependency and laziness where the individual regards others and not him/herself as primarily responsible for their own well-being. The essential idea of an 'enterprise culture' emerged first in Britain during the 1980s (Morris 1991) and, according to Keat (1991: 1), functions to represent classic liberal arguments in cultural terms. The concept of 'enterprise culture' typically conveys a number of different meanings. On the one hand it is a culture that encourages the acquisition of enterprising qualities such as self-help, self-reliance, initiative, energy, independence, boldness, a willingness to take risks, and to accept responsibility for one's actions and so on (Keat 1991: 3). On the other hand it elevates the model of the business enterprise as the preferred model for economic and social reconstruction. It also involves a sustained attempt to neutralise those qualities which are inimical to business values. This charge that the welfare state 'kills off enterprise' is one of the most popular and widespread arguments levelled against it (Keat 1991, Peters, 1992).
4. *Modernism-postmodernism*: The postmodernist argument advances yet another version of the thesis that 'things have moved on since the days of the welfare state'. The shift from modernism to postmodernism parallels in many ways the shift from Fordism to post-Fordism, and from the Keynesian welfare state to neo-liberalism. The postmodernist argues against the very idea of a central state on the grounds that such an institution is 'centrist' and 'totalistic' and cannot possibly claim to represent, let alone interpret, the needs and interests of the complex and multiple realities that constitute the social domain. In this the postmodernist opposes all integrating and unifying narratives displaying a preference for the values of 'difference', 'dispersion', 'localism', and 'plurality' (Yeatman 1990, Young 1990).

The postmodernists's opposition to centrism can be illustrated with reference to Foucault's distinction between 'total' and 'general' history (Sheridan

1980: 92). Whereas total history explains all phenomena in relation to a single centre, 'general history employs the space of dispersion', and operates in terms of the principle of difference. For the postmodernist, then, the modernist conception of history and society imposes a false unity on the cultural formation by searching for its central organising principle — whether 'the state', or 'the economy', or 'social classes'. The ultimate effect, says the postmodernist, is to underemphasise the essential plurality of the social order. The upshot of this form of theorising has been to usher in a new form of anti-statism.

Towards a revised, non-bureaucratic model of the welfare state

Neither the post-Fordist nor the postmodernist arguments seriously undermine the possibility of a new welfare state. The post-Fordist thesis has in fact been accused by Gregor McLennan of being misleading pop sociology.

> The solidaristic effects of being a wage-earner, even today, remain in my view full of political potential in the face of extraordinary predatoriness of international capital; work itself (and its absence) still dominates the lives and potentials of people like *nothing else.* (McLennan 1993: 110) (emphasis in original)

In addition to this, in spite of the fact that it constitutes a form of analysis stemming from the left, it tends almost by implication to suggest that the ascendency of neo-liberalism is in some sense 'inevitable' and 'could not have been otherwise'. It also suggests that it has emerged as a direct consequence of deeper changes in society and thus ends up by suggesting that neo-liberal options are an inevitable and necessary development. Notwithstanding such inferences, it can be argued that the developments that the post-Fordist identifies constitute an argument for rather than against the construction of a new welfare state. If work is to be of a more 'temporary' and 'varied' nature, and characterised by constant changes and a need for 'perpetual retraining', this would seem to me to create an indispensable case for the existence of some agency which can mediate the growing unpredictability of the relationship between individual human beings and the demands of capital accumulation.

The difficulties with the argument that the welfare state encourages dependency rather than enterprise are numerous. One is the abstractness of the claim. While it may conceivably have some validity in some situations with regard to some forms of state policy, it is difficult to understand as a blanket claim how all forms of welfare policy erode enterprise values. How, for instance, does universal health provision relate to enterprise? Should we all be self-reliant with respect to health care or medical treatment? The absurdity of such a possibility also highlights the fact overlooked by neo-liberals that all human beings are reliant on the structures of state support at one time or another. It is easy to overlook the profundity of this fact. Let me state it as a general principle. *All individuals depend at some stage in their lives on the structures of social support and on resources that they have not personally owned or created.*

Related to this, a second issue is concerned with the fact that people vary in respect to the extent in which they need support and assistance from the state. A person with multiple disabilities who is confined to a wheelchair may require greater assistance than the daughter of a multi-millionaire who has just won a scholarship to Harvard. A single mother with three small children may require forms of assistance that her ex-partner who owns a successful business does not. There are both *subgroups* of people as well as *critical periods* in all people's lives where welfare rights may be required. The existence of welfare rights in relation to health or education, or for people when they are sick or have special needs, does not signal 'dependence' as opposed to 'self-reliance' but rather indicates specific forms of dependence in a world where all people are dependent at some stage upon the structures of social support. The illusion of self-reliance simply indicates a privileged position in relation to the opportunity and reward structures of our society. As a consequence, it can be seen that the representation of the issue as being one of either 'dependency' or 'enterprise' is a false polarity. People do differ in the extent to which they rely on their own resources, but the neo-liberal needs to acknowledge that such resources are often achieved with social and institutional support. And just as every one of us has at some stage been dependent upon the resources of society, so too every one of us is potentially in need of assistance again.

Thirdly, a welfare state need not discourage enterprise, and hence a welfare state can also be an 'enterprise culture'. Unlike the neo-liberal conception of enterprise, however, the welfare liberal's view of enterprise is not limited to forms of 'busnocratic rationality' (Marshall 1995). Rather, 'enterprise' is defined more broadly to include both business and nonbusiness forms of initiative and creativity. It may include financially unrewarding activities such as art, scholarship, or child-rearing. In this sense, the concept of 'enterprise' may co-exist and be consistent with a need for various forms of assistance.

Fourthly, in that the welfare state allows a significant private-sector market, there is plenty of scope for individual business enterprise of the sort the neo-liberal likes.

Fifthly, the 'dependence/enterprise' dualism of neo-liberalism fails to recognise that some people, or groups of people, can experience bad luck, and that groups within society can be disadvantaged, just as it fails to recognise that the apparent self-reliance of some individuals and groups within society is based upon resources that were socially given.

The globalisation argument has some implications for the prospects for a new welfare state in as much as the increasing internationalisation of capital may well affect the ability of the nation state to act unilaterally. To this extent the contradiction between capital accumulation and democratic legitimation (Offe 1984) will increasingly weight the power imbalances in favour of capital. Yet this in itself must not mean that a legally independent sovereign nation-state should give up in despair. Politics, after all, is the 'art of the impossible'.

The concern with the issue of central planning may have some validity. It may well be, as the postmodernist argues, that the traditional welfare state has been unduly insensitive to local minorities and oppressed groups. It may also have been overly centrist and monolithic. Much of the tenure of postmodernism, like post-Fordism, and like neo-liberalism, has been against the forms of monist communitarianism where an overarching central state exerts its hegemony over the entire society.

There is no reason why a revised welfare state should be statist or overly centralised, however. Many of the left in recent years have acknowledged problems with statism and many have searched for non-statist formulae which force a democratisation of the public good rather than via neo-liberal private instrumentalism and market anarchy. The development of forms of 'associational socialism' (Martell 1992, Hirst 1990) or of decentralised democratic socialism (Bobbio 1987) have called for radical, democratic, socialist alternatives based on citizenship, parliamentary democracy, the rule of law, the strengthening of the institutions of civil society and liberal democracy, as well as decentralisation. This model of democratic socialism has much to teach welfare liberals who have traditionally supported the institutions of liberal democracy. Essentially, the future for a revived welfare state lies in its commitment to democratisation through new forms of decentralisation, citizenship and participation. Such commitments can also, under certain circumstances, imply the extension of democracy from the polity to the economy and to civil society. As Bowles and Gintis (1986) point out, it is one of the glaring contradictions which neo-liberals don't like to talk about too much, that they support democratic control and decision-making in relation to the political system but not in relation to the economic system. The welfare state liberal, then, can support the strengthening of the institutions of civil society, from parent involvement in Boards of School Trustees to consumer representatives on the boards of large business enterprises, through to new radical, pluralist, decentralised and participatory forms of democracy.

The welfare state liberal thus has a different response to the crisis of the state than does the neo-liberal. Rather than abandon ideas of the common good and of collectivism, the welfare state liberal's response to statism is not to abandon the state in preference for the abstract individual or to abandon public goods in favour of privatisation and markets but rather to bring them under greater democratic control. As Hirst (1990) has observed, democracy is the best answer the left has to the right. This might conceivably mean decentralising state powers into civil society; strengthening controls and checks on central government and on employers and all corporate actors; promoting a more active role for citizenry; and promoting a commitment to 'positive' as well as 'negative' liberty. Controls on government can be extended through legal and constitutional safeguards, through extending the separation and devolution of state powers, through promoting a vibrant civil society, increasing the number and strength of counteracting centres of power to the state, and promoting a strong role for independent associations. Activities of specific individuals or groups of individuals will only be restrained to the extent they conflict with the rights of other individuals or with certain democratically negotiated public goods.

In Britain, Luke Martell is one recent author who has advocated a theory of associational democracy (Martell 1992, 1993). While his own thesis is developed in relation to a broader examination of new models of socialism, the general idea of strengthening the associations of civil society, of devolving state powers and of increasing checks and controls on the state power can contribute towards a model of a revived welfare state. In Martell's theory, associations (such as teachers' unions, for instance) can provide the institutions appropriate to participatory democracy. First, associations can provide forums for the active popular participation of individuals at accessible decentralised levels. Second, an inclusive corporatist polity comprised of associations representing the plurality of interests is capable of negotiating agreed social priorities. Third, the state can decentralise functionally, bringing democracy down to small-scale, local levels. Fourth, associations, being corporate entities, can check the power of other corporate entities, including the state. Such a solution, says Martell, is neither statist nor *laissez-faire*.

Education

The provision of public education is based on a number of historically important rights and claims. The 'positive' rights associated with social democratic liberalism entailed that a universal and free education was the indispensable prerequisite to the freedom of the individual. Such education was to be compulsory because children needed to be protected against the individual self-interest of their parents. Such rights underpinned the goals of a democratic society to ensure its reproduction through a common set of skills and values. Public education thus served the community by addressing social needs. Schools provided students with a common set of values and knowledge, thus creating the basis for citizenship and the democratic functioning of society. Schooling also contributed to scientific and cultural progress and played an important role in economic and social growth, ensuring the conditions for full employment.

The public benefits of education cannot simply be seen as the sum of individual private benefits. Norms such as political or civic tolerance, literacy, or the values required for democratic functioning adhere to the quality of a community and are not reducible to the psychological characteristics of individuals. In short, essential to producing the public benefits of schooling, all children must experience certain common benefits which are not safeguarded for by a privatised education without the regulation and monitoring of the state. In a private system some parents will not be able to obtain schooling for their children at all; others might seek schooling that reinforces sectarian religious, political, ethnic or cultural ends. As a consequence, certain social benefits are not safeguarded and important issues to do with the regulation and control over such things as the 'quality of teacher training' or 'the nature of the curriculum' are not protected. Universal and compulsory education established common uniform features in order to guarantee skills such as universal literacy and numeracy as the universal common basis necessary for active citizenship and democratic participation.

By the intrinsic nature of their social organisation, private schools, argues Levin (1989), are also likely to neglect areas concerned with specific aspects of schooling, such as the curriculum, which are necessary to public benefits such as tolerance or citizenship. This is so, he argues, because private schooling is less likely to introduce students to, and encourage in them, a tolerance of diverse cultures and values. In a related sense, reflecting the specific social attributes on which they are based, they are likely to undermine the level of social and cultural integration, thus exacerbating differences in relation to class, race and religion within the community.

In that private schooling cannot provide for important social benefits, a suitably public-provided education can account for individual 'choice' through the provision of a greater variety of options and offerings within the public system. To this extent a publicly provided education can adapt itself flexibly to individual preferences thus reconciling the twin goals of preserving the 'public goods' of education and protecting individual rights (which have historically given to parents the ability to decide exactly how and where their children will be educated, and to withdraw them from the state system if they so wish). For the welfare liberal, the ideals of public education depend on a conception of schooling as a shared experience rather than based on 'choice'. Hence I would argue that while a public system can produce private benefits (such as individual qualifications and skills), a private system cannot provide for the social benefits which are necessary to the functioning of a democratic society and which education under the welfare state has historically provided. In fact, extensive privatisation is likely to undermine the public basis of a democratic, literate society itself.

Community

The model of a decentralised welfare society advanced here is compatible with the notion of 'community', which has been advocated as the basis of a revived welfare state since the 1970s (LeGrand 1982, Joppke 1987). The model is compatible too with Peters and Marshall's notion of an 'empowerment community' which they argue is consistent with a genuine state of participatory democracy (Peters and Marshall 1988a, 1988b, 1988c, 1988d, 1988e, 1989). Such a notion of community embodies the strengthening of the institutions of civil society and an increase in the possibilities for democratic participation. In relation to education, Robinson (1988) has argued in this respect that *Picot* presented possibilities for democratic participation that had not previously existed in schooling practices.

There is nothing inherently wrong with arguments for devolution of authority to schools or other community agencies. Such a devolution must be accompanied however, as Marshall (1981) has argued, by theories of participatory structures that are genuinely democratic. This would entail moves towards a more responsive, community-based, service delivery welfare state which might involve power-sharing and devolution, as well as forms of community-based public ownership of business enterprises (along the lines of the Trustee Savings Banks in New Zealand, for example). Such a conception is consistent with those that advocate a conceptual shift from the notion of a 'welfare state' to that of a 'welfare society' in which family, voluntary societies, local bodies, trade unions and employers play a greater role (Davey and Dwyer 1984). It is a welfare state which is sensitive to institutional abuses of power, which is committed to the twin goals of full employment and equality of opportunity as well as to universal welfare entitlements and Keynesian demand management. It is a welfare state which constitutes a viable alternative to the bureaucratic welfare state. In Joppke's words (1987: 250), 'it pursues the egalitarian project of a non-bureaucratic decentralized and self-reliant welfare society'. Consistent with Peters and Marshall's 'empowerment community', it is based on the values which encourage and promote cooperative rather than competitive behaviour and which make for a sense of cohesion and community. As Peters and Marshall put it,

> This is tantamount to arguing simply that a welfare state ought to be concerned with developing a sense of *communal* rather than *self* interest, that values of the private and the individual ought not to be privileged or aggrandized over those of the public and the community; and that collective provision based on communal interest is potentially more egalitarian, socially responsible and democratic than similar services provided by the free market. (1990: 81) (emphasis in original)

This is a far cry from the neo-liberal's conception. It rejects the notion of the market as a superior mechanism for allocating resources in society or as the instrument of a self-regulating or spontaneously ordered social system. It supports the notion that the real purposes of central planning are the creation of a genuinely free society, and that collective powers of the state are used only to protect individual rights and to enable individuals to 'pursue their own goals in their own way' (Hindess 1990: 10).

It supports the idea, too, that such a welfare society is committed to the principle of equality, although it acknowledges that the concept of equality, and its relationship to liberty, needs careful theorising. I am not so convinced that the traditional concern with equality needs ditching, as Gregor McLennan (1993: 109) has suggested, although if it could be shown that the concept generated undesirable features then these could be acknowledged and the welfare state's conern with equality could be modified accordingly. For McLennan, any merits in the concept can be recast in more precise terms which include a focus on 'access', 'needs fulfilment', 'social justice', and 'self-realisation'. In addition, the term sometimes conflates concerns such as equality of opportunity with universal provision and with equality of outcomes.

Equality itself has not been the failing of socialist or welfare states. The failing has been identified as having more to do with means rather than ends (Martell 1992), and in this sense tends to focus on the failings of the state (such as central planning and the encroachment of liberty). I have already questioned whether this association is not itself ideologically in support of a certain conception of property relations and class interests. Yet to abandon a concern for equality is, in my view, to abandon a concern for the welfare state, and in a world of dangerous arms stocks, starvation, huge extremes of wealth and poverty, it would seem to me that nothing could be more needed than a doctrine that stresses equality, community and the public good. In short, the concept of equality performs an important political function. Equality in all of its different senses is a precondition for freedom. Equality is a basis for an increase in the sum of liberty as well as in its equal distribution. Ultimately, as far as most people are concerned, a state that ignores the issue of equality is more coercive than a state that takes no action. In addition, the cumulative and compounding nature of the inequalities that the market generates relates to all of the different senses that McLennan mentions and yet it still means that such inequalities need to be rectified by distributional political decisions. Such a commitment need not entail a subordination of individual liberties in preference for extreme forms of communitarianism. Indeed, such egalitarianism is not, in my view, the same thing as 'uniformity', and in fact is fully compatible with pluralist politics and liberal democracy. What is important for liberal democracy is not to abolish the state in preference for market anarchy, nor to abolish liberty in preference for an all-powerful state, but to 'rescue the middle ground' (Martell, 1993). In the final analysis, it is the inability to adopt a balanced perspective that stamps neo-liberal restructuring as an extreme doctrine.

Conclusion

The welfare state, then, can assure a degree of both equality and community in a number of politically important respects. More specifically, it assures a number of important functions. As Bertram (1988: 135) suggests, it

> improves resource allocation, minimises qualitative differentiation of service, is politically sustainable because of the wide spread of beneficiaries, and performs an important socially integrative function by underpinning rights of citizenship.

In addition, it is suggested that problems of administrative inertia or of various forms of 'capture' can be overcome by the institutionalisation of quality checks and controls, through ongoing research, by the decentralisation of services, by the establishment of countervailing associational networks of power which can mediate and represent the diverse interests of individuals, and through publicly provided education.

Notes

1. The most important of these policies were the Picot Report (1988); the Meade Report (1988); Tomorrow's Schools (1988); the Lough Report (1988); the National Curriculum of New Zealand (1991); the New Zealand Curriculum Framework (1993); the Hawke Report (1988).
2. In bracketing various neo-liberal writers together, I am not wishing to deny that there are important differences between their theories. This is especially so in respect to the libertarian political philosophy of Nozick. Yet it is

claimed that the common features that their works stress (anti-statism, individualism, priority on liberty, priority on the market) have generally contributed to the ascendency of a neo-liberal hegemony, and in this respect their common features become germane to understanding the decline of the welfare state. Having said this, specific analysis will focus principally on Hayek's formulations.

3. In this respect (again) the arguments of writers like Friedman (1962, 1980), Buchanan (1975) and Nozick (1974) are similar.

References

AMIN, A. (1994) Models, fantasies and phantoms of transition, in A. Amin (ed.) *Post Fordism: A Reader* (Oxford: Blackwell), 1–40.

BATES, R. (1990) Educational policy and the new cult of efficiency, in S. Middleton, J. Codd and A. Jones (eds) *New Zealand Education Policy Today: Cultural Perspectives* (Wellington: Allen & Unwin).

BERLIN, I. (1969) *Four Essays on Liberty* (Oxford: Oxford University Press).

BERTRAM, G. (1988) Middle class capture: a brief survey. *Future Directions, Vol. III, Part II: Report of the Royal Commission on Social Policy*, April (Wellington: Government Printer), 109–70.

BOBBIO, N. (1987) *The Future of Democracy* (Cambridge: Polity Press).

BOWLES, S. and GINTIS, H. (1986) *Democracy and Capitalism* (London: Routledge).

BRUS, W. (1972) *The Market in a Socialist Economy* (London: Routledge & Kegan Paul).

BUCHANAN, J. (1960) *Fiscal Theory and Political Economy* (Chapel Hill: University of North Carolina Press).

BUCHANAN, J. (1969) *Cost and Choice* (Chicago: Markham).

BUCHANAN, J. (1975) *The Limits of Liberty: Between Anarchy and Leviathan* (Chicago: University of Chicago Press).

BUCHANAN, J. and TULLOCK, G. (1972) *The Calculus of Consent: Logical Foundations of the Constitution of Democracy* (Ann Arbor: University of Michigan).

BURCHELL, G. (1993) Liberal government and techniques of the self, *Economy and Society*, 22(2), 267–81.

CODD, J. (1990a) Policy documents and the official discourses of the state, in J. Codd, R. Harker and R. Nash (eds) *Political Issues in New Zealand Education* (Palmerston North: Dunmore Press), 133–49.

CODD, J. (1990b) Educational policy and the crisis of the New Zealand state, in S. Middleton, J. Codd and A. Jones (eds) *New Zealand Educational Policy Today* (New Zealand: Allen & Unwin).

DAVEY, J. and DWYER, M. (1984) *Meeting Needs in the Community: A Discussion Paper on School Service* (New Zealand: New Zealand Planning Council).

DICKINSON, H. (1933) Economics of socialism. *Economic Journal*, 11 (3), 237–250.

DOBB, M. (1955) *On Economic Theory and Socialism* (London: Routledge & Kegan Paul).

FORBES, I. (ed.) (1986) *Market Socialism: Whose Choice?* (London Fabian Society: Fabian Tract 516).

FRIEDMAN, M. (1962) *Capitalism and Freedom* (Chicago: University of Chicago Press).

FRIEDMAN, M. (1980) *Free to Choose* (Harmondsworth: Penguin).

GERGEN, K. (1985) The social constructionist movement in modern psychology. *American Psychologist*, 40, 266–75.

GORDON, C. (1991) Government rationality: an introduction, in G. Burchell, C. Gordon and P. Miller (eds) *The Foucault Effect* (London: Harvester Wheatsheaf).

GORDON, L. (1992) The state, devolution and educational reform in New Zealand. *Journal of Education Policy*, 7(2), 187–203.

GORDON, L. (1993) 'Rich' and 'poor' schools in Aotearoa. Paper presented at the Annual Conference of the New Zealand Association for Research in Education, Hamilton, December.

GOULD, B. (1985) *Socialism and Freedom* (London: Macmillan).

HABERMAS, J. (1975) *Legitimation Crisis* (trans. T. McCarthy) (Boston: Beacon Press).

HACKING, I. (1995) *Rewriting the Soul: Multiple Personality and the Sciences of Memory* (Princeton: Princeton University Press).

HALL, S. (1988) Brave new world. *Marxism Today*, October, 24–29.

HATTERSLEY, R. (1987) *Choose Freedom: The Future for Democratic Socialism* (Harmondsworth: Penguin).

HAYEK, F. (ed.) (1935) *Collectivist Economic Planning* (London: Routledge & Kegan Paul).

HAYEK, F. A. (1944) *The Road to Serfdom* (London: Routledge & Kegan Paul).

HAYEK, F. (1945) The use of knowledge in society. *American Economic Review*, 35 (4), 519–530.

HAYEK, F. (1960) *The Constitution of Liberty* (London: Routledge & Kegan Paul).

HINDESS, B. (1990) Liberty and equality, in B. Hindess (ed.) *Reactions to the Right* (London: Routledge).

HIRST, P. (1990) Democracy: socialism's best answer to the right, in B. Hindess (ed.) *Reactions to the Right* (London: Routledge).

JESSOP, B. (1994) Post-Fordism and the state, in A. Amin (ed.) *Post Fordism: A Reader* (Oxford: Blackwell), 251–79.

JOPPKE, C. (1977) The crisis of the welfare state: collective consumption and the rise of new social actors. *Berkeley Journal of Sociology*, 32, 237–60.

KEAT, R. (1991) Introductions: Starship Britain or universal enterprise, in R. Keat and N. Abercrombie (eds) *Enterprise Culture* (London: Routledge).

KELSEY, J. (1993) *Rolling Back the State: Privatization of Power in Aotearoa* (Wellington: Bridget Williams Books).

LANE, R. (1993) *The Market Experience* (Cambridge: Cambridge University Press).

LANGE, O. (1939) *On the Economic Theory of Socialism* (ed. B. Lippincott) (Minneapolis: University of Minnesota Press).

LEGRAND, J. (1982) *The Strategy of Equality* (London: Allen & Unwin).

LEGRAND, J. (1987) The middle class and the use of British social services, in R. Goodin and H. LeGrand (eds) *Not Only the Poor* (London: Allen &Unwin).

LEGRAND, J. and ESTRIN, P. (1989) *Market Socialism* (Oxford: Clarendon).

LEGRAND, J. and ROBINSON, R. (1984) Privatisation and the welfare state: an introduction, in J. LeGrand and R. Robinson (eds) *Privatisation and the Welfare State* (London: Allen & Unwin).

LEVIN, H. (1989) Education as a public and private good, in N. E. Darins (eds.) *Public Values, Private Schools* (New York: Falmer).

MACCALLUM, G. G. (1967) Negative and positive liberty. *Philosophical Review*, 76, 312–34.

MCLENNAN, G. (1993) The concept, history, situation and prospects of social democracy: a modest overview. *Sites*, 26, Autumn, 103–14.

MACPHERSON, C. B. (1962) *The Political Theory of Possessive Individualism* (Oxford: Clarendon Press).

MACPHERSON, C. B. (1973) *Democratic Theory: Essays in Retrieval* (Oxford: Oxford University Press).

MARSHALL, J. (1981) *What is Education?* (Palmerston North: Dunmore Press).

MARSHALL, J. (1995) Skills, information and quality for the autonomous chooser, in M. Olssen and K. Morris Matthews (eds) *Democracy, Reform and Education: Proceedings of Special NZARE/RUME Conference*, 25 June, Auckland College of Education.

MARSHALL, J. and PETERS, M. (1990) The insertion of new right thinking into education: an example from New Zealand. *Journal of Educational Policy*, 5(2), 143–56.

MARTELL, L. (1992) New ideas of socialism. *Economy and Society*, 21 (2), 152–72.

MARTELL, L. (1993) Rescuing the middle ground: neo-liberalism and associational socialism. *Economy and Society*, 22(1), 100–113.

MORRIS, P. (1991) Freeing the spirit of enterprise: the genesis and development of the concept of enterprise culture, in R. Keat and N. Abercrombie (eds) *Enterprise Culture* (London: Routledge), 21–37.

NEW ZEALAND TREASURY (1984) *Economic Management: Brief to the Incoming Government* (Wellington: Government Printer).

NOVE, A. (1983) *The Economics of Feasible Socialism* (London: Allen & Unwin).

NOZICK, R. (1974) *Anarchy, State and Utopia* (New York: Basic Books).

NUTI, D. (1981) Socialism on earth. *Cambridge Journal of Economics*, 4, 391–403.

O'CONNOR, J. (1973) *The Fiscal Crisis of the State* (New York: St Martin's Press).

OFFE, C. (1984) Some contradictions in the modern welfare state, in C. Offe (ed.) *Contradictions of the Welfare State* (Cambridge, MA: MIT Press).

OLSSEN, M. and MORRIS MATTHEWS, K. (eds) (1995) 'Education, Democracy and Reform: An Introduction'. *Education, Democracy and Reform* (New Zealand Association for Research in Education/Research Unit for Maori Education, University of Auckland, Auckland).

PETERS, M. (1992) Starship education: enterprise culture in New Zealand. *Access: Critical Perspectives on Education Policy*, 11 (1), 1–12.

PETERS, M. and MARSHALL, J. (1988a) Social policy and the move to community, in *Report of the (NZ) Royal Commission on Social Policy, III, Pt 1* (Wellington: Government Printer), 655–76.

PETERS, M. and MARSHALL, J. (1988b) Social policy and the move to 'community': practical implications for service delivery, in *Report of the Royal Commission on Social Policy, III, Part 1* (Wellington: Government Printer), 677–702.

PETERS, M. and MARSHALL, J. (1988c) Te reo o te Tai Tokerau: community evaluation, empowerment and opportunities for oral Maori language reproduction, in *Report of the Royal Commission on Social Policy, III, Pt 1* (Wellington: Government Printer), 703–43.

PETERS, M. and MARSHALL, J. (1988d) Empowerment and the ideal learning community: theory and practice in Tai Tokerau, in C. Wylie (ed.) *Proceedings of the First Research into Educational Policy Conference*, Wellington, 17–19 August.

PETERS, M. and MARSHALL, J. (1988e) The politics of 'choice' and 'community'. *Access*, 7, 84–109.

PETERS, M. and MARSHALL, J. (1989) Education and empowerment: postmodernism, humanism and critiques of individualism. Paper presented at the New Zealand Association for Research in Education Annual Conference, Educational Research: Can It Make a Difference in the Classroom?, 30 November–3 December, Wellington.

PETERS, M. and MARSHALL, J. (1990) Education, the new right and the crisis of the welfare state in New Zealand. *Discourse*, 11 (1), 77–90.

PETERS, M., MARSHALL, J. and MASSEY, L. (1994) Recent educational reforms in Aotearoa, in E. Coxon, K. Jenkins, J. Marshall and L. Massey (eds) *The Politics of Learning and Teaching in Aotearoa-New Zealand* (Palmerston North: Dunmore Press Ltd).

PLANT, R. (1988) *Citizenship Rights and Socialism* (London: Fabian Society).

POLANYI, K. (1969) The birth of the liberal creed, in K. J. Rea and J. T. McLeod (eds) *Business and Government in Canada* (Toronto: Methuen).

POPPER, K. R. (1961) *The Poverty of Historicism* (London: Routledge).

REA, K. J. and MCLEOD, J. T. (eds) (1969) *Business and Government in Canada* (Toronto: Methuen).

ROBINSON, V. (1988) An opportunity for participatory democracy. *Access*, 7, 16–26.

ROSE, N. (1993) Government, authority and expertise in advanced liberalism. *Economy and Society*, 22(3), 283–99.

SHERIDAN, A. (1980) *Michel Foucault: The Will to Truth* (London: Routledge).

SHONFIELD, A. (1965) *Modern Capitalism: The Changing Balance of Public and Private Power* (London: Oxford University Press).

SMITH, G. (1991) Reform and Maori educational crisis: a grand illusion Keynote Speech at PPTA Conference, Otautahi.

SNOOK, I. (1995) Democracy and education in a monetarist society. *Education Philosophy and Theory*, 27(1), 55–67.

TOMLINSON, J. (1990) Market socialism: a basis for socialist renewal, in B. Hindess (ed.) *Reactions to the Right* (London: Croom Helm).

WOOTTON, B. (1945) *Freedom Under Planning* (London: Allen & Unwin).

YEATMAN, A. (1990) A feminist theory of social differentiation, in L. J. Nicholson (ed.) *Feminism/Postmodernism* (New York: Routledge), 281–99.

YOUNG, I. (1990) The ideal of community and the politics of difference, in L. J. Nicholson, *Feminism/Postmodernism* (New York: Routledge), 300–23.

[21]

J. EDUCATION POLICY, 1996, VOL. 11, NO. 1, 27–51

Rethinking decentralization and state/civil society distinctions: the state as a problematic of governing [1]

Thomas S. Popkewitz
University of Wisconsin-Madison

In a variety of national contexts, there have been discussions about the changing relations of the state to the educational arena. Often, these discussions talk about centralization and decentralization of the state or of the devolution of power, the latter referring to shifts in the loci of power to geographically local contexts, for example through community governance of education. These discussions, it is argued in this essay, tend to position state power as dualistic, pitting one set of actors against another without inquiring into the patterns that locate different actors. The structuring of oppositions between state and civil society, public and private, government and economy does not adequately characterize the diverse ways that rule is exercised. The purpose in this essay is to relocate the problem of the state in the problematic of governing; to consider the state as networks of relations among various actors and discursive strategies that regulate and discipline the citizen. Pedagogy is explored as a particular site of governing patterns of the state through its systems of distinctions and differentiation. Pedagogy provides a site to explore how the governing patterns produce inclusions/exclusions through the inscriptions of subjectivities. The distinctions are not overt but occur through the production of reason and the 'reasonable' person. Changes in Russia, South Africa, Sweden and the USA are examined as different state traditions in the regulation of school practices.

Introduction

In a variety of national contexts, there have been discussions about the changing relations of the state to the educational arena.[2] Often, these discussions centre on issues concerning the centralization and decentralization of the state or the devolution of power, the latter referring to shifts in the loci of power to geographically local contexts, for example, through community governance of education. The discussion posits the state as a 'real' entity in opposition to civil society (public vs private, government vs economy). At a different level are discussions about the 'privatization' and 'marketization' of social policy, concepts which indicate a major change in the relation of the state to civil society. These sets of distinctions accept political rhetoric as the presuppositions of analysis rather than making that rhetoric itself the focus of what is to be understood and explained.

The purpose of this essay is to locate the problem of the state in the problematic of regulation. I argue that the changes in the educational arena mentioned above are examples of changes in the production of social regulation at two different but related layers. One of these is the reconstitution of relations among actors in governmental agencies *and* civil society. I use the concept of 'arena' to think about two related layers. One is the state as the patterns of relations in which certain actors are authorized to organize, classify and administer school practices.[3] A second layer of regulation involves the governing systems that organize and classify the objects for scrutiny and action in the arena. In the 19th century, Foucault (1979) argues, there occurred a new relationship between state governing practices and individual behaviours and dispositions. If the state was to be responsible for the welfare of its citizens, he argues, the identity of individuals had to be linked to the administrative patterns found in the larger society. This embodied a power/knowledge relation. New institutions of health, labour, education tied the new social welfare goals of the state to the self-reflective and self-governing principles of individuality (Donald 1992, Rose and Miller 1992, Shapiro 1992, Hunter 1994). Governing, then, is used to focus on historically specific practices through which individuals can think of, conduct and evaluate themselves as productive individuals. The 'socialization', as is Bourdieu's (1984) and before him Durkheim's and Weber's *habitus*, is not of the anthropological universe of functional sociology but of the outcome of specific social practices through which subjectivities are constructed. It also entails a change from a sovereignty notion of governing to one of governing people and things.

I explore the problem of the state as a system of regulation at three levels. First, I look at the relation of actors and discourses in the educational reforms of four apparently different countries – Russia, South Africa, Sweden and the USA. I draw maps of similarities and differences in the constructions/reconstructions in the educational arena. Of concern is how the subjectivities of various actors are historically constituted through the patterns of relation produced. *I argue that the effects in the governing patterns are not only related to the child and teacher but to the field of actors in the educational arena.* Second, I look at homologies between the construction of the teacher and the child in the educational arena and changes occurring in politics, the arts and economics. My purpose at this level of analysis is to explore an amalgamation of non-causal intersections in the patterns of governing. Third, I consider pedagogy as a specific site which relates political rationalities to the capabilities of the individual. The aforementioned governing, however, does not occur on a level playing field in the sense that there is an uneven distribution of eligibility for participation and action. The systems of distinctions and differentiation in pedagogy, I argue, produce systems of inclusion/exclusion as local, partial knowledges are inscribed as universal and global. 'Constructivist' pedagogy, given prominence in the USA and international reforms, is an exemplar of the production of such differentiations.

While public discussions about school reform are populist and sometimes evangelical – reforms ostensibly promote local, individual choice, empowerment, and democracy – I argue that reforms are governing technologies that order the possibilities of action and self-reflection. Such governing is not a linear story but one of fluctuation, uneven movements and unpredictable transformations as political rationalities are brought into the pedagogical discourse through multiple capillaries; capillaries that traverse distinctions between state and civil society.

Constructing the problem-solving citizen

The past two decades involve important changes in the state governing of the educational arena in Sweden and the USA, two industrialized countries which on the surface are historically different. In this section, I compare the educational arenas of these two countries to explore the transformations. My discussion problematizes a discussion that begins with Hegelian to post-Kantian moral and political philosophy and continues into the present. Its underlying premise is the idea that the state is not only the regulation of the legitimized forms of political and economic action, but the modes of action that act on the dispositions, sensitivities and awareness that enable individuals to be productive and self-autonomous actors. The subjectivity of the person, then, becomes 'not only *subject to* the play of forces in the apparatus of the social but also acts as author and *subject of* its own conduct' (Donald 1992: 14).

In focusing on the state as patterns of regulation, I engage a notion of power that has been prominent in postmodern discussions about the politics of knowledge. This concern is to understand how power is deployed through multiple capillaries that produce and constitute the 'self' as an agent of change (Young 1990, Barrett and Phillips 1992, Shapiro 1992, Butler 1993). My use of the concept of the educational arena is to interpret power relationally and historically as an amalgamation of institutional and discursive practices that function as 'a collective assemblage of disparate parts on a single social surface' (Crary 1990: 6).

The discussion refocuses the notion of power from that of *sovereignty* which seeks to identify the 'origins' or roots of power through classifying those groups which structurally dominate and which are repressed. While the notion of sovereignty provides certain insights, it ignores or misrecognizes the disciplining and productive qualities of power in the construction of the self-autonomous and self-reflective person. I have discussed the problems of the *sovereignty* notion of power in the study of schooling elsewhere (Popkewitz 1991, Popkewitz and Brennan in press). For now, suffice it to say here that the sovereign notion of power as an historical narrative posits unified, often evolutionary processes and structures; however, power tends to be constructed, visioned and deployed in a manner that is historically contingent, and with multiple, fluid boundaries. In a prominent category of traditional analysis, while one can posit a generalized condition of capitalism as a background to the organization of power, this positing does not provide an adequate theoretical grounding for understanding how the capillaries of power work in contemporary societies. There is no one model of capitalism; neither is its history one of a single, unified development (for different discussions related to this, see, e.g. Boyer 1989, Crary 1990, Sousa Santos 1995).

Governing at a distance: reconstituting the Swedish arena

The construction of the modern Swedish welfare state in the 1920s and 1930s transformed a network of diverse and often antagonistic voluntary associations, trade unions, political parties and local municipal bureaucracies into the centralized professional and administrative apparatus of the 'welfare' state.[4] This type of governing embodied certain principles and ideals of social engineering, that is, the application of a universal rational knowledge and the apparently 'neutral' professional expertise to calculate and regulate social, economic and moral affairs. That 'welfare' state was to ensure high levels of employment, economic progress, social security, health and housing (education as a state activity came much earlier in Sweden).

The major responsibility for planning and evaluation belonged to the central state ministry and bureaucracies, not to the teacher. Detailed parliamentary instructions to teachers were legislated. The Swedish Board of Education, for example, was constructed with this bureaucratic, social engineering approach to social progress. Further, the educational sciences were mobilized, particularly in the post-Second World War period, in the administrative development of schooling, and in the production of self that brought the process of rationalization to a disciplined, autonomous self-reliance and moral inner-directed individual.[5]

The past two decades have seen important shifts in the governing patterns which constitute the Swedish educational arena. By the 1970s, the centralized school system had produced a number of unsolved problems and developed a great deal of 'inertia'. Demands emerged for more flexible local responses to education, such as those provided historically by parish and later municipal schools (see, e.g. Kallos 1995). In fact, there was a common move to increase the scope of action of municipal school boards during the 1970s whose consequences are 'visible' in the reforms of the 1980s and 1990s. By 1991, the Board of Education was replaced with a new agency, the Swedish National Agency for Education (Skolverket). The latter is a small entity that has both regional and central concerns in the administration of schools. *In one sense, the construction of the Swedish educational agency, Skolverket, is a parliamentary effort to undo the strongly centralized and uniform school bureaucracy. At the same time, Skolverket is located within historically contingent changes in the educational arena that are neither evolutionary nor reducible to the conscious intentions of Parliament.*

I explore the changes in the educational arena by recognizing that the revisioning of the 'welfare' state is less the beginning of a new form of state than the construction of a new mode of inscribing political rationalities in the self-government of the individual. The changing patterns of regulation are examined through the repositioning of actors and problem solving produced in the educational arena.

The new problem solving embodies a revisioning of the Swedish state curriculum (*Läroplan*) that is reformulated as a goal-driven conception of the state *vis-à-vis* the educational arena (Carlgren in press a). General curriculum goals are set by the central government to provide local school districts with flexibility and a certain degree of autonomy in developing implementation plans. In return, the central state bureaucracy monitors outcomes and content through psychometric measurements rather than processes. If we view the current situation from one view of the state, the Swedish National Agency for Education establishes what is legitimate and reasonable for the conduct of education, but localities and teachers have the responsibility for evaluating and, in some cases, choosing from the many goals.

While the word stayed the same, the *Läroplan* embodies a restructuring of the 'problem-solving' capabilities of the teacher and local administrative authorities. The 'new' teacher who participates in the modern state is one who is flexible, responsive to changes and acts with greater autonomy in finding solutions to social problems.

Although there is debate about the reforms, the categories that are used to construct the teacher are generally not made problematic. The governing practices of the new *Läroplan* embody sets of assumptions related to the importation of two Anglo-American words: 'curriculum' and 'professionalism' (see, e.g. Kallós and Lundahl-Kallós 1994, Kallós and Nilsson 1995). The word 'curriculum' brings into focus distinctions about teaching, and helps to construct a teacher who has self-autonomy and capabilities in local planning, organizing, managing and evaluating school knowledge. The call for professionalism relates to a re-visioning of occupational identity. It gives value to school work that includes greater teacher responsibility and flexibility in implementing goal-governed approaches of the state.[6]

The importation of the words 'curriculum' and 'professionalism' represents more than a simple process of borrowing words to express desired 'states' of the future teacher. Instead these words embody 'rules of reasoning' about the self-examination and capabilities of teachers, educational researchers, bureaucrats and teacher educators. 'Curriculum' and 'professionalism' are concepts drawn from Anglo-American governing traditions in education where a 'weak' central bureaucracy historically interacts with civil organizations, local school districts and professional groups to produce pedagogical practice. These traditions provide a stark contrast with previous continental European state practices (Popkewitz 1993a).[7] However, they have relevance in the current reconstitution of the Swedish educational arena.

The Swedish reception of notions of 'curriculum' and 'professionalism' is that they are not 'merely' brought into its educational arena as 'fixed entities'. They are given interpretation within the patterns of relations in the educational arena that have a specific historical horizon. For example, the words 'curriculum' and 'professionalism' are nuances through continental European (Danish and German) educational traditions associated with Herbart, and an outlook about an educated class that is different from, but intermixes with, the Anglo-American notions of expert knowledge.

These changes in the problematic of regulation are not only of 'the rules' about teachers and students; they effect the subjectivities of the various actors in that arena. For example, there is a self-problematization of the bureaucracy. The former governmental official who monitored the school operated with the assumption that the rules of schooling were clearly defined within an hierarchical authority. This is no longer so, and the bureaucratic official needs to operate in a more fluid, pragmatic and locally defined problem-solving context. In this sense, the bureaucrat who 'administers' the school is defined and understood in the reconstitution of the governing principles of the educational arena.

Contemporary Swedish university and teacher education also involves a visioning/re-visioning of the production of knowledge and expertise. At one level, there has been a disbanding or weakening of governmental agencies which had previously coordinated and monitored the universities. In this new schema, universities occupy a changed relationship relative to other actors in the educational arena as there is greater internal control over faculty positions and budget. Contemporary political rhetoric speaks (either positively or negatively, depending on the ideological position of the speaker) about the 'new' Swedish university as responsible to some mythical notion of 'market' that is flexible to changing conditions, although the 'nature' of faculty involvement is often prescribed through the rationalities of 'self-government' and financial strategies of the central government that govern organizational matters.

Epistemologically, state-centred analyses in education have been challenged by a more pragmatic outlook that focuses on problems of teachers and didactics, with a greater use of 'qualitative methods' to assess local implementations of reforms and on teachers' problem-solving abilities. At the same time, centralized statistical information about children's achievement, school 'resources' and reform implementation has been authorized as the central government 'finds' itself with different requirements for 'information' about school outcomes. The production of the latter type of information has become a recognizable industry within the university as new national tests are being constructed to monitor governmental programmes.

Epistemological shifts in this arena involve the appearance of two 'new' sets of authorized actors. One of these is the psychometricans who have been present in the educational arena since the early 1950s but are given a new credibility in the current restructuring.

A different grouping of actors is teacher educators who had previously had little authority in the research community. I will call them the 'local' researchers. They focus on knowledge that is deemed 'usable' to regional authorities, the 'decentralized' teacher education programmes, and local parents. The 'local' evaluators see themselves as 'practically' orientated to respond to 'demands' about the use of reform programmes. With an emphasis on 'qualitative' methods, the new evaluations focus on teacher practices related to goal-governed educational steering.

The 'local' researchers are themselves positioned in relation to a re-emergence of didactics in the study and training of teachers. The didactics brought into current programmes, however, are different from those of the German idealism of earlier professional educational schematas.[8] The new didactics give importance to relations between the teachers, learners and the academic content of school subjects through constructivist psychologies (the latter are called 'progressivist' in Sweden). The emphasis is on a teacher who is a 'problem solver' and who works in a flexible environment that contains a constant flux.

The changes in the construction of the teachers do not occur through formal governmental directives but instead through changes in programme and discourses, as certain strategies are brought into play as 'professional education'. These include notions such as 'the reflective teacher' and 'action research' (Kallos and Selander 1993). The latter emerges through an increased emphasis on instruction in classroom evaluation. These strategies govern at a distance through the art of self-examination. Without arguing a correspondence, it can be seen that strategies described here as didactics and the 'autonomous' professional teacher who is 'self-reflective' are related to the teaching dispositions inscribed in the governmental 'goal-steering' practices discussed earlier.

The discourses about curriculum, professionalization, didactics and action research, among others, are positioned within a set of relations whose governing patterns comprise the state. The resulting patterns of relations, however, cannot be adequately understood as a reconstruction of what was dismantled by the 1920s, but instead as a reconstitution of power whose relations comprise the educational arena. The new governing practices are themselves being debated and the outcome is not clear.

Governing at a distance: the USA

Similar reform discourses can be seen in the USA. However, the reform discourses are embodied in different historical sets of relations in the educational arena.[9] From the 19th century, the governing of the school was organized through complex patterns that included commercial textbook publishers, municipal financing of and hiring in schools, and a strong local school district administration. In some discussions, the role of the state in the USA has been viewed as 'weak' in comparison with Sweden's 'strong' state tradition. The US Department of Education had little if any role in the construction of schooling until after the Second World War and the reform movements beginning in the late 1950s. In fact, most educational histories and research accept implicitly the idea of a 'weak' state through various categories of interpretation, such as descriptions of the US system as decentralized and localized, school outcomes through psychological 'learning' theories, micro-ethnographies of the classroom culture, and the principal as the key to school reform.

The notions of 'weak' and 'strong' states, however, have little analytic value when considering the problematic of governing. In fact, such language tends to be more misleading than helpful. One needs to look no further than current US policy discourses about 'virtuous' subjectivities to understand the USA embodies a strong set of institutional relations and discourses that govern subjectivities. Current debates about the regulation of smoking and the labelling of foods to discipline the dietary habits of individuals, for example, point to strong 'rules' that relate governmental legislation to the moral deportment of citizens. This inscription of the harmonizing of administrative patterns and individual 'self-government' transcends ideologies. National discourses about abortion and child's rights, women's abuse, teenage pregnancies and welfare 'reform', constructed with different ideological agendas, converge through the acceptance of the harmonization of political rationalities with the moral deportment and behaviours of individual subjects.

The differences between Sweden and the USA are in how governing patterns are constructed rather than in such labels of 'weak' or 'strong'. The linking of political rationalities with subjectivities in US schools during the 19th and early 20th centuries, for example, involved different trajectories from those described previously in Sweden. Certain discourses about the pedagogy of the 'child', 'childhood', school administration, and measurement of achievement, for example, circulated nationally to construct the object and subject of schooling. The rules of 'curriculum' and childhood inscribed notions of progress that tied social engineering approaches to child development to the construction of 'self'. At the same time, an academized knowledge of the 'teacher' in teacher education and the development of management techniques to hire, organize and assess teacher performance were woven together with other practices to govern the teacher and child. The amalgamation of ideas, technologies and institutions that formed the governing systems were not 'weak', decentralized or evolutionary.

The current reforms can be understood as a reconstitution of the patterns that have governed the school arena. Captured in the recently used phrase of 'systemic school reform', new sets of relations among governmental agencies, professional teaching groups in the various school subjects, research communities and regional authorities have emerged. As in Sweden, the new governing strategies move among multiple sets of actors whose patterns of governing constitute the state in education. The discourses of standards and professionalism appear within a context of building strong US government monitoring and steering systems, such as national curriculum goals, assessment techniques (e.g. portfolio assessments) and a national teacher certification test. The discourses about national standards and teacher professionalism emerge from coalitions among groups within state agencies, professional groups, foundations and teacher unions. The national discourses about standards are joined with discussions about site-based management, 'shared decision making', teacher education reforms concerning a 'reflective teacher', and a constructivist pedagogy. A consequence, I will argue in the last section, is a revision of the problematic of the governing of the 'self' through the applied reasoning.

The sets of actors being mobilized and the relations established in the educational arena of Sweden and the USA involve a reconstitution of the 'problem-solving' field for the possibilities of action, but in different historical national conditions. In neither instance can we assume that educational change involves a linear and evolutionary process in which a stable and consistent group of actors is suddenly challenged by a newly emerging group. Such an account of the reform process ignores the assemblage of techniques and images that intersect to create subject positions and to position and reposition 'actors'. The 'bureaucratic' actor who practises social engineering in Sweden is a different bureaucratic 'actor' in the current 'problem-solving' context. In an important sense, actors who might appear on some level to be the same are, in fact, transformed as they compete in different patterns and through different epistemological rules of engagement. Concepts such as 'markets' and 'privatization' that are offered in both countries to explain change leave unscrutinized the field of relations being produced in the educational arena.

Changing regimes and the patterns of regulation: Russia and South Africa

Whereas changes in Sweden and the US governments relate to party policies, the case of Russia and South Africa involves changes in the rationalities and rules of politics and citizenship associated with their regimes.[10] Yet both countries are engaged in educational reform programmes that have certain similarities to those of Sweden and the USA. But the historical conditions in each country involve different sets of relations in order to consider the meaning of the state in education. My focus on those relations here is twofold: to historicize the notion of state through exploring the intersection of changing actors and epistemologies in changes of political regimes; and to locate the production of a 'problem-solving' to govern social practices. The letter requires attention given to experted-mediated knowledge in the construction of governing patterns. The tying together of actors and discourses, again, is to offer a multilayered, relational and historical notion of the state.

Russia and South Africa are both witnessing a change in their political regimes. In both countries discussions are emerging about constructing a 'civil society' (through non-governmental organization – NGOs), an ideological focus within international agencies and policy discussion. Civil society, it is believed, provides intermediary social institutions between the individual and state that can democratize society and reduce or eliminate the authoritarian practices of the previous regimes (see, e.g. Fukuyama 1995, Zakaria 1995). Further, Russia and South Africa have policies that point to a decentralization that coincides with a centralization ('nation-building') that, on the surface, seems similar to that which was discussed in regard to Sweden and the USA. The former countries, for example, have developed a rhetoric of decentralization, site-based management and reforms which focus on didactics through the incorporation of a psychological constructivism.

In Russia, a liberal political and capitalist economic regime is replacing the system of centralization organized by the Communist Party. The previous Soviet regime, for example, had no governing actors outside the infrastructure of the formal governmental agencies and the party from which strong hierarchical systems of regulation were constructed and monitored. The rapid emergence of the Soviet system after the revolution resulted in a combination of Czarist and Communist policies that had prevented a viable civil society or public associations from forming. In all respects, the Party dominated the political, social and cultural activities. (In the language of international funding agencies, there were no viable NGOs in the former Soviet Union.)

We can contrast the transformations currently taking place in Russia with those in South Africa as the apartheid system is politically dismantled. Although it was authoritarian in its technologies that suppressed dissent, South Africa's apartheid system had a strong capitalist economic system and relatively strong social, academic and labour movements. Even during the worst moments of apartheid, Black labour unions were strong, and certain community groups functioned even though the economic consequences of racial discrimination often destroyed the fabric of family life. Furthermore, groups in exile challenged South Africa from outside. Although the educational system was segregated, there was an educated Black élite which came mainly from missionary schools. Academics could contribute to the local sciences through study abroad and domestically (sometimes they could read books considered as 'subversive' in special sections of libraries). The academic situation of South African intellectuals, then, presents a stark contrast with Soviet social and educational scientists for whom theoretical and methodological development was severely restrained. In South Africa a consequence of the functioning of these different groups outside and inside the country was developed administrative capabilities that could be brought into the restructuring of governing patterns once apartheid ended.[13]

It is within this political context that we can think historically about a mobilization of a social engineering that 'slept' during the apartheid years – some intellectuals were exiled, or lived in fear of reprisals if they acted out of concert with governmental policy. As apartheid began to be officially dismantled, the 'sleepers' in South African civil society could be awakened. They had the necessary skills (mentalities) to work as 'planning groups' alongside official governmental bodies.

With the Soviet Union's collapse, there were no such 'sleepers' except from the old party system. The Communist Party was so encompassing in its control (and fear) mechanisms that there was no developed civil society to interrelate with the formal governmental agencies in the construction of governing patterns.[11] Equally important was the fact that people did not have the dispositions and 'civilizing rules' of capitalistic modernity in which to negotiate the complexities of their new situation. It is no accident that many of the people who make decisions in Russia are the same people who were party bureaucrats in the old system, but now act within the 'new' epistemic spaces of institutional reforms that emphasize 'choice' and individuality (Kerr in progress).

Both instances of changes in regimes entailed a production of an expertise to govern reason and 'reasonable' people. The struggles over the new citizen and polity are most dramatically illustrated in the conflict between the Russian Parliament and the Russian President. However, these struggles are just as profoundly embodied in the reshaping of the educational arena. The Russian educational problem is, among other things, the need to develop an 'expertise' necessary for managing a more fluid and less bureaucratically centralized administration of schools. This expertise is not, however, 'merely' technical competence. It also involves a reconstitution of the teacher: how one feels, thinks, 'sees' and acts as a competent subject in schooling.

As in Sweden and the USA, the governing of teachers and children is central to the construction of the educational arena. On the surface, the new regimes in Russia and South Africa need to produce more teachers, retrain existing teachers and construct a new 'content' in the curriculum.[12] But the reform practices are more than recruitment practices or changes in curriculum foci; the map of the educational arena is also being reordered through the relations established.

Let me explore this through the work of the SOROS Foundation, a New York philanthropic agency investing large sums of money in Eastern Europe to facilitate changes towards a market economy. This foundation has been working with the Russian Ministry of Education to produce new high school textbooks concerning the new 'imagined communities' of nationhood and the citizen inscribed with western liberal philosophy and histories of ideas.

Previously, Soviet teachers worked from well-scripted 'lesson' plans that chronologically detailed an exact sequence for each lesson. The styles of presentation for materials were ritualized – everyone in the country was to use them in a standardized manner. The SOROS textbooks, in contrast, were intended to construct 'mentalities' that combined different Russian approaches to pedagogy with western liberal and progressive notions of 'child-centred' education. While the discursive constructions are not monolithic, 'New Teacher' was one who could act autonomously, using 'problem-solving' capabilities. In other words, this teacher is the embodiment of the 'problem solving' teacher that I discussed in a previous section.

However, the task of constructing a new, imagined community is more than 'merely' writing textbooks. It involves reconstituting the 'author' as a subject and object of scrutiny. When SOROS located authors to write such textbooks, the project planners realized that the authors did not have the requisite skills. A statist 'mentality' associated with the previous communist regime was embodied in the textbook 'authors'. To produce the textbooks, the SOROS Foundation held workshops to 'teach' the authors how to think about, and organize, curriculum content, didactics and assessments. The teacher's guides provided teachers with a choice of activities, and had visual and psychological appeal for children – 'things' that are taken for granted in western countries. Less explicit but on the horizon of the curriculum construction were Russian views about spirituality and specific religious outlooks that have become part of the discourses of schooling.

The practices of the SOROS Foundation provide one point of entry into the changing relations of different actors and the struggles over the production of 'reason'. The rewritten textbooks occupy a problematic position in relation to other school and teacher practices that centre on the mastery of school content embodied in the examination systems provided by the Russian Ministry of Education in Moscow. A more geographically localized context of school management with regional authorities and finances also redefines the 'planning' and the production of knowledge embodied in the Russian Academy of Education and Teacher Education. At present neither of these agencies has a monopoly in the production of the teacher or the epistemological systems that construct the curricula, didactics and the teacher. As in Sweden, there is a new 'local' researcher/evaluator.

The map of the South African arena has a different historical construction. As the South African negotiations for a change-over in regimes came closer, the African National Congress, with private internal and external foundation assistance, set up policy-making units to rival those functioning within the formal government controlled by the Afrikaaner National Party.

One such academic group in education produced the NEP (National Educational Plan). Whereas previously policy was dominated by Afrikaan academics and a 'Fundamental Pedagogics' that legimized apartheid, the NEP was intended to appraise and develop goals for a new multicultural system of education. Implementation of this plan resulted in the production of a series of polished booklets that outlined the purposes and directions of a multicultural curriculum, administration and economics of a new educational system. The NEP assumed a strong role by the state in steering South Africa towards national goals. This process, as found in Sweden, was coupled with developments in local government and teacher autonomy, expressed as professionalization.

If one expunges a particular rhetoric related to South Africa from the NEP documents (such as references to apartheid and equity and democracy), the texts embody universalized discourses about calculating and managing change that are also found in other countries, such as the USA and UK. The NEP also inscribes many of the priorities of inter-state agencies, such as the World Bank, through its definition of problems and options for problem solving.[14]

The NEP documents were produced by a new group of academic experts drawn from previously marginalized groups within the English and Indian universities as well as from Coloured and Black South Africans trained in postgraduate education outside the country (these distinctions are themselves the effects of power in the apartheid system which are still productive in its dismantling). Less visible and rarely acknowledged are foundations and inter-state agencies: these consist of not only SORO in Russia, but also other institutions such as the World Bank, USAID, Swedish SIDA, and the OECD, as well as 'non-governmental' institutions such as the Ford, Rockefeller and McArthur Foundations which operate within Russia, South Africa, Sweden and the USA. (See, e.g. Lagemann 1989, Fisher 1993.)

My argument to this point is that if we narrowly view the state as only confined to governmental agencies in the current historical conjuncture, we misrecognize the power relation through which the governing practices are forming. While similar reform practices in respect of decentralization circulate among the four countries, there are historical distinctions in the constituting of relations and power in the educational arena. Various actors within civil society and government have no 'essential', unchanging attributes but are defined through the systems of relations established. The reforms emerge through multiple trajectories and are given authority through different sets of actors that are located both in the state and civil society. My focus on Russia and South Africa, however, was also to bring the position of academic scientific actors into sharper relief in the governing principles used to construct the teacher and the child in schooling and teacher education. But even here, we cannot assume the academic actors are a single unified group. Only certain groupings of academics are authorized to speak. Understanding the patterns of regulation requires that we consider the notion of 'actor' as problematic; that we understand empirically the relations among groupings in their arena of practice and consider the knowledge systems that give direction and interpretation to those practices. The latter bring the problem of governmentality to the fore to understand how epistemological rules of problem solving position and are positioned by the various actors in the educational arena.

Pedagogy, and reconstituting the regulatory patterns as the US state

In this section, I focus directly on pedagogy in order to consider the rules and standards of problem solving. My purpose is to make problematic what many policy analysts assume when they focus on actors in 'decision making' or on the ideological 'origins' of policy statements – that is, *the practical technologies of pedagogy that order, evaluate and discipline educational practices and its individuals.* (See, Ball 1990, Marshall 1995 as counter-examples.) *My example is US constructivist pedagogical research about teaching school subjects, an exemplar explored for multiple reasons.*[15] This type of research is produced through multiple capillaries that are not restricted to the formal agencies of state government and civil society. That is, the particular epistemological rules governing constructivist research are authorized through the intersection of different sets of actors. In the USA, constructivist research programmes are sanctioned through federal, state government and foundational grants as well as through professional organizations.[16] This authorization is important, I will argue, not only in the educational arena but in relation to changes in the regulating patterns of other arenas. These arenas include politics, as I mentioned earlier, as well as the economy and the arts in ways that I discuss later. Finally, constructivist discourse is influential in all of the countries mentioned earlier, although in some cases it goes by different names, such as 'activity theory' in Russia and 'historical-materialist' psychology in South Africa.

Reforms as the governing of the teacher

In contrast with the reform movement of the 1960s/70s which sought to rationalize curriculum content, current US reforms seek to regulate by opening up the 'minds' of teachers through reworking the notions of teacher competence, skills and knowledge about school subjects. *The central focus is on how teachers' and students' capabilities and dispositions towards knowledge.* Pedagogical discourses normalize the dispositions and capacity of individuals who regularize their own conduct as 'autonomous' actors. One strong current in teacher and teacher education reforms, for example, gives attention to 'constructivist' research programmes that construct teachers who operate with a certain degree of semi-autonomy and flexibility. This type of research, often supported by federal and foundational grants, defines the knowledge of teaching as pragmatic and with negotiated 'meanings' organized through the practices of the classroom. The flexibility claimed by constructivist researchers refers to the way in which children learn concepts and is in contrast with earlier curriculum reforms that organized the disciplinary structures of knowledge according to strictly defined teachers' competencies, such as the ability to effect the 'conceptual mastery' of children.

If we place the various reform discourses in relation to each other, a number of different actors emerge in the construction of the 'identity' of the teacher. At the national level, US curriculum standards, a movement towards the steering of education by the federal government, not dissimilar to that in Sweden, provide frameworks (goal-steering) for local school staff (Celis 1993). Efforts by professional organizations to develop national curriculum standards are supported through federal legislation and foundational grants. The work of the National Council for Social Studies and The National Council for Teachers of Mathematics are two examples that inscribe constructivist education and research. The standards referred to in this type of discourse are indeed to 'remake' the teachers (and students) into problem-solving, 'empowered', autonomous and personally flexible individuals who act in contexts that have no clear set of boundaries or singular answers.

While we can point to the uneven processes through which the reforms are produced, there are differentiated actors who have become part of the governing processes. If we examine the national standards, for example, professional organizations have assumed the responsibilities of monitoring compliance through working with textbook publishers, state departments of education and testing institutions. This monitoring is not done through any legal process but instead through the construction of a network of actors that interrelate civil associations and governmental agencies.

At a different level, a range of management practices intended to liberalize the school have been introduced to increase teacher responsibilities in instruction; here I am thinking of site-based management of schools, 'shared decision making' in school governance, and a concept of teacher education which places a premium on teachers designing curriculum, and working collaboratively within local communities (the latter concept is found in programmes that emphasize teaching for diversity and multiculturalism). 'Action research', an important element in recent efforts to reform teaching and teacher education, can be seen historically in relation to the above reforms. Its purpose is to have teachers learn how to study systematically and reflect about the way their practices relate to curriculum goals.

If we think of the reform practices as occurring within an arena, the seemingly different practices above are constructed within patterns of relations whose effects are to reconstitute the way teachers are to think about and assess their performance. The different reform practices embody practices concerning the capabilities and dispositions of teacher as they think of themselves as capable and able professionals in schools.

It is important to note that the professional responsibility to monitor standard compliance in the USA is historically related to the development of a welfare state in the USA at the turn of the century. The US governing process has consistently woven together governmental and non-governmental administrative agencies in the production of regulations. Recent US Congressional legislation, for example, has established a standards commission to monitor the implementation of national goals. The commission is a semi-independent agency rather than one within the formal governmental bureaucracy. The construction of quasi-administrative agencies to regulate education is an historical part of state development in the USA, no different than the creation of a federal aviation agency, a federal transportation agency or the federal regulatory agency for stocks and bonds (Skowronek 1982).

The reformulation and coordination of reform practices is described by the slogan of 'systemic school reform. 'Systemic school reform' makes a rhetorical claim that researchers have identified the necessary components of successful schools and that the role of the central government is to coordinate federal, local and professional practices through a coherent policy (Smith and O'Day 1990). This 'coordinating' is not neutral, however, as it is part of the construction of patterns of governing that relate various sets of actors and discourses in the school arena. School boards, professional associations and local school districts, for example, are linked to a new expertise ordered through the categories and distinctions that define the 'successful' school, including those embodied in the constructivist approaches to teaching school subjects. Where debates do occur, they tend to ignore issues concerning pedagogy as a technology of governing that constructs the object and subject of schooling and focus instead on macro-level debates such as the relative merits of national versus local control of schooling, the need for equity and inclusion, or the benefits of a multicultural education.

Cognitivism and the reconstruction of the teacher

There is a particular set of epistemological rules around which the teacher is defined in current reform practices.[17] These rules often evolve around a label of 'constructivism' which draws on psychology and social-interactional perspectives. Constructivist strategies are intended to enable teachers to have the 'correct' dispositions and capabilities for effecting school reform. Knowledge and subjectivities are viewed as contingent and plural. They can be represented through the following equation:

'I understand it' + 'I can do it' + 'I care about it' = 'capacity'.[18]

But the constructivist pedagogies are not neutral strategies to teach 'problem solving'; they politicize the body through connecting power/knowledge. *There is a shift from the individual defined by having particular sets of competencies, skills and knowledge (such as those for cognitive mastery) to the individual who embodies pragmatic capabilities and dispositions.* The 'capabilities' of the teacher are 'self-confidence, self-discipline, problem-solving, and a willingness to learn'.

If we examine the Holmes Group (1986, 1990), organized by deans of leading schools of education in the USA to produce change in teacher education, a constructivist psychology is offerred as a template for improving the quality of teaching in professional development schools. Constructivism is brought to bear on the formation of teachers when it is asserted that 'the generic task of education' consists of 'teaching students how to make knowledge and meaning – to *enact culture* . . . ' or when it is argued that it is necessary for institutional networks to develop multiple models of reform 'rather than a template for a single conception' (Holmes Group, 1990; 10, 6).

In a different aspect of the current school reforms, that of national curriculum standards, constructivism is privileged as a technology to further the national goals of modernizing the school. The National Council for Teachers of Mathematics, for example, has developed teaching standards that are heavily influenced by cognitivist research. Using language which sounds as if it has been borrowed from a psychology text, proponents of curriculum standards propound the need to involve children as 'active individuals who construct, modify and integrate ideas . . . '. The constructivism in the Mathematics Standards is further supported by reference to Dewey's notion of knowledge as 'doing'.

The rhetorical constructions in the constructivist approaches to didactics are seductive. The new approaches to teaching capture a democratic impulse. The pedagogical reforms are intended to help teachers construct a professional identity through collaboration and individual initiative.[19] The teacher is to be a 'self-governing' professional who has greater local responsibility in implementing curriculum decisions within boundaries of state goal steering. The Professional Development School of the Holmes Report and school mathematics standards posit knowledge that is contingent and plural, with the 'new' teacher and student as a problem-solving, flexible 'self' whose boundaries are seen as continually changing.

At the same time, the rules of thinking are presumed democratic as they are presented as if they were universal and applicable to all children. The constructivist 'map' of reasoning seems applicable to all, as the categories of learning are laid out in a neutral way, without any time or space dimensions. The problem is how to provide efficient lessons so all children can solve problems in flexible ways.

While it is easy to laud the self-actualization which constructivist pedagogy claims to provide to every individual, certain power relations are brought to the fore. One element in the production of power is the obscuring of the historical and social mooring of knowledge. Constructivism naturalizes the expert-mediated knowledge that is brought into the school, while searching for the multiple ways that such knowledge can be learned. Science and mathematics are treated as universal 'things' of logic, rather than as systems of reasoning that are historically formed and contested. While the history of disciplinary knowledge is replete with examples of debate about the principles that are to organize problem solving, the constructivism in mathematics, for example, is a method of problem solving based on the idea of stable principles of proof and axioms that are learned through employing multiple teaching strategies.

Elsewhere, I have called the transformation of knowledge into school subjects an 'alchemy', as it involves the transfer of knowledge from one social field (the 'community' of scientists) into another social space, that of schooling (Popkewitz 1993b). The alchemy 'transfers' the disciplinary work of science, mathematics, social science, for example, into problems of learning, child development and school management. The alchemy leaves unquestioned the way in which the disciplinary categories in school subjects are themselves representations that are socially constructed and linked to a power/knowledge configuration – that is, mathematics, science, social science are competing methods and multiple paradigms for governing how the world should be viewed, understood and acted on. The alchemy makes it seem that thought and reason have no expression outside one's personal 'negotiations', group learning or individual 'problem solving'.

Focusing on constructivism in Swedish reforms, Carlgren (in press a) argues that previous reforms viewed the teacher as an 'object of change', as a non-thinking doer (in press b). This can be understood, for example, in the curriculum reform movement of the 1960s which sought 'teacher proof' materials that could not be undermined through incompetent instruction. The current reforms have rediscovered the teacher as a thinker as well as a doer, Carlgren argues, but this 're-introduction of the thinking teacher was, however, connected with a conception of the teacher as a planning and evaluating technical rational "expert"'. The conception of teacher, Carlgren concludes, includes not only a division between teachers' thoughts and actions, but also a dissociation of means from ends, and theory from practice.

At this point, one might suggest that school curriculum is a normative discourse and that there is an obligation to assert certain types of problem solving as worthwhile and appropriate. The didactic principles, it can be further argued, drawn from constructivist psychologies, are just one example of taking normative purposes of schooling and placing them into the professional obligations toward the improving of instruction. My argument, however, does not reject the normative qualities of school curriculum and teaching, or the general responsibilities of schools to regulate the types of problem solving. My argument, in contrast, is to explore how governing systems are deployed through multiple capillaries within the school arena, from the educational science, governmental agency, philanthropic, professional and reform registers. In the following section, I point to trajectories in other social arenas where there are homologies in the dispositions and sensitivities constructed.

Global systems, the capabilities of the individual and educational reforms

The restructuring of the patterns of regulation in education, as my previous comments indicate, needs to be understood historically and globally. At one level, these discourses are elements of an 'international' circulation of ideas about appropriate practices and interpretations of school change. The circulation of international discourses occurs not only through formal institutions concerned with policy, but through professional associations, journals, conferences and the mobility of academics around the globe.[20] Nor is the globalization restricted to particular 'hegemonic' groups of nations, as 'post-colonial' literatures have illustrated the hybridity of discourses (see, e.g. Appiah 1992, Young 1995).

We can also think about 'globalization' through homologies between the regulatory patterns of education and those of other arenas.[21] I use the term 'homologies' to consider relations of education with other social practices in a manner that is neither causal nor suggests a single origin of the changes. This second dimension of globalization enables me to extend the discussion of the regulatory norms of constructivism through situating the 'sensitivities' of the teacher to other transformations in the patterns of politics, culture and economy which schooling both expresses and influences.

The shift from bureaucratic centralism (rule governing) to 'goal steering' is occurring not only in Sweden but also in many other European countries. The changes can be related to a tendency for political projects to become more local and less class focused, such as in the Green movements and the politics of feminism in the past decade. Several years ago a member of the Swedish Parliament, for example, talked about the feminist movement as too important to be left to women; today that view of the state is no longer prevalent. 'Localized' practices are also found in academic discourse, with an emphasis on pragmatic knowledge, local social histories, and rejections of universal histories and generalization (Lloyd 1991).

The administrative-legal reorganization of the national governments is also related to changes in the relation of global and regional economies whose patterns of regulation are homologous to the educational arena. The new corporate structure is less hierarchical and pyramidal than it was in the past, and it has eliminated many middle layers of management. The language of the business pages of major newspapers is similar to that of the professionalization literature in teaching: the new business organization, for example, is 'the law of the microcosm', which postulates that the most agile and flexible companies are those which are most likely to survive. The new business entails a work condition which involves 'problem-solving' – where highly variable customer demands, new technologies, multi-centred business structures and 'horizontal' structures organize workers into groups concerned with specific projects that do not have the old layers of management. The smaller units are to 'empower' workers and to develop flexible, responsive environments that can respond quickly to customer (read 'corporate') demands.

This corporate restructuring embodies changing patterns of governance in respect to work and productivity. In examining efforts to increase production, Donzelot (1991) argues that there are increasing efforts to break previous psychological ties which define individual identity according to fixed notions of work and production. The new approaches accent the relation of the individual's autonomy, and capacity to adapt and to be an agent of change in a changing world as integral to one's self-fulfilment. 'Instead of defining the individual by the work he [*sic*] is assigned to, [the new psychology] regards productive activity as the site of deployment of the person's personal skills' (1991: 252).

In certain crucial ways, the dispositions of the person that Donzelot identifies are homologous to the constructivism which we have seen in the Holmes Reports and the national curriculum standards discussed earlier, as well as in the conceptual change literature associated with constructivist teaching of school subjects. Individual goals are now tied more closely and directly than before to institutional and corporate goals.

The individualism of constructivism is homologous to the changing conceptions of 'individuality' that Donzelot describes and which exist as well in culture practices, philosophy and politics. It is a world of instabilities, pluralities and a need for pragmatic actions as individuals interact with communication systems. It is a world of contingent qualities in contexts that quickly change. The pedagogical changes in how a teacher 'sees', appreciates and acts in the world are related to other social changes, but not in correspondence to other social arenas.

The significance of the strategies of reform in the problem of governing are in their intrusive qualities. The potential of constructivist discourses results from their linking people's knowledge of the world with institutional 'goals' in a manner which enables them to feel satisfied that the process will effectively reap personal as well as social ends. Inscribed in the concrete technologies of pedagogy are the correct *dispositions* and capabilities to be self-regulating and policing, so that the individual teacher is, to use expressions from the educational literature, not only 'able' but also 'inclined' (see, e.g. Barth 1986, Cazden 1986, Newmann *et al.* 1989). But the intrusive, regulatory quality is not a reflexive element of the discourse. The sense of 'doing' and 'wanting' are uncritically accepted as a prescription for action. *Thus, when we consider the shift in educational discourses from the individual defined as having particular sets of competencies, skills and knowledge (such as those for cognitive mastery) to the individual who embodies pragmatic capabilities and dispositions, these changes in the loci of regulation are related to changes in arenas other than those in education.*

Knowledge as a governing system of inclusion/exclusion

Early in this essay, I suggested that the construction of governing systems does not occur on level playing fields. *The same subjectivities are not constructed for all through the governing patterns that constitute the state.* The governing constitutes an economy that enables and disenables subjectivities through the inscription of different rules of participation and action. Here, then, I pursue briefly how the rules of 'reason' in pedagogical constructivism normalize and inscribe subjectivities that exclude as well as include.

We can think of the principles of pedagogy as constructing 'an imagined community'. Its systems of classification draw boundaries with regard to what is included on the 'map' through its ordering and dividing practices. This can be thought of as analogous to a map of a country that identifies 'citizens' within its territory. The inclusions not only define but have historically redefined identities (e.g. calling those who are Ibos as 'Nigerians') and excluded through not being given representation (such as not identifying areas as reclassifying all US Spanish speakers in Hispanic).

In pedagogy, the 'maps' are of reason, achievement, competence and capabilities drawn through the rules of classification. The rules classify 'reason' that normalizes particular dispositions and sensitivities of the individual who is in school. The normativity does not appear directly but through the rules of the normal which appear universal and applicable to all. Thus, we can look at contemporary ideas about educational reform in the USA as constructing distinctions that separate the 'normal' from the not-normal. Distinctions concerning 'inner-city' youth, learning styles, remediation, cultural diversity, ostensibly to give value and to help children who have not succeeded in schooling, involve such normalization.[22] The 'reasoning' establishes a silent set of norms that positions the child named as an 'Other'. Relations of sameness/difference are established. The 'at-risk' and 'diverse' child is interned and enclosed as different, not having competence, achievement and the capabilities of those classified as normal.

It is in this context of normalization that we can explore how pedagogy includes/excludes through the classifications of 'problem solving'. The constructivist pedagogy presumes, as do the systems of ideas that define the 'inner-city' child, a silent normativity which is obscured as 'problem solving' is seen as universal and 'natural' for all groups of children who come to school. Where diversity is assumed, it is a populational notion of diversity that constructs a continuum of value and divisions from which to compare the individual child. The problem of instruction is how to provide efficient lessons so that all children can solve problems in flexible ways; or so that teachers can be 'reflective' about their practices, with 'reflection' seeming to have a logic to it that is independent of historical time or social location. The rules are assumed to be 'natural' and universal.

But the 'reflections', thinking and problem solving which are presumed by constructivism to be universal are not global characteristics but local. A variety of research, for example, enables us to understand that the notions of problem solving that we take as 'universal' emerge from groups within a society that have 'cultural capital', to borrow from a term from Bourdieu, to insert their sensitivities, tastes and cognitive ordering as authoritative (see, e.g. Bourdieu 1984, also Hertfeld 1992, Zerubavel 1993).[23] The universalizing of reason is an inscription of power through taking what is 'locally' produced and making it appear 'global', natural and essential.

Why is the change from local to global important to the notion of the state? The distinctions represented as universal, to continue with the example of constructivism, are partial and exclude those whose capabilities and dispositions are different. The processes of inclusion/exclusion can be likened to a broader discussion called 'the two-thirds solution'. Commentaries about social policies in Europe have suggested that these may produce divisions in societies (see, e.g. Wagner 1994). The two-thirds society consists of those people whose subjectivities embody the sentiments and dispositions to create 'opportunities', where the 'Other'/others embody a different habitus that excludes them from 'the main spheres of society in which social identities can be formed' (Wagner 1994: 167).

The inclusions/exclusions are not in the categorical constructions that are associated with labelling theories, such as calling a child 'socially disadvantaged', 'at risk' or from 'the inner city'. Rather, the inclusions/exclusions are embedded in the systems of recognition, divisions and distinctions that construct identities. The systems of recognitions generate the normalcies by which individuals are to 'see', conduct and evaluate themselves as 'normal' and 'reasonable people'. The production of subjectivity is historically specific and inscribed within the subject relations of the arenas of social practices.

My argument is that systems that are to include are never universal, and they produce simultaneous exclusions. The universalizing of reason in constructivism has a duality: its governing systems are intended to open possibilities for those who have the appropriate dispositions and sensitivities to capitalize on the new curriculum, while those who do not are excluded. Thus, instead of opening up spaces for those who are different, the reform systems may instead place them in an oppositional or marginal space. This occurs as constructivism names the children who need remediation or special assistance while, at the same time, asserting a universalism in its systems for classifying how thinking occurs. As Dumm argues in a different context, the discourses of the social sciences are normalizing practices that classify marginalized groups such as people of colour as different from the norm and who, *at best*, can be 'like the normal person'. Particular groupings of people are enclosed and interned (Dumm 1993). Thus, the production of governing principles and actors also involves systems of inclusion/exclusion through the subjectivities produced.

But this issue is not only one of internal differentiation. As Badie and Burnbaum (1994) suggest in a recent paper on the state, the rise of transnational relations and the crisis in the machinery for regulating inter-national relations have imposed new regulatory patterns. I want to suggest here that the distinctions in the reconstruction of inter-national may not be made at the national-territory level but through the production of distinctions and differentiations related to subjectivities. In a recent review of the policies of international lending agencies towards the restructuring of teacher education, distinctions were produced among the teachers in 'First' World and 'Second'/'Third' World countries (Carnoy *et al.* in press). Whereas 'First' World countries emphasized university education and scientific cultures in the education of teachers, international funding agency policies towards non-industrialized countries gave preference to the practical, school-based training of teachers.

These differences in approaches in teacher education are ostensibly to save money in the educational sector, but the financial rules also intertwine the deployment of power with the production of distinctions. But if we focus not on the World Bank as a sovereign 'actor' but on 'the rules of reasoning' about educational practices, the educational practices can be understood as part of a broad set of discourses and practices intended to reconstruct the way teachers think about and assess their performance. The differences among countries are not only in what is overtly learned, but in the distinction, dispositions and sensitivities produced in social practices. My earlier discussion of the linking of work and 'leisure', the homologies between the dispositions associated with 'constructivist' pedagogy to other transformations within industrialized societies, and national differentiations among groupings, pointed to the deployment of power through the construction of particular styles of 'thinking' and 'acting'. Thus while we may talk about a universalized school as do Meyer and his associates (1992), we must historicize the construction of pedagogy to understand how distinctions and differentiations are the effects of power.

At a different layer of discussions about the state, it has been popular to label the changes as a 'conservative restoration', labels that I believe miss the long term historical processes that underlie these changes; some occurring as early as the 1940s and 1950s – well before Thatcher in Britain or Reagan in the USA (see, e.g., discussion in Popkewitz 1991, Whitty in progress). If we examine current rhetoric about neoliberal slogans of 'markets' and 'privatization' that emerged as political slogans and that have been brought into social scientific concepts, we realize that the changes do not start with recent policies but are part of more profound social changes that have been moving in uneven ways during at least the past four decades. At one level is the breakdown of the Fordist compromise in post-war Europe and the United States. As Fordism lost its efficiency with technologies and markets, there also occurred a collapse in the compromise among workers, industrialists and the state which produced a division of labor and mechanization in exchange for a favourable wage formula and the implementation of a state welfare system. The organizations of work that we are now witnessing is in part a response to the lack of efficiency of Fordist mass production as well as new technologies in production itself.

But, the changes in governing have no single origin that can be reductible to 'ideology', economy, or hegemony; but embody multiple historical trajectories.

There are a range of other challenges to the mechanism of social government that emerged during these same decades from civil libertarians, feminists, radicals, socialists, sociologists and others. These reorganized programmes of government utilise and instrumentalise the multitude of experts of management, of family life, of lifestyle who have proliferated at the points of intersection of socio-political aspirations and private desires for self-advancement (Rose and Miller 1992; 201).

If I pursue Rose and Miller's argument, the problem of the state is the constitution of governing practices. This position transposes much contemporary analyses which define the state as an 'object' that dispenses power rather one of a set of relations through which governing and government are produced. It is interesting to note here that contemporary discussions about 'bringing back the state' in social and educational theories tend to incorporate 19th century historicist and structural distinctions in the theoretical deliberations. The distinctions evoke images of the past that, I have argued, are inadequate for understanding the changing patterns of governing discussed above. (For a general discussion of 19th century epistemologies and contemporary social theory, see Wallerstein 1991; in education, Popkewitz, in press a.)

Some concluding notes

My interest in the state has been to consider the problem of governing in education as relational, historical and comparative. Two different but related intellectual strategies guided the essay. One related to the concept of an educational arena. The idea of an arena directed attention to the position of different actors as analogous to players in a game; it is also important to recognize that some players have more resources and 'capital', in Bourdieu's sense, than do others. Embedded in the notion of an arena was a second move, the exploration of the relation of actors to the construction of systems of regulation. This concept drew on Foucault's notion of 'governmentality' to direct attention to the rules of the game that discipline 'reason' and the self-governing of 'reasonable' people. While the disciplining is never totally coercive, the production of knowledge positions and produces power through the regulatory principles applied as 'reason' and 'truth'.

The meaning of the state lies, then, in relation of these two sets of empirical problems as they change over time and at its multiple levels. Russia, South Africa, Sweden and the USA provided examples of changes in the relations that constitute their educational arenas. *My examples focused on the actors who are authorized to 'speak' about the object and subject of education and the social relations where intelligibility concerning speaking is found. Attention was focused on the proximity among different groupings of actors in the production of the categories and distinctions.* The state, then, was treated as an epistemological category to empirically consider the patterns of governing.

My concern, however, was not only with patterns of relations but also practices of governing as producing systems of inclusion/exclusion. Governing to include/ exclude occurs through the reasoning applied rather than in any 'overt' systems of exclusion. Here, attention to 'reason' as an effect of power is, I believe, an important contribution of postmodern feminist theory and political analyses to our understanding of the micro-practices of schooling.

Three different dimensions in the study of policy, power and schooling can now be addressed. First, we cannot assume that the actors and their positions in the educational arena are stable and fixed categories. The categories of actors are at times the effects of power themselves. Further, the actors in the educational arena are not monolithic and universalized groups but are instead historically formed and reformed groupings. In fact, the grouping and position of actors does change over time even as their labels may stay the same. As an example, while we can say that educational researchers are positioned in the arena in which power is produced, that groupings and position change as the regulatory patters are reconstituted. In this sense, *there are neither old nor new actors who hold power, just patterns of relations.*

The production of power, then, can be understood as relational to the patterns in which the actor is constructed and constituted. While most analyses of the politics of reform apply structural concepts of power (i.e. questions about who rules and is ruled), the subjectivities in the educational arena are formed through an amalgamation of ideas, technologies and relations that are historically contingent. In other words, the 'reasonable' governmental bureaucrats who 'monitor' the reforms, the educational research community which produces systems of reflection and self-reflection, as well as the teacher and children who classify their practices are not, as they might appear to be, universal and neutral categories, but are instead situated in time and space. The refusal to make the subject problematic is one of the major difficulties of policy and studies of education.

My second focus is on pedagogy as a technology of power. Pedagogy links political rationalities to autonomous self-examination, self-reflection and self-care of the individual. But its importance in the problem of governing is not only that of production. It also inscribes systems of differences and distinctions that include and exclude. This occurs, I have argued, through practices of normalization that applied 'local' dispositions and sensitivities as universal and 'natural' to all. The normalizations and practices of inclusion/exclusion in pedagogy should not be viewed as an epi-phenomenon of other, more primary 'causes'. The exploration of homologies in politics, art, economics and the educational arenas as well as the governing technologies of constructivist pedagogy suggest relations that are not of correspondence or evolutionary, but of multiple historical trajectories in which the technologies that govern subjectivities are constructed that have no single origin.

I thus return to a point where I started. Discussions about conservative restorations, privatization and marketization, state/civil society obscure the changes occurring through the systems of reasoning applied. These categories are often constructed within a field of political rhetoric and are brought into social and educational sciences as the distributions to explain the phenomena. The 'reasoning' applied, however, assumes the state as a 'real entity' with stable actors. Further, such analyses assume what has to be made problematic – that is, the subject of the state as government. The assemblage of actors, techniques and images that intersect in the construction of governing are left unscrutinized. This assemblage is neither evolutionary nor structural, but historically contingent. I have argued that there are long-term shifts in the problems of governing which require different analytic distinctions to interpret the alternatives offered than those of the state as a sovereign entity related to its territory. While it is clear that the moral and political rhetoric of educational struggles have shifted, such analyses beg the question of the changes in the historical conditions through which power is constructed and deployed. Again, if the comparative discussions about homologies among politics, arts, science, economics and education *and* the constructions of educational arenas among different nations are historically appropriate, the changes that we now witness in the school arena are changes that involve uneven movements over a long duration in multiple arenas, long before Reagan and Thatcher took office.

Notes

1. This paper was originally given as a lecture at the University of Granada, Spain. I wish to thank the following people for the comments as I wrote and rewrote drafts: Lynn Fendler, Dory Lightfoot, Fran Varvus, Miguel Pereyra, Lizbeth Lundahl-Kallós, Daniel Kallós, Michael Shapiro, Ingrid Carlgren, Eva Aström, Ulla Johannson, Christina Segerholm, Bob Tabachnick, Geoff Whitty and the seminar group at Pedagogik Instititionen, Umeå University, Sweden and the Wednesday Seminar at Madison. I also appreciate the comments of the two anonymous reviewers for this journal.
2. I use arena to think of educational practices as occurring in a field of changing relations. These relations entail positions among actors and discursive practices. I use arena, therefore, as an historical concept to consider the changing social positions and power within education. The concept is discussed in Popkewitz and Pereyra (1993). The notion of arena borrows from Bourdieu's (1984) view of 'field'; and the notion of discourse is related to Foucault's (1979) arguments about science as both a normalizing and a disciplining practice. My particular way of relating these two concepts is discussed as a social epistemology in Popkewitz (1991).
3. I use the notion of actor to speak about social grouping in the arena. I am not concerned with actors in the individual sense or from the perspective of structural theory.
4. To cite a few statistics in education to illustrate (Kallós 1995):There were 2700 municipalities as late as 1957, and in 1995, there were only 286. The Ministry of Education in 1967 had a staff of 90, the National Board of Education had 550 and the Office of the Chancellor of the Universities about 100. The National Board of Education in 1977 allocated approximately 60% of all educational financing.
5. In the USA, for example, educational science received institutional 'pushes' through its ties to normal (teacher training) schools during the rapid expansion period of mass schooling at the turn of the century and during the First World War in which there was a great demand for military discipline. Psychologists were deeply involved in the problems of recruitment and training; as well in the search for ways to develop peaceful, democratic dispositions after the war (for the latter, Freedman 1987, also O'Donnell 1985).
6. It is interesting to note that many Scandinavian countries have a Germanic tradition in which the word 'profession' tended not to be used in talking about educated occupations such as law or medicine. Also the strong government-centred tradition tended to make the educated occupations tied more closely to the government with a less autonomous civil society. It is also important to note that hidden in discourses of professions is the relation of the government, the development of capitalism, and issues of gender (e.g. Popkewitz 1993a).
7. My assumption, borrowed from Giddens (1990), is that professional knowledge plays an important role in mediating between social changes and those in which the person interprets and acts in modernity. Further, I also view the concept of professionalism as a particular one associated with state developments (Popkewitz 1993a).
8. For a discussion of distinctions in traditions of didactics in the USA, Germany and Sweden, see Hoffmann and Riquarts (1995).
9. This discussion is drawn from Popkewitz (1991, 1993b).
10. My involvement in Russian education started in 1976, when attending a US–Soviet seminar in Washington, continued during a Fulbright in 1981 when I spent a semester with the Soviet Academy of Pedagogical Sciences, and on into the present. My observations about South Africa are related to an Oppenheimer fellowship given to me to lecture in universities and meet with its academic communities in May–June 1993. I provide this 'credentialling' with great hesitation as I recognize that the situations within these countries are far more complex than I can grasp here.
11. Russians have had to construct laws with which they had no experience since the first decades of the century: on private property, banking, finance, bankruptcy, private schools and so on.
12. For insightful discussions of the changes in South Africa, see Muller and Cloete (1993); in Russia, Kerr (in progress).
13. The rationalizing that involved various set of actors in the construction of regulation may have been necessary if only to prevent a civil war, which, to this point, has been successful.
14. During the political negotiations among the South African parties, a member of a teacher's union commented to me that much of the discussion about restructuring the educational system existed using categories related to the priorities set by the World Bank. Even though the Bank would not be involved in South African reforms until the transitional period, the Bank, the unionist thought, was part of the horizon of negotiation. The two major parties wanted to be able to say to the electorate that they had access to World Bank money in the restructuring.
15. In these countries, there are different labels for didactics research which may obscure a similar epistemological structuring of didactics knowledge; at the same time, we need to be aware that the concepts about reform in each national context are articulated in different traditions of state problem solving and in different sets of relations in which the educational arena is formed. In the USA and Russian, for example, there are strong traditions of constructivist research which are associated with high-status researchers who previously studied learning

but now study teaching and teacher education. What I call 'constructivist' in the USA would have a different label in Russia. The Russian discussion would be framed around a longstanding tradition of didactics research which is related to 'knowing activities' and the work of the psychologist, Lev Vygotsky. This imposes different nuances in discussion than found in the United States where the Russian psychological tradition is brought into constructivist psychologies that are also employed to direct school didactics. The USA maintains a legacy with Piaget. In both the Russian and the US research traditions, there is no distinction between the reformist intent on research and science (e.g. Popkewitz in press.) The USA provides another interesting contrast with most European intellectual discussions. Whereas constructivism is positioned as a problem of psychology in the USA and historically positioned in relation to an American utilitarianist research, European constructivism tends to be social and historical. See the work of Bourdieu and Wacquant (1992). While there is internal debate with the pedagogical reform movement about 'constructivism', there are also certain general epistemological rules which dominate in the US discussion.

16. When one looks at the titles of research at the American Educational Research Association Annual meeting over the past five years or at contemporary school reform literature or discussions about 'systemic reform', there is a strong presence of an assumption that reform practices require a 'constructivist' approach.
17. While we can understand 'constructivist' as encompassing many different views about teaching and learning, there are particular epistemological standards and rules from which the diversity occurs. My use of 'constructivist', therefore, is to focus on the general standards and rules, paying only partial attention to its inner distinctions. In certain ways, my focus on constructivism can be likened to Thomas Kuhn's (1970) discussion of the problem solving with a paradigm of 'normal science'.
18. I draw this distinction from an International Labour Organization discussion about the changing characteristics of metal-working skills and the labour of metal working. They compare the new conditions of work with those of a 'Fordist' model that focused on the competences of the worker rather than on the capabilities. While I use this formulation, my intent is to signal changes that are cultural and social as well as economic. Many of these changes, as Wagner argues, occur within social movements that cannot be reduced to economic changes (Wagner 1994).
19. It might seem that individual initiative and collaboration are mutually exclusive, but anyone aware of Russian research during the past few decades finds that the two can, in fact, coexist (e.g. Roubtsov, 1991).
20. The mobilization of intellectuals is evident if we consider the movement historically. Whereas previously only the élites of intellectual life moved in international circles, today it is commonplace; the European Community's ERASMUS programme is an official recognition of such mobility. One can also examine the increased use of 'English' as the 'lingua franca' of scientific communities, as well as the increased and quick translations of social scientific texts occurring from English and into English.
21. I use the word 'homology' to suggest an historical relation among events and discourses. It is not meant as a causal relation.
22. I recognize that the calls for multicultural curriculum and education which appreciates cultural diversity have multiple agendas in reorganizing the governing patterns of the subjectivities produced in schooling. My argument is that the discursive practices are located within rules of pedagogical reasoning that position children as 'the other' within a sameness. For example, see Young (1990) for a discussion of this notion of colonialization as it crosses liberal and 'oppositional' left discourses.
23. These differences are in the production of different 'habituses', and occur through distinctions and 'manners' available to different groups, from tastes in what is eaten, read, watched, bought, talked about and 'seen' as valuable and useful. They are found in the 'tastes' that we have in the reading of newspapers, the movies that we see, the books we buy, as well as the food eaten and the manner of eating. These sensitivities, distinctions and differentiations construct power.

References

APPIAH, K. (1992) *In my Father's House; Africa in the Philosophy of Culture* (New York: Oxford University Press).

BADIE, B. and BIRNBAUM, P. (1994) Sociology of the state revisited. *International Social Science Journal*, 139, 153–167.

BALL, S. (1990) *Foucault and Education: Disciplines and Knowledge* (London: Routledge).

BARRETT, M. and PHILLIPS, A. (1992) *Destabilizing Theory: Contemporary Feminist Debates* (Stanford, CA: Stanford University Press).

BARTH, R. (1986) The principal and the profession of teaching. *The Elementary School Journal*, 86, 471–492.

BOURDIEU, P. (1984) *Distinction: A Social Critique of the Judgement of Taste* (Cambridge: Harvard University Press).

BOURDIEU, P. and WACQUANT, L. (1992) *An Invitation to Reflexive Sociology* (Chicago: University of Chicago Press).

BOYER, R. (1989) The capital labor relations in OECD countries: From the Fordist 'golden age' to contrasted national trajectories. In J. Schor (editor), *Capital Labor Relations*.

BUTLER, J. (1993) *Bodies that Matter: On the Discourse Limits of 'Sex'* (New York: Routledge).

CARLGREN, I. (in press a) Professional cultures in Swedish teacher education. In A. Goodson and A. Hargreaves (eds) *Professional Lives* (London: Falmer Press).

CARLGREN, I. (in press b) National curriculum as social compromise or discursive politics: some reflections on a curriculum-making process. *Journal of Curriculum Studies* (forthcoming).

CARNOY, M. L., FENDLER, L., POPKEWITZ, T., TABACHNICK, B. and ZEICHNER, K. (in press) *Teacher Restructuring: Some Trends and Implications* (Geneva: International Labour Organization).
CAZDEN, C. (1986) Classroom discourse. In M. Wittrock (ed.), *Handbook of Research on Teaching*. 3rd edn (New York: Macmillan), 432–463.
CELIS, C. (1993) The fight over national standards. *Educational Life: The New York Times*, 1 August, 14–16.
CRARY, J. (1990) *Techniques of the Observer: On Vision and Modernity in the Nineteenth Century* (Cambridge, MA: MIT Press).
DONALD, J. (1992) *Sentimental Education: Schooling, Popular Culture and the Regulation of Liberty* (London: Verso).
DONZELOT, J. (1991) Pleasure in work. In G. Burchell, C. Gordon and P. Miller (eds) *The Foucault Effect, Studies in Governmentality* (Chicago: University of Chicago Press), 251–280.
DUMM, T. (1993) The new enclosures: racism in the normalized community. In R. Gooding-Williams (ed.) *Reading Rodney King: Reading Urban Uprising* (New York: Routledge), 178–195.
FISHER, D. (1993) *Fundamental Development of the Social Sciences: Rockefeller Philanthropy and the United States Social Science Research Council* (Ann Arbor, MI: University of Michigan Press).
FOUCAULT, M. (1979) Governmentality. *Ideology and Consciousness*, 6, 5–22.
FREEDMAN, K. (1987) Art education as social production: culture, society and politics in the formation of the curriculum. In T. Popkewitz (ed.) *The Formation of School Subjects: The Struggle for Creating an American Institution* (London: Falmer Press), 63–84.
FUKUYAMA, F. (1995) *Trust: The Social Virtues and the Creation of Prosperity* (New York: Free Press).
GIDDENS, A. (1990) *The Consequences of Modernity* (Stanford, CA: Stanford University Press).
HERTFELD, M. (1992) *The Social Production of Indifference: Exploring the Symbolic Roots of Western Bureaucracy* (Chicago: University of Chicago Press).
HOFFMANN, S. and RIQUARTS, K. (1995) Starting a dialogue: issues in a beginning conversation between Didaktik and the curriculum traditions. *Journal of Curriculum Studies*, 27, 3–12.
HOLMES GROUP (1986) *Tomorrow's Teachers* (East Lansing, MI: Holmes Group).
HOLMES GROUP (1990) *Tomorrow's Schools* (East Lansing, MI: Holmes Group).
HUNTER, I. (1994) *Rethinking the School: Subjectivity, Bureaucracy, Criticism* (New York: St Martin's Press).
KALLÓS, D. (1995) Reflections on decentralization as a concept in education policy analyses. Paper presented at the Second Comparative Education Policy Seminar: New Policy Contexts for Education: Sweden and the United Kingdom, Centre for Educational Studies, King's College, London, 27–29 April, 1995.
KALLÓS, D. and LUNDAHL-KALLÓS L. (1994) Recent changes in teachers' work in Sweden: professionalization or what? In D. Kallós and S. Lindblad (eds) *New Policy Contexts for Education: Sweden and United Kingdom* (Umea, Sweden: Pedagogiska institutionen, Umea universitet), 140–168.
KALLÓS, D. and NILSSON, I. (1995) Defining and redefining the teacher in the Swedish comprehensive school. *Educational Review*, 47, 173–188.
KALLÓS, D. and SELANDER, S. (1993) Teacher education and teachers' work in Sweden: reform strategies and professional reorientation. In T. Popkewitz (ed.) *Changing Patterns of Power: Social Regulation and Teacher Education Reform* (Albany: State University of New York Press), 211-262.
KERR, S. T. (in progress) When the center cannot hold: the devolution and evolution of power, authority, and responsibility in Russian education. In T. Popkewitz and A. Kazamias (eds) *Educational Knowledge: Changing Relations Between the State, Civil Society, and the Educational Community* (Albany: State University of New York Press).
KUHN, T. (1970) *The Structure of Scientific Revolutions*, 2nd edn (Chicago: University of Chicago Press).
LAGEMANN, E. (1989) *The Politics of Knowledge: The Carnegie Corporation, Philanthrophy, and Public Policy* (Middletown, CT: Wesleyan University Press).
LLOYD, C. (1991) The methodologies of social history: a critical survey and defense of structurism. *History and Theory: Studies in the Philosophy of History*, 30, 180–219.
MARSHALL, J. (1995) Needs, interests, growth and personal autonomy: Foucault on power. In W. Kohli (ed.) *Critical Conversations in Philosophy of Education* (New York: Routledge), 364–378.
MEYER, J., RAMIREZ, J. and SOYSAL, Y. (1992) World expansion of mass education, 1870–1980. *Sociology of Education*, 65, 128–149.
MULLER, J. and CLOETE, N. (1993) Out of Eden: modernity, post-apartheid and intellectuals. *Theory, Culture and Society*, 10, 155–172.
NEWMANN, F., GRIFFIN, D. and COLE, M. (1989) *The Construction Zone: Working for Cognitive Change in Schools* (Cambridge: Cambridge University Press).
O'DONNELL, J. (1985) *The Origins of Behaviorism: American Psychology, 1876–1920* (New York: New York University Press).
POPKEWITZ, T. (1991) *A Political Sociology of Educational Reform: Power/Knowledge in Teaching, Teacher Education, and Research* (New York: Teachers College Press).
POPKEWITZ, T. (1993a) Professionalization in teaching and teacher education: some notes on its history, ideology and potential. *Teacher and Teacher Education*, 10, 1–14.
POPKEWITZ, T. (1993b) US teacher education reforms: regulatory practices of the state, university, and research. In T. Popkewitz (ed.) *Changing Patterns of Power: Social Regulation and Teacher Education Reform* (Albany, NY: State University of New York Press), 263–302.

POPKEWITZ, T. (in press) Systems of ideas in social spaces: postmodernism conditions, and cultures/history in a Vygotskian psychology. In V. Rubstov (ed.) *Cultural and Historical Theory of 1. Vygotsky: The Past, The Present and The Future* (Moscow: Russian Academy of Education Sciences) (in Russian).

POPKEWITZ, T. and BRENNAN, M. (in press) Restructuring social and political theory: Foucault, and a social epistemology of school practices. In T. Popkewitz and M. Brennan (eds) *Governmentality through Education: Foucault's Challenge to the Institution Production and Study of Knowledge* (New York: Teachers College Press).

POPKEWITZ, T. and LIND, K. (1989) Teacher incentives as reform: implications for teachers' work and the changing control mechanism in education. *Teachers College Record*, 90, 575–594.

POPKEWITZ, T. and PEREYRA, M. (1993) An eight country study of reform practices in teacher education: an outline of the problematic. In T. Popkewitz (ed.) *Changing Patterns of Power: Social Regulation and Teacher Education Reform* (Albany: State University of New York Press), 1–52.

ROSE, N. and MILLER, P. (1992) Political power beyond the state: problematics of government. *British Journal of Sociology*, 43, 173–205.

RUBTSOV, V. (1991) *Learning in Children: Organization and Development of Cooperative Actions*, edited by L. Martin, trans. M. J. Hall (New York: Nova).

SHAPIRO, M. (1992) *Reading the Postmodern Polity: Political Theory as Textual Practice* (Minneapolis: University of Minnesota Press).

SKOWRONEK, S. (1982) *Building a New American State: The Expansion of National Administrative Capacities, 1877–1920* (New York: Cambridge University Press).

SMITH, M. and O'DAY, J. (1990) Systemic school reform. *Politics of Education Association Yearbook*, 233–267.

SOUSA SANTOS, B. (1995) *Toward a New Common Sense: Law, Science and Politics in the Paradigmatic Transition* (New York: Routledge).

TOULMIN, S. (1990) *Cosmopolis, the Hidden Agenda of Modernity* (New York: Free Press).

WAGNER, P. (1994) *Sociology of Modernity: Liberty and Discipline* (New York: Routledge).

WHITTY, G. (in progress) New school for new times? Educational reform in a global context. In T. Popkewitz and A. Kazamias (eds) *Educational Knowledge: Changing Relations Between the State, Civil Society, and the Educational Community* (Albany: State University of New York Press).

YOUNG, R. (1990) *White Mythologies: Writing, History and the West* (New York: Routledge).

YOUNG, R. (1995) *Colonial Desire: Hybridity in Theory, Culture and Race* (London: Routledge).

ZAKARIA, F. (1995) Bigger than the family, smaller than the state: are voluntary groups what make countries work? Book Review, *New York Times*, 13 August, Section 7, 1, 25.

ZERUBAVEL, E. (1993) *The Fine Line: Making Distinctions in Everyday Life* (Chicago: University of Chicago Press).

[22]

Teachers' Work, Restructuring and Postfordism: Constructing the New 'Professionalism'

Susan L. Robertson

Introduction

> In 1885 teachers were trained in classrooms to perform the specific functions of instruction and control. Over the course of the next century they had become highly educated professionals. By 1985, while still continuing with classroom instruction and control, teachers had become a body of people who were highly knowledgeable with regard to educational theory and practice, sociology, social theory, child psychology, learning theory and so on. They had become experts in their subject content; they had won the right, as a professional body, to be centrally involved in the determination and development of curriculum content, schooling practices and educational policy in general.
>
> By 1995 they are likely to have lost, in a single decade, most of the gains made in a single century. (Kevin Harris, 1994, p. viii)

While some teachers remain committed to the belief they can shut out change by closing the classroom door, others agree that this is too simple a description of the relationship between their work as teachers and the wider society. As evidence, they point to the dramatic changes occurring outside of the classroom, and the impact on the terms and conditions of their work inside. A quick scan of the educational jargon reveals just how much. Notions such as inputs, equity, centralized bureaucracy, mass education, seniority and unionization which defined post-world-war mass schooling have been replaced by a new language: outputs, performance, added-value, choice, markets, quality, competencies, excellence, flexibility, deregulation, and school–business partnerships.

The cause? Over the past decade, teachers in countries such as Australia, Canada, the United States of America, United Kingdom and New Zealand have experienced the winds change. Hyper-liberalism, neo-conservativism and economic rationalism are just a few of the labels writers have used to describe the economic nature of these shifts (Ball and Goodson, 1985; Carlson, 1992; Harris, 1994; Barlow and Robertson, 1994; Panitch, 1994). Whatever the term, as Freedman has observed in a recent newspaper editorial, 'the evidence of the shift is everywhere reaching beyond the ballot box and deep inside the culture . . . there gusts a headwind, *blowing right*' (my emphasis) (1995, p. 47).

Teachers agree this wind has penetrated deep inside the classroom, bringing into sharp focus the 'thrill and dread of a world in which "all that is solid melts into air"' (Berman, 1982, p. 13). Within a decade, the industrial and pedagogic achievements of public-sector teachers have been reversed. The consequences have been decisive and tangible: wage roll-backs, an overall decline in salaries, increased funds to the private sector, larger class sizes, more administration, massive budget cuts, the deregulation of wages setting, teacher licensing, to name a few. A chilling wind indeed, as 'ideological compliance and financial self-reliance' defines the new reality facing teachers (Hargreaves, 1994, p. 5). Caught in this post-modern post-Fordist maelstrom, where '(s)igns and tokens of radical changes in labour processes, in consumer habits in geographical and geopolitical configurations, in state powers and practices, and the like, abound' (Harvey, 1990, p. 121), teachers have been swept along. The juxtapositions of hope, despair, opportunity, and dismay fill the staffrooms and classrooms, as one of the central institutions of late modernity and monopoly capitalism — the educational bureaucracy — is systematically dismantled and replaced with devolved forms of school-based management, new technologies and school–business–community partnerships.

Clearly this is no ordinary storm. Rather, as national states and corporate capital experiment with new markets, technology and forms of work organization (Barlow and Robertson, 1994) to compete in the global economy, the spotlight has inevitably turned to the role of education and the work of teachers in this transition. Despite the obvious dislocations within education, some reform analysts have argued the current crisis offers a perfect opportunity for teachers to have their 'professionally-preferred cake and to eat it too'; an opportunity to move beyond the organizational paradigm which has structured modern schooling — of 'eyes front, lips-buttoned, sit-up-straight classroom cottages' (Ashenden, 1992, p. 5) — which has dominated much of this century. Teachers could, according to Ashenden, adopt new patterns of work organization which challenge the cottage model of mass education. In learning to work in smarter ways, such as delegating some tasks to other (cheaper) education workers or using a range of alternative teaching approaches, teachers would have a real chance to move in from the margins and become real professionals.

Ashenden is not alone in arguing that the current round of restructuring offers teachers new hope for that elusive title of 'professional' (Porter, 1990). In fact, the educational restructuring proposals in Australia and elsewhere, for example, have been liberally sprinkled with the promise of a new professionalism for teachers (Robertson and Trotman, 1992). Not surprisingly, many Australian teachers have found this rhetoric seductive, particularly in such hard times. This, despite the growing body of evidence that crucial aspects of the restructuring, such as self-management, have been little more than a 'deliberate process of subterfuge, distortion, concealment and wilful neglect as the state seeks to retreat in a rather undignified fashion from its historical responsibility for providing quality education' (Smyth, 1993, p. 2).

The current round of changes to teachers' work, including proposals such as those offered by Ashenden, must be investigated and debated by the educational community. Critics from the left have long argued that the industrial model underpinning public schooling, with its privileging of ruling-class culture, has provided limited scope for critical teacher practice (Aronowitz and Giroux, 1985). The question is, can the reorganization of time and space within schools be transformed to more democratic ends? This chapter seeks to contribute to that debate through an analysis of the restructuring of teachers' work and the proposed conditions for this new 'professionalism'. In particular I ask: Have the current restructuring initiatives, in the name of a new professionalism, created the conditions for teachers to work as autonomous intellectuals? The focus in this chapter will be directed toward a critical examination of the restructuring of teachers' labour in Australia on the premise that — given the historical specificity of both the State and the capital–labour compromise — developments in one polity cannot be read off against another.

My analysis draws upon three theoretical bodies of work. Firstly, that of the French regulation school and in particular the work of Alain Lipietz (1992) and Bob Jessop (1989, 1990, 1993) who analyse transformations in the welfare State and political economy within western capitalism toward what they argue is a new post-Fordist economy.[1] Although others have insights into this complex process, the French regulation school has gone furthest in developing those concepts useful for my purpose.

Secondly, I draw upon the work of Larson (1977, 1988) and others concerned with understanding the complex phenomena of professionalization and its crucial links to the restructuring of society. In particular, I have found Larson's (1988) elaboration of professionalism, based upon Foucault's analysis of the knowledge–power relations, helpful. Larson observes that professionals have their authority constituted within a discursive field which is infused with power relations. Discourses are about what can be said and thought, but also about who can speak, when and with what authority (Ball, 1990, p. 2). Seeing teacher professionalism as constituted within a discursive field of knowledge-power helps us understand the way in which words and concepts which define teachers' work can change and how teachers can be discursively repositioning as non-experts by powerful and vested interests. Further, Larson argues that some groups within an occupational field are located in the core region and therefore are positioned as more expert than others. These theoretical insights help us pinpoint not only the centrality of discourse to understanding the positioning of teachers, but also the fact that there are unequal relations between teachers which can be manipulated for strategic purposes.

Finally, I draw upon Christer Fritzell's (1987) analysis of relative autonomy within educational theory to illuminate the complex relationship between the internal structuring of schooling and the educational functions of social reproduction within capitalist economies. In particular, Fritzell's development of structural, functional and critical forms of correspondence between schooling and the economy are a useful heuristic in understanding the kinds of relationships between teachers, the State and the economy. Fritzell (1987) describes structural forms of correspondence as those relationships where the properties or internal relations of one system can be derived from the corresponding features in another, for example, the process of streaming which structurally equates to the primary and secondary division of labour. Functional forms of correspondence describe the internal penetration of one system by another external system of control, for example the production of skilled workers for the economy. In both cases of correspondence described so far, they can take on positive and negative forms. That is, as a set of direct (or positive) relationships from one site to the other, such as hierarchical authority relations, or by excluding or preventing (or negating) certain potentially critical tendencies, such as the scope for conflict.

Critical correspondence, on the other hand refers to the potentiality for social change. This potentiality can be realized when the dynamics of contradictions are made explicit. When teachers stand to lose many of the extrinsic (for example, status and wages) and intrinsic rewards (such as relationships with students) which teachers associate with teaching, as is the case during periods of crisis and transition, a critical correspondence between schooling and the economy is more likely to emerge. This opens the space for teachers to hold a more critical view of the proposed reform. Within this framework we can see how teachers' class allegiance might change with time as the contradictions within the system of reproduction become most apparent.[2] As the crisis deepens and the terms of the new settlement struggled over, teachers, whose role is crucial as knowledge producers/reproducers, are an increasingly unreliable ally.[3] This period of transition, because it offers scope for counter-hegemony, must be carefully managed by the State. This chapter explores precisely how this process has been 'managed' within Australia in the implementation of the post-Fordist accumulation regime.

Before turning to this task, however, I want to suggest that it is important to maintain a sense of historically located perspective with regard to the changing nature of teachers' work. For one thing, it is easy to romanticize the past and the 'golden years' in education and in doing so, overlook the rigidities of bureaucratic control and the limitations of professional ideology which have also shaped teachers' work during this period (Hargreaves, 1994, p. 10). For another, an historically located perspective helps bring into sharper focus the way in which new discourses, structures and struggles about the nature of teachers' work are layered upon and between old ones. Teachers, while active agents, are also constituted as subjects within a particular socio-political and historical context (Connell, 1985). The outcome of this struggle, despite a powerful ideology of professionalism which has produced considerable compliance and which has also been used by teachers for their own ends (Grace, 1987, p. 195), can never be predetermined. Finally, as Harvey notes, there is a real danger in confusing the transitory and ephemeral with more fundamental transformations in political and economic life (1990, p. 124). Viewing critically what is left behind as well as understanding the concreteness of what is, allowing us to see more clearly the distinctions between the ephemerality of 'reform rhetoric' and the substance of 'reform action' and thus the precise nature and the extent of the changes (Ginsburg and Cooper, 1991, p. 370). In this way, a counter-hegemonic (Aronowitz and Giroux, 1985) or reconstructivist (Harris, 1994) position will be informed by an understanding of the past.

Restructuring Teachers' Work: The Case of Australia

The unambiguous message over the past decade in Australia has been that schools and teachers must change. And radically! These pressures for change to teachers' work have emerged from the complexity of the present political and economic crises confronting most advanced nations. The result has led to fundamental transformations in the productive sector at the level of the global economy and the firm (McGrew, 1992), the development of new trading and cultural alliances (Harvey, 1990; Jessop, 1993), and the changing architecture of the nation State (Cerny, 1991; Lipietz, 1992; Jessop, 1993). Translated by an array of self-styled school-reform gurus, the message goes something like this. Schools are large, bureaucratic organizations. Like all bureaucracies, schools have top-heavy hierarchies, limited accountability, and a myriad of rules and regulations. Teachers are not only out of date, they fail to demand that the basic skills in education are covered. In short, teachers are out of touch with the needs of kids, the community and the nation at large. Efficiencies in the provision of educational services will be made if people (as consumers), not government, determine how their money is to be spent. It is only when the principles of the market-place are allowed to operate that teachers will have greater freedom for relevant teaching and community involvement. This will lead to a genuine teacher professionalism. We need to reinvent government and restructure our organizations to provide flexibility, diversity and choice within the marketplace.[4]

This rhetoric, at first glance, is powerful. Of course teachers want fewer regulations, less hierarchy, more opportunities for relevant teaching and a chance to regain the public's respect! However, as I will outline, the potential demise of teachers as bureaucratic workers and their reconstitution as a smaller cadre of flexible and professional teachers supported by a large group of deskilled teachers with the new label of 'cheaper educational worker', needs to be understood against a backdrop of shifts toward a post-Fordist development model. Closer scrutiny of this model, I will argue, expose real dangers facing public-sector educators. To understand the precise nature of these shifts, I would like to turn to a brief analysis of teachers as bureaucratic workers during the post-war period in Australia.

Teachers as Bureaucratic Workers and the Fordist Development Model

The prolonged boom following World War II — the 'golden era' — which saw a dramatic expansion in the provision of mass education had largely collapsed by the

1970s. The development model which underpinned the period following World War II consists of what Lipietz (1992, p. 2) describes as 'three legs of a tripod'. This model is widely referred to as the Fordist development model. These three legs or aspects of development refer to:

- a labour process model based upon Taylorist principles of scientific management;
- a regime of accumulation where macro-economic relations are based upon mass production and mass consumption; and
- a mode of regulation involving all of those mechanisms which try to adjust the contradictory and conflictual behaviour of individuals and workers to the collective principles of the regime of accumulation.

The later difficulties facing the Fordist model of development, which by and large was spectacularly successful within the developed nations, can be captured by the notion of rigidity. With the saturation of markets and over-accumulation, capital soon came to realize that the Fordist system was particularly rigid (Harvey, 1990, p. 142). Labour relations, consumer markets and methods of production all needed to be more flexible to facilitate exploitation of limited and unstable markets. This meant substituting the principle of 'just-in case' with the principle of 'just-in-time'.

The principle of 'just-in case' was central to the development of mass schooling. The post-war State undertook an important role in not only producing future workers and consumers for the mass-production society, but in creating the conditions for the reproduction of the capitalist relations of production. The values of the new post-war liberalism — equity and rationalization — were given a parliamentary face through welfare legislation (Beilhartz, 1989, pp. 141–2). The provision of public schooling, embedded within the welfare State, was crucial to this process. In large part, the State was able to guarantee the structural and functional correspondence of education to the economy through a mass expansion of education and through universal access. Despite the rhetoric of equity and uniformity, the streaming of students into 'ability' categories of academic (middle- and upper-class) and non-academic (poorer working-class) learners within the rapidly growing secondary comprehensives throughout this period paralleled the wider stratification of labour into primary and secondary labour markets. However, the dynamics underpinning the growth of schooling were not just economic. As Connell *et al.* (1982) observed of the time:

> The coalition favouring growth had a number of elements. People of a liberal mind had long been urging that more education meant social uplift. Critics and researchers in the 1940s pointed out the class biases in the education system, and a natural response was to eliminate them by extending more schooling to those who had been excluded . . . Above all, there was popular support. For most people in the 1940s, more education was

> one of the hopes they had for a better and more equal postwar world. (Connell *et al.*, 1982, p. 19)

The expansion of schooling, underpinned as it was by the contradictory social relations of efficient accumulation (the commodity form) and the pursuit of common democratic and general interests (the non-commodity form), created the conditions for conflict. Nowhere was this more apparent than in the growing inequality of schooling outcomes. Despite two decades of rhetoric about uniformity and equity within public education, a convincing body of evidence by the late 1970s pointed to the facts. Schools were active producers of inequality (Rist, 1970; Anyon, 1980), exposing 'a thinly strung welfare safety-net', rather than a set of arrangements recognizing citizens as active agents, not passive objects, of welfare (Beihartz, 1989, p. 141).

These debates on schooling inequality placed teachers on centre-stage. Were teachers agents of the State and capital? What was teachers' class location? Did the ideology of professionalism politically immobilize teachers? What was teachers' status *vis-à-vis* other professional groups? Throughout the post-war period teachers in Australia had consistently sought social recognition and economic reward from the State in exchange for their possession of scarce knowledge and skills. In fact, teachers' right to bargain for better working conditions had been accepted in all provincial states within Australia by the late 1940s. However teacher unions increasingly sought settlement through a system of arbitration rather than direct employer negotiation (Spaull, 1990, p. 12). This resulted in the highly centralized unions of this period largely being incorporated into most state educational apparatus, effectively neutralizing them.

The capacity of public-sector teachers to create a protected institutional market for their services, in comparison to doctors and lawyers, has only ever been partially successful and teachers remained on the periphery in relation to other professional occupations. The reasons for this are crucial to understanding the 'border' existence for teachers as a 'core' profession in Australia. To begin, teaching in Australia, as in many other countries, is a feminized occupation. Around two-thirds of teachers are female, with the bulk of women located in the elementary and early childhood areas of teaching (Schools Council, 1990, p. 34). Further, teaching is widely conceived as structurally equating to the labour of females in the household — caring for children. Clearly then, as Larson (1988, p. 25) reminds us, individuals and groups have differential capacities to appropriate authoritative and authorizing discourse, and it is 'this differential capacity [which] constitutes a singular and characteristic dimension of social inequality' both within professions and between different occupational groups. Within education, those teachers (i) whose knowledge embodies the rationality of science, (ii) who are in male-dominated areas, and (iii) in close proximity to authority and power (as in private schools), have greater authority to speak as educational professionals. Foucault (1980) refers to this as the knowledge–power relation. Within education, discipline areas dominated by males, such as science and mathematics (buoyed by powerful professional associations), or teachers in private schools, have been more successful in claiming and being constituted as more 'learned' and therefore more expert. The professional teacher during this period, armed with the ideology of scientific management and an array of objective instruments for promoting reason and testable outcomes, embodied the logic of science.

A second reason for the border-line status of public-sector teachers flows from the fact that the public sector has traditionally attracted to it fractions of the upper working and lower middle classes in what has been an important avenue for social mobility (Connell, 1985, p. 199). Up until 1973, higher education in Australia was not free. Students either funded their way through winning scholarships, or were required to pay substantial tuition fees. Through a system of bonding to the State, whereby the cost of tuition was paid in exchange for a specified period of service following graduation, students could enrol in college-based teacher-training programmes staffed and administered by the Department of Education. Teachers were trained for a minimal period of time, exiting with a two-year diploma and were obligated to take up an appointment wherever the State required. This cheaper alternative to university-based training provided around three-quarters of the teachers for the system. It is hardly surprising that 'bonding' (an almost feudal relationship between the State and the future worker) was an attractive occupational route for working class and female students; many would have faced considerable difficulties in accessing a 'respectable' career. The decision by the socially progressive federal Labor[5] government, elected in 1973, to remove higher education fees, provide federal funding to teacher-training colleges and grant a measure of autonomy to the college sector, went some way to opening up the teacher-training programme to a diversity of intellectual ideas (including a critique of meritocracy and an analysis of the links between schooling and stratification).

This period marked a temporary shift away from the strictly prescribed regimen of bureaucratically based rationality: rules, routines and regulations in the name of system uniformity and equity. The fact remained, however, that despite some freeing up of the system of teacher training, the majority of teachers still acquired their expert knowledge in the lower-status college rather than the university system of the higher education binary in Australia. Nonetheless, the (illusory) promise of professionalism was sufficient to guarantee the co-option of many teachers to the hegemonic project, thereby preventing large numbers of teachers from seeing that their interests were the same as that of the labouring classes. Thus teachers entered into a set of class relations by offering their expertise to a system which, legitimized by the ideology of meritocracy, continued to reproduce the unequal social relations of capitalism (Connell, 1985, p. 192).

This is not to suggest that all teachers in Australia are mere agents at the behest of the State and capital. As in all settlements, the total subordination of workers to the systemic requirements is never completely successful, and for teachers it was no different. By the early 1970s, teacher unions had successfully argued for the removal of barriers, such as marriage and family responsibilities, to permanent employment for women (Spaull, 1990, p. 12). In addition, teacher unions across Australia increasingly became embroiled in a number of public and electoral opinion campaigns over a range of issues, such as federal government funding to private schools (Spaull, 1990, p. 12), and formed a strategic alliance with other unions under the umbrella of the Australian Council for Trade Unions (ACTU). On the agenda were issues such as wage parity for females. The decision by the Federal Arbitration Commission in 1974 to increase female wages to approximately 80 per cent of male wages was to have important political and economic ramifications in Australia. A flight of capital at a time of global recession was accompanied by a hastened process of de-industrialization, as industries dependent upon cheap female labour (for example in the footwear and clothing industries) sought new havens for profitability (Catley, 1978). The popularist government stepped up its public-sector spending in an effort to inject much needed funds into the system and at the same time meet the demands of its large constituency of voters. However, the imminent fiscal crisis of the State and the resultant political turmoil not only forced the controversial dismissal of the Whitlam government in 1975, but laid the foundations for a highly pragmatic form of politics within the Labor party on its return to power in 1983 (Beilhartz, 1994).

The early 1970s heralded a period of political ferment in Australian education (Beilhartz, 1989). The increasingly obvious economic inequalities and social injustices produced by the system of public and private education were not lost on some teachers (Connell *et al.*, 1982, p. 197). The views of a number of the teachers in Connell's study examining the complex relations of gender and class and educational inequality were clearly at odds with the dominant ideology of meritocracy. However, teachers still resisted seeing inequality in class terms (Connell, 1985, p. 198). This fact is crucial in understanding the barriers to teachers' potential for class action. Despite this, the significant injection of federal funds to state-funded schools, underpinned by the twin ideologies of socially progressivism and centralist federalism, did have an important impact upon the work of teachers by providing an opportunity for some change within schools.[6] For a brief period, federal funds provided a mechanism for innovative teachers to side-step the weight of bureaucratic regulation at the State level. A small band of active and committed teachers and principals seized the opportunity, creating school environments where innovation, creativity, pedagogy and collegiality culminated in a grass-roots school-development reform movement (Robertson, 1990). Recasting the knowledge–power relation, these scattered groups of practitioners committed themselves to make a difference to those students the system had succeeded in marginalizing. However, as Beilhartz (1989) notes, at best the Whitlam reforms were only an enlightened liberalism, where 'positive equality remained essentially meritocratic liberalism bathed in a rosy hue — the focus on health and education as preconditions of individual achievement and social performance . . . For Whitlam this meant, in naive yet touching pathos, that every child should have a desk, a lamp and privacy in which to study' (1989, p. 144). In other words, the essential message was about opportunities within the existing social relations.

As a result, the more pressing problems of teachers, such as problems of authority, dilemmas of curriculum content and student motivation refused to go away. The failure to substantially renovate the curriculum, despite a massive injection of funds, meant large numbers of children encountered either useless or irrelevant knowledge. Added to this were twin realities; first, that teachers had been drawn into competition for credentials as a profession but had limited means to win higher prices for their services, and second, that their 'uncertain professional self-images were insulted by conditions of work that routinely included overcrowded classrooms and staffrooms, temporary buildings, and bureaucratic control by their employer' (Connell *et al.*, 1982, p. 23). This resulted in a heightened level of volatility, militancy and widespread strikes in Victoria and New South Wales. While some teachers clearly realized that their interests and that of their students lay in an association with other workers, for the most part the insidious controls of professionalism and 'being a good teacher' were largely unproblematic and went unchallenged (Watkins, 1992, p. 46).

Given, as Larson has observed, the 'complex social project of modern professional reform thus intertwined market and non-market orientations, disparate intellectual and ideological resources that feed back on each other' (1988, p. 27), then the brief but politically more open environment of this period provided some space for a diversity of discourses amongst teachers and teacher educators. In an effort to co-opt criticism and dissent, some state education departments attempted to manage the process by implementing limited forms of community participation, decentralization, reviewing the relevancy of curricular, and implementing more progressive teaching methods (Connell *et al.*, 1982, p. 16). Educational provision had briefly become a more critical discursive field made up of experts and a lay public, often with conflicting points of view, but nonetheless unified by a common concern: the social and economic education of children.

However, the relationship of schools to the labour market had changed by the late 1970s, leading Connell and his colleagues to observe that 'a programme for a drastic reform of schooling in a socially conservative direction is emerging' (1982, p. 16). It was increasingly difficult to disguise that the effective displacement of growing numbers of people, including youth, into the category of socially redundant (and unemployed) with no place in society was the product of a poor work ethic.

Teachers as Flexible Workers and the Post-Fordist Development Model

Following the collapse of the Fordist grand compromise, the whole of the education system — including teacher education — was under the political microscope. Critics launched successively more vicious attacks on teachers' competence, while teachers' vulnerability over their alleged failure to be more scientific, and therefore professional, was exploited. A profession which could not make explicit the scientific basis of its knowledge and practices was no profession at all! The fact was, the rules of the game had changed.

At the heart of the attack was the need to reorient schooling, and therefore the work of teachers, to the emerging model of development observers have called post-Fordist (Harvey, 1990; Lipietz, 1992; Jessop, 1990; 1993). This new model is based upon the crucial 'triad': a global regime of capital accumulation based upon the principle of flexibility as a result of intensified competition for diminishing markets; an increasingly flexible labour process centred in the principles of core, contracted and contingency labour and a new set of production concepts based upon teamwork, self-management and multiple but basic skills; and, finally, modes of regulation which are in the main governed by the ideologies of the free-market, individualism and private charity. The crucial issues facing the State and corporate capital were now two-fold: firstly, how to align the schooling system with the new system requirements, and secondly, how to limit the margin for manoeuvre of teachers — and therefore the potential for resistance and contestation — in an environment where teachers would seek to claim expertise and have their authority constituted.

Writing about post-Fordism more generally, John Holloway (1987) has identified three phases in its evolution. First an initial Keynesian and social-democratic phase which seeks to coordinate the efforts of managers, government and workers toward growth and productivity. However, recognition of the difficulties faced, and the less than satisfactory outcome of this approach, usually results in a second phase; a more macho approach by industrialists and politicians aimed at reasserting managerial power and facilitating a new strategy for growth. According to Holloway, the second phase is largely a transitional one, 'well suited to destroying the vestiges of Fordism/Keynesianism but not suitable for establishing the . . . patterns of the brave new world' (1987, p. 157). The aim of the third phase is to build upon the defeats achieved in the second phase in constructing a new consensus and new forms of integration, based upon the new division between core and marginalized workers.

This three-phase process can clearly be detected in the implementation of the post-Fordist development model in Australia and the reconstruction of teachers' labour. However, the implementation of this model has been politically mediated by an Accord involving corporate capital, peak interests within the labour movement and the State. Since 1983, the Prices and Incomes Accord has been the centrepiece of Labor's electoral strategy and a mechanism to guide Australia through the social and economic crisis (Watts, 1989, p. 104). The Accord has influenced the pace, direction and immediate outcome of the transition to post-Fordism. This strategy of 'progressive competitiveness', as an alternative to 'hyper-liberal globalization', has been described by Panitch as conforming to the principles of global competitiveness but which is also linked to the interests of peak social groups.

> In this way, key social groups that would otherwise become dangerously marginalised as a result of the state's sponsorship of global competitiveness may become attached to it by the appeal a progressive competitiveness strategy makes, especially through the ideology and practice of training, to incorporating working people who are unemployed and on welfare (or who soon might be) as well as the leaders of unions, social agencies and other organizations who speak for them. (Panitch, 1994, p. 84)

This strategy of progressive competitiveness is clearly evident in the reorganization of teachers' labour in Australia. A number of the key initiatives to restructure teachers' work have taken place under the auspices of the Accord partners. As a result, in comparison to the aggressive restructuring that has taken place in New Zealand and Great Britain, the process in Australia has been somewhat more muted. However, as Panitch also observes, this strategy has not offered an alternative to the logic of global competitiveness but rather is a 'subsidiary element in the process of neo-liberal capitalist restructuring and globalization' (1994, p. 85). In essence, the strategy of progressive competitiveness, while a more humane version, is typically a cosmetic means of buying off domestic opposition. Its effect at the school-level has been to produce teachers in a state of 'subdued agency'; a consensus seeking teacher who lays out the available options and facilitates a process of choice (Harris, 1994, p. 4).

Clearly teachers are a potential source of opposition during a period of transition. The potential for conflict arises during periods of fundamental restructuring when the prevailing ideology of an occupational group differs sharply from that of the new regime. Having been steeped in more than three decades of the ideology of the welfare state and notions of 'social uplift', teachers are likely to question those reforms which legitimize private rather than public interests, and which might lead to further inequity and social injustice. This poses potential problems for the new regime. For one, not all teachers can be dismissed for non-compliance. For another, training programmes cannot be hastily reshaped without some struggle. Thus, regulatory mechanisms are sought which significantly increase the degree of control over teachers, thereby limiting the space available for reflection, critique and contestation. Given that teachers are to implement the new reforms, what is required is greater control over the margin of discretion in their work. Further, the majority of teachers must be encouraged to embrace the new reforms. Three key regulatory tools have been crucial in this process in Australia: first, the promise of a new level of professionalism given concrete form by the introduction of new work practices (largely administrative); second, the implementation of a competency-based, outcome-oriented pedagogy which corresponds functionally to the world of work; and third, school–community (and business) partnerships. These tools have worked together, reinforcing each other.

Implementing Change

At one level, effecting change in teachers' work is no easy task. Teachers are one of the largest and most unionized occupational groups in Australia. They also make up approximately 3 per cent of the total labour force (Schools Council, 1990, p. 34). A quarter of a million teachers teach in around ten thousand primary, pre-primary and secondary schools spread across seven states and territories. Politicians, ever mindful of the pragmatics of party politics (which generally means staying in office), could be swayed by a powerful teachers' lobby. At another level, teachers' sensitivity to their marginal professional status can be used to impose an agenda which is, in reality, antithetical to their interests as autonomous workers. As it happened, when events unfolded in the 1980s, the reassertion of managerial power in the form of devolved administrative practice and the

Table 2.1: Policy Directions and Discursive Shifts in Restructuring Teachers' Work in Australia

Periodization	First wave Late 1970s	Second wave Early 1980s	Third wave Mid to late 1980s	Fourth wave 1990s
Focus	System	System	System/School	School/Classroom
Policy Directions	Keynesian • curricula adjustment • teacher supply • community confidence • professional development	Destabilization of existing settlement	Macro-restructuring • devolution • centralization • performance management	Micro-restructuring • labour flexibility • deregulation of schools
Discourse	• community • change • professionalism	• quality • outcomes • efficiency	• quality • outcomes • efficiency • professionalism • collegiality • entrepreneurialism	• quality • outcomes • professionalism • flexibility • work teams • competency
Outcomes	• system maintenance	crisis of confidence in teachers	• managerial control • standardization • market driven • labour intensification • greater managerial responsibility	• deregulation of labour • tiered labour structure • market driven • pedagogical deskilling • greater managerial responsibility • differentiation (student and curriculum)

imposition of school–community partnerships under the banner of professionalism, distracted teachers and concealed from them the fact that power had been further centralized. More importantly, many teachers did not connect these developments to the real agenda: a class war that had resulted in the restructuring of workplaces across the country. The result was that many teachers failed to understand the potential gravity of the changes within Australian society (Robertson and Soucek, 1991).

The restructuring of teachers' work which pushed teachers into the new world of post-Fordist flexibility appears to follow the evolution detailed by Holloway (1987) above. I have identified four phases (see Table 2.1) in the restructuring of teachers' labour in Australia (see also Robertson, 1994).

The first phase, coming at the end of the 1970s, was largely directed toward system maintenance. In the context of the curriculum, the official state line was that if teachers were engaged in work-experience programmes, better career counselling, school-to-work transition programmes, and highlighting the value of the work ethic and good manners — in other words, tinkered around the edges — that this would be sufficient to reorient the structural and functional relationship between schools and the economy (c.f. the Williams Report, 1979). With regard to teacher education, a series of reports focused their concerns upon issues such as teacher supply, managing change, community confidence and the professional development of teachers. In large part, however, the reports were underpinned by the Keynesian solution of altering the supply factors to alter the educational outputs. Many educators failed to be impressed by what was implied in these reports; that they had produced the crisis in education. So were some provincial governments; some refused to accept the generous federal programme funds, although the conflict was largely the result of federal–provincial tensions, rather than a more substantive critique of federal educational policy.

Destabilizing the Teaching Profession

The second phase of the restructuring grew from the failure to align schooling provision to shifts within the productive sector. The fiscal crisis of the State, a result of the diminution of the State's capacity to draw in a share of corporate profits as a result of de-industrialization and financial deregulation, together with the growing burden of unemployment (Watts, 1989, p. 106), saw the State turn to pruning a range of citizenship entitlements within the social-policy arena, including education. Despite the fact that Labor governments dominated federal and provincial politics throughout the 1980s, and that teachers had actively campaigned for the Australian Labor Party, it did not curtail the attack on education. Restructuring education, the State argued, was essential to produce a skilled and flexible labour force enabling Australia to become internationally competitive (Dawkins, 1988). However, there is also no doubt that the State's capacity to drive down education expenditures was limited by the current wage-award structures which underpinned teachers' wages. As in other parts of the workforce, wage flexibility was now viewed as central to market flexibility and global competitiveness.

This required a more radical change both in the organization and the terms and conditions of teachers' work. In other words, the labour process of teachers' work needed to be reworked. This could only be done by destabilizing the existing cultural and regulatory frameworks surrounding teachers' labour through an ideological attack on teacher competence. The most significant of the reports was the 1985 Federal *Report of the Quality of Education Review Committee* chaired by Professor Peter Karmel. While acknowledging the lack of supporting evidence, the Report nonetheless argued that teachers lacked the skills to develop fundamental competencies in students (reading, writing, conversing, calculating), rigour in teaching, and curriculum consistency (1985, p. 119). In other words, an efficient or professional teacher was concerned with the 'science' of teaching and learning for greater economic returns. This science could find concrete expression in measured student outcomes, public accountability through standards, and attention to the basic skills. Teacher professionalism was now constituted within a very different framework which was linked to changes within the economy.

Implementing the New Regime and Managing Dissent

Under the guidance of the corporate sector and key interests within the State (Pusey, 1991) the intent of the third phase (which was well underway by the late 1980s in almost all provincial states of Australia) was to spearhead an aggressive implementation of new managerialism within the administrative structure of education. Not only did it wipe out the potential for internal dissent, as those within the bureaucracy scrambled for jobs, but many of the new appointees at senior level were members of the technocracy; a professional managerialist class with no allegiance to teachers. This occurred concurrently within the federal and provincial arenas. In bureaucratic parlance this phase became known as the 'reorg' (Ashenden, 1990).

The intended purpose of this phase was to embed the tools (such as strategic planning, performance monitoring, site-based management and student outcomes) central to the new post-Fordist regime (efficiency, markets, entrepreneurialism) within education through a reassertion of managerial control and professional imperative. State-level devolutionary reforms in Australia tended to follow a similar pattern where the contradictory logics of corporate managerialism (flatter structures, decentralized decision-making, management information systems) and the professional imperatives of educational and organizational progressivism (school–community partnerships, site-based management, collegiality, self-determination) were grafted together. But as Harris notes, within this 'larger process of adopting forms and processes of corporate managerialism, professionals such as teachers are being redefined as straight-out contracted workers subject to direct management and becoming positioned in such a way that their expertise and professional knowledge is decreasingly called upon with regard to decision-making in areas central to the needs and requirements of those whom they teach and serve' (1994, p. 3).

Some teachers were wooed by the promise of a new professionalism. Others were forced to embrace the new practices when the new ideology found definition in the system of 'merit' promotion. However, in a remarkable show of solidarity, huge numbers of teachers went on strike in protest (Robertson and Soucek, 1991; Luzeckyj, 1992; Isaacs, 1993). They received little sympathy from the media who presented their dissent as the expected outpourings of over-paid, over-holidayed and underworked public servants. With teachers' claim to expert knowledge marginalized in the public mind, teachers' capacity to mobilize the laity — and therefore some support to their cause — was diminished. However, as Spaull has argued, 'the breadth of teacher union politics, and their willingness to prosecute them on as many fronts as are available, is certainly a new feature of contemporary unionism' (1990, p. 14). In an interesting turn of events, while other unions have declined in number, teachers' unions have increased. Spaull suggests that a combination of factors are involved in this, including the realization by teachers that they need to protect their working conditions, that they might be able to exploit the politics of devolution to increase control over their work situation, and that they can and should be social critics of society. Indeed, Isaacs (1993) draws upon evidence gathered in Victoria to argue that in comparison to the post-war period, Victorian teachers, at least, display a shift in class affiliation from the middle- to the working-class.

The solidarity of teachers was certainly apparent during the period of 1989 to 1993 in traditionally conservative states such as Western Australia. Despite the general lack of public support, outraged teachers and principals rallied in massive numbers (Robertson and Soucek, 1991). In some of the largest demonstrations in Australia since the troubled days of the Vietnam war, teachers took to the streets. In an ongoing campaign of active resistance, huge numbers of teachers waged a bitter battle of strikes, work-to-rules, lockouts, and the length of the working day. The struggle over the working day, as Harvey notes (1990, p. 230), has long been the familiar landscape of industrial capitalism in battles over minutes and seconds, and the intensity of work schedules. Rifts soon appeared between teachers, nourished by the image of the 'good teacher' who ignored the time-clock and remained dedicated to the organization, no matter what. But the failure of teacher unions to deliver either public acknowledgment of teachers' efforts as competent professionals or political recognition of their increased productivity by way of salary increases, resulted in many teachers losing the momentum which they had mobilized. The crucial issue for teachers seems to be that while their numbers have grown and their class affiliation has shifted, they must also develop a political programme to influence the course of events and construct their own futures (Harris, 1994).

Embedding the new post-Fordist rules has had the effect of tightening of the structural correspondence between education and the economy. In essence, the changes have meant teachers can participate in making decisions over a limited range of technical issues, not the big ticket items such as: What is it that we want children to know? How do we provide opportunities for students to genuinely participate in the learning process? What does it mean to educate a critical citizenry? Instead teachers have been left to dream up schemes as to how they can work smarter to increase student performance, compete for scarce students with neighbouring schools, raise money from the business sector, or access new technology for the school through school–business partnerships. At the same time it has marginalized teachers' dissenting voices and reduced their scope for critical practice and autonomy. Harris describes this as a process of repoliticizing of teachers 'away from the broader concerns of determining curricula, formulating educational goals and promoting social reconstruction and toward the realm of efficient school management within an educational marketplace' (1994, p. 4). This is not to suggest that some teachers are not able to see the extent to which markets and managerialism have eroded their already precariously balanced marginal autonomy. Examples of teachers protesting these changes are numerous. Teachers have pointed out the contradictions between good nutrition and the installation of Coke and Pepsi machines on the school grounds and have successfully campaigned to have McDonalds banned from forming school–business partnerships. However, the really insidious controls over the work of teachers have slipped in, as if they were invisible.

It is important at this point to reflect upon precisely what it is that teachers have lost control over. The work of Derber (1982) is useful here in understanding the dual forms of control over workers like teachers. He terms these two forms of control: ideological and technical. The loss of autonomy in these two spheres can be described as 'ideological' and 'technical proletarianization' (Derber, 1982, p. 30). The former involves teachers losing control over the goals, objectives and policy directions of their work. The latter refers to a loss of control over the skills, content, rhythm and pace of their work, for example with the introduction of various forms of technology in the classroom.

The loss of ideological control has occurred in a number of ways in the current round of restructuring. For example, the government has typically refused to engage in any level of prior consultation with teachers, their unions or teacher educators on the precise shape of key administrative, organizational or curriculum changes within education. The consultation which has occurred has been tightly managed and after the fact. The fact is, the goals, objectives and policy directions for schools are not for teachers to determine. Rather, the organization of schooling and teachers' work must take its cue from the needs of industry. An array of committees and forums, such as the Finn Committee under the chairmanship of Brian Finn (IBM General Manager) reviewing post-compulsory schooling, the Meyer Committee to implement the competency-based curriculum under the Chairmanship of Eric Meyer (National Mutual Life Insurance), the Industry Education Forum with representatives from all the large transnational corporations, and the federal Economic Planning and Advisory Council (a coalition of state, corporate capital and peak unions) have all laid out the ideal worker for the new regime: multiskilled, efficient, self-reliant, team-oriented, adaptable and flexible. The task for teachers is to develop new approaches to teaching which efficiently produce the ideal worker.

There are many instances which illustrate the technical proletarianization of teachers as well. For example, teachers have increasingly lost the scope to choose methods for determining how well students meet predefined goals. Rather, a national curriculum and standardized testing to monitor through student performance are the mechanisms by which teachers are now controlled. The advance of computer technology, as well as the onslaught of corporate-funded television programming for students in schools, are further instances of technical proletarianization.

The intensification of teachers' labour, an outcome of this third wave of educational restructuring, has certainly limited the opportunities for teachers to engage critically with their students. In a study on the impact of devolution on teachers in Western Australia, teachers reported the need to constantly attend meetings as a result of collegial and managerial demands, the escalation of accountability and control initiatives, the pressure to be more entrepreneurial, and an increasing scarcity of resources which led to intense rapid politicization. All of these activities took considerable time. In order to meet their commitments teachers worked longer hours per day and more days of the week (Robertson and Soucek, 1991).

The compression of time and space leading to an intensification of teachers' labour has resulted from a complex of factors. These include bigger classes, the addition of new managerial tasks at the school level, new technology such as fax machines moving information in and out of the school, new information systems in the school which monitor student and map school performance, increased activity around business partnerships, more intense entrepreneurial activity, a constant cycle of assessments, to name but a few (Smyth, 1993). The intensification of teachers' work inevitably leads to the prioritizing of those activities which are rewarded over those that are not. This is only human. Given that the reward structures for teachers are now based upon being able to generate market competitiveness, it is obvious where the sacrifices will be made. However, the more distant teachers become from their students, the more depersonalized their teaching. This leads inexorably to an even further alienated relationship between themselves and their students. Their relationship takes on all of the characteristics of the commodity form (Grace, 1989). It is the logic of the market — the commodity form — which has penetrated deep inside the schools, and constituted the authority of the new professional. The new professional has embraced a new science; the commodity form in the schooling market-place.

The commodity form can be seen in a myriad of ways: the direct involvement of business in the school by funding computer equipment and sponsoring industry-based scholarships, the encouragement of entrepreneurial teachers in the school, the development of niche courses such as aeronautics and art/fashion, and in marketing of the school's performances to the wider community. The outcome is that niche schools are able to provide, under the guidance of the corporate sector, a small band of suitably skilled workers to work in specialized industries. This trend toward market specialization in schools, based upon the principle of 'just-in-time', 'marks a bid by a new ideological configuration . . . educators are asked to base the curriculum on market trends which in turn are grounded in market forecasting' (Aronowitz and Giroux, 1985, p. 192).

The emerging entrepreneurial culture within the schools has not advantaged all teachers in the same way. We found winners and losers in our study of the effects on teachers of devolution (Robertson and Soucek, 1991). The winners were teachers who embraced the market, new managerialism and technology, setting into place the structural and functional correspondence between schools and the economy. They were the new entrepreneurs — the new professionals amongst teachers. Their values corresponded to the values of the post-Fordist regime, and they were rewarded accordingly. The losers were those teachers who failed to exploit the new opportunities, either for ideological reasons or because they were in areas where their expertise was no longer needed or valued. These teachers had fewer resources and marginal influence.

However, responding to market niches raised problems for teachers which had not been anticipated. The highly specialized programmes in the school attracted an *élite* group of male-student outsiders. Their presence in the school increased the divisions within the school resulting in conflict between the *élites* and the local 'lads'. In order to counter an emerging gender imbalance, the school offered a programme of specialized science and technology to an *élite* group of females. Again the programme attracted mainly outsiders. These female imports, however, were unhappy about establishing themselves in this new environment, and the programme was disbanded. In both cases, the idea of importing students did not sit well with all teachers. In our interviews, some teachers were firmly committed to the idea of a school servicing its local community. This view stands in opposition to the competitive school which provides specialized services within the educational market-place.

Embedding the New Commonsense

A final phase in the restructuring of teachers' work in Australia — beginning in the 1990s and still underway — is concerned with embedding the new commonsense of the post-Fordist model of development. Here the labour process, regime of accumulation and modes of regulation must work together to close the hegemonic circle. With ideological controls in place through the new management framework, thereby limiting the possibility for critique and autonomous action by teachers, the corporate sector and reform technocrats have challenged willing schools and teachers to 'trial' and 'experiment' with new work practices which might carry the new curriculum (National Project on the Quality of Teaching and Learning, 1991).

This phase has been paralleled by crucial changes to the industrial-relations legislation. The conditions for the deregulation of wage bargaining, pressed for by the corporate sector, took form in March 1987 when the federal Industrial Relations Commission (IRC) handed down their historic decision that wage increases were conditional upon productivity gains (Niland, 1992, p. 33). This marked a turning point in Australian industrial relations. Wage increases over the past century in Australia have rested in the judicial principles of uniformity across industries. This decision has opened the way for the deregulation of wage bargaining.

By late 1993 the new industrial-relations legislation was in force. Teachers in Victoria faced massive lay-offs, extensive school closures, and the deregulation of all wage bargaining. Western Australia is rapidly following suit. Wages are now determined in the market-place, with no guarantee of a bottom-line or safety net.

The thin strings of the welfare state have been severed altogether. For teachers, the outcome has been fear and compliance. The new professional must now sit up straight, with lips buttoned and eyes forward! The flight of teachers from provincial to federal awards offers teachers short-term protection. However, if teachers are covered on one federal award, teachers *en masse* are likely to be highly vulnerable to a change in political party. Despite the limitations of federal–state relations, the politics which flow from this relationship have sometimes been a source of protection from some forms of political control.

A crucial ideological theme in this phase of the restructuring is the notion of flexibility and adaptability. However, flexibility now has a very particular meaning. In outlining the federal government's view of flexibility, the Schools Council locates flexibility within a managerial and market-oriented framework rather than a pedagogical one. That is, flexibility is:

> . . . the skilful *management* of human and physical resources in response to identified educational needs which results in increased *effectiveness* (e.g., improved student learning outcomes) and *productivity* (e.g., improved school performance. (my emphasis) (Schools Council, 1992)

The teacher is now constituted as the 'manager' of resources which might lead to pre-specified learning outcomes and targeted performances. And while learners are to be enterprising, self-directed, work in multi-level groups, and progress on an individualized basis (Schools Council, 1989, 1992), their endeavours within school are almost exclusively directed toward their 'flexible' participation world of work rather than participation within the wider society. Here the functional requirements of the economy are made explicit. Further, the School Council outlines a structural alignment or correspondence between the organization of teachers' labour and the organization of labour within the wider workforce; the increased segmentation in teachers' work to enable staffing flexibility and cost efficiencies (Schools Council, 1992, p. 16).

However, there is no discussion by the School Council of the more dysfunctional relations within schools and which affect teachers' work; in essence, the contradictions that are revealed by the growing number of economic and social losers in the system. For example, how should teachers cope with the increased levels of stress in the classroom — the result not only of hunger, violence, abuse, and drugs, but an intense sense of hopelessness and alienation amongst an increasing number of students. The fact is, many of these students are never likely to enter the core or contract labour market. Rather they will be unceremoniously directed toward an insecure contingency labour market with basic skills and few chances but a healthy dose of the new ideology: adaptability and market flexibility. Teachers, with their reconstituted professional status authorized within the market-place, will be expected to play a key role as agents in this process.

And this outcome is precisely what the federally funded National Schools Project (NSP) is intended to achieve; to embed a new set of work practices within schools which works toward realizing the industry-endorsed worker competencies, while at the same time aligning the organization of schooling with the organization of the workplace. This requires that teachers review those work practices which are now dysfunctional and replace them with new ones directed to achieving the new system imperatives. However, providing a context for teachers to experiment with these new practices is quite a challenge. The brief for individual schools around Australia has been to investigate how changes in work practices can lead to improved student outcomes whilst working within current levels of resourcing.[7]

The NSP has several distinct features. Project schools operate in a 'deregulated zone' where the regulatory framework for teachers and their work is suspended. Further, the Project framework is also tightly prescribed — further evidence of ideological proletarianization. Teachers must accept a model of curriculum which is outcome-oriented and concerned with workplace competencies.[8] In addition, the focus for reforms must be on work practices rather than on the curriculum. The unit of change, to use the NSP jargon and borrowed directly from the post-Fordist literature, must be the 'systems work unit'. However, reframing teachers' central concerns as those of management rather than pedagogy has caused considerable unease, as is evident from this NSP teacher:

> To effect change for education for the 21st Century we need to change the relationship between teachers and students. But when we probed . . . (NSP official) on this point in terms of pedagogy he said the project was not about pedagogy, it's about work organization. His argument was that you can change pedagogy all you like and change teachers' professional development and have wonderful new programs going but they only last as long as teachers' interest in them. Whereas what he wants is change embedded in the organization. I think they have to go hand in hand. I can't see that just a change in structure is going to have a significant influence on student learning outcomes unless you have an associated complimentary change in the process. This is why I'm becoming more convinced that the only way to go is to adopt the philosophy of student centred learning, because if we do everything in terms of that, then we will both achieve. (Chadbourne, 1992, p. 51)

The teacher in Chadbourne's study reported above can see the need for changes to the organization of schooling. However, what is clear is that state officials believe pedagogical change should flow only from managerial change, rather than the other way around. In other words, it is still the case of the managerial tail waving the pedagogical dog. The crucial change is that the rhythm of the new managerial tune is now determined by the post-Fordist market-place!

The NSP's strategic separation of pedagogical concerns from managerial processes represents confused thinking about what ought to be the central and real interests of teachers. Teachers cite their immediate concerns such as problems of student literacy and numeracy, student behaviour, oversized classrooms, lack of resources, and the overtly top–down approach to innovation and change as the more significant barriers to learning (Chadbourne, 1992, pp. 30–1). Were teachers in the NSP to tackle issues such as what to do about growing student alienation within schooling, or what might constitute a set of outcomes for students which are linked to socially oriented goals, then teachers could be said to be moving toward creating the space for some intellectual autonomy. The fact that teachers have largely failed to do this, despite their increased level of unionization, is evidence of a further diminution of their already reduced capacity for critical autonomy.

By far the NSP's most controversial proposal for regulatory change has concerned the flexible deployment of non-teaching staff to assist teachers in a more diverse array of tasks. These propositions are also at the core of Ashenden's (1992) proposals. To begin, Ashenden argues that teachers' work is badly designed and managed, and there are too many trivial tasks. However, these 'trivial' tasks, like writing letters to parents about a student's behaviour, arise not so much as a result of the way in which teachers' work is organized, but as a result of the organization of schooling in general. Schools, as institutions, are structures of power. Further, many of the constant infractions arise as a result of the contestation of class/gender/ethnic relations within the school (see Connell *et al.*, 1982). This affects teachers' relationships with students. And as Ashenden himself reminds us (1992, p. 57), relationships with students can be spectacularly conflicting, upsetting and humiliating. These relations border on a constant movement in the classroom from consent to coercion, from resistance to compliance and pragmatism (Connell *et al.*, 1982). Unless the proposed changes to the organization of schooling confront the underlying relations of power, then little will alter.

Ashenden also argues that unless staffing is made more flexible, teachers will be unable to deliver increased student productivity (measured in student outcome terms). Ashenden proposes to reduce the number of professional staff in the school by more than one-third, and use the surplus funds to employ a range of other flexible educational workers in para-professional roles (parents, student teachers, consultants, teacher aides) on a casual or short-term contract basis. According to Ashenden, teachers do too much busy-work which is not real teaching. Teachers would also be encouraged to explore new options for the delivery of education, including the use of large groups, new technologies, learning packages, and peer tutoring.

What can be seen emerging here is a core and peripheral workforce typical of post-Fordism: a core of trained teachers and the periphery made up of expendable units of semi-skilled and cheaper labour, in this case parents, the unemployed and interns (c.f. Harvey, 1990). The remaining teachers would be required to do more of the 'real' teaching, while those skills which can be separated off will be embedded in a machine or given to cheaper workers to perform. It is this process, described so graphically by Braverman (1974), centred on the deskilling and devaluing of labour power which describes the essential features of proletarianization; the 'economic process of devaluation of labour power from skilled to average levels' (Harris, 1994, p. 1). While it is to be hoped that the peripheral workforce that operates within the school remains dedicated and available to the school, the low rates of pay make this doubtful. If it is the case that they stay, the school will be able to devote its main energies to curriculum as opposed to staffing issues. If not, these energies will be dissipated, and the school will operate on a constant training cycle.

In a study which explored teachers' views on these proposals (Chadbourne and Robertson, 1992) in a junior primary school, we found that most staff would like the support of para-professionals. However, teachers opposed increased salaries if it meant an erosion of other conditions, such as an increase in class sizes or an escalation in the number of multiple-ability groups. These teachers argue that moving to larger classes would reduce their contact with students and limit their teaching strategies and relationships with students. They argued that an inevitable outcome of these changes would be a burgeoning managerial (and supervisory) role for teachers, taking them out of the classroom and interaction with students. These teachers were reluctant to see a further division in their labour, arguing that there was very little which could be further delegated without significantly deskilling them and eroding their relationships with the students. The proposed expansion of technology within the school also worried them. Aside from the costs of computer technology being outside of the reach of many financially constrained schools, teachers also observed that the software available was educationally limited.

Some elements of the Ashenden proposal have merit. For too long teachers have engaged in teacher-centred pedagogy. A shift away toward a more learner-centred pedagogy would be a highly desirable move. But this would have to take the form of a shift toward a critical pedagogy which is built upon a relationship of trust and a genuine interest in the child as citizen, rather than as a commodity in the market-place. Unless the underlying relations of power upon which schooling is built are confronted, then the sorts of proposals offered by Ashenden will only momentarily obscure the social relations which schools are asked to reproduce. The problem with Ashenden's proposal, and his is the only one example amongst a growing number in the same vein, is that the model is essentially undemocratic. These proposals begin with the system imperatives of adaptability and flexibility for the economy rather than the needs of the life world and the child.

A New Professionalism for Teachers?

The evidence is overwhelming. The current restructuring initiatives — in the name of a new professionalism — have not created the conditions for teachers to work as autonomous intellectuals. Rather, I have shown that teachers have become a special target for control, because of their crucial role in the production of knowledge and labour power for the new post-Fordist settlement. As Harris (1994) reminds us — in a single decade, teachers have lost a great deal! The outcome of the reorganization of teachers' work is increased segmentation for the purposes of organizational flexibility, pedagogical deskilling, a new conception of professionalism linked to managerial activity, the reconstruction of teacher as learner-manager, an expansion of tasks to include management activity, and tighter external controls. These developments create a qualitatively different terrain on which teachers must work. The development model which underpinned Fordism has given way to a new post-Fordist ethos: the authority of the highly competitive market-place. Teachers' workplace is also now a market-place, as education takes on the commodity form. Teachers are the new saleswomen and salesmen for the economy; the only catch is that like in all market-places, not all buyers have equal power if the full force of labour deregulation and labour flexibility take their toll.

Teacher flexibility and professionalism have been cast in a new light in the new settlement. Flexibility in schools is not driven by pedagogical concerns, depite the fact that the rhetoric borrows heavily from the critique of schooling launched almost three decades ago. The fall-out for schools already includes larger classes, the increasing use of technology within the school, business–school relationships, the privatization of key services, and a segmented and cheaper teaching force. There is little scope in the promise of professionalism to wrest a degree of autonomy because the crucial margin for determination — that is ideological control — has been unceremoniously split from teachers' work and placed in the firm hands of administrators, politicians and transnational capital. The margin of indetermination is now located at the level of decisions to meet the system-specified outcomes, rather than at the point of judgment about what might constitute an adequate framing of knowledge. Gains to teachers are thus largely illusory. Teachers will be weighed down by the pressure of management, time constraints, larger classes and the management of other workers. What flows from this is a depersonalized authority — an outcome teachers have confused with professionalism. Teachers have not been provided or promised an opportunity to negotiate the changing shape of their work. Rather, their work has increasingly been moulded by economic imperative and expediency, and is the outcome of the State's need to establish the new conditions for accumulation.

Reconceptualizing the Space for Teacher Autonomy

The period of transition creates the conditions for a critical correspondence between teachers, the State and the economy. The dramatic curtailing of teacher autonomy in order to control teachers reveals a further erosion of teachers' already licensed autonomy. This period creates a unique space in which to insert an agenda which seeks to have the voices of teachers also constituted as those with authority to speak in the educational interests of children. But a crucial question remains to be addressed. Are the objective conditions created by the increased tendency toward proletarianization sufficient for teachers to mobilize and act in counter-hegemonic ways. I wish to argue that while Derber's (1982) two forms of proletarianization, technical and ideological, are useful in beginning to conceptualize the erosion of teacher autonomy, it is insufficient to help us understand neither the precise nature of that autonomy, nor the basis from which the possibility for educational change might emerge. That is, a notion of autonomy versus proletarianization does not fully reveal the kind of relationship between teachers, the economy and their students. Can we argue, for example, that a teacher who participates in a forum to discuss the outcomes of a particular set of policies but who has been blinkered by an ideology of professionalism, is acting autonomously? At one level it might appear to be the case. But at another level, the failure of the teacher to interrogate the basic relationships between schooling and the economy, such as the principle of meritocracy, would suggest otherwise. Dale has called this 'regulated autonomy' (Dale, 1982, p. 146). In this case, the basic character of the relationship between the teacher and the State has been mediated by an ideology of professionalism which results in a positive correspondence between schooling and the economy. On the other hand, if the basic character of the relationship between the teachers and the economy is one of critical correspondence, that is, where the teacher is able to see the penetration of the commodity form into the organization of their labour and classroom practice, then this, together with the objective conditions of proletarianization, are more likely to lead to forms of critical resistance and intellectual autonomy.

My argument is that the processes which lead toward the proletarianization of teachers' work, particularly during periods of crisis and transformation, may provide the conditions for, but will not necessarily lead to, a more critical practice within schools. Rather, the shift toward intellectual autonomy and a more critical practice will occur only when teachers are able to recognize and conceptualize the various ways in which the proletarianization of their work is the result of the penetration of the commodity form into schooling and the labour process. This project should be the starting point for future political action by all educators and intellectuals.

Notes

1 Peter Watkins provides a very good account of the different post-Fordist positions, including the French regulation school (1994).

2 I am accepting here that while teachers do occupy a contradictory class location, it is more useful to ask the question that Connell *et al.* (1982) poses: What class relations do teachers enter into? In this way teachers' class relations are seen as more fluid and dynamic rather than being necessarily overdetermined by the material relations of production.

3 John Hinkson (1991), however, argues that schools are increasingly less important as sites of socialization as this role is increasingly taken on by the mass media and television culture.

4 See for example J. Lewington and G. Orpwood, (1993) *Overdue Assignment: Taking Responsibility for Canada's Schools*, Ontario, John Wiley and Sons; A. Nikiforuk (1990) *Schools Out: The Catastrophe in Public Education and What We Can Do About It*, Toronto, Macfarlane Walker and Ross; J. Chubb, T. Moe (1990) *Politics, Markets and America's Schools*, Washington, DC, The Brookings Institute.

5 The Australian Labor Party was formed almost one hundred years ago to represent the interests of labour. In the main its constituency is drawn from the laboring classes and segments of the middle classes.

6 Ironically, it was the federal ideology of political centralism, infused with an economically derived nationalism, which has later profoundly impacted upon the nature of teachers' work in Australia. By 1988, the Federal Government had proposed a national curriculum, national testing and standards, and National Teaching Council. This despite the fact that the Federal Government has no constitutional authority for its

involvement in schooling provision, and that teachers' salaries and appointments are provincial rather than federal affairs.

7 In 1992, over 60 schools joined the NSP. There is funding however for time release for key staff in each of the schools.

8 As identified in the Finn, Mayer and Carmichael reports. The limitation of the overtly economic focus thus is picked up in the construction of these new school cultures and patterns of work organizations.

References

ANYON, J. (1981) 'Social class and the hidden curriculum of work', in GIROUX, H., PENNA, A. and PINAR, A. (Eds) *Curriculum and Instruction: Alternatives for the Future*, Berkeley, McCuthchan.

ARONOWITZ, S. and GIROUX, H. (1985) *Education Under Siege*, Massachusetts, Bergin and Garvey.

ASHENDEN, D. (1990) 'Award restructuring and education', *QTU Professional Magazine*, **8**, 1, pp. 8–13.

ASHENDEN, D. (1992) 'New forms of work organisation for teachers and students: Some developments and possibilities', IARTV Seminar Series, Melbourne, Incorporated Association of Registered Teachers in Victoria.

ANYON, J. (1980) 'Social class and the hidden curriculum of work', *Journal of Education*, **162**, pp. 67–92.

BERMAN, M. (1982) *All That is Solid Melts into Air*, New York, Verso.

BALL, S. (1990) 'Introduction Monsieur Foucault', in BALL, S. (Ed) *Foucault and Education: Disciplines and Knowledge*, London, Routledge.

BALL, S. and GOODSON, I. (1985) *Teachers' Lives and Careers*, Basingstoke, Falmer Press.

BARLOW, M. and ROBERTSON, H. (1994) *Class Warfare: The Assault on Canada's Schools*, Toronto, Key Porter Books.

BEILHARTZ, P. (1989) 'The Labourist tradition and the reforming imagination', in KENNEDY, R. (Ed) *Australian Welfare*, China, Macmillan.

BEILHARTZ, P. (1994) *Transforming Labor: Labour Tradition and the Labor Decade in Australia*, Australia, Cambridge University Press.

BRAVERMAN, H. (1974) *Labour and Monopoly Capital: The Degradation of Work in the Twentieth Century*, New York, Monthly Review Press.

CARLSON, D. (1992) *Teachers and Crisis: Urban School Reform and Teachers' Work Culture*, New York, Routledge.

CATLEY, B. (1978) 'Socialism and reform in contemporary Australia', in WHEELWRIGHT, E. and BUCKLEY, K. (Eds) *Essays in the Political Economy of Australian Capitalism: Volume Two*, Sydney, Australian and New Zealand Book Company.

CHADBOURNE, R. (1992) *The National Schools Project at Belmont Senior High School: A Formative Review of the First Nine Months*, Perth, International Institute for Policy and Administrative Studies.

CHADBOURNE, R. and ROBERTSON, S. (1992) *Dean Ashenden's Proposal for Restructuring Teachers' Work: A Junior Primary Perspective*, Perth, International Institute for Policy and Administrative Studies.

CERNY, P. (1991) *The Changing Architecture of Politics: Structure, Agency and the Future of the State*, Wiltshire, UK, Sage Publications.

COMMITTEE OF ENQUIRY INTO EDUCATION AND TRAINING (Williams Report) (1979) *Education, Training and Employment, Vols 1 and 2, Report* (B. Williams, Chair), Canberra, AGPS.

CONNELL, B., ASHENDEN, D., KESSLER, S. and DOWSETT, G. (1982) *Making the Difference*, Sydney, Allen and Unwin.

CONNELL, B. (1985) *Teachers' Work*, Sydney, George, Allen and Unwin.

DAWKINS, J. (1988) *Strengthening Australia's Schools*, Canberra, AGPS.

DALE, R. (1982) 'Education and the capitalist state: Contributions and contradictions', in APLE, M. (Ed) *Cultural and Economic Reproduction in Education*, London, Routledge and Kegan Paul.

DERBER, C. (1982) *Professionals as Workers: Mental Labour in Advanced Capitalism*, Boston, Massachusetts, G. K. Hall.

FOUCAULT, M. (1980) *Knowledge/power: Selected Interviews and Other Writings*, New York, Pantheon Books.

FRITZELL, C. (1987) 'On the concept of relative autonomy in educational theory', *British Journal of Sociology of Education*, **8**, 1, pp. 23–35.

FREEDMAN, J. (1995) 'New Right tackles social wrongs under guise of cultural warriors', *The Edmonton Journal*, 5 February, pp. A7.

GINSBURG, M. and COOPER, S. (1991) 'Educational reform, the State and the world economy: Understanding and engaging in ideological and other struggles', in GINSBURG, M. (Ed) *Understanding Educational Reform in Global Context*, New York, Garland.

GRACE, G. (1987) 'Teachers and the State in Britain: A changing Britain', in LAWN, M. and GRACE, G. (Eds) *Teachers: The Culture and Politics of Work*, East Sussex, Falmer Press.

GRACE, G. (1989) 'Education: Commodity or public good', *British Journal of Educational Studies*, **37**, 3, pp. 207–21.

HARGREAVES, A. (1994) *Changing Teachers, Changing Times*, Wiltshire, Cassells.

HARRIS, K. (1994) *Teachers: Constructing the Future*, Basingstoke, Falmer Press.

HARVEY, D. (1990) *The Condition of Postmodernity: An Enquiry into the Origins of Cultural Change*, Oxford, Basil Blackwell.

HINKSON, J. (1991) *Postmodernity, State and Education*, Geelong, Deakin University Press.

HOLLOWAY, J. (1987) 'The red rose of Nissan', *Capital and Class*, **32**, pp. 147–65.

ISAACS, D. (1993) 'Shifting class identity and industrial practice: The case of Victoria secondary teachers', *Discourse*, **14**, 1, October, pp. 65–74.

JESSOP, B. (1989) 'Conservative regimes and the transition to post-Fordism: The cases of Great Britain and West Germany', in GOTTDIENER, M. and KOMNINOUS, N. (Eds) *Capitalist Development and Crisis Theory: Accumulation, Regulation and Spatial Restructuring*, Macmillan, London.

JESSOP, B. (1990) 'Regulation theories in retrospect and prospect', *Economy and Society*, **19**, 2, pp. 153–216.

JESSOP, B. (1993) 'Towards a Schrumpeterian workfare state?: Preliminary remarks on post-Fordist radical economy', *Studies in Political Economy*, **40**, Spring, pp. 7–39.

LARSON, S. (1977) *The Rise of Professionalism: A Sociological Analysis*, Berkeley, University of California Press.

LARSON, S. (1988) 'In the matter of experts and professionals, or how impossible it is to leave nothing unsaid', in TORSTENDAHL, R. and BURRAGE, M. (Eds) *The Formation of Professions: Knowledge, State and Strategy*, Newbury Park, Sage.

LIPIETZ, A. (1992) *Toward a New Economic Order: Post-Fordism, Ecology and Democracy*, New York, Oxford University Press.

LUZECKYJ, M. (1992) 'Teachers and industrial relations in South Australia', in RILEY, D. (Ed) *Industrial Relations in Australian Education*, Wentworth Falls, Social Science Press.

MCGREW, A. (1992) 'A global society?', in HALL, S., HELD, D. and MCGREW, T. (Eds) *Modernity and its Futures*, Oxford, The Open University Press.

NATIONAL PROJECT ON THE QUALITY OF TEACHING AND LEARNING (1991) *The National Schools Project*, Canberra, NPQTL Secretariat.

NILAND, J. (1993) 'The light on the horizon: Essentials of an enterprise focus', in RILEY, D. (Ed) *Industrial Relations in Australian Education*, Wentworth Falls, Social Science Press.

PANITCH, L. (1994) 'Globalisation and the State', in MILIBAND, R. and PANITCH, L. (Eds) *Between Globalism and Nationalism: Socialist Register 1994*, London, The Merlin Press.

PORTER, P. (1990) 'World restructuring has put education in crisis', *QTU Magazine*, **8**, 1, pp. 3–7.

PUSEY, M. (1991) *Economic Rationalism in Canberra: A Nation-building State Changes its Mind*, Sydney, Cambridge University Press.

RIST, R. (1970) 'Student social class and teacher expectations: The self-fulfilling prophecy in Ghetto Education', *Harvard Education Review*, **40**, 3, pp. 411–51.

REPORT OF THE QUALITY IN EDUCATION REVIEW COMMITTEE (1985) *Quality of Education Review* [Chair: Professor P. Karmel], Canberra, AGPS.

ROBERTSON, S. (1990) 'The corporatist settlement in Australia and educational reform', Unpublished doctoral thesis, University of Calgary.

ROBERTSON, S. (1994) 'An exploratory analysis of post-Fordism and teachers' labour', in KENWAY, J. (Ed) *Economising Education: Post-Fordist Directions*, Deakin University Press, Geelong.

ROBERTSON, S. and SOUCEK, V. (1991) 'Changing social realities in Australian schools: A study of teachers' perceptions and experiences of current reforms', A paper presented at the Comparative and International Education Society Conference in Pittsburgh, Pennsylvania.

ROBERTSON, S. and TROTMAN, J. (1992) 'A spoke in the wheels of professionalism', *Education Links*, **42**, pp. 23–9.

SCHOOLS COUNCIL (1989) *Teacher Quality: An Issue Paper*, Canberra, AGPS.

SCHOOLS COUNCIL (1990) *Australia's Teachers: An Agenda for the Next Decade*, Canberra, AGPS.

SCHOOLS COUNCIL (1992) *Developing Flexible Strategies in the Early Years of Schooling*, Canberra, AGPS.

SMYTH, J. (Ed) (1993) *A Socially Critical View of the Self-managing School*, Basingstoke, Falmer Press.

SPAULL, A. (1990) 'Is there a new teacher unionism?', A paper presented to the Annual Meeting of AERA, Boston.

WATKINS, P. (1992) *Class, the Labour Process and Work: A Focus on Teaching*, Geelong, Deakin University Press.

WATKINS, P. (1994) 'The Fordist/post-Fordist debate: The educational implications', in KENWAY, J. (Ed) *Economising Education: Post-Fordist Directions*, Deakin University Press, Geelong.

WATTS, R. (1989) 'In "fractured times": The Accord and social policy under Hawke, 1983–7', in KENNEDY, R. (Ed) *Australian Welfare*, China, Macmillan.

[23]

State and Education Revisited: Why Educational Researchers Should Think Politically About Education

CARLOS ALBERTO TORRES
University of California, Los Angeles

This chapter argues that theories of the state, the nature of the state, and the nature of public policy have substantive importance for an understanding of the political nature of education and public policy formation. Defining the "real" problems of education and the most appropriate (e.g., cost-effective, ethically acceptable, and legitimate) solutions depends greatly on the theories of the state that underpin, justify, and guide the educational diagnoses and proposed solutions. Thus, this chapter reviews classical theories of the relationship between the polity and education; liberal, neoconservative, and neoliberal reformulations of these theories; and neo-Marxist, poststructuralist, and postmodernist critiques of these formulations. The analysis is further enriched by examining the contributions of feminist theories and by exploring how all of the above theories relate to such issues as multiculturalism. Any analysis of the relationships between education and the state should take into account the multilayered, complex, and dynamic nature of these relationships, revealing the multitude of tensions and contradictions that emerge out of the historical and social force buffeting political and educational institutions. Finally, the discussion of state and education is placed in the context of the globalization of economies, cultures, and societies.

A PERSONAL INTRODUCTION

Writing is an intellectual journey of discovery and dialogue.[1] I wrote this synthetic and yet analytical article while traveling to several places during the summer of 1994, teaching, attending conferences, lecturing, and engaging in dialogue with old and new colleagues and friends. Beginning writing at home in Agoura, in the dry heat of Southern California, I continued writing in Bielefeld, Germany; in Mexico City, before the Mexican elections; in tropical Managua, Nicaragua, in the midst of a transportation strike; in futuristic Brasilia, a dream (and for some a nightmare) of urban planning for those who believe in Le Corbusier's utopia; in the cold, gray, and busy city of São

Paulo, the financial core of capitalist Brazil; in the sunny, hot, and humid city of Rio de Janeiro; and in the cool winter of the avant-garde city of Buenos Aires, Argentina.

Cornel West has said that people do not live on arguments, although they might be influenced by arguments. West is right when he claims that people live on love, care, respect, and touch. While writing this article, as situated and dated as it is, I was very much influenced by people's love, care, touch, and respect. I have always been influenced by what West has defended so eloquently, that we should always preserve in our intellectual work a "nuanced historical sense" (West, 1993a). That is the reason why I was so impressed with the sense of agony and tragedy reflected in the perils of a major transportation strike in Managua that lasted virtually the entire last week of August when I was in Nicaragua studying the impact of neoliberal political economy after the Sandinista experience. The strike was itself a testimony to the contradictions of a country with more than 60% unemployment and extraordinarily divided political loyalties. The role of the post-Sandinista state was at the center of any attempt to try to make a nuanced historical sense of the strike.

A week later, I was collaborating on the workings of the Brazilian National Conference on Education for All, which formulated, by consensus of Brazilian nongovernment organizations, mass movements, teachers' unions, and municipal, state, and federal governments, the 10-Year Plan for Education for All in Brazil. Beginning in Brasilia, and later in São Paulo, I witnessed a political scandal of the Brazilian state that rocked the souls and hearts of many citizens. A former university professor and seasoned Brazilian diplomat, Rubens Ricupero, then minister of finance and the Brazilian candidate (with the support of all Latin American countries) for the presidency of a new international organism that will implement the Global Agreement on Tariffs and Trade (GATT), unintentionally disclosed to the public a number of his private thoughts on the Brazilian economy and politics. While Ricupero was waiting for the repair of a technical problem for what was going to be a public television interview, his private conversation with a journalist was picked up by open microphone. The conversation was (apparently) involuntarily aired and captured with unfiltered noises by parabolic antennas in several places in Brazil. What was labeled as "the crisis of the parabolic antennas" by the Brazilian media (see "Sucessão," 1994) showed that technology is not only social regulation but can be used for empowerment. Among other things, Ricupero said that he had no qualms about hiding economic information that may damage the campaign of the candidate supported by the government, sociologist Fernando Henrique Cardoso. He also was inclined to deceive the public about economic indices, boosting that he was extremely useful to the TV network Rede Globo, a network representative of the most conservative sectors of the Brazilian bourgeois. This was so because—according to Ricupero—instead of giving its open public support to Cardoso, the network simply reported Ricupero's arguments, as minister of finance, supporting the project of economic stabilization launched by Cardoso as the previous minister of finance. No one would question the word of Ricupero, a distinguished public official.

Needless to say, this private conversation shocked the public sphere, and Ricupero had to resign 2 days later. The implications of this affair are still looming in Brazilian politics. Ricupero had the demeanor and reputation of an extremely honest politician, a public servant who was above and beyond the fray of competing interests and mediocrity. He was always projected as a mystical, monklike figure among the Brazilian elite. Until that infamous conversation, his ethics and reputation as a state functionary were impeccable.

Many Brazilians of different social conditions and political affiliations felt deceived and betrayed. The whole political discourse was vitiated, casting shadows on the legitimacy of the upcoming government. This episode underscored, for me, as an educational researcher, the importance of discussing the relationships between state and education when facing complex moral choices concerning public policy. After all, a public interview by a public official is usually considered a pedagogical act of educating (or forming) public opinion. The art of persuasion is a pedagogical art. Not by chance, Foucault insisted that a good teacher is a great seducer. The interview also reinforced my concern for continuing a critical scrutiny of state affairs based on a healthy skepticism of state rhetoric. The same applies, from a perspective of critical theory, to every level of action exchanges and narratives in the public sphere and civil society. Finally, it reinforced my conviction that authentic moral indignation is a most relevant political weapon for cultural criticism and practical politics. Moral indignation, however, cannot be construed as "another" narrative. It is authentic only when it is nourished by anger and hope, two of the most important sentiments for a true renewal of states and civil societies in this critical time.

Reading Cornel West's (1993a) *Prophetic Thought in Postmodern Times* helped me to revisit, once again, why we conduct educational research, or at least why we should. West (1993a, p. 16) argues that there is an undeniable cultural decay in America that frightens him more than anything else: "By unprecedented cultural decay I mean the social breakdown of the nurturing system for children. The inability to transmit meaning, value, purpose, dignity, decency to children." While historically situated, his remarks, I believe, apply to many societies.

Facilitating the nurturing and learning of children, youths, and adults is what public education, along with the family and a few other societal institutions, is supposed to do. That is what educational research should be about: understanding the indissoluble linkages of theory and practice. This is another practical reason why, periodically, we should revisit theoretically the relationship between the state and education.

THE STATE: PROBLEMS OF DEFINITION

> Nations may have passed a long life before arriving at this their destination, and during this period, they may have attained considerable culture in some directions. . . . But it is the State which first presents subject-matter that is not only adapted to the prose of history, but involves the production of such history in the very progress of its own being. (Hegel, 1857, p. 62)

The legal state was conceived by Plato (1941), a philosopher prone to speculate about the deep-seated presence of mythical thought in human endeavors as the administrator of justice. The state is the general regulatory principle of order, unity, and lawfulness of what many centuries later Rousseau defined as the *volonté générale* or "general will." For Hegel, the state was the supreme and most evolving reality of history, the "spirit of the world," the real incarnation of the "Idea," and the producer of history. Thus, in the rich tradition of political philosophy that extends from Plato to Hegel, the state has been conceived as the personalization and guarantor of collective wishes. Hence, discussions about theories of the state are part of a heritage preoccupying generations of thinkers, philosophers, political activists, and common citizens concerned with definitions of the nation and the state and how these concepts relate to notions of democratic culture, power, and citizenship.

Max Weber (1964) provides a clear discussion of some of the central features of the states in modern societies:

> The primary formal characteristics of the modern state are as follows: It possesses an administrative and legal order subject to change by legislation, to which the organized corporate activity of the administrative staff, which is also regulated by legislation, is oriented. This system of order claims binding authority, not only over the members of the state, the citizens, most of whom have obtained membership by birth, but also to a very large extent, over all action taking place in the area of its jurisdiction. It is thus a compulsory association with a territorial basis. Furthermore, today, the use of force is regarded as legitimate only so far as it is either permitted by the state or prescribed by it. . . . The claim of the modern state to monopolize the use of force is essential to it as its character of compulsory jurisdiction and of continuous organization. (p. 156; see also Bendix, 1962.)

I will discuss the Weberian formula below, particularly Weber's notion of the state as a monopoly of force, compulsory jurisdiction, and continuous administrative organization. It is important to identify the relevance of the notion of the democracy and citizenship in the context of the relationships between the state and education.

The notion of democracy entails the notion of a democratic citizenship in which agents are responsible and able to participate, choose their representatives, and monitor the performance of these representatives. From liberal or neo-Marxist perspectives, these are not only political but also pedagogical practices, since the construction of a democratic citizen implies the construction of a pedagogical subject. Individuals are not, solely by their nature, ready to participate in politics. They have to be educated in democratic politics in a number of ways, including normative grounding, ethical behavior, knowledge of the democratic process, and technical performance. The construction of the pedagogic subject is a central conceptual problem, a dilemma of democracy. To put it simply: Democracy implies a process of participation in which all are considered equal. However, education involves a process whereby the "immature" are brought to identify with the principles and forms of life of the "mature" members of society. Thus, the process of construction of the democratic pedagogic subject is a process of cultural nurturing, but it also involves manipulating principles of pedagogic and democratic socialization in subjects who are neither tabula rasa in cognitive or ethical terms nor fully equipped for the exercise of their democratic rights and obligations.[2] Yet, in the construction of modern polities, the constitution of a pedagogical democratic subject is predicated on grounds that are a precondition but are also the result of previous experiences and policies of national solidarity (including citizenship, competence building, and collaboration). With this brief clarification of the importance of democracy for a political culture and the role of the state, I continue with the discussion about the definition of the state.

The state is usually defined as the totality of the political authority in a given society. In Roman law, *potestas* denoted official legal power, which is distinct from *auctoritas,* "which means influence or prestige, and ensured that one's view would be accepted" (Vincent, 1987, p. 32). Several key elements define institutionally and functionally the notion of the state. First, the state is a set of institutions manned by the state's own personnel or bureaucracy. These institutions vary from those responsible for law and order (and hence violence and coercion), including the courts, police, and the army, to those responsible for symbolic and ideological functions, including institutions linked to social policy and education. State institutions are geographically located in a bounded territory (hence the notion of the nation-state). The relationship between the state and the civil society is located within the same boundaries as well: "The state monopolizes rule making within its territory. This tends towards the creation of a common political culture shared by all citizens" (Hall & Ikenberry, 1989, pp. 1–2).

From a critical modernist position (see Morrow & Torres, 1995), two of the problems in defining state power from functional, legal, and institutional standpoints involve history and culture. Historically, not every state has controlled civil society and national boundaries and markets or enjoyed the monopoly of legitimate force as portrayed in the Weberian formula (Bendix,

1962; Weber, 1945, 1968). The Weberian definition begs the question What is or should be understood by "legitimate force"? If, as Boudon and Bourricaud (1989) argue, we substitute monopoly of force with monopoly of power, then it is evident that legitimate if not effective powers other than the state exist in every society. For instance, the Indian uprising in Chiapas on January 1, 1994, exposed the collusion of interest between ranchers and their so-called "White" armies (salaried vigilantes working for private ranchers in southern Mexico), bureaucratic groups of the ruling party, and elements of the Mexican state. Indeed, ranchers shared this monopoly of force with the Mexican government. Another example is imperialist intervention in domestic policies. Influenced either by multinational corporations such as AT&T during Allende's presidency in Chile or by direct action of colonial powers such as France or Belgium in several African or Asian nations—including the endless story of interventions of the United States government and the former Soviet Union and its specialized agencies in many areas of the globe—imperialist interventions have deeply undermined the power of postcolonial states. Not only imperialism but domestic and international institutions constrain the power of the state. While historically nation-states have attempted to control (through law, ideology, and coercion) what goes on in their own territories, other institutions have historically disputed that control (e.g., the Catholic Church in the European and Latin American Christendom trying to exercise cultural control and, on occasion, political hegemony) (Torres, 1992). Current "national" economic policies are deeply affected (challenged and sometimes plainly determined) by the globalization of economics, culture, and society and by outside economic forces (this issue will be discussed at length later).

The concept of a common culture (and hence of a common cultural heritage, a basic literacy, and a political culture nurturing all citizens) may apply, to a certain extent, to specific state experiences (e.g., Sweden, Denmark, and, to some extent, Japan) but fails to capture the reality of other state experiences as expressed in the debates on multiculturalism in the United States or in the experience with hybrid cultures in Latin America. Thus, the *common culture* argument is usually articulated by conservatives viewing culture as a forum of consensus and harmony rather than a process of disputed citizenship. Historical and regional variability; the elusiveness of racial identity; power differentials based on class, gender, race, ethnicity, religion, and sexual orientation; and the complexity of intergroup relations within formal institutions all conspire against the notion of a common culture, the blueprint for an official knowledge, and the social construction of a political culture (Apple, 1993b; Arnot, 1994; McCarthy & Chrichlow, 1993a; McLaren, 1994; McNeil, 1988).

Modern political philosophers have seen the state as half-beast and half-human. According to Machiavelli, the state reflects simultaneously the pattern of the fox and the lion:

A prince ought to know how to resemble a beast as well as a man, upon occasion: and this is obscurely hinted to us by ancient writers who relate that Achilles and several other princes in former times were set to be educated by Chiron the Centaur: that as their preceptor was half-man and half-beast, they might be taught to imitate both natures since one cannot long support itself without the other. Now, because it is so necessary for a prince to learn how to act the part of a beast sometimes, he should make the lion and the fox his patterns: for the lion has no cunning enough of himself to keep out of snares and toils; nor the fox sufficient strength to cope with a wolf: so that he must be a fox to enable him to find out the snares, and a lion in order to terrify the wolves. (Cassirer, 1946/1969, p. 150)

The dual nature of the modern prince has worried educators, preventing to some extent a systematic analysis of the implications of theories of the state in education. Educators have tried—I am afraid unsuccessfully—to place the world of politics and the state strictly outside the realm of education and schools. This is a futile attempt to prevent the clever (and yet elusive) nature of the fox and the sanguinary (although at times passive) nature of the lion from undermining the noble purposes of education. Does it matter that the mythological Chiron the Centaur was himself an educator of rulers? Does this dual nature of the state, half-beast and half-human, make it possible, theoretically, to think of school socialization as part and parcel of processes of indoctrination, ideological manipulation, and/or the formation of a "common sense," as Antonio Gramsci has suggested?

Gramsci proposed a suggestive hypothesis: Education, as part of the state, is fundamentally a process of formation of "social conformism." Educational systems, and schools in particular, appear as privileged instruments for the socialization of a hegemonic culture. In Gramsci's perspective, the state as an "ethical state" or as an educator assumes the function of constructing a new civilization or level. The state thus constitutes an instrument of rationalization. Schools in the Gramscian analysis (which, along with churches, are seen as the largest cultural organizations in each country) ultimately produce hegemony, that is, a process of intellectual and moral leadership established as a consensus shared on the basis of common sense. This consensus, however, is dynamic rather than static. It invariably emerges from a struggle or confrontation among social forces, ideologies, philosophies, and general conceptions of life. Despite Gramsci's antinomies (Anderson, 1978), he understood hegemony as a process of social and political domination in which the ruling classes establish their control over the classes allied to them through moral and intellectual leadership. Hegemony acquires a pedagogical character. But Gramsci (1980) also referred to hegemony as the dual use of force and ideology to reproduce social relations between the ruling and subaltern classes.[3] If Gramsci's hypothesis is plausible, examination of the relationships between state and education becomes central for understanding politics and culture in capitalist societies.

EDUCATION AND THE STATE

Almost all analyses of educational problems have implicit in them a theory of the state, but few tell us what this theory is. (Carnoy, 1992, p. 143)

Why is the notion of the state so important in an understanding of educational policies and practices? There is no simple answer to this question. For an approximation of the contours of the problem, we need to explore a triple context: the relationships between education and government, the relationships between education and the economy, and the relationships between education and citizenship building.

Theories and research on the state show that an analysis of the educational system cannot be separated from some explicit or implicit analysis of the role, purpose, and functioning of the government. During the 20th century, education has become increasingly a function of the state. Educational systems and practices are sponsored, mandated, organized, and certified by the state. Indeed,

public education is not only a state function in terms of legal order or financial support; the specific requirements for degrees, teachers' requirements and qualifications, mandated textbooks, and required courses for basis curriculum are controlled by state agencies and designed under specific public policies of the state. (Torres, 1985, p. 4793)

Similarly, it has been argued that the state played an important role in linking education and the economy. Proponents of human capital theory have argued that school expansion fosters economic growth (Hanushek, 1986; Psacharopoulos, 1988). However, those advocating theories of credentialism and political economy theories challenged the basic premises of human capital theories.[4] Facing the criticism of credentialism theorists, human capital scholars hypothesized that certain conditions must be met before educational expansion can have an appreciable and positive effect on economic growth. First, a standard curriculum should be in place, and a sizable number of children in the age cohort beyond Grade 6 should be enrolled in school. Second, there should be fluid linkages between education and the economy. Third (and a precondition for the first two relationships to succeed), the state must ensure quality of education over time. Using the case of France in the late 19th century, it has been argued that an active state plays an important role in linking education and economy, securing standard curriculum, and ensuring the quality of educational offerings. The French case has then been compared with findings in the United States that are considered consistent (Hage, Hage, & Fuller, 1988).

Notwithstanding the difficulties in identifying exactly the contributions of education to economic growth, it is clear that the state, through public policy and public expenditures, contributes a great deal to facilitating the linkages between the educational system and the economy. Hence, the nature of the state and the political regime and explicit state intervention (or lack thereof) will have decisive consequences for educational development and economic growth.

An educated citizenry is seen as a prized asset from all political perspectives (Meyer, 1977). Educational institutions are said to socialize individuals in peculiar ways, creating specific political orientations toward democratic or nondemocratic structures. The political culture is a set of "attitudes towards the political system and its various parts, and attitudes toward the role of the self in the system. It is a set of orientation towards a special set of social objects and processes" (Almond & Verba, 1963, p. 13). Whether pursuing explicit corporatist goals or seeking to develop a political culture based on the modern creed of democracy, the state is said to play a major role, providing for the socialization of the citizenship and creating the appropriate symbolic conditions for nurturing the political culture of the people.[5]

The relationships among education, politics, and the state cannot be discussed only from the perspective of mainstream political culture. Despite what those advocating "technocratic" or "technicist" views of educational research, curriculum, and educational policy would like to believe, education is neither politically neutral nor technically "objective." As Paulo Freire has consistently claimed in his work, there is an inherent "politicity" of education that has epistemological, analytical, and ethical implications. McLaren (1994, p. 321) notes: "Not only is it impossible to disinvest pedagogy of its relationship to politics, it is theoretically dishonest." This politicity relates foremost to the explicit but also the subtle linkages between education and power. At the same time, it is related to the political nature of the state and public education as contested arenas and sites for exchanges of goods and services and competition involving political-economic projects (Freire, 1994).

In summary, prevailing notions of the state held by policymakers and researchers influence the dominant research agenda, the analysis of educational problems, and policy prescriptions. Theories of the state also influence educational research per se. At a concrete and practical rather than abstract level, theories of the state held by government coalitions and educational bureaucracies will influence not only research but the planning and operation of educational systems. Discussions about theories of the state and education encompass a broad range of theories regarding the relationships among education, the state, and civil society. By implication, theories of the state define the nature, purpose, and role of educational research, policy, and practices. Therefore, any discussion of educational reform; relationships among teachers, students, and administrators; curriculum policy and work; teacher training; educational financing; or educational policy in general involves competing and contradictory views and perceptions of the relationships between individual and community, which represent a basic tension in the constitution of Western thought (Wolin, 1960). Different notions of community, in turn, relate to different notions of the state and involve different views of what democratic governance of societies and schools should entail, including notions of power, participation, representation, and democratic decision making. It is appropriate, then, to define in detail the concept of the state and its implications for theories of the multiple relationships among the state, society, and education.

THE CONCEPT OF THE STATE

> Wherever, therefore, any numbers of men so unite into one society, as to quit every one of his executive power of the law of nature, and to resign it to the public, there, and there only, is a political, or civil society. (John Locke, cited in Carnoy, 1984, p. 18)

The concept of the state is different from the concept of government, political system, or political regime. The importance of the concept of the state has been eloquently argued by Atilio Boron (1994; see also Boron, 1995):

> The concept of the state has become one of the very few in contemporary social sciences endowed with the capacity to foster a rich theoretical and methodological debate, not to mention the inflamed political controversy raised by its practical existence. This is all the most surprising because, for some time before this impressive comeback, the concept of the state had been excommunicated from the academy, its theoretical value condemned due to its allegedly inherent vagueness and formalistic bias as well as its equally reproved heuristic worth. It was in 1953, the times of the end of ideology, of the miraculous capitalist recovery after the war, and of the institutionalization of the class struggle, when David Easton eloquently voiced the prevailing consensus among the social scientists by saying that "neither the state nor power is a concept that serves to bring together political research." However, in less than three decades the real movement of history has made of this author an astonished witness of the "resurrection" of the concept, "now risen from the grave to haunt us once again." (p. 1)

Thus, the notion of the state has gained new recognition as a key concept in the history of political research. Discussions about theories of the state acquired new vigor in the early 1970s, as a result of debates concerning the Marxist political theory of the state and the work of Antonio Gramsci, and in the 1980s, in mainstream political science discussions of the autonomy of the democratic state (Easton, 1981; Nordlinger, 1981; see also Carnoy & Levin, 1985), and the process of redemocratization in authoritarian societies (O'Donnell, Schmitter, & Whitehead, 1986; Stepan, 1988). In addition, recent discussions on state-education relationships have incorporated debates around issues of racial, ethnic, class, and sexual identity; political choices; nationhood; democratic theory; and notions of social regulation derivative of Foucault's approach.

There is a need, at this point, to clarify the concepts of the state, political regime, political system, civil society, and public sphere. These concepts, which are subject to intense debate, are familiar to specialists trained in political science or sociology but may not be used commonly by educational specialists and practitioners. Given the scope, intensity, and complexity of these concepts and related debates, it will be possible only to outline the broadest contours of their definitions with the purpose of clarifying terminology rather than producing an exhaustive taxonomy or glossary of terms.

The notions of state and government are not synonymous, and the complexity of the modern state cannot be reduced to the notion of "the government." Likewise, the notion of government cannot be defined in purely descriptive terms as merely a collection of agencies, organisms, and offices that, without coherence or unity, carry out administrative chores and tasks in administering the government's business in society (the so-called "public good"). Neither the government nor the state can be conceived of as a collection of institutions and/or individuals merely performing roles and functions that are deemed necessary for the functioning of contemporary societies, including the administration of justice, economy, defense, and parliamentarism (Boron, 1990/1991). In this regard, Weber's definition suggested that the notion of the state must be considered as something more than the notion of the government.

The notion of the state—despite different competing interpretations (as shown below)—is generally seen as more comprehensive than that of the government. The state involves but cannot be restricted to the workings of the government. Theda Skocpol (1979, p. 29) argues that

> the state properly conceived . . . is a set of administrative, policing, and military organizations headed, and more or less coordinated by, an executive authority. Any state first and fundamentally extracts resources from society and deploys those to create and support coercive and administrative organizations. . . . Political systems . . . also contain institutions through which social interests are represented in state policy making as well as institutions through which non-state actors are mobilized to participate in policy implementation. Nevertheless, the administrative and coercive organizations are the basis of state power.

The notion of the state also interacts with (and sometimes includes) the notion of the political system. Thus, the state is an institutional structure that includes

> the incumbents within this structure, and body of law that makes up the public sector. It thus includes the government (in the sense of the head of state and the immediate political leadership that surrounds the head of state), the public bureaucracy, the legislature, the judiciary, public and semi-public corporations, and the legal system. (Collier, 1979, p. 403)

In theoretical terms, the notion of political system refers to the overall configuration of the model of governance in the context of a specific political regime, including the dominant coalition and public policy that characterize political life in a given society. Hence, different traditions in political science distinguish between different types of political systems, including democratic, authoritarian, and totalitarian regimes. These political systems certainly differ in dominant ideology, patterns of political representation and participation, and leadership style.

Notions of government and state have usually been subsumed in political theory under the concept of political society, which is counterpoised to the notion of civil society. Whereas the concept of civil society cannot be separated from the concept of the state,

> the latter, by providing the overall legal framework of society, to a significant degree constitutes the former. Nonetheless, it is not unreasonable to claim that civil society retains a distinctive character to the extent that it is made up of areas of social life—the domestic world, the economic sphere, cultural activities, and political interaction—which are organized by private or voluntary arrangements between individuals and groups outside the direct control of the state. (Held, 1989, pp. 180–181)

Sometimes the notions of political society and civil society are translated into an opposition of concepts: the public sector and the private sector. Public refers to the Roman notion of res publica, an artificially constructed community that preserves the overall rights and interests of practically or historically constituted communities or any aggregate of individuals per se. For political philosophers such as Hobbes and Rousseau (even preserving the differences between them), the raison d'être of the state as the political society and the embodiment of the public is to preserve the liberty of individuals, even at the risk of having to regulate, in the view of many, the exchanges of individuals who interact in the private sphere of voluntary arrangements and domestic interactions. While private and public are seen as distinct and opposite poles and private interests are seen (and even glorified in the figure of the market), by many, as more important than public interests, W. L. Weinstein's (1971) analogy draws a useful distinction: The notions of publicness and privateness are analogous to the layers of an onion. Just as a layer that is outside one layer will be inside another, then something that is public in terms of one sphere of life may be private in terms of another. Yet, the notion of public sphere is relevant in clarifying the relations between theories of the state and education.

Public sphere is a concept elaborated by Jürgen Habermas (1989b) in *The Structural Transformation of the Public Sphere*. Different intellectual traditions use different terms to refer to similar concepts that, in turn, are supposed to account for specific phenomena of reality. A social phenomenon, however, is actually constructed and given life through our conceptualization (in itself an interpretation or understanding) of it. With this short and obviously incomplete word of epistemological caution, I must say that, from the beginning, the notion of public sphere could be seen as overlapping but distinct from the notion of civil society in classical 18th-century philosophy.

To avoid an extensive discussion of the notion of public sphere, I quote Nancy Fraser (1994), who, with her customarily sharp analysis, captures critically the dimensions of Habermas's proposal:

> [The public sphere] designates a theater in modern societies in which political participation is enacted through the medium of talk. It is the space in which citizens deliberate about their common affairs, hence, an institutionalized arena of discursive interaction. This arena is conceptually distinct from the state; it is a site for the production and circulation of discourses that can in principle be critical of the state. The public sphere in Habermas' sense is also conceptually distinct from the official economy; it is not an arena of market relations but rather one of discursive relations, a theater for debating and deliberating rather than for buying and selling. This concept of the public sphere permits us to keep in view the distinction between state apparatuses, economic markets, and democratic associations, distinctions that are essential to democratic theory. (p. 82)

Hence, the public sphere is distinct from the state; in Habermas's definition—which Fraser criticizes as not wholly satisfactory—it is a body of private individuals constituting a public through deliberation and discursive interaction. The concept of the public sphere, as Fraser (1994) aptly notes, cannot be equated with the concept of community because the latter

> suggests a bounded and fairly homogenous group, and it often connotes consensus. "Public," in contrast, emphasizes discursive interaction that is in principle unbounded and open-ended, and this in turn implies a plurality of perspectives. Thus the idea of a public, better than that of a community, can accommodate internal differences, antagonisms, and debates. (p. 97)

Given the scope, cultural diversity, and complexity of late capitalist societies, a fundamental question is as follows: Where exactly is the locus of the public sphere? The public cannot be subsumed under the operation of the state, nor can the realm of the public and public opinion be premised in the operation of the mass media, which are general privately owned and operated for profit. The media report and form opinion but also circulate and construct views that are particular rather than universal. The notion of commodification of cultures, knowledge, and the role of media and advertisement precludes the media per se from embodying the locus of the public. Indeed, the media reflect, construct, and signify a consumer culture and life-style (Featherstone, 1991). Moreover, the views of minorities and groups traditionally excluded culturally are not represented in the political economy portrayed by the media as often or with the full range of deliberation that occurs in community and public settings.

Although a discussion of the public sphere is not the focus of this chapter, three comments are in order. First, it is dangerous to assume, as Habermas does, that the public sphere is a mere space for deliberation. There are institutions, rules, practices, and behavior that transcend discourses and cannot be subsumed under narratives or exchanges. Second, it is dangerous as well to assume that the public sphere can be restricted to a homogeneous definition of citizenship without recognizing the large number of exclusions (based on race, ethnicity, gender, class, religion, sexual preference, etc.) that prevail in the practice of realpolitik in capitalist societies and its structural-historical dynamics. Despite Marx's suggestion that the experience of modernity is marked by the fact that "all that is solid melts into air,"[6] there is no reason to assume that if the Habermasian formulas of constitution of public spheres and ideal speeches can be practically implemented, these practices and narratives of exclusions, prevailing structural hierarchies and powers, and homogenizing definitions of citizenship will simply go away without a fight. Third, it is clear that a public sphere cannot be created without contributions from the democratic state (i.e., a state working to enhance the role of democracy in capitalism while intervening to ameliorate structural trends of social inequality).

The preceding discussion should not distract one from the central focus of this chapter. Whatever the locus of the public sphere, schools have been considered, in traditional terms, part of the state because they are supposedly engaged in helping students gain the knowledge and skills necessary for citizenship. The notion of citizenship, however, cannot be considered self-explanatory and nonproblematic, and this is a point where the notion of public sphere becomes useful. From a critical perspective, the notion of citizenship is a concept that should account for the plural and hybridized nature of capitalist societies, including the diversity of social subjects. Critical pedagogy is seen as a form of cultural politics arguing for the need to struggle for schools as democratic public spheres (Giroux, 1988; Giroux & McLaren, 1994). Moreover, "critical pedagogy is more than a desacralization of the grand narratives of modernity, but seeks to establish new moral and political frontiers of emancipatory and collective struggle, where both subjugated narratives and new narratives can be written and voiced in the arena of democracy" (McLaren, 1991, p. 172). As part of the democratic public sphere (and not only as part and parcel of the state's legal action), schools could constitute arenas of discourses integrating diverse knowledge-guiding interests, including empirical-analytical, historical-hermeneutic, and critical-emancipatory knowledge.[7]

It is imperative now to return to a discussion of political philosophy. Any analysis of the relationships among democracy, the state, citizenship, and education should consider the classics, particularly classical theories of the state, including liberalism and Marxism.

CLASSICAL THEORIES OF THE STATE AND EDUCATION: FROM LIBERALISM TO MARXISM

> Look, I know wherein our most basic value judgments are rooted—in compassion, in our sense for the suffering of others. (Marcuse, cited in Habermas, 1985, p. 77)

The state in liberal political philosophy constitutes the supreme political authority within precise limits (Held, 1989). The liberal idea of the state rests on the notion of public power as different from the ruling and the ruled. Indeed, for this approach the state has great independence from civil society, which enables "it to serve as an arbiter or conciliator among the social classes" (Easton, 1981, p. 308). The liberal state argues that it is above the fray of interests and societal conflicts; represents a neutral terrain ready to be occupied by different political parties (or alliances) according to shifting voting patterns; acts independently from particular groups or interests; legislates, preserves, and enforces the law without prejudice or particularistic goals; and, above all, represents the public interest.

This classical liberal perspective of political authority can be discussed from contemporary traditions in political science. A major tradition of liberal political analysis focuses primarily on questions of state sovereignty and citizenship. A second tradition of liberal democracy focuses on problems of political representation and accountability, that is, how the actions of individuals, institutions, and state agencies can be subject to checks and balances while the rules that regulate but also reflect the actions of individuals, institutions, corporations, or state agencies find their legitimacy in the democratic pact or "social contract." Questions of state legitimacy, representation, and participation relate to how social and political practices of individuals and institutions are regulated within the framework of the democratic pact, thus enhancing rather than diminishing the democratic tradition of political negotiation. Tensions and contradictions between individual rights and collective rights (or the general will) are central theoretical constructs in discussions about political participation, representation, and legitimacy. A third tradition emphasizes the question of state power, particularly state actions that relate to class structures, including means, models, and institutions of political coercion. Indeed, the state is seen as institutionalized political power. A basic assumption is that political life is not divorced from the basic determinants of social and economic life. Therefore, domination, exploitation, oppression, inequality, and discrimination are an intrinsic part of state activities, reverberating in the constitution and exercise of state power. While the characteristics of the political regime play a major role in the exercise of state power, its nature is intrinsically related to the role and function of the state in capitalist societies. The processes of obtaining, securing, and reproducing consensus and implementing measures that guarantee interest representation cannot be exempted from coercion and force. In the same vein, consensus building does not remain unrelated to relationships of domination and exploitation between individuals and among individuals, social regulations, structures, and institutions. The illustrious presence of Max Weber marks the study of the institutional mechanisms of the operation of the state, especially the exercise of state authority, and the role of bureaucracy (including instrumental, legal, and bureaucratic rationality) in state actions. State action refers both to the actions of the state regarding the individuals and communities that define and play out their different interests, passions, and ideologies within the context of the nation and to the interactions between states in the world system (Held, 1983, 1989, 1991; Sonntag & Valecillos, 1977; Vincent, 1987). While Weber viewed the notion of domination as central to his analysis, notions of exploitation or oppression were outside his analytical framework.

For critical perspectives of classical liberalism, both those that are an extension of liberalism (including theories of democracy and political sociology) and those that are a critical reelaboration of liberalism (including neo-Marxism), the discussion of the state acquires a new profile. At first glance, the notion of the state appears as a heuristic instrument, a concept that radically differs from the classic notions of government, political regime, public power, and public sector. As a heuristic concept, the notion of state reflects the condensation of power and force in society. The power of the state is exercised through a specialized apparatus and implies actions of force and coercion of civil society. For instance, individuals may voluntarily pay taxes, but the regulatory and coercive powers of state agencies enforce the probability that they do so. The notion of condensation of force refers to another central component of the notion of state: The state not only represents the exercise of legitimate political authority but exercises its authority in a vast array of domains and activities. The notion of the state as the condensation of force refers to the ambivalent nature of state power, which appears to be relatively independent of the main social actors in civil society. At times, state power is exercised at least in consonance with, if not on behalf of, key demands of special interest groups and classes. Thus, without resorting to conspiracy theories (which refer to purposeful, singular, and coordinated actions of actors, groups, or institutions), some branches of political theory argue that state power may reflect a specific political project or a class alliance and, as such, may represent specific social, economic, cultural, ethical, and moral interests. The state appears as an alliance or a pact of domination in which, through elective affinities but not necessarily through preordained or concerted actions, certain interest groups or elites in civil society may exercise undue influence in the production of public policy.

An understanding that domination is always disputed, resisted, and challenged is central to a view of the state from the perspective of domination. That is, political domination is a historical process; it is rarely completely achieved, and therefore social control is never completely consummated. Challenges to political domination and hegemony may come from outside of the ruling alliance (i.e., by contestatary social movements or classes), but they also may result from disputes within the dominant clique or ruling alliance.

Domination and hegemony as theoretical notions suggest that the constitution of the state as a pact of domination is continually and invariably a work in progress. The state, then, appears as a contested terrain, as an arena of confrontation of political projects. As such, the state reflects not only the vicissitudes of social struggles and the tensions in the agreements and disagreements between social groups and elites but also the difficulties and contradictions resulting from attempts to establish a coherent and unified action within the framework of a given cultural, social, and political project. Public policy, as part of a project of domination, is both an arena for struggle and a sounding board for civil society. When public policy is defined and implemented, tensions, contradictions, and agreements and disagreements among social movements, elites, bureaucratic groups, individuals, and communities are played out daily. This explains the definition that Nicos Poulantzas formulated of the state and state power as social relationships. The state is the condensation of social power but, at the same time, has power and relative autonomy from social classes and interests or power groups.

The state appears as an arena for confrontation of social classes. According to Poulantzas, the capitalist state is an arena of class struggle. Poulantzas, departing from Althusser's (1971) interpretation of Gramsci, believes that the distinction between state practices of consensus and state practices of coercion is too subtle and does not reflect the practical operation of the state. It becomes difficult to identify both dimensions separately at the level of social practices. It is not possible to govern merely by force; there is always a need for a minimum of consensus. Likewise, it is impossible to establish repressive practices (and institutions) without an ideological base. Repressive activities count on the ideological support of those in charge of the repression and various sectors within civil society. Finally, in the presence of divergent and contradictory interests, there is no consensus that can be established without force, either at the level of actual implementation of physical force to achieve a given end or in terms of the probability of exercising physical force. Similarly, no ideological or scientific rhetoric can, by itself, justify and sustain indefinitely state action.

Poulantzas views Althusser's interpretation of Gramsci as too limited because of his emphasis on the negative and restrictive aspects of state action. In his latest work, Poulantzas (1980) argues that Gramsci's view of the state as part of the ideological hegemony of the dominant classes, along with the coercive state apparatus (policy, the army, the judicial system, and the prison system), should be reconstructed. Poulantzas quite eloquently argues that the capitalist state is part of the class struggle, playing a decisive role in the reproduction of the conditions of production. The state has a very important role as a capitalist relation, increasing the capacities for accumulation and legitimation of the capitalist system (Carnoy, 1984; Torres, 1985).

However, to understand the state strictly as an actor in class struggle is to downplay other important variants of its social action. The reason is that the state not only is a central actor in preserving (or challenging) class distinctions but is crossed by and is the location of a host of other key social struggles based on race and ethnicity, gender, geographical location, and ethical, moral, religious, and sexual preference. These differences generate social relations, and the state is forced to intervene as a legislator, regulator of social exchanges, executor of laws, or coercive disciplinarian.

From a critical theory perspective, Claus Offe takes as the central question for state action the contradictions between capital accumulation and legitimation. The state has to promote capital accumulation, which, in a capitalist structure, always generates inequalities. At the same time, the state has to promote and sustain the legitimacy of the overall political and economic system. Offe incorporates theories of systems and Gramsci's and Poulantzas's analysis of the state as a social relation into a new theoretical synthesis. The state acquires specific functions while trying to mediate in the basic contradiction of capitalism: the growing socialization of production and the private appropriation of surplus value. To be able to mediate in this fundamental contradiction, the state, in late capitalism, has to expand its traditional institutional functions and role (Torres, 1989).

For Offe, the state is a self-regulating administrative system. It is the condensation of legal foundations, rules, and regulations, as well as the formal and informal institutions and codes that have become crystallized historically in capitalist societies. A capitalist state does not necessarily respond to the ruling elite that may control the government in a given political regime, nor does such a state necessarily completely respond—in democratic regimes—to the will of the elite or dominant classes. Although the state appears as a pact of domination trying to mediate and avoid recurrent crises of capitalist production and trying to prevent threats to the conditions of production and reproduction of the system, a class perspective of the state does not rest in the ability of the state to represent the specific sectoral interests of a group or class or to represent the will of specific groups in control of the institutions of government (Carnoy, 1984). On the contrary, the specific class component of the capitalist state results from the structural and historical imperatives of the capitalist system and its reproduction and depends on its own secular dynamics as a regulatory institution in capitalism.

These regulatory functions are as follows. First, the state, considering that it cannot control or regulate capitalist production itself (given that capital accumulation takes place in units of private production), creates the conditions for the continuation of private relations of production. Second, the social actors that control the apparatus of the state depend, for their survival and the achievement of their political objective, on resources that, via taxes, can be extracted from private capitalist production. When there is a crisis of capital accumulation, state resources diminish. Third, the state has not only the authority but the "mandate" to sustain and create the conditions for capital accumulation and social reproduction and for the capitalist social relations of production. Finally, given that the political personnel who control the state do not themselves hold power but instead require a mandate for action, the notion of a state that represents the generalization of social interests can be justified.

According to Offe (1973), the state can only function as a capitalist state appealing to symbols and resources that conceal its nature as a capitalist state. In other terms, its very existence above the fray of social conflict depends on its systematic denial of its capitalist nature. The legitimation of the capitalist state and of the capitalist system implies that state institutions and state bureaucracies strive to reconcile the just-mentioned regulatory functions in promoting capital accumulation while struggling to implement the democratic demands of their citizens, demands already established in the democratic framework. Thus, the state must undertake political, ideological, social, cultural, and economic actions to counter the legitimacy deficit of late capitalism (Torres, 1989, 1991).

This legitimacy deficit is sometimes expressed as the ungovernability of democratic systems. The notion of governability of democratic systems is discussed by Offe (1984) in the following terms:

> Its connotations are "rising expectations" on the part of competing interest groups and parties, disseminated by the media; a resulting "over-load" of the state bureaucracies which find themselves, under the impact of fiscal constraints, unable to satisfy such expectations; a breakdown of government authority which would be required for a firm resistance to proliferating demands; an increasing level of distrust, suspicion and frustration among the citizens in their attitudes vis-à-vis the state, and a creeping paralysis of the foundations of economic stability and growth potential. (p. 164)

The state performs its basic functions, including the execution of a preventive strategy of crisis management, the establishment of a system of priorities with respect to social needs and eventual threats, and the creation of a long-term avoidance strategy, to diffuse future threats to political stability while building consensus. The notion of compensatory legitimation refers to the state's need to cope with a deficit of legitimacy in the overall system. This crisis of legitimation has several sources. One of the most important is the disparity between growing social demands on welfare policies and diminishing fiscal revenues to meet those demands. To confront the crisis of legitimation, the state calls on scientific and technical knowledge and expertise, increasing policies of participation, and legalization of educational policies with a growing role for the judicial system in education as a last resort to settle disputes in the educational arena (Torres & Puiggrós, 1995; Weiler, 1983). Therefore, education as compensatory legitimation implies that the state may use educational policies as a substitute for political rights and for increased material consumption while creating a system of legitimizing beliefs that will ensure the loyalty of its citizens. In synthesis, the state is a pact of domination and a set of self-regulating institutional apparatuses, bureaucratic organizations, and formal and informal codes seeking to represent the public and private spheres of society. A central role of the state is that of mediator in the context of the crisis of capitalism, especially in the contradictions between accumulation and legitimation.

Martin Carnoy (1992) has argued that most analyses of educational problems have implicit in them a theory of the state but that seldom are the fundamentals of that theory recognized or spelled out in educational research and practice. Becoming self-reflective about our own assumptions seems to be a precondition for solid scholarship. Alas, since the role of the state has become even more complex and problematic in contemporary societies, this new role poses new conceptual problems for theoretical analysis and the development of state theories and creates more practical problems as well. David Harvey (1989) has correctly argued that

> the state is now in a much more problematic position. It is called upon to regulate the activities of corporate capital in the national interest at the same time as it is forced, also in the national interest, to create a "good business climate" to act as an inducement to transnational and global finance capital, and to deter (by means other than exchange controls) capital flight to greener and more profitable pastures. (p. 170)

Changes in the nature of the alliance controlling the state and in the nature of the state itself are reflected in the logic of public policy and state action. At the same time, changes in the character of the state and public policy may reflect new visions of what democracy should look like. They may also reflect new visions of what education can do for a certain definition of democracy and whether and how schooling and nonformal education should intervene in the constitution of the democratic political culture. Finally, an important question is whether changes in educational systems and educational policies are compatible with the globalization of capitalism in the world system. Before addressing this question, the next section will provide a systematic overview of different perspectives on the state and education.

CONTEMPORARY EDUCATIONAL THEORIES AND THE CAPITALIST STATE

The Liberal State and Education

> The Enlightenment philosophers wanted to utilize this accumulation of specialized culture for the enrichment of everyday life, that is to say, for the rational organization of everyday social life. (Habermas, 1990, p. 348)

Liberal-pluralist theories of the state conceive of the state as a political system, as an autonomous political institution independent from the system of production and class structure. The state appears, then, as a neutral referee overseeing and regulating the clashes between interest groups. State intervention takes place either when different interest groups and eventually elites competing for resources conflict with the general interest of all citizens or when the state, pursuing independent activities, attempts to modernize society.

The liberal view suggests that the state is the collective creation of its individual members, providing a set of common social goods, including defense, education, a legal system, and the means of enforcing that system to all or the majority of citizens and legal residents (Arroni, 1992; Evans, 1991; Hall & Ikenberry, 1989; Held, 1983, 1991). This normative rather than analytical position was epitomized by Thomas Jefferson when, in 1776, he began the American Declaration of Independence with these famous words:

> We hold these truths to be self-evident, that all men are created equal; that they are endowed by their Creator with certain inalienable rights; that among these are life, liberty, and the pursuit of happiness. That, to secure these rights, governments are instituted among men, deriving their just powers from the consent of the governed.

There is a principle of autonomy in liberalism (shared to some extent by Marxism as an offspring of earlier classical liberal thought), and this autonomy is well expressed in Held's (1989, p. 165) synthesis: "Individuals should be free and equal in the determination of the rules by which they live; that is, they should enjoy equal rights (and accordingly, equal obligations) in the specification of the framework which generates and limits the opportunities available to them throughout their lives."

Two key meanings of the principle of autonomy should be highlighted: the notion of the autonomy of individuals aptly discussed by Held, and the notion of state autonomy and the independence of state bureaucracy (Carnoy, 1984, 1992). There are several implications of this principle of autonomy, particularly if one remembers that Kant equated the principle of autonomy with free will. First, "citizenship theory was grounded in the primacy of the practical politics of universal social obligations and rights" (Culpitt, 1992, p. 6). This assumption has implications for the role and functions of the state (as discussed below). Second, the state should remove any impediment to the full exercise of freedom and facilitate the pursuit of happiness by all individuals. Hence, liberalism emerges as the champion of tolerance and the archenemy of despotism (e.g., totalitarianism and authoritarianism). Finally, the state should work to remedy or prevent confrontations that could alter the nature of the social pact.

State autonomy "allows the state to translate its preferences into authoritative actions to the degree to which public policy conforms to the parallelogram of the public officials' resource-weighted preferences" (Nordlinger, 1981, p. 19). Indeed, the state in classical liberalism was conceived of as an arena in which "societal conflicts are fought out, interests mediated, and the ensuing results authoritatively confirmed" (Nordlinger, 1981, p. 5). Yet, Nordlinger goes on to argue that a state-centered view of the liberal democratic state shows, whether from a pluralist or a neopluralist perspective,[8] that public officials have societally unconstrained volitions; therefore, public officials not only witness the struggle for resources, the definitions of societal needs, and the adequation of preferences but also intervene authoritatively in pursuing specific goals. For a state-centered tradition, the liberal democratic state plays a critical role in balancing, aggregating, and reconciling conflicting demands, acting continuously as a broker and mediator and facilitating the acceptance of policy compromises. The development of the welfare state highlights the highest level of autonomy of the liberal democratic state in the achievement of the democratic pact.

The welfare state is a particular form of the democratic liberal state in industrialized societies. Its origins have been associated with Scandinavian state experiences at the turn of the century, particularly Sweden's social democracy, and the industrial and financial reconstitution of the post-Depression era in the United States based on a "social pact" (the New Deal) and coordination of policies between employers and labor (Moran & Wright, 1991; Offe, 1984, 1985; Therborn, 1980; Torres & Puiggrós, 1995). A striking feature of the welfare state is its interventionist role in the economy, including increased public spending in both productive and nonproductive sectors. Welfare policies are defined as government protection of minimum standards of income, nutrition, health, housing, and education. As Wilensky (1975, 1976) argued, these welfare benefits are assured to every citizen as a political right rather than as charity (see also Popkewitz, 1991).

In this century, schooling has reflected the key features of the liberal state in public policy. While education was perceived by 19th-century liberals as a tool for enlightenment and as the great equalizer, in the 20th century schooling has played a key role in the actions of the welfare state. School expansion has been associated with the extension of citizenship rights and welfare policies to the majority of citizens.[9] Central concerns for liberal and social-democratic planners have been how to analyze social and economic changes, how to conceptualize the functional relationship between schools and society, and, when societies become more specialized and diversified, what implications might follow from the transformations in schooling that have accompanied changes in the division of labor (Arnove, Altbach, & Kelly, 1992).

The analysis of the role of schooling in the liberal perspective of the welfare state was supported by an almost complete neglect of the contradictory aspects of the division of labor, including class conflict, and a very truncated conception of individualization implied by theories of socialization popularized by key functionalist theories, particularly the work of Parsons (see Morrow & Torres, 1995). The manifest and a limited number of latent functions of education were stressed, and positive functions were analyzed to the exclusion of negative or dysfunctional ones. In addition, there was an uncritical acceptance of assumptions such as the high level of systemic integration of society and the methodological principle that the "whole" served by the "part" (i.e., education) was indeed society as a whole rather than some powerful class, dominant ethnic groups, or castes within society taking advantage of positions of wealth, influence, and power.[10]

Post–World War II euphoria facilitated liberal and social-democratic options portraying a vision of equality of opportunity and educational reform in democratic societies. This vision was considered certainly an option to the equally unacceptable choices of Bolshevism and fascism. Parallel and complementary economic doctrines in the form of Keynesian economic theory paved the way for a mixed economy balanced by central fiscal and monetary policies (indicative planning), as well as the theory of human capital, which justified educational expenditures as part of a long-term strategy of economic growth. Thus, educational planning in industrial advanced societies played a central role in the conception of the interventionist welfare state that was necessary for controlling the self-destructive tendencies of capitalist growth. The emergence of the postcolonial state, sizable worldwide economic surpluses, and modernization theories, coupled with the diffusion of human capital theory for educational planning, helped to fuel educational expansion in the developing world to levels without precedent (Carnoy, 1977; Carnoy & Samoff, 1990; Fagerlind & Saha, 1983; Fuller, 1991; Russell, 1989; Selowsky, 1980; Torres, 1990).

Liberal educators see educational systems as performing three major functions: cognitive and moral socialization, skills training, and certification. These functions contribute to a rational allocation of resources and social mobility (Banks, 1989; La Belle & Ward, 1994). Educating people with universal cognitive skills is held as essential, while economic and political socialization functions are decisive in the welfare of individuals, communities, and the overall society. Educational systems perform an allocative function, preparing individuals for their roles in the division of labor, thus facilitating an efficient distribution of talent through competitive selection. The economic function, conceived primarily as producing human capital, links education to higher levels of productivity by individuals in the labor force. Finally, the role of schooling in political socialization is acknowledged as indispensable to social integration and social control. With the notion of social differentiation, ascriptive statuses are legitimated through academic achievement by converting them into acquired statuses.

Perhaps the best example of liberal policies in the U.S. educational system is that of the programs of the War on Poverty. These programs were based on a set of several assumptions. First, the elimination of poverty in the United States requires simply helping children born in poor families to escape from their situation (under the presupposition that there is no falling back into poverty). Second, the principal reason why children do not escape poverty is that they do not acquire the basic cognitive competencies for succeeding in the world. Finally, the best and most efficient mechanism for breaking the vicious circle of poverty is educational reform based on compensatory programs for families and neighborhoods to keep them above a minimal acceptable threshold (Jencks et al., 1972).

Because the dominant theory of the state held by liberal policy planners is the welfare state, the transmission and legitimation of inequality may have resulted as a (latent) function of the school, perpetrated by curricular and teaching practices. For instance, the debate on tracking highlights how school experience varies by social class, resulting in ability grouping and curriculum grouping, which perpetuate segregationist practices in U.S. schools to the detriment of students of color, women, immigrants, and working-class students (Oakes, 1985).

Thus, through educational planning and social engineering, liberal functionalist theories of educational reform advanced personal and civil rights, including a movement toward equality of opportunity and economic redistribution. In the United States, particularly, liberal education confronted the issue of unequal status attainment and the effects of race in education. At the same time, through a functionalist theory of stratification, liberalism provided a rationale for a hierarchy of rewards, rejecting notions of absolute equality while paradoxically placing equality of educational opportunity at the center of social efficiency and civil rights movements. The failure of functionalist educational theory stemmed therefore from its inability to fully explain the causes of inequality and problems of unequal opportunity, let alone suggest a plausible strategy for dealing with the role of the educational process in perpetuating social inequalities.

The general disillusionment with North American "liberalism" either led social theorists back toward a more pessimistic neoconservative position or led them to an emergent, if marginal and divided, democratic socialist left. In other advanced, liberal democratic societies (all characterized by the existence of a significant social democratic party with roots in labor and, in some cases, a significant communist party), the reception and appropriation of functionalist theories of education were rather different. In Europe, generally speaking, the existence of a conservative tradition in education and politics allowed the American combination of progressive education, comprehensive secondary schools open to all, and a tertiary system with relatively open admission standards (which evolved from functionalist education theory) to be associated with progressive reform. Hence we find the irony of European labor parties supporting policies rationalized, partly because of their effectiveness against the claims of defenders of traditional elitist education, in accordance with American functional theory, empirical mobility, and status attainment research (Morrow & Torres, 1995).

Most significant here was the case of Britain, where the sociology of education had its roots in the work of Karl Mannheim, who was exiled in England, and that of T. H. Marshall. The influential analysis of Marshall on the welfare state and the principle of citizenship gave hope for the reconciliation of liberty and equality in a democratic society, a theme that had been complemented in Mannheim's work on social planning (Marshall, 1950, 1983). Although the existence of a powerful labor movement made equality of opportunity a central theme, the problem of efficiency and the wastage of human resources were also central (Karabel & Halsey, 1977).

The fusion of social-democratic politics, technocratic functionalism, and empirical research in education did not take into account either the relationship between school outcomes and societal structures or the cultural processes involving education. Also, it did not seriously consider the implications of implementing a radical democratic educational policy within a welfare state subject, to some extent, to the contradictions of capitalist development. Research continued to show that "policies, informed by sociological understandings, did not in fact remove inequalities. On the contrary, they seemed to produce, with monotonous regularity, the same or similar educational outcomes" (Baron et al., cited in Morrow & Torres, 1995).

Liberalism was at a cross fire from the left and right. Various social forces undermined the educational agenda of liberalism. From the left, reproduction theories linked education with the social and cultural reproduction of capitalist societies, challenging key assumptions of educational liberalism. Reproduction theories emphasize that power and knowledge are always intertwined in education. Thus, educational policies, classroom practices, and curriculum are an integral part of a contradictory process of socialization of children and youth into a given social order, while educational sites, policies, and practices may develop forms of resistance to a hegemonic culture.[11] From the right came the growing dissatisfaction with the welfare state, particularly its fiscal performance. In addition, the liberal rhetoric on equality of educational opportunity was counterbalanced with rhetoric about educational achievement and excellence in the United States and a neoconservative rhetoric emphasizing individual rights over public obligations and social rights (neoconservative preoccupations, themes, and rhetoric are present in a number of works; e.g., see Adler, 1982; National Commission on Excellence in Education, 1983).

Central flaws of liberal reformers and researchers are their lack of a historical-structural analysis of educational processes in capitalist societies (i.e., their lack of a political economy of education); their refusal to tackle head on the implications of domination and exploitation in capitalist societies and, by implication, in education; and particularly their acritical acceptance of the role of the state as promoting citizenship on the bases of the primacy of the practical politics of universal social obligations and rights while a set of exclusions (based on economics, race, ethnicity, or gender) remains stubbornly in place. Nancy Fraser (1994) says it very nicely:

> Liberal political theory assumes that it is possible to organize a democratic form of political life on the basis of socioeconomic and sociosexual structures that generate systemic inequalities. For liberals, then, the problem of democracy becomes the problem of how to insulate political processes from what are considered to be nonpolitical or prepolitical processes, those characteristic, for example, of the economy, the family, the informal everyday life. The problem for liberals, thus, is how to strengthen the barriers separating political institutions that are supposed to instantiate relations of equality from economic, cultural, and sociosexual institutions that are premised on systemic relations of inequality. (p. 82)

A theory of the state that does not address the nature and distribution of power in society is seriously flawed. Indeed, if we assume that power in Western societies—as criticized by Miliband—is competitive, fragmented, and diffused and if everybody, directly or in organized groups, may have some power, how can the liberal state effectively regulate the appropriation and usufruct of power, influence, and wealth on behalf of all citizens? Can public education charged with the mandate to facilitate egalitarian social change be an effective tool in the presence of established social hierarchies, economic structures, and interest groups?

If institutional democracy, including universal suffrage, free and regular elections, representative institutions, and effective citizenship rights, is preserved, then both individuals and groups will take advantage of these rights under the protection of the law and an independent judiciary. For liberal multicultural researchers and policymakers, however, the political culture is not homogeneous but diverse; hence, intergroup relations become a problem to be addressed. The goal of multiculturalism "is to reform the school and other educational institutions so that students from diverse racial, ethnic, and social-class groups will experience educational quality" (Banks, 1993, p. 3).[12] The liberal state and its attempt to change individual preference as the preferred means to solve the dilemmas posed by multiculturalism have been contested by neoconservatives, neoliberals, those advocating reproduction and parallelist theories, and critics of official knowledge.

The Neoconservative State and Education: Choice, Cultural Pluralism, and Multiculturalism

> It is not a very satisfactory and plausible hypothesis to think of human culture as the product of a mere illusion—as a juggling with words and a childish play with names. (Cassirer, 1946/1969, p. 22)

Traditional conservativism emerged as a response to the French Revolution and the politics and ideology of the enlightenment. As such, conservatism opposes progressivism. The concepts of nation, family, duty, authority, standards, traditionalism, self-interest, competitive individualism, and antistatism have usually been linked to traditional conservatism, representing a clear reaction to the basic values of liberalism (Apple, 1993b; Bobbio & Matteucci, 1981). The neoconservative ideology and the neoconservative state have usually been associated with drastic political economy shifts away from the welfare state in the 1980s, including Margaret Thatcher's program of government (Thatcherism), Ronald Reagan's "conservative revolution" (Reaganomics), and Brian Mulroney's Progressive Conservative Party agenda in Canada. The bases of the model were forceful privatization of state enterprises and large sections of public property, loosening of regulations of the market and private enterprise, control of inflation rather than support for full employment, and the growing importance of the executive branch with the corresponding decline in the role of Congress or Parliament (Therborn, 1989).

There are, however, differences among the British, American, and Canadian neoconservative experiments, resulting in contradictory policy outcomes. For instance, opportunity structures, including institutions, political alignments, and ideology, vary across nations, and the personality, personal style of government, and general ideological profile of each leader are remarkably different. For instance, Margaret Thatcher developed a bitterly intransigent conservative approach to governing that involved taking to task trade unions, local governments, the political opposition, and virtually anyone who challenged or questioned her program (even from within the ranks of her own party). Ronald Reagan's supply-side economics was embellished with moral conservatism in social issues, with the rising importance of neoconservative forces such as the moral majority. Despite Brian Mulroney's admiration for and friendship with Thatcher and Reagan, his neoconservatism was tempered by his pragmatic nature as a broker politician; by the opportunity structure of Canada, with its decentralized policy orientation; by the entrenchment of equality rights in the Canadian Charter of Rights; and by the heterogeneous configuration of ideological positions within his coalition (with western Canada and Quebec representing distinct positions in a host of issues). Likewise, the contradictions between program rhetoric and program implementation became evident in Reagan's supply-side economic solution that included a massive budget deficit and increasing national debt (Stockman, 1986). Despite these differences and contradictions, privatization and market-driven policies became centerpieces of the neoconservative agenda.

Privatization and market-oriented reforms are appealing to the neoconservative state for a number of reasons. On one hand, they help to release some of the pressures on fiscal expenditures. On the other hand, they provide a convenient avenue for depoliticizing the regulatory policies of the state in important areas of public policy formation. Transferring public services outside the direct administration and/or control of the state helps to avoid conflictive exchanges with stakeholders and consumers. Privatization plays a pivotal role in the neoconservative model because

> purchase of service contracting is both an administrative mechanism for addressing the particular issues of the social legitimacy of the state involved in direct social services and an attempt to borrow from the managerial ethos of private enterprise (and entrepreneurial development) systems of cost-benefit analysis and management by objectives. (Culpitt, 1992, p. 94)

Neoconservatives have argued that "the state" and "the market" are two diametrically opposed social systems. They are considered clear choices in the organization of production as well as in the delivery of services (Moran & Wright, 1991). Why favor the market over the state? Neoconservatives consider markets more versatile and efficacious than the state's bureaucratic structures for a number of reasons. Markets respond more quickly to changes in technology and social demands than does the state. Markets are more efficient and cost-effective in providing services than public sectors, and market competition will produce greater accountability in "social investments" than bureaucratic politics. The argument is not merely economic but moral, as Milton Friedman let us know: "Every act of government intervention . . . limits the area of individual freedom directly and threatens the preservation of freedom indirectly" (Friedman, cited in Dahrendorf, 1975, p. 5). Similar arguments have been defended by von Hayek (1960).

Is this drive toward the market an indication of changes in the constitution and operation of capitalism per se? Capitalism moved in the 1970s, and clearly consolidated with the conservative governments in the 1980s, into a stage that David Harvey characterizes as "flexible accumulation." This late capitalist model

> rests on flexibility with respect to labor processes, labor markets, products, and patterns of consumption. It is characterized by the emergence of entirely new sectors of production, new ways of providing financial services, new markets, and above all, greatly intensified rates of commercial, technological, and organizational innovation. (Harvey, 1989, p. 147)

A central outcome of the economic process is the growing polarization in income distribution between the haves and have-nots in capitalist democracies (Przeworski, 1991; Reich, 1991; Thurow, 1992). Harvey (1989) sees these changes in flexible accumulation giving rise to a peculiar culture characterized as postmodernist, with its emphasis on "ephemerality, collage, fragmentation, and dispersal in philosophical and social thought [that] mimics the condition of flexible accumulation . . . all of this fits in with the emergence since 1970 of a fragmented politics of divergent special and regional interest groups" (p. 302). Notwithstanding Harvey's insights, flexible accumulation as a mode of production highlights a parallel process of concentration and centralization of economic power, with an increasing role of multinational corporations in the process of capital accumulation and production in the world system. The cultural features of ephemerality, collage, and fragmentation seem to fit better the description of what is happening to social classes, social movements, and subordinate cultures than the description of what is happening to transnational corporations in the world system.[13]

These cultural changes are not independent from the experience of social struggles in industrial advanced democracies and the developing world, including the feminist and women's movements, peace movements, antinuclear movements, and liberation movements *tout court.* Nor are such changes totally independent of specific ideologies. Hence, there is a neoconservative backlash to the "excesses" of liberalism and state intervention (or, conversely, in some areas lack of or timid intervention) in culture and education.

Neoconservatives in the United States see the origin of the contemporary crisis not in the economy or politics but in the moral and cultural spheres. For them, the social pact that brought together labor and capital at the turn of the century and, particularly, the democratic New Deal have run their course. Paradoxically, neoconservatives view the rise of the welfare state as the weakening of class conflict by providing a safety net and benefits resulting in the declining political significance of social class in postindustrial societies (Clark, Lipset, & Rempel, 1993).[14]

For U.S. neoconservatives, the philosophical premises of liberalism are bankrupt. From this principle follows that the liberal tradition has exhausted its ability to respond to the cultural and moral demands of the day. Liberals strategically placed in the mass media, schools, arts, and humanities and "tenured radicals" in higher education are blamed for the moral and cultural decay of capitalist America. Their moral permissiveness and refusal to sustain the traditional heterosexual family have resulted in increased teenage pregnancy, academic truancy, sexual promiscuity, and gang behavior and in gay and lesbian movements requesting recognition of alternative life-styles and sexual preferences. Neoconservatives see the liberals' contempt for authority, their disdain for cultural and historical traditions, and their reliance on "big" government and welfare policies as the roots of the crisis evolving in America.

The fiscal crisis of the state is seen as proof of what neoconservatives have been claiming all along in the United States: Society cannot sustain a social welfare safety net with increasing costs in entitlement programs because the system will be financially bankrupt and will create dependency. Individuals will rely on state support rather than on their own efforts and work ethic and will avoid the performance of their individual duties and obligations while pressing for their rights. Hence, the seeds of moral and cultural bankruptcy are planted.

Solving the cultural crisis will entail the creation of a legitimate system based on individual responsibility rather than state handouts. Dismantling the heavy welfare state programs, deregulating the private sector, and privatizing the public sector are considered appropriate recipes for America to remain competitive internationally and to thrive economically and politically in an enriched cultural atmosphere emanating not from decaying liberals but from "newborn" Christians (Boron, 1981; Coser & Howe, 1977; Habermas, 1989a, 1989b, 1990; Torres, 1986). There are thus many different roles assigned to education in the neoconservative state. A central component of the neoconservative restoration is a critique of the liberal notion of autonomy and its implications for classroom practices. Autonomy is interpreted as lack of accountability. Thus,

> national curricula and assessment, greater opportunity for "parental choice," tighter accountability and control, the marketization and privatization of education—all of these proposals may be internally contradictory as a set of "reforms," but all are part of the conservative package that has been formed by the Neoliberal and Neoconservative wings of this movement. (Apple, 1993b, p. 5; see also Apple, 1993a)

The neoconservative state in education rests on two central claims, one of accountability and parental rights and one dealing with race and a particular appraisal of multiculturalism and diversity in the United States. School choice and vouchers are predicated as an attempt to link schools and markets. The proposals of John E. Chubb and Terry M. Moe's (1990) *Politics, Markets, and America's Schools* are part of school reform agendas that have been launched in the United States and elsewhere focusing on "restructuring" (i.e., altering the purposes, assumptions, and methods of school systems) rather than merely transforming the efficiency of existing systems (Darling-Hammond, 1993).

Not surprisingly, this reform agenda is taking place in times of serious financial retrenchment in public education everywhere. Because much of the "schools-are-failing" literature blames teachers, the relationships between teachers and educational authorities are also being reconsidered. Even where there is less focus on blame, there is a good deal of attention to competency testing, certification, and national exams, in short, diverse attempts to improve excellence in instruction and learning. Reducing expenditures in financially overburdened school districts and attempting to make the systems more cost-effective involve layoffs and substitution of more expensive, fully trained teachers with lower paid instructional personnel.[15] This situation and recent initiatives concerning school finance (e.g., vouchers) have placed teachers' organizations at the center of disputes on educational policy and practice.

Chubb and Moe's analysis is a pristine example of the neoconservative argument, which is based, ostensibly, on a libertarian political philosophy.

Theoretically, these authors rely on public choice theories and a secularized theology of free markets:

> Political control, rooted in public authority and the group and constituency pressures that surround it, inherently operates to bury the schools in bureaucracy, deny them autonomy, and inhibit the emergence of effective organization. Market institutions, rooted in the decentralized choices of those who use and produce educational services, inherently tend to discourage bureaucracy, nurture school autonomy, and promote effective organization. (Chubb & Moe, 1993, p. 222)

What is original about Chubb and Moe's approach is that they focus not so much on the operation of markets (for them, theories of markets are already well developed) but on theories of government, particularly those linking governments to schools. A theory of school government is needed because the "way to improve schools . . . is to decentralize, make them smaller, and promote community" (Chubb & Moe, 1993, p. 222). They argue that individual achievement gains are influenced by the quality of school organization and that schools should be considered government agencies. Hence, the question is whether market-driven schools are better than democratically controlled ones (Sujstorf, Wells, & Crain, 1993). Wells (1993) contends that the complexities of the school choice process are usually ignored by free-market school choice advocates. Behaving more like private, profit-driven corporations and responding in this way to consumers' demands ignores critical issues "that make the school consumption process extremely complex" (Wells, 1993, pp. 47–48).

At a theoretical level, by focusing on theories of the state we may find ways to criticize and even improve on public choice theory, particularly when "in this view individuals are rational utility maximizers and it is accepted that the pursuit of self-interest in the market place will yield socially and economically desirable outcomes" (Peters, in press). Yet, as Wells correctly points out, the neoconservative promise of school choice falls prey to a simple fallacy: Competition between schools will not necessarily lead to school improvement because other variables are beyond the control of school quality. Racial attitudes, alienation, powerlessness, parental involvement, and lack of accurate information are part of the social context of family life. Wells (1993) argues that school competition can do little (if anything) to surmount structural and subjective determinations.

If choice is the shining armor of the neoconservative state, multiculturalism is its nemesis. It is common knowledge that in the 1980s in the United States, race was effectively used by the Reagan/Bush administrations to construct and hold together a new neoconservative majority. In education, this strategy involves addressing the intractable issues of multiculturalism. No doubt, many neoconservatives are "Eurocentric" in that they deny or place in a secondary position the legitimacy of historical and symbolic constructions of ethnic and national groups other than the dominant White or European culture. However, as West so persuasively argues, opposing multiculturalism to Eurocentrism obscures the theoretical and political treatment of the issue. West (1993a) argues, in his textured and conversant style, that we must move beyond the debate about multiculturalism and Eurocentrism

> because it means from the very beginning we must call into question any notions of pure traditions or pristine heritages, or any civilization or culture having a monopoly on virtue or insight . . . the very terms themselves, multiculturalism and Eurocentrism, are not analytical categories, they are categories to be analyzed with a nuanced historical sense, and also a subtle social analysis. (p. 4)

Traditional arguments define the sources of Western thought in the production of European, male, and heterosexual thinkers, and the basic premise is the call for canonical texts as the foundations of liberal education. The recalcitrant, one-sided, and unidimensional versions of Eurocentrism once prominent in the neoconservative movement, while still very powerful, have been losing ground facing the issues of cultural diversity and multiculturalism in the United States. The dispute within neoconservative quarters regarding Proposition 187 in California is a good example.

Most recently, neoconservative intellectuals have tried to reconceptualize in more subtle ways the importance of multiculturalism for American education, arguing for the advantages of ethnic multiculturalism over the dangerous trends of cultural pluralism. While accepting that multiculturalism in the United States is a "recognition of the sensitivities of ethnic or racial minorities, [it should not] be confused with *cultural pluralism* . . . ethnic groups should be maintained as identifiable constituents of the American nation because of the unique contributions they make to the richness and variety of American culture" (Safran, 1994, p. 69).

Neoconservatives accept that notions of cultural pluralism may have a racialist dimension because they blur together race, culture, and nationality; however, for them, cultural pluralism is not ethnoracial, like the majority of approaches to multiculturalism:

> While most proponents of cultural pluralism fully accept a "national" culture—usually that of the majority—as superordinate, that is, as one that serves a vehicle of interethnic communication, multiculturalism often tends to be culturally isolationist or "separatist." Moreover, many proponents of multiculturalism believe that their minority ethnic culture is not only equal but superior to that of the majority. While cultural pluralism is conservative, multiculturalism is radical in that it rejects long-established cultural traditions that the dominant as well as minority elites have wished to conserve. Yet cultural pluralism may be a force for modernity because it accords a place to ethnic minority cultures that may in certain instances be more advanced than the culture of the majority, whereas multiculturalism is antimodern to the extent that it stresses affirmative action and ascriptive (as opposed to merit-based) recruitment. (Safran, 1994, pp. 69–70)

Needless to say, this position contrasts starkly with James Banks's argument that multicultural education strives to ensure that all students—regardless of their gender, ethnicity, race, culture, social class, religion, or exceptionality—experience educational quality in the schools. In addition, multiculturalism, as predicated by Banks (1993), seeks to eliminate school discrimination, placing multiculturalism as a reform movement growing out of the civil rights and protest movements of the 1960s and 1970s and constituting an international reform movement trying to help students and teachers to develop positive attitudes toward racial, cultural, ethnic, and language diversity.

Not surprisingly, in the neoconservative vision multiculturalism is a unified movement; however, muticulturalism should more appropriately be viewed as an expression of cultural diversity and political programs and as an arena for confrontation of alternative views of agency and structural relationships, particularly race, ethnicity, culture, class, and gender in American education. Thus, ethnoracial multiculturalism (i.e., a view of multiculturalism anchored in notions of the social construction of ethnicity, race, culture, and nationality) for neoconservatives is antimodern because it skews meritocracy and credentialism and states its claim based on ascriptive status, tradition, and the politics of identity. Saffran's approach resonates with the common neoconservative complaint that multiculturalism is parochial, lacks universalism, and constitutes another instance of the force of the political correctness movement in academia and educational settings.

The use of race as part of the divide-and-conquer strategy of the neoconservative state has not been subtle. Giving the complexities of curriculum in multilingual, multiethnic, and multicultural societies like the United States, neoconservatives had to agree that teaching about heroes, holidays, and achievements of an ethnic minority has a wide appeal to ethnic pride. Yet, the debate on multiculturalism and the promotion of a multicultural curriculum is, in the view of neoconservatives, purely self-serving and opportunistic:

> These policies may provide jobs for ethnic minority intellectuals and administrators; in order to justify their positions—and the maintenance of the new ethnic minority bureaucracy—they may seek to attract a large enough clientele by appealing to the lowest common denominator, for example, by offering courses on Chicano cuisine and dance (vestigial or nostalgic ethnicity) and socioeconomic problems in the *barrio* (oppression studies) rather than the Spanish language and literature. In order to gain tactical allies, the purveyors of multiculturalism often make common cause with non-ethnic multiculturalists by mixing courses on ethnic culture with those on gender-specific (for example, feminist) culture and the culture of alternative life styles. While these approaches seek to undermine the dominance of the majority culture, they are ultimately counterproductive for the ethnic minority because they may cancel each other out and undermine the clarity and prestige of *its* culture. (Safran, 1994, pp. 69–70)

Lamenting the loss of "purity" and "prestige" of a culture or its social efficacy, the multicultural strategy of neoconservatives highlights differences, accepting the notion of diversity as long as multicultures agree to shape their identities in reference to an acceptable canon. This canon can be defined in terms of prescribed cultural literacy, a superordinate culture, or acceptable and recommended political fervor and behavior such as patriotism. Borrowing a page from the liberal prescription on tolerance in cultural encounters, pragmatic/utilitarian neoconservatives (as opposed to doctrinaire ones) define the war of cultures in the United States as creating insurmountable contradictions in the construction of uniform identities, unless we choose the only option to avoid the chaos resulting from cultural strife: identifying firm principles or foundations that every culture may refer to in the national context.

The neoconservative argument welcomes internal and self-destructive strife among minority groups, as well as any attempt to define monolithic, singular cultural identities. A careful exploration of theories of the state in education helps us to identify and criticize the pitfalls and analytical gaps of positions embraced by neoconservative intellectuals. It is particularly instructive to see how multiculturalism in education is considered a separatist movement damaging the social fabric of American society. Taking into account these weak aspects of the neoconservative argument makes it clear how neoconservatives see cultural pluralism as making use of the resources of multicultural societies while still selecting individuals according to achievement and performance. What is fascinating about secular and moderate neoconservatives is that, like neoliberals, they advocate free trade and the globalization of cultures and economies because globalization improves the mobility of capital. But to their dismay, globalization also increases the mobility of labor. Thus, it is paradoxical that they resent immigration and multiculturalism, which represent the other side of the coin of promoting globalization of economies. To be sure, globalization does not necessarily mean global-mindedness. Moreover, for Christian fundamentalists and other extremely conservative factions within neoconservatism, globalization is not a welcome process but another expression of the contradictions within the movement.

Multiculturalism as a vehicle of selective social mobility cannot be avoided in the logic of the neoconservative state. For neoconservatives, despite their privatizing ethos, the resolution of the debate on multiculturalism cannot, paradoxically, be left to the operation of the logic of the market. Neoconservatives seek to establish a basic, official knowledge to which every culture should be exposed, molding cultural understandings while keeping the culture's folkloric character. However, as a critic stated, every definition of knowledge is a site for conflict "over the relations between culture and power in class, race, gender, and religious terms" (Apple, 1993b, p. 5). For neoconservatives, individual responsibility and choice are the basis for cultural performance in dynamic markets. Here is, however, an important tension: If the market is left unchecked and a vigorous debate occurs in the different scenarios of culture, the moral commitments of different cultures could eventually mold individual responsibility and choice.

Because neoconservatives have used the politics of race as an effective tool for disintegration and fragmentation, as a policy of divide and conquer, the notion of "otherness" has been used as a wild card in "exporting" the blame for the failure of neoconservative policies to less powerful communities. Fragmentation and conflict between different factions of multicultural movements are acceptable and even encouraged from neoconservative quarters; multiracial coalitions and social movements for equality and radical democracy are not (Apple, 1993a; Darder, 1991; hooks & West, 1991; McCarthy & Crichlow, 1993b; West, 1988, 1992, 1993b). Critical multiculturalists are deemed separatists by neoconservatives.

There are certainly many analytical and political alternatives available to confront the dilemma of unity in diversity. First and foremost is to explore the degree of hybridization of cultures and the notion that every social subject is constituted by multiple identities. Recognition of the complexities posed by the process of hybridization and the notion of multiple identities in the social and psychological construction of the pedagogical subject should challenge any attempt to essentialize differences based on race, gender, class, nationality, and religious or sexual preferences. Second, rather than dealing with differences in ethical and political commitments as primary contradictions, one may see them as secondary contradictions, as conflicting loyalties in the social construction of identity. This opens up areas of negotiation in the context of progressive alliances based on multiple identities. A fundamental premise is to avoid any essentialization of cultural struggles. Also, however, an important ethical position is to recognize that there are a number of insights in neoconservative and neoliberal arguments. For instance, from a very different vantage point than that of neoconservatives, Cornel West (1993a, p. 196) and a number of Black intellectuals are concerned with "cultural breakdown and escalating self-destructive nihilism among the poor and very poor."

While the debate on neoconservatism has been vigorous in the United States, the influence of neoconservative educational policies reaches beyond U.S. borders. Neoconservative developments in curriculum, textbooks, and teaching, like changes in the international division of labor and the dynamics of the marketplace, were observed by Carnoy and Torres (1994) in Costa Rica in the mid-1980s. Costa Rican policymakers tried to solve the dilemma of lower enrollment, increased student dropout, and dissatisfied teachers by blaming teachers publicly for "mediocre" education. Blaming teachers would give teachers' organizations less support in their demands for higher salaries and would legitimize alternative (non-teacher-centered) means of improving education. This was precisely the policy advocated by the Reagan/Bush administrations in the United States.

Thus, while criticizing teachers and school personnel in general, a new Costa Rican administration launched a back-to-basics educational "modernization" reform shortly after it took office in 1986. The reform proposal, consisting of three specific projects, was intended to improve the "efficiency" of educational production. The first project involved the introduction of microcomputers in the classroom. Second, a national testing system was created for the first, second, and third cycles that included tests in mathematics, Spanish, science, social studies, and English and a test for high school seniors. A passing grade in all subjects, including a foreign language, writing and orthography, grammar and literature, science, mathematics, and social studies, was a prerequisite for graduation. Third, Costa Rican scientific colleges for gifted children were created to improve the international competitiveness of Costa Rica through advances in science and technology.

In addition, a number of controls were imposed on teachers and students. These controls included, among others, a canon of the minimum content to be taught, mandatory reintroduction of cursive writing for all pupils, the same uniform for students in all public schools, compulsory daily written lesson plans for teachers, more quizzes and semestral examinations, and a longer school calendar. Emphasis on rationalization of educational administration; a more efficient accounting and administrative system, database, and school registry; and functional decentralization by regions—despite the small size of the country—were also part of the package.

In Brazil, in a move similar to the neoconservative reaction to the threat posed by multiculturalists, neoliberal governments at the state and local levels have promoted educational policies of "quality control" based on North American and Japanese models of managerial efficiency and accountability. These moves have encountered opposition from the left, which advances the notion of "public popular schooling," seeking to address the specific cultural experience of the poor. In Brazil, too, neoconservatives argue that teachers' lack of technical expertise and the inefficiency of administrators are the main causes of school failure.

Despite the power of the neoconservative proposal, neoconservatives have accepted the notion of citizenship rights and obligations intrinsic to a welfare state model. Thus, neoconservatives

> cannot easily retreat from welfare . . . the overall pattern is that structural obligations remain. . . . What seems inevitable, despite the enormous power of the Neoconservative argument, is that social and economic survival depends in part on further resolving the classic political problem of the proper relationship between individual autonomy and public obligations. (Culpitt, 1992, pp. 192–194)

While the neoconservative state is strong in its cultural critique, many of its key economic and social proposals reemerge in neoliberal pragmatic models.

The Neoliberal State and Education: The Question of Autonomy

> The mere existence of state autonomy poses grave problems for liberal-democratic theory. (Boron, 1990/1991, p. 108)

While neoconservatives struggle with the dilemma of promoting individual autonomy and public obligations, neoliberal political economy implies a related contradiction between individualistically conceived preferences and rational social choice (MacIntyre, 1988). This contradiction is aptly presented by Williams and Reuten (1993):

> Though markets aggregate individual preferences in a way agnostic to any particular notion of the public good, like democratic political aggregation, they only work when there is considerable convergence in the preference orderings of the individuals—they do not reconcile fundamental conflict; rather they are *premised* on a stable structure of behavioral norms, supported by a mature state. (p. 82)

Williams and Reuten use Arrow's paradox to convey the full meaning of this problem. If the place of the individual in the capitalist economy is crucially and solely as a preference ordering subject, there is a serious questioning of the liberal idea of the state as a site for bargaining between individuals with autonomous preferences. In other terms, why should individuals subject themselves to any order, less so to the rule of the state? Moreover, why accept that there are social needs to be met?

The answer of the welfare state to these questions was quite straightforward. Welfare policies were concessions to the working class after a lengthy period of social upheaval in exchange for more predictable economic outcomes during the model implemented by Henry Ford, or Fordism (e.g., prevention of work stoppages or strikes). A perceived "social peace" and public investment in job creation strategies will bring prosperity for all. More satisfied, better educated workers will be more productive. They will prosper and with them their communities and society at large. Social expenditures were an insurance against class conflict. Yet, with the growing need to locate the place of the individual vis-à-vis the notion of the greatest societal good, the liberal state will defend its welfare policies as attempts to create solidarity and community and provide basic social goods and services.

Are there any connections between the neoconservative and the neoliberal state? Michael Apple has argued that both are wings of the same rightist movement. In agreement with Apple's argument, I would like to extend it, arguing that, taking a world system approach based on Wallerstein's work, the distinction of metropolitan, semiperipheral, and peripheral countries plays an important role in designating the nature of the state (for useful discussions of these categories, see Chirot, 1977; Wallerstein, 1979). Neoconservative political economy has emerged, partly, as a reaction to welfare states in metropolitan state formations. Many of these state formations have been characterized as industrially advanced societies or late capitalism. Indeed, the majority of neoconservative experiences have taken place in states that have not been historically subject to colonization.[16] Moreover, with few exceptions, these states have been colonizers themselves, profiting from colonizing regions of the world later identified as Third World states.[17] Culturally speaking, the tradition of conservatism, or more generally the social forces associated with the right in Europe, Canada, the United States, Australia, and New Zealand (i.e., countries of the North), is quite different from the political experience of the right in the Third World (e.g., countries of the South). Countries in the South have experienced authoritarian governments, military dictatorships, and authoritarian populisms with rightist affiliations. With the exception of fascism or authoritarian corporatist experiences, the right in metropolitan countries, despite the growing power of the executive function in neoconservatism, has negotiated its differences with liberalism within the framework of parliamentarism. This is not the experience of the Third World, where parliamentarism itself, given the power of the executive and strong caudillos, has often been a nominal rather than a substantive political practice.

In sum, differences in historical traditions, social and economic endowments, and political culture affect the theory and practice of democracy. The lack of a lasting (rather than an ephemeral), truly liberal democratic tradition in many of the countries of the South, the lack of an extensive welfare state experience, and the strong presence of corporatism and populism account for important differences in the configuration of the right vis-à-vis countries in the North. Differences can also be noted between a rightist movement with no oligarchical past in the United States and the right connected with the experience of feudalism and nobility in Europe.

Neoliberals, while still drawing from the tradition of liberalism but having serious reservations about the theory of democracy, have joined neoconservatives in their criticisms of the welfare state. A key component of the critique is the notion that the fiscal crisis of the state is the result of state overload, of an "overburdened" state trying to satisfy increased demands from citizens, thus creating a gap between increasing fiscal expenditures and decreasing fiscal revenues. These disparities and the dissatisfaction of taxpayers because of the higher taxes needed to pay for entitlements result in the ingovernability of democracies. Ingovernability stems from the institutionalized arrangements of mass democratic reforms in a welfare state, including the creation of state handouts that result in disincentives for workers and squeeze profits via taxes from corporations and individuals.

The notions of neoliberalism and the neoliberal state appear to be "exported" from the center to the periphery and semiperiphery. The point can be illustrated with a discussion of the Latin American experience. Neoliberalism and the neoliberal state are terms commonly used to designate a new type of state that has emerged in Latin America and regions of the South in the last few decades. No doubt, a neoliberal ideology and narrative are consolidated in the central countries. Given the implications of the liberal past of metropolitan societies, the specific debates within the political parties (e.g., the discussion in the United States regarding the role of the new right in the Republican party), and the influence of neoconservative economics in globalization, the notion of neoliberalism in central countries appears almost interchangeable with the notion of neoconservatism in political economy. This is not the case in terms of cultural, social, or ethical preferences.

An early example of economic neoliberalism in Latin America is usually associated with the policies implemented in Chile after 1973. Neoliberal policies advocate for free trade and small public sectors and against excessive state interventionism and tight regulation of markets. Lomnitz and Melnick (1991) argue that, historically and philosophically, neoliberalism has been associated with structural adjustment programs. Structural adjustment, in turn, is usually described as a broad range of policies recommended by the World Bank, the International Monetary Fund, and other financial organizations. Although the World Bank differentiates among stabilization, structural adjustment, and adjustment policies, it acknowledges that the general use of these terms "is often imprecise and inconsistent" (Sarnoff, 1990, p. 21).

This model of stabilization and adjustment has resulted in a number of policy recommendations, including reduction of government expenditures, currency devaluations to promote exports, reduction in import tariffs, and an increase in public and private savings. Key aims of the model are a drastic reduction in the state sector, the liberalization of salaries and prices, and the reorientation of industrial and agricultural production toward exports. The overall purpose of this policy package is, in the short run, to reduce the size of fiscal deficits and of public expenditures, to drastically reduce inflation, and to reduce exchange rates and tariffs. In the medium term, structural adjustment relies on exports as the engine of growth. To that extent, structural adjustment and subsequent policies of economic stabilization seek to liberalize trade, to reduce any distortion in price structures, to end "protectionist" policies, and, therefore, to facilitate the rule of the market in Latin American economies (Bitar, 1988).[18]

What are the differences between neoconservatism and neoliberalism in terms of the political sociology of education? The neoconservative state is partly a backlash against the so-called "excesses" of the welfare state and its fiscal crisis. The model of the neoconservative state under the Reagan/Bush administrations attempted to place the United States in hegemonic position in the context of fast-changing international systems. These administrations faced the growing economic competition of Germany and Japan and an overblown fear of the military might of the former Soviet Union. Education was associated with national security and economic competitiveness in the world system. The neoconservative vision of educational reform reflects an attempt to socialize American children and youth for the exercise of power and domination on a global scale. It is a project that distances itself from the singular idea of an education for democracy, as originally defended by liberalism and its pedagogical counterpart, progressivism (hence the emphasis on the quality of education and the support for science and technology in the schools). Central players in the context of neoconservatism are the Business Roundtable (an organization of business executives), private foundations, state governors, and professional associations seeking to develop standards for teaching of disciplines.

Neoliberalism offers similar prescriptions. The politics of neoliberalism, when transported to the countries of the periphery, constitute a set of proposals that refer to the condition of the countries of the South in the international context, particularly in the division of labor. Neoliberalism strives to pass the cost of educational services to clients through user fees, increasing the participation of the private sector in education (i.e., privatization), and promoting decentralization of educational services as a means of redefining the power and educational relations among federal, provincial, and municipal governments. These standard policy prescriptions overlap heavily with neoconservatism.

Is there an alternative to neoconservative or neoliberal analyses of the role of the state in educational development? Neo-Marxist analyses differ from the theoretical accounts of neoliberalism and neoconservatism. Neo-Marxist theories analyze the interactions between state and education in historical context, trying to show the contradictory dynamics occurring between economic and political structures and human agencies. Regarding schooling, neo-Marxism focuses on the role of official knowledge as a state practice and develops a parallelist analysis of race, class, and gender as independent but interactive dynamics.[19]

Parallelist Theories and Official State Knowledge: Neo-Marxist Theories of the State

> The concrete is concrete because it is the synthesis of multiple determinations, hence unity in diversity. (Marx, 1973, p. 101)

Neo-Marxist theories discuss the state as intimately related to notions of power and its distribution in society. Ralph Miliband (1969), one of the most prominent Marxist political scientists of this century, said it nicely:

> A Theory of the State is also a theory of society and of the distribution of power in that society. But most Western "students of politics" tend to start, judging from their work, with the assumption that power, in Western societies, is competitive, fragmented and diffused: everybody, directly or through organized groups, has some power and nobody has or can have too much of it. In these societies, citizens enjoy universal suffrage, free and regular elections, representative institutions, effective citizenship rights, including the right of free speech, association and opposition; and both individuals and groups take ample advantage of these rights, under the protection of the law, and independent judiciary and a free political culture. (p. 2)

Michael Apple (1993b) has highlighted the difficulties of classical Marxism in the treatment of class, race, and gender. This position is defined by McCarthy and Apple (1988) as a "nonsynchronous parallelism." Apple (1986) argues that

> a paradigm case in point here is the criticism leveled against traditional Marxist interpretations by feminist authors. Many of their arguments have been devastating to orthodox assertions . . . , so much so that many people on the left believe that any attempt at understanding our social formation that does not combine *in an unreductive way* analyses of class and gender together is only half a theory at best. . . . The same, of course, needs to be said of race as well. The rejection of major aspects of the received orthodox Marxist tradition and the emerging sensitivity to the truly constitutive nature of gender and race demonstrate not a weakness but the continued growth and vitality of a tradition of critical analysis that is attempting to deal honestly and openly with the complexity of life under present conditions of domination and exploitation. (pp. 320–321)

Nonsynchronous parallelist theories, while not sidelining the importance of class in sociology of education, avoid essentializing class in theories of social and cultural reproduction. Michael Apple, discussing the work of Basil Bernstein, argued that class itself is increasingly becoming gendered and raced. Thus,

> we cannot marginalize race and gender as constitutive categories in any cultural analysis. If there is indeed basic cultural forms and orientations that are specifically gendered and raced, and have their own partly autonomous histories, then we need to integrate theories of patriarchal and racial forms into the very core of our attempt to comprehend what is being reproduced and changed. At the very least, a theory that allows for the contradictions within and among these dynamics would be essential. Of course, this is one of the multiple areas where Neo-Gramscian and some post-structuralist positions that have not become cynically depoliticized intersect. (Apple, 1992, p. 143)

What, then, in this theoretical reconstruction is the role of the state in cultural reproduction and schooling? To begin with, the state is a site of multiple conflicts based on class, gender, race, and ethnicity struggles. Apple (1992, p. 141; see also Apple, 1989) suggests that, as a locus of ideological struggle, "to win in the state you must win in civil society," and that the politics of common sense of neoconservatives reflect a new consensus. This new consensus has been aptly characterized by Apple (1993b, p. 21) as an "authoritarian populism" building a new social accord. Apple (1992) notes that Bernstein contributes to our understanding of

> market-oriented visible pedagogies where educational policy is centered around programs of school choice. This, [Bernstein] correctly believes, is but a "thin cover" for a restratification of schools, students, and curricula. . . . The issue of restratification also points to the crucial role the state plays as a sponsor of such market-oriented programs and as a site of class conflict. (p. 142)

Better textbooks and teacher-proof curricula are seen as an imperative to restore order in classrooms and achieve excellence in education. Apple (1992, pp. 36–37) argues that "it is the history of the state, in concert with capital and a largely male academic body of consultants and developers, intervening at the level of practice into the work of a largely female workforce." Apple (1988b, p. 37) suggests that to understand the dynamics of the history of curriculum, "one must integrate an analysis of the state, changes in the labor process of state employees, and the politics of patriarchy." In order to do so, a dialectical approach is necessary. Privatization and market-oriented policies, "especially if they have been articulated through the State, are the results of conflicts, compromises, and accords within various levels of the State, and between the State and a wide array of social movements and forces in the wider society" (Apple, 1992, p. 142; see also Apple & Weis, 1986). The call is for a more subtle analysis of the state, "one that parallels the advances currently being made on the study of gender and race in economy and politics. This would certainly complement the current discussions of the central place of democratic conflicts in the State itself" (Apple, 1988a, p. 122; see also Carnoy, 1984). Such a study would offer a comprehensive analysis of the four trends that Apple (1993b) identified in the conservative restoration in the United States and in Britain: privatization, centralization, vocationalization, and differentiation.

Changes in state formation entail a change in the production of hegemony and commonsense interpretations of everyday life and, particularly, a change in the political alliances controlling the state, from liberalism to neoconservatism and neoliberalism. Replacing the role of the state with the logic of the market in determining educational policy is criticized as a class strategy in the neoliberal state (S. Ball, 1993; Dale, 1989). A similar argument is made in considerations of the withdrawal of state investment in public education in Latin America and how that would affect the constitution of citizens as pedagogical subjects (Puiggrós, 1990; Torres & Puiggrós, 1995). Changes in the labor process relate to the move away from a mode of production defined as the transformation of Fordism to a post-Fordist model (with implications for the process of skilling and deskilling of the labor force and the logic of technical control in curriculum) (Apple, 1982).

The post–World War I model of industrial development was mass production, superseding the 19th-century craft paradigm. Fordism as a mass production model was concerned with the production of standardized commodities for stable mass markets. Fordism and Taylorism were systems of production based on capital-intensive industrial manufacturing, scientific management, increases in plant use and productivity through stringent control over labor, the use of time-motion and control studies of labor work inside the factory, intense fragmentation of work tasks based on the separation of conception and execution, the acceleration of productive operations, and the famous Ford assembly line, which restructured the technical division of labor inside the factory (Braverman, 1974; Clarke, 1990; Gramsci, 1980; Manacorda, 1977).

Post-Fordism is characterized by flexible specialization and labor flexibility:

> Whereas work under the mass production paradigm was characterized by an intense division of labor, the separation of conception and execution, the substitution of unskilled labor for skilled labor and special purpose for universal machines; the quest for specializations prompts a more flexible organization of production based on collaboration between designers and reskilled craft workers to make a wide variety of goods with general purpose machines. (Tomaney, 1990, p. 30)

While Fordism and Taylorism were characteristic of industrial development in the United States, flexible specialization is characteristic of changes in labor management models in Japan and Germany. The distinction between conception and execution of tasks has been deliberately blurred by a reliance on teamwork, with foremen regarded as part of the work teams serving as representatives to management. In addition, there is extensive job rotation to familiarize workers with the context of their work and increase their flexibility (Piore & Sabel, 1984). Quality circles, in which labor and management teams work cooperatively to improve the different phases of production, were implemented around the mid-1960s. In Germany, with more trained workers on the shop floor, there is an explicit effort to eliminate the distinctions between blue-collar and white-collar workers. The overall model of institutionalization of long-term employment is not based so much on contract agreements in negotiations between labor unions and management under the supervision of the state but, particularly in Japan, on workers' dependence on the company for lifetime employment, family welfare, and welfare provision. This model, however, calls for job rotation and team working, which intensify the levels of commitment and productivity of workers and often involve overtime work on short notice to meet production shortfalls. There are, of course, other areas of job enhancement and flexibility, including the institutionalization of unregulated labor activities through nonformal or informal labor markets and the like. Quality control and just-in-time production are other salient traits of the Japanese model.[20]

Political economists have seen these changes in the workplace as attempts not only to increase productivity relative to wages but, more important, to discipline labor. The neoconservative approach that seeks to bring school expansion and practices in line with a disciplined labor force is seen as part and parcel of a general process of struggle over control of workplaces and schools (Carnoy & Levin, 1985). There are a number of implications for teacher training and curriculum reform. The obvious one is the erosion of teacher autonomy through the push for "prepackaged" curricula, textbooks, and computer/video technology that would be more "predictable" than individual craft implemented in the classroom when the door is closed. More control is sought through implementation of managerial techniques associated with labor flexibility including total quality control (hence the emphasis on standardized testing). A second direction is to promote the direct presence of the marketplace in the classroom through direct advertisement and linkages between corporations and schools (e.g., the presence of groups such as the Business Roundtable pressing for educational reforms or the implementation of Channel One [a news and education source] in public schools mixing commercial messages with educational instruction).

Michael Apple (1989) lists several educational policies gaining momentum in the United States that have been instrumental in shifting the debate toward the pastures of the right, reconstituting the prevailing common sense in education:

> (1) proposals for voucher plans and tax credits to make schools more like the idealized free market economy; (2) the movement in state legislatures and state departments of education to "raise standards" and mandate both teacher and student "competencies" and basic curricular goals and knowledge, thereby centralizing even more at a state level the control of teaching and curricula; (3) the increasingly effective assaults on the school curriculum for its supposedly anti-family and anti-free enterprise bias, its "secular humanism," its neglect of the "western tradition," and its lack of patriotism; and (4) the growing pressure to make the needs of business and industry into the primary goals of the educational system. (p. 27)

A primary goal is centralizing and making flexible teachers' training through a unified curriculum that is compatible with total quality models. A desirable by-product—and indeed a precondition—is that of curbing the power of trade unions. This is important because, given the present process of teachers' certification, teacher unions and the teacher profession per se are among the few unions and professions in capitalism somewhat protected from international competition. However, as Picciotto (1991) argues, the state must not counter the trend of internationalization:

> The capitalist state, although territorially defined, was born and develops a loose network of interrelated and overlapping jurisdictions. The regulatory framework for corporate capitalism which emerged from the last part of the 19th century was based on the nation state but involved emulation and transplantation of forms, as well as international coordination; and it facilitated international ownership of capital through the transnational corporation which became the dominant form in the 20th century. Transnational corporations have favored minimal international coordination while strongly supporting the national state, since they can take advantage of regulatory differences and loopholes. Processes of international coordination of state functions, relying on national legitimation, have taken the form of bureaucratic-administrative corporatist bargaining through a motley network of informal structures as well as the more visible and grand organizations. The glowing globalization of social relations has put increasing pressure on both national and international state structures. (p. 43; see also Ruccio, Resnick, & Wolff, 1991)[21]

The growing internationalization of the state is still an open question in terms of its scope and dynamics. Likewise, the implications of this internationalization and globalization for educational policies, textbooks, and curriculum are hitherto lacking empirical and theoretical research. There are exceptions. In an eight-country study of reform practices in teachers' education, Popkewitz and Pereyra (1993) argued that international organizations, such as the Organization for Economic Cooperation and Development (OECD), and the European community are playing crucial roles in promoting changes in regulations of teacher education.

The role of international organizations in the process of globalization and the nation-state has been aptly discussed by Joel Samoff, who studied the World Bank's logic of lending in education. By any account, the World Bank is one of the most prominent regulatory agencies of the capitalist system. Samoff argues persuasively that the World Bank is a major player in an intellectual and financial complex pursuing the transnationalization of knowledge and expertise, using a community of experts for hire in a process where there is a strong confluence of research and educational financing. The World Bank is seen as having a pivotal role in the network of power and decision making in education worldwide, influencing in peculiar ways research and policy-making in developing countries as well as influencing the international discourse in education by different means. First and foremost is the commission of long-term research with abundant budgets. In this process, the World Bank is considered an intellectual and financial complex because it is extremely influential in defining and selecting the themes, variables, and dominant terminology in research on international development in education. This terminology, as presented in most of the World Bank's documents, is based mostly on a neoclassical economy of education, human capital theory, and a theory of the firm applied to education. Through its financial weight and operational reach, the World Bank also influences the methods of analysis considered appropriate and legitimate (e.g., cost-benefit analysis, input-output analysis, and rates of return), defends a technocratic instrumental rationality rather than a politically and historically informed policy orientation, and confers legitimacy to hypotheses and research findings that its experts deem useful and necessary for educational investment and development. Samoff (1992, 1993) would agree that there is a diversity of theoretical perspectives within the ranks of the World Bank's researchers. But he points out that the organization's logic is implacably applied in the context of its lending and that the workings of its managers in charge of lending are distant from the theoretical and empirical analysis of its researchers. The World Bank's logic of analysis cannot be characterized as pluralistic. Although not free from tensions and contradictions, the organization is quite monolithic (Samoff, 1992, 1993). Similarly, in studying the influence of the World Bank in higher education throughout the world, Daniel Schugurensky has argued that the World Bank plays a role at an international level similar to the one played by the Business Roundtable in the United States with its agenda for educational reform. In short, there is an elective affinity between the policies promoted by the World Bank and the many neoliberal and neoconservative proposals emanating from the Business Roundtable (Schugurensky, 1994).

Social Regulation, the Public Sphere, and State Intervention: Postmodern Perspectives on the State and Education

> If power were never anything but repressive, if it never did anything but to say no, do you really think one would be brought to obey it? What makes power hold good, what makes it accepted, is simply the fact that it doesn't only weigh on us as a force that says no, but that it traverses and produces things, it induces pleasure, forms knowledge, produces discourse. It needs to be considered as a productive network which runs through the whole social body. (Foucault, cited in T. Ball, 1992, p. 28)

Classic principles of liberal political theory that conceive of the state as a great conciliator of divergent interests are challenged not only by critical modernist political theories but also by postmodernist criticism.[22] Thomas Popkewitz, for instance, would argue that, in a postmodern world, the state does not necessarily represent the public interest and professional knowledge is not privileged over common sense. With the collapse of the modernist project and, by implication, the collapse of the established modernist educational reform agendas, specific social movements, limited agendas, and particularistic claims represent the focus of politics (see Popkewitz, 1991).

Postmodernist analyses are based on explicit views of power as fragmented in capitalist society. Despite this fragmentation, as Miliband points out, the state remains firmly at the center of debates on the articulation of power in civil society and the constitution of democratic communities and democratic political cultures. One may add that any definition of the relationships between power and state should consider the role of education and its potential contribution to political representation, participation, and citizenship in late capitalism. Let us, however, examine some of the premises of postmodernism and how theories of the state and power are accounted for in recent postmodernist analysis.

Postmodernism argues that there is a "new" epoch in society and, thus, a new cultural paradigm. For current purposes, some of the key sociological implications of postmodern society and culture can be summarized as involving various processes of *fragmentation* as follows: (a) a decentering and fragmentation of power that calls into question theories of domination and hegemony; (b) an uncoupling of material interests and subjective expressions in collective action, resulting in the shift of the demands of social movements from distributional to cultural-ethical issues; (c) the emergence of heterogeneity as opposed to the homogenization that has been previously characteristic of the world system; and (d) a growing distrust and disillusionment with democracy resulting from the fragmentation of political communities and identities.

Consider briefly each of these points. Postmodernism argues that power has become decentered and fragmented in contemporary societies. Thus, to suggest the notion of a ruling elite conducting its business and having decisive influence in the formulation of public policy or education will obscure—in a postmodern view—the multiplicity of powers that interact in society and its policy outcomes (Bowles & Gintis, 1986). How does one define power that is fragmented and lacking a unifying principle? Does this fragmentation undermine the nonsynchronous, parallelist conception of the relations of class, gender, and race in cultural reproduction? Does, in short, the fragmentation of power undermine conceptual frameworks and "grand narratives" such as hegemony and domination?

The so-called death of grand narratives poses political and epistemological questions. For Foucault, truth depends on strategies of power rather than epistemological criteria. This is a central concern for a theory of the state and power. Does this mean that if we rely on skeptical poststructuralist accounts, we cannot define some "master signifier" that helps us to ground, ethically and politically, political action? Otherwise, we cannot validate ex ante any policy recommendation in education from a theoretical standpoint, nor can we validate ex post facto the same principles for political action. The most obvious implication is the lack of direction and the absence of a political program. One possible consequence of this is "a false radicalism which engages in constant but ultimately meaningless transgression of all defended viewpoints" (Hulme, 1986, p. 6). This political activism highlights Harvey's concern that we may end up with philosophical and social thought characterized by ephemerality, collage, fragmentation, and dispersion.

Political activism based on "false radicalism" does not challenge the fragmented politics of divergent special and regional interest groups. This situation adds to the secular internecine struggles of progressive groups, the structural and historical action of the capitalist state, and actions from the right and undermines the communities of learning and political action, hindering the ability of progressive groups to challenge preponderant differential resources (influence, power, and wealth) of elites and dominant classes in education. This transgressive activism may challenge the narratives of neoconservative and neoliberal projects in education (which is not a minor accomplishment considering the power of the "commonsense" narrative of the right), but it offers few if any guidelines for practical politics. The problem is compounded when social subjects are considered to be politically decentered.

The notion of the decentering of social subjects implies an uncoupling of the close link between objective social interests and subjective expressions (e.g., class consciousness) assumed by much modernist social theory. The resulting contradictory loyalties of individuals increasingly undermines a central organizing principle of struggle. One oft-noted consequence of this relative uncoupling of social position and political action is that the "new" social movements are more concerned with cultural (and ethical-political) demands than distributional ones. Decentered individuals are not supposed to have "class consciousness" in classical terms, yet they strive to achieve "self-actualization" in Giddens's (1991) social psychological analysis.

Postmodernism argues that nation-states are now being dimmed in the context of a growing interdependent world and in the context of more local struggles. Yet, as Immanuel Wallerstein (1991) argues, the (capitalist) world system has witnessed a historical trend toward cultural heterogeneity rather than cultural homogenization. Thus, the fragmentation of the nation in the world system is happening at the same time that there is a tendency toward cultural differentiation or cultural complexity (i.e., globalization). Globalization and regionalization seem to be dual processes occurring simultaneously. This fact has not been overlooked by certain strands of postmodernism, providing an avenue for understanding the rise of ethnicity and nationalism along with globalization, not necessarily as contradictory but as related phenomena.

In this increasingly more complexly organized multicultural and multilingual world system, the bases of traditional forms of political community have been eroded. There is an emerging theory and practice of distrust in democracy. Hence, the previous models of democratic checks and balances, separation of powers, and democratic accountability no longer work, not even at the level of formal rather than substantive democracy. Distrust in democracy and democratic theory as part of a modernist discourse cannot be associated with all postmodernist strands per se. However, it poses problems for the changing patterns of power in education and raises concerns about the narrowing of the meaning of democracy. The redefinition of democracy needs to be extricated from the forming of patterns of social regulation because "not only have the interests represented been narrowed; participation exists within a restricted range of problems and possibilities" (Popkewitz, 1991, p. 215).

Any redefinition of the notion of democracy again situates the school at the center of the modernist-enlightenment project. Postmodernists would argue, however, that the ethical, substantive, and procedural elements of democratic theory should be reexamined in consideration of postmodern culture. The challenge for educators, parents, students, and policymakers is to think critically about the failures of the past and about the myriad of exclusionary practices that still pervade schooling, hence bringing to the forefront issues of power and domination, class, race, and gender. The validity of the notion of instrumental rationality guiding school reform should also be examined because it gives attention to administration, procedures, and efficiency as the prime criteria for change and progress and because it assumes that there is a common framework structuring the experience of all people (Popkewitz, 1987; Torres, in press).

On a different front, professionalization, as Foucault has argued, defines also the limits of governmentalization and the different realms of governance. "The Foucauldian perspective suggests that those cognitive and normative elements that operate to establish the boundaries between associations of professional experts and the state must be viewed, in terms of process, as means of negotiation used by discourses that define the possible realms of governance" (Johnson, 1993, p. 150). Popkewitz (1994a) argues, in a similar vein, that the state "entails a variety of actors in the educational arena including government agencies and professional and social organizations which organize and administer policy." According to Popkewitz, state reorganization reconstitutes the patterns of social regulation and is clearly expressed in the decentralization process that, on the surface, is changing the patterns of state regulation of schooling. Another set of patterns of social regulations relating to Foucault's "governmentality" is described by Popkewitz (1994a):

> A second form of regulation and one which ties together different layers of social/political life is the construction of scientific discourses by which the individuals manage the "self" in the social world. I argue that there is a governmentality as certain reform discourses internationally circulate to shape and fashion teachers' dispositions towards practices, such as those found in constructivist psychologies that reform didactics. The construction of school reform discourse are practices that normalize social relations through the strategies for constructing and organizing the "objects" of schooling. (p. 21)

In short, from a postmodernist perspective such as that of Popkewitz (drawing from Foucault and Bourdieu), the state must be seen as a historical and relational concept that is multilayered. He presses his claim by stating that

> while most state theories have focused solely on actors and structures, my argument has sought to consider the state as an historical problem of relations; considering the production of social regulation through the position of actors and the deployment of discourses in the educational arena. This view of the state is one of an epistemological concept that is continually historicized. (Popkewitz, 1994a, p. 24; see also Popkewitz, 1994b)

This research agenda offers a path for a microanalysis of power, the state, and education that could be politically useful. In such an approach, Foucault's "pedagogical devices" and discursive relations may have their own independent power of macrostructural relations and discourses. There is always a risk of delinking microanalysis from macrodynamics of a structural and historical nature and hence losing the "nuanced historical sense" of the phenomena being analyzed; however, there should be no doubt that a multilayered approach such as the one proposed by Popkewitz opens up avenues for exploring the discourses of educational reform as social regulation and the patterns of transformation of the state and schooling as school rituals change (with strong implications in the discourses and practices [e.g., the pedagogical devices] that regulate the construction of language, discourse, and the social construction of "self").

Recent innovative comparative and international work shows the importance of this dual pattern of state regulations and how it is changing the practice of teacher education both at the level of the nation-state and globally (Popkewitz, 1991, 1993). Expert knowledge appears as a deployment of power. For Popkewitz, a historical view of the state—and a global perspective on international organizations regulating capitalism—should be seen as two strategies or patterns of regulation, one a product of the practices (ideologies, discourses, narratives, and social action) of the actors in the arena of education and one a product of the discourses themselves (with a growing internationalization of the rules that regulate the discourses of educational reform). These discourses deploy power and, in education, usually affect the lives of teachers, most of whom are women.

Against the Patriarchal State? Feminism and the Color of the State

> There is nothing about "being" a female that naturally binds women. There is not even such a state as "being" female, itself a highly complex category constituted in contested sexual scientific discourses and other social practices. Gender, race or class consciousness is an achievement forced on us by the terrible historical experience of the contradictory social realities of patriarchy, colonialism, and capitalism. (Haraway, 1984, p. 179)

Feminist theories can be classified in terms of theories of difference, theories of inequality, and theories of oppression (Lengermann & Niebrugge-Brantley, 1992). Theories of difference include biosocial, institutional, and social psychological explanations of the differences between men's and women's experiences and situations. Theories of inequality refer to the explanations of why women have fewer privileges and resources in relation to men (as analyzed by liberal and Marxist theories). Connell (1983, 1987) distinguishes three models of feminist analysis—class first theory, social reproduction theory, and dual systems theory—exemplifying the wide array of theoretical approaches explaining women's inequality in education and the role of the state.

Class first theory argues that capitalism is the root cause of all inequalities and that class struggle is primary. The social reproduction model, under the influence of structural Marxism, suggests that "the family, sexuality or gender relations at large were the site of *reproduction* of 'relations of production' " (Connell, 1987, p. 43). Hence, this theory suggests a systemic connection between the subordination of women and economic exploitation of capitalism. Dual systems theory (see Eisenstein, 1979; Hartmann & Sargent, 1981) argues that the basic idea is that capitalism and patriarchy are distinct and equally comprehensive systems of social relations that meet and interact.

Theories of oppression imply that women are oppressed by men, not merely that they are unequal to or different from men. Psychoanalytic, socialist, radical, and third-wave feminism have addressed these issues in different ways. With the growing presence of postmodernist discourse and its implications for feminism, third-wave feminist theories are offering one of the most compelling theoretical arguments (hooks & West, 1991). Third-wave feminism looks at the notion of "difference" and focuses on women of color in industrially advanced societies and on women in the Third World, assuming that one cannot use the concept of "women" as a generic category in stratification. Third-wave feminism focuses instead on the factual and theoretical interpretations of differences among women: "The differences considered are those that result from an unequal distribution of socially produced goods and services on the basis of position in the global system, class, race, ethnicity, and affectional preference as these interact with gender stratification" (Lengermann & Niebrugge-Brantley, 1992, p. 341).

What has happened with feminism and women's movements during the experience of neoconservative and neoliberal states? In comparison with the gains achieved in the liberal welfare state, the feminist and women's movement agendas have fared differently in the recent neoconservative agendas. A recent assessment of women's movement outcomes in legislative and judicial commitments in Canada, the United States, and Britain studied decisions regarding equal rights legislation, including legislative and judicial commitments to women's equality; reforms to family laws (including divorce policy affecting women and children); choice and reproduction policies, particularly women's access to safe and affordable abortion services; violence against women, including domestic violence and rape; and employment rights, including equal pay for equal work, affirmative action policies, and child-care delivery (Bashevkin, 1994). This study showed that, between 1971 and 1980, approximately 75% of legislative and judicial outcomes in Britain and the United States and 56% in Canada were favorable to women and feminists. A most striking reversal of this trend was found during the Reagan administration, with legislative and judicial decisions going against feminist positions: "From a success to failure ratio of 24:7 before Reagan's election, these figures dropped to 13:15 afterwards" (Bashevkin, 1994, p. 289). Some decisions seen as favorable to women's demands resulted from Reagan's efforts "to off load responsibilities from federal to state government and to reduce public spending on social welfare" (Bashevkin, 1994, p. 289). In Britain and Canada, the feminist agenda did much better; this was particularly true in Canada, with a success rate of 80% (even though feminists were marginalized in their access to federal elites during the Mulroney years). This analysis, however, considered only judicial and legislative decisions in the three governments, a small portion of the policy context. Major budget cuts in housing, child care, and education during the Reagan administration; Thatcher's policies undermining trade unions and local government; and the budget cuts of the federal government in Canada that affected women's groups were not evaluated. If these sectoral policies had been included, the analysis would have shown the negative impact of sectoral outcomes and budgetary policy on the feminist and women's movements.

It is clear that, particularly in the United States, despite its practical difficulties and pervasiveness of male chauvinism in politics, the women's movement thrived in the 1960s and 1970s in comparison with the neoconservative administrations of the 1980s. As a result of the struggles of women, the liberal state promoted women's equality through antidiscriminatory policies in employment, salary, and wages; women's reproductive rights and child-care provisions; and prevention of violence against women. These policies were highly favorable to women and to the feminist movement. The neoconservative state undermined some of those gains, and the women's and feminist movements learned not to take the state for granted, particularly when patriarchy was brought to the fore.

Patriarchal relations—and their representation in education—are a central concern for the feminist movement (Zaretsky, 1983). It is known that Marx devoted just a few pages of his magnum opus to the study of the situation of women and children. Marx saw women as wage workers and wage earners or, conversely, as unproductive labor. Their significance for capitalism was the generation of surplus value. Working women were perceived as part of the general category of proletariat. Hence, they were "perceived as exploited rather than oppressed and there was no sense of patriarchal structuring of the economy" (Coole, 1993, p. 181).

Nelly Stromquist (1991) argues that patriarchal states are at the root of the oppression of women. Looking at the relationship between gender and education and analyzing data on illiteracy and higher education, Stromquist (1991) concludes that all states, no matter what model of governance or mode of production they represent,

> engage in activities that either continue to assign domestic responsibility to women or leave undisturbed social representations of women's "proper" role in society. These representations, though maintained through ideological forces, have a clear material foundation and are supported by an implicit coalition of men and women of upper and middle classes that permits wealthier women to share some benefits with men while extracting resources from lower-class women. (p. 111)

Feminist theory of color points to the role of the state and class in the discrimination, exploitation, and oppression of women of color and working-class women. This is an important point when, according to Diana Coole (1993, p. 179), some postmodernist feminists "have shifted attention to [the] cultural aspect with little attempt to integrate the economic aspects of sexual politics." This charge cannot be applied in toto to the different varieties of postmodernist feminism, including expressions as different as those represented in the work of Dorothy Smith (1987), Nancy Fraser (1989), and Judith Butler (1993). The paradox is how to move away from a Hegelian concept of universality and, at the same time, define the universal features of feminist struggles facing patriarchal states.

Drawing from Hegel, one of the peculiarities of the Marxist concept of class was its inherent universalism: The working class was destined to be the class to end all classes. There was little basis for the hardening of class *difference* into anything more than a recognition of different trajectories of socialization and experience. The decline of the notion of a universal class left open the question of the ultimate meaning of class differences. The partial decline of class concepts in post-Marxist theory reflects the loss of any sense of anchorage that would allow some external attribute (e.g., participation in wage labor or productive vs. unproductive labor) to define an essential category of humanity. As neo-Marxist critics point out, however, this undermines the basis for collective strategies of change and creates a theoretical vacuum in thinking of the role of the state in social reproduction from a feminist perspective. Paradoxically, the emergence of gender, ethnicity, and race as central components of the reproduction of domination has suffered a similar but quite distinctive fate. As subjects of suppressed and colonized identities, women and racial minorities clearly have a need to recognize and celebrate their inevitable differences (at least those not contaminated by domination itself).

If, at the level of social theory (and metatheory), feminist theory calls for historical specificity, the same analytical logic calls for a structural and historically specific analysis of the form of state that is considered the embodiment of patriarchy. A definition of the nature and praxis of the state as patriarchal is just the beginning of an integrative and historically informed explanation. It is imperative to analyze the historical configuration of the state as a social formation, its dominant symbolic narrative (with its contradictions), and its modes, means, and methods of patriarchal (and classist and racialist) action (Block, 1989; Gordon, 1989; Jessop, 1983; Morrow & Torres, 1994; Torres, 1990). For theoretical as well as practical reasons, we need a concrete examination of the patriarchal role of the state in capitalist societies in terms of its limits and capacities, including institutional and economic endowment, the nature of the policy process, the social history of the state apparatus, the distinction between levels of state intervention, intersections and contradictions (e.g., among federal, state, and municipal levels), and historical specificities, including location in the world system, the challenge of scale, colonial/postcolonial experiences, and the nature of race, ethnicity, gender, and religion relations.

An integrative theory of the patriarchal state and its influence in gender discrimination may be difficult to accomplish in the current conditions of social theorizing. However, specific, timely, historically informed cross-cultural and comparative studies of the interrelations between patriarchy and capitalism in modern states and how those relationships affect schooling and educational policies per se are not only feasible but crucial for political action. Gender, race, and class need to be linked in any historically informed study of gender discrimination and state practices. Limitations of middle-class feminist theorizing were evident in the early emancipation movements in the United States that failed to recognize the claims of lower class women and those of color: "The convenient omission of household workers' problems from the programs of 'middle class' feminists past and present has often turned out to be a veiled justification—at least on the part of the affluent women—of their own exploitative treatment of their maids" (Lorde, cited in Grant & Sleeter, 1986, p. 196; see also Grant & Sleeter, 1988; hooks, 1990; hooks & West, 1991; Jelin, 1990; Lengermann & Niebrugge-Brantley, 1992; Lorde, 1984; Sternbach, Navarro-Aranguren, Chuchryk, & Alvarez, 1992). Feminist theory and particularly third-wave feminism have provided insights for a thorough understanding of the praxis of new social movements and the practice of the state in the Third World and in industrial advanced societies (Jelin, 1990; Scott, 1990).

Despite their increasing historical specificity, and because of their normative and analytical orientations, critical perspectives have, by and large, focused on the nation-state as the locus of politics and education. The notion of globalization, however, has transformed the debate, raising the stakes for emancipatory politics in education.

FROM THE NATION-STATE TO GLOBALIZATION: WHITHER THE STATE AND PUBLIC EDUCATION?

> The passage from the state of nature to the civil state produces in man a very remarkable change, by substituting in his conduct justice for instinct, and by giving his actions the moral quality that they previously lacked. (Rousseau, 1976, p. 22)

Globalization has been defined as "the intensification of worldwide social relations which link distant localities in such a way that local happenings are shaped by events occurring many miles away and vice versa" (Held, 1991, p. 9). Among other things, Held suggests that globalization is the product of the emergence of a global economy, expansion of transnational linkages between economic units creating new forms of collective decision making, development of intergovernmental and quasi-supranational institutions, intensifications of transnational communications, and the creation of new regional and military orders.

The process of globalization is seen as blurring national boundaries, shifting solidarities within and between nation-states, and deeply affecting the identities of national and interest groups. Neil Smelser (1993) captures the spirit of this theme quite well:

> A convenient starting-point for depicting the world situation is to consider the status of the nation-state. Once commonly supposed to be the natural and sovereign focus of the loyalty and solidarity of its citizens, this idea of the state has recently been challenged with respect to all of these constituent elements. The international boundaries of the state have become permeable through the greater globalization of production, trade, finance, and culture with a resultant loss of control of all states over their own fortunes. The sovereignty of states has been further compromised through shifting patterns of regional political federations and alliances. At the sub-national level, the state has found itself challenged by the efflorescence and revitalization of solidarity groupings with multiple bases—regional, linguistic, religious, ethnic, gender, and life-style—as well as a bewildering array of novel social movements that generate their own solidarity. All of these compete with the state for the loyalties of peoples and sometimes for jurisdiction over territory. In a word, the contemporary state has been pressured from both above and below by contested boundaries and shifting solidarities. (p. 5)[23]

If globalization is deeply undermining the position of nation-states in the concert of the world system, with movement of labor across national boundaries through immigration, globalization is also reshaping the social milieu of societies and, as a corollary, increasing their diversity. If multiculturalism is the result, at the level of the nation-state, of the globalization of culture and society, this has immediate implications for theoretical debates and practical policies relating to the constitution of bicultural and multicultural identities, multilinguism in schools, and the new cultural demands on curriculum, teaching and learning, evaluation, and intergroup relations in schools. These policies of national solidarity were historically developed through welfare policies, including education. These public policies, in turn, were developed, mandated, supervised, and regulated by the modern state and played a major role in the welfare state.

Emile Durkheim (cited in Bardis, 1985) argued that the state was central in moving societies from mechanical into organic solidarity:

> Even when society relies most completely upon the division of labor, it does not become a jumble of juxtaposed atoms, between which it can establish only external, transient contacts. Rather the members are united by ties which extend deeper and far beyond the short moments during which the exchange is made. There is above all, an organ upon which we are tending to depend more and more; this is the state. The points at which we are in contact with it multiply as do the occasions when it is entrusted with the duty of reminding us of the sentiment of common solidarity. (pp. 271–272)

Echoing Durkheim, several political scientists like Peter Flora (Flora & Alber, 1991) have argued that the nation-state is the main source of solidarity. The nation-state as provider of solidarity in the European context goes back to the 19th century but has a predecessor: the Roman Catholic Church, which provided welfare for the needy (e.g., see von Ketteler, 1981). The transformation of solidarity by the nation-state brought about the subject of citizenship. Gunnar Myrdal, as early as 1950, argued that large-scale systems like the nation-state are national and therefore related to citizenship and to ethnicity and cultural identity (Myrdal, 1960, 1973). Thus, the main (but not by any means the only) source of solidarity in the welfare state is related to the creation of citizenship rights and the attempt to build a homogeneous society, and the nation-state appears as the framework for institutionalized solidarity. One may ask why, otherwise, should the rich be in solidarity with the poor? Why should there be solidarity between generations? Between different neighborhoods or regions within the nation-state? Between individuals of different genders and occupational categories? Or among citizens (either by birth or nationalization) vis-à-vis illegal residents?

If the constitution of the state, as Rousseau suggests, implies forcing individuals to adapt to a social and democratic pact, then what motive do individuals have for creating relations of solidarity beyond certain limits of self-interest? What interest should they have in creating the conditions for minimum levels of tolerance and social articulation through organic rather than mechanical integration? Moreover, who will be able to enforce legitimately this limited solidarity? These are important questions if one considers Rousseau's views. For Rousseau, in the end people should be forced to become democratic. When individual protest is suppressed, we are forcing the individual to be free. Rousseau (1976) argues, in *The Social Contract,* that

> it will be asked how a man can be free and yet forced to conform to wills which are not his own. How are opponents free and yet subject to laws they have not consented to? I reply that the question is wrongly put. . . . The unvarying will of all members of the State is the general will; it is through that they are citizens and free. . . . Had my private opinion prevailed, I should have done something other than I wished; and in that case I should not have been free. (p. 113; see also Chapman, 1956)

A number of situations are affecting the process of solidarity. In the Western world, there is increased competition among powers. With the erosion of U.S. hegemony in international relations in the post–Cold War era, the competition among Japan, Germany, and the United States shows not only different capitalist states competing for markets (and multinational corporations usually associated with their national origins) but also different types of capitalism and democratic states (Omal, 1990; Przeworski, 1991; Reich, 1991; Thurow, 1992).

In Eastern Europe, the collapse of an organized system of solidarity calls for the establishment of another system of solidarity, but this time one that can be regulated through the market. The question arises, on one hand, of how to do away with a welfare system that, despite its inability to preserve freedom of choice, did in fact guarantee a minimum level of housing, employment, education, and health care subsidized or provided by the state. State conversion toward market exchanges will certainly be plagued by difficulties. On the other hand, an important problem, given the cultural and historical configuration of several artificially constructed Eastern European societies, is that of establishing the bases for solidarity beyond what is mostly ethnicity and national identity. The conflict in Bosnia is a tragic yet telling example of the sharp division along ethnic lines in several Eastern European societies. Finally, the creation of the European union implies a different type of solidarity, perhaps at a metanational level, that will alter the equilibrium of the world system.

Globalization and the worldwide division of labor imply that solidarity is organized at the nation-state level but also imply that tensions and determinants generated within the process of globalization are affecting the constitution of solidarity at the level of the nation-state without having any institution replacing social welfare in the international system. Despite these issues, the process of globalization, usually associated with movement of capital and labor, may not be the new phenomenon that it seems.

If market-oriented democracies exist in many forms (Wilensky, 1994) and the process of globalization is also part of the process brought about by changes in technology, communications, and trade, what changes can, in fact, be attributed to globalization (Gourevitch, 1986)? There are different institutional varieties of nation-states, not only with regard to differences in performance but with regard to the way forces external to nation-states command power in the context of the world system (i.e., multinational corporations, bilateral and multilateral international agencies). The corporatist arrangement among management, labor, and the welfare state has also been dramatically altered. Economic performances explain shifts in trade and taxation, but we should not underestimate the importance of power, ideology, and political parties in contemporary democracies. In short, according to Wilensky, globalization underscores labor policies that have been fully in place at least since the 1960s.

Another issue is the relationship between the process of globalization and the transnationalization of identity. While it is indeed debatable whether globalization is a planetary event, new notions of social marginality cut across the duality of North-South relationships. Thus, key issues of politics of solidarity, including governance, accountability, and citizenship, enter into conflict with the historical process of centralization that has been embedded in national territories. With globalization, there is a perceived denationalization of territories defined by the growing power of transnational corporations, interventionism of foreign states, and a pervasive transnational culture through mass media, all of which seem to prevail over peripheral nation-states, domestic capital, and local, regional, or national cultures. Such a process of denationalization is exemplified well in the recent Chiapas conflict and in the struggle of the Zapatista Liberation Front to establish an Indian identity (and rights) beyond and indeed opposed to the legal commitments accepted by the Mexican state, reflected in the North American Free Trade Agreement (Marcos, 1994).

There are multiple circuits of globalization, including an upper and lower circuit of globalization in terms of capital accumulation. The lower circuit refers to international migration, transnational identities, and the struggle of women and people of color. The upper circuit refers to new technologies and the mobility of capital. There are, thus, different forms of social control and regulation present in the upper and lower circuits of globalization. A good example is currency markets "out of control" because technology involves a speed of transactions that escapes existing forms of state regulation and control. This is fascinating when technology itself is designed not only as a form of exchange but as one of control. These are, however, forms of control that are not easily handled by governments and are "reversals of fortune" in the use of technology by governments, such as the episode of former minister Ricupero in Brazil illustrates. But still, it is possible for one to question whether or not new technologies are contributing to an overriding of traditional loyalties to the nation-state and historical forms of citizenship. Globalization has implications for issues of power and legitimacy at several levels, and most certainly, in light of debates about liberal education and human emancipation, it has implications for what West (1993a, p. 32) so properly calls "the irreducibility of individuality within participatory communities," a basic premise of democratic pragmatism, American style.

Economic globalization creates a relocation of certain components of power and authority. In so doing, new forms of nonstate power, legitimation, and authority appear. These new forms are ambiguous at best but indeed affect educational policies. The examples are the International Monetary Fund, the World Bank, GATT, and other international organizations that have acquired, in the last decade or so, new roles and legitimacy. Although the ability of national elites and scientific communities to deal with regulatory institutions of capitalism like the World Bank and their educational proposals is quite limited, the legitimacy of these institutions does not go uncontested. Nevertheless, such international institutions have become especially prominent in these times of economic retrenchment and fiscal crisis in the Third World. Exemplary of how these international economic players can create nonstate forms of power is the reaction of bond markets to the industrial incentive package that the Clinton Administration tried to pass on taking office. The perception that accelerated economic activity will lead to higher inflation, which in turn will lead to higher interest rates, created worrisome expectations for conservative, long-term investors holding bonds. Since an overheated economy and inflationary pressures will lead to higher interest rates, they will induce a massive sell off of bonds, increasing the fiscal pressure of the government. Bond markets and their economic logic have set clear limits for new economic policies of a new administration in the United States that had inherited a large fiscal deficit and internal debt. Is the allegiance (and overall strategic formulation) of these new forms of nonstate authority related to specific national policies or to transnational, abstract formulas of world system integration? Such questions are, again, of the utmost importance in considering the formulation of national educational policies in the context of globalization and declining economic resources.

Returning to Popkewitz's and Apple's analyses, globalization also relates to the new role played by professional associations in setting national standards in the United States and other industrially advanced countries (Apple, 1988; Popkewitz, 1993). Is this process of social regulation through professional associations operating independently of the ideologies outlined above (e.g., neoconservatism and neoliberalism)? Is the process a specific form of building hegemony in defining occupational and educational futures, as postmodernism seems to imply?

WHY SHOULD EDUCATIONAL RESEARCHERS THINK POLITICALLY ABOUT EDUCATION? THEORETICAL AND PRACTICAL IMPLICATIONS OF THEORIES OF THE STATE AND EDUCATION

> The answer is blowing in the wind. (Bob Dylan)

> The single minded pursuit of production for profit by large and small business, and the state's unquestioned support for this objective in the name of economic growth, sets a highly limited political agenda: it creates a situation in which public affairs become concerned merely with debating different means—the end is given, that is, more and more production. Depoliticization results from the spread of "instrumental reason"; that is, the spread of the concern with the efficiency of different means with respect to pregiven ends. (Held, 1989, p. 104)

A Troubled Beginning

The state is nothing "but the *sancta simplicitas* of the human race" (Cassirer, 1946/1969, p. 4). This warning by neo-Kantian German political philosopher Ernst Cassirer appeared in the opening pages of his last book, *The Myth of the State,* posthumously published in 1946. Cassirer, witnessing the rise of the totalitarian state in Germany, viewed the emergence of the power of mythical thought undermining rational thought as the most alarming feature of the time. As a myth, the state is nothing but the product of "primeval stupidity" (Cassirer, 1946/1969, p. 4).

Whether myths or rational creations, state and education posed serious concerns for me in writing this chapter. How should the elusive state-education relationship be approached, and how could all of the nuances (historical as well as theoretical) involved be accounted for? Coming to a full circle, I shall argue, reformulating Cassirer's claim, that the state is not a myth but that educators find ways to mythologize and mystify the relationships between state and education. I could have started from Theodore R. Sizer's (1992) admonition that

> the major elements of schooling are controlled outside the teachers' world. The state, or its contractor firms, writes the tests. The state mandates when each subject is to be taught; it and the district controls that key coinage of school, the time of teachers and students. Evaluations of school and teachers, the union contract, the departmental division, all run according to traditional formulas. (p. 8)

However, rather than looking at the empirical expressions of state action in schooling or educational policies, I have chosen to look at the state from the perspective of a political philosophy of education informed as well by a political sociology of education.

Pressing Questions

What kind of heuristic construct or notion of the state is implied when educators blame the state for educational problems? What type of state do they have in mind when they think of an educational reform seeking to improve the quality of education, testing, curriculum, or instruction? How do educational theorists, researchers, and teachers perceive the interplay of power, politics, and education in the context of educational reform? These are some of the questions implicit in the preceding discussion. I am aware that I have not offered a systematic answer to each one of them, knowing very well that most of the answers need to be elaborated in contextual rather than normative ways. Answers to these questions are not exclusively political-philosophical but historical, dependent on ideological debates, shifting intellectual paradigms, the constitutions of intellectual communities, and conjunctural and structural changes occurring simultaneously at the levels of the nation-state and the global economy. I believe a thorough review of theories of the state-education relationship is helpful in laying the groundwork for addressing these questions. Below I summarize the arguments outlined throughout this chapter.

The Classics

The question of why educational researchers should think politically about education and why they should consider theories of the state can be answered in part by listening to the voices of the classics of political philosophy, for which the question of education has never been separated from the question of power. Paideia, pedagogy, and politics have always gone hand in hand. Education has always been considered—from Aristotle to Plato, to Jean-Jacques Rousseau, to John Dewey, and to Paulo Freire, to name but a few—an extension of a political project (Apple, 1983; Gadotti, in press). A failure to recognize the intersections of education and power (and, in practical terms, the role of the state) is a result of a failure to consider the relevance of theories of the state for education and, of course, to heed the classics of political philosophy.[24]

Metanarratives

Theories of the state are interwoven with any attempt to constitute a pedagogical subject, even in the most radical postmodernist expressions of the constitution of decentered subjects. Likewise, theories of the state give substance to the range of moral and ethical dimensions (and roles) attributed to education and schooling in the process of cognitive socialization and construction of cultural identities. Moreover, theories of the state (and their precepts regarding the linkages among power, state, and society) will guide the constitution of national, regional, or local educational policies of schooling, including job training programs, and the knowledge that is deemed legitimate and official.

The construction of metanarratives (with the playfulness of colorful rhetorics interplaying in the debates about dichotomous choices, with questions of emphasis, direction, and scope) is marked by political rationales of education and power explicit and implicit in theories of the state. In simpler terms, debates about dichotomous choices for educational reform include excellence versus equity, educational quality versus educational expansion, centralization versus decentralization, and market-oriented versus state-sponsored programs. Despite their apparent pragmatic or technical nature, all rest on differential (sometimes antagonistic) theories of the state and education. What is at stake here is a discussion about the only organized set of state institutions in capitalist societies: schooling and nonformal education. Dexterity and practical skills, key moral and ethical values, and official and counterhegemonical knowledge are negotiated as an integral component of the democratic political accord. Ignoring the importance of theories of the state underlying these debates is dangerous for any serious attempt to advance educational theory and practice.

Debates about theories of the state should be undertaken with serious consideration of the importance of cultural studies. The notion of growing fragmentation (cultural as well as political) of the polity will direct attention to curriculum, teaching, and learning in schools. These are also contested terrains of social regulation. The notion of autonomy, so entrenched in the discourse of liberalism, is either neglected or criticized in the neoconservative and neoliberal approaches to state and education. For these reasons, a metatheoretical framework of theories of the state and education helps to identify the normative-ethical, practical-political, and epistemological-philosophical issues involved.

Any systematic criticism of social theory resting on a metatheoretical framework will identify critical theoretical transformations in the sociology of education. Theories of the state and education are crucial for a discussion of the social and cultural reproduction theories that remain extremely relevant to any analysis of education. First, although the actual term *reproduction* has tended to slip out of sight, Morrow and Torres have recently suggested that the basic problem of social and cultural reproduction remains a central preoccupation of critical theories of the relationships among state, schooling, and society. Second, a new model, the parallelist model (i.e., social action as the product of parallel determinations stemming from class, gender, and race)—while highly sensitive to history, agency, and social practices—still involves structuralist methodological strategies. Nevertheless, the parallelist model has effectively encouraged the exploration of the independent effects of class, gender, race, and other forms of domination in the context of schooling. Third, despite the analytical progress made by the parallelist model of analysis, it has failed to address adequately three fundamental issues: (a) that each form of domination has a significantly different systemic character with crucial consequences for its conceptualization, (b) that analysis of the interplay of these "variables" has been obscured by the language of "relative autonomy" left over from structuralist Marxism, and (c) that even though the explanatory objectives of parallelist reproduction theory are necessarily more modest and historically contingent than envisioned by classic, structuralist reproduction theories, they serve to avoid the postmodernist tendency to endlessly fragment and pluralize conflicts and differences as if no systematic links exist among them.[25]

Power

I have already argued, drawing from critical traditions in the sociology of education, that a critical theory of power and the state is a necessary starting point in the study of policy-making,

> hence moving the analysis from the strict realm of individual choice and preference somehow modeled by organizational behavior, to a more historical-structural approach where individuals indeed have choices, but they are prescribed or constrained by historical circumstances, conjunctural processes, and the diverse expressions of power and authority (at the micro and macro level) through concrete rules of policy formation. (Morrow & Torres, 1995)

The relationships among power, complex organizations such as schooling, and the state should be understood from a combined perspective of the political economy and political sociology of education.

The influence of neoconservative policies extends well beyond U.S. borders and, through neoliberal policies of economic stabilization, has reached the so-called Third World. The role of international organizations, such as the World Bank, in setting the agenda for educational reform worldwide calls into question the autonomy of the nation-state and has projected neoliberalism as the standard mainstream ideology in education. However, growing struggles over the politics of education, textbooks, and teaching are molding the political discussions in nation-states regarding the role of education for democracy and, indeed, molding the dominant discourse of educational research.

Contestation from below and conflict and contradictions from above mark the life of neoconservative and neoliberal states. A prominent contradiction in the political philosophy of neoconservatism and neoliberalism is the dilemma of promoting individual autonomy while simultaneously supporting public obligations. In terms of economic rationality, a similar dilemma occurs between individualistically conceived preferences and rational social choice. These dilemmas add complexity to the nature of the state as an arena displaying interactions of domestic and international actors. The state, then, is a microcosmic condensation of power relations in society. Schools are part of these dynamics as well, subject to changes in state policies and changes in the division of labor. Educational systems and settings, however, also develop, with relative autonomy from the state and the division of labor, their own institutional and political behavior and governability.

New Departures

Nonsynchronous parallelist and relational theories, neo-Marxism, postmodernism, and feminism offer alternative views to traditional political philosophy. The state seen as a historical, multilayered, and relational concept is at the center of the production of social relationships in education. A multilayered concept of the state will consider not only the action of actors but also the deployment of strategies of power, including expert knowledge.

Capitalism, while historically specific, has become intertwined with patriarchy, and the capitalist state can be defined as a patriarchal state. According to feminist analyses, the patriarchal state encapsulates and/or does not adequately challenge conventional gender representations and specific sexist (and racist and classist) practices in education. Whether we move toward a new institutionalized form of the nation-state in the context of capitalist globalization or toward a model of interdependency in which the nation-state will be gradually muted, theories of the state continue to be decisive in understanding changes in the division of labor, society, and education.

Nuanced Historical Sense or Depoliticization

The apparent elusive relationships between theories of the state and educational reform convinced Martin Carnoy and Henry Levin (1985), in their analysis of the U.S. educational system, that learning about previous struggles for equity and democracy will guide educational reform from progressive perspectives. Their words, written a decade ago, provide inspiration for people who care about the democratic education of children, youth, and adults:

> Continuing struggle, together with the failures of existing policies to meet the larger concerns of a democracy, will increase the power of democratic coalitions for fairness, equity, and participation. Democratic struggles for just and meaningful schooling are effective counters to the economic forces that are attempting to gain primacy over American schools and the formation of our youth. A study of the past supports our optimism for the future. (Carnoy & Levin, 1985, p. 267)

In addition to the number of arguments listed above, there is another reason why educational researchers should think politically about education. If our goal is an education for political and economic democracy and community empowerment, theories of the state and education should be continually revisited, in theoretical and practical terms, and actively used in educational research. The eloquent analysis of Herbert Marcuse in the mid-1960s, criticizing the fetishism of technology and the unidimensionalization of politics in late capitalism, warned about the risk of depoliticization of educational researchers dominated by instrumental reason. To paraphrase Held, researchers obsessed with technique, productivity, and efficiency are likely to consider their work free of any political interest and independent of the state and the forces of civil society. Unfortunately, the consequences of depoliticization are not better research findings but the eventual eradication of political and moral questions from schools and public life.

NOTES

[1] I am indebted to a number of friends and colleagues who tolerated my obsessive interest in discussing the relationships between state and education, even at the price of spoiling a good meal or a pleasant conversation. Many of them, indeed, reminded me that politics is a human endeavor continually linking political and civil society. They suggested that this article should focus on the state but should also revisit theoretically the interaction between state and civil society (and the public sphere) in discussing education, power, and politics. Within the available space constraints, I have tried to incorporate this suggestion. I am grateful to María Cristina Pons, Raj Pannu, Thomas S. Popkewitz, David Wilson, Moacir and Rejane Gadotti, José Eustaquio and Nailé Romão, Benno Sanders, Walter Garcia, Paulo Freire and Ana María Freire, Marcela Mollis, Adriana Puiggrós, Michael W. Apple, Gustavo Fischman, Pilar O'Cadiz, David Victorin, David Plank, Pat McDonough, and a number of presenters at the Bielefeld Congress of Sociology and at the seminar "Pos-Neoliberalismo: As Politicas Sociais e o Estado Democrático" who helped me clarify the relationships between globalization and the nation-state. Robert Arnove and Atilio

Boron, as consulting editors, offered invaluable advice, sharing with me their conversant knowledge. Raymond A. Morrow, with whom I have spent the last decade discussing and writing about sociological theory and education, provided, as always, insightful and critical suggestions. I put finishing touches on this article in between jogs on the beaches of Guarujá and Rio de Janeiro in Brazil. It may sound trivial, but the majestic and yet frightening beauty of the Atlantic Ocean and its relentless murmuring served as a source of inspiration while I was wrestling with difficult conceptual problems and indomitable phrases. The candor and gentleness of Brazilians and Argentineans, with their many demonstrations of love and care for people, helped me to go back constantly to the Latin adagio "ad fontes." That is, we should always come back to our senses of humanity, compassion, and love, true sources of intellectual inspiration.

[2] I am thankful to Walter Feinberg for this suggestion.

[3] For a commentary on Gramsci, education, and the state, see Torres (1990, 1992). For a good discussion on the relationships among education, common sense, and hegemony, see Apple (1993b).

[4] Two of the best examples of credentialist theories are those of Ronald Dore (1976) and John Oxenham (1984). Several political economists succeeded in casting doubt on the premises of human capital theory, arguing that the contribution of education to growth is much smaller than the early human capital theorists and development economists thought. In addition, the correlation between earnings and education includes many other influences on earnings that are also correlated with schooling but should not be attributed to it (Carnoy, Lobo, Toledo, & Velloso, 1979; Carnoy, Levin, Torres, & Unsicker, 1982; Torres, Pannu, & Bacchus, 1993).

[5] Corporatist Portugal offers an invaluable illustration of a process of conservative modernization propelled from the state, with specific roles assigned to the educational system. Stoer and Dale (1987) argued that "the State became increasingly concerned in the educational domain with the ideological contribution of education to a definition of national development . . . the state embarked upon a course that led to a very high degree of centralization of power and control over teachers and to the extreme ideologisation and elitisization of schooling" (p. 405). Offe and Preuss (1991) have argued that the notion of democracy increasingly appears to be "a secularized version of the most elementary tenets of Christian theology" (p. 146).

[6] I refer here, of course, to the analyses of Marx and modernity as discussed by Marshall Berman (1982).

[7] I refer here to Habermas's three knowledge-guiding interests (for a discussion, see Morrow & Torres, 1995).

[8] The former differs from the latter on a number of issues, particularly that a few interest groups are especially able to influence the state and that "the ineffectiveness of the others is further diluted because they are underutilized" (Nordlinger, 1981, p. 157).

[9] The institutionalist approach argues that public education plays a major role in the legitimation of political systems and in the integration and modernization of countries. Compulsory schooling has been associated with different theories of Westernization, modernization, social control, and status group competition. The institutionalist approach instead argues that educational development is not the result of domestic (internal) processes arising from economic and social differentiation, especially industrialization and urbanization. Likewise, mass schooling did not develop as a deliberate attempt to establish social control (over the lower classes or immigrants) or to reorient traditional attitudes of populations. Institutionalists argue, instead, that mass schooling "is a prominent consequence of the development of the cultural

framework of the West as a whole" (Boli & Ramirez, 1992, p. 28). This Western framework implies developing the notion of the nation-state, a modern conception of citizenship that is seen as a source of compulsory mass schooling. Hence, schooling serves as a "ceremonial induction" in modern society, as "an extended initiation rite that symbolically transforms unformed children into enhanced individuals authorized to participate in the modern economy, polity, and society, and it does so by definition" (see Boli & Ramirez, 1992, p. 30).

[10] A paradigmatic analysis of this approach has been presented by Parsons (1961). To be sure, there are critics within and outside the tradition that developed positions connected with the previous work of Durkheim but in a direction very different from the Durkheimian interpretation introduced by Parsons (see Merton, 1968). Outside the functionalist tradition, the work of Basil Bernstein and Pierre Bourdieu stands out (see Bernstein, 1973, 1977; Bourdieu, 1968, 1977; Bourdieu & Passerson, 1967, 1977).

[11] Samuel Bowles and Herbert Gintis's work is exemplary of preoccupations of radical economists with educational functions in liberal societies in the 1970s (see Bowles & Gintis, 1976, 1981). For critical yet sympathetic commentaries, see Cole (1988) and Apple (1988c). It is instructive to mention, however, that a central critique of Bowles and Gintis's approach, in addition to its perceived mechanistic views of the relationships between school and societies and their economicism, is their lack of a theory of the state in their argument criticizing schooling in capitalist societies. It is this theoretical flaw in their argument that prevented them from accounting for contradictory trends toward equality and democracy in education (i.e., correspondence and contradiction as organizing principles structuring social life and schooling) (Carnoy & Levin, 1985). For a systematic analysis of reproduction theories, see Morrow and Torres (1995).

[12] Notably, this otherwise commendable analysis of race and class relations in education makes no mention of the state, theories of the state in education, or the contradictions of public policy formation in the context of debates on multiculturalism in the United States. Typically, these omissions reflect both an epistemological perspective still influenced by positivism and multivariable analysis and a political perspective focusing on clearly defined educational boundaries for educational research, without the "contamination" of political philosophies and structuralist or poststructuralist analysis of public policies.

[13] In Latin America, and perhaps in other areas of the world, García Canclini (1993) defines the neoconservative models as a contradictory process of selective modernization and regressive cultural and social decadence.

[14] Clark, Lipset, and Rempel (1993) argue that, in addition to the rise of the welfare state, what accounts for the declining political significance of class is the diversification of the occupational structure, rising affluence, changing political party dynamics, the rise of dual labor markets, and the rise of other institutions of aggregation of interests beyond class.

[15] I am grateful to Joel Samoff for bringing this to my attention.

[16] This claim has verisimilitude in terms of the legal foundations and historical experience of the nation-state. The experience of "people" within the boundaries of the nation-state is altogether a different matter. Consider, for instance, the exploitation of labor through the slavery of Blacks, the treatment of Latinos and women, and so forth.

[17] The terms *Third World, Third World states, Southern countries,* and *countries of the South* are used interchangeably.

[18] There are variations in the implementation of these models of economic liberalization and structural adjustment. Some countries benefit from their economic endow-

ments or aggressive policies and successful performance of their export commodities (e.g., Chile), others benefit from specific free trade deals within larger regional markets (e.g., Mexico), and still others, such as Argentina's capital markets, benefit from the political instability of Eastern Europe.

[19] Up to this point, I have constructed my discussion of the liberal, neoconservative, or neoliberal state in empirically grounded and informed experience, linking that to political philosophical theories. The following discussions of parallelist theories, postmodernism, and feminism are largely theoretically derived. Because of space limitations, I will not discuss transitional states (e.g., transitions from capitalism to socialism or from socialist experiences to capitalism) and socialist state experiences per se.

[20] The model includes special industrial arrangements (i.e., "special relationships") between buyers and supplier companies, with a specific role played by the Ministry of International Trade and Industry (Hirst & Zeitlin, 1991; Jessop, 1988; Oliver & Wilkinson, 1988).

[21] There is a debate in neo-Marxism political economy regarding the ability of the state to rule because of the process of globalization and internationalization of capitalism (see Pooley, 1991). In his article, Pooley argues with Poulantzas on the intersection of transnational capital and nation-states. There is, however, an important contradiction. While, in the logic of internationalized capital, nation-states are the potential basis for international economic regulation, the location of international capital within nation-states makes them still subject to popular politics. In other words, while there is an interpenetration of nation-state and international capital, this alliance is affected by domestic (and popular) politics. This eventually may produce rivalry and collusion between nation-states and transnational corporations (see Pitelis, 1991).

[22] In this section, I borrow from my work with Raymond Morrow (1995).

[23] This is well documented in the sociological literature. The XII World Congress of Sociology, held in Bielefeld, Germany (in July 1994), had as its central theme "Contested Boundaries and Shifting Solidarities" (see Smelser, 1993).

[24] I am aware that "the classics" of political philosophy reflect, by and large, male, European, and heterosexual views and therefore cannot be made uncritically a cultural canon of any sort; however, I will contend that, properly deconstructed and analyzed with a nuanced historical sense, they continue to be an invaluable source for thinking and praxis.

[25] A more detailed explanation of this argument can be found in Morrow and Torres (1994).

REFERENCES

Adler, M. (1982). *The Paideia proposal.* New York: Macmillan.

Almond, G., & Verba, S. (1963). *The civic culture.* Princeton, NJ: Princeton University Press.

Althusser, L. (1971). *Lenin and philosophy and other essays.* New York: Monthly Review Press.

Apple, M. W. (1982). Curricular form and the logic of technical control: Building the possessive individual. In M. W. Apple (Ed.), *Cultural and economic reproduction in education: Essays on class, ideology, and the state* (pp. 247–274). London: Routledge & Kegan Paul.

Apple, M. W. (1983). *Education and power.* New York: Routledge.

Apple, M. W. (1986). Curriculum, capitalism, and democracy: A response to Whitty's critics. *British Journal of Sociology of Education, 7,* 320–321.

Apple, M. W. (1988a). Facing the complexity of power: For a parallelist position in critical educational studies. In M. Cole (Ed.), *Bowles and Gintis revisited: Correspondence and contradiction in educational theory* (pp. 112–130). London: Falmer Press.

Apple, M. W. (1988b). *Teachers and texts: A political economy of class and gender relations in education.* New York: Routledge.

Apple, M. W. (1988c). Standing on the shoulders of giants: Class formation and capitalist schools. *History of Education Quarterly, 28,* 231–241.

Apple, M. W. (1989). The politics of common sense. In H. Giroux & P. McLaren (Eds.), *Critical pedagogy, the state, and cultural struggle* (pp. 32–49). Albany: State University of New York Press.

Apple, M. W. (1989). Why the right is winning: Education and the politics of common-sense. *Strategies, 2,* 24–44.

Apple, M. W. (1992). Education, culture and class power: Basil Bernstein and the neo-Marxist sociology of education. *Educational Theory, 42,* 127–145.

Apple, M. (1993a). Constructing the other: Rightist reconstructions of common sense. In C. McCarthy & W. Crichlow (Eds.), *Race, identity and representation in education* (pp. 24–39). New York: Routledge.

Apple, M. W. (1993b). *What post-modernists forget: Cultural capital and official knowledge.*

Apple, M. W. (1993c). *Official knowledge: Democratic education in a conservative age.* New York: Routledge.

Apple, M. W., & Weis, L. (1986). Seeing education relationally: The stratification of culture and people in the sociology of school knowledge. *Journal of Education, 168,* 7–33.

Arnot, M. (1994). Male hegemony, social class, and women's education. In L. Stone (Ed.), *The education feminism reader* (pp. 84–104). New York: Routledge.

Arnove, R. F., Altbach, P. G., & Kelly, G. P. (Eds.). *Emergent issues in education: Comparative perspectives.* Albany: State University of New York Press.

Ball, S. J. (1993). Educational markets, choice and social class: The market as a class strategy. *British Journal of Sociology of Education, 14,* 3–19.

Ball, T. (1992). New faces of power. In T. E. Warteberg (Ed.), *Rethinking power* (pp. 14–31). Albany: State University of New York Press.

Banks, J. A. (1989). Multicultural education: Characteristics and goals. In J. A. Banks & C. A. McGee Banks (Eds.), *Multicultural education: Issues and perspectives* (pp. 3–28). Boston: Allyn & Bacon.

Banks, J. A. (1993). Multicultural education: Historical development, dimensions, and practice. In L. Darling-Hammond (Ed.), *Review of research in education* (Vol. 19, pp. 3–49). Washington, DC: American Educational Research Association.

Bardis, P. D. (1985). *Dictionary of quotations in sociology.* Westport, CT: Greenwood Press.

Bashevkin, S. (1994). Confronting neo-conservatism: Anglo-American women's movements under Thatcher, Reagan and Mulroney. *International Political Science Review, 15,* 275–296.

Bendix, R. (1962). *Max Weber: An intellectual portrait.* New York: Doubleday/Anchor Books.

Berman, M. (1982). *All that is solid melts into air: The experience of modernity.* New York: Simon & Schuster.

Bernstein, B. (1973). *Class codes and control. Vol. 1: Theoretical studies towards a sociology of language.* London: Paladin.

Bernstein B. (1977). *Class, codes and control: Towards a theory of educational transmission* (2nd ed., Vol. 3). Boston: Routledge & Kegan Paul.

Bitar, S. (1988). Neo-conservatism versus neo-structuralism in Latin America. *CEPAL Review, 34,* 45–62.

Block, F. (1989). *Revising state theory: Essays in politics and postindustrialism.* Philadelphia: Temple University Press.

Bobbio, N., & Matteucci, N. (Eds.). (1981). *Dicionario de Política* [Dictionary of politics]. Mexico City: Siglo XXI.

Boli, J., & Ramirez, F. O. (1992). Compulsory schooling in the Western cultural context. In R. Arnove, P. G. Altbach, & G. P. Kelly (Eds.), *Emergent issues in education: Comparative perspectives* (pp. 25–38). Albany: State University of New York Press.

Boron, A. A. (1981). La crisis Norteamericana y la racionalidad neo-conservadora [The U.S. crisis and neoconservative rationality]. *CIDE Cuadernos Semestrales, 9,* 31–58.

Boron, A. A. (1990/1991). Estadolatria y teorías "estadocéntricas": notas sobre algunos análisis del estado en el capitalismo contemporáneo. *El Cielo por Asalto, 1,* 97–124.

Boron, A. A. (1994). *The capitalist state and its relative autonomy: Arguments regarding limits and dimensions.* Unpublished manuscript.

Boron, A. A. (1995). *The state, capitalism and democracy in Latin America.* Boulder, CO: Lynne Rienner.

Boudon, R., & Bourricaud, F. (1989). *A critical dictionary of sociology.* London: Routledge.

Bourdieu, P. (1968). Structuralism and theory of sociological knowledge. *Social Research, 35,* 681–706.

Bourdieu, P. (1977). *Outline of a theory of practice* (R. Nice, Trans.). Cambridge, England: Cambridge University Press.

Bourdieu, P., & Passerson, J. (1967). Sociology and philosophy in France since 1945: Death and resurrection of a philosophy without a subject. *Social Research, 34,* 162–212.

Bourdieu, P., & Passerson, J. (1977). *Reproduction in education, society, and culture* (R. Nice, Trans.). Beverly Hills, CA: Sage.

Bowles, S., & Gintis, H. (1976). *Schooling in capitalist America: Educational reform and the contradictions of economic life.* New York: Basic Books/Harper.

Bowles, S., & Gintis, H. (1981). Education as a site of contradictions in the reproduction of the capital-labor relationship: Second thoughts on the "correspondence principle." *Economic and Industrial Democracy, 2,* 223–242.

Bowles, S., & Gintis, H. (1986). *Democracy and capitalism.* New York: Basic Books.

Braverman, H. (1974). *Labor and monopoly capital.* New York: Monthly Review Press.

Butler, J. P. (1993). *Bodies that matter: On the discursive limits of sex.* New York: Routledge.

Carnoy, M. (1977). *Education and employment: A critical appraisal.* Paris: International Institute for Educational Planning.

Carnoy, M. (1984). *The state and political theory.* Princeton, NJ: Princeton University Press.

Carnoy, M. (1992). Education and the state: From Adam Smith to perestroika. In R. F. Arnove, P. G. Altbach, & G. P. Kelly (Eds.), *Emergent issues in education: Comparative perspectives* (pp. 143–159). Albany, NY: State University of New York Press.

Carnoy, M., & Levin, H. (1985). *Schooling and work in the democratic state.* Stanford, CA: Stanford University Press.

Carnoy, M., Levin, H., Sumra, S., Nuget, R., Unsicker, J., & Torres, C. A. (1982). *The political economy of financing education in developing countries.* Ottawa, Ontario, Canada: International Development Research Centre.

Carnoy, M., Lobo, T., Toledo, A., & Velloso, T. (1979). *Can educational policy equalize income distribution in Latin America?* London: Saxon House.

Carnoy, M., & Samoff, J. (Eds.). (1990). *Education and social transition in the Third World.* Princeton, NJ: Princeton University Press.

Carnoy, M., & Torres, C. A. (1994). Educational change and structural adjustment: A case study in Costa Rica. In J. Samoff (Ed.), *Coping with crisis: Austerity, adjustment, and human resources.* Paris: ILO-UNESCO Task Force on Austerity, Adjustment, and Human Resources.

Cassirer, E. (1969). *The myth of the state.* New Haven, CT: Yale University Press. (Original work published 1946).

Cerroni, U. (1992). *Política: Método, teorías, procesos, sujetos, instituciones y categorías* [Politics: method, theories, processes, subjects, institutions, and categories]. Mexico City: Siglo XXI.

Chapman, W. (1956). *Rousseau, totalitarian or liberal?* New York: Columbia University Press.

Chirot, D. (1977). *Social change in the twentieth century.* New York: Harcourt Brace Jovanovich.

Chubb, J. E., & Moe, T. M. (1990). *Politics, markets, and America's schools.* Washington, DC: Brookings Institution.

Chubb, J. E., & Moe, T. M. (1993). The forest and the trees: A response to our critics. In E. Rasell & R. Rothstein (Eds.), *School choice: Examining the evidence* (pp. 219–239). Washington, DC: Economic Policy Institute.

Clark, T. N., Lipset, S. M., & Rempel, M. (1993). The declining political importance of social class. *International Sociology, 3,* 293–316.

Clarke, S. (1990). New utopias for old: Fordist dreams and post-Fordist fantasies. *Capital and Class, 42,* 131–155.

Cole, M. (Ed.). (1988). *Bowles and Gintis revisited: Correspondence and contradiction in educational theory.* London: Falmer Press.

Collier, D. (Ed.). (1979). *The new authoritarianism in Latin America.* Princeton, NJ: Princeton University Press.

Connell, R. W. (1983). *Which way is up? Essays on sex, class and culture.* Boston: George Allen & Unwin.

Connell, R. W. (1987). *Gender and power: Society, the person and sexual politics.* Stanford, CA: Stanford University Press.

Coole, D. (1993). *Women in political theory: From ancient misogyny to contemporary feminism.* Bolder, CO: Lynne Rienner.

Coser, L., & Howe, I. (Eds.). (1977). *The new conservatives: A critique from the left.* New York: New American Library.

Culpitt, I. (1992). *Welfare and citizenship: Beyond the crisis of the welfare state?* Newbury Park, CA: Sage.

Dahrendorf, R. (1975). *The new liberty: Survival and justice in a changing world.* Stanford, CA: Stanford University Press.

Dale, R. (1989). *The state and education policy.* Philadelphia: Open University Press.

Darder, A. (1991). *Culture and power in the classroom: A critical foundation for bicultural education.* Westport, CT: Bergin & Garvey.

Darling-Hammond, L. (1993). Introduction. In L. Darling-Hammond (Ed.), *Review of research in education* (Vol. 19, pp. xi–xxiii). Washington, DC: American Educational Research Association.

Dore, R. (1976). *The diploma disease: Education, qualification and development.* Berkeley: University of California Press.

Easton, D. (1981, August). The political system besieged by the state. *Political Theory,* pp. 303–325.

Eisenstein, Z. R. (Ed.). (1979). *Capitalist patriarchy and the case for socialist feminism.* New York: Monthly Review Press.

Evans, M. (1991). The classical economists, laissez-faire and the state. In M. Moran & M. Wright (Eds.), *The market and the state: Studies in interdependence* (pp. 1–23). New York: St. Martin's Press.

Fagerlind, I., & Saha, L. (1983). *Education and national development: A comparative perspective.* Oxford, England: Pergamon Press.

Featherstone, M. (1991). *Consumer culture and postmodernism.* Newbury Park, CA: Sage.

Flora, P., & Alber, J. (1991). Modernization, democratization and the development of welfare states in Western Europe. In P. Flora & A. J. Heidenheimer (Eds.), *The development of welfare states in Europa and America.* New Brunswick, NJ: Transaction Books.

Fraser, N. (1989). *Unruly practices: Power, discourse, and gender in contemporary social theory.* Minneapolis: University of Minnesota Press.

Fraser, N. (1994). Rethinking the public sphere: A contribution to the critique of actually existing democracy. In H. Giroux & P. McLaren (Eds.), *Between borders: Pedagogy and the politics of cultural studies* (pp. 74–98). New York: Routledge.

Freire, P. (1994). *Cartas a Cristina* [Letters to Cristina]. São Paulo: Paz e Terra.

Fuller, B. (1991). *The Western state builds Third-World schools.* New York: Routledge.

Gadotti, M. (in press). *Pedagogy of praxis.* Albany: State University of New York Press.

García Canclini, N. (1993, October–December). Una modernización que atrasa. La cultura bajo la regresión neoconservadora [Modernity that goes backwards: The culture under conservative regression]. *Revista de Casa las Américas,* pp. 3–12.

Giddens, A. (1991). *Modernity and self-identity: Self and society in the late modern age.* Stanford, CA: Stanford University Press.

Giroux, H. A. (1988). *Schooling and the struggle for public life: Critical pedagogy in the modern age.* Minneapolis: University of Minnesota Press.

Giroux, H., & McLaren, P. (Eds.). (1994). *Between borders: Pedagogy and the politics of cultural studies.* New York: Routledge.

Gordon, L. (1989). Beyond relative autonomy theories of the state in education. *British Journal of Sociology of Education, 10,* 435–449.

Gourevitch, P. A. (1986). *Politics in hard times: Comparative responses in international economic crisis.* Ithaca, NY: Cornell University Press.

Gramsci, A. (1980). *Selections from the prison notebooks of Antonio Gramsci* (Q. Hoare & G. N. Smith, Eds. and Trans.) New York: International Publishers.

Grant, C. A., & Sleeter, C. E. (1986). Race, class and gender in education research: An argument for integrative analysis. *Review of Educational Research, 56,* 195–211.

Grant, C., & Sleeter, C. E. (1988). Race, class, and gender and abandoned dreams. *Teachers College Record, 90,* 19–40.

Habermas, J. (1985). Psychic thermidor and the rebirth of rebellious subjectivity. In R. J. Bernstein (Ed.), *Habermas and modernity* (pp. 67–77). Cambridge, MA: MIT Press.

Habermas, J. (1989a). *The new conservatism* (S. W. Nicholsen, Ed. and Trans.). Cambridge, MA: MIT Press.

Habermas, J. (1989b). *The structural transformation of the public sphere: An inquiry into a category of bourgeois society* (T. Burger & F. Lawrence, Trans.). Cambridge, MA: MIT Press.

Habermas, J. (1990). Modernity versus postmodernity. In J. C. Alexander & S. Seidman (Eds.), *Culture and society: Contemporary debates* (pp. 342–354). Cambridge, England: Cambridge University Press.

Hage, G., Hage, J., & Fuller, B. (1988). The active state, investment in human capital, and economic growth: France 1825–1975. *American Sociological Review, 53,* 824–837.

Hall, J. A., & Ikenberry, G. J. (1989). *The state.* Milton Keynes, England: Open University Press.

Hanushek, E. A. (1986). The economics of schooling: Production and efficiency in the public schools. *Journal of Economic Literature, 24,* 1141–1178.

Haraway, D. (1984). A manifesto for cyborgs: Science, technology, and socialist feminism in the 1980s. In E. Weed (Ed.), *Coming to terms: Feminism, theory, politics* (pp. 130–143). New York: Routledge.

Hartmann, H., & Sargent, L. (Eds.). (1981). *The unhappy marriage of Marxism and feminism: A debate on class and patriarchy.* London: Pluto Press.

Harvey, D. (1989). *The condition of postmodernity.* Oxford, England: Basil Blackwell.

Hegel, G. W. F. (1857). *Lectures on the philosophy of history* (J. B. Baillie, Trans.). London: Henry G. Bohn.

Held, D. (Ed.). (1983). *States and societies.* Oxford, England: Martin Robertson.

Held, D. (1989). *Political theory and the modern state.* Stanford, CA: Stanford University Press.

Held, D. (Ed.). (1991). *Political theory today.* Stanford, CA: Stanford University Press.

Hirst, P., & Zeitlin, J. (1991). Flexible specialization versus post-Fordism. *Economy and Society, 20.*

hooks, b. (1990). *Yearning: Race, gender, and cultural politics.* Boston: South End Press.

hooks, b., & West, C. (1991). *Breaking bread: Insurgent Black intellectual life.* Toronto: Between the Lines.

Hulme, P. (1986). *Colonial encounters: Europe and the native Caribbean, 1492–1797.* London: Methuen.

Jelin, E. (1990). Citizenship and identity: Final reflections. In E. Jelin (Ed.), *Women and social change in Latin America* (J. A. Zammit & M. Thomson, Trans., pp. 184–207). London: Zed Books.

Jencks, C., Smith, M., Adaud, H., Bane, M., Cohen, D., Gintis, H., Heyns, B., & Michelson, S. (1972). *Inequality: A reassessment of the effect of family and schooling in America.* New York: Basic Books.

Jessop, B. (1983). Accumulation strategies, state forms, and hegemonic projects. *Kapitalistate, 10/11,* 89–111.

Jessop, B. (1988). Regulation theory, post-Fordism, and the state. *Capital and Class, 34,* 147–168.

Johnson, T. (1993). Expertise and the state. In M. Gane & T. Johnson (Eds.), *Foucault's new domains* (pp. 139–152). London: Routledge.

Karabel, J., & Halsey, A. H. (Eds.). (1977). *Power and ideology in education.* New York: Oxford University Press.

La Belle, T. J., & Ward, C. R. (1994). *Multiculturalism and education: Diversity and its impact on schools and society.* Albany: State University of New York Press.

Lengermann, P. M., & Niebrugge-Brantley, J. (1992). Contemporary feminist theory. In G. Ritzer (Ed.), *Contemporary sociological theory* (3rd ed., pp. 308–357). New York: McGraw-Hill.

Lomnitz, L., & Melnick, A. (1991). *Chile's middle class: A struggle for survival in the face of neoliberalism.* Boulder, CO: Lynne Rienner.

Lorde, A. (1984). *Sister outsider.* Trumansburg, NY: Crossing Press.

MacIntyre, A. (1988). *Whose justice? Which rationality?* London: Duckworth.

Manacorda, M. A. (1977). *El principio educativo en Gramsci: Americanismo y conformismo* (L. Legaz, Trans.). Salamanca, Spain: Ediciones Sígueme.

Marcos. (1994). Marcos: ¿De qué nos van a perdonar? [Marcos: For what are they going to forgive us?]. *Proceso,* 1, 13.

Marshall, T. H. (1950). *Citizenship and social class and other essays.* Cambridge, England: Cambridge University Press.

Marshall, T. H. (1983). Citizenship and social class. In D. Held (Ed.), *States and societies* (pp. 248–260). Oxford, England: Martin Robertson.

Marx, K. (1973). *Grundisse.* New York: Vintage Books.

McCarthy, C., & Apple, M. W. (1988). Race, class and gender in American educational research: Toward a nonsynchronous parallelist position. In L. Weiss (Ed.), *Class, race and gender in American education* (pp. 9–39). Albany: State University of New York Press.

McCarthy, C., & Chrichlow, W. (Eds.). (1993a). *Race, identity and representation in education.* New York: Routledge.

McCarthy, C., & Crichlow, W. (1993b). Theories of identity, theories of representation, theories of race. In C. McCarthy & W. Crichlow (Eds.), *Race, identity and representation in education* (pp. xiii–xxix). New York: Routledge.

McLaren, P. L. (1991). Schooling the postmodern body: Critical pedagogy and the politics of enfleshment. In H. A. Giroux (Ed.), *Postmodernism, feminism, and cultural politics: Redrawing educational boundaries* (pp. 144–173). Albany: State University of New York Press.

McLaren, P. (1994). Critical pedagogy, political agency, and the pragmatics of justice: The case of Lyotard. *Educational Theory, 44,* 319–340.

McNeil, L. M. (1988). *Contradictions of control: School structure and school knowledge.* New York: Routledge.

Merton, R. (1968). *Social theory and social structure.* New York: Free Press.

Meyer, J. (1977). The effects of education as an institution. *American Journal of Sociology, 83,* 55–77.

Miliband, R. (1969). *The state in capitalist society.* New York: Basic Books.

Moran, M., & Wright, M. (1991). *The market and the state: Studies in interdependence.* New York: St. Martin's Press.

Morrow, R. A., & Torres, C. A. (1994). Education and the reproduction of class, gender and race: Responding to the postmodernist challenge. *Educational Theory, 44,* 43–61.

Morrow, R. A., & Torres, C. A. (1995). *Social theory and education: A critique of theories of social and cultural reproduction.* Albany: State University of New York Press.

Myrdal, G. (1960). *Beyond the welfare state: Economic planning and its international implications.* New Haven, CT: Yale University Press.

Myrdal, G. (1973). *Against the stream: Critical essays on economics.* New York: Pantheon Books.

National Commission on Excellence in Education. (1983, April 27). A nation at risk: An imperative for educational reform. *Education Week,* pp. 12–16.

Nordlinger, E. A. (1981). *On the autonomy of the democratic state.* Cambridge, MA: Harvard University Press.

Oakes, J. (1985). *Keeping track. How schools structure inequality.* New Haven, CT: Yale University Press.

O'Donnell, G., Schmitter, P. C., & Whitehead, L. (Eds.). (1986). *Transitions from authoritarian rules: Comparative perspectives.* Baltimore: Johns Hopkins University Press.

Offe, C. (1973). The capitalist state and the problem of policy formation. In L. N. Lindberg, R. Alford, C. Crouch, & C. Offe (Eds.), *Stress and contradiction in modern capitalism* (pp. 125–144). Lexington, MA: Heath.

Offe, C. (1984). *Contradictions of the welfare state.* London: Hutchinson.

Offe, C. (1985). *Disorganized capitalism. Contemporary transformation of work and politics.* Cambridge, MA: Polity Press.

Offe, C., & Preuss, U. K. (1991). Democratic institutions and moral resources. In D. Held (Ed.), *Political theory today* (pp. 143–171). Stanford, CA: Stanford University Press.

Oliver, N., & Wilkinson, B. (1988). *The Japanisation of British industry.* London: Basil Blackwell.

Omae, K. (1990). *The borderless world: Power and strategy in the interlinked world economy.* New York: Harper Business.

Oxenham, J. (Ed.). (1984). *Education versus qualifications? A study of relationships between education, selection for employment, and the productivity of labour.* London: George Allen & Unwin.

Parsons, T. (1961). The school as a social system: Some of its functions in American society. In A. H. Halsey (Ed.), *Education, economy and societey: A reader in the sociology of education* (pp. 434–455). New York: Free Press.

Peters, M. (in press). Introduction. In M. Peters (Ed.), *Lyotard education and the postmodern condition.* Westport, CT: Bergin & Garvey.

Picciotto, S. (1991). The internationalisation of the state. *Capital and Class, 43,* 43–63.

Piore, M., & Sabel, C. (1984). *The second industrial divide.* New York: Basic Books.

Pitelis, C. (1991). Beyond the nation-state?: The transnational firm and the nation-state. *Capital and Class, 43,* 131–152.

Plato. (1941). *Republic* (F. M. Cornford, Trans.). Oxford, England: Clarendon Press.

Pooley, S. (1991). The state rules, OK? The continuing political economy of nation-states. *Capital and Class, 43,* 65–82.

Popkewitz, T. S. (1987). Knowledge and interest in curriculum studies. In T. S. Popkewitz (Ed.), *Critical studies in teacher education: Its folklore, theory and practice* (pp. 335–354). London: Falmer Press.

Popkewitz, T. S. (1991). *A political sociology of educational reform: Power/knowledge in teaching, teachers' education, and research.* New York: Teachers College, Columbia University.

Popkewitz, T. S. (Ed.). (1993). *Changing patterns of power, social regulation and teacher education reform.* Albany: State University of New York Press.

Popkewitz, T. S. (1994a). *Decentralization, centralization and discourses in changing power relationships: The state, civil society, and the educational arena.* Mimeographed document.

Popkewitz, T. S. (1994b). *Systems of ideas in historical spaces: Vigotsky, educational constructivism and changing patterns in the regulation of the self.* Mimeographed document.

Popkewitz, T. S., & Pereyra, M. A. (1993). An eight country study of reform practices in teacher education: An outline of the problematic. In T. S. Popkewitz (Ed.),

Changing patterns of power: Social regulation and teacher education reform. Albany: State University of New York Press.

Poulantzas, N. (1980). *State, power, socialism.* London: New Left Books.

Przeworski, A. (1991). *Democracy and the market: Political and economic reforms in Eastern Europe and Latin America.* New York: Cambridge University Press.

Psacharopoulos, G. (1988). Critical issues in education and development: A world agenda. *International Journal of Educational Development, 8,* 1–7.

Puiggrós, A. (1990). *Sujetos, disciplina y curriculum en los orígenes del sistema educativo argentino* [Subjects, discipline, and curriculum in the origins of the educational system in Argentina]. Buenos Aires: Galerna.

Reich, R. B. (1991). *The work of nations.* New York: Vintage Books.

Rousseau, J. J. (1976). *The social contract and discourse on the origin of inequality.* New York: Pocket Books.

Ruccio, D., Resnick, S., & Wolff, R. (1991). Class beyond the nation-state. *Capital and Class, 43,* 25–42.

Russell, D. G. (1989). *Planning education for development.* Cambridge, MA: Harvard University Press.

Safran, W. (1994). Non-separatist politics regarding ethnic minorities: Positive approaches and ambiguous consequences. *International Political Science Review, 15,* 61–80.

Samoff, J. (1990). *More, less, none? Human resource development: Responses to economic constraint.* Mimeographed document.

Samoff, J. (1992, July). *The financial intellectual complex.* Paper presented at the World Congress of Political Science, Buenos Aires, Argentina.

Samoff, J. (1993). The reconstruction of schooling in Africa. *Comparative Education Review, 37,* 181–222.

Schugurensky, D. (1994). *Global economic restructuring and university change: The case of Universidad de Buenos Aires.* Unpublished doctoral dissertation, University of Alberta, Edmonton, Alberta, Canada.

Scott, A. (1990). *Ideology and the new social movements.* London: Unwin Hyman.

Selowsky, M. (1980). Preschool age investment in human capital. In J. Simmons (Ed.), *The educational dilemma* (pp. 97–111). London: Pergamon Press.

Sizer, T. R. (1992). *Horace's school: Redesigning the American high school.* Boston: Houghton Mifflin.

Skocpol, T. (1979). *States and social revolutions: A comparative analysis of France, Russia and China.* Cambridge, England: Cambridge University Press.

Smelser, N. (1993). *International Sociological Association Bulletin, 60,* 5.

Smith, D. E. (1987). *The everyday world as problematic: A feminist sociology.* Boston: Northeastern University Press.

Sonntag, H. R., & Valecillos, H. (1977). *El estado en el capitalismo contemporáneo* [The state in contemporary capitalism]. Mexico City: Siglo XXI.

Stepan, A. C. (1988). *Rethinking military politics: Brazil and the Southern Cone.* Princeton, NJ: Princeton University Press.

Sternbach, N. S., Navarro-Aranguren, M., Chuchryk, P., & Alvarez, S. (1992). Feminisms in Latin America: From Bogotá to San Bernardo. *Signs: Journal of Women in Culture and Society, 17,* 393–433.

Stockman, D. A. (1986). *The triumph of politics: Why the Reagan revolution failed.* New York: Harper & Row.

Stoer, S. R., & Dale, R. (1987). Education, state, and society in Portugal, 1926–1981. *Comparative Education Review, 31,* 400–418.

Stromquist, N. (1991). Educating women: The political economy of patriarchal states. *International Studies in Sociology of Education, 1,* 111–128.
Sucessão: Crise parabólica. (1994, September 7). *Journal ISTOE,* p. 21.
Sujstorf, E., Wells, A. S., & Crain, R. L. (1993). A final word on Chubb and Moe. In E. Rasell & R. Rothstein (Eds.), *School choice: Examining the evidence* (pp. 245–246). Washington, DC: Economic Policy Institute.
Therborn, G. (1980). *What does the ruling class do when it rules?* London: Verso.
Therborn, G. (1989). Los retos del Estado de Bienestar: la contrarrevolución que fracasa, las causas de su enfermedad y la economía política de las presiones del cambio [The challenge of the welfare state: The failure of the counterrevolution, the causes of the illness, and the pressures of the political economy of change]. In R. Muñoz de Bustillo (Ed.), *Crisis y futuro del estado de bienestar* (pp. 81–99). Madrid: Alianza Universidad.
Thurow, L. (1992). *Head to head: The coming economic battle among Japan, Europe, and America.* New York: William Morrow.
Tomaney, I. (1990). The reality of workplace flexibility. *Capital and Class, 40,* 29–60.
Torres, C. A. (1985). State and education: Marxist theories. In T. Husén & T. N. Postlethwaite (Eds.), *International encyclopedia of education: Research and studies* (Vol. 8, pp. 4793–4798). Oxford, England: Pergamon Press.
Torres, C. A. (1986). Nation at risk: La educación neoconservadora. *Nueva Sociedad, 84,* 108–115.
Torres, C. A. (1989). The capitalist state and public policy formation: A framework for a political sociology of educational policy-making. *British Journal of Sociology of Education, 10,* 81–102.
Torres, C. A. (1990). *The politics of nonformal education in Latin America.* New York: Praeger.
Torres, C. A. (1991). State corporatism, education policies, and students' and teachers' movements in Mexico. In M. Ginsburg (Ed.), *Understanding reform in global context: Economy, ideology, and the state* (pp. 115–150). New York: Garland.
Torres, C. A. (1992). *The church, society, and hegemony: A critical sociology of religion in Latin America* (R. A. Young, Trans.). Westport, CT: Praeger.
Torres, C. A. (in press). Adult education and instrumental rationality: A critique. *International Journal of Educational Development.*
Torres, C. A., Pannu, R. S., & Bacchus, M. K. (1993). Capital accumulation, political legitimation and education expansion. *International Perspectives on Education and Society, 3,* 3–32.
Torres, C. A., & Puiggrós, A. (1995). The state and public education in Latin America. *Comparative Education Review, 39,* 1–27.
Vincent, A. (1987). *Theories of the state.* Oxford, England: Basil Blackwell.
von Hayek, F. A. (1960). *The constitution of liberty.* Chicago: University of Chicago Press.
von Ketteler, W. E. (1981). *The social teachings of Wilhelm Emmanuel von Ketteler: Bishop of Mains (1811–1877)* (R. J. Ederer, Trans.). Washington, DC: University Press of America.
Wallerstein, I. (1979). *The capitalist world economy.* Cambridge, England: Cambridge University Press.
Wallerstein, I. (1991). The national and the universal: Can there be such a thing as world culture? In A. D. King (Ed.), *Culture, globalization and the world-system* (pp. 91–106). Binghamton: State University of New York at Binghamton.
Weber, M. (1945). *From Max Weber.* London: Routledge & Kegan Paul.

Weber, M. (1964). The fundamental concepts of sociology. In T. Parsons (Ed.), *The theory of social and economic organizations* (pp. 421–423). New York: Free Press.
Weber, M. (1968). *Economy and society.* New York: Bedminster Press.
Weiler, H. N. (1983). Legalization, expertise and participation: Strategies of compensatory legitimation in educational policy. *Comparative Education Review, 27,* 259–277.
Weinstein, W. L. (1971). The private and the public: A conceptual inquiry. In J. R. Pennock & J. W. Chapman (Eds.), *Privacy* (pp. 32–35). New York: Atherton.
Wells, A. S. (1993). The sociology of school choice: Why some win and others lose in the educational marketplace. In E. Rasell & R. Rothstein (Eds.), *School choice: Examining the evidence* (pp. 47–48). Washington, DC: Economic Policy Institute.
West, C. (1988). Marxist theory and the specificity of Afro-American oppression. In L. Grossberg & C. Nelson (Eds.), *Marxism and the interpretation of culture* (pp. 17–29). Urbana: University of Illinois Press.
West, C. (1992). The postmodern crisis of the Black intellectuals. In L. Grossberg, C. Nelson, & P. Treichler (Eds.), *Cultural studies* (pp. 689–705). New York: Routledge.
West, C. (1993a). *Prophetic thought in postmodern times.* Monroe, ME: Common Courage Press.
West, C. (1993b). *Race matters.* Boston: Beacon Press.
Wilensky, H. L. (1975). *The welfare state and equality. Structural and ideological roots of public expenditures.* Berkeley: University of California Press.
Wilensky, H. L. (1976). *The new corporatism: Centralization and the welfare state.* Beverly Hills, CA: Sage.
Wilensky, H. (1994). *Tax and spend: The political economy and performance of rich democracies.* Manuscript in preparation.
Williams, M., & Reuten, G. (1993). After the rectifying revolution: The contradictions of the mixed economy. *Capital and Class, 49,* 77–112.
Wolin, S. S. (1960). *Politics and vision: Continuity and innovation in Western political thought.* Boston: Little, Brown.
Zaretsky, E. (1983). The place of the family in the origins of the welfare state. In D. Held et al., *States and societies.* Oxford, England: Martin Robertson.

Manuscript Received September 15, 1994
Revision Received and Accepted December 14, 1994

Part IV
Race, Development and Culture

[24]

J. EDUCATION POLICY, 1993, VOL. 8, NO. 2, 105–122

Marketing education in the postmodern age

Jane Kenway with Chris Bigum and Lindsay Fitzclarence
Faculty of Education, Deakin University, Victoria, Australia, 3215

This paper demonstrates that Australian public education is taking up a series of market identities and raises a number of selected matters that caused us concern as we both surveyed the field and the available critical literature and considered the social justice issues which are raised by markets in education. These matters are, first, the inadequacy of current conceptual frameworks for categorizing various developments and, second, the relative blindness of commentators to the connections between the growth of markets in education and certain wider cultural as opposed to economic shifts. It seems to us that some more recent forms of education markets raise social justice issues that the literature has either not engaged or has engaged in a rather restricted manner. We will identify some of these in the process of exploring the possibilities which theories about postmodernity provide both for explaining the rapid momentum and acceptance of the market lexicon in education in Australia and elsewhere and for predicting possible future trends. Much of what we say arises from research-in-progress. It is therefore tentative, exploratory, speculative and open ended. Our purpose in raising these matters at this stage is to generate discussion which will assist us all to answer at least some of the pressing questions posed by the marketization of education.

Introduction

Since the mid-1980s, Australia has experienced rapid and extensive changes in education at both the Commonwealth and state levels. Such changes have impinged to varying degrees on almost every sector and aspect of education. Education is now constituted and represented according to a language which is entirely different from that associated with previous governments, Labor or Liberal. Observers of educational politics tend to agree that at the Commonwealth and state levels, economic restructurinmg is the master discourse which informs all policy decisions and corporate management is the master discourse which informs all administrative processes. Most observers also recognize that underlying policy are two central strategies which are deployed in order to ensure that education will cost the state less and serve the economy more. One strategy involves intensified government intervention in education. The other strategy, perhaps paradoxically, involves the privatization and commercialization of public education. These two strategies come together in the sense that the state produces the frameworks within which privatization and commercialization will happen, it promotes certain values to guide these processes and undertakes the ideological work necessary to ensure they are publicly accepted. Social justice is included on this agenda in a subordinate but important way (see further Fitzclarence and Kenway, in press).

A pivotal concept in many of the proposed changes is *the market*. This concept is central to a number of discourses which constitute the current policy agenda. This may not seem remarkable to observers of educational politics from countries where a 'mixed economy' of schooling is the norm. However, Australians are used to high degrees of centralization and regulation in their education systems. This is the case even in those institutions which define themselves as independent and, to put it more crudely than they

0268–0939/93 $10·00

would, market driven. Under these circumstances then, the movement towards a market model represents a policy shift of some magnitude; a shift worth documenting and exploring with care for, in the view of many, it represents the end of an era in which the state sought to ensure equal and universal provision and the beginning of a period of considerable dislocation and uncertainty placing many long-held and worthy educational values at risk.

The market, or more particularly *markets in their considerable variety*, is/are the topic of this paper, which arises from our current research project titled 'Educational Markets in the Information Age'. Our concern here is threefold: to demonstrate that Australian public education is taking up a market identity or a series of market identities, to identify a selected number of issues which arise in connection with this almost paradigmatic shift, and to explore ways of understanding the imperatives which have brought it about. Generally, the paper explores the possibilities which a particular theoretical framework provides for explaining the rapid momentum and acceptance of the market lexicon in education in Australia and elsewhere.

Marketing education

A key concept in education in Australia in the late 20th century is *the market*. As we will demonstrate, education is now to be thought of in market terms and markets of various sorts are to guide priorities and funding. What will become evident from the short list of examples to follow is not simply the centrality of the concept *market* but its extremely flexible and imprecise usage. The term is in fact applied to a range of processes and practices which, it would seem, are very different in character.

In a very broad sense, education is expected to service the national and international market economy. It is to do so by preparing students for particular sectors of the labour market which will in turn service the export market. Students are to enter the work-force with marketable skills and value is accorded to knowledge, skill and various forms of production according to whether they satisfy market demand and enhance the market economy. Knowledge is to be regarded as an investment which 'pays off' for individuals in a job, for industry in a better trained labour force and for the nation in economic growth. Further, business and industry are increasingly encouraged to 'invest' in education and training both financially and in order to shape educational programmes, emphases and directions. As a result, they have developed and participated in any number of 'think tanks' and 'business round tables', all designed to influence education policy in a particular direction. They have also sponsored a number of Chairs in universities, and hybrid educational forms are developing as universities and companies make joint arrangements. Further, 'School/industry links' are encouraged and the technical and further education (TAFE) sector has, for some time, been undergoing a radical restructure in order that it may serve and better profit from the training needs of industry by developing marketable competencies in students that are oriented towards the labour markets which will supposedly enhance economic growth. Education is increasingly subsumed under the concept 'training'. Although not particularly forthcoming with money, the profile of business and industry has never been so high. Of course, such an economistic conceptualization of education if far from new. With varying degrees of intensity, it has guided the motives of many educational policy makers since the introduction of state-provided secondary education in Australia. However, never before has this view been so wide-ranging in its focus and promoted with such intensity.

Education for economic recovery and expansion is the only game permitted in policy circles and this has contributed significantly to some more recent and new forms of marketization.

In an economic climate dominated by enthusiasm for growth and for budget cuts, the public sector generally and the public sector of education particularly are juxtaposed against the private/market sector and found wanting (see Kenway 1990). As a result, genuine market forms, rather than just orientations towards labour and commodity markets, are encouraged in state educational institutions and activities. And, further, education is increasingly to be steered by market forces within as well as beyond education. The production of market forms in public education in Australia includes the transfer of certain costs from the state to the 'consumer' via various 'user pay' and loan schemes. The public tertiary sector is gradually reintroducing fees in various disguises for undergraduates and a number of full-fee-based post-graduate courses have developed and these are strongly encouraged. Some state schools are also introducing a form of 'voluntary' fees. In the interests of export earnings and profits to subsidize their other activities, public universities and TAFE are expected to sell education off- as well as onshore. In the tertiary sector particularly, many individual institutions and faculties are currently either in search of a 'niche' in the offshore market (business education is popular in this regard) or trying to identify or open up new markets overseas but also in Australia. Many students have been encouraged onshore not just by full-fee-based courses in public institutions but also by English-language intensive courses for overseas students (ELICOS) and these courses have been mounted by entirely private bodies. Competitive self-interest is now what characterizes relationships between tertiary institutions and increasingly amongst academics, who are 'encouraged' to market their 'intellectual property' to sponsors from business and industry. Such 'encouragement' partly takes the form of proposals to deregulate the academic labour market. Already, market-based salary loadings are paid to academics in certain fields. State and Commonwealth governments are not discouraging, and subtly encouraging, the development of private or semi-private universities. Further, an apparent, some would say manufactured, crisis of confidence in state schooling has led to a significant shift in enrolments from the public to the private sector. The public sector educated 78.9% of school students in 1977 but by 1990 it educated 72.1% (Marginson 1991). As a result state governments have decided to market (promote) state schools to parents and the community.[1] The devolution of certain management functions to schools is part of this trajectory allowing principals to 'contract out' certain school-related work, to buy in certain educational 'resources' and 'services', and to 'target' local 'consumers'. Dezoning in various forms is seen to expose state schools to market forces which in turn is supposed to enhance their quality.

Certainly, the state continues to attempt to hold the reins in these marketization processes. In the tertiary sector it has used financial rewards and penalties to reshape the system, at the same time as orienting it towards labour, commodity and educational markets. The enclosure of the tertiary and schooling sectors within corporate management frameworks can also be understood as a mechanism designed to steer the direction for public sector involvement in educational markets. Further, for schools, the rapid moves towards national curriculum frameworks and profiles and the development of the Curriculum Corporation can be seen to represent new disciplinary technologies for educational markets (see further, Kenway 1992). The Curriculum Corporation is a national body, servicing national corporate objectives, in part, through the development and marketing of educational materials. None the less, despite these centrifugal forces, the market metaphor heads up a new policy and administration lexicon in education which includes such terms as *educational property, educational enterprise, entrepreneurial approaches to education, educational services, products, packages, sponsors, commodities and consumers, value-added education, user pays, choice* and so on. These and other terms both reflect and are helping to bring into effect a relatively new and different era in public education in Australia, one in which state-provided, institutional education takes on many features of commercial markets.

A market imperative in state educational policy and administration is only part of the story, for what we are also seeing is a new player in the field of education which has the potential to recast education in ways as yet almost unimaginable. Various media, information and communications technologies, in particular broadcasting, publishing and modern computing and telecommunications, are converging to increasingly become integral to the operations of many education (and other) markets. Evident here is a strikingly new and unfamiliar nexus between education, markets and marketing discourses and information technology (Hinkson 1991). Because of their increasing use of various information and communications technologies, state educational institutions are providing an expanding market for commercial markets. For example, fierce competition developed in schools at all levels when the first commercially available microcomputers appeared. Schools were identified as key sites in the commercial contests between computer vendors (Bigum *et al.* 1987) and, as a result, many have been reconstructed to suit better the interests of those who sell the products of the new information technologies (Bigum 1991). Establishing an electronic 'beachhead' of compliant public and private consumers is clearly regarded as important if schools are to be implicated in the logic of the emergent global selling of the new information technologies and their products. And, on the other hand, educational institutions are using their relationships with information technologies in their own marketing enterprises. Some institutions are seeking to promote themselves on the basis of their use of such technologies in the curriculum and others are using such technologies to offer new forms of pedagogy which increase their market reach both nationally and internationally. A key example in this respect is distance education, a field which is, to some extent, at the cutting edge of the nexus of formal education, the new information technologies and educational and other markets. Equally, a number of institutions, technology high schools for instance, are redefining their practices in order to concentrate on preparing their students for employment in high-tech labour markets. In this framework, education is seen as providing a product or 'output' which is a necessary 'input' of human resources to maintain and develop new high-technology systems. More broadly, much current intellectual energy is being spent in exploring more and more sophisticated ways in which education, markets and information technology can come together efficiently and profitably. The Department of Employment, Education and Training's (DEET) recently formed National Open Learning Policy Unit is a case in point here. So too are the new, fee-charging 'open learning' degree courses sold on public television. There is no doubt that the technologized market momentum will continue to build in the future. Already there is a range of indications about the directions which future combinations of education, markets and the new information technologies might take and, although we will elaborate a little on these later, it is pertinent to note here that they tend to be commercially initiated and therefore guided entirely by the logic of sectional profit.

The intensification of market forms in state education is not a uniquely Australian experience. Literature from the UK and the USA demonstrates clearly that it is happening in these two countries and, as Geoff Whitty (1991) suggests, it is happening in Japan and elsewhere too. It is doubtful that this literature documents the full extent to which a market discourse is reshaping education in a range of countries as well as internationally; nevertheless, all the signs are that we are going through global educational adjustments of increasing force and magnitude.

From the preceding discussion it is evident that more traditional education markets, the archetypal cases here being the private school market (Kenway 1991) and the credential market for the labour market and the economy, are being caught up in and overtaken by a range of new market modes which in many cases mesh with information technologies in various ways which are becoming increasingly complicated and to some extent difficult to predict. Also, as noted earlier, despite its centrality, the concept 'market' has many meanings and applications. Further, there are a number of implied assumptions in its varied usage. One assumption is that educators, educational policy makers and administrators understand how markets in education (as opposed to other markets) operate and that they all share common understandings. Given the quite recent rise of the term in education and the relative dearth of sustained and serious research in the area neither is likely to be the case. Another common set of assumptions is that certain lines of thought from economics, business and liberal political philosophy can be unquestioningly transposed on to education and that they will have predictable consequences. There is no convincing evidence to demonstrate that this is so. A further assumption is that education, markets and information technology can and will come together in almost automatically mutually beneficial ways. Again, there is no convincing evidence to demonstrate this. However, despite the lack of conceptual clarity and supportive research evidence the marketization of Australian education without, with and through information technology proceeds apace. In the light of the rapid growth of market forms in education and the sparsity of relevant research evidence, a strong warrant exists for serious, sustained and far-sighted research into the various types of market in operation; the role that the new information technologies play in these markets; the different processes which generate, sustain and flow from them; and the educational, social, cultural and economic benefits and costs involved.

Meanwhile, how are we to understand what is going on? What conceptual frameworks are available to help us do so? How is the recent emergence of market forms in education to be explained and what are its implications? These are questions which a small number of policy analysts, of various persuasions, have been grappling with for some time. However, in our view, they have barely scratched the surface of this phenomenon. The reasons for this are many, not the least being that the pace of change constantly outstrips our capacity to describe it, let alone to explain it theoretically. The process will not stop still long enough for us to pin it down. It is not simply that old market forms are now accompanied by new, it is also that there is now a proliferation of types assembling the familiar and the unfamiliar in ways which would have been difficult to predict a decade ago. The pace of change in this area is 'white hot', as Giddens would say, and this suggests that a decade from now the likelihood is that we will be trying to come to grips with forms that we cannot even imagine at this stage. Clearly then, those who wish both to explore and to explain the emergence of markets in education and to identify current and likely future patterns are confronted with a research agenda of some magnitude. And what of those who remain to be convinced about the educational and social benefits of marketing education? If we are sceptical about the truth claims of market advocates and worried about the educational and social consequences of marketing education, then we are also faced with a matter of some political urgency. There is little doubt that what is at risk is the maintenance of a viable and vital public sector capable of sustaining universal provision of resources and services.

We will now raise a number of selected matters that caused us concern as we both surveyed the available critical literature and considered the social justice issues which are raised by markets in education. These matters are, first, the inadequacy of current conceptual frameworks for categorizing various developments and, second, the relative blindness of commentators to the connections between the growth of markets in education and certain wider cultural shifts. The third point relates to, and is contained in our discussion of the second. It seems to us that some more recent forms of education markets raise social justice issues that the literature has either not engaged or has engaged in a rather restricted manner. We will identify some of these. Much of what we are about to say arises from research work-in-progress; it is therefore tentative, exploratory, speculative and open ended. Our purpose in raising these matters at this stage is to generate discussion that will assist us all to answer at least some of the pressing questions posed by the marketization of education.

Interpreting the market

Conceptual frameworks

As education is overtaken by market modes, there is an increasing number of commentators documenting the ways in which this is happening. However, there has not been a corresponding amount of effort put into the development of a conceptual framework which helps to classify the range of ways that markets are manifest. An examination of the literature reveals that many commentators continue to use the concept 'privatization' to describe the emergence of educational markets and that they use the term in a global way without either attempting to disaggregate and classify the different types of privatization that are occurring or to ask themselves if what they are talking about can actually be defined as privatization. Rather than identify the tardy in this regard, we will discuss the work of those who have made at least some attempt to classify different market orientations, imperatives and forms. Before we do so, however, it is worth identifying the various dimensions of privatization that are mentioned in other policy literature and seeing what aspects of education may be located there. We draw here from a publication by the Labor Resource Centre (1987) which draws from the work of Heald (1983) who identifies four overlapping components of privatization.

1. *Denationalization and load shedding* which involves 'the sale of public assets and the transfer of existing state functions to the private sector' (p. 33). In education this involves the sale of land, buildings and plant which have been used for educational purposes. This is often the result of the 'residualization' (see Preston 1984) of a state school in a locality where state-funded private schools have flourished.
2. *The privatization of production* which includes: 'the subsidization of private sector arrangements that undermine public sector provision' (p. 33); contracting out and voucher distribution. In education this refers to financial support for private educational providers and this can include anything from subsidized 'in-service' for private school teachers, to research grants to staff at private universities, to educational institutions or systems engaging the services of private consultants or local cleaning or building contractors. In Australia its most obvious form is the considerable amount of funding which the state pays to the private schools; funding which, as any number of

observers has demonstrated, contributed to the dramatic expansion of private sector education and to the stigmatization of the state sector leading to a crisis of morale and confidence in state schools. The Labor Resource Centre calls this 'privatization by stealth' (p. 36).

3. *Liberalization/deregulation* involves the relaxation of 'statutory monopolies, licensing arrangements or other regulatory mechanisms which prevent private sector firms entering markets exclusively provided by the public sector' (p. 33). It was such deregulation which allowed for the establishment of a number of private English language intensive courses for overseas students in Australia which proved to be a disaster for many overseas parents and students and an international embarrassment for the government (see Bartos 1990).
4. *The privatization of finance*, in which the 'service continues to be produced by the public sector but is not funded (fully) by taxation' (p. 33). Any user-pays scheme fits into this category but primarily those goods and services which were previously provided free of charge.

Richard Pring is one commentator who continues to document the range of market forms in education under the concept 'privatization'. However, he does argue that various forms of privatization can be categorized under two broad headings.

> ... the purchasing at *private* expense of educational services within the *public* system, and ... The purchasing at *public* expense of educational services in private institutions. (Pring 1987: 11)

In the first instance, Pring draws our attention to the problem of finding a defining line between what the state should and need not provide. However, his implication is that over recent years the line has shifted dramatically, and the cost of many provisions and services which might once have been considered basic or essential have been transferred to parents within the state sector and redefined as enrichment or 'extras'. The increasing demands placed on schools to raise money and to solicit unpaid parental labour fit into this trajectory (see, for other examples, Walford 1989). (But does school sponsorship fit in here? Is business buying consumers, taught to be so by the school?) Pring's latter case refers to instances where the state is 'promoting the private at the expense of the public sector – it is a shifting of resources, an alteration of the overall structure of education' (Pring 1987: 11). In Australia, as indicated above, state aid fits under this heading. In the UK the 'assisted places scheme' can be thus categorized, so can voucher proposals as well as the myriad of other major and minor ways in which the state supports private provision (see further, Pring 1987). As Chitty (1992) observes, processes whereby the state system is starved of resources thus encouraging parents into the private sector could be defined as a more subtle form of privatization.

Pring's categories have the benefit of alerting us, in an elegantly simple way, to the ebb and flow of resources across the public/private divide and to the ways in which this happens which pose the greatest threat to the public sector and to equitable and universal forms of provision. However, despite the helpfulness of Pring's categories, it seems to us that they are unable to account for the range of marketization processes under way in education at the moment. They are too general to be able to make some important fine distinctions. For instance, when we talk of the private expense of public education it is important to know whose expense and what aspect of education they are purchasing. If local schools are raising money from business sources through sponsorships then this is likely to have a rather different set of ramifications than if it is raising money directly from parents. Similarly, if nation-state borders are crossed in order to permit the private purchase of public education, then a different set of complexities arises. This leads to the important questions: 'What is being purchased, by whom, on what scale, at what cost and with what implications for the education provided?' Further difficulties arise with Pring's framework and these include its emphasis on buying and selling (purchase), its reliance on the private/public dualism and its focus on transactions across the private/public divide. It is thus unable to account for the ways in which education is commodified which do not involve funds or purchase in the strict sense. (We use the term commodification here to mean the movement which turns complex social relationships and processes into objects and inserts them into the sphere of market exchange and values.) It thus cannot attend to the various developments which draw, in one way or another, on the concept of 'human capital'. Equally, it has difficulty in accommodating those structural, financial and ideological shifts *within* the state system, which encourage some aspects of a market mode. These include certain forms of devolution; a highly elaborated emphasis on choice, competitiveness and individualism; school effectiveness research and so forth but which, again, do not necessarily involve the transfer of costs. Such shifts position education in a consumer/product discourse. They encourage institutions to 'market' their speciality and exceptionality. They also encourage an emphasis on image rather than substance and indeed a confusion between the two. The concept of privatization is inadequate in other ways too. Because it is state-centric and because it is only concerned with formal institutionalized education, it does not allow into the frame non-institutional education forms which arise from commodity markets, and neither does it seem to permit discussion of the influence of material commodity markets on both state and private institutionalized education.

How have other policy analysts dealt with the limitations of the concept of privatization? Marginson (1991: 1) argues that the term and the binary oppositions upon which it rests (public/private and non-market/market relations) are no longer adequate to the task – if indeed they ever were. Drawing on feminist thinking he points to a number of instances in which the public/private dualism does not hold up. He suggests that the term commercialization more adequately accounts for many developments in education at the moment and describes it thus:

> Commercialisation takes place when production assumes some or all of the forms of market (exchange-based) production: sale of goods or services, scarcity and competition, profit making etc. (p. 1)

He makes the significant point that both privatization (which he wants to define primarily as the transfer of production or assets or reputation across the binary) and commercialization are often related.

> Commercial production in the public sector may form new markets in which private sector production later flourishes. Privatisation encourages competition and scarcity and weakens the influence of political factors in production. Under specific circumstances, commercialisation and privatisation may together lead to full market production. (p. 20)

So for Marginson the 'privatization of finance' would probably be classified more as commercialization than privatization, as would deregulation. Stephen Ball (1991) makes a somewhat similar distinction, except that he uses the term marketization saying simply that this involves 'the introduction of market forces into education' (p. 86). He focuses particularly on the local management of state schooling in the UK which was brought about by a number of Education Acts in the 1980s, and argues that 'the elements of this market are choice, competition, diversity' (p. 61) and particularly types of funding and organization (see further pp. 60–69). Implied in Ball's work is a further distinction between the macro-markets in education generated by the educational and economic priorities of the state and micro-markets. He is concerned to identify the micro-markets which develop in and around schools as policy is rearticulated within local educational and other politics. From his data he makes the point that:

> ... there is no one 'market in education' and no one set of market conditions. Schools operate in relation to multiple markets, usually local, which have very specific conditions, constraints and histories. Importantly too, schools are increasingly finding themselves implicated in other markets and their attendant regulatory legislation, e.g. leisure, financial and labour markets, each of which impinges upon the other and upon the 'educational markets that emerge out of local responses to' policy. (Ball, work in progress)

We believe that yet further conceptual work is required. Clearly a number of education markets are developing within the state sector as Ball's work shows and, as Marginson's work illustrates, many different state/private hybrid markets have emerged over the last two decades or so. However, any adequate discussion of markets in education must also accommodate the increasing range of fully private non-institutional commodity and image forms and those markets which are no longer contained within nation states. Different markets involve different types of exchange – various 'investments' and 'dividends'. They also involve a considerable range of forms and patterns of production, representation and consumption. Our empirical and conceptual work should help us to identify these.

Earlier, we alluded to the fact that markets in education have increasingly included information and communications technologies in their processes of production, representation and consumption. Investing in various ways in such technology is now regarded as common sense in many education markets – and seen to pay dividends in a number of ways: extending market reach and market share, capturing preferable employment options, enhancing learning and so forth. There is no doubt that these technologies are being employed in traditional education markets in quite familiar sorts of ways; for instance in the micro-markets that Ball discusses and in the development of magnet schools such as technology high schools and the like. But, as indicated, the markets/education/technology triad is also generating markets which in many senses are unfamiliar. In our view, such markets are a sign both of the times we are going through and those yet to come. They are in many senses 'post-modern markets' (Hinkson 1992). In order to explain what we mean by this term, we will briefly discuss postmodernism and, in the process, make the case that even though only some markets can be classified as postmodern, the rapid rise of the market form in education is best understood as a postmodern phenomenon.

Postmodernism

Some writers claim that in the late 20th century we live in social and cultural conditions which differ markedly from those of the early 20th and late 19th century (see further, Sharp 1985). Others go so far as to argue that these changes are so fundamental that the current condition must be named in order that it may be distinguished from earlier periods – hence the nomenclature 'the postmodern age (or condition)' (see Baudrillard 1981, Jameson 1984, Lyotard 1984). While recognizing the controversy that surrounds such claims we believe that the marketization of education generally and, more particularly, the newer technologically dependent and driven markets are best understood if we can identify some of the key features of the postmodern age. One such key feature is what has been described as the communications revolution which has arisen from what has been called the techno-scientific revolution (see Baudrillard 1981, Hinkson 1987).

Developments in science have brought about the communications revolution, scientific rationality has been its legitimating ideology and both have clearly had a pervasive influence over many aspects of our life form. New technologies of information and communication have significant implications for culture, society and the economy, and thus for social interaction and human subjectivity. It is appropriate that we identify a number of these implications because they all have a bearing, in different ways, on the education markets alluded to earlier.

Of particular pertinence to this paper are the implications of the techno-scientific and communications revolution for the nation-state. New technologies interact with economic matters to help facilitate transnational enterprises, the operations of which challenge the capacity of nation-states to control their own economies, and cultural and natural environments. Indeed, new technologies of communication are demonstrating an increasing potential to bypass state boundaries. The state thus attempts to steer but is also to some extent steered by the cultural and economic logic of the new technologies of communication. Nowhere is this more evident than in relation to international money markets (see Knightley and Fay 1986).

Broadly, from this point of view, the power of the nation-state, and its capacity for better or worse to control its subjects and their form of life is significantly reduced. As states struggle to transform their national economies and as they direct their resources accordingly, what we see is a shedding of welfare responsibilities. In the case of education, then, what we see is a transfer of certain responsibilities and costs away from the state to civil society. Accompanying this shift is an organizational and psychological reorientation of the education community within the state, encouraging a market/consumer orientation which feeds into the state-sponsored privatization momentum, which then feeds back into it. What also becomes evident is that information and communications technologies and scientific discourses are deployed to promote and legitimate such adjustments. Policy making becomes increasingly caught up in the marketing and policing of images and the differences between the image and 'the real' becomes difficult to determine as the state variously uses and abuses media outlets and is used and abused by them. Indeed, images and meaning have been generated and circulated which not only attract and attach people to this market discourse but which also persuade them that it is working in the interests of all. It is in this way that national and international education markets are classified and framed, as Bernstein would say. Let us explain this point.

The techno-scientific revolution has facilitated a certain shift in the nature of economic production itself and has also generated a preference on the part of policy makers that this shift become the basis for a major structural change. The actual and preferred move is from industrial towards postindustrial; from 'rust bucket' towards 'sunrise' industries and from primary towards service industries. This is most commonly described as a shift from Fordism to post-Fordism. While allowing for the range of post-Fordisms, Bagguley (1991) offers a succinct account of what this shift is said to entail, saying:

> Since the 1970s, it is claimed, Fordist forms of economic organization have entered a period of crisis, and the resolution of this crisis lies in the emergence of a new set of economic institutions which would ensure economic growth. This new arrangement, post-Fordism, would be characterized by short run batch-type production in small or decentralized firms, by the rolling back and partial privatization of the welfare state and by a decline in the membership of trade unions and of their industrial and political power. (p. 151)

He notes that the key features of ideal-type post-Fordism, other than the above, are:

> . . . fragmented niche markets, general flexible machinery, multi-skilled workers, 'human relations' management strategy, decentralized local or plant level bargaining, geographically new industrial districts, flexible specialist communities. (p. 155)

Both accompanying and facilitating this shift in the nature of economic production has been the development of a new form of social labour. Indeed, at the very heart of this transformation is the work of the 'intellectually trained', those:

> ... who apply established intellectual and scientific skills in work geared to the ends laid down by the owners or controllers of large scale industrial and administrative complexes. (Sharp and White 1968: 15)

The 'intellectual techniques' which such people deploy are abstract and portable. They have many applications and are thus, in many senses, universal (see Sharp 1985). Mental labour both replaces and displaces manual labour. It is clear that policy makers in many 'developed' nations believe that this segment of the work-force must be expanded to ensure international competitiveness. 'Really useful knowledge', that worth national and personal investment, has increasingly been defined as either technical and scientific, or that which services and expands the market economy. Hence students are steered towards maths, science, technology, commerce, business studies and Asian languages. Education institutions are to gear themselves accordingly and put the weight of their efforts and their funds in these directions.

But this is clearly not the end of the matter for, as Bagguley (1991) points out, post-Fordism also brings with it reorientations in the practices of management and industrial relations involving processes of de-centring. Let us explore this point a little through the work of Steven Ball. Ball (1991) makes the case that recent crises in capitalist accumulation and as a result in nation-states have brought about a *new* correspondence between education and the economy. As he says 'education is made more subordinate to and less autonomous from the commodity form ... [which] penetrates the form, content and delivery ... of schooling' (p. 81). Privatization, marketization, differentiation, vocationalism and the proleterianization of the teaching service in the UK are, as he demonstrates in some detail, reflections of this. And, with regard to vocationalism, he makes the point that the industrial lobby and economically oriented education policy makers are keen that schools not only produce 'enterprising' individuals for the 'enterprise' culture they are trying to effect, but also produce the types of individuals who have the attitudes and competencies appropriate to an emergent and anticipated post-Fordist economy. Hence this 'lobby' has developed a critique of 'narrow, abstract, academic and elitist' (p. 102) forms of curriculum and assessment and formed an ideological alliance with progressivist theories of learning and motivation (a process orientation, co-operation, problem solving, open-ended investigation and the like). Vocationally oriented education ('vocational progressivism') is to develop in students 'flexible competencies and a predisposition to change' (p. 102). The long and short of Ball's argument is that educational institutions are not only to produce the post-Fordist, multiskilled, innovative worker but to behave in post-Fordist ways themselves; moving away from mass production and mass markets to niche markets and 'flexible specialization'. His case is, first, that a post-Fordist mind-set is currently having implications in schools for management styles, curriculum, pedagogy and assessment and, second, that this mind-set is largely the result of the ways in which fractions of capital and factions within the state have responded to the crises mentioned earlier and engaged in profoundly successful discursive and interdiscursive work in order to reshape political and public opinion along post-Fordist lines.

As Ball and many others show, a considerable array of economic and political forces have converged to encourage the marketization of education in the UK and elsewhere. Popular educational and economic sentiments and concerns have been reworked and attached to the discursive ensembles of the neo-liberal and libertarian strands of the New Right whose ideas have been adjusted and rearticulated by policy makers in accordance with broader state imperatives. However, this does not fully explain why such ideas seem to have made their way so readily into popular consciousness and gained such acceptance.

We therefore believe it is necessary to move beyond explanations which focus on post-Fordism and beyond those which focus on the discursive politics of dominant fragments and fractions of labour, capital and governments. Neither engages sufficiently with some other significant cultural shifts which, in our view, help to explain why markets in education have found such a receptive audience. These shifts are more usually associated with postmodernism. Whitty (1991) takes up this point and suggests that it is possible to read the devolutionary and deregulatory imperatives associated with marketing education as part of a broader and deeper cultural shift – as a 'wider retreat from modern, bureaucratized state education systems' now seen to be 'inappropriate to societies of the late twentieth century', and as representing 'new ways of resolving the core problems facing the state' (p. 41) as a result of changes in capital accumulation. He further observes that the diversification of provision, and its associated notion of choice and so on, need not be seen as solely a reflection of a new Trinity between sections of the New Right, governments and industry but that such themes resonate strongly both with the cultural pluralism associated with the decline of totalizing meta-narratives of whatever sort and with the rise of cultural projects premised on notions of difference and fragmentation. Such projects, he says, are practised through pragmatic, shifting and short-lived alliances in relation to particular local struggles; 'unprincipled alliances' based in 'changes in the mode of social solidarity' (p. 8). None the less, Whitty is sceptical that such changes, to the extent that they exist, actually challenge structural inequalities in any significant way. To imagine this is otherwise, he suggests, is perhaps to mistake 'phenomenal forms for structural relations' and is also to replace the meta-narratives associated with social planning and social intervention (e.g. Keynesian economics and social democracy) with another meta-narrative – the market.

In our view, the dominance of markets, or more particularly intensified commodity forms, is one defining feature of postmodernity. The techno-scientific and communications revolutions have helped to facilitate the cultural dominance of the commodity. They have done so by revolutionizing processes of production and so reducing the need for manual work but also by invading people's lives with a flood of both commodities and seductive images which generate desire. As a result, people now are increasingly coming to define themselves less as workers and more as consumers. Non-market relationships are redefined according to the logic of the market. And, as Ranson (1990) argues, markets require a shift in focus from the collective and the community to the individual, from public service to private service, and from other people to the self. They redefine the meaning of such terms as rights, citizenship and democracy. Civil and welfare rights and civic responsibility give way to market rights in consumer democracy. Clearly, in promoting the marketization of education, policy makers seek to promote and tap into a cult of educational selfishness in the national interest. Educational democracy is redefined as consumer democracy in the educational supermarket. *Buying* an education becomes a substitute for *getting* an education. Consumers seek the competitive edge at the expense of others and look for value-added education. Increasingly, information technolgoy is seen to be the best value to add. That aside, by altering the relationship between space and time, new technologies have changed our patterns of communication and integration. The face-to-face has been replaced by more abstract and global ways of relating (see further, Hinkson 1991). This leads us back to our earlier point about postmodern markets in education.

Postmodern markets in education

John Hinkson (1991) argues that the communications revolution 'elaborates and facilitates markets' through a process of social extension; constructing 'settings for relations that go beyond the face to face' (p. 117). He goes so far as to argue that the market is 'crucially influenced by the communications revolution' which has indeed created a new phenomenon: the 'postmodern market'. There are four distinguishing features of postmodern markets, Hinkson argues, and these are:

1. swift and wide-ranging transactions facilitated by information technology (the international money market is the paradigm case here);
2. the assimilation of previously non-market spheres of life as a result of technological intervention;
3. the centrality of the image through the mass media;
4. a dramatic increase in the flow of commodities with implications for cultural production and self-production.

This postmodern market is made possible, he notes, by the application of the intellectual techniques discussed earlier, techniques produced by currently favoured and promoted segments of formal education systems.

There are clearly currently many market forms in education and as Ball's (1990) evidence with regard to the micro-markets in schools in the UK demonstrates, many do not take on any features of the postmodern form as described by Hinkson, even if they have, as we argued earlier, emerged, to some extent, as the remote result of the changed cultural conditions of postmodernity. None the less, as we also argued earlier, new forms are emerging which have all or some of the features of postmodern markets and it is highly probable that more such markets will develop in education. It is even possible that the education/technology/markets triad has the potential to change the shape of education as we know it. How might this happen?

Rotman (1987) describes the path that money has taken from gold to paper to magnetic marks on a disk. Modern computing and communication networks facilitated this most recent historical shift to, in his view, postmodern money or xenomoney. The education/markets/technology triad may well be bringing into effect a similar chain of events; it is possible that in the not too distant future magnetic marks on a disk may come to constitute the core of education and that we will then be in the era of xeno-education. Already there are signs of emergent forms which do not merely extend the somewhat better known interactions of the new information technologies, markets and education which we mentioned earlier. Indeed, there are some early indications that the state's monopoly over education is being discreetly challenged by such technologies which are bringing into effect new modes of de-institutionalized education guided entirely by market logic. It may well be that the educational centre of gravity is in the process of shifting; that education policy has not only been de-centred by the processes of devolution and the marketization of public services but by informal, technologically and commercially mediated learning. This form of 'education' certainly has the potential to challenge the pedagogical primacy in students' lives of institutionalized, formal and face-to-face learning. As the home increasingly becomes the focus for the delivery of information and education, there is no doubt that students' informal learning will be increasingly dispersed across the fleeting, shifting but life-dominating webs of information which are spun by communications technologies. In an electronic ecology, computer-based games in the home far outnumber their more serious counterparts in use in formal educational settings.

When numeric superiority is coupled with the eventual emergence of a virtual reality system (Rheingold 1991) in the home for various purposes, the threat to traditional schools, teachers and teaching will be serious. Meanwhile, the embryonic mass electronic media categories of *infotainment* and *edutainment* point to some of the possible new forms that education may take. Science and technology parks point to another.

However, at the moment full-fee, off-shore, distance education is a paradigm case of a postmodern market. The phone, fax, E-mail, and the satellite have brought space and time into new realignments. Relationships in this educational mode are abstract and fleeting, mediated by the market and the technology (see further, Fitzclarence and Kemmis 1988). And, if current trends are any indication, this is what the pundits would call a 'growth area'. While Hinkson's work is useful in identifying the central features here, a more complete understanding of the context in which these particular markets are developing is provided by the thinking of postmodern geography. To understand the context is to get some sense of the likely future directions of this genre of market in education. But it is also to recognize that exporting education puts significantly new issues on the educational and political agenda. These will become evident as we proceed.

It is postmodern geographers who explore what happens when new communication and information technologies, markets, post-Fordism and neo- and postcolonialism (see Ferguson *et al.* 1990) come together. Offshore education markets also bring such processes together. So it is pertinent to ask what postmodern geography has to say that might illuminate current and future offshore markets in education. In tentatively answering this question we will draw particularly on the work of Kevin Robins (1989, 1991).

A central theme in discussions of postmodern geography is that new technologies in association with the international restructuring of capitalist economies break down the forms of organization which have arisen as a result of geography and, as Robins (1991) points out, introduce new and competing 'centrifugal and centripetal forces' (p. 24). In Robins' view, global capital and new technologies have brought about the emergence of a new 'global–local nexus'; more specifically in the drive to capture world-scale advantage, in a world of continuous innovation, giant transnational corporations have become 'flexible', polycentric and deterritorialized; Robins shows that on the one hand globalization involves flexible forms of corporate association giving 'maximum integration on a world scale' and the possibility of responsiveness at a local level. This is made possible through new computer communications systems which create a new and abstract electronic space across pre-existing physical and social geographies – the 'network firm' creates a new 'electronic geography'.

One tendency here is towards global cultural convergence, the production of both universal cultural products and global market consumers. The impulse is towards a borderless 'placeless geography of image and simulation' (1991: 29) where time and space horizons are compressed and where communication is instant and depthless. This is created by new global cultural corporations such as NBC and Sony. However, as Robins shows, the globalization of culture is not necessarily about repressing local difference and particularity; it is about assembling, displaying, celebrating, commodifying and exploiting it. 'The local and "exotic" are torn out of place and time to be repackaged for the world bazaar' (p. 31) – delocalized. The other side of the global/local nexus is post-Fordist 'flexible specialization', and the 'revitalization and revalidation' (p. 34) of a strong sense of place in economic, cultural and self production – a renaissance of place-bound traditions and ways of life. However, this localization imperative is, according to Robins, in many cases a form of relocalization – 'place-making' and marketing in 'placeless times'; it is 'about new and intricate relations between global space and local space' (p. 35). While positive in some senses, he argues that this should not be romanticized or attributed with too much agency for, in this context, the local can mean what the global wants it to mean and it can be seen as useful today and useless tomorrow. The defining features of this global/locus nexus then are:

> ... new relations between space and place, flexibility and mobility, centre and periphery, 'real' and 'virtual' space 'inside and outside', frontier and territory. (Robins 1991: 41)

What are the implications of all this for education? If we think of education in the broadest possible sense as what we learn informally as we live, then the implications of this are immense. In global terms such education is already in the hands of transnational corporations and their myriad subsidiaries, and the question is how does what they do and the way they do it shape and reshape our individual and collective identities as we plug in, at various points, to their cultural and economic communications networks? This is the meta question for social theory and certainly not one we can engage adequately here. However, it does suggest that the commodity and the image will increasingly become the structuring forces of our lives, creating the conditions in which we learn how to be, who to be and what to value. As Schwartz, cited in Brand (1988) argues, mass finance (commodity) and entertainment (image) will shape computers and communication. And, in a very broad sense, this does lend further support to the point we made earlier about the commodification of our culture and its capacity to dispose us favourably towards markets. As work, place and community shape our identity less and less, then the commodity and the image slip into the lacuna.

Clearly the global/local nexus also raises questions about the role that the nation-state plays in identity formation. Notions of citizenship, rights, justice and so forth have long been connected to governments and thus to the state/nation. What meaning do these terms have in a global economy and culture? As Ted Wheelwright (1992) says:

> ... the globalization of capital does not necessarily change its character, except in one respect; it becomes less susceptible to the checks and balances of the nation state and national trade unions and movements. Its freedom to expand and contract, to exploit and relocate is greatly enhanced and its tendency to foster inequality is accentuated, for there is no world government, no world taxing authority, no global minimum wage or welfare state. World capitalism is therefore more unstable and creates more inequality within and between nations because there is no countervailing politically responsible power to offset it. (p. 74)

And, as any number of commentators have indicated, the image turns us inwards and outwards; on the one hand privatizing us and on the other directing us towards a distant and often seductive 'out there', which is often not there; or at least not there in the ways represented. For example, the simulacrum (see Baudrillard 1981) of the 'pleasures' of life in a market economy no doubt played a role in the recent fall of governments in Eastern Europe and the former Soviet Union. Now, many people in many instances are finding to their cost that the image was all there was. Doubtless, this is one example of a myriad which would demonstrate the power and emptiness of the image. None the less, the image has led people to distrust the evidence of their senses. These days it seems that the image does not have to prove itself – the senses do. And sometimes this evidence has to be considerable before it is accepted as sense. Let us take an example. In the recent UK election, the 'look around' factor was deliberately brought into play. People were told to turn away from their screens and *see around them* the damaging effects of the recession and the Tory government. To make the point more clearly the market and the image reinforce and hide each other. Robins (1989) makes this point well when he talks of image markets. In certain senses for consumers, the market is a simulacrum; it layers promise upon promise, but it has no centre of accountability.

Getting back to distance education and the new global/local nexus, there are many questions about the future worth asking. What is the place of distance education in this new geography? And, will it eventually model itself along the lines outlined above and map itself onto current network firms and electronic geographies? If so, will this mean that competing transnational education corporations with world-wide subsidiaries will develop and operate outside the nation-state? Will these new education corporations maximize their accumulation by creating and intensifying demand and achieving world-scale advantage by the continual denial of gratification? Will we have life-long education on a global scale which exists for no reason other than profit for the 'teacher'? Robins (1991: 28) argues that the command centre or 'strategic nodes' of world-wide electronic grids and their associated economies are such global cities as New York, Tokyo and London. Will these become the centres for the development of the postmodern, post-Fordist curriculum? And what will constitute the global curriculum? Will we have world-wide intellectual convergence and/or flexible specialization; will it be post- or neo-colonial? What is the place here for local knowledges? Indeed, what sort of curriculum is created for 'a world of flows, images and screens': a world of electronic space with its depthlessness and instantaneity (Robins 1991: 29)? If image and education become one, how do we learn to tell one from the other? Is that the end of 'reality'? And finally, is there any place in this future place-less educational economy of the sign for matters of ethics and justice?

Markets are not premised on the assumption of fairness or equality. While their proponents make the claim that there is general benefit from competitive self-interest, they also argue that those who play according to the rules and are best at the game deserve the greatest rewards. Ultimately, markets operate according to the logic of profit, only in certain sets of interests and let the 'weak' go to the wall. They work to produce a selfish, individualistic culture in which the main moral imperative is gratification, not the collective good. Of course critical policy analysts have been making this point for some time, although obviously not to much avail. None the less, the point stands and is supported. However, we are concerned that postmodern markets in education will both generate and obscure forms of injustice that are significantly different from those noted above. We suspect that certain of these injustices will be even more difficult to address precisely because the global markets which generate them stand outside the state and therefore outside our normal channels of redress. In many senses this is a devil we do not know. Or do we know it in another form? Do the operations of international money markets give us a hint? In the postmodern financial jungle 'the market is a predator. It looks around for a vulnerable currency and strikes it, unmercifully, like a cobra' (Knightley and Fay, *The Age, Sunday Extra*, 18 January 1986, p. 3).

Conclusion?

Education is not a field of practice that stands outside its context. It helps to shape and is shaped by that context and so contains traces of the old, the new and the in-between. The same can be said about markets in education. They too are a sign of their times and, as we have argued, some, either fully or partially, are a sign of 'new times', postmodern times, yet-to-be-known times. None the less, it does seem as if we are 'inside the belly of this monster', as Donna Haraway (1991) would say. Our current concern is to understand much more fully what we are inside and up against. However, we also hope to be able to move beyond the radical pessimism evident above to talk of other things, such as, for example, educational possibilities and oppositional politics within and against postmodern markets in education. Those who are interested in exploring ideas with us can do so by E-mail.[2] What does that say?

Notes

1. Interestingly, the rise of the market in state education has led to a concomitant intensification in the private school sector. A number of private schools now employ public relations officers in various guises and fund-raising specialists and collectively conduct quite large-scale marketing enterprises such as Information Fairs. A recent Fair was held in the World Trade Centre in Melbourne and was promoted through a 12-page supplement in a major newspaper (see *The Age* Classified Advertising Feature, Wednesday 19 February 1992, pp. 1-12).
2. cj@ deakin OZ AU or ljf@ deakin OZ AU.

References

BAGGULEY, P. (1991) 'Post-fordism and enterprise culture: flexibility, autonomy and changes in economic organization', in R. Keat and N. Abercrombie (eds) *Enterprise Culture* (London: Routledge), pp. 151–171.

BALL, S. (1990) 'Education inequality and school reform', Inaugural Lecture, Centre for Education Studies, Kings College, London University.

BALL, S. (1990) *Politics and Policy Making in Education* (London: Routledge).

BARTOS, M. (1990) 'The education exports fiasco', *Australian Society*, pp. 18–19.

BAUDRILLARD, J. (1981) *For a Critique of the Political Economy of the Sign* (St Louis: Telos Press).

BAUDRILLARD, J. (1981) *Simulations*, Semiotext(e) (Columbia University, New York: Foreign Agents Series).

BIGUM, C. (1991) 'Schools for Cyborgs: educating aliens', *ACEC '91, Ninth Australian Computers in Education Conference*, Bond University, Computer Education Group of Queensland, pp. 21–34.

BIGUM, C. *et al.* (1987) *Coming to Terms with Computers in Schools: Report to the Commonwealth Schools Commission* (Geelong: Deakin Institute for Studies in Education, Deakin University).

BRAND, S. (1988) *The Media Lab: Inventing the Future at MIT* (Harmondsworth, UK: Penguin).

CHITTY, C. (1992) 'The privatization of education', in P. Brown and H. Lauder (eds) *Education for Economic Survival: From Fordism to post-Fordism* (London: Falmer Press).

CORNER, J. and HARVEY, S. (1991) 'Mediating tradition and modernity: the heritage/enterprise complete', in J. Corner and S. Harvey (eds) *Enterprise and Heritage: Cross Concepts of Natural Culture* (London: Routledge), pp. 45–76.

FERGUSON, R. *et al.* (eds) (1990) *Out There: Marginalisation and Contemporary Cultures* (New York: The Museum of Contemporary Art, and Cambridge: MIT Press).

FITZCLARENCE, L. and KEMMIS, S. (1988) 'Education at a distance', *Arena*, 84, pp. 152–157.

FITZCLARENCE, L. and KENWAY, J. (1992) 'Education and social justice in the post-modern age', in B. Lingard, J. Knight and P. Porter (eds) *Re/forming Education in Hard Times* (London: Falmer Press), in press.

HARAWAY, D. (1991) 'The actors are Cygorg, Nature is Coyote, and the geography is Elsewhere: postscript to Cyborgs at large', in P. Constance and A. Ross (eds) *Technoculture* (Minneapolis: University of Minnesota Press).

HEALD, D. (1983) *Public Expenditure: Its Defence and Reform* (Oxford: Martin Robertson).

HINKSON, J. (1987) 'Post-Lyotard: A critique of the information society', *Arena*, 80, pp. 123–154.

HINKSON, J. (1991), *Post-Modernity and Education* (Victoria, Australia: Deakin University Press).

HINKSON, J. (1992) 'Misreading the deeper. current: the limits of economic rationality', *Arena*, 98, pp. 112–135.

JAMESON, F. (1984) 'Post-modernism, or the cultural logic of late capitalism', *New Left Review*, No. 146, pp. 53–93.

KENWAY, J. (1987) 'Left right out: Australian education and the politics of signification', *Journal of Education Policy*, 2 (3), pp. 189–203.

KENWAY, J. (1990) 'Education and the Right's discursive politics' in S. Ball (ed) *Foucault and Education* (New York: Routledge).

KENWAY, J. (1991) 'Conspicuous consumption: class, gender and private schooling', in D. Dawkins (ed) *Education, Power and Politics in Australia* (London: Falmer Press).

KENWAY, J. (1992) 'Into the zone of the unknown: profiles, markets and social justice', *Curriculum Perspectives*, 12 (1), pp. 66–72.

KNIGHTLEY, P. and FAY, S. (1986) *The Age, Sunday Extra*, 18 January, p. 3.

LABOR RESOURCE CENTRE (1987) *The Role of the Public Sector in Australia's Economy and Society Summary Report* (Sydney: LRC).

LYOTARD, J. (1984) *The Post-modern Condition: A Report on Knowledge* (Minneapolis: University of Minnesota Press).

MARGINSON, S. (1991) 'Implications of the emerging education markets', paper presented to the National Policy Conference at the University of NSW, July.

PRESTON, B. (1984) 'Residualisation: what's that? *The Australian Teacher*, 8 (May), pp. 5–6, 15.

PRING, R. (1987) 'Privatisation', keynote address to the British Educational Management and Administration Society Conference, Southampton.

RANSON, S. (1990) 'From 1944–1988: education, citizenship and democracy', in M. Flude and M. Hammer (eds) *The Education Reform Act 1988: Its Origins and Implications* (London: Falmer Press).

RHEINGOLD, H. (1991) *Virtual Reality* (London: Secker & Warburg).

ROBINS, K. (1989) 'Reimagined communities, European images, spaces, beyond Fordism', *Journal of Cultural Studies*, 3 (2), pp. 145–165.

ROBINS, K. (1991) 'Tradition and translation: behavioral culture in its global context', in J. Corner and S. Harvey (eds) *Enterprise and Heritage: Cross Currents of National Culture* (London: Routledge), pp. 21–25.

ROTMAN, B. (1987) *Signifying Nothing: The Semiotics of Zero* (London: Macmillan).

SCHWARTZ, P. (1988) cited in S. Brand *The Media Lab; Inventing the Future at MIT* (London: Penguin).

SHARP, G. (1985) 'Constitutive abstraction and social practice', *Arena*, 80, pp. 48–82.

SHARP, G. and WHITE, D. (1968) 'Features of the intellectually trained', *Arena*, 15, pp. 30–33.

WALFORD, G. (1989) *Privatization and Privilege in Education* (London: Routledge).

WEXLER, P. (1987) *Social Analysis of Education; After the New Sociology* (London: Routledge).

WHEELWRIGHT, T. (1992) 'Global capitalism now: depression in the 1990s', *Arena*, 98, pp. 63–76.

WHITTY, G. (1991) 'Recent education reform: is it a post-modern phenomenon?', paper presented to a conference on Reproduction, Social Inequality and Resistance: New Directions in the Theory of Education, University of Bielefeld, Germany.

[25]

The Politics of 'Modernisation': Education Policy-Making at the Periphery

Eve Coxon

School of Education
University of Auckland

Introduction

The focus of this chapter is the education policy-making process within the 'modernising–developing' context of a small island state at the extreme periphery of the global political economy. It maintains that an understanding of the contextual dynamics of education policy-making in such a setting requires critical analysis of the implications for the policy process of the power relations between international political and economic forces and those of the nation-state on the one hand and the articulation[1] of the socio-cultural forces of local 'tradition' and global 'modernity' on the other. Accordingly, it first sets out to make sense of the dominant discourses which inform the conceptualisation of 'modernisation' centred within the development and the education policy agenda that are carried to the periphery by the external agencies on which peripheral states depend for advice and funding, and which assume an increasingly significant role in peripheral states' policy-making processes (Dale, 1994; Samoff, 1994; Jones 1992). The fact that the global hegemony is less secure at the periphery is often attributed to the persistence of local 'traditions' despite the establishment of 'modern' institutions, such as the nation-state and education, so how 'tradition' and 'modernity' are conceptualised within the discourses is a key theme of the discussion. A central line of argument is that although the state and the school are significant political and cultural institutions of modernity, with each institution being exemplified by global similarities in form and ideology, adequate conceptualisations must take into account the different historical conditions of their development and their incomplete integration into the global political economy. It is argued that the employment of an adequate concept of culture is fundamental to the development of a non-reductionist, dialectical theorisation of local and global, traditional and modern; one which recognises the social relations and historical forces within which culture is embedded. Issues arising from the 'localized complexity' (Ball, 1993) of the education policy process are then discussed by drawing on participant-observation research undertaken within the peripheral state of Samoa. The establishment of an education policy process in which the interaction of 'top-down' and 'bottom-up' forces enabled 'locally appropriate' policy decisions rather than the application of a 'global formula' (Samoff, 1994: 4) is the focus of the discussion.

Modernisation Revisited

Theories of 'development' were generated in response to the associated post-second World War processes of decolonisation and United States economic and political ascendency, as a bid to explain and control the process of integrating 'developing' countries into the world capitalist system. They were based largely on the nineteenth century social evolutionism which justified colonialism and which has helped shape the ongoing processes of globalisation.

'Developmentalism' conceptualised social change as either a succession of stages, movement from one pole of a dichotomy to another, or the presence or absence of a critical variable (Pieterse, 1991). Underlying all these conceptualisations of social change was the biological metaphor of growth – social change/evolution was natural, progressive and unilinear with a known destination. The theories formulated to explain and predict social transition – from 'traditional society' to 'modern society' – within the newly independent states of the post-colonial periphery were underpinned by the evolutionist and dichotomous theories of the same transition in Western Europe (particularly those of Tonnies, Marx, Durkheim and Weber), and thus can be justifiably charged as ethnocentric, ahistorical and teleological.

Developmentalist discourse informs and shapes the predominant development perspective of modernisation. During the 1950s and 1960s organised programmes of development – planned economic and social change – financed with external assistance via aid funds and soft loans, were introduced to and rapidly expanded throughout the periphery. The capitalist west was keen to convince the leaders of the emerging post-colonial states that their economic and social development would be best served through their participation as producers and consumers within the world market system; but in order to fulfil these roles they would have to 'modernise'. The hegemonic intent of the resultant development programmes is revealed in the sub-title of American economist Rostow's influential theory of modernisation, *A Non-Communist Manifesto*, which crudely appropriated the Marxist stage theory it was constructed to refute (Rostow, 1960; Lasch, 1991). His and other modernisation theories espoused a unilinear and dichotomous view of history – that all societies could progress from being undeveloped/backward to becoming developed/advanced, and that to do so they must all follow the same evolutionary process. The process was not seen as inevitable however, so the realisation of development required the conscious abandonment of traditional values and institutions, perceived as antagonistic to the modern values and structures necessary for progress and development. Modernisation theory's conceptualisation of the interrelationship between economic, political and cultural determinants led to the development of comprehensive typologies of the sort produced by structural-functionalist sociologist Talcott Parsons (1951) which presented an evolutionary progression of social types from 'primitive' to modern with each being attributed a set of 'functional imperatives' and 'action systems' whereby a 'values consensus' would be maintained, thus ensuring the equilibrium and order of the system. The prerequisites for the economic and technological achievements accepted as the hallmarks of modern society were political and, especially, cultural changes. The belief was that such changes, and therefore their end result of economic growth, could be accelerated in underdeveloped societies through the diffusion of modern (western) political and cultural institutions and values, and the transfer of western technology and expertise.

The Global Diffusion of Modern Institutions

The typologies and ideologies of modernisation provided an agenda for the acceleration of the globalisation of modernity through the expansion of western institutions such as the nation-state and education in non-western societies. The process was facilitated by the modernisation programmes initiated during the decolonisation era and continued by the newly independent peripheral states. Development programmes promoted and financed through the international organisations and sectoral agencies of the United Nations' system were formulated according to the precepts and objectives of modernisation, as were bilateral aid arrangements. The peripheral state was positioned as the central player in determining and driving social and economic development, and education was attributed a significant and specific role in overall development at the periphery.

The Peripheral State

The modernisation theories of the 1950s and 1960s assumed the worldwide expansion of an increasingly homogeneous political culture and perceived the post-colonial states which became participants within the interstate system – the hierarchically structured system within which interstate consensus according to a common ideological framework is formulated (Cox, 1987: 254) – as key actors in the process of constructing a global political order. The new states were awarded a central role at the interface of international and national systems, which required the transformation of international consensus into national policy. The means whereby this could happen necessarily involved two sets of relationships: with the international agencies and other 'friendly' states (particularly former colonial powers) and with their citizens. The perception of how both sets of relationships impacted on the peripheral state's capacity to maintain legitimacy at both global and local levels, constitutes the core of changing conceptions of the state upheld by the modernisation perspective.

Initially, the state was awarded an unproblematically conceived role in promoting the transition from 'traditional' to 'modern values' and institutions, in maintaining order and integrating the various functions of the social system, as 'neutral arbiter' of relationships between external aid donors and citizens; in the process of internal resource distribution, and deciding and implementing the policies which would ensure the state's comparative advantage within the global economy (Higgot, 1983). The objectives of state-led development policy were taken for granted: psychological change at the individual level and economic growth at the national level. The emphasis was on the various inputs required to shape a socio-psychological environment conducive to modernity. There was no sense of limitation on what states could or could not do; the expectation was that policies projected from the west and formulated within state structures would be straightforwardly implemented and unquestioningly accepted. The transference of knowledge to developing states through technical assistance from developed states was seen as promoting the interests of each insofar as it influenced the development policies of the recipient state and accelerated its transition to a modern 'rational' state. Carnoy

(1984: 172, 177) notes that the concept of both 'the state' and 'development' upheld by the modernisation paradigm was based on Schumpeter's view of capitalism as a civilising influence which would subdue the 'atavistic impulses' of traditional elements in peripheral societies.

By the late 1960s, growing critiques of existing theories of modernisation resulted in a lowering of expectations of the political objective for peripheral states which was now perceived as institutionally fragile and politically incapable, largely because of its responsiveness to 'irrational' societal demands. Throughout the 1970s the modernising of the peripheral state involved a shift of emphasis away from analysis of the inputs required, to a focus on the development of a strengthened and further-centralised bureaucracy, which would ensure improved policy-making and implementation processes and increased efficiency in the production and measurement of outputs. The degree of state power became more important than its form. The bolstering of state authority and the separation of state from society were fundamental to the modifications within modernisation during this period. The policy process was rendered increasingly technocratic through the use of 'rational choice' models, 'devised in contexts isolated from the structural and cultural realities of the Third World' (Higgot, 1983: 97).

Education and the Peripheral State

Prior to the modernisation era, schooling on the periphery was controlled by missionary and colonial authorities but with the advent of the processes of decolonisation and modernisation, education took on a greater political and economic significance as a central site for the production of the state agents and skilled workers which would enable the catching-up progression from traditional to modern. Since that time, debates concerning peripheral education have focused on the education/development problematic and the education policies needed to achieve wider development objectives. Education has, therefore, been conceptualised largely in instrumental terms whereby learners become human capital.

In the early modernisation theories, education was widely touted as the vehicle for modernisation: the central means for organising social transition and the precondition for overall development. Education's contribution to development was perceived as threefold and unproblematically leading to economic growth. Schools as modern institutions would promote modern characteristics such as individualism and competitiveness thus transforming their students from traditional to modern individuals, motivated by the achievement objectives of capitalism and an awareness of the instrumental value of education as a commodity. Schools would promote state formation, national integration and the notions of citizenship that would enable rational economic planning, and schools could provide the skills and vocational training required as a result of the incorporation of the emerging economy into the world market system (Dale, 1982). Modernisation's prescription for education underpinned the education programmes developed by the newly independent peripheral states under the patronage of multilateral and bilateral aid agencies. The policy implications of this – the expansion of formal education at all levels and the promotion of the particular sorts of knowledge and skills which would make the graduates of the system responsive to world market signals – were eagerly picked up by peripheral states' leaders anxious to meet post-colonial demands for better standards of living, and conscious of the limited availability of resources other than human. 'Manpower planning', the forecasting of the labour skills required for new economic activities and the post-colonial state structures, became an integral part of national economic planning and the rhetoric of self-sufficiency. Investment in the educational structures needed to implement the manpower plan led to greatly increased educational expenditure, most of it from external sources, through bilateral arrangements with former colonisers, or international agencies such as the World Bank.

Disillusion with manpower planning's capacity to identify and deliver the labour skills assumed to be the trigger for the increasingly elusive economic growth, and the need to curb state expenditure on education (and suppress the demand for its expansion), led in the early 1970s to a shift of emphasis to short-term planning aimed at ensuring a greater rate of return from educational investments, through rational-choice policy decisions based on efficiency in the allocation of resources. A significant policy consequence of this shift was the promulgation of dualist systems of education: the maintenance of conventional 'academic' schools for the privileged minority, and the development of less formalised, 'relevant' education programmes for the subordinate majority. Despite these modifications to how the relationship between education and development was perceived to be best activated, however, the central notion informing the modernisation perspective on education and development remained (and still remains) constant. The notion that education can produce the psychological changes and technical solutions required for economic growth continued to be upheld by peripheral state leaders, aid agencies. foreign consultants and all others involved in the education aid industry.

The Neoliberal Shift: From State-Led to Market-Led Development

The contestations of 'development' which arose within academia during the 1960s, while to some extent engaged with by international development agencies and peripheral states' leaders during the 1970s, did not have any lasting effect on the development programmes promulgated by the agencies or the development policies of the peripheral states. One explanation for this could be the lack of acceptable policy options offered by the alternative perspectives. Another could be the role of international development agencies in restricting the parameters of the dominant development discourse to preclude possible policy alternatives. An increasingly economistic policy continuum modified from within the modernisation paradigm: from the macrosociological Parsonian approach of the 1960s, through the rational-choice approach of the 1970s, to the public policy approach of the 1980s and the neoliberalism of the 1990s, means that development policy for peripheral states continues to be defined according to the theoretical precepts of modernisation. The links between the early and present-day modernisation models have been identified by Samoff (1994) as based on four enduring premises: the initial premise locates the causes of 'backward' states as within them, the result of obstacles from their past; the second posits modernisation as largely a technical-administrative process in which development can be achieved through the application of knowledge and the manipulation of inputs; the third requires that the technical-administrative process be managed by a modernising middle-class imbued through western education with the necessary skills and values; the fourth promotes a political form in which modern expertise is privileged and from which non-modern sectors (viewed as obstacles to progress) are largely excluded (ibid: 246–7).

Structural Adustment and Peripheral States

Within the rejuvenated modernisation discourse, increased integration into the global economy is accepted as the only effective development strategy for peripheral states. The establishment and promotion of the mechanisms whereby this can proceed is the role undertaken by the World Bank and IMF – as instruments for the mediation of the neoliberal order across the globe and especially to peripheral states where the hegemony is weakest. Although initially conceived in the late 1970s as a response to the 'debt crisis' at the periphery, structural adjustment programmes have now become an effective mechanism for ensuring the universal application of neoliberal policies; the means whereby the market paradigm has gained momentum around the globe, pushing countries further into the global market place, reducing the sovereignty of the state and permeating the social terrain (George, 1994). Central to structural adjustment programmes is the demand that the state's role in development be reduced in favour of market-led development. Associated with a reduction in the size and cost of the public sector is an increasing centralisation of administrative power and authority, which for peripheral states often includes a direct role in policy-making by the aid agencies. The external assistance essential to peripheral states' existence has become contingent on their acceptance of structural adjustment to further their integration into the global economy, and their only available development option.

The evidence from many of the world's poorest states is that the adjustment measures have done nothing to alleviate economic and social crises, and in fact have exacerbated them. The overriding structural adjustment philosophy of 'earn more, spend less' means that the first victims of the policies prescribed are those who benefit most (women and children) from social services such as education and health. Critics deny any possibility of equitable and sustainable social or economic development through the adoption of structural adjustment programmes, especially for the states on the extreme periphery.

Structural Adjustment and Education Policy in Peripheral States

In peripheral states, because education is the public service which most immediately affects a large proportion of the population and because it soaks up a relatively large amount of public expenditure, it also tends to be the area of public policy of most concern to the citizenry of that state. While education at the periphery has always been strongly influenced from outside, within the context of structural adjustment the inevitable implications for education of reduced public expenditure combined with continued perceptions of education as a key agent of modernisation/development, means that the educational systems of many peripheral states are subjected to an increased degree of external influence, specifically that of the World Bank. The Bank is the largest single supplier of external finance to education and a major player in the 'network of global influence [which] limits the discretion of peoples to shape their own educational destinies' (Jones, 1992: xiv). The education discourse emanating from the combination of the rejuvenated modernisation and the context of structural adjustment, presents an education policy formula, standardised as a technical-administrative process according to the rules and norms of the Bank, for global application (Samoff, 1994). The increased need for donor assistance as a result of reduced education expenditure, the increased participation of donor agencies in national policy-making processes and the reduction of the parameters of the discourse within which 'development' is conceptualised, provide the means whereby this education policy formula has become increasingly prescribed as the solution to educational problems wherever they are found.

The distorting effects of economistically derived and universally applied education policy solutions for peripheral states, in which little or no reference is made to the conditions in which teaching and learning processes actually occur, have been widely researched and detailed (e.g. Samoff, 1994). These accounts emphatically deny the possibility of equitable and sustainable educational development resulting from the application of a top-down macroeconomic policy prescription. Rather, they point to the need for a bottom-up process which takes account of the local historical and cultural foundations of education and which allows for popular participation.

Modernisation: Globalisation

Within current globalisation discourse the term 'globalisation' is used to refer to both the historical processes which have led to the construction of the world as a single place, and a conceptual change – a global human condition shaped by the economic, political and cultural aspects of globalisation. Parallel to the globalising processes that began with colonialism, were accelerated through the modernisation programmes of the so-called decolonising and the post/neocolonial eras, and have been further accelerated within the neoliberal climate of the 1990s in a process described by some commentators (e.g. George and Sabelli, 1994) as 'recolonisation', was the elaboration of theories purporting to explain the 'cultural' effects of globalisation. Although earlier theories predicted a global cultural convergence and eventual homogeneity as the cultural outcome of the modernisation/development processes undertaken by peripheral states, the cultural heterogeneity that characterises the (post)modern world despite the global diffusion of modern institutions is regarded by many contemporary globalisation theorists (e.g. Giddens, 1990; Robertson, 1991) as testimony to the efficacy of cultural agency in mediating the processes of globalisation. They seek to avoid the reductionism of notions of globalisation as a monolithic uncontested process by emphasising the continuous dialectic between globalising processes and local contexts as the means of explaining the co-existence of local/global, tradition/modernity. So whereas globalisation is presented as a fundamental consequence of the world-wide expansion of modern institutions, the complexity of the dialectic between tradition and modernity through the processes of globalisation is theorised as having produced a critical response to modernity's limitations; one which may lead beyond modernity.

The connections drawn between globalisation and modernity/postmodernity are not disputed here, but how the process is theorised is. A dual line of argument exists in globalisation discourse: first there is the perception of the globalisation of modernity as inherent in the dynamism of modernity itself; then the acknowledgement that global hegemony is more secure in the nation-states where it originated than in those on the periphery of the world system. Explanations of these two problematics usually rely on a more or less dichotomised conceptualisation of tradition and modernity, which privileges the latter in perceiving, either negatively or positively, tradition as an obstacle to the attainment of modernity. Notwithstanding their protestations about the totalising and universalising tendencies in modernism, it is maintained here that many of today's globalisation theorists work from the same basic precepts as those within the modernisation paradigm, in which the particular and local becomes a reaction to and product of the universalism implicit in the global. While the co-existence of tradition and modernity is acknowledged, for many globalisation theorists the former exists only as a reaction to the latter. Giddens goes so far as to claim that, in the contemporary world, tradition 'is tradition in sham clothing and receives its identity only from the reflexivity of modern life' (1990: 38), a view congruent with the developmentalism that informs modernisation. In each case there is the perception that non-western cultures, which are equated with tradition, are static and irrational in contrast to the dynamism and rationality of modern, western, culture, and that so-called tradition can survive in the face of modernisation only if it serves some function requisite to modernisation.

In order to account adequately for how global modernity articulates with local tradition an appropriate concept of culture must be employed; one which is irreducible to globalising processes and which recognises the agency of peripheral people in mediating global culture, in indigenising global modernity. The primary characteristic of culture is not the unthinking maintenance of continuity in the face of change or the wholesale abandonment of continuity in favour of change, as suggested by the tradition/modernity dichotomy, but creativity in articulating continuity within change (Austin-Broos, 1987). An adequate concept of culture, it is maintained, is one that perceives culture as integral to the development process, as unable to be abstracted from its socio-historical and material conditions of existence and which accepts that an understanding of how development, including education development, is shaped by the articulation of tradition and modernity can be arrived at only by looking from the bottom-up – from the point of view of the local.

The Policy Context: the Extreme Periphery

In terms of the global political economy, the context under question is literally at the extreme periphery. The 20 small Pacific Island states comprise a significant proportion of the smallest states in the world as measured by population, land area, and per capita GNP. Their total land area of less than 90,000 sq. kms scattered over 27 million sq. kms of ocean means they are remote from each other and the markets on which they rely for the export of their few primary products and the import of consumption goods, and also renders them vulnerable to both natural disasters and external market fluctuations. Despite these difficulties, most Pacific Islands people enjoy a good standard of living with access to adequate health and education services, their availability being largely dependent on the very high levels of multilateral and bilateral development assistance they receive. Because of the ongoing injections of aid, combined with the emigrant remittances which finance consumption at the level of family and village and the availability of agricultural and fishing resources for subsistence and some cash cropping, low GNP measurements are not of major concern to most people. Of more concern is the maintenance of the diversity of cultural traditions, based on the customary norms and forms of regulation of premodern times, which still effectively structure the lives of most people in the region. These 'traditional' institutions and values powerfully influence the socio-economic practices which determine such things as political leadership, ownership and access to land and fisheries, and care of the needy. They cannot easily be accommodated by, indeed are highly resistant to, the framework of development promoted by the top-down forces of global modernity.

During the 1990s, the World Bank has marked its growing influence in the Pacific Island region with the release of two documents (1991, 1993) each consisting of a report on the overall performance of the six regional member countries and a country-specific survey on each. Although they acknowledge the relatively high living standards of Pacific Island countries and that their social indicators compare favourably with other developing countries at the same or even higher income levels, they express disappointment at the lack of measurable economic growth (Slatter, 1994). Neither report contains any analysis of the structural bases of the region's economic difficulties, instead attributing them to excessive state regulation of the economy and inward-looking development strategies, and 'the persistence of traditional patterns of economic development'. The usual structural adjustment formula is presented unproblematically as the solution to the perceived problems with no reference to the social and economic benefits arising from the traditional economy's ethics of inclusiveness, redistribution and reciprocity.

The Samoan State: A Brief Profile

The south-west Pacific state of Western Samoa[2] joined the international state system after 62 years of colonisation by Germany (1900–14) followed by New Zealand which administered Western Samoa under both a League of Nations mandate and a United Nations trusteeship. The 1830 arrival of missionaries into an autonomous and self-sufficient society and the subsequent rapid christianisation of Samoa had been accompanied in the following decades by civil strife among various factions of the Samoan polity, interspersed with attempts to establish a form of central government as a means of controlling the increasing encroachment of western economic and political interests. These were ultimately ineffectual and under an 1899 treaty the islands of Samoa were divided with Germany assuming control of the western islands and the United States the eastern. The boundaries established by the treaty define the respective territories of western and eastern (American) Samoa today; with that of Western Samoa comprising 2,934 sq. kms made up of two large volcanic islands and seven smaller ones, within 120,000 sq. kms of ocean.

The struggle to regain independence persisted throughout the period of colonial rule, peaking with the formation of a nationalist movement, the *Mau*, under the slogan *Samoa mo Samoa* (Samoa for Samoans) during New Zealand's administration. Their campaign of comprehensive passive resistance which employed traditional political strategies as well as more modern techniques such as petitions, protest marches and non-payment of taxes, culminated in Western Samoa becoming the first Pacific Island country, and first UN trust territory, to enter the post-colonial period. What distinguishes the *Mau* from anti-colonial movements elsewhere is that, rather than fight for the creation of a new social order with new sources of power, their struggle was for a form of state governance inclusive of their traditional decentralised political institutions (Meleisea, 1992). The main concern of the decolonisation era was the establishment of an inclusive and participatory process whereby the agreement of all Samoans to a state structure that would create enduring linkages between two co-existing forms of political authority could be reached (Davidson, 1967). The constitution declaring 'The Independent State of Western Samoa' to be founded on the *fa'aSamoa* (the Samoan way of life) established all the structures of a 'modern' nation state but in conjunction with 'traditional' structures specific to the Samoan state – a franchise which included only those holding *matai* (chiefly) titles, the protection of land under customary title, and a Head of State position which could be occupied only by holders of at least one of the four *tama a 'aiga* (paramount) chiefly titles.

The Samon population today numbers approximately 165,000, virtually all of Polynesian heritage with a common language, culture and religious (christian) affiliation. The majority (approx. 80%) live a semi-subsistence lifestyle in one or other of the 300 small *nu'u* (villages) positioned around the coastlines of the two main islands. Each village maintains a high degree of autonomy under the governance of a village *fono* (council) made up of the village *matai* who head the *'aiga* (cognatic descent groups) which collectively own the village and associated lands. Social, political and economic practices within the village – the control of land and distribution of resources; election to titles and offices, ceremonial occasions etc. – are structured by the *fa'aSamoa*. Over 80% of the land of Western Samoa is still held according to customary title under *mata'i* authority with agricultural production absorbing about 60% of the workforce and accounting for approximately 50% of GDP, two-thirds of that being utilised for subsistence purposes. Most of the remaining 20% (35,000) of the population live in the capital of Apia (albeit many in *nu'u* within its boundaries) which was built by Europeans as a trade centre in the mid-nineteenth century, prospered as a port town and became the seat of government. Today it is largely a service centre containing government offices, educational and health facilities, retail stores, a large produce market, hotels and restaurants, with some small industry and manufacturing concerns found mainly on the outskirts of the city.

Since independence Samoa has taken its position in the international political and economic systems at both global and regional levels – for the former as a member of the United Nations, the Commonwealth and the South Pacific Forum; for the latter through membership of the World Bank, the IMF and the Asian Development Bank – and has also entered a number of bilateral relations, significantly with former colonial administrator, New Zealand, with whom a Treaty of Friendship was signed soon after independence. New Zealand is still Samoa's major trading partner and the main destination for Samoan emigrants; today Samoans constitute New Zealand's second largest (after Maori) ethnic minority, numbering about 100,000.

Despite receiving the attention and advice of the IMF and World Bank to a greater extent than any other Pacific Island state the Samoan economy has been in decline for the past two decades. Today Samoa ranks as the second most indebted country in the region with one of the lowest per capita GDPs (low enough to be one of the three in the region classified by the UN as among the world's thirty-five ' least developed countries') and has become increasingly dependent on external aid and the money and goods remitted from emigrants. Only 12.5% of the population are in the paid workforce and more than half that number earn less than $US1500 per year. The devastation caused by two cyclones in the early 1990s and a blight that destroyed the taro crop (an important source of subsistence and a major export earner) exacerbated pre-existing economic problems. The present government, in power since 1988, has attempted to address these problems through the implementation of structural adjustment policies. Although the 1993 World Bank report refers to Samoa as one of the two 'front-line market-friendly states' in the region, further adjustments were urged including tax reforms, export incentives and the individualisation of title to communally held land. Because of perceived threats to the *fa'aSamoa* and excessive aid donor influence, the post-cyclone economic restructuring programme has been the subject of considerable public debate and dissension.

Samoan Education: A Brief Historical Overview

The development of 'western' education[3] in Samoa is firmly anchored in the historical structures shaped by the articulation of the sociocultural forces of local tradition and the processes – colonisation, decolonisation and post/neocolonialism – of global modernity. When the London Missionary Society arrived in Samoa in 1830, no time was wasted in establishing the formal schooling perceived as necessary to achieve their objective of creating a 'civilised' and christian Samoan society and village pastor schools were set up throughout the country (the Samoans having refused to follow the usual missionary-instigated procedure of leaving their villages and moving to central mission stations).[4] The process of evangelising through the development of literacy was greatly accelerated by the establishment of a seminary in 1845 which combined general education with theological training and 'added an aristocracy of education to the Samoan social structure' (Davidson, 1967: 37) through graduating pastor/teachers of high social standing. By the end of the nineteenth century there were mission schools in all villages and almost 100% literacy in the Samoan language.

The only significant change arising from German colonialism was the establishment of three schools in Apia: one for expatriate and local European children; another for Samoan children which the villages around Apia offered to construct if the government provided the site, materials and teachers; and a boarding school for boys established in response to a request from the *matai* that some of their older sons should attain knowledge of the German language and the training that would enable them to work as government officials (Ma'ia'i, 1957: 172). These beginnings of a dual schooling system were continued under the New Zealand administration which assumed much of the control of and responsibility for schools, but whereas in rural areas villages provided and maintained the school buildings which were staffed with state-trained teachers who taught a locally devised curriculum, the Apia schools were built and maintained by the administration and much more closely integrated into the New Zealand system, taking pupils as far as Standard 6 (Year 8) and the New Zealand end-of-primary examination. The result was a form of 'adaptation education' which prevented the creation of a western educated political élite which might threaten New Zealand's political authority. Samoan leaders recognised the objective of stifling their political aspirations and made continual objection to the education policies of the administration but their pleas for the establishment of more government primary schools, secondary education of the type that would enable them to participate in and eventually control the administrative structures of the country, and teacher education which would upgrade the standard of locally trained teachers, went unheeded. That the Samoan people were well aware of the politics of education was also demonstrated during the *Mau* resistance, when they withdrew their children from the government schools resulting in the temporary closure of many.

During the first post-second World War decade, New Zealand's Director of Education C.E. Beeby,[5] led two delegations of New Zealand educators to Western Samoa to discuss the educational direction required to produce the future leaders for self-government according to the terms of the UN trusteeship. The recognition of the consequences of New Zealand's educational neglect and the validity of Samoan political demands led to the conclusion that, rather than aim for the necessarily long-term comprehensive improvement of the whole system, what was needed was a short-term plan for the creation of an 'academic élite' by selecting a small group of pupils, on the basis of ability and leadership, for overseas education and training. This would provide both an able and educated public service necessary for self-government and the nucleus of qualified and trained teachers necessary for a secondary system of high standard (Barrington, 1968: 870; Beeby, 1992: 214). A scholarship scheme under which young Samoans were sent to New Zealand for secondary and/or tertiary education was inaugurated, and in 1953 the first secondary school, Samoa College, 'dedicated to the people of Western Samoa by the people of New Zealand in token of friendship and as a help towards self-government', was opened by Dr Beeby. The secondary curriculum on offer at Samoa College was closely modelled on the New Zealand curriculum and prepared a selected group for the New Zealand examinations followed by further selection for higher education in New Zealand while most students were provided with two years secondary in preparation for the public service, teaching, nursing, police force, clerical work. The consequences of the developing inequities between the provision and standard of the schooling available to urban and rural students was the subject of continual debate throughout the decolonisation period. The steady migration of rural families into Apia in order to access the educational facilities available to urban children led to calls for more and better rural education, both to keep people in their villages and to enable rural children to compete with those in the Apia primary schools for further educational opportunities.

Western Samoa became an independent state in 1962 with an education system dominated by the prescriptions of the New Zealand education system. By the end of the decade, dissatisfaction with the inherited educational structures was being expressed by educators concerned with the appropriateness of what the schools offered, and by politicians and bureaucrats concerned at the relatively large amount of resources being soaked up by the system. But the demand for increasing amounts of education, perceived as enhancing the prospects of joining the escalating migration trend in search of wage employment made increased provision politically imperative. Throughout the 1970s the major educational thrust was towards the expansion of school opportunities at every level of the system through the construction and equipping of school buildings and the provision of teaching personnel and resources. Government commitment to a country-wide school building programme, often initiated and financed by village *fono*, meant that by the end of the decade all Samoan children had access to nine years of primary schooling. Junior Secondary Schools were established in most districts and offered a three-year alternative secondary programme to those students who had not ranked highly enough in the national examination held at the end of their primary schooling to gain access to the senior secondary schools. The aim of these schools was to establish closer links between formal schooling and the rural life to which most students would return. Senior secondary places in both government and mission schools increased but remained highly selective. In 1979 two-year primary and three-year secondary teachers training programmes (for the preparation of junior secondary teachers) were instituted to cater for growing school enrolments, to improve the quality of classroom teaching and to decrease the dependence on overseas teachers. The main thrust of the 1980s was in the areas of curriculum and assessment, particularly at primary and junior secondary levels, and efforts to construct more 'relevant' curricula and an assessment system better suited to local 'needs'. At the same time, however, there were pressures on the senior secondary system to provide more places.

By the early 1990s the school system included approximately 50,000 primary, junior secondary and senior secondary students. The two cyclones that devastated the economy in the early 1990s had equally devastating educational effects – 85% of school buildings and virtually all school equipment and teaching materials were destroyed. The necessity for rebuilding the education system within the 1990s climate of economic decline, combined with reduced government expenditure resulting from structural adjustment measures and reduced community spending power as a result of decreased remittances from *'aiga* in metropolitan countries who are victims of the same economic policies, has had the effect of rendering Samoan education increasingly dependent on external assistance.

The Education Policy and Planning Development Project

In 1994 a New Zealand-funded project (the EPPDP) with the goal of 'the raising of the quality and relevance of education in Western Samoa and improvements in equity and efficiency' was initiated in response to a request from Samoa subsequent to a World Bank Education Sector Review undertaken in 1992, shortly after the second of two cyclones to hit Samoa within a period of two years. The project's three main objectives were a comprehensive policy framework, a strategic plan and a management information system and its focus was to be the strengthening of policy and planning capability within the Ministry of Education. Three 'technical assistants' (a policy adviser, an economist-planner and a MIS adviser) were provided through the NZODA programme.

In view of the difficulty of rehabilitating the education system within the severe economic conditions being faced following the cyclones, the Bank Review had recommended that the rebuilding of the system, necessarily dependent on external funding, take place within a long-term development strategy and that the government adopt the policy recommendations and implementation strategies detailed in the review with the least possible delay. These addressed two broad areas of concern: the need for increased 'cost effectiveness' through a 'restructured' and 'rationalised' education system (pointing out that Vote Education received 20% of the government's recurrent budget, with teacher salaries accounting for 95% of expenditure within that); and the need for 'improved management capacity and procedures' in schools and within the Ministry of Education. The identification of problems of quality, equity, relevance and efficiency in the Samoan system, and the solutions suggested for their redress, were generally congruent with the Bank's global formula. The development plan was costed at $US25,800,000.

Of interest to this discussion given the expressed need for a policy process which takes account of the local historical and cultural foundations of education, and which recognises the need for popular participation if the locally appropriate policy decisions necessary for equitable and sustainable educational development are to be arrived at, was Samoa's reluctance to accept the recommendations of the Review. The nominated tasks for the requested policy advisor – to facilitate a process of policy analysis of the Review recommendations and the development of a policy framework which would either incorporate them or formulate alternatives, and that this be undertaken within a participatory, consultative process – were indicative of unease with both the nature of the recommendations and the process through which they have been arrived at. These perceptions were confirmed by the following critical observations of the Bank Review offered by Samoan educators:

> It is typical of an economistic ideology which sees education as input and output, supply and demand … and that makes education so remote. It says next to nothing about what education is.

> I've seen the World Bank at work before. It doesn't make much difference to them what country they're in, they just see much the same problems – not enough resources, bad management, poor standard of teaching etc – so impose the same solutions all around the globe. But just because the problems are the same doesn't mean the reasons and answers are – many of the factors involved here are unique; they're the result of what's happened before …

The Political Backdrop

Of significance to the policy process established was that it took place against a backdrop of widespread political protest stemming from the introduction of the tax reforms prescribed by structural adjustment. The associated events provided a very immediate manifestation of localised resistance to the application of a policy formula standardised according to universalised notions of development, irrespective of the socio-historical particularities of the context.[6] A significant proportion of the population was mobilised under the leadership of groups of orator chiefs, whose predecessors had been the 'principal power wielders' within traditional political structures, in protest against a government seen as working in the interests of 'foreign capital, progress and power hunger' at the expense of most of the population and especially those in rural villages. The dialectic of tradition/modernity was played out through the appeal by the protest leadership to the ideals of the *fa'aSamoa* and the employment of traditional political structures, in undertaking a programme of political action modelled closely on that of the anti-colonial *Mau*, including protest marches of 15–20,000 people. The protestors' objective was stated as 'to bring massive public pressure expressed through traditional Samoan means' on the government. The complexity and dynamism of processes often presented in the globalisation/development discourses as monolithic and uncontested was clearly demonstrated.

For the education policy-makers the strength of the grassroot support mobilised through the decentralised traditional political structures contained a clear message – that the strength of the *fa'aSamoa* and the authority held within village and district-based political structures must be accommodated within the policy process and reflected in policy decisions. Furthermore, the constant mention of how the sales tax would impact on the costs associated with schooling for those least able to afford them, so exacerbating existing educational inequalities, served to highlight the most significant educational issue to be addressed by the policy process – the dual educational structures which continued to maintain and reproduce unequal provision and outcomes between rural and urban students. That these structures were anchored in the forms and expectations of education established through the articulation of the socio-cultural structures of the *fa'aSamoa* and the historical processes of globalisation/modernisation, spoke clearly to the need for a policy-making process that would ask the critical questions necessary to grasp the localized complexity of the policy context so arriving at the policy decisions that would lead to improved educational experiences for all groups of students.

Establishing the Policy Process

The body charged with analysing the recommendations of the World Bank Review and developing a policy framework, the Policy Planning Committee (PPC)[7] was agreed that the success of the project required the development of a process within which (in the words of one member):

> Policy issues must be debated thoroughly by all groups of Samoans in order to develop a vision – they have to focus on the critical issues in order to develop policies that are socially and politically appropriate.

In laying the foundations of a policy process which would ensure the above, the following steps were taken: a set of principles about the nature and process of policy itself was arrived at; a practical strategy for the analysis of existing and proposed policies, identifying policy needs, evaluating policy alternatives and formulating policy decisions was outlined; the key terms/concepts that would provide benchmarks for the policy process were defined; some philosophical understandings about education and its place within society, and a set of broad goals to guide the educational enterprise were defined; and the means whereby dialogue with interest groups could proceed were established.

It is not the purpose of this discussion to either explicate fully the issues and debates engendered by the policy process or to detail policy decision – suffice to say that none of the substantive recommendations of the World Bank Review were taken up; locally appropriate policy options were determined through the process outlined above. The following brief comments on selected aspects of the process are intended to illuminate how the contextual dynamics of the policy-making process.

Policy Principles

The principles established as guidelines for the process started from the position that the education policy is, first and foremost, educational; that the aim of revising education policies is to improve existing educational practices and conditions and that education policy decisions should lead to an improved education for all learners. Moreover, that for this to be the outcome of the education policy process, careful attention would be required to both the structures/practices of teaching and learning and the conditions under which teaching and learning take place (Prunty, 1984; Coxon *et al.*, 1994: 17–18). A clear focus on the educational mission of learning institutions was asserted as was the need to protect and enhance the professionalism of teachers. It was seen as crucial that educational personnel 'down the line' should not be seen as passive implementers of policy (Jones, 1992: 239) but that they should be involved as shapers of policy in order to ensure their 'ownership', and the successful implementation, of policy decisions.

While it was accepted that education policy is about change, it was asserted that it should also be about continuity in that it needs to recognise and build on the strengths of the existing system – so identification of what should be continued in the existing system was as important to the policy process as identifying what should be changed. Concern was also expressed that the policy decisions arrived at be implementable; that simple rather than complex changes be proposed and that the process of implementation be conceived as gradual 'with long time horizons' (Samoff, 1994: 250). The formulation of policies constructed according to the need for continuity in change was also perceived to require that education policy be seen as context-specific. Although it was agreed that international trends in education should be heeded, the view was held that globalised policy formula must be treated with circumspection as the solutions they advance often preceded any analysis of contextual problems; so the extrapolation of an externally-generated set of policies would be inappropriate and counter-productive if imposed on the Samoan system. It was viewed as fundamental to a successful process that the policy process be firmly planted in the local setting. In elaborating this principle, it was also emphasised that although education must be the focus of educational policy, it could not be considered apart from its situatedness. It was necessary, therefore, that context-specific education policies should be crafted according to a process of analysis and formulation whereby problems and their solutions would be considered within the full historical, socio-cultural, political and economic conditions in which the education system exists (Peters and Marshall, 1993); and that because historically-developed educational forms and expectations constrain and determine policy possibilities they must be thoroughly understood.

A further principle arose around the discussion of the tension between the internationalisation of education and so-called universal education values with their focus on the individual, and the *fa'aSamoa* values of community coherence and a collective identity. These were not seen as contradictory educational goals. It was maintained that Samoan students have been and could continue to be educated in such a way that they are able to develop their individual potentials and needs, contribute to their communities and wider society, and be prepared for life beyond Samoa. What was required was an education policy process and policy decisions responsive to the needs and workings of both the individual and society and aimed at social integration. It was also felt that while policies must attend first to individual, community and national needs as defined by the Samoan context, due attention should be paid to the fact that learning institutions must also prepare their students for membership of an international community.

It was accepted that the process established should be consultative and ensure the participation of all groups within society, particularly those most affected by policy decisions. This principle is central to the *fa'aSamoa* decision-making process of *soalaupule* described by Le Tagaloa (1992:123) as an inclusive and consultative process involving all the appropriate people and the only effective means of arriving at public policy decisions. It was also considered important that in a context with two official languages, one (English) in which the policy documents were being written, and the other (Samoan) being the mother tongue for the vast majority of those affected by the policy decisions, they should be presented in such a way that they would be understood by all sectors of the community. This would require not only translation into Samoan but also dialogue according to the *fa'aSamoa*, particularly through village *fono*.

Defining the Key Terms

Corson (1988) argues that the failure to treat the key terms underpinning policy issues as problematic, and the failure to agree on their meaning at the start of the policy process so all actors in the process have a shared understanding of them, is a major weakness in policy debate and a significant factor in education policy failure. He maintains that these terms should be defined in such a way that they communicate the overall objectives of the policy-makers in being explicitly spelt out in the policy text (ibid.: 258). The World Bank Review identified 'quality', 'access', 'equity', 'relevance' and 'efficiency' as 'key issues' informing the policy recommendations that make up their strategy for 'rebuilding the system' (1992: 15–18), and there was general agreement among the PPC members that these were indeed key issues for education in Samoa. In light of Corson's argument and realising the Bank's tendency for slippage – especially between quality and efficiency, and access and equity – it was decided that the key terms needed to be defined in ways clearly applicable to the Samoan context before proceeding with the policy process, and that they would be used in only one explicitly stated sense in the policy text.

Discussion of the term *equity* began with clarification of how it differs from that of 'equal opportunity', the notion that providing all individuals with equal access to schooling ensures a fair system, which has underpinned educational policy in Samoa since the 1950s. Equity, however, goes beyond access to maintain that all students must also be treated fairly in terms of treatment, pinpointing inequitable systems as those characterised by policies which advantage some groups and disadvantage others thereby leading to differential outcomes. It was decided that the term access should be subsumed within that of equity. The PPC members agreed with the Bank Review that inequities throughout the existing system for rural students were a priority but were concerned that, in their analysis of senior secondary structures, the review had not addressed gender inequities arising from the fact that of the three government senior secondary schools one was a single-sex boys school. The distribution of educational resources was seen as a central issue in the achievement of equity, and the obvious tension between the demand for equity and the availability of the resources to meet that demand, within a situation of tight financial constraint, was acknowledged. It was felt that if equity was to be integral to policy decisions, the only means of redressing inequities was to either employ redistributive policies which shift resources from the advantaged groups to the disadvantaged or to acquire additional resources through external sources which would be dedicated to the disadvantaged groups – girls at senior secondary level and rural schools at primary and junior secondary level.

In defining *quality*, the PPC's first consideration was how the Bank Review was using the term: the perception was that the Bank's focus on quantifiable 'inputs', on education as a 'delivery system' (Samoff, 1994: 225), equated quality with the efficiency of an education system. While it was agreed that efficient management and administrative practices have an effect on educational quality as measured by 'outputs' such as examination results, retention rates etc, what was questioned was that they define quality. Also questioned was the apparent faith which the Bank attached to the technical and material aspects of education and the relative downplaying of the process aspects of education. Agreed was that the quality of education rested on teaching and learning as an interactive process heavily dependent on teachers; that the effectiveness of the classroom teacher is the most significant determinant of educational quality. Improvements in quality were seen as thus necessitating critical attention to the structures of learning and teaching – curriculum, pedagogy, evaluation – especially the socio-cultural assumptions on which these structures are based. Focusing on the school as the key organisational unit in the education system, strengthening school-community links and promoting the cultural and social foundations of education were all pinpointed as issues of educational quality that should inform policy decisions.

The starting point for defining *relevance* was the recognition that it is most often associated with the provision of an appropriate quantity and type of workforce skills, and that it is usually used in debates about education as an example of what schools do not do. The PPC reported that one of the most common criticisms of schooling in Samoa is that of its 'irrelevance' but that attempts to initiate what is usually defined as 'relevant' have been overwhelmingly unsuccessful with a direct consequence being an inequitable dual secondary system. The fact that the Bank Review prioritised policies aimed at improving 'the relevance of education to the labour market' as a priority (1992: 32) was seen as problematic given the Samoan context with its limited opportunities for wage/salary employment where most school leavers become part of their village labourforce, undertaking duties as directed by the *'aiga* and village *fono*. But also noted was that the level of migration to metropolitan countries means an education programme too closely aligned with the student's immediate environment may also be irrelevant. Although it was accepted that schools should impart the knowledge, skills and attitudes upon which occupation-specific preparation can be built, whether labour market preparation should be seen as a specific function of the school was keenly disputed. It was agreed that education should be viewed as more than a means to the end of economic development. A notion of education as intrinsically worthwhile and as having socio-cultural and political as well as economic ends was upheld, with the most relevant type of schooling being accepted as a general one for all students: a sound academic grounding in the conventional subjects supplemented by creativity in arts subjects and applied work in practical areas; a programme that was planted firmly in the Samoan context while maintaining an international perspective.

Because of the confusion created by the Bank's conflation of 'efficiency' and 'quality', the PPC concern was to define *efficiency* in such a way that there was a clear distinction between them. It was well recognised that the technical/material factors discussed by the Review are important in the achievement of both quality and equity and that this takes on additional importance in an extremely financially constrained context like Samoa, so it was decided that the definition of efficiency should be based on the effective and equitable management and allocation of resources. The upholding of realistic, manageable and sustainable policy recommendations that take into account the constraints on both human and material resources, however, also gave rise to the perception that many of the Review's recommendations were unsustainable and likely to lead to inefficiency and/or increased aid dependency.

Concluding Comments

Not only were the policy decisions arrived at by the PPC more appropriate to the local context than the globally-derived recommendations of the World Bank Review, they were much more cost-effective. The Bank recommendations would have meant an extensive restructuring of the existing system and required large loans to implement, which even at the concessional rates available to LDCs would have been an unacceptable addition to the already considerable debt-burden sustained by the Samoan government The PPC recommendations, by contrast, while adhering to the principles established and proposing policies which met the contextual definitions of the key terms underpinning the process, were implementable insofar as they were concerned to build on what already existed and affordable within existing volumes of aid assistance. What could be deemed the most enabling outcome of the EPPDP is that it gave the Samoan decision-makers a coherent policy framework, well-supported with detailed plans and statistical data, within which aid-funded projects could be co-ordinated; thus going some way towards equalising the power relations of donor and recipient. An important achievement, too, given that the project as developed within the NZODA programme was characterised by the same managerial approach as promoted by the World Bank, was the extent to which teaching and learning issues were centred in the process, a reflection of the PPC's collective professional commitment to the grounded educational interests of students and teachers. But perhaps the most significant aspect of the education policy-making process in the peripheral state under discussion was that, although facilitated through external assistance, it was locally -driven by people who live the *fa'aSamoa* – a sociocultural system which has articulated with 'modern' state structures to the extent that it cannot be ignored by externally-conceived programmes of 'development'. In Samoa, the possibilities for the forces of global 'modernisation' to determine state policies are very definitely circumscribed by the culture history of local 'tradition'.

Notes

1. The term 'articulation' is being used in Hall's (1986: 53–4) sense as a form that *can* make a unity of two different elements under certain conditions but not as determined, absolute and essential for all time.
2. In 1997, 'Western' was dropped from the title.
3. I am using the term 'western education' to distinguish the particular form of schooling introduced by the missionaries and developed since, from pre-existing forms of indigenous education. I am not suggesting that the form of education found in Samoa today is 'western'; it is as much shaped by the imperatives of the *fa'aSamoa* as any global 'modernising' imperative.
4. Davidson maintains that 'Samoan protestantism never became the LMS ideal' – because Samoans would not move from their villages, *fono* decisions and *matai* opinion had to be taken seriously by the village pastors and their missionary supervisors, with the result that church structures took on 'a distinctively Samoan character' (1967: 36).
5. In the years following, Beeby advised many developing countries on education policy and in 1966 published the widely read *The Quality of Education in Developing Countries*. He sources the ideas encapsulated in this and later writings to his experiences in Western Samoa (Beeby, 1992).
6. The following information comes from coverage of the protests as reported in local newspapers and personal observation.
7. The Policy Planning Committee (PPC) consisted of the Director of Education, four Assistant Directors, the Principal of the Teachers' College and the Principal of a non-government school in Apia (a well-respected palagi educator, an Apia resident of many years), with the Policy Advisor and the Economist-Planner as *ad hoc* members for the duration of the project. Collectively, the Samoan membership of the PPC represented three high-ranking *matai* titles, the president of the Public Service Association, the president and secretary of the teachers' union, three ex-principals of senior secondary schools and one of a junior secondary and three graduates of Unesco's International Institute for Educational Planning.

References

Austin-Broos, Dianne J. (ed.), 1987. *Creating Culture*. Sydney: Allen & Unwin
Ball, Stephen J., 1993. 'What is policy? Texts, trajectories and toolboxes', *Discourse: The Australian Journal of Educational Studies*, **13**, No. 2: 10–17
Barrington, J.M., 1968. 'Education and National Development in Western Samoa'. Unpublished PhD Thesis, Victoria University

Beeby, C.E., 1966. *The Quality of Education in Developing Countries*. Massachusetts: Harvard University Press
Beeby, C.E., 1992. *The Biography of an Idea. Beeby on Education*. Wellington: New Zealand Council of Educational Research.
Carnoy, Martin, 1984. *The State and Political Theory*. New Jersey: Princeton University Press
Corson, David, 1988. 'Making the language of education policies more user-friendly'. *Journal of Education Policy*, **3**, No. 3: 249–260
Cox, Robert, W., 1987. *Production, Power, and World Order*. Columbia University Press: New York
Cox, Robert W., 1994. 'The Crisis in World Order and the Challenge to International Organisation'. *Cooperation and Conflict*, **29**, No. 2: 99–113
Coxon, Evelyn, Kuni Jenkins, James Marshall and Laura L. Massey, 1994. *The Politics of Learning and Teaching in Aoteavoa – New Zealand*. Palmerston North: Dunmore Press
Coxon, Evelyn, 1996. 'The Politics of "Modernisation" in Western Samoan Education'. Unpublished PhD Thesis, University of Auckland
Dale, Roger, 1982. 'Learning to be ... What? Shaping Education in "Developing Societies"'. In, Alavi, Hamza and Teodor Shanin (eds), *Introduction to the Sociology of Developing Societies*. London: Macmillan
Dale, Roger, 1994. 'Constructing a New Education Settlement: Neo-Liberal and Neo-Shumpeterian Tendencies'. Paper presented to NZARE Conference, Auckland
Davidson, J.W., 1967. *Samoa mo Samoa: the Emergence of the Independent State of Western Samoa*. Melbourne: Oxford University Press
George, Susan, 1994. 'Market Policies and Development Problems in the Third World'. Seminar paper presented at the University of the South Pacific, Suva, Fiji.
George, Susan, and Fabrizio Sabelli, 1994. *Faith and Credit. The World Bank's Secular Empire*. London: Penguin
Giddens, Anthony, 1990. *The Consequences of Modernity*. UK: Polity Press
Hall, Stuart, 1986. 'On Postmodernism and Articulation'. *Journal of Communication Inquiry*, **10**, No. 2: 45–60
Hau'ofa, Epeli *et al.*, 1993. *A New Oceania. Rediscovering Our Sea of Islands*. Suva: School of Social and Economic Development, University of the South Pacific
Higgot, Richard A., 1983. *Political Development Theory*. London: Croom Helm
Jones, Phillip, W., 1992. *World Bank Financing of Education*. London: Routledge
Lasch, Christopher, 1991. *The True and Only Heaven*. New York: W.W. Norton and Co.
Le Tagaloa, Aiono Fanaafi, 1992. 'The Samoan Culture and Government'. In, Crocombe, Ron *et al.*, *Culture and Democracy in the South Pacific*. Suva: University of the South Pacific
Ma'ia'i, Fanaafi, 1957. 'A Study of the Developing Pattern of Education and the Factors Influencing that Development in New Zealand's Pacific Dependencies'. Unpublished MA Thesis, Victoria University
Meleisea, Malama, 1992. *Change and Adaptation in Western Samoa*. Christchurch: Macmillan Brown Centre for Pacific Studies
Parsons, T., 1951. *The Social System*. London: Routledge and Kegan Paul
Peters, Michael and James Marshall, 1993. 'Education Policy Analysis and the Politics of Interpretation. The Search for a Well-Defined Problem'. *Evaluation Review*, **17**, No. 3: 310–330.
Pieterse, J.N., 1991. 'Dilemmas of Development Discourse: The Crisis of Developmentalism and the Comparative Method'. *Development and Change*, **22**: 5–29
Prunty, John J., 1984. *A Critical Reformulation of Educational Policy Analysis*. Melbourne: Deakin University Press
Robertson, Roland, 1991. 'Social Theory, Cultural Relativity and the Problem of Globality'. In, King, Anthony D. (ed.), *Culture, Globalization and the World-System*. London: Macmillan Press.
Rostow, Walt W., 1960. *The Stages of Economic Growth. A Non-Communist Manifesto*. Cambridge: Cambridge University Press
Samoff, Joel, (ed.), 1994. *Coping with Crisis. Austerity, Adjustment and Human Resources*. London: Cassell and Unesco
Slatter, Claire, 1994. 'Banking on the Growth Model? The World Bank and market policies in the Pacific'.

In Emberson-Bain, Atu (ed.), *Sustainable Development or Malignant Growth? Perspectives of Pacific Island Women*. Suva: Marama Publications
World Bank, 1991. *Towards Higher Growth in Pacific Island Economies: Lessons from the 1980s*, **1**, Regional Overview; **2**, Country Surveys. Washington
World Bank, 1992. *Western Samoa: Rebuilding the Education System*, Education Sector Review. East Asia Region
World Bank, 1993. *Pacific Islands Economies: Towards Efficient and Sustainable Growth*. **1**, Regional Overview. Washington

[26]

Comparative Education *Volume 33 No. 1 1997 pp. 117–129*

REVIEW ARTICLE

On World Bank Education Financing

PHILLIP W. JONES

World Bank (1995) *Policies and Strategies for Education: a World Bank review* (Washington DC, World Bank)

Introduction

On four occasions since its lending for education began in 1962, the World Bank has published a comprehensive policy statement outlining its views on educational development. On each occasion, these much-anticipated and much-discussed statements have had a dual purpose. First, they have provided the bank with an opportunity to outline its views on education and development. The bank's hope here is that governments, other multilateral and bilateral aid agencies and the education and academic community will be persuaded of its views and will adopt them. Second, the statements provide the bank with opportunities to publicise its own priorities for lending. Thus, they indicate not only the Bank's preferred view of educational futures, but also how it might back those views with finance. From the executive directors' initial education policy formally adopted in 1963, the sequence of formal policy statements—in 1971, 1974, 1980 and 1995—provides a useful framework for analysing evolving bank views of educational development and of its own priorities for lending.

In mid-1995, the executive directors of the World Bank approved the text of the latest bank statement of education policy, since published as *Priorities and Strategies for Education: a World Bank review* (World Bank, 1995). This review article attempts to place the statement in a historical and policy context. It locates it within the framework of the bank's evolving approach to education over the past 35 years and interprets it in the light of the most significant developments facing the bank over the past decade, in particular structural adjustment strategies and the end of the Cold War. Each has caused the bank to sharpen its thinking about the economic, political and social preconditions for educational development.

I have argued elsewhere that bank policies in education have never been static (Jones, 1992). Many examples can be found of countries repaying loans for purposes since questioned or even discredited by the bank. Despite its proven dexterity, whose prime driving force is the need to stay in business, the bank nevertheless operates within fairly firm parameters. The discipline imposed by its sources of loanable funds—the international financial community—locates the bank firmly within global economic structures, of which the bank provides a rare example of visibility. Market place realities impose on the bank the need to appear technically sound, confident and decisive. The price paid has been heavy, as

Correspondence to: Phillip W. Jones, Faculty of Education, The University of Sydney 2006, Australia.

0305-0068/97/010117-13 $7.00

simplicity has tended to accompany this need. What has changed is the bank's perception of its own role, the most dramatic changes being corrections of earlier arbitrariness rather than any shift in fundamentals. This should be kept in mind when the following overview of bank education policy development is presented: the bank's rationale has barely changed in 35 years, a celebration of the elegance of human capital theory.

As stated above, two broad avenues exist for the bank to indicate its policies. First, they can be explored by examining the loan negotiation and approval process, which reveal what the bank is actually prepared to lend for. Here can be seen the bank at its most flexible, prepared to concede for one government what it might not be prepared to concede for another. While loan covenants—'leverage' in bank parlance—also provide key insights into broader policy stances, their significance in reality should not be overstated. Borrower after borrower simply ignores them once signed. Second, there is the array of formal policy statements, analysis, rhetoric and research publications whereby the bank attempts to influence prevailing climates of opinion about education and development. In the battle of ideas, the bank is a keen participant.

Bank Policies in Education 1963–1990

The establishment of a portfolio in education—marked by caution, containment and arbitrariness—saw bank policy from 1963 to 1968 limited to the kinds of educational provision thought most likely to lead to increased worker productivity and economic expansion, best understood in the light of the bank's prior experience in supporting the physical infrastructure of production.

> In most developing countries . . . the most urgent need is for (a) an expression of vocational and technical education and training at various levels, including technical schools, agricultural schools and schools of commerce and business administration; and (b) an expansion of general secondary education, to provide middle-level management for government, industry, commerce and agriculture, more candidates for higher education and for specialized vocational training, and more teachers for the primary schools. (World Bank, 1963, p. 1)

Despite its caution, the extent of bank lending and the size and scope of its projects quickly escalated, so that by 1968 $US243 million had been lent to 23 countries for 25 projects. The allocation of loan funds was almost completely devoted to construction and equipment, the bank confining its interest in education policy and effectiveness to loan covenants (side-conditions). While it is something of a myth that in the 1960s the bank was solely interested in the expansion of educational facilities (a 'bricks and mortar' concern) it is nevertheless pertinent that bank staff in education were overwhelmingly architects, the United Nations Educational, Scientific and Cultural Organisation (UNESCO) providing the educational expertise needed for project identification and design.

The arbitrariness of bank lending policy stemmed in large measure from the bank's president, George Woods, whose departure permitted a liberalisation of policy. When Robert McNamara took up office in April 1968, he quickly initiated a dramatic increase in the size and scope of bank lending and advisory work. An expanding bank quickly became a more diverse bank, which education department director, Duncan Ballantine, was quickly able to exploit following years of frustration under Woods. Ballantine appointed Harvard economist Edward Mason to conduct a sector review as soon as Woods' departure was certain. Mason's February 1968 report politely pointed to the desirability of broadening the scope of bank lending, adding general (and not just technical) higher education, primary education, adult education and a concern for 'new techniques of teaching and learning'. The Mason report led directly to the executive directors' approval of the landmark document *Lending in Education* in August 1970, providing a policy framework for the remainder of the McNamara years (to 1980). McNamara, ever polite, nevertheless slammed the limitations of his predecessor's approach to education policy.

> . . . we should broaden the scope of projects considered and we should determine priorities and select projects on the basis of a thorough examination of the education system as a whole rather than by *a priori* designated areas of eligibility. . . . We should continue to emphasize projects which, like vocational training, produce trained manpower directly but we should also consider for financing other types of projects with less direct relation to the short-run training of manpower which would have important long-term significance for economic development. (World Bank, 1970, p. 4)

This set the scene for the bank education policy published in September 1971—the *Education Sector Working Paper* (World Bank, 1971). As the first public statement of education lending criteria, the paper achieved wide circulation, also providing the first published summary of project experience. The major point of interest was not so much the bank's views on how governments should construct their education systems and policies. Rather, it was looked to as an indication of what the bank itself was prepared to lend for and how it defined its own role. For many borrowers, the unprecendented levels of finance available through the bank could only sharpen their thinking along bankable lines, the mere availability of bank finance shaping to a considerable extent their policies and priorities. Explicitly included in a considerably expanded set of education subsectors was a list giving the McNamara bank an image of liberality and responsiveness to need.

(1) Primary education.
(2) Secondary education.
(3) Post-secondary education for middle-level employment.
(4) University education.
(5) Teacher education.
(6) Adult vocational training and non-formal education.
(7) Technical assistance.
(8) Staff and student housing.
(9) Educational technology.
(10) General support (including textbooks, equipment, research, planning and management).

The McNamara bank was one which actively debated the optimal means for guiding the rapid expansion of lending, not only in education but across the board. The much-trumpeted poverty focus, whereby redirecting investment to the poor formed the basis for the McNamara focus on 'redistribution with growth' (RWG), has been widely misunderstood. Within his bank, RWG was pitted against another policy contender, a 'basic human needs' (BHN) approach which had generated considerable support within an increasingly liberal atmosphere within the bank. The years 1970–1973 saw unusually noisy in-house battles between an RWG perspective which saw economic expansion as the key means of alleviating poverty and a BHN outlook which demanded more fundamental assessments of the causes of poverty. The prevailing RWG policy framework nevertheless permitted McNamara to speak tirelessly of the bank's determination to address the poverty of the world's poorest—the 40% of developing country populations living in 'absolute poverty', heavily concentrated in South

Asia. In brief, RWG constituted the softest redistributive policy option available, by reallocating the focus of investment in favour of the poor, while rejecting any need to reallocate resources within an economy or across economies (Chenery *et al.*, 1974; Jones, 1992, pp. 111–124).

Although RWG strategies as conceived by the McNamara bank had little to say about education, in 1973 and 1974 Ballantine was quick to seize upon the poverty focus and with his deputy Mats Hultin forged for education an accommodation with the spirit of the BHN approach. What emerged in December 1974 was the second published statement of bank education policy, a far more wide-ranging and innovative discourse. The new *Education Sector Working Paper* (World Bank, 1974), unlike its 1971 predecessor, which had merely summed up bank policies for lending, was more speculative about potential bank lending and invited discourse on the global future for education. It became part of the McNamara bank's self-perception and image—a flexible and responsive bank eschewing arbitrary and standardised policies. It made much of mass education, 'to enable the masses that have been unaffected by the growth of the modern sector to participate in the development process as more productive workers' (World Bank, 1974, p. 15) and thereby opened up prospects for more focus on rural populations and the education of women and girls. Adult, youth, non-formal and informal education were all actively incorporated in the name of balanced educational development and poverty alleviation (World Bank, 1974, pp. 14–15). Through the paper, Ballantine attempted to shape bank and borrower thinking in five key areas.

(1) Skill development and its potential for productivity increases.
(2) Mass participation in education and development.
(3) Education and equity.
(4) Increasing the efficiency of education.
(5) Improving educational planning and management.

At the time, there was much bank-inspired rhetoric about the revolutionary nature of these new formulations, seen as constituting a decisive break with the past. The notion of a basic education for all, however, was a virtual re-run of UNESCO's approach in the 1940s and 1950s of 'fundamental education', although the bank failed to echo UNESCO's central concern with basic education as a vehicle for democracy (Jones, 1988, pp. 47–87). What this educational articulation of RWG permitted was a dramatic expansion of bank lending without the need to rethink priorities or fundamentals. It permitted the grafting on of new possibilities for lending without upsetting earlier bank rationales for support, i.e. applications of human capital perspectives in the name of forging economic expansion through increased worker productivity. The real McNamara revolution was to broaden the scope and size of bank operations, a revolution which was set in place on his first day of office. In sum, the key to understanding the McNamara period is increased lending—the larger and busier bank was more readily a diversifying bank.

At the same time, it needs to be acknowledged that bank financing came to be less exclusively focused on the construction and equipping of educational institutions. Projects also came to address innovations, the management of change, curriculum development and improved methods of teaching and learning. Tracer studies sought evidence about educational effectiveness and the salaries and status of teachers were active concerns. Multipurpose education institutions were supported. Surprisingly little was lent for adult literacy, for applying new technologies in education and for textbook development and supply. The poorest countries, too, did not take long to reach the various limits of their borrowing capacity, the poorest of them borrowing 73.4% of bank education funds in 1976, but only 32.1% 2 years later.

At all points, personalities and institutional dynamics played their part in how the bank policies in education evolved. For example, the structural reorganisation of the bank in 1972 saw the demise of the single education department under Ballantine, a department which had been responsible for both policy formulation and project operations and a department completely dominated by the forceful Ballantine. The reorganisation saw responsibility for loan and project operations shifted to five regional departments, Ballantine retaining responsibility for a small policy department. This shift is reflected in the way in which the sweep of the 1974 *Education Sector Working Paper* is not apparent in that of 1971. Ballantine, with operations no longer his responsibility, could be far more expansive about what the bank could do. From this point there emerged the widening gap between bank rhetoric in education and the more limited realities of its lending operations.

By the end of the McNamara period, two influential reviews—one internal and one external—of the bank's work in education had been completed. The internal review of 1978, led by independently minded bank staffer Ralph Romain, provided a robust and strident critique of many past orthodoxies, a critique attacked by many in the bank as being overwhelmingly sympathetic to borrowing country perspectives (World Bank, 1978). Two major areas were emphasised: the bank's failure to involve its borrowers adequately in the identification and preparation of projects and insufficient bank concern to build up borrowers' capacities 'to plan, manage, research and develop their education systems' (World Bank, 1978, p. iv). The review set the scene for the bank to become less focused on institution strengthening than on systematically addressing the 'broader needs' of education systems (World Bank, 1978, p. ix).

The external review panel was established by Ballantine's successor (1977–1987), former Ethiopian education minister Aklilu Habte, who, with his subordinate Wadi Haddad, was to dominate bank policy in education throughout the 1980s. Unlike the Romain review, the external panel was one Aklilu was able to control, through its chair David Bell, executive vice-president of the Ford Foundation. In addition, unlike the Romain review, the Bell panel was less concerned with the bank's performance and shortcomings than with the broad shape of future policy directions. It reflected the conventional wisdom of the day by arguing for a view of education broader than its capacity to increase worker productivity and had much to say about regional and country variations in how best to promote educational development. The Bell panel strongly argued for a bank prepared to offer country-by-country advice, for a bank prepared to learn from its past arbitrariness and for a bank committed to researching difficult policy matters (External Advisory Panel on Education, 1978).

The scene was set for the last of the conventional statements of bank education policy, the 1980 *Education Sector Policy Paper* (World Bank, 1980), which characterised the 1980s bank. As with each of its counterparts, it can only be understood in terms of the evolving institutional character of the bank, its internal dynamics as much as its external relations. Much of the paper resembles a textbook-style discussion of education and development, rather than being an explicit statement either of bank lending criteria or its views on how governments should behave in the education sector. It was not a policy prescription to drive bank operations forward with vigour and purpose. It projected a milder policy rhetoric, despite the fact that the conditions and constraints under which the bank operated had not changed. The continuity with its 1974 predecessor is apparent in this set of principles, addressing what the paper termed the 'second generational' issues of educational development.

(1) Basic education should be provided for all children and adults as soon as the available resources and conditions permit. In the long term, a comprehensive system of formal and non-formal education should be developed at all levels.

(2) To increase productivity and promote social equity, efforts should be made to provide education opportunities, without distinction of sex, ethnic background or social and economic status.
(3) Education systems should strive to achieve maximum internal efficiency through the management, allocation, and use of resources available for increasing the quantity and improving the quality of education.
(4) Education should be effectively related to work and environment in order to improve, quantitatively and qualitatively, the knowledge and skills necessary for performing economic, social and other development functions.
(5) To satisfy these objectives, developing countries will need to build and maintain their institutional capacities to design, analyze, manage, and evaluate programs for education and training. (World Bank, 1980, p. 10)

How these principles came to be applied was not won easily within the bank. The most obvious shift in lending patterns fought for by Aklilu and Haddad was the absolute priority of primary education. Armed with bank economist George Psacharopoulos' rate-of-return analyses (Psacharopoulos, 1973, 1981) they embarked on nothing less than a crusade to convince the international community that public investments in education should be dominated by primary education, the proportion of public investments in education ideally declining as one proceeded up the 'education ladder'. Aklilu in particular was trenchant in his critique of public subsidies for higher education in the poorest countries, with their inequitable participation patterns, unrealistic curriculum orientation and élitist functions. A second obvious shift was spearheaded by Haddad, who by the late 1970s was somewhat courageously questioning bank conventional wisdom in promoting diversified school curricula, whereby the general content was bound up with the vocational content. Haddad was convinced that both personal and social returns from general education eclipsed those from both diversified and vocational curricula and pushed for bank researchers to find substantiating evidence (Psacharopoulos & Loxley, 1985; Haddad, 1987).

Despite these emphases, the bank entered the 1980s without a comprehensive policy to drive forward its education lending. Such policy vagueness could not last for long, given the escalating debt crisis and the rapidly deepening recession affecting much of the developing world. The bank and its twin agency, the International Monetary Fund (IMF), saw their roles as increasingly interventionist as the crisis of the 1980s worsened. The official view that they needed to respond assertively, even aggressively, contrasted sharply with the softer and vaguer style of Aklilu. Education could not remain innocent for long.

In general terms, the conceptual bases for the bank's approach to education policy were most convincing in contexts or periods of economic growth. Human capital theory, first conceived as an explanation for economic growth, came to be applied as a set of assumptions about how to foster it (Schultz, 1961, 1963). Designed to stimulate economic growth, bank strategies often took growth as given, looking to means of increasing the rates of expansion. In practice, the entire post-war experience in borrowing countries had been one of best managing already apparent economic growth.

The 1980s bank was confronted with a developing world very different from the one it felt most comfortable with. By 1990, the bank's *World Development Report* was painting a grim picture of the 1980s record in tackling poverty. Not only was much of the developing world in the grip of abiding recession and debt; by nearly every indicator the poorest segments of the developing country populations were the most severely affected and for whom levels of public expenditure for services had generally fallen (World Bank, 1990b, pp. 7–38). In low-income countries in particular, stagnant public investment in educational infrastructure and participation was becoming far more than a temporary setback: long-term development prospects were being seriously threatened. By 1985 the bank was estimating that 100 million school-aged children were in fact not attending, of whom 70% were from the low-income countries, a clear majority being female. The average length of schooling and the quality of schooling were noticeably declining throughout low-income countries, where public systems of primary education were increasingly propped up by contributions in cash and kind from families and local communities.

The dilemma facing the bank's education policy officials was a particularly acute one. For years, they had been arguing and accumulating evidence that public educational investments, notably at the primary school level, paid off handsomely in economic terms, for both individuals and in the aggregate. In particular, it was the poorest countries, with low baselines of basic education, for which investment was most beneficial. Their dilemma was how to promote such arguments when the bank and the IMF were mounting with increasing assertiveness that solutions to prolonged recession and debt were to be found through the kinds of structural adjustments to economies which necessitated radical rethinking about the role of governments in providing such social infrastructures and services as health and education. To risk oversimplification, the answer to the dilemma was to continue arguing the case for public commitments to universal primary education of decent duration and quality and for reducing public commitments as students proceeded up the education ladder, fostering privatisation and user-pays approaches. In practice, the severity of structural adjustment programmes in low-income countries was such that the basic provision of health and education services could not escape the knife. Finance ministers the world over could be forgiven for thinking they were receiving 'mixed messages' from the bank, a bank to which many borrowers were indebted for purposes since discredited by the lender.

The 1980s bank saw unprecedented debate about the best balance between project lending and programme lending. From the very beginning, the bank, with its focus on physical infrastructure, had deemed programme lending as too vague, intended for purposes too difficult to control and monitor. The World Bank–IMF perceptions of prolonged recession and indebtedness, however, opened up the possibility of bank and fund support (i.e. loans and credits) for programmes of reform, across entire economies or within such particular sectors as education. Their perceptions of economic reform were generally limited to means of reducing foreign debt, notably by increasing foreign exchange earnings through imports. Structural adjustment, it must be emphasised, revolved around this overarching goal of keeping foreign-exchange loan repayments on schedule and generally required a set of domestic policy reforms that addressed deteriorating terms of trade, changing international relative pricing and falls in the net inflow of foreign capital. Reducing public sector indebtedness was a hallmark of such strategies. Lending for structural adjustment tended to focus on improving a country's balance-of-payments position, aiming to increase the production of exportable goods and commodities, through such strategies as trade liberalisation, the removal of subsidies and the promotion of user charges for public services. By the mid-1980s, sober assessments were on the way in, such as this conclusion from the Overseas Develpment Council in 1986:

> While there still can be widespread agreement on the need for greater selectivity and care in public investment and for greater efficiency and consistency in economic management in general, there are major debates about strategy and tactics in particular country cases. And both in general and in the case of particular countries, there is fundamental political as well as professional disagreement on matters such as the overall role of the state, the scope for private enterprise, the degree of

> 'outward orientation', and the distribution of income . . . Just as the IMF has been criticized for the oversimplicity and inflexibility of its short-term models and approaches, the Bank now attracts criticism for the generalized character of the development policies it now recommends. Certainly its general approaches can be defended only if they are flexibly applied; as universal rules they are neither economically nor politically acceptable. (Helleiner, 1986, pp. 53–54)

As far as education was concerned, the import of structural adjustment programmes revolves around convictions about the preferred economic functions of the public sector. Structural adjustment could only effect major changes to the contexts in which education systems were located, bearing heavily on both the scope and extent of public sector activity. Given the prevalence of military governments throughout the developing world and their reluctance to reduce military capital and recurrent expenditures, public-sector social spending became especially vulnerable. Structural adjustment programmes, then, are both a sign of deteriorating prospects for developing education as well as an instrument which, at least in the immediate sense, makes educational development extremely difficult to promote. Again, the dilemma for the bank's education sector was acute: adjustment strategies were only tangentially and indirectly related to economic growth strategies, more to do with the preconditions for economic expression. The dilemma was how to serve the need for addressing those preconditions yet stopping short of jeopardising prospects for growth. By the mid-1980s, the bank's education sector was publishing conclusions that reform programmes appeared best suited to the middle-income countries least in need of them, those with reasonable debt-servicing and reform management capacities (Johanson, 1985).

The poorest countries, notably those of sub-Saharan Africa, were prominent in the bank's rationale for aggressive adjustment policies and reasonably so. The cascade of bank strategy papers addressing African reform, including educational reform, constituted an energetic response to the continent's rapidly deteriorating position. Again, the bank was content to publicise reform prescriptions for worldwide application, as if their general as well as localised pertinence was as clear as night is from day. Not a few middle-income countries found themselves questioning the insistence with which the bank and IMF were urging reform, given their ongoing moderate economic successes, despite temporary setbacks. The World Bank–IMF motives, however, did not take long to become obvious.

For education policy, the front-line issue which emerged was the financing of education, which again could only be understood in the light of the profound political questions raised by austerity strategies concerning the role of the public sector and its economic relationship with the private sector. The educational implications of austerity could not be hidden in contexts where up to 30% public outlays were devoted to education. Accordingly, Aklilu's education department could not ignore the policy challenge of continuing to promote education as a dynamic arena for public and private investment, while also addressing declining public sector education budgets and the need to foster user charges in education. These policy imperatives Aklilu skilfully combined with other priorities, not least the department's commitment to universal primary education, its concern to promote equity (especially of access) and its escalating concerns about educational quality and effectiveness.

The major product of the internal bank's discussions was a policy note issued in January 1986, published in a blander form as a kind of discussion paper (World Bank, 1986). Being too controversial, its contents prevented its issue as a statement of formal bank policy, although all subsequent loan negotiations have been dominated by the policy note's insistence on the reforms laid out in the policy. Compliance has been considerable, especially concerning privatisation. The fundamental assumptions of the policy note were threefold.

(1) Governments 'do not tap the willingness of households to contribute resources directly to education'.
(2) 'Current financing arrangements also result in the misallocation of public spending on education', with heavy subsidisation of higher education at the expense of primary education.
(3) 'In schools resources are not being used as efficiently as they might be, [a] problem reinforced by the lack of competition between schools.'

As should cause no surprise, the bank projected the assumption that these policy assumptions be applied universally, perhaps with variable force and with the usual rider acknowleding that some country-by-country variation could be tolerated. On the whole, however, the policy was intended for global application as part of the emerging role of the bank as a promoter of an integrated world economy.

(1) Recovering the public cost of higher education and reallocating government spending on education towards the level with the highest social returns.
(2) Developing a credit market for education, together with selective scholarships, especially in higher education.
(3) Decentralizing the management of public education and encouraging the expansion of non-government and community-supported schools (World Bank, 1986, p. 2).

The policy implications were most convincing when addressing the balance of public-sector investments in education, exposing the grossly inequitable support for higher education students in many poor countries. The aim of releasing finance for less resourced but developmentally dynamic parts of the education system was easy to promote, but difficult to sell given the politics of higher education in low- and middle-income countries.

The policy assumed much else, that in many instances teachers were being paid salaries 'above market levels' and that public education systems failed to be subject to appropriate accountability. It hinted strongly that the unit costs in public education were higher than in private education and that decentralisation of education decision making was conducive to incentive, competition and quality. It assumed, in particular for low-income countries, that significant levels of finance were available for transfer to the education system and that privatisation, quality, economic relevance and equity went hand-in-hand, whereas public education was marked by inefficiences, declining quality and waste. For low-income countries in particular, the bank's policies of privatisation and of quality enhancement were incompatible and contradictory. Although for a time there were divisions within the bank about the extent to which development was a process requiring careful and pronounced government planning and regulation (as opposed to sufficient deregulation to permit market forces to hold sway), in time institution-wide agreement could be detected over the broad goals projected and their relationship with the World Bank–IMF measures for adjustment and reform. At the end of the 1980s, fewer and fewer bank education loans were free of obligations to promote the privatisation of education and the expansion of user charges. Bank-promoted subsidisation of private schools increased, even to the point where public sector capacities to monitor and ensure the quality of the educational provision for all citizens were severely jeopardised.

Perhaps nothing has changed the World Bank—or at least its self-image—as much as the end of the Cold War and the entry of the Soviet bloc at the end of the 1980s and early 1990s. The so-called 'transition economies' were clearly bound to resist reform rhetoric originally designed to conquer policy intransigence and absolute poverty in poorest Africa. Most of the new members boasted proud records in economic growth strategies and in the provision of public services. For them, the World Bank and IMF language needed to be explicit, centring on their need to integrate with the global economy as a means of promoting and consolidating the dynamics of open-market economic behaviour (Heyneman, 1994; World Bank, 1994b). In short, with eastern Europe under their wing, the World Bank and IMF could afford to describe with clarity their global agenda for economic change—the worldwide adoption and consolidation of one particular model to guide economic, political and social policy, a model for which the discipline of the open market was more reliable than that of public planning and responsibility, whose role needed to be defined in terms of how market-oriented economies should ideally function. With policy positions emerging with such explicitness, the bank, which for so long had promoted an image of care in avoiding political prescriptions in favour of the technical, could no longer conceal its agenda. While nothing fundamental had changed, the fundamentals were now more visible.

The 1980s presidencies of Clausen and Conable are noteworthy for their focus on structural adjustment, initially promoted as a considered response to protracted recession and debt, particularly in the low-income countries. With the need to integrate the transition economies into the global economic system, structural adjustment strategies became more explicitly understood as a means of ensuring as little variation as possible in worldwide economic (and, hence, political) fundamentals. As the 1990s began, the education reform dilemma was particularly acute, yet the 'Education for All' initiative of the World Bank, the United Nations Development Programme (UNDP), UNESCO and the United Nations Children's Fund (UNICEF) was able to emphasise the need for sectoral adjustment policies in education as much as for a sharp focus in public expenditures on universal primary education (Inter-Agency Commission, 1990). The initiative enabled the bank to promote its poverty alleviation image while at the same time pushing ahead with its programme of global economic integration. The early 1990s also saw the Jomtien initiative followed up by a sharp rise in bank loan approvals in education. As far as education policy statements were concerned, the early 1990s saw a departure from the bank's practice of addressing comprehensively issues of educational development in all-embracing policy papers, as in 1971, 1974 and 1980. Subsectoral policy papers appeared for all areas except secondary education: primary education (World Bank, 1990a), vocational and technical education (World Bank, 1991) and higher education (World Bank, 1994a). In arguing that the 1995 statement *Policies and Strategies for Education* contains little detail about key subsectors in education, it has to be acknowledged that this prior set of statements was intended to meet that need. Any analysis of current bank education policy needs to involve an analysis of the set of papers as a whole.

The 1995 Statement

Notwithstanding the previous sentence, the 1995 policy paper is noteworthy in that it is more concerned with the preconditions for educational development than with the core matters of educational processes themselves (see also Bennell, 1996; Burnett, 1996; Burnett & Patrinos, 1996; Lauglo, 1996; Samoff, 1996). These preconditions can only be understood in the following terms.

(1) The bank's role as a bank and its location in the international financial marketplace.
(2) The evolution of bank views on both development and of education.

(3) The intellectual grounding of the bank's education commitment in human capital theory.
(4) The discipline of austerity and its effects on public provision of educational services.
(5) An ideological stance, now explicit, in promoting an integrated world economic system along market lines.

In painting a picture of the preconditions for successful educational development, the bank is in effect depicting its view of the ideal economy. It is an economy which at best can only tolerate public education:

> Public intervention in education can be justified on several counts: it can reduce inequality, open opportunities for the poor and disadvantaged, compensate for market failures in lending for education, and make information about the benefits of education generally available. But public spending on education is often inefficient and inequitable. (World Bank, 1995, p. 3)

It is an economy in which the management of education 'by central or state governments . . . allows little room for the flexibility that leads to effective learning' (World Bank, 1995, p. 6). Again, a limited view of public involvement in education becomes plain.

> The main ways in which governments can help improve the quality of education are setting standards, supporting inputs known to improve achievement, adopting flexible strategies for the acquisition and use of inputs, and monitoring performance. (World Bank, 1995, p. 6)

It is an economy in which 'educational priorities should be set with reference to outcomes, using economic analysis, standard setting, and measurement of achievement through learning assessments' (World Bank, 1995, p. 8). The kind of economic analysis looked to in this key task is made explicit, expressed in terms of a cost–benefit analysis.

> Economic analysis usually compares benefits (in labour productivity, as measured by wages) with costs, for individuals and for society. It identifies as priorities for public investment those investments for which the social rate of return is highest and the level of public subsidization is lowest. (World Bank, 1995, p. 8)

It is an economy in which a growing premium is placed on what is euphemistically termed 'household involvement' in education, understood in terms of maximising household choice in education. The 'risks' involved are easily identified and it is, accordingly, an economy in which fundamental difficulties and obstacles to equity can be easily managed:

> - Implementation of systemwide education policies can be more difficult.
> - Enforcement of broader national objectives can be hampered.
> - Social segregation may increase if schools become polarized between élite academies and schools for the children of the poor and uneducated.
> - Equity may be reduced if schools and institutions accept students on the basis of their ability to pay rather than on academic entrance qualifications.
> - Parents may lack the information they need to make judgments about quality.
>
> The first four risks can be mitigated relatively easily through policies for the provision of public funding. Such funds can be made available only to schools that follow certain practices, can be higher per student for poor children, and can be

> accompanied by restrictions on fee levels. The fifth risk can be reduced through government efforts to provide open and independent information about school quality. (World Bank, 1995, p. 12)

It is always an economy which can afford to pass to communities and households some of the costs of education. 'Even very poor communities are often willing to contribute toward the cost of education, especially at the primary level' (World Bank, 1995, p. 105). Further,

> Since upper-secondary-school graduates will have higher earnings than those who leave school earlier, selectively charging fees for public secondary school can help to increase enrollments. Cost-sharing with communities can be encouraged at the secondary, as well as the primary, level. Fees can usually be charged without affecting overall enrollments. (World Bank, 1995, p. 106)

However,

> The charging of fees at one level can affect enrollments by other family members at other levels. A poor family that has to pay fees for an upper-secondary student may not be able to enroll other children in primary school because the younger children's work is needed to generate the income from which the fees are to be paid. (World Bank, 1995, p. 106)

It is an economy about which we can relax: such threats to equity can be readily addressed.

> This dilemma is precisely why fee charging must be accompanied by targeted stipends to enable the enrollment of students from poor families. Fees used without compensatory measures will have a negative impact on the enrollment of such children. (World Bank, 1995, p. 106)

It is an economy which has shed the disagreeable effects of centralised control over education. Centralised control only fosters centralised teachers' unions, for example, which 'can disrupt education and sometimes lead to political paralysis' (World Bank, 1995, p. 137). Central tendencies mar higher education also.

> The relationship between higher education students and the government can be oppositional, as well. The conflict arises because of the centralized nature of university financing and governance and because higher education students, who come disproportionately from upper socioeconomic households, are a vocal and articulate political constituency. When students have grievances, usually only national governments can address them. (World Bank, 1995, p. 138)

It is an economy in which decentralisation fosters reform, in which parental and community control, 'when accompanied by measures to ensure equity in the provision of resources, can offset much of the power of vested interests, such as teachers' unions and the élite' (World Bank, 1995, p. 140). At least in urban areas, decentralisation 'can be enhanced by the use of market mechanisms that increase accountability and choice' (World Bank, 1995, p. 140).

It is an economy of which we only catch a glimpse in *Priorities and Strategies for Education*. The full picture comes into view when we examine the overall goals of the World Bank worldwide. For the first time there is an unambiguous consonance between those economic, political and ideological goals and those of the bank's education sector.

REFERENCES

BENNELL, P. (1996) Using and abusing rates of return: a critique of the World Bank's 1995 education sector review, *International Journal of Educational Development*, 16, pp. 235–248.

BURNETT, N. (1996) Priorities and strategies for education—a World Bank review: the process and the key messages, *International Journal of Educational Development*, 16, pp. 215–220.

BURNETT, N. & PATRINOS, H.A. (1996) Response to critiques of priorities and strategies for education: a World Bank review, *International Journal of Educational Development*, 16, pp. 273–276.

CHENERY, H.B., AHLUWALIA, M.S., BELL, C.L.G., DULOY, J.H. & JOLLY, R. (1974) *Redistribution With Growth: policies to impove income distribution in developing countries in the context of economic growth* (London, Oxford University Press for the World Bank and the Institute of Development Studies, University of Sussex).

EXTERNAL ADVISORY PANEL ON EDUCATION ('BELL EXTERNAL PANEL') (1978) *Report of the External Advisory Panel on Education to the World Bank (the "Bell report")* (Washington DC, World Bank).

HADDAD, W.D. (1987) *Diversified Secondary Curriculum Projects: a review of World Bank experience 1963–1979* (Washington, DC, World Bank).

HELLEINER, G.K. (1986) Policy based program lending: a look at the Bank's new role, in: R.E. FEINBERG (Ed.) *The World Bank's Next Decade*, pp. 47–66 (New Brunswick, NJ, Transaction Books for the Overseas Development Council).

HEYNEMAN, S.P. (1994) *Education in the Europe and Central Asia Region: policies of adjustment and excellence* (Washington, DC, World Bank).

INTER-AGENCY COMMISSION (1990) *Meeting Bank Learning Needs: a vision for the 1990s* (New York, Inter-Agency Commission, World Conference on Education for All).

JOHANSON, R. (1985) *Sector Lending in Education* (Washington, DC, World Bank).

JONES, P.W. (1988) *International Policies for Third World Education: UNESCO, literacy and development* (London and New York, Routledge).

JONES, P.W. (1992) *World Bank Financing of Education: lending, learning and development* (London and New York, Routledge).

LAUGLO, J. (1996) Banking on education and the uses of research: a critique of World Bank priorities and strategies for education, *International Journal of Educational Development*, 16, pp. 221–233.

PSACHAROPOULOS, G. (1973) *Returns to Education: an international comparison* (Amsterdam, Elsevier).

PSACHAROPOULOS, G. (1981) Returns to education: an up-dated international comparison, *Comparative Education*, 17, pp. 321–341.

PSACHAROPOULOS, G. & LOXLEY, W. (1985) *Diversified Secondary Education and Development: evidence from Colombia and Tanzania* (Baltimore, Johns Hopkins University Press).

SAMOFF, J. (1996) Which priorities and strategies for education?, *International Journal of Educational Development*, 16, pp. 249–271.

SCHULTZ, T.W. (1961) Investment in human capital, *American Economic Review*, 51, pp. 1–17.

SCHULTZ, T.W. (1963) *The Economic Value of Education* (New York, Columbia University Press).

WORLD BANK (1963) *Proposed Bank/IDA Policies in the Field of Education* (Washington, DC, World Bank).

WORLD BANK (1970) *Lending in Education* (Washington, DC, World Bank).

WORLD BANK (1971) *Education Sector Working Paper* (Washington, DC, World Bank).

WORLD BANK (1974) *Education Sector Working Paper* (Washington, DC, World Bank).

WORLD BANK (1978) *Review of Bank Operations in the Education Sector* (Washington, DC, World Bank).

WORLD BANK (1980) *Education Sector Policy Paper* (Washington, DC, World Bank).

WORLD BANK (1986) *Financing Education in Developing Countries: an exploration of policy options* (Washington, DC, World Bank).

WORLD BANK (1990a) *Primary Education: a World Bank policy paper* (Washington, DC, World Bank).

WORLD BANK (1990b) *World Development Report 1990* (Washington, DC, World Bank).

WORLD BANK (1991) *Skills for Productivity: policies for vocational and technical education in developing countries* (Washington, DC, World Bank).

WORLD BANK (1994a) *Higher Education: the lessons of experience* (Washington, DC, World Bank).

WORLD BANK (1994b) *Russia: education in the transition* (Washington, DC, World Bank).

WORLD BANK (1995) *Priorities and Strategies for Education: a World Bank review* (Washington, DC, World Bank).

[27]

Where Have All the Public Intellectuals Gone? Racial Politics, Pedagogy, and Disposable Youth

Henry A. Giroux

Rise of the "New" Public Intellectual

The crisis of meaning and politics facing the United States is, in part, strikingly evident in the emergence of a new breed of aggressive right wing public intellectuals who have given new importance to expanding the politics of the pedagogical into the diverse spheres of media and popular culture. Such intellectuals have redefined the meaning of cultural pedagogy as a potent force for social and political change in both the old and new electronic media. Public intellectuals such as Rush Limbaugh, Pat Robertson, Christina Hoff Sommers, and William Kristol—utilizing popular cultural sites such as talk radio, television news programs, op-ed columns in nationally syndicated newspapers, well-financed conservative magazines, and other public spheres—consistently and aggressively wage rancorous attacks on civil rights legislation, welfare reform, and social policies designed to benefit subordinate groups. Not only have such intellectuals given a radically different ideological slant to the notion of what it means to be a public intellectual, they have also created new sites of learning from which to shape popular opinion and provide the ground for retrograde public policy. The new conservative public intellectuals have put a low priority on children and the poor while simultaneously producing a public discourse that revives the disgraceful principles of Social Darwinism and the dictates of a racist science that links race and cognitive ability.[1]

Financed largely by well-funded foundations such as Olin, Scaife, and the Coors family, conservative public intellectuals travel with ease between the commanding heights of media culture and the highest reaches of political power.[2] The effects on democratic public life have been devastating. Across the nation, the dismantling of the welfare state appears to go hand-in-hand with the development of a growing right-wing culture of hate that promotes violence against women, gays, lesbians, and racial minorities.[3] At the state level, fear and racial hatred appear to be inspiring a major backlash against the gains of the civil rights movement as affirmative action is openly attacked and anti-immigration legislation, such as Proposition 209 in California, sweep the nation.[4] Financial cutbacks and the restructuring of the labor force have weakened unions and vastly undercut social services for the most vulnerable, including women with infants, children of the poor, and older citizens who rely on medicare and other such benefits.[5] Similarly, the assault on youth and the increasing instances of racial and gender discrimination are being accompanied by aggressive attacks on the arts and public funding coupled with assaults on those public sites instrumental in fighting AIDS, poverty, and the destruction of the environment.

One of the most incessant and insidious attacks waged by conservative public intellectuals has been on poor and black youth in the United States. Blamed for drug abuse, exploding crime rates, teenage pregnancy, spiraling cigarette addiction, and a host of other social and economic problems, youth are repeatedly scapegoated by politicians, the dominant media, and numerous liberal and conservative intellectuals. Examples of such scapegoating youth have become so commonplace in the media that they suggest the emergence of a new literary idiom. For example, commenting on contemporary youth in *Wired*, right-wing sensation Camilia Paglia bashes young people for their inability to think critically about any serious political issue. She writes:

> I think [young people] become hysterical. They become very susceptible to someone's ideology. The longing for something structured, something that gives them a worldview, is so intense that whatever comes along, whether it's fascism or feminist ideology (which to me are inseparable), they'll glom onto it and they can't critique it. You see the inability of the young...to think through issues like date rape. (Pagila and Brand 79)

Paglia simply reinforces and legitimates what has become a standard perception of young people in American culture, one that is echoed in Hollywood films such as *Dumb and Dumber* (1994), *Clerks*(1994), *Clueless* (1995) *Bio-Dome* (1995), and *Kids* (1996). In these films and others, kids are portrayed either as vulgar, disengaged, pleasure seekers or as over-the-edge violent sociopaths. Similarly, consider television sitcoms such as *Friends* that portray young people as shallow, unmotivated, navel-gazing slackers intent on making do without the slightest interest in a larger social and political world. While many of the characters frequently experience unemployment, low-wage jobs, and high credit debts, such experiences become at best fodder for comic relief and at worst completely nullified by their sporting hundred dollar haircuts, expensive makeup, and slick Greenwich Village-like apartments. These white middle-class youth are defined largely through their role as conspicuous consumers, their political indifference, and their intense lack of motivation to engage a world beyond their own self-indulgent interests.

On the other hand, represented through a celluloid haze of drugs, crime, and sex, black youth—as in a slew of recent Hollywood films including *Boyz N the Hood* (1991), *Sugar Hill* (1993), *Menace II Society* (1993), and *Clockers* (1995)—are viewed as menacing and dangerous. In addition, popular representations of youth in the music press take on a decidedly racial register as they move between celebrating the politics of cynicism and rage of white singers such as Alanis Morrisette and Courtney Love, on the one hand, and giving high visibility to the violent-laden lyrics and exploits of black rappers such as Snoop Doggy Dog and the recently deceased Tupac Amaru Shakur.

Caught between representations that view them as either slackers, consumers, criminals, or sell outs, youth increasingly are defined through the lens of commodification, scorn, or criminality. If not demonized, youth are either commodified or constructed as consuming subjects. For instance, in the world of media advertising prurient images of youth are paraded across high gloss magazines, pushing ethical boundaries by appropriating the seedy world of drug abuse to produce an aesthetic that might be termed "heroin chic." Capitalizing on the popularity of heroin use in films such as *Trainspotting* (1996), fashion designers such as Calvin Klein portray barely dressed, emaciated youthful models with dark circles under their eyes as part of an advertising campaign that combines the lure of fashion and addiction with an image of danger and chic bohemianism.

Market researchers represent one of the few groups that appear attentive to how youth think, feel, behave, and desire. One such company, Sputnik, sends "youthful spies" to seventeen cities to find out what youth wear, like, buy, and desire. Identifying five youth subcultures, it offers its "research" findings to clients such as Reebok, Levi Strauss and Pepsi-Cola. Whether seen as a market for commodities or commodified as in the recent Calvin Klein underwear ads, kids are stripped of their specificity, agency, and histories.[6] And yet, the popular press rarely takes up how children are exploited through a market logic that grinds up youth in order to expand the margin profits of the corporations. Such exploitation may constitute a more familiar, less sensational form of violence being waged against kids in the dominant media, but it is a violence that is rarely acknowledged as such.[7]

Yet, the corporate exploitation of youth does not account for the insurgent racism that breeds a different register of violence against young people. Racism feeds the attack on teens by targeting black youths as criminals while convincing working class white youth that blacks and immigrants are responsible for the poverty, despair, and violence that have become a growing part of everyday life in American society. Racism is once again readily embraced within mainstream society. As the gap between the rich and the poor widens and racism intensifies, neo-conservatives and liberals alike enact legislation and embrace policy recommendations that undermine the traditional safety nets provided for the poor, the young, and the aged.[8] As the reality of high unemployment, dire poverty, inadequate housing, poor quality education, and dwindling social services are banished from public discourse, white and black youth inherit a future in which they will be earning less, working longer, and straining to secure the most rudimentary social services.

In addition to being demonized by certain elements of the media, young people often find themselves inhabiting a postmodern world of cyberspace visuals, digitally induced representations of reality and a social landscape consisting mainly of malls, fast food restaurants, and convenience stores, punctuated by economic downsizing and escalating unemployment. The adult world provides few markers for negotiating this terrain; instead, it offers youth a world in which social mobility, the promise of economic security, and the house in the suburbs provide an increasingly irrelevant set of referents for gauging one's relationship to the so-called American dream. As evidence of the nation's diminishing commitment to equality of opportunity, working-class and youth of color are increasingly warehoused in educational institutions where rigid discipline and defunct knowledge are coupled with a cultural addiction to excessive individualism, competitiveness, and Victorian moralism.

One measure of the despair and alienation youth experience can be seen in the streets of our urban centers. The murder rate among young adults 18 to 24 years old increased 65 percent from 1985 to 1993. Even more disturbing, as James Alan Fox, the Dean of the College of Criminal Justice at Northeastern University, pointed out recently is that "murder is now reaching down to a much younger age group—children as young as 14 to 17. Since the mid-1980s, the rate of killing committed by teenagers 14 to 17 has more than doubled, increasing 165 percent from 1985 to 1993. Presently about 4,000 juveniles commit murder annually" (19). With soaring indices of poverty among children, a changing world economy characterized by subcontracting, an explosion in domestic sweatshops, and the proliferation of low-wage factory jobs, the most notable feature about the crisis of democratic public life appears to be the expendability of youth.

In a society gripped by the desire to lose itself in a rendering of mythic past and an equally strong desire to relinquish responsibility for the future, youth become one of the main casualties of such a crisis. As a case in point, the assault on youth is happening without the benefit of adequate rights, fair representation, or even public outcry. Children can't vote, but they can be demonized, deprived of basic rights, spoon fed an ethos of excessive materialism and forced to put up with a glut of commodified violence in the media. Contrary to the logic of a conservative dominated congress, building more prisons will not solve the problem; neither will reducing student loans, or privatizing public schools. What can academics, cultural workers and other public intellectuals do in light of such an onslaught against children's culture? What pedagogical and political possibilities exist within and outside of schools for progressives to address the economic, political, and racial problems destroying the hopes of a decent future for the next generation of youth? The effects of such an assault on both young people and the fabric of democratic life poses an urgent challenge for educators to redefine the connection between their roles as public intellectuals and their responsibility to address the major social problems facing young people today. Such a task means, in part, addressing how strategies of interpretation, critique, and intervention might be fashioned within those institutional and pedagogical spaces that provide representations for how youth defined themselves and how they are defined by adult society.

Public Intellectuals, Youth, and the Politics of Culture

If higher education represents one crucial site to educate young people to address the central problems of unemployment, racism, and the major political dilemmas faced by a generation of poor white and black youth, academics will have to address the nature of the current assault on education and its relationship to a broader attack on the basic foundations of democracy. The threat posed by the increasing vocationalization of education and the ongoing attempts by liberals and conservatives to remove all obstacles to the regulation of corporate practices and eliminate the language of equity and social justice from broader discussions about public life suggests that public intellectuals must begin to join together to create a national movement for the defense of public education and other public goods.

Rather than exclusively serving the stripped-down needs of the multinationals, educators and other cultural workers need to develop counter-public spheres and transformative pedagogical conditions in a variety of sites. Such a task would aim at enabling students to critically engage diverse forms of literacy, writing, and knowledge production through the broader lens of public problem solving in order to better understand and transform the political, economic, and ideological interests that shapes the post-industrial world they will inhabit.[9] Central to such an effort would be developing a new discourse for making visible those historical narratives that recount the important struggles for democracy that have unfolded in social movements extending from the civil rights struggles of the 1950s to the oppositional politics waged by organizations such as Act Up in the 1990s. Such movements need to be studied both for the pedagogies and politics at work in the struggles against injustice and engaged as transformative forms of knowledge to be incorporated into the curriculum.

Academics and cultural workers must also redefine the purpose of public and higher education not as a servant of the state nor to meet the demands of commerce and the marketplace but as a repository for educating students and others in the democratic discourse of freedom, social responsibility, and public leadership. At the heart of such a task is the need for academics and other cultural workers outside of the university and other educational sites to join together and oppose the transformation of the public schools and higher education into commercial spheres largely responsible for "the training and credentializing of the growing technical-professional managerial work force" (Strickland 2).[10] This means not only waging battles against the new professionalism with its rather gutless retreat into a version of post-war new criticism within higher education, or challenging the forces of privatization that threaten public education, but also vigorously opposing those institutional and pedagogical instances of power, discourse, and social practice that silence education for citizenship, abstract learning from public life, and remove politics from questions regarding ownership over means for the production of knowledge. Schools need to provide students with conditions for learning acts of citizenship and a sense of democratic community. And, as Robert Hass, the Poet Laureate of the United States, elegantly reminds us: "The market doesn't make communities. Markets make networks of self interested individuals" (19). Schools have a more noble political and pedagogical role which is to "refresh the idea of justice, which is going dead in us all the time" (22).

At the same time, progressives must revive critical attention to conflicts within the terrain of culture and representation that lay at the heart of struggles over meaning, identity, and power, particularly as they address issues regarding how youth are constructed and increasingly demonized within a broader public discourse. Unfortunately, many progressives have viewed the struggle over culture as less significant than what is often referred to as the "concrete" world of material suffering, hunger, poverty, and physical abuse. While such a distinction suggests that representations of homelessness and its actual experience cannot be confused, it is also imperative to understand how physical reality and discourse interact. The struggle over naming and constructing meaning also concerns how we constitute moral arguments and judge whether institutions, social relations, and concrete experiences open up or close down the possibilities for democratic public life. Struggles over popular culture, for instance, represent a different but no less important site of politics. For it is precisely on the terrain of culture that identities are produced, values learned, histories legitimated, and knowledge appropriated.

Culture is the medium of public discourse and social practice through which children fashion their individual and collective identities and learn, in part, how to narrate themselves in relation to others.[11] Culture is also the shifting ground where new and old literacies—ways of understanding the world—are produced and legitimated in the service of national identity, public life, and civic responsibility. As a site of learning and struggle, culture becomes the primary referent for understanding the multiple spheres in which pedagogy works, power operates, and authority is secured or contested.

At stake here is a rejection of the increasingly fashionable notion that such struggles are merely viewed as a stand-in for some "real" politics that are at worst inevitably replaced or at best delayed. Instead such struggles should be viewed as "a different, but no less important, site in the contemporary technological and postindustrial society where political struggles take place" (Gray 6). This should not suggest that academics or other cultural workers engage cultural texts as the privileged site of social and political struggle while ignoring either the historical contexts in which such texts are produced or the underlying economic and institutional forces at work in producing, legitimating and distributing such texts. Clearly cultural texts must be addressed and located within the institutional and material contexts of everyday life without reducing the issue of politics, pedagogy, and democracy to simply questions of meaning and identity.[12] At the risk of overstating the issue, I want to emphasize that I am not suggesting public intellectuals reduce the politics of culture to the politics of meaning, but recognize that any progressive notion of cultural politics and pedagogy must be concerned with "relations between culture and power because...culture is a crucial site and weapon of power in the modern world" (Grossberg 142).

If educators and others are to develop a cultural politics that links theoretical rigor and social relevance, they also must further the implications of such a politics by acknowledging the importance of those diverse educational sites through which a generation of youth are being shaped within a postmodern culture where information and its channels of circulation demand new forms of understanding, literacy, and pedagogical practice. This suggests progressives address how and where politics are being constructed and used in a global world steeped in visual and electronically mediated technologies that are refashioning the control and production of new information-based knowledge systems. Kids no longer view schools as the primary source of education, and rightfully so. Media texts—videos, films, music, television, radio, computers—and the new public spheres they inhabit have far more influence on shaping the memories, language, values, and identities of young people. The new technologies that influence and shape youth are important to register not merely because they produce new forms of knowledge, new identities, new social relations, or point to new forces actively engaged in new forms of cultural pedagogy, but also because they point to public spheres in which youth are writing and creating their histories and narratives within social formations that are largely ignored or only superficially acknowledged in trendy postmodern symposiums on music, youth, and performance.

Popular culture represents more than a weak version of politics or a facile notion of innocent entertainment. In its various registers—from cinema to fanzine magazines—popular culture constitutes a powerful pedagogical site where children and adults are being offered specific lessons in how to view themselves, others, and the world they inhabit. In this sense, the cultural texts that operate within such spheres must be addressed as serious objects of social analysis by anyone who takes education seriously. But recognizing that Hollywood films, for instance, function as teaching machines demands more than including them in the school curricula as a matter of relevance; it also demands that educators interrogate such texts for the connections they propose between epistemology and ethics. For instance, as Geoffrey Hartman has argued, there is a pedagogical connection between "how we get to know what we know (through various, including electronic media) and the moral life we aspire to lead" (Hartman 28).

Raising ethical questions about cultural texts is not meant to deny that such texts register different readings for youth. On the contrary, I am proposing that popular culture texts have important pedagogical consequences. Difficult as it may be to gauge what is precisely learned from reading, listening, or engaging such texts, educators need to analyze how popular texts function as public discourses. Further, educators must be critically attentive to how such texts work intertextually, either resonating or conflicting with ideologies produced in other sites which serve to legitimate or resist dominant policies, and social relations. Educators cannot treat popular texts as if they were hermetic or pure; such approaches often ignore how representations are linked to questions of power and broader social struggles. Reading popular texts through a political and ethical lens means educators, students, and others refuse to limit their analyses to formalist strategies designed to decipher a text's preferred meanings. Instead, educators should ascertain how certain meanings under particular historical conditions become more legitimate as representations of reality and take on the force of common sense, in turn shaping a broader set of discourses and social arrangements. By focusing on representations of popular culture as public discourses, it becomes possible to shift our attention away from an exclusive focus on narrow, formalistic readings of texts in order to explore the ways in which such texts bear witness to the ethical dilemmas that animate broader debates within the dominant culture. Such pedagogical inquiries become particularly important when raising questions about the political limits of representation—particularly when they portray children in degrading terms, legitimate the culture of violence, and define agency and desire outside of the discourse of compassion and moral responsibility. Expanding the political importance of the pedagogical also raises the crucial issue of what role academics and other cultural workers might play as critical agents, that is, as public intellectuals willing, as Raymond Williams argues, "to make learning part of the process of social change itself" (158).

As the right wing wages war against sex education, condom distribution in schools, free speech on the Internet, and school libraries that carry allegedly "pornographic" books, there is a curious silence from progressives and other radical cultural workers about the ways in which children are portrayed in films, advertising, and media culture in general. Little is said about how the media floods popular culture with representations of senseless violence, misogynist images of women, and black men as lazy, drug-crazed and dangerous. While it is important for progressives to continue to argue for freedom of expression in the defense of films or other cultural forms that might be deemed offensive, they also need to provide ethical referents within such discourses in order to criticize those images and representations that might be destructive to the psychological health of children or serve to undermine the normative foundations of a viable democracy.

Appeals to the First Amendment, the right of artistic expression, and the dignity of consent are crucial elements in expanding cultural democracy, but they are insufficient for promoting an ethical discourse that cultivates a politics of non-violence, self-responsibility, and social compassion. Progressives must begin to demonstrate a strong commitment to exposing and transforming structures of domination that operate through the media and particularly through those spheres that shape public memory and children's culture. That children derive meaning from the media suggests a broader concern for making those who control media culture accountable for the pedagogies they produce. Larger-than-life violence, sensationalism, and high tech special effects in the media can promote a "psychic numbing" and moral indifference in children. Sanctioned cruelty and racism in the popular media often hides behind what Theodor Adorno discerns as an "an obscene merger of aesthetics and reality" (Adorno in Hartman 27).

Zygmunt Bauman is correct in arguing that "there is more than a casual connection between the ability to commit cruel deeds and moral insensitivity. To make massive participation in cruel deeds possible, the link between moral guilt and the act which the participation entails must be severed" (148). All too often this is precisely what happens when culture is completely commodified, when popular culture is viewed as morally neutral or irrelevant, and when subordinate groups are excluded as moral subjects within dominant regimes of representation. But rather than being addressed by the progressive educators and others, such issues are often rearticulated by right-wing fundamentalists whose basic aim is to close down rather than expand the imperatives of a social and cultural democracy. Progressive educators need to build upon a significant body of theoretical work in which popular culture is not exempt from the discourse of political analyses and moral evaluation. At the very least, popular culture as an important site of contestation and struggle should not be handed over to conservatives such as Bob Dole and William Bennett who find in such a sphere a convenient scapegoat for reasserting a Victorian inspired morality and a nostalgic rendering of the past in which young rappers would have been turned over to the "cold war" police and teen mothers would have been forced to put their offspring in state sponsored orphanages. In opposition to such a discourse, progressives must neither romanticize nor dismiss popular cultural texts. On the contrary, such texts along with other forms of traditional knowledge (high-cultural texts) must become serious objects of critical analyses both within and outside of academia.

Education as a Performative Practice

In what follows, I want to explore briefly how elements of a performative pedagogy might be constructed within a radical project so as to affirm the critical but refuse the cynical, establish hope as central to political practice but eschew a romantic utopianism. Pedagogy in this context becomes performative because it opens a space for disputing conventional academic borders and raising questions "beyond the institutional boundaries of the disciplinary organization of question and answers" (Grossberg 145). Performativity reclaims the pedagogical as a power relationship that participates in authorizing or constraining what is understood as legitimate knowledge, and links the critical interrogation of the production of symbolic and social practices to alternative forms of democratic education that foreground considerations of racial politics, power, and social agency.

As a performative practice, the pedagogical opens up a narrative space that affirms the contextual and the specific while simultaneously recognizing the ways in which such spaces are shot through with issues of power. Referencing the ethical and political is central to a performative and pedagogical practice that refuses closure, insists on combining theoretical rigor and social relevance, and embraces commitment as a point of temporary attachment that allows educators and cultural critics to take a position without becoming dogmatic and rigid. The pedagogical as performative also draws upon an important legacy of theoretical work in which related debates on pedagogy and popular culture can be understood and addressed within the broader context of social responsibility, civic courage, and the reconstruction of democratic public life.[13] Cary Nelson's insight that cultural politics exhibits a deep concern for "how objects, discourses, and practices construct possibilities for and constraints on citizenship" provides an important starting point for designating and supporting a project that brings together various educators, academics, and cultural workers within and outside of the academy (Nelson and Gaonkar 7).

At stake here is a notion of the pedagogical that provides diverse theoretical tools for educators and cultural workers to move within and across disciplinary, political, and cultural borders in order to raise new questions to provide the context in which to organize the energies of a moral vision, and to draw upon the intellectual resources needed to understand and transform those institutions and forces that keep "making the lives [young people] live, and the societies we live in, profoundly and deeply antihumane" (Hall 18).

At the risk of overstating the issue, young people inhabit a society that is not only indifferent to their needs but scapegoats them for many of the problems caused by the forces of globalization, downsizing, economic restructuring, and the collapse of the welfare state. Those youth who have come of age during the culture of Reaganism that began in the 1980s are increasingly used as either bait for conservative politics—blamed for crime, poverty, welfare, and every other conceivable social problem—or "defined in relation to the processes and practices of commodification" (Grossberg 27). The attack on youth coupled with an insurgent racism in America have transformed the field of representations, discourse, and practices that shape today's youth into a battleground. Targeted as trouble and troubling, dangerous and irresponsible, youth face a future devoid of adult support, maps of meaning, or the dream of a qualitatively better life for their own families.

At issue is how youth and race are constructed within new realities that offer both a warning and a challenge to all educators concerned about furthering political and economic democracy in the United States. This is more than a matter of naming or bringing to public attention the scandal that constitutes the conservative attack on youth and the insurgent racism that parades without apology across the American landscape. There is also the matter of what Jacques Derrida calls "performative interpretation." That is, "an interpretation that transforms the very thing it interprets" (51). As a pedagogical practice, "performative interpretation" suggests that how we understand and come to know ourselves and others cannot be separated from how we are represented and imagine ourselves. How youth and race are imagined can best be understood through the ways in which pedagogy weaves its "performative interpretation" of youth within all those myriad educational sites in which electronic technologies are redefining and refiguring the relationship among knowledge, desire, and identity. Youth and racial identity are constituted within and across a plurality of partially disjunctive and overlapping communities—such communities or public spheres offer creative possibilities even as they work to constrain and oppress youth and others through the logic of commodification, racism, and class discrimination.[14] Educators must begin to reclaim the political as a performative intervention that links cultural texts to the institutional contexts in which they are used, critical analysis to the material grounding of power, and cultural production to the historical conditions that give meaning to the places we inhabit and the futures we desire.

At a time when racism and violence against young people has become a growth industry, it is necessary for educators to begin to understand the ways in which the concepts of youth and race function within particular pedagogical and political discourses. At stake here is more than simply providing a critical reading of different cultural texts or the languages that construct them. On the contrary, as I have repeatedly stressed, I am more concerned with how such texts contribute to our understanding of the expanding pedagogical and political role of cultural spheres that are often dismissed as mere entertainment or a showcase for consumer goods. Central to such a concern is how such spheres can be rearticulated as crucial pedagogical sites actively shaping how youth are named and produced in this society. Youth in this instance becomes more than a generational marker; it also becomes an ethical referent reminding adults of their political, moral and social responsibility as public citizens to prepare future generations to confront a world we have created.

The growing demonization of youth and the spreading racism in this country indicate how fragile democratic life can become when the most compassionate spheres of public life—public schools, health care, social services—are increasingly attacked and abandoned.[15] Part of the attempt to undermine those public spheres that provide a safety net for the poor, children, and others can be recognized in the ongoing efforts of the right to "reinstall a wholly privatized, intimate notion of citizenship" (Nelson and Gaonkar 7). Such a constrained notion of citizenship reinforces and legitimates right-wing attempts to shift policy initiatives at the local, state, and federal levels away from investments in social services to policies that support widespread efforts aimed at surveillance and containment. Such policies have resulted in the proliferation of laws passed in nearly a thousand cities to either inaugurate or strengthen curfews designed to keep youth off the streets and to police and criminalize their presence within urban space.

In the new world order, citizenship has little to do with social responsibility and everything to do with creating consuming subjects. Such a constrained notion of citizenship finds a home in an equally narrow definition of pedagogy and the racial coding of the public sphere. In the first instance, pedagogy is defined by conservatives so as to abstract equity from excellence in order to substitute and legitimate a hyper-individualism for a concerted respect for the collective good. In the second instance, it is presumed in both the media and in the representations that flood daily life that the public sphere is almost exclusively white. Blacks are rarely represented as a defining element of national identity or as an integral presence in the various public spheres that make up American life. Reduced to the spheres of entertainment and sports, blacks occupy a marginal existence in white America's representation of public life, largely excluded from those public spheres in which power and politics are negotiated and implemented. While the immediate effects of this assault on public life bear down on those most powerless to fight back—the poor, children, and the elderly, especially those groups that are urban and black—in the long run the greatest danger will be to democracy itself—and the consequences will affect everyone.

If public intellectuals are to address the interrelating problem of racism and the scapegoating of young people in this society, pedagogy as a critical and performative practice needs to be addressed as a defining principle of their work. That is, those cultural workers—journalists, performance artists, lawyers, academics, media representatives, social workers, teachers, and others-who work in higher education, public schools, the mass media, the criminal justice system, the social services, and related fields need to make those issues that bear down on youth in their daily lives a central and mediating concern of their work. The forces that construct, shape, produce, and legitimate the identities, spaces, values, and opportunities that give meaning to how poor white youth and youth of color imagine themselves and their relationship to the future must be addressed and linked to broader struggles for recognition, civil rights, social justice, and equality. While such concerns may appear too sweeping for some, it is precisely around the discourse of rights, recognition, and social justice that many academics and other cultural workers have rallied to the support of other subordinate and oppressed groups attempting to overcome the hierarchies of race, class, gender, and ethnicity.

Ignoring the attack on a generation of young people who appear to have become utterly dispensable to the dominant governing and cultural institutions of society does not bode well for the future of democracy. Demonizing youth not only absolves adults and academics of their civic responsibilities as critical citizens, it also weakens the conditions for carrying on pedagogical and political struggles crucial for a healthy democracy. Addressing the problems of youth both within and outside of the academy suggests reclaiming the space of political and pedagogical work so as to find ways to inspire students to address the pressing problems of joblessness, segregated schools, overcrowded classrooms, inadequate child care and health coverage as well as the economic, gender, and racial basis of injustice and inequity that permeate contemporary society. Such a project implies a fundamental redefinition of the meaning of pedagogy as a political discourse and the role of academics as public intellectuals. Defining themselves less as marginal, avant-garde figures or as professionals acting alone, educators must recover their role as critical citizens and organize collectively in order to address those economic, political, and social problems that must be overcome if young people are going to take seriously a future that opens up rather than closes down the promises of a viable and humane democracy.

Pennsylvania State University
University Park, Pennsylvania

Notes

[1]For instance, see the work of Richard J. Herrnstein and Charles Murray, Dinesh D'Douza. While an extensive list of sources documenting the growing racism in the dominant media and popular culture is too extensive to cite, some important examples include: Jimmie L. Reeves and Richard Campbell, John Fiske, Jeff Ferrell and Clinton R. Sanders, Herman Gray, Michael Dyson, and Giroux's *Fugitive Cultures*. For a summary of the double standard at work in the press coverage of rap music, see Art Jones and Kim Deterline.

[2]For a recent commentary on the funding of the right, see Robert Parry. For an extensive historical analysis of the rise of right-wing movements and politics in the United States, see Sara Diamond.

[3]On the resurgence of the right in American politics, see Chip Berlet.

[4]On the politics of race and blame in the United States, see Kofi Buenor Hadjor.

[5]See, for instance, Ruth Sidel.

[6]For a specific analysis of Calvin Klein's commodification of youth, see Giroux, *Channel Surfing: Race Talk and the Destruction of Today's Youth.*

[7]I address this issue in *Disturbing Pleasures: Learning Popular Culture.* See also, Stephen Kline, Ellen Seiter, and Michael F. Jacobson and Laurie Ann Mazur.

[8]On the politics and economics of wealth, welfare, and race, see Melvin L. Oliver & Thomas M. Shapiro.

[9]For an excellent analysis of these issues, see Harry C. Boyte.

[10]Strickland lays out specific strategies for addressing the particulars of such a struggle within the university itself.

[11]It is hard to believe that any serious scholar of contemporary youth can ignore the political importance of the cultural terrain in shaping the identities of young people. For one such instance, see Mike A. Males. Males believes that how young people learn to imagine themselves, others, and their place in the world is determined almost exclusively by generational forces and economic considerations. The political and pedagogical force of cultural institutions simply drops out of his account of young people.

[12]For an analysis of this issue, see Lawrence Grossberg.

[13]In this case, I am referring to work in the art world in which the performative, pedagogical, and political mutually inform each other. For instance, see Catherine Ugwu, Guillermo Gomez-Pena, Suzanne Lacy, Nina Felshin, or Carol Becker.

[14]I discuss this issue in more detail in *Disturbing Pleasures*, *Fugitive Cultures*, and in *Channel Surfing: Race Talk and the Destruction of Today's Youth.*

[15] See Stanley Aronowitz, *The Death and Rebirth of American Radicalism.*

Works Cited

Aronowitz, Stanley. *The Death and Rebirth of American Radicalism.* New York: Routledge, 1996.

Bauman, Zygmunt. *Life in Fragments.* Oxford and Cambridge USA: Basil Blackwell, 1995.

Becker, Carol. *Zones of Contention.* Albany: State U of New York P, 1996.

Berlet, Chip. *Eyes Right! Challenging the Right Wing Backlash.* Boston: South End P, 1995.

Boyte, Harry C. "Citizenship Education and the Public World." *The Civic Arts Review* (1992): 4-9.

Derrida, Jacques. *Specters of Marx.* New York: Routledge, 1994.

Diamond, Sara. *Roads to Dominion: Right-Wing Movements and Political Power in the United States.* New York: Guilford P, 1995.

D'Souza, Dinesh. *The End of Racism: Principles for a Multiracial Society*. New York: The Free P, 1995.

Dyson, Michael. *Between God and Gangsta Rap*. New York: Oxford UP, 1996.

Felshin, Nina, ed. *But Is It Art? The Spirit of Art Activism*. Seattle: Bay P, 1995.

Ferrell, Jeff and Clinton R. Sanders, eds. *Cultural Criminology* Boston: Northeastern UP, 1995.

Fiske, John. *Media Matters*. Minneapolis: U of Minnesota P, 1994.

Fox, James Alan. "A Disturbing Trend in Youth Crime." *The Boston Globe*. 1 June 1995. 19.

Giroux, Henry A. *Channel Surfing: Race Talk and the Destruction of Today's Youth*. New York: St. Martin's P, 1997.

—. *Disturbing Pleasures: Learning Popular Culture* New York: Routledge, 1994.

—. *Fugitive Cultures: Race, Violence and Youth*. New York: Routledge, 1996.

Gomez-Pena, Guillermo. *The New World Border*. San Francisco: City Lights, 1996.

Gray, Herman. *Watching Race*. Minneapolis: U of Minnesota P, 1995.

Grossberg, Lawrence. "Toward a Genealogy of the State of Cultural Studies." *Disciplinarity and Dissent in Cultural Studies*. Eds. Cary Nelson and Dilip Parameshwar Gaonkar. New York: Routledge, 1996.

Hadjor, Kofi Buenor. *Another America*. Boston: South End P, 1995.

Hall, Stuart. "Race, Culture, and Communications: Looking Backward and Forward at Cultural Studies." *Rethinking Marxism* 5 (1992): 10-19.

Hartman, Geoffery. "Public Memory and Its Discontents." *Raritan* 8 (1994): 24-40.

Herrnstein, Richard J. and Charles Murray. *The Bell Curve: Intelligence and Class Structure in American Life*. New York: The Free P, 1994.

Kline, Stephen. *Out of the Garden: Toys and Children's Culture in the Age of TV Marketing*. London: Verso, 1993.

Jacobson, Michael F. and Laurie Ann Mazur. *Marketing Madness*. Boulder: Westview, 1995.

Jones, Art and Kim Deterline. "Fear of a Rap Planet: Rappers Face Media Double Standard." *Extra* 7 (1994): 20-21.

Lacy, Suzanne, ed. *Mapping the Terrain: New Genre Public Art*. Seattle: Bay P, 1995.

Males, Mike A. *The Scapegoat Generation: America's War on Adolescents*. Monroe, ME: Common Courage P, 1996.

Nelson, Cary and Dilip Parameshwar Gaonkar, eds. *Disciplinarity and Dissent in Cultural Studies*. New York: Routledge, 1996.

Oliver, Melvin L. and Thomas M. Shapiro. *Black Wealth/White Wealth*. New York: Routledge, 1995.

Paglia, Camilia and Steward Brand. "Hollywood: America's Greatest Achievement." *Utne Reader* (1994): 79.

Parry, Robert. "Who Buys the Right?" *The Nation* (November 18, 1996): 5-6.

Pollick, Sarah. "Interview with Robert Hass." *Mother Jones* (March/April 1997): 19-22.

Reeves, Jimmie L. and Richard Campbell. *Cracked Coverage: Television News, The Anti-Cocaine Crusade, and the Reagan Legacy*. Durham: Duke UP, 1994.

Seiter, Ellen. *Sold Separately: Parents and Children in Consumer Culture.* New Jersey: Rutgers UP, 1993.

Sidel, Ruth. *Keeping Women and Children Last.* New York: Penguin, 1996.

Strickland, Ronald. "Curriculum Mortis: A Manifesto for Structural Change." *College Literature* 21 (1994): 2.

Ugwu, Catherine, ed. *Let's Get It On: The Politics of Black Performance.* Seattle: Bay, 1995.

Williams, Raymond. "Adult Education and Social Change." *What I Came to Say.* London: Hutchinson-Radius, 1989.

Educational Foundations, Spring 1997

Peter L. McLaren is a professor with the Graduate School of Education and Information Studies at the University of California, Los Angeles. *He presented this article as the R. Freeman Butts Lecture at the annual meetings of the American Educational Studies Association on November 8, 1996, in Montréal, Québec, Canada. Sections of this lecture will appear in Enrique Trueba and Yali Zou (Editors)* Ethnic Identity and Power *(Albany, NY: State University of New York Press, in press); Peter McLaren,* Revolutionary Multiculturalism: Pedagogies of Dissent for the New Millennium *(Boulder, CO: Westview Press, in press); Jim O'Donnell and Christine Clark,* Becoming White: Owning a Racial Identity *(Albany, NY: State University of New York Press, in press); Peter McLaren, "Decentering Whiteness,"* Multicultural Education *(forthcoming); and Joe Kincheloe and Shirley Steinberg,* White Reign: Learning and Deploying Whiteness in America *(forthcoming). The author also thanks Bernardo Gallegos and Diane Alvarez for their reading of this paper and their helpful commentary.*

Unthinking Whiteness, Rethinking Democracy:

Or Farewell to the Blonde Beast; Towards a Revolutionary Multiculturalism

Dedicated to the memory of Emiliano Zapata, *el líder campesino hecho martír en 1917* and *El Ejército Zapatista de Liberacíon Nacional.*

By Peter L. McLaren

The Price of freedom is death.
—Malcolm X (El Hajj Malik El Shabazz)

We don't want to be around that ol' pale thing.
—Malcolm X (El Hajj Malik El Shabazz)

El deber de cada revolucionario es hacer la revolución.
—Che Guevara

As the millennium draws closer and my time on this earth stretches within a whisper of half a century, I look back at my twenty-five years as an educator and social activist with few regrets. Yet I must confess a world-weariness has overtaken much of what I thought was my inviolate resolve, a feeling of anger and despair about living and dying in these new times, at this current and painful juncture in world history. I try to hide my despair and rage towards the system from my students, many of whom yearn to find in my writings and those of my colleagues some hard and fast ways to permanently dismantle structures of oppression that imprison the spirit and harden the hearts of so many of our brothers and sisters in struggle.

Despite the present social conditions that beset us, I am not in a perpetual state of dismay, forced to camouflage a secret despair. In my darkest hours I have on more than one occasion been graced by what could be described as a momentous shimmering of the human spirit, a slight breaking free from the deep inertia of this planetary soul. Occasionally light splinters the darkness in various shapes: a nascent social movement attempting to unite the barrios; a hip hop message that becomes a rallying cry for social justice in a community under siege; a million black men marching to Washington; a hundred thousand marchers striding down Cesar Chavez Avenue to protest Proposition 187 with a resolve so formidable that you could feel the sting of electricity in the air; hundreds of high school students in East Los Angeles defying their teachers and walking out of their classrooms to show their solidarity with the anti-Proposition 187 activists. Even a single pedagogical act, such as a group of students trying to undo the image of the Mexicano as the demon poster-boy by confronting white racists in a seminar, is enough to drive a tiny wedge between despair and cynical resignation.

Spaces of hope do appear. But rarely by historical accident. Sometimes they occur in the momentary indecision of the marketplace; sometimes in a rare paralysis of hate in the menacing machine of capital; but whatever the reason, these spaces need to be strategically seized. Spaces of hope offer encouragement to the forces of justice but they are not sufficient in themselves. Spaces—often private—must be made public. They must be expanded from spaces into spheres—from personal, individual spaces and private epistemologies into public spheres of hope and struggle and collective identities.

The specific struggle that I wish to address is that of choosing against whiteness. Yet is it possible for us to choose against whiteness given that, historically, the practice of whiteness has brought about such a devastating denial, dissassembly, and destruction of other races? One would think that such a choice against whiteness would be morally self-evident. However, precisely because whiteness is so pervasive, it remains difficult to identify, to challenge, and to separate from our daily lives. My message is that we must create a new public sphere where the practice of whiteness is not only identified and analyzed but also contested and destroyed. For choosing against whiteness is the hope and promise of the future.

Where do those of us, living in this vaunted western democracy, stand as a nation? Look around you, dear comrades; look inside as well as outside for the outside is really a mirror of who we are as a people. The Dickensianizing of post-modern megalopolises like Los Angeles (the enhancing of the personal wealth of the few who live in places like Beverley Hills at the expense of the many who live in places like Compton or East L.A.) is not a natural historical event (there is nothing natural about history). It is a politically contrived dismemberment of the national conscience. And it is comfortably linked to global economic restructuring.

Sustaining a meager existence is becoming frighteningly more difficult with the passage of time for millions of Third World peoples as well as First World urban dwellers, including millions of inhabitants of the United States. Global capitalism is excluding large numbers from formal employment while the poor, trapped within post-Fordist arenas of global restructuring and systems of flexible specialization, appear to be less able to organize themselves into stable and homogeneous social movements. Standardized forms of mass production, in which companies retool and keep production costs down in order to keep competitive in the international marketplace, are now disappearing. Economies of global efficiency are side-stepping the ability of nation states to mediate the control of money and information.

Labor markets are growing more segmented as full-time workers are replaced with part-time workers who are unable to secure even meager health or dental benefits. The days of high-wage, high-benefit mass production manufacturing are receding into the horizon as the First World bids farewell to industrialized regimes. Yet manufacturing has not completely disappeared from the United States. In Los Angeles, where I live, you can witness the Latinization of the Southland's working-class, as Latino/as now make up 36 percent of Los Angeles County's labor force in manufacturing (the nation's largest manufacturing base). And the exploitation of these workers continues to increase.

Stock options go up in companies that downsize and lay off thousands of employees. It used to be a sign that a company was in trouble when it laid off large numbers of workers. Now it's an indication of strength, making stockholders proud. Cutting costs is everything, as business moves farther away from even a peripheral engagement with the world of ethics. In fact, capitalism has made ethics obsolete. The buying and selling of labor power is all about aesthetics, which does share a hinge with ethics, true, but the latter is subsumed by reification's terrible beauty.

The war on poverty has given way to the war on the poverty-stricken—a war that is about as mean-spirited as wars can get. The average worker has to do without the luxury of decent living standards because to improve conditions for the majority of the population would cut too deeply into the corporate profitability of the ruling elite. Rarely has such contempt for the poor and for disenfranchised people of color been so evident as in the hate-filled politics of the last several decades.

The greed and avarice of the United States ruling class is seemingly unparalleled in history. Yet its goals remain decidedly the same. Michael Parenti writes:

> Throughout history there has been only one thing that ruling interests have ever wanted—and that is *everything*: all the choice lands, forest, game, herds,

> harvests, mineral deposits, and precious metals of the earth; all the wealth, riches, and profitable returns; all the productive facilities, gainful inventiveness, and technologies; all the control positions of the state and other major institutions; all public supports and subsidies, privileges and immunities; all the protections of the law with none of its constraints; all the services, comforts, luxuries, and advantages of civil society with none of the taxes and costs. Every ruling class has wanted only this: all the rewards and none of the burdens. The operational code is: we have a lot; we can get more; we want it all. (1996, p. 46)

As long as the small business lobby and other interests tied to capital successfully derail health care reform whenever the issue raises it's disease-ravaged face, as long as the bond market continues to destroy public investment, and as long as business continues to enjoy record-high profits, acquisitions, and mergers (with the aid of corporate welfare) at the expense of wages and labor, then prosperity in the United States, like its administration of social justice, will remain highly selective. And we all know who benefits from such selectivity. To remain in a state of political paralysis or inertia is to aid and abet the sickening suburbanization of the country—a suburbanization driven by a neo-liberal agenda designed to serve mainly Whites. Working under existing rules established by the National Labor Relations Act and the procedures carried out by the National Labor Relations Board, unions are being deprived of their right to organize, and this is contributing in no small way to wage decline. The situation reflects only too well what Parenti calls his "iron law of bourgeois politics": When change threatens to rule, then rules are changed (1996, p. 248).

Residents of the United States do not have a natural disposition to swindle the gullible, to target the poor more forcefully than a F-16 fighter locks onto an enemy "hunkered down" in the sands of Iraq, to scapegoat immigrants and to fashion them into *los olvidados* (the forgotten ones). The current evisceration of public protection programs, shamefully absent enforcement of environmental standards, rising health insurance premiums, drastic declines in salaries for working people, erosion of the primary sector proletariat, and steady increase of the chronically unemployed have catapulted the United States onto a tragic course towards social decay and human misery—a course that is far from inevitable.

It is possible that a quarter century from now Whites might be a minority in the United States. As they continue to feel that their civil society is being despoiled and to blame immigrants for their increasing downward mobility and the disappearance of "traditional" American values, Whites fall prey to the appeal of a reactionary and fascist politics of authoritarian repression. This is especially true at a time when Whites continue to feel removed from their ethnic roots and undergo what Howard Winant (1994, p. 284) has called "a racializing panethnicity as 'Euro-Americans.'"

The kindling of fascism lies in the furnace of United States democracy waiting for a spark to ignite a firestorm of state repression. Previous firestorms have occurred in the Watts rebellion of August 1965, the civil rights movement, and the anti-war movement of the 1960s, but also in more current forms such as the Los Angeles uprising of April 29, 1992, and the East L.A. high school walk-outs of 1994 over Proposition 187. We don't get many firestorms because, as Parenti (1996) has so presciently noted, fascism is already here on low-flame, which burns just fine with the occasional stoking from reactionary governors such as Pete Wilson.

The citizenry of the United States has been sold a damaged bill of goods in the Republican Contract with America. Parenti captures its ideology perfectly:

> The GOP socio-economic agenda is not much different from the kind pushed by Mussolini and Hitler: break the labor unions, depress wages, impose a rightist ideological monopoly over the media, abolish taxes for the big corporations and the rich, eliminate government regulations designed for worker and consumer safety and environmental protection, plunder public lands, privatize public enterprises, wipe out most human services, and liberal-bait and race-bait all those opposed to such measures. (1996, p. 42)

In the United States we are living at a time of undeclared war. Each day we negotiate our way through mine-sown terrains of confrontation and uncertainty surrounding the meaning and purpose of identity. American democracy faces Janus-like in two simultaneous directions: into a horizon of hope and co-existence and into the burning eyes of klansmen in sheets soiled with blood. While on the one hand this current historical juncture is witnessing an unprecedented growth of white supremacist organizations living on the fringes of social life, on the other hand establishment conservatives are stridently asserting nativistic and populist sentiments that barely distinguish them ideologically from their counterparts in racialist far right groups and citizen militias: The Ku Klux Klan, Posse Comitatus, The Order, White Aryan Resistance, Christian Identity, National Alliance, Aryan Nations, American Front, Gun Owners of America, United Citizens of Justice and militia groups have organizations in most, if not all, of the fifty states.

Young white males and females who may find these racist groups unappealing can still find solace in politicians such as Pete Wilson and Bob Dole whose anti-immigrant and Latinophobic policies and practices deflect their racializing sentiments through flag waving, jingoism, and triumphalist acts of self-aggrandizement—such as the disguising of Proposition 209 as a civil rights initiative—designed to appeal to frightened white voters who feel that growing numbers of Spanish-speaking immigrants will soon outnumber them. Politicians have become white warriors in blue suits and red ties dedicated to taking back the country from the infidel. Recently, amid headlines of Black churches in the south being razed by arson, a Los Angeles newspaper ran a photograph of Bob Dole at a Southland political rally. The magnetic allure of Dole's head, its skin a translucent blue, tensile; its shiny yellow tongue as if dipped in kerosene, seemingly wagging, appeared in metonymic relationship to his message: Anglos feel under siege from the most alien of alien nations—Mexico—and it is time that civilized white folks wrestle back the land from the barbarians.

Guillermo Gómez-Peña writes:

> This identity crisis translates into an immense nostalgia for an (imaginary) era in which people of color didn't exist, or at least when we were invisible and silent. The political expression of this nostalgia is chilling: "Let's take our country back." The far right, like Pete Wilson, Newt Gingrich, Jesse Helms, and Pat Buchanan, along with many Democrats, are in agreement on the following: This country must be saved from chaos and collapse into Third-Worldization; "illegal" immigrants must be deported; the poor should be put in jail (three strikes, you're out); welfare, affirmative action, and bilingual education programs must be dismantled; and the cultural funding infrastructure that has been infiltrated by "liberals with leftist tendencies" (the National Endowment for the Arts and the Humanities and the Corporation for Public Broadcasting) must be decimated. In the euphemistic Contract with America, ethnic "minorities," independent artists and intellectuals, the homeless, the elderly, children, and especially immigrants from the South, are all under close watch. (1996, p. 173)

On the day of General Colin L. Powell's address to the 1996 Republican Convention in San Diego, former Education Secretary and current director of Empower America, William J. Bennett, published a commentary in the *Los Angeles Times* entitled "Civil Rights is the GOP's mission" (Monday, August 12, 1996, B5). Evoking the figure of Dr. Martin Luther King Jr., Bennett called for the end of racial discrimination through the abolition of affirmative action. Bewailing the civil rights leaders of the past 30 years (with the exception of Dr. King, of course, whose symbolic power he seeks to conscript into his own agenda) whom he argued are a group of malcontents who have wielded a "racial branding iron," have "diminished the moral authority of the civil rights movement," have "fanned the flames of racial resentment," and have "helped Balkanize America," Bennett calls for the government to eliminate "race-based preferences" for people of color. He putatively wants African-Americans, Latino/as, and other ethnic minority groups to be judged by the "content of their character." He cites African-Americans such as Ward Connerly, chairman of the Civil Rights Initiative and General Powell as continuing "the great civil rights tradition of Dr. King."

However, Bennett's vision is perniciously short-sighted and malificent and effectively domesticates King's place in the Civil Rights struggle. And his logic is disturbingly flawed. It is similar to the conservative school board that abolishes school breakfast programs for hungry children because such programs are "anti-family." Since the children eat at school and not with their parents and siblings at home, they are apparently offending the values that made this country great. Supposedly, it is better to go hungry with your family than to be fed at school. Bennett's arguments are similarly confused. First, he appears to work under the mistaken assumption that U.S. society has reached a point of relative economic justice and affirmative action is no longer necessary. Second, he appears either to be unable or unwilling to fathom the nearly intractable reality of white privilege and uncontested hegemony in the arena of the economy. Thirdlý, he fails to realize that racist white people are going to be suspicious of African-Americans and Latino/as whether they are assisted by affirmative action initiatives or not. And fourthly, his vision is propelled by a nostalgic view of a United States as a middle-class suburban neighborhood in which people of color don't have so much "attitude" and where Whites are the uncontested caretakers of this prelapsarian nation of consensus and harmony. To be colorblind in Bennett's restricted use of the term is to be naive at best and ignorant at worst. Because not to see color in Bennett's view really amounts in ideological terms to be blind to the disproportionate advantage enjoyed by white people in nearly all sectors of society. Winant has argued:

> In many ways no African American, however affluent, can feel as secure as even the average White: for example, in an encounter with the police... Yet the malevolent attentions of floor walkers in Bloomingdales cannot be compared with those of the Los Angeles Police Department. (1994, p. 283)

Bennett's view is akin to conservative politicians who bemoan critics of tax breaks for the rich (welfare for the rich) for engaging in "class warfare." You don't have to be an economist to realize that since the Reagan administration, money has been transferred from the ranks of the poor into the coffers of the rich in record proportions. Yet conservative politicians resent people who label these practices as "unjust." After all, if rich (mainly white) people can work the system to their advantage, then all the more power to them. Bennett has turned the logic of Martin Luther King, Jr. upside down. He has replaced social analysis with homilies about "character." That a former Secretary of Education would take a position like this is especially telling, given the state of critical self-reflection among politicians in this country.

Politicians of Bennett's ilk want to increase the role of charitable institutions in this country. If economically disenfranchised people of color are to be helped, then it should be done by private individuals or organizations and not the government—or so the conservatives maintain. But wealthy private organizations have benefited from the hegemony of white privilege in the government and the marketplace for centuries. Unbridled capitalism in our present post-Fordist service economy is ruthlessly uncharitable to the poverty-stricken. Never the less, transferring the challenge of economic justice from the government into the hands of philanthropists who feel "pity" for the poor is not the solution. Bennett misses the crucial point: that not to have affirmative action for people of color in the present social structure amounts to a hidden affirmative action for white people. Bennett's position tacitly seeks the incorporation of racialized groups into the corporate ethics of consumption where white privilege increasingly holds sway. His ethics of racial tolerance can therefore work as a means of social control of populations of color. His motivated amnesia with respect to the history of capitalism causes him to ignore the macrostructures of inequality and injustice and the class-bound hierarchies and institutionalized racism of United States society and to act as if United States society already obtains on the issue of economic equality across diverse ethnic populations. There is a false assumption at work in Bennett's logic that views culture as essentially self-equilibrating, as providing similar sets of shared experiences to all social groups. The culture of diversity heralded by Bennett is a decidedly homogenized one, cut off from the contingencies of state power and economic practices. He fails to recognize the ideology of colonialism as a founding discourse of United States democracy and refuses to acknowledge that the skull and crossbones logic of imperial piracy that stole the land from its indigenous inhabitants is still largely with us both in domestic and foreign policy.

If Bennett is so intent on character building and fears that African Americans are now being viewed by white people as bearing the "stigma of questionable competence" because of affirmative action, why doesn't he, rather than dismantle affirmative action, place greater emphasis on improving the social practices of white people, by encouraging them not to stigmatize, demonize, and peripheralize people of color and women not only in the boardrooms but also in all walks of life.

It is precisely Bennett's stubborn unwillingness to recognize the asymmetrical allocation of resources and power that overwhelmingly favor white people as much now as during King's era, that effectively truncates Bennett's vision, fashioning it into a form of sound-byte histrionics.

In her article, "Whiteness as Property" (1993), Cheryl I. Harris makes the compelling case that within the legal system and within popular reasoning there exists an assumption that whiteness is a property interest entitled to legal protection. Whiteness as property is essentially the reification in law of expectations of white privilege. Not only has this assumption been supported by systematic white supremacy through the law of slavery and "Jim Crow" but also by recent decisions and rationales of the Supreme Court concerning affirmative action. Harris is correct in arguing that whiteness serves as the basis of racialized privilege in which white racial identity provides the basis for allocating societal benefits in both public and private spheres. Whiteness as a property of status continues to assist in the reproduction of the existing system of racial classification and stratification that protects the socially entrenched white power elite. According to Harris, rejecting race-conscious remedial measures as unconstitutional under the Equal Protection Clause of the Fourteenth Amendment "is based on the Court's chronic refusal to dismantle the institutional protection of benefits for whites that have been based on white supremacy and maintained at the expense of Blacks" (1993, p. 1767).

Current legal definitions of race embrace the norm of colorblindness and thus disconnect race from social identity and race-consciouness. Within the discourse of colorblindness, blackness and whiteness are seen as neutral and apolitical descriptions reflecting skin color, and unrelated to social conditions of domination and subordination and to social attributes such as class, culture, language, and education. In other words, colorblindness is a concept that *symmetrizes* relations of power and privilege and flattens them out so that they appear symmetrical or equivalent. But blackness and whiteness are not symmetrical; rather, they exist in society within a dependent hierarchy, with whiteness constraining the social power of blackness: by colonizing the definition of what is normal; by institutionalizing a greater allocation of resources for white constituencies; and by maintaining laws that favor Whites. According to Harris:

> To define race reductively as simply color, and therefore meaningless...is as subordinating as defining race to be scientifically determinative of inherent deficiency. The old definition creates a false linkage between race and inferiority, the new definition denies the real linkage between race and oppression under systematic white supremacy. Distorting and denying reality, both definitions support race subordination. As Neil Gotanda has argued, colorblindness is a form of race subordination in that it denies the historical context of white domination and Black subordination. (1993, p. 1768)

Affirmative action needs to be understood not through privatizing social inequality through claims of bipolar corrective justice between black and white competitors but rather as an issue of distributive social justice and rights that focuses not on guilt or innocence but on entitlement and fairness.

Bennett's faltering rhetoric and specious logic speak directly to the current crisis of democracy that has deported the hopes and dreams of growing numbers of minority populations across United States into an abyss of emptiness and despair. The crisis has exposed the infrastructure of American democracy to be made of Styrofoam, trembling spray-painted pillars of a Greek temple in an off-Broadway play. Democracy has been cut at the joints by events that are currently transpiring both locally and throughout the globe.

One of the tasks ahead for those of us who wish to reclaim the dignity offered by true justice, is to revivify democratic citizenship in an era of diminishing returns. It is to create critical citizens who are no longer content in occupying furtive spaces of private affirmation but who possess the will and the knowledge to turn these spaces into public spheres through the creation of new social movements and anti-capitalist struggle.

The struggle in these new times is a daunting one. Record numbers of disaffected white youth are joining citizen militias and white supremacist organizations at a time when black churches are burning in the South, and when cross-burnings are occuring at an alarming rate across the nation in Louisiana, Georgia, Pennsylvania, Oregon, Maine, Southern California, and elsewhere. As white youth search for identity in their lives, many are able to find meaning only in relation to their capacity to hate non-whites. While some postmodernists adventitiously assert that identities can be fluidly recomposed, rearranged, and reinvented towards a more progressive politics in these new "pluralistic" times, I maintain that this is a short-sighted and dangerous argument. It would take more than an army of Jacques Lacans to help us rearrange and suture the fusillade of interpolations and subject positions at play in our daily lives. My assertion that the contents of particular cultural differences and discourses are not as important as how such differences are embedded in and related to the larger social totality of economic, social, and political differences, may strike some listeners as extreme. Yet I think it is fundamentally necessary to stress this point.

We are not autonomous citizens that can fashionably choose whatever ethnic combinations we desire in order to reassemble our identity. While the borders of ethnicity overlap and shade into one another, it is dishonest to assert that pluralized, hybridized identities are options available to all citizens in the same way (Hicks, 1991). This is because class, race, and gender stratification and objective constraints and historical determinations restrict the choices of some groups over others. The division of labor linked to political organization and the politics of the marketplace regulate choices and often overdetermine their outcome (San Juan, 1996). Identity is more than the ideological trafficking between nationality and ethnicity, but rather the overlapping and mutual intereffectivity of discourses that are configured by the social relations of production. In other words, nationalism, ethnicity, and capitalist circuits of production can be seen moving into a shared orbit.

Rather than stressing the importance of diversity and inclusion, as do most multiculturalists, I think that significantly more emphasis should be placed on the social and political construction of white supremacy and the dispensation of white hegemony. The reality-distortion field know as "Whiteness" needs to be identified as a cultural disposition and ideology linked to specific political, social, and historical arrangements. This is a theme to which I shall return later in my talk.

A related theme that I would like to emphasize in the comments that follow is the need to incorporate, yet move beyond, the politics of diversity and inclusion when discussing multicultural education. The discourse of diversity and inclusion is often predicated on hidden assumptions of assimilation and consensus that serve as supports for neo-liberal democratic models of identity.

Neo-liberal democracy, performing under the banner of diversity yet actually in the hidden service of capital accumulation, often reconfirms the racist stereotypes already prescribed by Euro-American nationalist myths of supremacy—stereotypes that one would think democracy is ostensibly committed to challenge. In the pluralizing move to become a society of diverse voices, neo-liberal democracy has often succumbed to a recolonization of multiculturalism by failing to challenge ideological assumptions surrounding difference that are installed in its current anti-affirmative action and welfare 'reform' initiatives. In this sense people of color are still placed under the threshold of candidacy for inclusion into the universal right to self-determination, and interpolated as exiles from United States citizenship. After all, as a shrinking minority Whites are running scared, conscious of their own vulnerability, and erecting fortresses of social regulation while they still have the power to do so. Todd Gitlin declares:

> The Republican tilt of white men is the most potent form of identity politics in our time: a huddling of men who resent (and exaggerate) their relative decline not only in parts of the labor movement but at home, in the bedroom and the kitchen, and in the culture. Their fear and loathing is, in part, a panic against the relative gains of women and minorities in an economy that people experience as a zero-sum game, in which the benefits accruing to one group seem to amount to subtractions from another. Talk about identity politics! These white men, claiming they deserve color-blind treatment, identify with their brethren more than their wives or sisters, or minorities. (1995, p. 233)

Of course, one of the most hated groups among the poor in the Southland where I live are the Mexican migrant workers. Stereotyped as *crimmegrantes*, they have become the object of xenophobia par exellence. Ron Prince, one of the architects of Proposition 187, has remarked: "Illegal aliens are a category of criminal, not a category of ethnic group" (Gómez-Peña, 1996, p. 67). Gómez-Peña comments on the imbrication of borders as a perceived crisis-effect by white Americans:

> For many Americans, the border has failed to stop chaos and crisis from creeping in (the origin of crisis and chaos is somehow always located outside). Their worst nightmare is finally coming true: The United States is no longer a fictional extension of Europe, or the wholesome suburb imagined by the screenwriter of *Lassie*. It is rapidly becoming a huge border zone, a hybrid society, a mestizo race, and worst of all, this process seems to be irreversible. America shrinks day by day, as the pungent smell of enchiladas fills the air and the volume of quebradita music rises. (1996, p. 67)

The process of "Mexicanization" has struck fear into the hearts of the Euro-American who views this inevitability as an obdurate political reality. And this fear is only exacerbated by the media and anti-immigration activists. As Gómez-Peña notes:

> Now, it is the "illegal aliens" who are to take the blame for everything that American citizens and their incompetent politicians have been unable (or unwilling) to solve. Undocumented immigrants are being stripped of their humanity and individuality, becoming blank screens for the projection of Americans' fear, anxiety, and rage... Both the anti-immigration activists and the conservative media have utilized extremely charged metaphors to describe this process of "Mexicanization." It is described as a Christian nightmare ("hell at our doorsteps"); a natural disaster ("the brown wave"); a fatal disease or an

> incurable virus; a form of demographic rape; a cultural invasion; or the scary beginning of a process of secession or "Quebequization" of the entire Southwest. (1996, pp. 66, 67-68)

I remember the bestial hate mongering among Whites after the anti-187 march in East Los Angeles in 1994. The size of the crowd—approximately one hundred thousand protesters by some estimates—instilled such a fear of a brown planet that many white Angelenos fervently took to the streets in anti-immigration demonstrations. Too much "difference-effect" resulting from the borderization phenomena has created among previously stable white constituencies a type of fibrillation of subjectivity—a discursive quivering that eventually leads to a state of identity collapse. Wreaking havoc on the social landscape by creating a spectacular demonology around African-American and Latino/a gang members, welfare queens, undocumented workers, and gays and lesbians, members of the professional-managerial class made up primarily of cosmopolitan Whites have tried to convince White America that its identity is threatened and that white people now constitute the "new" oppressed. Can anyone take this claim seriously coming as it is from the most privileged group in history?

I believe that an emphasis on the construction of whiteness will help put a different and important focus on the problems surrounding identity formation at this particular juncture in our history. When North Americans talk about race, they inevitably refer to African-Americans, Asians, Latino/as, Native Americans, to the consistent exclusion of Euro-Americans. I want to challenge the prevailing assumption that in order to defeat racism we need to put our initiatives behind the inclusions of minoritarian populations—in other words, of non-Whites. I want to argue instead that in addition to making an argument for diversity, we need to put more emphasis on the analysis of white ethnicity, and the destabilization of white identity, specifically white supremacist ideology and practice. As David Roediger notes:

> Whiteness describes, from Little Big Horn to Simi Valley, not a culture but precisely the absence of culture. It is the empty and therefore terrifying attempt to build an identity based on what one isn't and on whom one can hold back. (1994, p. 137)

I am currently a citizen of a country who supplies the U.S. with a substantial group of undocumented workers—Canada. But you don't see the U.S. government militarizing its Northern border. I don't have to be too concerned about harassment from *la migra* if California's Propositions 187 or 209 someday take effect. Consider the vehemently racist comments directed against Mexican and other immigrants of color by Patrick Buchanan, a recent Republican candidate for the U.S. Presidency:

> If British subjects, fleeing a depression, were pouring into this country through Canada, there would be few alarms. The central objection to the present flood of illegals is they are not English-speaking white people from Western Europe; they

are Spanish-speaking brown and black people from Mexico, Latin America, and the Caribbean. (Bradlee Jr., 1996: 1 & 12)

I would ask you to consider Buchanan's remarks in light of United States history. I offer some comments made by Abraham Lincoln during a speech made in southern Illinois in 1858:

> "I am not," he told his audience, "nor ever have been, in favor of bringing about in any way the social or political equality of the white and black races.... I will say in addition that there is a physical difference between the white and black races which, I suppose, will forever forbid the two races living together upon terms of social and political equality; and in as much as they cannot so live, that while they do remain together there must be a position of the superiors and the inferiors; and that I, as much as any other man, am in favor of the superior being assigned to the white man." (Zinn, 1970, p. 148)

Another United States hero, Benjamin Franklin, wrote:

> "Why increase the Sons of **Africa**, by planting them in **America**, where we have so fair an Opportunity, by excluding all Blacks and Tawneys, of increasing the lovely White and Red?" (Cited in Perea, 1995, p. 973)

Or consider the views of Thomas Jefferson, who was concerned about the presence of Africans in America, whom he referred to as an impure "blot" on the purity of the land:

> ... it is impossible not to look forward to distant times, when our rapid multiplication will expand itself ... & cover the whole northern, if not the southern continent, with a people speaking the same language, governed in similar forms, & by similar laws; **nor can we contemplate with satisfaction either blot or mixture on that surface**. (Cited in Perea, 1995, p. 974)

Not only was Thomas Jefferson a mean-spirited racist and slave owner but he also can arguably be considered the central ideological founder of American Apartheid. He advocated an approach to democracy inspired by a mystical reading of the French Revolution, that justified mass slaughter in the name of liberty and justice for whites only. It's perhaps no coincidence that when Timothy McVeigh was arrested driving away from Oklahoma City on the day the Federal Building was bombed, he was wearing a T-shirt that bore the celebrated words of Jefferson: "the tree of liberty must be refreshed from time to time by the blood of patriots and tyrants." While Jefferson was surely against the practice of slavery, he unhesitatingly called for the banishment of free blacks from the Untied States since he believed that "nature, habit, opinion has drawn indelible lines of distinction" between white people and black people such that they "cannot live in the same government" (O'Brien, p. 57).

Jefferson preached against racism yet he had one of his many slaves, James Hubbard, severely flogged for escaping. In addition, he proposed an amendment to the Virginia legal code which would ban free Blacks from coming to Virginia of their own accord or taking up residence for more than a year. His amendment was rejected by his contemporaries as being too severe. Jefferson had even proposed that white women who had children by black fathers were to be ordered out of Virginia within a year of the child's birth. Failure to leave the state would place these women "out of the protection of the law" which meant, of course, that they could be lynched. Jefferson also suggested that the government purchase newborn slaves form their owners, and pay for their maintenance until the children could work off their debt up to their date of deportation to Santo Domingo (O'Brien, 1996). Fortunately, these other sugesstions were also rejected by his contemporaries.

Not to be outdone in the racist department, we have Senator John Calhoun, speaking on the Senate floor in 1848, where he oppossed annexation by the United States of land belonging to Mexico on the grounds of preserving a homogeneous white nation:

> I know further, sir, that we have never dreamt of incorporating into our Union any but the Caucasian race—the free white race. To incorporate Mexico, would be the very first instance of the kind of incorporating an Indian race; ... I protest against such a union as that! **Ours, sir, is the Government of a white race.** (Cited in Perea, 1995, p. 976)

Compare the ideological logic behind California's Proposition 187 with the statements provided by Calhoun, Jefferson, Franklin, and Buchanan. Compare, too, Proposition 187's logic to its precursor—California's 1855 "Greaser Act." The "Greaser Act" was an antiloitering law that applied to "all persons who are commonly known as 'Greasers,' or the issue of Spanish and Indian blood...and who go armed and are not peaceable and quiet persons" (cited in López, p. 145).

This is the same racist logic that fueled David Duke's 1992 comments: "...that immigrants 'mongrelize' our culture and dilute our values" (Cited in Lopéz, p. 143). Recent comments made by Duke during an appearance in California in 1996, were in support of Proposition 209, an anti-affirmative action effort at creating a 'colorblind' society. This effort has been orchestrated by Ward Connerly, an African-American, who is a University of California Regent and chairman of the Proposition 209 initiative. In addition to accusing minority men of raping white women "by the thousands" and claiming that black New Orleans police officers rape and kill local citizens, Duke remarked:

> I don't want California to look like Mexico...I don't want to have their pollution. I don't want the corruption. I don't want their disease. I don't want their superstition. I don't want us to look like that country. If we continue this alien invasion, we will be like Mexico. (Bernstein, 1996, A14)

Duke reflects a perspective that hasn't changed since the days of the Zoot Suit massacre, Operation Wetback, and when public Los Angeles swimming pools were frequently drained by Whites after they were used by Mexican-Americans.

It is a perspective also shared by the British extreme right, who sexualize racism in order to "generate fear among women and masculine protectiveness among men" in relation to the presence of black men in British inner-cities (Rattansi, 1994, p. 63). Such perspectives connote earlier ideas of the Empire as a dangerous place where white women need protection (Rattansi, p. 63). One example is a story that appeared in the National Front youth newspaper, *Bulldog*, which was titled: "Black pimps force White girls into prostitution" and which exhorted: "White Man! You have a Duty to Protect Your Race, Homeland and Family" (p. 63). Of course, this fear of the rape of the white woman is not projected solely onto the African-American male. Underwriting Duke's comments on Mexico, for instance, was the image of the Mexican as rapist and beast. In his discussion of the relationship between Dan Diegans and Tijuanenses, Ramón Gutiérrez describes how Tijuana—"as a place of unruly and transgressive bodies" (1996, p. 256)—has become fixed in the American Psyche. He reports that "Tijuana first developed as an escape valve for the sexually repressed and regulated American Protestant social body of San Diego" (p. 255). He writes that "the international boundary between Mexico and the United States has long been imagined as a border that separates a pure from an impure body, a virtuous body from a sinful one, a monogamous conjugal body regulated by the law of marriage from a criminal body given to fornication, adultery, prostitution, bestiality, and sodomy" (p. 255-256).

While the United States is constructed as a country governed by nature and the law, such codes of civility that regulate kinship and the body are thought not to exist in Mexico, where only unregulated desire and criminality exist to menace all who come into contact with Mexicans. The image of the undocumented worker as an illegal alien, as a "migrant" living in squalor, spreading disease, raping white women, extorting lunch money from white school children, creating squatter communities, hanging out in shopping centers, forcing Anglo schools to adopt bilingual education programs in order to accommodate the offspring of criminals and to appease the foreigner living on U.S. soil, has served to identify Mexicans with dirt, filth, and unnatural acts, while symbolically constructing Euro-American citizens as pure, law-abiding, and living in harmony with God's natural law (Gutiérrez, 1996).

One of the nation's relatively unblemished heroes of history is Woodrow Wilson. Many U.S. Citizens have little, if any, knowledge about Wilson's Palmer Raids against left-wing unions, his segregation of the federal government, and his military interventions in Mexico (eleven times beginning in 1914), Haiti in 1915, the Dominican Republic in 1916, Cuba in 1917, and Panama in 1918. Wilson also maintained forces in Nicaragua. Wilson was an unrepentant white supremacist who believed that black people were inferior to white people. In fact, Wilson ordered that black and white workers in federal government jobs be segregated. Wilson vetoed a clause on racial equality in the Convenant of the League of Nations. Wilson's wife told "darky" stories in cabinet meetings while Wilson's administration drafted a legislative program designed to curtail the civil rights of African Americans. Congress refused to pass it (Loewen, 1995). Wilson did manage to appoint southern Whites to offices traditionally given to Blacks. President Warren G. Harding was inducted into the Klu Klux Klan in a ceremony at the White House (Loewen, 1995). How many students can boast knowledge of this event? How can U.S. history books cover up these events, and hundreds of others, including the 1921 race riot in Tulsa, Oklahoma, in which Whites dropped dynamite from an airplane onto a black community, destroying 1,100 homes and killing 75 people (Loewen, 1995)?

How can we forget the evils of slavery, including the 10,000 native Americans shipped from Charleston, South Carolina, to the West Indies (in one year) in exchange for black slaves? Must we forget that the United States is a country conceived in slavery and baptized in racism?

The Protocols of the Learned Elders of Zion was a work that influenced another American hero—Henry Ford. His newspaper ran a series of anti-semitic articles in the 1920s that were made available to the public in book form under the title, *The International Jew.* In this particular sense the U.S. is not "post-Fordist" at all. At least in the case of rightwing Christian movements, many whom fervently believe that white people are the true Israelites, that Blacks are subhuman, and that Jews are the issue of Satan. The organization known as Christian Identity is linked to British Israelism which began as a white supremacist protestant organization in Victorian England. White Europeans were believed to be the twelve lost tribes of Israel. Like many post-millennial religions, Identity proclaims that God gave the Constitution of the United States to the white Christian Founding Fathers and only white Christian men can be true sovereign citizens of the Republic. Identity followers are set to destroy the "Beast"—the government of the United States, in order to hasten forth Armageddon (Southern Poverty Law Center, 1996). Members of Pat Robertson's Christian Coalition are aligned with the Patriot movement. This movement wants to establish God's law on earth, which in the view of some of the members of the movement, calls for the execution of homosexuals, adulterers, juvenile delinquents, and blasphemers (Southern Poverty Law Center, 1996).

Buchanan, Duke, Pete Wilson, and countless other conservative politicians currently enjoying considerable popularity among growing sectors of the United States population owe a great deal to the racist perspectives that they inherited from historical figures such as Jefferson, Franklin, and Lincoln who have been sanctified and haigiographied in the larger political culture. It appears that it is as patriotic now for white people to proclaim racist sentiments as it was 150 years ago. Today, however, one has to camouflage one's racism in deceptive and sophisticated ways by hiding it in a call for family values, a common culture of decency, and a "colorblind" society, but the racist formations underwriting such a call are clearly in evidence to the discerning cultural critic.

The concept of whiteness became lodged in the discursive crucible of colonial identity by the early 1860s. Whiteness at that time had become a marker for measuring inferior and superior races. Interestingly, Genghis Khan, Attila the Hun, and Confucius were at this time considered as "white." Blackness was evaluated positively in European iconography from the twelfth to the fifteenth centuries, but after the seventeenth century and the rise of European colonialism, blackness became conveniently linked to inferiority (Cashmore, 1996). For instance, during the sixteenth and seventeenth centuries, blood purity (*limpieza de sangre*) became raised to a metaphysical—perhaps even sacerdotal—status, as it became a principle used to peripheralize Indians, Moors, and Jews.

Blackness was not immediately associated with slavery. In the United States, the humanistic image of Africans created by the abolitionist movement was soon countered by new types of racial signification in which white skin was identified with racial superiority. Poor Europeans were sometimes indentured and were in some sense *de facto* slaves. They occupied the same economic categories as African slaves and were held in equal contempt by the lords of the plantation and legislatures (Cashmore, 1996). However, poor Europeans were invited to align themselves with the plantocracy as "white" in order to avoid the most severe forms of bondage. This strategy helped plantation owners form a stronger social control apparatus as hegemony was achieved by offering "race privileges" to poor whites as acknowledgment of their loyalty to the colonial land (Cashmore, 1996).

By the early twentieth century, European maritime empires controlled over half of the land (72 million square kilometers) and a third of the world's population (560 million people). Seventy-five million Africans died during the centuries-long transatlantic slave trade (West, 1993). The logics of empire are still with us, bound to the cultural fabric of our daily being-in-the-world; woven into our posture towards others; connected to the lenses of our eyes; folded into the sinewy depths of our musculature; dipped in the chemical reactions that excite and calm us; structured into the language of our perceptions. We cannot will our racist logics away. We need to work hard to eradicate them. We need to struggle with a formidable resolve in order to overcome that which we are afraid to confirm exists, let alone confront, in the battleground of our souls.

According to Alex Callinicos (1993) racial differences are invented. Racism occurs when the characteristics which justify discrimination are held to be inherent in the oppressed group. This form of oppression is peculiar to capitalist societies; it arises in the circumstances surrounding industrial capitalism and the attempt to acquire a large labor force. Callinicos points outs three main conditions for the existence of racism as outlined by Marx: economic competition between workers; the appeal of racist ideology to white workers; and efforts of the capitalist class to establish and maintain racial divisions among workers. Capital's constantly changing demands for different kinds of labor can only be met through immigration. Callinicos remarks that "racism offers for workers of the oppressing 'race' the imaginary compensation for the exploitation they suffer of belonging to the '*ruling* nation'" (1993, p. 39).

Callinicos notes the way in which Marx grasped how racial divisions between "native" and immigrant workers could weaken the working class. United States politicians take advantage of this division, which the capitalist class understands and manipulates only too well. George Bush, Jesse Helms, Pat Buchanan, Phil Gramm, David Duke, and Peter Wilson have effectively used racism to divide the working class. At this point you might be asking yourselves: Doesn't racism pre-date capitalism? Here I agree with Callinicos that the heterophobia associated with pre-capitalist societies was not the same as modern racism. Pre-capitalist slave and feudal societies of classical Greece and Rome did not rely on racism to justify the use of slaves. The Greeks and Romans had no theories of white superiority. If they did, that must have been unsettling news to Septimus Severus, Roman Emperor from AD 193 to 211, who was, many historians claim, a black man. Racism developed at a key turning point in capitalism during the seventeenth and eighteenth centuries on colonial plantations in the New World where slave labor stolen from Africa was used to produce tobacco, sugar, and cotton for the global consumer market (Callinicos, 1993). Callinicos cites Eric Williams who remarks: "Slavery was not born of racism; rather, racism was the consequence of slavery" (cited in Callinicos, p. 24). Racism emerged as the ideology of the plantocracy. It began with the class of sugar-planters and slave merchants that dominated England's Caribbean colonies. Racism developed out of the "systemic slavery" of the New World. The "natural inferiority" of Africans was a way that Whites justified enslaving them. According to Callinicos:

> Racism offers white workers the comfort of believing themselves part of the dominant group; it also provides, in times of crisis, a ready made scapegoat, in the shape of the oppressed group. Racism thus gives white workers a particular identity, and one moreover which unites them with white capitalists. We have here, then, a case of the kind of "imagined community" discussed by Benedict Anderson in his influential analysis of nationalism. (1993, p. 38)

To abolish racism, we need to abolish global capitalism. Callinicos is very clear on that point.

The educational left has failed to address sufficiently the issue of whiteness and the insecurities that young whites harbor regarding their future during times of diminishing economic expectations. With their "racially coded and divisive rhetoric," neoconservatives may be able to enjoy tremendous success in helping insecure young white populations develop white identity along racist lines. Consider the comments by David Stowe who writes:

> The only people nowadays who profess any kind of loyality to whiteness *qua* whiteness (as opposed to whiteness as an incidental feature of some more specific identity) are Christian Identity types and Ayran Nation diehards. Anecdotal surveys reveal that few white Americans mention whiteness as a

> quality that they think much about or particularly value. In their day-to-day cultural preferences—food, music, clothing, sports, hairstyles—the great majority of American whites display no particular attachment to white things. There does seem to be a kind of emptiness at the core of whiteness. (1996, p. 74)

Cornel West has identified three white-supremacist logics: the Judeo-Christian racist logic; the scientific racist logic and the psycho-sexual racist logic. The Judeo-Christian racist logic is reflected in the Biblical story of Ham, Son of Noah, who, in failing to cover Noah's nakedness, had his progeny blackened by God. In this logic, unruly behaviour and chaotic rebellion are linked to racist practices. The 'scientific' racist logic is identified with the evaluation of physical bodies in light of Greco-Roman standards. Within this logic, racist practices are identified with physical ugliness, cultural deficiency, and intellectual inferiority. The psycho-sexual racist logic identifies black people with Western sexual discourses associated with sexual prowess, lust, dirt, and subordination. A serious question is raised by West's typology in relation to the construction of whiteness: What are the historically concrete and sociologically specific ways that white supremacist discourses are guided by Western philosophies of identity and universality and capitalist relations of production and consumption? West has located racist practices in the commentaries by the Church Fathers on the Song of Solomon and the Ywain narratives in medieval Brittany, to name just a few historical sources. West has also observed that human bodies were classified according to skin color as early as 1684 (before the rise of modern capitalism) by French physician François Bernier. The famous eighteenth century naturalist, Carolus Linnaeus, produced the first major written account of racial division in *Natural System* (1735).

People don't discriminate against groups because they are different but rather the act of discrimination constructs categories of difference that hierarchically locate people as "superior" or "inferior" and then universalizes and naturalizes such differences. When I refer to whiteness or to the cultural logics of whiteness, I need to qualify what I mean. Here I adopt Ruth Frankenberg's injunction that cultural practices considered to be white need to be seen as contingent, historically produced, and transformable. White culture is not monolithic and its borders must be understood as malleable and porous. It is the historically specific confluence of economic, geopolitical, and ethnocultural processes. According to Alastair Bonnett (1996), whiteness is neither a discrete entity nor a fixed, asocial category. Rather, it is an "immutable social construction" (1996, p. 98). White identity is an ensemble of discourses, contrapuntal and contradictory. Whiteness—and the meanings attributed to it—are always in a state of flux and fibrillation. Bonnett notes that "even if one ignores the transgressive youth or ethnic borderlands of Western identities, and focuses on the 'center' or 'heartlands' of 'whiteness,' one will discover racialised subjectivities, that, far from being settled and confidant, exhibit a constantly reformulated panic over the meaning of 'whiteness' and the defining presence of 'non-whiteness' within it" (1996, p. 106). According to Frankenberg, white culture is a material and discursive space that

> is inflected by nationhood, such that whiteness and Americanness, though by no means coterminous, are profoundly shaped by one another...
>
> ...Similarly, whiteness, masculinity, and femininity are coproducers of one another, in ways that are, in their turn, crosscut by class and by the histories of racism and colonialism. (1993, p. 233)

Whiteness needs to be seen as *cultural*, as *processual*, and not ontologically different from processes that are non-white. It works, as Frankenberg notes, as "an unmarked marker of others' differentness—whiteness not so much void or formlessness as norm" (p. 198). Whiteness functions through social practices of assimilation and cultural homogenization; whiteness is linked to the expansion of capitalism in the sense that "whiteness signifies the production and consumption of commodities under capitalism" (p. 203). Yet capitalism in the U.S. needs to be understood as contingently white, since white people participate in maintaining the hegemony of institutions and practices of racial dominance in different ways and to greater or lesser degrees. Frankenberg identifies the key discursive repertoires of whiteness as follows:

> modes of naming culture and difference associated with west European colonial expansion; second, elements of "essentialist" racism...linked to European colonialism but also critical as rationale for Anglo settler colonialism and segregationism in what is now the USA; third, "assimilationist" or later "color- and power-evasive" strategies for thinking through race first articulated in the early decades of this century; and, fourth,..."race-cognizant" repertoires that emerged in the latter half of the twentieth century and were linked both to U.S. liberation movements and to broader global struggles for decolonization. (1993, p. 239)

Whiteness is a sociohistorical form of consciousness, given birth at the nexus of capitalism, colonial rule, and the emergent relationships among dominant and subordinate groups. Whiteness operates by means of its constitution as a universalizing authority by which the hegemonic white bourgeois subject appropriates the right to speak on behalf of everyone who is non-white, while denying voice and agency to these Others in the name of civilized humankind. Whiteness constitutes and demarcates ideas, feelings, knowledges, social practices, cultural formations, and systems of intelligibility that are identified with or attributed to white people and which are invested in by white people as "white." Whiteness is also a refusal to acknowledge how white people are implicated in certain social relations of privilege and relations of domination and subordination. Whiteness, then, can be considered as a form of social amnesia associated with certain modes of subjectivity within particular social sites considered to be normative. As a lived domain of meaning, whiteness represents particular social and historical formations that are reproduced through specific discursive and material processes and circuits of desire and power. Whiteness can be considered to be a conflictual sociocultural, sociopolitical, and geopolitical process that animates commonsensical practical action in relationship to dominant social practices and normative ideological productions. Whiteness constitutes the selective tradition of dominant discourses about race, class, gender, and sexuality hegemonically reproduced. Whiteness has become the substance and limit of our common sense articulated as cultural consensus. As an ideological formation transformed into a principle of life, into an ensemble of social relations and practices, whiteness needs to be understood as conjunctural, as a composite social hieroglyph that shifts in denotative and connotative emphasis, depending upon how its elements are combined and upon the contexts in which it operates.

Whiteness is not a pre-given, unified ideological formation, but is a multi-faceted collective phenomenon resulting from the relationship between the self and the ideological discourses which are constructed out of the surrounding local and global cultural terrain. Whiteness is fundamentally Euro- or Western-centric in its episteme, as it is articulated in complicity with the pervasively imperializing logic of empire.

Whiteness in the United States can be understood largely through the social consequences it provides for those who are considered to be non-white. Such consequences can be seen in the criminal justice system, in prisons, in schools, and in the board rooms of corporations such as Texaco. It can be defined in relation to immigration practices and social policies and practices of sexism, racism, and nationalism. It can be seen historically in widespread acts of imperialism and genocide and linked to an erotic economy of "excess." Eric Lott writes:

> In rationalized Western societies, becoming "white" and male seems to depend upon the remanding of enjoyment, the body, an aptitude for pleasure. It is the other who is always putatively "excessive" in this respect, whether through exotic food, strange and noisy music, outlandish bodily exhibitions, or unremitting sexual appetite. Whites in fact organize their own enjoyment through the other, Slavoj Zizek has written, and access pleasure precisely by fantasizing about the other's "special" pleasure. Hatred of the other arises from the necessary hatred of one's own excess; ascribing this excess to the "degraded" other **and indulging** it—by imagining, incorporating, or impersonating the other—one conveniently and surreptitiously takes and disavows pleasure at one and the same time. This is the mixed erotic economy, what Homi Bhabha terms the "ambivalence" of American whiteness. (1993: 482)

Whiteness is a type of articulatory practice that can be located in the convergence of colonialism, capitalism, and subject formation. It both fixes and sustains discursive regimes that represent self and "other"; that is, whiteness represents a regime of differences that produces and racializes an abject other. In other words, whiteness is a discursive regime that enables real effects to take place. Whiteness displaces blackness and brownness—specific forms of non-whiteness—into signifiers of deviance and criminality within social, cultural, cognitive, and political contexts. White subjects discursively construct identity through producing, naming, "bounding," and marginalizing a range of others (Frankenberg, 1993, p. 193).

Whiteness constitutes unmarked patriarchal, heterosexist, and Euro-American practices that have negative effects on and consequences for those who do not participate in them. Inflected by nationhood, whiteness can be considered an ensemble of discursive practices constantly in the process of being constructed, negotiated, and changed. Yet it functions to instantiate a structured exclusion of certain groups from social arenas of normativity. Coco Fusco remarks: "To raise the specter of racism in the here and now, to suggest that despite their political beliefs and sexual preferences, white people operate within, and benefit from, white supremacist social structures is still tantamount to a declaration of war" (1995, p. 76).

Whiteness is not only mythopoetical in the sense that it constructs a totality of illusions formed around the ontological superiority of the Euro-American subject, it is also metastructural in that it operates across specific differences; it solders fugitive, break-away discourses and re-hegemonizes them. Consumer utopias and global capital flows rearticulate whiteness by means of relational differences.

Whiteness is dialectically reinitiated across epistemological fissures, contradictions, and oppositions through new regimes of desire that connect the consumption of goods to the everyday logic of Western democracy. The cultural encoding of the typography of whiteness is achieved by remapping Western European identity onto economic transactions, by recementing desire to capitalist flows, by concretizing personal history into collective memory linked to place, to a myth of origin. Whiteness offers a safe "home" for those imperiled by the flux of change.

Whiteness can be considered as a conscription of the process of positive self-identification into the service of domination through inscribing identity into an onto-epistemological framework of "us" against "them." For those who are non-white, the seduction of whiteness can produce a self-definition that disconnects the subject from his or her history of oppression and struggle, exiling identity into the unmoored, chaotic realm of abject otherness (and tacitly accepting the positioned superiority of the Western subject). Whiteness provides the subject with a known boundary that places nothing "off limits," yet which provides a fantasy of belongingness. It's not that whiteness signifies preferentially one pole of the white-non-white binarism. Rather, whiteness seduces the subject to accept the idea of polarity itself as the limit-text of identity, as the constitutive foundation of subjectivity.

Whiteness offers coherency and stability in a world in which capital produces regimes of desire linked to commodity utopias where fantasies of omnipotence must find a stable home. Of course, the "them" is always located within the "us." The marginalized are always foundational to the stability of the central actors. The excluded in this case establish the condition of existence of the included. So we find that it is impossible to separate the identities of both oppressor and oppressed. They depend upon each other. To resist whiteness means developing a politics of difference. Since we lack the full semantic availability to understand whiteness and to resist it, we need to rethink difference and identity outside of sets of binary oppositions. We need to view identity as coalitional, as collective, as processual, as grounded in the struggle for social justice.

While an entire range of discursive repertoires may come into play, jostling against, superceding, and working in conjunction with each other, white identity is constructed in relation to an individual's personal history, geopolitical situatedness, contextually specific practices, and his or her location in the materiality of the racial order. In other words, many factors determine which discursive configurations are at work and the operational modalities present.

In his important volume, *Psychoanalytic-Marxism* (1993), Eugene Victor Wolfenstein describes the whiteness of domination as the "one fixed point" of America's many racisms. He argues that whiteness is a social designation and a "history disguised as biology" (1993, p. 331). Whiteness is also an attribute of language. Wolfenstein claims that:

> Languages have skin colors. There are white nouns and verbs, white grammar and white syntax. In the absence of challenges to linguistic hegemony, indeed, language *is* white. If you don't speak white you will not be heard, just as when you don't look white you will not be seen. (1993, p. 331)

Describing white racists as "virtuosos of denigration" (p. 337), Wolfenstein maintains that the language of white racism illustrates "a state of war" (p. 333). Yet the battles are fought through lies and deceit. One such lie is the idea of "color blindness."

Wolfenstein notes that colorblindness constitutes more than a matter of conscious deceit:

> White racism is rather a mental disorder, an ocular disease, an opacity of the soul that is articulated with unintended irony in the idea of "color blindness." To be color blind is the highest form of racial false consciousness, a denial of both difference and domination. But one doesn't have to be color blind to be blinded by white racism. ...Black people see themselves in white mirrors, white people see black people as their own photographic negatives. (1993, p. 334)

Wolfenstein suggests that two epistemological tasks be undertaken. Black people need to look away from the white mirror; white people need to attempt to see black people as they see themselves and to see themselves as they are seen by other black people. Wolfenstein links white racism to what he terms "epidermal fetishism." Epidermal fetishism reduces people to their skin color and renders them invisible. It is a form of social character that is formed within a process of exchange and circulation. As such, whiteness represents the super-ego (the standard of social value, self-worth, and morality). Since the ego is affirmatively reflected in the super-ego, it also must be white. What is therefore repressed is blackness which "becomes identified with the unwanted or bad parts of the self" (p. 336). Wolfenstein writes:

> At the level of social character, white racism is self-limiting for white people, self-destructive for black people. White people alienate their sensous potentialities from themselves. They are devitalized and sterilized. Blackness, officially devalued, comes to embody their estranged life and desire. They are able, however, to see themselves reflected in the mirrors of selfhood. But if black people have their selfhood structured by the whitened-out form of social character, they become fundamentally self-negating. Their blackness, hated and despised, must be hidden away. Hair straighteners and skin lighteners testify to the desire to go further and eradicate blackness altogether. (1993, pp. 336-337)

The incorporeal luminescence of whiteness is achieved, according to Wolfenstein, by the subsumption of blackness within whiteness. What cannot be subsumed and digested is excreted. White people both despise and lust after blackness. Wolfenstein describes some forms of inter-racial romantic hetero-sexual relationships as epidermally mediated erotic domination, as an epidermalized sexual rebellion against a repressive social morality, and as an epidermally mediated double violation of the oedipal incest taboo. In order to resist epidermal fetishism, oppressed people need a language and a politics of their own.

It is important to recognize that white racism is neither purely systemic or purely individual. Rather, it is a complex interplay of collective interests and desires. White racism in this instance "becomes a rational means to collective ends" (p. 341) when viewed from the standpoint of ruling class interests. Yet for the white working class it is irrational and a form of false consciousness. White racism also circumscribes rational action for black people in that they are encouraged to act in terms of their racial rather than class interests.

Alastair Bonnett notes that a reified notion of whiteness "enables 'white' people to occupy a privileged location in anti-racist debate; they are allowed the luxury of being passive observers, of being altruistically motivated, of knowing that their 'racial' identity might be reviled and lambasted but never actually made slippery, torn open, or, indeed, abolished" (1996, p. 98). Bonnett further notes:

> To dismantle "blackness" but leave the force it was founded to oppose unchallenged is to display both a political and theoretical naivety. To subvert "blackness" without subverting "whiteness" reproduces and reinforces the "racial" myths, and the "racial" dominance, associated with the latter. (1996, p. 99)

Ian F. Haney López's book, *White by Law*, offers a view of white transparency and invisibility that is at odds with the thesis that Whites are growing more conscious of their whiteness. López cites an incident at a legal feminist conference in which participants were asked to pick two or three words to describe themselves.

All of the women of color selected at least one racial term, but not one white woman selected a term referring to her race. This prompted Angela Harris to remark that only white people in this society have the luxury of having no color. An informal study conducted at Harvard Law School underscores Harris's remark. A student interviewer asked ten African Americans and ten white Americans how they identified themselves. Unlike the African Americans, most of the white Americans did not consciously factor in their "whiteness" as a crucial or even tangential part of their identity.

López argues that one is not born white but becomes white "by virtue of the social context in which one finds oneself, to be sure, but also by virtue of the choices one makes" (1996, p. 190). But how can one born into the culture of whiteness, one who is defined as white, undo that whiteness? López addresses this question in his formulation of whiteness. He locates whiteness in the overlapping of *chance* (*e.g.*, features and ancestry that we have no control over, morphology); *context* (context-specific meanings that are attached to race, the social setting in which races are recognized, constructed, and contested); and *choice* (conscious choices with regard to the morphology and ancestries of social actors) in order to "alter the readability of their identity" (1996, p. 191).

In other words, López maintains that chance and context are not racially determinative. He notes:

> Racial choices must always be made from within specific contexts, where the context materially and ideologically circumscribes the range of available choices and also delimits the significance of the act. Nevertheless, these are racial choices, if sometimes only in their overtone or subtext, because they resonate in the complex of meanings associated with race. Given the thorough suffusion of race throughout society, in the daily dance of life we constantly make racially meaningful decisions. (1996, p. 193)

López's perspective offers new promise, it would seem, for abolishing racism since it refuses to locate whiteness only as anti-racism's "other." I agree with Bonnett when he remarks that "to continue to cast 'whites' as anti-racism's 'other,' as the eternally guilty and/or altruistic observers of 'race' equality work, is to maintain 'white' privilege and undermine the movement's intellectual and practical reach and utility" (1996, p. 107). In other words, Whites need to ask themselves to what extent their identity is a function of their whiteness in the process of their ongoing daily lives and what choices they might make to escape whiteness. López outlines—productively in my view—three steps in dismantling whiteness. They are worth quoting in full:

> First, Whites must overcome the omnipresent effects of transparency and of the naturalization of race in order to recognize the many racial aspects of their identity, paying particular attention to the daily acts that draw upon and in turn confirm their whiteness. Second, they must recognize and accept the personal

> and social consequences of breaking out of a White identity. Third, they must embark on a daily process of choosing against Whiteness. (López, 1996, p. 193)

Of course, the difficulty of taking such steps is partly due to the fact that, as López notes, the unconscious acceptance of a racialized identity is predicated upon a circular definition of the self. It's hard to step outside of whiteness if you are white because of all the social, cultural and economic privileges that accompany whiteness. Yet, whiteness must be dismantled if the United States is to overcome racism. Lipsitz remarks:

> Those of us who are "white" can only become part of the solution if we recognize the degree to which we are already part of the problem—not because of our race, but because of our possessive investment in it." (1995, p. 384)

An editorial in the book, *Race Traitor*, puts it thus:

> The key to solving the social problems of our age is to abolish the white race. Until that task is accomplished, even partial reform will prove elusive, because white influence permeates every issue in U.S. society, whether domestic or foreign... Race itself is a product of social discrimination; so long as the white race exists, all movements against racism are doomed to fail. (Ignatiev & Garvey, 1996, p. 10)

I am acutely aware that people of color might find troubling the idea that white populations can simply reinvent themselves by making the simple choice of not being white. Of course, this is not what López and others appear to be saying. The choices one makes and the reinvention one aspires to as a race traitor are not "simple" nor are they easy choices for groups of whites to make. Yet from the perspective of some people of color, offering the choice to white people of opting out of their whiteness could seem to set up an easy path for those who don't want to assume responsibility for their privilege as white people. Indeed, there is certainly cause for concern. David Roediger captures some of this when he remarks: "whites cannot fully renounce whiteness even if they want to" (1994, p. 16). Whites are, after all, still accorded the privileges of being white even as they ideologically renounce their whiteness, often with the best of intentions. Yet the possibility that Whites might seriously consider nonwhiteness and antiwhite struggle is too important to ignore, to dismiss as wishful thinking, or to associate with a fashionable form of code-switching. Choosing not to be white is not an easy option for white people, as simple as deciding to make a change in one's wardrobe. To understand the processes involved in the racialization of identity and to consistently choose nonwhiteness is a difficult act of apostasy, for it implies a heightened sense of social criticism and an unwavering commitment to social justice (Roediger, 1994). Of course, the question needs to be asked: If we can choose to be nonwhite, then can we choose to be black or brown? Insofar as blackness is a social construction (often "parasitic" on whiteness) I would answer yes. Theologian James H. Cone, author of *A Black Theology of Liberation*, urges white folks to free themselves form the shackles of their whiteness:

> ...if whites expect to be able to say anything relevant to the self-determination of the black community, it will be necessary for them to destroy their whiteness by becoming members of an oppressed community. Whites will be free only when they become new persons—when their white being has passed away and they are created anew in black being. When this happens, they are no longer white but free... (1986, p. 97)

But again I would stress that becoming black is not a "mere" choice but a self-consciously political choice, a spiritual choice, and a critical choice. To choose blackness or brownness merely as a way to escape the stigma of whiteness and to avoid responsibility for owning whiteness, is still very much an act of whiteness. To choose blackness or brownness as a way of politically disidentifying with white privilege and instead identifying with and participating in the social struggles of non-white peoples is, on the other hand, an act of transgression, a traitorous act that reveals a fidelity to the struggle for justice. Lipsitz sums up the problems and the promise of the abolition of whiteness as follows:

> Neither conservative "free market" policies nor liberal social democratic reforms can solve the "white problem" in America because both of them reinforce the possessive investment in whiteness. But an explicitly antiracist pan-ethnic movement that acknowledges the existence and power of whiteness might make some important changes. Pan-ethnic, antiracist coalitions have a long history in the United States—in the political activism of John Brown, Soujourner Truth, and the Magon brothers, among others—but we also have a rich cultural tradition of pan-ethnic antiracism connected to civil rights activism...efforts by whites to fight racism, not out of sympathy for someone else but out of a sense of self-respect and simple justice, have never completely disappeared; they remain available as models for the present. (1995, p. 384)

George Yúdice gives additional substance to Lipsitz's concerns related to coalition-building when he points out some of the limitations of current identity politics:

> The very difficulty of imagining a new social order that speaks convincingly to over 70 percent of the population requires critics to go beyond pointing out the injustices and abuses and move on to an agenda that will be more effective in transforming structures. What good is it to fight against white supremacy unless whites themselves join the struggle? (1995, p. 268)

The key, Yúdice maintains, is to center the struggle for social justice around resource distribution rather than identity:

> Shifting the focus of struggle from identity to resource distribution will also make it possible to engage such seemingly nonracial issues as the environment, the military, the military-industrial complex, foreign aid, and free-trade agreements as matters impacting local identities and thus requiring a global

politics that works outside of the national frame. (p. 280)

Because ethnic identity is constructed diacritically, whiteness requires the denigration of blackness and brownness (López). Therefore I do not argue for the construction of a positive white identity, no matter how well intentioned. Rather, I argue against celebrating whiteness in any form. As López notes, whiteness retains its positive meanings only by denying itself. I call for the denial, disassembly, and destruction of whiteness as we know it and advocate its rearticulation as a form of critical agency dedicated to social struggle in the interests of the oppressed.

The work of critical multiculturalists attempts to unsettle both conservative assaults on multiculturalism and liberal paradigms of multiculturalism, the latter of which in my view simply repackage conservative and neo-liberal ideologies under a discursive mantle of diversity. In undertaking such a project, I have tried in a modest way to advance a critical pedagogy that will service a form of postcolonial hybridity.

It is true that the concept of hybridity has been used in a powerful way to counter essentialized attempts at creating monolithic and "authentic" forms of identity (McLaren, 1995; Hicks, 1991). However, Fusco rightly reminds us:

> Too often...the postcolonial celebration of hybridity has been interpreted as the sign that no further concern about the politics of representation and cultural exchange is needed. With ease, we lapse back into the integrationist rhetoric of the 1960s, and conflate hybridity with parity. (1995, p. 76)

Since not all hybridities are equal, we must attach to the term an ideological tacit nominal qualifier (Radhakrishnan, 1996). In making this assertion, Ragagopalan Radhakrishnan provides us with an important qualification. He maintains that we should distinguish between a metropolitan version of hybridity and postcolonial hybridity. Whereas the former is a ludic form of capricious self-styling, the latter is a critical identitarian mode. Metropolitan hybridity, notes Radhakrishnan, is "characterized by an intransitive and immanent sense of jouissance" while postcolonial hybridity is marked by a "frustrating search for constituency and a legitimate political identity" (1996, p. 159). Metropolitan hybridity is not "subjectless" or neutral but is a structure of identitarian thinking informed by the cultural logic of the dominant West. Postcolonial hybridity, on the other hand, seeks authenticity in "a third space that is complicitous neither with the deracinating imperatives of Westernizaton nor with theories of a static, natural, and single-minded autochthony" (p. 162). It is within such a perspective that educators are called to create *una pedagogia fronteriza*.

Critical multiculturalism as a point of intersection with critical pedagogy supports the struggle for a postcolonial hybridity. Gómez-Peña captures the concept of postcolonial hybridity when he conceptually maps what he calls the "New World Border":

> a great trans- and intercontinental border zone, a place in which no centers remain. It's all margins, meaning there are no "others," or better said, the only true "others" are those who resist fusion, *mestizaje*, and cross-cultural dialogue. In this utopian cartography, hybridity is the dominant culture; Spanish, Franglé, and Gringoñol are *linguas francas*; and monoculture is a culture of resistance practiced by a stubborn or scared minority. (1996, p.7)

A revolutionary multiculturalism must engage what Enrique Dussel (1993) calls "the Reason of the Other." The debates over modernity and postmodernity have a different set of valences in Latinoamerica for *los olvidados*, for the peripheralised, for the marginalized, and for the wretched of the earth. Dussel writes about this distinction, from his own Latin American context:

> Unlike the postmodernists, we do not propose a critique of reason as such; but we do accept their critique of a violent, coercive, genocidal reason. We do not deny the rational kernel of the universalist rationalism of the Enlightenment, only its irrational moment as sacrificial myth. We do not negate reason, in other words, but the irrationality of the violence generated by the myth of modernity. Against postmodernist irrationalism, we affirm the "reason of the Other." (p. 75)

Whites need to do more than remember the history of colonialism as it affected the oppressed; they need to critically re-member such history. As Homi Bhabha (1986, p. xxiii) reminds us: "Remembering is never a quiet act of introspection or retrospection. It is a painful re-membering, a putting together of the dismembered past to make sense of the trauma of the present." This means piercing the vapors of mystification surrounding the objectification of human relations within bourgeois consciousness in order to construct new forms of subjectivity and agency that operate within a socialist political imaginary.

What I am advocating, dear brothers and sisters in struggle, is a revolutionary multiculturalism that moves beyond the ludic, metrocentric focus on identities as hybrid and hyphenated assemblages of subjectivity that exist alongside or outside of the larger social totality. Revolutionary multiculturalism, as I am articulating the term, takes as its condition of possibility the capitalist world system; it moves beyond a monoculturalist multiculturalism that fails to address identity formation in a global context, and focuses instead on the idea that identities are shifting, changing, overlapping, and historically diverse (Shohat, 1995). Revolutionary multiculturalism is a politics of difference that is globally interdependent and raises questions about intercommunal alliances and coalitions. According to Ella Shohat, intercommunal coalitions are based on historically shaped affinities and the multicultural theory that underwrites such a coalitionary politics needs "to avoid either falling into essentialist traps or being politically paralyzed by deconstructionist formulations" (1995, p. 177). Shohat articulates the challenge as follows:

> Rather than ask who can speak, then, we should ask how we can speak together,

> and more important, how we can move the dialog forward. How can diverse communities speak in concert? How might we interweave our voices, whether in chorus, in antiphony, in call and response, or in polyphony? What are the modes of collective speech? In this sense, it might be worthwhile to focus less on identity as something one 'has,' than on identification as something one 'does.' (1995, p. 177)

Revolutionary multiculturalism recognizes that the objective structures in which we live, the material relations tied to production in which we are situated, and the determinate conditions that produce us, are all reflected in our everyday lived experiences. In other words, lived experiences constitute more than subjective values, beliefs, and understandings; they are always mediated through ideological configurations of discourses, political economies of power and privilege, and the social division of labor. Revolutionary multiculturalism is a socialist-feminist multiculturalism that challenges the historically sedimented processes through which race, class, and gender identities are produced within capitalist society. Therefore, revolutionary multiculturalism is not limited to transforming attitudinal discrimination, but is dedicated to reconstituting the deep structures of political economy, culture, and power in contemporary social arrangements. It is not about reforming capitalist democracy but rather transforming it by cutting it at its joints and then rebuilding the social order from the vantage point of the oppressed.

Revolutionary multiculturalism must not only accomodate the idea of capitalism, it must also advocate a critique of capitalism and a struggle against it. The struggle for liberation on the basis of race and gender must not remain detached from anti-capitalist struggle. Often the call for diversity and pluralism by the apostles of postmodernism is a surrender to the ideological mystifications of capitalism. The fashionable apostasy of preaching difference from the citadels of postmodernist thought has dissolved resistance into the totalizing power of capitalist exploitation. In this regard, Ellen Meiksins Wood rightly warns:

> We should not confuse respect for the plurality of human experience and social struggles with a complete dissolution of historical causality, where there is nothing but diversity, difference and contingency, no unifying structures, no logic of process, no capitalism and therefore no negation of it, no universal project of human emancipation. (1995, p. 263)

The challenge is to create at the level of everyday life a commitment to solidarity with the oppressed and an identification with past and present struggles against imperialism, against racism, against sexism, against homophobia, against all those practices of unfreedom associated with living in a white supremacist capitalist society. As participants in such a challenge you, dear comrades, become agents of history by living the moral commitment to freedom and justice, by maintaining a loyalty to the revolutionary domain of possibility, and by creating a collective voice out of the farthest reaching "we"—one that unites all those who suffer under capitalism, patriarchy, racism, and colonialism throughout the globe.

Comrades, at times we must allow our faith in revolutionary praxis to overwhelm the cynical reason of our age, a reason that lies halfway between wakefulness and a fitful sleep, a reason that contributes to ensuring the dissymmetry of power between the rich and the poor. We must advance toward an unconditional assent to struggle, to victory, to life. *Hasta la victoria siempre.*

Living in Los Angeles is like being encysted in a surrealist hallucination. Yet as I look at the city from this cafe widow, things don't seem that bad: Kid Frost pulsates through the airwaves, a 1964 Chevy Impala cruises the street in all its bravado lowrider beauty; the sun is shining bountifully on brown, black, and white skin (albeit prematurely aging the latter); my gas tank is full and the ocean is reachable before the heat gets too heavy and the streets get too packed. I'll take Olympic Boulevard towards Venice, searching for that glimmer of light in the eyes of strangers, seeking out that fertile space to connect, picking through that rag-and-bone shop of lost memories, and seizing that splinter of hope at the faultline of the impossible where the foundation of a new public sphere can be fashioned out of the rubble of concrete dreams.

References

Balibar, Etienne & Wallerstein, Immanuel. (1993). *Race, Nation, Class: Ambiguous Identities*. London & New York: Verso.

Balibar, Etienne. (1996). "Is European Citizenship Possible?" *Public Culture*, No. 19, pp. 355-376.

Bannerji, Himani. (1995). *Thinking Through*. Toronto, Canada: Women's Press.

Barrs, Rick (1996). "The Real Story about how the use of Crack Cocaine Exploded in South-Central." *New Times*, Sept. 12-18, Vol. 1, No. 4, p. 9.

Bauman, Zygmunt. (1992). *Mortality, Immortality & and Other Life Strategies*. Stanford, CA: Stanford University Press.

Bauman, Zygmunt. (1996, May). "On Communitarians and Human Freedom, or, How to Square the Circle." *Theory, Culture and Society*, Vol. 13, No. 2, pp. 79-90.

Bennett, William J. (1996). "Civil Rights is the GOP Mission." *Los Angeles Times*, Monday, August 13, 1996. B5.

Bernstein, Sharon. (1996). "Storm Rises Over Ex-Klansman in Deabate." *Los Angeles Times*, Wednesday, September 11, A3, A14.

Bhabha, Homi. (1986). "Remembering Fanon." Foreword to Frantz Fanon, *Black Skin, White Masks*. London: Pluto Press.

Bhachu, Parminder. (1996). "The Multiple Landscapes of Transnational Asian Women in the Diaspora." In Vered Amit-Talai & Caroline Knowles, eds., *Re-Situating Identities: The Politics of Race, Ethnicity, and Culture*. Peterborough, Canada & Essex, London: Broadview Press, pp. 283-303.

Boggs, C. (1995, Dec. 22-28). "The God Reborn: Pondering the Revival of Russian Communism." *Los Angeles View*, 10(20), 8.

Unthinking Whiteness, Rethinking Democracy

Bonnett, Alastair. (1996). "Anti-Racism and the Critique of White Identities." *New Community*, 22(1): 97-110.
Bradlee Jr., B. (1996). "The Buchanan Role: GOP Protagonist." *Boston Sunday Globe*, March 3, 1996, Vol. 249, No. 63, pp. 1 & 12.
Callinicos, Alex. (1993). *Race and Class*. London: Bookmarks.
Cashmore, Ellis. (1996). *Dictionary of Race and Ethnic Relations* (fourth edition). London & New York: Routledge.
Chomsky, Noam. (1996). *Class Warfare: Interviews with David Barsamian*. Monroe, ME: Common Courage Press.
Cone, James H. (1986). *A Black Theology of Liberation*. New York: Orbis Books.
Connell, Rich (1996). "2,000 Protest Alleged U.S.Role in Crack Influx." *Los Angeles Times*, Sept. 29, p. B1, B4.
Connolly, William. (1995). The Ethos of Pluralization. Minneapolis, MN & London: University of Minnesota Press.
Cruz, Jon. (1996). "From Farce to Tragedy: Reflections on the Reification of Race at Century's End." In Avery Gordon & Christopher Newfield, eds., *Mapping Multiculturalism*. Minneapolis, MN & London: University of Minnesota Press, pp. 19-39.
Dussel, Enrique. (1993). "Eurocentrism and Modernity." *Boundary 2*, Vol. 20, No. 3, pp. 65-77.
Fanon, Frantz. (1967). *Black Skin, White Masks*. New York: Grove Press.
Feagin, Joe R., & Vera, Hernan (1995). *White Racism*. London and New York: Routledge.
Frankenberg, Ruth. (1993). *The Social Construction of Whiteness: White Women, Race Matters*. Minneapolis, MN: The University of Minnesota Press.
Fraser, Nancy. (1993). "Clintonism, Welfare, and the Antisocial Wage: The Emergence of a Neoliberal Political Imaginary." *Rethinking Marxism*, Vol. 6, No. 1, pp. 9-23.
Fusco, Coco. (1995). *English Is Broken Here: Notes on Cultural Fusion in the Americas*. New York: The New Press.
Gallagher, Charles A. (1994). "White Construction in the University." *Socialist Review*, Vol. 1 & 2, pp. 165-187.
Gardiner, Michael. (1996, May). "Alterity and Ethics: A Dialogical Perspective." *Theory, Culture and Society*, Vol 13, No. 2, pp. 121-144.
Gatens, Moria. (1996). *Imaginary Bodies*. London & New York: Routledge.
Giroux, Henry. (1993). *Border Crossings*. London & New York: Routledge.
Giroux, Henry. (1996). "Race and the Debate on Public Intellectuals." *International Journal of Educational Reform*, Vol. 5, No. 3, pp. 345-350.
Gitlin, Todd. (1995). *The Twilight of Common Dreams: Why America Is Wracked by Culture Wars*. New York: Metropolitan Books.
Goldberg, David Theo. (1993). *Racist Culture: Philosophy and the Politics of Meaning*. Cambridge, MA & Oxford, England: Blackwell Publishers.
Gómez-Peña, Guillermo. (1996). *The New World Border*. San Francisco, CA: City Lights Bookstore.
Gutiérrez, Ramón. (1996). "The Erotic Zone Sexual Transgression on the U.S.-Mexican Border." In Avery Gordon & Christopher Newfield, eds., *Mapping Multiculturalism*. Minneapolis, MN: University of Minnesota Press.
Harris, Cheryl I. (1993). "Whiteness as Property." *Harvard Law Review*, Vol. 106, No. 8, pp. 1709-1791.

McLaren

Haymes, Stephen Nathan. (1995). *Race, Culture, and the City: A Pedagogy for Black Urban Struggle*. Albany, NY: State University of New York Press.

Hicks, Emily. (1991). *Border Writing*. Minneapolis, MN: University of Minnesota Press.

Holston, James & Appadurai, Arjun. (1996). "Cities and Citizenship." *Public Culture*, No. 19, pp. 187-204.

Ignatiev, Noel. (1995). *How the Irish Became White*. London & New York: Routledge.

Ignatiev, Noel & Garvey, John. (1996). *Race Traitor*. New York & London: Routledge.

Kahn, Joel S. (1995). *Culture, Multiculture, Postculture*. London, Thousand Oaks, CA & New Delhi: Sage Publications.

Kincheloe, Joe & Steinberg, Shirley. (In press). *Changing Multiculturalism: New Times, New Curriculum*. London: Open University Press.

Laclau, Ernesto. (1992). "Universalism, Particularism, and the Question of Identity." *October*, Vol. 61 (Summer), pp. 83-90.

Lash, Scott. (1996, May). "Postmodern Ethics: The Missing Ground." *Theory, Culture and Society*, Vol. 13, No. 2, pp. 91-104.

Lipsitz, George. (1995). "The Possessive Investment in Whiteness: Racialized Social Democracy and the 'White' Problem in American Studies." *American Quarterly*, Vol. 47, No. 3, pp. 369-387.

Lipsitz, George. (1996). "It's All Wrong, but its All Right: Creative Misunderstandings in Intercultural Communication." In Avery Gordon & Christopher Newfield, eds., *Mapping Multiculturalism*. Minneapolis, MN & London: University of Minnesota Press, pp. 403-412.

López, Ian F. Haney. (1996). *White by Law*. New York & London: New York University Press.

Loewen, James W. (1995). *Lies my Teacher Told Me: Everything Your American History Textbook Got Wrong*. New York: Touchstone.

Lott, Eric. (1993) "White Like Me: Racial Cross-Dressing and the Construction of American Whiteness." In Amy Kaplan & Donald E. Pease (eds.), *Cultures of United States Imperialism*. Durham, NC & London: Duke University Press, pp. 474-498.

Luhrmann, T.M. (1996). *The Good Parsi*. Cambridge, MA & London, England: Harvard University Press.

Macedo, Donald & Bartolome, Lilia. (forthcoming). "Dancing with Bigotry: The Poisoning of Racial and Ethnic Identities." In Enrique Torres Trueba & Yali Zou, eds., *Ethnic Identity and Power*. Albany, NY: State University of New York Press.

Martin-Barbero, Jesus. (1993). *Communication, Culture and Hegemony*. London, New Park, & New Delhi: Sage Publications.

McLaren, Peter. (1995). *Critical Pedagogy and Predatory Culture*. London & New York: Routledge.

McLaren, Peter. (in press). *Revolutionary Multiculturalism: Pedagogies of Dissent for the New Millennium*. Boulder, CO: Westview Press.

Miles, Robert. (1982). *Racism and Migrant Labour: A Critical Text*. London: Routledge.

Miles, Robert. (1993). *Racism After "Race Relations."* London: Routledge.

Miles, Robert. (1994). "Explaining Racism in Contemporary Europe" in Ali Rattansi and Sallie Westwood (eds.), *Racism, Modernity and Identity*. Cambridge, MA & Cambridge, UK: Polity Press.

Miles, Robert & Torres, Rudy. (1996). "Does 'Race' Matter? Transatlantic Perspectives on Racism after 'Race Relations,'" in Vered Amit-Talai & Caroline Knowles (eds.),

Re-Situating Identities. Toronto, Canada: Broadview Press.
Moore, Joan, & Pachon, Harry. (1985). *Hispanics in the United States*. Englewood Cliffs, NJ: Prentice-Hall.
Moraes, Marcia. (1996). *Bilingual Education: A Dialogue with the Bakhtin Circle*. Albany, NY: The State University of New York Press.
Novik, Michael. (1995). *White Lies, White Power: The Fight Against White Supremacy and Reactionary Violence*. Monroe, ME: Common Courage Press.
O'Brien, Conor Cruise. (1996). "Thomas Jefferson: Radical and Racist." *The Atlantic Monthly*, October, pp. 53-74.
Omi, Michael & Winant, Howard. (1993). "The Los Angeles 'Race Riot' and Contemporary U.S. Politics," in Robert Gooding-Williams (ed.), *Reading Rodney King*. London & New York: Routledge, pp. 97-114.
Parenti, Michael. (1996). *Dirty Truths*. San Francisco, CA: City Lights Books.
Perea, Juan, F. (1995). "Los Olvidados: On the Making of Invisible People." *New York University Law Review*, Vol. 70, No. 4, pp. 965-991.
Radhakrishnan, R. (1996). *Diasporic Mediations*. Minneapolis, MN & London: University of Minnesota Press.
Rattansi, Ali. (1994). "'Western' Racisms, Ethnicities and Identities in a 'Postmodern' Frame." In Ali Rattansi & Sallie Westwood, eds., *Racism, Modernity and Identity on the Western Front*. Cambridge, MA & Oxford, UK: Polity Press, pp. 403-412.
Ridgeway, James. (1995). *Blood in the Face*. New York: Thunder's Mouth Press.
Roediger, David. (1993). *The Wages of Whiteness*. London & New York: Verso.
Roediger, David. (1994). *Towards the Abolition of Whiteness*. London & New York: Verso.
Rugoff, Ralph. (1995). *Circus Americanus*. London & New York: Verso.
Said, Edward. (1985). *Orientalism*. London: Penguin.
San Juan, Jr., E. (1995). *Hegemony and Strategies of Transgression*. Albany, NY: State University of New York Press.
Sarup, Madan. (1996). *Identity, Culture and the Postmodern World*. Athens, GA: The University of Georgia Press.
Shohat, Ella & Stam, Robert. (1994). *Unthinking Eurocentrism*. London & New York: Routledge.
Shohat, Ella. (1995). "The Struggle Over Representation: Casting, Coalitions, and the Politics of Indentification." In Román de la Campa, E. Ann Kaplan, & Michael Sprinker, eds., *Late Imperial Culture* (pp. 166-178). London & New York: Verso.
Simon, S. (1996, January 2). "Job Hunt's Wild Side in Russia." *Los Angeles Times*, pp. 1, 9.
Sleeter, Christine E. (1996). "White Silence, White Solidarity" in Noel Ignatiev & John Gavey (eds.), *Race Traitor*. London & New York: Routledge.
Southern Poverty Law Center. (1996). *False Patriots: The Threat of Antigovernment Extremists*. Montgomery, AL: Southern Poverty Law Center.
Stowe, David W. "Uncolored People: The Rise of Whiteness Studies." *Lingua Franca*, Vol. 6, No. 6, 1996, pp. 68-77.
The Boston Globe, January 26, 1990.
Time. Banker to Mexico: "Go get 'em." February 20, 1995, Vol. 145, No. 7, p. 9.
Trembath, Paul. (1996). "Aesthetics without Art or Culture: Toward an Alternative Sense of Materialist Agency." *Strategies*, Vol. 9/10, pp. 122-151.
Tsing, Anna Lowenhaupt. (1993). *In the Realm of the Diamond Queen*. Princeton, NJ:

Princeton University Press.
Visweswaran, Kamala. (1994). *Fictions of Feminist Ethnography*. Minneapolis, MN & London: University of Minnesota Press.
Wallace, Amy. (1996). "Less Diversity Seen as UC Preferences End." *Los Angeles Times*, Wednesday, October 2, A1, 18.
Webb, Gary. (1996). "Unholy Connection." *New Times*, Sept. 12-18, vol.1, no. 4, pp. 10-24.
Welsch, Wolfgang. (1996). "Aestheticization Processes: Phenomena, Distinctions and Prospects." *Theory, Culture and Society*, Vol. 13, No. 2, pp. 1-24.
West, Cornel. (1993). *Keeping Faith: Philosophy and Race in America*. New York & London: Routledge.
Williams, Raymond. (1974). *Politics and Letters*. London: Verso.
Winant, Howard. (1994). *Racial Conditions: Politics, Theory, Comparisons*. Minneapolis, MN & London: University of Minnesota Press.
Winant, Howard. (1994). "Racial Formation and Hegemony: Global and Local Developments." In Ali Rattansi & Sallie Westwood, eds., *Racism, Modernity, and Identity on the Western Front*. Cambridge, MA & Oxford, U.K.: Polity Press, pp. 266-289.
Wolfenstein, Eugene Victor. (1993). *Psychoanalytic-Marxism: Groundwork*. New York & London: The Guilford Press.
Wood, Ellen Meiksins. (1995). *Democracy Against Capitalism: Renewing Historical Materialism*. Cambridge, United Kingdom: Cambridge University Press.
Yudice, George. (1995). "Neither Impugning nor Disavowing Whiteness Does a Viable Politics Make: The Limits of Identity Politics" in Christopher Newfield & Ronald Strickland (eds.), *After Political Correctness. The Humanities and Society in the 1990s*, pp. 255-285.
Zamichow, N. (1996, January 23). "Captains Courageous Enough Not to Fight." *Los Angeles Times*, pp. 1, 9-10.
Zinn, Howard. (1970). *The Politics of History*. Boston, MA: Beacon Press.

[29]

The Politics of Culture: Understanding Local Political Resistance to Detracking in Racially Mixed Schools

AMY STUART WELLS
IRENE SERNA
Graduate School of Education and Information Studies, UCLA

In this article, Amy Stuart Wells and Irene Serna examine the political struggles associated with detracking reform. Drawing on their three-year study of ten racially and socioeconomically mixed schools that are implementing detracking reform, the authors take us beyond the school walls to better understand the broad social forces that influence detracking reform. They focus specifically on the role of elite parents and how their political and cultural capital enables them to influence and resist efforts to dismantle or lessen tracking in their children's schools. Wells and Serna identify four strategies employed by elite parents to undermine and co-opt reform initiatives designed to alter existing tracking structures. By framing elite parents' actions within the literature on elites and cultural capital, the authors provide a deeper understanding of the barriers educators face in their efforts to detrack schools.

Research on tracking, or grouping students into distinct classes for "fast" and "slow" learners, has demonstrated that this educational practice leads to racial and socioeconomic segregation within schools, with low-income, African American, and Latino students frequently placed in the lowest level classes, even when they have equal or higher test scores or grades (see Oakes, 1985; Oakes & Welner, 1995). Furthermore, being placed in the low track often has long-lasting negative effects on these students, as they fall further and further behind their peers and become increasingly bored in school. Partly in response to this research and partly in response to their own uneasiness with the separate and unequal classrooms created by tracking, educators across the country are beginning to respond by testing alternatives to tracking, a reform we call "detracking."

Harvard Educational Review Vol. 66 No. 1 Spring 1996

0017-8055/96/0200-093 $1.25/0

Over the last three years, our research team studied ten racially and socioeconomically mixed schools undergoing detracking reform, and attempted to capture the essence of the political struggles inherent in such efforts.[1] We believe that an important aspect of our qualitative, multiple case study is to help educators and policymakers understand the various manifestations of local political resistance to detracking — not only who instigates it, but also the ideology of opposition to such reforms and the political practices employed (see Oakes & Wells, 1995).

This article focuses on how forces outside the school walls shaped the ability of educators to implement "detracking reform" — to question existing track structures and promote greater access to challenging classes for all students. More specifically, we look at those actors whom we refer to as the "local elites" — those with a combination of economic, political, and cultural capital that is highly valued within their particular school community.[2] These elites are most likely to resist detracking reform because their children often enjoy privileged status in a tracked system. The capital of the elites enables them to engage in political practices that can circumvent detracking reform.

In order to understand the influence of local elites' political practices on detracking reform, we examine their ideology of entitlement, or how they make meaning of their privilege within the educational system and how others come to see such meanings as the way things "ought to be." According to Gramsci (cited in Boggs, 1984), insofar as ruling ideas emanating from elites are internalized by a majority of individuals within a given community, they become a defining motif of everyday life and appear as "common sense" — that is, as the "traditional popular conception of the world" (p. 161).

Yet we realize that the high-status cultural capital — the valued tastes and consumption patterns — of local elites and the resultant ideologies are easily affected by provincial social contexts and the particular range of class, race, and culture at those sites (Bourdieu, 1984). In a study of social reproduction in a postmodern society, Harrison (1993) notes that "the task is not so much to look for the global correspondences between culture and class, but to reconstruct the peculiarly local and material micrologic of investments made in the intellectual field" (p. 40). Accordingly, in our study, we particularize the political struggles and examine the specific ideologies articulated at each school site. Because we were studying ten schools in ten different cities and towns, we needed to contextualize each political struggle over detracking reform within its local school community. These local contexts are significant because the relations of power and domination that affect people most directly are those shaping the social contexts within which they live out their everyday lives: the home, the workplace,

[1] Our three-year study of ten racially mixed secondary schools that are detracking was funded by the Lilly Endowment. Jeannie Oakes and Amy Stuart Wells were coprincipal investigators. Research associates were Robert Cooper, Amanda Datnow, Diane Hirshberg, Martin Lipton, Karen Ray, Irene Serna, Estella Williams, and Susie Yonezawa.

[2] By "school community," we mean the broad and diverse network of students, parents, educators, and other citizens who are connected to these schools as institutions.

the classroom, the peer group. As Thompson (1990) states, "These are the contexts within which individuals spend the bulk of their time, acting and interacting, speaking and listening, pursuing their aims and following the aims of others" (p. 9).

Our research team used qualitative methods to examine technical aspects of detracking — school organization, grouping practices, and classroom pedagogy — as well as cultural norms and political practices that legitimize and support tracking as a "commonsense" approach to educating students (Oakes & Wells, 1995). Our research question was, What happens when someone with power in a racially mixed secondary school decides to reduce tracking? Guided by this question, we selected ten sites — six high schools and four middle schools — from a pool of schools that were undergoing detracking reform and volunteered to be studied. We chose these particular schools because of their diversity and demonstrated commitment to detracking. The schools we studied varied in size from more than three thousand to less than five hundred students. One school was in the Northeast, three were in the Midwest, one in the South, two in the Northwest, and three in various regions of California. Each school drew from a racially and socioeconomically diverse community and served significant but varied mixes of White, African American, Latino, Native American/Alaska Native, and/or Asian students. We visited each school three times over a two-year period. Data collection during our site visits included in-depth, semi-structured tape-recorded interviews with administrators, teachers, students, parents, and community leaders, including school board members. In total, more than four hundred participants across all ten schools were interviewed at least once. We also observed classrooms, as well as faculty, PTA, and school board meetings. We reviewed documents and wrote field notes about our observations within the schools and the communities. Data were compiled extensively from each school to form the basis of cross-case analysis. Our study ran from the spring of 1992 through the spring of 1995.[3]

Descriptions of the "Local Elites"

The struggles over tracking and detracking reforms are, to a large extent, concerned with whose culture and lifestyle is valued, and, thus, whose way of knowing is equated with "intelligence." Traditional hierarchical track structures in schools have been validated by the conflation of culture and intelligence. When culturally biased "truths" about ability and merit confront efforts to "detrack," political practices are employed either to maintain the status quo or to push toward new conceptions of ability that would render a rigid and hierarchical track structure obsolete (see Oakes, Lipton, & Jones, 1995).

While we acknowledge that many agents contribute to the maintenance of a rigid track structure, this article examines the political practices of local elites in the school communities we studied. The elites discussed here had children enrolled in the detracking schools and thus constitute the subgroup of local

[3] For a full description of the study and its methodology, see Oakes & Wells (1995).

elites active in shaping school policies. Their practices were aimed at maintaining a track structure, with separate and unequal educational opportunities for "deserving" elite students and "undeserving" or non-elite students. Our analysis of elite parents' ideology of privilege and the resultant political practices therefore includes an examination of "corresponding institutional mechanisms" (Bourdieu & Wacquant, 1992, p. 188) employed to prevent structural change that would challenge their status and privilege.

Our intention is not to criticize these powerful parents in an unsympathetic manner. Yet, we believe that too often the cultural forces that shape such parents' agency as they try to do what is best for their children remain hidden from view and thus unquestioned. Our effort to unpack the "knapsack" of elite privilege will expose the tight relationship between the "objective" criteria of the schools and the cultural forces of the elite (McIntosh, 1992).

Detracking, or the process of moving schools toward a less rigid system of assigning students to classes and academic programs, is a hotly contested educational reform. In racially mixed schools, the controversy surrounding detracking efforts is compounded by beliefs about the relationship among race, culture, and academic ability. In virtually all racially mixed secondary schools, tracking resegregates students, with mostly White and Asian students in the high academic tracks and mostly African American and Latino students in the low tracks (Oakes, 1985; Oakes, Oraseth, Bell, & Camp, 1990). To the extent that elite parents have internalized dominant, but often unspoken, beliefs about race and intelligence, they may resist "desegregation" within racially mixed schools — here defined as detracking — because they do not want their children in classes with Black and Latino students.

Efforts to alter within-school racial segregation via detracking, then, are generally threatening to elites, in that they challenge their position at the top of the hierarchy. The perceived stakes, from an elite parent's perspective, are quite high. They argue, for instance, that their children will not be well served in detracked classes. And while these stakes are most frequently discussed in academic terms — for example, the dumbing down of the curriculum for smart students — the real stakes, we argue, are generally not academics at all, but, rather, status and power. For example, if a school does away with separate classes for students labeled "gifted" but teachers continue to challenge these students with the same curriculum in a detracked setting, the only "losses" the students will incur are their label and their separate and unequal status. Yet in a highly stratified society, such labels and privileged status confer power.

In looking at the ability of the upper strata of society to maintain power and control, Bourdieu (1977) argues that economic capital — that is, income, wealth, and property — is not the only form of capital necessary for social reproduction. He describes other forms of capital, including political, social, and cultural (Bourdieu & Wacquant, 1992). In our analysis of resistance to detracking reforms, we focus on cultural capital and its relationship to dominant ideologies within our school communities because of the explicit connections between cultural capital and educational achievement within Bourdieu's work. According to

Bourdieu (1984), cultural capital consists of culturally valued tastes and consumption patterns, which are rewarded within the educational system. Bourdieu discusses "culture" not in its restricted, normative sense, but rather from a more anthropological perspective. Culture is elaborated in a "taste" for refined objects, which is what distinguishes the culture of the dominant class or upper social strata from that of the rest of society. In order for elites to employ their cultural capital to maintain power, emphasis must be placed on subtleties of taste — for example, form over function, manner over matter. Within the educational system, Bourdieu argues, students are frequently rewarded for their taste, and for the cultural knowledge that informs it. For instance, elite students whose status offers them the opportunity to travel to other cities, states, and countries on family vacations are often perceived to be more "intelligent" than other students, simply because the knowledge they have gained from these trips is reflected in what is valued in schools. When high-status, elite students' taste is seen as valued knowledge within the educational system, other students' taste and the knowledge that informs it is devalued (Bourdieu & Passeron, 1979). In this way, high-status culture is socially constructed as "intelligence" — a dubious relationship that elites must strive to conceal in order to legitimize their merit-based claim to privileged status. In other words, what is commonly referred to as "objective" criteria of intelligence and achievement is actually extremely biased toward the subjective experience and ways of knowing of elite students. Similarly, Delpit (1995) describes the critical role that power plays in our society and educational system, as the worldviews of those in privileged positions are "taken as the only reality, while the worldviews of those less powerful are dismissed as inconsequential" (p. xv). The education system is the primary field in which struggles over these cultural meanings take place and where, more often than not, high-status cultural capital is translated into high-status credentials, such as academic degrees from elite institutions (Bourdieu & Passeron, 1977).

Thus, socially valuable cultural capital — form and manner — is the property many upper class and, to a lesser extent, middle-class families transmit to their offspring that substitutes for, or supplements, the transmission of economic capital as a means of maintaining class, status, and privilege across generations (Bourdieu, 1973). Academic qualifications and high-status educational titles are to cultural capital what money and property titles are to economic capital. The form and manner of academic qualifications are critical. Students cannot simply graduate from high school; they must graduate with the proper high-status qualifications that allow them access to the most selective universities and to the credentials those institutions confer.

Through the educational system, elites use their economic, political, and cultural capital to acquire symbolic capital — the most highly valued capital in a given society or local community. Symbolic capital signifies culturally important attributes, such as status, authority, prestige, and, by extension, a sense of honor. The social construction of symbolic capital may vary from one locality to another, but race and social class consistently play a role, with White, wealthy, well-educated families most likely to be at the top of the social strata (Harrison, 1993).

Because the cultural capital of the elite is that which is most valued and rewarded within the educational system, elite status plays a circular role in the process of detracking reform: parents with high economic, political, and cultural capital are most likely to have children in the highest track and most prestigious classes, which in turn gives them more symbolic capital in the community. The elite parents can then employ their symbolic capital in the educational decision-making arena to maintain advantages for their children. Educational reforms that, like detracking, challenge the advantages bestowed upon children of the elite are resisted not only by the elites themselves, but also by educators and even other parents and community members who may revere the cultural capital of elite families. The school and the community thus bestow elite parents with the symbolic capital, or honor, that allows them political power.

The status of the local elites in the ten school communities we studied derived in part from the prestige they and their children endowed to public schools simply by their presence. The elite are the most valued citizens, those the public schools do not want to lose, because the socially constructed status of institutions such as schools is dependent upon the status of the individuals attending them. These are also the families most likely to flee public schools if they are denied what they want from them. For example, at Grant High School, an urban school in the Northwest, the White, upper-middle-class parents who sent their children to public schools held tremendous power over the district administration. Many of them were highly educated and possessed the economic means to send their children to private schools if they so chose.

While the elites at each of the schools we studied held economic, social, and political capital, the specific combination of these varied at each site in relation to the cultural capital valued there. Thus, who the elites were and their particular rationale for tracking varied among locations, based on the distinctive mix of race, class, and culture. For instance, at Liberty High School, located in a West Coast city, many of the White parents were professors at a nearby university. As "professional intellectuals," they strongly influenced the direction of Liberty High; although they were generally not as wealthy as business executives, they were nevertheless imbued with a great deal of high-status cultural capital. Meanwhile, educators and White parents at Liberty noted that most of the Black and Latino students enrolled in the school came from very low-income families. Many of the people we interviewed said there was a sizable number of middle-class Black families in this community, but that they did not send their children to public schools. This school's social class divide, which some educators and Black students argued was a caricature, allowed White parents to blame the school's resegregation through tracking on the "family backgrounds" of the students, rather than on racial prejudice.

In the midwestern town of Plainview, the local White elites worked in private corporations rather than universities. Here, the high-status cultural capital was, in general, far more conservative, pragmatic, and less "intellectual" than at Liberty. Nonetheless, the elite parents here and at each of the schools we studied strove for the same advantages that the elite parents at Liberty High demanded for their children.

The African American students in Plainview comprised two groups — those who lived in a small, working-class Black neighborhood in the district and those who transferred into Plainview from the "inner city" through an inter-district desegregation plan. At this site, however, the social class distinctions between the two groups of Black students were blurred by many White respondents, particularly in their explanations of why Black students from both groups were consistently found in the lowest track classes. For instance, teachers could not tell us which Black students lived in Plainview and which rode the bus in from the city. Some teachers also spoke of Black students' — all Black students' — low levels of achievement as the result of their families' culture of poverty, and not the result of what the school offered them. Despite the relative economic advantages of many African American students who lived in the Plainview district as compared to those who lived in the city, all Black students in this mostly White, wealthy suburban school were doing quite poorly. While African Americans constituted 25 percent of the student population, less than 5 percent of the students in the highest level courses were Black. Furthermore, a district task force on Black achievement found that more than half of the Black students in the high school had received at least one D or F over the course of one school year.

In other schools, the interplay between race and class was more complex, especially when the local elite sought to distinguish themselves from other, lower income Whites. For instance, in the small midwestern Bearfield School District, which is partly rural and partly suburban, wealthy, well-educated, White suburban parents held the most power over the educational system because they possessed more economic and highly valued cultural capital than rural Whites or African Americans. When a desegregation plan was instituted in the 1970s, it was Black and poor rural White children who were bused. As the Bearfield Middle School principal explained, "As our business manager/superintendent once told me, the power is neither Black nor White; it's green — as in money. And that's where the power is. Rich people have clout. Poor people don't have clout."

Still, the less wealthy and less educated rural Whites in Bearfield, while not as politically powerful as the suburban Whites, remained more influential than the African American families. When the two middle schools in the district were consolidated in 1987, Whites — both wealthy suburban and poor rural — were able to convince the school board to close down the newly built middle school located in the African American community and keep open the older middle school on the White side of the town.

Although the interplay between class and culture within a racially mixed community is generally defined along racial lines, we found that was not always the case. For example, King Middle School, a magnet school in a large northeastern city, was designed to attract students of many racial groups and varied socioeconomic status. A teacher explained that the parents who are blue-collar workers do not understand what's going on at the school, but the professional and middle-class parents frequently call to ask for materials to help their children at home. Educators at King insisted that middle-class and professional parents were not all White, and that there was very little correlation between income and race at the school, with its student body composed of more than twenty racial/ethnic groups, including Jamaican, Chinese, Armenian, Puerto Rican, African American, and various European ethnic groups. While we found it difficult to believe that there was no correlation between race/ethnicity and income in this city with relatively poor African American and Latino communities, it is clear that not all of the local elites at King were White.

Thus, the layers of stratification in some schools were many, but the core of the power elite in all ten communities consisted of a group of parents who were more White, wealthy, and well-educated relative to others in their community. They were the members of the school communities with the greatest economic and/or high-status cultural capital, which they have passed on to their children. The schools, in turn, greatly rewarded the children of these elite for their social distinctions, which were perceived to be distinctions of merit (DiMaggio, 1979).

The Political Ideology of Tracking and Detracking: "Deserving" High-Track Students

Bourdieu's concepts of domination and social reproduction are particularly useful in understanding the education system, because education is the field in which the elite both "records and conceals" its own privilege. Elites "record" privilege through formal educational qualifications, which then serve to "conceal" the inherited cultural capital needed to acquire them. According to Harrison (1993), "What is usually referred to as equality of opportunity or meritocracy is, for Bourdieu, a "sociodicy"; that is, a sacred story that legitimates the dominant class' own privilege" (p. 43).

The political resistance of the local elite to detracking reforms cannot, therefore, be understood separately from the "sociodicy" or ideology employed to legitimize the privileged place elites and their children hold in the educational system. Ideology, in a Gramscian sense, represents ideas, beliefs, cultural preferences, and even myths and superstitions, which possess a certain "material" reality of their own (Gramsci, 1971). In education, societal ideas, beliefs, and cultural preferences of intelligence have found in tracking structures their own material reality. Meanwhile, tracking reinforces and sustains those ideas, beliefs, and cultural preferences.

According to Thompson (1990), ideology refers to the ways in which meaning serves, in particular circumstances, to establish and sustain relations of power that are systematically asymmetrical. Broadly speaking, ideology is *meaning in the service of power.* Thompson suggests that the study of ideology requires researchers to investigate the ways in which meaning is constructed and conveyed by symbolic forms of various kinds, "from everyday linguistic utterances to complex images and texts; it requires us to investigate the social contexts within which symbolic forms are employed and deployed" (p. 7).

The ideology of the local elites in the schools we studied was often cloaked in the "symbolic form" that Thompson describes. While the symbols used by politically powerful people to express their resistance to detracking differed from one site to the next, race consistently played a central, if not explicit, role.

Although local elites rarely expressed their dissatisfaction with detracking reform in overtly racial terms, their resistance was couched in more subtle expressions of the politics of culture that have clear racial implications. For example, they said they liked the concept of a racially mixed school, as long as the African American or Latino students acted like White, middle-class children, and their parents were involved in the school and bought into the American Dream. At Central High, a predominantly Latino school on the West Coast with a 23 percent White student body, the local elite consisted of a relatively small middle class of mostly White and a few Latino families. No real upper middle class existed, and most of the Latino students came from very low-income families; many were recent immigrants to the United States. A White parent whose sons were taking honors classes explained her opposition to detracking efforts at Central, exposing her sense of entitlement this way:

> I think a lot of those Latinos come and they're still Mexicans at heart. They're not American. I don't care what color you are, we're in America here and we're going for this country. And I think their heart is in Mexico and they're with that culture still. It's one thing to come over and bring your culture and to use it, but it's another thing to get into that . . . and I'm calling it the American ethic. They're not into it and that's why they end up so far behind. They get in school, and they are behind.

This construct of the "deserving minority" denies the value of non-White students' and parents' own culture or of their sometimes penetrating critique of the American creed (see Yonesawa, Williams, & Hirshberg, 1995), and implies that only those students with the cultural capital and underlying elite ideology deserve to be rewarded in the educational system. Yet because the political arguments put forth by powerful parents in the schools we studied sounded so benign, so "American," the cultural racism that guided their perspective was rarely exposed. Consequently, both the racial segregation within the schools and the actions of parents to maintain it were perceived as natural.

We found many instances in which elite parents attempted to distance their children from students they considered to be less deserving of special attention and services. For instance, at Rolling Hills Middle School, located in a southeastern metropolitan area with a large, county-wide desegregation plan, one wealthy White parent said she and her husband purchased a home in the nearby neighborhood because Rolling Hills and its feeder high school are two of the handful of schools in the district that offer an "advanced program." She said several people had told her that in the advanced program the curriculum was better, fewer behavior problems occurred in the classes, and students received more individualized attention from teachers. She also said that had her children not been accepted into the advanced program, she and her family would not have moved into this racially mixed school district, but would have purchased a home in one of the Whiter suburbs east of the county line. Interestingly enough, this parent did not know whether or not the White suburban schools offered an advanced program. Also of interest in this district is the creation of the advanced program in the same year as the implementation of the desegregation plan.

The White, well-educated parents at Grant High School often stated that the racial diversity of the student body was one characteristic they found most appealing about the school. They said that such a racially mixed environment better prepared their children for life in "the real world." One parent noted that "the positive mixing of racial groups is important to learning to live in society." But some teachers argued that while these parents found Grant's diversity acceptable — even advantageous — their approval was conditioned by their understanding that "their children [would] only encounter Black students in the hallways and not in their classrooms." Grant's assistant principal noted that "many upper class, professional parents hold occupational positions in which they work toward equity and democracy, but expect their children to be given special treatment at Grant."

This ideology of "diversity at a distance" is often employed by White parents at strategic moments when the privileged status of their children appears to be threatened (Lareau, 1989). In our study, the parents of honors students at Grant successfully protested the school's effort to eliminate the "tennis shoe" registration process by which students and teachers jointly negotiated access to classes.[4] Some of the faculty had proposed that the school switch to a computer registration program that would guarantee Black and Latino students greater access to high-track classes. The parents of the honors students stated that they were not protesting the registration change because they were opposed to having their children in racially mixed classes, but because "they [felt] that their children [would] learn more in an environment where all students are as motivated to learn as they are — in a homogeneous ability classroom."

Respondents at Grant said that parents assumed that if any student was allowed into an honors class, regardless of his or her prior track, it must not be a good class. The assumption here was that if there was no selectivity in placing students in particular classes, then the learning and instruction in those classes could not be good. Parents of the most advanced students "assumed" that since the language arts department had made the honors and regular curriculum the same and allowed more students to enroll in honors, the rigor of these classes had probably diminished, despite the teachers' claims that standards had remained high.

At Liberty High School, where the intellectual elite were more "liberal" than the elite in most of the other schools, parents also frequently cited the racial diversity of the school as an asset. For instance, one parent commented that it was the racial and cultural mix — "the real range of people here" — that attracted her to Liberty High. She liked the fact that her daughter was being exposed to people of different cultures and different socioeconomic backgrounds: "We took her out of private school, where there's all these real upper

[4] During the "tennis shoe" registration, teachers set up tables in the gymnasium with registration passes for each of the classes they will be offering. Students have an allocated time slot in which they are allowed into the gym to run from teacher to teacher and ask for passes for classes they want. Under this system, teachers are able to control who gets into their classes, and the children of the elite, who hold more political power in the school, are more likely to get the high-track classes that they want.

middle-class White kids." Yet, despite this espoused appreciation for diversity among White liberal parents at Liberty, they strongly resisted efforts to dismantle the racially segregated track system. According to another White parent of a high-track student at Liberty:

> I think the one thing that really works at Liberty High is the upper track. It does. And to me, I guess my goal would be for us to find a way to make the rest of Liberty High work as well as the upper track. But it's crucial that we not destroy the upper track to do that, and that can happen . . . it really could. . . . I feel my daughter will get an excellent education if the program continues the way it is, if self-scheduling continues so that they aren't all smoothed together.

In all of the schools we studied, the most interesting aspect of elites' opposition to detracking is that they based their resistance on the symbolic mixing of high "deserving" and low "undeserving" students, rather than on information about what actually happens in detracked classrooms. For instance, an English teacher at Plainview High School who taught a heterogeneous American Studies course in which she academically challenged all her students said that the popularity of the Advanced Placement classes among the elite parents was in part based upon a "myth" that "they're the only classes that offer high standards, that they're the only courses that are interesting and challenging. And the myth is that that's where the best learning takes place. That's a myth."

At Explorer Middle School, located in a mid-sized northwestern city, the identified gifted students — nearly all White, despite a school population that was 30 percent American Indian — were no longer segregated into special classes or teams. Rather, "gifted" students were offered extra "challenge" courses, which other "non-gifted" students could choose to take as well. The day after a grueling meeting with parents of the "gifted" students, the designated gifted education teacher who works with these and other students in the challenge classes was upset by the way in which the parents had responded to her explanation of the new challenge program and the rich educational opportunities available in these classes:

> And they didn't ask, "well what are our kids learning in your classes?" Nobody asked that. I just found that real dismaying, and I was prepared to tell them what we do in class and here's an example. I had course outlines. I send objectives home with every class, and goals and work requirements, and nobody asked me anything about that . . . like they, it's . . . to me it's like I'm dealing with their egos, you know, more than what their kids really need educationally.

What this and other teachers in our study told us is that many elite parents are more concerned about the labels placed on their children than what actually goes on in the classroom. This is a powerful illustration of what Bourdieu (1984) calls "form over function" and "manner over matter."

Notions of Entitlement

Symbols of the "deserving," high-track students must be juxtaposed with conceptions of the undeserving, low-track students in order for strong protests against detracking to make sense in a society that advocates equal opportunity. Bourdieu argues that "impersonal domination" — the sociocultural form of domination found in free, industrial societies where more coercive methods of domination are not allowed — entails the rationalization of the symbolic. When symbols of domination are rationalized, the *entitlement* of the upper strata of society is legitimized, and thus this impersonal domination is seen as natural (Harrison, 1993, p. 42).

In our study, we found that elite parents rationalized their children's entitlement to better educational opportunities based upon the resources that they themselves brought to the system. For instance, parents from the White, wealthy side of Bearfield Middle School's attendance zone perceived that the African American students who attended the school and lived on the "other" side of town benefited from the large tax burden shouldered by the White families. One White parent noted, "I don't feel that our school should have, you know, people from that far away coming to our school. I don't think it's right as far as the taxes we pay. . . . They don't pay the taxes that we pay, and they're at our schools also. Um, I just don't feel they belong here, no." According to the superintendent of the school district, this statement reflects the widely held belief among Whites that they are being taxed to pay for schools for Black students, "and therefore, the White community . . . should make the decisions about the schools . . . because they are paying the bill." These perspectives explain in part why the consolidation of the district's two middle schools resulted in the closing of the mostly Black but much more recently built school, and favored the old, dilapidated Bearfield building as the single middle school site.

At the same time, these parents balked at the suggestion that their own social privilege and much of their children's advantages had less to do with objective merit or intellectual ability than it had to do with their families' economic and cultural capital. Harrison (1993) expands upon Bourdieu's notion that culture functions to deny or disavow the economic origins of capital by gaining symbolic credit for the possessors of economic and political capital. Harrison argues that the seemingly legitimate and meritocratic basis upon which students "earn" academic credentials is an important aspect of the dominant class' denial of entitlement as a process in which inherited economic and political power receives social consecration. In other words, the elite parents must convince themselves and others that the privileges their children are given in the educational system were earned in a fair and meritocratic way, and are not simply a consequence of the parents' own privileged place in society. "The demonstration that the belief of merit is a part of the process of social consecration in which the dominant class's power is both acknowledged and misrecognized, is at the core of Bourdieu's analysis of culture" (Harrison, 1993, p. 44).

There is strong evidence from the schools we studied that students frequently end up in particular tracks and classrooms more on the basis of their parents' privilege than of their own "ability." A school board member in the district in which Rolling Hills Middle School is located explained that students are placed in the advanced program depending on who their parents happen to know.

Because the advanced program was implemented at the same time as the county-wide desegregation plan, it has become a sophisticated form of resegregation within racially mixed schools supported by conceptions of "deserving" advanced students. The school board member said that parents of the advanced students are very much invested in labels that their children acquire at school. When children are labeled "advanced," it means their parents are "advanced" as well. In fact, said the board member, some of these parents refer to themselves as the "advanced parents": "There is still an elitist aspect as far as I am concerned. I also think it is an ego trip for parents. They love the double standard that their children are in Advanced Placement programs."

Similarly, several elite parents of students in the advanced program at Grant High School expressed regret that the school had such a poor vocational education department for the "other" students — those who were not advanced. Their lament for vocational education related to their way of understanding the purpose of the high school in serving different students. One of these parents, for example, stated that the role of the honors classes was to groom students to become "managers and professionals" and that something else should be done for those kids who would grow up to be "workers."

According to Harrison (1993), the elite seek to deny the arbitrary nature of the social order that culture does much to conceal. This process, which he calls "masking," occurs when what is culturally arbitrary is "essentialized, absolutized or universalized" (p. 45). Masking is generally accomplished via symbols — culturally specific as opposed to materially specific symbols (Bourdieu & Wacquant, 1992). For example, standardized test scores become cultural symbols of intelligence that are used to legitimize the track structure in some instances while they are "masked" in other instances.

An example of this "masking" process was revealed to us at Grant High School, where elite parents of the most advanced students approved of using test scores as a measure of students' intelligence and worthiness to enroll in the highest track classes. But when children of the elite who were identified as "highly able" in elementary school did not make the test score cutoffs for high school honors classes, the parents found ways to get their children placed in these classes anyway, as if the tests in that particular instance were not valid. The educators usually gave in to these parents' demands, and then cited such instances as evidence of a faulty system. The so-called faults within the system, however, did not lead to broad-based support among powerful parents or educators to dismantle the track structure.

Similarly, at Explorer Middle School, where the wealthy White "gifted" students were all placed in regular classes and then offered separate challenge classes along with other students who chose to take such a class, the principal collected data on the achievement test scores for the identified gifted students and other students in the school. She found huge overlaps in the two sets of scores, with some identified "non-gifted" students scoring in the 90th percentile and above, and some "gifted" students ranking as low as the 58th percentile. Yet, when the mostly White parents of children identified by the district as "gifted" were presented with these data, they attributed the large number of low test scores among the pool of gifted students to a handful of non-White students participating in that program, although the number of non-White "gifted" students was far lower than the number of low test scores within the gifted program. The White parents simply would not admit that any of their children did not deserve a special label (and the extra resources that come with it). According to the teacher of the challenge classes, one of the most vocal and demanding "gifted" parents was the mother of a boy who was not even near the top of his class: "I still can't figure out how he got in the gifted program; he doesn't perform in any way at that high a level. . . . She is carrying on and on and on . . ."

Despite evidence that the "gifted" label may be more a form of symbolic capital than a true measure of innate student ability, the parents of students who had been identified as gifted by this school district maintained a strong sense of entitlement. For instance, a White, upper middle-class father of two so-called gifted boys told us he was outraged that the "gifted and talented" teacher at Explorer spent her time teaching challenge classes that were not exclusively for gifted students. This father was adamant that the state's special funding for gifted and talented (G/T) programs should be spent exclusively on identified G/T students. He noted that at the other middle school in the district, the G/T teacher worked with a strictly G/T class, "whereas at Explorer, the G/T teacher works with a class that is only 50 percent G/T." In other words, "precious" state resources for gifted and talented students were being spent on "non-deserving" students — many of whom had higher middle school achievement test scores than the students who had been identified by the school district as gifted many years earlier.

At Plainview High School, the English teacher who created the heterogeneous American Studies class began reading about the social science research on intelligence, and concluded that our society and education system do not really understand what intelligence is or how to measure it. When the principal asked her to present her research to parents at an open house, her message was not well received, particularly by those parents whose children were in the Advanced Placement classes. According to this teacher, "If you were raised under the system that said you were very intelligent and high achieving, you don't want anyone questioning that system, OK? That's just the way it is." She said that what some of the parents were most threatened by was how this research on intelligence was going to be used and whether the high school was going to do away with Advanced Placement classes. She recalled, "I used the word 'track' once and debated whether I could weave that in because I knew the power of the word, and I didn't want to shut everyone down. It was very interesting."

Political Practices: How the Local Elite Undermined Detracking

The ideology and related symbols that legitimate local elites' sense of entitlement are critical to educational policy and practice. As Harrison (1993) and Harker (1984) note, Bourdieu's work is ultimately focused on the strategic practices employed when conflicts emerge. In this way, Bourdieu identifies "practices" — actions that maintain or change the social structures — within strategically oriented forms of conflict. These strategic actions must be rooted back into the logic or sense of entitlement that underlies these practices. In other words, we examined political practices that are intended to be consistent with an ideology of "deserving" high-track students. These practices were employed by elite parents when educators posed a threat to the privileged status of their children by questioning the validity and objectivity of a rigid track structure (Useem, 1990).

According to Bourdieu, when seemingly "objective" structures, such as tracking systems, are faithfully reproduced in the dispositions or ways of knowing of actors, then the "arbitrary" nature of the existing structure can go completely unrecognized (Bourdieu & Wacquant, 1992). For instance, no one questions the existence of the separate and unequal "gifted and talented" or "highly advanced" program for children of the local elites, despite the fact that the supposedly "objective" measures that legitimize these programs — standardized tests scores — do not always support the somewhat "arbitrary" nature of student placement. This arbitrary placement system is more sensitive to cultural capital than academic "ability."

In the case of tracking, so-called objective and thus non-arbitrary standardized tests are problematic on two levels. First, the tests themselves are culturally biased in favor of wealthy, White students, and therefore represent a poor measure of "ability" or "intelligence." Second, scores on these exams tend to count more for some students than others. Elite students who have low achievement test scores are placed in high tracks, while non-White and non-wealthy students with high test scores are bound to the lower tracks (see Oakes et al., 1995; Welner & Oakes, 1995). Still, test scores remain an undisclosed and undisputed "objective" measure of student track placement and thus a rationale for maintaining the track structure in many schools.

When these undisclosed or undisputed parts of the universe are questioned, conflicts arise that call for strategic political practices on the part of elites. As Harrison (1993) states, "Where the fit can no longer be maintained and where, therefore, the arbitrary nature of the objective structure becomes evident, the dominant class must put into circulation a discourse in which this arbitrary order is misrecognized as such" (p. 41). When the arbitrary nature of the "objective" tracking structure becomes evident, detracking efforts are initiated, often by educators who have come to realize the cultural basis of the inequalities within our so-called meritocratic educational system.

Within each of our ten schools, when educators penetrated the ideology that legitimizes the track structure (and the advantages that high-track students have within it), elite parents felt that their privileges were threatened. We found that local elites employed four practices to undermine and co-opt meaningful detracking efforts in such a way that they and their children would continue to benefit disproportionately from educational policies. These four overlapping and intertwined practices were threatening flight, co-opting the institutional elites, soliciting buy-in from the "not-quite elite," and accepting detracking bribes.

Threatening Flight

Perhaps nowhere in our study was the power of the local elite and their ideology of entitlement more evident than when the topic of "elite flight" was broached, specifically when these parents threatened to leave the school. Educators in the ten schools we studied were acutely aware that their schools, like most institutions, gain their status, or symbolic capital, from the social status of the students who attend (Wells & Crain, 1992). They know they must hold onto the local elites in order for their schools to remain politically viable institutions that garner broad public support. As a result, the direct or indirect threat of elite flight can thwart detracking efforts when local elite parents have other viable public or private school options.

At Liberty High School, the liberal ideals and principles that are the cornerstone of this community were challenged when local elites were asked to embrace reforms that they perceived to be removing advantages held by their children. In fact, discussions and implementation of such reforms — for example, the creation of a heterogeneous ninth-grade English/social studies core — caused elite parents to "put into circulation a discourse" that legitimized their claim to something better than what other students received. Without this special attention for high-track students, elite parents said, they had little reason to keep their children at Liberty. As one parent of a high-track student noted in discussing the local elite's limits and how much of the school's equity-centered detracking reforms they would tolerate before abandoning the school:

> I think it happens to all of us; when you have children, you confront all your values in a totally different way. I mean, I did all this work in education, I knew all these things about it, and it's very different when it's your own child 'cause when it's your own child your real responsibility is to advocate for that child. I mean, I might make somewhat different decisions about Liberty High, though probably not terribly different, because as I say, I would always have in mind the danger of losing a big chunk of kids, and with them the community support that makes this school work well.

The power of the threat of elite flight is evident in the history of the creation of tracking structures in many of our schools, where advanced and gifted programs began to appear and proliferate at the same time that the schools in these districts were becoming more racially mixed, either through a desegregation plan or demographic shifts. This shift toward more tracking as schools became increasingly racially mixed follows the long history of tracking in the U.S. educational system. Tracking became more systematized at the turn of the century, as non-Anglo immigrant students enrolled in urban high schools (Oakes, 1985). At Grant High School, which is located in a racially diverse urban school district surrounded by separate Whiter and more affluent districts, the highly advanced and "regular" advanced programs were started shortly after desegregation at the insistence of local elite parents who wanted separate classes for their children.

One teacher noted that the advanced programs were designed to respond to a segment of the White community that felt, "Oh, we'll send our kids to public school, but only if there's a special program for them."

At Grant, the chair of the language arts department, an instigator of detracking reform efforts, said that the parents of the "advanced" students run the school district:

> They scare those administrators the same way they scare us. They're the last vestiges of middle-class people in the public schools in some sense. And they know that. And they flaunt that sometimes. And they scare people with that. And the local media would spit [the deputy superintendent] up in pieces if she did something to drive these parents out of the school district. So, yeah. I'm sure she's nervous about anything we're doing.

Similarly, at Rolling Hills Middle School, where the Advanced Program began in the late 1970s, shortly after the county-wide desegregation plan was implemented, the mother of two White boys in the program noted, "If I heard they were going to eliminate the Advanced Program, I would be very alarmed, and would seriously consider if I could afford a private school." She indicated that she thought that most parents of students at Rolling Hills felt this way.

At Central High School, White flight consistently paralleled the influx of Latino immigrant students into the school. Administrators said they hoped that the relocation of the school to a new site in a more middle-class area of the district would allow Central to maintain its White population. But many educators said they felt that what keeps White students at Central is the honors program, which would have been scaled back under detracking reform. This reform effort has been almost completely derailed by political roadblocks from both inside the school and the surrounding community.

Suburban, midwestern Plainview High School was the school in which we perhaps noted the *perceived* threat of elite flight to be most powerful. There, the concept of "community stability" was foremost on the minds of the educators. Many of the teachers and administrators in the Plainview district, particularly at the high school, came to Plainview from the nearby Hamilton School District, which experienced massive White flight two decades earlier. Essentially, the population of the Hamilton district shifted from mostly White, upper middle class to all Black and poor in a matter of ten years — roughly between 1968 and 1978. According to these educators and many other respondents in Plainview, the status of the Hamilton district and its sole high school plummeted, as each incoming freshman class became significantly darker and poorer. Once regarded as the premier public high school in the metropolitan area, Hamilton suddenly served as a reminder of the consequences of White flight. The large numbers of White residents and educators who came to Plainview after fleeing Hamilton kept the memory of White flight alive, and used Hamilton as a symbol of this threat.

Of all the educators in the district, it was the Plainview High School principal, Mr. Fredrick, who appeared most fixated on issues of community "stability" and the role of the schools in maintaining it:

> Here's my problem, what I'm doing at Plainview High School is essentially trying to make it stable enough so that other people can integrate the neighborhood. Now if other people aren't integrating the neighborhood, I'm not doing it either. I'm not out there working on that, I don't have time to be out there working on that, I've got to be making sure that what we're doing in Plainview High School is strong, we're strong enough, and have the reputation of, so that as we integrate, which I'm hoping is happening, that Whites won't get up and flee . . . when they come in and say, I hope you're here in eight years, that is a commitment those White people are gonna be there in eight years.

Fredrick argues that an academically strong high school led by a principal who maintains a good relationship with the community will help stabilize the whole community. As he explains, "I believe we can keep stability in Plainview while still being out in front of education. Now that's what I feel my job is." Fredrick's goal of maintaining racial stability in the community is noble in many respects, but we learned during our visits to Plainview that his focus on White flight has resulted in intense efforts to please the elite White parents. These efforts to cater to elite parents have consistently worked against detracking reforms in the school. While some of the teachers and other administrators continued to push for more innovative grouping and instructional strategies, Fredrick has advocated more Advanced Placement courses and encouraged more students to take these classes. In this way, the threat of White elite flight has helped maintain the hierarchical track structure and an Advanced Placement curriculum that many teachers, students, and less elite parents argue is not creative or instructionally sound.

Co-opting the Institutional Elites

The threat of flight is one of the ways in which local elites provoke responses to their institutional demands. This threat, and the fear it creates in the hearts of educators, is related to the way in which the "institutional elites" — that is, educators with power and authority within the educational system — become co-opted by the ideology of the local elites. Both Domhoff (1983, 1990) and Mills (1956) write about institutional elites as "high-level" employees in institutions (either private corporations or governmental agencies, such as the U.S. Treasury Department) who see their roles as serving the upper, capitalist-based class. At a more micro or local level, we find that the institutional elites are the educational administrators who see their roles as serving the needs and demands of the local elites. Indeed, in most situations, their professional success and even job security depend on their ability to play these roles.

For instance, in small-town Bearfield, the new superintendent, who is politically very popular with elite parents and community members, has developed a less than positive impression of detracking efforts at the middle school. Yet his view is based less on first-hand information about the reform through visits to the school or discussions with the teachers than on the input he has received from White parents who have placed their children in private schools. To him, the educators at Bearfield Middle School have "let the academics slide just a little bit." Because of the superintendent's sense of commitment to the powerful

White, wealthy parents, the principal of Bearfield indicated that he feels intense pressure to raise standardized test scores and prove that academics are not sliding at the school. Thus, some degree of "teaching to the test" has come at the expense of a more creative and innovative curriculum that facilitates detracking efforts by acknowledging, for example, different ways of knowing material. In a symbolic move, the teaching staff has rearranged the Black History Month curriculum to accommodate standardized test prepping in the month of February.

The relationship among the institutional elites at urban Grant High School, its school district office, and the local elite parents, however, demonstrates one of the most severe instances of "co-optation" that we observed. At the district's main office and at the high school, many of the educational administrators are African American. Still, these administrators frequently have failed to push for the kinds of reforms that would benefit the mostly African American students in the lowest track classes. Several respondents noted that Black educators who have been advocates for democratic reform have not survived in this district, and that those who cater to the demands of powerful White parents have been promoted within the system.

At the end of the 1993–1994 school year, the African American principal of Grant, Mr. Phillips, rejected the language arts department's proposal to detrack ninth-grade English by putting "honors" and "regular" students together in the same classes and offering honors as an extra credit option for all students. The principal claimed that it was not fair to do away with separate honors classes when the proposal had not been discussed with parents. His decision, he explained, was based on frequent complaints he received from the mostly White parents of high-track students that changes were being made at the school, particularly in the language arts department, without their prior knowledge or consent. According to the language arts department chair, when her department detracked twelfth-grade electives, it "really pissed people off." Also, when these elite parents were not consulted about the proposal to change the school schedule to an alternative four-period schedule, they protested and were successful in postponing the change.

Furthermore, a recent attempt by Grant's history department to do away with separate honors classes at the request of some students was thwarted by the parents of honors students, who, according to one teacher, "went through the roof." Some of the teachers in other departments indicated that they suspected that the history department's move to eliminate honors classes was not sincere, but rather a political tactic designed to generate support among powerful elite parents for the honors program. In fact, the history department chair, who opposes detracking, noted that his only recourse to stop the detracking reform was to go to the parents and get them upset "because they had the power to do things at school."

At Grant, administrators at the district office have historically been very responsive to the concerns of White parents, and thus regularly implement policies designed to retain the White students. For instance, the district leadership convened an all-White "highly capable parent task force" to examine issues surrounding the educational advanced programs for "highly capable" students. The task force strongly recommended self-contained classrooms for advanced students, making detracking efforts across the district more problematic. According to one of the teachers at Grant, school board members would not talk about the elitism around this program because they were "feeling under siege."

At several schools in our study, educational administrators, especially principals, have lost their jobs since detracking efforts began, in part because they refused co-optation and advocated detracking. At Liberty High School, despite the principal's efforts to make detracking as politically acceptable to the elite parents as possible, in the end he was "done in" by the institutional elites at the district office who would not give him the extra resources he needed to carry out detracking in a manner local elites would have considered acceptable.

Buy-in of the "Not-Quite Elite"

In an interesting article about the current political popularity of decentralized school governance and growth of school-site councils with broad decisionmaking power, Beare (1993) writes that the middle class is a very willing accomplice in the strategy to create such councils and "empower" parents to make important decisions about how schools are run. He notes that it is the middle-class parents who put themselves forward for election to such governing bodies. Yet he argues that in spite of this new-found participatory role for middle-class parents, they actually have little control over the course of their children's schools, because such courses are chartered by a larger power structure. As Beare states, "In one sense, then, participative decision-making is a politically diversionary tactic, a means of keeping activist people distracted by their own self-inflicted, busy work. The middle class are willing accomplices, for they think they are gaining access to the decision-making of the power structures" (p. 202).

The ideology of the local elite's entitlement is so pervasive and powerful that the elites do not necessarily have to be directly involved in the decisionmaking processes at schools, although they often are. But between the local elites' threats to flee, co-optation of institutional elites, and ability to make their privilege appear as "common sense," such school-site councils will most likely simply reflect, as Beare (1993) points out, the broader power structure. In this way, the "self-inflicted busy work" of the not-quite elites, which, depending on the context of the schools, tend to be the more middle- or working-class parents, is just that — busy work that helps the schools maintain the existing power relations and a highly tracked structure. This is what Gramsci (1971) would refer to as the "consensual" basis of power, or the consensual side of politics in a civil society (see Boggs, 1984; Gramsci, 1971).

We saw a clear example of how this co-optation plays out at Plainview High School, where a group of about thirty predominantly White parents served on the advisory board for the most visible parent group, called the Parent-Teacher Organization, or PTO (even though there were no teachers in this organization). The PTO advisory board met with the principal once a month to act as his "sounding board" on important school-site issues, particularly those regarding discipline. We found through in-depth interviews with many of the parents on the PTO board that these parents were not the most powerful or most elite parents in the one-high-school district. In fact, as the former president of the advisory board and the mother of a not-quite-high-track student explained, "The Advanced Placement parents don't run the president of the PTO. As a matter of fact, I'm trying to think when the last time [was] we had a president of the PTO whose kids were on the fast track in Advanced Placement. I don't think we've had one in quite a few years."

She did note, however, that there were "a lot of parents on the [district-wide] school board whose kids are in the Advanced Placement classes." Interestingly, in the Plainview school district, the school board and the central administration, and not the school-site councils such as the PTO advisory board, have the power to change curricular and instructional programs — the areas most related to detracking reform — in the schools.

Furthermore, despite the past president's assertion that the Advanced Placement parents do not run the PTO advisory board, the board members we interviewed told us they were unwilling to challenge the pro-Advanced Placement stance of the principal. Still, several of the PTO board members said they believed there was too much emphasis on Advanced Placement at Plainview, and that they were at times uncomfortable with the principal's constant bragging about the number of Advanced Placement classes the school offers, the number of students taking Advanced Placement exams, and the number of students who receive 3's, 4's, or 5's on these exams. Some of these parents said that, in their opinion, a heavy load of Advanced Placement classes is too stressful for high school students; others said the curriculum in the Advanced Placement classes is boring rote memorization. But none of these parents had ever challenged the principal in his effort to boost the number of Advanced Placement classes offered and students enrolling in them. According to one mother on the PTO board:

> I think parents have seen that there are so many pressures in the world, they realize that this is high school and they're fed up with all the competition. At the same time they know you have to play the game, you know. . . . And again, it's hard to evaluate with some of the top, top students, you know, what's appropriate. . . . I think a lot of this has to do with Plainview as a community, too. Now, for example, where I live right here is in Fillburn, and that is a more upscale community [within the Plainview district]. Two houses from me is the Doner school district, which is a community of wealthier homes, wealthier people, many of whom have children in private schools.

During interviews, most of the not-quite-elite parents at all of the schools in our study discussed their awareness of the demands that families with high economic and cultural capital placed on the schools. They cited these demands as reasons why they themselves did not challenge the push for more Advanced Placement or gifted classes and why they were not supporters of detracking efforts — even when they suspected that such changes might be beneficial for their own children. For instance, at Grant High School, the chair of the language arts department formed a parent support group to focus on issues of tracking and detracking. This group consisted mostly of parents of students in the regular and honors classes, with only a handful of parents of very advanced students in the highest track. The department chair said she purposefully postponed "the fight" with more of the advanced parents. "We thought if we could get a group of parents who are just as knowledgeable . . . as we were, they should be the ones that become the advocates with the other parents. So that's probably our biggest accomplishment this year is getting this group of parents that we have together." But one of the few parents of advanced students left the group because she said her concerns were not being addressed, and the advisory group disbanded the following spring.

We saw other examples of "not-quite-elite" buy-in at schools where middle-class minority parents had become advocates of tracking practices and opponents of detracking efforts, despite their lament that their children were often the only children of color in the high-track classes. For instance, a Black professional parent at Rolling Hills Middle School, whose two children were in the advanced program, noted that a growing number of African American parents in the district were upset with the racial composition of the nearly all-White "advanced" classes and the disproportionately Black "comprehensive" tracks within racially mixed schools. He said, "So you have segregation in a supposedly desegregated setting. So what it is, you have a growing amount of dissatisfaction within the African American community about these advanced programs that are lily White." Despite his dissatisfaction, this father explained that he is not against tracking per se. "I think tracking has its merits. I just think they need to be less rigid in their standards."

Similarly, at Green Valley High School, a rural West Coast school with a 43 percent White and 57 percent Latino student population, a professional, middle-class Latino couple who had sent their children to private elementary and middle schools before enrolling them in the public high school said that the students at Green Valley should be divided into three groups: those at the top, those in the middle, and those at the bottom. The father added that those students in the middle should be given more of a tech prep education, and that an alternative school might be good for a lot of kids who won't go to college.

Detracking Bribes

Another political practice employed by local elites in schools that are attempting detracking reforms is their use of symbolic capital to bribe the schools to give them some preferential treatment in return for their willingness to allow some small degree of detracking to take place. These detracking bribes tend to make detracking reforms very expensive and impossible to implement in a comprehensive fashion.

Bourdieu (in Harrison, 1993) would consider such detracking bribes to be symbolic of the irreversible character of gift exchange. In exchange for their political buy-in to the detracking efforts, elite parents must be assured that their children are still getting something more than other children. In the process of gift exchange, according to Bourdieu, gifts must be returned, but this return represents neither an exchange of equivalents nor a case of cash on delivery:

> What is returned must be both different in kind and deferred in time. It is within this space opened up by these two elements of non-identity [of the gifts] and temporality [deferred time] that strategic actions can be deployed through which either one actor or another tries to accumulate some kind of profit. The kind of profit accumulated is, of course, more likely to be either symbolic or social, rather than economic. (p. 39)

In the case of the detracking bribes, the elite parents tend to profit at the expense of broad-based reform and restructuring. Yet, detracking bribes take on a different shape and character in different schools, depending upon the bargaining power of the local elite parents and the school's resources. As Bourdieu notes, in the case of the gift exchange, it is the agent's sense of honor that regulates the moves that can be made in the game (Harrison, 1993).

For instance, at King Middle School, located in a large northeastern city, the bribe is the school itself — a well-funded magnet program with formal ties to a nearby college and a rich art program that is integrated into the curriculum. Because King is a school of choice for parents who live in the surrounding area of the city, it is in many ways automatically perceived to be "better than" regular neighborhood schools, where students end up by default. Still, an administrator noted that King must still work at getting elite parents to accept the heterogeneous grouping within the school: "The thing is to convince the parents of the strong students that [heterogeneous grouping] is a good idea and not to have them pull children out to put them in a gifted program. It is necessary to really offer them a lot. You need parent education, along with offering a rich program for the parents so that they don't feel their children are being cheated."

At Rolling Hills Middle School, where African American students are bused to this otherwise White, wealthy school, the detracking bribe comes in the form of the best sixth-grade teachers and a "heterogeneous" team of students, which is skewed toward a disproportionate number of advanced program students. For instance, the heterogeneous team is comprised of 50 percent "advanced" students, 25 percent "honors" students, and 25 percent "regular" students, while the sixth grade as a whole is only about one-third "advanced" students and about one-half "regular" students. Thus, detracking at Rolling Hills is feasible when it affects only one of four sixth-grade teams, and that one team enrolls a disproportionate number of advanced students and is taught by the teachers whom the local elite consider to be the best. The generosity of the "gifts" that the school gives the elite parents who agree to enroll their children in the heterogeneous team are such that this team has become high status itself. The "parent network" of local elites at this school now promotes the heterogeneous team and advises elite mothers of incoming sixth-graders to choose that team. According to one wealthy White parent, "the heterogeneous team is 'hand-picked'." Another White parent whose daughter is on the heterogeneous team noted, "It's also been good to know that it's kind of like a private school within a public school. And that's kind of fair, I hate to say that, but it's kind of a fair evaluation."

Of course, Rolling Hills does not have enough of these "gifts" to bribe all of the local elite parents to place their children on a heterogeneous team. In other words, Rolling Hills will never be able to detrack the entire school as long as the cost of the bribe remains so high and the elite parental profit is so great. By definition, the "best" teachers at any given school are scarce; there are not enough of them to go around. In addition, the number of Advanced Placement students in the school is too small to assure that more heterogeneous teams could be created with the same skewed proportion of advanced, honors, and comprehensive tracks.

At Grant High School, the bribe for detracking the marine science program consists of this unique science offering, coupled with the school's excellent science and math departments and one of the two best music programs in the city. These are commodities that elite parents cannot get in other schools — urban or suburban. As one teacher explained, "So what options do these parents have? Lift their kids out of Grant, which they love? They can't get a science program like this anywhere else in the city." Although the school itself is highly tracked, especially in the history department, the marine science classes enroll students from all different tracks. A marine science teacher noted that parents of the advanced students never request that their kids be placed in separate classes because curricula in this program are both advanced and unique.

Interestingly, the detracking bribe at Liberty High, as the school moved toward the ninth-grade English/social studies core classes, was to be smaller class sizes and ongoing staff development. Unfortunately, the district administration withheld much of the promised funding to allow the school to deliver these gifts to the parents of high-track students. Whether or not these parents were ever committed to this bribe — whether they thought the school was offering them enough in return — is not really clear. What we do know is that the principal who offered the gift was, as we mentioned, recently "let go" by the district. His departure may have been the ultimate bribe with the local elites, because, as Bourdieu (in Harrison, 1993) argues, the kind of profit accumulated is, of course, more likely to be either symbolic or social, rather than economic.

Conclusions

When our research team began this study in 1992, we initially focused on what was happening *within* the racially mixed schools we were to study. Yet as we visited these schools, it became increasingly evident to us that the parents had a major impact on detracking reform efforts. Over the course of the last three years, we came to appreciate not only the power of this impact but its subtleties as well. In turning to the literature on elites and cultural capital, we gained a deeper understanding of the barriers educators face in their efforts to detrack schools.

As long as elite parents press the schools to perpetuate their status through the intergenerational transmission of privilege that is based more on cultural capital than "merit," educators will be forced to choose between equity-based reforms and the flight of elite parents from the public school system.

The intent of this article is not simply to point fingers at the powerful, elite parents or the educators who accommodate them at the ten schools we studied.

We understand that these parents are in many ways victims of a social system in which the scarcity of symbolic capital creates an intense demand for it among those in their social strata. We also recognize the role that the educational system writ large — especially the higher education system — plays in shaping their actions and their understanding of what they must do to help their children succeed.

Still, we hope that this study of ten racially mixed schools undertaking detracking reform is helpful to educators and policymakers who struggle to understand more clearly the political opposition to such reform efforts. Most importantly, we have learned that in a democratic society, the privilege, status, and advantage that elite students bring to school with them must be carefully deconstructed by educators, parents, and students alike before meaningful detracking reforms can take place.

References

Beare, H. (1993). Different ways of viewing school-site councils: Whose paradigm is in use here? In H. Beare & W. L. Boyd (Eds.), *Restructuring schools: An international perspective on the movement to transform the control and performance of schools* (pp. 200–214). Washington, DC: Falmer Press.

Boggs, C. (1984). *The two revolutions: Gramsci and the dilemmas of western Marxism.* Boston: South End Press.

Bourdieu, P. (1973). Cultural reproduction and social reproduction. In R. Brown (Ed.), *Knowledge, education, and cultural change* (pp. 487–501). New York: Harper & Row.

Bourdieu, P. (1977). *Outline of a theory of practice.* Cambridge, Eng.: Cambridge University Press.

Bourdieu, P. (1984). *Distinction: A social critique of the judgment of taste.* Cambridge, MA: Harvard University Press.

Bourdieu, P., & Passeron, J. C. (1977). *Reproduction in education, society and culture.* Beverly Hills, CA: Sage.

Bourdieu, P., & Passeron, J. C. (1979). *The inheritors: French students and their relation to culture.* Chicago: University of Chicago Press.

Bourdieu, P., & Wacquant, L. J. D. (1992). *An invitation to reflexive sociology.* Chicago, IL: University of Chicago Press.

Delpit, L. (1995). *Other people's children: Cultural conflict in the classroom.* New York: New Press.

DiMaggio, P. (1979). Review essay: On Pierre Bourdieu. *American Journal of Sociology, 84,* 1460–1472.

Domhoff, W. G. (1983). *Who rules America now? A view for the 80s.* Englewood Cliffs, NJ: Prentice-Hall.

Domhoff, W. G. (1990). *The power elite and the state: How policy is made in America.* New York: A. deGruyter.

Gramsci, A. (1971). *Selections from the prison notebooks.* New York: International Publishers.

Harker, K. (1984). On reproduction, habitus and education. *British Journal of Sociology of Education, 5*(2), 117–127.

Harrison, P. R. (1993). Bourdieu and the possibility of a postmodern sociology. *Thesis Eleven, 35,* 36–50.

Lareau, A. (1989). *Home advantage.* London: Falmer Press.

McIntosh, P. (January/February, 1992). White privilege: Unpacking the invisible knapsack. *Creation Spirituality,* pp. 33–35.

Mills, C. W. (1956). *The power elite.* London: Oxford University Press.

Oakes, J. (1985). *Keeping track: How schools restructure inequalities.* New Haven, CT: Yale University Press.

Oakes, J., Oraseth, T., Bell, R., & Camp, P. (1990). *Multiplying inequalities: The effects of race, social class, and tracking on opportunities to learn mathematics and science.* Santa Monica, CA: Rand.

Oakes, J., Lipton, M., & Jones, M. (1995, April). *Changing minds: Deconstructing intelligence in detracking schools.* Paper presented at the annual meeting of the American Educational Research Association, San Francisco.

Oakes, J., & Wells, A. S. (1995, April) *Beyond sorting and stratification: Creative alternatives to tracking in racially mixed secondary schools.* Paper presented at the annual meeting of the American Educational Research Association, San Francisco.

Thompson, J. B. (1990). *Ideology and modern culture.* Stanford, CA: Stanford University Press.

Useem, B. (1990, April). *Social class and ability group placement in mathematics in transition to seventh grade: The role of parental involvement.* Paper presented at the annual meeting of the American Educational Research Conference, Boston.

Wells, A. S., & Crain, R. L. (1992). Do parents choose school quality or school status? A sociological theory of free-market education. In P. W. Cookson (Ed.), *The choice controversy* (pp. 65–82). Newbury Park, CA: Corwin Press.

Welner, K., & Oakes, J. (1995, April). *Liability grouping: The new susceptibility of school tracking systems to legal challenges.* Paper presented at the annual meeting of the American Educational Research Association, San Francisco.

Yonesawa, S., Williams, E., & Hirshberg, D. (1995, April). *Seeking a new standard: Minority parent and community involvement in detracking schools.* Paper presented at the annual meeting of the American Educational Research Association, San Francisco.

An earlier version of this article was presented at the American Educational Research Association's 1995 Annual Meeting in San Francisco.

[30]

Racial Stratification and Education in the United States: Why Inequality Persists

JOHN U. OGBU
University of California, Berkeley

The primary objective of this article is to explain (1) the persistence of inequality between blacks and whites in spite of the changes that have taken place in the opportunity structure since 1960; and (2) why a gap persists in the school performances of the two racial groups. I argue that inequality persists for two reasons. The first is that changes have occurred mainly in one aspect of racial stratification, barriers in opportunity structure, but not in other domains; moreover, the changes have been uneven in the black community, favoring middle-class blacks. The other reason is that white treatment of blacks has been the target of public policies and intervention efforts but not black responses to racial stratification. I argue that the school-performance gap persists because the forces of racial stratification—white treatment and black responses—that created it continue to some degree. However, before explaining why the inequality and school-performance gap persist, I define what I mean by social stratification and distinguish class from racial stratification. One implication of my distinction, which is reflected in subsequent analysis, is that racial stratification between blacks and whites has not been changed to class stratification. Therefore, it is not meaningful to call any segment of the black population in the United States "underclass." This article is not about public policy or intervention; however, readers can arrive at their own conclusions about both.

INTRODUCTION

I have heard both white and black Americans on several occasions ask (1) why racial inequality persists and (2) why black Americans continue to lag in school performance and educational attainment after all the improvements in race relations since 1960. They point to new employment opportunities in the private and public sectors for blacks who have a good education, and to the growing number of middle-class blacks. The belief that *things should be different now* because of improved opportunity structure can be seen in the number of black and white social scientists asserting that social class, rather than race, is now the important factor determining the life chances of black Americans.[1] They further argue that the emergence of an "underclass" phenomenon is the reason for the current problems facing blacks in education, employment, housing, and the like.

The shift from race to class explanation of the economic, educational, and social problems is attractive to both white Americans and middle-class

Teachers College Record Volume 96, Number 2, Winter 1994

0161–4681–94/9602/264$1.50/0

black Americans. For the whites it is compatible with their model of the United States as a society stratified by class. For middle-class blacks it gives a sense of achievement and reinforces their eagerness to distance themselves from those who have not made it or cannot make it. In the past the problem was "racism" and was blamed on whites; today the problem is "poverty" and is blamed on the underclass. A closer examination of the situation indicates, however, that the changes in opportunity structure have not gone far enough or lasted long enough to undo instrumental barriers, let alone other untargeted barriers of racial stratification, and that class has not replaced race as the chief determinant of the life chances of black Americans.

In this article I will argue that the racial inequality persists because changes have occurred mainly in one aspect of racial stratification, in barriers in opportunity structure, but not in other domains; moreover, middle-class and college-educated blacks have been and continue to be the beneficiaries of "a sponsored social mobility" in a labor-market and status mobility system that has not yet become color-blind. Another reason is that mainly white treatment of blacks has been targeted for change but not black responses to racial stratification. I also argue that the school-performance gap persists because the forces of racial stratification that created the gap in the first place continue to maintain it to some degree. Before taking up these two tasks I will define social stratification and distinguish racial stratification from stratification by social class.

CLASS STRATIFICATION VERSUS RACIAL STRATIFICATION

WHAT IS SOCIAL STRATIFICATION?

When people talk about black-white inequality they often talk in terms of class inequality. But as I will argue, the inequality between blacks and whites is one not of class stratification but of racial stratification. A part of the reason for thinking that it is a class problem lies in the simplistic definition of social stratification and the tendency to confuse social stratification with social inequality and social ranking. Conventional definitions of social stratification with emphasis on the instrumental or economic aspect of stratification, coupled with the cult of quantification in some schools of thought, have resulted in the neglect of symbolic and relational aspects of social stratification.

It is not evident from the literature that social inequality is not the same thing as social stratification. For this reason, it is important to start with this distinction. Social inequality is a universal phenomenon; social stratification is not. The most common bases for social inequality are age and sex. Social ranking of individuals, which exists in stratified societies, should also be distinguished from social stratification. The ranking of individuals *as individuals* does not constitute or result in social stratification.

A society is stratified *when and only when* its individual members from different social groups are ranked on the basis of their membership in specific social groups that are also ranked, or when they are placed in such ranked social groups. It is always groups that are hierarchically ranked in social stratification, not individuals. Social stratification, then, is an arrangement of social groups or social categories in a hierarchical order of subordination and domination in which some groups so organized have unequal access to the fundamental resources of society.[2]

A stratified society is a society in which there is a differential relationship between members of its constituent groups and the society's fundamental resources, so that *some people (e.g., white Americans), by virtue of their membership in particular social groups, have almost unimpaired access to the strategic resources,* while *some other people (e.g., black Americans), by virtue of their own membership in other social groups, have various impediments in their access to the same strategic or fundamental resources.* In addition, the different social groups in the hierarchy are separated by cultural and invidious distinctions that serve to maintain social distance between them. In a stratified society there is usually an overarching ideology, a folk or/and scientific "theory" embodying the dominant group's rationalizations or explanations of the hierarchical ordering of the groups.[3] Subordinate social groups do not necessarily accept the rationalizations of the system; however, they are not entirely free from its influence.[4]

There are several types of social stratification that may coexist within the same society, such as American society. They include social class, ethnic, racial, caste, and gender stratifications. The bases for formation of the different types of stratification are economic status, cultural heritage, and social honor or esteem. Different systems of stratification may be compared with regard to the following features: basis or reasons for stratification (from the society or dominant group's point of view), presumed source of the factor on which stratification is based (such as whether it is extrinsic or intrinsic to the groups and their members), mode of recruitment of members, status summation, mobility across strata, symbols of identity, and degree of internal stratification.[5] In this article I focus only on social class and racial stratifications.

CLASS STRATIFICATION

Conventional Perspectives

There is no commonly accepted definition of class, although we can generally distinguish between two perspectives: Marxist and non-Marxist.[6]

In the Marxist view, social class refers to a group's relation to the means of production and power struggle.[7] The ideas of "class conflict," "class struggle," and "economic exploitation" are important ingredients in the Marxist notion of class stratification. There are difficulties in using the Marxist class perspective to explain racial inequality in the United States.

One problem is that the Marxist framework is so dependent on relation to means of production and economic status that it ignores the existence of other types of social stratification. Some justify the lack of recognition of other forms of stratification by claiming that the ultimate source of inequality in U.S. society is corporate capitalism. The latter makes social class the fundamental form of stratification and inequality because it is based on economic differences and exploitation. They argue that racism, castism, and sexism are merely expressions of economic or class inequality.[8] The problem with this view is that anthropologists have documented the existence of caste and other forms of stratification in precapitalist societies and in societies without corporate capitalism.[9] Furthermore, class stratification based on economic status and stratification based on noneconomic factors can and do coexist in the United States, Britain, India, Japan, and elsewhere.[10]

Another problem is that the Marxist framework erroneously assumes that the labor market is color-blind, caste-blind, and gender-blind. On the contrary, there is ample evidence that "the corporate economic market" has not historically treated blacks, other racial minorities, and females like their white male peers.[11] Nor do "exploited" white workers treat black and other racial minority co-workers as co-sufferers and equal. This has been fully documented in the case of Chinese workers in California, and in the case of black workers nationwide.[12]

For non-Marxists, social classes are synonymous with socioeconomic status (SES) groups. A social class refers to a segment of society's population differentiated by education, occupation, and income, the interaction of which is believed to result in a particular life-style and a set of power relations. By defining social classes as SES groups, researchers usually assume that individuals who meet the criteria of their class index (namely, education, income, and jobs—instrumental criteria) belong to the same social class (e.g., upper class, middle class, working class, lower class, underclass, etc.) *and* that the individuals so included will manifest some assumed appropriate class behavior. The main research approach is *correlational* because of the belief that members of the same SES group will manifest the same values and patterns of behavior.[13]

One problem in applying class stratification to the analysis of racial inequality lies in the temporality of class membership in contrast to the permanence of racial group membership. Consider, for example, that on July 19, 1982, Dan Rather reported on CBS evening news that in one year,

1981, about 2 million Americans "fell" into or joined the underclass because their income slipped below the official poverty line. No such sudden mass recruitment has ever been reported between racially stratified groups. Furthermore, note that some of the 2 million "new recruits" of the underclass included retired middle-class people whose pension income fell below the poverty line because of inflation. I do not believe that these "former" middle-class Americans would immediately assume underclass values and behaviors. The new recruits to the underclass also included temporarily unemployed skilled workers whose unemployment benefits ran out. They, too, would not suspend their own values and behaviors to take up those of the underclass "temporarily" until they returned to their former life-style when the economy improved. So assigning people to different social classes, especially to the underclass, because of income and a few other instrumental criteria at a particular point in time may not be very meaningful.

We encounter more serious problems when people from different ethnic, racial, caste, and gender groups are lumped into the same SES groups because they have similar education, jobs, and wages. It is quite possible that the members of the different groups differ in some other ways that interfere with the influence the measured values and behaviors assumed to be determined by SES.

An Alternative Perspective

Class stratification is but one type of stratification. Its distinguishing feature is that *it is based on economic status, an acquired characteristic.*[14] Because the basis for membership in class groups can be acquired by an individual during a lifetime, social classes are open entities. Although they are more or less permanent, the entities have no clear boundaries; furthermore, their membership is not permanent because people are continually moving in and out of them. Children can move up or down the different class strata and thereby can belong to different strata than their parents. Furthermore, children of an interclass mating can affiliate with the class of either parent. In a system of social class, occupational, social, and political positions are often based on training and ability rather than ascriptive criteria—at least this appears to be the case in the United States. Vertical mobility, upward or downward, from one ranked stratum to another is legitimated in a class system. Usually, there are built-in means of achieving such mobility.

RACIAL STRATIFICATION

Racial stratification is the hierarchical organization of *socially defined "races" or groups* (as distinct from biologically defined "races" or groups) on the basis of assumed inborn differences in *status honor* or *moral worth*, symbolized in the United States by skin color. The amount of the status honor that members of a given racial group are purported to have is usually determined by the value that members of the dominant group attach to skin color and is interpreted by them as an inherent or intrinsic part of the subordinate racial group and its individual members. The latter are believed to possess this lifelong attribute already at birth. This is in contrast to the extrinsic nature of the attributes of social classes and their members (e.g., economic status), which can be acquired or lost during a lifetime.[15]

Recruitment into the racial strata, that is, the ranked racial groups, is by birth and descent. Racial groups are permanently organized hierarchically into more or less endogamous groups. In the past, marriage between blacks and whites was prohibited; even now that it is legally permitted the rule of descent has not changed. There is *a culturally sanctioned rule* that children of black and white mating, within or outside marriage, must affiliate with blacks. Throughout the history of the United States, all children of known black-white matings have been automatically defined as black by law and/or custom. In very rare cases do some blacks covertly become whites, through the painful and *nonlegitimated process* of "passing."[16] There have been some attempts in recent years by some individuals to have the U.S. courts reclassify them from black to white or vice-versa.[17] Thus, it is not very meaningful to point to increasing interracial marriage as evidence that race no longer matters. In a system of racial stratification people are prohibited from changing their group membership. The prohibition is usually rationalized in the dominant group's ideology. In short, membership in racially stratified groups is permanent. The permanent racial groups are visible, recognized, and named. Social integration may occur, but assimilation is *not* an option, at least for black Americans.

In a racially stratified society, each racial stratum has its own social classes. The social classes of component strata are parallel but not equal. The reasons for the unequal social classes are that the origins of the classes may be different and that members of the racial groups do not have equal access to societal resources that enhance class development. For example, black Americans did not begin their social, occupational, and political differentiation because of differences in training, ability, or family background as did white Americans. Instead, blacks were initially collectively relegated to menial status as slaves without regard to individual differences. For almost a century after emancipation from slavery they also experienced a high degree of status summation. That is, their occupational and other roles depended more on their membership in a subordinate racial group than on individual education and ability. They were restricted from competing for desirable jobs and social positions. This is an important reason why black Americans are preoccupied with the civil rights "struggle" for equal social, economic, and political opportunities. Here is an important difference between blacks as a subordinate racial stratum and lower-class whites as a subordinate economic stratum. At least in the contemporary United States, there is no conscious feeling on the part of members of any social class in the general population that they belong to a corporate unity or that their common interests are different from those of other classes.[18] American lower-class people do not, for instance, share a collective perception of their social and economic difficulties as stemming from class subordination. Perhaps it is because of the absence of such perceptions and interpretations that I have not observed over the last thirty-two years white lower-class members engaged in a "collective struggle" for better employment, credit rating, housing, political participation, and other opportunities.[19] In contrast, most black Americans see racial barriers in employment, education, housing, and other areas as the primary causes of their menial positions and poverty.

Black Americans, like white Americans, are stratified by class but their social classes are not equal in development and they are qualitatively different. They are unequal in development because, as I have noted, blacks have had less access to jobs and training associated with class differentiation and mobility. As a result, until the 1960s, the people who made up the upper class among blacks were from a few professions, such as law, medicine, business, teaching, and preaching, with the last two comprising almost two-thirds of that class. These were professions that served primarily the needs of the black community. Blacks were largely excluded from other higher-paying professions such as architecture, civil engineering, accounting, chemistry, and management. Before 1960, the black upper class tended to overlap with the white middle-class segment and the black middle class overlapped with the white upper-lower class. The lower class among blacks was made up of an unstable working class, the unemployed, and the unemployable.[20]

The social classes among blacks are qualitatively different because the historical circumstances that created them and the structural forces that sustain them are different from those that created and sustained white social classes. I noted earlier the narrow base of black class differentiation during slavery. After slavery, racial barriers in employment—a job ceiling—continued for generations to limit their base of class differentiation and mobility.[21] These collective experiences resulted in the evolution of shared perceptions among blacks of all social classes that they lack equal opportunity with whites and that it is much more difficult for blacks to achieve economic and social self-betterment.[22]

Another reason for the qualitative difference is that before the civil rights revolution of the 1960s blacks were forced to live in ghetto-like communities.[23] Whites created and maintained the ghettos as clearly defined residential areas of the cities to which they restricted the black population.

Blacks of all social classes were forced to share the ghetto life. This shared involuntary residential experience generated a shared feeling of oppression that transcended class boundaries.[24]

RACIAL STRATIFICATION AND INEQUALITY

RACIAL STRATIFICATION IN THE UNITED STATES: THE TWO SIDES OF THE PHENOMENON

In the last section I noted the differences between class stratification and racial stratification. In this section I will focus on racial stratification in the United States. Specifically, I want to discuss the factors that make up the stratification—treatments of blacks by whites and responses of blacks to their treatment. White treatments and black responses may be grouped in three domains: *instrumental, expressive, and symbolic and relational.* I have described them in detail elsewhere,[25] and will provide only a summary here.

White Treatments

White instrumental treatments take several forms: economic, political, social, and educational. I use the concept of *job ceiling* to show how economic discrimination works. A job ceiling consists of both formal statutes and informal practices followed by white Americans to limit black Americans' access to desirable occupations, to truncate their opportunities, and to channel narrowly the potential returns they can expect from their education and abilities.[26] Whites have historically used the job ceiling to deny *qualified blacks* free and equal competition for the jobs they desire and to exclude them from certain highly desirable jobs that require education and in which education pays off. Whites based their action on (1) the belief that blacks were incapable of doing certain jobs and (2) the idea that permitting blacks in certain positions would result in social equality.[27] The result was that before 1960, blacks *were not permitted* to obtain their proportional share of such jobs. Further, as a consequence, employment inequality developed in which a disproportionate portion of the black population was restricted to menial jobs below the job ceiling. Other discriminatory instrumental treatment of blacks resulted in inequality in housing, political participation, and education.[28]

Symbolic and relational treatments have to do with white denigration (put down) of blacks culturally, linguistically, intellectually, and socially. Whites tend to believe that there is some undesirable biological, linguistic, cultural, and intellectual inferiority that sets blacks apart. Such beliefs were strong enough that in the past white Americans took steps to protect themselves from contamination by erecting barriers between themselves and black Americans through prohibition of intermarriage and through residential and social segregation. Whites also used blacks for scapegoating and psychological relief by projecting onto them undesirable traits that created aversion to blacks and the belief that they are inferior. The aversion and belief in racial inferiority are probably important reasons for forcing children born of "mixed couples" to affiliate with blacks.

Black Responses

Equally important in maintaining racial stratification are black Americans' perceptions and responses, which also fall into *instrumental, expressive,* and *relational* domains.

Instrumentally, blacks developed their own folk theory to explain how American society works differently for them compared with whites. Public pronouncements aside, blacks still believe that there is an institutionalized discrimination against them, so that a black person cannot advance as far as a white person; nor do they really believe that black people get ahead merely by getting an education or acting like a white person.[29] This was brought home to me in 1969 while attending a workshop on black history and culture at the University of California, Los Angeles. One of my teachers, a black actress, described an incident that expressed this view. She said that she was trying to get blacks into a training program for technicians in the movie industry. One applicant was rejected because she did not speak standard English. The actress said that the applicant was rejected because of racial discrimination and insisted on her admission. She explained that before the late 1960s black people who spoke standard English could not get certain jobs in the movie industry and could not rent or buy homes in parts of Westwood. She concluded by saying that inability to speak standard English or behave like mainstream white Americans in other ways was not the reason for lack of self-advancement among blacks.

During my ethnographic research in Stockton, California (1968–1970), I found similar beliefs among middle-class blacks. The beliefs were expressed, for example, in their stories about the difficulty they faced in trying to buy homes in the more desirable neighborhoods. In 1963 the average cost of homes in North Stockton neighborhoods was about $16,500. Many blacks who were refused the right to buy homes in those neighborhoods were professionals, including teachers, social workers, and medical doctors. They had an average annual family income of about $12,000, far above the city average. They had completed median school years far above the city average. Many white families living in those neighborhoods had incomes well below $12,000 and much less education.[30] Twenty black families successfully crossed the residential caste line in 1963 by buying homes directly from civil rights–minded white residents. Some of these black pioneer residents whom I interviewed in 1969 and 1970 repeatedly recounted the stiff white opposition to their presence and the personal indignities they suffered after moving into their new homes.[31]

Because of such collective experiences of discrimination, blacks appear to believe that they cannot make it merely by following rules of behavior for achievement or the cultural practices that work for white people. So they developed their own "folk theory" of "making it" that goes beyond the strategy of pursuing educational credentials for mainstream employment strategies or saving money to be able to live in desirable neighborhoods, to include several *survival strategies.* Among the survival strategies that I have observed locally and nationally is "collective struggle" or collective action to change the rules that do not work well for them in education, employment, housing, and other areas. The belief that there is an institutionalized discrimination and the use of collective struggle to eliminate, reduce, or circumvent the barriers so that individual blacks can have access to jobs, housing, and so forth, commensurate with their training and ability continue to some degree.

Black symbolic response to white denigration of their languages and cultures was not simply the adoption of white language and culture. Nor was it merely the development of a different language (e.g., black English vernacular) and culture, or the retention of African cultural and language elements. It also included the development of a distinct black cultural/language *frame of reference* that is more or less oppositional vis-à-vis what they perceived as the white cultural/language frame of reference. Because black customary behaviors and speech are often erroneously attributed to their lower-class or underclass status, I will discuss their origins and form in detail.

The customary behaviors and communication patterns of blacks fall under what I call "secondary cultural/language differences vis-à-vis white American culture and language."[32] Usually, in a racial stratification, the cultural/language differences that existed at the beginning of racial domination are reinterpreted by the subordinate racial group in opposition to the customary behaviors of the dominant group for several reasons. One is that the subordinate group may be prohibited from behaving like the dominant group, forced to do so, or denied the rewards that go with such behaviors. Black Americans experienced all three treatments.

Black Americans brought from Africa precontact cultural/language differences with white Americans.[33] Later, however, they developed secondary cultural differences because of the way they perceived and interpreted their "social reality." Both during slavery and in postslavery subordination, blacks developed some distinct customary behaviors and assumptions permeating various domains of their lives, including religion, subsistence, language and communication, politics, folklore, and social relations. These were often in opposition to white American customary behaviors and assumptions in the same areas.

Black responses in religion and language will serve as examples. Reverend Calvin Marshall described in an interview with *Time* magazine the perceived "social reality" giving rise to the black version of Christianity and church institution. According to him,

> the man [White Americans] systematically killed your (i.e., black) language, killed your culture, tried to kill your soul, tried to blot you out—but somewhere along the way he gave us Christianity and gave it to us to enslave us. But it freed us because we understood things about it and we made it work for us in ways that it never worked for him.[34]

Holt suggests that black Americans developed their church into an institution within which to resist "the dehumanizing oppression, degradation, and suffering of slavery."[35] The black church promoted self-worth, dignity, and a viable identity among them and helped them overcome their fears. It became a forum where blacks developed unique language codes and communication styles to conceal their true feelings and aspirations from whites, deceive whites, maintain their sense of collective identity and self-worth, and put down whites "without Whites knowing that they are the real objects of ridicule."[36]

Black English vernacular provides another example of the emergence of an oppositional frame of reference. During slavery blacks were forced to speak English rather than their native African languages because white slave owners feared that blacks might conspire to revolt. However, the slaves learned to speak English in such a way that the slave-owners *still* did not know what was going on.[37] The slaves used certain words that had different and opposite meanings to them and to the slave-owners to keep the latter off guard. This practice continued after slavery so that even today blacks still use their English language to keep white society off guard. For example, a black person may use the word *bad* when he actually means *good*.

Under racial stratification the subordinate racial group develops an oppositional cultural adaptation by inventing new customary behaviors with new codes or norms *and* by reinterpreting its presubordination customary behaviors. Both are accomplished through "cultural inversion." Cultural inversion is a process whereby subordinate group members come to define certain forms of behaviors, events, symbols, and meanings as inappropriate for them because these are characteristic of their oppressors. At the same time they define other forms of behaviors, events, symbols, and meanings, often the opposite, as appropriate for them. What is appropriate for racial minority group members tends to be defined in opposition to what is considered appropriate for the dominant racial group, their "oppressors." For this reason, the issue of cultural and language differences between the two racial strata is no longer merely that members of each group behave or speak differently so that they do not understand each other. It is not merely that members of the subordinate racial group do not know or do not have access to the cultural practices of the dominant group. Rather, the issue is that members of the oppressed or subordinate racial group have come to ascribe *secondary meanings* to the differences in the customary/language behaviors and, as a result, the latter have become symbols of affiliation or opposition. That is, the minorities now interpret their members' participation in certain activities, behaving in certain ways, possessing certain objects, expressing certain ideas, or being in certain situations either as evidence of a bona fide membership in the minority group or as evidence that the individual has lost his or her black identity and has "assimilated" into white cultural identity or as evidence of disloyalty and collusion with the enemy.[38]

The target areas in which an oppositional cultural frame of reference is applied appear to be those traditionally defined as prerogatives of white Americans, first defined by whites themselves and then acceded to by blacks. These are areas in which it was long believed that only whites could perform well, and few blacks were actually given the opportunity to try or were rewarded well when they succeeded. They are also areas in which the criteria for performance have been established by white Americans, and competence in performance is judged by white people or their black representatives, and reward for performance is determined by white people according to white criteria. Intellectual performance (IQ test scores), scholastic performance, and performance in high-status jobs in mainstream economy represent such areas.[39]

The evidence for this problem comes from autobiographies, accounts of personal experiences, and research among blacks in academia and in the corporate world. A number of authors explicitly state that they themselves or other blacks they know or have studied view successful participation in mainstream culture or the white cultural frame of reference as threatening to their cultural identity.[40] According to Taylor, some blacks in corporations find it in their best interests to embrace overtly the behavior of whites, but "the flight into White role behavior is . . . highly costly" because for a black person to be accepted in the top echelons of corporations, he or she must think, manage, behave like a majority person and "be white, except in external appearance."[41] Writing about black female executives, Campbell states that these women are forced to pull away from their black cultural identity, and consciously modify their speech, laughter, walk, mode of dress, and choice of car to conform to mainstream requirements. And as the women rise in the corporate ladder "they become isolated from those in their old world."[42] Davis and Watson also repeatedly remark on the "phenomenal estrangement of corporate Blacks from Black cultural traditions, their own families and communities and their own pre-corporate life styles, ways of dressing and sense of humor."[43] We shall see later how this problem is perceived in education.

It is true that today many black Americans appear to behave like mainstream white Americans in many areas of life and that many speak standard English. I have also found that many of the same people behave and talk differently—"behave black" and "talk black"—in appropriate contexts. But the point I wish to stress is that other black Americans who practice mostly the black customary behaviors and talk black vernacular most of the time are not doing so because of their lower-class or underclass status. The differences between blacks and whites in customary behaviors and language are not merely class differences. Nor are the differences confined to adolescents. They are found among adults in the community.[44]

For my purpose, the most significant feature of black relational responses to racial stratification is the degree of distrust of white Americans. The history of black-white relationships abounds with many episodes that have left blacks with the sense that they cannot trust white Americans or trust the societal institutions controlled by whites.[45]

CIVIL RIGHTS REVOLUTION, SOCIAL CHANGE, AND PERSISTENCE OF RACIAL INEQUALITY

CHANGES IN WHITE TREATMENT

People think that the civil rights revolution of the 1960s changed the opportunity structure of black Americans. For that reason, blacks and whites ought to be equal by now. Some researchers compile statistics from the census to study the gap between blacks and whites in education, high-status jobs, income, housing, and middle-class status and they often find that the gap is not closing.[46]

A favorite explanation of the persisting inequality is that it is now due to class status, rather than racial barriers. According to this school of thought, macroeconomic changes (e.g., "industrial restructuring") have eliminated many unskilled jobs that blacks formerly did and created new types of jobs requiring education and skills that blacks do not have. Furthermore, the exodus of educated and middle-class blacks from the black community or ghetto has created a concentration of poverty that, in turn, has produced an underclass population not capable of acquiring the education and skills with which to take advantage of the new job opportunities.[47]

One should reject this explanation because it is not based on studies of *actual experiences* of black Americans in the opportunity structure. Rather, it is based on studies of "changes in American institutions," "economic restructuring," and the assumed new work-skill requirements. Research focusing on actual black experience shows that blacks still face employment barriers where economic restructuring has taken place and where it has not; that well-educated blacks and those with less education face more employment barriers than do their white peers; and that the passage of legislation for equal opportunity is one thing, and implementation and compliance are another. Moreover, blacks who are employed still face more barriers in advancement.[48]

An alternative explanation considers several factors. First, the civil rights revolution of the 1960s did not improve the opportunity structure for all segments of the black community. The people who benefited most through "a sponsored social mobility" are college-educated and middle-class blacks. They were and continue to be the target of affirmative action and other special programs in education, employment, promotions, positions in community programs, special appointments, and the like. Blacks without college education, lower-class blacks, and/or inner-city blacks are largely unhelped by these programs.[49]

Second, the civil rights revolution did not usher in an era of color-blind labor-market forces causing blacks to be hired above the job ceiling because they have the education and ability or skills required by the restructured economy. *A close examination of the situation shows that black advancement since 1961 has been primarily due to noneconomic forces.* The evidence comes from case studies of hiring practices and treatment of blacks in specific industries as well as in federal, state, and local government agencies throughout the nation. Indeed, the evidence suggests that economic restructuring and mainstream market forces had almost nothing to do with the changes in black employment.

What are the nonmarket forces and noneconomic forces that have brought about gains in black employment since 1961? They include *executive actions* (e.g., President Kennedy's Committee on Equal Employment Opportunity, 1961; affirmative action programs); *legislative actions* (e.g., Title VII of the Civil Rights Act of 1964; the war on poverty; etc.); *pressures applied by civil rights groups* and *collective struggle* of the black community (e.g., civil rights suits filed by the National Association for the Advancement of Colored People, boycotts and sit-ins, etc.); the *Vietnam War*, which caused labor shortages; *efforts by various public institutions*, such as public schools and universities, especially institutions receiving state and federal monies, to "racially balance" their personnel; and an increase in *social programs* for the poor and minorities.

Some noneconomic forces had direct or indirect impact on the employment practices of private business establishments, especially among those with federal contracts. It was largely because of these noneconomic factors that American corporations increased their recruitment visits to colleges and universities, including black colleges, beginning in the later part of the 1960s, to recruit black college graduates.[50] I observed the influence of the noneconomic forces during my ethnographic research in Stockton, California (1968–1970). At that time, Stockton public schools and other local agencies receiving state and federal funds periodically sent representatives to recruit Mexican-Americans from the Southwest and blacks from the South in order to meet their "racial/ethnic balance" requirements. The noneconomic forces still operate today in the public and private sectors under various concepts.

The effects of these noneconomic, nonmarket forces can be seen in the increases in black representation in high-level jobs. Thus, between 1960 and 1971 the number of blacks in the two top occupational categories nearly doubled.[51] In the top category, *the professional and technical occupations*, the increase was about 128 percent for blacks, whereas it was only 49 percent for the general population. In the second highest-paying occupational category—*managers, officials, and proprietors*—the number of blacks increased almost 100 percent, although the increase for all employees was only 23 percent. Most of the increases in black employment above the job ceiling happened after 1966, that is, after Title VII of the Civil Rights Act of 1964 became law. I conclude from these observations that blacks did not make their new advances because of normal market or economic forces or because mainstream employers decided to ignore race and change their hiring and promotion practices. In fact, subsequent studies of the experiences of blacks hired above the job ceiling show that many employers were merely complying with the law and that black employees were aware of this.[52]

Furthermore, studies of actual experiences of blacks on the job indicate that in many instances they are neither advancing nor getting adequate opportunity for on-the-job training for future advancement in comparison with their white peers.[53] This was also the experience of the "new middle-class" blacks working in *Fortune 1000 companies.*[54] In 1989 *The New York Times* reported complaints by black school superintendents that they were not evaluated as individuals on the basis of education, ability, and performance but as members of a collectivity—as blacks; black lawyers interviewed by Matuso in Washington, D.C., in 1989 complained that they lagged behind their white peers in opportunity structure. In a study of black elites, including university professors, Benjamin found that many still face "the color line" in advancement.[55] Individual black professionals write about their frustrations and in some cases the result is tragic. Consider the case of a black manager reported by Davis and Watson. The manager "was passed over for promotion three times—the last time by a less-educated, less experienced white male whom he had trained. The Black manager killed himself."[56] Other "racial" problems facing contemporary middle-class blacks have been reported by Cose.[57] I conclude from my own research and other studies focusing on actual experience of blacks that even among the highly educated and skilled, racial stratification is still a factor determining their instrumental treatment.

Some changes have also taken place in the symbolic and relational treatments of blacks. A poll conducted by *Newsweek* in 1978 showed that although whites' beliefs in black inferiority had been decreasing significantly since 1960, a large portion of whites still believed that blacks are inferior to whites. About 25 percent of the whites polled said that blacks had less intelligence than whites; about 15 percent thought that blacks were inferior to whites.[58] According to Sniderman and Prazza, some whites still believed this in the 1980s.[59] Intermarriage between blacks and whites, especially among highly educated blacks, is increasing; usually it is the well-educated black males who marry out.[60] It should be added that some of the black males marrying out are at times the only "successful" members of their own families. For example, we encountered one mother in my current ethnographic research who complained that the only one of her nine children who finished college married a white woman and disappeared; another black mother with six children told a similar story. Then, the offspring of the "mixed couples" are still compelled to affiliate with blacks. From the point of view of these mothers and other blacks in the community, interracial marriages are not necessarily a sign of positive change. Finally, blacks who move into "white communities" find that they face "assimilation blues."[61] The persistence of other symbolic and related treatment has been reported by Cose.[62]

CHANGES IN BLACK RESPONSES

There have also been some changes in black responses since the 1960s, but not always in the expected direction. Consequently, these changes have not really enhanced equality in terms of education, employment, and income or class status. In the instrumental domain, black response has varied. Among well-educated middle class blacks, some began to think that social class has replaced race in determining the life chances of blacks, and that equally *qualified* blacks and whites now have equal opportunity in employment, advancement, and remuneration. Often proponents of this view forget that they may owe their high-status positions to the nonmarket forces described earlier. For example, some may have been recruited to their positions because of "affirmative action" or "extraordinary opportunity" to recruit "underrepresented minorities." They may have been recruited because their institutions were directly or indirectly pressured to hire them. Although they have the academic and professional qualifications for their positions, the actual attainment of those positions may have been "sponsored." Other middle-class blacks continue to encounter racial barriers in employment, advancement, and remuneration; as such, they believe that race is still a significant factor.[63] As for the masses, most of whom have not experienced any significant improvements in their opportunity structure, they continue to respond instrumentally as before, often resorting to survival and alternative strategies, including drug dealing.[64]

The change in black symbolic response has also not all been in the expected direction. Prior to the 1960s, black quest for identity took at least three forms: accommodation and acquiescence, or at least nonovert opposition in the tradition of Booker T. Washington; ambivalence and opposition expressed in struggle for integration in the tradition of DuBois; and oppositional identity expressed in separatist movements in the tradition of Garvey and the Black Muslims.[65]

The civil rights mobilization of the 1960s increased and reinforced the oppositional qualities of black collective identity. For blacks the mobilization removed the stigma of being black, increased race pride, and generated much-needed ideology, namely, that "black is beautiful," to minimize the fear of other social costs to those black Americans who wanted to express openly or to be what they had always felt covertly. Public acknowledgement and expression of oppositional identity were not limited to activists or to the grass roots. It has reached every segment of the black community, although the change occurred more slowly in some segments. For example, I found during my research in Stockton (1968–1970) that middle-class blacks had difficulty identifying themselves as "black" or accepting the slogan "Black is beautiful" and wearing their hair "natural." When I returned to Stockton for a restudy eleven years later, this was no longer the case. Most middle-class blacks in the city identified themselves as black and were wearing their hair natural. Thus, whereas in 1969 when the Black Teachers Alliance was formed, fifty-five of the one hundred black teachers in the Stockton Unified School District did not join because the word "black" symbolized being "militant," by 1981 almost all the black teachers in the city were members of the alliance.

The change in the direction of opposition has permeated the work of black artists and scholars. Baker reports that in the field of theater there has been a replay of the course of some events that occurred during the Harlem Renaissance of the 1920s. At that time black dramatists stopped trying to please white audiences; they instead directed their attention to the black folk tradition and to contemporary issues of black life. He goes on to say that during the second half of the 1960s a significant portion of black Americans became disillusioned with the goals of integration, abandoned time-honored middle-class values, and instead adopted Black Power as a vehicle for spiritual liberation.[66] After the civil rights revolution, blacks also began to revise their history, so that new interpretations of the role and contributions of African and African-American heritages to American culture began to emerge.[67] At least among the masses, cultural and language frames of reference have probably not become less oppositional, as can be seen in some ethnographic studies.[68]

Two changes in relational responses are worth mentioning. Both are related to the so-called social dislocation of the ghetto.[69] It has been argued that with the decline of racial barriers, increase in employment opportunities in high-status jobs for blacks with college education and skills, and decline in housing discrimination, middle-class blacks moved out of the ghetto. The consequences are the dislocation of the ghetto, the concentration of poverty, and the emergence of the "underclass."

An alternative interpretation is that because blacks "were forced" to live in the ghetto for so long, some have come to interpret educational and economic success as "tickets" to disaffiliate with their community and to affiliate with mainstream whites, both physically and socially. Behavior of some middle-class blacks tends to create tension between "successful" ones who move out of or flee from the ghetto and the less successful ones who remain behind. Based on my ethnographic studies in the community, my impression is that people who remain in the ghetto, especially the youth, do not admire those who socially disaffiliate. Thus, the problem of role models for contemporary inner-city youths is not that there are no middle-class blacks physically resident as neighbors; rather the problem is that the people in the inner city interpret the social disaffiliation with the community negatively.[70]

PERSISTING CLASS ANALYSIS OF BLACK-WHITE INEQUALITY IN THE UNITED STATES

Neither the changes in the white treatments of blacks nor in the black responses are sufficient to move blacks and whites toward equality, even in the instrumental domain, which has been the focus of public policies and where most changes have occurred. But public policies have not had a significant impact in changing white treatments of blacks in the symbolic and relational domains. And public policies and intervention programs hardly recognize black instrumental, symbolic, and relational responses.

Class analysis, I contend, cannot throw much light on the persistence of racial inequality. But why does class analysis continue as the basis for explaining the persistence of the inequality? I have discussed some of the reasons elsewhere, and will summarize them here.[71] One reason lies partly in two misconceptions of the race situation in the United States. One misconception is the extension of European immigrants' experiences to racial minorities, especially involuntary minorities who did not come to the United States with expectations similar to those of European immigrants.

The other misconception is the confusion of socioeconomic success with "assimilation" into the mainstream white American society. There are, for instance, people who argue that when blacks acquire "basic cultural knowledge and specific educational skills" they will not only get better jobs than their parents but also become assimilated into the mainstream society and achieve full citizenship.[72] However, they present no evidence that white Americans *want* to assimilate blacks who have good education, skills, and good jobs. On the contrary, there is plenty of evidence that white Americans *do not want* to assimilate blacks. The latter was pointed out decades ago by Myrdal. According to him, white Americans consider black Americans to be *unassimilable* in the sense that it is not desirable to assimilate blacks in the way that European immigrants were assimilated.[73] As some contemporary middle-class blacks have learned when they tried to assimilate, assimilation is neither a matter of a black person's choice nor a pleasant experience.[74] Achieving socioeconomic success is not synonymous with assimilation and a minority person does not have to assimilate to be successful. From my comparative study of minority groups I have found that some groups (e.g., Chinese-Americans, East Indians, etc.) have achieved socioeconomic success without being assimilated.

Another reason for preferring class analysis is the influence of egalitarian ideology and the mythology of individualism, based primarily on white American experience. Maquet has correctly noted that such an ideology and such a mythology tend to form a screen that prevents their bearers from seeing the system that underlies their own behaviors in conforming to superior and inferior roles.[75] Still another reason is the belief that poverty is primarily the result of instrumental barriers: lack of access to good jobs, education, housing, and the like. Such instrumental barriers are, of course, the easiest target for public policy and remedial efforts. But this perception ignores the symbolic and relational barriers erected by whites against blacks as well as black people's own responses to such barriers.

I conclude from the preceding discussion that class analysis is not an adequate guide if one wants to understand why the inequality persists. The inequality between blacks and whites is due to racial stratification. Racial stratification does not rest alone on instrumental barriers erected by the whites; it also depends on white relational and symbolic treatments of blacks *and* on black Americans' own instrumental, relational, and symbolic responses. For these reasons, targeting and removing instrumental barriers will reduce but not entirely undo the racial stratification. Furthermore, to progress at a satisfactory pace toward equality, blacks, like some other minorities, must begin to distinguish between instrumental success and assimilation and between instrumental means or behaviors toward their goals and noninstrumental means or behaviors compromising their cultural identity.

EDUCATIONAL CONSEQUENCES OF RACIAL STRATIFICATION

CLASS ANALYSIS OF SCHOOL-PERFORMANCE GAP

As in the case of racial inequality in general, the preferred mode of analysis of the educational gap between blacks and whites is class.[76] While researchers may treat race as one "variable," there is usually no reference to racial stratification. Indeed, this concept does not appear in the index of some of the most influential books on public policies and programs in minority education since the 1960s.

We can identify two forms of class analysis corresponding to the non-Marxist and Marxist concepts of class stratification respectively: correlational and cultural reproduction/resistance analyses. In correlational analysis social class is equated with socioeconomic status (SES). Correlational analysts appear to believe that children's school success depends on appropriate family background or attributes that can be correlated with school adjustment and performance. Because middle-class children are more successful in school, these researchers assume that middle-class attributes are more conducive to school success than lower-class or underclass attributes. And since they classify most black children as belonging to the lower class, they attribute the lower school performance of black children to their lower-class or underclass background.[77]

One major difficulty with correlational studies is that they cannot explain why black and white children from similar social-class backgrounds perform differently in school. Correlational studies using black and white samples show two things: (1) within the black sample, as within the white sample, middle-class children do better in school and on standardized tests than do lower-class children; (2) however, when black children and white children from similar SES are compared, black children at every class level do less well than white children.[78] That correlational studies cannot explain the gap in the school performance of blacks and whites of similar social class is illustrated by the following study.

This was a study of a southeastern suburban elementary school located in an area where black households had higher educational attainment, better job status, and higher income than white households; yet the school performance of black children lagged behind that of the whites. Specifically, in this suburban community about twice as many black adults as whites had college degrees and about one and one-half times as many blacks as whites held managerial and professional jobs; black unemployment was almost the same as white unemployment. The average annual income of a black household was about 39.1 percent higher than the average annual income of a white household, a difference of about $10,000 per household in favor of blacks. In terms of class status, most black parents were of higher socioeconomic status than white parents. Still, black children lagged behind their white peers in the school district in academic achievement. Thus, in 1980–1981, the third-grade students at the elementary school (80 percent black), scored at the 2.6 grade equivalent level, or about the tenth percentile nationally, while the county or school district average was 3.1 in grade-level-equivalent score. In the same year, the fifth-grade students at the elementary school scored at 4.7 grade equivalent level or about the thirty-eighth percentile nationally, whereas the school district average was 5.2.[79]

The cultural reproduction/resistance school is usually associated with Marxist-oriented researchers. One version, which points to some resistance or opposition in the relationship between school culture and that of the students, suggests a more useful approach. As this theory is reformulated by Willis, working-class students fail in school because they consciously or unconsciouly reject academic work as being effeminate (recognizing manual labor as masculine and ideal). These students repudiate school by forming a counterculture, which eventually impedes their school success and their chances of getting high-status jobs after leaving school. Working-class students are said to reject school knowledge because they do not believe that the kind of education they are receiving will solve their problem of subordination.[80] The Willis study introduced "resistance" as a force of human agency in the process of the reproduction of class inequality through schooling. As Weis points out, this has helped researchers shift their attention to the day-to-day attitudes and behaviors or "lived culture" of students.[81] It is precisely because of the introduction of students and school personnel as human agents actively involved in the process of cultural reproduction or resistance that this kind of study is relevant to the educational problems of racially stratified groups.

However, although resistance theory goes some way toward explaining the school failure of working-class youths, it too has some problems when applied to racial minorities. For example, in her study of black youths in Philadelphia, Weis found a paradox: Black youths accepted academic work and schooling, but behaved in ways that ensured that they would not, and did not, succeed. Weis recognized the difficulty of explaining black students' behavior within the framework of social class and repeatedly referred to "racial struggle" in black American history. Nevertheless, she still ended up explaining the school failure of black youths within the framework of "class struggle," saying that the problem ultimately arises from "the material conditions" of blacks.[82]

There are two problems with the Marxist class analysis. One is that by and large Marxist researchers avoid explaining the discrepancies in the school performance of children from different racial/caste origins who belong to the same SES groups. Alternately, they erroneously treat the lower school performance of different types of subordinate groups as the result of resistance of an exploited working class. On the other hand, the cultural reproduction/resistance researchers are silent about the school success of Asian-American working-class students. On the whole, Marxist-oriented researchers do not have a satisfactory explanation for the paradox of both high educational aspirations and lower school performance among black students.

Cross-cultural comparisons suggest that class analyses do not shed much light on the educational experiences of racial and castelike minorities, not only in the United States but also in Britain, Japan, and elsewhere.[83] A more satisfactory approach must take into account the unique features of the stratification systems that distinguish racial minorities from social classes.

SCHOOL PERFORMANCE GAP TRANSCENDS TIME AND CLASS BOUNDARIES

An enduring educational gap is one major consequence of the racial stratification between blacks and whites. However, in contemporary thinking the tendency is to discuss the academic problems of black children as if they are the product of black underclass status, or inner-city environment, or both. The assumption is also that these are "new problems" that emerged when the "better class" of blacks moved out of the ghetto.[84] A closer look at the evidence suggests otherwise. The historical and persistent nature of the lower school performance of black children is well reflected in two school movements: *school desegregation* and *compensatory education.*

The school desegregation movement had as one of its goals the improvement of black school performance. Note, however, that a few years before *Brown* v. *Board of Education* several southern school districts began to publish the test scores of blacks and whites, and to use the lower test scores of blacks to oppose school desegregation.[85] In relatively affluent urban black communities, like Durham, North Carolina, and relatively poor ones like Memphis, Tennessee, black students lagged behind their white peers; and in both cities desegregation was intended to close the performance gap. It did not necessarily do so.[86] In the North the situation was no better.[87]

Compensatory education to improve the school performance of urban blacks began in St. Louis in 1956 and was operating in New York City by 1959. By 1961 this intervention strategy had spread to many other northern cities, even though there was no strong evidence that it was closing the gap between black and white children in school performance.[88]

Another educational consequence of racial stratification is that even today the school-performance gap is not limited to poor blacks living in the inner cities. *And it never was.* As I pointed out earlier, it is true that among blacks, as among whites, middle-class children do better than those from the lower class. But even this type of *within-group comparison by social class* shows some racial difference. *The correlation between SES and academic performance is not as strong among blacks as it is among whites.* For example, a study of some 4,000 high school graduates in California in 1975 found that among blacks and Mexican-Americans, children from affluent and well-educated families were not benefiting from their parents' achievement. Like children from poorer families, the middle-class children had difficulty achieving academic qualification for college admission.[89] In their analysis of the 1987 California statewide test results, Haycock and Navarro found that eighth-grade black children whose parents had completed four or more years of college did less well than other black children whose parents had attended but not finished college.[90] Of particular note is that when blacks and whites come from similar SES background, at every level blacks consistently perform lower than their white counterparts.[91]

The performance of blacks on professional examinations such as teacher certification exams provides additional evidence that the problem is not confined to poor blacks.[92] I was once attending a professional meeting where there was an extensive discussion of a state-mandated test for licensing. Many in attendance who had doctoral degrees said they failed the test several times and passed it only after the norm was lowered for minorities. But as would be expected, when we began to discuss black educational issues in general, my colleagues spoke as if the difficulty of passing academic and standardized tests were limited to the black underclass.

The problem of the school performance gap is found among blacks who live in affluent suburbs, including such places as Alexandria County, Virginia; Arlington County, Virginia; Fairfax County, Virginia; Montgomery County, Maryland; and Prince George's County, Maryland. In my current research in Oakland, California, black students attending the city's elite high school, Skyline, have an average GPA of 1.92 and an average GPA of 1.62 in the courses required to get into the University of California system. The comparable figures for Chinese and white students in the same school are 2.97/2.74 and 2.74/2.48 respectively.[93] I need to add that many of the affluent school districts have an impressive array of remedial programs intended to close the gap in the school achievement.

There are three worrisome features of black school performance. First, while all minorities may start lower than their white peers in the early grades, Asian students improve and even surpass their white peers eventually; for black students, on the other hand, the progression is in the opposite direction: The gap widens between them and their white peers in subsequent years.[94] Second, of all subgroups that I have studied, black males fare the worst. Third, not only are the average black GPA and other test scores lower than those of their white counterparts, but black students are often disproportionately underrepresented in courses that would enhance their chances of pursuing higher education.[95]

HOW RACIAL STRATIFICATION ENTERS INTO BLACK EDUCATION

The school-performance gap was created by forces of racial stratification: white treatment of blacks in the educational domain and black responses to schooling. The gap remains as long as these forces remain. How do these forces get into black education and maintain the gap?

There are three weays in which racial stratification enters into and adversely affects black education. One is through societal educational policies and practices. The societal channel includes denying blacks equal access to education through unequal resources, segregation, and the like—common phenomena in the past. This ensures that blacks do not receive equal education in terms of quantity and quality. If the U.S. society or one of her local communities provides blacks with less and inferior education, then blacks cannot perform as well or go as far as whites in school. This societal and community practice of unequal access was instrumental in the school desegragation movement.[96] The practice appears to be largely reversed, as the federal, state, and local school systems provide extra funds for special programs to improve minority educational achievement.

The other societal practice is denying blacks equal rewards with whites for their educational accomplishments through a job ceiling and related barriers, as discussed in the section on stratification and inequality. This probably historically discouraged blacks from developing "effort optimism" in the pursuit of education. It may also have forced some to seek self-advancement through nonacademic routes.

The second way that racial stratification enters into black education lies in the way black students are perceived and treated in the specific schools they attend. These treatments include tracking, testing and misclassification, representation or nonrepresentation in textbooks and curriculum. Cultural, linguistic, and intellectual denigration is also part of the problem. I have described elsewhere the within-school treatment of black children in the schools I studied in Stockton, California, and how such treatment affected their adjustment and performance.[97] One incident will illustrate how the perception and treatment may result in an unequal educational outcome. In early 1969 I discovered with some neighborhood people that first-grade children in the neighborhood elementary school had not started to learn to read the book designated for that grade. On inquiry we were informed that the children's performance on the "reading-readiness test" showed that they were not yet ready to read; they might be ready to read in March. On the other hand, first-grade children in the white middle-class schools in other parts of the city started on the same reader in September. In May of 1969 both groups of children would be given a state-mandated test based on the same reader. It does not take a great deal of imagination to see how poor black and Mexican-American children in my study school would perform on that test.

Racial stratification also enters into and adversely affects black education through *black people's own perceptions and responses* to their schooling in the context of their overall experience of racial subordination. The factors involved in this, third process is what I call *community forces.* I will elaborate on this mechanism because it is the least recognized, studied, or discussed.

Black Americans have not been helpless victims of racial subordination, as can be seen in the well-documented history of their "collective struggle."[98] The way they have responded or adapted to their minority status, discussed in the earlier part of this article, has to some extent generated educational orientations and strategies that may not necessarily enhance school success, in spite of people's verbally expressed wish to succeed, namely, to get good grades in their schoolwork and obtain good school credentials for eventual good jobs and decent wages as adults.[99]

The community forces arise from the three domains of black adaptation described earlier. The instrumental adaptation generates perceptions of opportunity structure that affect how blacks perceive and respond to schooling. For example, until the civil rights revolution of the 1960s, many black people did not see people around them who "had made it" because of their education, contrary to the claims of "underclass" theorists. In Stockton, California, hardly any of the adolescents I studied in the late 1960s knew anyone, except teachers, who had "become somebody" or become successful because of their education. Yet there had been no "exodus" of educated and professionally successful middle-class blacks from the city.[100] Many black parents in Stockton explained that they did not continue their education because "education did not promise to pay." One father said that he grew up in a town in Florida where college-educated blacks worked in the post office and at other low-prestige jobs; so he decided to go into the Navy. In my research both in Stockton and in Oakland, California, I have come across middle-class blacks who said that if they were white they "would have been farther along" or more successful. Blacks compare themselves *unfavorably* with whites and usually conclude that, in spite of their education and ability, they are worse off than they should be because of racial barriers, rather than lack of education or qualification.[101]

One professional interviewed by Matusow in Washington, D.C., illustrates this problem. He was a young lawyer who grew up in Alabama, believing that the civil rights revolution of the 1960s had indeed brought equal opportunities for blacks and whites. He took his education seriously, attended Princeton University, and eventually became a lawyer. But when he began to practice he began to feel that he could not be as successful as his white peers.[102]

It is true that in spite of the historical experience of blacks in the opportunity structure, black folk theories for getting ahead stress the importance of education. But this verbal endorsement is not to be accepted at face value. It is often not accompanied by appropriate or necessary effort. I have previously mentioned the paradox of high educational aspiration and inappropriate academic behaviors discovered by Weis in her research in Philadelphia.[103] My students and I encounter the same phenomenon in various locations in California: The students verbally assert that making good grades and obtaining school credentials are important. They also say that in order to make good grades, one must pay attention in class, do what teacher says, answer questions in class, and do homework. However, from our observations in the classroom, in the family, and in the community I must conclude that many do not do these things.[104] I have suggested that the reason for this lack of adequate and persevering effort is probably that, historically, blacks were not adequately rewarded for their educational achievement. So they may not have developed a widespread effort optimism or a strong cultural ethic of hard work and perseverance in pursuit of academic work.[105] Furthermore, the folk theories stress other means of getting ahead under the circumstances that face black people. But these alternative or "survival" strategies appear to detract from and conflict with their pursuit of formal education.

There are also factors arising from symbolic adaptation that do not particularly encourage striving for school success among lower-class as well as middle-class blacks. One such factor is how blacks perceive or interpret the cultural and language differences they encounter in school. I suggested earlier that black culture embodies a kind of oppositional cultural frame of reference vis-à-vis white American culture. Thus, for some blacks cultural and language differences between blacks and whites are consciously or unconsciouly interpreted as symbols of group identity to be maintained, not barriers to be overcome. Moreover, they tend to equate the school culture (e.g., the curriculum and required behaviors) and standard English with white culture and language. They therefore perceive school learning not as an instrumental behavior to achieve the desired and verbalized goal of getting a good education for future employment, but rather as a kind of linear acculturation or assimilation, detrimental or threatening to collective identity. Some are afraid to behave according to what they see as the white cultural frame of reference for fear it may result in loss of minority cultural identity. This problem has been reported in studies of black students in high school, junior college, and graduate school and parents in adult school.[106] A black professor told Weis that "a lot of Black students see [academic work] as a White world. (If I tell students, 'you're going to be excellent—often times excellence means being—White—that kind of excellence is negative here.'"[107] Based on his research findings in New York City, Labov explains that for some black youth accepting school values is equivalent to giving up self-respect because academic participation is equated with giving up black cultural identity.[108]

Apparently, some black educators and others agree with this interpretation that academic work is "white" because they, too, complain that the school curriculum and language of instruction are "white." A careful study of the writings of some black scholars who are proposing changes in the education of black children indicates that their proposals are more or less based on the assumption that the school curriculum, standard practices, and standard English are white and detrimental to black children's cultural identity. Among them are advocates of Afrocentric curriculum and cultural infusion.[109] I think that Claude Steele, a black psychologist at Stanford University, expresses the assumption of these black educators very well in a 1992 article in *The Atlantic Monthly*:

> One factor is the basic assimilationist offer that schools make to Blacks: You can be valued and rewarded in school (and society), the schools say to these students, but you must first master the culture and ways of the American mainstream, and since that mainstream (as it is represented) is essentially White, this means you must give up many particulars of being Black—styles of speech and appearance, value priorities, preferences—at least in mainstream setting. This is asking a lot.[110]

The equation of the school curriculum, the standard classroom behaviors and instructional language, the standard English, with white American culture and language results in conscious or unconscious opposition or ambivalence toward learning and using instrumental behaviors to make good grades and obtain the school credentials that the students say they need and want. This phenomenon, which has to do with identity choice, is a dilemma that cuts across class lines. It may partly explain the low school performance of some middle-class black students.

Racial stratification also affects black education through black *relational adaptation*. I will briefly point out two aspects of this. First, the deep distrust that blacks have developed for the public schools and those who control them—white Americans or their minority representatives—adversely affects communication between blacks and the schools and black interpretations of and responses to school requirements. Second, among blacks themselves, the practice of physical and social disaffiliation with the community by the academically and professionally successful middle class raises the question in the mind of community people about the real meaning of schooling.

IMPLICATIONS

From a comparative perspective, the persistence of black-white inequality in general and in education in particular is due to racial stratification, not class stratification. The barriers to equality caused by racial stratification go beyond those of jobs, income, housing and the like. These are the most obvious and are targets of public policies and efforts to achieve equality. There are other complex and subtle aspects of racial stratification in white treatment of blacks and black perceptions of and responses to their social reality, including their responses to schooling, that need to be better recognized, understood, and targeted for change.

Focusing on education, to promote a greater degree of academic success and good social adjustment, (1) it is essential to recognize, understand, and remove the obstacles from society and within the schools described earlier; and (2) it is equally necessary to recognize, understand, and attend to the community forces or the obstacles arising from black responses to racial stratification described above. At the moment, the role of community forces is the least known and the knowing is most resisted. Yet it is among the things that most distinguish immigrant minorities who are doing relatively well in school from nonimmigrant minorities who are not doing as well. There are two parts to the problem of the school-performance gap. Community forces constitute one part.

Notes

1 Michael B. Katz, ed., *The "Underclass" Debate: Views from History* (Princeton: Princeton University Press, 1993): C. Jencks and P. E. Peterson, eds., *The Urban Underclass* (Washington, D.C.: The Brookings Institute, 1991); Joint Center for Political Studies, "Defining the Underclass: Researchers Ask Who is Included and What Are the Policy Implications," *Focus*, June 1987; "The Black Conservatives," *Newsweek*, March 9, 1991, pp. 29–33; "What Black Conservatives Think of Reagan: A Symposium," *Policy Review* 34 (Fall 1985): 27–41; "Redefining the American Dilemma: Some Black Scholars Are Challenging Hallowed Assumptions," *Time*, November 11, 1985, pp. 33–36; W. J. Wilson, *The Declining Significance of Race* (Chicago: The University of Chicago Press, 1978); idem, "The Declining Significance of Race: Revisited But Not Revised," in *Caste & Class Debate*, ed. C. V. Willie (Bayside, N.Y.: General Hall, 1979), pp. 159–76; and idem, *The Truly Disadvantaged: The Inner City, the Underclass, and Public Policy* (Chicago: The University of Chicago Press, 1987).

2 Gerald D. Berreman, "Race, Caste, and Other Invidious Distinctions in Social Stratification," *Race* 13 (1972): 385–414; Morton Fried, "On the Evolution of Social Stratification and the State," in *Culture and History: Essays in Honor of Paul Radin,* ed. Stanley Diamond (New York: Columbia University Press, 1960), pp. 313–731; and Arthur Tuden and L. Plotnicov, eds., *Social Stratification in Africa* (New York: Free Press, 1970), pp. 1–29.

3 Tuden and Plotnicov, *Social Stratification in Africa.*

4 Gerald D. Berreman, "Caste in Cross-Cultural Perspective: Organizational Components," in *Japan's Invisible Race: Caste in Culture and Personality,* ed. George DeVos and Hiroshi Wagatsuma (Berkeley: University of California Press, 1967), pp. 275–307.

5 Gerald D. Berreman, "Social Inequality: A Cross-Cultural Analysis," in *Social Inequality: Comparative and Developmental Approaches,* ed. G. D. Berreman (New York: Academic Press, 1981), pp. 3–40.

6 See John U. Ogbu, "Class Stratification, Racial Stratification and Schooling," in *Class, Race and Gender in U. S. Education,* ed. L. Weis (Buffalo: State University of New York Press, 1988), pp. 163–82.

7 S. Aronowitz, *The Crisis in Historical Materialism* (New York: Praeger, 1981); S. Bowles and H. Gintis, *Schooling in Capitalist America: Educational Reform and the Contradictions of Economic Life* (New York: Basic Books, 1976); and O. C. Cox, *Caste, Class and Race: A Study in Social Dynamics* (New York: Monthly Review Press, 1959; orig. pub. 1948).

8 Cox, *Caste, Class and Race*; E. W. Gordon and C. C. Yearkey, "Review of *Minority Education and Caste,*" *Teachers College Record* 81 (Summer 1980): 526–29; and C. C. Yearkey and G. S. Johnson, "Review of *Minority Education and Caste,*" *American Journal of Ortho-psychiatry,* 49 (1980): 353–59.

9 See C. Hallpike, *The Konso of Ethiopia* (Oxford: Clarendon Press, 1968); J. J. Maquet, *The Premise of Inequality in Ruanda* (London: Oxford University Press, 1961); N. S. Nadel, "Caste and Government in Primitive Society," *Journal of Anthropological Society of Bombay* 8 (1954): 22; John U. Ogbu, "Education, Clientage, and Social Mobility: Caste and Social Change in the United States and Nigeria," in *Social Inequality,* ed. Berreman, pp. 277–306; D. Richter, "Further Consideration of Caste in West Africa: The Senufo," *Africa* 47 (1980): 37–44; and D. M. Todd, "Caste in Africa?" *Africa* 47 (1977): 398–412.

10 John U. Ogbu, *Minority Education and Caste: The American System in Cross-Cultural Perspective* (New York: Academic Press, 1978); and idem, "Education, Clientage, and Social Mobility."

11 See Bennett Harrison, *Education, Training, and the Urban Ghetto* (Baltimore: Johns Hopkins University Press, 1972); G. Myrdal, *An American Dilemma: The Negro Problem and Modern Democracy* (New York: Harper, 1944); Paul H. Norgren and Samuel E. Hill, *Toward Fair Employment* (New York: Columbia University Press, 1964); Ogbu, *Minority Education and Caste;* Stephan Thernstorm, *The Other Bostonians: Poverty and Progress in the American Metropolis, 1880–1970* (Cambridge: Harvard University Press, 1973); and Phyllis Wallace, ed., *Equal Employment Opportunity: The AT&T Case* (Cambridge: MIT Press, 1977).

12 S. Chan, *Asian Americans: An Interpretive History* (Boston Twayne Publishers, 1991); and E. C. Sandmeyer, *The Anti-Chinese Movement in California* (Urbana: University of Illinois Press, 1973); P. S. Foner, *Organized Labor and the Black Worker, 1619–1973* (New York: International Publishers, 1974); and William B. Gould, *Black Workers in White Unions: Job Discrimination in the United States* (Ithaca: Cornell University Press, 1977).

13 Richard J. Herrnstein, *I.Q. in the Meritocracy* (Boston: Little, Brown, 1973); C. Jencks et al., *Inequality: A Reassessment of the Effects of Family Schooling in America* (New York: Basic Books, 1972); Melvin L. Kohn, "Social Class and Parent-child Relationships: An Interpretation," in *Life Cycle and Achievement in America,* ed. R. Laub Coser (New York: Harper, 1969), pp. 21–48; and M. M. Tumin, ed. *Readings in Social Stratification* (Englewood Cliffs, N.J.: Prentice-Hall, 1967).

14 Berreman, "Social Inequality."

15 Ibid.

16 Berreman, "Race, Caste, and Other Invidious Distinctions."

17 John H. Burma, "The Measurement of Negro Passing," *American Journal of Sociology* 52 (1947): 18–22; and E. W. Eckard, "How Many Negroes 'Pass'?" *American Journal of Sociology* 52 (1947): 452–500. For an example of recent attempts by some people to be racially reclassified by the courts, see V. R. Dominguez, *White by Definition: Social Classification in Creole Louisiana* (New Brunswick, N.J.: Rutgers University Press, 1986).

18 Myrdal, *An American Dilemma.*

19 Ibid.; and Ogbu, "Class Stratification, Racial Stratification and Schooling."

20 St. Clair Drake and Horace R. Cayton, *Black Metropolis: A Study of Negro Life in a Northern City,* vols. 1 & 2 (New York: Harper 1970); Ogbu, *Minority Education and Caste*; and idem, *The Next Generation: An Ethnography of Education in an Urban Neighborhood* (New York: Academic Press, 1974).

21 R. Higgs, *Competition and Coercion: Blacks in the American Economy, 1865–1914* (Chicago: The University of Chicago Press, 1980); Arthur M. Ross and Herbert Hill, *Employment, Race, and Poverty: A Critical Study of the Disadvantaged Status of Negro Workers from 1865 to 1965* (New York: Harcourt, 1967); Norgren and Hill, *Toward Fair Employment*; and Ogbu, *Minory Education and Caste.*

22 B. Matusow, "Together Alone: What Do You Do When the Dream Hasn't Come True, When You're Black and Middle-Class and Still Shut Out of White Washington, When It Seems Time to Quit Trying?" *Washingtonian,* November 1989, pp. 153–59, 282–90; C. T. Rowan, "The Negro's Place in the American Dream," in *The American Dream: Vision and Reality,* ed. J. D. Harrison and A. B. Shaw, (San Francisco: Canfield Press, 1975), pp. 19–23; J. Sochen, ed., *The Black Man and the American Dream: Negro Aspirations in America, 1900–1930* (Chicago: Quadrangle Press, 1971); and idem, *The Unbridgeable Gap: Blacks and Their Quest for the American Dream, 1900–1930* (Chicago: Rand McNally, 1972).

23 St. Clair Drake, "The Ghettoization of Negro Life," in *Negroes and Jobs,* ed. L. A. Ferman, J. L. Kornbluh, and J. A. Miller (Ann Arbor: The University of Michigan Press, 1968), pp. 112–28; and Ogbu, *Minority Education and Caste.*

24 Drake, "Ghettoization of Negro Life"; and R. E. Forman, *Black Ghetto, White Ghetto, and Slums* (Englewood-Cliffs, N.J.: Prentice-Hall, 1971).

25 Ogbu, *Minority Education and Caste*; idem, "Diversity and Equity in Public Education: Community Forces and Minority School Adjustment and Performance," in *Policies for America's Public Schools: Teachers, Equity, and Indicators,* ed. (Norwood, N.J.: ABLEX, 1988), pp. 127–70.

26 R. A. Mickelson, *"Race, Class, and Gender Differences in Adolescent Academic Achievement Attitudes and Behaviors"* (Ph.D. diss., Graduate School of Education, University of California, Los Angeles, 1984); and Ogbu, *Minority Education and Caste.*

27 V. W. Henderson, "Region, Race, and Jobs," in *Employment, Race, and Poverty,* ed. *Ross and Hill,* pp. 76–139.

28 See Ogbu, *Minority Education and Caste*; idem, "Structural Constraints in School Desegregation," in *School Desegregation Research: New Directions in Situational Analysis,* ed. J. Prager, D. Longshore, and M. Seeman (New York: Plenum Press, 1986), pp. 21–36; and idem, "Castelike Stratification as a Risk Factor for Mental Retardation in the United States," in *The Concept of Risk in Intellectual and Psychological Development,* ed. D. C. Farran and J. D. McKinney, (New York: Academic Press, 1986), pp. 19–56.

29 Matusow, "Together Alone"; and Ogbu, *The Next Generation.*

30 Bernard Meer and Edward Freedman, "The Impact of Negro Neighbors on White Homeowners," *Social Forces* 45 (1966): 11–19; Ogbu, *The Next Generation,* p. 44; idem, "Racial

Stratification and Education: The Case of Stockton, California," *IRCD Bulletin*, 12 (Summer 1977): 10.

31 Ogbu, "Racial Stratification and Education," pp. 10–11.

32 John U. Ogbu, "Minority Status, Cultural Frame of Reference, and Schooling," in *Literacy: Interdisciplinary Conversations*, ed. D. Keller-Cohen (Cresskill, N.J.: Hampton Press, Inc., 1994), pp. 361–84; and idem, "From Cultural Differences to Differences in Cultural Frame Of Reference," in *Cross-Cultural Roots of Minority Child Development*, ed. P. M. Greenfield and R. R. Cocking, (Hillsdale, N.J.: Lawrence Erlbaum, 1994), pp. 365–91.

33 M. J. Herskovits, *The Myth of the Negro Past* (Boston: Beacon Press, 1990; orig. pub. 1941).

34 *Time*, April 6, 1970, p. 71; cited in Grace S. Holt, "Stylin Outta the Black Pulpit," in *Rappin' and Stylin' Out: Communication in Urban Black America*, ed. T. Kochman, (Urbana: University of Illlinois Press, 1972), p. 189.

35 Ibid.

36 Ibid., p. 190.

37 C. E. Becknell, *Blacks in the Workforce: A Black Manager's Perspective* (Albuquerque, N.M.: Horizon Communications, 1987), p. 35; Grace S. Holt, " 'Inversion' in Black Communication," in *Rappin and Stylin' Out*, ed. Kochman, pp. 152–59.

38 D. Holland and J. Valsiner, "The Ontogeny of Culture: Cognition, Symbols, and Vygotskys Developmental Psychology (Unpublished ms., Department of Anthropology, University of North Carolina at Chapel Hill, 1988).

39 Ogbu, "Minority Status," p. 372.

40 Houston A. Baker, *Blues, Ideology, and Afro-American Literature: A Vernacular Theory* (Chicago: The University of Chicago Press, 1981); F. Campbell, "Black Executives and Corporate Stress," *The New York Times Magazine*, Dec. 12, 1982, pp. 1–42; G. Davis and C. Watson, *Black Life in Corporate America: Swimming in the Mainstream* (Garden City, N.Y.: Anchor Books, 1985); Jacqueline Mitchell, "Reflections of a Black Social Scientist: Some Struggles, Some Doubts, Some Hopes," *Harvard Educational Review* 52 (1982): 27–44; and S. A. Taylor, "Some Funny Things Happened on the Way Up," *Contact* 5 (1973): 12–17.

41 Taylor, "Some Funny Things Happened," pp. 16, 17.

42 Campbell, "Black Executives," pp. 68–69, 70.

43 Davis and Watson, *Black Life in Corporate America*, pp. 5, 10–11, 38–39.

44 See Becknell, *Blacks in the Workforce*; T. Kochman, *Black and White Styles in Conflict* (Chicago: University of Chicago Press, 1982); and L. Luster, "Schooling, Survival, and Struggle: Black Women and the GED" (Ph.D. diss., School of Education, Stanford University, 1992).

45 P. R. Abramson, *The Political Socialization of Black Americans: Critical Evaluation of Research on Efficacy and Trust* (New York: The Free Press, 1977); E. F. Frazier, *The Negro in the United States* (New York: Macmillan, 1957); Alice Stanback, "The Testing of a New Integrative Model of Cognition within the Context of a Continually Existing Educational Problem" (Ph.D. diss., Biola University, 1992), and R. C. Twombly, *Blacks in White America since 1865: Issues and Interpretations* (New York: David MacKay, 1971).

46 R. Farley and W. R. Allen, *The Color Line and the Quality of Life in America* (New York: Oxford University Press, 1989); G. D. Jaynes and R. M. Williams, eds., *A Common Destiny: Blacks and American Society* (Washington, D.C.: National Academy Press, 1989); and W. L. Reed, ed., *African Americans: Essential Perspectives* (Westport, Conn.: Auburn House, 1993).

47 W. J. Wilson, "The Declining Significance of Race: Revisited but Not Revised," in *Caste & Class Controversy*, ed. C. V. Willie, (Bayside, N.Y.: General Hall, 1979), pp. 159–74.

48 P. Moss and C. Tilly, *Why Black Men Are Doing Worse in the Labor Market: A Review of Supply-Side and Demand-Side Explanations* (New York: Social Science Research Council,

1991); U.S. Civil Rights Commission, *Unemployment and Underemployment: Clearinghouse Publications, No. 74* (Washington, D.C.: Government Printing Office, 1982); and B. B. Williams, *Black Workers in an Industrial Suburb: The Struggle against Discrimination* (New Brunswick, N.J.: Rutgers University Press, 1987).

49 Ogbu, "Structural Constraints in School Desegregation."

50 Wilson, "Declining Significance of Race."

51 A. F. Brimmer, "Economic Development in the Black Community," in *The Great Society: Lessons for the Future*, ed. E. Ginzberg and R. M. Solo, (New York: Basic Books, 1974), pp. 146–73.

52 A. M. Ross, *The Negro Employment in the South: Vol. 3, State and Local Governments* (Washington, D.C.: Government Printing Office, 1973).

53 Williams, *Black Workers.*

54 E. W. Jones, "Black Managers: The Dream Deferred," *Harvard Business Review*, May-June 1986, pp. 84–93.

55 *New York Times* 1989; Jones, "Black Managers": Matuso, "Together Alone"; L. Benjamin, *The Black Elite: Facing the Color Line in the Twilight of the Twentieth Century* (Chicago: Nelson-Hall, 1991); Davis and Watson, *Black Life in Corporate America*, p. 3; and J. Nelson, *Volunteer Slavery: My Authentic Negro Experience* (Baltimore: Penguin, 1993).

56 Davis and Watson, *Black Life in Corporate America*, p. 74.

57 E. Cose, *The Rage of a Privileged Class: Why Are Middle-Class Blacks Angry? Why Should America Care?* (New York: Harper-Collins, 1993).

58 *Newsweek*, "Black Youth: A Lost Generation?" August 7, 1978, pp. 22–34.

59 P. M. Sniderman and T. Prazza, *The Scar of Race* (Cambridge: Harvard University Press, 1993), p. 40.

60 *San Francisco Examiner*, October 17, 1993, p. A1.

61 J. Johnson, "Poll Finds Blacks and Whites 'Worlds Apart' on Race Issues," *The New York Times*, January 12, 1989, p. 17; B. D. Tatun, *Assimilation Blues: Black Families in a White Community* (Westport, Conn.: Greenwood Press, 1987); and L. Williams, "An Uneasy Mingling: When Talk at Parties Turns to Racial Issues," *The New York Times*, October 31, 1988, pp. B1, B12.

62 Cose, *Race of a Privileged Class.*

63 Benjamin, *Black Elite*; Davis and Watson, *Black Life in Corporate America*; Jones, "Black Managers"; and Matusow, "Together Alone."

64 Ogbu, "Education, Clientage, and Social Mobility."

65 R. L. Hall, *Black Separatism in the United States* (Hanover, N.H.: University of New England Press, 1979); and S. Sygnnertvedt, *The White Response to Black Emancipation: Second Class Citizenship in the United States since Reconstruction* (New York: Macmillan, 1972).

66 H. A. Baker, Jr., *Blues, Ideology, and Afro-American Literature: A Vernacular Theory* (Chicago: The University of Chicago Press, 1984).

67 See H. A. Baer, *The Black Spiritual Movement: A Religious Response to Racism* (Knoxville: The University of Tennessee Press, 1984); and J. E. Holloway, *Africanisms in American Culture* (Bloomington: Indiana University Press, 1990).

68 S. Fordham and John U. Ogbu, "Black Students' School Success: Coping with the Burden of 'Acting White,'" *The Urban Review* 18 (1986): 176–206; Luster, "Schooling, Survival, and Struggle."

69 W. J. Wilson, "Cycles of Deprivation and the Underclass Debate," *Social Service Review*, Dec. 1985.

70 John U. Ogbu, "School Achievement of Urban Blacks" (Paper prepared for the Committee on Research on the Urban Underclass, Social Science Council, San Francisco, Calif., March 8–9, 1991).

71 Ogbu, *Minority Education and Caste*; and idem, "Diversity and Equity in Public Education."

72 Joint Center for Political Studies. "Poverty and Public Policy: Recent Experiences in the U.S., Canada and Western Europe" (unpublished ms. Washington, D.C., 1989), p. 23.

73 Myrdal, *An American Dilemma*, pp. 154–55.

74 Matusow, "Together Alone"; and Tatun, *Assimilation Blues*.

75 Maquet, *Premise of Inequality in Ruanda*.

76 C. C. Bond, "Social Economic Status and Educational Achievement: A Review Article," *Anthropology and Education Quarterly* 12 (1981): 227–57; J. S. Coleman et al., *Equality of Educational Opportunity* (Washington, D.C.: Government Printing Office, 1966); Ogbu, "Review" (*American Journal of Orthopsychiatry*); F. Mosteller and D. P. Moynihan, eds., *On Equality of Educational Opportunity* (New York: Random House, 1972); R. Rist, "Student Social Class and Teacher Expectations: The Self-fulfilling Prophecy in Ghetto Education," *Harvard Educational Review* 40 (1970): 411–51; and W. J. Wilson, "Race, Class and Public Policy in Education" (Unpublished Lect., prepared for the National Institute of Education, Vera Brown Memorial Seminar Series, Washington, D.C., 1980).

77 G. C. Bond, "Social, Economic Status and Educational Achievement: A Review Article," *Anthropology and Education Quarterly* 12 (1981): 227–57.

78 Ogbu, "Class Stratification, Racial Stratification, and Schooling," pp. 163–82.; M. L. Oliver, C. Rodriguez, and R. A. Mickelson, "Brown and Black in White: The Social Adjustment and Academic Performance of Chicano and Black Students in a Predominantly White University," *The Urban Review* 17 (1985): 3–24; and M. Slade, "Aptitude, Intelligence or What?" *The New York Times*, October 24, 1982, p. 22E.

79 S. P. Stern, *School Imposed Limits on Black Family Participation: A View from Within and Below* (Paper presented at the eighty-fifth annual meeting of the American Anthropological Association, Philadelphia, December 4–7, 1986).

80 Paul Willis, *Learning to Labor: How Working-Class Kids Get Working-Class Jobs* (New York: Columbia University Press, 1977).

81 L. Weis, *Between Two Worlds: Black Students in an Urban Community College* (Boston: Routledge & Kegan Paul, 1985).

82 Ibid., see also Ogbu, *The Next Generation*; and Jennifer Johnson-Kuhn, "Working Hard/Hardly Working: Motivation and Perceptions of Success in a Fifth-Grade Classroom" (Honor Thesis, Department of Anthropology, University of California, Berkeley, 1994).

83 M. A. Gibson and J. U. Ogbu, *Minority Status and Schooling: A Comparative Study of Immigrant and Involuntary Minorities* (New York: Garland Publishing, 1991); Ogbu, *Minority Education and Caste*; John U. Ogbu, "Equalization of Educational Opportunity and Racial/Ethnic Inequality," in *Comparative Education*, ed. P. G. Altbach, R. F. Arnove, and G. P. Kelly (New York: Macmillan, 1982), pp. 269–89; idem, "Immigrant and Involuntary Minorities in Comparative Perspective," in *Minority Status and Schooling*, ed. Gibson and Ogbu, pp. 3–33; and N. K. Shimahara, "Social Mobility and Education: The Burakumin in Japan," in ibid., pp. 327–53.

84 Wilson, "Race, Class and Public Policy."

85 "Under Survey," *Southern School News*, 3 (1952): 2.

86 D. C. Clement et al., *Moving Closer: An Ethnography of a Southern Desegregated School. Final Report* (Washington, D.C.: The National Institute of Education, 1978); T. W. Collins and G. W. Noblitt, *Stratification and Resegregation: The Case of Crossover High School. Final Report* (Washington, D.C.: The National Institute of Education, 1978); John U. Ogbu, "Desegregation in Racially Stratified Communities—A Problem of Congruence," *Anthropology and Education Quarterly* 9 (1979):290–94; and idem, "Structural Constraints in School Desegregation."

87 H. A. Ferguson and R. L. Plaut, "Talent: To Develop or to Lose," *The Educational Record* 35 (1954):137–40; and Ogbu, *Minority Education and Caste*.

88 E. W. Gordon and D. A. Wilkerson, *Compensatory Education for the Disadvantaged: Programs and Practices: Preschool to College* (New York: College Entrance Examination Board, 1966); and Ogbu, *Minority Education and Caste.*

89 K. P. Anton, *Eligibility and Enrollment in California Public Higher Education* (Ph.D. Diss., Graduate School of Education, University of California, Berkeley, 1980).

90 R. Haycock and S. Navarro, *Unfinished Business: Report from the Achievement Council* (Oakland, Calif.: The Achievement Council, 1988).

91 M. Slade, "Aptitude, Intelligence or What?"

92 L. Bond, Personal Communication, April 15, 1994; "Second Lawsuit Filed against California Teacher Test," *FairiTest Examiner* 7 (1993):14; J. A. Hartigan and A. K. Wigdor, eds., *Fairness in Employment Testing* (Washington, D.C.: National Academy Press, 1989); and M. A. Rebell, "Disparate Impact of Teacher Competency Testing on Minorities: Don't Blame the Test Takers—or the Tests," in *What Should Teacher Certification Tests Measure?*, ed. M. L. Chernoff, P. M. Nassif, and W. P. Gorth (Hillsdale, N.J.: Lawrence Erlbaum, 1987), pp. 3–34.

93 Alexandria County Public Schools, *1992–1993 ITBS/TAP Achievement Test Results, July 1993* (Alexandria, Va.: Alexandria County Public Schools, Monitoring and Evaluation Office, 1993); Arlington County Public Schools, *Report on the Achievement and Participation of Black Students in the Arlington Public Schools, 1986–1990* (Arlington, Va.: Division of Instruction, Office of Minority Achievement, 1991); Fairfax County Public Schools, *Annual Report on the Achievement and Aspirations of Minority Students in the Fairfax County Public Schools, 1986–87* (Fairfax, Va.: Office of Research, 1988); Montgomery County Public Schools, *School Performance Program Report,* (Rockville, Md.: Office of Evaluation, 1993); *Success for Every Student Plan: Second Annual Report on the Systemwide Outcomes* (Rockville, Md.: Office of Evaluation, 1993; Prince George's County Public Schools, *Black Male Achievement: From Peril to Promise, Progress Report, December 1993* (Upper Marlboro, Md.: Office of Research and Evaluation, 1993); *1993 Maryland School Performance Program Report* (Upper Marlboro, Md.: Office of Research and Evaluation, 1993); and Ogbu, "School Achievement of Urban Blacks."

94 Berkeley Unified School District, *An Equal Education for All: The Challenge Ahead. A Report to the Berkeley Board of Education by the Task Force on School Achievement, June 12, 1985* (Berkeley: Board of Education, 1985).

95 Prince George's County Public Schools, *Black Male Achievement: From Peril to Promise. Report of the Superintendent's Advisory Committee on Black Male Achievement* (Upper Marlboro: Office of the Superintendent, 1990), p. 65.

96 H. A. Bullock, *A History of Negro Education in the South: From 1619 to the Present* (New York: Praeger, 1970); and Ogbu, *Minority Education and Caste*, U.S. Office of Civil Rights, *Racial Isolation in the Public Schools: A Report,* Vol. 1 (Washington, D.C.: Government Printing Office, 1968).

97 Ogbu, *The Next Generation*; and idem, *Minority Education and Caste.* See also C. M. Payne, *Getting What We Asked For: The Ambiguity of Success and Failure in Urban Schools* (Westport, Conn.: Greenwood Press, 1987); and Rist, "Student Social Class."

98 A. Lynch, *Nightmare Overhanging Darkly: Essays on Black Culture and Resistance* (Chicago: Third World Press, 1992); A. D. Morris, *The Origins of the Civil Rights Movement: Black Communities Organizing for Change* (New York: The Free Press, 1984); Dorothy K. Newman et al., *Protest, Politics, and Prosperity: Black Americans and White Institutions, 1940–75* (New York: Pantheon Books, 1978); and Ogbu, *Minority Education and Caste.*

99 See Johnson-Kuhn, "Working Hard/Hardly Working"; Luster, "Schooling, Survival, and Struggle"; John U. Ogbu, *Understanding Community Forces Affecting Minority Students' Academic Efforts* (Report prepared for the Achievement Council, Oakland, California, 1984); idem, "Variability in Minority School Performance: A Problem in Search of an Explanation," *Anthropology and Education Quarterly* 18 (1987): 312–34; idem, "Overcoming Racial

Barriers to Equal Access," in *Access to Knowledge: An Agenda for Our Nation's Schools*, ed. J. I. Goodlad and P. Keating (New York: The College Board, 1990), pp. 59–89; and Weis, *Between Two Worlds*.

100 Ogbu, *The Next Generation*.

101 See Ogbu, "Racial Stratification and Education"; Johnson-Kuhn, "Working Hard/Hardly Working"; Luster, "Schooling, Survival, and Struggle"; J. U. Ogbu, "Minority Education Project: a Preliminary Report, 1994" (unpublished ms., Department of Anthropology, University of California, Berkeley); and Ogbu, *The Next Generation*.

102 B. Matusow, "Together Alone: What Do You Do When the Dream Hasn't Come True, When You're Black and Middle-Class and Still Shut Out of White Washington, When it Seems Time to Quit Trying?" *Washingtonian*, November 1989, pp. 153–59, 282–90.

103 W. A. Shack, *On Black American Values in White America: Some Perspectives on the Cultural Aspect of Learning Behavior and Compensatory Education* (Paper prepared for the Social Science Research Council, Sub-Committee on Values and Compensatory Education, 1970–71).

104 Weis, *Between Two Worlds*; J. Mitchell, "Visible, Vulnerable, and Viable: Emerging Perspectives of a Minority Professor," in *Teaching Minority Students*, New Directions for Teaching and Learning, No. 16 (San Francisco: Jossey-Bass, 1983), pp. 17–28; and Luster, "Schooling, Survival, and Struggle."

105 Ibid.; pp. 100–01.

106 Weis, *Between Two Worlds*; Mitchell, "Visible, Vulnerable, and Viable": and Luster, "Schooling, Survival, and Struggle."

107 Weis, *Between Two Worlds*, pp. 100–01.

108 W. Labov, "Rules for Ritual Insults," in *Rappin' and Stylin' Out: Communication in Urban Black America*, ed. T. Kochman (Urbana: University of Illinois Press, 1972), pp. 265–314.

109 See A. W. Boykin, "The Triple Quandary and the Schooling of Afro-American Children," in *The School Achievement of Minority Children: New Perspectives*, ed. U. Neisser (Hillsdale, N.J.: Lawrence Erlbaum, 1986), pp. 57–92; E. M. Clark, *A Syllabus for an Interdisciplinary Curriculum in African-American Studies* (Oakland, Calif.: Merritt College and Berkeley Unified School District, 1971); A. G. Hilliard, "Why We Must Pluralize the Curriculum," *Educational Leadership* 49 (December 1991-January 1992): pp. 12–16; A. G. Hilliard, L. Payton-Stewart, and L. O. Williams, *Infusion of African and African American Content in the School Curriculum: Proceedings of the First National Conference, October 1989* (Morristown, N.J.: Aaron Press, 1991); A. W. Nobles, "The Infusion of African and African-American Content: A Question of Content and Intent," in *Infusion*, ed. Hilliard, Payton-Stewart, and Williams, pp. 4–26; and Portland Public Schools, *African-American Baseline Essays* (Portland, Oreg.: Portland Public Schools, 1990).

110 C. M. Steele, "Race and the Schooling of Black Amerians," *The Atlantic Monthly*, April 1992, pp. 68–75.

[31]

New Mythologies in Maori Education

Graham Hingangaroa Smith and Linda Tuhiwai Smith

Introduction

Since 1984, New Zealand has undergone considerable educational and economic reform. In this climate of flux and change, Maori interests have been made highly vulnerable to appropriation by non-Maori interests. Of particular concern is the way in which the educational reforms have been 'bought' into uncritically by many Maori and the seemingly passive acceptance of these vital changes, despite the fact that they may be no better off, or might indeed be worse off. This chapter undertakes a critical investigation of the way in which the 'new speak' of the educational reforms has been constructed to appeal to and to ensure Maori compliance with the new economic vision underpinning the reforms. Thus a major focus of this work is on exposing the ways in which 'meanings' and 'interpretations' of key ideas driving the reforms have been specifically targeted to engender the support, participation and co-operation of Maori. It is argued that much of the symbolic rhetoric giving impetus to the education reforms – for example, 'choice', 'less state and more parental control', 'accountability', 'efficiency' and 'privatisation' – has been carefully selected to sell the reforms. Many of the ideas encapsulated within these short statements have a direct and distinct appeal to many Maori people, who historically have had few options, little cultural influence, poor achievement outcomes and only a minor decision-making role within schooling and education. It is as a result of these marginalised circumstances that there is an inevitable attraction to the promise of 'real' social, political and economic betterment contained in rhetoric which appears to align with Maori cultural aspirations and needs.

An effort is made here to unpack the ways in which the reforms have been construed ideologically as 'common sense', as 'reasonable' and as 'acting in the best interests of Maori'. Of significance is why the educational reforms for a long while remained mostly unquestioned by Maori, despite the fact that there was little or no change to their existing dire circumstances. There was very little critical commentary offered by Maori which challenged educational policies. The apparent domestication of Maori dissent can be understood theoretically as the control over the meanings and interpretations of key terms and ideas. Such ideological control provides a fundamental way by which dominant interests are able to be sustained within society. These meanings are produced and reproduced by a range of official sources as well as an array of media outlets. A key accomplice to the educational reforms of the 1980s in New Zealand has been a largely uncritical media who have been mostly happy to accept the critiques of education and schooling by government and big business interests and to subsequently attack schools, the curriculum, teachers, unions, administration and academics.

In the last decade, Maori people have paid a high price for both the free-market driven economic and educational reforms. Unemployment and other social indices still place Maori in a vulnerable and politically unstable position within New Zealand society. Despite this kind of reality, it can be claimed that at one level, select Maori interest groups and individuals have participated with and given consent to many aspects of the reforms. One effect of such consent is that the reforms have been given a degree of legitimacy internationally as serving minority group interests.

This chapter begins by examining the ways in which Maori consent has been manipulated and co-opted on the one hand, and Maori dissent has been managed and marginalised on the other. This discussion is followed by an analysis of four 'myths' which have been an important 'selling' point of recent educational reforms to Maori. The larger question being asked here is whether or not these educational reforms have meaningfully addressed Maori educational crises or have they simply reformulated these crises within a different educational model which will continue to produce the same or worse outcomes for Maori.

Hegemony

A key theoretical notion in understanding the arguments presented here is that of hegemony and its role in weakening Maori opposition to the prescriptive will of dominant interests. In particular, the ways in which Maori resistance to cultural oppression and economic exploitation is dissipated and undone can be significantly explained within Antonio Gramsci's (1971) notion of 'hegemony'. Gramsci employed this critical tool within his writings to help explain the rise of fascism in Italy under Mussolini. Gramsci was seeking to explain why the rigid and austere social, political and economic conditions created by the Fascist state developed by Mussolini were not openly resisted by the citizenry given that such conditions should have contradicted their common-sense cultural conditioning. In this sense, Gramsci was attempting to theorise how the oppressed are co-opted into forming and contributing to their own domination. A subtlety to be understood here is the extent to which the oppressed take on, as common sense, understandings which are contradictory and thereby sustain their oppression and exploitation. A distinction is drawn between external, coercive forces such as the police, the army, regulatory legislation and so on to enforce conformity, versus an internalised, ideological formation of 'common-sense' acceptance of dominant will.

What is important in the New Zealand social context of unequal power relations between dominant Pakeha and subordinate Maori interests is that a critical interrogation employing the concept of hegemony reveals how assimilation, colonisation, oppression, exploitation and/or domination is both produced and reproduced. The struggle for ideological consensus has been an historically important factor in the politics of Maori-Pakeha relations since early contact. In more recent times, the struggle to establish the new economic shape of education and schooling, following the 1986 Picot Review of Educational Administration, has resulted in making more overt the previously submerged function of schooling and education – its role as a key site for the insertion of dominant hegemony.

Creating the Conditions for Reform

The history of Maori involvement in, and resistances to, education have already been well documented (Walker, 1990). By 1984, Maori frustrations with education had converged around some key criticisms of the 'system'. These were the continuing underachievement of Maori children in mainstream schooling; the lack of recognition given to Maori language and culture; and the lack of autonomy Maori had in educational decision-making at all levels. Different strategies were associated with each of these areas of criticism but they also fed off and into each other. For example, arguments about underachievement tended to focus on the cultural exclusiveness of formal examination structures such as School Certificate; on the marginalisation of Maori in school structures through streaming; or on the narrow curriculum choices offered to Maori students which was further exacerbated by 'tokenistic' curriculum bridging programmes such as 'Taha Maori' (Walker, 1984).

Arguments relating to Maori language and culture were often framed around the urgency for the revitalisation of Maori language in the face of its imminent demise and the future needs of children who were emerging from Te Kohanga Reo (preschool immersion centres) which had begun in 1982. Meaningful and effective decision-making opportunities with respect to significant input into formal education were seldom available to Maori and mostly non-existent. As a response to this lack of decision-making power, the 1980s, building on the success frameworks established by Te Kohanga Reo, saw increasing calls for 'tino rangatiratanga' (self-determination) within education and schooling. These calls were being made by a variety of different groupings of Maori: parents, iwi representatives, community workers, Te Kohanga Reo parents, academics, advisers, teachers and principals. The alternative educational developments building on the preschool initiative of Te Kohanga Reo, Kura Kaupapa Maori (Immersion Primary Schools), Kura Tuarua (Immersion Secondary Schools), Waananga (Maori Institutions of Higher Learning) emphasised the cry for increased Maori control over key educational decision-making. Thus critical analyses of education and schooling by Maori began to converge with other forms of educational critique, such as those developed from both the 'left' and the 'right' of the political spectrum. The political conditions for educational reform by 1984 could not have been more favourable. The incoming Labour government was to seize on this opportunity of a legitimation crisis of state education and schooling (a significant part of this crisis relating to Maori underachievement) to promote its radical reforms based on free market economics.

At the same time, however, the mounting Maori critique of education needs to be read within a wider context of Maori 'development' which was also being promoted by the new Labour government under the guise of the increased 'devolution' of power and control to local community or iwi level. Ostensibly, this was done in order to give Maori increased autonomy over their own affairs; these programmes were generally embraced within the policy framework of 'Iwi Development'. Issues of Maori economic development were high on the agenda of the fourth Labour government, which was elected in 1984. These issues were discussed at the Hui Taumata, a summit on Maori economic development convened in October 1984 as one of the first major initiatives for Maori by the Labour government. At this conference, the failure of the state to deliver socioeconomic success for Maori was highlighted (Henare, 1994). The failure of education and failures in other 'social' policy areas were identified as major barriers to Maori development. While the linking of economic development to education was not a new idea by any means, what was new was the situating of Maori economic development in a more global context. Countering the critique of 'state interests and control' was the confidence that many Maori had the capacity to develop more successful models of development given the opportunity, the autonomy and the restoration of iwi resources. This confidence was reframed hegemonically in terms of 'Maori must do it for themselves'.

There are several layers to this idea. First, there is a distinction between the idea that 'Maori want to do it *ourselves*' and 'Maori want to do it *themselves*'. The transference from the first meaning, as defined by Maori, to the second meaning, as reformulated by New Right interests, at its most innocent implies an affirmation by Pakeha of Maori aspirations. This can also be regarded, however, as a transference of the right of determination from Maori (that is, doing it for ourselves) to Pakeha (that is, doing it on behalf of, or to, Maori). Second, there is a layer of meanings which pertains to the conditions needed for Maori to be able exercise greater autonomy. This relates to questions such as: over what is autonomy to be exercised? With what resources, expectations, or accountabilities? What Maori interest groups would be involved? How would they be constituted? Such conditions do not entirely, or indeed primarily, involve the creation of a set of conditions which enable Maori to have greater control over Maori cultural customs, Maori language or Maori knowledge forms. Greater autonomy over the conditions within which Maori have to live involve greater participation in and determination over much wider issues, ones which are nationally and internationally significant and ones which have traditionally been the preserve of dominant ruling interests.

An important ideological link between the view that the state had failed, and the view that Maori could do things better, was the idea that Maori people were deeply dependent on the state and that this dependency was a major impediment to Maori development and autonomy. The idea of state dependency was significant. Whilst not exactly placing the blame on Maori as many earlier analyses had done, it did imply that Maori had been made dependent by the state and had lost their initiative in the process. It suggested that the state had not only failed but had deliberately hindered development and implied that Maori would be better off without state interference. This view gave a mandate for restructuring the relationship between Maori and the state which at one level occurred around state initiatives related to recognition of the Treaty of Waitangi and, at a more submerged level, around far-reaching attacks on the welfare state. Whilst many Maori invested considerable faith and energy in the restoration of the Treaty of Waitangi as a mechanism for delivering more autonomy and greater opportunity, this focus came at the expense of attention which needed to be paid at the other end of the scale, namely, the high cost to Maori of economic reforms, and the manipulation of Maori by New Right interests in order to legitimate a wider raft of reforms.

It is easy to see now, in the late 1990s, why Maori desires for reform in 1984 could converge with and add strength to the reformist agenda of the New Right. The very targets of Maori frustration loosely labelled as 'the system' or 'the government' and the strategies to overcome such frustrations, such as greater autonomy and less state interference, appeared to complement the critique of the state being mounted by the New Right. This apparent complementarity of aims created the space for different kinds of strategic alliances between Maori, whose rhetoric was around iwi development and the survival of Maori language and culture, and corporate interests, whose interests centred on privatisation and entrepreneurial culture. The pivotal mechanism for raising the profile of Maori rights in the last decade has been the emergence of the significance of the Treaty of Waitangi. The reductionist economic logic of the New Right has had great difficulty in accommodating the Treaty of Waitangi and what it implies for Maori. The reasons behind a Maori commitment to the Treaty of Waitangi are profoundly different from the interests the New Right may have in the Treaty of Waitangi. Whilst many Maori see the Treaty as providing a permanent and embedded arrangement for the way New Zealand is governed, New Right supporters see national interests as no longer sovereign because they have been superseded by a global marketplace in which the rules of the market determine society. At another level, libertarian idealism posits individual freedoms and rights as being of prior importance over and above group or collective rights and advocates notions such as 'consumer sovereignty'. Furthermore, within the logic of libertarian economics, treaties with indigenous peoples as national settlements are seen as being contradictory and potential impediments to the idea of a 'free market'.

There have been several contradictory tendencies which have occurred as a consequence of economic reforms. One of these is that in the restructuring and privatisation of state assets, Maori have seen their resource base alienated yet again, that is, from the state to private ownership. Maori who have opposed such moves have sometimes clouded the wider implications of privatisation for all New Zealand citizens to be marginalised and their opposition has simply been seen as another example of Maori radical politics. On the other side, Maori who have supported economic restructuring have often given legitimacy to economic reform, not for the reasons Maori have argued for but for the logic and larger picture of New Right economics. Many Maori leaders who have participated in the formation of new economic settlements have entered into negotiations with a belief that they could influence outcomes in ways which made the policies more sympathetic to Maori. Others have been perceived by Maori opposition as self-interested and not to be trusted. One of the problems within which Maori are frequently trapped is the idea that 'we have to be in to win', or put another way, we have to participate if we are to influence outcomes. This belief, if assumed as a general rule, can be easily co-opted as a principle for consulting with Maori. In other words, if Maori can be convinced that matters are urgent and have to be settled within a tight time-frame, then Maori participation can be co-opted and, more importantly, contained. Much of the educational reforms relating to Maori issues following the Picot review were carried out in this 'ad hoc', 'tight time-frame', 'limited budget' manner by the Ministry of Education and the Iwi Transition Agency. In this way, multiple layers of urgent decision-making involving major implications for Maori have effectively kept a Maori leadership busy, distracted and fragmented. Within this situation of bureaucratic chaos, an illusion of proper consultation with Maori was created. However, the reality was that it provided a suitably distracting climate in which the vested interests of government were able to structure policy to suit themselves.

Whilst Maori consent has been manipulated and co-opted through the reinflection of hegemonies and the sheer scale of economic change, Maori dissent has been carefully managed. One may argue that all dissent in New Zealand has been marginalised and/or silenced completely but Maori dissent has still been visible. One reason for such visibility is that Maori dissent has been organised around a set of oppositions which are clearly different. Oppositional discourse involves the strategic use of language, imagery, values, objectives and networks. For Maori, such strategies have been easily situated within a history of colonialism and an alternative world-view which is capable of generating culturally different interpretations of events, policies and official discourses. Whilst Maori consent to economic restructuring has been highly visible, so has Maori dissent been visible. Kelsey (1993) has argued that 'the most sustained challenge to the liberal reforms came from Maori' but that Maori were, in turn, regarded as 'an equal, if not greater, threat to the New Zealand economy and the New Zealand way of life than those who were ringing in the changes'. Managing Maori dissent has been as important to the legitimation of reforms as the manipulation of consent.

One key way in which Maori dissent has been managed has been through the processes which have enabled the government to play a leading, if somewhat paternalistic, role in relation to the Treaty of Waitangi. The management of consultation, mediation, negotiation and information have been significant means through which dissent has been controlled. By taking hold of the Treaty of Waitangi debate and accepting a responsibility in the 'settlement of grievances', the state, under both Labour and National governments, has exercised a form of moral leadership which has allowed state interests to first, dictate the parameters of what counts as valid Treaty issues, that is to attempt to reduce the Tiriti to a set of core principles, and second (and subsequently), to determine the pace and resourcing of Treaty of Waitangi claims and settlements. Through their public displays of 'good will' and 'commitment' to the Treaty of Waitangi, government ministers and their top officials have appeared publicly to be supportive of Maori claims for greater autonomy with some hint that this may involve 'rangatiratanga'. Considerable fanfare was made in the education arena that Maori initiatives in relation to Maori language, Te Kohanga Reo and Kura Kaupapa Maori were being funded and supported by the state. However, it should be noted here that the 'rangatiratanga' being expressed here was simply the free-market notions of 'devolution', 'privatisation' and 'individual freedoms'. This public image of 'reasonableness' was countered behind the scenes with a raft of mainstreaming policies and clever financial management which in effect has seen a renewed emphasis on cultural assimilation. Selected Maori programmes such as Te Kohanga Reo and Kura Kaupapa Maori are therefore 'co-opted' as proof of government support of Maori aspirations but are also used to disguise other policies, for example, mainstreaming, which have in fact continued the 'status quo' situation of ongoing assimilation.

In terms of dissenting voices, Maori who have publicly criticised the government and these negative tendencies implicit within official policies, have generally been positioned as unreasonable radicals and activists who are not only on the outside of mainstream Pakeha New Zealand but outside of mainstream Maori society as well. When the dissenting voices have become too loud, Maori leadership has been called upon to exercise more control over 'their people'. Maori 'negotiating' relationships with the state are also silenced by the possible threat that any criticism would lengthen considerably the ongoing negotiations with the state. The coercion embedded in this 'big stick' approach needs to be seen as the other side of reasonableness.

Creating the Conditions for Hegemony

Recent reforms in New Zealand education have to be read within the broader aims of social and economic restructuring. The important point here is the inextricable link between economic reform and social reform. Thus the reform agenda, including those elements specifically targeted at education and schooling, need to be seen as forming two distinct impulses: an economic reform movement couched within libertarian economic principles and a social reform programme couched within conservative and authoritarian retrenchment idealism. The context of struggle between dominant Pakeha and subordinate Maori interests within the new reforms ought to be understood as occurring concurrently in both the economic and social domains. A further dynamic adding to the complexity of this situation is the simultaneous action of *deconstructing* prevailing ideologies and practices while at the same time promoting and *constructing* the 'new' reform agenda. Thus the approach to economic reform in New Zealand in the 1980s has involved the dual concerns of dismantling the welfare state on the one hand and promoting the new economic agenda of the 'free market' on the other. Associated with free-market principles is a growing emphasis placed on key ideas such as 'individual rights and freedoms', 'competition', 'choice', 'efficiency and accountability'. Such emphases on free-market values can be generalised as being contradictory to a Maori cultural propensity toward values such as 'collectivity', 'group responsibility', 'co-operation', 'consensus' and so on.

The binary opposition of 'deconstruction' and 'reformation' is an important concept to understand in analysing how and why hegemonies are promoted and sustained. Thus with respect to Maori, it is important to know where Maori 'are at' or have 'come from' in order to compare or understand the full significance of what new reforms might offer. For the most part, the current crises endured by Maori people across a range of social indicators (e.g. in comparison to non-Maori, Maori suffer disproportionate levels of poorer health, rates of incarceration, educational underachievement, short life expectancy, etc.) are not acceptable to Maori themselves and therefore, as a group, Maori are extremely open to seeking change of these conditions. In this sense, the urgent desire for change has made Maori more susceptible to the promises contained in these new ideologies and practices.

The attack on the welfare state and its associated ideals by New Right reformists has also been waged through hegemonic practices and beliefs. Many Maori have supported these beliefs uncritically and have succumbed to its controlling influence. Some examples which are employed to undermine the credibility of the welfare state are:

- 'New Zealand is living beyond its means and needs to cease living on borrowed money'
- 'New Zealand can no longer afford to pay for the welfare state'
- 'Let those who use public services, such as health and education pay for the service'.

The problem with promulgating such beliefs is that contrary to the implied assumptions, not everyone starts on an equal footing. Those who are already well off economically will be able to cope better with the consequences of the 'user pays' principles embedded in these comments, while those already socially and economically disadvantaged will continue to struggle. The economic 'level playing field' is a myth, the reality of which is cunningly disguised and concealed within hegemonic discourse. Thus, in Gramsci's terms, hegemonies are formed when the socially and economically disadvantaged take on the false consciousness of these ideologies as acting in their best interests as 'common sense', when in reality, by accepting the logic of these beliefs, they are in fact contributing to their ongoing exploitation and oppression.

Hegemony has played a vital role in promoting and sustaining the new free-market driven reforms within education and schooling. For example, a few of the commonly accepted beliefs are given here (although many of these hegemonies have begun to fall apart as the promises implied have failed to materialise):

- 'schooling and education has been captured by the professionals such as teachers'
- 'schooling and education has become overly bureaucratic'
- 'parents must have more control and power in the education of their children'
- 'there is a need to ensure that pupil consumers get value for the money which has been invested in education'
- 'parents ought to have real choices for the schooling of their children'.

Education and schooling reform was sold to parents on the promises similar to those implied above: more control over schools, more say in children's schooling, more school choices, improved curriculum options and so on. While some of these items have indeed occurred, many have not. For example, many parents believed that they would have power and control over their local school through the new Board of Trustees structure. In fact, what has happened is that there has been an illusion of power and control shifting to parents and local communities (Johnston, 1993). While parents have gained management *responsibility* of schools, *real power* and *control* remains within a streamlined central bureaucracy which continues to exercise power through other structural means. An example is the way in which funding to schools has been controlled and by directly diminishing parental influence over the learning domain by prescribing almost 90 per cent of school charters in non-negotiable regulations. Add to this the multiple accountability regulations which pertain to schools, principals, teachers, administrators, Boards of Trustees members and parents, then the freedoms implied in the new reforms begin to fade. Hegemony also operates in this situation when parents genuinely believe that they have gained power and control over the schooling of their children. The subtle distinction to be made here is that what parents have in fact got is more responsibility and accountability upon themselves; the central bureaucracy has neatly abdicated this role (and the financial burden associated with it under the old system of Education Boards) without relinquishing power, control and authority. Hegemony operates when many parents still buy into the Boards of Trustees structures believing that they have a good deal of autonomy and power to influence education.

Developing New Myths

The co-operation of Maori in maintaining their own oppression and exploitation is attained through hegemony. Within education, new 'myths' which contribute to the ongoing domination, marginalisation and assimilation of Maori have evolved within the educational reforms of the 1980s. These ideologies are taken for granted as acting in the best interests of Maori and are accepted unproblematically. Some examples of hegemony which have been inserted within Maori communities and which uphold the new economic restructuring of education and schooling as being positive, useful and transforming for Maori are identified here.

The Myth of 'Tino Rangatiratanga'

This myth has arisen out of the free-market reforms and the restructuring strategy of 'devolution'. Devolution as a social policy implied the shifting of increased power and control from the central bureaucratic structures to local communities. Two key areas where devolution was a key strategy for inserting free-market reforms were education and Maori affairs. In education, more power and control was ostensibly to pass to Boards of Trustees of schools. In Maori affairs, a new programme termed 'Iwi Development' (tribal development) was initiated with the principal aim being to 'downsize' the central bureaucratic structure of the Maori Affairs Department and to replace this with a small central office while iwi or tribes would constitute local committee structures to exercise more self-management and control.

Iwi development was carried out as an overt restructuring initiative but was also aided by many Maori influenced by hegemony. Examples of these hegemonies included:

- 'Maori would have more power and control to exercise tino rangatiratanga – self-determination and autonomy over their own lives'
- 'that economic resources would be more evenly shared across Maoridom and that tribes would be able to develop a measure of economic self-sufficiency'.

What in fact has happened is that iwi have restructured themselves into small bureaucracies (as required by the state authorities) and which subsequently have a dependency relationship through these local bureaucratic structures to the central government agency, the Ministry of

Maori Policy, which controls funding flows, sets policy and controls accountabilities.

A number of hegemonies have emerged which have a common link to illusions of assuming some form of 'tino rangatiratanga'. Many Maori (and Pakeha) operating within Boards of Trustee structures for example, have mistakenly assumed that these structures give them some form of autonomy or 'tino rangatiratanga' with respect to being able to exercise control on behalf of Maori interests within schooling and education sites. However, the outcome, based on bitter experience, has exposed the strong influence and control maintained by the Pakeha-dominated state. State control is also apparent in the ostensibly totally Maori educational sites of Te Kohanga Reo preschools and Kura Kaupapa Maori schools.

Bulk funding and voucher systems for Maori create a similar illusion of giving tino rangatiratanga to the consumer (hence consumer sovereignty). The problem of state-derived funding and the necessary accountabilites associated with this will ensure central state control and power being maintained by ruling-class interests.

The Myth of the Autonomous Chooser

This myth derives from the free-market context. It implies that within a free-market structure, consumer sovereignty and therefore consumer 'demand' will shape the 'supply' end of the market. In this meritocratic view, competition will create an atmosphere where the strongest and best will come to the forefront. This approach is to be seen underpinning the new developments in both the health and education sectors where individual health units and schools are expected to compete against each other for clients. When this approach is linked with 'user pays' (consumer sovereignty), market forces will determine which agencies will get more support and funding. In this logic, there is a correlation between what counts as 'successful' and the numbers of fee-paying clients.

The free market attempts to create choice for the consumer. It is argued that consumer sovereignty will save costs if social services are organised around principles of consumer demand. Unnecessary spending can be better controlled because of the user-pays principle; if you do not use the services, your contribution is significantly diminished. For many people, particularly Maori, the notion of the autonomous chooser is a myth. There are many other variables which impact on an individual with respect to choices being 'freely' made. For example, important variables related to 'race', class and gender may heavily influence what choices are in fact available. As well, the myth of the 'level playing field' is often taken for granted by adherents of choice theory – the assumption being that everyone has an equal choice with respect to such things as access to schooling, health provision and so on. The reality for most Maori is that they do not have the same choices with respect to schooling options if you live in west Auckland as opposed to Epsom in central Auckland for example. You certainly have restricted schooling options if you are a solo parent with limited income and do not have a car to transport children to a school of your choice.

The hidden dimension of choice theory is that it provides another means of abrogating responsibility by the state. School-related problems become the fault of the schools, the parents, the families or the individual learners themselves. For example, from the official point of view, a lag in capital works in a school is more likely to now be interpreted as due to school mismanagement with regard to prioritising the expenditure of the school budget rather than a lack of sufficient capital funds from the central authority. Similarly, learning difficulties and underachievement are more likely to be explained as poor school choices made by the student and parents rather than a structural anomaly related to issues such as the curriculum being a reflection of culturally selected forms of knowledge.

The Myth of Maori Language Revitalisation

A third myth relates to the support which has been given by the state for the revitalisation of Te Reo Maori. This myth supports the concept of choice and simultaneously serves the purpose of being seen to address the needs of minority and/or indigenous education. Support for Te Reo Maori gives people who desire education through the medium of Te Reo Maori an opportunity, in theory, to choose such an option. In reality, the choice is not so clear-cut. Apart from the demands such expectations place on small communities with only a single primary school, there is a question which relates to the wider implications of such a choice. What else is being chosen when parents opt for either a dual medium or immersion Maori education? Measured, even crudely, in terms of curricula resources and trained teachers, there has been systematic underdevelopment of this area of education (Davies and Nicholl, 1993). What is known already by communities who wish to develop a Kura Kaupapa Maori for example, is that: there is an ongoing struggle within the community over the use of any existing school facilities; there is a waiting list for state funding; there are few trained and available teachers; there are few curricula materials in Te Reo Maori; there are no Maori language assessment or diagnostic tools; there are few if any support agencies, such as educational psychologists, who can give assistance; there is no support for the whanau education programme, which is a fundamental aspect of Kura Kaupapa Maori. Choosing such an option then, is to choose something which has many known drawbacks. Many parents simply want to choose a quality education which is delivered through the medium of Te Reo Maori. The 'myth' of Maori language revitalisation is that it is a viable educational choice which will serve Maori aspirations and is of equal status and support with other types of educational programmes.

The other purpose which is served by state support for Maori language revitalisation is that it is seen to cater for minority, indigenous and/or multicultural education. This is an important selling point of the reform agenda as it seems to demonstrate that diverse needs can be recognised and accommodated within the new market model of education. It is simply a matter of choice and demand. Official support for Te Reo Maori is used in the international arena to demonstrate that New Zealand is doing something positive for indigenous people and is supporting the survival of indigenous language and culture. In this respect, such support fills an important legitimation role. What needs to be examined more critically, however, is the extent to which this support is a carefully managed exercise in window dressing or an exercise in the further marginalisation of Maori aspirations and demands. Not all Maori educational needs can be met by support for Maori language. At present, the majority of Maori still attend conventional schooling. Truancy, suspension and expulsion rates for these schools are still disproportionately high for Maori children. Achievement rates for Maori when compared to non-Maori have not improved in any substantial way in the last decade (Davies and Nicholl, 1993). There are still far too few Maori teachers teaching across the curriculum, especially in secondary schools. To expect that the expenditure allocated for Maori language will transform existing school achievement patterns for Maori is a false expectation. However, the media and less sympathetic interests equate the funding of targeted Maori programmes with such outcomes. This produces some of the backlash strategies that individual schools are forced to confront. These strategies cover a range of issues. For example, there may be a reluctance by a Board of Trustees to acknowledge that the achievement of Maori students is an issue which needs to be addressed systematically or there are issues related to the establishment of a bilingual unit in which Maori students are 'dumped' with the expectation that this programme will 'get rid of the Maori problem'. Accountability for inadequate programmes can be shifted from the state to the school and from the school to the community. In reality, all three groups are implicated in the continuing underachievement of Maori.

In summary, this myth is important because it uses Maori aspirations for the survival of Te Reo Maori to co-opt Maori consent for other aspects of educational reform which are not necessarily sympathetic to Maori interests. Increased costs for education resulting from user-pays policies, for example, make the prospect of sending children on to tertiary education an enormous burden for Maori families who have experienced continuing poverty as a direct consequence of economic and social reform. Choices for Maori have already been structured in ways which make some of those choices highly risky and unequal.

The Myth of Credentialism

The final myth to be discussed here is linked to unemployment and the attempts by the state to restructure the economy whilst dealing with the consequences of high and sustained unemployment. The hegemonic aspect of this myth is that people are unemployed because they do not have the right qualifications and training, that is, it is their own fault. Embedded in attempts to address unemployment has been a critique of the relationship between education and work. Both schools and the unemployed themselves have been identified as 'failing' in some way to address the changing role of the economy and the needs of the marketplace. Considerable emphasis has been placed, in recent years, on changing the school curriculum, on establishing better relationships between schools and the workplace and on bringing the needs and expertise of the business world into the world of education. An important goal of the reform process has been increased competition. One of the functions of schools is to turn individual learners into individualised and competitive units who can operate in the world of work or in the marketplace. The myth of credentialism is that increased and improved credentials will lead to a more highly skilled workforce and to increased work opportunities. The reality is that by rapidly increasing the number of credentials, the actual value of credentials decreases. This leads to the need to acquire more credentials. This process is also known as overcredentialling.

If we examine Maori unemployment figures since the economic reforms of the Labour government over a decade ago, it is clear that the rate of Maori employment was directly affected by the restructuring of such sectors as the forestry and the meat industry and has not, in the intervening years, improved (see Chapters 3 and 11). The rates of unemployment for Maori are disproportionately higher than for Pakeha. Although at one level this can be linked to educational achievement, it is also linked to the structure of the labour market and the economy. The huge increase in Maori unemployment in the mid-1980s did not occur because there was a sudden change in educational achievement patterns. If anything, the rate of Maori educational achievement was slowly improving, although the gap between Maori and non-Maori remained wide. Increased unemployment was related to a much wider set of changes both in the global economy and in the legacy of previous economic policies by New Zealand governments.

One of the major interventions in the high unemployment rate for Maori has been through the provision of training programmes. Over the years, these programmes have undergone several name changes and have become far more refined in terms of expectations and outcomes. The basic goal, however, is to provide training which will lead to employment. For the most difficult group of unemployed, those with no or minimal secondary school qualifications or those who have been long-term unemployed, training programmes are meant to lead into jobs. The reality, however, is that single, short-course programmes simply lead into further single, short-term courses. Incentives and disincentives, for example around childcare subsidies, ensure that people take the courses. Once on a course, they are removed from the register of unemployed thus creating the illusion that there is less unemployment. With each new course they complete, trainees receive more and more course certificates which outline their skills and understandings. These do not lead inevitably to employment. They simply lead to more certificates.

Supporting the myth of credentialism are the current attempts to create a single framework which co-ordinates, recognises, controls, ranks and gives legitimation to the different types of qualifications, certificates, diplomas and degrees. There are major implications of such an approach for Maori intellectual and cultural property rights. Qualifications in aspects of Maori language, culture and knowledge already exist in the New Zealand Qualifications framework. The details of the curriculum, the content of actual lessons and forms of assessment are given their legitimacy by the New Zealand Qualifications Authority. This effectively hands over control of Maori knowledge to the state therefore giving the state the power to credential, or to legitimate, what counts as Maori knowledge and culture.

Conclusion

These four myths show the complex ways in which ideas claimed to work at one level for Maori interests can work against those same interests either at another level or in relation to the wider context of educational reform. One of the dangers for Maori education is that while concentrating on the details and specifics of policies which are developed around Maori education, we lose sight of the directions in which education generally is heading. In the last decade, educational reform, like health and other social policy reforms, have kept people busy reacting and repositioning themselves in order to cope with constant change. This has included having to learn and unlock a new 'corporate' language and a new state ideology. It is time now to reflect on the consequences of change for Maori education. Are any changes that do exist the result of the wider reform process? Are these changes an improvement? Has the gap in achievement levels between Maori and non-Maori changed for the better? Has the quality of education improved for Maori children? Is there commitment to long-term development of Maori language education and greater control by Maori over their education, or are these temporary measures put in place until Maori can be reassimilated into a new order? Consideration of these questions will help to make sense of the long-term implications for Maori of radical educational and economic reform.

References

Davies, L. and Nicholl, K. (1993), *Te Maori i roto i nga Mahi Whakaakoranga Maori in Education*, Wellington: Ministry of Education.

Gibson, R. (1986), *Critical Theory and Education*, London: Hodder and Stoughton.

Gramsci, A. (1971), *Selections from the Prison Notebooks of Antonio Gramsci* (edited and translated by Hoare, Q. and Smith, G.), New York: International Publishers.

Henare. D. (1994), 'Social Policy Outcomes Since the Hui Taumata', *Kia Pumau Tonu, Proceedings of the Hui Whakapumau Maori Development Conference*, Massey University, Department of Maori Studies. [289]

Johnston, P. (1992), 'Enabling, Encouraging or Empowering? Maori Members on School Boards of Trustees', *ACCESS*, 11 (2), pp. 1–17.

Kelsey, J. (1993), *Rolling Back the State*, Wellington: Bridget Williams Books.

Walker, R. (ed.) (1984), *The Maori Education Development Conference*, Auckland: Department of Continuing Education, University of Auckland.

Walker, R. (1990), *Ka Whawhai Tonu Matou: Struggle Without End*, Auckland: Penguin. [290]

Part V
Social Justice, Literacy and New Technologies

[32]

Poverty and Education

R. W. CONNELL
University of California, Santa Cruz

In this article, R. W. Connell reexamines the schooling of children in poverty in several industrial countries. He suggests that major rethinking is due that draws on two assets that have not been considered by policymakers in the past: the accumulated practical experience of teachers and parents with compensatory programs, and a much more sophisticated sociology of education. Connell uses these assets to question the social and educational assumptions behind the general design of compensatory programs, to propose an alternative way of thinking about children in poverty that is drawn from current practice and social research, and to explore some larger questions about the strategy of reform this rethinking implies. He goes on to demonstrate that compensatory programs may even reinforce the patterns that produce inequality, since they function within existing institutions that force children to compete although the resources on which they can draw are unequal. At the core of this process, according to Connell, is the hegemonic curriculum and control over teachers' work. He argues that changing the industrial conditions of teachers' work is central to addressing issues of poverty and education because teachers are the most strategically placed workers to affect the relationship between poor children and schools, and because teachers of the poor have a capacity for strategic thinking about designing reform strategies that has been largely overlooked. Connell concludes by grounding his discussion in the larger realization that targeted programs are unlikely to have a major impact unless they are part of a broader agenda for social justice.

How schools address poverty is an important test of an education system. Children from poor families are, generally speaking, the least successful by conventional measures and the hardest to teach by traditional methods. They are the least powerful of the schools' clients, the least able to enforce their claims or insist their needs be met, yet the most dependent on schools for their educational resources.

Since modern school systems persistently do fail children in poverty, a sense of outrage runs through much educational writing about disadvantage. Several authors have recently added a note of urgency to this discussion. Natriello, McDill, and Pallas (1990) give their survey of U.S. practice the subtitle, "Racing

Harvard Educational Review Vol. 64 No. 2 Summer 1994

0017-8055/94/0500-0125 $1.25/0

against Catastrophe." Kozol's (1991) book, *Savage Inequalities,* presents an even bleaker portrait of willful neglect and deepening tragedy. Korbin (1992) speaks of the "devastation" of children in the United States. This note has also been heard outside education in discussions of the urban "underclass" and is given strength by the 1992 violence in Los Angeles and the rise of neo-fascism in Europe.

In its first year, the Clinton administration signalled no sharp break from the educational policies of the 1980s. But Clinton's election has created a political space in the United States for reconsidering compensatory programs, which were already gaining renewed support after a period of skepticism and narrowed horizons.[1] The secretary of education speaks, for instance, of a "revolutionary" plan for "reinventing" Chapter I, the major U.S. compensatory program (Riley, 1994). Rhetoric aside, there is certainly a need to rethink the underlying logic of compensatory programs, which have not changed in their basic design and political justification, either in the United States or in other countries, since the 1960s. Meanwhile, child poverty has grown dramatically, and the difficulties faced by some parts of the school system have reached crisis proportions.

Such rethinking can draw on two assets that were not available in the 1960s. The first is the accumulated practical experience of teachers and parents with compensatory programs. A great fund of such experience is found outside the United States, which Weinberg (1981) has documented in a vast "world bibliography." A more international perspective can help one to see both the deeper roots of the problems and a broader range of responses; however, participants in the debate in the United States rarely consider it.

The second asset is a much more sophisticated sociology of education. In discussion of how inequalities are produced, the focus has gradually shifted from the characteristics of the disadvantaged to the institutional character of school systems and the cultural processes that occur in them. Compensatory programs cannot be reinvented in isolation; the rethinking leads us inevitably to larger questions about education.

Education used to be represented in political rhetoric as a panacea for poverty. This is now rare, but education for the poor is still an arena for confident pronouncements by many economists and businesspeople, welfare specialists, and political and cultural entrepreneurs of various persuasions — some of whom are startlingly naive about the educational effects of what they propose. I hope to show that teachers' experience and educational reasoning are central to a strategy for reconstruction.

The purposes of this article are to question the social and educational assumptions behind the general design of compensatory programs; to propose an alternative way of thinking about the education of children in poverty, drawn from current practice and social research; and to explore some broad questions about the strategy of reform this rethinking implies. My focus is on the educational

[1] The term "compensatory" has been rightly criticized for its association with deficit notions about the poor. However, it is the only common term for the special-purpose programs that are the focus of the policy discussion. It continues in official use, so I, too, use it.

systems of industrialized, predominantly English-speaking, liberal-capitalist states (Australia, Britain, Canada, and the United States), though in broad outline the argument should also apply to other countries with comparable economic and political systems.

Poverties and Programs

"Poverty" is not a single thing, nor a simple concept. On a world scale, distinctly different situations are embraced in the term. MacPherson (1987) speaks of five hundred million children living in poverty in developing countries, most in rural settings. The quality of the schooling that reaches them is debated; Avalos (1992), for example, argues that the formal pedagogy conventional in their schools is profoundly inappropriate. Poverty in agricultural villages is different from poverty in the explosively growing cities, from Mexico City to Port Moresby, that now dominate the politics of the developing world. It was in the context of migration into such urban settings that Lewis (1968) formulated the idea of a "culture of poverty," which has had a profound effect on compensatory education in wealthy countries.

In industrial capitalist countries with high average incomes, poverty is the effect of unequal distribution, rather than the effect of absolute level of resources. Even in these countries, welfare researchers have pointed to the diversity of situations. As early as 1962, in *The Other America,* Harrington distinguished the aged, minorities, agricultural workers, and industrial rejects as belonging to different "subcultures of poverty." Such complexity is reemphasized in more recent and more systematic welfare research (for example, Devine & Wright, 1993).

There is complexity in two senses, first in the very definition of poverty. Low incomes are part of everyone's concept of poverty, but incomes vary in character as well as amount: some are regular and others are intermittent; some are paid all in money and some are partly "in kind"; some are shared in a household (or a wider group) and some are individual. Further, people's economic situations depend on what they own, as well as on their current incomes. The distribution of wealth is known to be markedly more unequal than the distribution of income, so a simple income measure of poverty is likely to underestimate the severity or extent of deprivation. Further, there are other types of resources beyond income and wealth that cannot be cashed out on an individual basis, but where inequality is materially significant: for example, access to public institutions such as libraries, colleges, and hospitals; to public utilities; and to safety and community health.

Official statisticians generally throw up their hands at this complexity, and settle for a single index that allows a "poverty line" to be drawn. The most widely used is an austere income-based poverty line adopted in the United States in 1964 (based on earlier government calculations about emergency food needs for families), and subsequently applied in other countries. The great virtue of a poverty-line approach is that it allows a straightforward calculation of the number of people living in poverty. For example, in 1991 the United States counted fourteen million children in poverty (U.S. Bureau of the Census, 1992); extrapolating to the industrial capitalist countries as a group (United Nations Development Programme, 1992), we might estimate they have about thirty-five million children in poverty, which might be regarded as the potential target group for compensatory education.[2] The great disadvantages of the poverty-line approach are that it ignores important dimensions of deprivation and inequality, and that it readily leads to political misperceptions of poverty, as I explain below.

The second form of complexity is that economic deprivation, however defined, is shared by people who are very different in other respects. Ethnic background is far from homogeneous. The poverty of indigenous peoples, still grappling with the consequences of invasion and colonization, is different from the poverty of recent immigrant groups. Political debate on poverty in the United States mainly addresses African-American urban "ghettos," but the majority of the people marked off by the poverty line in the United States are White. In a disadvantaged inner-city Australian school, there may be ten or twelve languages spoken on the playground. Further, poor people are not all of one gender. To note this is not merely to say we must count women as well as men. As with race relations, gender relations affect the creation of poverty and affect people's responses to poverty. Thus, women's overall economic disadvantage vis-à-vis men shapes the demography of poverty: female-headed households have higher poverty rates than male-headed households. The ways children and teenagers deal with gender affect their schooling. This is a familiar general point (Thorne, 1993). It should not be forgotten that it applies to children and teenagers in poverty; for both girls and boys, gender relations shape their difficult relationships with their schools (Anderson, 1991; Walker, 1988).

Schooling designed specifically for the poor dates back to the charity schools of the eighteenth century, and to the ragged schools of the nineteenth century that were established to tame the children of "the perishing and dangerous classes" (Clark, 1977). Modern compensatory programs date from the 1960s and have a specific history. Earlier in this century, most educational systems were sharply and deliberately stratified: they were segregated by race, by gender, and by class; tracked into academic and technical schools; divided among public and private, Protestant and Catholic. A series of social movements expended enormous energy to desegregate schools, establish comprehensive secondary systems, and open universities to excluded groups. As a result of this pressure, the expanding educational systems of the mid-century generally became more accessible. The idea of education as a right, which was crystallized in the 1959 United Nations Declaration of the Rights of the Child, was interpreted internationally as implying equal access to education (with notable exceptions like South Africa).

[2] I have counted the U.N. Development Programme's group of "industrial countries," excluding the communist or former communist countries. A more sophisticated calculation could adjust for known differences in the rates of child poverty — the United States appears relatively high — but a poverty line in any case has an element of arbitrariness; the order of magnitude would remain the same.

Poverty and Education
R. W. CONNELL

Yet equal access was only half a victory. Children from working-class, poor, and minority ethnic families continued to do worse than children from rich and middle-class families on tests and examinations, were more likely to be held back in grade, to drop out of school earlier, and were much less likely to enter college or university (for example, Curtis, Livingstone, & Smaller, 1992; Davis, 1948). Documenting this *informal* segregation within formally unsegregated institutions was the main preoccupation of educational sociology in the 1950s and 1960s. A mass of evidence built up, ranging from national surveys like the 1966 Coleman report in the United States (see his retrospective account in Coleman, 1990) to case studies like Ford's (1969) *Social Class and the Comprehensive School* in Britain. The evidence of socially unequal outcomes continues to mount; it is one of the most firmly established facts about Western-style educational systems in all parts of the world.

Compensatory education programs were designed in response to this specific historical situation: that is, the failure of postwar educational expansion, despite its principle of equal access, to deliver substantive equality. The educational movement occurred within a broader context of social welfare reform. In the United States, the civil rights movement, the rediscovery of poverty by the intellectuals, and the political strategies of the Kennedy and Johnson administrations led to the War on Poverty. Its main designers were welfare economists, and its main success was the reduction of poverty among the elderly — not among children (Katz, 1989).

Education was brought into the welfare picture through the correlation between lower levels of education on the one side, and higher rates of unemployment and lower wages on the other. The idea of a self-sustaining "cycle of poverty" emerged, where low aspirations and poor support for children led to low educational achievement, which in turn led to labor market failure and poverty in the next generation. Compensatory education was seen as a means to break into this cycle and derail the inheritance of poverty.[3] Thus the failure of equal access was read outward from the institutions to the families they served. Families and children became the bearers of a deficit for which the institutions should compensate. This maneuver protected conventional beliefs about schooling; indeed, a wave of optimism about the power of schooling and early childhood intervention accompanied the birth of compensatory education.

With this rationale, publicly funded programs were set up in the 1960s and 1970s in a number of wealthy countries, starting with the United States and including Britain, the Netherlands, and Australia.[4] While the details of these programs vary from country to country, they do have major design elements in common. They are "targeted" to a minority of children.[5] They select children or

[3] Useful histories of the compensatory idea have been written by Jeffrey (1978) and Silver and Silver (1991).

[4] For their stories see Connell, White, and Johnston (1991); Halsey (1972); Peterson, Rabe, and Wong (1988); and Scheerens (1987).

[5] In Australia, which is particularly explicit on this point, national compensatory education funds reach about 15 percent of school-age children. In the United States, where the situation is more complex, the figure appears to be about 11 percent, according to a careful estimate of the early 1980s (Kennedy, Jung, & Orland, 1986).

their schools by formulae involving a poverty-line calculation. They are intended to compensate for disadvantage by enriching the children's educational environment, which they do by grafting something on to the existing school and preschool system. And, finally, they are generally administered separately from conventional school funding.

The False Map of the Problem

The circumstances of the birth of compensatory programs and the political means by which some have survived — not all did — produced a false map of the problem. By this I mean a set of assumptions that govern policy and public discussion but are factually wrong, doubtful, or profoundly misleading. Three are central: that the problem concerns only a disadvantaged minority; that the poor are distinct from the majority in culture or attitudes; and that correcting disadvantage in education is a technical problem requiring, above all, the application of research-based expertise.

The Disadvantaged Minority

The image of a disadvantaged minority is built into compensatory education via the poverty line by which target groups are identified. Whatever the formulae used to measure disadvantage (they vary from country to country, from state to state, and from time to time, with a running controversy over the method), the procedure always involves drawing a cut-off line at some point on a dimension of advantage and disadvantage. Where the cut-off comes is fundamentally arbitrary. This is a familiar problem with defining poverty lines. In compensatory programs, determining the cut-off point leads to unending dispute over which children or schools should be on the list for funds. The procedure could label 50 percent of the population "disadvantaged" as logically as it could 10 percent or 20 percent. In practice, however, the cut-off point is always placed so as to indicate a modest-sized minority. This demarcation is credible because of the already existing political imagery of poverty, in which the poor are pictured as a minority outside mainstream society.[6] The policy implication is that the other 80 or 90 percent, the mainstream, are all on the same footing.

However, this is not what the evidence shows. Regardless of which measures of class inequality and educational outcomes are used, gradients of advantage and disadvantage typically appear across the school population as a whole (for one example among hundreds, see Williams, 1987). We can identify an exceptionally advantaged minority as well as an exceptionally disadvantaged one, but focusing on either extreme is insufficient. The fundamental point is that class inequality is a problem that concerns the school system *as a whole.* Poor children are not facing a separate problem. They face the worst effects of a larger pattern.

[6] The emergence of the modern concept of poverty is traced by Dean (1991), and its impact on welfare policy by Katz (1989).

The Distinctiveness of the Poor

That the poor are not like the rest of us is a traditional belief of the affluent. This belief affected the design of compensatory education mainly through the "culture of poverty" thesis, where the reproduction of poverty from one generation to another was attributed to the cultural adaptations poor people made to their circumstances (Lewis, 1968; for a later review see Hoyles, 1977).

Though framed within the discourse of anthropology, this idea was immediately given a psychological twist. Cultural difference in the group meant psychological deficit in the individual; that is, a lack of the traits needed to succeed in school. With this twist, a very wide range of research could be read as demonstrating cultural deprivation, from studies of linguistic codes to occupational expectations to achievement motivation to IQ, and so on. In the 1960s and 1970s, the cultural deficit concept became folklore among teachers as well as policymakers (Interim Committee for the Australian Schools Commission, 1973; Ryan, 1971).

It was this tendency to reduce arguments about different situations to the idea of a cultural deficit that Bernstein (1974) protested against in a famous critique of compensatory education. Culture-of-poverty ideas were strongly criticized by anthropologists, linguists, and teachers, not to mention poor people themselves, yet these ideas have had tremendous resilience, persisting through two decades of changing rhetoric, as Griffin (1993) has recently shown in a detailed survey of youth research. The ideas survive partly because they have become the organic ideology of compensatory and special education programs. The very existence of such programs now evokes the rationale of deficit, as Casanova (1990) illustrates in heartbreaking case studies of two Latino children in a U.S. school system: battered by the system's languages policy, inserted into "special education" programs — with mandated, rigid, teacher-centered methods — these children's education was massively disrupted and their social selves assaulted with labels like "learning-disabled." More broadly, deficit ideas also survive because they fit comfortably into wider ideologies of race and class difference.

But the facts of the matter do not require us to adopt cultural deficit concepts. The bulk of evidence points to cultural *similarity* between the poorest groups and the less poor. This might be expected from facts about the demography of poverty not widely known to educators. Studies such as the U.S. Panel Study of Income Dynamics (PSID), which has followed the same families since 1968, show large numbers of families moving into and out of poverty (as measured by the poverty-line approach). Over a twenty-year period, nearly 40 percent of the families in the PSID spent some period in poverty, when the rate of poverty in any one year was only 11 percent to 15 percent (Devine & Wright, 1993). We should, then, expect those in poverty at any one time to have a lot in common with the broader working class, including their relations with schools. For example, attitude surveys produce little evidence that the poor lack other people's interest in education or in children (for a recent example in England, see Heath, 1992).

In the United States, the argument over cultural deficit has been refocused by the concept of the "underclass," which is defined as inhabitants of urban centers marked by massive unemployment, environmental decay, high numbers of births to single mothers, community violence, and the presence of the drug trade. It is clear that the most severe concentrations of poverty have the most severe impact on education (for statistical evidence, see Orland, 1990). Ethnographies in inner-city settings (Anderson, 1991) and in communities of the rural poor (Heath, 1983) show ways of life that do not mesh with the practices of mainstream schooling. Ogbu's (1988) argument that this bad mesh has roots in the history of imperialism, with "involuntary minorities" such as conquered indigenous peoples and enslaved labor forces resisting the institutions of White supremacy, is attractive.

But ethnography may not be the best guide to this issue. As a research method, it assumes the coherence of the group being studied, and ethnographic writing understandably tends to emphasize what is unique or distinctive about its subjects' way of life. We must counter-balance this by considering the interplay and interconnection of poor people with other groups. The cultural inventiveness of poor people (including the American "underclass"), and their interplay with wider popular culture, is hardly to be denied — witness music from jazz to rap, new wave rock, punk fashion, contemporary street styles, and so on. And further, close-focus research on schooling, using interviews and participant observation, documents a vigorous desire for education among poor people and ethnic minorities (for example, Wexler, 1992, from the United States; Angus, 1993, from Australia). Yet there is massive educational failure. Something is malfunctioning, but hardly the culture of the poor.

The Nature of Reform

The belief that educational reform is, above all, a technical question, a matter of assembling the research and deducing the best interventions, is embedded in the education world through the very hierarchy of teaching institutions. At the apex of this hierarchy are the universities, which both produce education research and train administrators for the schools in education studies programs. The dominant ideology in education studies is positivist. The 1966 Coleman Report (Coleman, 1990) was a monument to technocratic policy research, and the "effective schools" and national testing movements continue to promote the belief that quantitative research will generate good policy more or less automatically. Teachers are defined within this framework as receiving guidance from educational science, rather than as producing fundamental knowledge themselves. The structure of educational funding in federal systems, where local institutions provide bread-and-butter school finance while higher level institutions fund policy innovation, further encourages a view of school reform as based on outside expertise.

While these are general conditions in educational policymaking, their effect on policy about poverty is especially strong. The poor are precisely the group with the least resources and the least capacity to contest the views of policymaking elites. Social movements of the poor can win concessions, but only by widespread mobilization and social disruption, as shown in the classic study by Piven and Cloward (1979). Mobilization and disruption do not generally develop around the education of the poor.

As a consequence, policy discussions about education and poverty have frequently been conducted in the absence of the two groups most likely to understand the issues: poor people themselves, and the teachers in their schools. A striking example is the 1986 conference held by the U.S. Department of Education to reconsider Chapter I programs, which was entirely composed of academics, administrators, and policy analysts (Doyle & Cooper, 1988). Teachers are expected to implement policies, but not to make them, while poor people are defined as the objects of policy interventions rather than as the authors of social change.

The broad effect of this "map" of the issues has been to locate the problem in the heads of the poor and in the errors of the particular schools serving them. Meanwhile, the virtues of other schools are taken for granted. The consequences of this policy, as Natriello et al. (1990) have perceptively pointed out, has been an oscillation among strategies of intervention that are mostly technocratic, all narrowly focused, all within a context of massive under funding, and none making a great difference to the situation.

Re-Mapping the Issues

What can we offer instead — "we" meaning researchers, teacher educators, students, and administrators, the typical audience for academic journals in education? We cannot continue to offer what we usually do: proposals for fresh, expert interventions and for more research to support them. The exemplary research by Snow, Barnes, Chandler, Goodman, and Hemphill (1991) shows the limits that have been reached by this approach. This careful and compassionate study, which sought practical lessons for literacy teaching by comparing good and bad readers among poor children in a U.S. city, found on returning four years later that hopeful differences were overwhelmed by what one can only read as the structural consequences of poverty. The enrichments these researchers proposed certainly improved the children's quality of life, but they were not capable of altering the forces shaping the children's educational fates.

There are no great surprises in the research on poverty and education, no secret keys that will unlock the solution. If there is a mystery, it is the kind that Sartre (1958) called a "mystery in broad daylight," an un-knowing created by the way we frame and use our knowledge. Descriptive research on poor children by psychologists, sociologists, and educators will certainly continue — spiced by occasional claims from biologists to have found the gene for school failure. But that kind of research is no longer decisive. What we need, above all, is a rethinking of the pattern of policy, a reexamination of the way the issues have been configured.

This rethinking should start with the theme that comes through insistently when poor people talk about education: power. This issue leads to the institutional form of mass education, the politics of the curriculum, and the character of teachers' work. I develop each of these themes in the discussion that follows.

Power

Educators are uncomfortable with the language of power; to talk of "disadvantage" is easier. But schools are literally power-full institutions. Public schools exercise power, both in the general compulsion to attend and in the particular decisions they make. School grades, for instance, are not just aids to teaching. They are also tiny judicial decisions with legal status, which cumulate into large authoritative decisions about people's lives — progression in school, selection into higher education, employment prospects.

Poor people, like the rest of the working class, by and large understand this feature of schools. It is central to their more dire experiences of education. An example is Wexler's (1992) description of students' experiences at Washington High, where tardiness is policed by an intrusive patrolling of corridors, leading to the bureaucratic processing of students for expulsion.

Once again we must recognize that what students in poverty experience is not unique. Mass schooling systems were created in the nineteenth century as state intervention into working-class life, to regulate and partly take over the rearing of children. Legal compulsion was needed because this intervention was widely resisted.

From this history, public schools and their working-class clientele inherit a deeply ambivalent relationship. On the one hand, the school embodies state power; hence the most common complaint from parents and students is about teachers who "don't care" but cannot be made to change. On the other hand, the school system has become the main bearer of working-class hopes for a better future, especially where the hopes of unionism or socialism have died. Hence the dilemma, poignantly described by Lareau (1987), of working-class parents who want educational advancement for their children but cannot deploy the techniques or resources called for by the school. The extent to which school routines presuppose a gender pattern based on a certain level of affluence, the unpaid labor of a mother/housewife, is particularly noteworthy.

To deal with powerful institutions requires power. Some of the resources that families need to handle contemporary schools are the bread and butter of positivist research on children: adequate food, physical security, attention from helpful adults, books in the home, scholastic know-how in the family, and so on. Generally absent from positivist research (because they are hard to quantify as attributes of a person) are the collective resources that produce the kind of school system that favors a particular home environment for success. These resources are put into play when property owners cap taxes supporting public schools; or when university faculty dominate curriculum boards and corporations create textbooks; or when the professional parents at an upper income school meet with routine responsiveness from principal and teachers.

In the false map already discussed, poverty is constantly taken as the sign of something else, such as cultural difference, or psychological or genetic deficit.

Educators need to be more blunt and see poverty as poverty. Poor people are short of resources, individually and jointly, including many of the resources that are deployed in education. The scale of material shortages is easily shown. For instance, an Australian study of household expenditure in families with dependent children found high-income couples spending an average of $8.82 per week on books and periodicals, while sole-parent pensioners (roughly equivalent to AFDC recipients in the United States) spent $2.06 (Whiteford, Bradbury, & Saunders, 1989).

Such differences in income and expenditure, not to mention the greater inequalities of wealth, mean both shortages of resources in the home and vulnerability to institutional power — such as derogatory labelling in the welfare system, and streaming or tracking in the education system. There is no mystery about this to poor people. As an activist in a Canadian immigrant women's group put it:

> Streaming of low income, immigrant children is obvious. More well-to-do parents make sure their children are directed in the proper direction, they have much more pro-active involvement in the school system. Poor working-class families don't have the time or the wherewithal to fight. (quoted in Curtis et al., 1992, p. 23)

Poverty and alienation are likely to mean material disruptions of life, one of the points emphatically made in the "underclass" discussion. Disruptions can also be seen outside the United States: witness Robins and Cohen's *Knuckle Sandwich* (1978), about youth and violence in England, and Embling's look at *Fragmented Lives* (1986) in Australia. We do not need to assume cultural difference to understand the damaging effects of poverty on young people's lives. We certainly need to think carefully about power in order to understand the violence that has long been an undercurrent in schools for the urban poor, and which has taken a dramatic turn with the advent of guns in U.S. high schools.

Serious violence is more common from boys than from girls, not because of their hormones, but because Western masculinities are socially constructed around claims to power. Where this claim is made with few resources except physical force, and where boys have been habitually disciplined by force, "trouble" in the form of violence is eminently likely. A familiar course of events frequently develops where boys' masculinity comes to be defined or tested in their conflict with the state power embodied in the school, a conflict that can turn violent. Losing this conflict, which is inevitable, is likely to end the boys' formal education.[7] The power relations of gender thus play out paradoxically in a context of poverty. To grapple with such a process means directly addressing the politics of masculinity — an issue, as Yates (1993) notes at the end of her review of the education of girls, still absent from educational agendas.

The School as an Institution

The young people who fight the school and find themselves bounced out on the street are meeting more than the anger of particular teachers and principals.

[7] See, for example, the life histories of unemployed young men discussed in Connell (1989).

They are facing the logic of an institution embodying the power of the state and the cultural authority of the dominant class. Fine's (1991) study of a New York inner-city school shows the dull bureaucratic rationality of encouraging students to drop out. In a school facing great difficulties in teaching and establishing its legitimacy, and with no prospect of the resources it needs or a change in its working methods, "discharge" of a student becomes the routine solution to a wide range of problems.

The role of institutional power in shaping pupil-teacher interactions has been clear in close-focus studies of schools for some time. It was vividly portrayed, for instance, in Corrigan's (1979) study of the struggle for control in two schools in a declining industrial area of England. What "school ethnographies" cannot show, however, is the institutional shape of the education system as a whole. Selectiveness at upper levels (selection cuts in at different ages in different countries) means a narrowing offer of learning that forces unequal outcomes, whether or not the system attempts to equalize opportunity. For instance, if a university system trains only one in ten of a particular age group, which is the current average for industrial countries (United Nations Development Programme, 1992), then nine must go without degrees. If unequal outcomes are forced, a struggle for advantage results, and the political and economic resources that can be mobilized in that struggle become important. The poor are precisely those with the least resources.

Policies to increase competitive pressures within the school system — including mandatory objective testing, parental choice plans, and "gifted and talented" programs — have a transparent class meaning, reinforcing the advantages of the privileged and confirming the exclusion of the poor. The fact that such policies deliver class advantages is not new knowledge; similar observations on the class meaning of testing programs have been made for half a century (for example, Davis, 1948). It seems to be a fact that has to be constantly rediscovered.

The legitimacy of educational competitions depends on some belief in level playing fields. Economic facts have been marginal in discussions of educational disadvantage, though educators periodically justify compensatory programs as contributing to a well-trained work force. In the United States, however, Kozol (1991) has recently made an issue of differences in school funding. Taylor and Piché (1991), in a study of per-pupil expenditure by U.S. school boards, found a range from $11,752 in the richest district to $1,324 in the poorest, with many states having a 2.5-to-1 or 3-to-1 ratio between high-expenditure and low-expenditure groups of districts. Further, current per-capita spending is likely to understate differences, because background capital expenditure has also been unequal. And beyond public finance, as already noted, there are stark inequalities in what can be privately spent on educational resources.

Other wealthy countries have more centralized, and thus more uniform, funding of schools than the United States, but a more exclusive system of student selection for higher education. This, being more costly, weights overall per-capita expenditure back in favor of advantaged groups who enter higher education in greater proportions. On the face of it, differences in the total social investment in the education of rich children and poor children appear to be much larger than any redistributive effect of compensatory education funds.

Curriculum

The importance of curriculum for issues of educational inequality has long been argued by Apple (1982, 1993), and the point is highly relevant to strategy about poverty. Compensatory programs were intended to lever disadvantaged children back into mainstream schooling. The success of these programs is conventionally measured by pupil progress in the established curriculum, especially as evidenced by the closing of gaps to system norms. This logic has been taken to a startling extreme in a program in Cleveland, Ohio, which consists of awarding pupils $40 for getting an A, $20 for a B, and $10 for a C (Natriello et al., 1990).

When progress in the mainstream curriculum is taken as the goal of intervention, that curriculum is exempted from criticism. However, the experience of teachers in disadvantaged schools has persistently led them to question the curriculum. Conventional subject matter and texts and traditional teaching methods and assessment techniques turn out to be sources of systematic difficulty. They persistently produce boredom. Enforcing them heightens the problem of discipline, and so far as they are successfully enforced, they divide pupils between an academically successful minority and an academically discredited majority. (Connell, Johnston, & White, 1992; Wexler, 1992).

To teach well in disadvantaged schools requires a shift in pedagogy and in the way content is determined. A shift towards more negotiated curriculum and more participatory classroom practice can be seen in compensatory education in Australia, where it is a broad tendency in disadvantaged schools, not just a matter of isolated initiatives (Connell, White, et al., 1991). The effectiveness of similar practice in U.S. elementary classrooms is demonstrated by Knapp, Shields, and Turnbull (1992). However, such practices do not seem to be the main tendency in the United States. A survey of U.S. middle schools by MacIver and Epstein (1990) suggests a more conventional pedagogy, with less commitment to active learning methods and exploratory courses in disadvantaged schools than in advantaged schools. The push for "standards" and "basic skills" has fostered a rigid, teacher-centered pedagogy in compensatory and special education programs (for a striking illustration, see Griswold, Cotton, & Hansen, 1986).

To see "mainstream" curriculum as a key source of educational inequality raises the question of where it comes from. We are beginning to get an answer from the new social history of the curriculum produced by Goodson (1985, 1988) and others. The very concept of "mainstream" must be called into question, as it suggests reasoned consensus. What we are dealing with, rather, is a dominant, or hegemonic, curriculum, derived historically from the educational practices of European upper class men. This curriculum became dominant in mass education systems during the last hundred and fifty years, as the political representatives of the powerful succeeded in marginalizing other experiences and other ways of organizing knowledge. It has been reorganized from time to time by struggles among interest groups; thus classics was replaced by physical science as the highest prestige knowledge, without disturbing the "subject" organization of knowledge. The competitive academic curriculum sits alongside other kinds of curriculum in the schools — such as practical knowledge in music or in manual arts — but remains hegemonic in the sense that it defines "real" knowledge, is linked to teacher professionalism, and determines promotion in the education system (Connell, Ashenden, Kessler, & Dowsett, 1982).

The apparently remote discipline of curriculum history has made a key contribution to rethinking the issues of poverty and education. It has de-mythologized the hegemonic curriculum and shown it to be *only* one among a number of ways knowledge could have been organized for the schools (Whitty, 1985; Whitty & Young, 1976). Without this historical perspective, proposals for alternative curricula are easily discredited as abandoning real knowledge and educational quality. Different versions of this claim were made in turn by the "Black Papers" neoconservatives in England in the 1960s and 1970s, cultural literacy entrepreneurs in the United States in the 1980s, and professors attacking assessment reform in Australia in the 1990s. We can now see that the work of teachers in disadvantaged schools implies not a shift to different content (though there will be some of that), but, more decisively, a different organization of the field of knowledge as a whole.

Teachers' Work

Teachers are strikingly absent from much of the policy debate about schooling and poverty (so much so that a recent book reviewing the subject does not even list teachers in its index). This absence is an important consequence of the deficit interpretation of disadvantage and the technocratic style of policymaking.

But teachers are the front-line workers in schools. If exclusion is accomplished by schools, it is certainly in large measure through what teachers do. We may not wish to blame teachers, but we also cannot ignore them. Education as a cultural enterprise is constituted in and through their labor. Their work is the arena where the great contradictions around education and social justice condense.

Teachers' work has been studied in an international literature (surveyed by Ginsburg, forthcoming; Seddon, forthcoming), which, like curriculum history, has been little noticed in discussions of poverty. Nevertheless, its significance is clear. Lawn (1993), for example, shows the complexity of teachers' relationships to state power and the importance of teacher professionalism as a system of indirect control. Professionalism is an important factor attaching teachers to the hegemonic curriculum. The question of the "de-skilling" of teachers through tighter management control and packaged curricula is highly relevant to the prospects for good teaching in disadvantaged schools, which requires maximum flexibility and imagination.

Some activities included under the name "compensatory education" expand teachers' options and call for higher levels of skill. Others, as a condition of funding, constrict methods and de-skill teachers, generally pushing them towards more authoritarian styles. Where compensatory programs are accompanied by an active testing program, for example, a familiar pressure is created to teach to the test and thus narrow the curriculum. "Pull-out" classes are likely to disrupt the supportive classroom dynamics that good teachers try to establish. The whole model of expert intervention tends to disempower teachers. Given all these effects, it is likely that some compensatory interventions have worsened the educational situation in disadvantaged schools, not improved it. It is almost impossible for embattled schools to resist offers of resources, but the consequences are not always beneficial. (See the uneasy discussions in Doyle & Cooper, 1988; Knapp, Shields, & Turnbull, 1992; Savage, 1987; Scheerens, 1987.)

By looking at the industrial conditions of teachers' work, we might also begin to understand the paradox of the evaluations of compensatory education (for example, Glazer, 1986). In a nutshell, most intervention projects produce little change when measured in conventional ways, while those that do produce change follow no clear pattern. The technocratic approach to policymaking should be deeply embarrassed by this situation, though the usual reaction is to call for more research.

I suspect these findings reflect a Hawthorne effect in poverty programs, along the following lines.[8] Teaching practice is governed mainly by the institutional constraints of the school as a workplace. Compensatory interventions are generally far too small to change these constraints, a point that has been made throughout their history (see, for example, Halsey, 1972; Natriello et al., 1990). Accordingly, most educational practice in disadvantaged schools is routinely like practice in other schools (for evidence, see Connell, 1991), and produces the usual socially selective effects. Those programs that do produce changes happen to have found one of the variety of ways — which may be situational and temporary — of bolstering teachers' agency, increasing their capacity to maneuver around constraints and grapple with the contradictions of the relationship between poor children and schools.

Towards a Strategy of Change

Given a remapping of the issues along these lines, our concept of what constitutes a solution must also change. Solutions cannot consist of expert interventions from a central place. The educational authority that defines "expertise" must itself be contested. People in disadvantaged schools and poor communities do not lack knowledge. They do, however, often lack ways of putting their knowledge to use.

Does this mean that academics should simply get out of the way? There is a lot to be said for breaking the routines by which science legitimates intrusions

[8] The "Hawthorne effect" is named for the factory where a famous experiment found industrial workers increasing output no matter how their work was arranged by the experimenters. The researchers finally realized that it was the experiment itself, not the manipulations within it, that was creating a supportive group and boosting the workers' morale.

in the lives of the poor. Nevertheless, researchers often do have information, resources, and skills that poor people and their teachers can use.

Rather than vacate the field, then, we should rethink the relationship between professional intellectuals and disadvantaged communities — as is done, for instance, in participatory action research in the welfare field (Wadsworth, 1983). It is possible to support strategic thinking in the schools rather than substitute for it, though the balance is not an easy one. That is to say, it is possible for researchers to refine, criticize, inform, and disseminate attempts to achieve educational purposes defined from below. In this spirit, I will briefly explore four issues that necessarily arise for democratic education strategies concerned with poverty: the goals of action, the direction of change in curriculum, the work force, and the political conditions of change.

Formulating Goals

Most statements of purpose for educational reform treat justice in distributional terms. That is, they treat education in much the way arguments about economic justice treat money: as a social good of standard character that needs to be shared more fairly. Even if the criteria for fair shares vary from one policy sphere to another, as in Walzer's (1983) sophisticated model of justice, the distributional approach governs the discussion of education.

If we have learned one thing from research on the interaction of curriculum and social context, it is that educational processes are not standard in this sense. Distributing equal amounts of the hegemonic curriculum to girls and boys, to poor children and rich children, to Black children and White children, to immigrants and native-born, to indigenous people and their colonizers, does not do the same thing for them — or to them. In education, the "how much" and the "who" cannot be separated from the "what."

The concept of distributive justice certainly applies to material resources for education, such as school funds and equipment. But we need something more to deal with the content and process of education: a concept of curricular justice (Connell, 1993). This idea is closely connected to the lesson curriculum history teaches: that there are always multiple ways to organize the knowledge content of schooling.

Each particular way of constructing the curriculum (i.e., organizing the field of knowledge and defining how it is to be taught and learned) carries social effects. Curriculum empowers and disempowers, authorizes and de-authorizes, recognizes and mis-recognizes different social groups and their knowledge and identities. For instance, curriculum developed from academic institutions controlled by men has, in a variety of ways, authorized the practices and experiences of men and marginalized those of women.[9] Curriculum defined by representatives of a dominant ethnic group is liable to exclude or de-authorize the knowledge and experience of dominated groups, or to incorporate them on

[9] For an excellent account of this process and the complexities of contesting it, see chapter five in Yates (1993).

terms that suit the dominant group.[10] Curricular justice concerns the organization of knowledge, and, through it, the justice of the social relations being produced through education.

There is nothing exotic about this idea. It is implied in a great deal of practical teaching that goes on in disadvantaged schools, teaching that contests the disempowering effects of the hegemonic curriculum and authorizes locally produced knowledge. This is the kind of "good teaching" Haberman (1991) has recently contrasted with the "pedagogy of poverty." As he observes, the challenge is how to institutionalize "good teaching" in disadvantaged schools. Initiatives of this kind remain marginal and are easily dismantled, unless they can be linked to larger purposes.

I think a concept of curricular justice makes the link to larger purposes possible and should be at the heart of strategic thinking on education and disadvantage. It requires us to think through curriculum-making from the point of view of the least advantaged, not from the standpoint of what is currently authorized. It requires us to think about how to generalize the point of view of the least advantaged as a program for the organization and production of knowledge in general.

Taking an *educational* view of poverty and education thus pushes us beyond the goal of "compensation" and towards the goal of reorganizing the cultural content of education as a whole. This goal is intimidating, given the difficulties encountered with much more limited goals. Yet clear thinking is helped if we put local initiatives in the perspective of the larger agenda they imply.

The Direction of Curriculum Change

Compensatory programs have mainly supplemented the hegemonic curriculum, adding extra activities or small group instruction in core areas of conventional teaching — principally, mathematics and language skills. Add-on programs do not change the main patterns of teaching and learning in the school. A strategy that takes curriculum change seriously would base itself on another approach found in compensatory programs, the whole-school change approach, which uses compensatory funds to redesign the major activities of the school.

How we understand curricular change depends on what we take the basic social effects of education to be. Wexler (1992) sees the main effects as the discursive formation of identities. This would focus strategies for justice on respect for diversity, and on producing identities that are rich and solid — not far, indeed, from the concerns of multicultural education. I would argue, however, for a broader conception of educational effects as the development of capacities for social practice (Connell, forthcoming). The social practices addressed by schooling include the winning of livelihood, a theme whose importance for youth still in school is documented by Wilson and Wyn (1987); the construction

[10] For a striking historical example of debate within the dominant group about this issue, see Ball (1984).

of gender and negotiation of sexuality (Frank, 1993); and the mobilization of social power, which is a familiar theme in adult literacy work (see Lankshear, 1987). Perhaps learning how to mobilize and use power is the clearest example of how a course of learning can open up ways of transforming the situation of the poor. The same point was made by the Australian Schools Commission, in stating objectives for its national compensatory education program; the objectives included:

> To ensure that students have systematic access to programs which will equip them with economic and political understanding so that they can act individually or together to improve their circumstances. (Australian Schools Commission, 1985, p. 98)

The idea of helping the poor "act . . . together" to change things is directly opposed to the divisive effects of a competitive assessment system. The link between exclusionary curricula and competitive assessment is very close. It is no accident that the Blackburn report on post-compulsory education in the Australian state of Victoria, which pursued the principle of a socially inclusive curriculum, also laid the groundwork for an important democratic reform of secondary assessment (Ministerial Review, 1985). This report drew on the experience of disadvantaged schools to formulate a policy for the state's school system as a whole.

Curriculum and assessment reforms are not cheap, especially in the time and human energy they require. The level of material resources for schools serving the poor still matters, even if one agrees that the quality of education does not depend on the freshness of paint on the school buildings. Measures of current per-capita funding are, as I have already suggested, inadequate measures of total social investment in the education of different groups of children. Given the educationally relevant inequalities of resources around schools, the consequences of unequal family and community wealth and income, distributive justice would require much higher levels of funding to the schools of the poor, and higher funding to working-class schools in general.

A curriculum focus, similarly, does not erase issues about the school as an institution. The curriculum as it is taught and learned, not just as it is in the manual, is the labor process of pupils and teachers, and, like other forms of labor, is powerfully affected by the surrounding social relations. Expanding the agency of teachers means moving towards industrial democracy at the level of the school. This is not easily achieved, as teachers' unions know; for a situation like that found in Britain after a decade of new-right government, it may sound utopian. But if we are serious about educational enrichment, then we need to produce the industrial conditions for richer forms of teaching.

The students, too, are working in more than a metaphorical sense. Democratization means expanding the agency of those normally overwhelmed by the agency of others or immobilized by current structures. Good teaching does this in an immediate, local way — as is vividly shown in the adult education for empowerment described by Shor (1992), where the teacher functions as problem-poser and a critical dialogue replaces teacher-talk. An agenda for change must concern itself with how this local effect can be generalized.

The Work Force

Given the institutional and cultural forces that make for inequality in education, the case can be made that more can be done outside schools than inside them. This seems to be implied by postmodernist readings of educational politics by authors such as Giroux (1992). Acknowledging the cultural changes to which this reading responds, I would nevertheless argue that the profoundly ambivalent relationship between working-class people and educational institutions is central to contemporary cultural politics in industrial countries. This relationship has grown in importance with the growing weight of education as a part of the economy and the culture. Teachers in schools are the workers most strategically placed to affect the relationship. I have argued already for bringing teachers' work to the center of discussions of disadvantage. If the education of children in poverty is to be changed, teachers will be the work force of reform. This conclusion has two important corollaries.

First, teachers should be centrally involved in the design of reform strategies. Giroux (1988) earlier called our attention to the sense in which teachers are intellectuals. A capacity for strategic thinking certainly exists among the teachers of the poor. The Disadvantaged Schools Program in Australia, partly because of its decentralized design, encouraged the growth of an activist network that included teachers' unions and a group of experienced teachers in poor districts. This informal network, more than any formal agency, has transmitted experience and provided the forum for intense policy debates (White & Johnston, 1993). Such groups exist in other countries, too. A notable example is the network around the magazine *Our Schools/Our Selves,* which has brought teachers across Canada into a series of debates about educational reform. An intelligent approach to policymaking would regard such teacher networks as a key asset.

Second, a reform agenda must concern the shaping of this work force: the recruitment, training, in-service education, and career structures of teachers in disadvantaged schools. The 1966 Coleman report, to its credit, raised this issue and collected data on teacher training, but the issue almost vanished from later discussions of disadvantage. In a recession, where education budgets are under pressure, funds for teacher preparation, and especially for in-service training, are likely to be cut. To an extent, compensatory programs themselves function as teacher educators. A potentially cost-effective reform would be to expand these programs' capacities to train teachers, to circulate information, to pool knowledge, and to pass on expertise.

The work force is not static. Families move into and out of poverty, and teachers move into and out of disadvantaged schools. For both reasons, issues about poverty *should* concern teachers in all parts of a school system. I would argue that these issues should be major themes in initial teacher training, and that competence in work with disadvantaged groups should be central to the idea of professionalism in teaching.

Political Conditions: The Poor and the Less Poor

Targeted compensatory education programs are based on definitions of disadvantage, which are always to some degree arbitrary and may also be stigmatizing — especially where, as in the United States, issues about poverty are interwoven with a volatile politics of race.

Special programs for the disadvantaged are most easily accepted where inequalities can be seen as accidental, or as consequences of neglect. They are not so easily accepted where the inequalities are intended. A recent court case showed the school system in Rockford, Illinois, to have been operating a covert system of racial segregation — via tracking, scheduling, and special programs — that subverted official desegregation policies to a startling degree ("'Integrated' Schools," 1993). This is a conspicuous example, but institutional racism is, of course, not unusual (for a recent British example, see Tomlinson, 1992.) We also cannot ignore the intention behind other forms of inequality and exclusion, whether along lines of class or gender or nationality.

Disadvantage is always produced through mechanisms that also produce advantage. The institutions that do this are generally defended by their beneficiaries. The beneficiaries of the current educational order are, broadly speaking, the groups with greater economic and institutional power, greater access to the means of persuasion, and the best representation in government and in professions. No one should imagine that educational change in the interests of the poor can be conflict-free.

That change happens at all is due to two facts. First, advantaged groups are far from monolithic. They are internally divided in a number of ways: for example, professionals versus capitalists, regional elites versus multinational elites, elite women versus elite men, new wealth versus old. These divisions affect educational stances, such as support for public expenditure on schooling. Members of advantaged groups differ in their judgments of short-term versus long-term interests, and in their willingness to take stances based on a notion of the common good. Their views of long-term interests are affected by pressure from below. United States elites, as Domhoff (1990) argues, conceded reforms in the 1960s and early 1970s — including compensatory education — under pressure of social disruption from the civil rights and other social movements. The reassertion of conservatism in U.S. public policy followed the decline of this pressure.

Second, the interests of the poor are not isolated. I emphasized earlier the statistical evidence that the most severe disadvantage is part of a much broader pattern of class exclusion. The poorest groups share an interest in educational reform with a broader constituency in the working class, even in very wealthy countries. However, it is not automatic that shared interest will be turned into any kind of practical alliance. Racism, regionalism, the weakening of the union movement, and the impact of new-right educational politics all stand in the way.

Targeted programs, however well-designed and lively, are unlikely to have a major impact unless they are part of a broader agenda for social justice. The problem of breadth is familiar in debates over social policy (see, for example,

Skocpol, 1991). Narrowly targeted benefits appear more cost-effective than universal benefits, especially in a context of budget-cutting. But narrow targeting is likely to stigmatize the targeted group; the current political hostility to welfare dependents in the United States is a prime example. Because their beneficiaries are stigmatized minorities, the programs are politically weak, and the level of benefits is held down to a minimum. Continuing poverty is a common result. Broad entitlements to benefits (as illustrated by age pensions and health insurance in countries with universal systems) create larger constituencies and mobilize more political strength. Paradoxically, then, *less* targeted benefits (including universal benefits) are often more effective in producing redistribution: they "level up."

In education the case is somewhat different because the universal benefit already exists — compulsory schooling. The problem, as I have argued throughout this article, is that this universal benefit contains powerful mechanisms of privilege and exclusion; it does not *function* in a universal way. A social justice program in education must attempt to reconstruct the service that is formally available to everyone. Once we recognize this, the same strategic principle applies as in welfare politics: the broader the agenda, the more chance of a social justice outcome. The task is easier than welfare reform in that the idea of common schooling is well established, and more difficult in that the unequal functioning of education systems is defended by a formidable combination of class interest, professional routine, and institutional hierarchy.

To accomplish the institutional change needed by children in poverty requires greater social forces than poverty programs themselves generate. At the end of the day, then, the educational problems of compensatory education are political problems. Their long-term solution involves social alliances whose outlines are still, at best, emerging. Yet work on education can be one of the ways these very alliances are created.

References

Anderson, E. (1991). Neighborhood effects on teenage pregnancy. In C. Jencks & P. E. Peterson (Eds.), *The urban underclass* (pp. 375–398). Washington, DC: Brookings Institution.

Angus, L. (Ed.) (1993). *Education, inequality and social identity.* London: Falmer Press.

Apple, M. W. (1982). *Education and power.* Boston: Routledge & Kegan Paul.

Apple, M. W. (1993). *Official knowledge: Democratic education in a conservative age.* New York: Routledge.

Australian Schools Commission. (1985). *Quality and equality.* Canberra: Commonwealth Schools Commission.

Avalos, B. (1992). Education for the poor: Quality or relevance? *British Journal of Sociology of Education, 13,* 419–436.

Ball, S. J. (1984). Imperialism, social control and the colonial curriculum in Africa. In I. F. Goodson & S. J. Ball (Eds.), *Defining the curriculum: Histories and ethnographies* (pp. 117–147). London: Falmer Press.

Bernstein, B. B. (1974). A critique of the concept of "compensatory education." In D. Wedderburn (Ed.), *Poverty, inequality and class structure* (pp. 109–122). Cambridge, Eng.: Cambridge University Press.

Casanova, U. (1990). Rashomon in the classroom: Multiple perspectives of teachers, parents and students. In A. Barona & E. E. Garcia (Eds.), *Children at risk: Poverty, minority status, and other issues in educational equity* (pp. 135–149). Washington, DC: National Association of School Psychologists.
Clark, E. A. G. (1977). The superiority of the "Scotch system": Scottish ragged schools and their influence. *Scottish Educational Studies, 9*, 29-39.
Coleman, J. S. (1990). *Equality and achievement in education*. Boulder: Westview.
Connell, R. W. (1989). Cool guys, swots and wimps: The interplay of masculinity and education. *Oxford Review of Education, 15*, 291–303.
Connell, R. W. (1991). The workforce of reform: Teachers in the disadvantaged schools program. *Australian Journal of Education, 35*, 229–245.
Connell, R. W. (1993). *Schools and social justice*. Philadelphia: Temple University Press.
Connell, R. W. (forthcoming). Transformative labor: Theorizing the politics of teachers' work. In M. B. Ginsburg (Ed.), *The politics of educators' work and lives*. New York: Garland.
Connell, R. W., Ashenden, D. J., Kessler, S., & Dowsett, G. W. (1982). *Making the difference: Schools, families and social division*. Sydney: Allen & Unwin.
Connell, R. W., Johnston, K. M., & White, V. M. (1992). *Measuring up: Assessment, evaluation and educational disadvantage*. Canberra: Australian Curriculum Studies Association.
Connell, R. W., White, V. M., & Johnston, K. M. (1991). *"Running twice as hard": The disadvantaged schools program in Australia*. Geelong, Australia: Deakin University.
Corrigan, P. (1979). *Schooling the Smash Street kids*. London: Macmillan.
Curtis, B., Livingstone, D. W., & Smaller, H. (1992). *Stacking the deck: The streaming of working-class kids in Ontario schools*. Toronto: Our Schools/Our Selves Education Foundation.
Davis, A. (1948). *Social-class influences upon learning*. Cambridge, MA: Harvard University Press.
Dean, M. (1991). *The constitution of poverty: Toward a genealogy of liberal governance*. London: Routledge.
Devine, J. A., & Wright, J. D. (1993). *The greatest of evils: Urban poverty and the American underclass*. New York: Aldine de Gruyter.
Domhoff, G. W. (1990). *The power elite and the state: How policy is made in America*. New York: Aldine de Gruyter.
Doyle, D. P., & Cooper, B. S. (Eds.). (1988). *Federal aid to the disadvantaged: What future for Chapter I?* London: Falmer Press.
Embling, J. (1986). *Fragmented lives: A darker side of Australian life*. Ringwood, Australia: Penguin.
Fine, M. (1991). *Framing dropouts: Notes on the politics of an urban public high school*. Albany: State University of New York Press.
Ford, J. (1969). *Social class and the comprehensive school*. London: Routledge & Kegan Paul.
Frank, B. (1993). Straight/strait jackets for masculinity: Educating for "real" men. *Atlantis, 18*(1-2), 47–59.
Ginsburg, M. B. (Ed.). (forthcoming). *The politics of educators' work and lives*. New York: Garland.
Giroux, H. A. (1988). *Teachers as intellectuals: Toward a critical pedagogy of learning*. Granby, MA: Bergin & Garvey.
Giroux, H. A. (1992). *Border crossings: Cultural workers and the politics of education*. New York: Routledge.
Glazer, N. (1986). Education and training programs and poverty. In S. H. Danziger & D. H. Weinberg (Eds.), *Fighting poverty: What works and what doesn't* (pp. 152–173). Cambridge, MA: Harvard University Press.
Goodson, I. F. (Ed.). (1985). *Social histories of the secondary curriculum: Subjects for study*. London: Falmer Press.
Goodson, I. F. (1988). *The making of curriculum: Collected essays*. London: Falmer Press.
Griffin, C. (1993). *Representations of youth: The study of youth and adolescence in Britain and America*. Cambridge, Eng.: Polity Press.

Griswold, P. A., Cotton, K. J., & Hansen, J. B. (1986). *Effective compensatory education sourcebook.* Washington, DC: U.S. Department of Education.
Haberman, M. (1991). The pedagogy of poverty versus good teaching. *Phi Delta Kappan, 73,* 290–294.
Halsey, A. H. (Ed.). (1972). *Educational priority: Vol. I. E. P. A. Problems and policies.* London: Her Majesty's Stationery Office.
Harrington, M. (1962). *The other America.* New York: Macmillan.
Heath, A. (1992). The attitudes of the underclass. In D. J. Smith (Ed.), *Understanding the underclass* (pp. 32–47). London: Policy Studies Institute.
Heath, S. B. (1983). *Ways with words: Language, life and work in communities and classrooms.* Cambridge, Eng.: Cambridge University Press.
Hoyles, M. (1977). Cultural deprivation and compensatory education. In M. Hoyles (Ed.), *The politics of literacy* (pp. 172–181). London: Writers and Readers Publishing Cooperative.
"Integrated" schools kept races separate. (1983, November 9). *San Francisco Chronicle.*
Interim Committee for the Australian Schools Commission. (1973). *Schools in Australia.* Canberra: Australian Government Publishing Service.
Jeffrey, J. R. (1978). *Education for children of the poor: A study of the origins and implementation of the Elementary and Secondary Education Act of 1965.* Columbus: Ohio State University Press.
Katz, M. B. (1989). *The undeserving poor: From the War on Poverty to the war on welfare.* New York: Pantheon.
Kennedy, M. M., Jung, R. K., & Orland, M. E. (1986). *Poverty, achievement and the distribution of compensatory education services: An interim report from the national assessment of Chapter I.* Washington, DC: U.S. Department of Education, Office of Educational Research and Improvement.
Knapp, M. S., Shields, P. M., & Turnbull, B. J. (1992). *Academic challenge for the children of poverty: Summary report.* Washington, DC: U.S. Department of Education, Office of Policy and Planning.
Korbin, J. E. (1992). Introduction: Child poverty in the United States. *American Behavioral Scientist, 35,* 213–219.
Kozol, J. (1991). *Savage inequalities: Children in America's schools.* New York: Crown.
Lankshear, C. (1987). *Literacy, schooling and revolution.* New York: Falmer Press.
Lareau, A. (1987). Social class differences in family-school relationships: The importance of cultural capital. *Sociology of Education, 60*(2), 73–85.
Lawn, M. (1993, April). *The political nature of teaching: Arguments around schoolwork.* Paper presented at American Educational Research Association Conference, Atlanta, 1993.
Lewis, O. (1968). *La vida: A Puerto Rican family in the culture of poverty — San Juan and New York.* London: Panther.
MacIver, D. J., & Epstein, J. L. (1990). *How equal are opportunities for learning in disadvantaged and advantaged middle grade schools?* Baltimore: Johns Hopkins University, Center for Research on Effective Schooling for Disadvantaged Students.
MacPherson, S. (1987). *Five hundred million children: Poverty and child welfare in the Third World.* Brighton, Eng.: Wheatsheaf.
Ministerial Review of Postcompulsory Schooling (Blackburn Committee). (1985). *Report.* Melbourne: Education Department, Victoria.
Natriello, G., McDill, E. L., & Pallas, A. M. (1990). *Schooling disadvantaged children: Racing against catastrophe.* New York: Teachers College Press.
Ogbu, J. U. (1988). Cultural diversity and human development. In D. T. Slaughter (Ed.), *Black children and poverty: A developmental perspective* (pp. 11–28). San Francisco: Jossey-Bass.
Orland, M. E. (1990). Demographics of disadvantage: Intensity of childhood poverty and its relationship to educational experience. In J. I. Goodlad & P. Keating (Eds.), *Access to knowledge: An agenda of our nation's schools* (pp. 43–58). New York: College Entrance Examination Board.

Peterson, P. E., Rabe, B. G., & Wong, K. K. (1988). The evolution of the compensatory education program. In D. P. Doyle & B. S. Cooper (Eds.), *Federal aid to the disadvantaged: What future for Chapter I?* (pp. 33–60). London: Falmer Press.

Piven, F. F., & Cloward, R. A. (1979). *Poor people's movements: Why they succeed, how they fail.* New York: Vintage.

Riley, R. W. (1994, January 27). Reinventing Chapter I deserves full support. *San Francisco Chronicle*, op ed page.

Robins, D., & Cohen, P. (1978). *Knuckle sandwich: Growing up in the working-class city.* Harmondsworth, Eng.: Penguin.

Ryan, W. (1971). *Blaming the victim.* New York: Vintage Books.

Sartre, J. P. (1958). *Being and nothingness.* London: Methuen.

Savage, D. G. (1987). Why Chapter I hasn't made much difference. *Phi Delta Kappan, 68,* 581–584.

Scheerens, J. (1987). *Enhancing educational opportunities for disadvantaged learners: A review of Dutch research on compensatory education and educational development policy.* Amsterdam: North-Holland Publishing.

Seddon, T. (forthcoming). Teachers' work and political action. In N. Postlethwaite & T. Husen (Eds.), *International encyclopedia for educational research.* Oxford, Eng.: Pergamon.

Shor, I. (1992). *Empowering education: Critical teaching for social change.* Chicago: University of Chicago Press.

Silver, H., & Silver, P. (1991). *An educational war on poverty: American and British policy-making, 1960–1980.* Cambridge, Eng.: Cambridge University Press.

Skocpol, T. (1991). Targeting within universalism: Politically viable policies to combat poverty in the United States. In C. Jencks & P. E. Peterson (Eds.), *The urban underclass* (pp. 411–436). Washington, DC: Brookings Institution.

Snow, C. E., Barnes, W. S., Chandler, J., Goodman, I. F., & Hemphill, L. (1991). *Unfulfilled expectations: Home and school influences on literacy.* Cambridge, MA: Harvard University Press.

Taylor, W. L., & Piché, D. M. (1991). *A report on shortchanging children: The impact of fiscal inequity on the education of students at risk.* Washington, DC: U.S. House of Representatives, Committee on Education and Labor.

Thorne, B. (1993). *Gender play: Girls and boys in school.* New Brunswick, NJ: Rutgers University Press.

Tomlinson, S. (1992). Disadvantaging the disadvantaged: Bangladeshis and education in Tower Hamlets. *British Journal of Sociology of Education, 13,* 437-446.

United Nations Development Programme. (1992). *Human Development Report 1992.* New York: Oxford University Press.

U.S. Bureau of the Census. (1992). *Poverty in the United States: 1991.* Washington, DC: Government Printing Office.

Wadsworth, Y. (1983). *Do it yourself social research.* Melbourne: Allen & Unwin.

Walker, J. C. (1988). *Louts and legends: Male youth culture in an inner-city school.* Sydney: Allen & Unwin.

Walzer, M. (1983). *Spheres of justice: A defense of pluralism and equality.* New York: Basic Books.

Weinberg, M. (1981). *The education of poor and minority children: A world bibliography.* New York: Greenwood.

Wexler, P. (1992). *Becoming somebody: Toward a social psychology of school.* London: Falmer Press.

White, V., & Johnston, K. (1993). Inside the disadvantaged schools program: The politics of practical policy-making. In L. Angus (Ed.), *Education, inequality and social identity* (pp. 104–127). London: Falmer Press.

Whiteford, P., Bradbury, B., & Saunders, P. (1989). Inequality and deprivation among families with children: An exploratory study. In D. Edgar, D. Keane, & P. McDonald (Eds.), *Child poverty* (pp. 20–49). Sydney: Allen & Unwin.

Whitty, G. (1985). *Sociology and school knowledge: Curriculum theory, research and politics.* London: Methuen.

Poverty and Education
R. W. CONNELL

Whitty, G., & Young, M. (Eds.). (1976). *Explorations in the politics of school knowledge.* Driffield, Eng.: Nafferton Books.
Williams, T. (1987). *Participation in education.* Hawthorn: Australian Council for Educational Research.
Wilson, B., & Wyn, J. (1987). *Shaping futures: Youth action for livelihood.* Sydney: Allen & Unwin.
Yates, L. (1993). *The education of girls: Policy, research and the question of gender.* Hawthorn: Australian Council for Educational Research.

My thinking on these issues has been profoundly influenced by my colleagues on the national study of the Disadvantaged Schools Program in Australia, Ken Johnston and Viv White, and by the other contributors to that project. This article is based on the 1992 Paul Masoner International Education Lecture; I am grateful to the University of Pittsburgh for the invitation to deliver this lecture and thus bring these ideas together for a North American audience.

[33]

Oxford Review of Education, Vol. 19, No. 2, 1993

Trends in Access and Equity in Higher Education: Britain in international perspective

A. H. HALSEY

INTRODUCTION

The papers in this issue, with their focus on access and equality in British higher education, make it clear that the structure of access to education has shifted since the end of the 1940s. Before the Second World War the main European preoccupation with educational equity was focused on entry to secondary schools. This was the decisive point of selection in traditional education systems and remained so, for example, when OECD staged its first major review and conference on the issue of equity in 1961 at Kungalv in Sweden (OECD, 1961). But in the past two or three decades, with secondary schooling becoming universal, attention has perforce shifted onto entry to higher education or, more accurately, entry into some form of post-compulsory schooling, a stage of mass tending to universal provision, whether classified as training or further or higher education. Crucial selection now occurs at the transition out of secondary education. The underlying idea of meritocratic society gives tertiary schooling a new significance.

The 'meritocratic' question itself remains in debate. Definition and measurement apart, it cannot be maintained that qualifications from schooling exactly determine market rewards. Other factors, including luck and the function of prices as signals of profitable shortages, may be in play, though a typical path analysis usually shows the highest coefficient for some measure of education where income or occupational status is the dependent variable. Market rewards accrue from occupational as well as educational experience and have no necessary relation to merit. The concept of merit is, however, more apt for analysing access to advanced forms of education than for measuring the justification or defensibility of variations in income.

Within the frame of fairness or desert, the balance of social interest has also shifted in the ensuing period of spectacular educational expansion. Rightly or wrongly the major focus of traditional concern was with social class as the largest obstacle to mobilising the productive power of nations and realising a more acceptable social equity in the distribution of opportunity. More recently attention has shifted to gender and to ethnicity. Class, gender and ethnicity are now the three giants in the path of aspirations towards equity, though awareness of other obstacles, including rurality and religion has persisted. And most significantly, there are strong signs, in discussion as well as in research, of heightened awareness that educational achievement and life-chances generally are fundamentally shaped by the structure of family upbringing. A picture of advanced industrial countries is beginning to emerge which links economic growth to regimes of low fertility. The two features of modernised society are correlated in some way with the decline of the traditional family, at least in the

Western world. Research by demographers and sociologists is therefore directed onto more concentrated analysis of family background. No comprehensive attempt to cover this line of research is possible here (Coleman *et al.*, 1991; Kiernan, 1992). In the sections below we shall see some reflections of this underlying transformation of industrial society in considering the trends in access to higher education of the genders, the classes and the ethnic minorities.

TRENDS IN BRITAIN

The papers below enable us to carry the analysis further, at least in the sense of bringing the description up to date. We must, however note cautiously that they use different definitions of what is meant by access. Most refer to any form of higher education aimed at a degree or equivalent qualification: but one (Blackburn & Jarman) restricts its attention to the universities and another (Paterson) is concerned with the Scottish universities. Moreover, the papers employ a variety of methods of measuring equity. There are good reasons and a rich tradition in the social sciences of concern with exact methods here if only because of preoccupation with answering questions about social justice. It is relevant to recall A. B. Atkinson's assertion that all measures of inequality involve social as well as statistical judgements (Atkinson, 1974). Interpretation is always necessary: and Professor Harvey Goldstein has wise guidance to offer to non-statisticians on the pitfalls in wait. Thus those who, like Heath or Halsey or Cheng or Egerton, have been associated with the Nuffield studies of social mobility tend to use odds ratios as the measure most apt for log linear analysis. Modood uses levels of representativeness (equivalent to the index of association) favoured by the Commission on Racial Equality. Blackburn and Jarman have their own Cambridge peculiarities, though it should be noted that results based on the technique of marginal matching are similar to those using odds ratios. Paterson has non-intrusive but sophisticated techniques, including multi-level logistic regressions, to proceed from description to explanation of variations in localism.

We draw attention here to these methodological variations for two other particular reasons. First is to underline the errors inherent in using sample surveys to estimate the state of populations. There are differing sampling errors. Second, there are different classifications (such as ethnic minority status), and, especially in combination, the two variations may mislead. Thus, Modood's important and bold finding that all ethnic minority groups in Britain outdo the native whites in their admission proportions to higher education might be modified by shifts in definition or sampling ratios. Indeed, we know from Cheng and Heath that Irish-born admissions are lower than whites: but Modood includes the Irish-born among the white population and thereby underestimates the white performance. Not until 1990 did the UCCA and PCAS statistics offer reliable information about the entry of ethnic minority candidates to the universities and colleges. It now seems clear that the ex-polytechnics have recently been more successful in attracting ethnic minority students. But differences between minorities remain and it may be that some of the population estimates may overestimate ethnic minority success.

Nevertheless, it may be asserted that social scientists are in accord in their broad appraisal of 'what is going on' in British higher education. Gender inequalities have decreased rapidly over the past two decades and feminist advocacy has moved somewhat towards inequality of access to the higher echelons of the professions and business management. The expansion of higher education has propelled many more women into new opportunities but with a skewed distribution towards the less prestigious courses and institutions.

With respect to ethnicity it appears that very considerable advances have recently been made in the accessibility of degree courses. It may even turn out on further evidence that ethnicity *per se* is not a barrier: only the asymmetric fit of race to class produces apparent inequality of access, and the case for positive discrimination may be solely on behalf of the disadvantaged working class. To be sure the working class child has had increased absolute chances of going on into some form of higher education, though in competition with women and those from the ethnic minorities. But class inequalities, measured in relative terms, have apparently remained stable for the past three generations. Egerton's analysis confirms several other studies and also confirms the continuation of stable class inequality established for earlier in the century by the Oxford mobility study (Halsey *et al.*, 1980).

It emerges that expansion has had and is having two further effects of some relevance to the general question of equality of access. Expansion has been disproportionately in favour of cheaper and less prestigious forms of institution offering degree courses or their equivalents. Women have become more concentrated in the ex-polytechnics and the colleges concerned. It is also noticeable that ethnic minority recruitment has tended to become concentrated on particular colleges and universities, as may be seen from Modood's paper. Moreover, and with its own separate fascination, there is the pattern demonstrated by Paterson for Scotland that the ancient linkages of particular universities to an origin in a locality and a destination in the priesthood or schools of that locality has been only recently eroded while newer institutions take over the localist role.

How then do these British developments appear in the wider context of advanced industrial countries generally?

THE WILENSKY ANALYSIS

The enlargement of educational access, which in principle raises the chances of all social groups, is heavily concentrated in the richer countries. As part of my international study of access to higher education (funded by the Spencer Foundation) my research officer, Muriel Egerton, has carried out a path analytic study analogous to the study by Harold Wilensky of the determinants of social spending by governments (Wilensky, 1975).

Comparative research on the development of welfare provision takes place against a background of competing conceptions of modernisation. Wilensky (1975) puts forward the thesis that industrialised societies, despite differing cultures, politics and ideologies, converge in welfare provision as a means of ensuring political stability and economic growth. He argues that industrial development is more important than political ideology or beliefs in determining welfare expenditure. Wilensky tested this hypothesis on a sample of 64 countries, using the following variables:

1. Social security expenditure as a percentage of gross national product (GNP) as the dependent variable.
2. GNP per capita, the average age of various social security systems, and population

proportion of elderly people as independent variables, measuring industrial bureaucratic and demographic development.

3. A fourfold classification of regimes as liberal democratic, totalitarian, authoritarian oligarchic, or authoritarian populist, as the basis for independent dummy variables measuring political effects.

This political categorisation was based on the degree of coerciveness of the state, crossed with the degree of popular participation in the affairs of the state. The two most important categories for his analysis were liberal democratic and totalitarian states. Two-thirds of the countries included in the liberal democratic category were advanced industrial ones; and all the countries included in the totalitarian category were industrial states in Eastern Europe, with the addition of the USSR as it then was. Authoritarian oligarchic states included Spain and Taiwan. Authoritarian populist states included Mexico and Iraq.

Wilensky concluded on the basis of a path analysis of these variables (Wilensky, 1975, pp. 20–27) that economic development was a more important predictor of welfare expenditure than political ideology. The effects of type of polity were minimal except among the rich countries. In so far as political system apart from economic level shaped the process of welfare state development, the two dominant modern systems, totalitarian and liberal democratic, exercised influence in the same direction (upwards) through their effects on demographic structure. Totalitarian countries, being more centralised, were slightly more effective in this limited positive influence. Wilensky excluded expenditure on education from welfare expenditure on the grounds that education expenditure redistributes opportunities rather than resources. He suggested that education systems are characteristically meritocratic, with the criteria of merit being set by the technical requirements of the state and the economy.

Of course the role of the state in determining the relation between education and the distribution of life-chances as well as the productive performance of the nation remains at issue. Thus, Hufner *et al.* (1987), in a wide-ranging view of comparative education research give education policy and the development of education systems a more comprehensive role than opportunity allocation. They argue that governments and international organisations concerned with development see education as the key to successful economic competition and/or modernisation. This strategy, which has its roots in the dynamics of the development of both communist and liberal democracies, values both equality and progress. So, given that both liberal democracies and centrally planned Marxist states use education policy to gain these objectives, it is to be expected that type of state will influence educational outcomes.

We have, therefore, tested Wilensky's model, using enrolment in tertiary education as the dependent variable. Data were available for 85 countries for this analysis. Both GNP per capita and school enrolment in 1970 have strong relationships, while the percentage of the population in the 20–24 year age cohort has a weak relationship (not statistically significant at the 0.05 level), with tertiary enrolment. A path analysis of these variables was carried out following Wilensky's model and is illustrated in Fig. I. School enrolment in 1970, used as a proxy for the weight of bureaucratic interests, and GNP per capita, have direct effects of 0.61 and 0.25 respectively. GNP per capita and type of polity have indirect effects through school enrolment.

Thus, this model gives a broad outline of the relationship between polity, wealth, and a universal system of primary and secondary education and the relationships are as predicted in my original research proposal to the Spencer Foundation.

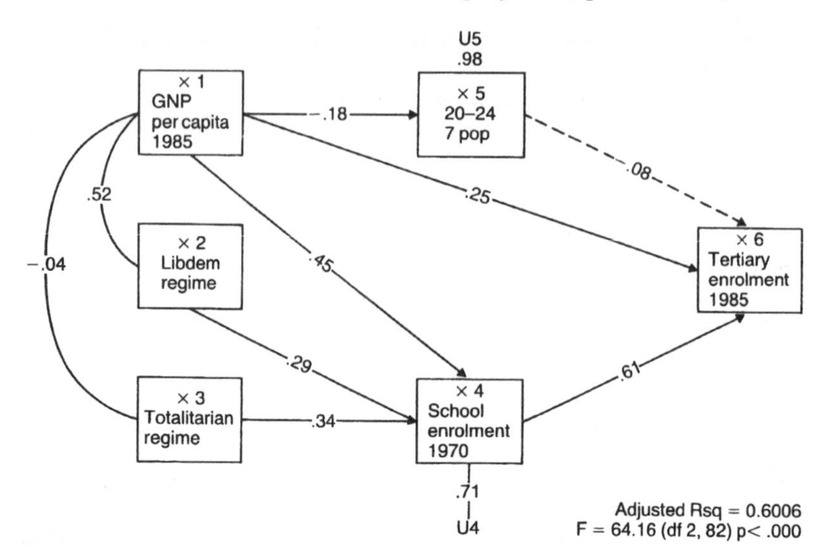

FIG. I. Path diagram of direct effects on tertiary education in 85 countries.

ACCESS TO HIGHER EDUCATION IN EUROPE

Narrowing the focus onto the European countries it appears that the period after the Second World War saw a growth in enrolment, a diversification of curricula, and a crisis in relation to the labour market destination of alumni (from both the education and the training systems and at both the secondary school and the tertiary college level) in the mid-1970s. The post-war period came to an end in the economic and political turmoil of that time. Then there was a phase of reconstruction in the 1980s in which access and selection were increasingly influenced by manifold difficulties in the political economies of Europe, including public expenditure and unemployment and the rise or resurgence of economic-liberal doctrines of state management. Put crudely, the 1980s were the decade of the market and the expansion of higher education had to proceed under conditions of fiscal constraint which led to much redefinition of the structure and purposes of the university. Conspicuous among these developments was a pronounced weakening of the traditionally close link between the academic secondary school and educational institutions. The upper secondary school in all countries became, in effect and instead, a free-standing institution rather than a conveyance of selected minorities from common elementary schooling to élite advanced education. Most secondary pupils now leave at 18 years, many postponing entry to higher education, others choosing part-time or full-tiome attendance at some other form of tertiary education, and still others going straight into employment (Husen *et al.*, 1992).

Nonetheless, entry to higher education in Europe and in most developed countries is still generally straight from school, sometimes from a particular type of school at which the student has concentrated in academic subjects. Italy has a very specialised structure, particular types of school leading to certain higher education categories. In the UK, as in Japan and the USA, the examination required for higher education entry can be taken at any type of establishment which provides for post-compulsory schooling. In other countries (and in Northern Ireland and some other parts of the

UK), children may be selected for entry to different types of secondary education although there is provision for transfer at later stages: the higher education entry examination is then usually taken in the more academic schools.

Each country has a specific national education qualification which forms the main basic requirement for entry to higher education. The qualification generally covers at least five subjects, some compulsory, and usually including mathematics, the native language and one modern language. England, Wales and Northern Ireland are unusual in limiting the number of subjects more narrowly and thus specialising earlier. At least five passes at GCE are required for degree level courses, of which two must be of A level standard, although most candidates for entry attempt three A-level subjects and already have at least 6 O-level passes. Special arrangements exist for mature students.

In her article in this issue Nina Wakeford is looking at a new development in the UK which is designed to offer a novel avenue of access to those who had not passed to higher education in the traditional way.

Entry to higher education depends mainly on gaining the appropriate entry qualification, although limits on places may mean that a further selection process takes place either for certain types of course, or for certain institutions which experience strong demand from students. In the UK entry to all institutions is competitive.

More generally in Europe the state has increasingly controlled entry to higher education since Napoleonic times, either through defining examination content and standards or through varied means of student financial support or through special schemes of encouragement for particular social categories of student by positive discrimination or, more usually, by setting up barriers to entry. Some countries like Belgium, France or Germany use one uniform national examination. Sweden attempts the ranking of students by marks weighted according to the courses taken and work experience (which tacitly introduces age as a selective barrier). The American system of standardised attainment tests is not used in Europe. Positive discrimination in favour of candidates with working-class backgrounds has been used in Hungary, Poland and Czechoslovakia, though examination performance has also been part of the entrance procedure. Entrance examinations have been widely used with higher requirements in medicine, science and law. Such procedures obtain in the highly prestigious institutions such as Oxford and Cambridge in the UK and the Grandes Ecoles in France, but also in the East European Communist states where, at the same time, at least a quarter of the places have been reserved for working-class students. Even the lottery is not unknown. In The Netherlands and Germany the problem of excessive demand has been overcome by its use. A lottery has been operated in which an individual's chances have been weighted by marks attained in the secondary school leaving examinations.

Nevertheless, the automatic right of entry to the university which is the privilege of those who obtain a baccalaureat or the abitur, still gives admission in France and Italy, though not to other forms of higher education. The consequences are seen in high failure or drop-out rates in the first two years of undergraduate study. Some countries, like Belgium or Spain, never granted the prerogatives of the abitur. In France, however, in spite of several university reforms, including the Loi Savary of 1984, the right of entry of a bachelier has never been modified. Of course, the highly selective Grandes Ecoles continue to cream off the best 15% of the candidates. And the *numerus clausus* has been increasingly applied in France and Germany so that we can now describe the right as nominal. It gives all qualified people a place; but it does not guarantee a place in any particular faculty of any particular university.

In summary, it appears that the evolution of the admissions system since the Second World War moved the point of selection upwards from the upper secondary school and its examinations to the admissions offices of the institutions of higher education. The traditional system was essentially controlled by teachers in universities. Control now is much more in the hands of politicians and budgetary administrators. Diversity is to be found at both the secondary and tertiary levels and the unique role of the baccalaureat, the abitur and their equivalents in other European countries as the *rite de passage* to university education, is no more.

Instead there have developed alternative modes of entry to a diverse set of post-compulsory educational and training institutions with the parallel development of vocational equivalents to A level, the baccalaureat and the abitur. In France there is a technical baccalaureat with 12 options as well as the traditional one with eight sections and a proposed 30 option practical baccalaureat which, it is expected, will be taken in one form or another by 80% of the secondary school leavers by the end of the century.

In all countries most students first enter higher education aged between 18 and 21. However, older students are also admitted everywhere; in Germany a quota of places is reserved for them. Reasons for starting first study in higher education later in life are many; some students pursue lower level further education full-time or enter employment; others may retake entry examinations and so increase the range of institutions which will accept them.

There has been a notable recent advance in comparable statistics arising out of the initiative of *Education at a Glance* (OECD, 1992). An illustration of the comparisons now possible is shown in Table I which sets out the graduation rates in various OECD countries in 1988.

In some OECD countries, non-university tertiary education is almost non-existent. The full-time equivalent participation ratio is below 5% in Austria, Italy, Luxembourg and Spain. In other countries, participation ratios reflect a substantial number of non-university students enrolled in tertiary-level institutions. The full-time non-university participation level is 20% or higher in Belgium, Canada, Japan and the USA. In each of the anglophone countries with the exception of Ireland (e.g. Australia, Canada, New Zealand, the UK and the USA), part-time participation is the predominant mode for non-university tertiary education. Part-time and full-time participation levels are similar in Switzerland and Ireland. In the remainder of the countries, the part-time participation ratio is less than half the full-time level. In the Pacific area (Australia, Japan and New Zealand), as well as in Denmark and Germany, the full-time participation level is twice as high for females as for males. The part-time participation level is only half as high for females as for males in New Zealand and a quarter as high in Switzerland.

The full-time university participation ratio is 15 or higher in eight OECD countries. Austria, Finland and Spain have the highest participation ratios. In most countries, full-time male and female participation ratios are similar. The major exceptions are Japan and Turkey where the ratios for females are only half those for males. The females ratios are also about a third lower than those for males in Belgium, Germany and Switzerland. In most countries part-time university enrolment is quite rare. The highest part-time levels are reached in Australia, Canada, New Zealand and the USA. As may be seen from Table I, the graduation rate of the UK in 1988 was behind that of Canada, the USA, Austria, Japan, Ireland and Finland. Britain's tertiary system was distinctive in the period before 1990 in that it was binary. There was a short, high-cost and efficient sector of restricted but socially open universities attended full time for

TABLE I. *Ratio of public and private higher education (university) graduates to population at the theoretical age of graduation (1988).* Source: *Education at a Glance: OECD indicators* (OECD, Paris, 1992)

	Degree taken into account (ISCED 6)	Theoretical age of graduation	Graduation ratio		
			F+M	M	F
North America					
Canada	Bachelor	22	25.4	23.3	27.7
USA	Bachelor	22	25.6	24.4	26.9
Pacific area					
Australia	Bachelor	22	19.5	18.6	20.4
Japan	Gakushi	22	26.3	37.7	14.4
New Zealand	Undergraduate Bachelor	21	15.7	16.8	14.5
Central and Western Europe					
Austria	Diplom	23	7.2	8.1	6.3
Belgium	Licence	22	11.6	13.9	9.2
France	Licence	21	12.1	12.1	12.0
Germany	Staats-Diplomprüfung	22	13.3	16.1	10.3
Ireland	First degree	21	17.2	19.2	15.0
The Netherlands	Doctoraal examen	23	11.4	14.2	8.5
Switzerland	Licence	25	7.6	10.1	5.0
UK	Bachelor	21	16.3	17.0	15.5
Southern Europe					
Italy	Laurea	23	7.7	8.0	7.4
Spain	Diplomado/Licenciado	21/23	17.0	14.0	20.1
Turkey	Lisans	23	5.8	7.4	4.1
Northern Europe					
Denmark	Bachelor	22	10.1	12.6	7.4
Finland	Master	23	18.6	20.6	16.6
Norway	Master and Cand. mag.	22	23.6	16.3	31.4
Sweden	Undergraduate Bachelor	23	12.7	10.8	14.8

F, female; M, male.

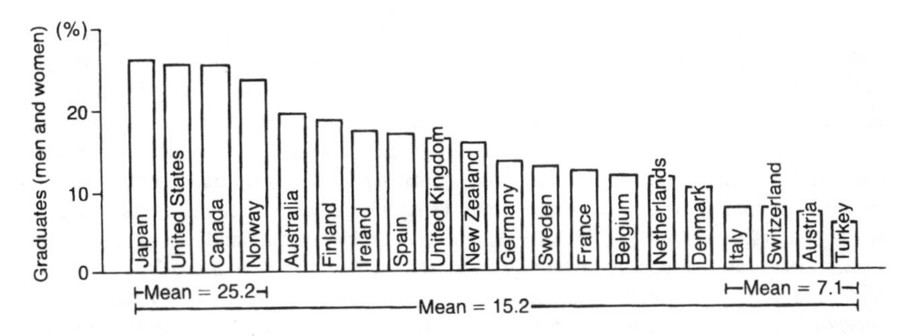

three years; and a diversified, localised, part-time vocational sector with rather tenuous connections to the universities.

Reform since 1990 may bring Britain more into line with its European and American competitors. Yet the consequences for social distribution of access cannot be predicted with confidence. It may turn out that a principal historical feature of post-war higher education in Europe was the elaboration of alternatives to the university. As part of an ambitious programme of expansion, 'doubling in a decade' as the progressive slogans of the 1950s had it, the terms of entry and the definition of what was to be learned in a university were altered all over Europe. The old stereotype of entry through completion of the baccalaureat or equivalent leaving certificate from a lycée or other upper secondary school into a full-time course of three or more years in pure science or pure arts was to be transformed into a large variety of courses, typically vocational or preparatory to professional training, and offered in a wider range of institutions, residential and non-residential. The development of mass higher education was dawning in Europe, increasing participation to significant proportions of the young and, in effect, replacing the older idea of the university in Europe by a much more expansive and, as many would argue, a diluted conception of tertiary rather than higher education.

SOCIAL SELECTIVITY AND STRATIFICATION

Walter Muller's study of nine European countries, because based on the Casmin data sets, pertains largely to the earlier post-war years (Muller & Karle, 1990). Blossfield's data show the experience of young people in the 1980s as well as in the earlier years of the century (Blossfield, 1990). The results of the two studies are complementary and consistent. They confirm that German higher education expanded from a low point immediately after the Second World War and that in the process there was a reduction in social selectivity for the population as a whole and for women but no serious change in the relative chances of children from the disadvantaged classes. Tertiary education remained linked characteristically to the superior and professional end of the service class with respect to recruitment and also to placement in an occupational career. This was the essential shape of meritocratic development in Europe and the role of the university within an expanding and elaborating system. The picture is complicated, not least by variation between countries in demography, the structure of the economy and the historical peculiarities of national arrangements for access to the stages of education, their curricular content, the type and availability of student financial aid, and the articulation between educational qualifications and entry to professions and trades. Thus, for example, where a country has had a large agricultural sector as in France or Poland, the significance of educational selection has been minimised for the sons of farmers. Where, as in the UK, education has been relatively loosely connected to qualifications in the labour market, it has been possible for relatively democratised access to the universities to emerge. Muller's analysis thus reveals the remarkable contrast between France and Britain that, adjusting for the difference in the shape of the occupational structure, it turns out that those who acquired a higher tertiary degree had service class origins of 55% in France and only 35% in England. So, at least in the earlier post-war years, the system of selection in France gave the offspring of the service classes—compared to children from other social backgrounds—better odds of surviving up to the highest educational level than they had in other countries. For his nine European countries Muller finds that, beginning at a less than 10% proportion of the pupils in primary school, the service class children grew to a cross-national average of about 45% among those who attained a higher tertiary degree.

England, Muller tells us, did not stand alone at the lower end of social selectivity but shared its relatively egalitarian position with Scotland and Northern Ireland. He also indicates an interesting contrast between Germany and France. By the end of compulsory schooling the proportion of service class children was highest in France and remained so through the successive stages or 'transitions'. In Germany, the proportion of service class children was lowest until the stage of an intermediate secondary degree, but then increased more than in most other countries until, at the end point of the educational career, Germany was placed in an intermediate position. Interestingly, the two command economies or Communist countries included by Muller were not among the most egalitarian from the point of view of class opportunity. Hungary in particular is near the top of the league for distributing most certificates of higher education to the higher social classes.

Like Blossfield, Muller identifies two important processes common to the countries which have inherited the European university. First education systems are organised so as to allow ever decreasing fractions of a student cohort to survive at each successive stage of education; and second, dropping out is socially selective though with decreasing severity. The outcomes are an interplay between these two processes. On the one hand the policies of expansion gradually move the systems of higher education through mass towards universal provision and *a fortiori* towards equality. On the other hand the selective forces continue to shape the composition of the student body.

Muller's study of an earlier period shows that already the European countries differed strongly in the extent to which they provided opportunities for obtaining educational qualifications to each successive cohort of young people. His data were collected in the early 1970s and the analysis relates to those aged 30 to 64, i.e. born between 1910 and 1947. They therefore had left their schools or universities mostly before 1970. Only a small proportion of them were affected in their educational careers by the reforms of the 1960s and 1970s in the Western European nations but, it must be noted, educational change in Eastern Europe had been initiated earlier. Thus, for our earlier years, Muller shows a pattern which is essentially binary. The UK and Sweden had a similar survival pattern from which Germany, Hungary, Poland and France differed. The sharpest contrast was between France and Germany. In Germany, 85% of pupils were surviving beyond compulsory schooling, in France only 30%. Hungary and Poland had the highest survival rates up to the end of a full secondary education. Yet, given the differences in survival rates between nations in early schooling, the remarkable feature of the systems as a whole is their similarity of outcome at the upper end. At that point, only France is distinctive with its exceptionally low fraction of the population obtaining a degree from an institution of higher education.

Within the context we have sketched, Muller draws attention to particular features of class selectivity. In Germany, Hungary and Sweden the upper service class appears to have given its children rather superior chances of educational survival. This finding fits with the observations of historians of the *Bildungsbuergertum*, a social stratum of civil servants, professionals and teachers in higher education, which has traditionally shared a set of common values associated with the experience of higher education and a relatively higher determination to pass on high standards of educational ambition and achievement to their children. The *Bildungsbuergertum* was probably most distinguished as a status group in Germany, but also existed in other countries that were influenced by the German tradition of higher education, such as Sweden and the Austro-Hungarian monarchy. English society in the early 20th century was distinctive in not having such a broad and educationally defined upper class. Entry to the upper echelons of British society was not so clearly restricted to educational channels.

In Britain, the 1970s saw little progress towards the democratisation of leisure which a modern system of higher or continuing education should represent. Instead the end of the decade saw governments, whether of the Left or of the Right, groping for solutions to external checks on economic growth, while the minority of the educated began to be more sophisticated about the nature of education as a positional rather than an investment or a consumption good, and the majority remained in blighted ignorance that education had anything seriously constructive to offer to either private or public life.

Nevertheless the story remains unfinished. Both economic fortunes and political pressure moved in the later 1980s. On the economic front, a much disputed restructuring of the economy with an also disputed movement towards integration with continental Europe had educational consequences. The achievement of competitive advantage impelled renewed educational expansion. Invidious international comparison in the preparations for '1992' excited almost hysterical reorganisation of training arrangements and reinforced pressure towards vocational education at all levels of schooling. From different standpoints and with different assumptions both the Conservative and Labour parties and the reformed Liberal Democrats began to share the view that a mass system of higher education was inevitable for 21st century Britain. In May 1991, the Conservatives, following the other parties, announced the beginning of the new educational era. Mass higher education would accommodate one school leaver in three (an extra 300,000 students over the next eight years), polytechnics could call themselves universities, the funding bodies would be dismantled and 'a single intelligence' would replace them, though with separate establishments in England, Scotland and Wales. The CNAA would be abolished. Quality would be assessed by the new academic audit unit which had recently been set up by the universities (Halsey, 1992).

It must be added immediately that plans for funding the new expansion remained vague. The drive towards increasing reliance on tuition fees will remain as a governmental stimulus of market forces. The government will also encourage universities and colleges to seek funds from the private sector, particularly from industry and commerce, benefactors and alumni. A fair share of public expenditure is guaranteed to higher education but the final emphasis is on further efficiency, which the embattled dons will realistically interpret as a levelling down of standards and still further reduction of staff/student ratios. The struggle will doubtless go on as Europe seeks ways to renew economic growth and escape from current recession. But one thing is sure. The British binary line has lost its official status and a post-binary system has begun.

REFERENCES

ATKINSON, A.B. (1974) *The Economics of Inequality* (Oxford).

BLOSSFIELD, H.P. (1990) Changes in educational opportunities in the Federal Republic of Germany, *EUI Working Paper*, SPS, No. 90/4.

COLEMAN, J. (1991) *Resources and Actions: Parents, their Children and Schools* (Chicago).

HALSEY, A.H. (1992) *Decline of Donnish Dominion* (Oxford, Oxford University Press).

HALSEY, A.H., HEATH, A.F. & RIDGE, J. (1980) *Origins and Destinations: family, class and education in modern Britain* (Oxford, Clarendon Press).

HUFNER, K., MEYER, J.W. & NAUMANN, J. (1987) Comparative education policy research: a world perspective, in: M. DIERKES, H. WEILER & A. B. ANTAL (Eds) *Comparative Policy Research: learning from experience* (Aldershot, Gower).

HUSÉN, T., TUIJNMAN, A. & HALLS, W.D. (1992) *Schooling in Modern European Society, A report of the Academia Europaea* (Oxford).

KIERNAN, K. (1992) Family disruption and transitions in young adulthood, *Population Studies*, 46.

MULLER, W. & KARLE, W. (1990) *Social selection in educational systems in Europe*, paper presented to the meetings of the International Sociological Association Research Committee on Social Stratification, XIIth World Congress of Sociology, Madrid, 9–13 July.

OECD (1961) *Ability and Educational Opportunity* (Ed. A. H. HALSEY, Paris).

WILENSKY, H.L. (1975) *The Welfare State and Equality* (London, University of California Press).

Correspondence: Professor A. H. Halsey, Nuffield College, Oxford OX1 1NF, UK.

[34]

International Studies in Sociology of Education, Vol. 7, No. 2, 1997

Producing and Practising Social Justice Policy in Education: a policy trajectory study from Queensland, Australia

BOB LINGARD & BARBARA GARRICK
University of Queensland, Australia

ABSTRACT This article provides a policy trajectory study of the Queensland Department of Education's Social Justice Strategy (1992-93) developed following the election of a State Labor government in late 1989. The paper considers the 'traditions' of social justice and their rearticulation under recent Labor governments. It then utilises research data to analyse the production of the Strategy within the Department and its reception within Brookridge, a secondary school located in a working class area. These analyses demonstrate the competing tensions within and upon both the production and reception of the Strategy, including the new managerialism within the Department and the concomitant reconstitution of Department/school relationships. Reasons for the 'refraction' of this state generated policy are also considered. In conclusion, the paper draws upon this policy trajectory study to reflect upon the politics of 'progressive' educational change and debates within the educational policy literature.

Introduction

There is a certain nostalgia about this article,[1] not for something that was ideal but for something which at least set a democratic context and discursive framework in which the many perplexing questions of social justice in schooling could be discussed, tried out, modified and developed. In Australia, under Labor governments at the Commonwealth level (1983-96) and at the Queensland State level (1989-96), and despite the commitment to a particular version of market liberal ideology and new managerialism, the discourse of social justice in education at least remained extant. These Labor governments sought, in their terminology to 'internationalise' the Australian economy, create a more competitive state and a 'freer market', refocus foreign and trade policy within Asia, create a just multicultural society, give effect to reconciliation with the Aboriginal people, and pursue social justice in a number of policy domains. There are palpable tensions between and within these sets of goals and we know that across this period Australia became a less egalitarian society with demands for 'recognition' perhaps having more political success [2] than those for 'redistribution' (Fraser, 1995). We also know that social justice has no essential meaning which remains inviolate, constant and uncontested across time, place and political regime (Troyna & Vincent, 1995; Rizvi & Lingard, 1996), and thus it was with the social justice approaches of these governments.

The conception of social justice which underpinned the policies of these Labor governments was distorted, reconstituted, weakened through its coupling with or subordination to the metapolicy status granted to the broader economic restructuring agenda (Yeatman, 1990) and the making of the competitive (Cerny, 1990), managerialist (Considine, 1988), 'postmodern state' (Lingard, 1996). As Marion Sawer (1989) has perceptively commented, putting those committed to market liberal economic ideology in charge of social justice policies is akin to putting mice in charge of the cheese shop! Thus, under Labor governments social justice was rearticulated through its alignment with market liberalism and new managerialism. Nonetheless, talk about social justice remained legitimate and its discourse framed specific state policies which allowed space and granted legitimacy to the practices of those in schools committed to social justice, but who at the same time were flooded with demands for other changes less conducive to such ends and to be achieved with reduced funds. With the change in political regimes at both Commonwealth and State levels during 1996, social justice has all but disappeared from policy discourse.

This article then attempts a number of things. The empirical section reports a study conducted throughout 1994 and 1995 of the implementation of the Queensland Department of Education's 1992-93 Social Justice Strategy in a large, outer suburban Brisbane secondary school located in a low socio-economic area (Garrick, 1995). We give the school the pseudonym of Brookridge State High School. More specifically as a policy trajectory study (Maguire & Ball, 1994),[3] the research aimed to describe and analyse the gestation and construction of the policy within the state and its reception within the school. The analysis of the policy text production also draws upon research reported elsewhere (Lingard, 1995) on the policy 'strategising' of equity workers inside the Queensland Department. We utilise the two pieces of research to reflect upon the policy sociology literature and upon questions concerning the relationships between policy and what we might call the 'politics of progressive change' in schools, a concept which has been destabilised somewhat by contemporary theoretical and political developments.

This short story of social justice within one Department of Education and its reception in one school will indicate why our nostalgia – "this bastard but pampered child" of history (Swift, 1983, p. 118) – for the immediate policy past in Australian schooling is somewhat muted. It also confirms Tom Crick's – the history teacher in Graham Swift's novel *Waterland* – perception of history: "It goes in two directions at once. It goes backwards as it goes forwards. It loops. It takes detours" (p. 117).

The Department

Queensland was governed for 32 years from 1957 until the Labor election victory in 1989 by conservative Coalition governments which transmogrified to some extent across this period from traditional conservative governments to ones influenced more by New Right ideology. This conservatism was manifest within the State Department of Education and in education policy. There was in the last years of these governments a substantial politicisation of the public sector, including within Education and the creation of a very conservative policy culture. Policy culture refers to 'the structures and policy goals, and dominant discourses and practices within public bureaucracies which frame the possibilities for policy' (Lingard, 1995, p. 146). Some new managerialist practices had begun to impact upon the State public sector from the late eighties, while most of the equal opportunity, affirmative action and freedom of information aspects of contemporary public sector management had not reached Queensland by the time Labor won government.

In terms of equity and social justice, any focus on these matters in schooling during the 1980s under Coalition governments was a result of Commonwealth specific policies and payments. As one senior bureaucrat interviewed in the research observed in relation to the Department of Education at that time, 'equity remained buried in the bowels of the Department'. Another indicator of the policy culture within the Department was the conservative government's opposition to the National Policy for the Education of Girls in Australian Schools (Schools Commission, 1987), a policy which had been endorsed by all the other State systems, as well as by Catholic systems and independent schools throughout the country. It needs to be stressed that Commonwealth support for social justice in schooling only tinkered at the edge of State Department culture which was moving in managerialist directions, but remained anti-equity.

The School

The research school was located in the Eastern corridor of Brisbane in a low socio-economic area with more than 70% of students from skilled, semi and unskilled working class backgrounds, where youth unemployment matched the national average, where incomes were low, where according to the 1991 census 66.6% of the area's employed adult population held no qualifications at all. The social infrastructure in the area is very poor and the area is isolated from the city by a green belt and poor transport. While Brookridge is largely residential in character, it is surrounded by a number of small factories, particularly in textiles, many of which have closed in the context of the globalisation of the economy, impacting on local employment prospects. A number of surveys, for example *Youth Profile 1994: Queensland young people, facts and figures,* suggests that the youth population in the district is on the increase and that many of these young people are experiencing social and economic difficulties.

The school was established in 1964 with 19 staff and an enrolment of 470, which peaked at 1100 in the late 1970s and is currently around 640 with 45 staff and growing again. The teachers at Brookridge were experienced – almost 60% had been teaching for more than 16 years – and most lived a long way from the school. Retention rates from Year 10 to Year 11 had increased, paralleling developments across the schooling system in the context of a policy push and the collapse of the teenage labour market, with an increase from 53% retention rate in 1988 to 70% in 1993.

In terms of social justice, from 1990 the school had attracted Commonwealth monies ($30,000 per year) from the Students at Risk (STAR) programme because of their comparatively poor student retention beyond the compulsory years. This programme was part of the Commonwealth's Social Justice package for young Australians introduced in the 1989/90 federal budget by the Hawke Labor government. The STAR programme meant that issues of social justice were discussed and debated at Brookridge well before the 1992-93 Social Justice Strategy of the State Department was to be 'implemented'.

The STAR funding also allowed for a 'social justice co-ordinator' in the school; this was an additional role *granted* to the resource teacher in the school. The STAR project also sought to broaden post-compulsory curricula, while attempting to keep options open for all students. These debates recognised that distributive justice questions to do with how much education different groups receive cannot be distinguished from consideration of what education actually is (Connell, 1993). There were very real tensions within the staff concerning such matters. The debate was basically one of commonality or diversity to cater for increased retention, which played out as whether or not all teachers or only specifically designated ones should be responsible for the post-compulsory schooling of all students. An attempt was made through extensive professional development for the teachers, funded out of STAR, to ensure that all teachers became responsible for the 'at risk' students who were the focus of the STAR programme. The proximity of a special school to Brookridge slowed the introduction of 'mainstreaming' of 'special needs' students at Brookridge, but this had begun at the time of the research. The social justice co-ordinator played an important role in seeking to resolve these matters of inclusion, but her presence also allowed some teachers to absolve themselves from responsibility for them.

The Research

Research on the difficulties faced by state equity workers in the Queensland Department of Education drew upon documentation, access to relevant department files and archives, and lengthy interviews with most of these equity workers involved in the production of social justice policy in Queensland (Lingard, 1995).[4] Data on the reception of the 1992-93 Social Justice Strategy in Brookridge were collected via participant observation and interviews – conversations with a purpose (Burgess, 1984) – with a small group of administrators, six teachers, and three students (Garrick, 1995).[5] The interview with the principal was conducted first, acknowledging Simon's (1981, p. 29) observation that the timing of the Principal interview impacts upon the 'freedom' felt by other interviewees.[6] The interviews were complemented by a questionnaire on various aspects of the Strategy, developed from the work of Burnside (1992), and administered to the teaching staff of Brookridge to which there was an 80% response rate from the 45 teachers (Garrick, 1995). The questionnaire was finalised after the interviews had been conducted and was piloted with teachers at another school.

This case study thus describes one stage in the Strategy's evolution. Indeed, as the research was being conducted there was a change of Education Minister, the Department's Director of Equity (Studies and Workforce) resigned in April, 1993 and was replaced by an Acting Director who was never confirmed in the position, a second Strategy 1994-98 was being developed, and a small Department evaluation of the implementation of the Strategy was being conducted.

Conceptualising Social Justice and the Production of the Strategy

Social Justice

Social justice works politically as a 'condensation symbol' (Edelman, 1977), defying 'stipulative definition' (Troyna & Vincent, 1995, p. 149). Nonetheless, there have been various historical 'traditions' of social justice within Australian politics (MacIntyre, 1985) and within political theory more generally (Rizvi & Lingard, 1996). More recently these have been challenged by postmodern, poststructural and postcolonial criticisms of their formally universal character and ahistorical treatment (Foucault, 1984; Yeatman, 1994; Hall 1996). as well as their failure to account for difference (Fuss, 1989; Young, 1990).

The three dominant traditions have been liberal-democratic, liberal-individualist and social democratic. Rawls (1972) is perhaps the best known of the liberal-democratic theorists who argues that each person should have the most extensive personal liberty compatible with such liberty for all and that primary social goods should be distributed equally, unless unequal distribution benefits the least advantaged. This view has underpinned a range of affirmative action and redistributive policies and is linked to an activist role for the state. In contrast is Nozick's (1976) liberal-individualist (or market-individualist) conception of social justice which neglects issues of distribution and focuses instead on processes of accumulation of goods, arguing that it is how the competition is carried out which counts. As such, this view supports a minimal state which is only necessary to ensure fair competition, it also emphasises deserts. There are distinct differences between Rawls and Nozick, particularly in relation to the desirable functions of the state in relation to social justice, nonetheless both operate on the assumption that all individuals act in their own self-interest. In contrast the social democratic tradition stresses 'need' as a primary category. Peter Beilharz (1989, p. 94) notes: "it is qualitatively different to the preceeding understandings, in that need is viewed as a primary rather than a residual category, and it is this which sets this view off from the charity-based arguments about the 'needy' which are compatible with either the 'desert' or 'fairness' principles". This conception is based upon a more collectivist view of society and a different conception of the relationship between social justice and the market, arguing that some intervention against the market is necessary to its achievement.

Across the past decade under Labor governments the market individualist view of social justice has become more predominant and challenged the other two traditions within the Labor Party. As Fitzclarence & Kenway (1993, p. 90) have noted, in addition to "the amelioration of social disadvantage" social justice policy at the national level under Labor was required "to play a role in unifying the nation behind the cause of economic mobilisation". As such, a contradictory amalgam of the three conceptions underpinned their public policies. More accurately, this amalgam consisted of "Rawlsian redistributive principles and Nozickian entitlement theory" (Rizvi & Lingard, 1996, p. 19), with social democratic conceptions marginalised but pushed by critics inside and outside the government. Clearly, however, the Nozickian conception best complemented the priority given to the market over the state. Since the election in 1996 of conservative governments at both Commonwealth and State levels a market individualist notion of social justice has taken hold.

The Production of the Social Justice Strategy

This rearticulation of social justice by Labor governments provided part of the policy culture within which specific social justice strategies were developed. There is also a further rearticulation which occurs when such strategies are developed, because bureaucratic politics mediate policy production, ensuring that any particular text sutures together competing ideas and interests. This is the conception of policy as temporary 'settlement', a concept appropriately applied to any given policy text, here the Social Justice Strategy 1992-93, but which appears somewhat functionalist and too static a characterisation when applied to the ongoing 'policy cycle' (Bowe et al, 1992). The situation of social justice as a political condensation symbol and its rearticulation into a policy text acknowledges the politics inside the state involved in its production (Lingard, 1993); this reality also almost certainly ensures multiple readings when the text arrives in schools. There is also another 'slippage' here in the match or mismatch between the rearticulated policy discourse and the resourcing which pushes the policy either in a symbolic or material direction.

The conservative policy culture of the Department of Education when Labor won office in late 1989 has been described earlier. This was to change with the election of a Labor government which rapidly set about 'modernising' the Queensland public sector, introducing a range of progressive legislation and a full blown managerialism. In these 'reforms' education lost its previous *sui generis* character and was restructured along managerialist lines. The *Focus on Schools* (1991) report was centrally important here and was underpinned by Wilenski's (1986) progressive form of managerialism which attempted to achieve simultaneously greater efficiency and effectiveness, a more democratic and representative bureaucracy, and equitable policy outcomes. However, as a number of commentators have clearly demonstrated (e.g. Yeatman, 1990), given funding constraints and commitment to market ideology, the efficiency focus often became a fetish and the managerialist agenda overwhelmed the political one. So it was with social justice reforms within Queensland Education.

The *Focus on Schools* report saw the creation of an Equity Directorate within the Department which was both responsible for schooling (curriculum and students) and staffing. The first Director was a nationally respected 'femocrat'.[7] She was responsible for putting into practice Labor's range of equal opportunity and anti-discrimination legislation within the Department of Education and for developing the first Social Justice Strategy 1992-93. Confirming the earlier observation about the rearticulation of social justice when it is 'operationalised' into policy, the Director of Equity argued that the Strategy had to implement the broader across government legislative changes, as well as being framed strategically in ways which were achievable and measurable in the short term. There were potentially both good and bad outcomes here with managerialism's demand for performance indicators: a reduction of the social justice agenda to the readily measurable or a strengthened commitment to real change. The proof lay in the funding. The Equity Director argued that such a policy statement should not be a philosophical treatise about the 'ideal character' of social justice, thus recognising it as a condensation symbol. It needs to be stressed though, that she saw the first Strategy as simply the initial step of a long term approach. Thus the first Strategy focused upon the 'system' and system level change, locating individuals as responsible for its 'implementation', and establishing achievable and measurable goals. Given this approach and the time frame, the Strategy was produced in a very much top-down fashion with implications for its reception in schools.

Several interviews with senior bureaucrats within the Equity Directorate stressed the significance of its structural location within the Department, including membership of the Executive Management Committee for the Director, to its potential effectiveness. One woman commented: "membership of the Executive Management Team is profoundly important. And if it wasn't at that level they would run around and give the impression that it was ... it gives the issues legitimacy" (IT 12, 1992, p. 3). Later in the interview she added: "It's not just a symbol. Being a Director means one's able to intervene on everything and be informed on everything" (IT 12, 1992, p. 3). Another female interviewee indicated how material location had a symbolic effect in policy terms:

> *It just can't be underestimated how significant it is having the Equity Director on the Executive, both symbolically and materially. For example, there would hardly be a committee within this Department that would not have a representative from the Equity Directorate. (IT 1, 1991, p. 9)*

These comments confirm Cockburn's (1991, p. 232) research findings that getting the 'equality initiative placed in a high and secure place' is central to its effectiveness within bureaucratic organisations. However, the way in which this location framed the first Social Justice Strategy also meant its practice in schools was somewhat problematic.

It is significant that those responsible for the Social Justice Strategy 1992-93 were women, albeit women located within senior positions within the Department. Research has documented how such equity workers within the Australian state are by and large women which carries implications for the politics which surround the production of such Strategies inside the state (Eisenstein, 1996).

The political character of this work was acknowledged by one of the femocrats involved in the creation of the first Social Justice Strategy:

> *Well it's a profoundly political role because you're placed there to change the structures you're in, as well as the power relations in that structure and those that have put the structures there. So you're always working inside and outside the camp as it were. (IT 12, 1992, p. 7)*

This same interviewee noted that while the structures and personnel had changed with the Labor Government, much of the conservative policy culture remained intact. She also observed that politicisation of social justice issues and the anti-equity stance which dominated during the long period of conservative government (1957-89) carried implications for the practice of the Strategy in schools. She argued that situation had meant that there were those in the schools who had been 'strongly politicised' and who were aware of the issues and ready 'to run with them', given the legitimating umbrella of the Strategy; yet at the same time there were those who were unaware and sceptical of the issues and some opposed to them.

The Social Justice Strategy

Turning then to the actual Social Justice Strategy 1992-93; the document had a supporting Foreword by the Director-General of Education, noting that it was part of the Department's corporate plan and that as it was 'a whole-of-organisation strategic plan' all 'work units' within the Department should utilise the document in the development of their specific plans, including schools. The language of the Strategy was very much framed by the context of its production, including the residues of an old anti-equity culture, new managerialism and the restructuring of department/school relationships and a more managerialist definition of the role of school principals. The volume, pace and character of other changes occurring simultaneously with the production and distribution of the Strategy, which will be briefly documented below, probably ensured some refraction of its intentions in schools.

Section One of the Strategy outlined the central goal of maximising access, participation and outcomes for disadvantaged students, considered existing policies or programmes which now came under the rubric of the Strategy and noted how these applied to both staff and students. It is interesting that programmes for the so-called 'gifted and talented' were included; there was considerable contestation over this inclusion. Section Two lists 12 actions which were to be completed in 1993, a rationale for each action, a responsible person for the achievement of the action and expected 'output'. This very structure is managerialist in character and indicative of a 'rational approach' to policy production; an observation confirmed by Section Three which relates the Strategy to programme management, review and evaluation and to a reporting cycle. The 12 actions outlined in Section Two included: the development of a non-discriminatory language policy; the development of a policy on parent participation; documentation of the level of accessibility in Queensland schools for people with disabilities; establishment of a database on access, participation and outcomes for target students as a base for future developments within the Strategy; development of a Department standard for an inclusive curriculum; identification of the costs for students of schooling and determination of commensurate levels for student allowance schemes; a review of procedures for allocating human, financial and material resources to schools; development of an anti-racism policy and grievance procedures for both staff and students; identification of the need for interdepartmental co-operation in relation to social justice; development of a sexual harassment policy and grievance procedures for both staff and students; and finally development of socially just enrolment policies. This list gives some indication of the omnibus character of social justice within the Strategy. It also implies certain barriers which have to be overcome for social justice to be achieved. In that context, the use of the word 'strategy' is significant with respect to the policy; it seems to denote some political will about achieving its goals, but also implies that some things have to be changed. Table I summarises this aspect of the Strategy.

The barrier	The process	The solution
o language which discriminates	Action Statement One	o policy statement *and* guidelines concerning the use of non-discriminatory language
o some parents excluded from participation in their child's schooling	Action Statement Two	o policy statement re inclusive parent participation
o building design which excludes those in wheelchairs etc	Action Statement Three	o database and locality guide/directory on access to Queensland education facilities
o inequitable access, participation in schooling o inequity in funding and staffing of individual schools	Action Statements One to Twelve, but specifically Action Statements 4; 7; 8	o student database to monitor access and participation o revised policy for allocating human, financial and material resources to schools
o a hegemonic curriculum which excludes contributions and experiences of a number of social groups	Action Statement Five	o development of a Departmental Standard for Inclusive Curriculum
o financial demands placed on students and families which exclude access and participation	Action Statement Six	o database of the current costs of schooling o investigations to maximise allowances and resourcing
o racist attitudes and practice	Action Statement Nine	o development of an anti-racism and grievance policy
o bureaucratic boundary maintenance	Action Statement Ten	o mapping gaps in service delivery across departments
o sexism; patriarchy, discrimination on the basis of gender	Action Statement Eleven	o enacting legislation o sexual harassment policy and grievance procedure
o enrolment practices which exclude students	Action Statements One to Twelve, but specifically Action Statement Twelve	o a social justice enrolment statement

Table I. Barriers addressed by the Social Justice Strategy, 1992-93.

The strategy was not distributed to all schools until September, 1993 and only three copies were sent to Brookridge for a teaching staff of 45. By that time several of the Action Statements had been completed and 'marketed' separately to the schools; articles had appeared in the *Courier-Mail,* Queensland's daily newspaper, about the Strategy; directives about aspects of the Strategy had gone to schools from Regional Offices; and a large number of articles had appeared in *Education Views,* the Department's fortnightly newspaper. Even this brief documentation indicates that the assumption within rational approaches to policy of a discrete moment of the production of the policy text, and a clear delineation between such a text and its implementation, absolutely fails to encapsulate the 'messiness' of the policy cycle (cf. Ball, 1994, p. 10). As Martin Rein (1985, p. 115) has noted, policy production and implementation continually 'play off' each other.

The Contextual and Intertextual Relations of the Strategy

As noted, Labor on gaining office at the end of 1989 was strongly committed to 'modernising' the public sector. Some of the resultant legislation formed part of the intertextual context of the Strategy and included the Criminal Justice Act 1989, the Education (General Provisions) Act (1989), the Anti-discrimination Act of 1991, and Freedom of Information Act, Equal Opportunity in Public Employment Act, Judicial Review Act and Disability Services Act, all passed in 1992. Thus at the same time that the Strategy was being developed and sent to schools, the Department itself was being restructured and a plethora of legislation with implications for both the Department and the schools was enacted.

1992		
February	o	Aboriginal and Torres Strait Islander Early Childhood Education Policy
March	o	Gender Equity Policy
June	o	*Draft* Sexual Harassment Policy
September	o	Social Justice Strategy (1992 - 1993)
November	o	Equal Employment Opportunity Management Plan
1993		
February	o	Educational Provision for Students with Disabilities and Ascertainment Guidelines for Students with Disabilities and Learning Difficulties
March	o	Youth Policy Queensland
April	o	Gender Equity in School Sport Policy
	o	Sexual Harassment Policy and Grievance Procedures
	o	Suspected Child Abuse Policy
	o	Departmental Procedures for Responding to Allegations of Physical/Sexual Abuse of Students made against School Staff
June	o	Strategic Plan for Literacy and Numeracy
August	o	*Re-write* of Schools and Discipline: Managing Behaviour in a Supportive School Environment
	o	*Refined* Transfer Policy
September	o	Equal Employment Opportunity Management Plan
	o	Schools and Discipline: Managing Behaviour in a Supportive School Environment
	o	Education of Gifted and Talented Students Policy
November	o	HIV/AIDS Education Policy
1994		
April	o	*Draft* Anti-Racism Policy
May	o	Standard for Inclusive Curriculum

Table II. Educational policies directly related to the implementation of relevant state legislation in Queensland, 1992-94. *Source: Education Views:* 1992, 1993, 1994; *Metropolitan Regional Circulars:* 1992, 1993.

With each piece of legislation came a Department policy. Table II lists the policies developed which related either directly or indirectly to legislative changes and indicates something of the extent of the changes occurring within the Department. Teachers were 'bombarded' with materials to read in relation to these matters. A teacher interviewed for the research observed, 'you can't read it all and you can't internalise the whole thing'.

By September 1993 Brookridge State High School teachers had elected and trained two Sexual Harassment Referral Officers, had formed a Special Needs and Social Justice Committee and had discussed or been 'inserviced' on the Sexual Harassment Referral Process and the new Behaviour Management Programme. Issues of equity were also incorporated into the School Development Plan. One teacher interviewed for this research noted the intensification of teachers' work flowing from this situation:

> *...we seem to be confronted with more apparent decision making – and there are constraints on that decision making anyway ... it just seems that we seem to take up progressively more and more times in those areas and we still have the same amount of time in the classroom. (IT 5, 1994, p. 8)*

A very substantial number of managerialist changes were going on at the same time as the development of the Strategy and which in some ways sat in tension with it, but this new managerialism had already marked the character of the Strategy in terms of its construction and framing. Furthermore, some uncertainty began to surround the Strategy when the Director of Equity, who had 'driven' the Social Justice Strategy, resigned in April 1993 to take a new position interstate. The rumours about the likely abolition of the Equity Directorate were so strong that in her final article in *Education Views* the Equity Director stressed the necessity for the Directorate to be retained as the Strategy was still in its formative stages. The Director-General also saw it as necessary in *Education Views* articles to stress that the Directorate would not be abolished. A change of Minister in late 1992, who spoke a much more managerialist language and who implored principals to do MBAs, also altered the context of the Strategy. Cuts in the 1993 education budget exacerbated this situation. On the basis of projected reductions teachers took industrial action prior to this budget. In the schools there was considerable anxiety about the volume and pace of change.

Layered over these State level changes was an array of 'national' developments (Lingard & Porter, 1997). These included, *inter-alia,* the agreement to National Goals in Schooling (1989), moves towards national curriculum statements and profiles, the development of generic competencies, the push for the integration of schooling and training reform, agreement to a national equity strategy, and implementation of the National Policy for the Education of Girls in Australian Schools (1987) and the National Aboriginal and Torres Strait Islander Education Policy (1990). The appointment of the Wiltshire review of school curriculum in Queensland in November, 1992 related to these national moves and added to the sense of rapid policy change, while appearing to confirm Stephen Kemmis's (1990, p. 1) observation that policy was increasingly replacing education theory as the source of guidance for teachers. The Wiltshire report *Shaping the Future* (1994), while arguing that social justice was one of its core values, appeared to treat social justice as a policy element distinct from questions of curriculum (Lingard & Rizvi, 1995), at the same time failing to give any priority to the Social Justice Strategy. The internal bureaucratic politics of getting even some mention of social justice into *Shaping the Future* is another story, but is mentioned here to indicate the competing messages the educational policy community was receiving with respect to the extent of the political commitment to social justice.

It was in this context that the Social Justice Strategy 1992-1993 'hit' the schools. By then the Strategy was not the major priority for teachers who were also confronted by the impact of devolution, pressures for product accountability from the new managerialism, and deterioration in their conditions of work. One interviewee nicely encapsulated this situation:

> *... social justice in Queensland is a poor third to efficiency and devolution, ... because if it was important, if they felt it was something that really had to be done, they would do it. It would get a lot more response from the Department. They would be pushing it more, they would make sure they would have the money. (IT 3, 1994, p. 7)*

The Reception of the Strategy at Brookridge High School

The context of the production of the Social Justice Strategy has been outlined and some inkling given as to the difficulties with its reception in schools. Some refraction of the Strategy resulted from the conflicting and confusing measures coming from the Central Office and the rapidity of change already noted, while some clearly resulted from a 'residual conservatism', and some from the 'muddling through' or 'satisficing' (Ham & Hill, 1984, p. 84) evident in any policy 'implementation', but particularly so in a context of 'policy overload' and work intensification.

Only three copies of the Strategy were distributed to the school and the questionnaire indicated only about 56% of Brookridge teachers had actually seen it, while only about 43% had actually read it. Half of the staff who had actually read the Strategy were either considering promotion or actively seeking it.

Changes in educational funding had meant that there were staff reductions at Brookridge with a resultant work overload for teachers. In turn, this impacted upon the work of the resource teacher with responsibility for social justice; she was now regularly required to take replacement classes. This was significant given that, according to questionnaire responses, teachers saw the principal and resource teacher as the most relevant in achieving social justice within the school. Responses to the questionnaire demonstrated quite clearly that the teachers believed funding and staffing to be central to achieving social justice, just those factors which had been reduced around the time of the 'implementation' of the Strategy. Further, teachers regarded support from the school administration as the next most important factor, at the same moment there were increased demands upon the principal contingent upon managerialism and devolution.

Answers to the question of the 'most crucial enabler' for success of the Strategy showed that Brookridge teachers believed that "Training and Inservice programmes outlining the general concept of Social Justice and its role in the schooling process" were most crucial for ensuring the Strategy's success. The Department's own Social Justice Review (November, 1994) documented the paucity of professional development for teachers in relation to the Strategy. It is interesting that 'a more simply worded document' was the second most crucial enabler perceived by the staff. (Here the teachers were most likely confusing the first fairly austere Strategy with the wordier second draft Strategy.) This perception may have been a factor in the low readership of the document. The low ranking of curriculum assessment and review, combined with the debates in the school surrounding appropriate curricula for post-compulsory schooling, would seem to indicate that most teachers held to a distributive conception of social justice.

The questionnaire results indicated that the staff ranked the principal first with responsibility for social justice. Teacher interviews, however, questioned the strength of the commitment of the principal and deputy to social justice. The principal when asked in an interview who was responsible for social justice in the school replied, 'unfortunately me'.

The principal in interview outlined the myriad pressures upon him – from devolution, more financial responsibility, calls for greater efficiency and from the Social Justice Strategy. He noted the tension between the call for efficiency and for consultative leadership and a committee approach in the schools. He also pointed out that staff ownership of change through devolution and committee processes at school level was desirable, but that such processes were exceedingly time consuming so as to cause consequences which were 'more negative than the positive ones of ownership'.

The principal also argued that STAR was important in getting social justice and curriculum debates going within the school in an attempt to broaden curriculum offerings. In terms of his responsibility for the 'implementation' of the Social Justice Strategy he stated:

> *Well, ultimately it is my responsibility for seeing that it [Social Justice Strategy] is implemented but part of that process is to devolve it to committees and individuals and to educate staff on an ongoing, well I see it as, it's one, it's only one of many new policies the Department's putting out ... I've noticed that it is a 'corner stone' of the Department's, in fact the whole government's policies, but it's an evolutionary process and that's how I see it's being implemented – in an evolutionary rather than revolutionary way. And that people are gradually coming to grips with it, that they are gradually widening their understandings and their applications. (IT 1, 1994, p. 11)*

It is perhaps this view of the 'implementation' of the Strategy in Brookridge which 'encouraged' the staff perceptions of lack of support from the administration for social justice. The principal also acknowledged the avalanche of legislative and policy changes that he and the teachers at Brookridge had to cope with, indicating that he could not keep up the reading. The principal saw the classroom as the desired focus of teachers' work and that committee work detracted from this focus. In the interviews teachers repeatedly complained that policy initiatives emanating from Central Office took them away from their teaching duties, and consequently they saw the Social Justice Strategy as an 'add on', not central to their work.

Those teachers interviewed articulated a notion of social justice as 'fairness' and stressed the need for 'a fair competition'. In that way some argued that the Social Justice Strategy made no difference because they had always operated fairly to all students, with 'ability' as the explanation of the academic success or otherwise of students. As questionnaire responses indicated, the teaching staff basically agreed with the 12 Action Statements in the Strategy, with resourcing and staffing once again ranked very highly. The principal in his interview predicted quite accurately that teachers would not be so interested in the Action Statements to do with parent participation, inclusive curriculum and student costs.

Female staff tended to agree more with the Action Statements of the Strategy than did male teachers. Although one of the 10 maths/science teachers confirmed strong agreement with each of the Action Statements, and the science teacher interviewed displayed considerable understanding of the issues of social justice, the maths and science staff, along with administration and commercial staff were more likely to disagree with the Action Statements than other staff. Only two staff members overall rated their interest in the Social Justice Strategy as very high and no one ranked their participation as very high. When asked to rate the interest levels of others, staff felt that colleagues were less interested in the Strategy than they themselves were and participated less in its implementation. Staff believed that more than 80% of teachers had a minimum level of involvement with the 'practice' of the Strategy.

The interviews and the questionnaire suggested that the construction of social justice of the teachers and administrators at Brookridge was individualist – about fairness and fair competition. They used words and phrases such as 'ordinary kids', 'normal kids', 'adjustments', words which signify 'us and them', which practise 'othering' rather than inclusion. One teacher suggested that the thing he remembered most about the Social Justice Strategy was that 'it doesn't appear to cater for ordinary kids'. Most of the staff were tentative about 'mainstreaming'. The lack of relevant inservice was very significant here with the principal commenting that "the inclusions had run ahead of staff development".

Perhaps Brookridge's teachers' attitudes here are a reflection of their age, experience and period of teacher education, which parallel the general pattern amongst Australian teachers. One interviewee suggested that this mature and experienced teaching staff at Brookridge actually meant that they regarded "anything new automatically with a negativity" (IT 2, 1994, p. 2). However, apart from the 10-15% of teachers who interviewees believed were explicitly anti-equity – those who see social justice as a 'lot of hogwash', 'social engineering', who would not change their opinions even if 'hit by an atomic bomb' – most teachers at Brookridge State High School were beginning to redefine their roles in the school so as to be inclusive of the needs of all students. Student research interviews verified such a perception.

Conclusion

This conclusion does two things. First, it summarises factors central to the reception of the Social Justice Strategy at Brookridge. Secondly, drawing on this research and other work (Taylor et al, 1997), an attempt is made to raise some more general issues to do with policy sociology and the politics of 'progressive' educational change.

Understanding the 'Refraction' of the Strategy at Brookridge

While the two pieces of research reported in this paper have shown how micropolitics in relation to the Strategy were continually played out within both the central office and the school so that there was no distinct moment of policy text production and policy reception, the concept of 'refraction' remains useful given that we are dealing with a state generated policy text. A number of factors were responsible for the refraction of the Strategy at Brookridge. The competing discursive constructions of social justice were significant in this process, as the concept was contested in an ongoing fashion at the central state level and within the research school where a conception of social justice as simply 'fairness' predominated. This was a factor in the contingent relationship between the Strategy and its reception in the school. A distributive notion of social justice was supported by many teachers who were well able to separate the 'what' of education from the 'how much' individuals were able to access (Connell, 1993). There was also a sense in which social justice was regarded as something which applied to the so-called special needs groups. Both the development and reception of the Strategy were framed by a strong and lingering anti-social justice conservatism within the Department's 'policy culture'. At the same time, the Strategy's reception at the school was affected by an emerging 'tradition' of social justice work established by earlier Commonwealth equity policies and the availability of some funds. The Strategy was framed by new managerialism and 'more for less' rhetoric of steady funding against a backdrop of substantial change and reforms and greater expectations. Much of the first strategy also appeared to be somewhat tangential to the core concerns of classroom teachers as they perceived them. Its top-down production, probably inevitable given the political situation and legislative requirements, was another factor in its reception. To be fair, its focus was systemic change as the first step to a long term approach. The weakening of political commitment to the Strategy with a new Minister and resignation of the Director of Equity also sent certain signals to the schools, as did the non-formal endorsement of the second Strategy (1993-98).

When faced with reduced staffing, cuts to teacher release, preparation and correction time and to inservice for professional development, the teachers were understandably angry and resistant to the very substantial extra demands being made upon their time, including those stemming from the Social Justice Strategy, which was seen largely as an 'add on' rather than as central to practice. They were suffering from 'reform fatigue' and appeared to indicate that they would give less until they got more.

Connell (1993) has noted that it is a simple truism of educational policy that teachers make or break most attempts at reform. McLaughlin (1987) likewise has observed that the putting of educational policy into practice depends upon the smallest unit – the teacher in the class room. Teacher professional development is a significant element for ensuring policy practice. Extensive professional development was not available for teachers in relation to the Strategy; indeed at the moment of its 'implementation' the Department decided all teacher professional development had to be conducted in the teachers' own time. This is not to suggest, however, that all teachers would have been committed to the Strategy given the appropriate professional development.

The Brookridge principal was very important in framing the school's reception of the Strategy, as was the resource teacher. The research showed the use of 'a demonstrable commitment to social justice' as a criterion for appointment and promotion within the Department was an important factor in the extent of teachers' engagement with the Strategy. It is significant that the new Coalition Minister has abolished this criterion.

The articulation of a system-wide Social Justice Strategy is thus a necessary, but not sufficient condition for the practice of social justice in schools. This first Strategy contained no notion of 'local' school-based innovation within it. As Elmore & McLaughlin (1988) have noted:

> *Policies as we have seen, are useful but blunt instruments. Under the best of circumstances, they can influence the allocation of resources, the structure of schooling, and the content of practice; but those changes take time and have unexpected effects. (Elmore & McLaughlin, 1988, p. 60)*

The posting of the Strategy to the school is clearly not sufficient for its practice! Teachers need time, involvement in policy production, professional development, and a consideration of their interests for effective social justice changes in the schools. Policy is indeed a blunt instrument for change and change is not simply a technical matter.

One can see the reasons for our muted nostalgia for this moment in educational policy history. This small story of the policy cycle in one Department of Education also appears to confirm the veracity of Graham

Swift's observation that history goes backwards and forwards and takes detours – progressive educational change can never be taken for granted and is never simply linear in character. However, on a more optimistic note we would argue that many residues of the Strategy remain within the schools and the Department, as evidenced by the opposition when the new government moved to reject the discourse of social justice. Furthermore, those aspects of the Strategy which were backed by legislation, for example sexual harassment, still have real effects in the Department and the schools.

The Politics of Educational Change

In this section, we utilise the policy trajectory study reported in this paper to reflect generally upon the complex relationships and mediations between politics, policy and 'progressive change', as well as upon policy sociology debates.

This study has shown the significance of the external context to change within education. The election of a Labor government after thirty-two years of conservative rule provided the impetus for the Social Justice Strategy, but it did so in a post-Keynesian era of market liberal ideology and new managerialism. This new managerialism, including changing central office/school relationships, as well as the changing character of the work of principals and teachers, affected the production, character and reception of the Strategy. The study has demonstrated the significance of the internal dynamics of the Department of Education to these processes, including structural location within the central bureaucracy of those with responsibility for the Strategy and the stance of those with leadership responsibilities within the school. The research has clearly shown that the reception of a policy is also marked by the conditions of its production. The study has also indicated the need for a long-term approach to policy institutionalisation. This requires professional development across the system. Experienced teachers require particular forms of professional development.[8]

The research confirms that effective organisational change requires political will, structural and cultural change, and the appointment of new personnel (Wilenski, 1986). However, often more energy is expended in the internal state micropolitics necessary to the production of a policy text than to its institutionalisation. Such institutionalisation demands a long term strategy of embedding all elements of the policy into the structures, practices and culture of the organisation. It also needs the mobilisation of community support. The situation in the Queensland Department of Education with the first Social Justice Strategy was that the Equity Director constructed it to focus on systemic change as the first stage of a longer term approach, which would eventually focus on schools and take a more consultative and participatory mode of working, and also involve the community. The changing political circumstances ensured that this did not happen. The study would suggest that, given the inevitability of changing political contexts, work with teachers is the indispensable element in effective policy practice. We would also conclude that the mobilisation of community support is important in keeping issues such as social justice high on policy agendas. The research reported in this paper showed that the Social Justice Strategy only involved policy personnel and teachers to the exclusion of the community.

In terms of policy sociology, this study confirms a 'policy cycle' view of policy processes (Bowe et al, 1992), but one which recognises the significance of the changing postmodern state. Thus we would accept Stephen Ball's (1994) characterisation of policy:

> *Policy is ... an 'economy of power', a set of technologies and practices which are realized and struggled over in local settings. Policy is both text and action, words and deeds, it is what is enacted as well as what is intended. Policies are always incomplete in so far as they relate to or map on to the 'wild profusion' of local practice. Policies are crude and simple. Practice is sophisticated, contingent, complex and unstable. (Ball, 1994, p. 10)*

The state can take the lead in the policy process, as it did with the Social Justice Strategy, but can never mandate what happens with such policies in the schools. Furthermore, it would seem to be the case that the state is no less important than it once was, but rather that it now works in different ways with different priorities. A democratic and participatory reconsideration of the processes of policy – from production to practice and the relationships between them – can probably ensure a more enabling situation in schools for state developed policies. There will, however, always be resistances to 'progressive' educational policy changes at all levels of the educational system. The relationship between policy and change is mediated; the relationship between policy and 'progressive' educational change even more so.

We acknowledge that talk of 'progressive change in education' is somewhat problematic, given 'postmodern revisionings of the political' (Yeatman, 1994), but nonetheless remains an important normative political question. In this concluding comment, the register of the language of the paper will change, but will seek to maintain a stance of radical vulnerability and attempt to eschew the language of imperatives. Here we will make our own theoretical vulnerability public, but do so because we accept Bourdieu & Wacquant's (1992) observation that this ought to be central in academic presentations and the reporting of research [9] – an observation even more the case today, given current political and theoretical contexts.

Briefly then, we would argue that while education provides individual benefits and always will, it should always be part of working towards a 'truly civil society' (Cox, 1996), a society which emphasises the collective good and encourages relationships of equality and reciprocity. Some reference was made earlier in the discussion of the modernist traditions of social justice to their neglect of a politics of difference and their conceptualisation as 'ahistorical universals'. The politics of difference clearly requires a reconceptualisation of a 'truly civil society' and collective well-being, one which 'works together' a politics of recognition and a politics of redistribution (Fraser, 1995), and situated specifics and universals (Yeatman, 1994). Regarding this need to rework universalism, we concur with Yeatman's position:

> *If universalism does not reside in what is, or even what could be, but lies instead in a political, contestatory space that opens up in relation to existing wrongs and those who contest them in the name of equality, it is clear that this has radical implications for the nature of political vision. (Yeatman, 1994, p. ix)*

Such a specific political usage of universalism is comparable with Spivak's (1990, p. 109) talk of the 'strategic use of essentialism'.[10] Such a strategic essentialism remains important in terms of marginalised groups making policy claims upon the state, but needs to be tempered by an awareness of differences within categories and a recognition that each policy inclusion creates yet another exclusion (Yeatman, 1994). The global economy of the 'postmodern condition' has seen fragmentation within nations, a reworking of global/local relations and a restructuring of the 'postmodern state' to emphasise the market and international competitiveness, resulting in more inequality and a state *perhaps* more prepared to 'recognise' difference than the pressing need for redistribution. This is not the sort of postmodern state we have in mind here. Rather, we conceive of one which is concerned with equality and difference, with material inequalities and identities, that is, a modernist state reframed by postmodern revisionings of the political. Here we take 'post' to mean both 'after' and 'going beyond' (Hall, 1996, p. 253), taking a 'deconstructive relationship' to the universalism and rationalism of a modernist politics (Yeatman, 1994, p. vii). Thus we consider progressive educational change as that which contributes in the democratic struggle towards such ends. Discourses of social justice and state generated social justice policies remain important for making political claims and for providing an umbrella for debates around such matters as equality and difference as they are worked out in specific contexts of educational policy and practice.

Correspondence

Bob Lingard, Graduate School of Education, University of Queensland, Brisbane, Queensland 4072, Australia.

Notes

[1] We would like to thank the two referees for their perceptive comments and Fazal Rizvi, Cathryn McConaghy, Carolynn Lingard and John Knight who commented on earlier versions of this paper. The theorising about policy has developed out of engagement with the two sets of data and out of Bob Lingard's collaborative work on policy with Sandra Taylor,

Fazal Rizvi and Miriam Henry. See here Taylor et al (1997) *Educational Policy and the Politics of Change.*

[2] We recognise the postcolonial critique of the concept of 'recognition' which can paradoxically continue to 'other' difference. See Hall (1996).

[3] We are aware of the potential for trajectory studies to present too linear a conception of the relationship between policy production and policy practice or reception. However, in this paper we are dealing with a state generated policy text.

[4] The interviews were conducted in 1991 and 1992 and transcribed and numbered beginning at 1. In the text these interviews appear as IT (Interview Transcript), number, 1991 or 1992, followed by page.

[5] Little use is made in this paper of the student interviews.

[6] These interviews were conducted in 1993 and 1994 and transcribed and numbered beginning at 1. The same format is used in the paper as for the other set of research interviews.

[7] On the femocrat role and strategy see Eisenstein (1996)

[8] The Commonwealth funded National Schools Network (NSN), an initiative of the previous Commonwealth Labor government as part of the Accord it signed with the teacher unions, has provided some guidance here. The NSN has run fully funded, week-long professional development schools for groups of teachers during school vacations. These teachers work together on a particular 'policy and practice problem' with a 'teacher leader' and an academic with expertise in the relevant domain.

[9] Bourdieu & Wacquant (1992, p. 219) note: "A research presentation is in every respect the very opposite of an exhibition, of a *show* in which you seek to show off and to impress others. It is a discourse in which you *expose yourself*, you take risks."

[10] See the interview between Spivak and Ellen Rooney in the edited collection by Naomi Schor & Elizabeth Wood (1994) *The Essential Difference* for subsequent developments in her thinking about the dangers of both essentialism and anti-essentialism and the differences between a strategy and a theory. Also see Fuss (1989).

References

Ball, S. (1994) *Education Reform: a critical and post-structural approach.* Buckingham: Open University Press.

Beilharz, P. (1989) Social democracy and social justice, *Australian and New Zealand Journal of Sociology,* 25, pp. 85-99.

Bourdieu, P. & Wacquant, L. J. D. (1992) *An Invitation to Reflexive Sociology.* London: University of Chicago Press.

Bowe, R., Ball, S. & Gold, A. (1992) *Reforming Education and Changing Schools.* London: Routledge.

Burgess, B. (1984) *In the Field: an introduction to field research.* Sydney: Allen & Unwin.

Burnside, B (1992) Restructuring of Secondary Education in Western Australia: a case study of 'devolution' at work in a senior high school. Unpublished M.Ed Admin. thesis. The University of Queensland.

Cerny, P. (1990) *The Changing Architecture of Politics: structure, agency and the future of the state.* London: Sage.

Cockburn, C. (1991) *In the Way of Women: men's resistance to sex equality in organisations.* London: Macmillan.

Connell, R. W. (1993) *Schools and Social Justice.* Sydney: Pluto Press.

Considine, M. (1988) The corporate management framework as administrative science: a critique, *Australian Journal of Public Administration,* XLVII, pp. 4-19.

Cox, E. (1996) *A Truly Civil Society: Boyer lectures.* Sydney: ABC Books.

Edelman, M. (1977) *Political Language.* New York: Academic Press.

Eisenstein, H. (1996) *Inside Agitators: Australian femocrats and the state.* Sydney: Allen & Unwin.

Elmore, R. & McLaughlin, M. (1988) *Steady Work: policy practice and the reform of American education.* Washington: The Rand Corporation.

Fitzclarence, L. & Kenway, J. (1993) Education and social justice in the postmodern age, in B. Lingard, J. Knight, & P. Porter (Eds) *Schooling Reform in Hard Times*, pp. 90-105. London: Falmer.

Foucault, M. (1984) What is enlightenment? in P. Rabinow (Ed.) *The Foucault Reader.* Harmondsworth: Penguin.

Fraser, N. (1995) From redistribution to recognition: dilemmas of justice in a 'post-socialist' society, *New Left Review*, July-August, pp. 68-93.

Fuss, D. (1989) *Essentially Speaking: feminism, nature and difference.* New York: Routledge.

Garrick, B. (1995) Proximate solutions or strategic action? The implementation of the 1992 Queensland Education Department's social justice strategy in a Queensland high school. Unpublished M.Ed. Admin. thesis. The University of Queensland.

Hall, S. (1996) When was 'the post-colonial'? thinking at the limit, in I. Chambers & L. Curti (Eds) *The Post-colonial Question: common skies, divided horizons*, pp. 242-260. London: Routledge.

Ham, C. & Hill, M. (1984) *The Policy Process in the Modern Capitalist State.* Brighton: Wheatsheaf.

Kemmis, S. (1990) *Curriculum, Contestation and Change.* Geelong: School of Education, Deakin University.

Lingard, B. (1993) The changing state of policy production in education: some Australian reflections on the state of policy sociology, *International Studies in Sociology of Education*, 3, pp. 25-47.

Lingard, B. (1995) Gendered policy making inside the state, in B. Limerick & B. Lingard (Eds) *Gender and Changing Educational Management*, pp. 136-149. Sydney: Hodder.

Lingard, B. (1996) Educational policy making in a postmodern state, *The Australian Educational Researcher*, 23, pp. 65-91.

Lingard, B. & Porter, P. (1997) Australian schooling: the state of national developments, in B. Lingard & P. Porter (Eds) *A National Approach to Schooling in Australia?: essays on the development of national policies in schools' education.* Canberra: Australian College of Education.

Lingard, B. & Rizvi, F. (1995) Shaping the future through back to basics? The Wiltshire Review of the Queensland school curriculum, in C. Collins (Ed.) *Curriculum Stockade: evaluating school curriculum change*, pp. 59-70. Canberra: Australian College of Education.

MacIntyre, S. (1985) *Winners and Losers.* Sydney: Allen & Unwin.

Maguire, M. & Ball, S. (1994) Researching politics and the politics of research: recent qualitative studies in the UK, *International Journal of Qualitative Studies in Education*, 7, pp. 269-285.

McLaughlin, M. (1987) Learning from experience: lessons from policy implementation, *Educational Evaluation and Policy Analysis*, 9, pp. 171-178.

Nozick, R. (1976) *Anarchy, State and Utopia.* Oxford: Blackwell.

Rawls, J. (1972) *A Theory of Justice.* Oxford: Clarendon Press.

Rein, M. (1985) *From Policy to Practice.* London: Macmillan.

Rizvi, F. & Lingard, B. (1996) Disability, education and the discourses of justice, in C. Christensen & F. Rizvi (Eds) *Disability and the Dilemmas of Education and Justice*, pp. 9-26. Buckingham: Open University Press.

Sawer, M. (1989) Efficiency, effectiveness and equity? in G. Davis, P. Weller & C. Lewis (Eds) *Corporate Management in Australian Government*, pp. 138-153. Melbourne: Macmillan.

Schools Commission (1987) *The National Policy for the Education of Girls in Australian Schools.* Canberra: AGPS>

Spivak, G. (with S. Harasym) (1990) Practical politics of the open end, in S. Harasym (Ed.) *The Post-colonial Critic: interviews, strategies, dialogues*, pp. 95-112. London: Routledge.

Spivak, G. (with E. Rooney) (1994) In a word, interview in N. Schor & E. Weed (Eds) *The Essential Difference*, pp. 95-112. Bloomington: Indiana University Press.

Swift, G. (1983) *Waterland*. London: Picador.

Taylor, S., Rizvi, F., Lingard, B., & Henry, M. (1997) *Educational Policy and the Politics of Change*. London: Routledge.

Troyna, B. & Vincent, C. (1995) The discourses of social justice, *Discourse: studies in the cultural politics of education*, 16, pp. 149-166.

Wilenski, P. (1986) *Public Power and Public Administration*. Sydney: Hale & Iremonger.

Yeatman, A. (1990) *Bureaucrats, Technocrats and Femocrats*. Sydney: Allen & Unwin.

Yeatman, A. (1994) *Postmodern Revisionings of the Political*. London: Routledge.

Young, I. (1990) *Justice and the Politics of Difference*. New Jersey: Princeton University Press.

MEANINGS OF LITERACY IN CONTEMPORARY EDUCATIONAL REFORM PROPOSALS

Colin Lankshear

Language and Literacy Education
Queensland University of Technology

This essay will identify some dominant meanings of literacy within contemporary proposals for educational reform in North America, Britain, and Australasia. It will subject these meanings to critique, and begin to redress what is seen as a serious imbalance within the current reform "vision" for literacy education.

In general terms, reform implies deliberate efforts to improve something which is (or has become) flawed: to change it in desirable ways, by giving it a new form. At this general level of meaning, reform might be seen as occurring almost constantly in education as teachers, administrators, and others strive — individually, or in concert with others — to improve their techniques or results.[1] At a more formal level, however, educational reform is associated with attempts by governments and their administrations (local, state, and federal) to direct or steer changes in the practices and performances of educational institutions by framing policies, enacting legislation, and trying to ensure their implementation — in response to perceived weaknesses within the education system and notions of how to overcome them.[2]

At this formal level, educational reform has been an increasingly high profile political focus in many countries, including the United States, Canada, Britain, Australia, and New Zealand, since the early-mid 1980s. Indeed, in the United States, the period since 1983 is often identified by educationists as being characterized by "an unprecedented volume of [educational] policymaking."[3] The reform scene is extremely complex, especially when multiple countries are considered. In attempts to reduce undue complexity and locate patterns across states and countries, some commentators have distinguished discrete "waves" or "loci" of reform: notably, an emphasis on curricular aspects of reform (for example, policies establishing curriculum frameworks and controls, mandated testing, competency statements, and benchmarking practices), and an emphasis on structural-organizational aspects

1. R.M. Thomas, "Educational Reforms," in *International Encyclopedia of Education*, 2d ed., ed. Torsten Husén and T. Neville Postlethwaite (Oxford: Pergamon Press, 1994), 1152-57.

2. Hedley Beare and W.L Boyd, "Introduction," in *Restructuring Schools: An International Perspective on the Movement to Transform the Control and Performance of Schools*, ed. H. Beare and W.L. Boyd (London: Falmer Press, 1993).

3. Susan H. Fuhrman, Richard P. Elmore, and Diane Massell, "School Reform in the United States: Putting it into Context," in *Reforming Education*, ed. Stephen L. Jacobson and Robert Berne (Thousand Oaks, Calif.: Corwin Press, 1993), 4.

EDUCATIONAL THEORY / Summer 1998 / Volume 48 / Number 3

(such as school-based management approaches, administrative restructuring, school-community-business partnerships, and devolution of tasks and responsibilities). While the focus on literacy in this essay falls largely within the curricular emphasis, how literacy is framed within reform proposals is *also* inseparably linked to values, purposes, and initiatives (such as "technologizing"' social practices and maximizing efficiencies and accountability) inherent in larger "designs" (or "scripts") for reconstituting everyday structures and organizations across a wide front: from work to welfare, corporations to classrooms.[4]

Analysts of educational reform initiatives within Anglo-American settings over the past 10-15 years often discuss them in terms of three interrelated concerns: revitalizing economic competitiveness and advantage; maintaining a "viable" degree of cultural coherence and cohesion, while orchestrating "necessary" institutional change with an eye to the future; and preserving a sense of nationhood, and national allegiance and solidarity — in the face of escalating cultural and ethnic diversity within national borders, intensified international and transnational forms of organization, experience, and interchange, and postmodern celebrations of individuality with consequent erosion of more collective forms of identity.[5] Of these, says Thomas Toch,

> [The] quest for renewed economic competitiveness [was] the principal reason that the nation supported the push for excellence in education so strongly; more than anything else, it was the competitiveness theme that defined the education crisis in the nation's eyes.[6]

Toch's claim refers specifically to the United States, but holds equally for Australasia, Britain, and Canada. James Guthrie notes the extent of this trend across the Western world. He observes that modern economies "are not simply boosting or gently nudging an already initiated notion that education systems should enhance a nation's human capital resources." On the contrary, Guthrie provides evidence of the extent to which economic forces operating internationally have already begun

4. "Designs," "scripts," and "cultural models" are terms used by James Paul Gee in relation to enactive projects of reform. See also James Paul Gee, Glynda Hull, and Colin Lankshear, *The New Work Order: Behind the Language of the New Capitalism* (Sydney: Allen and Unwin, 1996).

5. See, for example, Thomas Toch, *In the Name of Excellence* (New York: Oxford University Press, 1991); Thomas Popkewitz, *A Political Sociology of Educational Reform: Power/Knowledge in Teaching, Teacher Education, and Research* (New York: Teachers College Press, 1991); James Guthrie and Julia Koppich, "Exploring the Political Economy of National Educational Reform," in *The Politics of Excellence and Choice in Education*, ed. W. Lowe Boyd and Charles Kerchner (London: Falmer Press, 1989) 235-47; and James Cibulka, "The Evolution of Educational Reform in Great Britain and the United States," in *The Reconstruction of Education: Quality, Equality and Control*, ed. Judith Chapman et al (New York: Cassell, 1996) 103-28.

6. Toch, *In the Name of Excellence*, 17.

COLIN LANKSHEAR is Professor and Research Director in the School of Language and Literacy Education, Queensland University of Technology, Victoria Park Road, Kelvin Grove, Queensland 4059 Australia. His primary areas of scholarship are philosophy of education, critical literacy, economic and educational change, and education policy.

"to reshape the forms of schooling across national boundaries." Moreover, "this 'human capital imperative' is only likely to intensify over time."[7] Indeed, Guthrie observes that its current intensity is such that many of the other purposes schools have traditionally been expected to meet — such as assisting social mobility, promoting individual fulfillment, encouraging artistic and aesthetic awareness and abilities, and enhancing social cohesion and civic order — are already "being forcefully subordinated to national economic development."[8] This dominance of the economic imperative is fundamental to my argument here. I will identify and critique some of its implications for how literacy gets framed within influential reform statements and recommendations, and argue the importance of adopting a larger perspective.

Before turning to meanings of literacy more specifically, let me stress that my concern is with meanings at the level of policy proposals and requirements bearing on literacy, *not* with meanings evinced in concrete implementations of proposals as actual programs. As is often observed, reform proposals are rarely implemented in practice as they are framed on paper.[9] The meanings of literacy we locate in reform proposals may differ significantly from those we might subsequently locate in concrete responses to these proposals. Hence, we cannot infer from meanings of literacy (or anything else) identified in reform proposals those meanings that will subsequently materialize "on the ground." Nonetheless, while our *ultimate* concerns as educationists are with what happens on the ground in schools and allied sites, it is very important to address and understand the extent to which, and ways in which, reform proposals and policies can influence the range of meanings and practices subsequently realized in these sites — and, indeed, well beyond them.

Although educational reform plays out most immediately and visibly around values, purposes, conceptions, and practices of teaching and learning within formal public institutional settings, its impact is ultimately on what we do and what we are as individuals and bearers of roles within social practices, including practices that are enacted and shape human life far beyond the school gates. Thomas Popkewitz speaks here of social reform initiatives being concerned with "mobilizing publics" around particular values, purposes, and modes of operation. From the standpoint of social regulation, reform initiatives are about "socially producing and disciplining the capabilities of individuals."[10]

Consequently, to investigate meanings of literacy in current educational reform discourse involves asking what these proposals would have us *mobilized* to understand, become committed to, and enact through our practice in the name of "literacy." Such "mobilizing" proposals are contained in a wide range of texts. These

7. James W. Guthrie, "School Reform and the 'New World Order,'" in Jacobson and Berne, *Reforming Education*, 234.

8. Ibid., 253.

9. Thomas, "Educational Reform" and Beare and Boyd, "Introduction."

10. Popkewitz, *A Political Sociology of Educational Reform*, 1, 3.

include: policy legislation;[11] official curriculum and syllabus statements and frameworks, mandatory tests, and achievement profiles developed in response to legislation;[12] formal reports of research projects, working parties, task forces, discussion/position papers and the like, commissioned by governments/administrations;[13] policy discussion and draft policy documents, official media reports of and commentaries on policy directions, policy related speeches released by or on behalf of government and administration officials;[14] and texts identified by scholarly commentators on educational reform as having been influential in shaping reform policy outcomes.[15] To interrogate such texts for meanings of literacy is to ask what we are being rallied and directed to *become* (and *not*) as teachers and learners of text production, transmission, and reception/retrieval, and what we are being enlisted to *make literacy into* (and *not*) as lived conceptions and practices.

11. Typical examples include United States Congress, *Goals 2000: Educate America Act*, 1993; Department of Employment, Education, and Training, Australia, *Australia's Language: The Australian Language and Literacy Policy — the Policy Paper* (Canberra: Australian Government Publishing Service, 1991); and Department of Education and Science, *The Education Reform Act 1988* (London: HMSO, 1988).

12. For example the California state-promulgated curriculum frameworks for Math, Science, History, and English; textbook-selection procedure policies for California, Texas, and Florida enacted in the early 1990s; Department of Education and Science, *The National Curriculum 5-16 (England and Wales) — A* Consultation Paper (London: DES, 1987), and *The Education Reform Act 1988: The School Curriculum and Assessment Circular 5/88* (London: DES, 1989); Education Department, Queensland, *The P-10 English Syllabus* (Brisbane: DEQ, 1994), and *The Year 2 Diagnostic Net* (Brisbane: DEQ, 1995); National Benchmarks for Literacy and Numeracy currently under development in Australia; Curriculum Corporation, *A Statement on English for Australian Schools* and *English — A Curriculum Profile for Australian Schools* (Carlton, Victoria: Curriculum Corporation, both 1994); and Australian Committee for Training Curriculum, *National Framework of Adult English Language, Literacy and Numeracy Competence* (Frankston: ACTC, 1994).

13. Examples include Irwin Kirsch et al, *Adult Literacy in America: A First Look at the Results of the National Adult Literacy Survey* (Washington, D.C.: U.S. Department of Education, Office of Educational Research and Improvement, 1993); National Commission on Excellence in Education, *A Nation at Risk. The Imperative for Educational Reform* (Washington D.C.: U.S. Department of Education, 1983); The Children's Literacy National Projects and Adult Literacy National Projects programs of the Australian Department of Employment, Education, Training and Youth Affairs; F. Christie et al, *Teaching English Literacy: A Project of National Significance on the Preservice Preparation of Teachers for Teaching English Literacy* (Canberra: DEET, 1991); Department of Education and Science, *Report of the Committee of Inquiry into the Teaching of English Language* (London: HMSO, 1988); S.T. Easton, *Education in Canada: An Analysis of Elementary, Secondary, and Vocational Schooling* (Vancouver: The Fraser Institute, 1988); and Premier's Council (Ontario), *Competing in the New Global Economy* (Toronto: Queen's Printer for Ontario, 1988).

14. For example, President Bush's State of the Union address, January 1990 and his subsequent *America 2000* proposals of April 1991; Terrell Bell, "Bill Pushes Education in Math and Sciences," *San Francisco Chronicle* (9 February 1990), and "'C' Stands for Company, Turned into Classroom," *Wall Street Journal* (1 March 1990); John Dawkins, "Strengthening Australian Schools: A Consideration of the Focus and Content of Schooling" (Canberra: DEET, 1988); Kirk Winters, "America's Technology Literacy Challenge" (Washington D.C.: U.S. Department of Education, Office of the Under Secretary, <k.winters@inet.ed.gov> posted on <acw-l@unicorn.acs.ttu.edu> 17 February 1996); and President Clinton's State of the Union address, 1996.

15. Classical examples from the United States include the Holmes Group's *Tomorrow's Teachers*; Diane Ravitch and Chester Finn, *What Do Our 17-Year-Olds Know?* (New York: Harper and Row, 1987); Carnegie Forum on Education and the Economy, *A Nation Prepared: Teachers for the 21st Century* (Washington D.C.: Carnegie Forum on Education and the Economy); NBPTS, *Toward High and Rigorous Standards for the Teaching Profession* — Report of the National Board for Professional Teaching Standards (Washington D.C.: NBPTS, 1988); E.D. Hirsch, *Cultural Literacy: What Every American Needs to Know* (Boston: Houghton Mifflin, 1987); and David Kearns and Denis Doyle, *Winning the Brain Race: A Bold Plan to Make Our Schools Competitive* (San Francisco: ICS Press, 1991).

From this perspective, the meanings of literacy in educational reform discourse and their associated modes of "doing and being around texts" are both *informed by* and intended to *inform* ideals and practices of literacy much more generally. They are also intended to permeate larger "social ways of doing and being" — such as being workers, citizens, parents, consumers, and members of organizations — that are mediated by texts. In all of this it is important to tease out why some meanings and sets of possibilities are being championed through reform, whilst others are being ignored, displaced, or marginalized. Hence, investigating meanings of literacy in educational reform proposals also involves asking what (and whose) perspectives, priorities, and world views prevail within them.

It is important to do this kind of work as a form of cultural critique. Reform proposals are like scripts, frames, or "cultural models."[16] They encode values intended to change people and social practices — and which *will* change people and practices to a greater or lesser extent depending on how fully they get implemented in practice. From this perspective we must look at educational reform proposals in terms of a much broader context than formal educational sites alone. For those who propose educational reforms intend them to mesh with "scripts" for "doing life as a whole." The key question here is: what kinds of "visions" for life, people, and practices more generally, are encoded in these scripts?

It is also important to approach reform proposals as *frames* that open up certain options and close down others at the level of lived meanings. How do particular reform proposals frame debate about social ideals and, in particular, what range of options do they put before the public? As Robert Reich has observed recently, in a sobering article on the framing of economic debate in the United States since the early 1990s, how options are framed and put before publics can ultimately be "more important...than the immediate choices made."[17] Reich argues that in the case of economic debate the frame was set around balancing the budget by 2002, cutting taxes, and reducing the welfare bill. Given this, certain options for "spending most of the unanticipated bounty" from the current economic recovery were, effectively, closed off. "Rather than dedicate it to what had been neglected and was most needed — universal health care, child care, better schools, jobs for the poor who would be shoved off welfare, public transportation, and other means of helping the bottom half of our population move upward — they devised the largest federal tax cut on upper incomes since Ronald Reagan signed the tax cut of 1981" — which is likely to divert almost half of the cut to the wealthiest 5% of Americans, and three quarters to the richest 20%.[18] This is a dramatic and disturbing example of the design implications of a particular frame; the encoding of certain values as opposed to others in a reform script.

Clearly, we should be engaging critically with such framings — including those of educational reform — long before they are played out in practical implementation.

16. See footnote 4 above. "Cultural models" is the designation preferred by Gee, since it makes explicit the sociocultural nature of enactive projects.

17. Robert Reich, "The Missing Options," *The American Prospect* (November-December 1997): 6.

18. Ibid.

Even if there *is* leeway for "customization" — or, for that matter, resistance — inside the parameters established by the frames of policy proposals, options are nonetheless already circumscribed, and room is established by the policies for introducing subsequent "enforcement" procedures. Moreover, it is important to take a long view. Options might not be curtailed at the practical level to a pronounced and visible extent in the short run, but the "knock on" effects of framing work done now can become enormous a decade or two down the line. Investigating meanings in reform proposals is a matter of interrogating and critiquing a *design* process as distinct from an *implementation* process. And it is crucial work. Reform proposals are enactive texts that are connected to projects to change how we think and act (by changing our cultural models of things like learning, teaching, and schooling). It behooves us to examine carefully the texts of these enactors and their projects before we "buy into them." This includes identifying the perils and possibilities actual implementations may face, and which implementors need to know before they "buy in."[19]

LITERACY IN EDUCATIONAL REFORM PROPOSALS

Our immediate question, then, is: How can the meanings of literacy in contemporary educational reform proposals be seen to encode values that define literacy as an ideal (or multiple ideals) to be realized in practice, establish the bases of its perceived worth, and set parameters for what counts as being literate and engaging in literacy as social practice? More generally, how are these encoded values liable to change people and practices to the extent that they are implemented?

Interestingly, the present educational reform moment coincides quite neatly with the "elevation" of literacy from being a marker of marginal spaces, used mainly in relation to "marginal people" ("illiterates"), to becoming a lofty mainstream educational ideal. Not surprisingly, then, literacy spans a wide spectrum of meanings, some of which remain close to its earlier connotative and denotative associations (as in lingering constructions of basic, functional, and remedial literacy), while others stretch to encompass sophisticated levels of analysis, abstraction, symbol manipulation, and theoretical knowledge and application — particularly in science, math, and technology (as in constructions of higher order literacies). Since the early 1980s, the earlier emphasis on "basics" within educational reform discourse has been complemented by increased concerns for "excellence," construed as higher levels and standards of achievement, with a strong emphasis on a range of "metalevel" understandings and applications.[20] Both emphases are evident in current reform constructions of literacy.[21] What do they *mean*, however, so far as visions of literate people and literacy practices are concerned?

19. Jim Gee, personal communication. See also Gee, Hull, and Lankshear, *The New Work Order*, chaps. 2, 3, and 7.

20. James Paul Gee, *Social Linguistics and Literacies: Ideology in Discourses*, 2d. ed. (London: Taylor and Francis, 1996). This book will be cited as *SLL* in the text for all subsequent references.

21. Department of Employment, Education, and Training Australia, *Australia's Language: The Australian Language and Literacy Policy — Companion Volume to the Policy Paper* (Canberra: Australian Government Publishing Service, 1991); Kirsch et al, *Adult Literacy in America*; National Commission on Excellence in Education, *A Nation at Risk*; and United States Congress, *Goals 2000*.

My approach has been to review an array of landmark reform texts, with an emphasis on United States and Australian exemplars. Over successive readings I have looked for recurring patterns relevant to meanings of literacy — in a *sociocultural* sense of "meanings" which includes conceptual accounts of literacy, values encoded in these accounts, and kinds of practices and relationships they prefigure for literacy within social, cultural, and institutional settings. Patterns emerging from these readings provide two useful ways of organizing meanings. First, the reform texts reveal a range of *types* of constructions of literacy: in other words, several "literacies" that can be seen to vary from each other significantly in kind or degree. Second, for all the differences between these constructions of literacy, they share more or less in common a number of *features* that are important and contentious from a normative perspective. I employ these two "axes" as a structure for identifying and critiquing dominant meanings of literacy in current reform proposals. They provide "leverage" for my critique of the agenda proposed for literacy in educational reform texts, as well as for reviving elements of an alternative agenda for literacy.

TYPES OF LITERACY CONSTRUCTIONS

Four different constructions of literacy have emerged in key reform texts. I call these the "lingering basics," the "new basics," "elite literacies," and "foreign language literacy." They are described in turn.

THE "LINGERING BASICS": RECOVERING "MARGINALS" FOR BASELINE INCORPORATION

Literacy conceived as mastery of fundamentals of encoding and decoding print texts (including elementary math operations) has an ambiguous position within reform discourse. On one hand, it is believed that survival level reading and writing competencies are no longer enough for effective participation in the economic and social mainstream. *A Nation at Risk* laments that "in some metropolitan areas basic literacy has become the goal rather than the starting point."[22] On the other hand, it is acknowledged emphatically that integration into public life demands, minimally, the ability to negotiate texts encountered in the course of everyday routines. A 1993 U.S. report cites statistics claiming that 21-23% — or between 40 and 44 million U.S. adults — would perform at the lowest level of prose, document, and quantitative proficiencies on the test used: ranging from those who could perform few or no items at all on the test, to those who could not perform above this level.[23] *Goals 2000* pledges more adult literacy programs to help improve "the ties between home and school, and enhance parents' work and home lives."[24]

Reform initiatives address basic and functional literacy competencies at both school and adult education levels, although the constructions differ between these levels. At school levels, basic literacy is framed in terms of mastering the building blocks of code breaking: knowing the alphabetic script visually and phonetically, and grasping the mechanism of putting elements of the script together to encode or

22. National Commission on Excellence in Education, *A Nation at Risk*, 14.

23. Kirsch et al, *Adult Literacy in America*, xiv.

24. U.S. Congress, *Goals 2000*, Goal 6 B (iv).

decode words, and to separate words or add them together to read and write sentences. Proposed approaches to remedial literacy work focus heavily on accuracy and self-correction in reading aloud exercises, and correct spelling in written work. Typically, they recommend that remedial learners be subjected to batteries of word recognition and dictation activities and tests, as well as letter identification and print concept exercises. Teachers are to be required to maintain accurate and comprehensive records for diagnosis, validation, accountability, and reporting purposes.

For adults, basic literacy is defined more in terms of baseline functional competencies or "life skills" all adults should have, emphasizing ability "to perform specific literacy-related tasks in the context of work, family, and other 'real-life' situations."[25] The literacy test involved in the 1993 U.S. study mentioned above operationalizes basic literacy in terms of "bottomline" prose, document, and quantitative proficiency. Level 1 *prose* proficiency tasks include identifying a country in a short article, and locating one piece of information in a sports article. Level 2 tasks include locating two pieces of information from a sports article, and interpreting instructions from an appliance warranty. *Document* proficiency tasks at Level 1 include signing one's name, and locating the expiration date on a driver's license; and, at Level 2, locating an intersection on a street map, and identifying and entering information on an application for a social security card. *Quantitative* proficiency task examples at Level 1 include totaling a bank deposit entry and, at Level 2, calculating total costs of a purchase on an order form, and determining the difference in price between tickets for two shows.

Basic literacy competence for *school* learners, then, relates to mastery of generalizable techniques and concepts that are presumed to be *building blocks for subsequent education* — decontextualized tools to serve as means for accessing subsequent content and higher order skills. By contrast, *adult* basic/functional literacy competence is seen to consist more in completing immediate tasks that are *their own ends*, and that are directly and functionally related to daily survival needs.

THE "NEW BASICS": APPLIED LANGUAGE, PROBLEM-SOLVING, AND CRITICAL THINKING

A central motif in educational reform proposals is that the "old" ("lingering") basics are no longer sufficient for effective participation in modern societies. Alleged qualitative shifts in social practices variously associated with the transition from an agri-industrial economy to a postindustrial information/services economy; from "Ford-ism" to "post-Fordism"; from more personal face-to-face communities to impersonal metropolitan and, even, virtual communities; from a paternal (welfare) state to a more devolved state requiring greater self-sufficiency, and so on; are seen to call for more sophisticated ("smart"), abstract, symbolic-logical capacities than in the past. Some see this in terms of a generalized shift toward a more "metalevel" modus operandi, captured in emphases on "higher order skills" as the norm. In this context, it is argued, the old base needs to be raised.

25. U.S. Congress Office of Technology Assessment, *Adult Literacy*, 32.

This sentiment is captured in claims that many school leavers "do not possess the higher order intellectual skills we should expect of them. Nearly 40% cannot draw inferences from written material; only one-fifth can write a persuasive essay; and only one-third can solve a mathematics problem requiring several steps."[26] Concerns are expressed that schools may be overemphasizing such rudiments as reading and computation at the expense of other essential skills like comprehension, analysis, solving problems, and drawing conclusions.[27]

"Critical thinking" is often used as a grab bag for such higher order skills as comprehension, problem solving and analysis, and conjoined with reading, writing, speaking, listening — or, in short, "communications" — to encapsulate the "new basic literacy." Judith Maxson and Billy Hair, for example, frame their conception of "critical literacy" in just this way: "Critical literacy, a relatively new term, combines the concepts of critical thinking and communications."[28]

In like vein, *Australia's Language: The Australian Language and Literacy Policy* identifies "effective literacy" for all Australians as its primary objective — its first goal being for all Australians "to develop and maintain effective literacy in English to enable them to participate in Australian society."[29] Effective literacy is defined as "intrinsically purposeful, flexible, and dynamic and involves the integration of speaking, listening, and critical thinking with reading and writing." It "continues to develop throughout an individual's lifetime," with "the support of education and training programs."[30]

Such constructions remain abstract until they are put into explicit contexts. Concrete embodiments are provided most regularly and graphically in terms of life on the floor of "new times" workplaces: with their demands for team work (requiring "communications skills"), self-direction (calling for "problem-solving" and "trouble shooting" capacities), and devolved responsibility throughout the entire enterprise for producing the efficiency and competitive edge (abilities to "innovate," "maintain quality," "continually improve") that enhances the success of the enterprise and, to that extent, improves workers' prospects of job security. In a well-known statement, Motorola's corporate vice-president for education and training observed that the rules of manufacturing and competition changed during the 1980s, and Motorola had to rethink their approach to workplace literacy and training. Line workers now have to "understand their work and equipment," "begin any trouble shooting processes themselves," "analyze problems and then communicate them." Hence, "from the

26. National Commission on Excellence in Education, *A Nation at Risk*, 9.

27. Ibid.

28. Judith Maxson and Billy Hair, *Managing Diversity: A Key to Building a Quality Workforce* (Columbus: National Alliance of Community and Technical Colleges, 1990), 1. See also Sean Brandon, *Workers as Thinkers in New Times: Critical Literacy Development in the Restructured Workplace*, unpublished Master of Education thesis (Brisbane: Queensland University of Technology, Faculty of Education, 1998).

29. Department of Employment, Education, and Training, Australia, *Australia's Language: The Policy Paper*, 4.

30. Ibid., 5, 9.

kind of skill instruction we envisioned at the outset, we moved out in both directions: down, toward grade school basics as fundamental as the three R's; up, toward new concepts of work, quality, community, learning, and leadership."[31]

"ELITE LITERACIES":
HIGHER ORDER SCIENTIFIC, TECHNOLOGICAL, AND SYMBOLIC LITERACIES

Reform proposals based on "education for excellence" affirm that post-elementary education must emphasize *academic* learning, and pursue greatly increased academic subject standards.[32] The key underlying notion here is that high-impact innovation comes from applications of theoretical knowledge. In 1983, the National Commission on Excellence in Education claimed that

> at a time when knowledge, learning, information, and skilled intelligence are the new raw materials of international commerce...our once unchallenged preeminence in commerce, industry, science, and technological innovation is being overtaken by competitors throughout the world.[33]

According to a 1984 National Academy of Sciences task force, "those who enter the workforce after earning a high school diploma need virtually the same competencies as those going on to college."[34] These sentiments have materialized recently in *Goals 2000* proposals where, for example, Goal 6 objective (v) states that the proportion of college graduates who demonstrate an advanced ability to think critically, communicate effectively, and solve problems will increase substantially. The same general scenario is evident in many other Western countries, and notably in Australia.

"Elite literacies" comprise high level mastery of subject or discipline literacies, understood in terms of their respective "languages" and "literatures."[35] The *language* of an academic subject/discipline is basically the "logic" and process of inquiry within that field. The *literature* of a subject/discipline consists of the accumulated attainments of people working in the field, who have brought its language to bear on its existing literature in order to extend knowledge, understanding, theory, and applications within everyday life.

Command of the language and literature of subject disciplines enables critique, innovation, variation, diversification, and refinement when applied to work. This ranges from producing entirely new approaches to managing organizations, or new kinds of computer hardware and software (from mainframe to PC; DOS to Windows; addition of sound and video), to producing new reporting processes for literacy attainment and new ways of conceiving literacy; from variations within architectural and engineering design, to variations on mass-produced commodities that provide a semblance of individuality or novelty.

31. William Wiggenhorn, "Motorola U: When Training becomes an Education," *Harvard Business Review* (July-August 1990): 71-72.

32. Toch, *In the Name of Excellence*, 1.

33. National Commission on Excellence in Education, *A Nation at Risk*, 7, 5.

34. National Academy of Science Task Force, *High Schools and the Changing Workplace: The Employers' View* (Washington D.C.: National Academy Press, 1984) xi.

35. Paul Hirst, *Knowledge and the Curriculum* (London: Routledge and Kegan Paul, 1974).

This is very much the literacy of Robert Reich's "symbolic analysis" and Peter Drucker's "knowledge work," which is alleged to be the real value-adding work within modern economies.[36] From this perspective, scientists, historians, architects, software designers, composers, management theorists, and electronic engineers are seen as manipulating, modifying, refining, combining, and in other ways employing symbols contained in or derived from the language and literature of their disciplines to produce new knowledge, innovative designs, new applications of theory, and so on. Such activity is seen as adding "maximum value" to raw materials and labor in the process of producing goods and services. Within reform proposals the *critical* dimension of knowledge work is valued mainly, if not solely, in terms of value-adding economic potential. This, however, is critical analysis and critical judgment directed toward innovation and improvement *within* the parameters of a field or enterprise, rather than criticism in larger terms that might hold the field and its applications and effects, or an enterprise and its goals, up to scrutiny.

FOREIGN LANGUAGE LITERACY: PROFICIENCY FOR GLOBAL DEALINGS?

Following decades of decline in percentages of students learning a foreign language in schools, colleges, and universities, reform discourse has given renewed attention to increasing second language proficiency.[37]

Justifications advanced in policy documents and supporting texts often foreground "humanist" considerations in support of foreign language proficiency and bilingualism: whether by increasing foreign language enrollments, or by maintaining community languages and ensuring ESL proficiency among linguistic minority groups. Sooner or later, however, economic motives generally emerge as the "real" reasons behind efforts to promote foreign language proficiency. *Australia's Language* gives as its first reason the fact that it enriches our community intellectually, educationally, and culturally; and second, that it contributes to economic, diplomatic, strategic, scientific, and technological development.[38] However, Australia's location in the Asia-Pacific region and its patterns of overseas trade are the only relevant factors explicitly mentioned with respect to developing a strategy that "[strikes] a balance between the diversity of languages which could be taught and the limits of resources that are available."[39] Elsewhere, influential statements are direct and unambiguous: for example, former U.S. Senator Paul Simon's reference to tongue-tied Americans trying to do business across the globe, in a world where there are 10,000 leading Japanese business persons speaking English to less than 1,000 Americans, and where "you can buy in any language, but sell only in the customer's."[40]

36. Robert Reich, *The Work of Nations* (New York: Vintage Books, 1992) and Peter Drucker, *Post-Capitalist Society* (New York: Harper, 1993).

37. Department of Employment, Education, and Training, Australia, *Australia's Language: The Policy Paper*, 15 and Toch, *In the Name of Excellence*, 8.

38. Department of Employment, Education, and Training, Australia, *Australia's Language: Companion Volume*, 14-15.

39. Ibid., 15.

40. Kearns and Doyle, *Winning the Brain Race*, 87.

Two main factors have generated the emergence of second language literacy education as a new (and pressing) capitalist instrumentality. First, trading partners have changed greatly for Anglophone economies, and many of our new partners have not been exposed to decades (or centuries) of colonial or neocolonial English language hegemony. Second, trade competition has become intense. Many countries now produce commodities previously produced by relatively few. Within this context of intensified competition, the capacity to market, sell, inform, and provide after-sales support in the customer's language becomes a crucial element of competitive edge.

While more could be said about each of these constructions of literacy found in current educational reform proposals, the descriptions provided are sufficient for immediate purposes. It is clear that Guthrie's point about educational reforms generally tending to subordinate wider educational purposes to a dominant *economic* purpose holds more specifically for literacy.[41] This tendency toward subordination reflects, of course, an emphasis at the level of *framing*, or *encoded values*. It remains open in principle to pursue wider purposes at the level of pedagogy. At the same time, however, we must recognize that how we come to value a practice has a strong influence on how we come eventually to practice it. In this regard, it is sobering to reflect on the extent to which our everyday talk and operations are in fact constrained by structured demands and processes in which economic purposes are heavily foregrounded; and the extent to which we may *already* be "walking and talking the economic walk and talk" in our everyday routines. (Are our courses "client centered?" Have they been sufficiently "rationalized?" Are we "adding value" through our research? What "income" are we "generating" this semester?) The ways in which and extent to which reform proposals frame and order educational purposes in reform proposals need to be *named*, or made *explicit*, if we are to contest values they encode — as opposed to taking our chances on how they work out in practice.

Interestingly, various tensions — if not potential contradictions — exist among some of the literacy constructions identified here: notably, between the "lingering basics" and the "new basics." As we enter the latest round of literacy crisis talk, emerging policy predilections for test-based benchmarking and batteries of standardized diagnostic, remedial, and reporting procedures cast strongly in a "lingering basics' mold, threaten new regimes of "teaching to the test." For those students adjudged "most at risk," there is a real possibility that time spent in diagnosis-remediation cycles may undermine their opportunities to acquire the "new basics."

Elsewhere, I have argued that we may be facing a potential emergence of a New *Word* Order, corresponding to differential access to social and personal goods

41. It is interesting, for example, to compare rationales for adult literacy provision from the 1970s, when a strong adult and community education ethos was in place, with mainstream current statements. In the 1970s considerable rhetorical play was made around personal enrichment, reading for pleasure, and like rationales. These, frankly, have been swamped recently by a powerful *functionality* motif which, increasingly, is cast in terms of *workplace* functional demands.

associated with mastery of the varying literacies identified above.[42] If the likelihood of such an outcome *is* enhanced by current framings of literacy within reform proposals, it has serious implications for agendas of access, equity, and inclusive education. To advance the argument, I will now consider various features associated with the constructions of literacy in question by way of further elaborating their meanings.

CHARACTERISTICS OF LITERACIES IN EDUCATIONAL REFORM DISCOURSE

A NEW *WORD* ORDER IN A NEW *WORK* ORDER?

Within post-industrial economies work is becoming increasingly dominated by polarized forms of service work: namely, "symbolic analytic services" on one hand, and "routine production" and "in-person" services on the other.[43] Furthermore, modern organizations aim to infuse a sense of responsibility for the success of the enterprise throughout the entire organization, and to push decision-making, problem-solving, and productive innovation as far down toward "front line" workers as possible.

As intimated in earlier discussion of "elite" literacies, symbolic-analytic work provides services in the form of data, words, and oral and visual representations: diverse problem-identifying, problem-solving, and strategic brokering activities, spanning the work of research scientists, all manner of engineers (from civil to sound), management consultants, investment bankers, systems analysts, authors, editors, art directors, video and film producers, musicians, and so on. Framed as substantial value-adding work within the postindustrial information economy, it is the best paid work. By contrast, beyond demands for basic numeracy and the ability to read, "routine" work often calls primarily for reliability, loyalty, and the capacity to take direction, and, in the case of in-person service workers, "a pleasant demeanor."[44] Seen as low value-adding work, and with huge (global) labor pools, this work is poorly paid.

This polarization broadly reflects the order of difference between elite literacies and the "lingering (old) basic" literacy. In between we find the complication introduced by the changed rules of manufacturing and competition, mentioned by William Wiggenhorn — such as the need for workers to solve a lot of their own problems, operate self-directing teams, and understand concepts and procedures of quality — seen as requiring mastery of the "new basics." While this work, like the previous category of "routine" work, is often not well paid, it presupposes a "higher order basics" than previously and, to the extent that it is not well paid entails economic exploitation (as, of course, does routine work calling only for "lingering basics").

42. Colin Lankshear, "Language and the New Capitalism," *International Journal of Inclusive Education* 1, no. 4 (1997): 307-21.

43. Reich, *The Work of Nations*, 177.

44. Ibid.

I would argue that insofar as reform proposals have, at worst, the potential to entrench a New *Word* Order more deeply in the structure of daily practices and, at best, do nothing significant to redress existing "word order entrenchments," they should be revealed as such, and contested at the level of *designs* that frame options (as well as at the level of implementation and, ideally, before matters even reach the level of implementation). This is especially important if *word* orders are imbricated with *work* orders — as I suspect they are, although considerable further investigation is needed here.

THE EMPHASIS ON STANDARD ENGLISH

In key reform statements literacy means, first and foremost, standard English.[45] Increasingly, the intended force of reform proposals is that standard English should become the sole medium of instruction and learning in all subjects other than foreign language education within mainstream classes. The rationale is that standard English proficiency has a vital bearing on the labor market prospects and general welfare of individuals, and is made absolutely explicit in much supportive rhetoric of educational reform.[46] The meaning of literacy as "standard English literacy" has two main origins. Migrants from non-English-speaking backgrounds (NESB) have a strong presence within our labor markets, especially in *routine* manufacturing and in-person service work sectors — generating a new capitalist instrumentality for standard English. In addition, standard (American) English has thus far emerged as *the* international language of the information age.

Potential implications here include the consequences of requiring NESB students to learn content and process knowledge through a second language at the time they are trying to *acquire* this language, as well as targeting NESB and other "non standard" students disproportionately for remedial work grounded in "lingering basics." We need to consider here the risks of both undermining these students' opportunities for equal access to activities highlighting "new basics" and denying them opportunities to demonstrate (for credentials and progress) mastery of concepts and processes involved in subject learning integral to mastering "elite literacies." Plainly, standard English does not have a mortgage on the attributes of "elite literacies." Hence, the option of educating "nonstandard" students for "elite" competencies via their first languages or dialects — or, better still, via high quality bilingual programs — and allowing the transition to standard English competence to emerge over time is real. The potential implications of denying, or subordinating, this option in favor of standard English include running the risk of structuring differential locations within the New *Word* Order ever more tightly and deeply into educational practice.

THE CLAMOR TO TECHNOLOGIZE LITERACY

Across each construction identified here literacy increasingly means computer-mediated text production, distribution, and exchange. This is a facet of our enforced

45. Department of Employment, Education, and Training, Australia, *Australia's Language: The Policy Paper*, 1.

46. See, for example, Kearns and Doyle, *Winning the Brain Race*, 86-87.

learned dependence on computer applications in work and other daily routines. Education reform proposals are an important integral part of this dynamic, with their prominent references to "technological literacy," technologized curriculum, and technologized administration. Stanley Aronowitz and Henry Giroux go so far as to claim that "the whole task set by contemporary education policy is to keep up with rapidly shifting developments in technology."[47]

Promoting technological literacies in tune with labor market *production* needs is part of the story here. In addition, however, we also have to reckon with *consumption* "needs"—as Ivan Illich has reminded us consistently for almost thirty years.[48] New electronic technologies directly and indirectly comprise key *products* of new capitalist economies. As "direct products," they include all manner of hardware and software, for which worldwide markets need to be generated and sustained. As "indirect products," new technologies include information and communications services, such as Internet access provision, online ordering and purchasing facilities, manuals, and guides, networking and repair services, web page design, and so on. Educational reform agendas serve crucially here as a means to creating and maintaining enlarged markets for products of the information economy—extending beyond curricular exhortations to advocate also the extensive use of new technologies within administrative tasks of restructured schools

President Clinton's "Technology Literacy Challenge" policy package of February 1996 is setting the standard and pace for initiatives across the West, and beyond. It is a direct response to such claims as that of the National Science Board that alarming numbers of young Americans are ill-equipped to work in, contribute to, profit from, and enjoy our increasingly technological society.[49] The "Challenge" asserts the goal of making all U.S. children "technologically literate" by "the dawn of the twenty-first century." Its strategy is to ensure that all teachers receive the necessary training and support "to help students learn via computers and the information superhighway"; to develop effective and engaging software and online learning resources as integral elements of school curricula; to provide all teachers and students with access to modern computers; and to connect every U.S. classroom to the Internet.[50]

We should maintain a cautious and informed skepticism toward such proposals, asking: "if we could not insure equitable access to "elite" and other powerful forms of literacy in the context of technologies as simple and readily available as the pencil, what grounds are there for believing things will be any different with new technologies?" New technologies mediate the New *Word* Order in parallel ways to those by

47. Stanley Aronowitz and Henry Giroux, *Education Still under Siege* (Westport, Conn.: Bergin and Garvey, 1993), 63.

48. Ivan Illich, *Deschooling Society* (New York: Harper and Row, 1971) and Ivan Illich, *Tools for Conviviality* (New York: Harper and Row, 1973).

49. Cited in Toch, *In the Name of Excellence*, 16.

50. Kirk Winters, "America's Technology Literacy Challenge," Washington D.C.: U.S. Department of Education, Office of the Under Secretary, <k.winters@inet.ed.gov> posted on <acw-l@unicorn.acs.ttu.edu> 17 February 1996.

which the pencil mediated older word orders. Equal access involves far more than availability of physical infrastructure alone, as the voluminous literature addressing the politics of literacy makes abundantly clear.[51] The point is not to eschew new technologies *per se* (as if we *could*): although questioning the extent of their current servitude to the logic of "manipulative institutional style" is the beginning of wise practice.[52] Rather, we need to think and act our way beyond the frames of education reform proposals and look to alternative cultural models of effective literacies and literacy pedagogies.

LITERACY AS INDIVIDUALIZED, STANDARDIZED, AND COMMODIFIED

Education reform proposals construct literacy as an intensely *individual* performance and, indeed, as an individual *possession*. Despite increased emphasis within work and civic domains, as well as much educational theory and research, on teamwork and participation in "communities of practice," literacy is strongly framed in reform proposals as measurable capacities of individual learners. Achievements are to be compiled as personal portfolios, to serve in part as an accountability mechanism and, for adults, as a fundamental criterion of employability. At a time when individuals in well-supplied labor market sectors must be prepared to move around to find employment, "portable certified literacy competence" acquires strong functional value.

This may be seen as encoding values of what Popkewitz calls "possessive individualism," a key operating principle of current reform discourse. According to Popkewitz, possessive individualism is grounded in a liberal conception of persons and society, wherein "society is composed of free, equal individuals who are related to each other as proprietors of their own capabilities. Their successes and acquisitions are the products of their own initiatives, and it is the role of institutions to foster and support their personal development" — not least because national revitalization — economic, cultural, and civic — will "result from the good works of individuals."[53]

51. Examples include Jenny Cook-Gumperz, "Dilemmas of Identity: Oral and Written Literacies in the Making of a Basic Writing Student," *Anthropology and Education Quarterly* 24, no. 4 (1993): 336-56; Ann Egan-Robertson and David Bloome, eds. *Students as Researchers of Culture and Language in Their Own Communities* (Cresskill, N.J.: Hampton Press, 1998); Nan Elsasser and Patricia Irvine, "English and Creole: The Dialectics of Choice in a College Writing Program," *Harvard Educational Review* 55, no. 4 (1985): 399-415; Harvey Graff, *The Literacy Myth* (New York: Academic Press, 1979); Shirley Brice Heath, *Ways with Words: Language, Life, and Work in Community and Classrooms* (Cambridge: Cambridge University Press, 1983); Sarah Michaels, "Narrative Presentations: An Oral Preparation for Literacy with First Graders," in *The Social Construction of Literacy*, ed. Jenny Cook-Gumperz (Cambridge: Cambridge University Press, 1986), 94-116; Brian Street, *Literacy in Theory and Practice* (Cambridge: Cambridge University Press, 1984); and Brian Street, ed., *Cross-Cultural Approaches to Literacy* (Cambridge: Cambridge University Press, 1993). For an account concerned specifically with literacy and new technologies, see Michele Knobel and Colin Lankshear, "Ways with Windows: What Different People Do with the Same Equipment," *Language, Learning, and Culture: Unsettling Certainties*, Conference Proceedings, first joint national conference of the Australian Association for the Teaching of English, the Australian Literacy Educators Association, and the Australian School Library Association, Darwin (8-11 July 1997), 182-202.

52. Illich, *Deschooling Society*, chap. 4.

53. Popkewitz, *A Political Sociology*, 150.

Education reform proposals also aim to *standardize* literacy performance against benchmarks and accountability criteria predicated on notions of economic efficiency and competitiveness, cultural cohesion, and national allegiance. A definite tendency toward standardization exists in requirements that teachers observe and map student progress using designated "tools," texts and tests. Here again, it does not follow from the proposals *per se* that they will necessarily result in highly standardized *practices* and outcomes. At the same time, we need to acknowledge that "teaching to the test" is already common practice. Under conditions of intensified accountability, burgeoning class sizes, fiscal restraint, and diverse student-linguistic populations, recourse to narrow definitions of outcomes backed by packaged methods and resources may well prove increasingly "attractive" to many teachers. In Queensland, for example, where a Year 2 "Diagnostic Net" has been introduced since 1995, there are already strong indications that many Year 1 and 2 teachers have begun teaching to the requirements of the "Net," despite a considerably wider brief defined by the English syllabus.

Many current reform proposals also encourage strongly *commodified* views of literacy, by promoting assessment, evaluation, and validation packages, remedial teaching and textbook packages, and teacher professional development packages. These hold out the promise of recipes and resources for securing required performance outcomes. In many cases, this is intensified by narrow and mechanistic models of literacy competencies, and by encouragement to public and private "providers" to "generate income" by "selling" professional development and literacy packages to "clients" in schools and workplaces.[54] In addition, identifying literacy largely, if not primarily, as an *exchange* value, to be cashed in as a credential or as forms of scarce expertise valued by employers, is to perceive and value literacy as a commodity.

There are strong theoretical, ethical, and political grounds for contesting these meanings of literacy. Framing literacy in individualist terms flies in the face of the fact that producing, receiving, and exchanging meanings is fundamentally a *social* practice. To paraphrase Paulo Freire, among others, the "I read/write" presupposes the "We read/write." To portray literacy as an individual capacity and possession, then, is ultimately incoherent. Without others there is nothing to read, write or say. Beyond this, to imbue literacy with individualist values invites further erosion of forms of solidarity and identifying with others' well-being that are integral to working against patterned distribution of places within "word orders" and associated hierarchies of access to social and personal goods. It is more obviously consistent with competitive, self-interested orientations, and "limited sympathies," than with cooperative stances and adopting extended sympathies toward others in the interests of mutual well-being.[55]

54. For a classic example, see National Board of Employment, Education, and Training, Australia, *Literacy at Work: Incorporating English Language and Literacy Competencies into Industry/Enterprise Standards* (Canberra: Australian Government Publishing Service, 1996).

55. For the ethical significance of "limited sympathies," see Geoffrey Warnock, *The Object of Morality* (London: Methuen, 1970).

Parallel arguments apply to the tendencies toward standardization inherent in many reform statements. There is a curious tension between advocating values like innovation, flexibility, diversity, and adaptability as being good for economic advantage, and stipulating requirements that practically invite standardization. At the ethical level, we should note also that if institutional practices tending toward standardization emerge as contingent outcomes of reform proposals, the very social groups who will be most disadvantaged by this are those *already* most marginal within educational, economic, and social life — since the "standards" in question reflect linguistic and cultural mainstreams.

Commodification is likewise problematic. The more we are invited to turn literacy teaching and learning into engagements with recipes and packages, the greater the risks of undermining many values seen as crucial to economic efficiency and viability: problem solving, innovation, applying theory to practice in "smart" ways, and "higher order" operations generally. The most obvious way to resolve this and similar tensions is to say that such "higher order" and "elite" capacities are really only needed by a minority of workers and citizens. This, however, is to concede any serious hopeful concern for equitable and democratic educational principles.

We do well also to recall Illich's arguments that to confuse learning with consuming packages — of competencies, remediation, resources, for example — is to commit the very category mistake that underwrites the ethical, existential, and environmental weaknesses of consumer societies.[56] Furthermore, proposals which encourage us to understand and value literacy as an exchange marginalize the significance of literacy practices as productions of use values of diverse kinds.[57] Practices which subordinate use values to exchange values beyond what participants find acceptable run the risk of *alienating* them. It is not for nothing that workers have resisted and, in many cases, rejected in droves, narrow economically functional programs of workplace education on the grounds that such programs do not meet many of their most powerful and pressing needs.[58]

"INCORPORATED" CRITIQUE

While many educational reform proposals emphasize "critical" forms of literate practice — couched in terms of a critical thinking component of effective literacy, or as text-mediated acts of problem solving — it is important to recognize the nature and limits of the critical literacies proposed. They are typically practices that permit subjecting *means* to critique, but take *ends* as given. References to critical literacy, critical analysis, critical thinking, problem solving, and the like, have, "in the

---

56. Illich, *Deschooling Society*.

57. Colin Lankshear and Michele Knobel, "The Moral Consequences of What We Construct through Qualitative Research." Paper presented to the annual conference of the Australian Association for Research in Education, Brisbane, November 1997.

58. See, for example, Sheryl Gowen, *The Politics of Workplace Literacy: A Case Study* (New York: Teachers College Press, 1992); Glynda Hull, ed. *Changing Work, Changing Workers: Critical Perspectives on Language, Literacy and Skills* (Albany: State University of New York Press, 1997); Peter O'Connor, *Making It Happen* (Sydney: ALBSAC, 1992), and "Spanner in the Works," *Critical Forum* 4, no. 2 (1995).

current climate...a mixture of references to functional or useful knowledge that relates to demands of the economy and labor formation, as well as more general claims about social inquiry and innovation."[59] The nearer literacy proposals approach the world beyond school, the more functional and instrumental critique becomes, with emphasis on finding new and better ways of meeting institutional targets (of quality, productivity, innovation, and improvement), but where these targets are themselves beyond question. The logic here parallels that seen by Concha Delgado-Gaitan as operating in notions of empowerment construed as "the act of showing people how to work within a system from the perspective of people in power."[60] The fact that standards are specified so tightly and rigidly within current reform proposals reveals the intention that the ends driving these standards be seen as beyond critique.

Of course, they are *not* beyond critique. Proposals are always open in practice to critique. Where they are not, in fact, subjected to critique, it is often because we either yield to the impression that they are beyond critique, fear the consequences of critiquing them (in terms of employment or promotion prospects), or are unsure what to advocate in their place. Fears of consequences of critique are often well founded, and there is little this essay can do to mitigate those — other than to recall that history is full of examples where the consequences of refusing to engage in critique have proved enormous in the long — and often not so long — run. In the case of contesting educational reform proposals, as elsewhere, the chances of minimizing unwanted fallout from practicing critique are likely to be indexical to the numbers involved in the practice. The imperative, then, for those opposed to the direction and values of current reform proposals, is to encourage commitment to critique and capacity for critique.

Contributions to this imperative include refusing the impression that proposals are beyond critique, identifying points at which they are open to critique and the grounds on which they are open to critique, and suggesting alternatives to what is being proposed. This essay has refused the impression and tried to identify points of and grounds for critique. I have argued that we need to frame and pursue more expansive and generous agendas for literacy and literacy education. In the final section I take a modest step in what I believe is a better direction.

LITERACY FROM A DIFFERENT POINT OF VIEW

What might literacy look like under some other agenda? What should those committed to a more expansive ideal than *economization* be struggling for in the name of literacy? The very question suggests an answer: namely, literacy practices that engage us in critique of proposals that regulate who and what we become individually and collectively. James Gee's account of liberatory (or "powerful") literacy in *Social Linguistics and Literacies* provides such an ideal. It acknowledges that discursive constructions of the good life are contingent and provisional, that to

59. Popkewitz, *A Political Sociology*, 128.

60. Concha Delgado-Gaitan, *Literacy for Empowerment* (London: Falmer Press, 1990) 2.

be educated is to be capable of critiquing dominant Discourses, and that every person is entitled to be educated in this sense.

Other accounts of liberatory literacy, similar in important respects to Gee's, have been advanced, notably by Freire.[61] Some of these accounts, and Freire's in particular, have been charged with aiming to overthrow a dominant discursive regime, or *order*, only to replace it with another.[62] While I have never been persuaded by such arguments against Freire's view, an important strength of Gee's approach is that he *explicitly* identifies the problem at issue, and develops his account at every point in ways that put it beyond reasonable charges of "colonial intent."

Gee's ideal of liberatory/powerful literacy builds on a distinctive account of Discourse and his appropriation of Stephen Krashen's distinction between "acquisition" and "learning." He defines Discourses in terms of playing socially meaningful "roles" and being identifiable as a member of some recognizable group, class, or network (*SLL*, p. 131). To be in a Discourse means that others can recognize us as being a "this" or a "that" (for example, a priest, a mother, or a teacher), or a particular "version" of a this or a that (for example, a *Jesuit* priest or *Marist* brother, a *traditionalist* teacher or a *progressivist* teacher, a *"middle class"* mother or a *surrogate* mother). Others can recognize us as such by virtue of how we are speaking, reading, writing, believing, valuing, feeling, acting, gesturing, and so on. Language is a dimension of Discourse, but only one dimension, and Gee uses discourse (with a small "d") to mark this relation.

Discourses are of two broad (or "ideal") types: primary and secondary. Our primary Discourse is how we learn to do and be (including speaking and expressing) within our family (or face-to-face intimate) group during our early life. It comprises our first notions of who "people like us" are, and what "people like us" do, think, value, and so on (*SLL*, p. 137). Our secondary Discourses are those we are recruited to through participation in outside groups and institutions, such as schools, clubs, workplaces, churches, and political organizations. These all draw on our resources from our primary Discourse, but they may be "nearer to" or "further away from" our primary Discourse — as in the case of children from marginal social groups who struggle to get a handle on the culture of school classrooms. Gee also distinguishes between dominant and subordinate Discourses in terms of what they make available in the way of "social goods" — status, income, and power. People who master dominant Discourses get more of these things than those who have mastered more subordinate Discourses. Hierarchical societies operate on the principle that some Discourses are dominant and others subordinate, and that opportunities to master dominant Discourses are not equal.

61. Paulo Freire, *Pedagogy of the Oppressed* (New York: Seabury, 1970); *Cultural Action for Freedom* (Harmondsworth: Penguin, 1973); *Education for Freedom* (New York: Seabury, 1973); *Politics of Education* (London: MacMillan, 1985); and Paulo Freire and Donaldo Macedo, *Literacy: Reading the Word and the World* (South Hadley, Mass.: Bergin and Garvey, 1987).

62. Peter Berger, *Pyramids of Sacrifice* (Harmondsworth: Penguin, 1977) and Jim Walker, "The End of Dialogue: Paulo Freire on Politics and Education," in *Literacy and Revolution: The Pedagogy of Paulo Freire*, ed. Robert Mackie (London: Pluto Press, 1980), 120-50.

Literacy is mastery or fluent control of a secondary Discourse. To be literate is to have mastered a secondary Discourse — which involves more than just its language aspect. Since there are many secondary Discourses, there are many literacies, and "people like us" (readers of this page) are multiliterate: we have mastered multiple secondary Discourses.

We gain access to and control of secondary Discourses via two "ideal" modes — acquisition and learning — in some mix or other that will vary from person to person. Variations depend on contingencies of the context and circumstances in which we are recruited to a Discourse, as well as in accordance with our prior experiences, the Discourses we already command, and the nature of the Discourse in question.

We acquire competence by exposure to competent models within natural and functional settings. There is no formal teaching as such. Rather, we know there is something to be mastered, and we "get it" by immersion in the setting through practice, trial and error, feedback, and the like. We get "on the inside" of the competence without having to know it for what it is. Children get their first language through acquisition, which is a largely subconscious process (*SLL*, p. 138). Learning, by contrast, is conscious. We learn either through formal instruction or through experiences that make us reflect on something, such that we gain conscious knowledge of it, and are able to analyze or explain it. When we *learn* something, we get some metaknowledge about it, as well as getting the "it" itself (*SLL*, p. 138). Hence, language *learning* occurs when we get (via instruction or reflection) knowledge of verbs, sound sentence structure, and the like along with new capacities to communicate things linguistically/textually.

From this perspective, there are two aspects to discursive competence: performance in the Discourse, and knowledge about that Discourse. Conceived as fluent control or mastery of a Discourse, as evinced in *performance* (that is, demonstrating the real thing, as though it comes naturally to us), literacy is usually "a product of acquisition, not learning" (*SLL*, p. 144). We get to perform Discourses fluently through abundant exposure to competent performance and opportunities to practice them within functional settings. Knowledge about the Discourse, gained through learning, can expand the range of our performance, and allow us to innovate and diversify, by extending our acquired fluencies into new combinations and variations. But this is necessarily performance *within* accepted parameters of the Discourse — since that is what we are exposed to within contexts of acquisition. This is the logic of "incorporated" critique. The more a context is one of pure acquisition, the more our recruitment to a Discourse is a matter of being colonized (*SLL*, p. 145).

Learning is essential for critique, for the practice of a liberatory or powerful literacy. A literacy (that is, a fluent control of a secondary Discourse) can be seen as powerful or liberating when we can use it to put us beyond colonization — including when we can use it to put us beyond forms of colonization that undermine our interests, and that otherwise produce consequences we would choose to prevent if we were aware of them. This involves using a literacy as "a meta-language or a meta-Discourse (a set of meta-words, meta-values, meta-beliefs) for the critique of other literacies and the way they constitute us as persons and situate us in society" (*SLL*, p. 144).

To get beyond colonized participation in/recruitment to a Discourse and incorporated critique, we need access to standpoints and perspectives from which we can seriously critique that Discourse, and position ourselves to promote and adopt others from an informed and principled base. This presupposes metalevel knowledge about the Discourse to be critiqued, together with experience and metalevel knowledge of the other Discourse(s) on the basis of which it will be critiqued (*SLL*, p. 145). Hence, powerful literacy presupposes learning and a commitment to exposing learners to diverse Discourses. The metalevel knowledge of Discourses that can become available through learning is knowledge *about* what is involved in recruitment to those Discourses. It is more than (merely) knowing *how* to perform them with fluent control. Beyond this knowing how, metalevel knowledge is knowing about the nature of a Discourse, its constitutive values and beliefs, its meaning and significance, how it relates to other Discourses, what it is about successful performance that makes it successful, and what some of the significant consequences are of that Discourse operating the way it does within the larger universe and hierarchy of Discourses.

Contrary to currently dominant educational reform D/discourse, with its forced recruitment to narrow and (for many people) interest-disserving practices, its attendant banalities of standardized competencies and strait-jacketed assessment, and even (*especially*?) its systematic undermining of sound pedagogy by denying acquisition its proper place — our ideal of powerful literacy presupposes discursive diversity, informed pedagogy, and a commitment to keeping options and critique open as the *sine qua non* of any genuinely open pursuit of the good life.

As a complex of dominant Discourses, current educational reform proposals are no more (or less) than an elaborate strategy for maintaining hierarchies, shoring up particular interests, and reproducing patterns of advantage and disadvantage - albeit in increasingly exacerbated and polarised forms. The ideal of powerful literacy presupposes an agenda of radical democracy, in which possibilities for future ways of doing and being are wilfully kept open, and where the commitment to hearing voices on an equal basis is genuine. Educational reform proposals should be among the first objects of critique within this agenda: an agenda to which this essay call us anew.

I AM GRATEFUL TO David Gabbard and Lawrence Erlbaum publishers for first prompting me to think as systematically as I can about meanings of literacy in educational reform proposals. I acknowledge Lew Zipin's collegiality in offering valuable feedback on my early efforts, and appreciate the very helpful directions provided by Nicholas Burbules and two anonymous reviewers for improving the original version of this essay. As always, Jim Gee and Michele Knobel have offered generous support and input throughout the development of this essay. None of those above have any responsibilities for whatever inadequacies remain, but can take much credit for any good that may lurk in these pages.

[36]

The Abuses of Literacy: Educational Policy and the Construction of Crisis

Allan Luke, Bob Lingard, Bill Green & Barbara Comber[1]

Introduction

> **Declining literacy skills for study**
> The impact of key teaching methods on how students learn to read and write will be the focus of the first national survey of children's literacy skills in more than a decade. ... Dr Kemp said that while 'different teaching methods do seem to suit different children', an alarming 10 to 20 per cent of primary school children did not have the basic literacy skills. (Carolyn Jones, *The Weekend Australian*, p. 8, April, 27–8, 1996)

One of the emergent themes of New Times has been the need for sustainable futures: for ecological and environmental sustainability, for new and hybrid communities, identities and life pathways, and for the redirection of post-war and industrial-era social institutions in what appear to be unprecedented economic conditions. How we can reinvent the traditions, practices and texts of print literacy – transforming them for new civic and economic institutions, new technologies and architectures, new ethnicities and cultures – is the focal curriculum debate at the end of the century (New London Group, 1996). In this context, we should welcome the move of the Australian and other OECD governments to afford literacy a central place in educational policy formation.

Unfortunately, among its well documented virtues and uses, literacy has become a sustainable object of political rhetoric, a movable feast with every political and civic group seated with its elbows on the table. For better and worse, literacy is what pollsters and political advisers call a 'hot button issue' and was such during the 1998 election year – an election which focused on significant issues about the very identity, sustainability and future of a polycultural Australian society and a globalised Australian economy. Literacy itself has become a nodal point for political discourse, a sign and symbol for the rallying of political and electoral force, energy and sentiments.

In his seminal postwar study of 'the uses of literacy', Richard Hoggart (1955) established the very grounds for contemporary cultural studies. Many of the critical issues he raised then remain focal, specifically the complex relationships between social class, mass schooling and discriminatory access to literacy. This chapter is a critical case study of a very different 'use of literacy' – specifically of the construction of a public crisis over teaching standards as a means for the destabilisation and disinvestment in state schooling. Hence our title – 'The Abuses of Literacy'. Since the Australian conservative Coalition government's strategic withdrawal from an educational agenda of social justice and equity – the persistent representation of literacy in terms of 'lack', 'deficit' and 'crisis' has been used to make the case for the restructuring and redirection of state and public schooling – an institution that is at the heart of modernity and industrial society. Such a reorientation of educational policy nationally and in several states has occurred, not coincidentally, as Australia enters a period of backlash, with the emergence of extreme right political forces opposed to, *inter alia*, immigration and multiculturalism, indigenous land rights, closer ties to Asia and economic globalisation.

In this context, we argue that what is needed is not a simple or uncritical defence of the *status quo*, of teaching and learning conditions and industrial and institutional conditions hard won in the 1980s and 1990s by teachers, teachers' unions and governments. The task facing literacy educators, educational researchers and policy development is to disentangle the very real demands for new levels and kinds of skills and competences, and the continuing need for equitable access and provision of these skills and competences for historically marginalised groups, from a more general 'panic' over schooling, youth and economic change – a task which has been complicated rather than facilitated by the recent government policy orientations documented here.

In April 1996 the Federal Minister for Schools, Vocational Education and Training, Dr David Kemp, announced a forthcoming National English Literacy Survey. Significantly, a *Weekend Australian* article reporting the planned study was entitled 'Declining literacy skills for study', setting a tenor of alarmist and negative reporting. Apparently even before the survey was finalised, the results were reported as a forgone conclusion. It was also reported as if it were an evaluation of teaching methods, when in fact it had not been designed or conceptualised as such by a senior and highly regarded team of Australian educational researchers who had worked at the project for several years.[2] The *Weekend Australian* report, one of many focusing on literacy in the last three years, deployed a vocabulary of crisis: a 'decline', 'problems', 'struggle', 'poverty', 'shame', 'blame', and 'deception'. Media attention peaked in September 1997, when the Minister released the 'results' of the survey and described them as 'a national disgrace'.

According to the report, 27% of Year Three and 29% of Year Five students did not meet the year-level standard for reading and 28% of Year Three and 33% of Year Fives did not meet the standard for writing. The weekend these results were made public, Minister Kemp appeared on '60 Minutes', a nationally televised current affairs television programme to proclaim his concerns about the 'scandalous' state of children's literacy and how 'parents are being deceived'. The '60 Minutes' segment described the Minister's 'crusade' and introduced a human-interest take on the issue, portraying the Minister's personal concern and family. The programme also noted associated 'threats' and 'warnings' to state Ministers, principals and teachers, that in the future Commonwealth (federal) funding would be tied to performance and that no 'excuses' would be heard. The release of the findings on a Sunday night current events programme attracted considerable media attention in the press over the following days. Several state Ministers publicly contested the interpretation of the results themselves, the pre-emptive media release before they had achieved consensus on an appropriate benchmark, and the suggestion that Commonwealth funding for state schools would be contingent on measurable outcomes in literacy performance.

Since the post-war period, literacy crises have come and gone in Australia and other 'Western' nations, evidence more of governments' and institutions' responses to major social, economic and cultural change rather than absolute declines in literacy *per se*. The current argument over literacy standards may serve to decoy attention from a more significant, structural reorientation in government policy. We pick up the story of what one journalist termed the 'literacy hysteria' (Martin, 1997) surrounding the public release of the survey results later in this chapter. However, that specific event has both a complex history and policy implications which may well have far-reaching effects on public education in Australia. Our aim here is to look at how the alleged crisis has been used to undermine the legitimacy of public belief in state schooling and at the same time to deflect attention away from material problems such as youth poverty and unemployment, problems that have resisted the ameliorative efforts of successive Labor and Coalition federal governments.

It will be ironic indeed if literacy – viewed by successive federal governments as necessary for social access and mobility – becomes a labelling device for a conservative backlash against equity-driven reforms in education. In the past two years, the changed names of the pertinent federal government equity programmes are revealing: the Disadvantaged Schools Programme (1974–94) became an element of the National Equity Programme (1994–96), and then evolved into the Grants for Commonwealth Targeted and National Priority Programmes (1997) as Disadvantaged Schools with literacy as a central priority. Under the Coalition government the Disadvantaged Schools Programme was transformed into a literacy programme for disadvantaged students. There also was an accompanying shift in its documentation, which now speaks of educationally disadvantaged students rather than of schools serving socio-economically disadvantaged communities. The unit of analysis and the focus of policy and intervention has changed. The focus is upon remediating the literacy deficits of individual students rather than changing whole school practices to better meet the needs of students from materially poor backgrounds (Lingard, 1998), with a parallel shift in funding and accountability from a focus on the quantification of 'needs' to an emphasis on the use of testing to identifying 'value-added student outcomes'. This is nothing less than a reinvention and return of the individual deficit subject in New Times: structural social problems, local community problems and intercultural pedagogic issues have been translated, yet again, into individual failings and weaknesses (Luke, 1997a).

In several states, schools, districts and regions have invested significant curriculum and professional development resources in specific literacy packages (e.g., First Steps, THRASS, Keys to Life),[3] moving away from approaches that would place a greater emphasis on culturally appropriate, whole school or school/community-based pedagogies. Ironically, then, the result may be renewed faith in yet another generation of new methods; a faith that has proven again and again in the inter and postwar periods that it cannot 'solve' the systemic social access and complex cultural problems that are part and parcel of literacy education. How many of the readers of this article, for instance, recall DISTAR or the Corrective Reading Programme, Reading 360, or any of the numerous comprehensive, packaged curriculum of the 1960s, 1970s and 1980s that, whether through phonics, word recognition, direct instruction, developmental sequencing etc., offered teachers definitive and scientific solutions? The recent history of literacy education, particularly since World War II, is a tradition of the new, a junkyard of once new and now failed curriculum products and packages, methods and tests that have purported to provide definitive solutions to the alleged 'problem'. Taken together, these successive curriculum reforms repeatedly seem to prove Basil Bernstein's (1972) axiom that 'education cannot compensate for society', which we take to mean that purely and simply technical approaches to pedagogy will not work unless they are based on a systematic analysis of the social and cultural basis of educational problems.

In this chapter we consider the history of the most recent literacy crisis in Australia, its articulation in educational policy and practice, and its political concomitants and consequences. Through an analysis of press releases and media events, we argue that the current crisis has been constructed as part of an explicit governmental critique and destabilisation of public education. Our concluding comments attempt to resituate the debate against the backdrop of the larger issues of governmentality, economy and culture in New Times. These, we conclude, are the real challenges for an Australian reinvention of literacy curriculum and of public schooling, not an alleged decay of normalising standards of reading and writing to be solved by a return to a 'basics' of curriculum benchmarks and standardised tests.

Not only does the educational measurement axiom that '*You don't fatten a cow by weighing it*' hold here. We would also add, mixing our metaphors further, that '*you can't prepare a cow for the next century by feeding it last century's fodder*'. In short, the kind of return to early and mid-century agricultural and crop yield techniques – which formed the basis for the 'test and treat' model of educational research popularised in America in the 1920s and 1930s – are inadequate policy responses to the kinds of complex economic, cultural and social challenges Australia faces. Following Giddens (1994), our position is that a positive direction for reinventing public schooling and other civic institutions today requires that we move beyond old tags of left and right, beyond simply defending the *status quo* in the face of regressive policies associated with 'manufactured uncertainties'. But while there is a genuine need to reconstitute literacy and literacy education in relation to new conditions, the Australian government's preferred pathways towards a nostalgic basics that might never have historically existed, towards simplistic 'test and treat' solutions do not provide a viable way forward.

When is a Crisis a Crisis? For Whom? In Whose Interests?

There are now two decades of comprehensive scholarship on the deployment of literacy myths and the systematic invocation of literacy crises to shift attention (and legitimation) from economic problems to moral and social arenas.[5] Yet it is crucial to resist the temptation to write off such claims as cyclical hysteria or simple backlash. It is imperative, rather, that we analyse each successive outbreak of crisis in terms of its material and discursive antecedents. The public rhetoric of crisis warrants careful and critical attention in relation to this particular crucial moment in Australian politics. We use it quite deliberately here, however, precisely because we want to highlight its character as *discourse*. That is, it needs to be understood semiotically, as a signifier which works socially in the domain of politics in the contemporary nation-state – a nation-state that, not incidentally, stands at the crossroads with regard to major questions about its governmentality (e.g., the debate over when and how Australia will become a republic), its economic and cultural alliances (e.g., with Asia in a globalised economy, as against its century-long ties with continental Europe and the UK), and in terms of how it will reconcile its cultural histories, identities and responsibilities (e.g., the debate over Aboriginal reconciliation and entitlements and Asian immigration). So no matter how much of a post-war 'broken record' the literacy debate might appear, it now needs to be reconsidered in light of these contemporary challenges to Australia. Why and how are 'crises' being constructed, deployed and invented? How do these crises work in relation to educational policy processes?

It needs to be noted at the outset that 'quite unambiguously that there is no general literacy crisis in Australia' (Lo Bianco and Freebody, 1997: xvi). That is by no means to deny that there are clear signs of 'systematic underperformance' and related problems of educational and social disadvantage, along with new challenges for literate practice, both print and electronic. Indeed, the findings of the recent National English Literacy Survey tell us once again what any one of a number of existing state sample and census tests, surveys and profiles have been telling state authorities for years: that students living in poverty, with a non-English speaking background and Aboriginal students are more likely than other groups of students to be represented in those *not* meeting benchmarks, wherever and however we set acceptable levels of performance. These are unsurprising results and comparable affiliations of lower literacy achievement with economic marginality and cultural subordination are common across post-industrial and rapidly industrialising nation-states. So our view is not that there isn't a literacy problem, but that the problem has been and continues to be intimately linked with a host of issues about educational institutions' capacity to contend with cultural diversity and poverty (Wilkinson, 1998), therefore about community access and economic enfranchisement, and, increasingly, about the emergence of local, national and global 'new work orders' (Holland, 1998; Gee, Hull and Lankshear 1996). It is not nor has it ever been a simple matter of the 'right' or 'wrong' pedagogy.

These patterns, the recent OECD adult literacy data would seem to indicate, are problems Australia shares with other advanced Western economies, as we jointly contend with the transitions from industrial to post-industrial work and technologies, and the persistent problems of socioeconomic disadvantage among minority, youth and rural populations.[6] More specifically, while the Australian school system has demonstrated apparent success at 'closing of the gap' between Aboriginal and NESB and 'mainstream' performance in secondary reading comprehension (Masters and Forster, 1997) and while mainstream performance on reading newspaper prose remains largely unchanged, the same survey indicated that the gap between male and female performance had increased – with boys' apparent comprehension declining. For its part, the adult literacy survey (Australian Bureau of Statistics/OECD, 1997) indicated that a significant proportion of adult literacy problems are aggregated among the aged and among recent migrants of NESB backgrounds. In this regard, we concur with the Minister and others who argue that federal and state educational policies need to systematically target resources, materials and educational efforts to address these patterns of 'underperformance' – problems that persist, we would note, even or rather especially in those countries which long ago put in place the kinds of national curriculum systems (e.g., UK following the Education Reform Act of 1988) and large-scale state testing systems (e.g., US, Canada) that are now offered up to the Australian public as panaceas. It is worth noting here that similar adolescent comprehension and adult functional literacy achievement patterns can be identified in most American states and Canadian provinces despite extensive and expensive testing systems, that the first evidence of a 'comprehension crisis' emerged in the American reading research literature in the 1960s, and that, across the UK, US, Canada and Australia, it shows no signs of abating in spite of successive large scale interventions that began with the US National Right to Read Programmes in the 1970s.

The relationship between literacy underperformance and its concentration among those longstanding groups identified in educational policy as requiring specialised support is beyond dispute. The question begged in the current debate is over the depth, dimension and (though all educational researchers should be rightly suspicious of any such oversimplifications) 'causes' of the problem. Simply put, analyses of differential achievement in school or institutionally based literacy achievement need to conceptualise changes in achievement in the first instance as something far more complex than simplistic epidemiological 'symptoms' of individual deficit or failed method. Changes in literacy achievement are always tied to: (a) cultural and social changes in population demographics (e.g., school-aged and adult populations consist of socio-economically, linguistically and culturally more diverse, and, in instances, more economically 'at risk' populations than 20 years ago); (b) changes in actual literate practices required and used in communities, workplaces and civic life (e.g., everyday cultural and workplace practices have shifted significantly with the advent of first and second wave new technologies), and (c) changes in differential access to a range of social institutions, including schools, churches, media, non-government community organisations and other agencies that act as 'institutional supports' for literacy (Heath, 1986). That is, changes in literacy achievement are indicators of, *inter alia*, changes in social and cultural, community and local contexts, and indeed the emergence of 'underperformance' has to do with systematic discrepancies between contexts of acquisition (e.g., homes, schools, curriculum) and contexts of use (e.g., communities, workplaces, other educational institutions). (Luke, 1994)

The logic of such an account suggests that what is needed is a systematic audit of new and old texts, practices and skills required by new media, technologies, by emergent and traditional workplaces, for civic and community participation (e.g., Hull, Jury, Ziv and Katz, 1996) – and a systematic analysis of the curriculum, then turning to account for systematic underperformance at key developmental transition points in students' transitions between community and school contexts, both in early childhood and in the ongoing, multiple transitions to community life, work and further study. While this is a far more delicate and complex empirical task than simple benchmarking and testing – it offers potential explanations and strategies for systematically addressing those pedagogical and experiential bases of underperformance in schools and other institutions that can be influenced and altered via policy (e.g., Wilkinson, 1998), rather than simply telling us again what we already know about at risk student populations and utilising a lot of public money to do so. Further, such an agenda would offer to use rather than discard the extensive 1990s' Australian research on competencies, on workplace and community literacy uses, and on the 'profiling' of individual students' literacy development (e.g., Cope *et al.*, 1994).

By any axiom of literacy research that views literacy as an historical, social practice and not as a universal set of skills in peoples' heads (Cole, 1997), attempts to reduce apparent underperformance to individual or group deficit are naive at best, if not educationally counter-productive. Further, to reduce underperformance to the failure of teachers or of this or that teaching method is, in measurement terms, to take one independent variable and treat it as *the* principal variable, in what remains, after all, a complex constellation of contexts and factors. Identifying for policy intervention which difference might make what difference is not a simple task, and, as the UK curriculum experience indicates, might lead to a misinvestment in major reform in search of an instructional 'magic bullet' for illiteracy.[7] Yet the ecological and contextual complexity of educational problems, of course, is neither 'good press' nor is it readily explicable in the sound-bites that government and public policy has come to be based on. As we know from the policy literature, policy is very often as much about constructing problems in given ways as solving them (Beilharz, 1989; Taylor, Rizvi, Lingard and Henry, 1997). By contrast, a moral epidemiology of group and individual deficits that are said to cause unemployment and lower socioeconomic life-pathways, deficits that can be 'solved' by teachers and methods acting properly and morally, has a simplicity and commonsense appeal. It also effectively deflects public attention from government, private sector or, indeed, community responsibility for youth and family poverty, for youth unemployment, for economic and social disenfranchisement of cultural and ethnic minority groups, for the social disinvestment of governments, and indeed for the confusion and frustration that surrounds the processes of globalisation. Our case here is that the politics of policy production create problems in particular ways and produce policies to supposedly solve the problem as created within the policy discourse – raising the question of whose values are authoritatively allocated within the policy text (Taylor, Rizvi, Lingard and Henry, 1997: p. 29).

Our questions, then, can be reframed. What does 'crisis' stand for? How can it usefully be seen within the context of 'the politics of contested meaning' (Yeatman, 1990: 160) surrounding educational policy? What is the *work* of the metaphor of 'crisis' as a specific, highly charged discourse category in the articulation of public policy? The rhetoric of 'crisis' historically has been associated with the phenomenon of large-scale social, cultural and economic *change* – whether viewed positively or negatively, as something to be embraced or something to be resisted (Green, Hodgens and Luke, 1997). In what follows, we ask what changes and challenges are at issue in current Australian policy contexts, and what competing interests are in play? More specifically, our concern here is how the rhetoric of literacy crises marks out a more fundamental policy shift in the formation of Australian state schooling.[8]

Literacy Crises and the Destabilisation of National Identity

If metaphors drawn from other sciences are the stock and trade of educational policy, for a moment it might be worthwhile to leave aside the idioms of medical epidemiology that seem so popular with the press and government ('disease', 'symptoms', 'plague') and try to invent a kind of social seismology. Literacy debates are always struggles over more than simply reading and writing. They act as Richter Scales of enduring and renewing social tensions, economic restructuring and cultural changes – and as such they provide discursive fields for the playing out of significant ideological and political issues. In post-war Australian educational history, different images and discourses of literacy, schooling and society have been put into circulation. These themes and tropes have tended to represent anxieties and projects of *identity*: relationships and tensions among distinctively Australian (distinctive even in their periodic mimicry of other national and post-colonial contexts) social, cultural and national identities.

Since World War II, different versions of the literate subject have been mobilised in public debate, from the (im)moral subject of the 1950s, through the (un)skilled and (in)competent subjects of the 1960s and 1970s, to the economic subject of 1980s and 1990s. In a documentary study, Green, Hodgens and Luke (1994) found that the first wave of literacy crises in post-war Australia arose in the early 1970s, at the historical point of unprecedented changes to Australian culture: the impact of Vietnam-war era student politics and the increasing influence of American popular and intellectual culture; the demise of the White Australia policy and the political and economic enfranchisement of Aborigines and Torres Strait Islanders, and the 'arrival' of the children of post-war migrants at secondary schools, colleges and universities. In this way, the initial post-war literacy crisis was in fact a crisis in national identity and culture at a particularly crucial faultline in Australian history – one that raised critical and, for some states, as yet unresolved issues for schools about what might count as a truly post-Anglo/colonial, Australian school curriculum. However, in terms of the actual preservation and extension of public education, the combined federal and state response in the 1970s to cultural change was an unprecedented expansion of education at all levels, including the foundation of the 'bush-unis', expansion of the College of Advanced Education system and of secondary schooling, and a peak of real funding provision. Note that this 1970s' governmental response to a 'first wave' literacy crisis occurred in a period of sustained economic growth and expansion – right at the end of the post-war economic boom and Keynesian policy settlements. Hence, a public discourse of 'crisis' actually encouraged and enabled the expansion of public educational infrastructure and the justification of this expansion through a nascent human capital rationale.

The politics of identity of the current literacy crisis are no less significant. Historically, the emergence of 'literacy crises' seems to have marked the destabilisation of cultural identity and economic destiny. In the current policy context, the 'unfinished business of difference' (Luke, 1997a), the problematics of increasing cultural, linguistic and demographic diversity raised in the early 1970s remain stubbornly and tenaciously on the table – in spite of the overt unwillingness in current educational policy to 'name' cultural, gender and social class difference as part of the issue. *Indeed the emphasis upon individual deficits has been used to annul and cancel notions of group diversity and disadvantage, at a time, not coincidentally, when the historical facts of systemic disadvantage of Aborigines, Torres Strait Islanders, particular migrant groups, and, indeed, girls and women have been called into question as forms of 'political correctness' and, even more significantly, when this conservative Coalition federal government is struggling to contend with electoral victories by minority parties to its political right that identify multiculturalism, Indigenous entitlements and immigration as principal causes of economic problems.*

In politics, timing is all. Is it curious that the literacy debate should arise simultaneously with an overt political debate around race pushed by the emergence of a right wing backlash that appears to have caught both the Labor and Coalition conservative parties by surprise? The last two years have been characterised by a succession of overt and more subtle policy moves that signal a federal government under Prime Minister Howard with what appears to be a questionable commitment to redefining cultural and economic affiliations around the symbols and images of a multicultural, multiethnic, multilingual Australian identity (Luke and Luke, forthcoming). The reopening of the national debate on immigration, the government's silence and loss of face in the region in response to the symbolic and real attacks on Asians and Indigenous Australians, the government's response to the 'stolen children' issue and national Reconciliation, and its use of Indigenous land rights as a key electoral strategy, as well as its attack on 'political correctness' (Luke, 1997b): taken together, these moves indicate that the government is moving towards at best an ameliorative, at worst an assimilationist approach to questions of national identity and diversity. Australia's future is seen to lie with our past; the conservative Prime Minister appears to desire a return to the cultural formation of the 1950s.

In this light, we can reconsider the timing and the substance of calls for the 'basics', literacy testing benchmarks, correct teaching methods, and increased standardised testing. Taken as a package, these share a technocratic approach to literacy[9] that disregards culture and context (whether conceived of as community or workplace, ethnic or global) as constitutive elements in the development, transmission and use of literate practices. It is, necessarily and typically, reductionist in its approach to and definitions of literacy as a corpus of universal, testable and transferable, trans-cultural and acultural 'basics' (Luke and Van Kraayenoord, forthcoming). In this way, the current crisis enlists literacy education, its alleged shortcomings *and* its apparent solutions, in the move towards a monocultural approach to education, curriculum and, indeed, national identity formation – right at an historical juncture when both new technologies and globalised economies have placed a premium on hybrid, trans-national and intercultural identities and communications. Specifically, the standardised testing and national curriculum agenda mark a return to a normalised, generic Australian literate, who is capable of basic skills and performance regardless of, in spite of, above and beyond, contextual, community, cultural and local background knowledges and standpoints, intercultural communications and power relations, globalised codes and semiotic systems. The government's policy response to the unfinished business of difference and the emergent business of new economies and cultures, then, is a return to the technocratic literate of the post-war, industrial era, the generic worker citizen who might, even on a good day, be ill-fitted for a globalised, multi-ethnic economy and culture. Whose practical benchmarks such a literate worker might meet and which economic and social worlds such a citizen might inhabit are interesting and unresolved questions that are not taken up in current policy debates.

For all its flaws, the policy orientation towards competence-based adult, vocational and secondary education that proliferated in Australian education in the 1990s attempted to identify and describe the contexts of both new and old workplaces, civic spaces, and new forms of community and institutional life (e.g., Cope *et al.*, 1994). Despite its overt aim to quantify the production of human capital, competency-based adult education in Australia was also an attempt by Labor governments at curriculum prescription for sustainable futures, based on a vision of what and how new workplaces and civic spheres could operate in the national interest, as against the prescription of decontextualised skills and knowledges that, fingers crossed, might prove to be of universal value – subject, of course, to successful transfer of training from pedagogical context to (unspecified) work and community contexts. A leap of faith indeed – particularly given the ongoing ethnographic evidence that transfer of training between institutional contexts of acquisition and contexts of use for literate practice is a persistent educational problem (e.g., Gerber and Finn, 1998). Our point here is that competency scales attempted to develop curriculum and assessment instruments based on the analysis of current and emergent workplace and civic domains of practice – an appropriate place, given a socio-cultural perspective on literacy, from which to begin. By contrast, current government policy has attempted to identify by political and professional consensus a set of universal 'skills' and 'behaviours', that can then be developed into *de facto* national assessment and curriculum. The latter approach risks creating rather than solving the archetypal transfer of training problem.

Which skills, competences and identities should be taught are central issues that are linked to general questions about the whole enterprise of schooling. In the current crisis, critiques of levels and kinds of literacy have been translated into a more general scepticism towards state government schooling. Moreover, just as what is clearly being marked out in public debates over literacy are deficiencies or forms of inadequacy and lack, so too schooling in such contexts and equations is systematically conceived in minimalist, reductionist terms. The key organising term that emerges in such debates is that of 'standards' – moreover, of literacy and schooling alike as *not* being up to scratch, or up to some arbitrary, always *imaginary* standard. Not that this is something that is simply fictional, or imagined, or somehow unreal. Rather, that it is ultimately, ontologically, a manifestation of the Social Imaginary, that order of the socio-symbolic realm – and of social practice – in which dreams and fantasies have material form and effect.

A central issue to be grasped here is the role and significance of the symbolic order, and the problems and anxieties associated with 'managing the symbolic'. We have already suggested that this latest manifestation of the literacy debate is not just something peculiar to Australia, but also has resonance elsewhere in the western world. In an account of literacy and educational politics in the UK, Donald and Grealy (1983: 88) noted that governmental policy and public debate had acquired 'the habit of treating social inequalities as if they were natural differences'. In what they described as the quite fascinating and intoxicating mixture of science and myth, nostalgia and arguments for 'modernisation', literacy is linked strongly and indeed obsessively to notions such as standards and skills. Moreover, this link is used as a kind of symbolic power that asserts the inevitability, the 'naturalness' of particular patterns of social inequality.

> A conservative conception of standards does not just impose a scale of values on forms of knowledge within the curriculum. It also discriminates among people. It ascribes value and legitimacy to certain class-based competences and habits of thought. More than that, it passes them off as natural attributes, as instances of individual excellence. (Donald and Grealy, 1983: 89)

They go on to conclude that 'what is at stake in education is the production and distribution of a society's symbolic values' (Donald and Grealy, 1983: 90) – something which applies with equal force, we suggest, to public debates over literacy and schooling. Seen in this light, then, literacy debates need to be understood as struggles over symbolic value, as struggles and battles over what is valued in education and indeed in the wider society, and over what is to be *imag(in)ed* as worthwhile and desirable forms of curriculum and schooling. Just as the Teacher is a powerful symbolic figure (Green, 1997), so too is the School. Schools matter, in our dreams and our imagination as much as in our daily working lives. Hence attempts to discriminate among schools, or school sectors, must also be understood as attempts to 'discriminate [...] among people', and hence between their different social groupings. Moreover, this 'discrimination must also be understood as working symbolically, as generating different social and educational visions, different images of constraint and possibility, as both the complement and the supplement of material differences and social division.

Labor Policies: Broadbanding and the Move to Accountability

Since the 1980s, the division of wealth in late capitalist nations has generated greater gaps between a small, concentrated upper class of people, a large and growing percentage in the lower middle and lower income levels, and an underclass of long-term underemployed and unemployed people (Bessant, 1993; Connell, 1994; Polakow, 1993; Varghese, 1995; Lash and Urry, 1994).[10] During this period, governments of all political orientations have been faced with the difficult problem of managing and caring for populations so divided, while increasing national competitiveness in globalised and regional economies that stand beyond the direct control or overt regulation of any particular nation-state. There is a tension between economic reform which aims to improve the performance of the nation and the need to provide for increased employment and enhanced living conditions. Despite the apparent shift of the discourses of American educational policy given the economic expansion of the late 1990s in that economy – how economic 'hard times' impact on educational policy (Lingard, Knight and Porter, 1993) and upon literacy education remains the persistent issue in Australia, particularly in light of its real economic ties with Southeast and East Asian countries.

In Australia, the late 1980s and early 1990s saw a proliferation of programmes and policies, supported by the National Labor Government (led first by Hawke [1983–91] and then by Keating [1991–96]), which purported to deliver both 'excellence' and 'equity' in order to produce a 'clever country'. As Bessant (1993) notes, the Australian Labor governments were highly adaptable in making their social justice, equity and economic policies 'add up'. To illustrate, youth unemployment and the resultant high levels of poverty amongst young people could in part be addressed through training programmes designed to make young people more employable. The rationale at work here is that increased levels of education and training increase employability, which decreases the likelihood of unemployment and poverty. Increased enrolment in such training schemes, further, would generate an actual decline in the numbers registering as unemployed. At the same time, by keeping young people in institutional training and education schemes longer, the government could be seen to meet its commitment to increasing the length of education for disadvantaged students. Increased levels of education participation, then, are taken as evidence of the government's social justice policies in action. In such cases, what came to count as 'social justice' clearly served political ends, in terms of providing the substantial appearance of action on behalf of unemployed youth, even though such actions held negligible real promise in increasing youth employment. Just as, as we argued earlier, illiteracy *per se* does not cause unemployment, training programmes *per se* cannot generate meaningful and significant employment. In this context there is a partial conflation of training for employability and welfare, with the emphasis upon employability rather than employment. In this framework, Labor commissioned the first National English Survey as part of its *Working Nation* policy.

The Labor government made education and training the centrepiece of its response to unemployment and economic restructuring (Taylor *et al.*, 1997; Bessant, 1995; Lingard *et al.*, 1993). In so doing, educational institutions were positioned as 'shock absorbers' for wider social and economic changes and problems (Green *et al.*, 1994, 1997). As for the central role of literacy, the linking of economic and equity agendas is evident in *Australia's Language*, the first national policy on language and literacy (Commonwealth of Australia, 1991):

> Apart from its obvious importance to the individual Australian's personal, social and cultural development, proficiency in English is central to the education, training and skill formation necessary to produce a more dynamic and internationally competitive Australian economy. The development of

> English skills is also fundamental to improving the quality of life and opportunities for disadvantaged members of our society. (*Australia's Language*, Companion Volume, Commonwealth of Australia, 1991, p. xiv)

Here the 'development of English skills' is linked with both the production of an 'internationally competitive Australia' and also the improvement of 'the quality of life and opportunities for disadvantaged members of our society'. Here literacy education was connected explicitly with the linked political goals of social justice and economic viability, which resulted in specific policy and infrastructure reforms.

One of these was the process of 'broadbanding', initiated by the federal Labor government, whereby Commonwealth Special Programmes, including amongst others the Disadvantaged Schools Programme, the Country Areas Programme, and the English as a Second Language Programme, were brought together under the National Equity Programme for Schools. Fazal Rizvi (1995) has discussed the various rationales for such a move. As he argues, there was the potential that this shift would override compartmentalised views of 'difference' and 'disadvantage', where gender, race, class, location, first language and so on were treated as separate, and that it would reconcile those bureaucratic structures and procedures that seemed to focus educators on their own particular clienteles and patches (Rizvi, 1995: 26).

> If the idea of broadbanding is intended to help schools become better equipped to tackle the issues of social justice in a more holistic manner, then the National Equity Programme would certainly represent a major advance on the current compartmentalised ways in which various equity programs are currently implemented. (Rizvi, 1995: 28)

However, Rizvi also stresses that any such improvement is contingent upon the programme being organised around a concept that is relevant to each of the target groups. He suggests poverty as such a concept, in that 'it can be justified on the strongest possible moral and political grounds' (Rizvi, 1995: 29). He notes that across the targeted groups it is students in poverty who should have the greatest claims to state support, and he makes the case that education must serve the interests of those groups who are most disadvantaged by the ways that society is arranged and distributes its goods.

Notwithstanding the possibilities of broadbanding as a bureaucratic instrument for delivery of equity-based policies and programmes, what is of interest here is how the broadbanding reform contributed to a particular set of pre-conditions for the incoming federal Coalition government in 1996. The key point here is that by the time the federal Coalition government took office in March 1996, the policy discourses, categories and institutional procedures were in place to allow a swift move towards increased performance-based 'accountability', the marginalisation of those policies affiliated explicitly with social justice, and an overt challenge to public schooling. The explicit yoking of social justice and economic viability under Labor paved the way for the coalition government to effectively re-read and reframe social justice as simply the efficient provision of literacy standards.

We would argue that it is no accident that the backgrounding of poverty in Australian politics has occurred at the same time as literacy has been foregrounded. In the absence of a strong and coherent federal government policy on specific equity issues and groups, and a public policy debate on material conditions and categories that might define an integrated concept of broadbanding, the government has moved to drastically reformulate the system for allocation of Commonwealth funds to schools. As outlined in the Coalition government's Grants for Commonwealth Targeted and National Priority Programmes: 'The new programme combines funding provided under the former Disadvantaged Schools and English as a Second Language (ESL) – General Support programmes, and also includes additional funding of $45 million over three years for a National Literacy and Numeracy Strategy' (283). The key point here is that 'literacy' has been relentlessly foregrounded in policy and media representations of childhood, while 'poverty' 'disadvantage' have effectively been eliminated as organising concepts. Furthermore, the shift in policy focus is to individuals rather than sociological concepts of group or community disadvantage. *In effect, poverty and its impact upon educational performance have been transformed into the literacy deficits of individuals*. What has occurred, then, is simple: a literacy and numeracy strategy has replaced the former funding allocations model based on material and educational disadvantage, and the Minister has indicated on several occasions government intentions that the distribution of funds would be contingent on performance according to Commonwealth determined accountability measures.

Before moving to the implications and outlining possible positive responses, we track how the current literacy crisis has been used to undermine community confidence in public schooling – largely a state responsibility, and to deflect attention and responsibility from material problems of poverty and youth unemployment. A key question here is how people in socioeconomically marginal communities stand to benefit or lose further ground when the an ethics of 'equity' is replaced with an ethics of individual 'choice'. While the former Labor government attempted to balance its economic rationalism with a social justice agenda resulting in a hybrid policy regime, the Coalition government's orientation has been towards market deregulation and individual choice.

Coalition Policies: Shopping in the Educational Marketplace

> **Report card on schools' job success**
> Data to help parents choose
> All Australian schools could be compelled to publish figures showing how many of their students find jobs. The Coalition's 'schools' league table' plan would arm parents with crucial extra data to help them choose a school for their children. Schools would publish data on literacy skills, job success and possibly expulsions – as well as lists of tertiary scores. The proposal is the brainchild of the federal Schools' Minister, Dr Kemp. (Matthew Denholm, *The Advertiser*, p. 1 April 14, 1997)

In this report of an interview with the Minister, key features of contemporary federal Coalition educational policy – parental choice, measurable outcomes, and literacy – are brought together. And the hint that 'expulsions' are being considered as another item for the comparative grid implies a covert concern with 'unruly youth'. Here public schooling is being asked to account for itself though the mechanism of holding individual schools as fully responsible for student performance, as though schools and their students were somehow all already equal in terms of their resources to perform on such measures. What 'parents want' features regularly in government speeches and press releases:

> Dr Kemp said parents deserved a much wider range of information to help them 'shop around'. ... 'At the primary level, parents have a right to know whether their child is going to be literate by the end of

> Grade Three', he said. 'And that sort of information is not available at the moment'. (Matthew Denholm, *The Advertiser*, p.1 April 14, 1997)

The strategy here is to position the government as a champion of parents' rights. In constructing the collective 'good parent' (as, more or less, a white, middle-class, educated, literate parent with the resources, time and mobility to 'shop around'), reports such as these actively capitalise on and galvanise the dissatisfactions of a number of different interest groups. Missing from this rhetoric, however, are any specifications about how such choice will be available to all parents. 'Choice' is presented as an unproblematic goal. Which parents can 'shop around'? Who is the Minister speaking to and for? And who will use 'that sort of information'? These kinds of public statements by the Minister have the effect of undermining confidence in public schools, and at the same time directing responsibility for 'job success' or lack of such, youth indiscipline and other social phenomena towards schools and teachers. It is this public criticism of teachers, public schooling and literacy outcomes which, we argue, stands to erode the credibility of the public education system, to directly and indirectly threaten federal funding and to redirect parents and students, particularly upper middle and upper class communities, towards other educational systems and markets. What is the logic of such a policy move? Perhaps it is driven by a genuine belief that market competition will strengthen public schools, perhaps by the genuine belief that public schools are indeed lacking in the aforementioned imaginary 'standard', or perhaps the marketisation of public schools, like that of universities and tertiary training, is part of an overall strategy of reduction of public expenditure that the Coalition government, like some of its overseas counterparts, has pursued consistently. To pursue these possibilities, let us further and more systematically track what is brought together in the name of literacy for all – or rather, what is accomplished through the production of the 'literacy crisis', and what is silenced in the process.

In what follows, we consider in more detail two key ministerial speeches. One is addressed directly to literacy in the context of schooling and 'the democratic challenge' (Kemp, 1996), while the other is focused more specifically on the question of 'Quality Schooling for All' (Kemp, 1997). Our interest here is on the *image* projected and produced of literacy and of schooling, and hence the symbolic work involved in this most current version of the literacy debate.

The following is a clear indication of the general tenor of the arguments here:

> ... problems in the classroom, the likelihood that a student will finish formal education before Year 12, and the likelihood of being unemployed after leaving school. Literacy problems are a significant contributing factor in youth unemployment. A democratic society cannot afford to have young people barred from full participation by inadequate literacy and numeracy skills. Improving literacy must be regarded by the community as a key issue in providing for social equity because illiteracy is the worst form of poverty. (Kemp, 1996: 5)

Literacy, discipline, school retention, and unemployment: adequate levels of literacy are linked here to the successful completion of twelve years of schooling, with the assumption being that the more one experiences schooling, the more one is likely to be 'literate', in these quite specific terms. On the other hand, discipline in the classroom is connected with employment opportunity, with a clear emphasis on education's primary role as a preparation for work via the production of appropriate social subjects. Literacy is thus highlighted as key to social success and national efficiency. This is directly linked to the notion of 'democracy', which is presented as the cornerstone of 'liberal' politics.

Illiteracy is framed as 'the worst form of poverty', renamed as the constituent cause of real material poverty. What happens in this and other government comments is that discussions of 'illiteracy' have replaced discussions of poverty in Australian politics, certainly in Australian educational policy. For instance, we do not see Australia's political leaders acknowledging that it is a 'national disgrace' that 12% of Australians (*at least 1.7 million people*) are estimated to live in poverty, or that about one fifth of sole parent families live on incomes below the poverty line, or that 13 of every 100 couple families with children were living on incomes below the poverty line, *or that in June 1997 751,000 people were unemployed or that 32% of teenagers in the fulltime job market were unable to find work* (Brotherhood of St Laurence, Poverty Update, August, 1997).

It is of course, politically, much safer to focus on literacy rates and 'democratic values':

> Democratic values hold that all people are of equal worth, that people have a right to participate in their forms of governance and to choose that governance. Democratic values prize tolerance, consider information as something to be shared and recognise diversity in a society. Democratic values treat people as rational, and hold them responsible for their actions. Enshrined in democratic values are the rights of free speech and freedom of religion and association. The right to choose is perhaps the most fundamental democratic right. (Kemp, 1996: 1)

Note that 'the right to choose' is a key metaphor in this particular version of democracy. Moreover, schooling ('beyond the family') is 'perhaps the single most important institution in determining the opportunities people will enjoy in life, and the quality of human relationships in the wider society'. Schools, indeed, are fundamental to democracy, and it is to schools that the community looks to 'strengthen the quality of Australian democracy' (Kemp, 1996: 1). Hence schooling is linked to informed citizenship. What is particularly significant is that this latter argument is framed in terms of access to knowledge and information, and hence presented as a matter of *rationality* above all else, of rational decision-making and rational choice: 'Improving knowledge about Australia's democratic tradition will be a key component of meeting the democratic challenge' (Kemp, 1996: 2). Why this is significant becomes clear later in the speech when reference is made to a 'cult of secrecy', related specifically to literacy and 'the collective educational attainment of our students' (Kemp, 1996: 7), whereby the community at large is said to have been kept uninformed about existing literacy standards and levels. In part, this assertion needs to be understood intertextually, as referring to the policies and practices of the previous government and of Labor educational policy, but it is also part of a broader political agenda organised around state minimalism, economic deregulation, and ethos of 'market' and 'choice', and the privatisation of educational provision. The 'right to choose', then, amounts to participation in an ostensibly deregulated free market for, among other things, social and educational services.

Further, literacy is directly linked here to what has been called 'the test paradigm' (Cook-Gumperz, 1986: 37). Literacy education is thus (re)defined in terms of testing and assessment, conceived expressly within the terms and forms of existing 'technologies' – both literally and metaphorically. That is, on the one hand, literacy is defined as traditional print competence, with little account taken of the distinctive challenges associated with new technologies and emerging literacies. On the other, assessment itself involves the use of particular conventional measurement technologies ('standardised tests', etc). In this way, literacy is defined in terms of a nexus of print skills and pencil-and-paper assessment technology.

This particular construction of school-based literacy is increasingly out-of-step with the emergence of a knowledge-based economy and new forms of techno-capitalism. Literacies and their technologies *are* changing, in accordance with new and emerging technological and cultural dynamics. With new forms of literacy and textuality, new literacy challenges are entering into public and professional calculations (Green and Bigum, 1997). Literacy education and literate practice must be re-envisioned accordingly, with due account taken of changing formations of culture and economy. Hence, even accepting the claim that, as one editorial noted, 'today's social and economic conditions demand greater literacy capabilities than ever' ('Literacy row obscures the real issue', *The Australian*, September 17, 1997, p. 12), it is crucial that the *differences* that are now emerging are not suppressed or glossed over, or misrepresented by increasingly inadequate and inappropriate modernist technologies and schooling and assessment. Simply, if the current policy position is to increase basic literacy in support of economic expansion and growth – and not simply an ambit claim against government education – the particular version of literacy it pursues may not be of particular or demonstrable functional value.

It is also clear that increased testing of the kind proposed provides for enhanced and strengthened forms of surveillance and control. A form of 'superpanopticism' is in operation across the social and educational landscape. Of course, like all forms of panoptic power, this has two aspects: a productive dimension, in that knowledge *is* useful, and a negative one, especially when organised by an insistent hierarchical managerialism, despite moves to devolution within the state systems of schooling (Lingard, Ladwig and Luke, 1998). Arguably, however, the balance shifts decisively to that latter negative dimension in the context of an economic-rationalist agenda and new social imperatives of accountability, efficiency and performativity.

Considerable work also is devoted to a *defence* of private schooling.[11] Much is made of the 'diversity' of Australian education, with reference specifically to both government and non-government sectors, and also to the value of collaboration between not only these sectors but also the school itself and the family – as well as, less obviously, the states and the federal government. Yet an effort is made explicitly to counter the view that private schools are to be associated with élite values and constituencies and with 'exclusivity and high fees'. Rather, in Australia, 'farsighted policy has opened educational choice to families from a broad range of cultural and socio-economic backgrounds' (Kemp, 1996: 4). This is connected to the ideology of choice, and hence to the democracy of the marketplace: a freedom to shop for education. Moreover, parents need information on school performance in order to make *rational* choices – something denied them under Labor, it is argued, including and perhaps especially 'Labor's restrictive New Schools Policy', a policy which sought to limit the growth of non-government schools and the resultant stress upon the public purse. In contrast:

> The [Liberal] Commonwealth Government does not favour one sector over another. The Government is committed to the school education of every child, regardless of where that child goes to school. Our fundamental principle is that parents should be able to decide on the best school for their children, whether this school is in the government or the non-government sector. (Kemp, 1996: 11)

Yet how might this issue of government and non-government schools connect with any perceived deficits in literacy education? By publicly highlighting a crisis in literacy education, the effect is to at least imply that the public schooling sector is significantly deficient, since it is its 'natural' constituency that is largely at issue here. Hence, emphasising and isolating literacy both directly and indirectly constitutes a government critique *against* public schooling, despite vigorous disclaimers of the even handedness of the critique. This powerful rhetorical strategy appears to work as follows:

- attack declining literacy standards as a threat to economy and democracy;
- attribute problems to schools and teachers;
- attribute unemployment and poverty to deteriorating standards of literacy;
- demand testing and public accountability that will enable ready comparison of schools and systems;
- defend public choice as the highest democratic virtue.

What this particular argument does is set up a public loss of faith and (justified) market disinvestment in public schooling and a market movement towards non-government providers as a logical, cost-effective and, most importantly, 'democratic' solution to the problems of poor achievement, unemployment, and indeed, poverty.

In a subsequent speech, the Minister sought to indicate 'some of the main directions in which schooling is moving in Australia', and to outline 'in particular a vision for government schools' (Kemp, 1997: 1). In direct response to the question 'Are Government schools in crisis?' he presented two reasons why this might be the case, although he suggested that the government system rather than being 'in crisis ... face[d] great challenges'. The first was the fact of 'a continuing drift of students to non-government schools', which he tied directly to the positive value of 'parents exercising choice' (Kemp, 1997: 2); the second was the mistaken and misguided perception that 'government funding policies [were] actually designed to fund the expansion of non-government schools at the expense of government schools' (Kemp, 1997: 3). The latter was sharply rebutted, arguing that the government sector was actually better off under the Coalition: 'The resources available to government schools from the Commonwealth will actually increase, not decline, under the legislation passed by the Federal Parliament [...]'. Hence: 'There is certainly no funding crisis for government schools as a result of Commonwealth decisions about school funding' (Kemp, 1997: 3). The Minister once again stated that the government had 'no preference for one sector of schooling over the other', suggesting that its educational objectives 'could equally well be met by a reversal of this flow, and by an increase in the proportion of parents choosing government schools' (Kemp, 1997: 4). The point was, rather, 'the right of parents to choose' – a key principle in Coalition educational policy – and the reality of the matter was that increasing numbers of parents *were* making a (rational, democratic) choice in this regard, with the result being that enrolments were indeed increasing in the non-government sector.

Although literacy is not explicitly referred to, it is clearly linked to this matter of parental choice, itself presented as inextricable from 'parental expectations about schooling' (Kemp, 1997: 4). Importantly: 'parents who choose are seeking quality educational experiences for their children', and hence, '[i]f we accept the fact of parents' desire to choose the best school for their child, as we must, then the task of good policy is to assist parents to make the most informed choice, and to ensure that schools are in the best position to respond to those choices' (Kemp, 1997: 6). Key to the information in question here is standardised testing as a general feature of 'responsible' schooling: 'Comprehensive reporting by schools on educational outcomes, both quantitative and qualitative, is a necessary concomitant of informed parental choice' (Kemp, 1997: 11). Given the view presented earlier, and elsewhere, that educational performance is 'fall[ing] short of objectives', especially with regard to 'some fundamentals, such as literacy and numeracy skills and on the relevance of schools not merely to university entry but to the job prospects of the majority of young people who are not going on to full-time tertiary study', it is clear that such reporting will be organised significantly around testing in precisely these areas. This is of course the focus of government initiatives already in place, following the National Commission of Audit and the historic agreement of the Ministerial Council to national standardised literacy testing, which has been described as 'a signifier of things to come' (Lingard and Porter, 1997: 13).

At this point it is appropriate to return to the extraordinary formulation that is at the very heart of the earlier speech, asserting 'direct connections between low levels of literacy, behavioural problems in the classroom, the likelihood that a student will finish formal education before Year 12, and the likelihood of being unemployed after leaving school'. It is remarkable because it effortlessly brings together a range of the key themes of the literacy debate. More than this, however, it evokes major fears and anxieties in this regard. These are arguably *excessive*, in that they are registers of important symbolic tensions and associated projections of the Other – to be identified specifically with those other schools, those other people ... *Them*, not *Us*. 'They' are unruly and undisciplined, illiterate, inadequately schooled, unemployable and hence 'non-productive' ... wandering the streets, seething with anger and certainly with disaffection. Unlike 'us'. In this way, class antagonisms and anxieties are clearly being mobilised. Forty years on, then, public policy debates reinforce Richard Hoggart's post-war analysis: the matters of literacy and schooling still need to be understood as matters of political struggle *par excellence*.

We have made the case here that the most recent 'literacy crisis' in Australia has been constructed in government policy and political strategy as part of a broader attack on *public* schooling. Literacy functions here as a metaphor for schooling more generally, but refers more specifically to the public schooling sector. Historically, state interventions in literacy and schooling have been motivated by a concern on the part of dominant-cultural groups to organise and regulate the lives and learning of the disadvantaged groups. That remains very much the case with the current 'crisis'. This is why there is relative silence in the public playing-out of such debates. What is at issue is not just literacy *per se*, and not just schooling by implication and extension, but rather the literacy practices and performances of certain social constituencies and certain schools and school systems as matched against, as Donald and Grealy argued, an imaginary social benchmark. As one commentator puts it:

> The unspoken assumption is that most of the schools that fail the literacy test will be government schools in the lowest socio-economic areas of the nation, and that the money 'freed up' can be passed on to the schools most successful in meeting Dr Kemp's standards, which just happen to be mainly private schools whose student populations are drawn from the highest socio-economic groups. (Kenneth Davidson, *The Age*, Thursday, October 16, 1997, p. 19)

This policy approach fits well with the larger concerns of the Coalition government, towards the deregulation and marketisation of social services and public sector activities. In his major study of the history of Australian educational policy, Marginson (1997: 133) points to clear articulations between the 'standards' debate, within which literacy figures heavily, and a pattern of government bias since at least the late 1970s towards private schooling, in accordance with the logic of economic rationalisation and reform.

To cut through the thicket of claims and counter-claims, we need to apply a simple strategy: to ask how debates such as these over the state of literacy and education, even when they move beyond simplistic denunciations of public schooling, teaching methods and teachers, continue to target certain homes and families as deficit, as lacking, as unproductive, rather than others. This is indicated, for instance, in editorial statements to the effect that while '[p]oliticians and parents find it easy to place the blame on poor teaching or other deficiencies in the school system', there is however 'another critical factor in the battle to improve literacy standards and that is the home' ('Literacy drive begins with family', *The Weekend Australian*, September 20–21, 1997, p. 16). But it is certainly not just *any*, let alone *all*, homes and families that are in question here, especially since '[t]he evidence is that the most literate parents produce the most literate children': 'The students who performed better at school were those who read books and newspapers at home, talked at home about events in their lives and did homework frequently'. Which students, and which families? No account is made here of socioeconomic or cultural disadvantage.

Literacy debates thus actively participate in the systematic *othering* and a simple caricature of certain social interests and differences. In this most recent Australian literacy campaign they effectively work to privilege those associated with private schooling at the expense of the public sector, both symbolically *and* materially. More homework and books in the house, whatever their educational virtues, will not suffice as systematic policy approaches to economic marginality and social divisions. In this way, this late twentieth century Australian literacy crisis, once its rhetorical circle closes, is not that much different from the myths and crises that linked poverty, youth and moral decay in, say late nineteenth century England or mid-century USA: it constructs a trail of quasi-medical symptoms and quasi-juridical evidence that leads back first to the blaming of faulty public institutions and educators, and, ultimately, to the blaming of faulty parents, families and communities for the failure of their children. What is more is that this particular construction of the problem of literacy offers the solution of market competition with an undermined and diminished public sector.

Contesting the 'Crisis' and Raising the Stakes

If there is a simple lesson from the policy analysis in this chapter, it would be about the historical character of literacy crises, about how they are manufactured and deployed for larger political and social ends. The current crisis is no exception. But, our position should not be construed as a simple defence of 'business as usual' in literacy education, curriculum and teaching, and schooling. To return to our starting point, while we have documented a host of problems in respect of current government policy towards public schooling – it is the silence of that policy about sustainable educational, cultural and economic futures that is of most concern to us.

In responding politically to the current manufactured crisis, the policies of previous Labor governments and those of the current Coalition government need to be reexamined in the broader political context of globalisation and its political, economic and cultural effects. However in the Australian political context, the adoption of market liberal ideology has been posed as the only viable policy option in the face of economic globalisation. As a result, government policies have attempted to assert 'the market' and market forces rather than the state as the major steering mechanism for desired policy outcomes. In such a model, the chief function of the (competitive) state then becomes ensuring the international competitiveness of the putatively national economy, with the production of a better educated and trained, more flexible and multiskilled workforce as a central policy goal of the state. The paradox, of course, is that these increased demands and expectations upon education have to be achieved within tighter funding parameters, within a context of social disinvestment. Furthermore, as opposed to the Keynesian state approach of increasing state expenditures to achieve desired policy outcomes, the performative state now valorises outcomes as measured through performance indicators (Lyotard, 1984). Such performativity usually ensures an emphasis upon 'productivism' rather than enhanced 'productivity' (Giddens, 1994). What we have, then, is the emergence of the competitive-performative post-modern state: complementary to an educational policy based on market forces, quantitative student performance indicators and benchmarks, and individual competitiveness and deficit. Further, as we have seen here, literacy is ideal for repackaging as an ameliorative educational commodity for sale on an educational free market, albeit subject to the product guarantees and state regulation of standardised testing.

The policy regime of the Conservative Coalition federal government differs from the hybrid approach of previous Labor governments that attempted to link market liberalism and social justice. That model at least recognised group disadvantage and attempted to ameliorate it, even while its economic policies ensured great insecurity in respect of employment/unemployment. The policy approach of the current government, in contrast, writes off the notion of group disadvantage, and has instead placed the individual deficit subject at the centre of its policies. The manufactured literary crisis and the policy approach to literacy adopted by the current government must be seen against this range of developments. The Coalition government's approach is a rote recitation of a modernist, industrial model of literacy: assuming and desiring cultural homogeneity and generic citizens, while being located and disoriented within emergent post-modernist and post-industrial economies, unprecedented intercultural complexity and hybridity.

There is much more to the empirical effects of globalisation than the market–liberal ideological reading of it. Globalisation works in a range of homogenising and differentiating ways in terms of culture, politics and identity, as well as reconstituting the place of the nation state and local/national/global relationships. A range of 'political' issues have come to the fore in Australia as a consequence of globalisation, requiring us to recontextualise the literacy crisis and rethink definitions of literacy. And thus re-read and critique the current government's solutions to their constructed literacy crisis. As mentioned at the outset, questions of governmentality have been prominent in relation to the Republic and a post-modern polity, including a rethinking of the nature of citizenship. Questions of identity have also been foregrounded in respect of the place of indigenous people in the Australian polity, as well as the place of their historical experiences in the national collective memory. Such representations are played out in the contestation between the so-called black armband and white 'blindfold' versions of Australia's history and imagined community. The sociodemographic facts of immigration, multilingualism and multiculturalism have brought the politics of diasporic identity and culture into every region and community in the nation, with the nation itself having been constituted as a white diasporia at the edge of empire. Finally, Australia's incorporation into the regional economies of Asia has placed squarely on the table a host of issues around culture, language and identity, and, indeed, education, that cannot be ignored or avoided. The Coalition's literacy policy based on the marketisation of educational 'basics' is silent on these issues and decidedly inward looking in its national and cultural orientation.

What construction of literacy underpins government policy in the face of hybrid identities and the need to re-imagine the diasporic and multicultural character of the Australian community? Monocultural literacy against multicultural and multilingual populations; another manifestation of backlash national chauvinism, not as strong an articulation as that mouthed by the voices of the emergent far-right which has seen some electoral success in a recent state election and pressured the Coalition government from its right and rural flanks, but a version of backlash national chauvinism nonetheless. And, as many have suggested, it is the silence of government policy and public dialogue on these issues that in many ways has encouraged the 'blaming' of economic problems on Asians, Indigenous peoples and, without a trace of irony, globalisation and 'economic rationalism', by Australia's emergent far right wing parties.

Clearly what is required in this post-modern, post-colonial globalised context is not a 'dumbing down' of the construction of literacy but an enhancement and rethinking of its very construction (New London Group, 1997; Prain, 1997; Cope and Kalantzis, 1997). At the same time, we need to debate the policy and financial support necessary to achieve effective outcomes in respect of such literacies for all students, including those from disadvantaged groups. Claims of the end of the nation-state notwithstanding, it is only the central state that retains the ostensive capacity and will for a redistributive approach to the funding of public institutions (Castells, 1997), including schools. The return of the individual deficit subject needs to be contested and resisted, while public schooling needs to be defended and redefined. However, we must move beyond a defence of the *status quo*. The current 'literacy crisis' will have done some good, somewhat ironically, if it spawns the sort of debate and rethink about literacy, public schooling and educational policy which, we suggest, is absolutely necessary if Australia is to become a post-modern pluralist democracy and productively diverse economy operating effectively, efficiently *and* fairly in a globalised world.

To conclude, it is no coincidence that the current literacy crisis has come at the same time as an identity crisis for the nation in the context of globalisation and its proliferating uncertainties. Yet the concepts of literacy underpinning the current policy constructions appeal to an earlier (supposed) universal Australian subject which denies the reality of difference as it is experienced in contemporary Australia. Both to contend with backlash and to find a way forward, what is needed is a debate about what appropriate contemporary literacies might look like in relation to these issues of citizenship, identity, culture, difference, economy and new workplaces, as well as to the new technologies which facilitate the time/space effects of globalisation.

The challenge of New Times, then, for Australian governments and oppositions present and future alike is to undertake an urgent and unprecedented curriculum debate about the future of literacy in the globalised, networked, intercultural economies and cultures of the next century. Retreat to a 1950s vision of literacy, to a 'test and treat' model of basic skills, couched in a defense of parental choice and the free market is, quite simply, a waste of valuable time and precious financial resources.

In policy terms, what this case study of the contemporary 'literacy crisis' in Australian education demonstrates is the way in which policy is as much about creating problems as solving them, and how particular issues are rearticulated within policy narratives across time. In the production of policy texts, policy definition is the first step in this contested process, brought to bear prior to the mobilisation of government action and policy settlement as articulated in a text or texts. The creation of the literacy crisis was very much about problem creation or definition so as to delimit the policy options, in this case to introduce a national 'test and treat' approach to literacy, while also destabilising government schooling as a move towards a more marketised competitive form of schooling between government and non-government sectors. This is why we have entitled this chapter 'The Abuses of Literacy'.

Our analysis demonstrates the need to understand more fully the societal (and indeed, global) context of policy production, that is, the need to see beyond the context constructed by policies. The federal government's literacy policies can only be understood against a contextual backdrop of contests over Australian identities past, present and future, in the face of rapid economic, political and cultural globalisation. In their own way, they are a version of backlash national chauvinism and can be seen to involve the imposition of modernist constructions of literacy on a society which has become other than that imagined (or desired) by the current conservative coalition government, at least in relation to questions of difference.

Notes

1. Authors' names are in reverse alphabetical order. This chapter has developed from an earlier one entitled 'Literacy Debates and Public Education: A Question of Crisis?' which appeared in A. Reid (ed.) (1998) *Going Public: Education Policy and Public Education in Australia*, Deakin West, ACT, Australian Curriculum Studies Association.
2. Putting issues of test validity aside for a moment, the tendency here as elsewhere is to construe ostensible changes in student performance as the direct consequence of (failed and/or successful) teaching methods rather than changes in the school, workplace and civic contexts and character of performance demanded, major demographic and sociocultural shift, large-scale technological and cognitive change and so forth.
3. Note that the processes of 'devolution' and 'school-based management' in Queensland, NSW, Western Australia and Victoria, with other states to follow shortly, have placed more discretionary funding for curriculum and professional development in the hands of local schools and districts. This hasn't escaped the notice of publishers and an emergent sector of independent and private professional development consultants. The very early signs are that this has increased the appeal of comprehensive and well-packaged literacy curriculum materials and approaches that purport to offer direct and immediate results.
4. In the UK context Giddens' work has been used to justify and sell what the Blair government calls a 'politics of the third way'. That is not our position here, but rather we are asserting the need for a new social democratic approach, whereas the Blair position seems to be one which is situated between Thatcherism and social democracy.
5. Such work historically has tended to take a Habermasian view that literacy crises entail the systematic displacement of economic crises to cultural institutions and systems. See, for example, Freebody and Welch (1993).
6. Note that the ABS Adult Literacy survey tends to dispel any large scale causal relationship between adult literacy levels and levels of national unemployment. While it indicates, as all adult surveys in the post-war era have, that long term unemployed are more likely to have lower levels of grade-level equivalent educational achievement and, relatedly, are more likely to experience performance-

related reading and writing problems in daily life – this does not establish a causal link between education, skill-level and unemployment. In fact, if we juxtapose overall national adult performance to unemployment levels (and more specifically indicators of structural and youth unemployment), a very different picture emerges. Several OECD countries with 'higher' adult literacy survey performance than Australia in several categories continue to suffer high or increasing levels of structural unemployment (e.g., Canada, Germany); the US, whose sample performs more poorly than the Australian sample in several areas, has just announced the lowest official levels of unemployment in over two decades. Axiomatically, in advanced post-industrial OECD economies, sector-specific job growth, global flows of capital, and, *inter alia*, the overall state of one's economy dictate employment levels, and specifically youth participation in employment – not increases or decreases in skill levels *per se*. The argument that levels of illiteracy cause unemployment is itself an artefact of 1960's human capital models which were relevant when OECD countries still faced severe shortages of skilled labour for expanding industrial and service sectors, prior to high and sustained levels of structural unemployment, economic globalisation and such post-industrial phenomena as the proliferation of entry-level service sector and rural employment for guestworkers and migrants.

7. It is revealing that after the major decade-long investment by Conservative governments in the National Curriculum and related testing systems, one of the first moves of the newly elected Labor government in 1997 was to declare a 'crisis' in literacy – revealing both for what it may say about the futility of large-scale investment in testing and national curriculum, and for what it says about the sustainability and political usefulness of literacy and educational 'crisis'.
8. In Australia schooling is a constitutional policy responsibility of the states and territories. However, since the late 1980s federal governments have achieved greater impact on schooling: during the Labor period which ended in 1996, through the development of a range of national policies in schooling (Lingard, 1993; Lingard and Porter, 1997), and since, under a coalition government, through the introduction of national testing in literacy and numeracy. The coalition government, with Dr Kemp as Minister, has sought greater influence over state controlled schooling through such testing and achieved the states' agreement to such testing through the creation of the literacy crisis which is the focus of this chapter. Further, through a number of other policies, the coalition federal government has attempted to introduce a more market driven policy approach to schooling.
9. Note that the now apparently deceased Mayer Competencies belatedly added 'cultural understandings' as the eighth key competency, stressing multilingualism and intercultural communication as necessary productive resources for the expansion of Australian competitiveness in a globalised economy (Luke, 1995). There is no mention of intercultural, interlingual or multilingual competence in the current benchmarks documents.
10. Many of the more traditional class-based analyses of structural economic changes have failed to acknowledge the emergence of 'trans-national' classes, that consists of routine participants and key players in a globalised economy. The policy literature is also now starting to speak of globalising bureaucrats and policy-makers and a global policy community.
11. About 30% of Australian students are schooled in 'non-government' or 'private' schools.

References

Australian Bureau of Statistics/OECD, 1997. *Adult Literacy Survey in Two Parts: Aspects of Literacy Profiles and Perceptions, and Aspects of Literacy Assessed Skill Levels 1996*, Survey co-ordinated by OECD and Statistics Canada, Canberra: Australian Government Publishing Service.

Beilharz, P., 1989. 'Social democracy and social justice', *The Australian and New Zealand Journal of Sociology*, **25**, 1, pp. 85–99.

Bernstein, B., 1972. 'Towards a critique of compensatory education'. In C. Cazden, V. John and D. Hymes, eds, *Functions of Language in the Classroom*. New York: Teachers College Press.

Bessant, J., 1993. 'Policy paradoxes: The disempowerment of young people under the Labor government, 1983-91', *Australian Journal of Social Issues*, **28**, no. 2, pp. 87–105.

Bessant, J., 1995. 'Consolidating an industry and prolonging dependency: Professionals, policies and young people', *Australian Journal of Social Issues*, **30**, no. 3, pp. 249–74.
Brotherhood of St Laurence, 1997. *Poverty Update August*. Melbourne: Brotherhood of St Laurence.
Castells, M., 1997. *Towards the Network Society*. Oxford: Blackwell.
Cole, M., 1997. *Cultural Psychology*. Cambridge: Cambridge University Press.
Commonwealth of Australia, 1991. 'Australia's Language, The Australian Language and Literacy Policy', and the Companion Volume to the Policy Paper, released by The Hon. John Dawkins, Minister for Employment, Education and Training, Australian Government Publishing Service, Canberra.
Connell, R.W., 1994. 'Poverty and education', *Harvard Educational Review*, **64**, no. 2, pp. 125–49.
Cook-Gumperz, Jenny, 1986. 'Literacy and Schooling: An Unchanging Equation?', in Jenny Cook-Gumperz (ed.), *The Social Construction of Literacy*, Cambridge: Cambridge University Press, pp. 16–44.
Cope, B. and Kalantzis, M., 1997. ' "Multiliteracies", Education and the New Communications Environment', *Discourse*, **18**, 3, pp. 469–78.
Cope, B., Kalantzis, M., Luke, A., McCormack, R., Morgan, B., Slade, D., Solomon, N. and Veel, N., 1994. *National Framework for Adult English Language, Literacy and Numeracy Competence*. Canberra: Australian Committee for Training Curriculum. ERIC Document.
Davidson, Kenneth, 1997. 'Plenty of room to advance in Kennett's schools', *The Age*, Thursday, October 16, p. 19.
Donald, James and Grealy, Jim, 1983. 'The Unpleasant Fact of Inequality: Standards, Literacy and Culture', in Anne Marie Wolpe and James Donald (eds), *Is There Anyone Here from Education?*, London: Pluto Press, pp. 88–101.
Freebody, Peter and Welch, Anthony R. (eds), 1993. Knowledge, *Culture and Power: International Perspectives on Literacy as Policy and Practice*, London and Washington, DC: Falmer Press.
Gee, J.P., Hull, G. and Lankshear, C., 1996. *The New Work Order*. Sydney, Allen & Unwin.
Gerber, S. and Finn, J.D., 1998. 'Learning document skills at school and at work'. *Journal of Adolescent and Adult Literacy*, **42**, 32–44.
Giddens, A., 1994. *Beyond Left and Right: The Future of Radical Politics*, Stanford, Stanford University Press.
Green, B., 1997. 'Born Again Teaching? Governmentality, "Grammar" and Public Schooling', in Thomas S. Popkewitz and Marie Brennan (eds), *Foucault's Challenge: Discourse, Knowledge, and Power in Education*, New York: Teachers College Press, pp. 173–204.
Green, B. and Bigum, C., 1997. 'Re-Tooling Schooling? Information Technology, Cultural Change and the Future(s) of Australian Education'. Commissioned Paper for the 'Voices on Culture and Schooling' Project, Flinders Institute for the Study of Teaching, Flinders University, South Australia.
Green, Bill, Hodgens, John and Luke, Allan, (1994). *Debating Literacy in Australia: A Documentary History, 1945–1994*, Melbourne: Australian Literacy Federation [2 vols].
Green, Bill, Hodgens, John and Luke, Allan, 1997. 'Debating Literacy in Australia: History Lessons and Popular F(r)ictions', *Australian Journal of Language and Literacy*, **20**, no. 1, pp. 6–24.
Heath, S.B., 1986. 'Critical Factors in Literacy Development'. In S. De Castell, A. Luke, K. Egan (eds) *Literacy, Society and Schooling*, Cambridge University Press.
Hoggart, R., 1955. *The Uses of Literacy*. Harmondsworth: Penguin.
Holland, C., 1998. *Literacy and the New Work Order: An international literature review*. Leicester: National Institute of Adult Continuing Education.
Hull, G., Jury, M., Ziv, O. and Katz, M., 1996. *Changing work, changing literacy? A study of the skill requirements and development in a traditional and restructured workplace*. Berkeley, National Centre for Research in Vocational Education and Centre for the Study of Writing and Literacy.
Kemp, D., 1996. 'Schools and the Democratic Challenge'. The Bert Kelly Lecture, Centre for Independent Studies, Perth, October 21.
Kemp, D., 1997. 'Quality Schooling for All'. 'Issues in Public Sector Change' Lecture Series, Centre for Public Policy, University of Melbourne, Melbourne, April 21.
Lash, S. and Urry, J., 1994. *Economies of Signs and Space*. London: Sage.
Lingard, B., 1993. 'Corporate Federalism: The Emerging Approach to Policy Making for Australian

Schooling', In B. Lingard, J. Knight and P. Porter (eds) *Schooling Reform in Hard Times*, London: The Falmer Press, pp. 24–35.

Lingard, B., 1998. 'The disadvantaged schools programme: caught between literacy and local management of schools', *International Journal of Inclusive Education*, **2**, 1, pp. 1–14.

Lingard, B. and Porter, P., 1997. 'Australian Schooling: The State of National Developments', in B. Lingard and P. Porter (eds), *A National Approach to Schooling in Australia? Essays on the Development of National Policies in Schools Education*, Canberra: Australian College of Education, pp. 1–25.

Lingard B. and Rizvi, F., 1995. 'Shaping the Future through Back to Basics?', in C. Collins (ed.), *Curriculum Stocktake: Evaluating School Curriculum Change*, Canberra: Australian College of Education, pp. 59–70.

Lingard, R. Knight, J. and Porter, P., (eds), 1993. *Schooling Reform in Hard Times*, Falmer Press: London.

Lingard, B., Ladwig, J. and Luke, A., 1998. 'School effects in postmodern conditions', in, R. Slee, G. Weiner and S. Tomlinson (eds), *School Effectiveness for Whom? Challenges to the School Effectiveness and School Improvement Movements*, London: Falmer Press, pp. 84–100.

Lo Bianco, J. and Freebody, P., 1997. *Australian Literacies: Informing National Policy on Literacy Education*, Canberra: Language Australia.

Luke, A., 1994. *The Social Construction of Literacy in the Classroom*. Melbourne: Macmillan.

Luke, A. , 1995. 'Getting our hands dirty: provisional politics in postmodern conditions', in, P. Wexler and R. Smith (eds) *After Postmodernism : Education, Politics, Identity*, London: Falmer Press, pp. 83–97.

Luke, A., 1997a. 'New narratives of human capital', *The Australian Educational Researcher*, **24**, no. 2, pp. 1–21.

Luke, A., 1997b. 'The material effects of the word: apologies, "Stolen Children" and public discourse', *Discourse*, **18**, no. 3, pp. 343–68.

Luke, A. and VanKraayenoord, C.E., forthcoming. 'Babies, bathwaters and benchmarks: Literacy assessment and curriculum reform'. *Curriculum Perspectives*.

Luke, C. and Luke, A., June, 1999. 'Theorising interracial families and hybrid identity: An Australian perspective. *Educational Theory*.

Lyotard, J.F., 1984. *The Postmodern Condition*, Manchester: Manchester University Press.

Marginson, S., 1997. *Educating Australia? Government, Economy and Citizen since 1960*, Cambridge: Cambridge University Press.

Martin, R., 1997. 'Manufacturing the literacy crisis', *The Australian Educator*, no. 9, Summer, pp. 9–11.

Masters, G. and Forster, M., 1997. *Mapping Literacy Achievement: Results of the 1996 National School English Literacy Survey*, Canberra: Department of Employment, Education, Training and Youth Affairs.

New London Group, 1996. 'A Pedagogy of Multiliteracies: designing social futures' *Harvard Educational Review*, **66**, 1, pp. 60–92.

Polakow, V., 1993. *Lives on the Edge: Single Mothers and their Children in the Other America*, The University of Chicago Press, Chicago.

Prain, V., 1997. 'Multi(national) Literacies and Globalizing Discourses', *Discourse*, **18**, 3, pp. 453–67.

Rizvi, F., 1995. ' "Broadbanding": Equity in Australian Schools', in M. Kalantzis (ed.) *A fair go in education*, Canberra: Australian Curriculum Studies Association & Australian Centre for Equity through Education.

Taylor, S., Rizvi, F., Lingard, B. and Henry, M., 1997. *Educational Policy and the Politics of Change*, London: Routledge.

Varghese, B., 1994. 'Schooling's shadow: poverty and education', in *Schooling What Future? Balancing the Education Agenda*, Deakin Centre for Education and Change, Deakin University, Waurn Ponds, Victoria.

Wilkinson, I.A.G., 1998. 'Dealing with diversity: Achievement Gaps in Reading Literacy among New Zealand Students', *Reading Research Quarterly*, **33**, 144–67.

Yeatman, A. 1990. *Bureaucrats, Technocrats, Femocrats: Essays on the Contemporary Australian State*, Sydney: Allen & Unwin.

[37]

A Post-Technocratic Policy Perspective on New Information and Communication Technologies for Education[1]

Nicholas C. Burbules
University of Illinois
Thomas A. Callister, Jr.
Whitman College

Deliberations over the potential benefits and limitations of new information and communication technologies for education highlight the ways in which policy choices often require a reframing of the issues at stake, and not simply a 'balancing' or 'trade-off' between assumed givens. We refer to this perspective as post-technocratic at two levels: first as a way of rethinking what the significance of new educational technologies might be, but also as a way of re-examining the techniques of policy debate itself, the manner in which choices are typically framed and the meliorative perspective that tends to dominate not only in educational policy debates but in reformist perspectives on social policy generally. In our view, the implications (for better *and* for worse) of new information and communication technologies for education offer a mixture of transformative potential and deeply disturbing prospects, not as 'benefits and costs' to be weighed against each other, but as inseparable dimensions of the type of changes these technologies represent (though we believe this perspective applies to many other areas of educational and social policies as well).

In this essay, we want to trace out some of the ways in which choices about new technologies in education are typically framed, explain why we think they are unhelpful, and propose a different way of thinking about such policy choices.

Versions of the Technocratic Dream

The first way in which technology issues are often framed can be called the 'computer as panacea' perspective: new technologies carry inherent possibilities that can revolutionize education as we know it. If we simply unleash this potential many educational problems will be solved. Computers can help alleviate overcrowded classrooms, computers can ease the burden of overworked teachers, or computers can make teachers unnecessary at all. Such views are promoted enthusiastically by those who have a commercial stake in encouraging the sale and use of their hardware or software. The education market is so large that if even a few states or districts can be persuaded that a particular new technology will take care of their difficulties, millions of dollars can be made on the deal. But because so many problems of education are the result of inadequate resources or the misallocation of resources, funneling more of the finite amount of funding available into one area of spending might actually exacerbate these problems, not remedy them.

Furthermore, the proclamation of panaceas is not simply a marketing ploy; it is a mantra long familiar to the educational scene. The history of education (in the United States, at least) can be traced from technical innovation to innovation, from pedagogical gimmick to gimmick, from reform to reform, all in the search for the One Best Way of Teaching, for the next New Thing that will help educators cope with the fundamentally imperfect and indeterminate nature of the teaching process itself.[2] Rather than acknowledge the inherent difficulty and imperfectability of the teaching–learning endeavor, rather than accept a sloppy pluralism that admits that different approaches work in different situations – and that no approach works perfectly all the time – educational theorists and policy-makers seize upon one fashion after another and then try to find new arguments, or new mandates, that will promote widespread acceptance and conformity under the latest Revolution. The Information Technology Revolution is just the latest in this long line of utopian dreams, and there will always be a ready audience in education for such over-promising.

To be fair, many computer producers and advocates have actually been among the forefront in trying to limit exaggerated claims for new information and communication technologies; those most familiar with these machines know best what they are and are not capable of. Ironically, it is often educational leaders who have raised the fevered sense of urgency that everything has to change, right now, before schools fall behind some perceived 'wave' of technological innovation.

One consequence of the search for panaceas is that when the Revolution does not come to pass, when the imperfections of each New Thing become all too apparent, there is typically an equally exaggerated rejection of the reform, not because it is of no use but because it falls short of the hyperbole marshaled in its favor. As a result, educational change lurches from one New Thing to another, with the shortest of memories about similar (or even identical) reforms tried in the past, failing to learn from experience and less able to integrate the partial benefits of multiple approaches, multiple technologies, into a pragmatic orientation that seeks workable approaches to different problems as they arise.

We are already seeing some of this backlash toward computers and related information and communication technologies. Schools that spent millions of dollars to purchase equipment and software in the first heady rush to be sure that they did not fall behind in some perceived race with what other schools were doing, find that much of this equipment is unused and already obsolete. Schools that are rushing now to purchase fast connections to the Internet are finding that this raises unexpected new difficulties, when students actually take advantage of the access provided but for purposes that authorities find troubling or inappropriate. The panacea-approach reinforces a certain naiveté in educators, and in the public that evaluates education, by suggesting to them that spending money to acquire new technical resources solves more problems than it creates, not realizing that the potential of information and communication technologies *increases* the need for imagination, careful planning, and coping on the fly with unexpected new challenges.

The second type of technocratic dream, much more subtle and seductive than the first, is the 'computer as tool' perspective. Advocates of this view rightly excoriate the 'panacea' perspective, and argue that it expects far too much of new information and communication technologies which are, as they say, merely tools that can be used for good or bad purposes. Tools carry within them neither the guarantees of success or failure, or of benefit or harm – it is all a matter of how wisely people use them.

Unfortunately, this technocratic dream simply errs in the opposite direction from the first. Where the panacea perspective places too much faith in the technology itself, the tool perspective places too much faith in people's abilities to exercise foresight and restraint in how new technologies are put to use. It ignores the possibilities of unintended consequences or the ways in which technologies bring with them inherent *limits* to how and for what purposes they can be used. A computer is not just an electronic typewriter; the World Wide Web is not just an online encyclopedia. Any tool changes the user, especially, in this instance, in the way in which tools shape the conception of the purposes to which they can be put. As the old joke goes, if you give a kid a hammer they'll see everything as needing hammering.

A slightly more sophisticated variant on this perspective is the 'computer as non-neutral tool' perspective. Yes, advocates say, every technology carries within it certain tendencies of how it is likely to be used and shapes the conception of purposes to which it can be put. Users should be reflective and critical, therefore, about the unexpected consequences of using these technologies, and should be prepared for the possibility that the benefits gained from the technology's usefulness may be tempered by unforeseen problems and difficulties created by its use (pollution caused by automobiles, for example).

This third version of the technocratic dream is probably where most thoughtful observers are today in regard to new information and communication technologies. It is a sensible, level-headed approach. It understands balancing costs and benefits, trade-offs, the mix of good and bad that comes from attempts at major reform. It understands the language of unintended consequences and accepts the imperfections of human rationality. It does not see technology as a panacea, nor does it imagine that technology is just a tool. Yet, we want to argue, it is still a variant of the technocratic dream. We will provide three arguments for why this is so.

Beyond the Technocratic Dream

First, the technocratic mindset maintains a clear distinction between the conception of a tool and the aims it serves. The 'computer as non-neutral tool' perspective represents a transitional step away from this, stressing that people do not simply use new tools to pursue old purposes more efficiently or effectively. New tools cause people to imagine new purposes that they had not even considered before. But the problem goes even further than this. It is not simply a matter of an unproblematic relation of means to ends (even new ends). People's conception of what constitutes 'success' is changed in light of the means used to pursue it. The technocratic mindset takes the *relation of means and ends* itself as given. A crude version (crude but still widely held in the field of education) simply defines problems as matters of relative efficiency or effectiveness in this relation. A less crude version sees changing purposes, even multiple or conflicting purposes, but still sees the relation of means to ends as given. Thinking beyond technocracy means seeing the means/ends relation itself as an artifact of a particular cultural and historical formation. A more dialectical perspective would regard the interpenetration of people's conceptions of means and ends, each continually refigured in light of the other.[3] It would regard new information and communication technologies, for example, not simply as means for doing what people used to do, better and faster, and not even simply as innovations that now allow people to do things they had never imagined before, but as artifacts that reshape people's perceptions of themselves as agents, their relations to one another, their perceptions of time and speed, their expectations of predictability, and so forth – all dimensions of *changing* people's ways of thinking about means and ends, purposes and efficacy. The point here is to see the relation of means to ends not as a given, but as itself a particular way of thinking, one subject to criticism and change like any other. The pursuit of 'success', defined as the effective and efficient attainment of specific goals, needs to be situated in the context of a less linear conception of actions and outcomes, intentions and effects.

A second aspect of moving beyond the technocratic mindset is to rethink the calculus of costs and benefits as a way of evaluating change. Once again, there are relatively crude and relatively subtle versions of cost/benefit analysis. Crude versions regard such decisions as basically a matter of drawing two columns and listing considerations *pro* and *con*. Perhaps these individual factors need to be given different weightings as to their importance in relation to one another. But then you add up each column and determine the result. A more subtle formulation of this mode of thinking would acknowledge that there are unintended consequences, to which values cannot be ascribed because they cannot be anticipated; it would acknowledge multiple consequences that may be difficult to isolate from one another or evaluate separately. Hence it might acknowledge that cost/benefit assessments are a matter of imperfect approximations, not a formal calculus.

But it is, again, a significant step beyond this mode of thinking to regard the 'cost/benefit' framework as itself artificial and simplistic. It would be a matter of seeing decisions as more than an issue of trade-offs or *pros* and *cons*. It would stress the value-laden character of even the most rudimentary identification of *pros* and *cons*: *pros* and *cons* for whom, within what time frame, relative to what *other* goals or values? In addition, it would stress the hubris that often underlies attempts to foresee discrete effects of complex social decisions. It is not only the problem of unintended consequences, not only the problem of multiple, conflicting consequences. It is the problem of a web of contingencies, caught up in complex relations of interdeterminacy; it is the obstinacy of circumstance, refusing to give people what they want without also giving them what they do not want. We want to emphasize that nowhere is this clearer than in the case of new information and communication technologies, which are continually confronting us with the inseparability of consequences, the desirable and the undesirable – and we will discuss a specific example of this phenomenon in a moment. But the final step beyond technocratic thinking and the cost/benefit mindset is perhaps the most challenging of all.

The assessment of means and ends, the weighing of costs and benefits, also assumes that people can distinguish and evaluate the 'good' and 'bad' aspects of different aims and consequences. The inseparability and interdependence of many consequences should begin to shake the faith that such determinations can be so readily made. But, again, the problem is more than this: the *very same* effects can be regarded as 'good' or 'bad', depending on other considerations, or when evaluated by different people, or when judged within alternative time frames. For example, the widespread use of antibiotics to eliminate infectious bacteria has, clearly, saved many millions of lives. This is a good thing. But it is also hastening the development of more and more virulent strains of bacteria, some of which now are resistant to all antibiotics. That is a very bad thing. Note that this is not a simple matter of intended and unintended consequences. The very same decisions that give rise to one set of effects give rise to the others. Nor is this a simple matter of weighing competing 'short-term' benefits against potential 'long-term' costs – for one thing, the 'long-term' costs of such policies might be of incalculable harm. The post-technocratic mode of thinking we are proposing here would stress the limits to human foresight and planning; the interdependency of multiple consequences; and the problematic attempt to sort out 'good' from 'bad' outcomes. Instead we want to stress the inseparability of good and bad in all complex human circumstances and the error of imagining that we can readily evaluate such matters individually and discretely. We must always keep in mind that new technologies are inherently dangerous, and not fool ourselves in imagining that we are their masters.

A Post-Technocratic Policy Perspective on Information and Communication Technologies

We mean these observations as comments on technological innovation and reform generally; but they apply to the field of new information and communication technologies especially. Why? Because they have shown themselves to be particularly susceptible to overpromising and hyperbole, especially but not only in their purported impact upon educational change. Yet if our arguments about multiple effects, the indeterminacy and inseparability of consequences, and the difficulty of isolating 'good' and 'bad' outcomes hold any weight generally, they apply with special force to these technologies.

First, the field of information and communication technologies is changing at an extremely rapid pace, one that appears to be accelerating even faster. These areas of innovation feed back on themselves in some unique ways. The increasing capacities of machines, programming languages and other software hasten the development of still further innovations. The very horizon of capabilities is continually re-invented, as new possibilities that were not imagined previously suddenly become within the reach of development, then soon within the scope of the taken-for-granted. This field of development is also socially, technologically, and commercially self-generating. For example, as operating systems and software become easier to use, and as more people then use them, this creates both a broader talent base and a widened scope of incentive to imagine and create new products. The problem field of these new technologies is, in a way, fundamentally about itself; in other words, it is uniquely self-reflexive in the way in which new developments make possible more and more developments. Yet this self-reflexive character makes it especially susceptible to defining its problems and goals hermetically, as technical objectives of value in and of themselves, apart from clear consequences for human society generally.

Second, and related to this point, because the object of information technologies is information, and the production, organization, and dissemination of information, there is a sense in which it is also continually re-inventing the perceptions of its use and purpose. All new technologies, as we discussed earlier, change people's understandings of what they can do, what they want to do, what they think they need to do. And when those technologies refer to the very raw material with which people imagine, plan, and evaluate change – that is, information – and the media through which they share information and deliberate about it, there arises an especially strong likelihood that what falls outside of the readily available raw material will fall outside the decision itself. Hence, as argued previously, a particular relation of means to ends needs to be situated in a larger constellation of what is known and what is not known; multiplied in this instance by a critical reflection on what the medium of information about what is known and not known can and cannot tell us.

Third, the various considerations about information and communication technologies which we have been discussing here press an even more radical conclusion about the indeterminacy of effects. In this instance, we would argue, the future lines of development are *literally* inconceivable – not only because of the rapidity and complexity of change in this field, and not only because of the self-reflexive nature of innovation, but because new developments in information and communication technologies are uniquely also new developments in our imaginings of capabilities and goals. Conventional descriptions of the enormity of these changes (the computer as the new Gutenberg printing press, and so on) are merely analogies. What made the printing press a momentous innovation was not only that it created a mechanism for a new kind of textual delivery. It was that by doing so it fundamentally changed the conditions for its own accessibility and uses. It created a mechanism for a new kind of production, organization and dissemination of information, a new medium of communication, and as such it created possibilities that were not, and could not have been, imagined previously. That is the scale of change represented by new information and communication technologies, and it should buttress our sense of humility to realize that we *cannot* know all of the changes they portend, and that what we might consider today 'good' or 'bad' prospects will certainly appear to others who have passed through those changes in a very different light. But we are not those others; or, at least, not yet.

For all of these reasons, we believe, reflections upon new information and communication technologies must proceed with a profound modesty and caution. They are, literally, dangerous. Yet they are dangerous precisely because they hold such tremendous potential – a potential that goes beyond our capacities to imagine it fully. Hence we need to go beyond the simplistic categories in which much current assessment of information and communication technologies has proceeded (especially, but not only, in the field of education). Douglas Kellner refers to the polarities of 'technophobic' and 'technophilic' perspectives.[4] Jane Kenway, similarly, describes 'utopian' and 'dystopian' alternatives.[5] Along with these commentators, and others, we want to press the need to go beyond such easy dichotomies, dichotomies that rely fundamentally on the illusion that we can easily separate and imagine 'good' and 'bad' effects in this field.

A great deal of rhetorical ink has been spilled excoriating the 'fraudulent' promises of new information technologies: books with titles like *Silicon Snake Oil* have gained a wide readership and have fundamentally shaped the perception of information and communication technologies among many groups, especially those with relatively little direct experience with these new technologies themselves. The fact that such accounts serve a popular taste for reports of scandal and fraud partly explain their appeal. Part of the explanation also must be yielded to people's anxieties about changes they do not entirely understand. And, we have argued, a certain healthy skepticism and caution is more than justified in this context.

But we believe that a more modulated position is necessary. For one thing, these changes are upon us and have a particular momentum of their own; one way or another, these are issues society will need to struggle with. Furthermore, we persist in believing that there are multiple potentials in these technologies, and it is yet to be determined what forms they will take and the purposes to which they will be put. Adopting a rejectionist position and yielding these decisions to others merely guarantees that the skeptics will be ignored and the enthusiasts given free rein. We want to push the policy debate beyond the false choices of rejectionism or boosterism. We want to suggest a distinctive tone or feel to what the post-technocratic stance might mean: not just weighing 'risks' and 'promises' against each other, but of seeing their fundamental inseparability. The dangers and possibilities of information and communication technologies are not opposed to one another – they are aspects of one and the same capacities. We cannot simplisticly choose one over the other.

In the final section of this essay, we want to discuss an example of a major policy issue that has arisen in current debates around information and communication technologies, and to show how the post-technocratic perspective we are proposing applies to thinking more carefully about the complex relations of cause and effect, of anticipated and unintended outcomes, of the difficulty of distinguishing 'good' and 'bad' effects where such matters are concerned.

A Case Study: The Dilemmas of Censorship

Even before the advent of new information and communication technologies, such as computers, censorship in schools was on the rise. More and more groups, from a variety of political agendas, have been challenging standard curricula, textbooks, library materials, and so forth. These moves toward censorship have been most visible recently in the coordinated efforts of interest groups such as the so-called Religious Right, but they have often gained wider acceptance as well. As schools have made heavier use of information and communication technologies, including connections to the Internet and CD-ROMs, there have been more and more calls to censor digital content even among groups who have not traditionally been pro-censorship; the usual rationale for such efforts is the fear that children will have ready access to pornographic or 'indecent' materials.

To our way of thinking, the major current policy responses to this situation typify the technocratic mindset. The equation is typically framed in simple, straightforward terms. Access to the Internet is a benefit because it connects students to enormous amounts of information; but the cost is that some of that information is inappropriate at best, pornographic at worst. How can we have the good without the bad? What are the appropriate balances between the benefits of free access to information and the costs of potential harm to children? Having defined the problem in terms benefits and the costs, the next step is apparently easy: eliminate or minimize the objectionable material without abandoning what is beneficial. The only question is a technical one: How?

One approach is to attack the problem on the side of supply. This was the approach in the

United States, for example, with the Communications Decency Act of 1997, recently ruled unconstitutional. With that ruling, censors have been looking for new ways to limit objectionable materials on the Internet. But there are good reasons to doubt whether the problem can ever be solved on the supply side, given the vast, decentralized nature of the Internet, the speed with which new provider sites can be established, the internationalization of content, which places many suppliers outside the grasp of national laws or regulations, and so forth. Yet the predominant response among censorship advocates has been merely to rewrite the CDA to see if it can withstand constitutional review. (Give a kid a hammer …)

The most highly touted alternative method of limiting access has been through the use of filtering software. This approach seeks to address the problem on the side of demand, through software that blocks searching for certain terms or visiting known sites that contain designated kinds of 'objectionable' material. However, early returns with this approach have revealed myriad cases of filters knocking out too much (for example, all pages mentioning 'breasts', so that people cannot access pages with information on breast cancer detection and treatment) or of applying filtering criteria that have other unintended effects (for example, the access provider in Vietnam that picked up tonal marks in Vietnamese, rendered as the letters 'sex', which knocked out 85% of all messages and overloaded the software). The predominant response has been that such software is in its infancy, and can be expected to improve with further development.

The problem with both the supply and demand approaches is that they abstract the technical problems from a larger social context; they analyze the problem as one of filtering out the 'bad' to protect the 'good'; and they both see the failure of technical solutions as simply requiring more and better technical solutions. Sometimes the results are merely laughable. On a deeper level, however, we want to argue that such approaches to censoring access to information reveal a deeply anti-educational bias and have the potential to cause real harm.

First of all, while the desire to protect young children from accidentally encountering crude or even dangerous material on the Internet is entirely understandable, as is the desire more generally of people not to have to deal personally with upsetting or offensive content, there is no general shortcut to solving these problems. The risk of exposure to unexpected and unwanted material is inherent to the structure of the Internet itself, and while there are specific things that informed users can do to limit such nuisances, they are as much a condition of this public space as they are with foul graffiti or overheard profanity in any other public space. For very young children it is possible to erect fairly reliable walls to limit their inadvertent contact with broad categories of material, but this is mainly due to the limits of children's abilities to exploit the technological resources. There is no way – *no way* – to prevent motivated, technically knowledgeable adolescents or teenagers from accessing such materials if they are determined to do so, especially when (as is often the case) they are pooling their skills and information and sharing what they find. This means that the only intervention that can have any significant impact on this issue is an educational approach: parents or teachers talking with them about their curiosities, interests, peer relations, sexual feelings, and how they act those out. Better technology or new censorship laws will not solve this problem.

Second, as discussed earlier, the attempt to neatly demarcate 'good' and 'bad' (or 'useful' and 'indecent' material) is fraught with difficulties. Part of the problem is with the vague and subjective connotations of terms like 'indecent' – which in fact was used in the CDA in place of terms like 'obscenity', which has a better-defined set of legal precedents for interpretation and application, precisely in order to broaden the range of what could be limited under the scope of the law. Such language inevitably brings in substantive social and political assumptions that are not merely technical in nature.

But this problem goes even further than simply calling for better-defined criteria. The Internet is a hypertextual, fundamentally relational information environment; its defining feature is the *link*, the association of material and the opening of multiple pathways of getting from point to point within the information space. Both attempts to limit the supply of content and filtering software will inevitably block access to unexpected sources of information because of that information's tangential relationship with subjects that someone believes to be objectionable. For example, attempts to prevent access to material about sex may inadvertently limit information about gender issues in general, about health care issues, or about equity issues in women's sports.

An additional danger, beyond the inability to obtain information, is that users who are denied access to information will probably never know it. For example, a student writing a term paper searches for references to 'abortion' and finds none. What does this mean to the student? Perhaps she will know the information has been censored or perhaps she will be left with the belief that the subject is not sufficiently important to warrant an entry. Or perhaps she will only find materials discussing the issue from a particular moral or political perspective. The user is in a perpetual quandary of not knowing whether some information does not exist, is not important, or has been censored. It is difficult to see what you are not seeing.

On a conventional level, this is not entirely different from other forms of censorship in schools and libraries – the book not assigned, the empty space on the shelf, or the space that isn't conspicuously 'empty' because there was nothing allowed there in the first place. However, in cyberspace censorship is much more difficult to discern. Given the nature of how information is stored, searched, and retrieved with hypertechnologies, the practice of censoring information tears holes in the fabric of knowledge and understanding. Knowledge, creativity, critical thinking, wisdom – these are not about the accumulation of 'facts', they are about the *relations* among ideas, information, ethics and culture. As one searches using hypertechnologies, points of information are not so much destinations as they are nodes – points that are linked to other points of information. Navigation proceeds from point to point based on the idiosyncratic interests or needs of the user, and suggests, or creates, new relations of significance. It is not that someone goes to 'abortion' so much as they move through 'abortion' on their way to somewhere else – somewhere where they (and perhaps only they) see an important connection. If we close the door marked abortion, we do not just close a door, we close off an entire hallway of possibilities.

Such censorship is antithetical to the sorts of educational and democratic ideals society holds for schools. How can students learn to discern, discriminate, synthesize or evaluate? How can they learn to make good choices, social and intellectual, if the choices are made for them by restricting the information they can and cannot see? Censorship in a technical environment does not just remove information, it unpredictably prevents access to other information.

Moreover, and at a deeper level, the development of skills of discernment, judgment, criticality, and so forth *require* that one encounter and deal with material that is unpleasant, misleading, offensive, and so forth. It is through engagements with such material that one can become more resistant to them: by making a *choice* that it is unworthy or immoral. Plato, in the *Republic*, famously argued that if certain topics or points of view were simply never presented to young learners they would never arise as issues. Not only is this demonstrably false, it is patently self-defeating; for the refusal to expose learners to 'infectious' material simply guarantees that they never develop the 'antibodies' against it. In an open society with widespread media, enormous diversity of viewpoints in public spaces, and the myriad content of the Internet at its disposal, any attempt to deal with these issues solely by censorship strategies must fail.

Attempts simply to censor suppliers of 'indecent' materials or the application of filtering software to limit demand will create as many problems as they will ever solve, because they are the wrong kinds of responses for the problems they attempt to address. These problems, in fact, cannot be 'solved'. The blanket approach of trying to weed out the bad while retaining the good cannot take into account the complexity of learning and knowledge, and the diversity and diverse needs of learners. This, then, is the educational challenge: helping students learn to operate in an environment that is inherently dangerous, to deal with what may be unexpected or unpleasant, to make critical judgments about what they find. Such a task cannot be framed as simply sorting out the 'good' from the 'bad', and excluding all that is 'bad'. *Educationally, we need some of the 'bad' in order to create some of the 'good'*. How else does someone develop the skills and dispositions of critical discernment?

The evaluation of information and communication technologies continually presents society with issues that cannot be analyzed in terms of simple dichotomies of good and bad. Such thinking promotes technocratic solutions that preclude the important (and difficult) educational questions that need be asked when discussing communication and the retrieval of information in hypertextual environments. Rather than discuss how to censor information from young people, policy-makers need to focus their attention on a host of issues, including society's attitude toward sexual matters, the question of what constitutes appropriate and inappropriate educational materials in general, how to help students to become more responsible and to learn to exercise critical judgment, and young people's rights to access some information whether adults want them to or not. It is not difficult to understand why most policy-makers have shied away from such controversies; but in shying away from them, they have shied away from the real educational issues at stake.

Notes

1. An earlier version of this essay was presented at the Pennsylvania State 'University Conference on Education and Technology, Autumn 1997', and entitled 'The Risky Promises and Promising Risks of New Information Technologies for Education'. It was published under that title in *The Bulletin of Science, Technology and Society*, **19**, No. 2 (1999): 105–112.
2. See Nicholas C. Burbules and David T. Hansen, eds., *Teaching and Its Predicaments* (Boulder Colorado: Westview Press, 1997).
3. Bertram Bruce calls this the 'transactional' perspective on new technologies: Bertram C. Bruce, 'Literacy Technologies: What Stance Should We Take?' *Literacy Research*, **29**, No. 2 (1997): 289–309.
4. Douglas Kellner, 'Multiple Literacies and Critical Pedagogy in a Multicultural Society', *Educational Theory*, **18**, No. 1 (1998): 103–122.
5. Jane Kenway, 'The Information Superhighway and Postmodernity: The Social Promise and the Social Price', *Comparative Education*, **32**, No. 2 (1996): 217–31.

[38]

British Journal of Educational Studies, ISSN 0007–1005
Vol. 45, No. 1, March 1997, pp 69–82

PRIVATISING THE PAST? HISTORY AND EDUCATION POLICY IN THE 1990s

by Gary McCulloch, *Division of Education, University of Sheffield*

ABSTRACT: A fundamental shift has taken place in the relationship between images of the past and educational policy making. In the 1930s and 1940s, a shared public past was incorporated in State policy to denote gradual evolution towards improvement in education and in the wider society. This consensual image has become fractured and less comforting especially since the 1970s. In particular, it has divided into a largely alienated or estranged public past, and personalised images of a reassuring and nostalgic 'private past'. This privatising of the past has exerted an increasing influence in education policy in the 1980s and 1990s, reflecting the concurrent trend towards an emphasis on 'choice and diversity' in education.

Keywords: history, policy, public, private, society, choice, diversity

1. Introduction

Education policies have often appeared to be lacking in historical perspective. The events and problems of the past tend to be treated as an irrelevant distraction to the problems at hand. Unmistakably, however, history continues to impinge on even the most historically unaware of education policies. David Tyack and Larry Cuban (1995), in the United States, argue that 'whether they are aware of it or not, all people use history (defined as an interpretation of past events) when they make choices about the present and future', and insist that the real issue is 'not whether people use a sense of the past in shaping their lives but how accurate and appropriate are their historical maps' (p. 6). This paper explores some of the key forms in which these interpretations and 'historical maps' have influenced education policy, and especially discusses recent and contemporary trends in Britain in the 1990s. It discerns a fundamental shift from the kinds of historical awareness that were evident earlier in the twentieth century to those that are characteristic of its closing years, based in an estrangement from a shared and supportive public past, and manifested in particular in a recourse to personalised, privatised notions of the past.

2. History, Culture, and Social Improvement

The kinds of historical consciousness that were prevalent in educational policies earlier in the twentieth century took several familiar forms. These tended to emphasise the close relationship between education and national culture and identity. They also served to promote the notion of continuous development or evolution towards social improvement through educational reform, development that might be gradual or rapid but which would be built upon earlier advances and achievements. These forms of historical awareness involved the endorsement by the State of a public history that both helped to legitimise educational policies and was ingrained within them.

Historical consciousness in education policy has often been expressed in terms of myth through which the complex relationships of historical change are selected and simplified to provide an idealised image of a national or local 'tradition' that education policy must continue to pursue. In Scotland, for example, as Anderson (1983) has documented, the notion of a distinctively democratic and egalitarian 'Scottish tradition' has developed to become a potent factor that itself influences the nature of reform. Anderson describes this Scottish tradition as a 'powerful historical myth', not in order to signify tht it is necessarily untrue or false, but to suggest its character as 'an idealization and distillation of a complex reality'. It assumes ideological and political force as it informs change, as Anderson remarks, 'interacting with other forces and pressures, ruling out some developments as inconsistent with the national tradition, and shaping the form in which the institutions inherited from the past are allowed to change' (p. 1). In New Zealand, too, historical awareness has also tended to be mythical in nature, grounded in ideals of 'equality' that are closely aligned with notions of the national character (McCulloch, 1990, 1991a).

Notions of an 'English tradition' in education were similarly employed to inform and justify specific forms of outlook, planning, or policy. In the nineteenth century, as Hobsbawm (1983) has demonstrated, the 'invention of tradition' was a means of establishing or reinforcing the status of particular social and political institutions, and of defining the ways they were to develop. Public schools and universities were notable in taking advantage of this method of sustaining their own authority, which in turn defined the role of other institutions in relation to them. In the 1920s, Cyril Norwood, at that time Head of Harrow School, attempted to articulate and defend an 'English tradition of education', in terms of the values and ethos of the public schools. According to Norwood (1929), the ideals of knighthood, chivalry, and the English gentleman, preserved through the public schools, constituted the 'highest English tradition', which needed to be maintained, broadened to include wider groups of pupils, and extended into the future (see also McCulloch, 1991b, Chs. 3–4).

A strong theme that was also evident in educational policies in England and Wales earlier in the twentieth century was a liberal notion of steady and gradual evolution towards social improvement. In this outlook, the past was usable because it was safe and domesticated; it provided a firm basis for shared values to be espoused and for existing developments to be continued. The Hadow Report of 1926 on the education of the adolescent expressed this position explicitly in the course of a lengthy historical discussion of the provision of education for children of eleven to fifteen years of age:

> As our survey shows, that problem has behind it a history extending back almost to the beginning of public education in England, and it has given rise, particularly in recent years, to more fruitful educational activity. It is on the basis of the experience thus obtained that further progress will now be made. The question is not one of erecting a structure on a novel and untried pattern, but of following to their logical conclusion precedents clearly set, and of building on foundations which have long been laid. (Board of Education, 1926, p. 70)

However, although the foundations that had been laid in the past were perceived as fundamentally sound, they could still be responsible for difficulties that needed to be addressed in the present.

In many respects, considerations of the national tradition and the wider culture were often regarded not merely as relevant to education policy but as an inescapable starting point for thinking about the nature of reform. The Hadow Report was especially forceful on this point as it decreed that 'in education, as in other departments of social policy, it is not impossible to proceed *per saltum*, that no generation ever has a clean sheet on which to write, that each generation must build with materials inherited from the past on pain of not building at all' (p. 77). The inheritance of entrenched social class divisions and inequalities was widely recognised as a central issue with which current educational policies needed to contend. Fred Clarke, a leading liberal reformer in the 1930s and 1940s, noted (1933) that 'class-feeling' was a particular characteristic of the English educational tradition, a *damnosa haereditas.* According to Clarke (1940, p. 31), this constituted a major 'historical determinant of English education' in the present, since 'the effects of a long past during which it was the rule that the many should be schooled for the service and convenience of the few are not thus easily to be thrown off, even if that past is no longer with us, as some would contend that it still is'. Sometimes an awareness of this 'social tradition' led educational reformers to counsel against too radical a break with the past, for example in the early 1950s when H. C. Dent (1952, p. 11) argued against the wider development of comprehensive schools on the grounds that 'at present English parents and teachers simply won't have it'. Indeed, Dent insisted, 'plan with the grain of the national character, and you have a reasonable assurance that things will go well; plan against it – and you've had it. And, what is more important – for no one need waste pity on incompetent planners – large numbers of unoffending souls will be put to enormous expenditure of time, effort, and nervous energy to tell you where you get off.' (p. 14).

The major cycle of education reform that took place in the 1940s, culminating in the Education Act of 1944, assumed in general a radical stance that was rooted in this awareness of continuous development. The Spens Report on secondary education, published in 1938, devoted much space to an historical critique of 'liberal' and 'vocational' approaches, arguing somewhat loftily that:

> As we see one view or theory of education subjected to criticism and in consequence modified or superseded by another, we may be able partially to understand and appraise the value and meaning of each successive phase, and to form opinions of our own which, although they cannot possibly claim to be final, may at least claim to be based on something more substantial than current opinion and popular views of the significance of what has occurred. (Board of Education, 1938, p. 1).

The committee was clearly aware that its own opinions 'cannot possibly claim to be final', that is, it realised that its own ideas would come to be 'subjected to criticism and in consequence modified or superseded'. In common with the educational reformers of the 1940s, by and large, their historical sense warned them that political fashions and social trends would continue to change, they assumed towards gradual improvement, and that educational reforms needed to accommodate themselves to these.

Another feature of the historical reforms of the 1940s was that this historical awareness was closely related to a sense of the social, cultural, and philosophical goals of education. The Fleming Report on the public schools, published in 1944, provided a detailed historical account of its subject on the grounds that 'the public schools, as living organisms with traditions in many cases lasting for centuries, can hardly be understood at all without some consideration of the past'. At the same time, and as part of this purpose, it attempted to come to terms with 'the social factors which have determined the development of these schools' (Board of Education, 1944, pp. 5–6). Meanwhile, the President of the Board of Education, R. A. Butler, could discuss (1942) the importance of the Greek philosopher Plato with the socialist intellectuals G. D. H. Cole and Harold Laski: 'Mr Cole and I discussed in an amiable manner what Plato had attempted to discuss before us, namely the best method of training the leaders of a community.' This treatment of education in relation to wider philosophical, social and cultural problems immediately raised issues involving its social and historical development.

During this period, then, roughly from the 1920s until the 1950s, a public history was incorporated and ingrained in state policy, validated by it and contributing actively towards it. This public history consisted of partial, selective, and often simplistic renderings of historical change designed for contemporary policy purposes. Its significance was often strongly contested among competing groups and ideologies, for example over the historical development of 'liberal' and 'vocational' approaches to education and the role of social class, but it helped to form the basis of widely shared collective values about the nature of education and of the further development of the education system (see also McCulloch, 1994). An important dimension of its potency, moreover, was that, despite its 'mythical' characteristics, this public history generally subsumed and incorporated individual experiences of educational change. The public history transmitted by leading figures such as Clarke, Tawney, Dent and Butler generally overrode their own personal stories. That is, there did not appear to be major discrepancies between 'official versions' of the past and lived, personal reality, or if there were these did not manifest themselves in the public arena.

3. The Estranged Past

This positive awareness of a progressive public past in education has been much less evident in the education policies of the past thirty years, and is conspicuous by its absence in the 1990s. In part, this was due to a general loss of confidence in the idea of a gradual evolution towards social improvement. By the 1960s and 1970s, the shared values on which earlier reforms had drawn were rather less clear, and social progress was called into question. In the 1980s, the past came to be viewed negatively rather than in terms of providing solid foundations for further development. The past became identified as the problem, an explanation for the failures of British society and the economy.

A hostile, negative view of the educational past developed during the 1980s that held the 'educational establishment' responsible for the problems that needed solving. The prevalent emphasis upon academic and liberal values in English education was held to explain the relative decline of British industry and economic productivity during the twentieth century (e.g. Wiener, 1981, Barnett, 1986, Aldcroft, 1992). The alleged excesses of 'progressive' education sanctioned in particular by the Plowden Report of 1967 were increasingly blamed for an alleged decline in standards (e.g. Clarke, 1992). This was a form of historical consciousness that influenced the major education reforms of the 1980s and early 1990s in its way just as much as the 'historical maps' of the 1930s and 1940s had helped to underpin the Education Act of 1944. Yet it also represented an estrangement from the past. History was no longer the ally of reform, nor was it safe or domesticated. Rather, it was now the enemy, something dangerous and alien, to be controlled or expunged. It was less the source of shared social and national values than the organ of failure and decline in society and industry. This image of the past as barren wilderness, filled with disappointments and betrayals, led directly to the education policies of the late 1980s, which attempted to change the culture of schooling itself. In particular, there was an estrangement from the public history that had earlier been ingrained in education policies, a process reflected in the marked absence of explicit historical discussion in most 'official' reports on education since the 1970s.

There remained some important vestiges of previous notions of historical awareness in particular areas of education policy, although these ideals were strongly challenged by more hostile and negative approaches to the past. At one level, for example, the National Curriculum introduced under the Education Reform Act of 1988 constituted a systematic attempt to rebuild the nation-state and to re-establish national identity and ideology, in response to fears of economic decline, cultural dissolution, and a loss of national power (e.g. Goodson, 1994, Ch. 7). It drew upon idealised traditions of English culture in order to become widely acceptable, in much the same way that earlier educational policies had also been grounded in social and cultural myth. At another level, even so, the National Curriculum also posed a series of challenges to a different and potentially opposing 'tradition' that had been cultivated as integral to the educational reforms of the 1940s, that of the idea of teacher professionalism defined in terms of autonomy and effective control in the curriculum domain.

In the development of the National Curriculum, these idealised notions with their underlying sets of assumptions about the past were vigorously contested among the different groups and constituencies involved in and affected by the reform (e.g. McCulloch in press, Ball, 1994). The former Prime Minister, Margaret Thatcher (1993), was able to draw on the received tradition or myth of teacher control in the curriculum area when she challenged the more prescriptive policies of Kenneth Baker as her Education Secretary: 'The fact that since 1944 the only compulsory subject in the curriculum in Britain had been religious education reflected a healthy distrust of the state using central control of the syllabus as a means of propaganda.' (p. 590). It was on this basis that Thatcher endorsed the view that the State should not try to 'regiment every detail of what happened in schools', and argued that the French 'centralised system' would 'not be acceptable in Britain' (p. 591). On the other hand, Baker and others preferred to see greater 'accountability' introduced into the system, and had little sympathy for these received ideals (Baker, 1993, p. 198).

These conflicting notions of the public past are also reflected in the marked absence of explicit historical discussion in most recent policy documents on education in England and Wales. This is a notable silence that provides a clear contrast for example between most White Papers on education since the 1970s, and those produced earlier in the century. The series of major Reports on education such as Hadow, Spens, Crowther and Newsom, which had emanated first from the Consultative Committee of the Board of Education, and then from the Central Advisory Council of the Ministry of Education, fell into abeyance in the 1970s. With it there lapsed a key means of approving and disseminating an official 'public history'. The public history was no longer a convenient or tractable tool of policy; on the contrary, it had become remote and estranged. It is as a response to this situation that the overt hostility to earlier trends in educational policy and the fragmenting of earlier national myths and traditions may be interpreted.

4. Private and Public Pasts

A fundamental shift in the relationship between history and policy is exhibited in the emergence of the personal self or private past as a version of historical awareness in the 1980s and 1990s. In this 'historical map', the politician or policy-maker derives lessons drawn from an interpretation of their own past, often from their own schooling or family history, or from the experiences and attitudes acquired by their contemporaries. These lessons tend to be self-justifying in nature, used in order to reinforce not only a particular policy goal but also the person's general political stance and aspirations. Moreover, this private past of the self and close circle is commonly posed in opposition to a more official or public past. The private past is nostalgic and comforting; the public past is threatening, hostile, and alien.

Personal experience, especially in childhood, has become a common device to criticise or challenge wider trends in education policy. Lord Callaghan, the former Labour Prime Minister, explains the background to his major Ruskin College speech on education in the following terms (1987, p. 409):

> I have always been a convinced believer in the importance of education, as throughout my life I had seen how many doors it could unlock for working-class children who had begun with few other advantages, and I regretted my own lack of a university education. I was also aware of growing concerns among parents about the direction some schools were taking and I was anxious to probe this.

Personal and private experiences of education are here posed against more general trends and changes in order to endorse a particular view of contemporary educational needs. The lessons derived from these experiences do not always seem to follow straightforwardly from the autobiographical account. For example, in Callaghan's case, the personal experience of lacking a university education is taken to strengthen the argument that the school curriculum should be related more closely to the concerns of industry. Even so, it attaches to the policy argument a certain moral force to augment its political potency.

The lessons drawn by Kenneth Baker from his autobiography (1993) exhibit similar tendencies. His experience of the 1960s highlights his hostility to comprehensive schools and his distrust of the 'educational establishment'. When the tripartite system of grammar, technical and modern schools was replaced with comprehensives, he recalls, 'I had been amazed that Britain had decided to abandon the structure of its education system in this way, and as each year passed it became clearer that the high hopes of the comprehensive movement had not been fulfilled.' (p. 165). He also invokes his own family background to help to justify his policies in relation to teachers:

> I have always been keenly aware of the crucial importance of teachers in our society, for the last three generations of my own family had all seized opportunities which only education had opened up for them. Moreover, my grandmother had been a teacher, one of my great aunts had run Catholic Education in south Wales in the early part of the century, several other relations were teachers, and my wife had been a teacher for over seven years.

The lesson that he derived from this set of experiences was that 'teachers' status should be enhanced in the eyes of the public'. This meant, he suggested, 'putting behind them – I hope forever – any thoughts of industrial action', which would allow them to 'look forward instead to an era when they were better paid, better trained, and working in better schools' (p. 254).

Lady Thatcher's notion of the role of the personal background in education policy is especially interesting in highlighting the dichotomy between the private and the public past. In relation to her own personal experience, she emphasises (1993) the importance of direct grant schools and grammar schools and the wider decline of these forms of schooling: 'It is my passionate belief that since the war we have . . . "strangled the middle way". Direct grant schools and grammar schools provided the means for people like me to get on equal terms with those who came from well-off backgrounds.' (p. 378). The policy goal that is endorsed as a result is the development of grant-maintained schools and the more active pursuit of competition and specialisation. Thatcher also discerns (1995) four distinct attitudes towards education among her fellow Conservatives, and these are all grounded in their different kinds of personal and family histories. The first group are 'those who had no real interest in state education in any case because they themselves and their children went to private schools'. This 'important group', she suggests, are 'all too likely to be swayed by arguments of political expediency'. The second group comprises 'those who, themselves or their children, had failed to get into grammar school and had been disappointed with the education received at a secondary modern'. Those in the third group 'either because they themselves were teachers or through some other contact with the world of education, had absorbed a large dose of the fashionable egalitarian doctrines of the day'. By contrast, the fourth group was made up of 'people like me who had been to good grammar schools, were strongly opposed to their destruction and felt no inhibitions at all about arguing for the 11-Plus' (p. 157). In this perspective, 'people like me', defined as such through their childhood and schooling experiences, are defended against the depredations of educational decline and the 'fashionable egalitarian doctrines of the day'.

The elevated private past that was thus ingrained and incorporated into the educational policies of the 1980s and 1990s lent itself to nostalgia, again all the more clearly when set against the hostile background of the public past. Michael Jones, political editor of *The Sunday Times*, for example, recalls (1991) the primary schools of his childhood, during the Second World War: 'Primary school was a happy time for me. About 40 of us sat at fixed wooden desks with ink wells and moved from them only with grudging permission. Teacher sat in a higher desk in front of us and moved only to the blackboard. She smelt of scent and inspired awe.' Then comes the intrusion of educational changes in the 1960s:

> The Plowden report changed all that in the 1960s, 20 years too late for me, thank God, but not alas, for the generations that followed. My children spent their primary years in a showpiece school where they were allowed to wander around at will, develop their individuality and dodge the three Rs. It was all for the best, we were assured. But it was not. In that, as in much of their dogmatic othodoxy, the disciples of the Plowden report served the nation ill.

According to Jones, this 'dogmatic orthodoxy' led directly to educational and social decline, and he was therefore a fervent supporter of the reforms of the 1990s.

A similar stance was adopted by John Patten as Secretary of State for Education (1993), although he made use of his own personal experience to criticise both the inequalities produced through the policies of the 1940s and the progressivism of the 1960s:

> My own school days neatly straddled the two reforms. The Sixties had opened with school boys and school girls patiently waiting to be tested at 11 and thereafter parcelled and graded like vegetables into grammar, technical or secondary [sic] children. They ended with the transmogrification of those uniformed and inky children into Biro-bearing 'Kids', for whom difference was abhorred, diversity damned, choice condemned.

This personal reminiscence again helped to justify Patten's contemporary purpose in pursuing radical education policies, as he concluded: 'We are now on another cusp between the second phase of post-war schooling and the third, just as in the Sixties I saw that similar switch from the world of the 11-plus to the comprehensive experience.' (Patten 1993). This in turn served to underpin the policies proposed in the major White Paper *Choice and Diversity*, published in July 1992.

5. Towards a Privatised Past?

Much of this kind of approach reflects a nostalgia for an idealised 'Golden Age', remote from the machinations of the 'education establishment', but vivid in the memories of educational reformers. This seemed apparent also in the sympathies of the Prime Minister, John Major, who, it was mischievously observed, 'seems to hanker after a Britain, circa 1955, when every summer was warm, every village had its bakery, life revolved round the Rotary Club and the Women's Institute and every child sat attentively in front of a teacher in a cardigan reciting Shakespeare's sonnets' (*The Sunday Times* 1993). At the same time, it betokened a splintering of the public past in education policy, into a mutually opposed private and public or collective past. Even where the public past still fostered sympathy and even nostalgia, for example the memory of the so-called 'Butler Act' of 1944 from the vantage point of the late 1980s, there were powerful tendencies to personalise the account and to draw a sharp distinction between the private and the public experience. Thus the Labour spokesperson on education, Jack Straw (1987), condemned the new Education Reform Bill by comparing it unfavourably with the 1944 Act, and yet at the same time could suggest that the Bill would 'recreate that segregated and divisive system' of the 1940s: 'Some of us remember what the 11-plus did to children, with bribes of bicycles, of holidays, of parental love and approval if they passed, and the humiliation and shame which families felt when children failed.' Again here the private past stands in contradiction to the collective, public past, and serves to obscure and undermine its meaning, not as a nostalgic reading in this case, but as a rebuke to the failings of public policy.

More broadly, too, these opposing images helped to develop the basic dichotomy between 'parent' and 'politician' experienced by public figures such as the Labour Party shadow minister for health Harriet Harman (*TES* 1996): the 'parent' drew on a private past that conflicted with an official public myth. This conflict, when Harman chose to send her son to a selective school rather than to a local comprehensive, helped to induce a debate in the early months of 1996 on what were seen as 'the shortcomings of the comprehensive legacy in education' (*The Independent* 1996a). Harman's stance was supported by those whose personal and family experiences similarly sat uncomfortably with an officially sanctioned public past. Bernie Grant, for example, noted that his own three children had gone to a comprehensive school in the Tottenham area of London and he now regretted it; the decision should be seen as 'a personal decision by Harriet and Jack and as such none of our business' (*The Independent* 1996b). In this instance, the private past comes into open conflict with one of the last remnants of a comforting public past and helps to undermine its credibility.

As in the earlier part of the century, then, education policies in the 1980s and 1990s continued to incorporate images of the historical past. The nature of these historical images, however, had fundamentally changed. From being safe, domesticated, and progressive, images of the public past had become threatening, estranged, and regressive. Rather than being mainly a source of stability, they were more often a source of dissension. Increasingly, they gave rise to a disjunction between the idealised personal experiences or myths of the consumers of education, and the collective history of the 'producers'. The experience of what Thatcher called 'people like me' was estranged from the failures and disappointments of the public past. A nationalised public past, so potent in the 1940s, had undergone privatisation.

The outcome can be viewed as constituting a choice and diversity in the range of 'historical maps' that were available on the basis of private and personal experience, to be tested against each other in the public forum towards contemporary political and policy goals. The more monolithic explanations of reform, evolution and improvement that had been endorsed and approved in the State policies of the 1930s and 1940s had largely given way to pluralistic, expressly subjective, competing notions of history. Such notions represented essentially privatised versions of the past, more comfortable and indeed more relevant to those who espoused them than was the public past. These afforded for policy makers in education a refuge from some aspects of history, a retreat into others, through a recourse into their own private experience. They provided, in short, a new way of ensuring what had perhaps always been true, that what was too painful to remember, they could choose to forget.

6. References

ALDCROFT, D. (1992) *Education, Training and Economic Performance 1944 to 1990* (Manchester, Manchester University Press).

ANDERSON, R. D. (1983) *Education and Opportunity in Victorian Scotland: Schools and Universities* (Edinburgh, Edinburgh University Press).

BAKER, K. (1993) *The Turbulent Years: My Life in Politics* (London, Faber and Faber).

BALL, S. (1994) Education, Majorism and the curriculum of the dead. In S. BALL, *Education Reform: A Critical and Post-Structural Approach* (Milton Keynes, Open University Press).

BARNETT, C. (1986) *The Audit of War: the Illusion and Reality of Britain as a Great Nation* (London, Macmillan).

BOARD OF EDUCATION (1926) *The Education of the Adolescent* (Hadow Report) (London, HMSO).

BOARD OF EDUCATION (1938) *Secondary Education* (Spens Report) (London, HMSO).

BOARD OF EDUCATION (1944) *The Public Schools and the General Educational System* (Fleming Report) (London, HMSO).

BUTLER, R. A. (1942) note of interview, 12 May (Board of Education papers, Public Records Office, Kew, ED/136/599).

CALLAGHAN, J. (1987) *Time and Chance* (London, Collins).

CLARKE, F. (1933) Some reflections on secondary education, *University of Toronto Quarterly*, 3(1), 74–86.

CLARKE, F. (1940) *Education and Social Change: An English Interpretation* (London, Sheldon Press).

CLARKE, K. (1992) Education's insane bandwagon finally goes into the ditch. *The Sunday Times*, 26 January.

DE (DEPARTMENT FOR EDUCATION) (1992) *Choice and Diversity: a New Framework for Schools* (London, HMSO, Cm 2021).

DENT, H. C. (1952) *Change in English Education: A Historical Survey* (London, University of London Press).

GOODSON, I. (1994) *Studying Curriculum* (Milton Keynes, Open University Press).

HOBSBAWM, E. (1983) Introduction: inventing traditions. In E. HOBSBAWM, T. RANGER (eds) *The Invention of Tradition* (Cambridge, Cambridge University Press).

JONES, M. (1991) At last, trendy teachers' days are numbered. In The Sunday Times, 8 December.

McCULLOCH, G. (1990) The ideology of educational reform: an historical perspective. In S. MIDDLETON, J. CODD and A. JONES (eds) *New Zealand Education Policy Today: Critical Perspectives* (Wellington, Allen and Unwin).

McCULLOCH, G. (1991a) 'Serpent in the garden': conservative protest, the 'New Right' and New Zealand educational history. *History of Education Review*, 20(1), 73–87.

McCULLOCH, G. (1991b) *Philosophers and Kings: Education for Leadership in Modern England* (Cambridge, Cambridge University Press).

McCULLOCH, G. (1994) *Educational Reconstruction: The 1944 Education Act and the 21st Century* (London, Woburn Press).

McCULLOCH, G. (in press) Teachers and the National Curriculum in England and Wales: socio-historical frameworks. In G. HELSBY, G. McCULLOCH (eds) *Teachers and the National Curriculum*, London, Cassell.

NORWOOD, C. (1929) *The English Tradition of Education* (London, John Murray).

PATTEN, J. (1993) A learning-by-choice revolution. In *The Independent*, 5 April.

HISTORY AND EDUCATION POLICY IN THE 1990s

STRAW, J. (1987) Speech in House of Commons debate on the Education Reform Bill, 1 December, *Hansard*, vol. 123 Parliamentary Debates 1987–88, col. 781.
THATCHER, M. (1993) *The Downing Street Years* (London, Harper-Collins).
THATCHER, M. (1995) *The Path to Power* (London, Harper-Collins).
THE INDEPENDENT (1996a) leading article, 'A painful lesson for Labour', 28 February.
THE INDEPENDENT (1996b) report, 'Blair appeal defuses revolt', 25 January.
TIMES EDUCATIONAL SUPPLEMENT (1996) leading article, 'Hounding Harriet', 26 January.
THE SUNDAY TIMES (1993) Darling buds of Major. Leading article, 7 February.
TYACK, D. and CUBAN, L. (1995) *Tinkering Toward Utopia: A Century of Public School Reform* (Cambridge, Mass., Harvard University Press).
WIENER, M. (1981) *English Culture and the Decline of the Industrial Spirit, 1850–1980* (Cambridge, Cambridge University Press).

Correspondence:
Professor Gary McCulloch
Division of Education
University of Sheffield
388 Glossop Road
Sheffield, S10 2JA

Date received: 18 January 1996
Date accepted for publication (*subject to revision*): 20 February 1996

Name Index